Introduction to
Comparative Politics
Political Challenges and Changing Agendas

SEVENTH EDITION

Mark Kesselman
Columbia University

Joel Krieger
Wellesley College

William A. Joseph
Wellesley College

Contributors

Ervand Abrahamian
Baruch College

Amrita Basu
Amherst College

Joan DeBardeleben
Carleton University

Louis De Sipio
University of California, Irvine

Shigeko N. Fukai
Chiba University

Haruhiro Fukui
University of California, Santa Barbara

Wade Jacoby
Brigham Young University

Halbert Jones
Saint Anthony's College, University of Oxford

Darren Kew
University of Massachusetts, Boston

Atul Kohli
Princeton University

Peter Lewis
Johns Hopkins University

Tom Lodge
University of Limerick

Alfred P. Montero
Carleton College

George Ross
Université de Montréal

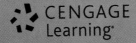
CENGAGE
Learning

Australia • Brazil • Mexico • Singapore • United Kingdom • United States

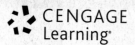

**Introduction to Comparative Politics:
Political Challenges and Changing
Agendas**, Seventh Edition

Mark Kesselman, Joel Krieger,
William A. Joseph

Product Team Manager: Carolyn Merrill

Associate Product Manager: Scott Greenan

Managing Developer: Joanne Dauksewicz

Content Developer: Kate Scheinman

Associate Content Developer: Amy Bither

Product Assistant: Abigail Hess

Senior Media Developer: Laura Hildebrand

Marketing Manager: Valerie Hartman

Content Project Manager: Cathy Brooks

Art Director: Linda May

Manufacturing Planner: Fola Orekoya

IP Analyst: Alexandra Ricciardi

IP Project Manager: Farah Fard

Production Service and Compositor:
Integra Software Services Pvt. Ltd

Text and Cover Designer: Rokusek Design

Cover Image: © Ints Vikmanis/
Shutterstock.com

For product information and technology assistance, contact us at
Cengage Learning Customer & Sales Support, 1-800-354-9706

For permission to use material from this text or product,
submit all requests online at **www.cengage.com/permissions**.
Further permissions questions can be emailed to
permissionrequest@cengage.com.

Library of Congress Control Number: 2014947987

ISBN-13: 978-1-285-86533-1

Cengage Learning
20 Channel Center Street
Boston, MA 02210
USA

Cengage Learning is a leading provider of customized learning solutions with office locations around the globe, including Singapore, the United Kingdom, Australia, Mexico, Brazil, and Japan. Locate your local office at **www.cengage.com/global**.

Cengage Learning products are represented in Canada by Nelson Education, Ltd.

To learn more about Cengage Learning Solutions, visit **www.cengage.com**.

Purchase any of our products at your local college store or at our preferred online store **www.cengagebrain.com**.

Printed in the United States of America
Print Number: 01   Print Year: 2014

Brief Contents

Contents

Contents

Contents

Contents

Contents

Contents

Contents

Contents

Contents

Contents

PART III   MIXED SYSTEMS

Contents

Contents

Contents

Contents

Contents

Contents

PART IV   AUTHORITARIAN REGIMES

Chapter 14 Iran   595

Ervand Abrahamian

Contents

Contents

Preface

The prefaces to several previous editions of *Introduction to Comparative Politics* (ICP) used Bob Dylan's words to observe that "the times, they are a–changin'." We reflect on how we began previous editions:

- "Politics throughout the world seems more troubled today than even a few years ago, when celebrations around the globe ushered in the new millennium."
  —*Introduction to Comparative Politics*, 3rd edition. © 2004.
- In recent years the "world of politics was as turbulent as at any time in recent memory, with clear-cut trends more elusive than ever."
  —*Introduction to Comparative Politics*, 4th edition. © 2007.
- "[We] have witnessed as much—or more—turmoil and uncertainty as the preceding years."
  —*Introduction to Comparative Politics*, 5th edition. © 2010.
- "The sixth edition of ICP... has been published soon after prodemocracy movements overthrew decades-old dictatorships in Tunisia and Egypt, and repressive regimes unleashed deadly force against similar movements in Algeria, Bahrain, Iran, Libya, Syria, and Yemen."
  —*Introduction to Comparative Politics*, 6th edition. © 2013

When it comes to the degree of uncertainty, and the range and depth of challenges faced by ordinary citizens who yearn for stability, less strife, and a widening circle of opportunities, the present edition is no different than its predecessors. We write these lines just days after a highly controversial referendum was held in Crimea on the question of seceding from Ukraine. Less than 24 hours later, the Crimean parliament voted for Crimea's annexation by Russia, and Moscow moved quickly to make that a fact. Russian forces had taken control of Crimea just a couple of weeks before following a pro-European revolution in Ukraine had ousted an unpopular pro-Russian president. Russia's intervention in Ukraine raises fears in other parts of the former Soviet Union, particularly in the other states in the Black Sea region—Armenia, Azerbaijan, and Georgia—that their hard-won independence is at risk.

The seventh edition of *Introduction to Comparative Politics* does not try to emulate the coverage of fast-breaking daily events by CNN, Fox News, and Twitter. Its mission is to provide students with a clear and comprehensive guide to these unsettled political times through comparative analysis.

Country-by-Country Approach and Thematic Framework

The methods of comparative analysis come alive as students examine similarities and differences among countries and within and between political systems. Our thematic approach facilitates disciplined analysis of political challenges and changing agendas within each country. Like previous editions of *Introduction to Comparative Politics*, this edition (ICP7) employs a country-by-country approach structured around four core themes:

1. **A Globalizing World of States** focuses on the importance of state formation, the internal organization of the state, and the impact of the interstate system on political development. We emphasize the interaction of globalization and state power.

2. **Governing the Economy** analyzes state strategies for promoting economic development and competitiveness, emphasizes the crucial role of economic performance in determining a state's political legitimacy, and stresses the interactive effects of economic globalization on domestic politics.
3. **The Democratic Idea** explores the challenges posed to the state by citizens' demands for greater participation and influence in democracies, mixed systems, and authoritarian regimes, and discusses the inevitable gap between the promise of democracy and its imperfect fulfillment.
4. **The Politics of Collective Identities** considers the political consequences of the complex interplay among class, race, ethnicity, gender, religion, and nationality.

Our approach to comparative politics stresses the analysis of each country's politics by applying these four themes within a context shaped by globalization. This approach strikes a balance between a fine-grained analysis of the richness of each country's distinctive pattern of political development and explicit cross-country comparative analysis. In so doing, our text teaches students that the study of comparative politics is defined by a method that investigates similarities and differences in cases and, at the same time, poses and attempts to answer searching questions that really matter in the lives of students as active citizens. These are questions embedded in the thematic scaffolding of ICP.

Five Critical Junctures in Politics

Chapter 1 helps students navigate through the text by introducing the book's thematic framework, which is combined with a thorough analysis of the political institutions and processes of each country in the chapters that follow. It sets the stage and previews the thematic focus by noting:

1. 1989, which symbolizes the end of the Cold War, and the eruption of capitalist democracies that transcend East versus West divisions in Europe and much of the world;
2. 9/11/01, which reframes globalization, shifting attention away from the development gap and to terrorism, security, and the use of force;
3. 2008, a year of intense financial and economic crisis around the world;
4. 2011, when prodemocracy movements confronted repressive regimes in North Africa and the Middle East, and Japan was rocked by a severe earthquake, tsunami, and nuclear disaster;
5. 2014, when Vladimir Putin's invasion of Ukraine threatened to destabilize the post-Soviet global order and created the very real possibility of a "back to the future" scenario of a new Cold War between Russia and the United States and its European allies.

Chapter 1 also describes the comparative method; presents in some detail our four-theme framework; discusses how we classify the political systems of the countries covered in this book; and provides an overview of the organization of the country chapters.

Consolidated Democracies, Mixed Systems, and Authoritarian Regimes

We classify the thirteen countries in this edition of ICP in three categories:

- *Consolidated democracies* (Britain, France, Germany, Japan, India, and the United States)
- *Mixed systems* (Brazil, Mexico, South Africa, Nigeria, and Russia)
- *Authoritarian regimes* (Iran and China)
- New to this edition is a chapter on the European Union, which, in addition to Britain, France, and Germany, is made up of twenty-five other member states that fall into the category of consolidated democracies.

In the Introduction, we define the three regime types and explain the rationale for the typology. In particular, we warn against assuming that there is a linear movement from authoritarian regimes to mixed systems to consolidated democracies. Democratization is often a protracted process with ambiguous results or reversals, rather than a clearly delineated path toward completion. Thus, we stress that the countries we classify as mixed systems are not riding a historical escalator mechanically leading to their transformation into stable or consolidated democracies. We call attention to "hybrid" regimes, in which some elements of democracy coexist with authoritarian practices.

We also emphasize that the boundaries dividing the three groups are not airtight. For one thing, politics is a moving target. Russia is a good example of a country on the cusp between a mixed system and an authoritarian regime. Furthermore, scholars disagree about the appropriate criteria for classifying regime types as well as about how to classify particular cases. Indeed, instructors may find it fruitful to encourage class discussion of alternative conceptual schemes for classifying groups of countries and how to best characterize the political system of given countries.

NEW! Seventh Edition Content

The content of this edition of ICP has been shaped by our survey of what instructors found appealing about previous editions of the book and their recommended changes. Based on this feedback, we have made the following improvements:

- **NEW!** Shortened country chapters compared to the previous edition. The result is a more streamlined text that strikes a balance between introducing comparative politics to students with little or no background in political science while maintaining coverage of the complexity of institutions, issues, processes, and events.
- **NEW! Focus questions** at the beginning of each major section heading in the country chapters introduce students to the section that follows.
- **NEW! Making Connections** questions at the end of each feature box encourage students to link the topic of the box to the content of the chapter.
- **NEW! Where Do You Stand?** questions at the end of each section in all chapters encourage students to develop and defend original arguments on controversial issues.
- **NEW! Chapter on the European Union (EU).** Given the unique importance of the EU in shaping the political and economic life of its member states, ICP7 has added a chapter on the EU. Although the outline of the chapter varies slightly from those for country chapters, we have tried to make the treatment of the EU as close as possible to other chapters. The chapter is written by George Ross, one of the most distinguished specialists on European and EU politics.
- **NEW! Subsections on Environmental Issues, The Political Impact of Technology, and Youth Politics and the Generation Gap** highlight the particular importance of these issues.
- **NEW! The thoroughly updated introduction and country chapters** provide analysis of major recent political developments throughout the world. For example, the chapters on France, India, Iran, Japan, Mexico, South Africa, and the United States extensively analyze the implications of recent elections in these countries. The chapter on Russia discusses the crisis in Ukraine and the annexation of Crimea. The China chapter analyzes the rise to power of Xi Jinping, who was installed as head of the Chinese Communist Party in November 2012 and as president of the People's Republic of China in March 2013.

Consistent Country Chapter Organization

At the beginning of each chapter, students will find a map, data on ethnicity, religion, and language specific to that country to aid in comparing countries, and some basic information about the country's political system. Each country chapter consists of five sections:

1. **The Making of the Modern State**, which begins with an opening vignette that illustrates an important feature of the country's contemporary politics. This is followed by a description of the country's

geographic setting, a discussion of the critical junctures in the historical development of the state, and an overview of how the book's four central themes relate to the country. This section concludes by noting the significance of the country for the study of comparative politics.

2. **Political Economy and Development** analyzes the relationship between the state, the impact of economic development on society, current environmental issues, and the country's position in the global economy,

3. **Governance and Policy-making** looks at the general organization of the state, the executive branch, and other state institutions, including the judiciary, subnational levels of government, and the military, police, internal security and other agencies of coercion. This section concludes with a description of the policy-making process.

4. **Representation and Participation** covers the country's legislature, party system, elections, political culture, citizenship, national identity, interest groups, social movements, and protest. The final subsection is a new one on the political impact of technology.

5. **Politics in Transition** begins by highlighting a recent important event that is influencing the country's politics and then proceeds to an analysis of the major political challenges facing the country. This is followed by the new subsection on youth politics and the generational divide. The chapter ends with some concluding thoughts about politics of the country in comparative perspective.

Special Features That Teach

Maps, tables, charts, photographs, and political cartoons enliven the text and present key information in clear and graphic ways. We have provided a more visually interesting presentation of data in a way that is intended to enhance cross-country comparative analysis. At the end of Chapter 1, various data is presented in a way that facilitates comparisons among the countries covered in this book.

Sidebar boxes in each country chapter highlight three interesting and provocative aspects of politics:

1. The **Profile** feature highlights biographies of important political leaders.
2. The **Global Connection** feature provides links between domestic and international politics.
3. The **U.S. Connection** feature compares an important feature of political institutions with its American counterpart or explores a crucial aspect of the country's relationship with the United States.

Key terms are set in boldface and defined in the margin of the page where the term is first introduced and in the complete glossary at the end of the book. The glossary defines many key concepts that are used broadly in comparative politics.

Student Research and Exploration. In Chapter 1, students are enabled to do further research using a sidebar box that discusses the use of the Internet in the study of comparative politics. It notes a variety of websites where students can find more information about the countries covered in the book. Each chapter concludes with a list of suggested readings and websites.

An end-of-chapter **Summary** highlights the major themes and facts in the chapter.

Supplemental Teaching and Learning Aids and Database Editions

Instructor Companion Website
ISBN: 9781285865416

This Instructor Companion Website is an all-in-one multimedia online resource for class preparation, presentation, and testing. Accessible through www.cengage.com/login with your faculty account, you will find the following available for download: book-specific Microsoft® PowerPoint® presentations; a Test Bank compatible with multiple learning management systems; an Instructor Manual; Microsoft® PowerPoint® Image Slides; and a JPEG Image Library.

The Test Bank, offered in Blackboard, Moodle, Desire2Learn, Canvas, and Angel formats, contains Learning Objective–specific multiple-choice and essay questions for each chapter. Import the test bank into your LMS to edit and manage questions, and to create tests.

The Instructor's Manual contains chapter-specific learning objectives, an outline, key terms with definitions, and a chapter summary. Additionally, the Instructor's Manual features a critical thinking question, lecture launching suggestion, and an in-class activity for each learning objective.

The Microsoft® PowerPoint® presentations are ready-to-use, visual outlines of each chapter. These presentations are easily customized for your lectures and offered along with chapter-specific Microsoft® PowerPoint® Image Slides and JPEG Image Libraries.

Instant Access Code for Cognero

ISBN: 9781285865478
Cengage Learning Testing Powered by Cognero is a flexible online system that allows you to author, edit, and manage test bank content from multiple Cengage Learning solutions, create multiple test versions in an instant, and deliver tests from your LMS, your classroom, or wherever you want. The test bank for *Introduction to Comparative Politics*, 7th Edition, contains Learning Objective–specific multiple-choice and essay questions for each chapter.

Student Companion Website

ISBN: 9781285865409
This free companion website for *Introduction to Comparative Politics* is accessible through cengagebrain.com and allows students access to chapter-specific interactive learning tools including flashcards, glossaries, and more.

CourseReader 0-30: Comparative Politics

Printed Access Code ISBN: 9781111477608
Instant Access Code ISBN: 9781111477622
CourseReader for Comparative Politics allows you to create your reader, your way, in just minutes. This affordable, fully customizable online reader provides access to thousands of permissions-cleared readings, articles, primary sources, and audio and video selections from the regularly updated Gale research library database. This easy-to-use solution allows you to search for and select just the material you want for your courses. Each selection opens with a descriptive introduction to provide context and concludes with critical-thinking and multiple-choice questions to reinforce key points.

CourseReader is loaded with convenient tools like highlighting, printing, note-taking, and downloadable PDFs and MP3 audio files for each reading. CourseReader is the perfect complement to any Political Science course. It can be bundled with your current textbook, sold alone, or integrated into your learning management system. CourseReader 0-30 allows access to up to 30 selections in the reader. Please contact your Cengage sales representative for details.

As our discussion of the critical junctures of 1989, 9/11/01, 2008, 2011, and 2014 suggests political change is a constant feature of our contemporary world. Not much is certain about what the future will hold—except that the political world will be endlessly fascinating and comparative analysis will continue to be an important tool for trying to make sense of it. Welcome aboard!

Acknowledgments

We are grateful to colleagues who have reviewed and critiqued past and current editions of ICP:

Joseph Ellis, *Wingate University*
Katharina Felts, *Loudoun Valley High School*
Gunther Hega, *Western Michigan University*
Kira Hoilman, *Potomac Falls High School*
Debra Holzhauer, *Southeast Missouri State University*
Anika Leithner, *California Polytechnic State University*

In addition, we thank the talented and professional staff who helped edit and publish ICP7: Scott Greenan, Associate Product Manager; Kate Scheinman, Senior Content Developer; Carolyn Merrill, Product Team Manager; Laura Hildebrand, Senior Media Developer; Amy Bither, Associate Content Developer; and Abigail Hess, Product Assistant.

M. K.
J. K.
W. A. J.

1

Introducing Comparative Politics

Mark Kesselman, Joel Krieger, and William A. Joseph

THE GLOBAL CHALLENGE OF COMPARATIVE POLITICS

▼ Focus Questions

- What are two examples of how comparison can bring to light features that might otherwise not be observed?

- Describe a discussion in which you used the comparative method to make a point.

It has been said that the personality of students and scholars tends to resemble the characteristics of what they study. We might stretch this observation to speculate that what fascinated you as a child might have attracted you to comparative politics. As a child did you love to observe the shape-shifting images through the lens of a kaleidoscope? If you did, then you are a natural for comparative politics—for you are sure to be fascinated by the endlessly shifting developments of the contemporary world of politics, and the range and depth of challenges faced by political elites and ordinary citizens around the world.

As a subject for study within political science, comparative politics is the only subfield within political science that defines a method in its name. Comparative politics is both a subject matter and a method of analysis. As a subject matter it studies the politics of your own and other countries and peoples by analyzing patterns of similarity and difference, primarily at the national (country) level.

The drumbeat of politics goes on and on, but as the French say, the more things change, the more they stay the same.

The current era of politics remains a combustible and volatile mix in which uncertainty alternates with stability, and movements for peace and justice confront demonic forces that often divide societies along every axis of collective identities and divisions.

- Young people desperate for jobs and educational opportunity sometimes sinking together with—and sometimes pitted against—middle-aged job-holders and pensioners are burdened by what feels like perpetual austerity, gross inequality, and a loss of faith that things will improve.
- Ordinary citizens in every corner of the globe, from Occupy Wall Street activists in the United States to people in authoritarian regimes throughout the world, demanding democratic governments and the chance to enjoy the fruits of liberty.
- Ethnic, racial, and national tensions enflamed by hard times and a tightly integrated globalized global order, strain national unity—a precious and increasingly rare commodity.

Like the Internet technology that speeds up and transforms our lives, creates vast far-flung social networks, and makes possible the cell phone images and messages that flash instantly around the globe—and partly as a result of this technology—the political world is changing rapidly too.

Cold War

The hostile relations that prevailed between the United States and the Soviet Union from the late 1940s until the demise of the USSR in 1991.

In a quarter century, we have witnessed the collapse of the Berlin Wall in 1989, which ushered in the end of the **Cold War** era; the attack on the World Trade Center towers in 2001, ushering in a new era of global insecurity in the face of mounting terrorism; and the Great Recession of 2008, which threw the global economy into a tailspin, heightened political conflict, and widespread anxiety about the future. More recently, we have witnessed bellicose rhetoric from Russian president Vladimir Putin, backed by military takeover of the Crimea, which prompted Western countries to expel Russia from the Group of 8 (G-8)—an exclusive club of the eight most industrialized nations in the world: Canada, France, Germany, Italy, Japan, Russia, the United Kingdom, and the United States. Despite overheated rhetoric, we are not on the precipice of a new Cold War—a nuclear confrontation akin to the Cuban missile crisis is unthinkable; and the financial integration of a globalizing world mitigates the likelihood of increasing hostility between Russia and the West.

Russian president, Vladimir Putin (seated second on right), along with Crimean officials, signs the treaty of annexation in Moscow on March 18, 2014. The agreement made the former Ukrainian territory part of the Russian Federation.

Anadolu Agency/Getty Images

[handwritten margin note: 2014 – Crimea annexed as part of Russian Federation violates sovereignty of Ukraine]

While the changes that have occurred in the past quarter century are momentous, they were not unique in magnitude. They were preceded by other—even more momentous—changes, notably the two world wars of the twentieth century. And they will doubtless be followed by other momentous changes in the not too distant future. How can we make sense of the bewildering march of world history? Our aim in *Introduction to Comparative Politics* is to provide the tools to help bring order out of the apparent chaos of kaleidoscopic political change.

Introduction to Comparative Politics studies how different countries both shape and are shaped by the world order created by watershed events such as those that occurred in 1989, 2001, 2008, 2011, and 2014. Each of these dates describes a particularly important moment—what we call a **critical juncture**—that helps define key transitional moments.

Chapter 1 helps students navigate through the text by introducing the book's thematic framework, which is combined with a thorough analysis of the political institutions and processes of each country. It sets the stage and previews the thematic focus by noting five important critical junctures in recent history.

1. 1989, which symbolizes the end of the cold war, and a wave of capitalist democracies that replaced the former East versus West divisions in Europe and much of the world;
2. September 11, 2001, which reframes globalization, shifting attention away from the development gap to terrorism, security, and the use of force;
3. 2008, a year that ushered in intense financial and economic crisis around the world;
4. 2011, when pro-democracy movements toppled repressive regimes in North Africa and the Middle East, and Japan was rocked by a severe earthquake, tsunami, and nuclear disaster;
5. 2014, when a resurgent Russia, under the increasingly authoritarian leadership of Vladimir Putin, annexed the Crimea and violated the sovereignty of Ukraine.

critical juncture

An important historical moment when political actors make critical choices, which shape institutions and future outcomes.

Making Sense of Turbulent Times

The flash of newspaper headlines, television sound bites, and endless tweets can make politics look overwhelming and chaotic. Through the study of comparative politics, we can better understand a rapidly changing world. Political analysis involves more than blogging, talking head debates, or Monday-morning quarterbacking. It requires both a longer historical context and a framework for understanding unfolding developments.

This book describes and analyzes government institutions, policy-making processes, and other key aspects of politics in a wide range of countries. By using a framework that facilitates analyzing and comparing similarities and differences in a representative sample of countries, we can understand longer-term causes of political changes and continuities within nations. Each chapter explores a country's political development by reference to four themes that are central for understanding politics in today's world:

- *The Globalizing World of States:* the historical formation, internal organization, and interaction of states within the international order
- *Governing the Economy:* the role of the state in economic management
- *The Democratic Idea:* the spread of democracy and the challenges of democratization
- *The Politics of Collective Identities:* the sources and political impact of diverse **collective identities**, including class, gender, ethnicity, nationality, and religion

collective identities

The groups with which people identify, including gender, class, race, region, and religion, and which are the "building blocks" for social and political action.

These themes, discussed below, help us make political sense of both stable and tumultuous times.

The contemporary period presents an extraordinary challenge to those who study comparative politics, but the study of comparative politics also provides a unique opportunity for understanding this uncertain era. In order to appreciate the complexity of politics in countries around the world, we must look beyond any single national perspective. Today, business and trade, information technology, mass communications and culture, immigration and travel, as well as politics, forge deep connections—as well as deep divisions—among people worldwide. We urgently need a global and comparative perspective as we explore the politics of different countries and their interaction and interdependence with one another.

There is an added benefit of studying comparative politics: by comparing political institutions, values, and processes in countries around the world, the student of comparative politics acquires analytical skills that can also be used at home. After you study comparative politics, you begin to think comparatively. As comparison becomes second nature, we hope that you will look at the politics of your own country differently, with a wider and deeper, more analytical, focus that will inspire new reflections, interpretations, and insights. The contemporary world provides a fascinating laboratory for the study of comparative politics. We hope that you share our sense of excitement in the challenging effort to understand the complex and ever-shifting terrain of contemporary politics throughout the world.

Where Do You Stand?

There are more than 200 countries in the world: is it time for other countries to take on more of the burdens of global leadership that the United States has shouldered since the end of World War II?

How do you think the study of comparative politics will change the way you understand the United States—or whatever country you call home?

WHAT—AND HOW—COMPARATIVE POLITICS COMPARES

To "compare and contrast" is one of the most common human mental exercises, whether in the classroom study of literature, politics, or animal behavior—or in selecting dorm rooms or arguing with friends about your favorite movie. In the observation of politics, the use of comparisons is very old, dating in the Western world from the ancient Greek philosopher, Aristotle, who analyzed and compared the city-states of Greece in the fourth century BCE according to whether they were ruled by a single individual, a few people, or all citizens. The modern study of comparative politics refines and systematizes this age-old practice of evaluating some features of country X's politics by comparing it to the same features of country Y's politics.

Comparative politics is a subfield within the academic discipline of political science as well as a method or approach to the study of politics.[1] The subject matter of comparative politics is the domestic politics of countries. Within the discipline of political science, comparative politics is one of four areas of specialization. In addition to comparative politics, most political science (or government) departments in U.S. colleges and universities include courses in political theory, international relations, and American politics.

Because it is widely believed that students living in the United States should study the politics of their own country in depth, American politics is usually treated as a separate subfield of political science. The pattern of separating the study of politics at home and abroad is also common elsewhere, so students in Canada study Canadian politics as a distinct specialty, and Japanese students master Japanese politics.

However, there is no logical reason why study of the United States should not be included within the field of comparative politics—and good reason to do so. Comparative study can make it easier to recognize what is distinctive about the United States and what features it shares with some other countries. This is why we have included a chapter on the United States in this book.

Special mention should be made of the distinction between comparative politics and international relations. Comparative politics involves comparing domestic political institutions, processes, policies, conflicts, and attitudes in different countries; international relations involves studying the foreign policies of and interactions among countries, the role of international organizations such as the United Nations, and the growing influence of global actors, from multinational corporations to international human rights advocates to terrorist networks. In a globalized world, however, domestic and international politics routinely spill over into one another, so the distinction between the two fields is somewhat blurry. Courses in international relations nowadays often integrate a concern with how internal political processes affect states' behavior toward other states, while courses in comparative politics highlight the importance of transnational forces for understanding what goes on within a country's borders. One of the four themes that we use to analyze comparative politics, the "globalizing world of states," emphasizes the interaction of domestic and international forces in the politics of all nations.

It still makes sense to maintain the distinction between comparative politics and international relations. Much of the world's political activity continues to occur within national borders, and comparisons of domestic politics, institutions, and

Focus Questions ▽

- What do we mean by globalization?

- How does increased cross-border contact among countries and peoples affect political, social, and cultural life?

comparative politics

The field within political science that focuses on domestic politics and analyzes patterns of similarity and difference among countries.

globalization

The intensification of worldwide interconnectedness associated with the increased speed and magnitude of cross-border flows of trade, investment and finance, and processes of migration, cultural diffusion, and communication.

processes enable us to understand critical features that distinguish one country's politics from another's. Furthermore, we believe that, despite increased international economic competition and integration (a key aspect of **globalization**), countries are still the fundamental building blocks in structuring most political activity. Therefore, *Introduction to Comparative Politics* is built on in-depth case studies of a sample of important countries around the world.

The comparative approach principally analyzes similarities and differences among countries by focusing on selected political institutions and processes. As students of comparative politics (we call ourselves **comparativists**), we believe that we cannot make reliable statements about most political situations by looking at only one case.

THE INTERNET AND THE STUDY OF COMPARATIVE POLITICS

The Internet can be a rich source of information about the politics of countries around the world. Following are some of the types of information you can find on the Web. We haven't included URLs since they change so often. But you should be able to find the websites easily through a key word search on Google or another search engine.

- **Current events.** Most of the world's major news organizations have excellent websites. Among those we recommend for students of comparative politics are the British Broadcasting Corporation (BBC), Cable News Network (CNN), the *New York Times*, and the *Washington Post*.
- **Elections.** Results of recent (and often past) elections, data on voter turnout, and descriptions of different types of electoral systems can be found at the International Election Guide (IFES), Elections by Country/Wikipedia, and the International Institute for Democracy and Electoral Assistance.
- **Statistics.** You can find data helpful both for understanding the political, economic, and social situations in individual countries and for comparing countries. Excellent sources of statistics are the Central Intelligence Agency (CIA), United Nations Development Program (UNDP), and **World Bank**[*].

There are many websites that bring together data from other sources. These enable you not only to access the statistics, but also to chart or map them in a variety of ways. See, for example, nationmaster.com and gapminder.com.

- **Rankings and ratings.** Many organizations provide rankings or ratings of countries along some dimension based on comparative statistical analysis. We provide the following examples of these in the data that appear at the end of this chapter: the UNDP **Human Development Index (HDI)**; the **Global Gender Gap**; the **Environmental Performance Index**; the **Corruption Perceptions Index**; and the **Freedom in the World rating**. Others you might consult are the UNDP's Gender-Related Development Index (GDI) and Gender Empowerment Measure (GEM); the World Bank's Worldwide Governance Indicators

Project; the Index of Economic Freedom; and the Press Freedom Index. *A note of caution: Some of these sites may have a political perspective that influences the way they collect and analyze data. As with any Web source, be sure to check out who sponsors the site and what type of organization it is.*

- **Official information and documents.** Most governments maintain websites in English. The first place to look is the website of the country's embassy in Washington, D.C., Ottawa, or London. The United Nations delegations of many countries also have websites. Governments often have English-language versions of their official home pages, including governments with which the United States does not have official relations, such as Cuba and North Korea.
- **The United States Department of State.** The State Department's website has background notes on most countries. American embassies around the world provide information on selected topics about the country in which they are based.
- **Maps.** The Perry-Castañeda Library Map Collection at the University of Texas is probably the best currently available online source of worldwide maps at an educational institution.
- **General comparative politics.** Several American and British universities host excellent websites that provide links to a multitude of Internet resources on comparative politics (often coupled with international relations), such as Columbia University, Emory University, Keele University (UK), Princeton University, and Vanderbilt University. Do a search for "comparative politics resources" with the university name to get to these websites.

MAKING CONNECTIONS How has easy access to the Internet changed the way you do research? Is there a down side?

[*]Definitions of key terms in this boxed feature appear in the Glossary, which begins on p. 697.

We often hear statements such as: "The United States has the best health care system in the world." Comparativists immediately wonder what kinds of health care systems exist in other countries, what they cost and how they are financed, how it is decided who can receive medical care, how effectively they deliver health care to their citizens, and so on. As we know from the ongoing controversies over the Affordable Care Act, there is little agreement about what "the Best" means when it comes to health care systems. Is it the one that provides the widest access? The one that is the most technologically advanced? The one that is the most cost effective? The one that produces the healthiest population?

None of us would declare the winner for best picture at the Academy Awards without seeing more than one—and even better, all—of the nominated movies! Shouldn't we be as critically minded and engaged when we are comparing and evaluating critical public policy issues decisions?

Some comparativists focus on comparing government institutions, such as the legislature, executive, political parties, or court systems, in different countries.[2] Others compare specific political processes, such as voting or policies on a particular issue, for example, education or the environment.[3] Some comparative political studies take a thematic approach and analyze broad topics, such as the causes and consequences of nationalist movements or revolutions in different countries.[4] Comparative studies may also involve comparisons of an institution, policy, or process through time, in one or several countries. For example, some studies have analyzed a shift in the orientation of economic policy that occurred in many advanced capitalist countries in the 1980s from **Keynesianism**, an approach that gives priority to government regulation of the economy, to **neoliberalism**, which emphasizes the importance of market-friendly policies.[5] And many comparativists study politics within a single country, often within a framework that draws on similarities and differences with other countries.[6]

Level of Analysis

Comparisons can be useful for political analysis at several different levels of a country, such as cities, regions, provinces, or states. A good way to begin the study of comparative politics is with **countries**. Countries are distinct, politically defined territories that encompass governments, composed of political institutions, as well as cultures, economies, and collective identities. Although countries are often highly divided by internal conflicts, people within their borders may have close ties to those in other countries, and business firms based in one country may have operations in many others. Countries have historically been among the most important sources of a people's collective political identity. They are the major arena for organized political action in the modern world.

Within a given country, the **state** is almost always the most powerful cluster of institutions. But just what is the state? The way the term is used in comparative politics is probably unfamiliar to many students. In the United States, it usually refers to the states in the federal system—California, Illinois, New York, Texas, and so on. But in comparative politics, the state refers to the key political institutions responsible for making, implementing, and adjudicating important policies in a country. Thus, we refer to the "German state" and the "Mexican state." The state is synonymous with what is often called the "government," or in the United States, the "administration." The state also implies a more durable entity. Governments may come and go, but the institutions that comprise the state generally endure (unless overthrown from within or conquered by other states in war).

comparativist

A political scientist who studies the similarities and differences in the domestic politics of various countries.

Keynesianism

Named after the British economist John Maynard Keynes, an approach to economic policy in which state economic policies are used to regulate the economy in an attempt to achieve stable economic growth.

During a recession, state budget deficits are used to expand demand in an effort to boost both consumption and investment, and to create employment. During periods of high growth when inflation threatens, cuts in government spending and a tightening of credit are used to reduce demand.

neoliberalism

A term used to describe government policies aiming to promote free competition among business firms within the market, including reduced governmental regulation and social spending.

country

A territory defined by boundaries generally recognized in international law as constituting an independent country.

state

The most powerful political institutions in a country, including the executive, legislative, and judicial branches of government, the police, and armed forces.

executive

The agencies of government that implement or execute policy.

cabinet

The body of officials (e.g., ministers, secretaries) who direct executive departments presided over by the chief executive (e.g., prime minister, president).

bureaucracy

An organization structured hierarchically, in which lower-level officials are charged with administering regulations codified in rules that specify impersonal, objective guidelines for making decisions.

legislature

One of the primary political institutions in a country, in which elected or appointed members are charged with responsibility for making laws and usually for authorizing expenditure of the financial resources for the state to carry out its functions.

judiciary

One of the primary political institutions in a country; responsible for the administration of justice and in some countries for determining the constitutionality of state decisions.

legitimacy

A belief by powerful groups and the broad citizenry that a state exercises rightful authority.

The most important state institutions are the **executive**—usually, the president and/or prime minister and the **cabinet**. Other key state institutions include the military, police, and **bureaucracy**. In some countries, the executive includes the communist party leadership (such as in China), the head of a military government (as in Nigeria until 1999), or the supreme religious leader (as in the Islamic Republic of Iran). Alongside the executive, the **legislature** and the **judiciary** comprise the institutional apex of state power. The inter-relationships and functions of these institutions vary from country to country and through time within countries.

States claim, usually, but not always with considerable success, the right to make rules—notably, laws, administrative regulations, and court decisions—that are binding for people within the country. Even democratic states—in which top officials are chosen by procedures that authorize all citizens to participate—can survive only if they can preserve dominance internally and protect their independence with regard to other states and external groups that may threaten them. Many countries have highly repressive states whose political survival depends largely on military and police powers. Even in such states, however, long-term stability requires that the ruling regime have some measure of political **legitimacy**; that is, the support of a significant segment of the citizenry (in particular, more influential citizens and groups) who believe that the state is entitled to demand compliance. Political legitimacy is greatly affected by the state's ability to "deliver the goods" to its people through satisfactory economic performance and at least a minimum distribution of economic resources. Moreover, as the upheavals in the Arab world in 2011 dramatized, legitimacy is much more secure when there is some measure of democracy.

Thus, *Introduction to Comparative Politics* looks closely at both the state's role in governing the economy and the pressures exerted on states to develop and extend democratic participation.

You will see from the country chapters in this book that the organization of state institutions varies widely, and that these differences have a powerful impact on political, economic, and social life. Therefore, we devote considerable attention to institutional variations, along with their political implications. Each country study begins with an analysis of how the state has evolved historically; that is, **state formation**. One critical difference among states involves the extent to which citizens in a country share a common sense of nationhood; that is, a belief that the state's geographic boundaries coincide with the political identity of the people who live within those boundaries, what can be described as a sense of solidarity and shared values based on being citizens of the same country. When state boundaries and national identity coincide, the resulting formation is called a **nation-state**. A major source of political instability can occur when state boundaries and national identity do not coincide. In many countries around the world, nationalist movements within a state's borders challenge existing boundaries and seek to secede to form their own state, sometimes in alliance with movements from neighboring countries with whom they claim to share a common heritage. Such is the case with the Kurds, an ethnic group whose members live in Turkey, Syria, and Iraq. Many groups of Kurds have fought to establish an independent nation-state of Kurdistan. When a nationalist movement has distinctive ethnic, religious, and/or linguistic ties opposed to those of other groups in the country, conflicts are likely to be especially intense. India and Nigeria, for example, have experienced particularly violent episodes of what has been termed ethnonationalist conflict. Tibet is an example of ethnic conflict within a country, China, whose population otherwise has a strong sense of national identity.

Young people were at the forefront of the democracy movements that shook the Middle East and North Africa in 2011.

Yahya arhab/epa/Landov

Causal Theories

Because countries are the basic building blocks in politics and because states are the most significant political organizations within countries, these are two critical units for comparative analysis. The comparativist seeks to measure and explain similarities and differences among countries or states. One widely used approach in doing such comparative analysis involves developing **causal theories**—hypotheses that can be expressed formally in a causal mode: "If X happens, then Y will be the result." Such theories include factors (the **independent variables**, symbolized by X) that are believed to influence some outcome (the **dependent variable**, symbolized by Y) that the analyst wants to explain.

For example, it is commonly argued that if a country's economic pie shrinks, conflict among groups will intensify. This hypothesis claims what is called an inverse correlation between variables: as X varies in one direction (the economic pie shrinks), Y varies in the opposite direction (political and economic conflict over the economic pie increases). This relationship might be tested by statistical analysis of a large number of cases (Large N Analysis) or by analyzing one or several country cases in depth to determine how relevant relationships have varied historically (Small N Analysis). Even when the explanation does not involve the explicit testing of hypotheses (and often it does not), comparativists try to identify significant patterns that help explain political similarities and differences among countries.

It is important to recognize the limits on just how "scientific" political science—and thus comparative politics—can be. Two important differences exist between the "hard" (or natural) sciences like physics and chemistry and the social sciences. First, social scientists study people who exercise their political will and may act in an

state formation

The historical development of a state, often marked by major stages, key events, or turning points (critical junctures) that influence the contemporary character of the state.

nation-state

A country in which the state and national identity coincide.

causal theories

An influential approach in comparative politics that involves trying to explain why "if X happens, then Y is the result."

independent variable

The variable symbolized by X in the statement that "If X happens, then Y will be the result"; in other words, the independent variable is a cause of Y (the dependent variable).

dependent variable

The variable symbolized by Y in the statement that "If X happens, then Y will be the result"; in other words, the dependent variable is the outcome of X (the independent variable).

unpredictable way, as the events of 2011 in the Middle East and North Africa power-fully demonstrate. This does not mean that people choose in a totally arbitrary fash-ion. We choose within the context of material constraint, institutional dictates, and cultural preferences. But there will always be a gulf between the natural and social sciences because of their different objects of study.

In the natural sciences, experimental techniques can be applied to isolate the contribution of distinct factors on a particular outcome. It is possible to change the value or magnitude of a factor—for example, the force applied to an object—and measure how the outcome has consequently changed. There is a lively debate about whether the social sciences should seek scientific explanations comparable to what prevails in the natural sciences, such as physics. An approach largely bor-rowed from economics, called **rational choice theory**, has become influential—and highly controversial—in political science, including comparative politics, in recent years.[7] Rational choice theory focuses on how individuals act strategically (that is, rationally) in an attempt to achieve goals that maximize their interests. Such actions involve varied activities like voting for a particular candidate or rebelling against the government. Proponents of rational choice generally use deductive and quan-titative methods to construct models of political behavior that they believe can be applied across all types of political systems and cultures. The appeal of rational choice theory lies in its capacity to provide theoretical and practical insights about comparative politics through formal models based on the assumption that individ-ual actors pursue goals efficiently. But this approach has been criticized for claim-ing to explain large-scale and complex social phenomena by reference to individual choices. It has also been criticized for dismissing the importance of variations in historical experience, political culture, identities, institutions, and other key aspects of the political world.

The study of comparative politics offers many challenges, including the com-plexity of the subject matter, the fast pace of change in the contemporary world, and the impossibility of manipulating variables or replicating conditions. As a result, most comparativists probably agree on a middle course that avoids either focusing exclusively on one country or blending all countries indiscriminately. If we study only individual countries without any comparative framework, compara-tive politics would become merely the study of a series of isolated cases. It would be impossible to recognize what is most significant in the collage of political charac-teristics that we find in the world's many countries. As a result, the understanding of patterns of similarity and difference among countries would be lost, along with an important tool for evaluating what is and what is not unique about a country's political life.

If we go to the other extreme and try to make universal claims, we would tend to ignore significant national differences and patterns of variation. The political world is incredibly complex, shaped by an extraordinary array of factors and an almost endless interplay of variables. Indeed, after a brief period in the 1950s and 1960s when many comparativists tried—and failed—to develop a grand theory that would apply to all countries, most comparativists now agree on the value of **middle-level theory**, that is, theories focusing on specific features of the political world, such as institutions, policies, or classes of similar events, such as revolutions or elections.

Consider an example of middle-level theory that would help us understand the developments of 2011—theories of transitions from authoritarian to more democratic forms of government. Comparativists have long analyzed the processes through which many countries with authoritarian forms of government, such as

---

rational choice theory

An approach to analyzing political decision making and behavior that assumes that individual actors rationally pursue their aims in an effort to achieve the most positive net result. Rational choice is often associated with the pursuit of self-interested goals, but the theory permits a wide range of motivations, including altruism.

---

middle-level theory

Seeks to explain phenomena in a limited range of cases, in particular, a specific set of countries with particular characteristics, such as parliamentary regimes, or a particular type of political institution (such as political parties) or activity (such as protest).

military **dictatorships** and one-party regimes, have developed more participatory and democratic regimes. In studying this process, termed **democratic transitions**, comparativists do not either treat each national case as unique or try to construct a universal pattern that ignores all differences.[8] Students of democratic transitions seek to identify the weak links in authoritarian regimes, such as declining economic performance, a weakening of the regime's repressive capacity, and a switch in loyalty by influential insiders, that result in the crumbling of the authoritarian regime.

We believe that students will be in a better position to consider these questions—and provide the most powerful answers—after gaining a solid grasp of political continuities and contrasts in diverse countries around the world. It is this goal that we put front and center in *Introduction to Comparative Politics*.

dictatorships

A form of government in which power and political control are concentrated in one or a few rulers who have concentrated and nearly absolute power.

democratic transition

The process of a state moving from an authoritarian to a democratic political system.

Where Do You Stand?

Is declining economic performance or political instability a greater threat to a regime?

Ten years from now will Edward Snowden be viewed as patriot defending civil liberties and conscious or a traitor who has damaged American security?

THEMES FOR COMPARATIVE ANALYSIS

 SECTION **3**

Our framework in *Introduction to Comparative Politics*, comprised of four core themes, provides a guide to understanding many features of contemporary comparative politics. But we urge students (and rely on instructors!) to challenge and amplify our interpretations. Further, we want to note that a textbook builds from existing theory but does not construct or test new hypotheses. That task is the goal of original scholarly studies.

Focus Questions ▽

- Which one of the four themes presented for comparative analysis seems the most important? Why? The least important? Why?

- Give an example of how, in one particular country, features of one theme can affect the features of another theme.

institutional design

The institutional arrangements that define the relationships between executive, legislative, and judicial branches of government and between the national government and subnational units such as states in the United States.

Theme 1: A Globalizing World of States

Our first theme, *a globalizing world of states*, focuses on the central importance of states in the understanding of comparative politics. International organizations, such as the United Nations, private actors like transnational corporations, such as Microsoft, and non-governmental organizations (NGOs), such as Amnesty International, play a crucial role in politics. But states provide security to their citizens, make and enforce laws, and to varying degrees provide citizens with social protection in times and circumstances of need.

Our globalizing world of states theme highlights that states are still the basic building blocks in world politics. The theme also analyzes the importance of variations among the way that states are organized, in other words, the mix of political institutions that distinguishes, for example, democratic from authoritarian regimes. Country chapters emphasize the importance of understanding similarities and differences in state formation and **institutional design.** We identify critical junctures of

World Trade Organization (WTO)

A global international organization that oversees the "rules of trade" among its member states. The main functions of the WTO are to serve as a forum for its members to negotiate new agreements and resolve trade disputes. Its fundamental purpose is to lower or remove barriers to free trade.

International Monetary Fund (IMF)

The International Monetary Fund is the global institution with a mandate to "foster global monetary cooperation, secure financial stability, facilitate international trade, promote high employment and sustainable economic growth, and reduce poverty." It has been particularly active in helping countries that are experiencing serious financial problems. In exchange for IMF financial or technical assistance, a country must agree to a certain set of conditions that promote economic liberalization.

North American Free Trade Agreement (NAFTA)

A treaty among the United States, Mexico, and Canada implemented on January 1, 1994, that largely eliminates trade barriers among the three nations. NAFTA serves as a model for an eventual Free Trade Area of the Americas zone that could include most nations in the Western Hemisphere.

state formation: key events like colonial conquest, defeat in war, economic crises, or revolutions that impact and shape states. We also study variations in states' economic management strategies and capacities, diverse patterns of political institutions, such as the contrast between presidential and parliamentary forms in democratic states, the relationship of the state with social groups, and unresolved challenges that the state faces from within and outside its borders.

The globalized world of states theme also emphasizes the interaction between the national and the international levels in shaping the politics of all countries. Here the theme points in two directions: One focuses on a state's influence in affecting other states and the international economic and political arena; the other focuses on the impact of international forces on the state's activities within the country's borders.

Regarding the first direction, states dwarf other influential actors, such as transnational corporations, in the exercise of power that matters, whether with regard to war, peace, and national security, or when it comes to providing educational opportunities, health care, and pensions (social security). The second dimension of the globalizing world-of-states theme underlines the multiple global forces that have significant impacts on the domestic politics of virtually all countries.[9] A wide array of international organizations and treaties, including the United Nations, the European Union, the **World Trade Organization (WTO)**, the World Bank, the **International Monetary Fund (IMF)**, and the **North American Free Trade Agreement (NAFTA)**, challenge the sovereign control of national governments within their own territories. Transnational corporations, international banks, and currency traders in New York, London, Frankfurt, Hong Kong, and Tokyo affect countries and people throughout the world. A country's political borders do not protect its citizens from global warming, environmental pollution, or infectious diseases that come from abroad.

Thanks to the global diffusion of radio, television, twitter and the Internet, and social media of all kinds, people nearly everywhere can become remarkably well informed about international developments. This knowledge may fuel popular demands that governments intervene to stop atrocities in, for example, faraway Kosovo, Rwanda, Libya, and Syria or provide aid to the victims of natural disasters, as happened after a devastating earthquake in China in 2008 and a tsunami in Japan in 2011 each killed many thousands of people. And heightened global awareness may encourage citizens to hold their own government to internationally recognized standards of human rights and democracy. Such awareness played a significant role in motivating people to join prodemocracy movements in North Africa and the Middle East in 2011.

A puzzle: To what extent can even the most powerful states (especially the United States) preserve their autonomy and impose their will on others in a globalized world? And in what ways are the poorer and less powerful countries particularly vulnerable to the pressures of globalization and disgruntled citizens?

Increasingly, the politics and policies of states are shaped by diverse international factors often lumped together under the category of globalization. At the same time, many states face increasingly restive constituencies within their country who challenge the power and legitimacy of central governments. In reading the country case studies in this book, try to assess how pressures from both above and below—outside and inside—influence a state's policies and its ability to retain citizen support.

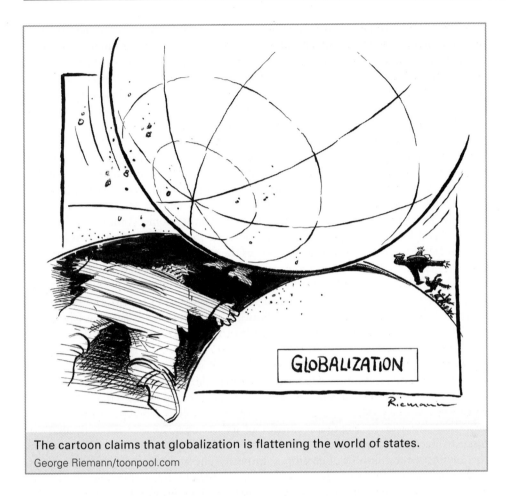

The cartoon claims that globalization is flattening the world of states.

George Riemann/toonpool.com

Theme 2: Governing the Economy

The success of states in maintaining sovereign authority and control over their people is greatly affected by their ability to ensure that enough goods are produced and services delivered to satisfy the needs and demands of their populations. Citizen discontent with communist states' inadequate economic performance was an important reason for the rejection of communism and the disintegration of the Soviet Union and its allies in Eastern Europe in 1989. In contrast, China's stunning success in promoting economic development has generated powerful support for the communist regime in that country.

Pursuing effective economic performance is near the top of every state's political agenda, and "governing the economy"[10]—how a state organizes production and the extent and nature of its intervention in the economy—is a key element in its overall pattern of governance. The core of governing the economy involves the strategies that states choose in an attempt to improve economic performance, deal with economic crises, and compete in international markets. A key contrast between various strategies is the relative importance of private market forces versus government direction of the economy.

political economy

The study of the interaction between the state and the economy, that is, how the state and political processes affect the economy and how the organization of the economy affects political processes.

The term **political economy** refers to the interaction between politics and economics, that is, to how government actions affect economic performance and how economic performance in turn affects a country's political processes. We place great importance on political economy in *Introduction to Comparative Politics* because we believe that politics in all countries is deeply influenced by the interaction between a country's government and the economy in both its domestic and international dimensions.

Is there a particular formula for state economic governance that produces maximum success in promoting national prosperity? In particular, is there an optimum balance between state direction of the economy and free markets, that is, the ability of private business firms to operate without government supervision and regulation? On the one hand, some economic winners and losers among the world's countries display a pattern of extensive state intervention in the economy. And, similarly, other winners and losers engage in relatively little state intervention. Thus, it is not the *degree* of state intervention that distinguishes the economic success stories from those that have fared less well. For example, a study of the world's affluent capitalist economies identifies quite different patterns of political economy that have been associated with strong economic performance.[11] Studies seeking to explain the East Asian "economic miracles"—Japan, Taiwan, South Korea, and more recently China—as well as the variable economic performance of other countries, highlight the diversity of approaches that have been pursued.[12]

Comparative analysis of how well different states govern their economies becomes even more complex when one considers the appropriate yardstick to measure economic success. Should economic performance be measured solely by how rapidly a country's economy grows? By how equitably it distributes the fruits of economic growth? By the quality of life of its citizenry, as measured by such criteria as life expectancy, level of education, and unemployment rate? What about the environmental impact of economic growth? These are very different measures. Although many are positively correlated, there is far from a complete correspondence. Recently, there has been much greater attention to the issue of **sustainable development**, the pattern that promotes ecologically sound ways to modernize the economy and raise the standard of living. (See "How Is Development Measured?") We invite you to consider these questions as you study the political economies of the countries analyzed in this book.

sustainable development

An approach to promoting economic growth that seeks to minimize environmental degradation and depletion of natural resources.

A puzzle: What is the relationship between democracy and successful national economic performance? This is a question that students of political economy have long pondered—and to which there are no fully satisfactory answers. Although all economies, even the most powerful, experience ups and downs, all durable democracies (with the exception of India) have been notable economic success stories. On the other hand, several East Asian countries with nondemocratic regimes—notably South Korea, Taiwan, and Singapore in the 1960s and 1970s, and Malaysia and Thailand in the 1980s and 1990s—achieved remarkable records of development. China, an authoritarian **communist party–state** that has enjoyed the highest growth rate among major economies in the world since the early 1990s, provides a vivid case of development without democracy. An influential study by political scientist Adam Przeworski and colleagues concludes, after an exhaustive comparison of the economic performance of democratic and authoritarian states, that there is no clear-cut answer to the question of which regime is better able to achieve superior economic performance.[13] Similarly, Nobel Prize–winning economist Amartya

communist party–state

A type of nation-state in which the communist party attempts to exercise a complete monopoly on political power and controls all important state institutions.

(handwritten margin notes: "How we measure a good economy", "poor democracy = development", "No poor democracy")

GLOBAL CONNECTION

How Is Development Measured?

As we have noted, we put particular importance on understanding the relationship between the political system and the economy in the study of the politics of any country and in our overall approach to comparative politics. Each of the country case studies describes and analyzes the role of the government in making economic policy. They also take special note of the impact of the global economy on national politics. This book makes frequent reference to two commonly used measures of the overall size or power of a country's economy:

- **gross domestic product (GDP)***: The value of the total goods and services produced by the country during a given year.
- **gross national product (GNP)**: GDP plus income earned abroad by the country's residents.

A country's GDP and GNP are different, but not hugely so. In this book, we usually use GDP, calculated according to an increasingly popular method called **purchasing power parity (PPP)**. PPP takes into account the real cost of living in a particular country by calculating how much it would cost in the local currency to buy the same "basket of goods" in different countries. For example, how many dollars in the United States, pesos in Mexico, or rubles in Russia does it take to buy a certain amount of food or to pay for housing? Many scholars think that PPP provides a relatively reliable (and revealing) tool for comparing the size of an economy among countries. In terms of annual total output according to PPP, the world's ten largest economies, in descending order, are the United States, China, India, Japan, Germany, Russia, Brazil, Britain, France, and Mexico.

Total GDP is a useful measure. It helps to understand a country's overall weight in the world economy. But because this measure does not take into account the size of the population, it does not reveal anything about the standard of living of the country's citizens. China and India are economic powerhouses according to their total GDP, but their citizens' average income ranks far below that of many countries in the world. A better way to measure and compare the level of economic development and citizens' standard of living in different countries is to look at annual GDP *per capita* (per person), in other words, to divide a country's total economic output by its population. Although China has the world's second-largest economy as measured by total output, it falls to 120th out of 227 economies in terms of its annual GDP *per capita* ($9,800); India, the world's third largest economy (with $4,000 *per capita* income) ranks 168th. The United States—by far the world's biggest economy—has the thirteenth highest GDP *per capita* ($52,800). Qatar ($102,100) and Liechtenstein ($89,400), with their tiny populations rank first and second in GDP *per capita*. Using GDP *per capita* provides a much better idea of which countries in the world are rich (developed) or poor (developing).

The comparative data charts at the end of this chapter provide total GDP and GDP *per capita* as well as other economic, geographic, demographic, and social information for our country case studies. The Comparative Rankings table also provides several ways of evaluating countries' economic, political, or public policy performance.

In 2014, an international team of scholars launched an important new comparative index that ranks countries according to what they call "social progress," which is defined as "the capacity of a society to meet the basic human needs of its citizens, establish the building blocks that allow citizens and communities to enhance and sustain the quality of their lives, and create the conditions for all individuals to reach their full potential." The **Social Progress Index (SPI)** is derived from twelve measures such as shelter, health and wellness, ecosystem sustainability, personal freedom and choice, and tolerance and inclusion. Out of 133 countries, the three with the highest SPI were New Zealand, Switzerland, and Iceland, while the three with the lowest were Chad, the Central African Republic, and Burundi. The countries covered in this book had the following SPI rankings: Brazil (46), Britain (13), China (90), France (20), Germany (12), India (102), Iran (94), Japan (14), Mexico (54), Nigeria (123), Russia (80), South Africa (69), and the United States (16).

MAKING CONNECTIONS As you look at the SPI rankings what two country rankings make you want to dig deeper because something about the ranking seemed surprising?

*Definitions of key terms in this boxed feature appear in the Glossary, which begins on p. 697.

Sen has argued, "There is no clear relation between economic growth and democracy in *either* direction."[14] As you read the country studies, try to identify why some states have been more successful than others in "governing the economy," that is, fostering successful economic performance.

Theme 3: The Democratic Idea

democracy

From the Greek *demos* (the people) and *kratos* (rule). A political system featuring: selection to public offices through free and fair elections; the right of all adults to vote; political parties that are free to compete in elections; government that operates by fair and relatively open procedures; political rights and civil liberties; an independent judiciary (court system); and civilian control of the military.

One of the most important and astonishing political developments in recent years has been the rapid spread of **democracy** throughout much of the world. There is powerful evidence of the strong appeal of democracy, that is, a regime in which citizens exercise substantial control over choice of political leaders and the decisions made by their governments.

According to statistical analysis of numerous measures of political freedom and civil liberties, the think tank Freedom House has calculated that in 1973, there were 43 countries that could be considered "free" (or democratic), 38 that were "partly free," and 69 that should be classified as "not free."[15] In 2014, the count was 88 free, 59 partly free, and 48 not free. In terms of population, 35 percent of the world's people lived in free countries in 1973, 18 percent in partly free, and 47 percent were citizens of countries ranked as not free. In 2014, the percentages were 40 percent free, 25 percent partly free, and 35 percent not free. (See Table 1.1.) Economist Amartya Sen has observed, "While democracy is not yet uniformly practiced, nor indeed uniformly accepted, in the general climate of world opinion, democratic governance has now achieved the status of being taken to be generally right."[16] As authoritarian rulers in countries from Albania to Zaire (now called the Democratic Republic of the Congo) have learned in recent decades, once persistent and widespread pressures for democratic participation develop, they are hard to resist. However, as brutal suppression of protesters in China (in 1989) and Libya and Bahrain (in 2011) demonstrated, dictators do not easily give up their power.

Table 1.1	The Spread of Democracy[a]		
Year	**Free Countries**	**Partly Free Countries**	**Not Free Countries**
1973	43 (35%)	38 (18%)	69 (47%)
1983	54 (36%)	47 (20%)	64 (44%)
1993[b]	75 (25%)	73 (44%)	38 (31%)
2014	88 (40%)	59 (25%)	48 (35%)[c]

[a] The number of countries in each category is followed by the percentage of the world population.

[b] In 1993, the large increase in the number of free and partly free countries was mostly due to the collapse of communist regimes in the Soviet Union and elsewhere. The main reason that there was a significant drop in the percentage of world population living in free countries in 1993 was that India was classified as partly free from 1991 through 1997. It has been ranked as free since 1998.

[c] The increase in the number of countries and percentage of people rated as not free countries in 2010 compared to 1993 reflects the fact that several countries, most notably Russia, were shifted from partly free to not free. Half of the world's "not free" population lives in China.

Source: Freedom House (www.freedomhouse.org)

What determines the growth, stagnation, or decline of democracy in a country? Comparativists have devoted enormous energy to studying this question. One scholar notes, "For the past two decades, the main topic of research in comparative politics has been democratization."[17] Yet, for all the attention it has received, there is no scholarly consensus on how and why democratization develops and becomes consolidated, remains incomplete, or is reversed. Just as there is no single route to economic prosperity, we have also learned that there is no one path to democracy, and that democratic transitions can be slow, uncertain, and reversible. Many of the country studies in *Introduction to Comparative Politics* analyze the diverse causes and sources of support for democracy; and some expose the fragility of democratic transitions.

In certain historical settings, democracy may result from a standoff or compromise among political contenders for power in which no one group can gain sufficient strength to control outcomes by itself. The result is that they "settle" for a democratic compromise in which power is shared. In some (but not all) cases, rival groups may conclude that democracy is preferable to civil war. Or, it may take a bloody civil war that produces stalemate to persuade competing groups to accept democracy as a second-best solution. Democracy may appeal to citizens in authoritarian nations because democratic regimes often rank among the world's most stable, affluent, free, and cohesive countries. In some cases, a regional demonstration effect occurs, in which a democratic transition in one country provokes democratic change in neighboring countries. This occurred in southern Europe in the 1970s, Latin America and parts of East Asia in the 1980s, Eastern and Central Europe in the 1990s, and in North Africa and the Middle East in 2011. Another important pressure for democracy is born of the human desire for dignity and equality. Even when dictatorial regimes appear to benefit their countries—for example, by promoting economic development or nationalist goals—citizens may demand democracy.

Is it possible to identify conditions that are necessary or sufficient for the democratic idea to take root and flourish? Comparativists have proposed, among such factors, secure national boundaries, a stable state, at least a minimum level of economic development, the widespread acceptance of democratic values, and agreement on the rules of democratic politics among those contending for power.

Institutional design also matters when it comes to producing stable democracies. Do certain kinds of political institutions facilitate compromise as opposed to polarization and hence greater stability? The balance of scholarly opinion suggests, for example, that parliamentary systems that tie the fates of the legislators to that of the prime minister tend to produce more consensual outcomes than do presidential systems, where the legislature and executive are independent from each other and often compete in setting national political agendas. As you read the country studies, note the patterns of similarity and difference regarding the degree of conflict or polarization in presidential systems (such as the United States and Mexico) and compare those cases to parliamentary systems (such as Britain).

Although certain economic, cultural, and institutional features enhance the prospects of democratic transitions and consolidations, democracy has flourished in unlikely settings. India, for example, is a long-established democracy that ranks in the bottom quarter of the world's countries in terms of per capita income. Hundreds of millions of Indians live in dire poverty. Yet, despite some important instances of undemocratic practices, India has had a vibrantly functioning democratic system since it became independent in 1947.

Democracy has also failed where it might be expected to flourish, most notably and with tragic consequences in highly educated and relatively wealthy Germany in the 1930s. Democracies vary widely in terms of how they have come into existence and in their concrete historical, institutional, economic, and cultural dimensions.

Displacing authoritarian regimes and holding elections does not guarantee the survival or durability of a fledgling democracy. A wide gulf exists between what comparativists have termed a *transition* to democracy and the *consolidation* of democracy. A transition involves toppling an authoritarian regime and adopting the basic institutions and procedures of democracy; consolidation requires fuller adherence to democratic principles and making democratic government more sturdy and durable. Below we further explore the important question of how to distinguish what we term *transitional democracies* from *consolidated democracies*. We consider the distinction of such great importance that it forms one basis for our scheme for classifying countries throughout the world.

The theme of the democratic idea requires us to examine the incompleteness of democratic agendas, even in countries with the longest experiences of representative democracy. Citizens may invoke the democratic idea to demand that their government be more responsive and accountable, as in the Civil Rights Movement in the United States. **Social movements** in some democratic countries have targeted the state because of its actions or inactions in such varied spheres as environmental regulation, reproductive rights, and race or ethnic relations. Comparative studies confirm that the democratic idea fuels political conflicts in even the most durable democracies because a large gap usually separates democratic ideals and the actual functioning of democratic political institutions. Moreover, social movements often organize because citizens perceive political parties—presumably, an important vehicle for representing citizen demands in democracies—as rigid and out of touch with the people.

A puzzle: Is there a relationship between democracy and political stability? Comparativists have debated whether democratic institutions contribute to political stability or, on the contrary, to political disorder.[18] On the one hand, democracy by its very nature permits political opposition. One of its defining characteristics is competition among those who aspire to gain political office. Political life in democracies is often turbulent and unpredictable. On the other hand, and perhaps paradoxically, the very fact that political opposition and competition are legitimate in democracies can deepen support for the state, even among opponents of a particular government. The democratic rules of the game may promote political stability by encouraging today's losers to reject the use of violence to press their claim to power. They may do so because they calculate that they have a good chance to win peacefully in future competition. Although deep flaws often mar democratic governance in countries that have toppled authoritarian regimes, a careful study finds that, once a country adopts a democratic regime, the odds are that it will endure.[19] As you learn about different countries, look for the stabilizing and destabilizing consequences of democratic transitions, the pressures (or lack of pressure) for democratization in authoritarian states, and the persistence of undemocratic elements even in established democracies.

Theme 4: The Politics of Collective Identities

How do individuals understand who they are in relation to the state and other citizens? How and why do they join in groups to advance shared political or other goals within a country? In other words, what are the sources of collective political identities? At one time, social scientists thought they knew. Scholars once argued that age-old loyalties of ethnicity, religious affiliation, race, and locality were being

social movements

Large-scale grassroots action that demands reforms of existing social practices and government policies.

dissolved and displaced as a result of economic, political, and cultural modernization. Comparativists thought that **social class**—solidarities based on the shared experience of work or, more broadly, economic position in society, had become the most important—indeed, nearly only—source of collective identity. They believed that in the typical political situation, groups formed on the basis of economic interest would pragmatically and peacefully pursue their interests. We now know that the formation of group attachments and the interplay of politically relevant collective identities are far more complex and uncertain.

In many long-established democracies, the political importance of identities based on class membership has declined. Economically based sources of collective identity do remain significant in influencing citizens' party affiliation and preferences about economic policy, and how the economic pie is divided and distributed. Especially in this era of austerity, the struggle over who gets what—and who decides who gets what—can be fierce. Indeed, these days class politics is making a comeback. But contrary to earlier predictions, in many countries nonclass identities have assumed growing, not diminishing, significance. Such identities are based on a sense of belonging to particular groups sharing a common language, region, religion, ethnicity, race, nationality, or gender.

The politics of collective political identity involves efforts to mobilize identity groups to influence political outcomes, ranging from the state's distribution of benefits, to economic and educational policy, the basis for political representation, and even territorial claims. Identity-based conflicts appear in most societies. Politics in democratic regimes (and, often in a more concealed way, in authoritarian regimes as well) involves a tug of war among groups over relative power and influence, both symbolic and substantive. Issues of inclusion, political recognition, representation, resource allocation, and the capacity to shape public policies, such as immigration, education, and the status of minority languages, remain pivotal in many countries.

Questions of representation are especially hard to resolve: Which groups should be considered legitimate participants in the political game? Who is included in a racial or ethnic community? Who speaks for the community or negotiates with a governmental authority on its behalf? Conflict about these issues can be intense because political leaders often seek to mobilize support by exploiting ethnic, religious, racial, or regional rivalries and by manipulating issues of identity and representation.

An especially important source of identity-based conflict involves ethnicity. And given the pace of migration and the tangled web of postcolonial histories that link colonizer to colonized, what country is not multiethnic? As political scientist Alfred Stepan points out, "…there are very few states in the entire world that are relatively homogeneous nation-states…."[20] In Britain, France, Germany, and the United States, issues of nationality, citizenship, and immigration—often linked to ethnic or racial factors—have often been hot-button political issues. Ethnic conflicts have been particularly frequent and intense in postcolonial countries, for example, in Nigeria, where colonial powers forced ethnic groups together when defining the country's boundaries and where borders were drawn with little regard to preexisting collective identities. The process of state formation has often sowed seeds for future conflict in many postcolonial nations.

Religion is another source of collective identity, as well as of severe political conflict, both within and among religious communities. Violent conflict among religious groups has recently occurred in India, Sri Lanka, and Nigeria. Such conflicts may spill over national boundaries and involve an especially ugly form of globalization. For example, leaders of al Qaeda targeted non-Muslim Western military forces stationed in what they regarded as the sacred soil of Saudi Arabia as a principal reason for the 9/11 attacks. At the same time, the political orientation of a particular religious

social class

A group whose members share common worldviews and aspirations determined largely by occupation, income, and wealth.

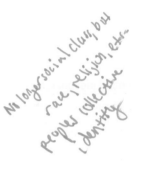

No longer social class but race, religion, etc. Peoples collective identity

community is not predetermined. The political posture associated with what it means to be Christian, Jewish, Muslim, or Hindu cannot simply be determined from holy texts. Witness the intense conflict *within* most religious communities today that pits liberal, secular elements against those who defend what they claim is a more orthodox, traditional interpretation.

distributional politics

The use of power, particularly by the state, to allocate some kind of valued resource among competing groups.

A puzzle: How do collective identities affect a country's **distributional politics**, that is, the process of deciding how resources are distributed, concretely, who gets what? when? how? Once identity demands are placed on the national agenda, can a government resolve them by distributing political, economic, and other resources in ways that redress the grievances of the minority or politically weaker identity groups?

Collective identities operate at the level of symbols, attitudes, values, and beliefs as well as at the level of material resources. The contrast between material- and nonmaterial-based identities and demands should not be exaggerated. In practice, most groups are animated both by feelings of attachment and solidarity and by the desire to obtain material benefits and political influence for their members. Nonetheless, the analytical distinction between material and nonmaterial demands remains useful. Furthermore, nonmaterial aspects of collective identities may make political disputes over ethnicity or religion or language or nationality especially divisive and difficult to resolve because in such cases it is harder to purchase peace through distributing material benefits.

These four themes provide our analytic scaffold. With an understanding of the method of comparative politics and the four themes in mind, we can now discuss how we have grouped the country studies in *Introduction to Comparative Politics* and how the text is organized to help students master the basics of comparative analysis.

Where Do You Stand?

Karl Marx wrote that the ruling ideas of an age are the ideas of the ruling class—in other words that those with power and wealth shape the values in a society. Do you agree—or do you think we are shaped more by the values we learn at home around the dinner table?

Are collective identities or economic interests more important to the understanding of comparative politics?

SECTION 4

CLASSIFYING POLITICAL SYSTEMS

▽ Focus Questions

- What are the advantages of using a typology based on levels of adherence to democratic practices? What are the disadvantages?

- What alternative would you propose?

There are more than 200 states in the world today. Although each state is unique, to avoid being overwhelmed by the sheer number, it makes sense to highlight categories of states that share some important features. It is useful to identify what distinguishes one category of relatively similar states from other categories, and to study how a state moves from one category to another as circumstances evolve. When comparativists classify a large number of cases into a smaller number of categories, or types, they introduce a **typology**. A typology is an analytic construct that helps us engage in comparisons that yield useful knowledge. In ICP we will employ a typology that distinguishes among consolidated democracies, mixed systems, and authoritarian regimes.

Typologies are also useful for making comparisons within the same political category. For example, Britain and the United States are consolidated democracies. But

Britain has a parliamentary form of government and the United States has a presidential one. What difference very different mixes of democratic institutions make in practice is the kind of important and intriguing question that lies at the heart of comparative politics.

As with many other important concepts, the meaning of democracy is a contentious subject among political scientists and citizens. Should democracy be defined solely on the basis of the procedures used to select top governmental officeholders? For a political system to be democratic, occupants of high office clearly must be selected on the basis of free and fair elections. However, are other elements also necessary for a system to qualify as democratic? For example, must there be respect for civil liberties; due process; the rule of law; freedom of expression and assembly; and the unfettered right to petition and criticize government? A narrow conception of democracy might not consider these elements as necessary. As a general matter, most comparativists, including ourselves, support a richer conception of democracy, one that includes additional core features as part of the definition of democratic.

Yet the matter does not end there, for it is necessary to translate abstract values to actual political practice. For example, we contend that democracy requires the right of privacy. However, how should this right be defined these days, in an era of routine mass surveillance and intercepts of communications by government? Another example: we believe that democracy requires an independent judiciary. Yet how is judicial independence to be guaranteed when judges are either elected—and therefore inclined to bow to public opinion; or appointed by elected representatives—and therefore inclined to defer to those who appoint them? It is also generally agreed that democracy requires freedom of religion—but this too might be hard to define in practice. Another element: we contend that democracy requires substantial gender equality. However, this requirement may also prove hard to define in theory and much harder to achieve in practice! A final element: many comparativists argue that democracy requires some leveling of the economic playing field. What, then, does this say about the quality of present-day American democracy, where the richest 1 percent of Americans own over one third of all U.S. wealth and the richest fifth own about 90 percent of all U.S. wealth?

We invite you to keep these issues in mind as you read the case studies of the **consolidated democracies**, which include Britain, France, Germany, Japan, India, and the United States. There is also a chapter on the European Union, which consists of consolidated democracies, including Britain, France, and Germany and the other countries of Western Europe, as well as democratic states that were established more recently, for example, in former communist party-states such as Poland and Bulgaria. Even in such long established democratic states, there remains a gap—often a substantial one—between the aspirations and ideals of democracy and the practice and results of the actually existing democracy. For example, police abuse and unequal legal treatment of citizens who are poor or from a racial or ethnic minority are all too common in countries generally considered high in the democratic rankings.

The reason why we highlight the importance of adhering to democratic procedures and institutional arrangements becomes apparent when we turn to the second category of democracy that we use in this book. In **mixed systems**, a façade of democratic institutions often conceals numerous practices that violate some core features of democracy. As a general matter, although there is usually greater legal protection of citizen rights and liberties in mixed systems than in authoritarian regimes—there

typology

A method of classifying by using criteria that divide a group of cases into smaller groups of cases whose members share common characteristics.

← what comparativists argue democracy required

consolidated democracies

Democratic political systems that have been solidly and stably established for an ample period of time and in which there is relatively consistent adherence to the core democratic principles.

mixed systems

Countries whose political systems exhibit some democratic and some authoritarian elements.

is considerably less than in consolidated democracies. The mixed systems that are covered in *Introduction to Comparative Politics* are Brazil, Mexico, South Africa, and Russia.

authoritarian regimes

A system of rule in which power depends not on popular legitimacy but on the coercive force of the political authorities.

How do we define **authoritarian regimes**—the third kind of political system in our typology? The simplest way is say that they lack most or even all of the features of a democracy. Thus, authoritarian regimes lack effective procedures for selecting political leaders through competitive elections based on universal suffrage; they include few institutionalized procedures for holding those with political power accountable to the citizens of the country; oppositional politics and dissent are severely restricted; people of different genders, racial groups, religions, and ethnicities do not enjoy equal rights; the legal system is highly politicized and the judiciary is not an independent branch of government capable of checking the power of the state or protecting the rights of citizens; and coercion and violence are part of the political process.

Clearly, then, authoritarian states are nondemocracies. But it isn't good social science to define something only by what it is not. The term *authoritarianism* refers to political systems in which power (or authority) is highly concentrated in a single individual, a small group of people, or a single political party, ethnic group, region, or institution. Furthermore, those with power are not selected by competitive elections, they claim an exclusive right to govern, and they use arbitrary force, among other means, to impose their will and policies on all who live under their authority.

As with states classified as democracies, there are an enormous variety of authoritarian regime types: communist party–states (e.g., China and Cuba); theocracies in which sovereign power is held by religious leaders and law is defined in religious terms (e.g., Iran); military governments (e.g., Thailand after the army overthrew the parliamentary government in 2014); absolute monarchies (e.g., Saudi Arabia); and personalistic dictatorships (e.g., Iraq under Saddam Hussein, North Korea under Kim Jong-un). Authoritarian regimes frequently claim that they embody a form of democracy, particularly in the contemporary era when the democratic idea seems so persuasive and powerful. For example, according to the Chinese Communist Party, the political system of the People's Republic of China is based on "socialist democracy," which it claims is superior to the "bourgeois democracy" of capitalist countries that favors the interests of wealthier citizens. But most political scientists would conclude that there is little substance to these claims and that in such states dictatorship far outweighs democracy. As the chapter on China will describe, the Communist Party monopolizes most decision making, and its leaders are chosen by self-selection rather than popular election.

Nevertheless, even countries classified as authoritarian may include democratic values and practices. In Iran, a theocratic authoritarian regime, there are vigorously contested multiparty elections, although the extent of contestation is limited by Islamic clergy who ultimately exercise sovereign power. In China, a form of grassroots democracy has been implemented in the more than 600,000 rural villages where just under half of the population lives. Even though the Communist Party still oversees the process, China's rural dwellers now have some real choice when they elect their local leaders. Such democratic elements in Iran and China are certainly significant in understanding politics in those countries; however, they do not fundamentally alter the authoritarian character of the state.

Our categories of consolidated democracies, mixed systems, and authoritarian regimes are not airtight, and some countries may straddle two categories. Consider Brazil, which we designate as a mixed system. Ever since democracy was

exception within authoritarian gov. →

restored in 1984, following a period of harsh military rule, Brazil has compiled a solid record of democratic practice. For example, since the return of civilian rule there have been several peaceful electoral alternations between dramatically different political coalitions. One might claim that Brazil should be classified as a consolidated democracy. We believe, however, that because of repeated violations of democratic procedures, political corruption, lack of entrenched democratic values, and extensive inequality (which is heavily coded in racial terms), Brazil remains a mixed system.

Another example of the difficulty of classifying states: We consider India a consolidated democracy because it has generally respected most democratic procedures identified above since it gained independence in 1947. There is intense political competition in India, elections are usually free and fair, and the Indian judiciary is quite independent. However, some might question our decision. For example, India has repeatedly experienced scenes of horrific communal violence, in which large numbers of Muslim, Sikh, and Christian minorities have been brutally massacred, sometimes with the active complicity of state officials.

A further point about our typology is that the boundaries among categories are fluid. Some of the countries classified as mixed systems are experiencing such political turmoil that they could very well fall out of any category of democracy. Take Russia, for example, which we classify as a mixed system but whose trajectory in the last several years years is in the authoritarian direction. Since Vladimir Putin's reelection as president in 2012, the Russian government has engaged in numerous undemocratic practices, including arbitrary detention and rigged trials of opponents, repeated violations of the constitution, and extensive political corruption. There are competitive but not fair elections, multiple parties but one dominant establishment party, terrible violations of civil liberties across the board, not to mention dangerously bellicose foreign policy and blatant disregard for the sovereignty Ukraine. We have kept Russia in the mixed system camp for now, but we are fully aware of the ominous tendencies that may move Russia into the authoritarian slot in our typology in the next edition of this book.

ORGANIZATION OF THE TEXT

SECTION 5

We selected the countries for the case studies in this book for their significance in terms of our comparative themes and because they provide an extensive sample of types of political regimes, levels of economic development, and geographic regions. Although each of the country studies makes important comparative references, the studies primarily provide in-depth descriptions and analyses of the politics of individual countries. At the same time, the country studies have identical formats, with common section and subsection headings to help you make comparisons and explore similar themes across the various cases. And each chapter emphasizes the four themes that anchor analyses in ICP and enables you to engage in cross-country comparisons.

The following are brief summaries of the main sections and subsections of the country studies.

Focus Questions ▼

- If you could choose one other country to study in a comparative politics course besides the thirteen included in this book, what would it be? Why?

- What would you like to know about politics in that country?

1: The Making of the Modern State

Section 1 in each chapter provides an overview of the forces that have shaped the state. We believe that understanding the contemporary politics of any country requires familiarity with the historical process of state formation. "Politics in Action" uses a specific event to illustrate an important political moment in the country's recent history and to highlight some of the critical political challenges it faces. "Geographic Setting" locates the country in its regional context and discusses the political implications of this setting. "Critical Junctures" looks at some of the major stages and decisive turning points in the state's development. This discussion should give you an idea of how the country assumed its current political shape and provide a sense of how relations between state and society have developed over time.

"The Four Themes and Country X" applies the text's key themes to the making of the modern state. How has the country's political development been affected by its place in position in the globalized world of states—its relative ability to control external events and its regional and global status? What are the political implications of the state's approach to governing the economy? What has been the country's experience with the democratic idea? What are the important bases of collective identity in the country, and how do they influence the country's politics? Section 1 ends by exploring the "Implications for Comparative Politics" in the study of the country.

2: Political Economy and Development

Section 2 analyzes the pattern of governing each country's economy, and it explores how economic development has affected political change. We locate this section toward the beginning of the country study because we believe that a country's economic profile has an important impact on its politics. Within this section, there are several subsections. "State and Economy" discusses the basic organization of the country's economic system, and focuses on the role of the state and the role of markets in economic life. It also examines the relationship between the government and other economic actors. "Society and Economy" examines the social implications of the country's economic situation. It describes the state's social welfare policies, such as health care, housing, and pension programs. It asks who benefits from economic change and looks at how economic development creates or reinforces class, ethnic, gender, regional, or ideological in society. The next subsection, "Environmental Issues," analyzes environmental politics and policies within the country. Section 2 closes by examining the country's relationship to "The Global Economy." How have international economic issues affected the domestic political agenda? How have patterns of trade and foreign investment changed over time? What is the country's relationship to regional and international economic organizations? To what degree has the country been able to influence multilateral policies?

3: Governance and Policy-Making

In Section 3, we describe the state's major government institutions and policy-making procedures. "Organization of the State" lays out the fundamental principles on which the political system and the distribution of political power are based, the country's constitution, key state institutions, and historical experience. The chapter also outlines the basic structure of the state, including the relationship among different levels and branches of government. "The Executive" encompasses the key offices (for example, presidents, prime ministers, communist party leaders) at the top of the political system, focusing on how they are selected and how they use their power to make policy. This subsection also analyzes the cabinet and the national bureaucracy, their relationship to the chief executive, and their role in policy-making. "Other State Institutions" examines the military, the judiciary and the legal system, semipublic agencies, and subnational government. "The Policy-Making Process" summarizes how public policy gets made and implemented. It describes the roles of formal institutions and procedures, as well as informal aspects of policy-making, such as the influence of lobbyists and interest groups.

4: Representation and Participation

Section 4 focuses on the relationship between a country's state and society. How do different groups in society organize to further their political interests, how do they participate and get represented in the political system, and to what extent and how do they influence policy-making? Given the importance of the U.S. Congress in policy-making, American readers might expect to find the principal discussion of "The Legislature" in Section 3 ("Governance and Policy-Making") rather than Section 4. But the U.S. Congress is an exceptionally powerful legislature. In most other political systems, the executive dominates the policy process, even when it is ultimately responsible to the legislature (as is the case in parliamentary systems). In most countries other than the United States, the legislature functions primarily to represent and provide a forum for the political expression of various interests; it is only secondarily (and in some cases, such as China, only marginally) a policy-making body. Therefore, although this section does describe and assess the legislature's role in policy-making, its primary focus is on how the legislature represents or fails to represent different interests in society.

"Political Parties and the Party System" describes the overall organization of the party system and reviews the major parties. "Elections" discusses the election process and recent trends in electoral behavior. It also considers the significance of elections (or lack thereof) as a vehicle for citizen participation in politics and in bringing about changes in the government. "Political Culture, Citizenship, and Identity" examines how people perceive themselves as members of the political community: the nature and source of political values and attitudes, who is considered a citizen, and how different groups in society understand their relationship to the state. The topics covered may include political aspects of the educational system, the media, religion, and ethnicity. We also ask how globalization affects collective identities and collective action. "Interests, Social Movements, and Protest" discusses how groups in civil society pursue their political interests outside the party system. What is the relationship between the state and such organizations and movements? When and how do citizens engage in acts of protest? And how does the state respond when they do? The final subsection is about "The Political Impact of Technology" and assesses, for example, how the growth of the Internet and social media influence politics and how the state uses technology as an instrument of power.

5: Politics in Transition

In Section 5, we identify and analyze the major challenges confronting each country and revisit the book's four themes. "Political Challenges and Changing Agendas" lays out the major unresolved issues facing the country and how they may play out in the near future. Many of these challenges involve issues that have generated intense conflicts around the world in the recent period—globalization, economic distribution, collective identities, human rights and civil liberties, the wars in Iraq and Afghanistan, and the consequences of America's exercise of global **hegemony**. "Youth Politics and the Generational Divide" is about how the concerns of the country's young people play out in political terms and shape the national agenda. "Politics in Comparative Perspective" highlights the implications of the country case for the study of comparative politics. How does the history—and how will the future—of the country influence developments in a regional and global context? What does this case study tell us about politics in other countries that have similar political systems or that face similar kinds of political challenges?

hegemony

The capacity to dominate the world of states and control the terms of trade and the alliance patterns in the global order.

Key Terms, Suggested Readings, and Suggested Websites

In the margin of the text, we briefly define key terms, highlighted in bold in the text, that we consider especially important for students of comparative politics to know. The key words in each chapter are also listed at the end of the chapter and all key terms, with definitions, are included in the Glossary at the end of the book. Each chapter also has a list of books that reflect important current scholarship in the field and/or that we think would be interesting and accessible to undergraduates. This Introduction ends with suggested readings that survey the scope and methods of comparative politics and illuminate important issues in the field. We also include a set of websites, which will help you track developments and acquire timely information in the ever-changing world of comparative politics.

We realize that it is quite a challenge to begin a journey seeking to understand contemporary politics in countries around the globe. We hope that the timely information and thematic focus of *Introduction to Comparative Politics* will prepare and inspire you to explore further the often troubling, sometimes inspiring, and endlessly fascinating world of comparative politics.

Where Do You Stand?

Are you optimistic or pessimistic about the spread of democracy around the world? Why?

Do you think globalization will continue to erode the nation-state as the basic building block of politics in the world? Why or why not?

WHAT'S IN THE COMPARATIVE DATA CHARTS?

The following charts and tables present important factual and statistical information about each of the countries included in this book. We hope most of this information is self-explanatory, but a few points of clarification may be helpful.

The social and economic data mostly come from the CIA *World Factbook*, the World Bank *World Development Indicators*, and the United Nations *Human Development Report*, all of which are issued annually. These statistics are available at the following websites:

- https://www.cia.gov/library/publications/ the-world-factbook/

- http://data.worldbank.org/
- http://hdr.undp.org/en/data

The data presented are as up-to-date as possible. Several important terms used in the data, including gross domestic product (GDP), gross national product (GNP), purchasing power parity (PPP), and Gini Index, are explained in the Glossary and/or the feature called "How Is Development Measured?" on page 15.

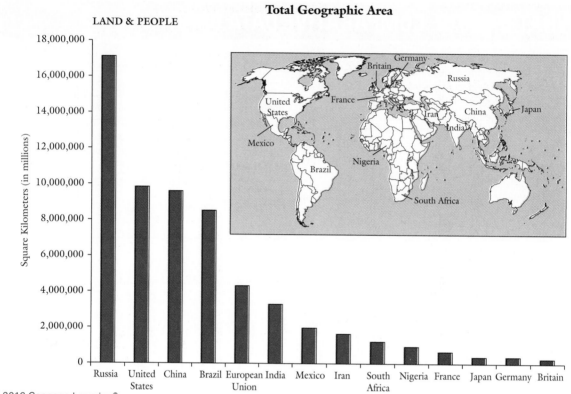

Total Geographic Area

LAND & PEOPLE

Square Kilometers (in millions)

18,000,000
16,000,000
14,000,000
12,000,000
10,000,000
8,000,000
6,000,000
4,000,000
2,000,000
0

Russia | United States | China | Brazil | European Union | India | Mexico | Iran | South Africa | Nigeria | France | Japan | Germany | Britain

© 2016 Cengage Learning®

	Brazil	Britain	China	France	Germany	India	Iran
Official name	Federative Republic of Brazil	United Kingdom of Great Britain and Northern Ireland	People's Republic of China	French Republic	Federal Republic of Germany	Republic of India	Islamic Republic of Iran
Capital	Brasilia	London	Beijing	Paris	Berlin	New Delhi	Teheran
Comparative Size	Slightly smaller than the US	Slightly smaller than Oregon	Slightly smaller than the US	Slightly smaller than Texas	Slightly smaller than Montana	Slightly more than 1/3 the size of the US	Slightly smaller than Alaska
Population growth per year	0.9%	0.8%	0.5%	0.5%	−0.18%	1.3%	1.3%
Major ethnic groups	White 47.7%; Mulatto (mixed White and Black) 43.1%; Black 7.6%; other (includes 0.5% Asian) 1.6%	White 87.1%; Black 3.0%; Asian Indian 2.3%; Asian Pakistani 1.9%; other Asian 2.8%; mixed 2.0%; other 1.0%	Han Chinese 91.6%; other nationalities 8.4% (includes 55 ethnic minorities, such as Zhuang, Manchu, Hui, Miao, Uyghur, Yi, Mongol, Tibetan, and Korean)	*It is illegal in France to collect data about ethnicity.*	German 89.9%; Turkish 4.0%; other 6.1%	*The government of India does not collect statistics on ethnicity.*	Persian 61%; Azeri 16%; Kurd 10%; Arab 3%; Lur 6%; Baloch 2%; Arab 2%; Turkmen and Turkic 2%; other 1%
Major religions	Roman Catholic 64.6%; Protestant 22.2%; other 5.2%; none 8.0%;	Christian 71.6% Muslim 2.7%; Hindu 1%; other 1.6%; unspecified or none 23.1%	Buddhist 18.2%; Christian 5.1%; Muslim 1.8%; unaffiliated 52.2% other 1.0% **Note:** officially atheist	Christian (almost entirely Catholic) 45%; no religion 35%; not stated 10%; Muslim 3%; other religions 7%	Protestant 34%, Roman Catholic 34%, Muslim 3.7%, unaffiliated or other 28.3%	Hindu 80.5%; Muslim 13.4%; Christian 2.3%; Sikh 1.95; Buddhist 0.85%; Jain 0.4%; other 0.6% not stated 0.1%	Muslim 99.4% (Shia 90–95%, Sunni 5–10%), other 0.3% (includes Zoroastrian, Jewish, Christian, and Baha'i); unspecified 0.4%
Major languages	Portuguese	English The following are recognized regional languages: Scots, Scottish Gaelic Welsh, Irish, Cornish	Standard Chinese or Mandarin based on the Beijing dialect; other major dialects include Cantonese and Shanghaiese. Also various minority languages; such as Tibetan and Mongolian	French	German	22 official national languages, of which Hindi is the primary tongue of about 30% of the people. English is the most important language for government and business.	Persian 53%; Azeri and Turkic dialects 18%; Kurdish 10%; Gilaki and Mazandarani 7%; Luri 6%; Balochi 2%; Arabic 2%; other 2%

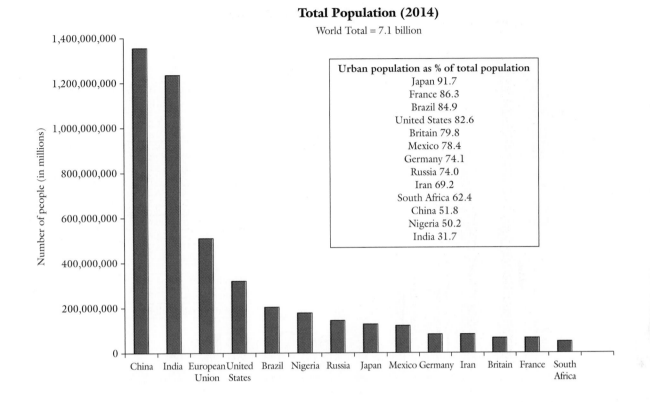

Total Population (2014)

World Total = 7.1 billion

Urban population as % of total population

Japan 91.7
France 86.3
Brazil 84.9
United States 82.6
Britain 79.8
Mexico 78.4
Germany 74.1
Russia 74.0
Iran 69.2
South Africa 62.4
China 51.8
Nigeria 50.2
India 31.7

	Japan	Mexico	Nigeria	Russia	South Africa	United States
Official name	Japan	United Mexican States	Federal Republic of Nigeria	Russian Federation	Republic of South Africa	United States of America
Capital	Tokyo	Mexico City	Abuja	Moscow	Pretoria	Washington, D.C.
Comparative size	Slightly smaller than California	Slightly less than three times the size of Texas	Slightly more than twice the size of California	Approximately 1.8 times the size of the US	Slightly less than twice the size of Texas	About half the size of Russia
Population growth per year	−0.2%	1.2%	2.8%	0.4%	1.2%	0.7%
Major ethnic groups	Japanese 98.5%; Koreans 0.5%; Chinese 0.4%; other 0.6%	Mestizo (Amerindian-Spanish) 60%; Amerindian or predominantly Amerindian 30%; White 9%; other 1%	More than 250 ethnic groups; the most populous and politically influential are: Hausa and Fulani 29%, Yoruba 21%, Igbo (Ibo) 18%, Ijaw 10%,	Russian 80.90%; Tatar 3.87%; Ukrainian 1.40%; Bashkir 1.15%; Chuvash 1.05%; Chechen 1.04%; other 10.59%	Black African 79.20%; White 8.90%; Colored 8.90%; Indian/Asian 2.50%; Other 0.50%	White 63.0%; Hispanic 13.9%; Black or African American 13.1%; Asian 5.1%; American Indian and Alaska Native 1.2%; Native Hawaiian and Other Pacific Islander 0.2%; two or more races 2.4%
Major religions	Shinto 79.9%; Buddhist 66.5%; Christian 1.5%; other 7.4% Note: Many Japanese practice both Shintoism and Buddhism	Catholic 84.9%; Protestant 8.2%; none 4.9%; other 2.0%	Christian 49.3% Muslim 48.8%; other 1.9%	Russian Orthodox 49.7%; Protestant 6.2%; Muslim 7.6%; Non-Religious 27.4%; Atheist 5.2%; other 3.9%	Protestant 36.6%; other Christian 36%; none 15.1%; Catholic 7.1%; other 2.3%; Muslim 1.5%; unspecified 1.4%	Christian 78.40% (Evangelical Protestant churches 26.3%; Mainline Protestant 18.1%; Catholic 23.9%; Historically Black Churches 6.9%; Mormon 1.7%) Unaffiliated 16.10%; Jewish 1.70%; other faiths 2.90%; don't know/refused 0.80%
Major languages	Japanese	Spanish only 92.7%, Spanish and indigenous languages 5.7%, indigenous only 0.8%, unspecified 0.8%	English (official), Hausa, Yoruba, Igbo (Ibo), Fulani	Russian, many minority languages	IsiZulu 22.7%; IsiXhosa 16%; Afrikaans 13.5%; English 9.6%; Sepedi 9.1%; Setswana 8%; Sesotho 7.6%; other 13.1%	Speak only English at home, 79.2%; speak only Spanish at home, 12.9%; speak only another language at home, 7.9%

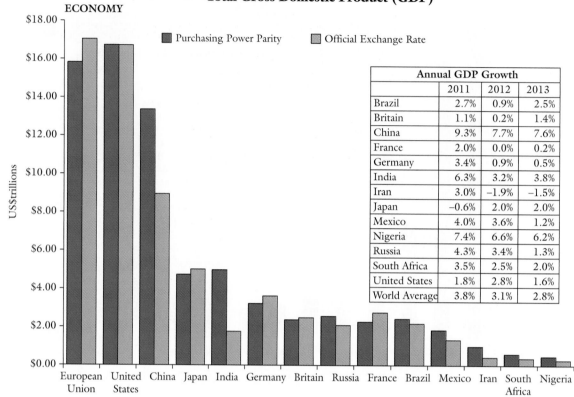

Total Gross Domestic Product (GDP)

ECONOMY

■ Purchasing Power Parity ■ Official Exchange Rate

Annual GDP Growth			
	2011	2012	2013
Brazil	2.7%	0.9%	2.5%
Britain	1.1%	0.2%	1.4%
China	9.3%	7.7%	7.6%
France	2.0%	0.0%	0.2%
Germany	3.4%	0.9%	0.5%
India	6.3%	3.2%	3.8%
Iran	3.0%	−1.9%	−1.5%
Japan	−0.6%	2.0%	2.0%
Mexico	4.0%	3.6%	1.2%
Nigeria	7.4%	6.6%	6.2%
Russia	4.3%	3.4%	1.3%
South Africa	3.5%	2.5%	2.0%
United States	1.8%	2.8%	1.6%
World Average	3.8%	3.1%	2.8%

	Brazil	Britain	China	France	Germany	India
GDP average annual growth: 2000–2013	3.4%	1.7%	9.9%	1.2%	1.3%	6.9%
GDP *per capita* average annual growth:						
2000–2013	2.2%	1.1%	9.2%	0.6%	1.3%	5.1%
1990–1999	0.1%	2.0%	8.8%	1.4%	1.9%	3.7%
1980–1989	0.8%	2.3%	8.2%	1.8%	Before German	3.4%
1970–1979	5.9%	2.3%	5.3%	3.5%	Reunification	0.6%
GDP composition by economic sector						
Agriculture	5.5%	0.7%	9.7%	1.9%	0.8%	16.9%
Industry	26.4%	20.5%	45.3%	18.7%	30.1%	17.0%
Services	68.1%	78.9%	45.0%	79.4%	69.0%	66.1%
Labor force by occupation						
Agriculture	15.7%	1.2%	34.8%	2.9%	1.5%	47.7%
Industry	13.3%	18.9%	29.5%	21.7%	28.3%	24.7%
Services	71.0%	78.9%	35.7%	74.9%	70.2%	28.1%
Foreign trade as % of GDP						
Exports	12.6%	31.6%	27.3%	27.4%	51.8%	23.8%
Imports	14.0%	33.8%	24.5%	29.7%	45.9%	31.5%
Inequality & poverty						
Household income or consumption by % share						
Poorest 10%	0.8%	3.4%	1.7%	3.0%	3.6%	3.7%
Richest 10%	42.9%	34.7%	30.0%	24.8%	24.0%	28.8%
GINI Index *(0–100; higher = more unequal)*	51.9	40.0	47.4	32.7	27.0	33.9
% of population in poverty						
National poverty line	21.4%	14.0%	13.4%	7.8%	15.5%	29.8%
International poverty line (below $2/day)	10.8%	–	27.2%	–	–	68.8%

Annual GDP per capita at Purchasing Power Parity (US$)

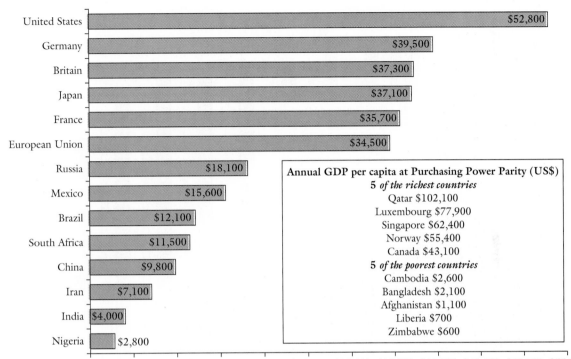

Annual GDP per capita at Purchasing Power Parity (US$)
5 of the richest countries
Qatar $102,100
Luxembourg $77,900
Singapore $62,400
Norway $55,400
Canada $43,100
5 of the poorest countries
Cambodia $2,600
Bangladesh $2,100
Afghanistan $1,100
Liberia $700
Zimbabwe $600

Iran	Japan	Mexico	Nigeria	Russia	South Africa	United States
3.8%	1.0%	1.9%	6.7%	4.9%	3.4%	1.9%
2.6%	0.92%	1.0%	3.8%	5.0%	?????	1.0%
2.9%	1.2%	1.7%	0.5%	4.8%	−0.8%	1.9%
−3.7%	3.1%	0.1%	−1.8%	Before Collapse	−0.3%	2.1%
2.9%	4.1%	3.3%	4.2%	of Soviet Union	1.0%	2.3%
10.6%	1.1%	3.6%	30.9%	4.2%	2.6%	1.1%
44.9%	25.6%	36.6%	43.0%	37.5%	29.0%	19.5%
44.5%	73.2%	59.8%	26.0%	58.3%	68.4%	79.4%
16.9%	3.7%	13.4%	70.0%	9.7%	4.6%	1.6%
34.4%	25.3%	24.1%	10.0%	27.8%	24.3%	16.7%
48.7%	69.7%	61.9%	20.0%	62.5 %	62.7%	81.2%
20.8%	14.7%	32.9%	55.4%	29.4%	28.3%	13.5%
12.7%	16.6%	34.5%	22.8%	22.1%	31.3%	16.9%
2.6%	1.9%	2.0%	1.8%	5.7%	1.2%	2.0%
29.6%	27.5%	37.5%	38.2%	42.4%	51.7%	30.0%
44.5%	37.6%	47.2%	48.8%	42.0%	63.1%	42%
18.7%	16.0%	52.3%	46.0%	11.0%	31.3%	15.1%
8.0%	–	4.5%	84.5%	–	31.3%	–

SOCIETY & POLITY

Life Expectancy at Birth (Years)

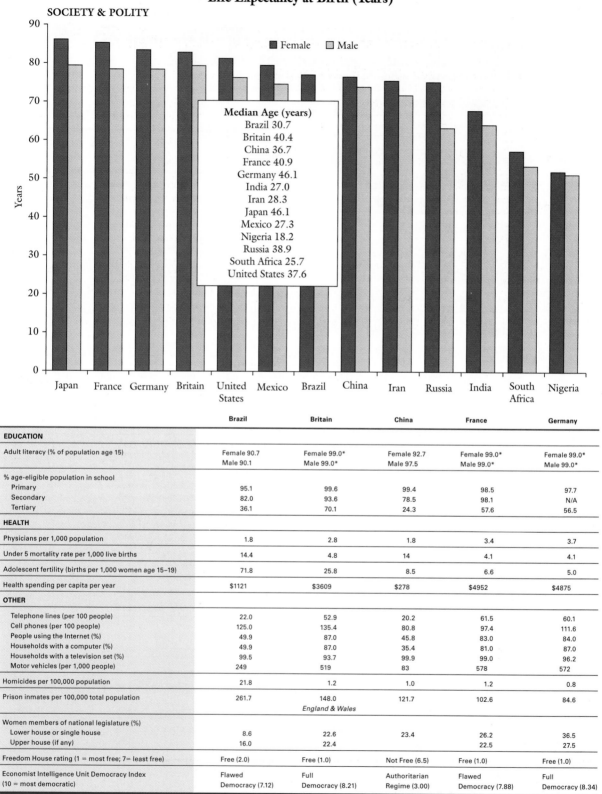

Median Age (years)
Brazil 30.7
Britain 40.4
China 36.7
France 40.9
Germany 46.1
India 27.0
Iran 28.3
Japan 46.1
Mexico 27.3
Nigeria 18.2
Russia 38.9
South Africa 25.7
United States 37.6

	Brazil	Britain	China	France	Germany
EDUCATION					
Adult literacy (% of population age 15)	Female 90.7 Male 90.1	Female 99.0* Male 99.0*	Female 92.7 Male 97.5	Female 99.0* Male 99.0*	Female 99.0* Male 99.0*
% age-eligible population in school					
Primary	95.1	99.6	99.4	98.5	97.7
Secondary	82.0	93.6	78.5	98.1	N/A
Tertiary	36.1	70.1	24.3	57.6	56.5
HEALTH					
Physicians per 1,000 population	1.8	2.8	1.8	3.4	3.7
Under 5 mortality rate per 1,000 live births	14.4	4.8	14	4.1	4.1
Adolescent fertility (births per 1,000 women age 15–19)	71.8	25.8	8.5	6.6	5.0
Health spending per capita per year	$1121	$3609	$278	$4952	$4875
OTHER					
Telephone lines (per 100 people)	22.0	52.9	20.2	61.5	60.1
Cell phones (per 100 people)	125.0	135.4	80.8	97.4	111.6
People using the Internet (%)	49.9	87.0	45.8	83.0	84.0
Households with a computer (%)	49.9	87.0	35.4	81.0	87.0
Households with a television set (%)	99.5	93.7	99.9	99.0	96.2
Motor vehicles (per 1,000 people)	249	519	83	578	572
Homicides per 100,000 population	21.8	1.2	1.0	1.2	0.8
Prison inmates per 100,000 total population	261.7	148.0 England & Wales	121.7	102.6	84.6
Women members of national legislature (%)					
Lower house or single house	8.6	22.6	23.4	26.2	36.5
Upper house (if any)	16.0	22.4		22.5	27.5
Freedom House rating (1 = most free; 7= least free)	Free (2.0)	Free (1.0)	Not Free (6.5)	Free (1.0)	Free (1.0)
Economist Intelligence Unit Democracy Index (10 = most democratic)	Flawed Democracy (7.12)	Full Democracy (8.21)	Authoritarian Regime (3.00)	Flawed Democracy (7.88)	Full Democracy (8.34)

Infant Mortality per 1,000 Live Births

■ Male   □ Female

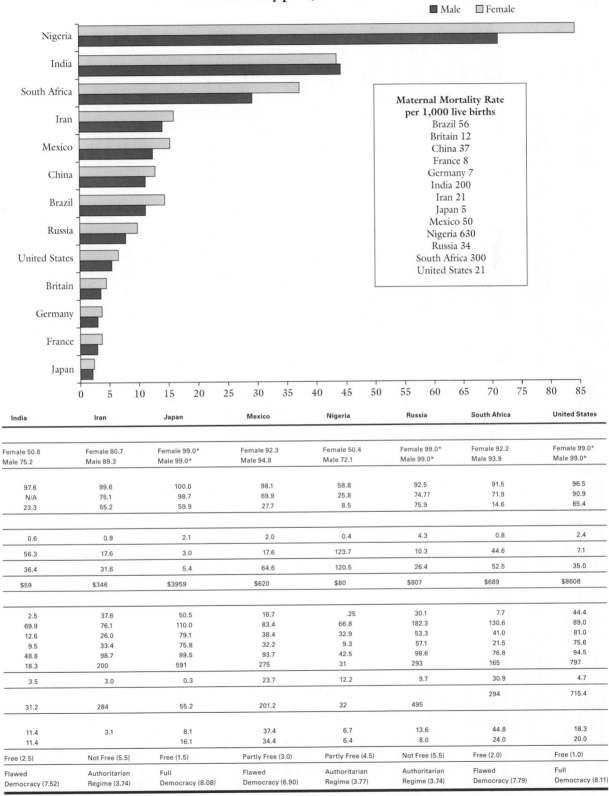

Maternal Mortality Rate
per 1,000 live births
Brazil 56
Britain 12
China 37
France 8
Germany 7
India 200
Iran 21
Japan 5
Mexico 50
Nigeria 630
Russia 34
South Africa 300
United States 21

India	Iran	Japan	Mexico	Nigeria	Russia	South Africa	United States
Female 50.8	Female 80.7	Female 99.0*	Female 92.3	Female 50.4	Female 99.0*	Female 92.2	Female 99.0*
Male 75.2	Male 89.3	Male 99.0*	Male 94.8	Male 72.1	Male 99.0*	Male 93.9	Male 99.0*
97.6	99.6	100.0	98.1	58.8	92.5	91.5	96.5
N/A	75.1	98.7	69.9	25.8	74.7?	71.9	90.9
23.3	55.2	59.9	27.7	8.5	75.9	14.6	85.4
0.6	0.9	2.1	2.0	0.4	4.3	0.8	2.4
56.3	17.6	3.0	17.6	123.7	10.3	44.6	7.1
36.4	31.6	5.4	64.6	120.5	26.4	52.5	35.0
$59	$346	$3959	$620	$80	$807	$689	$8608
2.5	37.6	50.5	16.7	.25	30.1	7.7	44.4
69.9	76.1	110.0	83.4	66.8	182.3	130.6	89.0
12.6	26.0	79.1	38.4	32.9	53.3	41.0	81.0
9.5	33.4	75.8	32.2	9.3	57.1	21.5	75.6
48.8	98.7	99.5	93.7	42.5	98.6	76.8	94.5
18.3	200	591	275	31	293	165	797
3.5	3.0	0.3	23.7	12.2	9.7	30.9	4.7
						294	715.4
31.2	284	55.2	201.2	32	495		
11.4	3.1	8.1	37.4	6.7	13.6	44.8	18.3
11.4		16.1	34.4	6.4	8.0	24.0	20.0
Free (2.5)	Not Free (5.5)	Free (1.5)	Partly Free (3.0)	Partly Free (4.5)	Not Free (5.5)	Free (2.0)	Free (1.0)
Flawed Democracy (7.52)	Authoritarian Regime (3.74)	Full Democracy (8.08)	Flawed Democracy (6.90)	Authoritarian Regime (3.77)	Authoritarian Regime (3.74)	Flawed Democracy (7.79)	Full Democracy (8.11)

* Developed countries have near universal adult *basic* literacy rates, but *functional* literacy among the working age population is lower. For example, in Britain it is 80%, in France 85%, Germany 86%, and the United States 86%.

COMPARATIVE RANKINGS

International organizations and research institutions have developed statistical methods to rate and rank different countries according to various categories of economic, social, political, and environmental performance. Such rankings can be controversial, but we think they provide an interesting approach to comparative analysis. Five examples of this approach are listed below. In addition to the countries included in this book (which are in bold), the top and bottom five countries in each of the rankings are also listed.

Human Development Index (HDI)

is a measure used by the United Nations to compare the overall level of well-being in countries around the world. It takes into account life expectancy, education, and standard of living.

2013 HDI Rankings:

Very High Human Development
1. Norway
2. Australia
3. United States
4. Netherlands
5. Germany
10. Japan
20. France
26. Britain

High Human Development
55. Russia
61. Mexico
76. Iran
85. Brazil

Medium Human Development
101. China
121. South Africa
136. India

Low Human Development
153. Nigeria
183. Burkino Faso
184. Chad
185. Mozambique
186. D.R. Congo
186. Niger

http://hdr.undp.org/en/data
Identical numbers indicate a tie in the rankings

Global Gender Gap

measures the extent to which women have achieved equality with men in five critical areas: economic participation, economic opportunity, political empowerment, educational attainment, and health and well-being.

2013 Gender Gap Rankings:

1. Iceland
2. Finland
3. Norway
4. Sweden
5. Philippines
14. Germany
17. South Africa
18. Britain
19. United States
61. Russia
62. Brazil
68. Mexico
69. China
85. Brazil
101. India
105. Japan
106. Nigeria
130. Iran
129. Ivory Coast
132. Mauritania
133. Syria
134. Chad
135. Pakistan
136. Yemen

http://www.weforum.org
/issues/global-gender-gap

Environmental Performance Index (EPI)

measures how close countries come to meeting specific benchmarks for national pollution control and natural resource management.

2014 EPI Rankings:

1. Switzerland
2. Luxemburg
3. Australia
4. Singapore
5. Czech Republic
6. Germany
12. Britain
26. Japan
27. France
33. United States
65. Mexico
72. South Africa
73. Russia
77. Brazil
83. Iran
134. Nigeria
118. China
155. India
174. Afghanistan
175. Lesotho
176. Haiti
177. Mali
178. Somalia

http://epi.yale.edu

International Corruption Perceptions Index (CPI)

defines corruption as the abuse of public office for private gain and measures the degree to which corruption is perceived to exist among a country's public officials and politicians.

2013 CPI Rankings:

1. Denmark
1. New Zealand
3. Finland
3. Sweden
5. Norway
12. Germany
14. Britain
18. Japan
19. United States
22. France
72. South Africa
72. Brazil
80. China
94. India
98. Mexico
127. Russia
144. Iran
144. Nigeria
173. South Sudan
174. Sudan
175. Afghanistan
175. North Korea
175. Somalia

http://www.transparency.
org/
Identical numbers indicate a tie in the rankings

Economist Intelligence Unit Democracy Index

categorizes four types of political systems based on five categories: electoral process and pluralism; civil liberties; the functioning of government; political participation; and political culture.

2013 Democracy Index:

Full Democracies
1. Norway
2. Sweden
3. Iceland
4. Denmark
5. New Zealand
14. Germany
16. Britain
21. United States
23. Japan

Flawed Democracies
28. France
31. South Africa
38. India
44. Brazil
51. Mexico

Authoritarian Regimes
120. Nigeria
122. Russia
142. China
158. Iran
163. Saudi Arabia
164. Syria
165. Chad
166. Guinea-Bissau
167. North Korea

http://www.eiu.com/public/

Key Terms

authoritarian regimes
bureaucracy
cabinet
causal theories
Cold War
collective identities
communist party–state
comparative politics
comparativist
consolidated democracies
Corruption Perceptions Index
country
critical juncture
democracy
democratic transition
dependent variable
dictatorships
distributional politics
Environmental Performance Index

executive
Freedom in the World Rating
Global Gender Gap
globalization
gross domestic product (GDP)
gross national product (GNP)
hegemony
Human Development Index (HDI)
independent variable
institutional design
International Monetary Fund (IMF)
judiciary
Keynesianism
legislature
legitimacy
middle-level theory

mixed systems
nation-state
neoliberalism
North American Free Trade Agreement (NAFTA)
political economy
purchasing power parity (PPP)
rational choice theory
social class
social movements
Social Progress Index
state
state formation
sustainable development
typology
World Bank
World Trade Organization (WTO)

Suggested Readings

Acemoglu, Daron, and James A. Robinson. *Why Nations Fail: The Origins of Power, Prosperity and Poverty.* New York: Crown Business, 2012.

della Porta, Donatella. *Mobilizing for Democracy: Comparing 1989 and 2011.* New York: Oxford University Press, 2014.

Diamond, Larry, Marc F. Plattner, and Philip J. Costopoulos, eds. *Debates on Democratization.* Baltimore: The Johns Hopkins University Press, 2010.

Hays, Jude C. *Globalization and the New Politics of Embedded Liberalism.* New York: Oxford University Press, 2009.

Krieger, Joel, ed. *The Oxford Companion to Comparative Politics.* New York: Oxford University Press, 2013.

Levitsky, Steven R., and Lucan A. Way. *Competitive Authoritarianism: Hybrid Regimes after the Cold War.* New York: Cambridge University Press, 2010.

Nooruddin, Irfan. *Politics and Economic Development.* New York: Cambridge University Press, 2011.

Norris, Pippa. *Making Democratic Governance Work: How Regimes Shape Prosperity, Welfare, and Peace.* New York: Cambridge University Press, 2012.

Tarrow, Sidney. *Power in Movement*, 3rd ed. New York: Cambridge University Press, 2011.

Stepan, Alfred, Juan J. Linz, and Yogendra Yadav. *Crafting State-Nations: India and Other Multinational Democracies.* Baltimore: The Johns Hopkins University Press, 2011.

Suggested Websites

CIA World Factbook
https://www.cia.gov/library/publications/the-world-factbook

U.S. Bilateral Relations Fact Sheets
http://www.state.gov/r/pa/ei/bgn/

Election Guide (Consortium for Elections and Political Process Strengthening)
http://www.electionguide.org/

Freedom House
http://www.freedomhouse.org/

NationMaster
http://www.nationmaster.com/

Politics and Government Around the World
http://www.politicsresources.net/

2 Britain

Joel Krieger

Official Name: United Kingdom of Great Britain and Northern Ireland
Location: Western Europe
Capital City: London
Population (2014): 63.7 million
Size: 244,820 sq. km.; slightly smaller than Oregon

THE MAKING OF THE MODERN BRITISH STATE

SECTION 1

Politics in Action

The first woman prime minister in Western Europe, Margaret Thatcher, was also remarkable for being the first British prime minister to win three general elections in a row since Lord Liverpool in the nineteenth century. Born in 1925, the daughter of a shopkeeper in Grantham (Think: Downton Abbey), she studied chemistry at Oxford, then law. Winning the leadership of the Conservative Party in 1975 against the odds, Thatcher served as prime minister from 1979 to 1990, the longest continuous stretch as prime minister in the twentieth century and a very memorable one. Thatcher's leadership as prime minister marks a critical dividing line in postwar British politics. Like few others before or since she set the tone and redefined the goals of British politics. The Thatcher government inaugurated a decisively right-wing regime and set out to divide and conquer trade unions. New revelations in 2014 have revealed that Thatcher was so determined to defeat the miners during the epic strike in 1984 that she secretly considered using the military and declaring a state of emergency.

Focus Questions ⍰

- How does its history of the empire still shape British politics today?

- Why did an electoral system designed to produce a stable single-party majority result in a Conservative–Liberal coalition government in 2010?

Margaret Thatcher's funeral procession.

Indigo/Getty Images

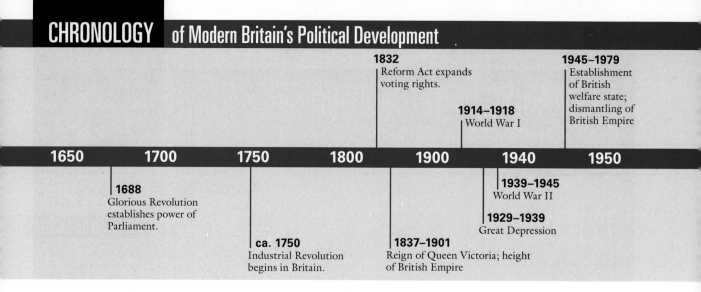

1832 Reform Act expands voting rights.

1914–1918 World War I

1945–1979 Establishment of British welfare state; dismantling of British Empire

1650 1700 1750 1800 1900 1940 1950

1688 Glorious Revolution establishes power of Parliament.

ca. 1750 Industrial Revolution begins in Britain.

1837–1901 Reign of Queen Victoria; height of British Empire

1929–1939 Great Depression

1939–1945 World War II

Despite all the trappings of a grandly staged funeral procession on a gun carriage when she died in 2013, with Queen Elizabeth in attendance, in London protesters on the left shouted slurs. Supporters decried President Obama's decision not to send any senior American officials to the funeral, despite Mrs. Thatcher's high-profile partnership with President Reagan and her role confronting the Soviet Union. The chant "Maggie, Maggie, Maggie, dead, dead, dead, dead!" could be heard as far away as Glasgow. (Thatcher never played well to the crowds in Glasgow.)

Geographic Setting

Britain is the largest of the British Isles, a group of islands off the northwest coast of Europe that encompasses England, Scotland, and Wales. The second-largest island includes Northern Ireland and the independent Republic of Ireland. The term *Great Britain* includes England, Wales, and Scotland, but not Northern Ireland. We use the term *Britain* as shorthand for the United Kingdom of Great Britain and Northern Ireland.

Covering an area of approximately 94,000 square miles, Britain is roughly two-thirds the area of Japan, or approximately half the area of France. In 2013 the British population was approximately 62 million.

As an island off the shore of Europe, Britain was for centuries less subject to invasion and conquest than its continental counterparts. This gave the country a sense of security. The separation has also made many Britons feel they are more apart from than an intrinsic part of Europe. This feeling complicates relations with Britain's EU partners.

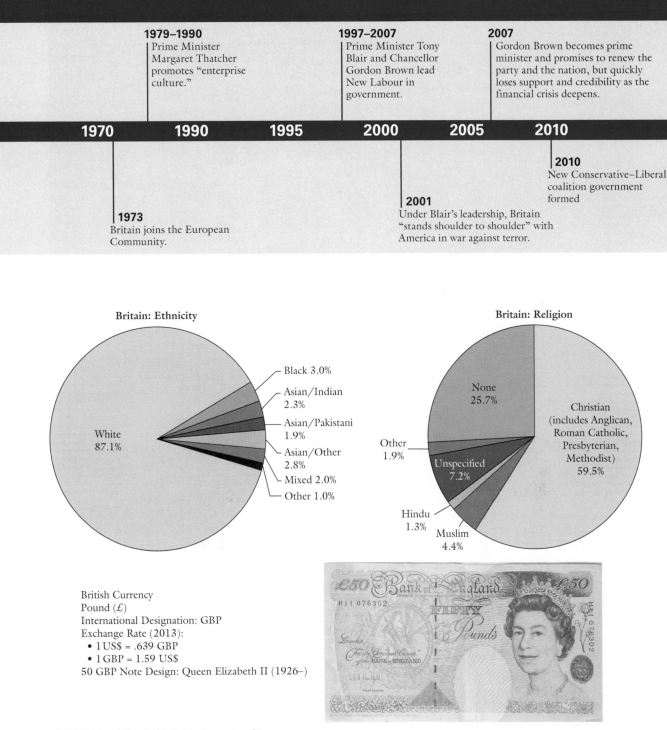

1979–1990
Prime Minister Margaret Thatcher promotes "enterprise culture."

1997–2007
Prime Minister Tony Blair and Chancellor Gordon Brown lead New Labour in government.

2007
Gordon Brown becomes prime minister and promises to renew the party and the nation, but quickly loses support and credibility as the financial crisis deepens.

1970   **1990**   **1995**   **2000**   **2005**   **2010**

2010
New Conservative–Liberal coalition government formed

1973
Britain joins the European Community.

2001
Under Blair's leadership, Britain "stands shoulder to shoulder" with America in war against terror.

Britain: Ethnicity

White 87.1%

Black 3.0%

Asian/Indian 2.3%

Asian/Pakistani 1.9%

Asian/Other 2.8%

Mixed 2.0%

Other 1.0%

Britain: Religion

None 25.7%

Christian (includes Anglican, Roman Catholic, Presbyterian, Methodist) 59.5%

Other 1.9%

Unspecified 7.2%

Hindu 1.3%

Muslim 4.4%

British Currency
Pound (£)
International Designation: GBP
Exchange Rate (2013):
- 1 US$ = .639 GBP
- 1 GBP = 1.59 US$
50 GBP Note Design: Queen Elizabeth II (1926–)

FIGURE 2.1 The British Nation at a Glance

Ben Molyneux/Alamy (for photo)

Britain

0   100 Miles

0   100 Kilometers

Shetland
Islands

Orkney
Islands

Outer Hebrides

Inner Hebrides

SCOTLAND

North Sea

★Edinburgh
•Glasgow

NORTHERN
IRELAND

Belfast★

Isle
of Man

Irish Sea

REPUBLIC
OF   Dublin★
IRELAND

Isle of
Anglesey

Manchester
•
•Liverpool

ENGLAND

WALES

•Birmingham

Thames

Cardiff
★   •Bristol   London   Chunnel

ATLANTIC
OCEAN

Southampton•

Isle of Wight

•Plymouth

English Channel

FRANCE

© Cengage Learning®

Critical Junctures

The Consolidation of the British State

The consolidation of the British state unified several kingdoms. After Duke William
of Normandy defeated the English in the Battle of Hastings in 1066, the Norman
monarchy eventually extended its authority throughout the British Isles, except for
Scotland. In the sixteenth century, legislation unified England and Wales legally,
politically, and administratively. Scotland and England remained separate kingdoms,
until the Act of Union of 1707. After that, a common Parliament of Great Britain
replaced the two separate parliaments of Scotland and of England and Wales.

Table 2.1	Political Organization
Political System	Parliamentary democracy, constitutional monarchy.
Regime History	Long constitutional history, origins subject to interpretation, usually dated from the seventeenth century or earlier.
Administrative Structure	Unitary state with fusion of powers. United Kingdom Parliament has supreme legislative, executive, and judicial authority. Limited powers have been transferred to representative bodies in Scotland, Wales, and Northern Ireland.
Executive	Prime minister (PM), answerable to House of Commons, subject to collective responsibility of the cabinet; member of Parliament who is leader of party or coalition that can control a majority in Commons (normally a single party but since 2010 as a two-party coalition [Conservative–Liberal Democrat]).
Legislature	Bicameral. House of Commons elected by single-member plurality system. Main legislative powers: to pass laws, provide for finance, scrutinize public administration and government policy. House of Lords, unelected upper house: limited powers to delay enactment of legislation and to recommend revisions. Since 2009, the judicial functions of parliament were transferred to the UK Supreme Court. Recent reforms eliminated voting rights for most hereditary peers.
Judiciary	Independent but with no power to judge the constitutionality of legislation or governmental conduct. UK Supreme Court, established in 2009, is the final court of appeal for all UK civil cases and criminal cases in England, Wales, and Northern Ireland.
Party System	Two-party dominant, with regional variation. Principal parties: Labour and Conservative; a center party (Liberal Democrat); and national parties in Scotland, Wales, and Northern Ireland; and United Kingdom Independence (UKIP).

© Cengage Learning®

Royal control increased after 1066, but the conduct of King John (1199–1216) fueled opposition from feudal barons. In 1215, they forced him to consent to a series of concessions that protected feudal landowners from abuses of royal power. These restrictions were embodied in the Magna Carta, a historic statement of the rights of a political community against the monarchical state. It has served as the inspiration for constitutions around the world that contain protections for citizens and groups from the arbitrary exercise of state power. In 1236, the term *Parliament* was first used officially for the gathering of feudal barons summoned by the king whenever he required their consent to special taxes. By the fifteenth century, Parliament had gained the right to make laws.

The Seventeenth-Century Settlement

By the sixteenth and seventeenth centuries Britain was embroiled in a complex interplay of religious conflicts, national rivalries, and struggles between rulers and Parliament. These conflicts erupted in the civil wars of the 1640s, and later forced the removal of James II in 1688. This was the last successful revolution in British history.

This "Glorious Revolution" of 1688 also resolved long-standing religious conflict. The replacement of the Roman Catholic James II by the Protestant William and

Mary ensured the dominance of the Church of England (or Anglican Church). To this day, the Church of England remains the established (official) church. By about 1700, a basic form of parliamentary democracy had emerged.

The Industrial Revolution and the British Empire

Industrial Revolution

A period of rapid and destabilizing social, economic, and political changes caused by the introduction of large-scale factory production, originating in England in the middle of the eighteenth century.

The Industrial Revolution from the mid-eighteenth century onward involved rapid expansion of manufacturing production and technological innovation. It also led to vast social and economic changes and created pressures to make the country more democratic. Britain's competitive edge also dominated the international order. The **Industrial Revolution** transformed the British state and society.

Despite a gradually improving standard of living throughout the English population in general, industrialization disrupted lives and shattered old ways of life. Many field laborers lost their jobs, and many small landholders were squeezed off the land.

The British Empire

hegemonic power

A state that can control the pattern of alliances and terms of the international order and often shapes domestic political developments in countries throughout the world.

Britain relied on imported raw materials, and by 1800, it sold the vast majority of finished goods overseas. Growth depended on foreign markets—not domestic consumption. This export orientation made economic growth much faster than an exclusively domestic orientation would have allowed.

Because Britain needed overseas trade, its leaders worked aggressively to secure markets and expand the empire. Backed by the British navy, international trade made England the dominant military and economic world power. Britain led the alliance that toppled Napoleon in the early nineteenth century, thus enabling the country to maintain its dominant position in the world.

By 1870, British trade represented nearly one-quarter of the world total (see Figure 2.2) and by 1900, Queen Victoria (1837–1901) ruled an empire that included 25 percent of the world's population, exercising direct colonial rule over 50 countries, including India and Nigeria. Britain also dominated an extensive economic empire—a worldwide network of independent states, including China, Iran, and Brazil. Britain ruled as a **hegemonic power**, controlling alliances and shaping domestic political developments in countries throughout the world.

*As compared with the average rate of productivity in other members of the world economy.

FIGURE 2.2 World Trade and Relative Labor Productivity

Source: From AFTER HEGEMONY by Robert O. Keohane

Industrial Change and the Struggle for Voting Rights

The Industrial Revolution shifted economic power from landowners to businessmen and industrialists. The first important step toward democratization began in the late 1820s, when the propertied classes and increasing popular agitation pressed Parliament to expand the right to vote. With Parliament under considerable pressure, the Reform Act of 1832 extended the vote to a section of the (male) middle class.

The reform was narrow. Before 1832, less than 5 percent of the adult population could vote—afterward, only about 7 percent. The reform showed the strict property basis for political participation inflamed class-based tensions.

The Representation of the People Act of 1867 increased the electorate to 16 percent but left cities significantly underrepresented. The Franchise Act of 1884 nearly doubled the electorate. The Representation of the People Act of 1918 finally included nearly all adult men and women over age thirty. How slow a process was it? The struggle to extend the vote took place mostly without violence, but it lasted for centuries.

World Wars, Industrial Strife, and the Depression (1914–1945)

State involvement in the economy increased significantly during World War I (1914–1918). The state took control of numerous industries, including railways, mining, and shipping. It channeled resources into war production. After World War I, the state remained active in managing industry, but in a different way. Amid tremendous industrial disputes, the state fragmented the trade union movement and resisted demands for workers' control over production. This government manipulation of the economy openly contradicted the policy of laissez-faire (minimal government interference in the operation of economic markets) that generally characterizes Britain's approach to governing the economy.

welfare state

A set of public policies designed to provide for citizens' needs through direct or indirect provision of pensions, health care, unemployment insurance, and assistance to the poor.

Tensions between free-market principles and interventionist practices deepened with the Great Depression—1929 through much of the 1930s—and with World War II (1939–1945). Fear of depression and yearnings for a better life after the war transformed the role of the state and led to a period of unusual political harmony.

Collectivist Consensus (1945–1979)

The term *collectivism* describes the consensus in politics after World War II, when most Britons and all major political parties agreed that governments should work to narrow the gap between rich and poor, and provide for basic necessities through public education, national health care, and other policies of the **welfare state** (the set of policies designed to provide health care, pensions, unemployment benefits, and assistance to the poor). They also accepted state responsibility for economic growth and full employment. British people came to expect that the state should be responsible for economic growth and full employment. In time, however, economic downturn and political stagnation unraveled the consensus.

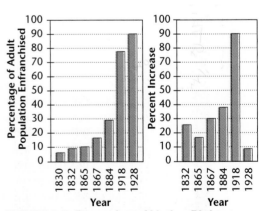

New Labour's Third Way

Under the leadership of Tony Blair from 1997 to 2007, the Labour Party was determined to modernize itself. Although its official name did not change, the party was rebranded "New Labour," promising a "third-way" alternative to Thatcherism and the collectivism of traditional Labour. New Labour rejected interest-based politics, in which unions and

FIGURE 2.3 Expansion of Voting Rights
Expansion of the franchise in Britain was a gradual process. Despite reforms dating from the early nineteenth century, nearly universal adult suffrage was not achieved until 1928.

Source: From RASMUSSEN. The British Political Process, 1E. © 1993 Cengage Learning.

working people tended to vote for Labour and businesspeople and the more prosperous voted for the Conservatives. Labour won in 1997 with support from across the socioeconomic spectrum.

Early in their careers, Tony Blair and Gordon Brown formed an alliance as rising stars in the Labour Party. Blair pushed the party to modernize and expand its political base well beyond its heritage as a labor party. Brown became shadow chancellor (the opposition party's spokesman on the economy).

But after Labour took office, Blair and Brown became rivals rather than partners. Blair won a third electoral victory in May 2005. Due mainly to the war in Iraq, his parliamentary majority was slashed by nearly 100 seats. In June 2007 Blair resigned and Gordon Brown became prime minister.

A strong finance minister, Brown was not a nimble campaigner and was never able to get out from under the shadow cast by New Labour's role in the war in Iraq, a war that was extremely unpopular in the United Kingdom.

Brown's effectiveness as chancellor (finance minister) for ten years and his highly praised efforts to stabilize the global economy during the "Great Recession" was soon forgotten. Nor could Brown—or any prime minister—reduce the fear of sudden terrorist attacks that ordinary people in Britain have felt ever since bombs were set off in the London transport system on July 7, 2005 (in the United Kingdom referred to as 7/7).

The Conservative–Liberal Coalition

There is a familiar maxim: In politics, a week is a long time. If that is true, thirteen years is an eternity. Ever since the Conservatives held power in 1990, many of the core principles of New Labour's approach have become widely shared across much of the political spectrum. When the Conservatives elected David Cameron as their party leader in 2005, he took the party in a familiar mainstream direction, appealing directly to youth for political support and championing modernization and pragmatism. Young (he was born in 1966), smart, and telegenic, Cameron seemed to consciously adopt, in both style and substance, much of Blair's early appeal, stealing the thunder of New Labour, and expanding the appeal of the Conservative Party by reaching out to youth and promoting agendas, such as climate change, citizen activism, and promises to reduce both the global development gap and the gap between rich and poor in the United Kingdom—issues that would have broad non-ideological appeal. As a result, when the May 2010 election produced what the British call a "hung parliament"—an outcome after a general election when no party can by itself control a majority of the seats in parliament—it was a stretch for the Conservatives and the Liberal Democrats to form a government, but it was not an unbridgeable gap.

The coalition government, like New Labour before it, has tried to capture the mood in Britain, by characterizing its governing objective as a commitment to reject ideological positions in favor of broad appeals to what Cameron and Clegg characterize as a radical, reforming government that attempts to blend the Conservative commitment to the dynamism of free markets with the Liberal Democrat commitment to decentralization. The result is captured in a new framework for governance, which the coalition partners call the "Big Society." The Big Society argues for wide-ranging initiatives to empower ordinary citizens to take control over their lives and shift the balance of power downward from the state to communities and individual citizens. Parents should be given the opportunity to start their own schools; citizens should be encouraged to take over the administration of post offices; to elect police commissioners; to recall MPs who violate the public trust. An innovative approach to governance in the United Kingdom, the Big Society is the "Big Idea"—the catchphrase and rebranding of politics demanded of all new governments in the United Kingdom. Thus far, the "Big Society" is, more than anything else, a catchphrase, but not yet a clear set of policies for encouraging local autonomy and citizen bottom-up activism, viewed by Conservatives as a much-needed corrective to New Labour's tendency toward the concentration of power away from the center, despite lip service to a governing vision create citizen stakeholders and devolve power away from the central government.

Critics have expressed skepticism about the Big Society, and supporters have not yet been able to clearly define what it means in policy terms or how to implement Big Society policies effectively. At a time when severe cuts in public spending demanded a rollback of government, it remains unclear whether the Big Society is a defining vision that will drive the agenda of a strong, stable, and effective coalition government, or that it will be remembered as a catchphrase that could not paper over the difficulties that a government would face once it was committed to making the broad, deep, and increasingly unpopular cuts demanded by the "great recession" that began in 2008. The challenges are all the greater for a young, untested, and divided government, which faces the special challenges of coalition government that emerged from the 2010 general election. Note that one-party government is very much the rule in Britain. How unusual is coalition government? Note that the last formal coalition government before 2010 was the wartime coalition government led by Winston Churchill, the indomitable leader who saved Britain from the Nazi juggernaut. It is no great insult to observe that David Cameron is no Winston Churchill. Who could be? As we will discuss throughout this chapter, these are very challenging times for any British government. The challenges are especially daunting in the case of a coalition government, which must contend with crosscutting pressures to keep the coalition intact—and must bring along an electorate that is instinctively uneasy about—if not hostile to—the very idea of coalition government. We are speaking about Britain, a country with the longest tradition of parliamentary democracy, and a populace that is inclined to privilege tradition and the British way of doing things over institutional change and the uncertainty that brings.

The Four Themes and Britain

Britain in a Globalized World of States

The first theme analyzes how a country's position in the globalizing world of states influences its ability to manage domestic and international challenges. A weaker international standing makes it difficult for a country to control international events or insulate itself from external pressures. Britain's ability to control the terms of trade and master political alliances during the nineteenth century confirms this maxim, but times have changed.

Through gradual decolonization Britain fell to second-tier status. Its formal empire shrank between the two world wars (1919–1939) as the "white dominions" of Canada, Australia, and New Zealand gained independence. In Britain's Asian, Middle Eastern, and African colonies, pressure for political reforms that would lead to independence deepened during World War II and afterward. Beginning with the formal independence of India and Pakistan in 1947, an enormous empire dissolved in less than twenty years. Finally, in 1997, Britain returned the commercially vibrant crown colony of Hong Kong to China. The process of decolonization ended Britain's position as a dominant player in world politics.

Is Britain a world power or just a middle-of-the-pack country in Europe? Maybe both. On the one hand, resulting from its role in World War II, Britain sits as a permanent member of the United Nations Security Council and a leading member of the world's select club of nuclear powers. On the other hand, Britain almost always plays second fiddle in its special relationship to the United States, which has exposed British foreign policy to extraordinary pressures, especially since 9/11. British governments also face persistent challenges in their dealings with the EU. Many countries in Europe, but not Britain, have adopted a common currency, the euro. Can Britain afford to remain aloof from such fast-paced changes of economic integration?

🪪 PROFILE

David Cameron

Christopher Furlong/
WPA Pool/Getty
Images

The King's Speech is a charming award-winning movie on both sides of the Atlantic, based on a true story about how an Australian speech therapist secretly aided King George VI, a stutterer, enabling him to speak quite clearly and forcefully over the radio—a remarkable technological innovation at the time—to rally the British people to stand together against Hitler's fascism as World War II erupted. As *The Economist*, an influential weekly noted, it is a movie with deep political–cultural resonance:

> "There are some lessons here for Britain's present rulers. This is a prickly, conservative and proud nation, in which grandeur must be offset with displays of humanity: David Cameron, a privileged chap who has suffered tragedies in his private life, knows this already."*

Born in 1966, in London, Cameron was brought up in Berkshire, a historic county near Oxford and the royal residence, Windsor Castle. He is the son of a stockbroker and followed generations of Cameron males who attended Eton, the historic boarding school for the privileged elite, and then Oxford, where he studied Politics, Philosophy, and Economics (PPE). Cameron graduated in 1988 with a first-class honors degree, a signal achievement affording great and lasting status.

A journalist once asked Cameron, just before he became leader of the Conservative Party in 2005, if he thought his pedigree and elite schooling would hurt him politically. Cameron sighed mightily and then offered a very revealing reply. "I don't know. You can try to be logical about it and say the upside is a terrific education, the downside is the label that gets attached and mentioned in every article," replied Cameron. "Or you can just think to yourself: I am what I am. That is what I had, I am very grateful for it."**

Cameron's elite education and step-by-step rise to political leadership from MP (member of parliament) to member of the Conservative Party research department, to opposition spokesman (member of the shadow cabinet with increasingly significant portfolios), to leader of the Conservative Party is very traditional, if unusually rapid. Nevertheless Cameron represents a new brand of Conservative, a "third-way" conservative who has tried to steal much of the thunder from Tony Blair, whom admirers liken to John Kennedy, and who characterizes himself as a compassionate conservative. If Cameron can lead Britain successfully through the tough economic and political times he inherited from New Labour in 2010, he will have achieved a lasting place in modern British politics—and he will have earned it the hard way.

MAKING CONNECTIONS Do you think David Cameron's elite pedigree is an asset or a hindrance to leadership of the nation in hard economic times?

*Bagehot, *The Economist*. January 15, 2011, p. 62 (Economist.com/blogs/Bagehot)

**Francis Elliott and James Hanning, *Cameron: The Rise of the New Conservative*, London: Harper Perennial, 2009, p. 25.

A second theme examines the strategies employed in governing the economy. Since the dawn of Britain's Industrial Revolution, prosperity at home has relied on superior competitiveness abroad. This is even truer today with intensified international competition and global production. Will Britain's "less-is-more" **laissez-faire** approach to economic governance, invigorated by partnerships between the state and key competitive businesses, sustain economic growth and competitiveness in a global context?

Our third theme assesses the potent political influence of the democratic idea, the universal appeal of core values associated with parliamentary democracy as practiced first in the United Kingdom. Even in Britain, issues about democratic governance, citizen participation, and constitutional reform have been renewed with considerable force. What are the implications of the election of May 2010 for democracy in Britain? In a sense no party won the election, but Labour was soundly defeated. The Liberal Democrats won five seats fewer than they had won in 2005 (down from 62 to 57), but won the opportunity to be the junior partner in the Conservative–Liberal Democrat coalition government; and the Conservatives, with 36.1 percent of the vote, a mere 3.7 percent increase over 2005, were unable to form a government on their own, but won the right to be responsible for shepherding the country through political uncertainty and a moment of severe economic challenges. The highly unusual outcome—the first peacetime coalition in 70 years—guarantees that 2010 will be remembered as a remarkable election, but the consequences for the democratic idea in Britain will take longer to tally.

The traditionally respected royal family, which has been rocked by improprieties, including tax scandals and infidelity over the past two decades, has seized on the marriage of Prince William as a moment of redemption. Few reject the monarchy outright, but questions about the finances and decorum of the monarchy have placed on the agenda broader issues about citizen control over government and constitutional reform. That William of Wales is now the knight in shining armor coming to the rescue of the royal family provides a graphic reminder that long-settled issues about the constitutional form and unity of the state have not been put to rest. Can the interests of England, Wales, Scotland, and Northern Ireland be balanced within a single nation-state?

The fourth theme, the politics of collective identity, considers how individuals define themselves politically through group attachments, come together to pursue political goals, and face their status as political insiders or outsiders. Through the immigration of former colonial subjects to the United Kingdom, decolonization created a multiracial and multiethnic society. Issues of race, ethnicity, and cultural identity have challenged the long-standing British values of tolerance and consensus. The concept of "Britishness"—what the country stands for and who makes up the political community—has come into question, especially since 9/11 and the bombings of the London transport system by British Muslims in July 2005.

Themes and Comparisons

Britain was the first nation to industrialize. For much of the nineteenth century, the British Empire was the world's dominant power, with a vast network of colonies. Britain was also the first nation to develop an effective parliamentary democracy.

British politics is often studied as a model of representative government. Named after the building that houses the British legislature in London, the **Westminster model** emphasizes that democracy rests on the supreme authority of a legislature—in Britain's

laissez-faire

A term taken from the French, which means "to let do," it refers to the pattern in which state management is limited to such matters as enforcing contracts and protecting property rights, while private market forces are free to operate with only minimal state regulation.

Westminster model

A form of democracy based on the supreme authority of Parliament and the accountability of its elected representatives; named after the Parliament building in London.

case, the Parliament. Finally, Britain has served as a model of gradual and peaceful evolution of democratic government in a world where transitions to democracy are often turbulent, interrupted, and uncertain.

Where Do You Stand?

Was Margaret Thatcher just what the doctor ordered to jump-start the British economy—or was she too divisive and ideological?

Tony Blair and Gordon Brown reinvented the modern Labour Party, severing its ties with the working class and emphasizing a cross-class coalition, which often seemed to tilt toward business. In this era of occupy movements and huge income inequality should Labour return to its historic roots?

SECTION 2

POLITICAL ECONOMY AND DEVELOPMENT

The pressures of global competitiveness and the perceived advantages of a minimalist government have encouraged the adoption in many countries of neoliberal approaches to economic management. A legacy from Thatcher's Britain, **neoliberalism** was a key feature of Tony Blair's and Gordon Brown's New Labour government. Its policies aimed to promote free competition, interfere with entrepreneurs and managers as little as possible, and create a business-friendly environment to attract foreign investment and spur innovation. Given that New Labour had long accepted the core principles of neoliberalism, the differences in economic policy between New Labour and the Conservative–Liberal coalition reflected changed circumstances—the economic crisis driven by the recession of 2008—more than ideological shifts.

✓ Focus Questions

- What are the similarities and what are the differences in New Labour's approach to governing the economy compared to that of Margaret Thatcher and John Major?

- What are the key elements of the coalition government's approach to economic management in the post-2008 context?

State and Economy

In the 1980s, economic growth in Britain was low and unemployment high. Britain was routinely called the "sick man of Europe." But from the mid-1990s to the "Great Recession" of 2008, Britain avoided the high unemployment and recession of many EU nations. The UK economy has run on a "two-track" pattern of growth. A strong service sector (especially in financial services) offset a much weaker industrial sector. Until the global downturn of fall 2008, the British economy exhibited overall strength. With low unemployment, low interest rates, low inflation, and sustained growth, the UK performance was one of the best among the leading industrial economies. Weeks before the collapse of Lehman brothers heralded the Great Recession, Brown warned at a meeting of Eurozone countries that the collapse of the U.S. housing market and the Great Recession to follow could be blamed on America, but insisted that global problems required coordinated global solutions. Thus far neither Britain nor other European economies have stepped up to the plate.

With the transition in 2010 from a New Labour to a Conservative–Liberal government, the policy orientation did not change at a stroke. Neoliberalism drove the economic policy of New Labour and, as a result, the economic performance of the

neoliberalism

A term used to describe government policies aiming to promote free competition among business firms within the market, including reduced governmental regulation and social spending.

UK economy today remains oriented to a patchwork neoliberal approach. Two central dimensions, economic management and social policy, capture the new role of the state and show how limited this new state role really is, partly by design and partly by the sheer force of changes demanded by the recession.

Economic Management Like all other states, the British state intervenes in economic life, sometimes with considerable force. However, the British state has generally limited its role to broad policy instruments that influence the economy generally (**macroeconomic policy**). How has the orientation of economic policy evolved during the postwar period?

The Consensus Era After World War II, the unity inspired by shared suffering during the war and the need to rebuild the country crystallized the collectivist consensus. The state broadened and deepened its responsibilities for the economy.

The state assumed direct ownership of key industries. It also accepted the responsibility to secure low levels of unemployment (a policy of full employment), expand social services, maintain a steady rate of growth (increase economic output or GDP), keep prices stable, and achieve desirable balance-of-payments and exchange rates. The approach is called Keynesian demand management, or **Keynesianism** (named after the British economist John Maynard Keynes, 1883–1946).

Before Thatcher became leader of the Conservative Party in 1975, Conservative leaders generally accepted the collectivist consensus. By the 1970s, however, Britain was suffering economically without growth and with growing political discontent. Investments declined, and trade union agitation increased. Industrial unrest in the winter of 1978–1979 dramatized Labour's inability to manage the trade unions. It seemed as if everyone was on strike. Strikes by truckers disrupted fuel supplies. Strikes by train-drivers disrupted intercity commerce and visits to granny. Some ambulance drivers refused to respond to emergency calls. Grave diggers refused to bury the dead. Thatcher came to power a few months later in May 1979. What was dubbed "the winter of discontent" destroyed Britain's collectivist consensus and discredited the Keynesian welfare state.

Thatcherite Policy Orientation The economic orientations of Thatcher and John Major, her successor, rejected Keynesianism. **Monetarism** emerged as the new economic doctrine. It assumed that there is a "natural rate of unemployment" determined by the labor market itself. State intervention to steer the economy should be limited to a few steps to foster appropriate rates of growth in the money supply and keep inflation low. Monetarism reflected a radical change from the postwar consensus regarding economic management. Not only was active government intervention considered unnecessary; it was seen as undesirable and destabilizing.

New Labour's Economic Policy Approach Gordon Brown as chancellor—and later as prime minister—insisted on establishing a sound economy. He was determined to reassure international markets that the British economy was built on a platform of stability (low debt, low deficit, low inflation) and that the Labour government could be counted on to run a tight financial ship. Only after he turned the public debt into a surplus did the "iron chancellor" reinvent himself as a more conventional Labour chancellor. Even then, Brown used economic growth to increase spending (rather than cut taxes).

macroeconomic policy

Policy intended to shape the overall economic system by concentrating on policy targets such as inflation and growth.

Keynesianism

Named after British economist John Maynard Keynes, an approach to economic policy in which state economic policies are used to regulate the economy to achieve stable economic growth.

monetarism

An approach to economic policy that assumes a natural rate of unemployment, determined by the labor market, and rejects the instruments of government spending to run budgetary deficits for stimulating the economy and creating jobs.

Artist: Chris Riddell. Published in The Observer, 13 Nov 2011. http://www .cartoons.ac.uk/record-request/95507. British Cartoon archive Kent

Brown claimed that since capital is international, mobile, and not subject to control, industrial policy and planning are futile if they focus on the domestic economy alone. Instead, government should improve the quality of labor through education and training, maintain labor market flexibility, and attract investment to Britain. Strict control of inflation and tough limits on public expenditure would promote both employment and investment opportunities. Economic policy should increase competitive strength through government–business partnerships and efforts to improve the skill of the workforce and therefore the competitiveness of British industry.

The Coalition Government's Economic Policy Approach The centerpiece of the coalition government's approach to economic policy is its overarching commitment to deficit reduction as the necessary precondition for stabilizing the economy. Very soon after taking office, the coalition government engaged in a comprehensive spending review and a predictably harsh retrospective critique of the state of the economy they inherited from New Labour. To say the least, Britain's chancellor of the exchequer (finance minister) George Osborne cast significant doubt on the way New Labour handled public finances. Cameron's speech to the Tory Party conference in October 2010 lambasted Labour, characterizing the result of Labour's economic policy and the urgent need for debt reduction this way:

> Back in May, we inherited public finances that can only be described as catastrophic.... This year, we're going to spend 43 billion pounds (68 billion dollars) on interest payments alone ... not to pay off the debt—just to stand still.... That's why we have acted decisively—to stop pouring so much of your hard-earned money down the drain.

Key cuts announced by the chancellor, which are scheduled to be in effect for four years, include cuts in government subsidies for public housing, increases in the age for pensions, a reduction in child benefits for middle-class families, a general reduction of about 10 percent in a range of social protection and welfare benefits, and a cut of roughly 20 percent in public spending across the board. Of course, the new economic course set by the coalition government spurred considerable controversy. Osborne insisted that the budget was "guided fairness, reform," while Labour critics characterized it as "a reckless gamble with people's livelihoods," and a threat to any economic recovery. On balance, the cuts were viewed as both necessary and regressive, hitting those in the lower end of the income distribution harder than those who are better off.

sounds like America →

Social Policy

Historically, in the United Kingdom welfare state provisions have interfered relatively little in the workings of the market, and policy-makers do not see the reduction of group inequalities as the proper goal of the welfare state. In fact, through changes in government there has been considerable continuity across the period of postwar consensus, despite differences in perspectives on the welfare state. The collectivist era enshrined the welfare state. Thatcher assailed the principles of the welfare state but accepted many of the policies as increased need triggered expanding welfare state budgets. New Labour attempted to link social expenditures to improving skills, making everyone a stakeholder in society, and tried hard—with only limited success—to turn social policy into an instrument for improving education, skills, and competitiveness.

In comparative European terms, the UK welfare state has offered few comprehensive services, and the policies are not very generous. At the same time—and the one exception—the National Health Service (NHS) provides comprehensive and universal medical care and has long been championed as the jewel in the crown of the welfare state in Britain, an exception to the rule in ordinary times because it provides fine, low cost medical care to all British citizens as a matter of right. Despite periodic infusions of cash to temporarily stabilize the NHS, the NHS is chronically underfunded, general practitioners are woefully underpaid, and the NHS faces some of the same challenges, which the Affordable Care Act in the United States is facing, such as the excessive use of emergency rooms and insufficient access to primary care physicians. According to a recent report of the European Commission, Britain has fewer doctors per capita than nearly all the other countries in the EU.

Society and Economy

New Labour rejected both the cutbacks in social provisions of Conservative governments that seemed mean-spirited as well as the egalitarian traditions of Britain's collectivist era that emphasized entitlements or what in the United States is called "tax-and-spend liberalism." Instead, New Labour focused its social policy on training and broader social investment as a more positive third-way alternative.

New Labour emphasized efficiencies and attempted to break welfare dependency. Its effort to identify comprehensive solutions to society's ills and reduce the tendency for government to let marginalized individuals fall by the wayside captures the third-way orientation of the New Labour project.

The economic upturn that began in 1992, combined with Major's moderating effects on the Thatcherite social policy agenda narrowed inequality in the mid-1990s. Attention to social exclusion in its many forms, and strong rates of growth were good omens for narrowing the gap between rich and poor. But even before the "Great Recession" of 2008 and despite New Labour's commitment to producing a more egalitarian society and reducing poverty, it has proven very difficult to achieve success.

A 2007 report by UNICEF compared twenty-one wealthy countries (members of the OECD) on their success in securing the well-being of children along six dimensions. Both the United States and the United Kingdom were in the bottom third for five of the six dimensions under review. In the summary table that presents the overall rankings, the United Kingdom came in dead last, just behind the United States. Despite repeated high visibility commitments by New Labour to eliminate childhood poverty, they were unable to make any sustained headway toward that laudable goal.

In a market-driven economy, it is extremely difficult for governments to effectively pursue targeted goals such as eliminating childhood poverty. The government may have the will, but it doesn't have the way (the policy instruments or the strategic capacity) to meet such goals. That said, the United Kingdom has moved up in the rankings since 2007, having risen from last place in 2000/2001 to a middle-of-the-pack position (sixteenth) in 2013, close to Portugal and the Czech Republic—not auspicious perhaps but, at least, in the middle, not the bottom of the rankings.

Inequality and Ethnic Minorities

Ethnic minorities disproportionately suffer diminished opportunity in the United Kingdom. Despite the common and often disparaging reference to ethnic minority individuals as "immigrants," members of ethnic minority groups are increasingly native-born. Today, fully one-third of the children born in England and Wales have at least one foreign-born parent. Americans are accustomed to characterizing themselves with pride as a nation of immigrants, but in empirical terms it is probably more appropriate to characterize Britain as a nation of immigrants—in fact, Britain is positioned to become the most ethnically diverse Western nation by 2050. Unfortunately, this does not mean that Britain has resolved the challenges of social exclusion and marginalization of its ethnic minority members.

Ethnic minority individuals, particularly young men, are subject to unequal treatment by the police and considerable physical harassment by citizens. They have experienced cultural isolation as well as marginalization in the educational system, job training, housing, and labor markets. There is considerable concern about the apparent rise in racially motivated crime in major metropolitan areas with significant ethnic diversity.

Poor rates of economic success reinforce the sense of isolation and distinct collective identities. Variations among ethnic minority communities are quite considerable, however, and there are some noteworthy success stories. For example, among men of African, Asian, Chinese, and Indian descent, the proportional representation in the managerial and professional ranks is actually higher than that for white men (although they are much less likely to be senior managers in large firms). Also, Britons of South Asian, especially Indian, descent enjoy a high rate of entrepreneurship. Nevertheless, the experiences faced by ethnic minorities remain grim, as is the case for younger workers. Minority individuals are twice as likely to be unemployed than whites. Government data indicate that in 2013 the gap in the unemployment rate for ethnic minority youth compared to whites rose to 13 percent as the average unemployment rate for young people in all minority groups hit 37 percent. The jobless rate for young Bangladeshi and Pakistani workers was 46 percent and the rate for young blacks was 45 percent. As if these data were not sufficiently concerning, the trend suggests even harder times ahead, since ethnic minorities are overrepresented in public sector jobs in health care and social work—which face significant cutbacks due to austerity measures.[1]

Inequality and Women

According to data from the Office of National Statistics (ONS) released in December 2013, for the first time in 5 years the gender pay gap has widened, reversing what had been a period of steady progress in narrowing the gap. Based on median hourly earnings for full-time workers the differential between men and women increased last year from 9.5 percent to 10 percent—and that is only part of the story. If all employees, including those in part-time work are included, the gender gap increased to just under 20 percent. In addition the gap is expected to widen as public sector cuts increase the number and percentage of women into the private sector—where the gender gap is greater than in the public sector. At the same time, a survey by a highly regarded management group concludes that a woman can be expected to earn roughly $678,000 less than a man over her career. Nor is the gender gap in economic rewards the only expression of gender bias in Britain. Despite the legal recognition of equality between women and men, and the growing empowerment of women in nearly all spheres of social and political life in the United Kingdom, readily observable differences in the treatment and experiences of women and men persist—and as every student reading this text knows instinctively, the terrain of gender in every society produces complicated and crosscutting evidence about the role of women in society. On the one hand, girls and young women routinely out-perform boys and young men at every educational level, yet more men than women are in the workforce (although the gap is narrowing).[2] Where family dynamics and cultural habits intercede, however, gender divisions remain strong. Women who work are far more likely than their male counterparts to work part-time (56–57 percent), compared to 86–87 percent for men, while women are far more likely to shoulder the additional burdens of childcare, eldercare, and housework, but recent UK policy has favorably impacted women's role. In 2013 the government implemented policies to provide early learning facilities for the 20 percent most disadvantaged 2-year-olds and in 2014 introduced early learning facilities for roughly 40 percent of all 2-year-olds. Clearly these policies reduce the strain on women (and increasing numbers of men) who juggle the responsibilities of work and family.

*[handwritten margin note: → * Pay gap increasing (increase more as women move to private sector because larger gap here than in public sector)]*

Environmental Issues

In Britain, as in much of America, extreme weather events in 2013–2014 have pro-voked intense debate about environmental issues. Britons have suffered through the worst storm and tidal surges in 60 years on the North Sea coastline, floods ruining Christmas. The most intense and unremitting rainfall in Somerset and Dorset in 250 years has inspired intensified and increasingly politicized hostile debate within the government and in the scientific community about the role of climate change in the rash of floods and storms.

More generally, the British public has expressed increasing concern about a vari-ety of environmental issues including acid rain, as pollution from coal-fired power plants endanger animals and plants. There is concern also about fracking, which involves drilling holes deep into the ground and then using high-pressure liquid to fracture shale rocks to release gas trapped inside. Environmentalists have strongly criticized the practice, warning of health risks to those in the surrounding area and the effect the method would have on surrounding areas. They have claimed it could have dire effects over the public's health. At the same time, Britain has environmen-talists who have long raised concerns about the safety of the food supply. Concerns have been raised about contaminated beef, the use of pesticides, the risk of salmonella, and the potential risks of genetically modified (GM) food. Environmental policy is hotly contested in the United Kingdom, perhaps most dramatically in the case of "climategate" in 2009, when scientists at the University of East Anglia were accused of manipulating data to overstate the dangers of climate change. In 2012 the UK government produced the first of what are intended to be 5-year climate risk assess-ment reports. In general, environmental policy has reflected a cross-party consensus, although Labour has been accused by critics of an urban bias, which played into the view of some that British governments, regardless of party, are slow and ineffective when it comes to addressing the needs of rural areas, a view exacerbated in 2013–2014 by the slow and ineffective response to extreme weather. Politicians have been accused of becoming little more than "flood tourists" who have visited the scenes of devastation in droves, producing endless photo opportunities, while the environ-ment agency responsible for flood protection and river management has been roundly criticized as ineffectual. These historic floods have provoked produced tension with rural interests, most significantly with the countryside alliance, a broad-based and extremely effective organization to promote traditional hunting and shooting, especially hunting with hounds, which was outlawed in 2005. In general there remains a tension between a growing desire of many in Britain, including Prime Minister Cameron, to "think Green" and the anti-regulatory bias that makes effective environmental policy more difficult, despite the professed cross-party commitment to effective environmental policy.

Britain in the Global Economy

foreign direct investment

Ownership of or investment in cross-border enterprises in which the investor plays a direct managerial role.

Foreign direct investment (FDI) favors national systems, like those of Britain (and the United States), that rely mostly on private contractual and market-driven arrangements. Because of low costs, a business-friendly political climate, government-sponsored financial incentives, reduced trade union power, and a large pool of potential nonunionized recruits, the United Kingdom is a highly regarded location in Europe for FDI. In 2013 Britain scored eighth globally in foreign direct investment inflows.

The United Kingdom scores well in international comparisons of microeconomic competitiveness and growth competitiveness. It has also achieved significant competitive success in particular pockets of science-based high technology industries. Even before the Great Recession, the picture of UK global competitiveness, however, was clouded by weak industrial performance.

Gordon Brown's Britain preached a globalization-friendly model of flexible labor markets throughout EU Europe, and its success in boosting Britain's economic performance in comparison with the rest of Europe won some reluctant admirers.

Under New Labour, Britain achieved an enviable record of growth, low inflation, and low unemployment in part because of its sustained commitment to attract foreign investment and to assume an outward-looking competitive profile. Of course, that international market-driven orientation of the British economy, combined with a hands-off antiregulatory approach exposed Britain to enormous risk and a very severe downturn, with reverberating political consequences, when the global recession engulfed Britain in 2008. Until the great recession, the British economy exhibited an enviable growth model that was fueled by ready access to consumer credit and by the simultaneous "fool's paradise" of low interest rates, inflated housing values, low inflation, and highly questionable lending practices.[3]

Under the woeful conditions that the coalition government faced from their first days in office, their options for governing the economy are very limited. Rejecting the temptation to stimulate the economy through government spending, budgetary cuts are the first, second, and third priority, and effective economic management will be a daunting challenge. Government leaders are resolute and plain-spoken about the challenges they face and in the early going have impressed many by their willingness to insist on radical cuts and tight budgetary control across the board. This is bitter medicine, but if they can maintain popular support and keep their coalition afloat, they may yet have an opportunity to benefit from the recovery they anticipate around the middle of the decade. The governor of the Bank of England, Mark Carney, a Canadian, a former executive at Goldman Sachs, and the first non-Briton to head the bank that governs the city of London, the United Kingdom's equivalent to Wall Street, is determined to end 5 years of stagnation, and keep Britain's interest rates low, if possible, below 7 percent. Broadly speaking this aligns the Bank of England and America's Federal Reserve.

GOVERNANCE AND POLICY-MAKING

SECTION 3

[handwritten margin note: not written & basically ancient]

Britain's constitution is notable for two features: its form and its age. Britain lacks a formal written constitution in the usual sense. There is no single unified and authoritative text (like the U.S. Constitution) that has special status above ordinary law and can be amended only by special procedures. Rather, the British constitution is a combination of statutory law (mainly acts of Parliament), common law, convention, and authoritative interpretations. Although it is often said that Britain has an unwritten constitution, this is not accurate. Authoritative legal treatises are written, of course, as are the much more significant acts of Parliament that define crucial elements of the political system. These acts define the powers of Parliament and its relationship with the monarchy, the rights governing the relationship between state and citizen, the relationship of constituent nations to the United Kingdom, the relationship of the United Kingdom to the EU, and many other rights and legal arrangements. In fact, "What distinguishes the British constitution from others is not that it is unwritten, but rather that it is part written and uncodified."[4]

The conventions and acts of Parliament with constitutional implications began at least as early as the seventeenth century, notably with the Bill of Rights of 1689, which helped define the relationship between the monarchy and Parliament. "Britain's constitution presents a paradox," a British scholar of constitutional history has observed. "We live in a modern world but inhabit a pre-modern, indeed, ancient, constitution."[5]

Constitutional authorities have accepted the structure and principles of many areas of government for so long that the very appeal to convention itself has enormous cultural force. Thus, widely agreed-on rules of conduct, rather than law or U.S.-style checks and balances, set the limits of governmental power. Absolute principles of government are few, but those that exist are fundamental to the organization of the state and central to governance, policy-making, and patterns of representation. It will become clear, however, that even the most time-encrusted principles of Britain's ancient constitutional traditions are subject to quick and potentially radical changes.

Organization of the State

The core of the British system is **parliamentary sovereignty**: Parliament can make or overturn any law; the executive, the judiciary, and the throne do not have any authority to restrict, veto, or otherwise overturn parliamentary action. In a classic **parliamentary democracy**, the prime minister is answerable to the House of Commons (the elected element of Parliament) and may be dismissed by it. That said, by joining the European Economic Community in 1973 (now known as the European Union), Parliament

Focus Questions

- What are the strengths and weaknesses of parliamentary democracy?

- How has the devolution of powers from the UK Parliament to Wales, Scotland, and Northern Ireland changed both the organizing principles of the state and politics in the United Kingdom?

parliamentary sovereignty

The doctrine that grants the legislature the power to make or overturn any law and permits no veto or judicial review.

parliamentary democracy

System of government in which the chief executive is answerable to the legislature and may be dismissed by it.

accepted significant limitations on its power to act. It acknowledged that European law has force in the United Kingdom without requiring parliamentary assent and that European law overrides British law. Parliament has accepted the authority of the European Court of Justice (ECJ) to resolve jurisdictional disputes. To complete the circle, the ECJ has confirmed its right to suspend acts of Parliament.

Second, Britain has long been a **unitary state**. By contrast to the United States, where powers not delegated to the national government are reserved for the states, no powers are reserved constitutionally for subcentral units of government in the United Kingdom. However, the Labour government of Tony Blair introduced a far-reaching program of constitutional reform that created a quasi-federal system. Specified powers have been delegated (the British prefer to say *devolved*) to legislative bodies in Scotland and Wales, and to Northern Ireland as well, now that the long-standing conflict there seems settled. In addition, powers have been redistributed from the Westminster Parliament to an authority governing London with a directly elected mayor. As part of New Labour's constitutional reform agenda, regional development agencies (RDAs), which are appointed bodies, were set up in 1999 to enhance development plans for regions throughout the United Kingdom.

Third, Britain has a system of **fusion of powers** at the national level: Parliament is the supreme legislative, executive, and judicial authority and includes the monarch as well as the House of Commons and the House of Lords. The fusion of legislature and executive is also expressed in the function and personnel of the cabinet. U.S. presidents can direct or ignore their cabinets, which have no constitutionally mandated function, but the British cabinet bears enormous constitutional responsibility. Through collective decision making, the cabinet—and not an independent prime minister—shapes, directs, and takes responsibility for government. This core principle, **cabinet government**, however, may at critical junctures be observed more in principle than in practice. Particularly with strong prime ministers, such as Thatcher and Blair, who can rally—or bully—the cabinet, power gravitates to the prime minister.

Britain is a **constitutional monarchy**. The Crown passes by hereditary succession, but the government or state officials must exercise nearly all powers of the Crown. Parliamentary sovereignty, parliamentary democracy, and cabinet government form the core of the British or Westminster model of government.

The Executive

The term *cabinet government* emphasizes the key functions that the cabinet exercises: responsibility for policy-making, supreme control of government, and coordination of all government departments. However, the term does not capture the full range of executive institutions nor the scale and complexity of operations. Nor does it capture the realities of a system in which power invariably flows upward to the prime minister. In addition, the executive reaches well beyond the cabinet. It extends from ministries (departments) and ministers to the civil service in one direction, and to Parliament (as we shall see in Section 4) in the other direction.

Cabinet Government

After a general election, the Crown invites the leader of the party that emerges from the election with control of a majority of seats in the House of Commons to form a government and serve as prime minister. The prime minister selects approximately two dozen ministers for the cabinet. Senior cabinet posts include the Foreign Office

---

unitary state

In contrast to a federal system, a system of government in which no powers are reserved for subnational units of government.

fusion of powers

A constitutional principle that merges the authority of branches of government, in contrast to the principle of separation of powers.

cabinet government

A system of government in which most executive power is held by the cabinet, headed by a prime minister.

constitutional monarchy

System of government in which the head of state ascends by heredity but is limited in powers and constrained by the provisions of a constitution.

(equivalent to the U.S. secretary of state), the Home Office (ministry of justice or attorney general), and the chancellor of the exchequer (finance minister). Unlike the French Constitution, which prohibits a cabinet minister from serving in the legislature, British constitutional tradition *requires* overlapping membership between Parliament and cabinet. A member of the cabinet must be either a member of parliament (MP) or less commonly, a member of the House of Lords.

The cabinet room at 10 Downing Street (the prime minister's official residence) is a place of intrigue as well as deliberation. From the prime minister's viewpoint, the cabinet may appear as loyal followers or as ideological combatants, potential challengers for party leadership, and parochial advocates for pet programs that run counter to the overall objectives of the government. By contrast, the convention of collective responsibility normally unifies the cabinet. In principle, the prime minister must gain the support of a majority of the cabinet for a range of significant decisions, notably the budget and the legislative program.

The only other constitutionally mandated mechanism for checking the prime minister is the government's defeat on a vote of no confidence in the House of Commons (discussed further in Section 4). Since the defeat of a government by parliament is rare and politically dangerous, the cabinet remains the only routine check on the prime minister.

Margaret Thatcher often attempted to galvanize loyalists in the cabinet and either marginalize or expel detractors. In the end, her treatment of the cabinet, which stretched British constitutional conventions, helped inspire the movement to unseat her as party leader. John Major returned to a more consultative approach.

Tony Blair, like Thatcher, narrowed the scope of collective responsibility. The prime minister, a few key cabinet members, and a handful of advisers made many important policy decisions in smaller unofficial gatherings. Under Blair, cabinet meetings were usually less than an hour and could not seriously take up (much less resolve) policy differences.

The decision to go to war in Iraq underscored the cabinet's weakened capacity to exercise constitutional checks and balances. Blair and his close aides seemed skeptical about the effectiveness and centrality of the cabinet as well as cabinet committees. Blair preferred to coordinate strategically important policy areas through highly politicized special units in the Cabinet Office.

How does David Cameron run his cabinet? Carefully, no doubt, since he presides over a potentially unstable coalition in which one wrong move could bring down the government. On balance, cabinet government represents a durable and effective formula for governance, although the United Kingdom has very little experience with coalition governments. The cabinet operates within a broader cabinet system, or core executive (see Figure 2.4), and the prime minister holds or controls many of the levers of power in the core executive. Because the prime minister is the head of the cabinet, his or her office helps develop policy, coordinates operations, and functions as a liaison with the media, the party, interest groups, and Parliament.

The cabinet is supported by a set of institutions that help formulate policy, coordinate operations, and facilitate the support for government policy. Acting within a context set by the fusion of legislature and executive, the prime minister enjoys a great opportunity for decisive leadership that is lacking in a system of checks and balances and separation of powers among the branches of government.

Cabinet committees (comprising ministers) and official committees (made up of civil servants) supplement the work of the cabinet. In addition, the treasury plays an important coordinating role through its budgetary control. The cabinet office supports day-to-day operations. Leaders in both the Commons and the Lords, the *whips*, smooth the passage of legislation sponsored by the government. Given that the government always has a working majority (except when the government declares

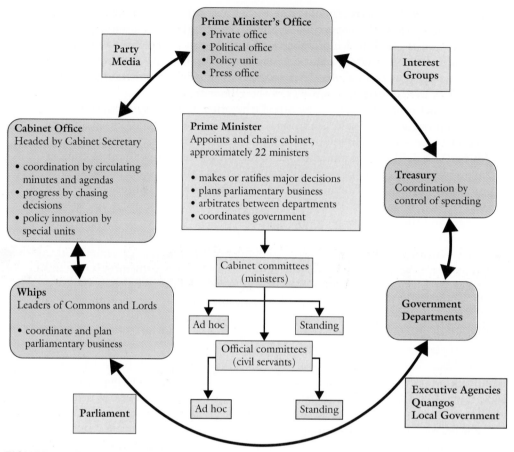

FIGURE 2.4 The Cabinet System
The cabinet is supported by a set of institutions that help formulate policy, coordinate operations, and facilitate the support for government policy. Acting within a context set by the fusion of legislature and executive, the prime minister enjoys a great opportunity for decisive leadership that is lacking in a system of checks and balances and separation of powers among the branches of government.

a "free vote," which signals that a matter is either too controversial or too inconsequential to be introduced on behalf of the government), the outcome of a vote is seldom in doubt.

Because the cabinet system and the core executive concentrate power at the top, London does not suffer from Washington-style gridlock. The risk in the United Kingdom is the opposite danger of excessive concentration of power by a prime minister who is prepared to manipulate cabinet and flout the conventions of collective responsibility.

Bureaucracy and Civil Service

Policy-making may appear to be increasingly concentrated in the prime minister's hands. When viewed from Whitehall (the London street where key UK units of government and administration are located), however, the executive may appear to be dominated by its vast administrative agencies. The range and complexity of state policy-making mean that the cabinet's authority must be shared with a vast set of unelected officials. Government departments are directed by members of the cabinet.

Ministers are assisted by a very senior career civil servant, called a permanent secretary, who has chief administrative responsibility for running a department. Other senior civil servants, including deputy secretaries and undersecretaries, assist the permanent secretaries. In addition, the minister reaches into his or her department to appoint a principal private secretary, an up-and-coming civil servant who assists the minister as gatekeeper and liaison with senior civil servants.

Since nearly all legislation is introduced on behalf of the government and presented as the policy directive of a ministry, civil servants in Britain do much of the work of conceptualizing and refining legislation. (In the United States committee staffers in the Congress often do this work.) Civil servants, more than ministers, assume operational duties.

As a result of the ongoing modernization of Whitehall, the civil service has been downsized and given a new corporate structure. Few at the top of these agencies (agency

THE U.S. CONNECTION

Comparing the U.S. Presidential System to the British Parliamentary System

Political scientists—especially those engaged in comparative politics—often discuss how the design of political institutions affects political outcomes.

Among the institutional differences that matter most is the distinction between presidential systems such as the United States and parliamentary systems such as the United Kingdom.

In a presidential system, the legislature and executive are *independent*. Both the legislature and the chief executive have their own fixed schedule for election and their own political mandate. Legislators and presidents have been elected independently of each other. They have different constituencies and often have different political agendas. Each may even gain credibility and support by opposing the other. In presidential systems the agenda and the authority of the president are often compromised when the president and the majority of legislators are from different parties—in fact this is the rule, rather than the exception in the United States and in many other presidential systems. Stalemates on key items of legislation are common. Between presidential elections, it is very difficult to remove a president, even one who has very little popular support or is suspected of acting unconstitutionally. It requires impeachment, which, in turn, requires a finding of extraordinary misconduct and a strong majority vote in the legislature.

Prime ministers, in contrast, must enjoy the support of the majority of the legislature to achieve office—and they must preserve that support to stay in office, since prime ministers and their governments can fall if they lose a vote of no confidence in the legislature. Furthermore, in a parliamentary system the timing of elections is typically not fixed (although the Cameron government has modified this rule). When riding high, the prime minister can call for a new election in an effort to win a new mandate and a deeper majority in parliament. When in trouble, a prime minister can be sent packing in an instant through a vote of no confidence.

In a parliamentary system like Britain's, because the legislators and prime minister sink or swim together, they tend to cooperate and work through differences. In a presidential system like America's, because the legislature and executive are mutually independent—one can swim, while the other sinks—the tendency for finger pointing and stalemate is much greater.

But the distinctions should not be exaggerated. Powerful prime ministers such as Thatcher and Blair were routinely criticized for being too presidential. And in Britain, the threat a prime minister faces of losing office through a vote of no confidence has all but disappeared—it has happened only once in more than 80 years. In fact, if recent history is a good predictor, an American president is more likely to face a bill of impeachment than a British prime minister is to face a serious vote of no confidence.

MAKING CONNECTIONS Is a parliamentary system more or less effective than a presidential system?

The analysis draws heavily from Alfred Stepan, with Cindy Skatch, "Constitutional Frameworks and Democratic Consolidation: Parliamentarism versus Presidentialism," in Mark Kesselman and Joel Krieger, eds., *Readings in Comparative Politics: Political Challenges and Changing Agendas* (Boston: Houghton Mifflin, 2006), pp. 284–293.

chief executives) are traditional career civil servants. There is growing concern that the increasing importance of special advisers (who are both political policy advisers and civil servants) is eroding the impartiality of civil servants. Key special advisers played critical roles in making the case in the famous "dodgy dossier" of September 2002 alleging that the threat of weapons of mass destruction justified regime change in Iraq.

Public and Semipublic Institutions

Like other countries, Britain has institutionalized "semipublic" agencies, which are sanctioned by the state but without direct democratic oversight. Examples include nationalized industries and nondepartmental public bodies.

Nationalized Industries The nationalization of basic industries—such as coal, iron and steel, gas and electricity supply—was a central objective of the Labour government's program during the postwar collectivist era. By the end of the Thatcher era the idea of public ownership had clearly run out of steam and most of these giant state enterprises were privatized, that is, sold to private large-scale investors or sold in small units to ordinary citizens, as was the case with British Telecom, the communications giant. More than 50 percent of the BT shares were sold to the public. When thinking of expanding state functions, we can look to a set of semipublic administrative organizations.

Nondepartmental Public Bodies Since the 1970s, an increasing number of administrative functions have been transferred to bodies that are typically part of the state in terms of funding, function, and appointment of staff, but operate at arm's length from ministers.

These nondepartmental public bodies (NDPBs) are better known as quasi-nongovernmental organizations or **quangos**. They take responsibility for specific functions and can combine governmental and private sector expertise. At the same time, they enable ministers to distance themselves from controversial areas of policy.

Alongside quangos, in recent years the government has looked for ways to expand the investment of the private sector in capital projects such as hospitals and schools. Thus New Labour continued the private finance initiative (PFI) it inherited from the Conservatives as a key part of its signature modernization program and as a way to revitalize public services. The results are controversial: Critics and supporters disagree about the quality of services provided and about whether taxpayers win or lose by the financial arrangements. In addition, the tendency of PFI initiatives to blur the line between public and private raise important and controversial issues.[6]

quangos

Acronym for *quasi-nongovernmental organizations*, the term used in Britain for nonelected bodies that are outside traditional governmental departments or local authorities.

Other State Institutions

The Military and the Police

Those involved in security and law enforcement have enjoyed a rare measure of popular support in Britain. Constitutional tradition and professionalism distance the British police and military officers from politics.

In the case of the military, British policy since the Cold War remains focused on a gradually redefined set of North Atlantic Treaty Organization (NATO) commitments. Still ranked among the top five military powers in the world, Britain retains a global presence. In 1999, the United Kingdom strongly backed NATO's Kosovo campaign and pressed for ground troops. According to Blair, global interdependence rendered isolationism obsolete and inspired a commitment to a new ethical dimension in foreign policy. Throughout the war in Iraq and its bloody aftermath, Blair persistently sought to characterize Iraq as an extension of Kosovo, an effort to liberate Muslims from brutal dictatorships, whether Serbia's Milosevic or Iraq's Saddam Hussein. Until Blair's decision to support the American plan to shift the main venue of the war on terror from Afghanistan to Iraq, the use of the military in international conflicts generated little opposition. It may be that the Iraq war is the exception that proves the rule that the United Kingdom can play an important role in the world of states, including the use of force, when justified, without losing public support. In 2011, the Cameron government played a leading role in the international effort, endorsed by the U.N. Security Council, to protect civilians and enhance the cause of rebels fighting the regime of Libyan dictator Muammar Gaddafi. In the early stages, Cameron enjoyed strong support for his decision to participate in the international coalition. In August 2013, however, despite strong pressure from the United States and Cameron's best efforts, parliament refused to authorize use of force to quell the violence in Syria.

The police have traditionally operated as independent local forces throughout the country. Since the 1980s, the police have witnessed growth in government control, centralization, and level of political use. During the coal miners' strike of 1984–1985, the police operated to an unprecedented, perhaps unlawful, degree as a national force coordinated through Scotland Yard (London police headquarters). Police menaced strikers and hindered miners from participating in strike support activities. This partisan use of the police in an industrial dispute flew in the face of constitutional traditions and offended some police officers and officials. During the 1990s, concerns about police conduct focused on police–community relations. These included race relations, corruption, and the interrogation and treatment of people held in custody.

The Judiciary

In Britain, the principle of parliamentary sovereignty has limited the role of the judiciary. Courts have no power to judge the constitutionality of legislative acts (**judicial review**). They can only determine whether policy directives or administrative acts violate common law or an act of Parliament. Hence, the British judiciary is generally less politicized and influential than its U.S. counterpart.

Jurists, however, have participated in the wider political debate outside court. They have headed royal commissions on the conduct of industrial relations, the struggle in Northern Ireland riots in Britain's inner cities, and the suspicious death of a UN weapons inspector who challenged Blair's case for the war in Iraq.

In recent years Britain has witnessed dramatic institutional changes in law and the administration of justice, most notably with the 2009 creation of the UK Supreme Court, which serves as the highest court of appeal, removing that authority from the House of Lords.

As a member of the EU, Britain is bound to abide by the European Court of Justice (ECJ). For example, with the passage of the Human Rights Act in 1998, Britain is required to comply with the European Convention on Human Rights (ECHR). Also, the adoption of the ECHR forced Britain to curtail discrimination against gays in the military.

judicial review

The ability of a high court to nullify actions by the executive and legislative branches of government that in its judgment violate the constitution.

Subnational Government

The United Kingdom is a state comprising distinct nations (England, Scotland, Wales, and Northern Ireland). Because the British political framework has traditionally been unitary, not federal, for centuries, no formal powers devolved to either the nations within the United Kingdom or to subnational (really subcentral or sub-UK) units as in the United States, Germany, or India. Historically, the UK Parliament asserted authority over all political units in the United Kingdom. No powers were reserved for any other units of government: There are no states, and no powers were reserved for nations within the United Kingdom, or for local government. Even so, nations were a significant aspect of collective identities in the United Kingdom, often exerting a powerful hold on their members. For many, to be Scottish or Welsh or English or Northern Irish was a core source of identity that created a sense of commonality and shared fates among members. Nations were not political units. But that is no longer true.

Recent constitutional reforms have introduced important modifications in the organizing principles of the United Kingdom. After referendums in Wales and Scotland in 1997, and in Northern Ireland, which is part of the United Kingdom, and in the Republic of Ireland (an independent country) in 1998, Tony Blair's Labour government introduced a set of power-sharing arrangements (what the British call "devolution") to govern the arrangements among the UK Westminster Parliament, the Welsh Assembly, the Northern Ireland Assembly, and the Scottish Parliament. And by the time you are reading this passage, a referendum on Scottish independence may have ratified the creation of an independent Scotland.

In general, the UK government retains responsibility for all policy areas that have not been devolved, and that are the traditional domain of nation-states. Westminster controls security and foreign policy, economic policy, trade, defense, and social security for the United Kingdom as a whole, except where it doesn't; that is, where specific powers have been ceded to Scotland, Northern Ireland, or Wales.

Of all the devolved nations and regions within the United Kingdom, Scotland and the Scottish government enjoy the most robust powers. Whereas Wales and Northern Ireland have relatively limited independent authority and have legislative arenas called assemblies, Scotland has a parliament, and the Scottish government is responsible for crucial areas of policy, including education, health, and the administration of justice. Clearly, devolution involves both an element of federalism and a carefully crafted compromise. The UK Parliament is still the mother of all parliaments, but it has some potentially restive offspring!

It is important to note that every power devolved from the UK Parliament to the Scottish Parliament or the Welsh or Northern Ireland assembly chips away at the very core of parliamentary sovereignty that lies at the heart of the Westminster model. Devolution has also sparked a controversy about the asymmetry in voting rights that devolution produces.

What right should a Scottish MP have to vote on laws that might relate to England or Wales, while English and Welsh MPs cannot vote on some matters related to Scotland, in areas where policy had been devolved from the Westminster Parliament to the Scottish Parliament?

Devolution within England is also part of the reform process. Regional Development Agencies (RDAs) were introduced throughout England in 1999 to facilitate economic development at the regional level. Even though they are unelected bodies with no statutory authority, they have opened the door to popular mobilization in the long term for elected regional assemblies. In addition, the Blair government placed changes in the governance of London on the fast track. The introduction of a directly elected mayor of London in May 2000 marked an important reform, leading to the direct election of mayors in other major cities, such as Birmingham and putting into practice a process of decentralizing power.

The Policy-Making Process

Parliamentary sovereignty is the core constitutional principle of the British political system. But for policy-making and policy implementation, the focus is not on Westminster but rather on Whitehall.

In the United Kingdom Parliament has little direct participation in policy-making. Policy-making emerges primarily from within the executive. There, decision-making is strongly influenced by policy communities—informal networks with extensive knowledge, access, and personal connections to those responsible for policy. In this private hothouse environment, civil servants, ministers, and members of the policy communities work through informal ties. A cooperative style develops as the ministry becomes an advocate for key players and as civil servants come perhaps to overidentify the public good with the advancement of policy within their area of responsibility.

This cozy insider-only policy process has been challenged by the delegation of more and more authority to the EU. Both ministers and senior civil servants spend a great deal of time in EU policy deliberations and are constrained both directly and indirectly by the EU agenda and directives. More than 80 percent of the rules governing economic life in Britain are determined by the EU. Decisions by the EU Council of Finance Ministers and the European Central Bank shape British macroeconomic, monetary, and fiscal policies in significant ways. Even foreign and security policy are not immune from EU influences. The increasing Europeanization of policy-making has been and promises to further become one of the most interesting and potentially transformative developments in British politics.

Where Do You Stand?

Which is a more effective form of government: American checks and balances or British parliamentary democracy?

Does the strength of the cabinet and the power of the prime minister risk turning Britain into an elective dictatorship?

REPRESENTATION AND PARTICIPATION

SECTION 4

As discussed in Section 3, parliamentary sovereignty is the core constitutional principle defining the role of the legislature and, in a sense, the whole system of British government. The executive or judiciary can set no act of Parliament aside, nor is any Parliament bound by the actions of any previous Parliament. Nevertheless, in practice, the control exerted by the House of Commons (or Commons)—the lower of the two houses of Parliament and by far the more powerful—is not unlimited. This section investigates the powers and role of Parliament, both Commons and Lords. It also looks at the party system, elections, and contemporary currents in British political culture, citizenship, and identity. We close by offering an analysis of surprising new directions in political participation and social protest.

Focus Questions ▼

- What are the political implications of the Conservative–Liberal coalition government?

- What are the constitutional implications of the Conservative–Liberal government?

The Legislature

Today, the Commons does not really legislate in a meaningful way. Its real function is to assent to government legislation, since (with rare exceptions such as the present coalition government) a single governing party has a majority of the seats and can control the legislative agenda and pass legislation at will. In addition, the balance of effective oversight of policy has shifted from the legislature to executive agencies.

The House of Commons

The House of Commons, the lower house of Parliament, with 650 seats at the time of the 2010 election, exercises the main legislative power in Britain. Along with the two unelected elements of Parliament, the Crown and the House of Lords, the Commons has three main functions: (1) to pass laws, (2) to provide finances for the state by authorizing taxation, and (3) to review and scrutinize public administration and government policy.

In practical terms, the Commons has a limited legislative function. Nevertheless, it serves a very important democratic role. It provides a highly visible arena for policy debate and the partisan collision of political worldviews. The flash of rhetorical skills brings drama to Westminster. One crucial element of drama, however, is nearly always missing. The outcome is seldom in doubt. MPs from the governing party (or as now, members of the Conservative–Liberal coalition) who consider rebelling against the leader of their respective parties or challenge the terms of the coalition agreement are understandably reluctant in a close and critical vote to force a general election. This would place their jobs in jeopardy. Only once since the defeat of Ramsay MacDonald's government in 1924 has a government been brought down by a defeat in the Commons (in 1979). Today, the balance of institutional power has shifted from Parliament to the governing party (or at present parties backing the coalition) and the executive.

The Legislative Process

Bills must be introduced in the Commons and the Lords, although approval by the Lords is not required. Ideas for legislation come from political parties, pressure groups, think tanks, the prime minister's policy unit, or government departments. Proposed legislation, on behalf of the government, is then drafted by civil servants, circulated within Whitehall, approved by the cabinet, and then refined by the office of Parliamentary Counsel.

In the Commons the bill usually comes to the floor three times. The bill is formally *read* upon introduction, printed, distributed, debated in general terms, and after an interval, given a *second reading*, followed by a vote. The bill then undergoes detailed review by a standing committee reflecting the overall party balance. It then goes through a report stage during which new amendments may be introduced. In the *third reading*, the bill is considered in final form (and voted on) without debate.

A bill passed in the Commons follows a parallel path in the Lords. There the bill is either accepted without change, amended, or rejected. The Lords passes bills concerning taxation or budgetary matters without alteration, but can add technical and editorial amendments to other bills (if approved by the Commons) to add clarity and precision. Finally, it receives royal assent (which is only a formality) and becomes an Act of Parliament.

The House of Lords

Traditionally the House of Lords (or Lords) was a wholly unelected body that was comprised of hereditary peers (nobility of the rank of duke, marquis, earl, viscount, or baron), and life peers (appointed on the recommendation of the prime minister or the recently institutionalized House of Lords Appointment Commission). The Lords also includes the archbishops of Canterbury and York and some two-dozen other bishops and archbishops of the Church of England. As part of a gradual reform agenda, in 1999, the right of all hereditary peers to sit and vote in the Lords was curtailed, and that right limited to 92, pending further reform. In 2014 there were about 760 members eligible to take part in the work of the House of Lords.

The Lords serves mainly as a chamber of revision, providing expertise in redrafting legislation, with the power to suggest amendments to legislation in the Commons. The Lords can debate, refine, and delay—but not block—legislation. For example, in 2006, to protect the civil liberties of British Muslims the Lords persuaded the Commons to water down a bill that prohibited incitement to violence, on the grounds that the bill might unfairly be used to target Muslim clerics. It is interesting that when it comes to parliamentary reform more attention has been paid in recent years to reform of the Lords—an issue that has repeatedly deadlocked with multiple versions of reform in play, including the possibility of an elected upper chamber, which would bear some kinship to the U.S. Senate. Increasingly the Lords engaged in unruly and inconclusive debate, challenging the coalition government on a variety of governance and substantive matters, for example, displaying firm resistance to reforms in the National Health Service and welfare benefits. It appears that in what might be the waning days of the House of Lords, members seem inclined to go out with a bang, not a whimper.

Reforms in Behavior

There have been a number of changes in the House of Common, which, ironically, have been tamer than the potential changes afoot in the House of Lords. Since the 1970s, backbenchers (MPs of the governing party who have no governmental office and rank-and-file opposition members) have been markedly less deferential. A backbench rebellion against the Major government's EU policy in 1993, which was viewed by Thatcherites as dangerously pro-European, weakened the prime minister considerably and divided the party. In addition, one-third of Labour MPs defected on key votes authorizing the use of force in Iraq in 2003—an historic rebellion.

Structural Changes: Parliamentary Committees

In addition to the standing committees that routinely review bills, in 1979 the Commons extended the number and responsibilities of select committees, which help Parliament exert control over the executive by examining specific policies or aspects of administration.

The most controversial select committees monitor the major departments and ministries. Select committees hold hearings, take written and oral testimony, and question senior civil servants and ministers. Their reports have included strong policy recommendations at odds with government policy. These reforms have complicated the role of the civil service. Civil servants have been required to testify in a manner that may damage their ministers, revealing official culpability or flawed judgments. More significant has been a tawdry scandal that has affected all the major parties concerning fraudulent claims by MPs (including ministers) for travel expenses and expenses for upkeep of extravagant homes away from London—in some cases, homes occupied by their lovers. The practice of fiddling expense accounts was widespread and improprieties over expense accounts in some cases resulted in jail time.

Political Parties and the Party System

Britain is often referred to as a two-party system, but as the 2010 election makes clear, that is a misnomer. It is true that from 1945 until the 2010 election, only leaders of the Labour or Conservative parties had served as prime ministers. And Conservative and Labour have been very closely matched. From 1945 through 2005, the Conservative and Labour parties each won eight general elections. In addition, throughout the postwar period, these two parties have routinely divided at least 85 percent of the seats in the Commons. But since the 1980s the Liberal Democrats (Lib Dems) have become an important alternative. Britain also has several national parties: the Scottish National Party (SNP) in Scotland and the Plaid Cymru in Wales as well as a roster of parties competing in Northern Ireland.

The Labour Party

Fifty years ago, those not engaged in manual labor voted Conservative three times more commonly than they did Labour. More than two out of three manual workers, by contrast, voted Labour. Britain then conformed to one classic pattern of a Western European party system: a two-class/two-party system.

Since the mid-1970s significant changes have developed in the party system, for example, the decline in class-based voting. It has also seen growing disaffection with even the moderate social democracy associated with the Keynesian welfare state and Labourism. The Labour Party suffered from divisions between its trade unionist and parliamentary elements, constitutional wrangling over the power of trade unions to determine party policy at annual conferences, and disputes over how the leader would be selected. Divisions spilled over into foreign policy issues.

The 1980s and 1990s witnessed relative harmony within the party. Moderate trade union and parliamentary leadership agreed on major policy issues. Labour became a moderate center-left party. Under the leadership of Tony Blair, Labour was rebranded as "New Labour," although its formal name remained the Labour Party. After the party's defeat in the 2010 election, two close-knit brothers who had served in the cabinet, David Miliband with close ties to Blair as foreign minister, and Ed Miliband with close ties to Brown and former Secretary of State for Climate Change, were the top contenders to succeed Gordon Brown. In a dramatic contest for leadership of the Labour Party in September 2010, Ed Miliband, the younger brother, prevailed in a very close election, signaling a turn away from New Labour and an effort to turn the party in a more progressive direction, without returning to "Old Labour." Miliband has tried with only moderate success to rally the base, particularly among trade unionists and public sector employees who are feeling the pinch the hardest under the austerity policies of the Coalition government.

The Conservative Party

The Conservative Party dates back to the eighteenth century. Its pragmatism, flexibility, and organizational capabilities have made it one of the most successful and, at times, innovative center-right parties in Europe.

In 2003, the combative and experienced Michael Howard took over as party leader. For a time, the Conservatives seemed revitalized. But it was not easy for Howard to translate his assured performances from the front bench in Parliament into popular support, as effective opposition to New Labour proved elusive. In fact, Conservatives made far less trouble for Labour Prime Minister Tony Blair on Iraq than did members of the Labour Party. Despite an energetic campaign in 2005, one likely to be remembered for the Conservatives' playing of the race and ethnicity card, electoral defeat led to his quick resignation. In December 2005, the Conservatives elected David Cameron as party leader in a landslide.

Cameron wasted little time in reorienting the party, modernizing its appeal, and reaching out beyond its traditional core values. He acknowledged that New Labour had been right in understanding the mood of Britain and right, also, to insist on achieving both social justice and economic success. Cameron promised to reduce poverty both in Britain and globally, take on climate change as a priority, and ensure security from terrorism. A testament to Blair's success, Cameron worked hard to reposition the Conservatives as a reforming more centrist party that could compete effectively with post-Blair New Labour across the economic and social spectrum.

Liberal Democrats

Through the 1970s, the Liberal Party was the only centrist challenger to the Labour and Conservative parties. Since the 1980s, a changing roster of centrist parties posed an increasingly significant threat to the two-party dominance of Conservative and Labour. In 1981, the Social Democratic Party (SDP) formed out of a split within the Labour Party. After the Conservative victory in 1987, the Liberal Party and most of the SDP merged to form the Social and Liberal Democratic Party (now called the Liberal Democrats or Lib Dems), which quickly emerged as a major political player.

In the 2001 general election the party increased its vote tally by nearly one-fifth and won fifty-two seats, the most since 1929. This success positioned the party as a potentially powerful center-left critic of New Labour. That said, at least until Blair's fortunes declined, Labour did not make it easy for them. As the Blair government began to spend massively to improve education and health care—an approach that would come to haunt them later—it narrowed the range of policy issues on which the Liberal Democrats could challenge New Labour. Party leader Charles Kennedy won the political gamble in spring 2003 by opposing the war in Iraq. But it was not easy to take electoral advantage of Blair's political weakness. For a time, the fortunes of the Liberal Dems declined. In December 2007, after two leadership turnovers, Nick Clegg, a 40-year-old ex-journalist and former member of the European Parliament, took over leadership of the Liberal Democrats. Clegg and his party faced an uphill battle to make the Lib Dems a serious contender in time for the 2010 election. But the country's fatigue with New Labour, post-9/11 and post-7/7 concerns about the erosion of civil liberties that played to the party's strength, and Clegg's energetic and confident leadership—in fall 2008 Clegg launched a campaign to knock on 1 million doors to connect with ordinary citizens—quickly catapulted the Liberal Democrats into serious contention. Today, in the context of the unfamiliar terrain of a coalition government, many are concerned that the two-party system is eroding. Some anticipate the emergence of a two-and-and-a-half party system, which may be evolving into a more fluid multiparty system, with an enhanced role for less mainstream parties. This prospect provokes considerable handwringing, notably with reference to the far-right British National Party, which placed their first members in the European Parliament in 2009 and UKIP (The United Kingdom Independent Party), which, drawing on a deep reservoir of Britain's Euroskepticism, pushed Labour into third place. Despite a broad but apparently not deep commitment to a green Britain, the Green Party performed badly, winning only one seat while the BNP and UKIP secured no seats in 2010. In comparative European terms, radical right parties have not had the success in Britain that they have enjoyed elsewhere.

Elections

British general elections are exclusively for seats in the House of Commons. The prime minister is not directly elected as prime minister but as a member of Parliament (MP) from a single constituency (electoral district). The Queen invites the leader of the party that can control a majority in the Commons to become prime minister. Constituencies vary widely in size, but the average number of voters remains roughly comparable. (In the 2010 election, the average number of voters in each constituency was roughly 68,000.)

Traditionally, Parliament had a maximum life of five years, with no fixed term. The 2010 coalition agreement proposed a fixed term of five years subject to dissolution by a 55 percent vote of members of parliament.

The Electoral System and the 2010 Election

Election for representatives in the Commons (members of Parliament, or MPs) is by a "first-past-the-post" principle in each constituency. In this single-member plurality system, the candidate who receives the most votes is elected. There is no requirement of a majority and no element of proportional representation (a system in which each party is given a percentage of seats in a representative assembly roughly comparable to its percentage of the popular vote).

This winner-take-all electoral system tends to exaggerate the size of the victory of the largest party and to reduce the influence of regionally dispersed lesser parties. This system is praised for increasing the chances that a party or coalition of parties will gain a majority of parliamentary seats and therefore form a stable government. Critics of the electoral system charge that it does not give adequate representation to minority opinion.

Contrary to the typical tendency of the winner-take-all electoral system, the 2010 election resulted in a **hung parliament** (a situation after an election when no single party comprises a majority in the Commons). Only after a quick set of negotiations, could an arrangement be found to form a coalition government. Thus, 2010 is one for the record books. On the one hand, it was the exception that proves the rule. Ordinarily Britain exhibits a stable two-party-dominant system (Conservative and Labour), with support for a third party (Liberal Democrat) spread widely across the country, but spread too thinly for the party to win a substantial number of seats. The Liberal Democrats needed an exceptional stroke of luck to buck the trend—and they got it in 2010.

hung parliament

A situation after an election when no single party comprises a majority in the Commons.

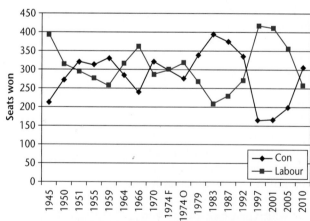

FIGURE 2.5 Comparison of Number of Seats Won by Conservative versus Labour in UK General Elections from 1945 to 2010

Source: http://ukpolitical.info.

The campaign by the Tories peaked early, failed to inspire, and could not convince the electorate that they had the experience or were equipped to handle the enormous challenges of the economic downturn. With Blair fatigue, an unpopular successor in Gordon Brown, and a failing economy, New Labour never really stood a chance to win the election outright. The first televised debates ever in UK politics certainly enlivened the campaign. They also initially fueled a surge in popularity for the telegenic and media-savvy Liberal Democratic leader, Nick Clegg, who stole the show in the first debate. In fact, for a time, "Cleggmania" produced polls showing the Lib Dems with an unprecedented one-third of the electorate behind them. For a brief moment, Britain enjoyed the unlikely spectacle of a three-party contest, but one in which Labour never really had a chance.

With a two-party dominant party system, the UK electoral system tends to produce a stable single-party government. That observation seems less certain now than it did before 2010, but it will take more than one hung parliament to make observers think that the UK party system has been fundamentally transformed into a multi-party system.

It is not clear whether the 2010 election returns signal the beginning of a critical realignment in the electoral system, but most observers recognize some grounds for improvement. For a start, the electoral system raises questions about representation and fairness. Like other winner-take-all systems, a close second place in a constituency (as in a U.S. electoral district) is simply a loss. The system reduces the competitiveness of smaller parties, like the Lib Dems, with diffuse pockets of support across the country.

In 2010 the Liberal Democrats with 23 percent of the vote won 57 seats. Labour with 29 percent of the vote won 258 seats. The Conservatives with 36.1 percent of the vote won 306 seats. Thus, the Liberal Democrats achieved a share of the vote that was roughly two-thirds that of the Conservatives, but won roughly one-fifth of the seats won by the Tories. Such are the benefits of an electoral system to the victor (as well as the second major party).

Is there any wonder why more than anything else the Liberal Democrats want what neither major party would give them: a change in the electoral system to proportional representation (PR), where the number of seats allocated to parties in Parliament would closely approximate the proportion of votes cast for a given party? PR would be a game changer, catapulting the Lib Dems into major party status and making them a potential kingmaker, tipping the balance in many close general elections to either the Conservatives or Labour. For that very reason, it is unlikely that such a fundamental change in the electoral system will be introduced any time soon. But parliamentary sovereignty means that any time there is a political will to change the electoral system, the electoral system can be changed by Parliament.

Under the terms of the 2010 coalition agreement, a referendum was held in May 2011 as follows: At present the United Kingdom uses the "first-past-the-post" system to elect MPs to the House of Commons. Should the "a vote" system be used instead (a system in which voters rank preferences among candidates)? If no candidate receives a majority of first-preference votes, then second-preference votes of the candidate who finished last are redistributed, and the process is continued until a candidate achieves a majority. The coalition agreement called for a referendum on exactly this question—and the referendum failed, preserving the first-past-the-post system.

Gender, Ethnicity, and Representation

The party and electoral systems contribute to the creation of a Parliament that has been and remains a bastion of white men, but it is becoming more diverse. The

2010 election produced a record number of ethnic minority MPs, with 27 elected, nearly double the number in 2005. Moreover there were a set of firsts: Labour's first Muslim female MP and first African MP; and for the Conservatives, their first Asian female MP. Also a record percentage of women were elected in 2010 (21.5 percent, up from 19.8 percent in 2005). But this increase is hardly a surge, and in comparative terms the United Kingdom has a long way to go when it comes to women's representation: It ranks 73rd in the world in female representation. Despite the general trend of increased representation of women and minorities, they remain substantially underrepresented in Parliament.

Trends in Electoral Behavior

Recent general elections have deepened geographic and regional fragmentation. British political scientist Ivor Crewe has referred to the emergence of two two-party systems: (1) Competition between the Conservative and Labour parties dominates contests in English urban and northern seats, and (2) Conservative-center party competition dominates England's rural and southern seats. A third two-party competition has emerged in Scotland, where Labour competes with the Scottish National Party.[7,9]

The national (that is regional) parties have challenged two-party dominance since the 1970s, but with only limited results. The Scottish National Party (SNP) was founded in 1934 and its Welsh counterpart, the Plaid Cymru, in 1925. The 2010 election showed the strength of Labour in Scotland, where it won 41 seats and 42 percent of the Scottish popular vote, an improvement over 2005. The Lib Dems came in a distant second with 11 seats, the SNP won six seats. The election demonstrated once more that the Conservatives have very little traction in Scotland. They walked away with a single seat. In Wales, the Conservatives fared better, gaining five more seats than they had won in 2005 for a total of eight seats at Westminster. The Plaid Cymru won three seats, one more than in 2005. Although Labour lost four seats compared to 2005, they walked away with a very strong showing, winning 26 out of 40 seats. The right-wing populist UK Independence party was the big winner in Britain in the European parliament elections in 2014. It won no seats but transformed the future electoral map in Britain, winning 27.5 percent of the ballots. It won 161 English council seats (up from a total of 30 seats combined in 2009 and 2012). By contrast none of the major parties did well. Labour fared better than the Conservatives, although below their expectations. The Liberal Democrats lost ten of their 11 seats in the EP and 310 council seats. The Conservatives benefited from Cameron's warnings of low expectations. With UKIP strongest in traditional Conservative constituencies it seems likely that UKIP's older, more conservative, more rural whiter conservative base may significantly challenge Tory electoral bastions in the years ahead. We will return to the increasingly dramatic and significant politics of the nations within the United Kingdom, notably Scotland, in Section 5.

Political Culture, Citizenship, and Identity

In their study of the ideals and values that shape political behavior, political scientists Gabriel Almond and Sidney Verba wrote that the civic (or political) culture in Britain was characterized by trust, deference to authority, and pragmatism.[8,10] But the 1970s became a crucial turning point in British political culture and group identities that challenged this view.

During the 1970s, the long years of economic decline culminated in economic reversals in the standard of living for many Britons. Also for many, the historic bonds of occupational and social class grew weaker. Both union membership and popularity declined. At the same time, a growing number of conservative think tanks and mass-circulation newspapers worked hard to erode support for the welfare state. New social movements such as feminism, antinuclear activism, and environmentalism challenged basic tenets of British political culture. Identities based on race and ethnicity, gender, and sexual orientation gained significance. These trends fragmented the political map and inspired a shift to the right.

Thatcher's ascent reflected these changes in political culture, identities, and values. Thatcherism rejected collectivism, the redistribution of resources from rich to poor, and state responsibility for full employment. It considered individual property rights more important than the social rights claimed by all citizens in the welfare state. Thatcherism set the stage in cultural terms for the new Labour consolidation of neoliberalism and the core political–cultural orientation in Britain.

Social Class

A key change in political culture in the last quarter-century has been the weakening of bonds grounded in the experience of labor. During the Thatcher era, the traditional values of "an honest day's work for an honest day's pay" and solidarity among coworkers were derided as "rigidities" that reduced competitiveness—a perspective that has continued through New Labour and the coalition government .

Being "tough on the unions" was a core premise of New Labour and a view that the Conservative-led coalition government has powerfully reinforced. In the context of the aggressive cuts in public spending, it looks like very tough days ahead for unions, particularly public sector unions, which have become a lightning rod, not only in the United Kingdom, but in the United States as well, for governments looking to cut budgets—and blame somebody for the need to make cuts. Collective bargaining has been largely relegated to declining private sector industries and the public sector.[9,11] Strike rates in the United Kingdom have generally been below the average of both the OECD and the EU in recent decades.

National Identity

Decolonization has created a multiethnic Britain. National identity has become especially complicated. Questions about fragmented sovereignty within the context of the EU, the commingled histories of four nations (England, Scotland, Wales, and Ireland/Northern Ireland), and the interplay of race and nationality have created doubts about British identity that run deep. Ethnicity, intra-UK territorial attachments, Europeanization, and globalization are complicating national identity. Can Britain foster a more inclusive sense of British identity?

Nearly 8 percent of the people who live in Britain are of African, African-Caribbean, or Asian descent. The authors of a landmark study of multiethnic Britain explained: "Many communities overlap; all affect and are affected by others. More and more people have multiple identities—they are Welsh Europeans, Pakistani Yorkshirewomen, Glaswegian Muslims, English Jews, and black British. Many enjoy this complexity but also experience conflicting loyalties."[10,12]

Despite many success stories, ethnic minority communities have experienced police insensitivity, problems in access to the best public housing, hate crimes, and accusations that they are not truly British if they do not root for the English cricket

team. In addition, harsh criticism is directed at immigrants and asylum seekers. Since this criticism comes in the wake of intense scrutiny of the Muslim community after 9/11 and 7/7, it contributes to the alienation of the ethnic minority community, particularly among some groups of Muslim citizens. Ordinary law-abiding Muslims have experienced intensified mistrust and intimidation. But it is also true that Muslim university graduates are assuming leading roles in the professions and that dozens of Muslim city counselors have been elected across the country.

Interest Groups, Social Movements, and Protest

In recent years, partly in response to globalization, political protest has been on the rise. Protesters demand more accountability and transparency in the operations of powerful international trade and development agencies. For example, in 1999 London became the site of protests timed to correspond with the Seattle meeting of the World Trade Organization (WTO). The London demonstration generated some 100,000 protesters.

The intensity of environmental activism has taken off with the growing attention to genetically modified (GM) crops in the late 1990s. In November 1999, the government announced a ban on commercially grown GM crops in Britain.

A quite different kind of activism spread to the countryside among a population not usually known for political protest. Farmers had been badly hurt by the "mad cow disease" crisis in 1996 and saw an urban bias at play in New Labour and the growing threat to fox hunting. They launched massive protests, and, even after a law banning the hunt went into effect in 2005, they kept up the heat with legal challenges.

A series of antiwar rallies were held in London before the United Kingdom and the United States launched the Iraq war. In September 2002, a huge protest rally was organized in London, led by the Stop the War Coalition and the Muslim Association of Britain. Both within the United Kingdom and among observers of British politics and society, many still endorse the view that British culture is characterized by pragmatism, trust, and deference to authority. This may be true, but the persistence of a wide range of protest movements, including reverberating protests in 2011 against the very significant cuts introduced by the Conservative–Liberal Democrat coalition government qualifies this story.

The Political Impact of Technology

Two recent developments have underscored the impact of technology on British politics. In a scandal that is still reverberating with global implications, a parliamentary committee released a report in 2012, disclosing that Rupert Murdoch, the Australian media mogul whose companies in 2011 accounted for the second largest media holdings in the world including the prestigious *Times of London* and *The Wall Street Journal* engaged in hacking. The hacking scandal, which involved the use of sophisticated electronic technologies to hack into emails and voice mails for the purpose of breaking major news stories ahead of the competition, created collateral damage for many news organizations and high-flying politicians. The scandal also implicated Tony Blair at a trial exposing the scandal, when it was revealed that the former prime minister secretly offered to advise the Murdoch empire as the scandal erupted—a scandal that besmirched reputations among members of Parliament in all three major parties and extended to allegations of corruption and kickbacks by senior police officials. Potentially more significant in this era of governmental use of sophisticated and often secret surveillance of ordinary citizens, it has been revealed that Government Communications Headquarters (GCHQ), the UK surveillance agency, has collected millions of webcam images in bulk from Yahoo users, some of which may have revealed pornographic images.

[handwritten margin note: Surveying ordinary citizens (Yahoo users) with webcams]

Where Do You Stand?

Is perpetual surveillance too high a price to be for security?

Nearly everyone in Britain wants Britain to go green. Why is the support for a Green Party so weak?

BRITISH POLITICS IN TRANSITION

SECTION **5**

Political Challenges and Changing Agendas

On July 7, 2005, four British suicide bombers, all Muslims, detonated a set of coordinated attacks on the London transport system during morning rush hour. Three bombs went off in quick succession on the London underground (subway) and one, an hour later, on a double-decker bus nearby. Fifty-six people were killed including the al-Qaeda–linked suicide bombers, and some 700 people were injured. The mayor and most inhabitants of the city, often invoking imagery of stoic Londoners withstanding the German blitz during World War II, remained calm and determined in the face of these devastating attacks. They insisted that London would remain an open and cosmopolitan city as it had been for centuries. And then the other shoe dropped.

Two weeks after 7/7, an entirely innocent Brazilian electrician, unconnected to the bombings, was shot dead by police who were under enormous pressure to prevent further attacks and mistakenly considered him responsible for the suicide attacks. The victim was traveling from his apartment to a job in Northwest London when he was killed. He was chased into a London subway station by roughly twenty police officers, where he was cornered, tripped, and shot seven times in the head and once in the shoulder. He was wearing a thick coat that, in the jittery aftermath of 7/7, raised suspicions that he might be hiding a suicide belt. He ran from the police when ordered to stop. A Brazilian could be mistaken for a person of Pakistani or Jamaican or Middle Eastern descent, as were the 7/7 bombers. Coming on the heels of 7/7, this tragic accident underscores how tense everyone is about security from terror attack and how race and ethnicity probably blinded even well-trained police officers into making an awful mistake.

As our democratic idea theme suggests, no democracy, however secure it may be, is ever a finished project. Even in Britain, with its centuries-old constitutional

Focus Questions ▽

- Is Britain best understood as four nations or one?

- How well is Britain's ancient political system adjusting to contemporary challenges?

The murder of an innocent Brazilian electrician by police officers shortly after 7/7 raised new and troubling questions about security and about ethnic and racial tension in Britain.

Alessandro Abbonizio/AFP/Getty Images

settlement and secure institutional framework, issues about democratic governance and citizens' participation remain unresolved.

Constitutional Reform

Questions about the role of the monarchy and the House of Lords have long been simmering on Britain's political agenda. Why should the House of Commons share sovereignty with the House of Lords? What is the role of the monarchy—a very expensive institution and one subject to periodic scandals—in a modern political system? In addition, the balance of power among constitutionally critical institutions raises important questions about a democratic deficit at the heart of the Westminster model. Britain's executive easily overpowers Parliament. Its strength in relation to the legislature may be greater than in any other democracy. Add to these concerns the prime minister's tendency to bypass the cabinet on crucial decisions and the bias in the electoral system that privileges the two dominant parties. Consider how tumultuous and volatile the contemporary political moment in Britain has become. The British have very little experience with coalition governments, and yet they presently have one. Moreover, not only is the capacity of the party system to produce the familiar one-party leadership in doubt, but the electoral system is under scrutiny and subject to potential change. The May 2011 referendum on the voting system—a key element in the coalition agreement—produced a decisive vote to preserve the United Kingdom's current system for electing MPs, but managed to upset the apple cart anyway. The Labour leader, Ed Miliband, who supported the "Alternative Vote" system, was chastened by its resounding defeat by the electorate, and by losses in Scotland in local government elections. But the outcome was even worse for Liberal Democrat leader, Nick Clegg, for whom electoral reform was a calling card issue and a key part of the Liberal Democrat rationale for joining the coalition government. As the dust settled on the referendum on the UK voting system, held on the same day as local elections throughout the United Kingdom, the fate of Clegg and the ultimate future of the coalition remained uncertain.

Identities in Flux

The relatively small scale of the ethnic minority community limits the political impact of the most divisive issues concerning collective identities. It is probably in this area that rigidities in the British political system most severely challenge principles of democracy and tolerance. Given Britain's single-member, simple-plurality electoral system, and no proportional representation, minority representation in Parliament remains very low. There are deep-seated social attitudes that no government can easily transform.

The issues of immigration, refugees, and asylum still inspire a fear of multiculturalism among white Britons. Since the London bombings by British Muslims on 7/7 that killed fifty-six people, intense scrutiny has been focused on the Muslim community, which faces endless finger pointing and harassment. According to police, the number of hate crimes primarily affecting Muslims soared 600 percent in the weeks after the bombings. Then, in 2007, Salman Rushdie, whose book, *The Satanic Verses*, had offended many Muslims around the world and forced him into hiding in the face of a formal death threat from Iranian religious leaders, was knighted by the Queen. The honor accorded Rushdie was widely held to be an affront to the Muslim community in Britain. There is increasing concern across the political spectrum that Britain needs to find a way to deepen the ties of shared political culture and values that hold society together as well as to ensure security.

But finger pointing at the Muslim community has intensified since 9/11 and 7/7, and positions are hardening against multiculturalism. In February 2011, Prime Minister Cameron explicitly challenged the long-standing cross-party support for multiculturalism at a high-visibility security conference in Munich. Cameron condemned a culture of "hands-off" tolerance in the United Kingdom and in Europe. He criticized immigrants, and particularly Muslims (whom he seemed to define as immigrants whatever their immigration status) for leading lives apart from mainstream society. In strong terms, he warned of the dangers of multicultural policy, which made it possible for Islamic militants to radicalize Muslim youth, some of whom were likely to become terrorists. And he concluded that Europe had to defeat terrorism at home, not exclusively by the use of force elsewhere, for example, in Afghanistan.

With the war in Iraq viewed across the political spectrum as a debacle forged by the thoughtless application of the special relationship, Cameron tried hard to recalibrate the special relationship by broadening its meaning to extend beyond its historic U.S.-UK definition and to include other key allies and critical trading partners with special historic ties to the United Kingdom, for example, India.

Youth Politics and the Generational Divide

It comes as no surprise but with considerable concern and regret that the recession that began in 2008 has produced a huge generational divide. Imagine that you were born in Britain between 1980 and 1990. If that were you, bad luck. It would

GLOBAL CONNECTION

Britain and the Legacies of Empire

At its height during the reign of Queen Victoria (1837–1901), the British Empire encompassed fully one-quarter of the world's population and exerted direct colonial rule over some four-dozen countries scattered across the globe. In a stunning reversal of Britain's global status and fortunes, the empire fell apart in the half-century of decolonization between the independence of India in 1947 and the return of Hong Kong to China in 1997. Apart from a few scattered dependencies, the sun finally set on the British Empire, but the legacies of empire lived on to shape its relationship to the world of states in important ways.

The end of empire did not bring the end of great power aspirations for Britain, but it shifted the emphasis as the British role in the globalizing world of states has been shaped by its determination to view its **"special relationship*"** with the United States as a dominant framework for foreign policy and global leadership, even at the expense of a full commitment to economic integration with and leadership in the European Union.

With the end of empire it was inevitable that the special relationship between the United Kingdom and the United States would become a relationship between unequal partners. As a result, U.S. interests have tended to exert a tremendous magnetic pull on British foreign policy, to the relative neglect of European partnerships and broader international influences.

Before 9/11 New Labour stood for a coherent and progressive foreign policy framework, one that linked globalization to a growing UK commitment to narrow the development gap and in the words of Robin Cook, Blair's first foreign secretary, "to be a force for good" in the world. The Kosovo war created the context for Blair's explicit linkage of globalization with foreign and security policy.

Blair's "doctrine of international community" gave new weight to the notion of global interdependence by asserting a responsibility to use military force when necessary to achieve humanitarian objectives and contain catastrophic human rights abuses. This doctrine, as well as Blair's Atlanticist leanings, conditioned his response to 9/11 and subsequently his determination to bring the United Kingdom into the war in Iraq.

But in the days following 9/11, the powerful attraction of the Atlantic Alliance, with Blair's distinctive inflections, took an irresistible hold over British foreign policy. At this critical juncture, several elements came together to forge the decision to support the U.S. administration, even when the venue of the war on terror changed from Afghanistan to Iraq:

1. A fear that if the United States were left to fight the war on terror by itself, then unilateralist forces in Washington would be strengthened, and the world would be worse off.[11]
2. Blair's conviction that Iraq should be understood, like Kosovo, as an exercise in humanitarian intervention to save Muslims from catastrophic human rights abuses.[12]
3. A particular reading of the special relationship that made it imperative that the United Kingdom support the U.S. war in Iraq, viewing it as a necessary part of the global war on terror.

In Blair's doctrine of international community, the reverberations of empire were unmistakable. The civilizing mission of empire and the right of the metropolitan power to use force against the weaker dependent or failed states were both understood as an exercise of humanitarian intervention. And the use of force, however it was justified, represented an exercise in great power politics. How will the Conservative–Liberal government under the leadership of David Cameron recast the United Kingdom's role in the world of states? It seems likely that the Liberal Democrats will be more inclined to align British interests with Europe, while the Tories will remain in the Euroskeptic camp, aloof from further integration with Europe, especially so long as many of the European economies remain troubled. Perhaps to allay European concerns as well as that of his coalition partners, Cameron's first trip abroad as prime minister was to Paris and Berlin. Equally revealing, to emphasize his concerns about security, Afghani president Hamid Karzai was the first foreign leader to meet Cameron as prime minister, and at a joint press conference with Karzai at the White House, President Obama was quick to confirm "the extraordinary special relationship between the United States and Great Britain." As a sign of the times and the shifting power among British allies, Cameron has also made clear that he regards a "new special relationship with India" as a critical element in UK foreign relations and trade policy. With a proliferation of "special relationships" it may be time to wonder if the United States is still the United Kingdom's BFF (Best Friends Forever) or just one of several special relationships.

MAKING CONNECTIONS Does the special relationship enhance Britain's standing in a globalizing world of states or lock Britain in to a set of problems not of its own making but rather determined in Washington?

*Definitions of key terms in this boxed feature appear in the Glossary, which begins on p. 697.

be very difficult for you to get a job. Unemployment for university graduates in your generation's shoes is close to 20 percent. For dropouts the unemployment rate is close to 50 percent. Hardly anyone can get a loan to finance their mortgage. Train fare for getting to work has eaten up roughly 8 percent of your income; the gas bill has gone up 15 percent a year. Although the cost of university/college in the United Kingdom is not nearly as high as it is in the United States, the costs have increased substantially, which produced riots outside parliament when tuition fees were tripled in 2010. Rents have been hitting record highs. If you were a young Briton in your 40s and with a job and starter house with a low mortgage, recession has barely hurt your life style. For those in retirement or facing retirement, record low interest rates have reduced their monthly income. The generation retiring today can complain that their pensions are squeezed, but many are the beneficiaries of traditional pension plans that guaranteed two-thirds salary in retirement.

British Politics in Comparative Perspective

Until the Asian financial crisis that began in 1997, it was an axiom of comparative politics that economic success required a style of economic governance that Britain lacks. Many argued that innovation and competitiveness in the new global economy required the strategic coordination of the economy by an interventionist state. But the United Kingdom escaped the recession that plagued the rest of Europe for much of the 1990s. Britain also outperformed most major world economies until the "Great Recession" of 2008 signaled a decisive downturn in Britain's economic fortunes.

In many countries throughout the world, politicians have been looking for an economic model that can sustain competitiveness while improving the plight of the socially excluded. For this reason, New Labour's third way—a political orientation designed to transcend left and right in favor of practical and effective policies—was carefully watched for more than ten years. Observers saw in New Labour a historic intellectual and political realignment, not only in Britain, but in Clinton's America and Cardoso's (and later Lula's) Brazil. Ten years is a very long time in politics, and for ten years it looked as if New Labour had found a way to mold a new political orientation that combined a sophisticated approach to competitiveness in the global economy with a pragmatic anti-ideological approach to governance. But in time, the bloom most decidedly came off the rose of New Labour, which could never recover from the war in Iraq. The electorate grew tired of Blair and never warmed up to Brown. When the financial and economic crisis struck in 2008, Britain was among the hardest hit of the core European economies.

Where Do You Stand?

Is Britain important enough and functioning well enough today to stand alongside the United States as one of the two great models of democratic government?

With Putin's Russia on the ascendant, America looking inward, and the EU facing tremendous economic and institutional challenges, is there an opportunity for Britain to play a greater role in a globalizing world of states?

Chapter Summary

Consider the decline of Britain's historic laissez-faire economic model, its refusal to participate in the Eurozone, and the unresolved legacies of empire, reflected in tumultuous debates and recriminations over race, ethnicity, and the meaning of "Britishness." Add to those tensions the surprising constitutional and institutional uncertainty about the role of the Commons and the Lords; and the possibility that Britons might have to get used to coalition governments and an independent Scotland; and perhaps a series of referendums on UK voting systems.

It is fair to say that Britain is experiencing a period of uncertainty across all four of our core themes as challenging as anything the country has experienced for generations.

Undoubtedly people in Britain today sense that the nation is divided on multiple fronts and, measured against the historic achievements of parliamentary democracy, empire, and Industrial Revolution—that Britain is in decline, with little confidence that renewal is in the cards.

Since 2008, Britain has been facing daunting challenges. Almost inevitably, economic downturn produces political challenges, but it also creates opportunities for change and renewal. A new generation of untested leadership in all the major political parties and, most importantly, at the helm of the coalition government will produce new political challenges, innovative policy directions, new approaches to solving old problems, and occasional policy U-turns. Will the coalition hold or will the strains and challenges of governing shatter the coalition of convenience between the Conservatives and Liberal Democrats? Across the globe, many electorates are asking for effective pragmatic leadership in hard times. If the

United Kingdom's coalition government, which came to office almost by accident and in very difficult times, stays intact and effectively manages from the center, it may last long enough to benefit both from the resourcefulness of an electorate and a country that is not easily daunted and from a rising economic tide. If that happens, it may build on the New Labour legacy of government judged on effectiveness, not ideology, and enjoy a long run in office. If not, the British distaste for coalition government will be confirmed. Perhaps more important for the future of the United Kingdom is the very basis of the union measured against the real possibility of a profound and fundamental institutional change with unknown consequences for the fate of Britain.

In September 2014, a referendum was held on the straightforward question: "Should Scotland be an independent country?" An incredible 97% of eligible voters registered to vote—a remarkable indication of the intensity of feelings on all sides. Polls leading up to the referendum indicated the prospect of an extremely close result. In the end, the "No" votes scored a rather decisive victory (55.3%), with the "Yes" vote tally at 44.7 %. The United Kingdom preserved its historic constitutional design, but at some cost. To secure the "No" vote, the leaders of all three Westminster parties, David Cameron, Nick Clegg, and Ed Miliband, promised extensive new powers to the Scottish parliament in regard to taxing, spending, and social welfare benefits. Within days of the referendum, prime minister Cameron also introduced plans to limit the voting rights of Scottish MPs on English issues, a sign that the referendum only began what seems likely to be an extended period of constitutional uncertainty.

Key Terms

cabinet government
constitutional monarchy
foreign direct investment
fusion of powers
hegemonic power
hung parliament
Industrial Revolution

judicial review
Keynesianism
laissez-faire
macroeconomic policy
monetarism
neoliberalism
parliamentary democracy

parliamentary sovereignty
quangos
special relationship
unitary state
welfare state
Westminster model

Suggested Readings

Bogdanor, Vernon. *The Coalition and the Constitution.* Oxford: Hart, 2011.

Brown, Gordon. *Beyond the Crash: Overcoming the First Crisis of Globalization.* New York: Free Press, 2010.

Elliott, Francis, and James Hanning. *Cameron: The Rise of the New Conservative.* Harper: 2009.

Flinders, Matthew V. *The Oxford Handbook of British Politics.* Oxford: Oxford University Press, 2011.

Howell, Chris. *Trade Unions and the State: The Construction of Industrial Relations Institutions in Britain, 1890–2000*. Princeton: Princeton University Press, 2005.

Kumar, Krishan. *The Making of English National Identity*. Cambridge: Cambridge University Press, 2003.

McLean, Iain. *Scotland's Choices: The Referendum and What Happens after It*. Edinburgh: Edinburgh University Press, 2013.

Modood, Tariq. *Multicultural Politics: Racism, Ethnicity, and Muslims in Britain*. Minneapolis: University of Minnesota Press, 2005.

Modood, Tariq. *Still Not Easy Being British: Struggles for a Multicultural Citizenship*. Stoke-on-Trent, UK: Trentham, 2010.

Parekh, Bhiku, et al., *The Future of Multi-Ethnic Britain: The Parekh Report*. London: Profile Books, 2000.

Thompson, E. P. *The Making of the English Working Class*. New York: Vintage, 1966.

Thompson, Noel. *Political Economy and the Labour Party*, 2nd ed. London and New York: Routledge, 2006.

Suggested Websites

The official UK government website
www.direct.gov.uk

The UK Parliament
www.parliament.uk

BBC
www.bbc.co.uk

The UK cabinet office
www.cabinet-office.gov.uk

Ipsos-Market & Opinion Research International (Mori)
Britain's leading polling organization
http://www.ipsos-mori.com/

The Scottish Parliament
www.scottish.parliament.uk

The Welsh Assembly Government
http://wales.gov.uk/

3 France

Mark Kesselman

Official Name: French Republic (*République Française*)

Location: Western Europe

Capital City: Paris

Population (2014): 66.3 million

Size: 634,427 sq. km.; slightly smaller than Texas

THE MAKING OF THE MODERN FRENCH STATE

Politics in Action

Focus Questions ▽

• What are two distinctive features of French history that have led scholars and French politicians to speak of French exceptionalism?

• What explains France's relative economic decline from the nineteenth century until World War II?

Dieudonné M'bala M'bala is a French citizen whose white mother is from Brittany, a region in Western France, and black father is from the Cameroun, a former French colony in West Africa. Dieudonné, as he is commonly known, usually performs to sold-out audiences—that is, when his performances aren't banned, as they often are. Why are they prohibited? And why has he been repeatedly prosecuted for his public statements? The reason is that his comedy routine is brazenly anti-Semitic—replete with crude, anti-Semitic jokes, denial of the Holocaust, and arm-outstretched parody of the Nazi salute.

Dieudonné has been convicted for violating French laws that prohibit denying the existence of the Holocaust, promote racism, and threaten to disturb public order. Such laws highlight a contrast between France and the United States regarding protection of free speech as opposed to other core values. France has no equivalent to the American Constitution's First Amendment that prohibits legislation restricting free speech.

Dieudonné is especially popular among two very different and opposing groups in French society—Muslim youth, who are often from immigrant backgrounds and live in large housing projects in shabby suburban towns, and native-born white supporters of the far right. Their support for Dieudonné suggests the erosion of a mainstream liberal consensus and increased support for bigotry.

By prosecuting Dieudonné, authorities have boosted his notoriety. Online videos of his performances have received millions of visits. And although his anti-Semitic routine is illegal, it provides a grim reminder of the bleakest moment in modern French history, when a fascist government (described below) energetically collaborated with Nazi Germany's anti-Jewish genocidal campaign during World War II. Dieudonné's popularity is a reminder that France is not simply a cradle of democracy, as mainstream political leaders often proclaim, but host to disturbing forces opposed to this inspiring heritage.

Geographic Setting

France is among the world's favored countries, thanks to its temperate climate, large and fertile land area, rich culture, and prosperous economy. Its natural beauty, superb architecture, vibrant culture, and world-class cuisine explain why it is the world's most popular tourist destination.

France occupies a key strategic position in Europe. It borders the Mediterranean Sea in the south and shares borders with Belgium, Switzerland, and Germany on the north and east. Spain lies to the southwest, Italy to the southeast. With a population over 66 million, France is among the most populous countries in Western Europe. But its large area—211,000 square miles—means that population density is low (about half that of Britain, Germany, and Italy).

France has a modern and productive economy. Most people work in the industrial and service sectors. No other French city rivals Paris, the capital, in size and

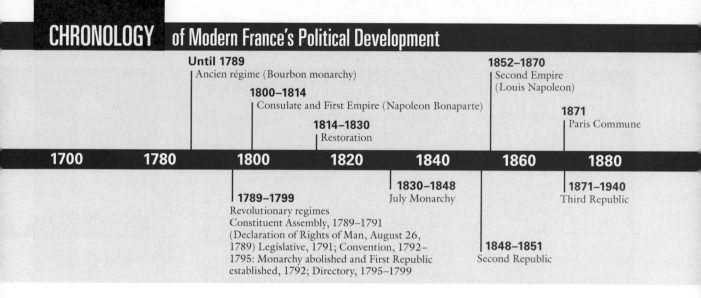

CHRONOLOGY of Modern France's Political Development

Until 1789	Ancien régime (Bourbon monarchy)
1800–1814	Consulate and First Empire (Napoleon Bonaparte)
1814–1830	Restoration
1852–1870	Second Empire (Louis Napoleon)
1871	Paris Commune

1700 — 1780 — 1800 — 1820 — 1840 — 1860 — 1880

1789–1799 Revolutionary regimes
Constituent Assembly, 1789–1791
(Declaration of Rights of Man, August 26,
1789) Legislative, 1791; Convention, 1792–
1795: Monarchy abolished and First Republic
established, 1792; Directory, 1795–1799

1830–1848 July Monarchy

1848–1851 Second Republic

1871–1940 Third Republic

influence. In fact, Lille, Lyon, and Marseille are the only other large cities. In 2013, the country's gross domestic product (GDP) was just over $2 trillion and per capita income was $30,277. France ranked 20th among 186 countries of the world in the 2013 United Nations Development Programme's Human Development Index.

Table 3.1	Political Organization
Political System	Unitary republic. Semipresidential system; popularly elected president, bicameral parliament, and prime minister and government officials who are appointed by president and are formally responsible to National Assembly (lower house of parliament) and informally responsible to president.
Regime History	Frequent regime changes, including five republics, since the French Revolution of 1789. A dictatorial regime based in Vichy collaborated with the Nazis during World War II; the Fourth Republic existed from 1946 to 1958; and the Fifth Republic, originating in 1958, is universally accepted.
Administrative Structure	Unitary, with twenty-two mainland and five overseas regions; and ninety-six mainland and five overseas departments (as of 2014). A major consolidation is planned.
Executive	Dual executive: president (five-year term); PM appointed by president, generally leader of majority coalition in National Assembly, and responsible to National Assembly (as well as informally responsible to president).
Legislature	Bicameral. Senate (upper house) has power to delay legislation passed by lower house and to veto proposed constitutional amendments. National Assembly (lower house) can pass legislation and force government to resign by passing a censure motion.
Judiciary	A system of administrative, criminal, and civil courts. At the top, a nine-member independent Constitutional Council named for nonrenewable nine-year terms; president of republic names three members, president of each house of parliament names three. The Constitutional Council exercises right of judicial review.
Party System	Multiparty. Principal parties: Union for a Popular Movement (UMP); Socialist Party (PS); National Front (FN); minor parties: Left Front; Parti Communiste Français (PCF); Green Party; many others.

© Cengage Learning®

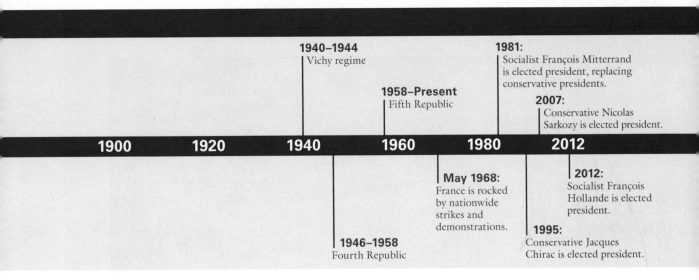

1940–1944
Vichy regime

1958–Present
Fifth Republic

1981:
Socialist François Mitterrand is elected president, replacing conservative presidents.

2007:
Conservative Nicolas Sarkozy is elected president.

| 1900 | 1920 | 1940 | 1960 | 1980 | 2012 |

May 1968:
France is rocked by nationwide strikes and demonstrations.

2012:
Socialist François Hollande is elected president.

1995:
Conservative Jacques Chirac is elected president.

1946–1958
Fourth Republic

France's extensive regional and cultural diversity makes the country vibrant and interesting but also prone to conflict. Charles de Gaulle, a former political leader described below, famously lamented, "How can you govern a country that has 246 varieties of cheese?" The consequence on a personal level is that, in a survey examining citizen happiness around the world, France ranked 64th out of 178 countries. (The United States ranked 23rd; Germany, 35th; and Britain, 42nd.)[1]

A related issue involves trust. When a 2014 World Values Survey asked respondents whether "most people can be trusted," 38 percent of Americans, 36 percent of Germans, and 20 percent of French agreed. On the other hand, the French were more likely than Germans to trust their neighbors and personal acquaintances.

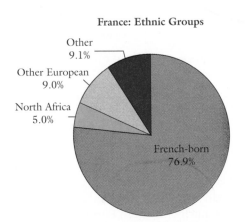

France: Ethnic Groups

Other 9.1%
Other European 9.0%
North Africa 5.0%
French-born 76.9%

France: Religions

Muslim 7.5%
Other Religions 1.5%
No Religion 28.0%
Christian (almost entirely Catholic) 63.0%

It is illegal in France to collect data about ethnicity or to ask respondents about their ethnicity in polls.

French Currency
Euro (€)
International Code: EUR
Exchange Rate (2013):
- 1US$ = 1.33EUR
- 1 EUR = 0.75US$

100 Euro Note Design: Baroque and Rococo (17th and 18th century) style arch

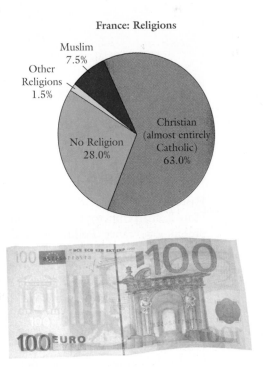

FIGURE 3.1 The French Nation at a Glance

© Labrador Photo Video/Shutterstock.com (for photo)

SECTION 1   The Making of the Modern French State   **83**

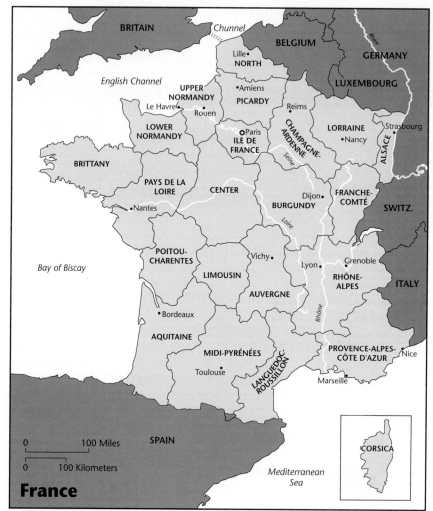

France

© Cengage Learning®

Critical Junctures

Creating Modern France

Historical surveys of modern France often begin with Charlemagne, who became Holy Roman emperor in 800 CE and dominated much of Western Europe, including present-day France. Following his death in 814, the empire disintegrated. Norsemen from Scandinavia established a duchy in Normandy, in northwest France. One of their rulers, William the Conqueror, invaded England in 1066 and defeated English troops at the Battle of Hastings. During the following centuries, French monarchs clashed with powerful provincial leaders and regions within present-day France. Challenges also came from outside. For example, the English nearly conquered the country during the Hundred Years' War (1337–1453). Joan of Arc, a peasant who believed she had a divine mission to protect her country, led French forces to defeat the English army. While the English captured and burned Joan at the stake, she remains a symbol of intense national pride.

During the sixteenth century, the Wars of Religion violently pitted Catholics against Protestants. In 1598, Henry IV helped end religious strife by issuing the

Edict of Nantes granting Protestants religious liberty. However, the bitter memory of religious conflict, as well as the powerful Catholic Church's repeated attempts to shape French society and culture, may help explain the development of a more militant form of **secularism** in France than in neighboring countries.

The seventeenth through early nineteenth centuries were the high point of France's economic, military, and cultural influence. During this period, France was the richest and most powerful country in continental Europe as well as Europe's artistic and scientific capital. In the eighteenth century, it was the center of the Enlightenment, the philosophical movement that emphasized the importance of scientific reason rather than religious belief or folk wisdom.

The Ancien Régime

A turning point in the struggle between French monarchs and provincial rulers came when Louis XIV (r. 1643–1715) created a powerful, modern state. France began to be centrally administered by state agents, some of whom directed administrative departments in Paris while others were posted to the provinces. A uniform legal code began to be applied throughout France.

An informal agreement between the monarchy and powerful landholding nobility promoted political stability. The nobles supported the monarchy; in return, they were lightly taxed. The Catholic Church—itself a large landowner and tax collector—also enjoyed privileged status. On the other hand, historian James Collins notes, the king "had to raise ever more money to feed his military...." The steep costs of foreign wars and the lavish lifestyle of the royal court stretched the monarchy's "financial capacity beyond its limits."[2] The response of Louis XIV and his successors was to raise taxes on the rising middle classes—the most productive sectors of the economy—and on peasants and urban workers, a policy that later backfired. These complex arrangements were later described as the *ancien régime*, or old regime.

From the mid-seventeenth to the mid-eighteenth century, France was usually at war. Further, while the French economy stagnated, Britain—a major rival—enjoyed the benefits of the Agricultural and Industrial Revolutions. In 1789, Louis XVI convened representative assemblies (the Estates General) that had not met for centuries in order to obtain their support for raising taxes. His decision fueled anti-royal opposition. On July 14, 1789, a Parisian crowd stormed the Bastille, a widely despised prison in Paris, and freed the prisoners. The event symbolized the crumbling of royal authority. Not long after, the monarchy and entire *ancien régime* toppled.

The Two Faces of the French Revolution, 1789–1815

The Revolution of 1789 was a *political* and a *national* **revolution**. It replaced the monarchy by a **republic**. It was an *international* revolution, inspiring national uprisings, often supported by French armed intervention, throughout Europe. It was *liberal*, and championed individual liberty in the political and economic spheres, as well as secularism and religious freedom. It was *democratic*, and proclaimed that all citizens have an equal right to participate in key political decisions.

Although the revolutionary regime proclaimed liberty, equality, and fraternity, it treated opponents brutally, beheading many at the guillotine. The regime's intolerance and hostility toward the Catholic Church divided French society.

The revolution that toppled the *ancien régime* replaced it with an even more centralized political system. Emperor Napoleon Bonaparte, the brilliant revolutionary general who seized control of the state and ruled from 1799 to 1814, created state institutions that survive to this day, for example, the system of administration in

secularism

The doctrine that mandates maintaining a strict separation between church and state; it holds that religious beliefs and practices should be confined to the private sphere, and should not play a role in public or political life. The French conception of secularism also demands that the state not regulate religious practices.

ancien régime

The monarchical regime that ruled France until the Revolution of 1789, when it was toppled by a popular uprising.

revolution

The process by which an established political regime is replaced (usually by force and with broad popular participation) by a new regime that introduces radical changes throughout society.

republic

In contemporary usage, a political regime in which leaders are not chosen on the basis of their inherited background (as in a monarchy).

prefects

French administrators appointed by the minister of the interior to coordinate state agencies and programs within France's territorial subdivisions known as *départements*.

which territorial *départements* or subdivisions are administered by a **prefect** appointed by the central government. Ever since the revolution, France has struggled to forge a satisfactory balance between state autonomy—the state's independence from groups within society—and democratic participation and decision making.

Many Regimes, Slow Industrialization: 1815–1940

Following Napoleon's defeat in 1815, France experienced steady decline through World War II. One cause was chronic political instability, involving a succession of ineffective regimes. The most durable was the Third Republic. Created after France's defeat in the Franco-Prussian War and a civil war that followed in 1871, it ended with France's defeat by Germany in World War II. The Third Republic involved an all-powerful parliament and weak executive—a sure-fire recipe to prevent decisive state action.

During the nineteenth century, while regimes came and went at a dizzying pace, economic change was gradual. Unlike Britain and Germany, France chose economic stability over the dislocations of modernization. In 1800 France was the world's second economic power; by 1900 it slipped to fourth. French manufacturers excelled in custom-made luxury goods, like silk and porcelain. But these did not lend themselves to mechanized production. In addition, slow population growth spelled stagnant demand and therefore low investment.

State policies contributed to economic stability. In order to offset political instability, the state shielded farmers, manufacturers, and artisans from foreign competition. France maintained some of the highest tariff barriers in Western Europe throughout this period. However, the state did promote some economic modernization. In the 1860s, it organized an efficient rail network and sponsored an investment bank to finance its development.

France's slow economic growth, internal divisions, and poor planning during the 1930s, when Hitler's Germany was rearming, help explain its crushing defeat by Germany in 1940—the second loss in less than a century. (The first was in 1870, when Germany defeated France in the Franco-Prussian War.)

Vichy France (1940–1944) and the Fourth Republic (1946–1958)

authoritarian

A system of rule in which power depends not on popular legitimacy but on the coercive force of the political authorities.

When Germany overran France in 1940, the French parliament appointed Philippe Pétain, an aged World War I military hero, to be prime minister. He sealed the Third Republic's destruction by signing an armistice with Hitler that divided France in half. Germany occupied and directly administered the North. For several years, until Germany imposed direct rule throughout France, Pétain led an **authoritarian** puppet state in central and southern France. Known as the Vichy regime, because its capital was Vichy, a city in central France, it violently repressed French opposition to Germany and sent well over 1 million French citizens to work producing goods in German factories. Vichy was the only government not directly under German occupation that actively targeted Jews: it sent 76,000 French and foreign Jews to Nazi death camps.

Most French passively accepted the Vichy regime and German domination. However, at enormous personal risk, some Communists, Socialists, and Catholic activists organized an armed opposition movement. Charles de Gaulle, a general and junior cabinet minister in the last Third Republic government before Pétain became prime minister, led the Resistance movement. His brilliant wartime leadership and on several other occasions during the following three decades have earned him the reputation as France's most influential politician of the twentieth century—and one of the most distinguished French leaders ever.

PROFILE

Bettmann/CORBIS

Charles De Gaulle

Charles de Gaulle was from a conservative Catholic background. He chose a conventional career path for someone of his background by attending St. Cyr, France's equivalent of West Point. However, he soon became a gadfly by publishing books proposing bold innovations in military doctrine and strategy. De Gaulle rejected French reliance on large troop concentrations and fixed fortifications—the strategy that resulted in 1.4 million French casualties in World War I. Instead, he advocated organizing a highly trained, mobile professional army making extensive use of tanks and swift personnel carriers. Although his proposal was rejected, he so impressed political leaders that in 1940 he was appointed a junior minister in a short-lived government formed after Nazi forces were sweeping through France.

When the German offensive succeeded and the Third Republic collapsed, de Gaulle bitterly opposed the decision by Philippe Pétain, leader of the Vichy regime, to sign an armistice dictated by Hitler signifying France's defeat.

During World War II, de Gaulle led most of the forces combating the Vichy regime and German Occupation. He headed the provisional government formed when France was liberated by Allied forces in 1944. However, he resigned within two years when he failed to gain sufficient parliamentary support to create a regime based on a strong executive—the critical ingredient whose absence, in his view, weakened the Third Republic and facilitated the Nazi military victory.

De Gaulle gambled that, given his stature as wartime leader, he would quickly be summoned back to office. When he was not, he sulked from the sidelines as the Fourth Republic, created in 1946, stumbled along without him. However, the Algerian crisis enabled his return to power in 1958. In order to forestall a military insurrection, parliament chose de Gaulle prime minister with power to organize a regime to replace the Fourth Republic. He used this golden opportunity to sponsor a draft constitution creating the centralized republic with a strong executive that he had long advocated. Voters approved the proposed constitution in 1959 and de Gaulle became the Fifth Republic's first president.

De Gaulle amply used the powers granted by the constitution, along with others not explicitly delegated. While his actions were often controversial, he succeeded in creating a strong state able to act forcefully within France and on the world stage. He was a frequent gadfly in relations with the United States, for example, passionately denouncing American intervention in Vietnam.

Ten years after de Gaulle returned to power, he experienced a major setback in May 1968 when the regime was rocked by weeks of nationwide strikes and anti-regime demonstrations. Although de Gaulle survived the challenge, he emerged much weaker. In an attempt to bolster his sagging legitimacy, he sponsored a referendum the following year to reform political institutions. When it was defeated—the first time after the previous four were approved in the Fifth Republic—he immediately resigned as president and withdrew from political life. (He died within a year.) However, the Fifth Republic survives to this day and remains de Gaulle's most influential legacy.

MAKING CONNECTIONS Why do some scholars consider Charles de Gaulle as a rebel whereas others regard him as a conservative? Which interpretation is more persuasive, and why?

The Fourth Republic (1946–1958) was created over de Gaulle's opposition and after he resigned from power after World War II. It embodied an extreme form of parliamentary rule and weak executive. As in the Third Republic, the constitution granted parliament a near monopoly of power. However, in practice, parliaments were often deadlocked because a large number of parties were represented in parliament and could not agree on policy initiatives. The **proportional representation (PR)** procedure used to elect members of parliament contributed to this outcome. PR is an alternative to the single-member district, first-past-the-post system used in the United States and Britain, where the party with the most votes in a given district wins the seat.

Because PR encouraged many parties to be represented in parliament, it was easier to assemble a majority to oppose than support the current government. Since the

proportional representation (PR)

A system of political representation in which seats within multimember constituencies are allotted to parties in proportion to the votes each party receives. The single-member district system tends to favor larger parties and thus reduces the number of parties represented in parliament.

constitution required a government to resign if opposed by a majority, governments were voted out of office about once every six months! And yet, as described below, the Fourth Republic helped reverse persistent economic stagnation by promoting economic modernization.

The Fourth Republic might have survived despite governmental instability. However, the regime toppled in 1958 when it was unable to resolve a crisis involving Algeria, a French colony in North Africa that the government considered an integral part of mainland France. When French military forces failed to crush an insurgent movement seeking Algerian independence, it was rumored that the government planned to negotiate peace with the insurgents. To prevent such a move, rebellious officers threatened to order troops stationed in Algeria to invade mainland France. At this critical moment, de Gaulle acted decisively by offering to use his influence with the army to forestall a coup on condition that parliament vote his return to power, scrap the Fourth Republic, and authorize him to propose a new regime. Although critics regarded de Gaulle's bold initiative as illegal, it succeeded.

De Gaulle used the opportunity to draft a new constitution whose centerpiece was a strong executive and weak parliament. It was approved in a **referendum** in 1959. The Fifth Republic has lasted ever since and promises to be the most durable regime in modern French history.

The Fifth Republic (1958 to the Present)

Critics of the Fourth Republic charged that it was all talk and no action. (As we discuss in Section 2, this overstates the case.) On the other hand, the Fifth Republic can be considered the reverse. The Fifth Republic is designed to empower political leaders to act decisively—too decisively, many claim—because the regime lacks a separation of powers, adequate checks and balances, and mechanisms to hold leaders accountable.

De Gaulle demonstrated the danger of a high-handed governing style as well as the potential cost incurred when political institutions stifle legitimate opposition. In May 1968, millions of students, workers, and others engaged in the largest general strike in Western European history. For weeks, France was immobilized. Although de Gaulle eventually regained control of the situation, he was discredited and resigned the following year. Whatever de Gaulle's failings, no subsequent French president has rivaled his national and international standing.

The **conservative** forces that supported de Gaulle's return to power in 1958 swept every major election until 1981. However, economic slowdown and divisions in the ruling coalition during the 1970s eventually enabled **Socialist** Party candidate François Mitterrand to win the 1981 presidential election on a platform promising sweeping economic and social reforms. The peaceful transition that followed demonstrated the ability of Fifth Republic political institutions to accommodate political alternation.

Mitterrand's Socialist government sponsored audacious reforms, including **decentralization**, expanded social benefits, and increased state economic control. The centerpiece involved a state takeover of many large industrial firms, banks, and insurance companies, with the aim of boosting economic efficiency and social equity. Although the reforms were partially successful, as described in Section 2, they were costly and controversial. When economic crisis loomed in 1983, Mitterrand ordered the reforms scaled back and partially reversed. His decision has been widely interpreted as demonstrating the futility of achieving radical reforms in industrialized democracies. Since the Socialist government's right turn, France has resembled other affluent capitalist countries, where moderate ideological conflicts typically pit parties of the center-left against those of the center-right. However, as the 2002 presidential

---

referendum

An election in which citizens are asked to approve (or reject) a policy proposal.

conservative

The belief that existing political, social, and economic arrangements should be preserved.

socialist

The doctrine stating that the state should organize and direct the economy in order to promote equality and help low-income groups.

decentralization

Policies that aim to transfer some decision-making power from higher to lower levels of government.

Students and workers unite in a mass demonstration on the Left Bank of Paris, May 27, 1968.

AP Images.

elections described below and Dieudonné's popularity demonstrate, ideological conflicts have not ended in France.

2002: The Le Pens' Bombshells

The 2002 presidential elections promised to be a remake of the alternating control of the presidency and parliament by center-left and center-right parties that had become familiar since the Socialist Party's centrist turn in 1983. Instead, they revealed a disturbing ideological fissure within French society not reflected in mainstream party competition.

French presidential elections are held according to a two-ballot system. Many candidates compete at the first ballot. If no candidate gains an absolute majority—the typical case—a runoff ballot is held between the two front-runners. In 2002, Lionel Jospin, the center-left Socialist prime minister, and Jacques Chirac, the center-right conservative president, running for re-election, were widely expected to be the runoff candidates. As predicted, Chirac came in first. However, confounding predictions, Jospin was nudged out for second place by Jean-Marie Le Pen, leader of the ultra-nationalist far-right Front National Party (also known as the FN). While Le Pen was a demagogue who targeted Muslim immigrants, Jews, and mainstream politicians, his performance qualified him to face Chirac in the runoff.

Chirac trounced Le Pen in the second ballot by adding to his own first-round supporters Jospin voters who reluctantly turned out for Chirac to prevent a Le Pen victory. The 2002 first round results remain a troubling memory in French politics.

The following two presidential elections resembled the earlier pattern of domination by mainstream parties, with the FN confined to the sidelines. However, the party achieved a remarkable comeback under the leadership of Le Pen's daughter, Marine Le Pen, who succeeded her father as head of the FN in 2011. In the 2014 elections to the European Parliament, the FN achieved the amazing exploit of coming in first among all parties. Most likely, Marine Le Pen will obtain enough votes in the 2017 presidential elections to reach the runoff ballot.

France after September 11

Since the terrorist attacks of September 11, 2001, France has been deeply involved in global conflicts. While it supported the U.S. military action against al Qaeda and the Taliban regime in Afghanistan in 2001, it strongly opposed the U.S. invasion of Iraq in 2003. In 2011, it took the lead—ahead of the United States—in organizing military intervention in Libya against the regime of former dictator Muammar el-Qaddafi.

France's relations with the United States have often been prickly. Indeed, groups throughout the French political spectrum share opposition to American culture and to the powerful role that the United States exercises in the international arena. However, a new era of cooperation between France and the United States began under President Nicolas Sarkozy, who was elected in 2007, and continued after the election in 2012 of François Hollande. When Hollande pledged French support for a possible military intervention with the United States in Syria in 2013, Secretary of State John Kerry referred to France as "our oldest ally." During Hollande's visit to the United States in 2014, a reporter asked President Obama whether France had replaced Britain as the United States' closest European ally. Obama gracefully replied that it was impossible to choose, just as he could not choose between his two daughters, since "both are wonderful in their own way." The days when Charles de Gaulle infuriated U.S. presidents were long past!

The French "Non"—Now or Forever?

France has traditionally been a leader in promoting cooperation among European Union (EU) members, the association described in Chapter 5 that seeks European economic integration and political cooperation. In 2005, France again took the lead—but this time in an opposite fashion. When French voters voted in a referendum whether to adopt a draft constitution strengthening the EU, they rejected the proposal. The decision staggered the EU. Many French, especially those with less education and low income, opposed the constitutional change because they blamed the EU for their difficulties. Two years later, President Sarkozy helped revive the process of European integration. However, France's membership in the EU proved a mixed blessing during the global economic crisis beginning in 2008, when France helped engineer a costly bailout for several financially strapped member states.

The Four Themes and France

Analyzing the four themes that frame *Introduction to Comparative Politics* reveals dramatic changes and suggests troubling questions about recent French politics.

France in a Globalized World of States

Although France is a middle-rank power, it is among the world's richest and most powerful countries. It is one of the five permanent members of the UN Security Council, a leader in the EU, and possesses advanced nuclear weaponry.

The French state has helped the country adapt to global economic competition. France is a world leader in telecommunications, aeronautics, and high-speed rail transport. It led the European consortium that developed the Airbus wide-bodied airplane. France has excelled at developing relatively safe and cheap nuclear power. (Three-quarters of all French electricity is generated by nuclear power.) The pattern of state economic guidance that prevailed in France since the end of World War II has been called **statism**. However, international economic competition, EU and other international commitments, ideological shifts, and citizens' demands for more autonomy have reduced the state's role in economic management in recent decades.

statism

A doctrine advocating firm and extensive state direction of the economy and society.

Governing the Economy

Compared to other industrialized capitalist countries, the French state has been exceptionally active in managing the economy. However, following the brief expansion of the state's economic role after 1981, and the right turn since 1983, the state has assumed a more modest role.

The Democratic Idea

France has passionately embraced two democratic currents. The first claims that citizens should participate directly in political decisions rather than merely voting to choose leaders. This idea nourishes protest movements like May 1968 and more recent ones discussed below. The second democratic current fears direct democracy on the grounds that it produces demagogic leaders and prefers representative government.

Politics of Collective Identity

French national identity has always been closely intertwined with the central position of the state and citizenship. In principle, all—native born and newcomers alike—are entitled to be citizens—but only on condition that they accept France's republican and secular values, and confine collective identities based on religion, ethnicity, or gender to the private sphere: these identities should play no role in the public arena. It is often claimed that multiculturalism violates the universalist/secular model of republican unity.

And yet France is also deeply divided by social, economic, and cultural cleavages. Recently, ethnic conflict, unemployment, the EU, and globalization have destabilized national identity, a situation skillfully exploited by the National Front.

Themes and Comparisons

French politics offers rich lessons for comparative politics. Scholars have coined the term *French exceptionalism* to highlight a prevalent belief by scholars and citizens that the country is distinctive. For example, President Jacques Chirac stated in his Farewell Address, "France is a country unlike any other. It has special responsibilities inherited from its history and the universal values that it has helped forge." One account identifies four elements comprising exceptionalism: the state's key role in economic and social life; extensive political and ideological polarization; the principle that citizens should regard themselves as individuals rather than as members of ethnic or religious groups; and the claim that French political culture, involving secularism, liberty, equality, and fraternity, has universal value.[3]

Where Do You Stand?

Do you agree—or disagree—with the widespread opposition to multiculturalism in French public opinion?

To what extent do the elements comprising French exceptionalism endure; to what extent have they declined?

SECTION

POLITICAL ECONOMY AND DEVELOPMENT

▼ Focus Questions

- What have been two major changes in the state's role in economic management in the Fifth Republic?

- What is one major strength and one major weakness of the state's approach to economic management since 1983?

Thanks to skill, clever state management, and favorable historical and geographic circumstances, France has the world's eighth-largest economy. After World War II, the French state played a key role in steering the economy. However, since 1983 the state has retreated. Private business firms now operate in less-regulated markets and receive less state financing and guidance. Accompanying the change has been a shift from an inward-looking economic posture to an export orientation. France has become a major global economic actor. However, French economic performance presents a mixed picture. For decades, economic growth has been sluggish, unemployment widespread, and economic challenges daunting.

State and Economy

The New French Revolution

During the nineteenth century, when Britain and Germany were engaging in rapid industrialization, the French state chose the more conservative course of preserving traditional society and economy. Predictably, France lagged behind her European neighbors and rivals. A turning point in the state's role occurred after World War II. The groups governing the newly created Fourth Republic gave highest priority to economic and social modernization. In order to achieve this goal, they created powerful new state agencies. One scholar described the result as "a new French Revolution. Although peaceful, this has been just as profound as that of 1789 because it has totally overhauled the moral foundations and social equilibrium of French society."[4]

French-Style Economic Management

After World War II, the state helped transform France's rural, stagnant economy into a modern, urban, industrial economy. A principal tool developed to promote economic and social modernization was **indicative planning**. A national Planning Commission of civil servants established national economic and social goals for the next several year. They also selected priority industries, sectors, and regions to receive extensive state assistance.

In the new scheme, the state was the chief economic player. State agencies were created and provided with ample capital to finance and supervise key industrial sectors

indicative planning

A term that describes a national plan identifying desirable priorities for economic and social development.

(this is known as **industrial policy**). Small and medium firms in important industries, including steel, machine tools, and paper products, were ordered to merge to achieve economies of scale. The state created and ran firms, dubbed "national champions," in high-tech sectors. They were designed to become leading competitors in French and world markets. Some were world class. For example, France became a leader in designing, building, operating, and exporting nuclear power installations. Statism is often viewed as socialist. However, many conservative leaders at the time, including de Gaulle, eagerly embraced statism as a way to modernize the French economy.

France's Economic Miracle

From 1945 to 1975, France's rate of economic growth was among the world's highest (see Figure 3.2). Average yearly income nearly tripled between 1946 and 1962. France leapfrogged into the twentieth century. However, the state's heavy-handed manner caused intense political and social conflict, most notably in May 1968.

New problems developed in the 1970s. The challenges of technological change and global competition required economic flexibility and decentralized economic decision making—the opposite of the centralized style that characterize statism. This structural problem, along with a slowdown in growth in the 1970s, eventually resulted in the electoral defeat of the conservative coalition that had governed France ever since the creation of the Fifth Republic. In 1981, Socialist candidate François Mitterrand was elected president on an ambitious platform that proposed to extend statist direction of the economy, increase social benefits, and expand personal liberty.

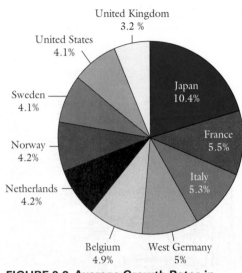

FIGURE 3.2 Average Growth Rates in Gross National Product, 1958–1973

Source: From THE FIFTH REPUBLIC AT TWENTY by William G. Andrews and Stanley Hoffmann (Eds). © 1981 State University of New York.

industrial policy

A policy that uses state resources to promote the development of particular economic sectors.

French Socialism in Practice—and Conservative Aftermath

The Socialist government sponsored a dizzying array of measures to revive the economy, create jobs, and recapture domestic markets. It substantially boosted the minimum wage, family allowances, old-age pensions, rent subsidies, and state-mandated paid vacations. It promoted cutting-edge technological development in biotech, telecommunications, and aerospace. A centerpiece of the program was **nationalization**, involving the state takeover of many privately owned industrial and financial firms. The Socialist reforms promoted social equity and helped modernize the French economy, society, and state in the long run. But in the short run, the high cost and opposition its reforms provoked drove France to the brink of bankruptcy. Deficits soared. France's international currency reserves ran low.

nationalization

The policy by which the state assumes ownership and operation of private companies.

The crisis cruelly demonstrated the limited margin of maneuver for a medium-rank power. In 1983, Mitterrand reluctantly ordered an about-face in economic policy. Political scientist Jonah Levy observes, "A leftist administration that had been elected just two years earlier on a campaign to intensify *dirigisme* [that is, statism] began instead to dismantle *dirigisme*."[5] Since 1983, the core elements of statism have been abandoned.

The French Socialist government's difficulties in the early 1980s were partly a result of changes in economic policy occurring elsewhere. Just when President Mitterrand was extending statism, British Prime Minister Margaret Thatcher and

"What!?? The president's a Socialist and the Eiffel Tower is still standing!??" "Incredible!"

Courtesy Plantu, Cartoonists and Writers Syndicate/ Cartoon Arts International, Inc., from *Le Monde*, May 1981.

American President Ronald Reagan were sponsoring **deregulation** and cutbacks in social benefits. France was apparently too small a country to buck the international tide. In any case, all governing parties in France, whether of center-left or center-right, have apparently reached this conclusion. The failure of the Socialist experiment dealt a body blow to France's traditional statist pattern.

France's Neoliberal Modernization Strategy

Since 1983, economic priorities have included **privatization**, deregulation, and liberalization. Privatization involves the sale of publicly owned financial and industrial firms to private investors. Deregulation reduces the state's role in setting prices and wage levels, allocating credit, and hiring and firing employees. Financial liberalization facilitates movements of capital in and out of France. This package of economic policies is often referred to as **neoliberal**. France's approach to governing the economy has now partially converged with that of other rich capitalist countries.

Yet differences persist. Political scientist Vivien Schmidt observes that France has not "abandoned its statist model.... Governments have not stopped seeking to guide business ... even as they engineer the retreat of the state."[6] State spending is 56 percent of the GDP, the highest in the Eurozone, compared to 44 percent in Germany and 40 percent in the United States. Statism therefore remains alive (if not altogether well). Socialist president François Hollande has conveyed contradictory signals about the pros and cons of statism.

France did weather the 2009 recession somewhat better than Britain and Germany, partly because France retained more extensive state economic regulation. A related reason is that France's strong safety net, discussed below, channeled resources to less-advantaged groups and thereby boosted economic demand. But although the French economy fared fairly well at the beginning of the recession, it fared worse later. In 2013, France's ailing growth rate and high level of unemployment led Britain's *Financial Times* to criticize France as the sick man of Europe—a term that an exasperated American secretary of state had used in the 1950s to describe France![7] In 2013, the EU threatened to penalize France for exceeding the EU's ceiling of 3 percent of GDP for maximum budgetary deficits. The EU warned that France was endangering the economic health of the entire EU. The EU and IMF periodically urge France to deregulate labor markets, and reduce social spending and budget deficits. However, France has adopted many reforms. For example, in 2014 President Hollande proposed a Responsibility Pact that involved cuts in business taxes and public spending in return for a commitment by employers to create jobs. Yet, as discussed in Section 5, government proposals to reduce social benefits have invariably generated fierce popular resistance.

Assessing French Economic Performance

Many factors impede French economic performance. France devotes fewer resources than other leading countries to technological innovation. There is a common pattern

deregulation

The process of dismantling state regulations that govern business activities.

privatization

The sale of state-owned enterprises or services to private companies or investors.

neoliberal

A term used to describe government policies that aim to promote private enterprise by reducing government economic regulation, tax rates, and social spending. The term *liberal* in Europe usually refers to the protection of individual political and economic liberty; in the United States, it often refers to government policies to distribute resources to low income groups.

of large budget deficits, heavy public debt, and high taxes. Moreover, as described later in this section, already costly social programs will consume more resources in coming years.

Among France's most acute economic problems is unemployment—exceeding 11 percent in 2014. France's extensive social programs, hefty labor costs, high taxes, and continued statism fuel unemployment and contribute to the country's lack of economic competitiveness. According to the Institute for Management Development, France is the 28th most competitive economy in the world. And yet the French economy remains strong. For example, there are more Fortune 500 companies located in France than in any other European country. Although full-time French workers have a shorter workweek than British and German workers, their hourly output is the highest in the world.

Society and Economy

According to Nobel Prize–winning economist Paul Krugman, it is misleading to regard France as an economic laggard. Rather, it has chosen a different path than other countries. Rather than giving sole priority to economic efficiency and output, France has sought to balance these goals with concern for citizens' quality of life, as evidenced by policies that favor early retirement, short workweeks, and long vacations.[8] Workers who are laid off are eligible for up to two years of unemployment insurance and job retraining. Although bitterly contested reforms since 2010 have raised the retirement age and tightened eligibility for pension benefits, the terms of retirement remain highly favorable.

France has among the world's most extensive welfare states. Dubbed the French social model, it reflects a widely held belief that the state should help citizens lead healthy, secure lives. Social services include free prenatal care for pregnant women, family payments, and subsidies enabling children to attend preschool. High school students who pass a stiff graduation exam are entitled to attend public universities where tuition is virtually free. Other social benefits include public housing and rent subsidies, five weeks of paid vacation annually, and near-universal coverage of medical care.

The results are impressive. In 2000, the World Health Organization ranked the French health care system first in the world. No wonder that Michael Moore's documentary film *Sicko* (2007) praised the French public health care system so highly!

Yet if social welfare programs and benefits are intensely popular, they are also flawed. For one thing, unequal access to social programs promotes what the French call *the social fracture*. Stably employed workers and pensioners are on the fortunate side of the divide. (Seventy percent of social spending goes for pensions and other benefits for the elderly.) On the other side, youth, part-time workers (who are often young), women, and those from immigrant backgrounds experience higher levels of unemployment and receive fewer social benefits. (However, those most in need are entitled to a minimum yearly income.)

Moreover, France's social programs are expensive: One-third of French GDP is devoted to social spending. And an aging population spells rising medical and retirement costs, along with shrinking revenue to pay the bill. Currently, three adults work for every retired worker. By 2050, the ratio will drop to 1.5 employed workers for every retired worker. For decades, governments have proposed cutting social benefits—only to encounter intense pushback that often succeeds in blocking change.

Labor Relations

Stormy relations between management and labor have traditionally been conflictual. Employers have viewed unions as opponents, and workers have responded by organizing strikes and enlisting state support for their cause. The labor movement has historically been quite weak: Under 10 percent of employees are currently union members and unions have quite little public support. However, when unions organize demonstrations to protest proposed government social cutbacks, citizens turn out by the millions. An important reason for France's poor competitive position internationally is the stormy climate of labor relations.

Inequality and Ethnic Minorities

France has long prided itself on being inclusive toward ethnic minorities. Public opinion polls find the French less fearful of immigrants from outside the EU compared to citizens in most European countries. Yet, the unemployment rate for those from immigrant backgrounds is double that of other French. A research project provided one dramatic reason. Researchers sent applications for job openings by two groups of fictitious applicants. "Thomas Lecomte" and "Guillaume Dupont" ("traditional" French names) were invited to one job interview for every 19 applications; "Youssuf Belkacem" and "Karim Brahimi" (obvious Muslim names), with identical credentials, were invited to one job interview for every 54 applications.[10]

Inequality and Women

France provides extensive social services enabling women to work outside the home (see Figure 3.3). Government spending for family payments, child care, and maternity benefits is about double that in other EU countries. Mothers are entitled to four to six months of paid maternity leave. Fathers receive two weeks of paid paternity leave. Laws mandate gender equality in the workplace and outlaw sexual harassment.

Nevertheless, gender inequalities in employment persist. The proportion of female managers and administrators is among the lowest of all industrialized countries. Women earn about 20 percent less than men for comparable work. The impact of a 2010 law mandating equal pay for equal work has not yet been measured. But

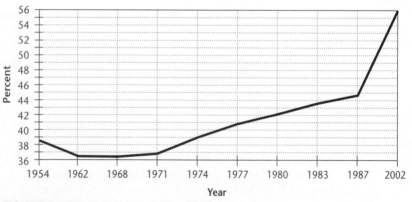

FIGURE 3.3 Women in the Labor Force

Source: INSEE, in Louis Dirn, *La Société francaise en tendances* (Paris, PUF, 1990), p. 108; 2002 data from INSEE, *Tableaux de l Économie Francaise, 2003–2004* (Paris: INSEE, 2003), p. 77.

a newspaper's bleak headline sums up the current situation all too accurately: "For Women in France, Dim Outlook on Equality."[11]

The Generation Gap

There is a wide generation gap in the French economy. Older workers are more likely to be employed and to receive good wages and social benefits. Because labor laws restrict dismissing workers, fewer new workers are likely to be hired. The result: over one-quarter of young workers were unemployed in 2014—double the proportion of older workers. In recent years, government measures to encourage early retirement and ease restrictions on scheduling work and dismissing workers have encouraged job creation, which especially benefits young workers. However, two-thirds of newly created jobs are temporary or part-time and provide lower wages and fringe benefits.

Environmental Issues

There is a keen awareness in France of environmental challenges. There are several Green parties; Hollande's government initially included two ministers from the Green Party. President Chirac sponsored a constitutional amendment in 2004 stating that new technology should not be introduced if there is significant uncertainty about possible environmental risks. (This is known as the precautionary principle.) On the other hand, France is firmly committed to nuclear energy, on which it depends for most of its electricity. It is a world leader in developing and exporting nuclear technology.

THE GLOBAL CONNECTION

France and the European Union

Since France helped create the European Union in 1957, it has been a leader of the organization. Three devastating wars in less than a century between France and Germany taught both countries that there was no alternative but to cooperate. The Franco-German tandem has largely shaped the pace and character of European integration. The EU has helped modernize the French and other European economies. It has fostered close ties between EU member states and has helped make Europe one of the most prosperous regions of the world.

The French economy and society have been profoundly reshaped by EU membership. The bulk of French international trade and investment are no longer with the country's former colonies in Asia and Africa. Nowadays, over 60 percent of French imports and exports are with other member states of the EU.

The EU provide France with many benefits during good economic times. For example, French farmers receive the largest share of the EU's generous agricultural subsidies.

However, when the economy turned sour in the 1980s, many citizens turned against the EU. The proportion of French supporting the EU declined from 70 percent in 1987 to 43 percent in 2004.[12]

In 2005, citizens expressed their discontent by rejecting a revised draft of the EU constitution. The vote revealed a wide chasm between many French voters and the governing parties, who lobbied for a yes vote.

The 2008 economic crisis created additional strains within the EU. Prosperous members, including France, who shared a common currency, the euro, with distressed members, notably Greece and Portugal, were obliged to provide bailouts. A refusal would have had disastrous consequences for the euro, Eurozone countries, and entire EU. The EU's near implosion illustrated how closely the EU's fate is linked to the economic well-being of its member states.

MAKING CONNECTIONS Has France's membership in the EU been a blessing or a curse?

France in the Global Economy

For much of the nineteenth and twentieth centuries, France was relatively isolated from the international economy. High tariffs limited foreign competition, protected French industry, and limited technological innovation. This cozy pattern is gone. France is now tightly integrated in the wider international economy and a major global economic player. Imports and exports account for over half of French GDP. Foreign investors, notably American pension funds, own nearly half of all shares traded on the Paris stock exchange. One-third of French workers work for firms partly or wholly foreign-owned. France ranks among the world's largest importers and exporters of capital. Yet participation in the EU and in the global economy has caused intense strains in domestic politics because the costs and benefits of participation are unequally distributed. Citizens with less education and job skills benefit least, which helps explain why so many support the FN, a party squarely opposed to the EU and globalization. When European citizens are polled about globalization, the French are most critical. In addition to the fact that the EU and globalization have been blamed for recent economic difficulties, there is a tendency in French political culture to cherish what is regarded as distinctively French and view with suspicion what is considered foreign. For example, in negotiations involving creation of the World Trade Organization (WTO), whose mission is to promote free trade around the world, the French government strenuously (and successfully) lobbied for what was called the cultural exception, that is, a government's right to subsidize and favor its domestic cultural sector, including film and television production. At the same time, the French are avid consumers of American films and popular culture. McDonald's highest European sales are in … France!

Where Do You Stand?

Were policy-makers wrong to weaken state capacity by scaling back statism?

Is the French social model an example to be copied—or rejected?

SECTION 3

GOVERNANCE AND POLICY-MAKING

▽ Focus Questions

- What are two advantages and two disadvantages of France's semipresidential system?

- What might be the consequences of replacing the present two-ballot procedure for electing the president with a single ballot plurality system?

Charles de Gaulle designed the Fifth Republic to enable a strong executive to govern without significant checks and balances. Critics suggest that he was too successful, for the result has been a relatively unaccountable executive and unduly weak parliament.

At the same time, three changes have reduced the executive's power. The first involves decentralization of the state. The constitution originally specified that the French Republic is "indivisible." However, the Socialist government transferred substantial governmental powers to subnational governments in the 1980s. A conservative government later extended the reforms and sponsored a constitutional amendment proclaiming that "the organization of the republic is decentralized."

Second, as Section 2 described, the state's relation to the economy has shifted. It now commands less, and consults and persuades more. The third change has limited both the executive and legislature. French democratic theory traditionally held that governments should govern freely because they were elected. Thus, neither the constitution nor unelected authorities should limit their power. However, the constitution of the Fifth Republic has now become the authoritative source for distributing power among political institutions. And the Constitutional Council now routinely exercises the power of judicial review, that is, the ability to nullify legislation and executive actions when it judges that they violate the constitution.

Organization of the State

The Fifth Republic is a semipresidential system. As described in the box feature on the U.S. connection, this pattern combines elements of presidential and parliamentary systems.

De Gaulle designed the semipresidential system in 1958 to bolster the power of the executive. It is a hybrid that combines an independent president and a prime minister responsible to parliament.

Since the 1980s, the constitutional framework has overcome two daunting political challenges. In 1981, Socialist François Mitterrand defeated conservative incumbent president Valéry Giscard d'Estaing, who sought re-election. Despite dire predictions of political instability due to the shift in political control (alternation) between opposing partisan coalitions, the system continued to function without disruption.

THE U.S. CONNECTION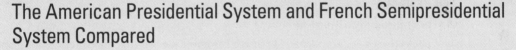

The American Presidential System and French Semipresidential System Compared

In a presidential system, such as in the United States, the executive and the legislature are elected separately. The two branches have independent powers. Neither selects the other, is directly accountable to the other, nor can dissolve the other. The legislature can, however, impeach and force the president to resign for treason or other grave misdeeds. The French Fifth Republic has a similar impeachment procedure, but it has never been used.

In a parliamentary system, by contrast, the executive and legislature are fused. Neither has powers independent of the other. The government is accountable to parliament and must resign if parliament votes no confidence. However, the government has substantial control over the parliamentary agenda and can dissolve parliament.

The Fifth Republic resembles a presidential system in that both the president and parliament are directly elected. Unlike both the presidential and parliamentary systems, however, the French system is directed by a dual executive—the president and a prime minister appointed by the president. The system is called *semipresidential*, not *semiparliamentary*, because every deviation from a purely parliamentary or presidential model strengthens the executive. The fusion of executive and legislative powers (as

in parliamentary regimes) enables the executive to control the parliamentary agenda and dissolve parliament. While the French parliament can vote to censure the prime minister—and thereby force him or her to resign—parliament cannot vote to censure the president.

The most important difference between the two systems involves executive-legislative relations. The American legislature is powerful and fiercely independent. Even when Congress is controlled by the same party as the president, members of Congress have their own base of power and are not dependent on the president. Further, elections to Congress occur at fixed intervals, which further reduces the U.S. president's influence. Because both branches are independent, agreement occurs not because one branch (that is, the president) commands—but because the two negotiate a compromise. By contrast, the French constitution renders the president powerful and parliament relatively humble.

MAKING CONNECTIONS Why do you think that many countries adopting new political systems in recent decades have chosen the semipresidential over the presidential or parliamentary system?

The second challenge involved divided institutional control, that is, when the president leads one political coalition and a rival coalition controls parliament. The French call this **cohabitation**, or power sharing. Many feared cohabitation would produce stalemate and crisis. The test did not arise for decades. However, five years into President Mitterrand's presidential term, conservative forces won the 1986 parliamentary elections. Mitterrand immediately bowed to political realities and appointed Jacques Chirac, leader of the conservative coalition, to be prime minister. The two seasoned politicians quickly devised workable solutions to manage the business of governing. However, cohabitation proved highly unpopular when it occurred again, starting in 1997, during Chirac's presidency, when a Socialist sweep of parliamentary elections forced Chirac to name a Socialist prime minister. In reaction, the major political parties supported a constitutional change in 2002, described below, that makes cohabitation less likely to recur.

cohabitation

The term used by the French to describe the situation when a president and prime minister belong to opposing political coalitions.

The Executive

France was the first major country to adopt a semipresidential system. After the fall of communism, Russia and many formerly communist countries in Eastern Europe were so impressed by France's example that they adopted it. Fifty countries have now chosen the semipresidential system, including Russia and postcommunist countries in Eastern Europe, Austria, Finland, Iceland, Pakistan, Portugal, Sri Lanka, and (most recently) Iraq.

The President

The French president typically possesses more power than the U.S. president within their respective political systems. He (there has never yet been a female president) directs the executive branch and is independent of the legislature. Yet he can dissolve parliament and controls its agenda. When the same party coalition wins the executive and legislative branches, the president is more powerful than the chief executive in virtually any other democratic nation.

The presidential office is so powerful because of (1) the towering personalities of Charles de Gaulle, founder and first president of the Fifth Republic, and François Mitterrand, Socialist president from 1981 to 1995; (2) the ample powers conferred on the office by the constitution; and (3) political practices of the Fifth Republic.

Presidential Personalities Charles de Gaulle was in a class by himself. As first president in the Fifth Republic, he set the standard for his successors. (Table 3.2 lists the Fifth Republic's presidents and their terms of office.) Thanks to his role as leader of the Resistance in World War II, he initially enjoyed wide popularity. He put his stamp on the presidential office by firm control of the government, executive, and entire political system.

Since de Gaulle, there have been six presidents in the Fifth Republic. However, only one—François Mitterrand—stands out. Mitterrand was president from 1981 to 1995, the longest term of any president in the

Table 3.2	Presidents of the Fifth Republic
President	**Term**
Charles de Gaulle	1958–1969
Georges Pompidou	1969–1974
Valéry Giscard d'Estaing	1974–1981
François Mitterrand	1981–1995
Jacques Chirac	1995–2007
Nicolas Sarkozy	2007–2012
François Hollande	2012–Present

© Cengage Learning®

Fifth Republic. He sponsored the Socialist government's initial radical reform agenda and later directed its about-face in 1983. Further, by demonstrating that the Left could govern effectively, he facilitated subsequent political alternation in the Fifth Republic.

The Constitutional Presidency The constitution of the Fifth Republic endows the president with the ceremonial powers of head of state. He resides in the resplendent Élysée Palace and represents France at international diplomatic gatherings. He derives immense power from being the only official elected by the entire French electorate.

A candidate for president must be a French citizen at least twenty-three years old. Presidents serve a five-year term. There are no limits to how many terms a president can serve. There is no vice president in France. If a president dies in office, the president of the Senate (the upper house of parliament) acts as interim president. A new presidential election is held within a short time.

Presidents are elected by a two-ballot procedure. A candidate can win on the first ballot by obtaining an absolute majority of those voting. If no candidate receives a first-ballot majority—the case in every presidential election to date—a runoff election is held between the two front-runners two weeks later.

The Constitution grants the president the following powers:

- The president names the prime minister, approves the prime minister's choice of other cabinet officials, and nominates high-ranking civil, military, and judicial officials.
- The president presides over meetings of the Council of Ministers (the government). Note that the constitution entrusts the president, not the prime minister, with this responsibility.
- The president conducts foreign affairs, through the power to negotiate and ratify treaties. He also names French ambassadors and accredits foreign ambassadors to France.
- The president directs the armed forces. A 1964 decree also granted the president exclusive control over France's nuclear forces.
- The president may dissolve the National Assembly and call new elections.
- The president appoints three of the nine members of the Constitutional Council, including its president. He can also refer bills passed by parliament to the Council to determine if they violate the constitution.
- Article 16 authorizes the president to assume emergency powers in a grave crisis. The only time this power has been used was when de Gaulle faced a military uprising. A 2008 constitutional amendment authorizes the Constitutional Council to limit the use of this clause.
- Article 89 authorizes the president, with the approval of the prime minister, to propose constitutional amendments. To pass, an amendment must be approved by both houses of parliament and then ratified either by a national referendum or by a three-fifths vote of both houses of parliament meeting together as a congress.
- Article 11, amended in 1995, authorizes the president to organize a referendum to approve important policy initiatives or reorganize political institutions. (This procedure is distinct from the process of amending the constitution—which, as we have just seen, may also involve calling a referendum.)
- Article 5 directs the president to be an arbiter to ensure "the regular functioning of the governmental authorities, as well as the continuance of the State." The precise meaning of this clause is unclear. But the president is the sole official delegated this power.

The Political President The constitution grants the president ample powers. But to be effective they must be translated into actual influence. Presidential preeminence is further limited by the fact that the constitution also grants the prime minister and government important powers.

A key factor affecting the extent of presidential leadership is whether the president's political allies control the government and parliament. When they do, he is supreme; when they do not (that is, during cohabitation), the president must share power.

The Prime Minister and Government

The constitution authorizes the president to appoint the prime minister. Presidents generally choose a senior politician from the party leading the majority coalition in the National Assembly. This ensures parliamentary support for the prime minister and government. The prime minister in turn nominates, and the president appoints, members of the cabinet or government, a collective body directed by the prime minister.

The reason why it matters whether the president can command a parliamentary majority is that the constitution authorizes the government, not president, to "determine and direct the policy of the nation. It shall have at its disposal the administration and the armed forces" (Article 20). Article 21 authorizes the prime minister to "direct the action of the government. He [the prime minister] is responsible for national defense. He assures the execution of the laws." Thus, a prime minister accepts the president's leadership because of political, not constitutional dictates, that is, because he or she is a political ally—a junior partner—of the president. In other words the president's preeminence results from *political dynamics* rather than *constitutional directive*. This situation becomes crystal clear during cohabitation, when presidents must deal with a prime minister and government who are political opponents.

This description highlights why the relationship between the president and prime minister is key. The relationship differs dramatically, between unified control, when the president and prime minister are political allies, and cohabitation, when they are rivals. When the president commands a parliamentary majority, and therefore can name a political ally as prime minister, the result is undisputed presidential supremacy. Loyal and effective prime ministers can provide the president with parliamentary support for the government's policies, sympathetic media treatment, and firm supervision of the state bureaucracy.

During cohabitation, the constitution authorizes the prime minister to direct policy-making and policy-implementation. Thus, the president must become a dignified and ceremonial head of state, while the prime minister gains responsibility for governing.

The last experience of cohabitation, in 1997–2002, provoked an important institutional reform. When the Socialist-led coalition won the 1997 parliamentary elections, Jacques Chirac, who had been elected president only two years earlier, was forced to name Socialist Party leader Lionel Jospin as prime minister. Cohabitation lasted five long years, and the frequent sniping between Jospin and Chirac was highly unpopular. The institutional reform devised to prevent a repeat performance was to reduce the president's term from seven to five years, the same length as that of the National Assembly, and to hold elections for the two several weeks apart, thus making it likely that the same political coalition will win both elections. This was in fact the outcome in 2007, when Nicolas Sarkozy won the presidency and his political allies gained a majority in the National Assembly. By appointing an ally as prime minister, Sarkozy had a free hand to govern. Similarly, when François Hollande was elected in 2012, he appointed a Socialist prime minister when the Socialist Party-led coalition won the parliamentary elections several weeks later. The reform has thus achieved its intended goal of producing unified party control.

To summarize the complex relationship between president and prime minister: During periods of unified control, presidents use their formal and informal powers to the hilt, and prime ministers play second fiddle. At these times, presidents can shape policy in virtually any domain they choose, while the prime minister is delegated responsibility for translating general policies into specific programs and supervising the implementation of policy. The prime minister shepherds government proposals through parliament, drums up popular support for the president, takes the heat on controversial issues, and supervises the bureaucracy. During cohabitation, the balance of power shifts toward the prime minister. While the president retains major responsibility for defense and foreign policy, the prime minister assumes control over other policy areas.

Most cabinet members, also known as ministers, are senior politicians from the dominant parliamentary coalition. Cabinet ministers direct the government ministries. Positions in the cabinet are allotted to political parties in rough proportion to their strength in the majority parliamentary coalition. An attempt is also made to ensure regional and, within recent years, gender balance.

The French cabinet is not an important forum for developing or debating policy. Cabinet meetings are occasions where constitutional requirements are met, such as formally authorizing appointment of key administrative officials. Important government policies are shaped at the Élysée or Matignon (official residence of the prime minister) or by interministerial committees directed by the president, prime minister, or their staff.

Bureaucracy and Civil Service

The bureaucracy is large and sprawling. An army of civil servants—approximately 2.3 million—performs the day-to-day work of the state. Another 2.7 million staff public hospitals and subnational governmental bureaucracies. About one in five French jobholders is a civil servant! Administrators appointed to the personal staffs of the president, prime minister, or cabinet ministers, in order to assist them in supervising the formulation and implementation of policy, are especially powerful.

The French bureaucracy is notorious for intervening extensively to regulate social and economic life. The Fifth Republic bolstered the executive's influence by limiting parliament's legislative power and granting the government authority to issue binding regulations with the force of law.

The top slots in the bureaucracy rank among the most prestigious and powerful positions in France. To qualify for a high-level position, one must earn a degree from an elite educational establishment called a *grande école*. Over 1 million students are enrolled in French higher education at any given time. Most study at public universities. A small minority—3,000 students—are admitted to the handful of highly competitive *grandes écoles*. The most prestigious are the École Polytechnique, which provides scientific and engineering training, and the École Nationale d'Administration (ENA), which trains top administrators. Children from culturally and economically favored backgrounds have an immense advantage in the fierce competition for admission to the *grandes écoles*.

Students who graduate at the top of their class at a *grande école* join an even more select fraternity, a *grand corps*. These small, cohesive networks help direct

grandes écoles

Prestigious and highly selective schools of higher education in France that train top civil servants, engineers, and business executives.

grands corps

Elite networks of graduates of *grandes écoles*.

government departments. Membership in a *grand corps* is for life and provides a fine salary, high status, and considerable power. Members may get plum jobs in the private sector after several years in the bureaucracy. Some run for public office and pursue political careers. Membership in a *grand corps* is a stepping stone to parliament or a cabinet appointment. Over half the prime ministers in the Fifth Republic and two former presidents have been members of *grands corps.*

Obtaining a position in the bureaucracy at any level provides lifetime employment, considerable prestige, and a fine salary. However, the increased power of the private sector, the reduce role of the state, and the power of the EU have all reduced the morale and prestige of the civil service.

Public and Semipublic Agencies

Since the Mitterrand government's turn from statism, there has been a steep decline in the number of state-owned enterprises. However, some giant, powerful semipublic agencies remain. For example, Electricity of France, the sole distributor of electricity throughout France, has been described as a state within the state. The French national railroad is another enormous public enterprise. However, like the civil service, semipublic agencies no longer enjoy the prestige and power of yesteryear. Many formerly state-owned bastions like France Télécom, Air France, and the Renault automobile company have been fully or partially privatized.

Other State Institutions

The Judiciary

The French system of Roman law differs substantially from the common law pattern prevailing in Britain and the United States. French courts pay little attention to judicial precedents. What counts are legislative texts and legal codes that regulate specialized fields like industrial relations and local government. When it comes to criminal law, a judicial official, the *juge d'instruction*, is delegated responsibility for preparing the prosecution's case. Criminal defendants enjoy fewer rights than in the U.S. or British system of criminal justice. In the French trial system, judges actively question witnesses and recommend verdicts to juries. The *Cours de cassation* is the top appeals court for civil and criminal cases; its role is quite technical and apolitical. A separate system of administrative courts, described below, hears charges of wrongdoing by the bureaucracy.

Through much of modern French history, the judiciary was considered an arm of the executive. In the past few decades, however, this pattern has dramatically changed. Independent administrative regulatory authorities have gained extensive power in telecommunications, stock market trading, and commercial competition. An additional important initiative was the creation of the Constitutional Council in the Fifth Republic.

The Constitutional Council

The Constitutional Council is the Cinderella of the Fifth Republic. One study observes, "Originally an obscure institution conceived to play a marginal role in the Fifth Republic, the Constitutional Council has gradually moved toward the center stage of French politics and acquired the status of a major actor in the policy-making system."[13] The Constitutional Council has often acted as a check on the legislature and, especially, on the executive. It became more powerful and independent after successfully claiming the right of judicial review. Unlike the U.S. Supreme Court, the council must review a bill within one month of its passage, after which it can no longer rule on the constitutional status of the law.

The nine members of the council serve staggered nine-year nonrenewable terms. The presidents of the National Assembly and Senate each appoint three members. The president of the republic names the remaining three members and designates the council's president. A 2008 constitutional amendment gave parliament a limited right to veto nominees to the council. The first woman was appointed to the council in 1992. Since then, seven other women were appointed. In all, eight women and 64 men have served on the council in the Fifth Republic.

In contrast to most constitutional courts, lower court judges are rarely appointed to the French Constitutional Council. Instead, most members are prominent politicians. Since conservative parties have controlled the presidency and parliament much of the time in the Fifth Republic, judges have usually been conservative politicians. At the same time, the Constitutional Council is considered a relatively nonpartisan body.

State Council

France has a system of administrative courts that hear cases brought by individuals alleging that administrative actions have violated their rights. These courts play an especially important role, given that the executive is so powerful. The most important administrative court is the *Conseil d'État* (State Council). It advises the government about the constitutionality, legality, and coherence of proposed laws that the government is drafting, as well as reviews administrative regulations and decrees.

Subnational Government

France has three levels of subnational elected governments: municipal, departmental, and regional. The government announced a proposal in 2014 to reduce the number of departments and regions.

Until the 1980s, local governments were quite weak. Responsibility for regulating local affairs was in the hands of nationally appointed field officers, such as prefects, civil engineers, and financial inspectors.

The Socialist government sponsored a fundamental reform in the 1980s to loosen the supervision of local governments by the national government. Regional governments were also created. Subnational governments were authorized to levy taxes and formulate education, transportation, social welfare, and cultural policy.

Decentralization has brought government closer to citizens but has also created new problems. For example, many local officials have been prosecuted for corruption in connection with awarding contracts to private firms.

The Military and the Police

Although a middling-rank power nowadays, France was once a world leader and it continues to wield significant influence. It is one of the five permanent members of the UN Security Council and a member of the nuclear arms club. Although the French military has intervened in domestic politics at some key moments in the past, it has remained under civilian control since 1958. France has negotiated military alliances with many of its former colonies in Africa, and its armed forces have often bolstered allied (and dictatorial) regimes engaged in conflicts with insurgents. Two such instances occurred in 2014: in the Central African Republic and in Mali.

Within France, the police operate with considerable freedom—too much, according to critics. Alongside local police forces, the ministry of defense directs a national police force. Judges and executive officials rarely rein in the police. The "forces of order," as they are called in France, have a reputation for engaging in brutal tactics, illegal surveillance, arbitrary actions, and racial profiling.

The Policy-Making Process

As discussed above, the policy-making process differs substantially between periods of unified control and cohabitation. In both cases, however, executive dominance sharply limits legislative and popular participation in the policy-making process, although special mention should be made of the role that protest can play in challenging executive policy-making. Further, the turn away from statism has enlarged the scope for interest groups and voluntary associations to shape policy.

France's participation in the global economy has deeply affected the executive and the French state more generally. EU commitments have limited France's freedom of action. Yet France's leading role within the EU has also enabled it to leverage its power.

Where Do You Stand?

Is there an adequate balance in the Fifth Republic between democratic participation and effective policy-making? Suggest one reform that could improve the balance.

Have decentralization reforms strengthened or weakened the state?

SECTION 4

REPRESENTATION AND PARTICIPATION

▼ Focus Questions

- Why do scholars claim that the French legislature does not adequately represent citizens and hold the executive accountable?

- What are two reforms that might promote checks and balances, empower the legislature, make it more representative, and enable it to hold the executive accountable?

Charles de Gaulle believed that political parties and parliament prevented vigorous executive leadership in the Fourth and Fifth Republics. In response, he designed the constitution of the Fifth Republic to limit popular participation, representation, and legislative autonomy. While he succeeded in muzzling parliament, he failed to curb parties. Indeed, de Gaulle's proposal to elect the president by popular suffrage has encouraged the development of strong political parties. In order to win the all-important presidential contest, formerly decentralized parties were forced to become centralized, unified organizations. Ironically, however, the development of strong parties has helped promote energetic executive leadership.

The Legislature

The French parliament consists of the Senate (the upper house) and the more powerful National Assembly. Parliament neither enjoys the independence that legislatures have in full presidential systems, nor can it hold the executive fully accountable, as parliaments can in parliamentary systems. (Recall that it can only censure the prime minister, not the president.)

The Constitution created a revolution in French constitutional law. Rather than providing parliament with an open-ended grant of authority, that is, parliamentary sovereignty, Article 34 enumerates the areas in which parliament *may* legislate and prohibits legislation on all other matters. The Constitution also authorizes the executive to issue influential regulations and decrees that do not require parliamentary approval. Even within the area of parliamentary competence, Article 38 authorizes the government to request parliament to delegate its authority to issue ordinances (regulations) with the force of law. Governments have used this controversial procedure to limit parliamentary debate and unwelcome amendments.

Even within the limited area of lawmaking, parliament lacks autonomy. The government initiates about 90 percent of bills passed into law. Parliament has limited control over the budget. The executive can dissolve the National Assembly before its normal five-year term ends. Although the executive cannot dissolve the Senate, this hardly matters since the Senate cannot pass legislation without the National Assembly's assent and it cannot force the government to resign by voting censure.

The government's control over parliament is further bolstered by Article 44, known as the package or blocked vote, which authorizes the government to require parliament to vote on a bill with only those amendments included that the government selects. Governments have used (or abused) the package vote to restrict debate on many key legislative bills.

An even more powerful and weapon is Article 49.3, described by political scientist Emiliano Grossman as "one of the most powerful instruments at the disposal of contemporary democratic government," authorizes the government to call for a confidence vote on its overall policies or a specific bill.[14] When it does so, the policies or bill are considered approved unless deputies (as members of the National Assembly are called) pass a censure motion by an absolute majority within twenty-four hours. Deputies who abstain or are absent are, in effect, counted as supporting the government. A 2008 constitutional reform specified that this controversial procedure can only be used once in each parliamentary session and only for matters involving finances or security.

Censure motions can also be initiated by deputies; again, passage requires an absolute majority of deputies to vote in favor. The Constitution limits the number of such parliament-initiated censure motions. In any case, since governments typically command a parliamentary majority, there is little risk of a successful censure vote. Only one has ever passed in the entire history of the Fifth Republic.

It should now be clear why parliament is widely regarded as a rubber stamp. Its debates are not widely reported and opposition parties cannot adequately air grievances. One result is that discontented groups express opposition in the streets rather than channel demands through parliament.

Parliamentary committees (called commissions) are not very powerful. Although they are authorized to review and propose amendments to draft legislation, the government can drop amendments it dislikes before putting the text to a vote.

The National Assembly is more powerful than the Senate for two reasons. It alone can censure the government, and it can pass laws despite the Senate's opposition. The Senate can only delay approval of legislation. However, its approval is required to pass constitutional amendments.

Modest reforms have been enacted in response to widespread calls to strengthen parliament. A constitutional amendment in 2008 requires parliament to approve nominations to key executive positions. Opposition parties were given control over the parliamentary agenda one day a month. Yet parliament continues to play a quite limited role in the French political system.

How a Bill Becomes a Law

The Constitution provides two procedures for passing laws. A rarely used provision authorizes the government to sponsor a referendum in which citizens are asked to vote on a government proposal. The typical procedure is for parliament to pass legislation. Following a bill's introduction in one of the two chambers (usually the National Assembly), a commission reviews the bill. The text is then submitted to the full house for debate, possible amendment, and vote. If approved, the same procedure is followed in the second chamber.

A bill becomes law if passed in identical form by both houses (unless nullified by the Constitutional Council). If the two houses twice vote different versions of a bill (or one time each if the government declares the bill a priority matter), a joint commission of members from both houses seeks to negotiate a compromise. If it succeeds, the revised text is voted upon by the two houses. If they fail to pass the text at this reading, the government can request the National Assembly to vote once more. If it approves the measure, the bill becomes law despite the lack of senatorial approval. This method has been used to by-pass the Senate on some important legislation.

Once a bill passes, the president of the republic, president of either legislative chamber, or sixty deputies or senators can refer the bill to the Constitutional Council within a month. The council can strike down the entire text or those portions that it judges violate the Constitution. After this period, the law can never be reviewed by the council save if a citizen successfully alleges that a law violates constitutionally protected rights.

Why might the two chambers hold different positions? Mainly because they are elected by different procedures and represent different interests.

Electing the Legislature

The 577 deputies the National Assembly are elected for a five-year term by a two-ballot single-member district procedure that resembles the procedure for electing the president. To be elected at the first ballot, a candidate must receive an absolute majority of the votes cast in a district. A few popular incumbent deputies are reelected at the first ballot, but most elections require a runoff the following week. Whereas in presidential elections, only the two front-runners can compete at the runoff ballot, in elections to the National Assembly, any candidate who receives at least 12.5 percent of the votes at the first round can compete in the runoff. However, most second-ballot elections pit a candidate on the left against one on the right because minority candidates typically support the best-placed major party candidate on their side of the left-right political divide. Thus, elections to the National Assembly contribute to polarization and increase the likelihood that a cohesive coalition will gain a parliamentary majority.

The 348 members of the Senate are elected for six-year terms by electoral colleges consisting of local elected officials from France's 101 *départements*. The fact that mayors and town councilors from small towns and villages are the largest group in these electoral colleges explains why the Senate usually has a conservative orientation.

Political Parties and the Party System

Contrary to de Gaulle's fear that political parties would prevent stable leadership, they have forcefully promoted it. Recently, however, ideological convergence between the major parties has provoked a backlash because so many French citizens feel unrepresented. The popularity of the far-right National Front and Dieudonné highlight citizen discontent with the mainstream parties.

The Major Parties

Coalitions led by the UMP and PS have dominated French political life for decades. At the same time, neither party has achieved a lock on power and both face a major challenge from the FN and from smaller parties throughout the ideological spectrum.

Union pour un Mouvement Populaire (Union for a Popular Movement—UMP)

Until de Gaulle reached power in 1958, right-wing parties were numerous and fragmented. De Gaulle's allies formed a party that unified many on the moderate right. The social base of the party—business executives, shopkeepers, professionals, elderly, wealthy, religiously observant, and highly educated—reflects its conservative orientation.

The Gaullist party—today known as the UMP—was the keystone of the early Fifth Republic. Although its fortunes flagged in the 1970s and 1980s, it regained dominance when Jacques Chirac was elected president in 1995. Chirac was reelected in 2002 and UMP dominance continued when Nicolas Sarkozy succeeded Chirac as president in 2007. However, François Hollande's Socialist Party gained power in 2012, and the UMP became badly divided following the election when UMP politicians competed for party leadership. The UMP's leader was forced to resign in 2014 when the party was rocked by financial scandal. Despite Sarkozy's announcement after his 2012 defeat that he would retire from political life, his renewed activism the following year fueled speculation that he might make another run for the presidency in 2017.

Parti Socialiste (PS)

A perpetual failure in the early Fifth Republic, the Socialist Party (PS) became a vanguard of newly modernized France in 1981. Under François Mitterrand's leadership, it swept the presidential and parliamentary elections that year on a platform promising far-reaching social, economic, and political reforms. Following its shift to a more moderate course in 1983, described in Section 2, it became a center-left pillar of the Fifth Republic. Ever since, until the FN's recent rise, the PS and the UMP vied for control of French political institutions.

Ségolène Royal, PS nominee for president in 2007, was the first female presidential candidate of a major party. Although she was a striking contrast to older, male—and stale—Socialist politicians, she lost to Nicolas Sarkozy in 2007. However, the PS rebounded when Socialist Party candidate François Hollande foiled Sarkozy's bid for reelection in 2012. Hollande's victory was mainly due to Sarkozy's erratic performance and the scandals that tarnished his presidency.

During the 2012 election campaign, Hollande promised that he would be a "normal" president—a swipe at Sarkozy's flamboyant style. However, Hollande's performance was singularly unimpressive. By 2014, his approval ratings plummeted to record lows. Reasons included his indecisive manner, persistent economic difficulties, and his private behavior.

While most French, unlike many Americans, believe that politicians' private lives should remain private—and should not influence judgments about their political performance—there are limits to this tolerant approach. Hollande exceeded that limit in 2014. The context: Hollande and Ségolène Royal were a stable couple for decades. However, they separated in 2007—the news was announced the evening of Royal's electoral defeat. The reason for their separation? The revelation that Hollande had been involved for years in a romantic relationship with another woman. Upon Hollande's election as president in 2012, she was officially designated First Lady and moved into the Élysée. However, Hollande soon began yet another clandestine liaison—clandestine, that is, until in 2014 a magazine published incriminating photos of the president driving a motor scooter on his way to a tryst with his new love. Following the revelations, Hollande's partner immediately moved out of the Élysée and entered a hospital, reportedly suffering from depression. These events drove Hollande's already unimpressive poll ratings to an historic low. The Socialist Party paid the price when it experienced a severe decline in the 2014 European elections; it came in third with a meager 15 percent of the vote.

The PS electoral base is composed of civil servants, low-income groups, and educated professionals. Although the UMP and PS represent different socioeconomic groups, their supporters mostly occupy secure positions French society. Unskilled workers, unemployed, school dropouts, and other marginal groups often support fringe parties.

Small Parties

While the UMP and PS have been the dominant parties, many others compete. The most influential nowadays include the National Front (FN); Les Verts (Greens); two centrist parties: Alternative and Democratic Movement; the Parti de gauche (Left Party); and the Parti communiste français (PCF). We describe the PCF, the most important historically; and the FN, the most important currently.

Communist Party (PCF)   The French Communist Party (PCF) was created after the Russian Revolution with the goal of promoting revolutionary change in France. For most of its history, the PCF loyally supported the Soviet Union. Its active role in the Resistance to the Vichy regime and Nazi occupation enabled it to become France's largest party after World War II. In addition to its electoral strength, it controlled France's largest trade union and local governments in working class areas. However, the PCF experienced a steady decline because of its authoritarian internal organization, rigid ideology, and pro-Soviet stance. PCF presidential candidates nowadays receive only a handful of votes. Thanks to an alliance with the PS, the PCF elected seven deputies to the National Assembly in 2012.

Front National (FN)   For decades the FN was conventionally classified as a fringe party because of its small size and anti-mainstream ideological stance. However, matters became more complicated following its breakthrough showing in the 2014 European elections, when it came in first and achieved a comfortable lead over the UMP and PS. This development signifies a substantial reorganization of the French party system.

The FN was among the first parties in Western Europe since World War II to openly promote racism. It first scored significant victories in local elections in the 1980s by scapegoating Muslim immigrants, especially Arabs from North Africa. The FN proposed withholding social benefits from documented immigrants and even deporting them—a bigoted response to unemployment, crime, and ethnic diversity.

Jean-Marie Le Pen led the party for decades. His crude humor and combative style dramatically contrasted with the polished manner of most French politicians. Beginning in the 1990s, Le Pen broadened the party's focus by blaming mainstream politicians for rising crime rates, unemployment, and what he charged was the EU's domination of France. He also adopted the traditional far-right theme of anti-Semitism (he characterized the Holocaust as an insignificant "historical detail"). And he claimed that the Nazi occupation of France during World War II was not especially harsh.

Le Pen's dramatic breakthrough occurred in the 2002 presidential election, when his second-place showing qualified him to compete with Chirac in the runoff ballot. Although the 2002 election was the high point of FN popularity for the next decade, the party achieved the amazing exploit of coming in first in the 2014 elections to the European Parliament, and it has now established itself as among France's major parties. Several factors explain this outcome.

First is the dynamism, skillful leadership and popularity of FN leader Marine Le Pen, who succeeded her father as head of the party. She modernized the party and downplayed anti-Semitic and homophobic themes in a successful effort to recruit youthful voters. At the same time, Le Pen continued to engage in Muslim-baiting, as when she compared Muslims praying in Paris streets to the Nazi occupation of France in World War II. A further reason why she ranks among the most popular politicians in France is her youthful dynamism, a powerful contrast to mainstream politicians. By receiving 18 percent of the vote in the 2012 presidential elections, she came in third. Polls suggest that in the 2017 presidential elections she may repeat her father's 2002 performance and reach the runoff ballot.

Second, the FN has profited from the fact that the governing UMP and PS have failed to bring down France's high unemployment rate or restore economic growth. It also links these problems to France's participation in the EU and globalization. In contrast to the mainstream UMP and PS, it champions economic nationalism, calling for French withdrawal from the Eurozone and the EU. The FN draws its strongest support from those who are most economically vulnerable: less educated and lower income voters.

Third, the FN has successfully positioned itself as a party of cultural conservatism, supporting law and order in opposition to alleged official laxity regarding crime, undocumented immigration, and corruption. The FN now represents the major source of opposition to France's mainstream parties.

Elections

France's most important elections are the legislative and presidential elections (see Tables 3.3 and 3.4). The following troubling developments indicate a crisis of political representation and the party system.

- Voting patterns have been increasingly unstable. In every one of the six legislative elections between 1981 and 2002, the governing majority swung between the center-left and center-right parties. When the UMP won the 2007 parliamentary elections, it was the first time in thirty years that alternation between competing coalitions did not occur. But alternation again occurred in the 2012 presidential and parliamentary elections, when the PS replaced the governing UMP.
- Voter turnout has generally been declining in both presidential and parliamentary elections.
- Fringe parties, above all the FN, but other parties throughout the ideological spectrum that oppose mainstream governmental parties.

Candidate	Dec 1965 Candidate	Ballot %	June 1969 Candidate	Ballot %	May 1974 Candidate	Ballot %	Apr–May 1981 Candidate	Ballot %	Apr–May 1988 Candidate	Ballot %	Apr–May 1995 Candidate	Ballot %	Apr–May 2002 Candidate	Ballot %	Apr–May 2007 Candidate	Ballot %	Apr–May 2012 Candidate	Ballot %
Extreme Right									J.M. Le Pen (FN)	14.4	J.M. Le Pen (FN)	15	J.M. Le Pen (FN)	17.0 (17.9)	J.M. Le Pen (FN) De Villiers	10 2	M. Le Pen (FN)	17.9
Center Right de Gaulle (Center-Right)	de Gaulle	43.7 (54.5)	Pompidou (UNR)	44.0 (57.6)			Chirac (RPR)	18	Chirac (RPR)	19.9 (46.0)	Chirac (RPR)	20.8 (52.6)	Chirac (RPR)	19.9 (82.1)	Sarkozy (UMP)	31 (53)	Sarkozy (UMP)	27.2 (48.4)
Center Lecanuet (Opposition-Center)	Lecanuet	15.8	Poher (Center)	23.4 (42.4)	Giscard	32.9 (50.7)	Giscard	28.3 (48.2)	Barre	16.5	Balladur (UDF)	18.9	Bayrou (UDF) Saint-Josse (CNPT) Madelin (PR)	6.8 64.3 3.9	Bayrou (UDF) Nihous (CNPT)	19 1	Bayrou (Mouvement Démocratique)	9.1
Center Left Mitterrand (Socialist-Communist)	Mitterrand	32.2 (45.5)	Defferre (PS)	5.1	Mitterrand (PS)	43.4 (49.3)	Mitterrand (PS)	25.8 (51.8)	Mitterrand (PS)	34.1 (54.0)	Jospin (PS)	23.3 (47.4)	Jospin (PS) Chevènement Mamère (Greens)	16.1 5.3 5.3	Royal (PS) Voynet (Greens)	26 (47) 2	Hollande (PS) Joly (Greens)	28.6 (51.7) 2.3
Left			Duclos (PCF)	21.5			Marchais (PCF)	15.3	Lajoinie (PCF)	6.8	Hue (PCF)	8.6	Hue (PCF) 3 candidates (Extreme Left)	3.4 10.6	Buffet (PCF) 4 candidates (Extreme Left)	2 7	Melanchon (Front de Gauche)	11.1
Abstentions		15.0 (15.5)		21.8 (30.9)		15.1 –12.1		18.9 (14.1)				20.6		27.9 (19.9)		16 (16)		20.5 (19.7)

Note: Numbers in parentheses indicate percentage of vote received in second ballot. Percentages of votes for candidates do not add to 100 because of minor party candidates and rounding errors.

Sources: John R. Frears and Jean-Luc Parodi, *War Will Not Take Place: The French Parliamentary Elections of March 1978* (London: Hurst, 1976), p. 6; *Le Monde. L'Élection présidentielle: 26 Avril–10 Mai 1981* (Paris: *Le Monde*, 1981), pp. 98, 138; *Journal officiel*, May 14, 1995; *Le Monde*, April 28 and May 12, 1998; *Le Monde*, May 5–6, 2002; *Le Monde*, May 7, 2002; www.electionresources.org/fr/president.php?election=2007%region=fr (accessed on June 18, 2007); 2012, Conseil Constitutionnel.

- Countless prominent politicians have been implicated in criminal misconduct. President Chirac was convicted in 2010 of using public funds to assist the UMP while he served as mayor of Paris in the 1970s. He avoided a prison sentence only because of ill health. Since 2010, President Sarkozy has been embroiled in financial scandals involving allegations of having received illegal campaign contributions from billionaire Liliane Bettencourt and former Libyan dictator Muammar el-Qaddafi.

The record for tawdry behavior, however, is doubtless held by Dominique Strauss-Kahn, a former Socialist finance minister. In 2011, Strauss-Kahn was managing director of the International Monetary Fund (IMF), highly popular, the likely Socialist party candidate in the 2012 presidential election, and favored to become next president. However, while on an IMF mission to New York, he was arrested for sexually assaulting a housekeeper in a posh hotel. Evidence soon emerged of his sordid behavior stretching back years. Such incidents help explain why a public opinion poll reports that 64 percent of the French regard most politicians as corrupt.[15]

Allegations of corruption by President Chirac.
Philippe Wojazer/Reuters/Corbis.

Table 3.4	Electoral Results, Elections to National Assembly, 1958–2007 (percentage of those voting)													
	1958	**1962**	**1967**	**1968**	**1973**	**1978**	**1981**	**1986**	**1988**	**1993**	**1997**	**2002**	**2007**	**2012**
Far Left	2%	2%	2%	4%	3%	3%	1%	2%	0%	2%	2%	3%	2%	1%
PCF	19	22	23	20	21	21	16	10	11	9	10	5	4	7
Socialist Party/Left Radicals	23	21	19	17	22	25	38	32	38	21	26	25	26	34
Ecology	—	—	—	—	—	2	1	1	1	12	8	4	3	—
Center	15	15	18	10	16	21*	19*		19*	19*	15*		8	6
Center-Right	14	14	0	4	7			42*				5*	4	—
UNR-RPR-UMP	18	32	38	44	24	23	21	—	19	20	17	34	40	27
Far Right	3	1	1	0	3	0	3	10	10	13	15	12	7	14
Abstentions	23	31	19	20	19	17	30	22	34	31	32	36	40	43

*Number represents the percentage of combined votes for Center and Center-Right parties.
Sources: Françoise Dreyfus and François D'Arcy, *Les Institutions politiques et administratives de la France* (Paris: Economica, 1985), 54; *Le Monde*, March 18, 1986; *Le Monde, Les élections législatives* (Paris: Le Monde, 1988). Ministry of the Interior, 1993, 1997. *Le Monde*, June 11, 2002; *www.electionresources.org/fr/deputies.php?election=2007&region=fr* (accessed on June 18, 2007); 2012, Conseil Constitutionnel.

More generally, French political leaders and institutions are held in pitifully low esteem. In a 2011 poll, 87 percent of the French judged all politicians to be dishonest. Few respondents expressed confidence in the government's ability to improve their personal situation.[16] France's ailing party system has contributed to the widespread belief that political institutions need serious overhaul. This is a principal reason for the FN's popularity. However, aside from angry protest, it is not clear what reforms are needed or how they might be achieved.

Political Culture, Citizenship, and Identity

Until the 1980s, two traditional subcultures powerfully shaped French political and cultural life. One subculture had a strongly working-class flavor. It was structured by the French Communist Party (PCF) and the PCF's powerful trade union ally. The other was a conservative subculture linked to the Catholic Church. The subcultures provided members with contrasting political orientations and social identities. Most French citizens identified with one or the other. In recent decades, however, both subcultures have disintegrated and the number of self-identified Communists and observant Catholics has plummeted. No new, broad-based networks have replaced them. Instead, French society has become both less polarized and more fragmented.

Social Class

For centuries, class cleavages produced intense political conflict in France. Class identification, however, rapidly declined in the 1970s, as a result of changes in the economy and ideological orientations. The most extensive demographic shift was a massive reduction in the number of manual workers, as basic industries, including steel, shipbuilding, automobiles, and textiles, drastically downsized the industrial workforce. This was matched by the rise of service sector employment. The scrambling of class boundaries has eroded traditional social identities while no new social anchors have developed to replace them. When combined with persistently high unemployment beginning in the 1970s, the result has been a widespread sense of insecurity. Since mainstream political parties, notably the UMP and PS, are blamed for failing to resolve the problems, this has provided fertile soil for the FN.

Ethnicity and Immigration

France has traditionally attracted large numbers of immigrants. Indeed, in 1930, it had a higher proportion of immigrants than the United States. A new wave of immigrants arrived after World War II when the government actively recruited foreign workers to help rebuild the French economy. At the high point of postwar immigration, one-ninth of the French population was foreign-born. After the economy slowed in the 1970s, the government began restricting further immigration. New arrivals since then have consisted of family members of immigrants already established in France, those occupying skilled positions, and the undocumented. However, France retains strong connections beyond its borders. One French person in four these days has at least one foreign-born grandparent.

Economic stagnation and high unemployment feed insecurity that the FN exploited to fan anti-immigrant flames. President Sarkozy partially mimicked the FN's anti-immigrant orientation. For example, in 2010 he ordered police to destroy Roma camps (the Roma are also known as Gypsies) and forcibly deport Romas to their native Romania and Bulgaria. The European Union's minister of justice announced that she was "appalled" by the government's campaign of ethnic profiling.

President Hollande has also targeted the Romas. In 2013, a middle school student whose family had overstayed their visa was removed from a school bus, escorted to the airport, and deported to her native Romania. Following a groundswell of protest, Hollande announced that he would reverse the decision—on condition that the girl return to France *without* her family!

Citizenship and National Identity

France's dominant approach to immigration, citizenship, and national identity is often described as the republican model. On the one hand, it is inclusive. No matter what newcomers' race, religion, or national background, all are welcome—on condition that they learn French and adopt prevailing French political values.

However, while the republican model claims to be nondiscriminatory, it includes exclusionary and potentially repressive elements by insisting that cultural identities and values—other than the French republican, secular ones—should remain private and play no role in the public sphere. The French often charge that the American conception of multiculturalism is dangerous and divisive because it encourages "identity politics" that fragments society and encourages conflicts among racial, ethnic, and religious groups.

The exclusionary aspect of the republican model is illustrated by the adoption in 2004 of legislation involving a dress code for Muslim women. The law bans displaying "conspicuous signs of religious affiliation" in public schools. Although the law also prohibits wearing the Jewish *yarmulke* (skullcap) and large Catholic crosses, its main purpose was to ban the *hidjab* (headscarf—or *foulard*, in French). An official estimate was that fewer than 2,000 of nearly 1 million Muslim schoolgirls wore the headscarf to school. Just the same, the government sponsored the law on the grounds that it was needed to preserve religious neutrality in public schools and combat Muslim **fundamentalism**.

In 2010, parliament went even further. Women were prohibited from wearing garments that concealed the face when they appeared in streets, parks, businesses, and government buildings and used public transportation. Most legislators, and according to one poll, over 80 percent of the French supported the measure.

The principal targets of the law were the *burqa*, the head-to-toe garment worn by some Muslim women, and the *niqab*, which covers most of the face. According to a police report, only about 2,000 of France's over 1 million Muslim women are veiled. However, supporters claimed that the ban was needed to preserve women's independence and protect secular values. President Sarkozy declared, "The *burqa* is not welcome in France because it violates our values and our ideals of a woman's dignity."

Another illustration: In 2008 administrators turned down a woman's application for citizenship on the grounds that, by wearing the *niqab*, she demonstrated her rejection of fundamental French values.

Historian Joan Scott suggests that the dress code reflects "the impotence and/or unwillingness of the government to ... adjust national institutions and ideologies ... to the heterogeneity of [France's] current population...."[17] The dress code reveals insecurity about French national identity and the relation of Islam to traditional French culture and values. Further, the government's action illustrates the French

fundamentalism

A term recently popularized to describe extremist religious movements throughout the world.

state's wide scope for regulating personal relations. In the United States, the Supreme Court would consider similar legislation as a violation of the First Amendment's constitutional protection of free speech.

France's republican model champions the value of individual merit. However, in practice, the policy of ignoring racial, religious, and ethnic differences often marginalizes minorities. The government has addressed racial and ethnic inequality indirectly, for example, by providing resources to what it designates as "sensitive areas," that is, impoverished urban neighborhoods that (not coincidentally) are often home to minorities. However, minorities remain severely underrepresented in many spheres. For example, only a handful of Muslims or people of color have occupied positions of political leadership. Most recently, the minister of justice in the Hollande government was a woman of color—yet she was often the target of racist slurs.

The French are intensely proud of their country's cultural heritage. But in an era of globalization, French identity and culture have lost their distinctive edge. Nowadays, confidence and pride in French exceptionalism and France's unique position in the world have been replaced by uncertainty about the meaning and value of French identity.

Gender

When French philosopher and novelist Simone de Beauvoir published *The Second Sex* after World War II, a book analyzing the social processes by which women are assigned a secondary role in society, it became a feminist trailblazer. In the 1960s and 1970s, French feminist theorists played a major role in reshaping literary studies around the world. And yet these noteworthy contributions did not make France a trailblazer in pursuing gender equality in the political sphere. However, a breakthrough occurred on this issue in 1999.

Women have traditionally been highly underrepresented in the French political system. Although they make up over half the electorate, there has never been a female president and only one prime minister. However, after decades of struggle by the women's movement, France adopted a constitutional amendment in 1999 that mandates gender parity for many elected offices. France was the first country in the world to require political parties to nominate an equal number of men and women for elected positions. Since then, over 100 other countries have followed France's lead.

parity law

A French law passed in 2000, following the adoption of a constitutional amendment in 1999, and subsequently extended, that directs political parties to nominate an equal number of men and women for many elections.

The **parity laws** require parties to nominate an equal number of male and female candidates for elected offices that are filled by proportional representation. Parties failing to do so can be disqualified. For offices, notably the National Assembly, filled by the plurality system in single-member districts, parties that do not nominate an equal number of men and women receive smaller public subsidies.

Following passage of the parity law, the number of women elected to town councils skyrocketed, and women now make up about half of these legislative bodies. However, women remain less than one-quarter of the Senate and are highly underrepresented in the National Assembly, whose members are elected from single-member districts. (France ranks lower than Britain and Germany with respect to the proportion of female members of the legislature.) The reason is that a party can comply with the requirements of the parity law by nominating women in districts where the party is weak and has little prospect of winning. Thus, while female representation in the National Assembly more than doubled from 12 percent in 2002 to 26 percent after the 2012 elections, the number of female deputies is only half the proportion of female voters. The parity law does not apply to the presidency, the most important elected position. However, pressure for parity may have indirectly helped Ségolène

Royal, PS president of a regional council, gain the PS nomination for president in 2007, the first time that a major political party nominated a female presidential candidate. However, Royal came in second behind Nicolas Sarkozy thanks to a lackluster campaign.

When Sarkozy was elected president, he appointed many women, including women of color, to his cabinet. For the first time, women directed some of the most powerful departments, including Interior and Finance. In 2012, Hollande went further and appointed an equal number of men and women to the cabinet. He also created the first ministry of women's rights with full cabinet status.

While women have achieved greater political representation, thanks to the parity law, changing values, and pressure from the women's movement, they continue to have unequal political, social, and economic representation.

Interest Groups, Social Movements, and Protest

Organized Interests

Compared to Britain, Germany, and the United States, interest groups in France are relatively weak. The French executive has typically developed policy by keeping interest groups at arm's length. There are exceptions, notably the farm lobby (the FNSEA) and Medef, the umbrella business association. They participate in consultative commissions and have easy access to policy-makers.

The development of a more modest state since the 1980s has encouraged an explosion of voluntary and advocacy associations, in areas like sports, leisure, feminism, environment, and civil liberties. One estimate is that the number of associations has doubled since the 1980s to 1 million today.

French Trade Unions

The French labor movement is quite weak. Far fewer workers belong to unions than is the case in other industrial democracies: less than 10 percent of the labor force, the lowest figure among comparable countries. This constitutes a steep drop from the period after World War II, when over 30 percent of workers belonged to unions.

The labor movement is further weakened by internal divisions. In many industrialized democracies, including Britain, Germany, and Japan, most unions belong to a single trade union confederation. France has four, along with several independent unions. Each confederation pursues its own agenda and competes with the others for members. Rival confederations rarely cooperate and sponsor joint activities. When they do, as occurred for example in demonstrations in 2010 opposing pension reform, the whole is much greater and more powerful than the sum of the parts.

Yet unions are not simply weak. They possess two important resources. First, they are represented on the governing boards of powerful public agencies, including the social security, health, pension, and unemployment insurance funds. Second, they can sometimes mobilize members and nonmembers alike. When unions organize demonstrations to oppose plant closings or proposed cutbacks in social benefits, large numbers of French often participate. At these times, feverish meetings are held between government administrators, business leaders, and union officials to restore order, a situation that may enable unions to obtain significant benefits for their members. When calm returns, unions again assume a marginal role—until the next explosion.

Social Movements and Protest

Fifth Republic institutions were designed to discourage citizens from acting autonomously. There are fewer organized interest groups and voluntary associations in France than in comparable countries. Those that exist, such as the trade union movement, are weak. This pattern helps explain why France's centuries-old tradition of direct protest persists. France is among the European countries where the highest proportion of citizens report having participated in demonstrations. This situation is a response to the fact that institutional channels of representation are meager. A partial list of groups that have engaged in strikes and demonstrations in recent years include farmers, postal workers, teachers and professors, high school and university students, truckers, railway workers, industrial workers, sanitation workers, health care workers, retired workers, the unemployed, homeless, immigrants, actors, research workers, and opponents of gay marriage!

To illustrate, in late 2010 between 2 and 3 million French turned out weekly to oppose the government's plan to increase the retirement age. Demonstrations were held in cities and towns throughout the country. France ground to a halt when workers in key industries like petroleum refining and trucking went on strike. Despite the inconvenience this caused, polls reported that most French supported the demonstrations. Protests of this kind widen the gulf between the French state and its citizens.

Crowds gather at a demonstration protesting the French pension reform on October 5, 2010.

AP Images/Claude Paris

The Political Impact of Technology

Like societies around the world, France is powerfully influenced by recent technological change. In a globalized world, countries failing to maintain a competitive technological edge are doomed to be followers. France has traditionally been at the forefront of technological change. However, it has slipped recently, both because it is a middling size country and because of a declining proportion of public and private resources devoted to R&D (research and development). One result has been a French brain drain of 60,000 scientists, engineers, and entrepreneurs who have migrated to California's Silicon Valley. They report moving there because of attractive salaries, light government regulation, and the greater availability of financial support for startups. Unless this trend is reversed, it bodes badly for France's future international economic position.

Where Do You Stand?

Is the balance in the values comprising French national identity more inclusive or repressive?

Does popular protest in France demonstrate the vibrancy or weakness of French democracy?

FRENCH POLITICS IN TRANSITION

SECTION 5

Focus Questions ▼

- What are two major challenges facing the French political system? Name one feature of French political institutions or culture that can help meet these challenges, and one feature making it difficult to meet the challenges.

- What are two features of French politics that have surprised you after reading this chapter, and why?

In November 2005, France erupted in flames following a tragic incident at a slum neighborhood outside Paris. Two adolescent boys of Algerian background were accidentally electrocuted at an electrical power substation while fleeing from the police. News of their deaths ignited riots in *cités* (impoverished neighborhoods) throughout France. For weeks, bands of young men roamed nightly through slum districts torching cars, schools, and public buildings. (Ten thousand cars were burned during the uprising.) The rebellion ended only after heavy police reinforcements occupied the turbulent neighborhoods.

Why did the young men's death provoke such widespread anger and destruction? An underlying cause is extensive unemployment among young men, especially Muslims. (Many of the rioters, although not all, were Muslim.) Another cause is the tense relations between the police and youth of immigrant background who live in what the French call "sensitive neighborhoods." A third cause is that, shortly before the uprising, then-interior minister Nicolas Sarkozy visited a suburban slum, publicly described juvenile delinquents as "scum," and proposed using a harsh cleaning product to disinfect the slums. (For years after the intemperate remark, Sarkozy was unable to visit poor neighborhoods because his presence attracted angry crowds.)

These disturbing events were not unique. They conform to a pattern of French political culture in which, rather than political institutions and policies promoting well-being and security, they have on too many occasions had the opposite impact.

Political Challenges and Changing Agendas

Integrating the Excluded

Not long after the suburban riots just described a government proposal triggered yet another massive wave of opposition. In 2006, the government sponsored a youth employment scheme designed to create jobs for young people, especially the less-educated. The prime minister used the 2005 urban riots as evidence of the need for the plan. However, labor unions and student organizations charged that the reform lowered labor standards by authorizing employers to hire workers at low wages and arbitrarily dismiss them. When parliament voted to approve the plan, it produced an explosion. In no time, half of all French universities were shut down by strikes and occupations. The conflict widened when unions joined the student movement. After 2 million citizens throughout France participated in demonstrations, the government admitted defeat and cancelled the CPE.

In 2010, not long after protests stymied the proposed youth unemployment plan, President Sarkozy proposed raising the retirement age. Again, millions turned out to protest, but this time Sarkozy did not budge. Weeks later a second nationwide demonstration was held, followed by a third and then a fourth. However, Sarkozy stood firm, and the reform was implemented.

In a replay of what has become a familiar scenario in French politics, President Hollande took a leaf out of Sarkozy's book when he sponsored a further reform of the retirement system in 2013 and changed the labor code to make it easier for employers to hire and fire workers. Once again, the proposals provoked giant demonstrations throughout France. The confrontations were especially noteworthy because they pitted a Socialist president against his core constituency. At the same time, they highlighted the wide distrust that exists between the state and society in France, and they served to further sour France's already gloomy social climate.

Reshaping the French Social Model?

An underlying cause of many of the intense confrontations described above is the government's attempt to cut social spending. A reporter identified the basic dilemma as follows: "In a more competitive world economy, the question is not whether the French social model is a good one, but whether the French can continue to afford it."[16] When governments have proposed social cutbacks, the reaction is swift. Protests have occurred over proposed reforms of the health care system, cultural institutions, pension benefits, and the electrical power and petrochemical industries. Conflict has been fueled not only by the cutbacks themselves but by the manner in which they were introduced. Britain, Germany, and other affluent countries have initiated social cutbacks in response to globalization, changing demography, ideological shifts, and economic stagnation. In these countries, however, organized consultation has smoothed the process of adjustment. In France, reforms have typically been imposed from above. The result has been wholly predictable in a country with a proud tradition of popular protest!

Oui to Roquefort Cheese, *Non* to Genetically Engineered Products

France is home to a flourishing antiglobalization movement comprised of far-leftists, intellectuals, farmers, and environmentalists. The movement's best-known leader has been José Bové, a former sheep farmer from southwestern France, where Roquefort cheese (made from sheep's milk) is produced. Small farmers like Bové oppose the standardized methods of farming that agribusiness corporations seek to impose, including using genetically modified seed, which the movement opposes as potentially risky and designed to boost corporate profits. Farmers also oppose corporate-controlled food processing and distribution. Bové became a popular hero after he ransacked a McDonald's construction site and served a six-week prison sentence. However, he failed to translate his popularity into political support. When he ran for president in 2007, he garnered a negligible 1.3 percent of the vote, although he remains a popular public figure.

Opposition to globalization is a major theme in French political discourse and has wide resonance in French public opinion. One reason is that many French regard globalization as threatening French culture and oppose the "invasion" of American companies, products, and values that threatens France's cherished way of life. Globalization is also blamed for exporting French jobs to low-wage countries. However, as discussed in Section 2, France is tightly integrated into the global economy, and an enormous number of jobs in France are devoted to producing goods and services for export.

The Challenge of the FN

The antiglobalization movement is one response to France's position in a changing world. Another is the National Front. The FN has reaped a political harvest from warning about the threat supposedly posed by the 5 million Muslims in France, the largest number of any country in Western Europe. Political sociologist Pierre Birnbaum observes, "What the National Front proposes to the French people … is a magical solution to their distress, to their loss of confidence in grand political visions of the nation."[18]

The FN attracts most of its support from native-born white citizens on the margins of French society. The party is often the first choice among working class voters. Yet, given the FN's popularity, it is surprising that French attitudes toward immigrants of Muslim backgrounds are more positive than is the case for citizens of neighboring countries. When French, Germans, and British citizens were asked whether "it is a good thing [that] people from the Middle East and North Africa [are] coming to your country," the French were most likely to answer yes. This result suggests yet another dimension on which French society is polarized and fragmented. The same poll found that French Muslims report feeling far less alienated from the dominant culture compared to Muslims in Britain and Germany.[19]

France Falling?

France has been wracked by self-doubt in recent years, as illustrated by best-selling books with titles like *France Falling*, *France's Disarray*, and *French Melancholy*. One poll found that 63 percent of the French believe their country is in decline. Indeed, one political analyst chides the French for being unduly self-critical![20]

France's political system is often described as rigid and unable to adapt. Yet, political scientist Peter A. Hall observes that "the economy, society and politics of France have changed … profoundly during the past 25 years…."[21] Recall important reforms that have involved the parity law, decentralization, and the health care, retirement, and industrial relations systems.

Another example involves policies involving sexual orientation. In 1999, legislation created the possibility of civil unions between unmarried couples, including gay couples. Known as the civil solidarity pact (*pacte civil de solidarité*, or PACS), it provides many legal rights and benefits enjoyed by married couples. The arrangement proved highly popular: nearly as many PACS are registered each year as marriages. (Most couples who register under the provisions of the PACS law are straight.) In 2013, the Socialist government further liberalized policies involving sexual orientation by passing legislation authorizing gay marriage. However, the measure was heatedly opposed by the conservative parties, who organized demonstrations for months.

Have recent changes in economic and social policies and practices promoted a welcome pluralism or a destructive fragmentation of French society? Many French regret that their country's distinctive way of life is under siege, as well as that French society seems destabilized. A key question on the agenda for the future is whether the positive features of France's past can be preserved while reforms are introduced to effectively address the country's economic, social, political, and cultural problems.

France's Relation to Terrorism

France's relationship to terrorism is quite different from that of the United States. The United States has experienced two terrorist attacks organized from abroad, both directed at the World Trade Center in New York—in 1993 and September 11, 2001. (On 9/11 the Pentagon was also attacked.) For decades before 9/11, however, France was the target of terrorist violence, often linked to its brutal colonial war in Algeria.

In recent years, there have been numerous violent incidents linked to al Qaeda and affiliated groups. In 2003, Richard Reid, a British citizen, was overpowered by other passengers when he tried to ignite explosives to bring down a plane flight he was on between Paris and Miami. Also in 2003, French antiterrorist police arrested eighteen Algerians and Pakistanis near Paris and charged them with ties to al Qaeda. In 2006, Zacarias Moussaoui, a French citizen, was sentenced to life imprisonment in the United States on charges that he helped plan the September 11 attack. In 2007, French antiterrorism police charged eleven people with participating in a network linked to al Qaeda.

In 2010, police ordered the evacuation of the Eiffel Tower and arrested a dozen people throughout France suspected of being affiliates of al Qaeda. They were charged with organizing bomb attacks. In 2011, two French citizens in Niger were taken hostage by a terrorist group and executed following an attempt by Niger's armed forces to rescue them.

France's Defense and Interior ministries house extensive intelligence and counterterrorist services. They claim to have foiled an average of two terrorist plots a year. However, these agencies operate in secret with little accountability, and critics charge that they have been guilty of corruption, human rights abuses, and religious and ethnic discrimination.

Youth Politics and the Generational Divide

Protests organized by high school and university students have often dramatically symbolized the existence of a generational divide in France. The May 1968 upheaval was in part a gigantic challenge by young French against what they regarded as hierarchical, conservative values. (One of the initial sparks that ignited the nationwide May Movement, as it was called, was a police intervention seeking to crush students protesting rigid regulations involving gender relations at a suburban university outside Paris.)

Young people have legitimate reasons to protest their situation. As discussed in Section 2, they are indirectly penalized by the generous social benefits and legal protections provided older citizens. Legal barriers to dismissing full-time workers may deter employers from hiring new—often young—workers. The result is that youth unemployment is distressingly high.

French Politics in Comparative Perspective

Is French politics becoming less exceptional? Recall the four elements comprising the exceptionalist model identified in the beginning of this chapter: the key role of the state in France's economic and social life; extensive political and ideological polarization; the obligation for citizens to identify in the political sphere as individuals rather than as members of groups based on bonds of race, ethnicity, or religion; and the claim that French political culture, involving secularism, liberty, equality, and fraternity, has universal value. Statism and ideological conflict, the first two features of the exceptionalist model, have markedly declined in recent years. However, as discussed in Section 2, although statism has declined, it has not been abandoned. And while traditional left-right divisions are less evident, ideological passions are far from a thing of the past. The third and fourth elements are also under siege, as evidenced by conflicts involving immigration, as well as declining confidence in the uniqueness and universal value of French political culture.

France lends itself to comparisons along the four dimensions that have framed this book. It can usefully be compared with countries where the state plays a less central role. France's statist style of economic management, even the currently more modest version, offers an interesting contrast to countries in which market forces are less regulated. The French theory and practice of democracy lend themselves to comparison with democracy elsewhere. And the ways that France deals with issues involving collective identity can usefully be compared with regimes adopting a different approach.

A second kind of comparison involves historical comparisons within France. For example, analyzing the extent and limits of the impact of the parity law provides an opportunity to study the relationship of political institutions to political and social change.

Where Do You Stand?

The criticism that French political institutions failed overlooks how successful they have been in meeting past challenges.

France's best days are behind it.

Chapter Summary

France is justly celebrated for its natural beauty, rich culture, and quality of life. But the country also has a turbulent past and deep socioeconomic and cultural divisions. For centuries, the state structured French political and social life. However, in recent decades the state has lost its preeminent role.

Following a century of relative economic stagnation, France reinvented itself after World War II. For several decades, the economy soared and most French benefited. The state played a central role in the French economic miracle. Eventually, however, the state proved less effective at steering an economy that demands decentralized and flexible decision making. The last attempt at state-sponsored development occurred under the Mitterrand presidency. The failure of the statist features of his reform agenda shifted the balance toward a more market-based economy. Even so, statism continues to play a larger role in France than in most other industrialized capitalist countries.

The French social model is a source of great pride, great benefits—and great costs. Additional economic burdens involve high unemployment, especially among youth and ethnic minorities; an aging population—whose costly medical care and pensions pose burdens for social welfare systems; and state budget deficits—the product of the high cost of financing social programs. France's close ties to the EU and the international economy more generally have produced great benefits but have also involved economic hardships and dislocations that fall especially hard on youth, immigrants, and the less educated.

France's semipresidential system has proved highly successful in achieving the goals that President de Gaulle sought when designing the Fifth Republic. However, the Fifth Republic lacks adequate mechanisms for representing citizens' interests. The result is a wide gap between the state and civil society.

While French society is a rich mosaic of many religious, ethnic, and racial groups, those from immigrant backgrounds are often second-class citizens. They are given less desirable jobs, or are not offered jobs at all. They often live in unattractive public housing projects located in suburban slums.

As a result of design flaws in public institutions and the rigidity of political culture, what may appear as a calm political situation in France has often turned out to be the calm before the storm. The pattern of disruptive popular protests is partly a product of design flaws in French political institutions.

Paradoxically, the Fifth Republic is about a decade shy of equaling the Third Republic's record for the longest-lived modern French regime. France occupies an enviable position in the world, and a majority of citizens enjoy a fine quality of life. However, despite these achievements, and the fact that France's political system and society possess ample resources to confront current challenges, the French are divided and troubled about the future. Nearly fifty years after youthful protesters chanted in May 1968, "The struggle continues," the words have lost none of their relevance.

Key Terms

ancien régime
authoritarian
cohabitation
conservative
decentralization
deregulation
fundamentalism
grandes écoles

grands corps
indicative planning
industrial policy
nationalization
neoliberal
parity law
prefect
privatization

proportional representation (PR)
referendum
republic
revolution
secularism
socialist
statism

Suggested Readings

Brouard, Sylvain, Andrew M. Appleton, and Amy G. Mazur, eds. *The French Fifth Republic at Fifty: Beyond Stereotypes.* New York: Palgrave Macmillan, 2009.

Chafer, Tony, and Emmanuel Godin, eds. *The End of the French Exception?* Basingstoke, Hampshire, UK: Palgrave Macmillan, 2010.

Cole, Alistair, Patrick Le Galès, and Jonah D. Levy, eds. *Developments in French Politics 4.* New York: Palgrave MacMillan, 2008.

Culpepper, Pepper D., Peter A. Hall, and Bruno Palier, eds. *Changing France: The Politics That Markets Make.* New York: Palgrave Macmillan, 2006.

Levy, Jonah, ed. *The State after Statism: New State Activities in the Age of Liberalization.* Cambridge: Harvard University Press, 2006.

Schmidt, Vivien A. *From State to Market? The Transformation of French Business and Government.* Cambridge: Cambridge University Press, 1996.

Scott, Joan Wallach. *The Politics of the Veil.* Princeton, NJ: Princeton University Press, 2007.

Shields, James G. *The Extreme Right in France: From Pétain to Le Pen.* London: Routledge, 2007.

Vail, Mark I. *Recasting Welfare Capitalism: Economic Adjustment in Contemporary France and Germany.* Philadelphia: Temple University Press, 2010.

Weil, Patrick. *How to Be French: Nationality in the Making since 1789.* Durham, NC: Duke University Press, 2008.

Suggested Websites

A blog by Art Goldhammer, a keen observer of French politics and society:
http://artgoldhammer.blogspot.com

Embassy of France in the United States:
www.ambafrance-us.org

French Ministry of Foreign Affairs
www.diplomatie.gouv.fr/en

French National Assembly
www.assemblee-nationale.fr/english

French government
www.gouvernement.fr/english

Le Monde (centrist newspaper—in French)
www.lemonde.fr

Liberation (center-left newspaper—in French)
www.libération.fr

Le Figaro (conservative French newspaper—English translation)
http://plus.lefigaro.fr/tag/lefigaro-in-english

4 Germany

Wade Jacoby

Official Name: Federal Republic of Germany (*Bundesrepublik Deutschland*)

Location: Central Europe

Capital City: Berlin

Population (2013): 80.8 million

Size: 357,021 sq. km.; slightly smaller than Montana

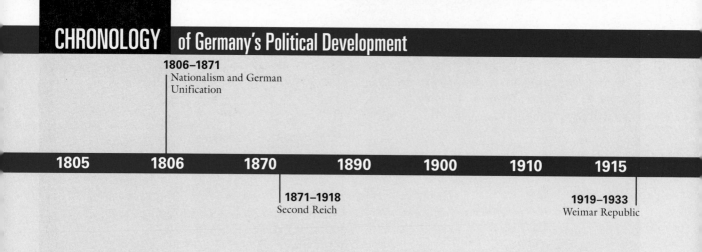

1806–1871
Nationalism and German Unification

| 1805 | 1806 | 1870 | 1890 | 1900 | 1910 | 1915 |

1871–1918
Second Reich

1919–1933
Weimar Republic

SECTION 1

THE MAKING OF THE MODERN GERMAN STATE

▼ Focus Questions

- Why did German politics take such a disastrous turn in the first half of the twentieth century?

- How successfully have German leaders since World War II provided for their citizens without destabilizing the rest of Europe?

Politics in Action

When the global financial crisis struck the United States in 2008, many Germans first thought this was strictly an American problem. The German press was filled with stories about how the German economy was unlikely to be deeply affected. In part, this sense of security flowed from the correct idea that the German economy was much less reliant on soaring profits in the financial sector compared to the United States and the United Kingdom. This interpretation was further strengthened by the clear problems in Europe's own financial center, London, and by worrisome losses in the few German banks that had bet heavily on exotic investment instruments that originated in the United States and the United Kingdom.

When the German economy also tanked in 2009, however, it undermined the idea that the financial crisis was strictly a "made in America" problem or that its pain would be limited to countries with risky new financing practices and lax regulation of banks. When global access to capital dried up, much of the financing for trade dried up with it. Since Germany exports high-quality machinery, chemicals, cars, and electronics, this decline in trade badly hurt Germany. It also turned out that German banks were neck-deep in very messy investments abroad. Suddenly, the mood shifted, and the fear in Germany was palpable. Even today, some Germans see financial instability through the prism of the 1920s, when hyperinflation damaged democracy and helped pave the way for the Nazi seizure of power.

As the crisis swept through Europe, falling exports soon threw the German economy into decline. GDP fell by about 5 percent in 2009. Some important features of German politics immediately came into clear view. First, Germans had little faith in the power of government spending to counteract the deep recession.

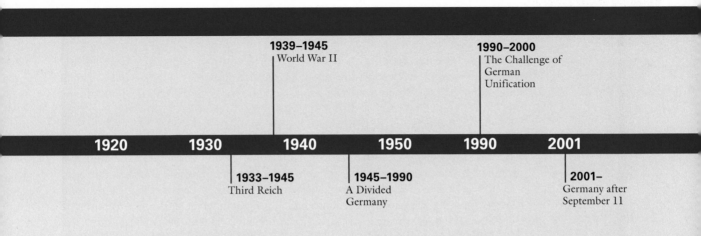

They worried far more (and far earlier) about government deficits than did other European governments. Second, even as orders fell, German firms generally held onto their workers rather than laying them off. Here, they were helped by the possibility of "short-time work," in which government paid part of the wages of workers who moved temporarily to part-time. This helped firms hold onto skilled workers in hopes of getting

Table 4.1	Political Organization
Political System	Parliamentary democracy.
Regime History	After the Third Reich's defeat in 1945, Germany was partitioned and occupied by the Allies. In 1949 the Federal Republic of Germany (FRG) was established in the west, and the German Democratic Republic (GDR) was established in the east. The two German states unified in 1990.
Administrative Structure	Federal, with sixteen states, including the city-states of Berlin, Hamburg, and Bremen.
Executive	Dual. Ceremonial president is the head of state, elected for a five-year term (with a two-term limit) by the Federal Convention. More powerful chancellor (prime minister) is head of government and is a member of the *Bundestag* and the leader of the majority party, which usually rules in a coalition with one other party.
Legislature	Bicameral. *Bundestag* (631 members after 2013 federal election) elected via dual-ballot system combining single-member districts and proportional representation. Upper house (*Bundesrat*) comprised 69 members who are elected and appointed officials from the 16 states.
Judiciary	Autonomous and independent. The legal system has three levels: Federal High Court, which is the criminal-civil system; Special Constitutional Court, dealing with matters affecting Basic Law; and Administrative Court, consisting of Labor, Social Security, and Finance courts.
Party System	Multiparty. Major parties are Christian Democratic Union (CDU), Christian Social Union (CSU), Social Democratic Party (SPD), the Greens, and Left Party (*die Linke*). Smaller parties are Free Democratic Party (FDP) and Alternative for Germany (AfD).

a fast start once the economy rebounded. Third, German companies were willing to accept lower profits than were most American companies. As a result, German households essentially enjoyed the same standard of living even as the economy shrank by 5 percent.

Almost as quickly as it crashed in 2009, the German economy recovered starting in 2010. As Germany boomed, however, other European states sank deeper into economic misery as a crisis of the Eurozone emerged and threatened the ability of several countries to pay their bills and, ultimately, to remain inside Europe's currency union (see Figure 4.1). How would the better-off states of the European Union (EU) respond? German governments had often spent generously to promote the EU.[1] Since the onset of the Eurocrisis, however, the German government's advice to troubled European countries can be summed up as "less risk and less debt." To an extent, this advice makes good sense. It implies both consumers and governments in struggling countries should spend less. Yet if other European states consume less, to whom will Germany sell its exports? Germany has steadily increased its trade outside Europe in recent years, yet the EU markets still matter greatly. Once Greece and then Ireland and Portugal needed emergency financing from the EU, Germany's role became especially difficult. German leaders worried that to bail them out might discourage reforms and enrage German voters. Yet to let these states go bankrupt might threaten the euro, the European currency that benefits Germany. There is no simple way out of this dilemma, then or now.

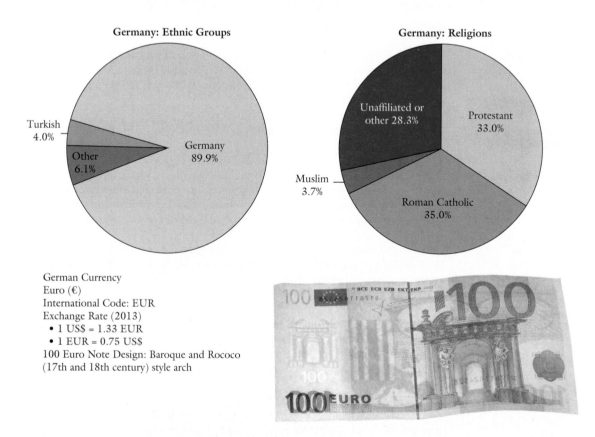

Germany: Ethnic Groups

Germany 89.9%
Turkish 4.0%
Other 6.1%

Germany: Religions

Unaffiliated or other 28.3%
Protestant 33.0%
Muslim 3.7%
Roman Catholic 35.0%

German Currency
Euro (€)
International Code: EUR
Exchange Rate (2013)
• 1 US$ = 1.33 EUR
• 1 EUR = 0.75 US$
100 Euro Note Design: Baroque and Rococo (17th and 18th century) style arch

FIGURE 4.1 The German Nation at a Glance
© Labrador Photo Video/Shutterstock.com (for photo)

Geographic Setting

Located in central Europe, Germany has often been at the heart of the best and the worst of European history. It has an area of 137,803 square miles (slightly smaller than Montana). Its population is 80.8 million, the vast majority of which are ethnic German but also including about 4 percent Turkish and a further 6.1 percent a mixture of Kurds, Italians, Poles, Russians, and many others. The country has roughly even proportions of Roman Catholics, Protestants, and religiously non-affiliated citizens. For hundreds of years before unification, large German communities settled across much of central and eastern Europe. Germany has the largest population in western Europe, second only to Russia in all of Europe. Since the 1960s, ethnic diversity has been increased by several million Turks and Kurds, who came to the Federal Republic as *Gastarbeiter* (**guest workers**)—foreign workers without citizenship.

Gastarbeiter (guest workers)

Workers who were recruited to join the German labor force in the 1960s and early 1970s, generally from Italy, Yugoslavia, and especially Turkey.

Germany

© Cengage Learning®

Recent immigration by about 3.4 million EU citizens has further increased cultural heterogeneity. In sum, about 7.4 million foreign citizens reside in Germany (about 9 percent of the population).

For a densely populated country, Germany has a high proportion of land in agriculture (54 percent). It consists of large plains in the north, smaller mountain ranges in the center, and the towering Alps at the Austrian and Swiss borders. The absence of natural borders in the west and east has been an important geographic fact, enhancing the possibilities for both commerce and conflict. Indeed, conflicts and wars with its neighbors were a frequent feature of German life until the end of World War II. Inadequate natural resources—aside from scattered iron ore and coal deposits—also shaped German history. Many of Germany's external relationships, both commercial and military, have involved gaining access to resources.

Critical Junctures

Nationalism and German Unification (1806–1871)

The first German "state" was the Holy Roman Empire (not the original Roman Empire). This was not a *nation*-state, however. Rather, the long-lasting empire (*Reich*) was a loose and fragmented collection of more than 300 sovereign entities, including the territories of much of present-day Germany, Austria, Italy, the Low Countries, Switzerland, Poland, the Czech Republic, and even a bit of France. Many of today's sixteen **federal states** (*Bundesländer*) in Germany correspond to historic German-speaking kingdoms and principalities (Bavaria, Saxony, and Hesse) or medieval trading cities (Hamburg and Bremen), while others are fragments from larger historical units (Mecklenburg–West Pommerania is a chunk of old Prussia).

Moving from loose empire to the modern German federal state was long and difficult. Napoleon's 1806 victories against Prussia and Austria killed off the Holy Roman Empire. France's hard-nosed military occupation then sparked German nationalism. Yet boundary disputes and fights between Protestant and Catholic areas made it hard for many German-speaking lands to cooperate. Still, Prussia—a powerful German-speaking state—led an alliance against Napoleon's France, leading to a new German confederation in 1815. In 1819, Prussian leaders created a tariff union that by 1834 included almost all of the German Confederation except Austria. Many Germans thus shared a market but not (yet) a state. At this point, the Prussian state was dominated by a reactionary group of noble landlords in eastern Prussia (*Junkers*), a patriotic military, and a political culture of honor, duty, and service to the state. This setting was quite hostile to free-market capitalism and democracy.

The year 1848 saw many prodemocracy uprisings across Europe, including in Berlin, Frankfurt, and Vienna. But these revolutionary movements "from below" were brutally suppressed. Instead, Germany was united several years later by a revolution "from above" led by Count Otto von Bismarck, who became minister-president of Prussia in 1862. Although a *Junker* himself, Bismarck realized that Prussia needed to industrialize to compete with Britain, France, and the United States. Bismarck despised democracy, and he created an unlikely (and thoroughly nondemocratic) coalition of northeastern rural *Junker* lords and northwestern Ruhr Valley iron industrialists (known as the "marriage of iron and rye").

These German "revolutionaries" were elites, with an appetite for a bigger state and bigger markets. Stressing Prussia's reliance on "blood and iron," Bismarck launched three short, successful wars—against Denmark (1864), Austria (1866), and

federal state

A state whose constitution divides power between a national (federal) government and lower units such as states, provinces, regions, *Länder*, or cantons.

Junkers

The land-owning nobility of Prussia, who were the grain (rye)-growing component of Bismarck's "marriage of iron and rye."

France (1870). These conquests, together with Prussia's annexation, intimidation, or inducements toward other German principalities led to the unification of Germany in 1871, when the so-called Second Reich was proclaimed. Prussia's king was made *Kaiser* (emperor).

The Second Reich (1871–1918)

Industrial and landed elites controlled the Second Reich. It had some democratic features, like universal male suffrage for the lower house of the legislature (*Reichstag*). However, this mattered little since the upper house (*Landtag*), which Bismarck controlled, made all key decisions.

Bismarck's primary goal was to achieve rapid industrialization, supported by state power and a powerful banking system that would foster large-scale industrial investment. By 1900 Germany had become a leading industrial power. The state pushed **heavy industries**, often at the expense of those producing consumer goods. Lacking a strong domestic consumer-goods economy, Germany had to export a substantial portion of what it produced.

Fast economic growth brought many challenges, including social dislocation as agricultural workers left villages for growing cities. A small middle class of professionals and small-business owners pressured the government—mostly unsuccessfully—to democratize and provide basic **liberal** rights. Industrialization also created a skilled manual working class and a militant Social Democratic Party (*Sozialdemokratische Partei Deutschlands*, SPD). The SPD's primary goals were economic rights in the workplace and mass participation in politics—democratization. The party was greatly influenced by revolutionary thinkers and activists Karl Marx and Friedrich Engels, whose socialist philosophy argued that workers, who produce society's goods and services, should also possess substantial economic and political power.

As German **chancellor**, Bismarck banned the SPD yet also created the first welfare state. He used it to blunt protests against the disruption from rapid economic growth. This "Bismarckian" welfare state included some basic health benefits and the world's first state-sponsored old age pensions. Bismarck also created a powerful and centralized German state. The *Kulturkampf* (cultural struggle) he initiated against the Catholic Church sought to remove educational and cultural institutions from church control and place them under the state.

By 1900, Germany's economic goal was obtaining raw materials and accessing world markets in which to sell its finished goods. Germany joined the imperial adventure, sometimes called "the scramble for Africa." But as a latecomer, Germany could colonize only resource-poor southwestern and eastern Africa. This experience pushed German leaders to develop the shipbuilding industry and a navy to protect and expand German economic and geopolitical interests.

Rivalries with its European neighbors eventually led to World War I, which Germany bears much responsibility for starting. After Bismarck was dismissed, subsequent German leaders had been far less skilled. The political system remained undemocratic and the colonies unprofitable. Meanwhile, Germany engaged Britain in a fierce naval rivalry and faced an aggressive and aggrieved France to the west. To the south, Germany's alliance with Austria-Hungary exposed it to the tinder keg of the Balkans, where many groups struggled to get free of Austrian rule. To the east, Germany perceived a threat from a growing Russia with its large army. When a Serb separatist assassinated the Austrian emperor's nephew, nationalists of all stripes were inflamed, including those in Germany.

heavy industries

The coal, iron, and steel sectors and the machinery, railroad, and armaments production associated with them.

liberal

Basic citizenship rights of speech, assembly, petition, religion, and so forth.

chancellor

An old German title now used by the German head of government and essentially the same as "prime minister."

Kulturkampf

Bismarck's fight with the Catholic Church over his desire to subordinate church to state.

Germany's leaders listened to aggressive voices in the army and elsewhere and declared war on Russia, France, and Belgium in the first week of August 1914. German leaders hoped to gain economic and political benefits from a quick victory in World War I. Instead, the long conflict cost Germany its few colonial possessions and its imperial social order. The Second Reich collapsed in November 1918 as Germany suffered a humiliating defeat in the war, leaving a weak foundation for the country's first parliamentary democracy.

The Weimar Republic (1918–1933)

Weimar Republic

The constitutional system of Germany between the end of World War I in 1918 and the Nazi seizure of power in 1933. So-named because the assembly to write the constitution occurred in the German city of Weimar.

Kaiser Wilhelm II abdicated after Germany's defeat, and the **Weimar Republic** replaced the Second Reich. The SPD, the only major party not discredited by the war, led Germany's first democracy. Its first task was to surrender to the Allies. The surrender was later used to discredit the party on the grounds that it had betrayed Germany by accepting defeat, even though, in fact, the war was already lost and it was the German generals who had forced the Kaiser to abdicate.

The new government was a **procedural democracy** (a system with formal procedures for popular choice of government leaders, notably free party competition). However, the Weimar Republic had a fatal flaw: It lacked broad public support because both the Conservative forces on the right and the Communists on the left rejected democratic government. Part of the right also accused the Weimar government of "stabbing Germany in the back" by surrendering in a war that was, in their mythology, never truly lost.

procedural democracy

A system with formal procedures for popular choice of government leaders (especially free party competition) but that may lack other democratic elements.

The Weimar Republic got off to a shaky start when SPD leaders foolishly asked the undemocratic military to guarantee order and stability. Communists had attempted to take control of some cities, and the right, including the little-known Adolf Hitler, attempted a coup. SPD leaders also signed the Treaty of Versailles, the peace treaty ending the war. Versailles required Germany to pay heavy reparations to the victorious allies. When the government printed money to buy foreign currency to pay these reparations, however, the value of the German currency crashed. Inflation raged until, in 1923, a glass of beer cost 4 billion marks, and a pound of meat was 36 billion. Wages were paid several times a day, so workers could spend their income before it became worthless. Although later governments controlled inflation and Germany returned to some prosperity for a few years, the Depression of the 1930s struck Germany especially hard.

Nazi

A German abbreviation for the National Socialist German Workers' Party, the movement led by Hitler.

Into this turmoil stepped Adolf Hitler, the leader of the **Nazi** Party. Exploiting the deepening economic crisis, the Nazis mobilized large segments of the population by preaching hatred of the left and of "inferior, non-Aryan races"—especially Jews. Yet the Weimar Republic persisted, strengthening its economy (often with loans from the United States) and improving its foreign relations. But the Great Depression dramatically reduced trade and, with it, German income.

The Great Depression also made Germany even more politically unstable. No parties could win a majority on their own or form lasting coalitions with other parties. Meanwhile, many conservative Germans underestimated Hitler's real intentions and considered his hate-filled speeches merely as political rhetoric. In early 1933 the Nazis and their conservative allies pressured President Paul von Hindenburg to appoint Hitler chancellor in a Nazi–Nationalist coalition. The Nazis then quickly banned other political parties and repressed the opposition. Hitler also got Hindenburg to grant—by emergency executive order—broad, sweeping powers to the Nazi-dominated cabinet. The Nazi regime quickly consolidated its hold on power.

The Third Reich (1933–1945)

After the Nazis obtained the chancellorship, they set out to get complete control. The Nazis used the military, paramilitary, and police to brutally suppress the opposition and used propaganda to mobilize large parts of the population. The Nazis set up the first concentration camps already in 1933, populated mostly with their political opponents.

Hitler's forces centralized power and rebuilt an economy devastated by the Depression. They concentrated all political authority in Berlin, removing any regional autonomy. After the regime banned free trade unions, industries forced workers into longer hours and less pay. Although some segments of big business had initially feared Hitler, most of German industry eventually endorsed Nazi economic policies. The Nazis also emphasized massive public works projects and, with the onset of war, gave industrialists access to slave labor from conquered territories.

Extolling a mythically glorious and racially pure German past, Hitler made scapegoats out of political opponents, homosexuals, ethnic and religious minorities, and, especially, Jews. Hitler blamed all political problems on Jews, this "external" international minority. Jews were quickly excluded from many professions, including

Hitler strides triumphantly through a phalanx of Nazi storm troopers (SA) in 1934.

ullstein bild/The Granger Collection

teaching, law, medicine, and the civil service, and were prohibited from marrying non-Jews. Of course, far worse measures would be adopted during the war.

Openly defying the Treaty of Versailles (some Weimar governments had cheated quietly), Germany began to produce lots of weapons and remilitarized the Rhineland, Germany's key coal and steel region. Hitler further claimed that a growing Germany needed increased space to live (*Lebensraum*) in eastern Europe. In 1938 he engineered a union (*Anschluss*) with his native Austria, most of whose leaders and citizens supported the pact with enthusiasm. His troops then occupied the German-speaking Sudetenland area of Czechoslovakia. When Poland resisted Nazi territorial claims, Hitler's forces attacked on September 1, 1939, beginning World War II with his soon-famous "*Blitzkrieg*" tactics. Britain, France, and eventually, the Soviet Union and the United States, formed an alliance to oppose Germany, which was allied with Italy and Japan.

Despite the Allied efforts, Hitler conquered much of Europe during 1939 and 1940. In 1941, despite an earlier friendship treaty with the USSR, Hitler attacked the Soviet Union, mistakenly calculating that it would fall as easily as his other conquests. The attack was a costly failure, and foreshadowed the Third Reich's defeat, though not until after an estimated 40–50 million Europeans lost their lives over the course of the war.

The most heinous aspect of the Nazi regime was the systematic extermination of 6 million Jews and the imprisonment in concentration camps of millions of Jews and other civilians. Prisoners were the target of extreme brutality, and large numbers were shot or died from starvation, disease, or overwork. The Nazis also ran "scientific" experiments on camp inmates and the mentally ill and disabled. During the war, the Nazis created extermination camps in occupied countries like Poland, equipped with gas chambers specifically for the purpose of murdering Jews and other inmates. This was the so-called Final Solution. Jews from countries controlled by Nazi allies generally survived in higher numbers than those in countries directly occupied by the Germans, very few of whom avoided transport to the death camps.

Early on, loot from conquered territory eased wartime hardship for the German "home front." As the military tide turned, however, civilian production was redirected to produce weapons, food rationing was introduced, and a fierce Allied bombing campaign killed about 300,000 civilians and razed major cities to the ground. About 2 million German civilians and 4.5 million German soldiers died from war, in a country whose prewar population was about 70 million.

Blitzkrieg

German battle tactics that began with aerial assaults to destroy enemy forces and infrastructure, followed quickly by a massive invasion of armored troops, with ordinary infantry mopping up resistance.

A Divided Germany (1945–1990)

Following Germany's total defeat in 1945, Cold War tensions led to the formal division of Germany: The Federal Republic of Germany (FRG) emerged in the west out of zones assigned to the western Allies (Britain, France, and the United States). Meanwhile, the communist German Democratic Republic (GDR) was formed out of a zone directed by the Soviet Union in the east. Postwar Germany was soon reshaped by the respective ideological visions of the two victorious sides. Democratic political institutions and a market economy were installed in the west, while the communist political system and command economy in the east was controlled by the Socialist Unity Party (SED).

The two Germanys became formal nation-states in 1949, and the Occupation ended. Yet large foreign military bases remained, and neither half of divided Germany was fully sovereign. The FRG deferred to the United States in international relations, as did the GDR to the Soviet Union. Neither of the two Germanys joined the Cold

War's international alliances—NATO (North Atlantic Treaty Organization) and the Warsaw Pact, respectively—until 1955.

The Federal Republic (West Germany) became a democracy with constitutional provisions for free elections, civil liberties and individual rights, and an independent judiciary (see Table 4.1). The FRG's democratic system produced rapid economic growth and remarkable political stability. Under center-right Christian Democratic chancellors Konrad Adenauer (1949–1963) and Ludwig Erhard (1963–1966), the FRG established a parliamentary regime, extensive social welfare benefits, a politically regulated market economy, and reestablished strong state governments.

Under center-left Social Democratic chancellors Willy Brandt (1969–1974) and Helmut Schmidt (1974–1982), West Germany initially had plenty of jobs, increased social services, and a diplomatic opening to the Warsaw Pact. But in the late 1970s, two recessions increased unemployment and forced Chancellor Schmidt to trim some benefits. Under Helmut Kohl, the Christian Democrats returned to power in 1982 as part of a center-right coalition with the Free Democratic Party (FDP) (*Time* Magazine's headline was "Germany Changes Helmuts").

As noted, the GDR was established in Soviet-occupied East Germany in 1949, a one-party state controlled by the SED. Although the state provided full employment, housing, and extensive social benefits, it was a rigid, Stalinist regime. The infamous *Stasi*, or secret police, was present everywhere. (At the regime's end, there was a full-time Stasi official for every 180 GDR citizens. By comparison, there was one Soviet KGB for every 595 people, and one member of the Nazi Gestapo for every 8,500). The Stasi kept close tabs on all East Germans and dealt ruthlessly with those suspected of opposing the regime.

Unsurprisingly, many East Germans emigrated west, and in 1961, the GDR built a wall entirely around the city of West Berlin to prevent further emigration. Over the next forty years, about 5,000 escaped through Berlin (early on, two young boys snuck out several weeks in a row to watch cowboy movies in West Berlin). Over time, sneaking out became very difficult, and at least 136 people lost their lives trying to flee the GDR through Berlin. Over the years, many creative escapes were tried, including a homemade hot air balloon, zip lines, hiding under carcasses of slaughtered cows, driving under a guard barrier in a sawed-off convertible, and flashing a smuggled membership card from the Munich Playboy Club, which (somewhat) resembled a diplomatic passport.

Though the wall allowed the GDR to hang onto more of its citizens, relatively easy access to Western TV signals meant the GDR population saw constant reminders of the growing prosperity and freedoms of the FRG. The GDR was the richest state in the Soviet bloc—but that mattered little to East Germans, who tended to measure their material lives and civil liberties against those in the FRG. For example, voting in East Germany consisted of dropping a ballot with a single Communist Party candidate name into the voting box. Those who preferred a different candidate had to use a different (non-private) booth, cross out the printed name, and write in their preferred choice. Most of those who took this step could lose privileges and even their jobs. In fact, fraudulent local government elections in spring 1989 contributed to citizen unrest that ended with the breaching of the Berlin Wall on November 9, 1989 and the collapse of the GDR.

The Challenge of German Unification (1990–2001)

When Soviet rule over communist regimes loosened throughout East Central Europe in 1989, the two German states at first envisioned a slow process of increased contacts and cooperation while maintaining separate sovereign states for the medium term. But German unification came rapidly, primarily because only reunification could convince East Germans not to migrate west. In 1990, the former East Germany was absorbed into the FRG as five new West German states (*Länder*).

Formal unification took place in 1990 to great fanfare. But unification euphoria did not last. The communist-planned economy was much weaker than had been recognized. East German technology was decades behind, and the unified German government spent huge sums just to rebuild communication networks and major roads that, for the first time in many years, allowed unrestricted traffic between East and West.

Aligning East Germany with the FRG was a daunting job and necessitated large tax increases. Unemployment soared, especially in eastern Germany—to approximately 20 percent—fueling ultra-right-wing political movements who blamed foreigners for taking away jobs. Skinheads and other extremist groups often targeted Turkish immigrants.

To win the support of eastern Germans, Chancellor Kohl sugarcoated the enormity of unification. To win the support of western Germans, he had to convince them that a costly "unification tax" would achieve economic integration. But the longer the unification process remained incomplete, the less patient the German electorate became. Even today, the average monthly wage in the five eastern states is $3,265, compared to $4,760 in western Germany, for comparable work.

An important aspect of unification involved extending the West German currency to East Germany. As European capital flowed into East Germany, raising the value of the currency, German manufacturers nervously observed the price of German exports rising with the Deutsche Mark (DM). This trend also increased their support for a European solution to national currency fluctuations.

Kohl, who had been uncertain about a European currency union, committed Germany to the idea, which France had long supported. Germany's leaders generally have been strong supporters of European integration. When the euro eventually replaced the currency of eleven European countries in 2002, however, many Germans wondered whether the EU and the euro would provide the same stability as the formidable DM and the inflation-fighting *Deutsche Bundesbank* (Germany's central bank). Many also worried about Germany's loss of domestic control of monetary and, to a lesser extent, fiscal policies.

After 16 years of Kohl's leadership, a political tidal wave occurred in the 1998 elections. SPD leader Gerhard Schröder convinced Germans that a change was necessary. He became chancellor, and the SPD formed a coalition government with the environmentalist Green Party that lasted nearly eight years.

Germany after September 11, 2001

There are no restrictions of movement on EU citizens between most member states, so as more and more countries joined the EU this highlighted the challenge that immigration poses for Germany. During the *Gastarbeiter* period of the 1960s, immigration to Germany was straightforward. Workers came from southern Europe and Turkey, supposedly for limited periods. What was not anticipated was that several generations of Turkish-Germans would remain. After 2000 a new wave of migrants seeking political asylum arrived from unstable and repressive countries in Africa and eastern Europe. Germany's sensitivity to the crimes of the Nazi regime had led to permissive asylum laws that allowed the majority of these migrants not only to stay but also to enjoy many benefits of Germany's generous social welfare system.

A small number of newcomers were (or became) Islamic radicals. The fact that several 9/11 terrorists had belonged to an al Qaeda cell in Hamburg raised thorny questions about the balance between freedom and security. After 9/11 the government increased domestic surveillance and made a series of arrests and detentions. Still, many Germans oppose government surveillance of residents, and Germany has strict laws regulating privacy. This combination created tension between Germany and the United States, which was widely seen to be pushing the German government to act more forcefully.

Tension with the United States ratcheted up when, during Gerhard Schröder's 2002 reelection campaign, he opposed the Bush administration's arguments for war against Iraq. The strong relationship between Germany and the United States was significantly weakened. While Schröder's foreign policy stance was popular, his government (in coalition with the Greens) lost support in a number of other areas. It was replaced in 2005 by a "Grand Coalition" of CDU-CSU and SPD. Schröder gave way as chancellor to CDU leader Angela Merkel, who then won reelection in 2009 with her preferred coalition partners, the Free Democrats (FDP). Together, these parties were focused on the economic and financial crisis, often choosing **austerity policies** that left other European leaders (and, on some occasions, U.S. President Barack Obama) visibly frustrated. A particular frustration for the United States has been Germany's very large export surplus. Many observers feel Germans love to sell but refuse to buy; the surplus reached a whopping 7.5 percent of GDP in 2013. Meanwhile, German frustrations with the United States reached a fever pitch in 2013 when NSA contractor Edward Snowden released material documenting that the United States had tapped Merkel's cell phone (the chancellor is a ferocious texter). Only upheavals in the Ukraine and new worries about Russia brought German anger over the NSA scandal down to a simmer.

Overall, Germany's foreign policy has become less predictable. It has broken with its quasi-pacifist stance to send many troops abroad in recent years. And yet it resisted efforts to impose a "no-fly zone" in Libya, abstaining from the vote on UN Resolution 1973. The CDU-FDP government ruled out military action against Syria in fall 2013, though it later transpired Germany had, under a civilian license, sold chemicals to Syria that could be used to make sarin gas. The CDU-SPD Grand Coalition foreshadowed few major changes in foreign policy, although it agreed to be more transparent about arms exports to authoritarian governments. Russia's policy toward Ukraine has split German opinion. Few support Russia, and most support the West, but a large minority would like to see Germany positioned between the two.

austerity policies

Spending cuts, layoffs, and wage decreases meant to address budget problems.

The Four Themes and Germany

Germany in a Globalized World of States

Germany's development can be understood in light of this book's four major themes. Consider the first theme: a globalizing world of states. Because of its history of militarism and authoritarian political culture, Germany's role in the globalizing world of states is controversial. In the nineteenth century, Germany's war-propelled unification caused anxiety among its neighbors. In the twentieth century, World War I and the crimes of the Third Reich during World War II intensified this fear. Today, although Germany's foreign policy is constrained by the EU, many Europeans remain wary of Germany's international role. A debate still rages over whether Germany is or should be a "normal" state. Many worry that German energy policy cooperates too much with Russia and too little with the rest of Europe. Inside Europe, many fear that Germany's remarkable success in economic globalization has made it less interested in its European neighbors.

As for the second theme, governing the economy, late unification and industrialization prevented Germany from starting the race for empire and raw materials until the late nineteenth century. The state's pursuit of fast economic growth and an awakened sense of German nationalism made the state aggressive. During the Third Reich, Hitler then sought to fuse state and economic power. In reaction, policy-makers after World War II tried to remove the state from running the economy, but there was a strong consensus in Germany that the economy needs an "order" that can only come from government. Thus, Germans are not as obsessed with "free" markets, as in the United States and the United Kingdom.

The postwar period saw the development of *Modell Deutschland* (the German model), a term often used to describe the Federal Republic's unusual economy. While successful for decades, it remains an open question whether these economic institutions will continue to function well in a unified Europe. The EU sometimes promotes free market practices faster than Germany can absorb them. Meanwhile, Germany often produces export surpluses faster than the rest of Europe can absorb them. Both imbalances often spark frustration.

The democratic idea, our third theme, developed late in Germany. Not until 1918 and the shaky Weimar Republic did Germany attain democracy. And despite a formally democratic constitution, Weimar was a prisoner of forces bent on its destruction. Lacking a stable multiparty political system, Weimar was plagued by a sharp polarization of political parties. Germany's descent into the most brutal form of authoritarianism in the 1930s destroyed every vestige of democracy.

The constitution of the Federal Republic in 1949 was designed to overcome both Weimar shortcomings and Nazi crimes. This was a delicate task since in the first system the state was too weak while in the second it was far too strong. But postwar constitution-making proved a resounding success, even if uncertainties and problems remain. Today, at a time when most Europeans are unimpressed by the quality of their politicians, Germans remain relatively satisfied. Every democratic system needs citizen support, and the Germans are in far better shape than many of their neighbors.

As for the fourth theme, the politics of collective identity, compared to other democratic countries, German political institutions, social forces, and patterns of life are more inclined to emphasize collective action rather than individualism.[2] This does not imply that German citizens have less personal freedom compared to those in other developed democracies or that there are no political conflicts in Germany. It means that political expression, in both the state and civil society, generally revolves around group representation and cooperative spirit. For example, although unions and employer associations have fewer members than in past decades, they continue to shape the workplace culture and practices of German firms in profound ways.[3]

Certainly, Germany's history from Prussian militarism through Nazism has led many to worry about the dangers of collectivist impulses. However, Germany is unlikely to embrace an individualistic democracy like that of the United States. Collectivism has deep roots in German political culture and many positive features. Germany's collective identity since 1945 also has been broadened by linking the country's fate to that of Europe. Germany is also the economic motor of the EU, and its participation in the EU also produced a more flexible understanding of what it means to be German. For example, many Germans readily describe themselves as "Europeans." And Germany's traditionally restrictive immigration law was changed in 1999 to enable those who had lived in Germany for decades to obtain citizenship. A big question going forward is how German voters' identification with Europe will affect their willingness to assist countries—like Greece and Ireland—hardest hit by the economic crisis.

Themes and Comparisons

Germany differs from many other developed countries. For example, like Japan, Germany was late to industrialize and late to democratize. Yet the Nazi past and the destruction caused by the Third Reich make Germany different from every other industrialized democracy. Although concerns about this period persist, they have been substantially allayed by Germany's stable democratic experience since 1949.

Germany's political patterns provide rich topics of significance for the study of comparative politics, including the contrast between its nationalistic history and democratization in an integrating Europe; its distinctive form of organized capitalism that is neither state-led nor laissez-faire; its successful representative democracy that combines participation and representation of the entire electorate in a stable parliamentary regime; and a politics of identity that builds on existing groups but leaves some room for newcomers.

Where Do You Stand?

Does the Nazi past still oblige Germans to behave differently from other people?

Is German anger about U.S. spying justified or just naive?

POLITICAL ECONOMY AND DEVELOPMENT

State and Economy

Germany's capitalist economy tries to capture the benefits of intense competition between firms *and* of close cooperation among firms. This is no easy trick, but Germany has proved highly successful at pursuing this goal: Germans' standard of living is among the highest in Europe, and Germany exports as much as the United States despite having just one-fourth the population. Moreover, the balance between cooperation and conflict extends beyond companies to include Germany's two main social classes, owners/managers and workers. The German economy faces a bevy of challenges including the rise of new competitors, the challenge of free market ideas, the continuing difficulties of German unification, and the burden of the financial crisis. But Germany has some important assets to meet these challenges, notably its great economic strength and (according to some scholars) its organized and cooperative form of capitalism.[4]

The Social Market Economy

After World War II, German economic policies took a different course from either Anglo-American laissez-faire policies (generally based on "freeing" the market from the state) or state-led economies in countries like France and Japan. Germany's state

Focus Questions ▽

- In what ways is a "social market economy" different from the kind of market economy found in the United States?

- What are the strengths and weaknesses of the German social market economy, and how are its traditional strengths challenged by the EU, neoliberal ideas, globalization, and economic crisis?

was important, but its role was indirect. It complemented rather than replaced the critical decisions taken by private groups like employers, trade unions, chambers of commerce, churches, and others. Broadly, this remains true today. Although the government sets guidelines, it encourages voluntary associations to play a key role. Subsequent negotiations among employers, banks, unions, and regional governments fill in key details whose aim is to fulfill the government's broad objectives.

The German state allows market forces to work relatively unimpeded within the general framework and rules set by the government. In short, this system regulates not the details, but the general rules of the game under which all actors must play. The pattern, known as **framework regulations**, has enabled German economic policy to avoid the abrupt lurches between laissez-faire and state-led economic policy that have characterized post–World War II Britain.[5] To be sure, some have criticized the system as rigid and cumbersome, a charge discussed below.[6] To its advocates, however, German economic policy is flexible and encourages private actors to cooperate to devise their own solutions. As a result, the German system is often able to produce agreement on major policy directions without much social upheaval and protest.

Since the time of Adenauer, the Germans have referred to this broad approach as the **social market economy** (*Soziale Marktwirtschaft*). The social component includes health insurance, unemployment, and pensions, as well as distinctive programs like subsidies for personal savings subsidies. The system of vocational training—part tech school, part junior college, and part on-the-job training—has helped create a deep pool of human capital that has enabled Germany to produce high-quality goods for decades.

The market component of the social market economy is equally critical. There is intense competition in the German economy. German firms are often world leaders in everything from cars and machine tools to kitchen appliances and chocolate bars. The typical pattern of high wages and high benefits has not prevented Germany from maintaining its international market position far better than most of its competitors. Even when the Euro goes up in value, Germans generally can still sell things.

Semipublic Institutions

By the late 1940s, the idea of a strong German central state was discredited for two reasons: the excesses of Nazism *and* the American occupation authorities' confidence in the private sector. Yet West German authorities faced a dilemma. How could they rebuild society if a strong public sector was prohibited? The answer was to create modern, democratic versions of those nineteenth-century institutions that blurred the boundaries between the public and private sectors (hence "semipublic").[7]

Semipublic institutions are responsible for much of Germany's economic policy-making. The most influential include the boards that manage the health insurance funds, pensions, and unemployment insurance systems, plus the employment agencies, the central bank, and the vocational education and training system. Cooperation between firms and the government requires compromise and encourages moderation. For example, Germany's Chambers of Industry and Commerce as well as its Council of Economic Advisors are both far less partisan (and arguably far more useful) than their openly partisan American counterparts. Similarly, union and employer representatives sit on the boards of the pension and unemployment systems. Another semipublic institution, the **health insurance funds** (*Krankenkassen*), brings all major health interests together to allocate costs and benefits through consultation and group participation. There is still disagreement, but the politics of health care is far less contentious than in the United States. Germany does not have "socialized medicine."

framework regulations

Laws that set broad parameters for economic behavior but that require subsequent elaboration, often through formal agreements between employers and employees.

social market economy

A system that aims to combine the efficiency of market economies with a concern for fairness for a broad range of citizens.

health insurance funds

Semipublic institutions that administer insurance contributions from employees and employers and thus pay for health care for covered participants.

The social market economy is part of the broader system of **democratic corporatism**, in which national (and state) governments delegate certain policy-making authority to private and semipublic institutions. In countries that had a guild system in the Middle Ages, democratic corporatism is common, and similar systems exist in the Netherlands, Belgium, the Scandinavian countries, Switzerland, Slovenia, and Austria. In return for access to power and a role in policy administration, groups representing a particular economic sector are expected to aggregate the interests of their own members and act responsibly. Semipublic institutions differ greatly from "pluralist" representation in countries such as the United States, where interest groups seek benefits from government agencies while keeping the implementation process at arm's length.

> **democratic corporatism**
>
> A bargaining system in which important policies are established and often carried out with the participation of trade unions and business associations.

The social market economy and the semipublic institutions both require effective labor and business organizations. German trade unions are powerful, representing 6.2 million workers—about one-fifth of the labor force. They are grouped into eight countrywide, multisectoral organizations. For example, the metalworkers union organizes all union members in sectors as diverse as autos (whether or not the worker actually works with metal!), machinery, and computer chips. Similarly, the main service sector union has members from over 1,000 different trades and professions.

German unions encompass a broad range of interests, so they can negotiate with associations of employers in those same broad sectors. This also means less *state* regulation of wages, working conditions, and employment. For example, unlike almost everywhere else in Europe, Germany has traditionally had no minimum wage (though the government pledged to introduce one of $11.57 per hour by 2015). At the same time, collective bargaining agreements enable German workers to enjoy high wages and ample fringe benefits.

The interplay of cooperation and conflict is not limited to the broad economy but also takes place *inside* each German firm through a system known as **co-determination** (*Mitbestimmung*). In the United States and United Kingdom, management makes most business decisions. By contrast, co-determination gives employees the right to participate in major decisions that affect their firms and industries. Although common in northern Europe, including the Netherlands and Scandinavia, co-determination is best known in Germany.

> **co-determination**
>
> The legal right of representatives of employees to help determine the direction of the company in which they work. Co-determination often takes place through elected works councils in each firm or factory.

Co-determination allows representatives of workers and trade unions in Germany to obtain voting seats on the supervisory boards of directors of firms with 2,000 or more employees. Separate provisions are made for smaller firms. Firm managers sometimes resent having to share management decisions with workers, but they often appreciate that co-determination helps them reach accommodation with workers. Ultimately, German managers recognize that rather than making their firms uncompetitive, this system often has had the opposite effect. Co-determination also has provided German workers with a broader and deeper knowledge of the goals and strategies of the firms for which they work.

Another German institution providing workers a voice is the **works councils** (*Betriebsräte*). While the first form of co-determination gives trade unions a voice outside the plant (that is, on the board), the works councils represent workers inside the workplace by addressing shop-floor and firm-level affairs. Whereas unions bargain over wages, hours, and working conditions, works councils concentrate on social, environmental, and personnel matters. They also handle bonuses, which are common. About two-thirds of works councilors are also union members, a fact that minimizes but does not always prevent tension between unions and works councils.

> **works councils**
>
> Firm employees elected by their coworkers to represent the workforce in negotiations with management at that specific shop or company.

Another useful semipublic institution is the vocational education system built on apprenticeship training. About 40 percent of German young adults attend university.

Most of the rest complete a three-year apprenticeship that combines school-based classes with four days a week devoted to working and learning in a company. By combining school and workplace-based learning, apprenticeships resemble a rigorous college internship, except that they usually benefit working class youth and last three years rather than three months. Many apprentices are later hired as permanent employees by the firm with which they trained. Long after manufacturing in the United States and Britain languished, nearly a third of the German economy remains engaged in manufacturing.[8] Young Germans' first jobs are often in industry rather than retail or fast food. Thus, "Do you want fries with that?" is not nearly as common an expression for young German workers as for young American ones.

With its highly skilled workforce, Germany long resisted the claim that it must lower wages to compete. Since 1995, German wages have grown at about the same (very slow) rate as in the United States. Germany's competitive advantage lies in raising product quality rather than slashing wages. This pattern has enabled Germany's highly skilled blue-collar workers to drive expensive cars, obtain high-quality medical care, and enjoy six weeks of paid vacation each year. By contrast, wages in much of the service sector are lower, and unemployment rates for the least skilled are over 20 percent in West Germany and up to 40 percent in the East.

Germany's research and development strategy supports these economic policies. Rather than seek breakthroughs in exotic technologies that take years to commercialize, German firms adapt existing technologies to boost already competitive sectors. During the postwar years, this policy enabled Germany to maintain competitiveness and a big trade surplus. In recent decades, the challenges have been, first, to integrate former GDR workers raised in an East German industrial culture that told workers to follow orders rather than apply initiative and, second, to invest in formerly communist countries where high skills and lower wages can be combined.

The relentless search for technical improvements also influences Germany's leading role in debates over global warming. German politicians from across the political spectrum have pushed for regional (EU) and global action (at Kyoto/Copenhagen) to limit and possibly reverse climate change. This position reflects a broad consensus among German voters about the reality and dangers of man-made global warming. Most Germans are shocked to hear that many Americans think global warming is a matter of opinion rather than a scientific certainty. German firms, including those in the all-important auto sector, generally accept regulations requiring cleaner technology. Therefore, they have a keen interest in requiring their competitors in other countries to face the same regulatory conditions. German firms and politicians also display confidence that they can meet bold targets for reductions in CO_2 emissions (partly because they got credit for shutting down dirty East German industries that were slated to close anyway). German business is also convinced it can make money selling green technology to other countries.

Current Strains on the Social Market Economy

Over time, the social market economy has faced many strains, including the rise of new competitors, the challenge of free market ideas (especially at the EU level and among employers), the difficulties of German unification, and the burden of the financial crisis.

Germany is a trading state, and globalization involves plenty of new competitors jostling German firms used to being world leaders. German firms face relatively high costs in wages, taxes, social contributions, and investments in apprenticeships and technology development, so they need high revenues to make a profit. Although making workers more productive is one way they have done this, it has not been enough for manufacturing firms facing ferocious competition from Asian auto and machine tool producers. Another solution for German firms is to procure supplies from lower-cost eastern and southern European countries rather than to maintain long-standing relationships with other domestic firms that were the lynchpin of the German model. Thus, even though Germany continues to run a trade surplus in Europe and globally, its formula for export success faces a number of strains.

More fundamentally, Germany's social market economy has been increasingly attacked at the level of ideas. For years, free-market proponents from abroad criticized the German model for the "clubby" relationships among the German social partners (business associations, labor unions, and federal and state governments). Critics charged that this pattern added costs and reduced flexibility for employers. Yet as we have seen, working with unions has not prevented German firms from maintaining (and often expanding) their competitive positions. For example, by keeping skilled workers on the payroll (with some help from the government and taxpayers), business was able to get a jump on the economic recovery after the 2009 slump.

Free market supporters also accuse the social market economy of a failure to create sufficient jobs. However, through much of the postwar period, this too was false: For nearly 25 years, German unemployment hovered around a remarkable 1–2 percent. Since the 1970s, however, unemployment has varied from 6 to over 10 percent. Since wages are high, employers limit part-time work and hold off hiring until the need for employees becomes acute. During recessions, however, employers tend to hold onto skilled workers. In fact, unemployment fell from almost 11 percent in 2005 to 5.2 percent by mid-2013, the lowest in two decades.

Unification in 1990 posed a particular challenge for the social market system. In the early 1990s, the Kohl government underestimated the costs of unification, which, by the early 1990s, was consuming 20 percent of Germany's budget. Moreover, employers and trade unions found their history of cooperation in the west difficult to transfer to eastern Germany. After the government privatized thousands of East German firms, the firms' new owners fired workers in droves. The problems in eastern Germany soon threatened to overwhelm the system.

In addition, the EU had already begun to disturb the intricate, mutually reinforcing pattern of German government and business self-regulation. EU rules disallowed some traditional state subsidies to promote economic development. In addition, some deregulation in European finance threatened Germany's distinctive finance-manufacturing links, which depend on long-term relationships between banks and companies, rather than short-term deals. These challenges, along with the high wages and taxes, stoked a long-simmering debate: "Is Germany a good place to do business?" Many Germans worried that the combination of domestic and international factors made Germany a less attractive place for investment.

Substantial policy changes eventually followed from these worries. Ironically, it was the SPD-Green (left-oriented) government that made labor law, pension policy, and unemployment insurance less generous. Many trade union members were furious at the SPD leadership. Financial reforms also weakened the policy of encouraging banks to maintain equity holdings in other firms. This brought the German model somewhat closer to the Anglo-American world of highly mobile capital investment, although German firms still rely far less than American firms on issuing stock to attract capital.

Finally, the financial crisis compounded anxieties. On the one hand, German voters and politicians were reassured that the German financial system seemed less prone to excesses than were, for example, those of the United States and the United Kingdom. On the other hand, some German financial institutions were badly burned by risky investments abroad (one bailout cost German taxpayers about $140 billion, and German banks still have many bad loans hidden in their books).

GLOBAL CONNECTIONS

Germany's Global Leadership

Each year the BBC polls 25,000 people worldwide on various countries' influence in the world. In 2013, 59 percent said Germany's role is "mostly positive," the highest figure in the world. When Germans hear such things about themselves, they are puzzled. Why are they so popular?, they wonder. Is it because of what they do? Or because of what they don't do?

British political scientists William Paterson and Simon Bulmer refer to Germany as a "reluctant hegemon." It doesn't want to lead but often feels other states want it to. Leadership is risky and expensive. Germans are cautious and fairly frugal. This was evident in the Eurozone crisis, but also in foreign policy more generally.* Take Germany's military. The *Bundeswehr* is a professional (all-volunteer) army in a country deeply skeptical of the use of force. Far fewer Germans display pride in their military (42 percent) compared to France (53), Britain (66), or the United States (87).**

Since 2002, however, the *Bundeswehr* has deployed 4000–4400 soldiers to Afghanistan in support of NATO operations, the largest deployment of German troops since World War II. While the mission began as one of peace building, reconstruction, and aid to civil society, it later turned into a combat mission.

As "warlike conditions" were reported in Afghanistan, however, public support for the mission fell (from 65 percent in 2005 to under 40 percent by 2011). By early 2014, Germany had drawn down to 3000 troops in Afghanistan, and all German combat operations there were supposed to end in

2014. Several hundred German soldiers should remain until 2016 to train and advise.

The Afghan deployment presented the *Bundeswehr* (and German politicians) with a steep learning curve. Many soldiers gained combat experience and confidence. The *Bundeswehr* developed a counterinsurgency doctrine and much tactical experience. It gained experience with drones, used to target Taliban fighters. At the same time, the *Bundeswehr* has faced severe and often justified criticism. Inadequate equipment and poor communication between soldiers and political leaders led to deadly fiascos in the field. Political restrictions on the military often incurred the ridicule of other NATO forces.

Part of Germany's popularity comes from not throwing its weight around. But many of Germany's friends wish it would take a far more active role. Would Germans prefer to be influential or popular?

MAKING CONNECTIONS If German interests are global, can their politics remain regional (European)? And what of ethics? Can Germans be pacifist and still supply arms to the rest of the world?

*Simon Bulmer and William Paterson, "Germany as the EU's Reluctant Hegemon?" *Journal of European Public Policy* 20, no. 10 (2013), 1387–1405.

**Thomas Buhlmann, "Bevölkerungsbefragung 2008: Sicherheits-und verteidigungspolitisches Meinungsklima in Deutschland," Sozialwissenschaftliches Institut der Bundeswehr, Strausberg, Germany, 2008.

Society and Economy

Booming economic growth after World War II provided a sound foundation for social programs. Until the 1990s, Germany provided generous social benefits to almost everyone, including support for public transit, subsidies for the arts, virtually free higher and vocational education, and a comprehensive welfare state.

Unlike in the United States, public services receive consistent cross-party support. There is no substantial German movement akin to the U.S. Tea Party. Public services dwarf those in the United States. From housing subsidies to savings subsidies, health care, and the rebuilding of the run-down cities and public infrastructure of the former GDR, public spending is remarkably generous in Germany. But the costs of unification, adjustment to the EU, and globalization have begun to challenge Germany's high standard of living and well-paid workforce. The primary workplace fault line lies between the core of mostly male, high-skilled blue-collar workers in the largest competitive industries and less-skilled workers, often employed in smaller firms with lower wages and part-time work. Immigrants and women are over-represented in the latter sector.

Ethnicity and Economy

Germany's only large ethnic minority originated in the *Gastarbeiter* program of the 1960s, when temporary workers were recruited from southern Europe (especially Turkey) on the understanding that they would return to their native countries if unemployment increased. However, the economic boom lasted so long that when the economy did turn down in the mid-1970s, many guest workers had lived in Germany for a decade. Many stayed, but because German citizenship was not granted to these workers or their children, they were in legal limbo. The clash between German and *Gastarbeiter* cultures increased in intensity in the 1980s, particularly in areas where Turkish workers were highly concentrated. However, the SPD-Green government in 1999 allowed some second- and third-generation immigrant descendants to obtain citizenship or maintain dual citizenship.[9]

Currently, about 3.75 million people of Turkish background live in Germany, though in recent years more have left Germany than have arrived. While early Turkish migrants supplemented industrial work with niche occupations in Turkish groceries and restaurants, these niches are declining. One partial replacement is caring for the elderly, especially Turkish elderly. Increasingly, some higher-paid service jobs are held by ethnic Turks (many now German citizens). Even so, about 40 percent of Turkish families are near or below the poverty line, and Turkish unemployment levels have risen well above those for Germans during the economic crisis. More than fifty years after the first *Gastarbeiter* arrived, 57 percent of young Turks in Germany have no professional qualifications (up from 44 percent in 2001). Yet especially since the financial crisis, more recent immigrants actually have *higher* educational qualifications on average than do native Germans.

Racist attacks against Turkish immigrants and other ethnic minorities have forced Germans to confront the possibility that over sixty years of democracy have not eliminated German xenophobia. Meanwhile, in addition to the *Gastarbeiter*, the Federal Republic for many years provided generous provisions for those seeking political asylum. The issue was exacerbated in the 1990s and 2000s by unification and European integration.

East Germans were raised in a closed society that did not value tolerance. Former GDR citizens, raised on a promise of guaranteed lifetime employment, suddenly faced a labor market that did not supply enough jobs. Yet they were expected to embrace a much more ethnically diverse society than they had ever known. Thus, many Germans who were falling through the cracks of the welfare state and were without jobs became susceptible to racist arguments blaming minorities for Germany's economic problems. Some smaller towns and villages in eastern Germany are literally no-go zones for immigrants.

Some immigrant labor does involve high skills. For example, Germany's changing economy produced a tech worker shortage in the early 2000s that led the Schröder government to recruit software specialists from India. However, this new wave of *Gastarbeiter* was arriving precisely when some Germans were increasingly agitated about the immigration boom, and a backlash quickly occurred. In 2012, Germany joined the EU's blue card scheme. Analogous to the U.S. green card, this allows highly skilled foreigners from outside the EU to live and work in Germany.

Table 4.2	Labor Force Participation Rates (Ages 20–64)					
	1992	1996	2000	2004	2008	2012
Male	80%	76%	77%	75%	80%	82%
Female	58%	58%	61%	63%	68%	72%

Source: Eurostat, 2014.

Gender and Economy

Until the late 1970s, men monopolized positions of authority in both management and labor (though unions subsequently made greater strides than management in expanding leadership opportunities for women). Although half of all German women were in the workforce by the late 1970s, their participation rate of 63 percent by 2004 was far lower than the male rate of 75 percent. In the wake of the economic crisis, however, rates for women surged a bit more than for men, in part because day-care funding is up (see Table 4.2).

Historically, women's benefits have been closely tied to their roles as mothers and wives. German women often face job discrimination, and though they are about as likely to work outside the home as American women, they are far more likely to work part-time. It is much harder for German women to achieve positions of power and responsibility than it is for their American counterparts.[10]

Environmental Issues

Germany is a resource-poor but highly industrialized country, which means it must strive for maximum efficiency. Moreover, it is a crowded country, so pollution can quickly affect daily life. When the country was poor after World War II, environmental worries ranked low. But since the 1970s, most citizens have come to embrace environmental concerns, and most see waste and pollution as big problems. Germans tolerate some of the highest energy prices in the world. To fill the 14.5 gallon tank of a Volkswagen Golf at $8.01 per gallon would cost a cool $116 in Germany, compared to about $53 in the United States (at $3.66 per gallon). Driving 150 mph may be *legal* (much of the Autobahn has no speed limit), but at $8 per gallon it's very *expensive*.

Energiewende

A policy to shift German energy consumption from fossil fuels and nuclear to sustainable sources such as wind, solar, hydro, and biomass.

Since 2010, Germany has embarked on a major reform of energy policy, known as the *Energiewende*. The objectives are to replace fossil fuels (oil and gas) and nuclear energy with renewable sources like wind, solar, biomass, and ocean power to increase energy efficiency, and to promote sustainable development. The goal is to reduce fossil fuel consumption by 80 to 95 percent by 2050, by which time at least 60 percent of German energy should come from renewables (the current figure is around 23 percent). The Russia-Ukraine crisis is likely to spur deeper efforts for energy efficiency, as about 30 percent of German energy comes from Russia.

The major German parties have roughly similar agendas in many areas of environmental policy, though they disagree a lot about the pace with which to require changes. German businesses have complained about rising energy prices, but an even greater concern is the need to build transmission networks from scratch between new (often decentralized) supply sources and the places where energy is consumed. Of course, part of the idea of the *Energiewende* is that more energy will be consumed closer to where it is produced (currently, in huge power plants often far from customers). Still, many new regional networks must be built to make the *Energiewende* a reality. Finally, new technologies are required, and part of the

German motivation is not just to be clean but to be first to the market for greener products. German companies hope to capitalize on these advances by selling them to the rest of the world.

Germany in the Global Economy

Germany's relationship to the regional and international political economy is shaped by two factors: the EU and globalization.

The European Union

As Europe's leading economic power, Germany has benefited from European integration. Behaviors that might once have been viewed by its neighbors as a German bid for domination are more acceptable when seen as Germany's participation in the EU. German exporters depend on markets in other parts of Europe, and German banks have made large profits in the rest of Europe. But Germany also had to adapt to some unfamiliar free-market economic regulations quite different from the rules of organized capitalism that emerged after World War II.

Several difficult issues challenge Germany's international position today. One is whether German-specific institutional arrangements, such as worker (and union) participation in management, tightly organized capitalism, and the elaborate system of apprenticeship training, will flourish in wider European and global contexts.

Before the economic crisis most thought Germany's institutional, political, or cultural patterns could not successfully transfer beyond the Federal Republic. Since then, however, admirers have pointed to its impressive employment performance during the crisis as evidence of the value of Germany's policies and practices. At the same time, some German investments in the rest of Europe have gone spectacularly sour, and Germany has felt obliged to bail out less prosperous Eurozone member states. A 2009 Constitutional Court decision sent shockwaves through the EU because it limited any deeper German integration with the EU and restricted German money for bailouts for other European countries. A 2014 decision on central bank rules caused further anxiety.

Germany in a Regional Context

After World War II, Germany faced two different criticisms. Many feared a too-powerful Germany since the country had run roughshod over its neighbors for much of the previous eighty years. Yet by the 1990s, Germany contended with an opposite problem: what was widely dubbed an economic giant–political dwarf syndrome in which Germany was accused of benefiting from a strong world economy while taking on too few political and military responsibilities.

Chancellors Kohl, Schröder, and Merkel all hoped an integrated Europe might solve both problems. Germany's postwar political leaders embraced European unity because they welcomed the opportunity that a more united continent would present. Germany remains the economic anchor of the EU, while Germany's membership in the EU has enabled it to take on political responsibilities that it would be unable to assume on its own, such as UN peacekeeping operations in the Balkans (which had borne the brunt of many of Germany's World War II–era crimes).

The biggest test of Germany's European leadership came with the euro. For decades, Germany's powerful economy contributed to a strong national currency, the famous Deutsche Mark (DM). Although the DM boosted postwar German economic performance and contributed mightily to German self-confidence, a strong DM also made German exports expensive. The DM's strength also sometimes frustrated other Europeans by enticing investment that might otherwise have flowed to other European countries.

Successive German chancellors judged that economic success for both Germany and Europe would require a stronger common foundation. This is where the euro came in. It promised to prevent European neighbors from weakening their currency at Germany's expense. In return, Germany's neighbors hoped to suffer less inflation and attract more investment capital. Kohl insisted that countries that used the euro must promise to control public spending and inflation (a promise many countries—including Germany—would subsequently break on several occasions).

Now used by over 300 million Europeans, the euro was introduced in most EU member countries in 2002. Gone was the redoubtable DM. For most of the time since its emergence, the euro's value has traded above the U.S. dollar. While this is an advantage for European tourists wanting to visit the United States, it is not so high that it prevents the export-oriented German economy from selling its goods in the Americas or Asia.

Eurozone

The 18 members of the EU (out of 28 total members) who share a common currency, the euro.

Between 2010 and 2012, however, Germany came under pressure to help bail out Greece, Ireland, and Portugal, members of the **Eurozone** who got in huge trouble, partly because the euro allowed them to borrow much more easily. Much larger Spain and Italy also have worrisome levels of debt. In summer 2012, faced with the possibility of the Eurozone breaking apart, Merkel reluctantly agreed to let the European Central Bank finance some state debt. German voters are angry, but German politicians fear that without the common currency, many of the old problems of export and capital imbalances would return. The euro may yet have to be reconfigured, although blowing it up entirely and going back to national currencies would be hugely expensive and politically destabilizing. This dilemma has no easy solution, so watch it carefully. Issues such as trade, economic competition with East Asia and North America, the euro, European economic integration, climate change, and patterns of financial regulation pose daunting challenges. More than most countries, Germany's economic fortunes are tied to globalization. Management and unions realize that exports represent both profits and jobs and therefore protectionism would be self-defeating. The growth in world trade has allowed German firms to export and prosper. Yet it involves large costs, as well. When global trade collapsed during 2009, Germany suffered badly. However, the recovery of trade boosted German exports into record territory since 2010.

Where Do You Stand?

What can Germany do to best alleviate tensions between immigrants and ethnic Germans?

Have Germany (and Europe) gone too far in efforts to protect the environment? Or not far enough? What case can be made for each position?

GOVERNANCE AND POLICY-MAKING

German politics is no less rule-driven than the German economy. Each has its own "constitutional order." Most Americans expect a constitution to be a single written document. In Germany, there is a single document, but it is not called a constitution (*Verfassung*). When West Germany was founded in 1949, the Cold War kept East Germany in the communist bloc. Thus, West Germany chose to adopt a more temporary-sounding "**Basic Law**" (*Grundgesetz*), hoping reunification would come soon and permit the writing of a true constitution. When reunification finally did come—forty years later—the Basic Law had been so successful that both the term and the document itself were kept, while the old GDR was added to the FRG in the form of five new *Länder*.

In what sense did the Basic Law succeed? The primary goals of the young Federal Republic were to avoid repeating the mistakes of the Weimar Republic and to lay to rest the legacy of the Nazi regime. The Basic Law aimed to deal with both failures, and it did.

Two fundamental institutional weaknesses undermined the Weimar government: (1) The fragmented party system prevented stable majorities in the *Reichstag*, and (2) the president's right to exercise emergency powers enabled him to centralize authority and suspend democratic rights. The first weakness (instability) encouraged the second (the use of emergency powers to break legislative deadlocks).

Since Weimar's weakness invited the Nazi takeover, the core reform after World War II aimed to minimize the risk of extremism and the abuse of executive power. These problems were dealt with by introducing federalism and a weak presidency, and by reforming electoral procedures to curb instability.

Organization of the State

After flourishing for over sixty-five years, the Federal Republic has clearly attained its most important goals. It has permitted successful alternations in power, although the Basic Law's provisions for federalism and divided powers tend to keep policy change slow and incremental. Undemocratic parties have received miniscule voter support despite occasional neo-Nazi threats and worrisome incidents of racial violence.

Government Institutions

The German state features a fairly weak president and a much stronger chancellor (prime minister), who is elected by the bicameral parliament's (more powerful) lower house (the *Bundestag*). Germany's parliamentary democracy resembles the parliamentary systems of Britain and Japan in that there is a fusion of powers where the chancellor (the executive or head of government) is also the leader of parliament's largest party. This contrasts with the separation of powers in the United States. Generally, the German executive dominates the lower house of the legislature (the *Bundestag*). Most parliamentary members of the governing parties support the chancellor at all times, since their own positions depend on a successful government. Party voting

Focus Questions

- What institutional changes aimed to fix the problems of Weimar fragmentation and Nazi autocracy?

- How does German federalism differ from federalism in the United States?

Basic Law

The 1949 proto-constitution of the Federal Republic, which continues to function today.

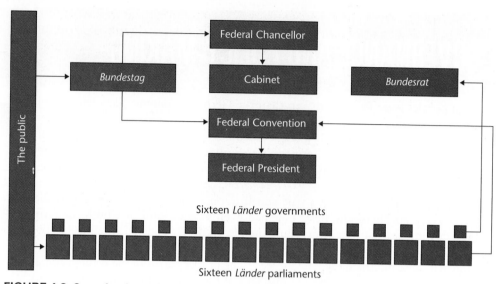

FIGURE 4.2 **Constitutional Structure of the German Federal Government**

rates in Germany are among the highest in Europe. An upper house (the *Bundesrat*) embodies Germany's unique form of federalism where the sixteen states have considerable powers (see Figure 4.2).

The Executive

The division between the head of government (the chancellor) and the head of state (the president) is firmly established, with responsibilities clearly distinguished between the two offices.

The President

The German president's role is largely ceremonial. The president is elected by the Federal Convention (*Bundesversammlung*), an electoral college of all *Bundestag* members and an equal number of delegates elected by the state legislatures. The presidential term is five years and most presidents serve only one term. No woman has been elected president. German presidents are usually senior politicians who are moderates within their parties and broadly acceptable to the electorate. However, if a political crisis were to prevent the chancellor from governing, the president could act as caretaker or help to engineer a new election.

The Chancellor

The Basic Law requires that the chancellor be elected by an absolute majority of the *Bundestag*. Germany has usually had coalition governments because no one party has typically commanded an absolute majority in the *Bundestag* (though Merkel's CDU-CSU came within five seats of doing so in 2013). The chancellor's ability to be a strong party (and coalition) leader is thus essential to the government's success. However, even weak chancellors can usually count on their majority coalition to support their remaining in office. Only once (1998) has a government been tossed out by German voters and replaced with an entirely new one.

The chancellor sets out the main direction of government, names cabinet ministers (in coordination with leaders of the coalition partner), and can reorganize the number and type of ministries. The chancellor has considerable authority to govern, thanks to the Federal Chancellery (*Bundeskanzleramt*). This "superministry's" wide-ranging powers enable the chancellor to oversee the entire government and mediate conflicts among other ministries.

Chancellors have a fair opportunity to implement their programs and take responsibility for success or failure because the interval between parliamentary elections is four years, and it is difficult to call snap elections (as in the United Kingdom). It is also hard to topple a government. Under the Weimar constitution, disparate forces could band together to unseat the chancellor but were then unable to agree on a replacement. Therefore, the Federal Republic's founders added a twist to the no-confidence vote familiar from most parliamentary systems. A German chancellor cannot be removed unless the *Bundestag* simultaneously elects a new chancellor (usually from an opposition party).

This **constructive vote of no confidence** provision strengthens the chancellor in two ways. First, chancellors can more easily reconcile disputes among cabinet officials because the dispute does not threaten the chancellor's position. Second, because the

constructive vote of no confidence

This measure requires the *Bundestag* to elect a new chancellor by an absolute majority in order to oust the current one.

PROFILE

Angela Merkel

Jens Buettner/Corbis Wire/ epa/Corbis

Angela Merkel was fifty-one years old in 2005 when she became the first female chancellor. A minister's daughter, a physicist, a latecomer to political life, an eastern German, a Protestant in a party dominated by Catholics, and a woman who does not champion feminist positions, Merkel is hard to predict or pigeonhole.*

Like many East Germans, her political awakening came in 1989 when she took part in pro-democracy protests as the Berlin wall came down. Merkel eventually joined the CDU and rose swiftly through the party ranks, catching the eye of Helmut Kohl. Positions as a *Bundestag* member, cabinet minister, and then party leader followed. In 2005, her CDU won a plurality, and Merkel became chancellor in a coalition with the SPD.

As the new chancellor, her talk of a "new social market economy" combined appeal to tradition with a promise of renewal. Her opposition to Turkish membership in the EU appealed to many voters, as did her suggestion that "multiculturalism" was a poor model for German society. In foreign policy, Merkel helped put climate change on the international agenda and helped rescue the EU's Constitutional Treaty after its rejection by French and Dutch voters. Her government responded to the 2008 economic crisis with two medium-sized stimulus bills and the original cash-for-clunkers program (2500 euro rebates for purchases of fuel-efficient new cars).

After the 2009 election, her CDU formed its preferred coalition with the Free Democrats, and Merkel remained chancellor. Her second term was defined by her approach to the economic crisis. She angered many other international leaders—U.S. officials were skeptical at the modest size of the German stimulus package while Greek and Irish leaders chafed at her lectures about fiscal responsibility—but she understood the suspicions of German voters.

Like Kohl, Merkel has successfully sidelined key opponents within her party. Thus, even when her popularity flagged in 2010–2011, there was no clear alternative CDU leader. In any event, she rebounded strongly and by the September 2013 elections her approval ratings were at 70 percent. Her party won a crushing victory, helped drive the FDP from parliament, and entered another Grand Coalition with a still-weak SPD. Together, the parties hold an unprecedented 80 percent of the seats in the *Bundestag* (504 out of 631).

MAKING CONNECTIONS What aspects of German politics helped Angela Merkel, an unlikely political figure, rise to the position of chancellor?

*Sarah Wiliarty, *The CDU and the Politics of Gender: Bringing Women to the Party* (New York: Cambridge University Press, 2010).

„ ... WENN DU GROß BIST, MUSST DU DAS BOOT DAHINTEN ZIEHEN ! "

A working-class figure tows a small boat of retirees upstream while noting to the child, "When you grow up, you get to pull the second boat." See discussion on pages 166, 172.

Waldemar Mandzel, www.w-mandzel.de

opposition must agree on concrete and specific alternatives to the existing government, this minimizes opposition for its own sake.

At the same time, chancellors face significant limits on their power. As will be discussed in Section 4, the *Bundesrat* (upper house) must ratify most important legislation passed in the *Bundestag* (lower house) unless overridden by a two-thirds vote of the *Bundestag*. In addition, since the *Bundesrat* implements much legislation, chancellors have to consider the position of the upper house on most issues.

The Cabinet

A government is formed after a majority of the *Bundestag* has nominated a chancellor. This usually follows a parliamentary election. The newly nominated chancellor consults with other party (and coalition party) officials to form the cabinet. Negotiations on the policies that a coalition will pursue often become heated. The choice of cabinet ministers is made on policy as well as personal grounds. The most significant ministries are those of finance, economics, justice, interior, and foreign policy. After the 2013 election, the SPD agreed not to demand the Finance Ministry that they coveted in exchange for policy concessions by the CDU. In many cases, chancellors rely on strong ministers; some chancellors have taken ministerial responsibility themselves in key areas such as economics and foreign policy. The economics and finance ministries always work closely with the European Central Bank (ECB), since the euro adoption has taken over the main functions of the old German Central Bank (the *Bundesbank*).

Ministers are important government actors. They have broad autonomy to set policy in their ministry, subject to the chancellor's overall authority to guide the government and the coalition agreement between the parties. Ministers are also collectively responsible for cabinet policy: they are expected to support the government's position and not publicly express disagreements or reservations about policy.

The Bureaucracy

The national bureaucracy is a key part of the executive branch of the government. In Germany, it is especially powerful, and its members are protected by civil service provisions that give them influence, prestige, and guaranteed employment for life. German **civil servants** believe their work is a profession, not just a "job."

Surprisingly, the federal government employs only about 25 percent of civil servants; the rest are employed by state and local governments. Today, most civil servants are university graduates and/or come from positions within the parties. Top-level federal bureaucrats are primarily policy-makers who work closely with their ministers and the legislature. State and local bureaucrats are the main agents of policy implementation. Under Germany's distinctive form of federalism, the states administer most policies, even those determined at the national level. Because of the close links among the various levels of the bureaucracy, public policies are often more consistent than in countries where federal and state governments are at odds with one another. Indeed, overlapping responsibilities on policy issues make it difficult to identify the exclusive responsibility of the three levels.

The German bureaucracy enjoys respect from the population. German bureaucrats have a well-deserved reputation for competence. Most civil servants are politically neutral. However, a few top federal officials are partisan, consistent with the idea that parties play a critical role in German democracy and so should be represented in society's main institutions. Most civil servants are chosen on the basis of merit, with elaborate licensing and testing for the highest positions. Civil servants can and do run for office. About one-third of the *Bundestag* is typically made up of civil servants, including many teachers. This contrasts with the United States, where few legislators have any experience as administrators.

civil servants

Employees of federal, state, and municipal governments.

Other State Institutions

In addition to the institutions discussed so far, the military, the judiciary, and subnational governments are essential institutions for governance and policy-making.

The Military and Police

From the eighteenth century through World War II, the German military was powerful and aggressive. After 1945 it was disbanded because of its role in the war. It was reconstituted in the 1950s, placed under strict civilian control, and tightly limited by law and treaty. Germany renounced any intention to acquire nuclear weapons (in contrast to Britain and France). Moreover, the Allied occupation and German Basic law long prohibited the armed forces from operating outside Germany. The military originally was to be used only for defensive purposes within Europe, and then in coordination with NATO authorities. Constitutional changes ended this prohibition, and Germany's *Bundeswehr* participated in the UN peacekeeping mission in Bosnia in 1995 (under a CDU-FDP government), the bombing of Serbia in 1999, and hostilities in Afghanistan after September 11, 2001 (both the latter decisions by SPD-Green governments). As decades pass, the post–World War II opposition to foreign deployment of the German army has somewhat eroded, although the CDU-FDP government avoided any contribution to the 2011 Libyan conflict and sent clear signals it would not support military action against Syria in 2013.

Germany's 2011 abolition of the draft made its army an all-volunteer professional force that is easier to deploy abroad. However, the military's role remains limited. Germany spends approximately 1.3 percent of its GDP on the military, less than most other large, industrialized countries. It also spends less on foreign aid than do France or the United Kingdom. The Ukraine crisis has heightened Germany's reputation for tentativeness in foreign policy, where it has come in for widespread criticism for not "leading." Observers suggest many reasons for Germany's reluctance to confront Russia more sharply, ranging from more cynical motives like trade, investment and energy ties with Russia to more practical ones like its small military. German voters also constrain its politicians. On the right, some think Putin's condemnation of homosexuality and decadence in the West is justified; on the left, some anti-Americanism (and plenty of anti-NSA) sentiment still exists. Many Germans simply think that given their history, it's not their role to pass judgment on the borders of other countries.

German police powers are organized on a *Land* basis and, because of the excesses of the Third Reich, strong provisions are in place to protect human and civil rights. To be sure, there have been exceptions. By far the worst police abuses came not from the West German police forces, however, but from East Germany's notorious secret police, the *Stasi*. The *Stasi* spied on virtually the entire society and arbitrarily arrested and persecuted thousands of citizens. They even had a mole in Chancellor Willy Brandt's office, which helped lead to his resignation in 1974. After unification, *Stasi* archives were opened because the government believed that full disclosure of *Stasi* excesses was essential. Making public the names of informants has often created bitter confrontations. Outstanding German films have treated these topics, including *Goodbye Lenin* (2003) and *The Lives of Others* (*Das Leben der Anderen*) in 2006. The latter deals with both full-time agents and part-time informants. By the GDR regime's end, there was one *Stasi* informant for every 6.5 citizens in the country! Many Germans' negative reaction to the NSA surveillance scandal becomes more understandable in light of the *Stasi*'s legacy.

German police have faced heightened challenges in the wake of 9/11. Police gained new powers, including surveillance, but courts later cut back some of these powers. Numerous members of al Qaeda, including several of the 9/11 bombers, lived in Hamburg and other German cities. Germany has seen a number of subsequent "near misses," including a 2006 plot by two Lebanese men to explode suitcase bombs on a crowded commuter train in Cologne. In 2007, German police uncovered a plan by two German converts to Islam and a Turkish national to drive explosives-laden trucks into U.S. military facilities. All three young men had trained in Pakistan. In 2011, a Kosovar worker at the Frankfurt Airport opened fire on U.S. airmen, killing two and wounding two others. A foiled 2013 plot involved two aeronautics students at the University of Stuttgart who planned to use explosives-filled remote-control planes as crude missiles.

The Judiciary

The judiciary has always played a major role in German government. During the Nazi regime, it issued numerous repressive decisions, banning non-Nazi parties, allowing the seizure of Jewish property, and sanctioning the deaths of millions. The Federal Republic's founders were determined to prevent further judicial abuses. The Basic Law charges the judiciary with safeguarding the democratic rights of individuals, groups, and political parties. In fact, the Basic Law enumerates twenty individual rights—more than exist in the U.S. Constitution or in British common law.

Germany's legal system differs from the legal tradition of Britain and the United States in other ways as well. The Anglo-American common law precedent-based systems are characterized by adversarial relationships between contending parties. The judge merely presides over a clash between opposing lawyers. In continental Europe, including France and Germany, civil law has roots in Roman law and the Napoleonic code. The judiciary acts as an aggressive administrator of the law rather than just an arbiter. In defining the meaning of laws and implementing their administration, German courts go considerably beyond those in the United States and Britain.

The Federal Republic's court system is three-pronged. One branch consists of the criminal-civil system, with the Federal High Court at the top. It is a unified system that tries to apply consistent criteria to cases in the sixteen states. The Federal High Court reviews appeals of lower court decisions, including criminal and civil cases, disputes among the states, and matters viewed as political in some countries, such as the abortion ruling.

The Special Constitutional Court deals with matters directly affecting the Basic Law. A postwar creation, it was created to safeguard the new democratic order. Because of Nazi abuses of the judiciary, the FRG founders added a judicial layer to ensure that the democratic order was maintained. The Constitutional Court is widely respected and has issued many landmark decisions, including one in 2009 that halts any further transfer of German power to the EU unless expressly ratified by the German parliament (not just the government). The Court has also deliberated on (and, so far, generally approved) key Euro-bailout programs of the European Central Bank (though it expressed great skepticism in a 2014 ruling on ECB purchases of government bonds).

The Administrative Court system is the third branch of the judiciary. It can check the bureaucracy's power, an important function since policy is often determined by the bureaucracy. Citizens can use administrative courts to challenge bureaucratic decisions, for example, with respect to labor, welfare, or tax policies.

The courts have sometimes come under fire. In the late 1970s, critics charged that courts did not restrain clandestine searches for leftist terrorists. These searches arguably violated the rights of citizens. More recently, the courts have been criticized for giving undue protection to neo-Nazis and potential al Qaeda terrorists. The judicial system must walk a fine line between maintaining civil rights in a democratic society and preventing extremist violence.

Subnational Government

Like the United States, Canada, Switzerland, and Austria, Germany is a *federal* republic. There are sixteen *Länder* (states); eleven constituted the old West Germany and five additional ones were made from former East Germany. These state governments enjoy considerable autonomy and independent powers. Each state has a regional assembly (*Landtag*) that functions much as the *Bundestag* does at the federal level. The governor (*Minister-Präsident*) of each *Land* is the leader of the largest party (or coalition) in the *Landtag* and forms a state government, just as does the chancellor in the *Bundestag*. State elections are held on independent, staggered four-year cycles, which generally do not coincide with federal elections. Subnational governments in Germany are powerful, important, and responsible for much national policy implementation, including most laws passed by the federal government. German states must also share a portion of their tax revenues, so states with stronger economies (grudgingly) support those with weaker economies and lower revenues.

The negative side of German federalism is its lack of flexibility. Since the Basic Law did not specify which powers were reserved for the federal level and which for the states, policymaking is cumbersome. Since different levels share responsibility, conflict often results. At times, opposition parties have used the upper house to "blockade" (that is, stalemate) the lower house. A 2006 reform tried to clarify the policy domains of the federal and state levels and reduce blockades. However, it has not been very effective.[11]

State politics is organized on the same basis as the national parties. However, the common party names and platforms at all levels let voters see the connection among local, regional, and national issues. Parties adopt platforms for state and city elections, so voters can see the differences among parties and not be swayed solely by personalities. The German party system encourages politicians to begin their careers at the local and state levels. Regional and local party members' careers are tied closely to the national, regional, and local levels of the party. This way, voters can reward ideological and policy continuity across levels.[12]

German local governments employ about 1.5 million people and assume a wide range of tasks, providing social services (often working with semipublic institutions), implementing environmental standards, and managing the transport network. Local governments can raise revenues by owning enterprises. Many Germans believe that publicly owned museums, theater companies, television and radio networks, recreational facilities, and housing complexes improve their quality of life. With the *Energiewende*, more localities now have incentives to develop energy grids and production facilities.

The Policy-Making Process

The chancellor and cabinet are responsible for policy-making, but the process is largely consensus-based. Contentious issues are debated within various public, semipublic, and private institutions. Although the legislature has some role in policy-making, the primary drivers are the cabinet departments (and sometimes the experts on whom they call). The Basic Law makes the upper house co-equal in all areas where state (*Land*) interests and/or administration play a central role. In practice, this came to mean almost any important piece of domestic legislation. Recent reforms tried to streamline these responsibilities, for example, attempting to remove the federal government entirely from higher education policy. It hasn't really worked.

Policy implementation is also a shared task. The *Bundesrat* plays a big role, along with corporatist interest groups and semipublic organizations noted earlier. EU policy is shaped by both national and regional governments and by private sector interests that use corporatist institutions to participate in the process. The states are guaranteed a role in shaping EU policies that affect them.

Both unification and the increasing importance of the EU (for example, the adoption of the euro and the rules associated with it) have challenged this informal style of policy-making.[13] Moreover, for all its system-maintaining advantages, the German consensual system is somewhat intolerant of dissent. This tendency helps explain why protest politics occasionally erupts in Germany, seemingly out of nowhere.

Where Do You Stand?

In light of the German experience, should constitution-writers be more worried about designing too strong a state or too weak a one?

Do you see foiled terror plots as evidence of success or of failure?

REPRESENTATION AND PARTICIPATION

SECTION 4

German parties represent well many established interests, yet parties and interest groups still struggle to give a voice to other major collective identities and interests. Partly, this is understandable. Incorporating disparate political cultures is a dilemma for any society, and east and west Germany are *very* different cultures. Yet the German party system is not particularly responsive to new interests and values bubbling up from society.

Focus Questions ▽

- How has the proliferation of new parties disrupted traditional parties' ways of doing business?

- How and why do protest politics work differently in Germany and the United States?

The Legislature

Like most parliamentary regimes, Germany "fuses" power rather than "separates" it. This means the executive is voted in by the legislature. Unlike many parliamentary systems that are tightly controlled by the government, however, both the lower house (*Bundestag*) and the upper house (*Bundesrat*) possess important partially independent powers. Both branches of the legislature are broadly representative of the major interests in German society, although some interests such as business and labor are somewhat overrepresented, whereas ecological and noneconomic interests are underrepresented.

The *Bundestag*

The lower house consists of 614 seats. German elections are by a two-ballot system, known as the **mixed member system**. This system blends the British and U.S. traditions of a single legislator representing one district and the European tradition of proportional representation, in which parties are allotted seats in the legislature in proportion to the percentage of popular votes they receive. To do this, the hybrid system asks each voter to cast two votes on his or her ballot: the first for an individual candidate in a voter's local district and the second for a list of national/regional candidates grouped by party affiliation. In this way, votes can help determine "constituency" relationships with their individual representatives and also help determine which parties will have the most influence in the *Bundestag*.

mixed member system

An electoral system in which about half of deputies are elected from direct constituencies and the other half are drawn from closed party lists. The *Bundestag* uses the mixed member system, which is basically a form of proportional representation.

Bundestag seats are allocated among parties by proportional representation—but with a twist produced by the single-member district feature. For every seat won by a party's candidate in an individual district, his or her party is allotted one less seat from the party's slate elected via list voting. In practice, the two large parties, the Social Democrats and the Christian Democrats, win virtually all of the district seats. In this way, the *Bundestag*'s composition is "mixed" between those deputies who are directly elected and those elected from party lists. This mix gives the system both a constituency logic but also a mechanism for parties to incentivize legislators to toe the party line. Once elected, the two groups of legislators sit together and have identical powers.

Most members of the *Bundestag* are middle-class male professionals. Through the 1983 election, fewer than 10 percent were women. Since 1987, however, the number of women has increased substantially, reaching 36.6 percent with the 2013 election (see Table 4.3). The addition of the ex-communist Left Party and the continued presence of the Greens has increased the variety of backgrounds among *Bundestag* members.

The proportional representation list system produces multiple parties, but it also helps strengthen parties. If legislators consistently defy their party, the leadership can punish them by assigning them a low list position in the next election. This greatly reduces their chances of being reelected. This is a powerful lever to promote party discipline. Party unity contributes to consistency in the parties' positions over a four-year legislative period and enables the electorate to identify each party's stance on issues.

5 percent clause

This rule obliges a party to get at least 5 percent of the "second votes" in order for its candidates to get seats in the *Bundestag* (or the state parliaments) as a party. This rule depresses votes for "splinter" parties unlikely to meet this threshold.

A key constitutional element of German politics is the so-called **5 percent clause**, which requires parties to obtain at least 5 percent of the nationwide vote to enter parliament and benefit from proportional representation. Five percent of the vote is also required in state or municipal elections for representation in those governments. This barrier matters! In 2013, the Free Democrats, who had been in the *Bundestag* since 1949, just missed getting 5 percent (4.8). A new party, the Alternative for Germany, received 4.7 percent and so also failed to crack the *Bundestag*. Both must do better in state elections in order to stay on voters' minds. Over time, many smaller parties have faded away. Thus, Germany has avoided the wild proliferation of parties that plagues some democracies, such as Italy and Israel, where coalitions are extremely difficult to form and sustain. The German Constitutional Court ruled the 5 percent clause unconstitutional for European (not national or state) elections, and this had a big effect on the 2014 elections to the European Parliament. As expected, the ruling CDU and SPD parties did best, with 34 and 27 seats, respectively (though the CDU/CSU had its worst European result in many years). The Greens were third with 11 seats, and the Left Party won 7. AfD also won 7 seats. But without the 5 percent clause, four other parties got into the European Parliament: the FDP had 3.5 percent and 3 seats, while the libertarian Pirate Party, the far-right National Democratic Party and the Animal Rights Party got one MEP each.

The tradition of strong, unified parties in the *Bundestag* has some drawbacks. New members must serve long stints as backbenchers, and individual legislators have few chances to make an impact. Many leaders have preferred to serve their political apprenticeship in state or local government, where they have more visibility. This system, in turn, does improve the skills of young politicians.

The executive branch introduces most (but not all) legislation and must initiate all federal budget and tax legislation. There is often a consensus within parties and within coalitions about what legislation should be introduced. When the executive proposes a bill, it first goes to the *Bundesrat* for comment. Thereafter, it has a quick first reading in the *Bundestag*—primarily to identify any contentious issues in the bill. It then goes to a relevant *Bundestag* committee for review, while the upper house is also notified. Most committee deliberations take place privately, and committee members have great latitude to shape the legislation. Committees generally consult with many groups, both pro and con. This makes it more likely that a consensus-oriented outcome will be achieved.

After the committee reports, the bill has two more readings in the *Bundestag*, with debate between governing parties and opposition generally most intense around the second reading. The primary purpose of the debate is to educate the public about the major issues of the bill. Following passage in the *Bundestag*, the *Bundesrat* must approve most bills for them to become law.

The *Bundesrat*

The *Bundesrat* (Upper House) really shapes the federal system. Made up of sixty-nine members from the sixteen state governments,

Table 4.3	Percentage of Women Members of the *Bundestag*		
Year	**Percentage**	**Year**	**Percentage**
1949	6.8	1983	9.8
1953	8.8	1987	15.4
1957	9.2	1990	20.5
1961	8.3	1994	26.3
1965	6.9	1998	30.2
1969	6.6	2002	32.2
1972	5.8	2005	31.8
1976	7.3	2009	32.8
1980	8.5	2013	36.6

Source: Bundeszentrale für Politische Bildung, 2014.

it is the arena where the national and state governments interact. When the government initiates a bill, it sends it first to the *Bundesrat* for comment. The *Bundesrat* can also initiate bills, and these must get the government's comment before passing to the *Bundestag* for consideration.

The *Bundesrat* can exercise an **absolute veto** on amendments to the constitution as well as all laws that affect the fundamental interests of the states, such as taxes, territorial integrity, and basic administrative functions. Historically, laws that affect fundamental interests of states and thus require *Bundesrat* approval have amounted to slightly over half (53 percent) of bills, although a 2006 constitutional reform dropped this to around 40 percent. The *Bundesrat* also can exercise a **suspensive veto**, which slows the passage of legislation. However, if the *Bundesrat* votes against a bill, the *Bundestag* can override it by passing the measure again by a simple majority. If, however, a two-thirds majority of the *Bundesrat* votes against a bill (a rare occurrence), the *Bundestag* must pass it again by a two-thirds margin.

Oddly, the Grand Coalition's staggering majority in the *Bundestag* is not replicated in the *Bundesrat*. The reason is that the political composition of the *Bundesrat* depends upon which parties control the sixteen state governments. Each state delegation casts its votes on legislation in a unified bloc, reflecting the views of the state's majority party or coalition. Consequently, the party controlling the majority of state governments can have a significant effect on what legislation is passed. Although states ruled by SPD, CDU-CSU, or Grand Coalitions can be expected to vote with the government, most states are ruled by *either* the CDU or SPD plus an opposition party (Greens, FDP, or the Left Party). Such states will often abstain from *Bundestag* votes. Crucially, such abstentions count as a "no." At the time of the Grand Coalition's formation, the government had only twenty-seven out of sixty-nine votes in the *Bundestag*. Because state elections usually take place between *Bundestag*

absolute veto

In areas that directly affect the states, the *Bundesrat* can veto any bill passed by the *Bundestag*.

suspensive veto

In policy areas with no direct effect on the states, the *Bundesrat* has the prerogative to make the *Bundestag* pass a bill a second time.

electoral periods, the *Bundesrat* majority often shifts during the *Bundestag's* four-year legislative period. Thus, although more states may see Grand Coalitions in coming years, there is no guarantee of this and thus no guarantee of smooth sailing for the government.

The *Bundesrat* introduces comparatively little legislation, but its administrative responsibilities are considerable. Most *Bundesrat* members are also state government officials, experienced in implementing laws. The *Bundesrat* is close to the concerns of the entire country and provides a forum for understanding how national legislation affects each state. Their expertise is frequently called on in the committee hearings of the *Bundestag*, which are open to all *Bundesrat* members. The *Bundesrat* also administers the world's largest public television network (ARD) and helps coordinate regional and national economic policies.

Finally, the *Bundesrat* plays a significant role in dealing with the EU. It has long advocated representation for the *Länder* in EU institutions, and it represents the German government in Brussels in some negotiations that centrally affect the states.

Political Parties and the Party System

party democracy

The constitutional guarantee that political parties have a privileged place in German politics, including generous subsidies for building party organizations.

Germany has often been called a **party democracy** because its parties are so important in shaping state policy. Until the early 1980s, Germany had a "two-and-a-half" party system, composed of a moderate-left Social Democratic Party (SPD), a moderate-right Christian Democratic grouping (CDU in all of West Germany except Bavaria, where it is called the CSU), and a small centrist Free Democratic Party (FDP).

During the 1980s and 1990s, two new parties emerged to challenge the "two-and-a-half" major parties. These were the Greens, generally on the left and favoring ecological, environmental, and peace issues, and the Party of Democratic Socialism (PDS), the former Communist Party of East Germany. In 2005, the latter formed *die Linke* (Left Party) with a group of left-wing ex-Social Democrats who believed Schröder's reforms undermined social democracy. The small right-wing National Democratic Party (*Nationaldemokratische Partei Deutschlands*, NPD) also emerged at this time. Much more conservative than the CDU/CSU, it emphasized nationalism and intolerance toward immigrants and ethnic minorities.[14] Thus far, it has failed to clear the 5 percent threshold to gain representation in the *Bundestag*, though it cleared that hurdle in two *Landtagen* in eastern Germany, where it is particularly strong. In 2013, the *Bundesrat* petitioned the Constitutional Court to ban the NPD after a terror group with NPD links was accused of murdering nine immigrants and a police officer.

The Christian Democrats

The CDU/CSU (two distinct, but closely allied parties) have dominated postwar German politics, governing, usually in coalitions, from 1949–1969, 1982–1998, and continually since 2005. The CDU and CSU unite Catholics and Protestants in confessional, catchall parties of the center-right. Christian Democracy champions the social market economy. Their social policies in the decades after World War II were paternalistic, but they sponsored the considerable expansion of the German welfare state. The party alliance has been a consistent advocate of European integration since Konrad Adenauer's leadership in the early postwar period. The most

18th Bundestag 2013
Party Seats and Percentage of the National Vote

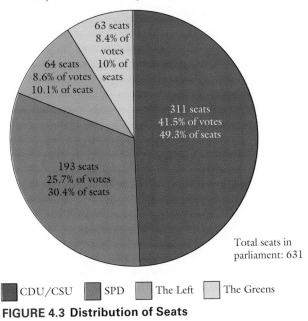

63 seats
8.4% of
votes
10% of
seats

64 seats
8.6% of votes
10.1% of seats

311 seats
41.5% of votes
49.3% of seats

193 seats
25.7% of votes
30.4% of seats

Total seats in
parliament: 631

■ CDU/CSU ■ SPD □ The Left □ The Greens

FIGURE 4.3 Distribution of Seats

significant and historic accomplishments of the long Kohl regime (1982–1998) are German unification and Germany's much deeper integration into the EU.

CDU leader Angela Merkel became Germany's first female chancellor after the 2005 election, when the CDU/CSU entered into a Grand Coalition with its arch-rival, the SPD. The 2009 election enabled Merkel to form her preferred coalition with the FDP, and in the 2013 elections, she came within five seats of capturing the first absolute majority since Adenauer's in 1957 (for more on Merkel, see the Profile box in Section 3). At present, Merkel faces few challenges from within the party. She is also extremely adept at gobbling up the SPD's preferred themes as she brings her party more to the center and away from the right.

The Social Democratic Party

The traditional leading party of the left, the SPD, was founded in 1875 in response to rapid industrialization and Bismarck's authoritarianism. Following World War I, it became the leading party—but without having a majority—of the early years of the Weimar Republic.

Despite being the second-largest party in postwar Germany, the SPD obtained only about 30 percent of the vote until the early 1960s and never succeeded in joining a national government. In an attempt to broaden its constituency, it altered its party program in 1959. De-emphasizing its reliance on Marxism and its working-class base, its new goal was to recruit voters from throughout the social structure, including the middle class and among Christians.

In 1969, the SPD was finally elected to office as the leading member of a majority coalition (with the FDP). It remained in power for thirteen years under chancellors Willy Brandt and Helmut Schmidt. The SPD brought to the coalition a concern for increased welfare and social spending, as well as an effort to ease strained relations with the USSR and other communist countries (*Ostpolitik*).

Ostpolitik

The policy developed by the SPD's Willy Brandt to promote contact and commerce with the Soviet Union and its communist allies during the Cold War.

Out of power from 1982 to 1998, the SPD failed to formulate winning alternative policies, though it governed many states. In 1998, the exhausted Kohl regime was voted out, and the SPD was able to form a coalition with the Greens. The early years of the second SPD-led regime were initially successful, but divisions within the party over economic reforms brought the second term of the SPD-Green government to an early end in 2005. After limping through a Grand Coalition for four more years, the SPD vote plunged to 23 percent in the 2009 elections, its lowest total ever. It lost seventy-six seats in the *Bundestag*. The SPD improved modestly in the 2013 elections, picking up forty-seven seats on 26 percent of the vote. Given the elimination of the FDP from parliament, however, this was easily enough to enter a Grand Coalition.

The Greens

The Greens entered the political scene in 1979 and have won seats at national and regional levels ever since. This heterogeneous party drew support from several constituencies in the early 1980s: urban-based **citizen action groups**, environmental activists, farmers, antinuclear activists, the peace movement, and small bands of Marxist-Leninists. After first overcoming the 5 percent hurdle in 1983 *Bundestag* elections, the Greens went on to win seats in most subsequent state and national elections by stressing noneconomic quality-of-life issues.

Electoral success generated division within this "antiparty party." The *realos* (realists) believed it was important to moderate the party's positions in order to win power; the *fundis* (fundamentalists) opposed any collaboration with existing parties, in order to avoid compromising the party's demands, even if this meant damaging their short-term electoral prospects. The squabbling between *fundis* and *realos* undercut the party's credibility, even though ecological problems in eastern Germany presented the Greens with a tremendous opportunity.

In 1998 the Greens got a chance to govern in a national coalition. The *fundi-realo* split soon emerged when Green foreign minister, Joschka Fischer, a *realo*, split the party by supporting Germany's participation in the NATO-led bombing of Serbia. Fischer explained that his generation was raised both to say "never again war" *and* "never again Auschwitz." When forced to choose, he insisted Germany must choose the latter in order to prevent Serbian tyrant Slobodan Milosevic from genocidal aggression against Kosovar Albanians.

Following the 2005 election, the Greens returned to opposition in the *Bundestag*. One indication of the complexity and volatility of German politics is that the CDU clearly sees the Greens as a serious competitor. Accentuating the CDU's difference with the Greens was one reason for Merkel's shift toward nuclear energy, a move that backfired after the post-earthquake Japanese nuclear crisis. In 2011, a Green became governor of a state for the first time. However, after the party reached nearly 20 percent in national polls, two political scientists unearthed a 1981 document signed by the current Green leader and calling for decriminalization of nonviolent sexual acts between adults and minors. Dragged down by this scandal and an unfocused campaign, the Greens' vote share fell to 8.4 percent in 2013.

The Left Party (*die Linke*)

In 2005, the former East German Communist Party (PDS) merged with a breakaway faction of the SPD to form the Left Party. While officially a new party concentrated

---

citizen action groups

Nonparty and often single-issue initiatives, often focused on concrete problems such as the environment, traffic, housing, or other social and economic issues.

in the former East Germany, the PDS had a long and volatile history. Beginning in the late 1940s, the Communist Party (SED) dominated all aspects of life in East Germany. The GDR led by the SED was probably the most Stalinist and repressive regime in Eastern Europe.

After unification in 1990, the SED demonstrated tactical agility by changing its name to the PDS and moderating its program. It often polled over 20 percent in the five *Länder* of the former East Germany and won a spot in the *Bundestag* in each election. The Left Party was formed when it merged with left-wing dissidents from the SPD who were based primarily in western Germany. The new arrivals provided electoral support for the PDS precisely where it was weakest.

The Left Party's strong showing is largely due to its opposition to cuts in social spending. With a growing base in the west (around 5 percent) and traditional eastern support (nearly 25 percent) it seems solidly entrenched. The Left Party's durability makes "coalition math" far more complicated than in the simple old days of either CDU-FDP or SPD-FDP alliances. The Left Party has been part of several coalitions at the state level. It is the only German party to consistently oppose the German-supported austerity policies in struggling Eurozone states.

The FRG is one of the few countries in western Europe that has not had a far-right and/or neofascist party gain seats in its national legislature. Because the Left Party's primary support in the east comes from marginalized and/or unemployed people in German society, it has provided a left-wing alternative for many voters who, in other west European countries, have turned to the far right. Many Left Party deputies are closely monitored by the federal and state (especially western German) constitutional protection officials.

The Free Democratic Party

For decades, the FDP specialized in turning modest numbers of votes into lots of power. However, in 2013 its luck ran out when it failed to clear the 5 percent threshold and crashed out of the *Bundestag*. This "swing party" allied with each of the two major parties (SPD and CDU/CSU) at different periods since 1949 and regularly held both the foreign and economics ministries in those coalitions.

The FDP could "swing" so easily because it contained two ideologies: economic liberalism (in the European sense of free market-oriented) and social liberalism (personal freedoms). In recent years, the FDP has become more explicitly free-market, emphasizing deregulation and privatization. The growth of the Green and Left Parties has diminished the "kingmaker" status of the FDP. In 2009, after polling an astonishingly high 15 percent, the FDP replaced the SPD in Merkel's CDU-led government coalition. However, the FDP's standing subsequently plummeted. In 2013, its weak performance in government combined with its voters' worries about German policies to rescue the euro and led many of its voters to abandon it. It must now limp along in state parliaments (and the European Parliament) until 2017.

Elections

Until recently, German voter turnout rates of 80 to 90 percent exceeded those in most other western European countries. Germany has enjoyed relatively stable electoral allegiance, despite the ups and downs of unification and European integration.

But the entry of two new parties (and very nearly a third) in the *Bundestag* in recent decades may now reflect higher volatility among voters and, hence, among parties. The danger is that the multiparty system may often result in inconclusive elections, in which no party is a decisive winner. After the vote, it may fall to the parties to haggle amongst themselves to choose among possible coalitions. Will voters then react with even greater frustration? And will parties turn to more and more adventurous coalitions in order to form majorities?

Political Culture, Citizenship, and Identity

With parties representing such a broad ideological spectrum, there is wide-ranging political debate. Germany's moderate right parties have integrated a broad swath of right-wing voters into democratic and even centrist politics. Among the democratic left, there is a strong participatory ethic, fostered by extensive participation at the workplace through the works councils. Moreover, the Greens have placed great emphasis on **grassroots democracy**—that is, rank-and-file participation. The Greens, and now the Left Party, have forced the traditional parties to engage in grassroots efforts to mobilize support.

Germany's educational system is steeped in tradition, though it has changed considerably in recent decades. Traditionally, only a small cohort went on to university—most children who eventually enrolled in higher education began the university prep track in the sixth grade!—while the rest went on to technical or vocational tracks. In recent years, German schools have been disappointingly middle-of-the-pack in comparative analyses.

The postwar universities long remained elitist and restrictive and often provided little critical analysis of Germany's bloody twentieth-century history. But widespread student mobilizations in the 1960s opened up the educational system to a much wider class spectrum and also caused many of the '68 Generation (1968 was the year of the most significant student demonstrations) to challenge their parents about attitudes shaped by the Nazi period and before. Far more Germans now attend universities, but few German universities are in the top rank globally. In the mid-2000s, some German states tried to charge tuition of €500 per semester—up to then, university tuition was free. In recent years, student resistance has ended this experiment in most states.

grassroots democracy

The idea that real democracy requires participation from rank-and-file members and not merely from organizational leaders.

Refugees, Immigration, and Migrant Labor

German crimes in the Holocaust and World War II—where many non-Jewish peoples and ethnicities also experienced German brutality—led postwar Germany to accept a special responsibility to Jews and other ethnic minorities. The new FRG government made large compensation payments to survivors of the Holocaust, their families, and the state of Israel. It also passed generous asylum laws to enable large numbers of those facing political persecution elsewhere to obtain German residency, although not citizenship. With the end of the Cold War and the opening up of east European borders, the trickle of asylum seekers turned into a flood. In response, the Kohl government restricted political asylum.

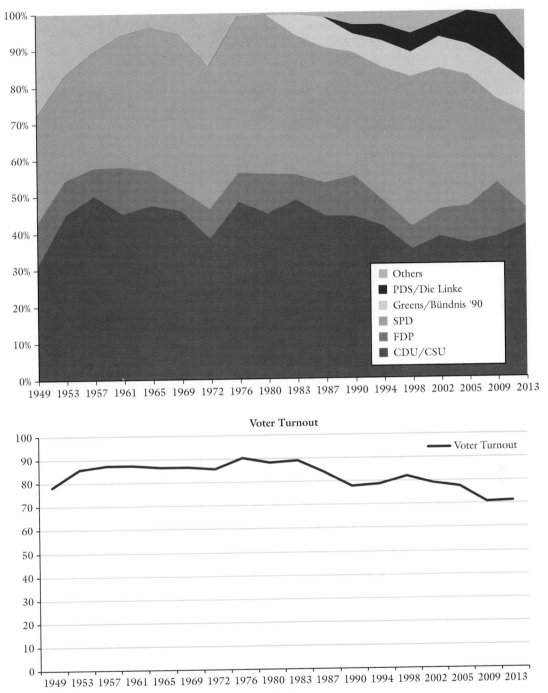

FIGURE 4.4 FRG Election Results, 1949–2009, 2013

Sources: German Information Center, 2005; Bundestagswahl, 2009, 2013.

At the same time, immigrants to Germany had little chance to obtain citizenship. The 1913 Immigration Law stipulated that citizenship was based on blood (*jus sanguinis*) and not naturalization (*jus solis*). This meant that German citizenship was easy to obtain for ethnic Germans whose families had lived in Russia or eastern Europe for generations and did not speak German, but difficult for the *Gastarbeiter* children born in Germany. Until the SPD-Green government eased citizenship rules in 1999, Germany's restrictive definition of identity looked insular and backwards in a Europe rapidly becoming more international.

Every European state faces a version of this dilemma: How can they protect national identity and still respond to the economic and ethical motives to allow some immigration and asylum? While some Germans are fearful immigration will weaken the traditional conception of "German," globalization has opened the country to increasing migration. One million people moved to Germany in 2012 alone (though not all will stay). Economic pressures to increase immigration go together with a demographic trend that, likewise, affects almost all European countries: a shrinking native-born population. The aging native population relies on a welfare and pension system financed by currently employed (that is, younger) workers. One partial solution to the fiscal demands of an aging population is young immigrant workers who will both revitalize economic growth and help fund pension and welfare obligations. To do so, however, requires that Germany—and many of its neighbors—reconsider who can be a citizen. The Grand Coalition has agreed to allow dual citizenship to anyone of foreign background who was born in Germany.

Until the 1960s, women had been politically marginalized in the FRG. Taking to heart the slogan *Kinder, Kirche, Küche* (children, church, and kitchen), few women held positions in society outside the home. Even with the social explosions of the 1960s and the spread of feminism since the 1970s, German women have generally lagged behind women in many west European countries in obtaining adequate representation in business and civil society. However, as the data in Table 4.3 show, German women have quadrupled their representation in the Bundestag from approximately 8 percent in 1980 to almost 37 percent in 2013.

Following unification, there were controversial differences between the Federal Republic and the former GDR on policy affecting women. Women in the former East Germany had more presence and influence in public life and in the workplace than did their counterparts in West Germany. To be sure, female employment was nearly obligatory in the GDR. Still, East German women enjoyed greater government provision for childcare and family leave. In fact, one of the hottest debates in Germany during the early 1990s was whether to reduce East German–style benefits to women in favor of the more conservative and restrictive ones of the Federal Republic. The West German practices and patterns prevailed after unification, to the frustration of many.

Germany's press is free, diverse, and vibrant. There are a wide variety of private TV cable and satellite channels, but the three main public channels provide a balance of major party positions. During election campaigns, each major party gets seven free 90-second ads on the public stations. The campaigns spend most of their limited campaign funds on billboards and posters, leaving television viewers largely unmolested by ads.

Newspapers appeal to a broad range of political opinion. The rough-and-tumble tabloid press has a populist tone and is quick to punish any signs of elitism on the part of politicians. The tabloids played a key role in mobilizing opposition to German financing of the Eurozone crisis after 2008. A few daily papers are partisan (for example, *Die Welt* on the right and *Tageszeitung* on the left). Germany also has widely read weekly papers, including the more inflammatory *Der Spiegel* and the more sober *Die Zeit*.

Interest Groups, Social Movements, and Protest

As discussed in Section 2, Germany remains a country of organized groups: major economic producer groups such as the BDI (Federal Association of German Industry), BDA (Federal Association of German Employers), and DGB (German Trade Union Confederation); political parties (in which authentic participatory membership remains higher than in most other countries); and social groups.

Interest groups in Germany operate differently than in the United States and Britain. In Germany, interest groups have a societal responsibility beyond representing the immediate interests of their members. Laws allow private interests to perform some public functions. Thus, interest groups are part of the fabric of society and are virtually permanent institutions. This makes it critical that they can adapt to new issues.

Despite the emphasis on negotiation and consensus, strikes and demonstrations do occur. In some cases, strikes and other conflicts act as mechanisms pressuring institutions to be responsive. Rather than being detrimental to democratic participation, such bottom-up protests contribute to a vibrant civil society.

In the best case, because they aggregate the interests of all their members, groups take a broader view of problems and solutions. The state neither remains distant, as in Britain and the United States, nor intervenes in the intensive fashion typical of France and Japan. Political scientist Peter Katzenstein observes that in Germany, the state is not an actor that "imposes its will on civil society," but rather a series of "relationships" mediated and solidified in semipublic institutions.[15] Katzenstein further notes that semipublic institutions have been assigned the role of "independent governance by the representatives of social sectors at the behest of or under the general supervision of the state."[16] In other words, organizations that would elsewhere be regarded as "mere interest groups" work with semipublic agencies to fill a critical role between state and society.

Many smaller groups fall outside this organized system, including political parties that fail to meet the 5 percent electoral threshold, such as the far-right NPD. The established party system also offered little to German voters angry at Eurozone bailouts. Founded by an economics professor in April 2013, the party Alternative for Germany (*Alternative für Deutschland*, AfD) won 4.7 percent of the vote in the federal election six months later. The AfD advocates Germany encouraging/pushing economically weak states to leave the euro.

Since the student mobilizations of the late 1960s, Germany has witnessed considerable protest and mobilization of social forces outside established channels. Among the most significant have been feminists, the peace movement, the antinuclear movement, and the church-linked protests in East Germany in 1989 that catalyzed the breakdown of the communist regime. Another catalyst was a 1988 Bruce Springsteen concert in East Berlin that shocked Communist Party officials by drawing so many people it overwhelmed the security staff. While not overtly political, Springsteen did open the show with "Badlands" and mused about a day when "barriers would be torn down." A year later, it was.[17]

When right-wing violence in West German cities claimed the lives of three Turks (including two children) in a house bombing in 1992 and five more in an arson fire in 1993, hundreds of thousands of Germans marched to show their sympathy for the victims.

Though Germany currently has no strong far-right parties, right-wing violence remains a problem. The Ministry of the Interior documented sixty killings by

About a year before the wall came down, 300,000 East Germans (about 200,000 without tickets) jammed into a park in East Berlin to hear a free Springsteen concert. For many, it was their first experience seeing East German security forces back off from a crowd of citizens.

ullstein bild/The Granger Collection, NYC

right-wing extremists from 1990–2001, with an additional 746 open cases of murder or attempted murder suspected to have right-wing involvement. The Ministry reported 17,134 right-wing motivated crimes in 2012 (a thousand more than in 2011), of which 802 incidents were violent.

The Iraq war issue produced an increase in social protest beginning in 2003, largely among forces to the left of the governing SPD-Green coalition. There have also been smaller right-wing protests against continued immigration, such as a May Day Hamburg riot in 2008, but these have not approached the violent episodes of the 1990s. Only the Left Party actively opposed German troop deployments to Afghanistan (fifty-four German soldiers have been killed since being deployed there since 2002). Most protests on this issue have been limited to hundreds rather than thousands of demonstrators.

The Political Impact of Technology

German politicians use Twitter, Facebook, texting, and blogging to reach out to voters in an attempt to emulate Obama's online campaigns, which used such tools to target swing voters. Such tactics are very difficult in Germany, however, because German law dictates that parties can only collect voter data with their consent. Unlike parties in the United States, Germany parties cannot combine consumer data with political information. They also do not have as much money as American parties and cannot afford vast data-collecting operations.[18]

THE U.S. CONNECTION

Comparing Anti-Nuclear Movements in the United States and Germany

Ever since a tsunami destroyed Japan's Fukushima nuclear plant, concerns about nuclear safety have increased in the United States and Germany. Both nuclear industries share some important features. Their relative size is roughly equal. The United States gets about 19 percent of its electricity from nuclear power, and Germany's nine remaining plants account for about 15 percent of its electricity. (France's fifty-eight plants produce 75 percent of its electricity). Both states debate whether to extend the life of existing plants and generally oppose building new plants. Both governments play a critical role in licensing and inspecting plants, subsidizing R&D, and insuring against risks. In both, private companies produce nuclear power, and the government is responsible for dealing with waste.

Both states also have selected a waste storage site that has never opened because of political opposition. In the United States, it involves tunnels bored into Yucca Mountain in the Nevada desert. In Germany, the potential dump is 1000 meters below the surface of a north German salt dome called Gorleben. Finally, in both countries an iconic nuclear accident (Three Mile Island in Pennsylvania in 1979 and Chernobyl in Ukraine in 1986) helped end construction of new nuclear plants. Yet alongside these similarities, there are striking differences in how the antinuclear movements work in both countries. The German antinuclear movement, which began in the early 1970s, has often been radical, even violent at times. It built on a cultural foundation of ecological activism, and, by forming the Green Party, it eventually "broke through" an electoral system that requires coalition government and has more space for small parties than in the United States.

In the United States, however, the antinuclear movement split, with neither faction resembling its German counterpart. One wing of the U.S. movement has focused on legal tactics, essentially challenging the nuclear industry (and often the government) in court. The other wing has been confrontational, but nonviolent.* Moreover, because Germans take global warming seriously, the antinuclear movement strongly supports policies involving alternative energies. In the United States, this is less true.

In Germany, the movement has been highly confrontational. Nuclear waste trains have been disrupted by protestors shooting fireworks and boarding the trains. The Japanese nuclear disaster only deepened scepticism, and Merkel's government eventually decided to phase out all German nuclear plants by 2022.

MAKING CONNECTIONS How do differences in the German and American electoral systems help account for differences in antinuclear movements?

*Christian Joppke, *Mobilizing Against Nuclear Energy: A Comparison of Germany and the United States* (Berkeley: University of California, 1993).

Certain aspects of the Obama campaign were copied: the SPD created a *mitmachen* ("participate!") website, where volunteers signed up to campaign door-to-door. As with electoral ads on television, however, most Germans are unnerved by the thoughts of campaigners visiting their homes. Parties tread very carefully, lest they turn off voters by too much intrusion.

During the sole televised electoral debate (viewed by 18 million people) between Merkel and SPD challenger Peer Steinbrück, more people tweeted about Merkel's red, black, and yellow necklace than about either candidate's arguments. Before the debate ended, a mock Twitter account for the necklace (*@schlandkette*, slang for "Germany necklace") had more than 6,000 followers.

Where Do You Stand?

Can Germans legitimately claim to support human rights yet still sell weapons to repressive governments?

Can citizen use of social media improve political decisions? Increase our enjoyment of politics?

SECTION 5

GERMAN POLITICS IN TRANSITION

▼ Focus Questions

- Does the European Union require Germany to be especially generous in order for the EU to function properly?

- How durable is the German economic model in the face of new regional and global competitors?

In June 2009, EU officials breathed an enormous sigh of relief as the German Constitutional Court gave its blessing to the Treaty of Lisbon, which reformed the EU's major institutions to attempt to improve the quality of decision making. Five years earlier, the EU member states had attempted another, more thorough-going treaty reform. Both French and Dutch voters had decisively rejected this so-called Constitutional Treaty. In the aftermath, Angela Merkel placed high priority on devising a new treaty that could succeed politically where the Constitutional Treaty had failed. Eventually, the Lisbon Treaty was negotiated and signed by all EU member states. But the day that it was ratified by the Bundestag, a CSU Bundestag member, acting in cooperation with the Left Party, challenged the Treaty in the Constitutional Court for harming parliamentary democracy and national sovereignty. If the Court had overturned German ratification, the treaty would be dead. Instead, the Court's decision was mixed. On the one hand, it found that Lisbon was acceptable because the EU's member states would remain in control of the EU. In other words, the Court did not see a federal "United States of Europe" emerging from the treaty—and the Court warned that such a federal state would violate the German Basic Law. On the other hand, the Court stated there were some policy areas where Germany could delegate no further powers to the EU since this would undermine national democratic and parliamentary control.

Since the 1950s, Germany has depended on European integration to solve many problems, from its inability to run an independent foreign policy to its need for foreign consumers to buy its huge export surpluses. To gain approval for these deals, the Germans generally made side payments to other states. But Germany's capacity and its will to do this have both waned. In addition to previously mentioned changes in mass and elite opinion, Germany is in debt, having gone from 20 percent of GDP to over 80 percent today (the EU limit is 60 percent).

Political Challenges and Changing Agendas

The future of German politics depends on how the country addresses the four themes identified at the outset: the globalizing world of states, governing the economy, the democratic idea, and the politics of collective identity. Germany long enjoyed a spiral of success that enabled it to confront these issues with confidence and resolve during the post–World War II period. For example, problems of collective identities were handled in a much less exclusionary way as women, nonnative ethnic groups, and newer political parties and movements contributed to a healthy diversity in German politics. Democratic institutions balanced participation and dissent, offsetting the country's turbulent and often racist past by fifty years of stable multiparty democracy. Germany's economic success has been significant and unique. Germany has confidently, and with the support of its neighbors and allies, taken a leading role in European integration.

Beginning with the globalizing world of states, Germany is now firmly anchored in western Europe but also has been uniquely positioned to shape the transition of the former communist central and eastern European states toward economic and political modernization and EU membership. After the collapse of communism, there were fears that German investors would "reconquer" eastern Europe. For a time, these states resisted German investment. But Germany emerged as a forceful advocate of both EU and NATO enlargement, and the postcommunist states also recognized that they desired both German investments and consumer goods. Today, Germany has generally friendly and mutually beneficial relations with the countries of the region. At the same time, most German politicians stress that their state is a "normal" state that should not be shamed into doing things because of its fascist past.

Germany's approach to governing the economy also faces challenges in the early twenty-first century. For many years, the German economy was characterized as "high everything," in that it combined high-quality manufacturing with high wages, high fringe benefits, high worker participation, and high levels of vacation time. Critics insisted that such a system could not last in a competitive world economy. Nevertheless, the German economy has remained among the world's leaders. But the huge costs of unification, globalization, and the fiscal crisis in Europe all challenge the German model anew.

Democracy appears well established after over sixty years of the Federal Republic. It features high (if declining) voter turnout and a healthy civic culture. Many observers believe that broad-based participation is part of the fabric of German political life. Yet the much more complex business of forming effective coalitions noted above is a big challenge, as is the assimilation of the five eastern states. Can eastern Germans who have lost jobs accept that ethnic minorities are not the main cause of their unemployment? Can tolerance and understanding offset a right-wing fringe that preaches hatred and blames scapegoats for the costs of unification? There is reason for optimism. On balance, eastern Germans have shown that they understand and practice democracy amazingly well.

In the area of collective identities, Germany faces many unresolved challenges. Turkish and other non-German guest workers remain essential to Germany's economy. Their long-term acceptance by the CDU/CSU, not to mention the smaller ultra-right parties, will likely be the key to a fundamental change in the concept of who is a German. More than two generations after the end of World War II, young Germans are asking what being German actually means. Changes in citizenship laws will complicate this issue, for although this search for identity can be healthy, and immigrants can help enrich and renew the meaning of German identity, these changes can encourage extremist groups to preach exaggerated nationalism and hatred of foreigners and minorities. By contrast, religious divides seem manageable: 35 percent of Germans are Catholic and 33 percent Protestant, with about 33 percent unaffiliated or other. Only about 4 percent of the population is Muslim. More difficult was the early-1990s influx of refugees and asylum seekers, which placed great strains on German taxpayers and increased ethnic tensions.

Is European Integration Stalled?

While European integration in the post–World War II period could usually rely on German support and even generosity, this is no longer the case. Germany has become far more ambivalent about European integration at the same time that the EU clearly needs further reform. German elites also were long free to make deals at the European level with almost no scrutiny from voters. This also is no longer true. To be sure, Germans have the highest percentage among Europeans of favorable views of the EU, according to a 2013 Pew poll (68 percent), but only about 44 percent feel the euro is a "good thing."

Euro-skepticism is also clearly evident in the political landscape. Even the CDU, the party intimately identified with Europe, has ceased to see further European integration as positive. Although most CDU supporters also do not want less integration, not all Germans feel this way. AfD voters don't want Germany to leave the EU, but they do want weaker states out of the Eurozone. East Germans are far more skeptical about the EU than West Germans, and perceive little benefit from membership. Further, given the enlargement of the EU to twenty-eight members, it becomes harder for the German-French tandem to shape EU integration as they did for so long.

Youth Politics and the Generational Divide

Germany's generation gap has two dimensions. First, many young people hold so-called postmaterialist values and focus more on lifestyle concerns—including ecology and personal freedom—than on bread-and-butter economic issues. Such people, however, have not been able to challenge the political dominance of the skilled working and middle class. Youth unemployment is around 8 percent, higher than adult unemployment but far below the European average of 23 percent. Still, many young Germans suspect they will not get all the benefits their parents' generation enjoyed.

The second aspect of the generation gap involves pensioners and older workers. The German birthrate fell markedly in the last decade of the twentieth century, particularly in the former GDR but also in the West. This placed great demographic pressure on the German welfare state because the low birthrate and increasing age of the baby boom generation meant that fewer younger workers now contribute to the welfare and retirement benefits of an increasing elderly population. (See cartoon on page 152.) Managers worry about worker shortages, and some have called for more immigration to fill the gap.

To encourage more children, former Family Minister Ursula von der Leyen (herself a physician and mother of seven) instituted policies making it easier for both mothers and fathers to take paid time off for the birth of a child. The ministry also increased federal daycare funding. Though more women now work, no increases in childbirths occurred. The German female fertility rate remains about 1.4 births per woman and is well below the 2.1 rate at which a population remains stable.

German Politics in Comparative Perspective

Germany offers important insights for comparative politics. First, it shows that an authoritarian past can be put to rest. Germany's impressive democratic experience during the first sixty years of the Federal Republic has clearly exorcised the ghosts of the Third Reich. Yet some critical questions remain open for now. To what extent do the educational system, civil service, and the media bear some responsibility for the rise of right-wing violence? Have educational reforms since the 1960s provided a spirit of critical discourse in the broad mainstream of society that can withstand far-right rhetoric if it increases further? Can judges effectively punish those who abuse ethnic minorities' civil rights? Will the news media continue to express a wide range of opinion and contribute to a healthy civic discourse? Or will strident, tabloid-style journalism stifle the reasoned debate that any democracy must have to survive and flourish?

Second, Germany's historical development illustrates how being late to achieve political unity and late to industrialize can have negative consequences. These two factors, combined with an unfavorable institutional mix, eventually helped produce a catastrophic first half of the twentieth century for Germany and much of the world. Yet the country's subsequent transition to a successful economy with a solid democracy can provide more positive lessons for other countries.

Third, Germany offers a distinctive model for combining state and market. Germany's social market economy blurs the distinction between the public and private sectors. The German state pursues development plans based on its cooperative interaction with a dense network of key social and economic participants, particularly in such areas as climate change or energy policy. This approach is neither as free market as in the United States nor as statist as in France or Japan. To succeed, it requires both a state with a light touch and an organized and self-confident society.

Fourth, while immigration politics are emotional and deeply rooted, Germany reminds us that countries can make fundamental changes here as well. For decades, German policy essentially said, in the words of a popular CDU slogan, "Germany is not an immigration country." But the Schröder government modified Germany's immigration policies to provide a path for long-time foreign workers to gain citizenship. Again, open questions persist. Can remaining ethnic tensions be resolved in a way that enhances democracy?

Finally, Germany shows us that middle-ranked powers can wield lots of clout, especially if they can emerge as regional leaders with attractive policies. For example, Germany has played an important role in debates over climate change, where its approach has broad support in the EU. In areas like energy policy, however, Germany tends to make its own deals with countries like Russia and thus has less clout in Europe.

Germany is facing intense pressures from within its borders, notably conflict among ethnic groups, and from a complex mix of external influences. Its role as both a major western and an eastern European power puts it in a unique position. What an ironic but inspiring twist if Germany, the country whose virulent nationalism caused the most widespread destruction and destabilization in the twentieth century, took the lead at the head of the supranational EU in promoting democracy, creativity, and stability in the twenty-first century.

Where Do You Stand?

Do you consider low birthrates a "problem" to be fixed? If so, how?

Or should Germans accept that their population will decline?

Chapter Summary

Germany's past never fully goes away, but measuring today's Germany exclusively by its past is a big mistake. Germany's turbulent history presented postwar policy-makers with two daunting challenges: the too-strong state and the too-weak one. On the one hand, policy-makers had to avoid re-creating a state that could destroy the freedom or indeed the very lives of those the regime saw as its opponents. On the other hand, policy-makers needed to avoid re-creating a state so fragmented and

weak it could not tackle Germany's problems. There is no doubt that these policy-makers handsomely succeeded in both these tasks. Germany is peaceful, democratic, and rich.

In the meantime, plenty of new challenges have arisen. From the ruins of World War II, Germany has built one of the world's strongest economies. With only 80 million people, Germany sometimes exports more goods than the 316 million Americans or 1.2 billion Chinese. Yet when trade declines, so do German standards of living. This means globalization can be a rollercoaster for a medium-sized economy like Germany's. Germany responds with a social market economy that differs from free market economies like the United States and statist economies like France. Government regulation establishes general framework regulations rather than detailed standards. A key role of the state is to force firms to compete. The government sets broad licensing and performance standards for most professions and industries. Once core state requirements are announced, the government trusts that private actors will respect those broad parameters (and checks to be sure they do). In contrast, the U.S. government often produces many layers of detailed—and sometimes contradictory—regulations in the wake of economic crises, banking failures, and financial abuses.

Germany's indirect approach to regulation is bolstered by the active engagement of unions and employers, in cooperation with state and municipal policy-makers. Semipublic institutions provide a forum in which these social partners help shape the German economy. At the same time, Germany is challenged to provide regional and global leadership on a wide range of issues, from the rescue of financially stressed European governments to global warming.

Germany's political system still struggles to generate effective policy. Its version of federalism has led to ferocious battles between the center and the states, while the EU has complicated policy-making at both national and subnational levels. Meanwhile, the Constitutional Court has made it difficult to delegate more power to the EU level. Germany's fragmenting party system has now generated at least six parties represented at the state or federal level with one more (AfD) on the cusp of such status. When more than one coalition may be mathematically and politically possible, parties will be more inclined to horse trade, a fact that is sure to turn off voters and cause their further alienation from parties. Moreover, German Grand Coalitions—such as the one that emerged in 2013—are notorious for boosting in the next round the electoral fortunes of the smaller parties who are left out.

Meanwhile, problems are not getting any simpler to solve. Like all European states, the German state and society must address immigration—in all its positive and negative complexity. It must do so, however, with relatively little experience in treating foreigners as potential citizens. The economic crisis, environmental and energy issues, and increasingly fierce tussles over the role of the EU all crowd the agenda in ways that parties seem increasingly unable to manage. The major advantage Germans have may lie in the remarkable capacity of German society to contribute to joint problem solving. This legacy of the earlier historical periods will be a critical asset as Germany faces the challenges ahead.

Key Terms

5 percent clause
absolute veto
austerity policies
Basic Law
Blitzkrieg
chancellor
citizen action groups
civil servants
co-determination
constructive vote of no
    confidence

democratic corporatism
Energiewende
Eurozone
federal state
framework regulations
Gastarbeiter
grassroots democracy
health insurance funds
heavy industries
Junkers
Kulturkampf

liberal
mixed member system
Nazi
Ostpolitik
party democracy
procedural democracy
social market economy
suspensive veto
Weimar Republic
works councils

Suggested Readings

Deeg, Richard. *Finance Capital Unveiled: Banks and Economic Adjustment in Germany.* Ann Arbor: University of Michigan Press, 1998.

Herrigel, Gary. *Manufacturing Possibilities: Creative Action and Industrial Recomposition in the U.S., Germany, and Japan.* Oxford: Oxford University Press, 2010.

Jacoby, Wade. *Imitation and Politics: Redesigning Modern Germany.* Ithaca, NY: Cornell University Press, 2001.

Katzenstein, Peter, *Tamed Power: Germany in Europe.* Ithaca, NY: Cornell University Press, 1997.

Kirschbaum, Erik. *Rocking the Wall: Bruce Springsteen: The Untold Story of a Concert in East Berlin That Changed the World*. New York: Berlinica, 2013.

Thelen, Kathleen. Varieties of Liberalism and the New Politics of Social Solidarity. New York: Cambridge University Press, 2014.

Röpke, Wilhelm. "The Guiding Principle of the Liberal Programme." In H. F. Wünche, ed., *Standard Texts on the Social Market Economy*. New York: Gustav Fischer Verlag, 1982.

Snyder, Timothy. *Bloodlands: Europe Between Hitler and Stalin*. New York: Basic Books, 2012.

Streeck, Wolfgang. *Re-Forming Capitalism: Institutional Change in the German Political Economy*. Oxford: Oxford University Press, 2009.

Suggested Websites

American Institute for Contemporary German Studies
www.aicgs.org/

Der Spiegel (in English)
http://www.spiegel.de/international/

Deutsche Welle (in English)
http://www.dw.de/

German Embassy, German Information Center
http://www.germany.info/gic/

German Institute for International and Security Affairs (SWP)
http://www.swp-berlin.org/en/

German Politics
http://www.tandf.co.uk/journals/fgrp

German Politics and Society
http://journals.berghahnbooks.com/gps/

German Studies Web
http://wess.lib.byu.edu/index.php/German _Studies_Web

Max Planck Institute for the Study of Societies, Cologne
http://www.mpi-fg-koeln.mpg.de/index_en.asp

WZB, Social Science Research Center, Berlin
www.wz-berlin.de/default.en.asp

5 European Union

George Ross

Official Name: European Union

Location: Comprised of twenty-eight countries in Western and Eastern Europe

Capital City: Brussels (Belgium)

Population (2014): 505 million

Size: 4,234,782 sq. km; less than one-half the size of the United States

THE MAKING OF THE EUROPEAN UNION

Politics in Action

Focus Questions ❓

• Why would the economic problems of the 1970s cause a retreat into "Eurosclerosis"?

• How did the end of the Cold War affect prospects for European integration?

On May 9, 1950, French Foreign Minister Robert Schuman proposed that France and Germany, plus any other democratic nation in Western Europe that wanted to join, should establish a transnational "community" to govern the coal and steel industries. France and Germany had been at war, or preparing for war, for most of the twentieth century, at huge cost. Schuman's announcement spoke to deeper issues:

> World peace cannot be safeguarded without creative efforts.... The contribution that an organized and vital Europe can bring to civilization is indispensable to the maintenance of peaceful relations.... Europe will not be made all at once, nor ... in a single holistic construction: it will be built by concrete achievements that will create solidarity in facts. To assemble European nations first demands that opposition between France and Germany be eliminated.... (first paragraph of the Schuman declaration, of May 9, 1950)

Robert Schuman came from Lorraine, a battleground area between France and Germany. Konrad Adenauer, first chancellor of the German Federal Republic and eager participant in the new European Coal and Steel Community (ECSC), had been mayor of Cologne before Hitler put him into Buchenwald prison. The primary author of the "Schuman plan" was Jean Monnet, a brilliant networker and technocrat who then headed France's economic planning commission. Leaders in the other ECSC countries were also veterans of war-making determined to change Europe.

Sixty-five years later, after huge efforts the European Union, direct descendant of the ECSC, has become something that its creators could never have imagined. There were six original ECSC members. Now there are twenty-eight EU members, over 500 million citizens, and the world's largest open market. The EU was built in peace, around democracy, and with respect for the rule of law.

Critical Junctures

European integration is a unique construction built by European states seeking peace. It quickly took on economic forms and expanded into other areas of its members' sovereignty but without weakening their national identities. This "new" Europe has grown in response to changing international conditions, rarely resting and always innovating, often in ways that outsiders have had difficulty understanding.

Integration emerged after World War II, a cataclysmic event in which tens of millions of Europeans perished. The war had broken the appeal of antidemocratic regimes that had earlier come to power and brought democratic ideals and sweeping social reforms. At this point the United States, the United Kingdom, France, and the Union of Soviet Socialist Republics (USSR) jointly occupied Germany and were

CHRONOLOGY of European Integration

1950
Schuman Plan for European Coal and Steel Community includes France, Germany, Italy, Belgium, the Netherlands, and Luxembourg.

1957
"Original six" agree to Rome Treaty creating European Economic Community.

1971 and after
EEC economic difficulties after United States ends Bretton Woods exchange rate regime; oil shocks.

1989
Fall of Berlin Wall, leading to German unification and end of Cold War

1965
Treaty unites ECSC, EEC, and Euratom in "European Communities."

1973
Enlargement to United Kingdom, Ireland, Denmark

1981
Greece joins EC.

1950 **1965** **1970** **1975** **1980** **1985** **1990**

1945–1948
Europe devastated; Cold War and Marshall Plan

1965
French precipitate "empty chair crisis," leads to "Luxembourg compromise."

1979
European Monetary System (EMS) begins; direct elections to the European Parliament

1986
Spain and Portugal join.

1985
Commission White Paper on Completing the Single Market, Single European Act

1961
French President de Gaulle vetoes British EEC application.

1975
European Council founded (summits of state and government heads)

determined to prevent anything like Nazism from recurring. The war left Europe economically devastated, however, without money to rebuild.

The Union of Soviet Socialist Republics and the United States, wartime allies, became enemies after 1945, leading to the Cold War and communist-dominated "Peoples' Republics" in eastern Europe. In the west, national efforts plus Marshall Plan help from the United States jump-started reconstruction. Overwhelming American military power made war between Western European countries inconceivable, and the North Atlantic Treaty Organization (NATO) provided territorial defense under American hegemony. Economic integration was paramount to removing the threat of war, however. If different national markets could be tied together, economic interests might in time acquire stakes in peaceful resolution of differences. This was the process begun by the European Coal and Steel Community (ECSC). The ECSC established a centrally regulated market of the coal and steel industries of six Western European countries, the traditional enemies, Germany and France, plus Italy, Belgium, the Netherlands, and Luxembourg, around a common European authority.

The six ECSC countries became more committed to European integration than anyone anticipated and in 1957 signed the Treaty of Rome creating a European Economic Community (EEC, or "Common Market") to abolish economic borders between them. The EEC started precisely when postwar economic reconstruction opened a period of prosperity. It supplemented national economies by creating a customs-free area between them, allowing national manufacturing firms to export more, plus a Common Agricultural Policy (CAP) to stimulate agricultural modernization. The EEC's external tariff imposed uniform duties on goods imported into the common market, sheltering EEC members from the international market and, in

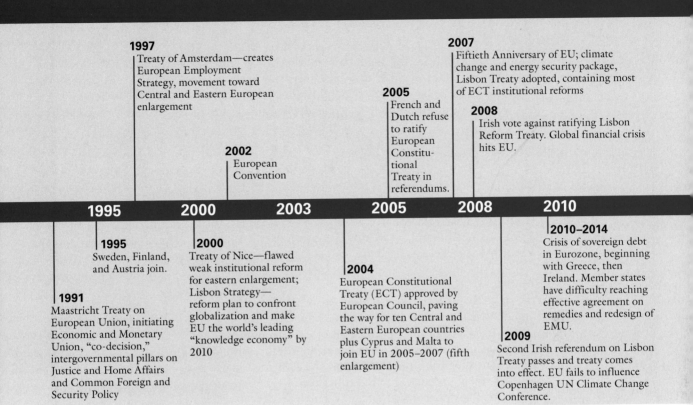

1997
Treaty of Amsterdam—creates European Employment Strategy, movement toward Central and Eastern European enlargement

2007
Fiftieth Anniversary of EU; climate change and energy security package, Lisbon Treaty adopted, containing most of ECT institutional reforms

2005
French and Dutch refuse to ratify European Constitutional Treaty in referendums.

2008
Irish vote against ratifying Lisbon Reform Treaty. Global financial crisis hits EU.

2002
European Convention

| 1995 | 2000 | 2003 | 2005 | 2008 | 2010 |

1995
Sweden, Finland, and Austria join.

2000
Treaty of Nice—flawed weak institutional reform for eastern enlargement; Lisbon Strategy—reform plan to confront globalization and make EU the world's leading "knowledge economy" by 2010

2010–2014
Crisis of sovereign debt in Eurozone, beginning with Greece, then Ireland. Member states have difficulty reaching effective agreement on remedies and redesign of EMU.

1991
Maastricht Treaty on European Union, initiating Economic and Monetary Union, "co-decision," intergovernmental pillars on Justice and Home Affairs and Common Foreign and Security Policy

2004
European Constitutional Treaty (ECT) approved by European Council, paving the way for ten Central and Eastern European countries plus Cyprus and Malta to join EU in 2005–2007 (fifth enlargement)

2009
Second Irish referendum on Lisbon Treaty passes and treaty comes into effect. EU fails to influence Copenhagen UN Climate Change Conference.

particular, from some of the economic power of the United States. Mass production, consumerism, and full employment followed, and EEC states redistributed some of their economic growth through national social programs for health care, housing, pensions, and education that were backed by social groups that had long been politically excluded. These EEC "postwar settlements" founded enduring representative democracy in much of Western Europe.

International economic turmoil in the 1970s ended this happy situation. EEC members—nine after the United Kingdom, Denmark, and Ireland joined in 1973—then faced home-grown inflation, oil shocks, and "stagflation," a combination of high inflation and low growth. They made things worse by their different national policies that endangered the EEC customs-free area and added to the exchange-rate fluctuations that followed the American ending of its Bretton Woods commitments to back the dollar by gold. Growth disappeared, Europe lost competitiveness, and unemployment returned. In an era characterized by "Eurosclerosis," an inability to move forward because of disagreements among member states brought European integration to a halt and endangered the Common Market. For a brief period after 1985 the EEC found new energy after member states agreed to "complete the single market" and create a Europe-wide "space without borders." The period culminated in the Treaty on European Union (TEU, ratified in 1993) when the EEC became the EU and its members agreed to form an **Economic and Monetary Union** (EMU, a Europe-wide monetary policy and single currency), build a **Common Foreign and Security Policy** (CFSP), and begin cooperation in **Justice and Home Affairs** (JHA) to facilitate free movement of people within EU borders. These large new commitments also brought institutional changes, in particular increased powers for the European Parliament.

Economic and Monetary Union

The 1991 Maastricht Treaty federalized EU monetary policy, created a European Central Bank and founded the Eurozone and its single currency, the euro.

Common Foreign and Security Policy (CFSP)

Commitment in the Maastricht Treaty for deeper cooperation in international affairs and defense.

Justice and Home Affairs (JHA)

Engagements to make legal and regulatory changes to allow free movement of EU citizens throughout the EU.

The post-Maastricht EU saw international conditions change dramatically again. Globalization came rapidly, fueled in part by new technologies that shrunk the manufacturing jobs that had been the key to earlier prosperity. European industrial production began migrating to lower labor cost areas elsewhere. The United States was already way ahead of the EEC in creating a new "knowledge economy."

The end of the Cold War posed new daunting challenges. After 1989, the EU had to rethink its security positions, beginning unhappily by its clumsy response to brutal warfare in the Balkans. Deciding what to do with the formerly communist countries of Central and Eastern Europe (CEECs) was another puzzle. Beginning in 1989 the EU sent aid, negotiated freer trade, and encouraged countries to apply for EU membership, but it was not until the later 1990s that it undertook the process of incorporating the CEECs, encouraging new democracy, organizing economic interdependencies, and transferring resources to help foster modernization. The prospect of enlargement also forced the EU to think seriously about remodeling its institutions.

Facing such challenges, Europeans turned inward. The EU was becoming more intrusive, eastern enlargement was confusing, and many Europeans felt they had not been adequately consulted and that there was an EU "democratic deficit." The Union then embarked on a decade-long effort to rebuild EU institutions to cope with newcomers, a process that proved difficult and painful. A first effort, the 2001 Nice Treaty, produced tensions between larger and smaller countries. Leaders then decided to sponsor wide-ranging public debate in a "European Convention" that in 2004 produced an ambitious "European Constitutional Treaty." When the new treaty was sent out for ratification, however, it was rejected in 2005 referendums by both the French and the Dutch. It took several years more before leaders hammered out an amended proposal that led to the 2009 **Lisbon Treaty**. The institutional changes that the new treaty initiated were put immediately to the test by the global financial collapse in 2007–2008, which threatened several Eurozone countries with national bankruptcy, beginning with Greece in 2009–2010. The EU then entered a deep crisis mode.

Themes and Comparisons

EU politics obliges EU member states to accept shrinking national sovereignty, making the EU the most significant modern workshop at transcending a world of independent states. Europe's states, earlier producers of world wars, learned to produce peace, economic success, and high levels of cooperation while maintaining their identities in a context of cultural diversity. The principal implications of the EU for comparative politics lie here. We are accustomed to thinking about a world of sovereign states interacting and competing with one another. By its very successes the EU transcends traditional assumptions of comparative politics, because it is based on cooperative decision making among governments. Its founders recognized that intergovernmental cooperation needed new institutions. The EU was endowed with a Commission with exclusive powers to propose legislation and a Court that could build a body of binding European-level law. Then came a directly elected **European Parliament** that "co-decided" proposed legislation as the representative of European peoples alongside the Council of Ministers that represented national governments. More recently, the institutional structure has

Lisbon Treaty

After a decade of efforts to redesign EU institutions in light of enlargement to Central and Eastern Europe, the treaty created new positions of the President of the European Council and High Representative for foreign and security policy and increased the powers of the European Council and European Parliament.

European Parliament

The Parliament of the European Union, which meets in Strasbourg and Brussels, "co-decides" EU law with the Council of Ministers, but it cannot initiate legislation.

been supplemented by the **European Council**, a regular summit of member state leaders that provides general strategy. The product is a political system that bears little resemblance to anything we know at a national level, an "unidentified flying political object."

Because the EU is not a state, and because of its unique institutions, understanding its role and function in a world of states is not easy. The EU mediates among national states primarily in economic governance. But it also mediates between its members and the broader globalized world in some areas. In foreign policy, EU members agree that some questions are to be handled by the EU and others remain national. Members that were great powers such as Britain and France insist on the capacity to act independently. On international trade, however, the EU Commission negotiates everything of significance, making the EU a significant global power in global trade. The EU has assumed its largest roles in market-building and regulating, in breaking down economic barriers, including the free circulation of people, legislating and enforcing rules to build a "single" market, and then setting up the Economic and Monetary Union (EMU). Once rules are legislated, the Commission monitors and enforces compliance. The politically independent European Central Bank (ECB) takes responsibility for EMU monetary policy. The EU has little power over national social spending (pensions, education, health care), the largest component of national budgets.

In the immediate postwar period European integration consolidated democracy and the rule of law in western European countries whose democratic pasts had been fragile. As the EEC enlarged in the 1980s, welcoming formerly authoritarian southern European countries (Spain, Greece, and Portugal), it insisted that they undertake reforms to demonstrate their democratic commitments. A decade later, when the time came to welcome the formerly communist countries of central and eastern Europe, the EU stipulated that candidate countries had to prove commitments to democracy, possess an effective judiciary dedicated to the rule of law, and establish a competitive modern market economy. Aspirants for EU membership had always been obliged to accept and adopt all of the norms, laws, and procedures of the European "club" they wanted to join, but the "Fifth enlargement" to the east refined this process by developing direct apprenticeships in democratic practices. Finally, as the contemporary EU began to reach beyond its own borders as an international actor in trade promotion, humanitarian aid and peace-keeping, environmental policy, and classical foreign policy, it presented itself as a "normative Europe" spreading its democratic DNA abroad.

The EU's politics of collective identity are works in progress. The EU has always made efforts to *combine* existing national identities with growing European identity. Since the 1993 Maastricht Treaty these efforts have institutionalized coexistence between national and European citizenships, each with specific rights and duties. There has been endless discussion about what being "European" means, however, and the larger the EU, the more the disagreement.

The EU has indeed been a massive force for peace on the European continent, but now that lasting European peace has been achieved, citizens take it for granted. There is an EU flag, anthem, passport and many EU programs designed to build European identity. To choose but one, the Erasmus program has subsidized millions of European students to study outside their own countries as a way of promoting their educational progress and deepening "European-ness." In the economic realm, as businesses and workers have participated in the EU's huge internal market, they became more "European." But becoming French, British, German, and so forth were historical projects that took centuries. We cannot expect ordinary Europeans to

European Council

The European Council is a regular summit meeting of heads of state and government, under an appointed president, to find grand strategies for resolving EU problems and delineating paths into the future.

embrace dual identities, one old, national, and familiar, and one new, European, and unclear, with ease or rapidly.

The EU has played an enormous rule in making Europe fully democratic and has united the European continent, both historic firsts. Yet, as Jacques Delors, president of the European Commission from 1985–1995 often observed, "people do not fall in love with a single market." The EU is difficult for ordinary Europeans to understand, steeped as they are in their native lands, particularly since the EU's policy backbone has been in matters of economic governance that are often difficult to penetrate. In addition, the EU has often been a convenient scapegoat for national politicians to blame for policies that national citizens do not like. Its moments of popular success have come when its policies have been experienced by citizens as providing real benefits. Depending on the popularity of policy outputs is precarious, however, because European public policies, like national ones, are often redistributive, satisfying some but upsetting others. Convincing citizens that European integration brings broad public benefits is a hard job, therefore, even if it may be the key to the EU's futures.

Where Do You Stand?

Being part of a fervent national community is a fundamental part of a person's identity. Is it dangerous to tamper with this, as the EU has done?

Should the EU become a state? What kind of a state?

SECTION 2
POLITICS AND ECONOMICS IN THE DEVELOPMENT OF THE EUROPEAN UNION

Focus Questions

- What have been the relative weights of international and European-domestic factors in the development of the EU?

- How would you assess the changing balance between "supranational" and member state institutions in EU history?

State and Economy: EU Economic Governance

A combination of international politics, national and local issues, and political creativity launched European integration, but economics quickly became the heart of things. Integration began as an ingenious plan to integrate coal and steel sectors in six continental western European countries under Cold War pressure. The movement for integration proved powerful enough to create the EEC "common market" in industrial and agricultural goods. Delegating sovereignty raised large issues, however, such as deciding what to delegate and how to administer what had been delegated.

Starting in the Cold War

The United States and the United Kingdom, concerned with rebuilding international trade after World War II, designed the Bretton Woods system. The United States committed to support the dollar with gold, there would be a World Bank to help fund postwar rebuilding, an International Monetary Fund (IMF) to stabilize international trading, and the General Agreement on Tariffs and Trade (GATT) to promote freer trade. Before a war-devastated, penniless Europe could trade, however, it had to rebuild. The Americans, worried about European political stability, responded with the Marshall Plan (1947) that provided billions of dollars to reconstruct European economies, coinciding with the outbreak of Cold War. In its central and eastern European sphere of influence, the USSR established "popular democracies" backed by Soviet troops. With Paris only a few hundred miles from a million Soviet troops and the political power of communists in some Western European countries, Americans feared that a Soviet westward offensive would be difficult to stop. Cold War rearmament indirectly spurred European integration. The United States pressed Western European nations to rearm through NATO, which would provide American-led western European territorial defense. It then decided to rehabilitate, rather than punish, postwar Germany, leading in 1949 to a new German Federal Republic (FRG). The Americans then insisted that this new FRG be rearmed.

Europeans knew that they needed to cease periodic bloodbaths, perhaps by integration. But what should European integration be? Federalists wanted a United States of Europe. "Intergovernmentalists" pressed for a method in which national states would retain power and make decisions. Their debates led to the Council of Europe, a human rights organization, but not to integration. Europe's immediate problem was to end chronic conflict between France and Germany. The French, overrun by the Germans three times in seventy-five years, initially wanted to fragment post–Nazi Germany and neutralize its heavy industrial power, goals that stood in the way of American insistence on rehabilitating Germany. The French leader closest to the German problem was Jean Monnet, who faced American pressure for a less punitive French policy on Germany. Monnet proposed integrating the French and German coal and steel industries in a European Coal and Steel Community, an idea that quickly became the "Schuman plan," when it was taken up by Robert Schuman, French foreign minister. The "original six," France, Germany, Luxembourg, the Netherlands, Belgium, and Italy (the British refused to participate), signed the ECSC treaty in 1951 and the new Community began in July 1952.

Monnet thought that integration could best begin with practical solutions to practical problems, fitting with his idea that transnational integration of coal and steel could prevent the rebirth of nationalistic German heavy industry. Monnet also thought that the interdependence of modern economies might mean that economic cooperation in coal and steel could spread into new areas. France and Germany were willing to accept the ECSC because both knew that the United States would impose a less attractive plan. French public opinion, deeply hostile to Germany after the war, might accept the ECSC because it promised to neutralize German threats. German industrial interests needed larger markets to grow. The ECSC that resulted had an appointed high authority to propose rules and policies that a Council of Ministers would then vote up or down. It also had an appointed parliamentary-like assembly that had to be consulted, but had little power. Finally, a Court of Justice could review ECSC processes and decisions for their conformity with the ECSC treaty.

Despite the 1954 failure of a more ambitious Monnet proposal for a European Defense Community (EDC), the idea of European integration had staying power. In Messina, Italy, in 1955, the ECSC six committed to a European atomic energy agency, another Monnet idea, plus a European Common Market, brainchild of the

Dutch and Belgians. The Treaties of Rome in 1957 established Euratom and the European Economic Community (EEC). The French wanted Euratom but were less enthusiastic about the Common Market, while the Germans knew that a trade liberalizing Common Market would help their economy grow and give legitimacy to the new FRG. The French eventually accepted the EEC in exchange for a common agricultural policy. The United Kingdom, which had not joined the ECSC, once again stayed outside, betting on a parallel European Free Trade Area (EFTA) that would not share sovereignty.

At its core, the Common Market was a customs union removing internal trade barriers for industrial goods with ambitions to end "obstacles to freedom of movement for persons, services, and capital," a common external tariff, and unified trade policies toward third countries. The treaty's other objectives included common antitrust, agricultural, and transport policies. On Common Market matters, member states were to harmonize their legal systems. There were also provisions for a European Social Fund, a European Investment Bank to help less prosperous regions, and association arrangements that allowed access to the Common Market for overseas ex-colonies. In institutional terms, there was an appointed **European Commission**, sited in Brussels—a subdued copy of the ECSC's high authority—with exclusive power to propose laws and rules, implement policy, and safeguard the treaty. A Council of Ministers representing each national government and coordinated by a presidency rotating every six months, was the EEC "legislature" that decided on Commission proposals. There was also a European Parliament, appointed rather than elected, empowered to bring suits before the ECJ against other EEC institutions for "failure to act" on Treaty commitments and pose questions to which the Commission had to respond, but not much more. Finally, there was a **European Court of Justice** (ECJ) to adjudicate in those areas where the Rome Treaty gave EEC law precedence over national statutes.

The Commission's job was to carve space from member state sovereignty to build the Common Market, and some countries objected when it tried to do this. Because the Commission was appointed, critics attacked it as an unelected "Brussels bureaucracy." And because the Council of Ministers acted behind diplomatic secrecy, it was criticized for lack of transparency. The European Court of Justice was vulnerable to those who opposed "judge-made law." Behind this there was disagreement about what the new EEC should be, often from France. French President Charles de Gaulle twice vetoed British applications for membership (in 1963 and 1967) because the United Kingdom was not sufficiently "European" (meaning too close to the United States) and paralyzed the Council of Ministers in the 1965 "empty chair" crisis to block Commission power-grabbing and prevent the shift from unanimity to **qualified majority voting** (which would allow some member states to be outvoted) foreseen in the Rome EEC Treaty. When the Commission proposed a liberal Common Agricultural Policy (CAP) that threatened French and German agricultural subsidies, it was replaced by a French-inspired plan that was protectionist and subsidized farmers at the expense of consumers and taxpayers. Commission attempts to promote common transport, regional, and industrial policies came to little, despite the goals of the Rome Treaty. The young EEC survived because it floated on buoyant economic conditions. Emulating the American model of consumerism and mass production, Western Europeans enjoyed new cars on new roads, household appliances for their new houses, seaside holidays, and television, built on an impressive 5 percent average economic growth of EEC member states in the 1960s. Internal EEC trade grew even faster.

European Commission

The EU executive, which has a legal monopoly on proposing EU legislation and overseeing its implementation as "guardian of the treaties."

European Court of Justice

EU Supreme Court that decides the legality of EU legislation and its implementation.

qualified majority voting

Method in the Council of Ministers for deciding most EU legislation that weights member state voting power depending upon size and defining how many votes constitute a majority.

Crisis and Renewal: 1970–1993

The 1969 Hague Summit of EEC leaders set out ambitious plans for more market opening, enlarging to new members, greater EEC budgetary powers, foreign policy coordination, and Economic and Monetary Union (EMU). The British, Irish, and Danes then joined in 1973. The EEC, which had initially depended on direct funding from its members, also acquired new revenues from agricultural levies, import duties, and national value-added taxes. An energetic future seemed ahead, but international storm clouds appeared. The United States, threatened by trade deficits, ended its commitment to the Bretton Woods dollar/gold standard, allowing the dollar to "float" against other currencies and fluctuating exchange rates that caused havoc in the international monetary system, making economic prediction difficult, slowing trade growth, and tempting governments to use revaluations as trading weapons. At the same moment oil price shocks engineered by OPEC in response to the 1973 Yom Kippur war caused inflation to spike in energy-dependent Western Europe—a gesture that OPEC repeated in 1979.

Conditions became treacherous for the multicurrency EEC. Member states reneged on economic and monetary union. Profits and investment declined. EEC industry began to lose competitive advantage. "Stagflation"—simultaneous inflation, sluggish growth, and rising unemployment, led to cutbacks in social programs and precarious public finances. Divergent national responses made things worse. Germany restructured in a context of stable prices. After 1981 France's new Socialist administration pursued statist inflationary policies. Margaret Thatcher's Britain went its own harsh liberal reforming way.

By the early 1980s European integration was in danger. Decision making was paralyzed by budget disputes, in particular by the United Kingdom, which had paid too high a price to join, demanding their money back. Greece, which joined in 1981, immediately demanded that the EEC cough up more development aid. Non-tariff barrier protectionism caused the Common Market to clog up. The infrequent EEC-level responses to problems came mainly from summits of leaders (after 1974 called the European Council) that proposed direct elections to the European Parliament, held for the first time in 1979, and a new European Monetary System (EMS), to limit currency fluctuations. Observers began commenting about "Eurosclerosis."

In early 1985 the new Commission President Jacques Delors asked the European Parliament, "… is it presumptuous to … remove all the borders inside Europe between now and 1992 …?" Then, after the Commission produced its White Paper on Completing the Internal Market replete with three hundred new market-opening measures, the EEC began to stir again. Internal border posts would disappear, cross-border formalities simplified, common European product standards developed, value-added and excise taxation harmonized, and other obstacles to cross-border trade removed, allowing the free movement in the EEC of goods, services, and capital. National leaders then called an "intergovernmental conference" (IGC) in May 1985, which produced the Single European Act (SEA, ratified in 1987). The SEA tied the single-market program to qualified Council majority voting, leaving unanimity for only the most sensitive matters (fiscal policy, external border controls, the movement of people, and workers' rights). It also empowered the European Parliament to propose amendments and expanded the EU's prerogatives to enhance regional development ("economic and social cohesion"), research and development, and environmental policy. It legally acknowledged the European Council (summits of government heads) and European Political Cooperation (foreign policy coordination), both of which had been unofficial earlier. Last but not least, the new treaty anticipated monetary integration. The single-market program played to political realities. The Germans wanted new European trade. The French wanted to enhance their diplomatic power and help domestic reforms move forward. The British favored liberalization and deregulation in principle. Big business wanted a single market. Organized labor, less enthusiastic about the single market for fear of "social dumping" (companies relocating to find lower overhead costs), was seduced by promises of new "social dialogue" between Euro-level "social partners."

The Delors Commission, after profoundly reforming the EU's budgeting methods and innovating in regional development funding, then turned to economic and monetary union. A blue ribbon Committee led by Delors and of central bankers proposed a federal monetary policy, a European Central Bank, a single currency, and open capital movement. EMU, the committee claimed, could make intra-European factor costs more transparent, reduce transaction costs, prod Europe's financial sector to restructure, make wages better reflect national productivity, bring national budgetary and fiscal policies closer to economic fundamentals, and give governments new reasons for needed economic reforms.

Maastricht Treaty

Treaty renegotiations (ratified in 1993) that gave the EU its present name, created the EMU and the CFSP, and granted the European Parliament power to "co-decide" EU legislation.

The drive to EMU culminated in the **Maastricht Treaty**, ratified in 1993. Agreement was helped by German unification. Germany had been reluctant about EMU, but its unification scared other Europeans, and the German government agreed to EMU to reassure them. In exchange, however, Germany demanded their kind of EMU, one that guaranteed price stability and national financial responsibility. The French, whose hope had been to use EMU to constrain German monetary power, gave in to a final bargain that proposed stiff "convergence criteria" obliging EMU applicants to lower budget deficits to 3 percent and longer-term debt to 60 percent of GDP. EU members that reached these targets would be eligible to join the new EMU on January 1, 1999.

The negotiations were complicated by Belgian and German insistence on parallel talks about "political union" (leading to the new title of "European Union"). Political union included a common EU foreign and security policy (CFSP), greater democratization and more power for the European Parliament, and more efficient, coherent institutions. "Justice and home affairs" (JHA)—matters relating to the free circulation of people—sought to broaden existing "Schengen" open border policies to all EU states and coordinate police information and action on "Europeanized" crime. Maastricht also established EU citizenship and common immigration and asylum policies. By far the most significant institutional result, however, was "co-decision" in which the European Parliament got equal weight to the Council of Ministers deciding Community legislation plus the right to vote on the membership of Commissions. There was a hitch, however. Negotiators deemed that the CFSP and JHA were too important for the traditional "community method" of decision making (Commission proposals, Council and Parliament decisions, and ECJ review) and insisted on separate intergovernmental "pillars" with unanimity decision rules.

Globalization and the EU

The years after Maastricht were meant to consolidate the new treaty's innovations, but things proved much more complicated. The GATT Uruguay Round, the first to include agricultural trade, came to a head just after Maastricht and would have failed without a 1992 CAP reform. The EU and the United States then transformed the GATT into the World Trade Organization. In Europe itself, however, citizens worried that EU changes had been too rapid and far-reaching, something that first appeared in difficulties ratifying Maastricht. The Danes voted against the treaty—approving it later after concessions, and a French referendum in September 1992 passed by only 1 percent. Then followed a sharp economic down-turn due to European monetary problems just when the single-market program, which led employers to shed labor, was worsening unemployment. After the down-turn, member states faced difficult growth compressing preparations for the EMU membership deadline in 1998—the 3 percent deficit and 60 percent debt criteria in particular.

In 1993 the Delors Commission tried to remobilize the EU with a new White Paper on *Growth, Competitiveness, and Employment* that sounded alarms about glo-balization and suggested changes in EU economic governance. The EU's interna-tional competitive position was worsening, it argued, and this necessitated labor market and educational changes, more flexible social policies, and new attention to productivity. EU members refused to follow the Commission's lead, however. Citizens were unenthusiastic, while governments opposed the EU debt programs the Commission wanted. The Union enlarged again in 1995 to include Austria, Sweden, and Finland (the Norwegians voted against membership for the second time), all against new incursions into their sovereignty. Finally, the Germans, skeptical about some eventual EMU members, imposed a Stability and Growth Pact (SGP, incorpo-rated into the treaty of Amsterdam in 1997) to continue EMU convergence targets, and relative austerity, after EMU began.

In autumn 1989 Europe had been divided so long that most thought that this was permanent, but when the Berlin Wall came down in November, divisions abruptly ended. The Commission welcomed German unification, even if British Prime Minister Thatcher and French President Mitterrand had reservations. Helping ex-socialist societies of Central and Eastern Europe to democratize and modernize, and, perhaps, eventually join the EU, was a big challenge, first of all to hopes for a common EU foreign and security policy. The end of the Cold War found most

GLOBAL CONNECTION

The EU's International Connections

The EU has been a formidably successful organiza-tion committed to market economics, standing with the United States in promoting an open world trading sys-tem. It worries seriously about terrorism, failed states, how to help poor countries develop, promoting the rule of law, holding repressive dictators to account, and fitting newcomers like China, India, Brazil, Russia, and South Africa into a peaceful world order. The EU has been deeply devoted to multilateral approaches to international affairs, a highly positive approach in a globalizing world where integrating and giving voice to different countries has been a wise way forward. The EU, the largest market in the world, is central to inter-national commerce. It is also one of the world's largest fully democratized regions, as well as the world's leading development aid donor and a pioneer in humanitarian aid and crisis management. Recent globalization has been a profound challenge, however. The EU's members sought, usually successfully, to build strong industrial econo-mies and protective social policies to allow its citizens to better themselves through education and growing incomes and live secure lives. Globalization has brought new competition from emerging markets with compara-tive advantages in lower labor and social policy costs, as well as financial volatility. The EU has tried to persuade its member states to adapt to these challenges. Whether or not it will succeed is not yet clear.

MAKING CONNECTIONS What dimensions of globalization most challenge the EU and its members?

EU members ready to confront a Soviet invasion as the Soviet Union was dying, but before they had time to reconsider their defense preparations, the Yugoslav Federation disintegrated. Belgrade launched brutal campaigns—the word *genocide* may be appropriate—against Croatia in 1990, and then against Bosnia-Herzegovina. The first European wars since 1945 were greeted by Euro-posturing—solemn statements, high-powered delegations, economic sanctions, and handwringing that made little difference. It took American brokerage to stop war in Bosnia. The lesson was clear. The United States could make credible threats and call shots, while Europe's threats were hollow.

Later in the 1990s the EU began to respond. Evasive wording on CFSP was clarified in the 1997 Amsterdam Treaty to help circumvent the vetoes inherent in Maastricht's confusing decision rules. Amsterdam also created a "Mr. CFSP" to lead the CFSP process. Squabbling with the United States over NATO was moderated with new arrangements for the EU to share some NATO assets, provided that EU ambitions remained modest. By the turn of the century the EU had a small military planning staff and new goals for international peace-keeping and crisis management, and a new goal of portraying the EU as a different, gentler and more humane military actor.

A different problem arose about what to do about the formerly communist countries of Central and Eastern Europe (CEECs). In the early 1990s, the EU began coordinating to them through a PHARE program that soon became the EU's major instrument to help CEECs to build infrastructure, business, education, training, and research, and fund new environmental protection. The 1993 Copenhagen European Council then declared that the EU was "conditionally" willing to accept new members if they built stable democratic institutions (the rule of law, human rights, and minority rights), a functioning market economy, and the capacities to cope with competitive pressures inside the EU. Past EU experience obliged new applicants to conform to an *acquis communautaire*, by 2000 an accumulation of 80,000 plus pages of EU rights, obligations, and processes touching every corner of applicants' lives. Enlarging thus involved massive reforms that imposed Western European norms. A detailed "pre-accession strategy" came in 1994, including regular meetings, preparing for the single market, and new policies on infrastructure, environmental policy, CFSP, and justice and home affairs. The strategy worked better in some CEECs than others, with problems in Hungary, Romania, and Bulgaria.

Ten new members joined the EU in 2005 (eight CEECs plus Cyprus and Malta), followed in 2007 by Bulgaria and Romania. The joy of the moment was tempered, however. To make an EU of twenty-seven members work (28 after Croatia joined in 2013), EU institutions had to be redesigned because what had worked, more or less, for six or nine, might have become a crowd shouting in a football stadium at twenty-seven. But changing EU institutions was not simple, however, because it upset existing power relationships. The result was a decade of debates that few citizens could follow, national referendum defeats on new treaty texts (Ireland 2002 and 2008, France and the Netherlands 2005), and much acrimony and confusion. Finally, in 2009 the Treaty of Lisbon was adopted.

The Great Recession and the Euro zone Crisis

By 2009 the EU faced the worst economic crisis since the Great Depression of the 1930s, originating in the financial sector and symbolized by the 2008 bankruptcy of Lehman Brothers in New York. Anglo-American risk-defying financial innovation had already spread widely in the EU, however. The Great Recession brought credit freezes, negative growth, mass unemployment, declining government revenues, and rising costs. The United States and EU leaders agreed that failing banks needed to be saved to provide credit supplies and that stimulus plans could help jump-start the real economy again. Central banks, including the new ECB, supplied liquidity to re-oil the financial machinery. The EU also advocated re-regulation of the global financial sector, through the G-20. All this helped avoid the worst, but the damage went very deep.

In the fall of 2009, George Papandreou, the new Prime Minister of Greece, confessed that his predecessors had lied about his country's budget deficit—double what had earlier been announced. Thus did the greatest crisis in EU history open. International bond markets, fearing Greek default, then raised interest rates on future borrowing, confronting the EU with stark choices. Should EMU member states help Greece or should Greece be allowed to default and leave the Euro zone, perhaps creating new and potentially disastrous problems?

Decisions about what to do would be made by the Euro group of EMU members and the European Council, the EU's strategic decision-maker since Maastricht. Both were inter-governmental, meaning that governments had to bargain in processes that were slow, cumbersome, and guaranteeing that the preferences of stronger member states would shape decisions. Germany, initially reluctant to help Greece, shifted its position once it realized that the existence of the Euro was threatened and agreed to conditional loans to Greece from a temporary European Financial Solidarity Facility (EFSF), armed with €750 billion from the EU budget, EMU member states, and the International Monetary Fund. The first Greek loan was not large enough, however, and its high interest rates worsened Greece's debt and its conditions were draconian. Greece had to reduce its deficit to 3 percent by 2014, cut public sector pay, increase taxes, freeze pensions, lower wages, reform labor markets, and privatize, a package that led to widespread Greek social protest. The loan did not calm the situation and the crisis spread to Ireland and Portugal, who had to borrow with the same harsh conditions. Germany was the powerhouse in this bargaining.

The crisis showed that Maastricht's EMU architecture and rules needed restructuring. During the first EMU decade, EMU members had regularly disregarded the rules, which were not backed by serious sanctions in any case. The Maastricht negotiators had anticipated that EMU members would converge economically, but the opposite happened. Finally, there were no provisions for emergencies or to aid EMU members in trouble. Germany insisted throughout on strict policies obliging bailout countries (Ireland, Portugal, and Greece, plus Spain and Italy in partial ways) to impose harsh "internal devaluations," monitored by a *Troika* of Commission, ECB, and IMF officials. The major goal of EMU reconstruction became more effective central controls over member state fiscal practices. Members had to submit budgets for EU-level scrutiny before they were nationally voted, with stronger, more detailed monitoring of national fiscal policies, quasi-automatic sanctioning for bad behavior, and new regulations for the financial sector. A 2011 "Euro Plus Pact" pledged member states to control wage growth, raise retirement ages, reduce payroll taxes on labor, and observe new EU debt and deficit rules, backed by stiff penalties for noncompliance. German insistence also produced private sector involvement (bondholder liability) for restructuring bailout country debt. Then in 2012 a "Treaty on Stability, Coordination, and Governance" enjoined signatories to make national balanced budget commitments—the "golden rule." Finally, members were committed to set up a "Banking Union" to exercise ECB supervisory control over most EMU banks, a new "resolution" authority to deal with failing banks, and an EMU deposit insurance system.

Every choice brought trade-offs between those who bargained for national goals and international financial interests, above all bond holders seeking favorable terms. What with miscalculations, myriad political tensions, and tawdry back-room deals, crisis after crisis ensued. At one point the *Economist*'s cover labeled EU and EMU leaders as a "gang that couldn't shoot straight." The interest rates of the 2010 Greek bailout deal were too high and repayment schedules too rapid, worsening Greece's debt problems and necessitating more Greek loans. A German proposal for "haircuts" on expected bond returns (that is, agreements to for financial interests to take far less than a hundred cents on the dollar) upset the ECB and caused new market agitation. Later discussions about a second Greek loan went on for months and helped to spread the crisis to Italy and Spain. In November 2011, French and German intervention helped fire Greek Prime Minister Papandreou and Italian Premier Berlusconi and replace them with EU-influenced technocrats, an experiment that did little to help economically but deeply angered Greeks and Italians. In 2013, when called upon to bail out Cyprus, EU leaders botched things by calling for deep haircuts even for small depositors.

Hesitations about moving to a banking union unsettled the situation again. By 2013 the crisis had calmed, mainly because of the ECB's policies. Calmer bond markets were to be distinguished from disgruntled EU citizens, however. Euro zone policies of harsh sacrifice and redistributive reform badly tarnished the EU's legitimacy. "Internal devaluations" left citizens in borrowing countries in protracted austerity and insecurity. They experienced negative economic growth and very high unemployment (25 percent in Spain in 2012, 19 percent in Greece, 14 percent in Ireland, 13 percent in Portugal). Long-standing labor market rules were changed at the expense of trade unions. Minimum wages and unit labor costs declined, social programs cut back, public sector employment slashed, and inequality, poverty, and social exclusion shot up. Finally, generalized European recession in 2013, the product of Euro zone austerity policies, made things even worse. The intergovernmental ways in which decisions were made also hurt EU legitimacy, mainly because some EU member states, Germany in the first instance, decided policies that were experienced by those hurt as an unpleasant and unwelcome imposition from outside. Issues of democratic legitimacy are less about statistics than about how groups of citizens understand events, however. Favorable opinions of the EU have declined, with the trends stronger in the most crisis-affected countries. In mid-2013, a majority thought that the worst was yet to come and worried about their own employment prospects. According to one report only 28 percent believed that European integration had helped their economies. Loss of confidence in the EU was particularly strong among younger people.

Where Do You Stand?

Does EU-style transnational cooperation in response to large economic challenges inevitably create profound political problems?

Some EU countries do better than others economically, even in crises as threatening as the recent global financial collapse. Why?

EU GOVERNANCE

The Maze of EU Institutions

In 1648, exhausted from the Thirty Years War, Europeans founded the Westphalian state system. The results over centuries were strong, powerful states—each with its own language, identity, and ways of doing things—that were rivals and sometimes fought one another. Sixty plus years ago, some of these states began to create what would become the European Union. Their experiment began tentatively, in particular areas, with members warily keeping most of their powers. The new institutions they built were not "statelike," but built to govern particular things. These institutions persist today, making the EU a unique and complex system of multilevel governance.

For much of its life, the EU has been primarily a triangle of **community method** institutions including the European Commission, the Council of (national) Ministers, and the European Parliament. As the EU matured, however, complexities blurred this model. Beginning in the 1970s, the European Council, regular summit meetings of heads of state and government, slowly became the EU's longer-term strategist and decision-maker of last resort. The 1993 Maastricht Treaty on European Union then expanded the Union's scope into new areas such as foreign policy, defense and security, criminal justice, and immigration. These new areas lay

Focus Questions ▽

- To what degree does the EU provide lessons for governance on a global scale?

- Why might citizens have trouble identifying with EU institutions?

community method

The EU method of making decisions in which the European Commission proposes, the Council of Ministers and European Parliament decide, and the European Court of Justice reviews European law.

📇 PROFILE

AP Images/Cornelius Poppe/NTB Scanpix/Pool

Jose Manuel Barroso, Herman Van Rompuy, Martin Schulz

The EU was awarded the 2012 Nobel Peace Prize because of its record in preserving European peace and because the Nobel Committee hoped to encourage EU leaders to work harder to surmount the Euro zone crisis. When the award was announced, however, no one knew which leader of which EU institution should go to Oslo. In the event, three of them, Jose Manuel Barroso—Commission President, Martin Schulz—President of the European Parliament, and Herman Van Rompuy—European Council President, mounted the stage together. Behind this lay serious questions. What was the "true" nature of the EU, and where was its institutional heart? Everyone could agree that the EU was central to European economic governance, sharing the job with its members. And everyone knew that the EU's prerogatives had

grown substantially beyond economic governance, although there were arguments about how much, where, and whether it was good thing. The three presidents on the Oslo stage stood for three different axes of government. The European Commission represented the regulatory governance ideals of Jean Monnet, one of the EU's main founding fathers. The European Parliament represented federalist ideals and the hope that eventually the EU might become something like a European state. The European Council of heads of state and government represented another ideal, that of a confederation of states in which important decisions were reached by intergovernmental bargaining. In fact, the EU was an unsteady mixture of all three.

MAKING CONNECTIONS Think about the reasons behind the complexity of the EU's institutions. What differences have this complexity made?

at the core of national sovereignty, however, and EU leaders initially decided that the Community institutional "triangle" was not the best place for them, opting instead for intergovernmental "pillars." Since then, the EU Community "triangle" has dealt with most things, but institutional power has steadily shifted toward the intergovernmental European Council and the member states. Before entering such complexities, however, we must first describe the EU's major institutions.

The European Commission

The 1957 Rome treaties gave the European Commission three prerogatives: It alone could propose Community legislation in the form of regulations, directives, and recommendations (laws binding on all members in the same terms, laws that have to be transposed into national legal codes, plus nonbinding "soft law"). Next, as the EU's executive, it supervised the implementation of Community policy. Finally, it was the "guardian" of the EU treaties, seeing to the observation of EU law and, if needed, bringing member states and private bodies before the European Court of Justice to oblige them to follow. On a different plane, its main job has been to help overcome the difficulties that national governments have in reconciling their differences by devising projects and ideas that express common European interests and goad member states to make collective commitments. It has been most successful when key member states—often France and Germany—agree that greater integration is desirable and encourage a strong Commission President. When key member states have wanted a weak Commission, as they have since 1995, they have appointed a weak Commission President. Since 2005, member states have also agreed that the Commission President, preferably a former prime minister, should share the political leanings of the majority in the most recently elected European Parliament.

European single market

Official title of the EU's barrier-free economic space created after 1985.

The Commission can initiate proposals only where the EU treaties explicitly allow it. It does have some policy competencies where it behaves much like a federal government, however. It administers EU competition (antitrust) policies, the Common Agricultural Policy (CAP), proposes rules for and administers the **European single market**, and manages plans to help the EU's poorer regions to develop. It also has a key role in European environmental policy and helps design European-level research and development programs. It draws up the draft EU budget, even if the draft is always rewritten by member states. Internationally, it represents the Union in trade matters and, until 2009, when the Lisbon Treaty created a High Representative Foreign and Security policy, in some international organizations, plus manages foreign aid programs and supervises EU diplomatic delegations.

Commissioners are appointed by member state governments for five-year terms coinciding with the electoral life of the European Parliament. The 2004–2007 enlargement gave each member state one commissioner, making twenty-eight in all today, too many for the number of important Commission jobs. The Commission has a president, nominated by the European Council and approved by the Parliament, plus several vice presidents who oversee different clusters of activities. Commissioners work together in a "college" in which each commissioner, whatever his or her specific tasks, participates equally in all decisions. The Commission president exerts influence from assigning specific tasks to commissioners and by "presiding" over the Commission and planning its agenda. Each commissioner politically supervises one or several of the Commission's "services" (General Directorates or DGs), but does not have completely independent powers over them, since tasks are undertaken in accordance with programmatic lines to which the entire Commission has agreed. Despite its reputation as a formidable "Brussels bureaucracy," the total Brussels-EU administration, of which the Commission is the largest part, is small, around 30,000 people—about the number in a mid-sized European city, and only a minority are real "Eurocrats," the "A-grade" officers. Such A-level posts are carefully allocated to member state nationals. Each major Commission service is headed by a general director, the Commission's highest administrative post. Commission jobs are interesting and well paid (A-level jobs, the top of the ladder, range from around $150,000 to over $250,000 yearly, have numerous perks, and are exempt from national taxes, even if the EU itself taxes them lightly).

The Commission's most important job is to design policy proposals and get them passed by the Council of Ministers and the European Parliament. It rarely proposes from scratch, however, and in most cases translates the desires of others, particularly the European Council, and the requirements of international agreements. The Commission thus spends much time sounding out politicians, national ministries, and other Euro-level institutions for openings to act. It is also the object of intense lobbying, mainly because its most important tasks involve economic governance. The implementation of most Community measures is left to the administrations of member states.

The Council of Ministers

The original EU system was relatively simple. Where the EU could act legally, the Commission proposed, and the Council of (national) Ministers disposed. The European Parliament had to be "consulted," but lacked real power. The European Court of Justice could then review decisions and proceedings to ensure conformity with the EU's treaties. Things changed rapidly beginning in the 1980s, however. The Single European Act allowed the Parliament to propose amendments, and it became a "co-decider" with the Council in the Maastricht Treaty. Maastricht also introduced two new intergovernmental "pillars" for CFSP and "justice and home affairs" that initially fell almost completely outside the Community. The 2009 Lisbon Treaty "communitized" most of what these pillars did, but progress at this has been slow.

For two decades, after a crisis precipitated by France in the 1960s, the Council decided unanimously on anything any member deemed in its vital national interest. The SEA (1987) opened quality majority voting (QMV) on almost everything in the program for completing the single market. The Maastricht, Amsterdam, and Nice Treaties extended QMV, but not to everything. The 2009 Lisbon Treaty replaced QMV with a "double majority" formula on most matters that required both a majority (55 percent) of member states with a majority (65 percent) of the EU population for approval.

The Council of Ministers, along with the European Council, is where member states express their preferences and negotiate. Composed of national ministers empowered to deal with European issues, its most important job is passing European laws. It also legally concludes international agreements for the EU, approves the EU budget (with the Parliament), and decides some issues in the CFSP and Justice and Home Affairs areas. A powerful Committee of Permanent Representatives (or COREPER), composed of member state ambassadors to the EU, does much of the preliminary work for the Council. COREPER, which relies on preliminary sorting of issues by 150–200 working committees composed of national civil servants, also coordinates high-level functional committees, including the political and security committee that prepares CFSP, a special agriculture committee, a trade committee, a committee for justice and home affairs matters, and an economic and financial committee.

The Council of Ministers traditionally worked behind closed doors. Except for leaks, the public never really knew what debates took place, what alternatives were considered, and the positions of different countries. Worries about legitimacy led to efforts to open the proceedings, however, including television broadcasts showing parts of meetings and public announcements of certain votes, although because the Council usually works on consensus rather than voting, this is less important than it seems. Inside knowledge remains limited because much of the Council's work is done in bilateral and multilateral discussions before things close to decision. Shrouding deliberations in diplomatic secrecy has facilitated the wheeling and dealing that can lead to decisions and allowed national governments to obscure their responsibility especially when they have had serious redistributive effects at national level. The 2009 Lisbon Treaty obliged the Council's actual decision-making sessions to be open, however, so some change is occurring.

Up until the Lisbon Treaty, the Council was organized by a presidency that rotated among member states every six months, which coordinated Council–Parliament interactions, including the "conciliation committees" for co-decision, and submitted the Council's annual program to the Parliament. It also prepared and presided European Council summits and spoke for the EU on foreign policy (excepting trade). After Maastricht, CFSP and JHA broadened the presidency's role, since it also coordinated the new noncommunity "pillars" where decisions were taken intergovernmentally. The member state that held the presidency also played the role of power broker, coalition builder, and program initiator. The presidency was not always effective, however, and sometimes there were leadership discontinuities, poor preparation, and ineptitude.

The European Council

Enlargement to twenty-seven members led the 2009 Lisbon Treaty to establish a president of the European Council. Prior to this, the European Council had been a summit reunion of heads of state and government plus one other minister (usually the foreign minister), the Council secretary-general, and the Commission president and secretary-general, that met twice during each six-month Council presidency. The relative intimacy of its meetings was meant to encourage open discussion on important matters of EU strategy. The final hours of intense work produced a "Presidency Conclusion," which provided the European Council's decisions, intentions, and goals. The importance of the European Council is clear from a partial list of its conclusions (see Table 5.1).

The European Council president—the first was Herman Van Rompuy, a former Belgian Prime Minister—serves for a two-and-one-half-year, once renewable, term. The Lisbon Treaty hoped to create a powerful new personal symbol of the EU and a more effective administrative leader than the rotating Council presidency had been. Lisbon also provided for a new M/Mme CFSP—Catherine Ashton was the first—to represent the EU internationally, consolidate the EU's different and divided foreign policy operations, and establish a new EU "External Action" (diplomatic) service. The Council of Ministers and the European Council rely on a 2,000-strong secretariat (several hundred A-level administrators), with a staff for the secretary-general, legal services, and seven general directorates. The Council secretary-general, with an international focus, and his assistant, who focuses on EU domestic matters, are important officials.

The European Parliament

The European Parliament (EP) lives a vagabond existence between Strasbourg, France, where it holds its plenary sessions, and Brussels, where it meets in groups

Table 5.1	Major Conclusions of Recent European Councils
European Council	**Product(s)**
Fontainebleau, 1984	Solved "British check" issue; Spain and Portugal; admitted appointment of Jacques Delors
Milan, 1985	Approved "1992" White Paper; decided intergovernmental conference leading to SEA
Brussels, 1987	Adopted first Delors budgetary package (reform of structural funds)
Madrid, 1989	Accepted Delors report on EMU
Dublin, 1990	Decided German East-West reunification within the EU
Maastricht, 1991	Maastricht Treaty
Edinburgh, 1992	Decided enlargement to European Free Trade Association countries
Essen, 1994	Began discussing enlargement to CEECs
Dublin, 1996	EMU Stability and Growth Pact
Amsterdam, 1997	Amsterdam Treaty
Berlin, 1999	Approved Agenda 2000 budgetary package to facilitate enlargement
Lisbon, 2000	Lisbon Strategy on competitiveness and knowledge society
Nice, 2000	Nice Treaty
Laeken, 2001	Called European Convention
Brussels, 2003	Ten countries signed treaty to join EU
Brussels, 2004	Agreement on new Constitutional Treaty derived from Convention
Brussels, 2005	New budgetary package for 2007–2013
Brussels, 2007	Adopted proposals on energy, the environment, and global warming. Agreement on Lisbon Treaty
Brussels, 2007	Initial EU responses to Great Recession
2010–2013	Grappled with Eurozone crisis
2013	New budgetary package for 2014–2020

and committees. Since 1979 the Parliament has been directly elected. (Table 5.2 shows the allocation of seats among member states as of 2014.) Candidates run on national party tickets and then, if elected, their national political groups usually join European-level party coalitions. Elections to the EP are meant to encourage debate between aspiring leaders and voters about future European policies, raise levels of political education and consciousness about European integration, and reinforce EU solidarities and identity. Up to now, however, votes for the EP have been second-order national elections, treated by national politicians more as important indicators of the relative strength of national parties than as important EU events.

The EP elects its president and executive bureau for two-and-one-half-year terms. The presidency has usually alternated between a Socialist and a Christian Democrat, most often the two largest groups. After the 2009 elections the presidential term was divided between a Polish Christian Democrat, who served until 2012, and a German Social Democrat who served until the 2014 elections. The president presides

Table 5.2	European Parliament, Seats per Country 2014 (alphabetical order of country's name in its own language)		
Country	**2014**	**Country**	**2014**
Belgium	21	Lithuania	11
Bulgaria	17	Luxembourg	6
Cyprus	6	Malta	6
Croatia	11	Netherlands	26
Czech Rep	21	Austria	18
Denmark	13	Poland	51
Germany	96	Portugal	21
Greece	21	Romania	32
Spain	54	Slovakia	13
Estonia	6	Slovenia	8
France	74	Finland	13
Hungary	21	Sweden	20
Ireland	11	United Kingdom	73
Italy	73		
Latvia	8	TOTAL	751

over parliamentary sessions, participates in periodic inter-institutional discussions with Commission and Council counterparts, and addresses member state leaders at European Council summits. The bulk of Parliament's work is done by seventeen permanent committees, which produce detailed reports in their functional areas, making them target for an army of lobbyists.

In the early years the Parliament was only "consulted" by the Commission, but it has slowly become more important. In the 1970s it won power over the Community's budget and discovered that it could delay decisions by juggling the required time limits for delivering its opinions. The real shift began in 1987, however, when the Single European Act (SEA) instituted a "cooperation" (amending) procedure for most single-market legislation, soon replaced at Maastricht by "co-decision," a term to be taken literally, because Parliament and the Council "co-decide" on Commission proposals as if they were two separate legislative houses. Each reads and sometimes amends Commission proposals twice. Then, if they do not agree, the proposal goes to a "conciliation committee" of the Council and Parliament. If the committee can agree, the measure goes back to Council and Parliament for a "third reading" when it is usually approved. Parliament also possesses "assenting" power over applications from prospective new members, international treaties, EMU arrangements, multiyear regional fund programs, and its own electoral procedures. In addition, the Rome Treaty gave Parliament the right to bring the Commission and Council before the ECJ for "failure to act" where the treaty seemed to oblige them to, supplemented later by a right to sue if the Council infringed on its powers. The Parliament also must approve the Commission's annual budget proposal and "discharge" completed budget years (retrospective auditing).

Growing parliamentary influence has been good for the EU. Parliaments are most effective when they pursue specific political platforms, as happens nationally when they deliberate proposals from elected governments. The EP has no right of legislative initiative, however, and deals with, but can only react to, proposals from the Commission. The Lisbon Treaty added new "yellow card" linkages between EU institutions and national parliaments, which allow the latter to indicate whether they believe an EU legislative proposal violates **subsidiarity**, the principle that decisions should be made at the lowest and least centralized competent authority. The Lisbon Treaty also established a **citizen initiative** procedure by which at least a million citizens across several member states can petition EU institutions to take up a specific piece of legislation, provided that it is legally within the remit of EU treaties. But none of these reforms have resolved a challenge at the heart of the EU—how to make ordinary citizens accredit the EU's legitimacy.

The Eurozone crisis was an earthquake that caused political aftershocks in the May 2014 European Parliament (EP) elections. The crisis multiplied protest and support for populist parties on the right and the left, and not only those hardest hit by the austerity policies. Anti-EU passions reinforced the existing political repertories of unconventional political forces, whether statist protectionism on the left or right-wing anti-immigrant xenophobia.

Low turnout for EP elections traditionally favoured protest voting, even if the result was usually a majority from traditional center-left and center-right parties. The 2014 election was a test of new Eurosceptic strength, however. Turnout was stable (43.09%), but the center-left and center-right parties did less well than in the past. The European People's Party (EPP; conservatives and Christian Democrats) remained the largest party group, but lost 6.6% of its 2009 vote (to 29.4%, down from 36%) and 44 seats (to 221). The Socialists and Democrats (S&D) gained 0.6% (25.6% from 25%) and 9 new seats (to 192). Alliance of Liberals and Democrats for Europe

subsidiarity

Principle consecrated by the 1991 Maastricht Treaty that the EU should seek decision making at the level of the lowest effective jurisdiction.

citizen initiative

Clause in 2009 Lisbon Treaty allowing citizens to propose referendums to initiate EU legislation, provided 1 million legal signatures have been obtained in a "significant number" of different EU member states.

lost 2.7% (8.7% from 11.4%) and 17 seats. Finally, anti-EU and antisystem candidates won more than 20% of votes and seats. The UK Independence Party, the French *Front National*, and the Danish Peoples' Party, in the intolerant right, along with new left Syriza in Greece, made breakthroughs while anti-EU rebels of all stripes did well.

What did this mean for the EP? Reduced support for the center-right EPP and the center-left S&D compels them to combine to create majorities, implying more compromise. Eurosceptical newcomers will make a great deal of noise, but because they disagree among themselves, the noise will be cacophonic. In addition, because of these disagreements, it is difficult for Eurosceptic parties to ally enough to form the official parliamentary groups that give greater access to financing, staffing, speaking time, and EP committees. Whether rebel voices grow louder and more coherent will depend on how the EU proceeds as the economic crisis eases, if it eases. If employment levels rise and growth returns, Eurosceptic threats could moderate. If austerity, low growth, and economic despair persist, there could be deeper political troubles.

The 2014 EP elections produced an additional aftershock, however. In their campaigns, the larger EP parties invoked a clause in the Lisbon Treaty enjoining member states to "take into account" EP election results in the choice of the next President of the European Commission and presented "leading candidates" for this presidency, in the hope of forcing the European Council to appoint the candidate from the party with the most votes, the EPP's Jean-Claude Juncker, ex-Prime Minister of Luxembourg and former chair of the Eurogroup. The broader goal was to connect the Commission presidency with electoral results to politicize and further legitimate the Commission while frustrating claims of the intergovernmental European Council's to be the EU's final decision maker. Member state leaders responded with a serious row. British Prime Minister Cameron, faced with a major Eurosceptic challenge inside his own party and committed to negotiating a repatriation of powers from the EU before an "in or out" national referendum in 2017, denounced Juncker as "too federalist" and forcefully stated that member states, not voters in EP elections, were the legitimate base of the EU. German Chancellor Merkel, whose Social Democratic Grand Coalition partner had been central in the "leading candidate" campaign, eventually came out for Juncker, leading many of Cameron's earlier allies to retreat and a European Council vote for Juncker. The decision did little to resolve uncertainty about the EU's future, however. How far would the Euro-parliamentary challenge to intergovernmental power in the EU actually go? Would it help citizens to see the "Community method" as more democratic?

The European Court of Justice

European law is based on the treaties that member states have signed over six decades, and EU action must spring from this "treaty base." European law is only part of the laws of European Union member states, but where it exists, it is superior to, and supersedes, their laws. The European Court of Justice (ECJ), born in the ECSC, has been the key to making this happen. The Court, located in Luxembourg, is composed of twenty-eight justices (one from each member state) and eight advocates-general. The advocates-general review cases and provide legal opinion to the justices but do not rule on fundamental legal matters. The Court can sit in plenary session when it wishes, but must do so when dealing with matters brought before it by a Community institution or member state. Otherwise, it subdivides its work into "chambers" (of three and five judges each), any one of which may refer matters to the full Court. The ECJ's decisions are binding on member states and their citizens. The Court's huge workload led the SEA to establish of a

Tribunal of First Instance, known since the Lisbon Treaty as the General Court (composed of one judge for each member state, each with six-year terms). The General Court covers complex matters of fact in litigation brought by individuals and companies. Its decisions concerning questions of law (but not fact) can be appealed to the full ECJ.

The ECJ can strike down laws from member states and EU institutions when it judges them contrary to the treaties and, in so doing, interprets the treaties and makes EU law with its rulings. Cases get to the ECJ in many ways. The most significant is "preliminary ruling" in which a national court, presented with a case that may involve European law, forwards it to the ECJ for advice, which then usually settles the matter. Next are "annulment proceedings" in which a European institution, government, or individual can ask the court to rule on the legality of European legislation and other EU measures. A third path involves the Commission or a member state asking the ECJ to decide whether or not a member state has failed to fulfill its EU legal obligations ("treaty infringement proceeding"). Member states, other EU institutions, or individuals may also bring cases against a particular institution for "failure to act" when it ought to have done so. Cases for damages against Community institutions are considered as well. Member states and EU institutions may ask for rulings on the compatibility of international agreements with EU law. In general, ECJ rulings have been central in the evolution of European integration as Table 5.3, listing landmark cases, shows. The 2009 Lisbon Treaty established an EU Charter

Table 5.3	Significant Decisions of the European Court of Justice
Decision	**Importance**
Van Gend and Loos, 1963	Ruled that the Community constituted a new order of international law, whose subjects were member states and their nationals, derived from limitations of sovereignty by member states.
Costa v. ENE, 1964	Central in establishing the supremacy of EU law itself.
Van Duyn v. Home Office, 1974	Gave individuals the same right to employment in another member state as nationals of that state.
Defrenne v. Sabena, 1976	Based upon Article 119 of the Rome Treaty enjoining equal treatment of men and women in employment. The case opened initiatives attenuating gender discrimination in EU labor markets.
Cassis de Dijon, 1979	Member states must accept goods from other member states on the principle of mutual recognition, assuming that all members have reasonable product standards.
Vereniging Bond van Adverteerders v. the Netherlands State, 1988	Obliged member states to open up national telecommunications services to competition.
Bosman, 1995	Made illegal local club rules and restrictions on the employment of football players, opening international movement for professional athletes.

of Fundamental Rights (with the United Kingdom, Poland, and the Czech Republic securing opt-outs), which is promoting substantial new litigation, particularly by individuals invoking Charter provisions to settle grievances. The Court will be called upon to decide their claims, implying a significant extension of EU jurisprudence.

Other Institutions

The EU has several other institutions. In Brussels there also two important "advisory committees": An Economic and Social Committee with delegates from business, labor, and other professions and a Committee of the Regions with representatives from the EU's regions. Both review and submit opinions on pending EU legislation and, informally, are useful places for organized interests to network and connect with the Commission, Council, and Parliament. There is also an official Court of Auditors that reviews EU spending, and a European Investment Bank that mobilizes investment loans for regional planning and development purposes. Finally, there are now thirty-three "community agencies" scattered across the member states (each member state has a claim) that work on informational and regulatory matters, from fish stocks and plant variety, Europol, maritime security, health and safety at work, disease prevention and control, the environment, food safety, railways, and many more.

Where Do You Stand?

EU institutions are much more difficult to understand than those of most democratic national states, to the detriment of European integration. If true, why?

Imagine you are a European trying to make sense of all this. Would you throw up your hands and revert to your national identity or would you dive headlong into the brave new world of Europe?

SECTION 4

THE EU AND ITS POLICIES

▼ Focus Questions

- Why does the EU have so many legitimacy problems?

- Is there a place for the EU as a new kind of "soft power" international actor?

The EU can only work where members have agreed by treaty to do so. The EU has grown because EU policy cooperation in one area has sometimes spilled over into others, as Jean Monnet had hoped. Sometimes spillover has happened via classic "community method" market building. Sometimes the Commission has quasi-governmental roles, as in Competition Policy, or, to a lesser degree, in agricultural policy. EU governance can also be federal, but not in a "community method" way, as with EMU. In many areas governance prerogatives are shared between EU and national levels. In some the EU, without formal power, can influence governance through soft law.

Building a European Market

The most important thing the EU has done has been integrating many national markets into one. After the Rome Treaties it built a "common market" customs-free area where manufactured goods could move freely, plus a common agricultural policy. The "community method" and the Commission's power to propose legislation were at this market-building core. After the first decades, however, it was clear that other problems needed resolving before the market was truly open. People could not circulate freely across borders, goods stalled in trucks at customs posts while drivers filed endless forms, professionals had difficulty working in other countries, financial and services markets remained national, and national sales taxes discouraged trade. In the 1970s, when economic times got tougher, members set up new nontariff barriers to trade.

The 1985 program to complete the single-market and open a "space without borders" revived, and may have saved, European integration. The program liberalized and deregulated national markets, promoted new trade between EU members and, ultimately, created one European market and economy. To do this, it established uniform standards and norms, stiffer competition rules and environmental policies, and integrated some forms of taxation. For example, when the EU enlarged to poorer countries, it devised new regional development policies to help them. Finally, pledges to establish fully the "four freedoms" of goods, services, capital, and people movement had to be fulfilled.

Initially, under the guidance of the commissioner for the internal market, the single-market program drafted proposals after consulting widely with interests, committees, national-level administrations, the Committee of Permanent Representatives (COREPER), and other bodies. The European Parliament, its new power of amendment in hand, examined these proposals, and the Council of Ministers made final decisions by new QMV procedures. The last step was for member states to "transpose" the new rules into national legal codes. One of the more daunting tasks was harmonizing technical standards and norms. When this had been tried earlier, multilateral negotiations often failed. The single-market program proposed instead to proceed by "mutual recognition" following the ECJ's 1979 *Cassis de Dijon* ruling that goods legally marketed in any member state should circulate freely throughout the EU as long as minimum standards were upheld. Last but not least, VAT (value-added) taxes had to be harmonized to prevent different levels and types of national taxes from distorting competition within the single market.

After 1992, the target date for completing the single-market program, change did not stop, but what remained was harder to do. Members disagreed, particularly about liberalizing the service sector—70 percent of European economic activity. The Union changed intellectual property laws; harmonized taxation on savings; liberalized public procurement; opened up telecoms, electricity, and gas provision to greater competition; and made it easier for service businesses to set up in other countries. Beginning in 1999, the Commission also proposed a major action plan to harmonize rules and open markets in securities, banking, and insurance. Opening up service markets was controversial, however, and protest about a 2005 Services Directive was central in referendums that defeated the proposed European Constitutional Treaty. Public services have been a particular problem. There has always been recognition that public services in health, education, public transportation, post offices, and utilities were different from grocery stores and law firms, but economic conditions change, and so have ideas about public services. Postal services, challenged by private delivery firms like FedEx and UPS and the Internet, have been privatizing. National pricing and access restrictions for what had once been "natural monopolies" (airlines, electricity, gas, and telecoms) needed lowering. It is not hard to foresee challenges to the public nature of health care and education in the future.

Single-market progress has often been blocked by entrenched special interests in national professional associations, powerful banks and financial service firms, employers, and unions. Enlargement to twenty-eight members brought the task of insuring that existing market rules and regulations were applied. The free movement of people has stirred deep national anxieties about immigration. Still, the Commission has calculated that the single market had increased EU GDP by 1.8 percent, created 2.5 million more jobs, increased exports and imports, lowered utility prices, and enhanced consumer choice.

Competition Policy

There would have been little point in opening the European market if companies and countries could then limit competition within it. The Rome Treaty declared that measures should be taken so that "competition in the internal market is not distorted" and granted the European Commission responsibility for this. Competition policy has since become one of the Commission's rare federal competencies, subject only to ECJ review. The Commission traditionally has done most of Europe's big antitrust work, leaving only small cases to national authorities. Anticompetitive firm behaviors—cartels, trusts, and monopolies—can be outlawed when judged to be against European interests, and since 1989, the Commission has overseen mergers and more recently played a key role in deregulating public utilities.

The Commission's antitrust powers are both negative—preventing illegal behavior—and positive—regulating and authorizing. Its Competition DG works with lawyers and economists who monitor company conditions, the business press, and market developments. It can request information from firms and carry out investigations, including "dawn raids" to obtain company documents. Because mergers in other parts of the world can have market-limiting effects in Europe, the Commission's merger control operations have international scope and DG Comp is among the most powerful competition authorities in the world. Its investigations of potential violations often end informally after the threat of sanctions leads to successful negotiations. But when informal dealing fails, the Commission may levy substantial fines. It ruled against Microsoft's practice of "bundling" software programs in Windows, for example, initially fining it €500 million and then fining it later even more for noncompliance. EU procedures for merger control involve proactive economic and legal judgments about how a proposed merger could restrain trade. Perhaps the most spectacular case occurred in 2001, when the Commission blocked an avionics merger between General Electric and Honeywell, even after U.S. authorities had already approved. More often, mergers go through after company plans are reformulated to meet DG Comp's concerns.

The issue of state aid to companies is more difficult because national companies, jobs, and votes are at stake and some member states have traditions of state-centered industrial policy. While the Commission uses its power to prevent state subsidies that could impair markets from working, it has also allowed state aid for projects such as well-defined one-off industrial restructuring in industries hurt by recessions or world market shifts. This power has been extensively used in the Great Recession and Euro zone crisis, almost always with the proviso that subsidies are phased out once crisis conditions are over. It has also allowed subsidies for large projects that might enhance the European market, like the English Channel tunnel, and to shore up regions hit by natural disasters.

EU competition policy is constantly evolving. National as well as corporate players push back and insist on their right to use instruments such as subsidies to promote social cohesion, economic growth, and job creation. The ECJ has also slapped down DG COMP when it has occasionally done its work badly. In recent years the

Commission has decentralized competition policy matters below a certain threshold of importance to national authorities, but following European rules.

Agriculture

The Rome Treaty proposed a Common Market for agricultural as well as manufactured products. The original Common Agricultural Policy (CAP) was a strange market, however, with price supports administered by the Commission to keep Community prices for agricultural goods higher than they might have been otherwise in the interests of food security and modernizing European agriculture. After only a few years, it had begun to encourage farmers to overproduce, overuse chemical fertilizers, pollute, and damage water tables. But farmers had been shrewd enough to build powerful groups and alliances with national agriculture ministers in order to protect the policy from reformers. The CAP, the largest single EU budget item, became redistributive from taxpayers and consumers to farmers and also moved a great deal of money from country to country, giving some members more than others. The CAP's incentives to produce more created surpluses that necessitated expensive EU-funded storage facilities and dumping on the international market. Finally, as economies of scale grew, there were disproportional additional transfers to larger, more efficient producers.

The CAP made DG Agriculture the largest administrative unit in Brussels. For much of the CAP's existence hundreds of technocrats measured carrots, rented barns, sold surpluses the world over, and proposed prices for a huge range of products that the Council of Ministers voted on by QMV (with the Parliament marginalized until the Lisbon Treaty). Because the DG proposed prices and regulations, it was heavily lobbied by farmers' organizations. Highly regulated markets also tempted fraud, leading DG Agriculture to police farmers to see that they actually produced what they claimed. Each product area had its own management committee, with the entire system tracked by an intergovernmental committee on agriculture, but implementation was left largely to member states, monitored by the Commission.

Reforming the CAP began not long after the CAP itself. "Net contributor" member states like Great Britain and the Netherlands disliked subsidizing French beet-sugar conglomerates and well-off Danes. The CAP's costs grew so fast that they threatened to crowd out other EU activities and discredit European integration. In response, cost control began in the 1980s and land "set asides" and direct income support came in 1992 and have since accelerated. There has been a lessening of EU international dumping, if not enough to satisfy farm producers elsewhere. Fitting the CAP to Eastern European agriculture has been another challenge. Making new member states full CAP participants, particularly Poland and its plethora of small farmers, might have expanded the budget more than anyone wanted. The result, Poles ended up with less than they expected and western farmers hung onto their benefits.

In tough negotiations about the EU's 2007–2013 budget package, the CAP, defended by the French, became part of the negotiating endgame. No one won much, but the CAP budget lost least. As had traditionally been the case, CAP reforms were made by raising the budget to placate farmers for incremental changes. More recently, budgets have been kept at a nominally steady state but slowly declining as a percentage of the EU budget. "Decoupling" CAP subsidies from price supports and shifting spending to rural development left the CAP budget more vulnerable in 2014, however, when a new EU budgetary package began. Farmers are a dwindling and aging part of EU population and the long CAP saga may be coming to an end.

Regional Development

Financing regional development through the "structural funds" is the EU's largest budgetary item after agriculture and an expression of solidarity between better-off and less-developed regions. There was recognition about regional development in the Rome Treaty, mainly to help Italy with its underdeveloped south. Then, after the EU enlarged in 1973 to the United Kingdom, Denmark, and Ireland, a European Regional Development Fund (ERDF) was created to help distressed and undeveloped areas. Enlargement in the 1980s to poorer countries like Greece in 1981, then Spain and Portugal in 1986, necessitated greater efforts and the SEA made "economic and social cohesion" a new common policy. The 1988 reform of the structural funds doubled financing over five years, with another doubling in the 1990s.

EU regional development prioritizes specific objectives and promotes "partnership" between the Commission (which vets projects and administers them) and national and regional levels, which must come up with cofinancing—the so-called principle of additionality. The priorities developed in the later 1980s were to assist underdeveloped regions (75 percent of the structural fund budget), help restructure deindustrialized regions, enhance skills and combat long-term and youth unemployment, and aid rural areas. The money went to multiannual, multitask, and multiregional programs, mainly in areas where average income was 75 percent or less than the EU average. The Maastricht Treaty added a "cohesion fund" to compensate Greece, Ireland, Portugal, and Spain for participation in the EU's environmental and transport policies. Enlargement to the CEECs has reshaped regional development policies, however, because the new members were almost all below the 75 percent threshold. By rights they should have received most of the money, but this did not happen immediately because older member states wanted to continue receiving what they had earlier.

THE EU BUDGET: A SIGNIFICANCE TEST?

In 2013 the EU spent €150.9 billion in the general categories shown in the table below. While this may seem large, it is only 1 percent of the GDP of its member states, whose national budgets are incomparably larger (44.5 percent of GDP on average). The budget grew through the 1980s and 1990s, stabilized, and has declined slightly recently, as member states try to keep the EU on a tighter leash. Many EU policies also entail large national spending. Almost all western EU members contribute more to the budget than they get back and poorer countries are "net beneficiaries." The EU budgetary process has two steps. The first is intergovernmental negotiation every five years on multiyear "financial perspectives"—a new deal was negotiated in 2013 for 2014–2020. The second involves annual European Parliamentary review of yearly budgets and EP "discharge" (approval) of the books after the year is completed.

Spending Category 2013	Billion Euros
Sustainable Growth, of which 77 percent is for regional development, the rest R&D and life-long education	70.5
Natural Resources, of which 90+ percent is for agriculture and rural development, the rest fisheries and climate change policy	60.1
Citizenship, Liberty, Security and Justice (Maastricht's JHA)	2.1
EU as a global player (CFSP, aid, development cooperation)	9.5
Administration	8.4
Total	150.9

The cumulative effects of EU regional programs are hard to calculate. Amounts given to any particular country are small in absolute terms, but can add up to 4 percent to local investment, particularly in infrastructural projects that might not have been affordable. Some, like Ireland and Spain, were spectacularly successful until the Great Recession, while others upgraded a great deal. The funds have also provided incentives to avoid "races to the bottom" through the use of cheap labor and minimalist social policies. Another bonus has been that regional levels of government have developed stakes in European integration and increased purchasing power in poorer areas is used to buy goods and services from the rest of the EU. The structural funds also provide incentives for reform. The CEECs, for example, with incomes of less than 40 percent of EU average, needed the money, and to get it they had to develop administrative capacity to absorb it productively. Funding improvement in roads, railroads, energy provision, telecommunications, airports, and ports brings rapid returns. But the biggest payoff, proven by experiences in Spain, Portugal, and Greece and the CEECs, all emerging from authoritarian regimes, is that EU regional development can help consolidate the rule of law and greater democracy. Finally, when countries have been reluctant to invest enough in such capacities, the threat of withholding structural funds—as recently for Romania and Bulgaria—can be sobering.

The Euro and EMU

Economic and Monetary Union (EMU), decided at Maastricht, began in 1999. Its importance for the EU, both positively and negatively, cannot be overestimated. For business, a single currency means more transparent costs and economic indicators. Ordinary Europeans and foreign tourists no longer have to exchange money every time they cross a border. Most importantly, the EU has built a single market that would have been hard pressed to manage fluctuations among national currencies if EMU and the euro had not been invented. EMU has done a very good job at maintaining price stability. In light of the Eurozone crisis, however, the record has been mixed.

How did EMU work prior to 2007–2008? Maastricht created a European System of Central Banks that included all member state central banks and charged it with maintaining price stability, designing and implementing EU monetary policy, managing foreign exchanges, holding reserves, and operating payments systems. Its core, very federal, institution is the European Central Bank (ECB) with a powerful president and six-member executive board plus a governing council of central bank governors from all EMU members. Located in Frankfurt, Germany, the ECB is statutorily independent from political influence. Its most important job is achieving price stability, defined as an inflation rate of 2 percent a year or less and tracked by targeting money supply and inflation levels and adjusting EMU-wide interest rates.

All EU members excepting those with explicit opt-outs (the UK and Denmark) were expected to join EMU eventually, but only those who have met Maastricht's convergence criteria have joined. EMU officially thus started at eleven members in 1999—now eighteen—and the ECB made its philosophy clear from the beginning. If some members had problems, it was their own fault and most likely caused by selfish market actors and imprudent governments. Economic growth in 1998–2000 allowed the ECB to dispel worries that its dedication to price stability might stifle new growth. Major early criticisms were that it had problems communicating and that the new euro fluctuated too much. The 1997 Stability and Growth Pact (reformed in 2005) bound EMU members to budgetary deficits of less than 3 percent, but after 2000 more than half of EMU members stopped observing this, indicating something amiss. EMU's "one size fits all" monetary policy lowered interest rates to smaller and poorer economies like those of Greece, Ireland, Portugal, and Spain, providing them with a windfall that encouraged debt-based development strategies that often fed housing bubbles.

EMU "federalized" monetary policy, but its members retained national taxing, spending, and budgeting. A "Eurogroup" of EMU finance ministers tried to promote coherence in these areas across the Euro zone, but with few tools to oblige members to comply. The absence of cooperative economic and financial governance helped create the situation that eventually exploded in the Euro zone crisis. As discussed earlier, the crisis demanded a reconfiguration of EMU's architecture involving a substantial increase in central oversight of national fiscal and budgetary policies backed by new enforcement powers, increasing the power of the ECB as policy-maker and regulator and the Commission as monitor and enforcer. The ECB performed well during the crisis, both as a tough negotiator in crisis summits and, most important, by implementing "nonstandard measures" such as providing funds to commercial banks at low interest rates to keep credit flowing, buying up bank debt, and buying up national debt on secondary markets, in all providing liquidity to the financial sector and member states that otherwise would not have been available. A pledge made by ECB President Mario Draghi in 2012 to "do what it takes," that is, to continue such policies, was widely credited as the turning point that finally calmed crisis.

Shared Policies

The EU is a mixed system of public policy-making. In some areas the EU has strong, "vertical" powers that directly shape national policies. In others it has more limited, "horizontal" power to generate ideas, set examples, delineate best practices, provide seed money, and cajole, but national policy-making remains central. The precise division of shared labor is determined by EU treaties and in the concept of "subsidiarity" written into Maastricht, according to which the public interest is best served when policy is undertaken at the lowest appropriate level.

Globalization and Competitiveness

To respond to globalization the EU has most often used its "horizontal" powers. EU policies to promote economic competitiveness stretch to the beginning of the European Coal and Steel Community (ECSC). Since then, the EU has often been involved in helping to reconfigure troubled industries and regions, providing financial aid, retraining, and temporary trade protection. Many of these actions were to ease the pain of regional deindustrialization. By the 1990s, however, EU focus had turned toward investment in high-end innovation.

Six decades ago Europe was far behind the United States, and the ECSC and Common Market were Western Europe's catch-up tools. After the economic difficulties of the 1970s, the United States jumped ahead again, while Japan and the Asian Tigers came onto the scene. The single-market program and EMU were meant to prevent Europe from falling behind, but the United States moved forward again in the 1990s, propelled by its financial power and vanguard position in information technology, while China, India, and other low-cost newcomers began gobbling up manufacturing markets in which Europe had earlier specialized. Today's EU Europe of 500 million people is the richest single market in the world, but it is not at the top of the league in economic competitiveness.

Key new areas like research and technological development (R&D) and industrial policy remain primarily national issues, but the EU can provide incentives for new cooperation. In the early 1980s, the EU began funding high-tech R&D, particularly for research in electronics. The SEA and the Maastricht Treaty allowed more EU activity in research and technological development to complement member states' efforts. The 2000 Lisbon European Council then called for the creation of a "European Research Area" that would raise spending on R&D—primarily national, but also EU-level—to 3 percent of EU GDP by 2010, a target still not met. The flagship vehicles for EU R&D have been multiyear research "framework programs" drawn up by the Commission and approved by the Council, designed to work with, rather than substitute for, national policies. The 2000 Lisbon strategy sought greater cooperation and convergence among member states around general European goals. Budgets have been relatively small—in the just-completed Sixth Plan the budget was €17.5 billion, and efforts have been hindered by national rivalries, but there has been greater European focus and coherence. One significant product has been trans-European scientific networks. The EU has also invested in areas of immediate trans-European importance—infrastructure, environmental research, and health and food safety, for example. There have also been major European "industrial policy" innovations in mobile phones, space technologies, and satellites that have "Europeanized" standards and helped security policy and air transport.

The 2000 "Lisbon Agenda" sought to make EU Europe the world's most advanced "knowledge economy" by 2010, by which point the EU was also to have restored full employment and preserved Europe's "social model"—welfare states and labor market policies—through reform. The Lisbon program also included new infrastructure, environmental policies for sustainable development, and upgraded "citizen competence" through education and training. The Lisbon architects, anticipating problems of cooperation, proposed an "open method of coordination" (OMC) that involved setting general European goals, encouraging member states to hold regular and open national discussions about achieving them, identifying best practices, building up comparative indicators of progress, and publicizing successes and failures—naming and shaming—from Brussels. The hope was that in the absence of harder tools, "soft law" would work. It did not, however, and in 2004–2005, the Barroso Commission refocused efforts more narrowly on structural reforms and liberalization, retreating from the OMC and reassigning responsibilities to member states. Proposals to open energy markets were hindered by opposition from national energy monopolies, making it difficult for the EU to have a European energy policy. Brussels moved on chemicals regulation (REACH) and climate change while talking a great deal about lightening its regulatory hand, but results have been limited. After a decade, consensus was that the Lisbon strategy fell short because it depended on voluntary coordination by member states.

By 2010 it was clear that reform was going on, but not enough, and the financial crises had set things back considerably. Unemployment had risen, and the EU was far from becoming the world's leading knowledge economy. But by then the EU was looking forward to its new "2020" strategy to follow the Lisbon project. Europe 2020 was a more modest affair—raising the employment rate that had dropped in the crisis, finally reaching Lisbon's 3 percent R&D target, reducing greenhouse gas and finding new non-carbon energy sources, and reducing school dropout and poverty rates.

Social Policy

Social policy best illustrates the EU's multilevel governance and subsidiarity issues. The EU has some influence to exhort countries, but little direct power, because welfare state and employment policies are national. The Treaty of Rome narrowly limited the EU to matters of labor market mobility within the common market, some occupational training, and equal opportunity for men and women. It created a European Social Fund with the vague purposes of making "the employment of workers easier, increasing their geographical and occupational mobility within the Community." In general, however, the great variety of social policy regimes within the EU today reflects the variety of its members, who protect their systems well.

Concern with inequality in the workplace between men and women translated into an article in the 1957 Rome Treaty, requiring "equal treatment." EU Europe has since developed progressive programs for advancing women's rights. The SEA added workplace health and safety to EU-level social policy prerogatives out of anticipation that lower national rules might be a source of comparative advantage. The SEA also included an article stating that "the Commission shall endeavor to develop the dialogue between management and labor at European ... level." This was elaborated into a "Social Chapter" at Maastricht and led to EU social policy directives on working time, consultative European Works Councils, parental leave, and "atypical work" (part-time and short-term contracts). By the later 1990s, however, member states had lost enthusiasm for EU social policy, and emphasis shifted to decentralized "soft" procedures and the open method of coordination (OMC) in the European Employment Strategy in the 1997 Amsterdam Treaty, followed by wider use of OMC to promote change in pensions, poverty policy, and other matters. By 2011 there were signs that the European Employment Strategy was helping, but OMC had by then been abandoned in other areas. Despite "soft" activities, the EU's direct influence over social policy has remained very limited.

Environmental Policy

When environmental issues exploded into the public consciousness in the 1960s and 1970s, they seemed a perfect fit for EU action. Acid rain, air and water pollution, transporting dangerous materials, protecting biodiversity, and managing the externalities of industrial development were problems that did not respect borders. The likelihood of EU action was enhanced by the political success of "green movements" in key EU countries like Germany, the Netherlands, and France. When in 1972 a member state summit invited the Commission to work in the environmental policy area, it responded eagerly, passing legislation including legal recognition of the "polluter pays" principle, promoting codes of conduct through "green labels" on products, requiring environmental impact assessments for large projects, and testing and grading beach water safety. Since then, the Commission and its DG Environment have proposed six ambitious multiyear environmental action programs, and are currently working on another. The EU's conversion to strong environmentalism was strengthened in the early 1980s after the European Parliament urged that environmental policy be placed in European Treaties. The Single European Act then established EU competence via a formula that enshrined subsidiarity.

The EU rapidly committed to transnational environmental protection, signing conventions on the Mediterranean and Antarctic, and by the later 1980s the Commission and many heads of state, attuned to growing awareness of climate change, decided to place the EU on the front line out of conviction that climate change could only be confronted globally and because they saw it a good issue to enhance the EU's image as a "soft power" international player. The EU then became a leader in promoting sustainable development with several large initiatives that began with its signature of the UN Framework Convention on Climate Change at Rio in 1992. It was also central in negotiating the Kyoto Protocol, and perhaps more important, in bringing it into legal operation. The EU cap-and-trade scheme for limiting greenhouse gas emissions quickly became the world's most advanced, albeit not without problems. In 2007–2008 it committed to a very ambitious "20-20-20" program that promised to cut EU greenhouse gas emissions by 20 percent, reach 20 percent use of renewable energy, and become 20 percent more energy efficient by 2020. This program imposed significant constraints on member states and was advertised as a "smart development" response to slow economic growth.

The 20-20-20 program was also meant to help launch a successor to the Kyoto Protocol. The 2009 UN Copenhagen climate change negotiations demonstrated how easily EU attempts to lead multilateral climate negotiating could be ignored, however. The EU brought 20-20-20 to the table and promised even more if others agreed to follow in an ambitious post-Kyoto bargain. Copenhagen ended with a very weak deal struck by the United States and China, with the EU on the sidelines, however, a resounding slap in the face for its climate change strategy. EU leaders had overestimated the openings for "soft-power" leadership on the environment. Moralizing had obvious limits, but more important was that multilateral negotiating had changed. Even with a new American president, there was no chance that the U.S. Congress would accept a new treaty modeled on EU objectives. Emerging market powers like China, India, Brazil, and others insisted on being heard. Some, like China, expressed willingness to undertake national actions but opposed binding international commitments in the name of sovereignty. Others, including African leaders, were unwilling to commit to new constraints unless the wealthy world agreed to subsidize the costs of climate change regulation. There was also suspicion that western-led pleading on climate change were in part new ways to deprive economic newcomers of comparative cost advantages just as they started to modernize.

This setback was followed by internal problems. It was unfortunate, but significant, that the EU had been able to band together to try to force the pace at Copenhagen but had never agreed on a coordinated energy policy itself. Europe was heavily dependent on imported energy, particularly oil and gas, but the EU's member states had chosen different strategies to cope with this, from North sea oil and gas Russian oil and gas that Germany and others sourced, expensive nuclear power, as in France, to "fracking," all variations on a go-it-alone theme prompted by needs to nail down present and future energy supplies. This led to a wide disparity in energy costs, even if most EU members paid a great deal more than other industrial countries for energy. The global financial collapse and the Eurozone crisis made things worse. High unemployment, low growth, and squeezed government revenue streams made it much harder for national governments to ask citizens to make sacrifices to mitigate climate change. The consequences have been new disagreements and confusion that have further deflated EU claims of global leadership and lowered EU ambitions on climate change issues.

Intergovernmental Europe

The EU's scope has grown substantially, encroaching ever more on national sovereignty. This has been especially true of Justice and Home Affairs (JHA) and the Common Foreign and Security Policy (CFSP), both hived off into two new intergovernmental pillars by the Maastricht Treaty to allow governments alone to control the pace of change. The 1997 Amsterdam Treaty the 2009 Lisbon Treaty both pledged to integrate these pillars further into the "community method." Movement has been slow, however.

Justice and Home Affairs

The Rome Treaty proclaimed "free movement of people" as a goal, but the EU did not do much about it for decades. After the single-market program made serious new commitment to opening borders, it became inevitable that organized crime—drug dealers, human traffickers, money launderers, and terrorists, and other evildoers—would "Europeanize" along with legitimate business. In the absence of new EU cooperation on visas, identification, asylum policy, and enhanced control at external borders, individual EU states would have been in the dark about who was wandering around and what they might be doing. On top of this, without increased legal cooperation, freedom of movement would leave perfectly respectable EU citizens faced with a bewildering array of national civil laws and baffled about their rights.

The issues were real, and even before the EU took them up, ad hoc groups of member states formed organizations on specific problems such as drugs and human trafficking. But it was the Schengen Group in the 1980s—originally France, Germany, and the Benelux countries, that first removed internal border crossings to allow free movement of their citizens. The Justice and Home Affairs (JHA) clauses at Maastricht were meant to bring these areas together in an intergovernmental pillar outside the community method—leaving only parts of visa policy a "community" matter. Detailed JHA business was done by COREPER and the Council of Ministers (via the K.4 Committee) with help from committees of national experts on immigration and asylum, police and customs cooperation, plus judicial cooperation on civil and criminal matters. Even though JHA decisions had to be made unanimously, there was considerable JHA activity in the 1990s. Europol built up police cooperation among EU member states, gathering, pooling, and circulating intelligence and information. JHA also built up data bases about the **Schengen area**, customs, asylum-seeking, and stolen property, even before the Amsterdam Treaty incorporated the full Schengen *acquis*.

Intergovernmentalism was slow, in part because ministers were secretive and zealously protected national interests. The 1997 Treaty of Amsterdam thus agreed to shift some JHA matters to the "Community Method" and qualified-majority voting, including asylum, parts of immigration, judicial cooperation in civil matters with cross-border implications, and common procedures at EU external borders. There was also a new *passarelle* clause that allowed member states, if they were unanimous, to shift new areas toward the community method and QMV. Highly sensitive matters of police and judicial cooperation remained intergovernmental, however. Amsterdam also committed the EU to build an "area of freedom, security, and justice." The change was meant to shift emphasis from mysterious intergovernmental police activities toward the rights of EU citizens and legal visitors (along with growing harshness for immigrants, part of a general shift in national political focus). Maastricht made citizens of EU member states automatic EU citizens, with equal rights of movement, residence, voting in European elections, and diplomatic protection abroad, and a broader Charter of Fundamental Rights was legalized in the 2009 Lisbon Treaty (with British, Polish, and Czech opt-outs). Amsterdam also proposed policy harmonization through "mutual recognition," better transnational readability of national

Schengen area

EU area, named after small city in Luxembourg, where freedom of transnational movement without border controls was first agreed in 1985. Schengen now includes all EU members except Romania, Bulgaria, Croatia, the United Kingdom and, Ireland. It also includes non-EU countries Norway, Iceland, and Switzerland.

policies, and more international cooperation on civil law matters like divorce and alimony, child visitation, and financial problems such as debt and bankruptcy.

Matters of the police, interior ministers, and criminal law have been difficult to follow because of closed doors and secretive actors, but there are now a number of monitoring and information agencies on drugs, discrimination, and fraud. There are also a European Police College, a European Police Chiefs Task force, and Eurojust, an organization of senior justice officials to facilitate cross-border prosecutions. After 2004 a common European arrest warrant has superseded complicated national extradition proceedings. Europol's antiterrorist coverage and budget were already expanding prior to 9/11 and grew substantially thereafter. There have been serious recent terrorist incidents in the EU as elsewhere, in Madrid in 2004 and London in 2005, for example. But there have been few American complaints about lack of European counterterrorist cooperation, meaning that Europeans have been doing a good job. On the other hand, American NSA spying, which includes the EU's leaders, has opened a serious rift with the EU.

The 2009 Lisbon Treaty further "communitarized" JHA by moving border and asylum control issues and minimal rules about crime and punishment for certain cross-border crimes (terrorism, drugs and arms trafficking, money laundering, sexual exploitation of women, cyber-crime) to qualified majority voting, co-decision, and ECJ review. The Lisbon Treaty also promised an increase in the speed and effectiveness of legal cooperation, in particular because of "mutual recognition" in which member states accepted the decisions of one another as valid. Passports and identity cards, family law, and further Europeanization of criminal law remained intergovernmental, however, to be decided only unanimously.

There are growing clouds over the spirit, if not the letter, of JHA, however. Immigration is a heated issue among across the EU, and citizens usually include internal economic migration from new EU members westward and economic migrants from the EU south in their grievances, which have grown because of unemployment and insecurity from recent conditions of economic crisis. These pressures have created an elite balancing act between defending the rights of Europeans, including free movement and the human rights of migrants, and recognizing anti-immigrant pressures that are sometimes openly xenophobic. The 2011–2012 Arab spring turned illegal immigration in the Mediterranean region into panic flight, overwhelming the EU's practical ability to cope with the surge of refugees. Then French President Sarkozy and Italian Premier Berlusconi both advocated limiting free movement inside the EU for non-EU citizens, a cry echoed by the Danish prime minister who even shut down the Danish border with Germany for a few days. There has also been widespread agitation and repressive responses to Roma migration. This may mean that JHA has been too effective and is feeding growing Euroscepticism.

Foreign and Security Policy

When Jacques Delors was Commission president, he often asked, rhetorically, whether the EU was happy being a "big Switzerland," an economic giant and foreign policy dwarf. The question remains pertinent. The EU has been an important actor in international trade from the beginning and as it grew became an "economic giant." But American hegemony and NATO kept it distant from important security matters and the diverging foreign policy goals of larger members prevented serious foreign policy action. After the Cold War, the Maastricht Treaty created another intergovernmental pillar for the new CFSP. Did the post–Cold War world demand a larger European international footprint? Many thought it did.

THE U.S. CONNECTION

The EU and the United States have had a long, sometimes quarrelsome, but intimate history. Without American policies after World War II European integration would not have begun, but American leaders were persistently annoyed with the early EU. The French were a bother about NATO and European defense, the Germans with *Ostpolitik*, the Common Agricultural Policy threatened American food exports, and there was wrangling about competition policy and exchange rates. U.S. governments favored European integration, but hoped for an obedient "special relationship" like that with Britain rather than what emerged. As the EU revived in the 1980s, the United States thought it too slow to copy American neoliberalism and too eager to keep its social programs. The EU persisted with Economic and Monetary Union despite the scepticism of American leaders who also believed that the Common Foreign and Security Policy could threaten NATO. Trade conflicts, exemplified by a long dispute about bananas that pit an EU determined to protect its former colonies against gigantic, politically influential American agro-corporations whose bananas actually came from Central and Latin America, were chronic. Larger U.S.-EU conflicts such as the EU's divided response to the Iraq war left bitter tastes. The EU's antitrust policies annoyed big American corporations and NSA spying on EU leaders annoyed European politicians. The picture changes if we step back, however. The United States and the EU have stood side-by-side on things that count like democracy, the rule of law, the need for open and free societies, human rights, and opposition to illiberal dictatorships.

MAKING CONNECTIONS The EU and the United States have always been close friends and faithful allies. Why has their connection been so fraught with controversy?

The EU is very important in international trade, and because of globalization, trade policy will structure world events for years to come. EU trade policy begins with a general mandate from the Council of Ministers that is then administered by the Commission and carried out by the International Trade Commissioner. The EU privileges its trade positions for "ACP" (African, Caribbean, Pacific) countries whose relationships are regulated separately, but open trade has also been extended to most of the world's poorer countries via free trade in "anything but arms." The EU has been more open to developing countries than other rich parts of the world, with agriculture a large exception. Of late, issues that were outside earlier trade talks such as health, environmental, and labor standards, public procurement, and intellectual property rights, are on the table because the EU has put them there. Private diplomacy by European economic interests and a lively international civil society composed of protest groups and nongovernmental organizations (NGOs) are also recent facts of life. Together with the United States, the EU engineered the Doha Development Round, the first WTO trade negotiations, aimed at bringing the poorest developing societies into global trade. Rapid development in Asia and Latin America has created other threats to established northern interests, however. The Doha Round has fallen far short of EU hopes, but trade diplomacy remains central to EU foreign policy. Most recently, post-Doha, the EU has sought new bilateral trade treaties such as that recently concluded with Canada, meant in part to be a door-opener to new negotiations with the United States. International trade policy will continue to be a bumpy, but essential, road for the EU.

Is the EU still a security dwarf in a world where global summits, bombs, and big battalions remain fundamental? At Maastricht, where the EU's CFSP originated, participants knew that cooperation would be difficult and that intergovernmentalism implied slow progress. They nonetheless had hopes that the Western European Union (WEU), a European defense arrangement originating in the 1940s, might grow to become the Union's defense arm. Europe's incoherence toward the former Yugoslavia in the 1990s demonstrated how difficult the issues were. Reflections then led to official focus on the WEU "Petersberg tasks" of humanitarian intervention and peacekeeping, which called for combat-ready, properly equipped European forces to manage crises in and outside Europe. The first challenge was building rapid-response capacities. The 1997 Amsterdam Treaty discussion of a "European Security and Defense Identity" included planning operations in the Council of Ministers, the appointment of a High Representative for CFS, and empowerment of the Council to develop common strategies. In December of that year, the French and British met in St. Malo and issued a "Joint Declaration on European Defense" to create ".... the capacity for autonomous action, backed up by credible military forces, the means to decide to use them, and a readiness to do so." This new determination was reinforced by what happened over Kosovo, where the United States called, and fired, most of NATO's shots to deter Serbian brutality.

The December 1999 Helsinki European Council announced "headline goals" for 2003 of a 60,000 man rapid-reaction force for crisis management, peace-keeping, and humanitarian aid that could be deployed within sixty days and stay for a full year, backed by warplanes and ships. The Council of Ministers then created mechanisms to plan and control these forces that included a Council Politics and Security Committee (COPS), an EU Military Committee that included the military chiefs of EU members, and a Brussels general staff of 150. Helsinki also underlined EU "determination to develop an autonomous capacity to take decisions and, where NATO as a whole is not engaged, to launch and conduct EU-led military operations in response to international crises." As a result, the EU took on new, if limited, military duties. By 2003, however, the new European Security Strategy had downsized the Helsinki goals to fifteen battalion-sized battle groups, mobilizable, with tactical support, in five days and able to operate for thirty days. This was not a "European army," for which neither money nor political commitment existed, but nonetheless a coordinated commitment for particular kinds of missions. More coordination and integration of the European defense industry was also needed, but this threatened national jobs and vested interests. The number of ready EU battalions is now close to full capacity, and there has been new investment in high-tech fighter planes, smarter weapons, new airlift capacity (the Airbus A400), and new satellites.

Since 2003 the EU has been involved in fourteen civilian, six military, and three mixed missions on three different continents, sometimes moving "out of area" in contingents of a few hundred. On the civilian side, the EU took over policing in Bosnia and Herzegovina from the UN, monitored elections in East Timor in 2005, worked in Iraq, Afghanistan, Palestine, and Moldova-Ukraine, and sent 3,000 people to help develop the rule of law in Kosovo in 2008. Militarily, it has engaged in joint missions with NATO in Macedonia and Bosnia and Herzogovina and, by itself, it has engaged in a 1,500-troop emergency mission to Goma in the Democratic Republic of Congo to calm a very troubled region, and in 2006 EUFOR RD Congo calmed Kinshasa during elections. More recently the EU has intervened in Chad and the Central African Republic in 2009, and been the mainstay of anti-piracy patrolling off Somalia.

Even tentative EU initiatives in defense and security inevitably spilled over into relations with the United States. Long arguments in the 1990s over the role of NATO ended up in an agreement in which the United States will give the EU access to some NATO assets for limited kinds of action, as long as NATO remains predominant, something that the EU's renunciation of the WEU facilitated. A French journalist has noted that Americans and Europeans "indulge in incompatible dreams. The U.S. wants to be number one.... Europeans want to keep the U.S. as the ultimate insurance policy as they evolve towards a common identity." The meaning of this became clearer after September 11, 2001. Europeans immediately and unanimously expressed massive support and sympathy for Americans, did all they could to assist U.S. intelligence services to beef up European counterterrorism, and EU member states fully participated in the U.S.-led NATO expedition to Afghanistan. Deep disagreements emerged over Iraq, however. When the United States decided to invade, the French and Germans were deeply opposed, while the British marched to Baghdad along with Spain, Italy, Portugal and several CEEC then-applicant EU members, in G. W. Bush's "coalition of the willing."

European nations, especially old imperial powers, have long-standing divergent foreign policy goals. Smaller EU countries worried about domination in security matters by bigger ones. Some, like Sweden, Finland, and Austria, had earlier been neutral. Others, like many CEECs, were strongly pro-American because of what the United States had stood for in the Cold War. The term "common foreign policy" thus could not mean a *single* European policy that would replace everything member states did. Building on long years of European Political Cooperation—constant diplomatic communication that could, on occasion, lead to joint statements—the Maastricht CFSP ambitions were more modest, demonstrated by Maastricht's intergovernmental pillar and Lisbon's "communitization" that left large matters for unanimity decision making. In the years since the turn of the century the EU has invested in "soft power" foreign policy areas like international environmental politics, partly because EU leaders were seeking new issues where the EU could agree and then take a global lead. EU enlargement itself has been "soft" foreign policy. The EU "club" has proved attractive to neighbors, and the prospect of joining has pushed many to democratize, commit to the rule of law, and cooperate for the European greater good, a process documented in the histories of Greece, Spain, and Portugal in the 1980s and formerly communist CEECs more recently. The EU has also tried this approach to offer partial benefits such as trade and development aid to "near neighbors" to the east (Turkey, the Ukraine, and others), and Mediterranean countries, but progress has not been smooth. The EU and Turkey continue to dance around one another without progress toward Turkish membership. A "Mediterranean Union" promoted by French president Sarkozy disappeared in the dust of the Arab spring. The EU's "neighborhood" policy has more recently run up against the brash toughness of Vladimir Putin in Ukraine, against which EU "soft power" was ineffective, particularly because member states were divided over its use.

EU humanitarian and development aid is part of this "soft" approach. The EU, long in the aid business, has expanded and concentrated its approaches. There is now a European Development Fund directed to ACP countries, special regional aid programs directed to the very poorest countries, a cluster of humanitarian aid programs often used to co-finance worthy NGO activities in poorer parts of the world, and sophisticated humanitarian aid operations for areas hit by natural disasters, population displacement, and deadly conflict. The EU (the Union and its member states taken together) gives 50 percent of the world's development aid, and is now more problem-targeted and conditional, seeking out infrastructure projects (transportation, water supply, schools, health care), trying to leverage its aid into better administration and governance in recipient countries.

The EU's "big Switzerland" position has never really been a contrast between muscular America and weakling EU. As a heavyweight in trade, environmental and sustainable development, a significant promoter of democratization, a well-equipped expert in humanitarian aid and crisis management, and a major player in the international exchange rate regime, the EU is difficult to overlook internationally. By smart bomb and big battalion measures, however, the EU remains a small power. Whether and how this will change in a perilous world that is becoming more "multipolar" is unforeseeable. The 2009 Lisbon Treaty created a new institutional foundation in foreign and security policy. The new High Representative for CFSP, Baroness Ashton, was "double hatted" as president of the CFSP Council in the Council of Ministers and vice president of the Commission and charged with combining the different and often rival administrative bodies presently dealing in foreign affairs, energizing the Council's fledgling security groups, developing a new EU diplomatic service out of disparate EU and national units, and being the public face for EU diplomacy. She has needed lots of energy and good fortune to get started, and the going so far has been tough.

Where Do You Stand?

The EU's institutional system seems to be too complicated to understand and does not work very well. Can the EU survive and thrive?

The EU institutions may not be democratically legitimate enough to sustain the EU's policies. What institutional changes might help to change this?

EURO-POLITICS IN TRANSITION

SECTION **5**

Analogies between the biographies of people and political systems are sometimes useful. The EU is now a "young adult" compared to many Western states. Young adulthood is often a perilous moment both for humans and states, however. The bloom is off initial patriotic and identity enthusiasms. Generations have changed and the facts of what went before have been forgotten. The less-than-glorious practices of real politics have started to puncture the rhetoric of happy talk. Finally, conflicts that obscured in the foundational period break through. At the EU's present age, the United States was moving toward the Civil War, the Soviet Union toward the gerontocratic stagnation that would lead to its demise, and Italy and Germany after World War I were embracing fascism. Young adulthood is often a time of crisis, and so it has been for the European Union.

The EU'S recent years have been tumultuous. Maastricht's new policies in foreign affairs and defense, internal affairs, the environment, market liberalization, and monetary union, at a moment when the EU was doubling its membership—have brought changes that EU citizens have often misunderstood and disliked. Economic globalization has challenged the EU's economy and destabilized its social contracts. The joys of uniting post–Cold War Europe were obscured by the conflictual reform of the EU's institutions to welcome new Central and Eastern European members. Last, but far from least, the Great Recession and **Eurozone crisis** put the EU in economic harm's way. The EU is in transition, and there is great uncertainty about what will come next.

Focus Questions ▼

- Why has adding new members to the EU caused so much difficulty?

- How can we explain the recent "retreat" of EU member states from commitment to European integration?

Eurozone crisis

Crisis of sovereign debt within Eurozone that broke out after 2009 that led to frantic emergency efforts by Eurozone members and the European Council to bail out Greece, Ireland, and Portugal and reconfigure EMU rules.

The EU's stars are out of line after the Eurozone crisis. Is there a way forward?

Martin Sutovec/Cagle Cartoons

The EU's problems defining new foreign and defense policies should not have been surprising. The CFSP was meant to coexist with those of member states rather than replace them. Member states continued to prioritize their own interests and goals, as seen in responses to the invasion of Iraq, policies toward Russia (of great importance in the energy realm), attitudes toward NATO and the United States, and responses to the risings in North Africa and the Middle East. The slow accretion of EU savoir-faire in peace-keeping and crisis management and military matters has run up against a world of hard-nosed territorial defense and force projection that remains resolutely national and coordinated by the United States and NATO. Rhetorical announcements about the nobility of the EU's "soft power" foreign policy DNA failed at the 2009 UN Copenhagen Climate Change Conference, had limited effects in the EU's "neighborhoods" in the eastern European borderlands, the Mediterranean, and the Middle East, and have been overwhelmed by economic globalization and new international multipolarity. The 2009 Lisbon Treaty's appointment of a Mr./Ms./Mrs. CFSP to establish order from the EU's existing dispersion of foreign, defense, development, and humanitarian aid policies has proceeded very slowly.

The institutional reforms connected with enlargement to the CEECS were turbulent because they opened a Pandora's box of reshuffling the relative power of different EU institutions and member states. The 2000 Nice Treaty that threatened smaller member states was rejected by the Irish in a 2002 referendum. There followed a European Convention in which delegates from EU institutions, member states, and civil society debated for almost two years before producing a European Constitutional Treaty (ECT). The ECT was then submitted for ratification in 2005 and rejected in French and Dutch referendums. Two years later the most important parts of the ECT were rewritten into a new treaty and then rejected by the Irish in another referendum. Leaders then cajoled the Irish to vote again and this time they approved, allowing the Lisbon Treaty to come into effect in 2009. This decade-long debate about EU institutions persuaded many citizens that the EU was not working very well. Declining turnout in elections to the European Parliament has been another sign of the EU's waning popularity

European economic fortunes greatly contributed to citizen skepticism. The EU's first period had seen high economic growth, full employment, and positive life changes. Its more recent programs have been sold as remedies for the lowered growth and higher unemployment in the globalization era. Although EU members had varying records of success and failure, promises made had not been redeemed even before the disasters of the Great Recession and the Eurozone crisis led to harsh and protracted austerity, very high unemployment, and unwanted social reforms, plunged the EU into a second recession, further tarnished the EU's already shaky legitimacy, deepened the EU's North-South divisions, and divided Eurozone from non-EMU countries.

The EU that had helped bring peace and prosperity seemed further and further in the past. In the present, many citizens sense that the EU is far away, top-down and bureaucratic, and not very effective at solving their problems. When asked about the EU, or asked to vote for a European Parliament they had trouble making sense of, they responded with negativity or indifference much more than they had in the past. Their puzzlement was connected, first of all, to lack of transparency and ineffectiveness in the EU's institutions. The "community method" seemed technocratic, depoliticizing, and baffling. More recently, it had receded in favor of a new intergovernmental confederalism led by the European Council that worked too slowly and clearly favored the preferences of more powerful EU members. Citizen negativity was also connected to EU responses to globalization. In the 1990s the EU had decided to be proactive and promote reform at all levels. Many Europeans, accustomed to middle-class lifestyles and extensive social protection, perceived this as threatening. Worse still, the new strategies did not rejuvenate European economic energies, restore growth, and alleviate unemployment. The global financial crisis that exploded in 2007–2008 accentuated widespread and growing citizen pessimism. The European integration experiment had always lived from crisis to crisis, often responding well. Its future could depend on how well it could distance itself from the financial crisis and rebuild its credibility.

Despite all this, the young adult European Union has been a fabulous success, well beyond any of its founders' dreams. It has bound together nations that earlier had gone regularly to war. Yet for younger generations that have not experienced European war, this is a fading memory. The EU has gone far beyond its original concerns in economic governance into European citizenship, monetary policy, foreign affairs, environmental regulation, and unifying Europe politically after the Cold War. Yet these changes have often caused greater uncertainty and confusion, particularly as success at economic governance became more difficult to achieve with the advance of globalization. The EU proved over and over again that multilateral negotiations between sovereign states in carefully designed and innovative institutions could build lasting and growing cooperation. It created European interests and identities where neither had existed. Its different citizens are unquestionably more comfortable with one another and more "European" than ever. But the EU remains an "unidentified political object," a strange combination of federation and confederation that does not resemble a state and is badly understood by citizens. It has coexisted with sovereign states that have learned to share power with others when cooperation made more sense than clinging to sovereignty, but this coexistence has had many rocky moments. The present period is one of the rockiest. The EU has a good record at responding to vast changes in the lives and social orders of its members and the international system. In a world filled with turbulence this is truly extraordinary, but today's uncertainty is very troubling.

Where Do You Stand?

Enlargement of the EU to include almost all European countries, ex-communist central and eastern European ones in particular, was bound to bring new difficulties. What are the most important of these difficulties, how has the EU responded to them, and how well have these responses worked?

The Eurozone crisis has left the EU in a difficult situation. EU member states are at odds, many citizens are unhappy, and economic conditions are not promising. How might the EU rekindly public enthusiasm for the cause of integration?

Key Terms

citizen initiative
Common Foreign and Security
   Policy
community method
Economic and Monetary Union
   (EMU)
European Commission

European Council
European Court of Justice
European Parliament
European single market
Eurozone crisis
Justice and Home Affairs (JHA)
Lisbon Treaty

Maastricht Treaty
qualified majority voting
Schengen area
subsidiarity

Suggested Readings

Bastasin, Carlo. *Saving Europe: How National Politics Nearly Destroyed the Euro* Washington Brookings, 2012.

Cini, Michelle and Nieves Perez-Solorzano Borragan. *European Union Politics,* 3rd ed. Oxford: Oxford University Press, 2010.

Dinan, Desmond. *Ever Closer Union,* 4th ed. Boulder: Lynne Rienner, 2010.

Eichengreen, Barry. *The European Economy Since 1945.* Princeton: Princeton University Press, 2007.

Kassim, Hussein, John Peterson, Michael W. Bauer, and Sara Connolly. *The European Commission in the 21st Century.* New York: Oxford University Press, 2013.

Rosamond, Ben. *Theories of European Integration.* Basingstoke, England: Palgrave, 2000.

Ross, George. *The European Union and Its Crises seen through the Eyes of the Brussels Elite.* Houndsworth: Palgrave-Macmillan, 2011.

_____. *Jacques Delors and European Integration.* Cambridge: Polity, 1995.

Scharpf, Fritz. *Governing in Europe: Effective and Democratic.* Oxford: Oxford University Press, 1999.

Wallace, Helen, Mark A. Pollack, and Alasdair Young, eds. *Policy-Making in the European Union,* 6th ed. New York: Oxford University Press, 2010.

Suggested Websites

Delegation of the European Commission to the USA
www.eurunion.org

European Union, official Brussels site
www.europa.eu

Bruegel, a good site for EU economics
www.bruegel.org

EUobserver, excellent daily EU bulletin from centrist-liberal group in the European Parliament
www.EUObserver.com

Notre Europe-Institut Jacques Delors (Paris); includes many documents in English
www.notre-europe.eu/en/

6 Japan

Shigeko Fukai and Haruhiro Fukui

Official Name: Japan
Location: Eastern Asia
Capital City: Tokyo
Population (2013): 127.1 million
Size: 377,930 sq. km.; slightly smaller than California

1867
Meiji Restoration inaugurates rapid Japanese industrialization and modernization.

1912–1926
Taisho Democracy period

1925
Universal Manhood Suffrage Law promulgated. Japan Trade Union Council formed.

1932
Military officers attempt but fail to take over government.

1945
Atomic bombs dropped on Hiroshima and Nagasaki. Soviet Union declares war on Japan. Japan surrenders. Allied occupation and reform of Japan begin.

1947
New Constitution of Japan, promulgated in 1946, comes into effect featuring a democratic government and a peace clause (Article 9) renouncing the right to make war.

1976
Lockheed scandal and arrest of former Prime Minister Tanaka Kakuei

1860	1900	1920	1940	1950	1960	1985

1900–1901
Constitutional Party of Political Friends (Seiyukai) formed

1889
Constitution of the Great Empire of Japan establishes a bicameral legislature, the Imperial Diet.

1941
Japan attacks U.S. naval base in Pearl Harbor. United States declares war on Japan.

1937
Japan invades China.

1931–1932
Japanese army takes control of Chinese Manchuria without orders from the government in Tokyo.

1955
Socialist parties unite to form Japan Socialist Party (JSP); conservative parties merge into Liberal Democratic Party (LDP).

1951
Japanese Peace Treaty and United States–Japan Mutual Security Treaty signed in San Francisco

1985
Telecommunications and tobacco industries privatized. Equal Employment Law enacted.

SECTION 1

THE MAKING OF THE MODERN JAPANESE STATE

Focus Questions

- How have the characteristics of Japan's natural resource endowment influenced its economic development and foreign policy strategies since the mid-nineteenth century?

- Which watershed events in Japanese history are particularly relevant to understanding government and politics in contemporary Japan?

Politics in Action

Sitting smack at the midpoint on the "Ring of Fire" horseshoe that runs along the entire length of the Pacific Rim from the southern end of New Zealand in the west to the southern end of Chile in the east, Japanese are thoroughly used to frequent, and often violent, earthquakes and tsunamis. On March 11, 2011, however, the nation's northeastern coast some 200 miles northeast of Tokyo was struck by a combination of an earthquake and tsunamis of unprecedented ferocity. The magnitude 9 earthquake and the tsunami waves cresting at over 70 feet at the shoreline left in their wake a trail of destruction and horror across the coastal communities: approximately 120,000 homes totally destroyed, 16,000 people dead, 2,600 missing, and nearly a half million displaced. The receding waves carried with them back to the Pacific Ocean a huge mass of debris, part of which would reach the west coast of North America within a few years. A ship used for marine science classes at a local

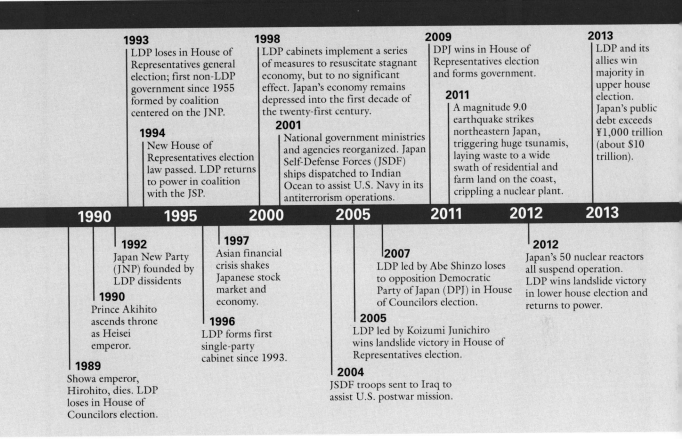

1993
LDP loses in House of Representatives general election; first non-LDP government since 1955 formed by coalition centered on the JNP.

1994
New House of Representatives election law passed. LDP returns to power in coalition with the JSP.

1998
LDP cabinets implement a series of measures to resuscitate stagnant economy, but to no significant effect. Japan's economy remains depressed into the first decade of the twenty-first century.

2001
National government ministries and agencies reorganized. Japan Self-Defense Forces (JSDF) ships dispatched to Indian Ocean to assist U.S. Navy in its antiterrorism operations.

2009
DPJ wins in House of Representatives election and forms government.

2011
A magnitude 9.0 earthquake strikes northeastern Japan, triggering huge tsunamis, laying waste to a wide swath of residential and farm land on the coast, crippling a nuclear plant.

2013
LDP and its allies win majority in upper house election. Japan's public debt exceeds ¥1,000 trillion (about $10 trillion).

1990 1995 2000 2005 2011 2012 2013

1992
Japan New Party (JNP) founded by LDP dissidents

1990
Prince Akihito ascends throne as Heisei emperor.

1989
Showa emperor, Hirohito, dies. LDP loses in House of Councilors election.

1997
Asian financial crisis shakes Japanese stock market and economy.

1996
LDP forms first single-party cabinet since 1993.

2007
LDP led by Abe Shinzo loses to opposition Democratic Party of Japan (DPJ) in House of Councilors election.

2005
LDP led by Koizumi Junichiro wins landslide victory in House of Representatives election.

2004
JSDF troops sent to Iraq to assist U.S. postwar mission.

2012
Japan's 50 nuclear reactors all suspend operation. LDP wins landslide victory in lower house election and returns to power.

high school was lost to the tsunami, reached a Crescent City beach in northern California in the spring of 2013, and was returned to the high school in October of the same year.

Potentially even more lasting in its devastating physical and psychological impacts on the nation was the crippling damage done to a waterfront nuclear power plant in Fukushima Prefecture, which bore the brunt of the pounding tsunami waves. They swallowed the whole plant, probably already wrecked by the earthquake, knocking out its power-operated cooling system, causing meltdowns at three of its six reactors, extensive radiation leaks, and wholesale evacuations of the towns and villages in the vicinity that had survived the earthquake and tsunami. The radioactive strontium released into the atmosphere reached in no time most of the downwind cities and towns, including the capital, Tokyo. Equally radioactive and lethal substances, mostly cesium leaked into and contaminated coastal waters, shutting down the local fisheries industry, the mainstay of the regional economy.

The radioactive contamination of the entire regional ecosphere and the destruction of the main sources of livelihood made it impossible for the majority of the evacuated survivors to return to their own homes, turning them into semipermanent "nuclear refugees," indefinitely stranded at public shelters or the homes of relatives and friends. Part of the radioactive fallout, like other debris, would cross the Pacific Ocean and reach the west coast of North America within a few days, if airborne, or within a few years, if waterborne. The March 2011 "triple disaster," as it has come to be known, thus turned out to be much more than a national disaster for Japanese alone, but also a major international environmental calamity.

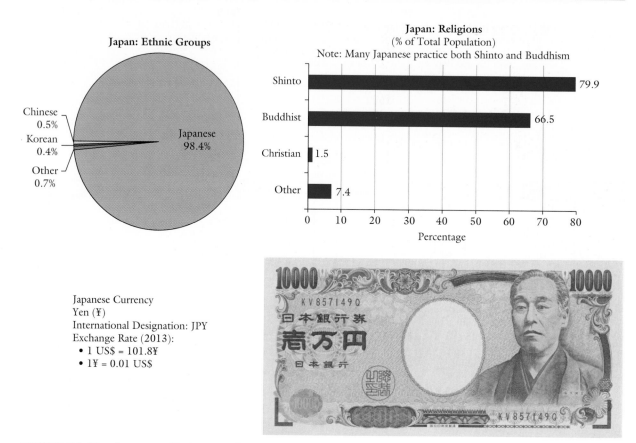

FIGURE 6.1 The Japanese Nation at a Glance

© Takeshi Nishio/Shutterstock.com (for photo)

Geographic Setting

Japan is an archipelago of 6,850 islands lying off the east coast of continental East Asia. To the west, across the Sea of Japan, it faces the Russian Far East and the two Koreas, and, across the East China Sea, the central coast of China. Eastward across the Pacific Ocean, it faces the west coasts of the United States and northern Mexico. Tokyo is about 5,600 miles due west of San Simeon National Park in central California. Japan's northernmost and southernmost cities are, respectively, due west of Portland, Oregon, and Isla Margarita Island in Baja California.

The Japanese archipelago covers a land area of about 146,000 square miles. Ninety-seven percent of the land area is within four islands—Honshu, Hokkaido, Kyushu, and Shikoku. The nation is slightly smaller than California and slightly larger than Montana. With about 127 million people, it is the tenth most populous nation in the world and about ten times as densely populated as the United States. About three-quarters of the people live in 285 cities with a population of 100,000 or more and about a quarter in 11 cities with 1 million or more.

Nearly all Japanese are descendants of immigrants from today's Southeast Asia, South Pacific islands, Siberia, China, and Korea, who have arrived in a series of waves and trickles since about 35,000 years ago, mostly during the period when the sea levels were about 300 feet lower than the present levels and today's Japan was connected by land with most of its neighboring regions and countries. The immigrants from the

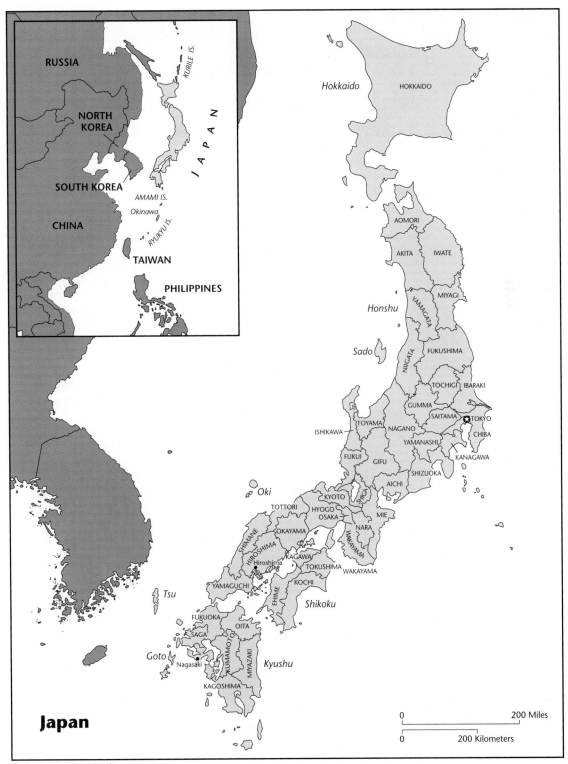

Japan

Table 6.1	Political Organization
Political System	Parliamentary democracy and constitutional monarchy, in which the emperor is merely a symbol of national unity.
Regime History	Current constitution promulgated in 1946 and in effect since 1947.
Administrative Structure	Unitary state, 47 intermediate-level subnational "prefectures," and 1,720 municipalities.
Executive	Prime minister selected by legislature; a cabinet of about twenty ministers appointed by prime minister.
Legislature	Bicameral. The upper house (House of Councilors) has 242 members elected for six-year terms. Half of the members are elected every three years. One hundred forty-six are elected from multiple-seat prefecture-wide districts; 96 are elected nationally by a party list proportional representation method. The lower house (House of Representatives) has 480 members elected for four-year terms, which may be shortened by the dissolution of the house. Three hundred lower house members are elected from single-seat constituencies; 180 are elected by party list proportional representation from eleven regional constituencies.
Judiciary	Supreme Court has fourteen judges appointed by the cabinet and the chief judge nominated by the cabinet and appointed by the emperor; all are eligible to serve until seventy years of age, subject to periodic popular reviews.
Party System	Stable one-party dominant (Liberal Democratic Party) from mid-1950s to mid-1990s, a quasi-two-party from 2007 to 2010, and unstable one-party dominant since. Major parties: Liberal Democratic Party, Democratic Party of Japan, Clean Government Party, Social Democratic Party, Japan Communist Party.

diverse sources and their descendants have intermingled and interbred to produce the genetically heterogeneous people of contemporary Japan.

Critical Junctures

Pre-Modern Japan

Recent works in phylogeographic research, popularly known as "genetic tracking," show that the Japanese archipelago began to be populated by immigrants from the surrounding areas, originally beachcombers, hunters, and gatherers, as early as 33000 BCE, during the last glacial period. By about 7000 BCE, some inhabitants began to build and live in small settlements and raise livestock. In the third century CE, newly arrived immigrants from Korea began to build much larger settlements, or proto-states, in the southwestern regions of the country. In the next several centuries, most of these proto-states were unified, either by force or negotiation, into a single state led by a legendary "heavenly sovereign," or "emperor," who claimed to be a descendant of the Sun Goddess, an obvious copy of the rulers of ancient China. This led to the founding of the world's oldest surviving monarchy.

Early Japanese rulers frequently sent emissaries to Korea and China to pay homage to their rulers, and they returned with a variety of goods and ideas. These included the teachings of the Chinese philosopher, Confucius (551–479 BCE), who exhorted reverence for ancestors and deference to authority, ideas that have had enduring effects on Japanese society. Buddhism, with its origins in India, also reached Japan via China and Korea in the middle of the sixth century. Commingled with the native Japanese religion, Shinto, Confucianism and Buddhism continue to shape Japanese people's everyday life.

A succession of emperors, and a few empresses, or their regents, ruled the ancient and early medieval Japanese state until the late twelfth century, when they began to lose effective control of both the territory and the people to multiple local landlords with armed farmers in their employ, who over time grew into professional warriors. A few of these became powerful warlords with their own vassals. This gave rise to a Japanese version of medieval feudalism contemporaneous with and very similar to its European counterpart. In the next few centuries, some of these warlords appropriated the title of **shogun** (general), claiming to be the emperor's military guardian.[1] In the early seventeenth century, one of these warlords, Tokugawa Ieyasu,* established a military government, or shogunate, in the new capital city of Edo, today's Tokyo, which lasted for the next 265 years. Figurehead emperors were left to reside in the old capital, Kyoto.

These events took place largely in isolation from developments in the rest of the world, thanks to Japan's geographical location. The isolation, however, was seriously broken twice in the mid-sixteenth century by the arrivals, first, of a couple of Portuguese sailors in possession of firearms, or matchlocks, on a Chinese ship stranded on an island off the coast of Kyushu, then, of a Spanish Jesuit missionary, Francis Xavier. The former event introduced the Japanese to the cutting-edge weapon of the era and led to the production of a half million local copies in the next few decades, while the second event ushered in a "Japan's Christian Century," when an estimated 130,000 Japanese were converted to Christianity.

Under the Tokugawa shogunate's iron-fisted rule, however, Japan was closed almost completely to the outside world by government order. The production and possession of guns, a potential source of physical threat to the ruling regime, was strictly regulated, and the practice and proselytizing of Christianity, a potential source of spiritual threat to the regime, were banned. The nation was divided into nearly 300 feudal domains, each under a local lord's rule and all under the shogunate's control. Within each domain, the people were divided into six classes—warriors, farmers, artisans, merchants, "filthy hordes," and "nonhumans." Warriors, called **samurai** (or *bushi*) in Japanese, made up about 8 percent of the total population and constituted a substratum of the ruling class. The last two classes were "outcastes." Members of the several classes were strictly segregated from each other, both occupationally and residentially. Women were treated as inherently inferior and subordinate to men and could not participate in public affairs. Most children from samurai families—and increasingly those of well-to-do farmers and merchants—received rudimentary school education. In addition to reading, writing, and arithmetic, these children learned Confucian teachings about the correct social order and proper personal behavior.[2]

Meiji Restoration and Taisho Democracy (1868–1925)

In 1868 a widespread insurrection toppled the Tokugawa regime, an event triggered by the forced entry in 1853 and 1854 of a small flotilla of U.S. warships under the command of Commodore Matthew C. Perry into a bay some 100 miles southwest of

shogun

The title, meaning general, assumed by a succession of hereditary leaders of the three military dynasties—the Minamotos, the Ashikagas, and the Tokugawas—that ruled Japan one after another from the late twelfth century to the mid-nineteenth century. Their government was called the shogunate.

samurai

The warrior class in medieval Japan, also known as *bushi*. The class emerged around the tenth century, and a dominant band of its members established Japan's first warrior government in the twelfth century. The last samurai government was overthrown in the Meiji Restoration of the mid-nineteenth century.

---

*In Japanese, the family name comes before the personal or given name.

Edo. Perry's intrusion violated the centuries-old official policy that forbade all foreigners, with the exception of a handful of authorized Chinese, Koreans, Ryukyuans (Okinawans), and Dutch, to enter Japanese territory. The shogun capitulated to Commodore Perry's demand that Japan open its ports to U.S. naval and merchant ships. This gave anti-Tokugawa local lords and their followers an excuse to revolt against the shogunate ostensibly to defend national honor and integrity.

The rebels installed a young heir to the imperial throne as the nation's new ruler and moved him and his court to Edo, which was renamed Tokyo ("eastern capital"). His reign title was Meiji ("enlightened rule"), and the insurrection came to be known as the Meiji Restoration. Over the next fifty years, Japan's government was led by a small group of erstwhile rebels and their friends, dubbed the Meiji oligarchy, who quickly transformed a feudal state into a modern industrial and military power.

The Meiji government replaced the feudal domains by prefectures and the six-class social structure by a three-class system. The samurai class was nominally retained, while farmers, artisans, and merchants were lumped into a single "commoner" class, and those in the two outcaste categories became a "new commoner" class. A national public education system, composed of universal primary schools and voluntary secondary schools and colleges, was introduced, opening new avenues for all citizens to improve their life opportunities on the basis of knowledge and academic performance.

The democratic idea was introduced to Japan for the first time and gave rise to a "freedom and people's rights" movement, led by two proto-political parties, the Liberals and the Reformists. The Meiji oligarchy responded to their demand in 1889 by issuing a constitution modeled after Prussia's and establishing a bicameral legislature, the Imperial Diet. The upper house, the House of Peers, consisted exclusively of hereditary and appointed members, such as adult male members of the imperial family, former feudal lords, and men credited with distinguished service to the state. The lower house, the House of Representatives, was elected by an all-male electorate of top-bracket taxpayers, who initially accounted for a little over 1 percent of Japan's total population, rising to about 5.5 percent by the early 1920s.

The 1889 constitution guaranteed civil rights and freedoms to the people "subject to the limitations imposed by law" and required every law to be enacted with the consent of the Imperial Diet. But the emperor held the formal right to approve and issue all laws; open, close, and adjourn the Diet; and declare war, make peace, and conclude international treaties. In his name, the oligarchy ruled the nation through several nonelective institutions of government, such as the Privy Council, the House of Peers, and the civil and military services.

Taisho democracy

A reference to Japanese politics in the period roughly coinciding with Emperor Taisho's reign, 1912–1926. The period was characterized by the rise of a popular movement for democratization of government by the introduction of universal manhood suffrage and the reduction of the power and influence of authoritarian institutions of the state.

During the reign of the Meiji emperor's successor, the Taisho ("great righteousness") emperor, Japan made significant progress toward political liberalization, in a period known as **Taisho democracy** (roughly 1912–1926). The two main political parties of the Meiji period were renamed Seiyukai (Constitutional Party of Political Friends) and Kenseito (Constitutional Government Party) and alternately formed a government through electoral competition. A Universal Manhood Suffrage Law was enacted in 1925, removing the tax payment requirement for the vote and quadrupling overnight the size of the electorate (males over the age of 25) to about 20 percent of the total population.

Rise and Fall of Militarist Nationalism (1926-1945)

Despite these important political changes, Taisho democracy was fundamentally superficial and fragile. Class inequalities still divided Japanese society. Rural Japan was dominated by a small class of wealthy landlords and urban Japan by a few giant industrial and financial conglomerates, known as *zaibatsu*. The government bureaucracy was controlled by graduates of a single government-run university. As the Japanese economy became mired in a long recession after World War I and then devastated by the Great Depression in the early 1930s, advocates of democracy at home and peace abroad increasingly faced savage attacks by the military and ultranationalist civilian groups.

Buoyed by victories in the Sino-Japanese War (1894–1895) and the Russo-Japanese War (1904–1905), the military's political influence grew steadily throughout the Meiji-Taisho eras. Under the new Showa ("enlightened peace") emperor's reign, which began in 1926, the military became increasingly independent from the civilian government in pursuit of its own policy goals. This eventually led to the Japanese invasion and occupation of northern Chinese provinces and the creation of a puppet state called Manchukuo in 1932.[3]

In that same year, a group of young naval officers attacked several government offices in Tokyo and shot the prime minister to death in an abortive coup d'état. In a similar attempt in February 1936, bands of army troops murdered the finance minister and several others and occupied a whole block in central Tokyo for four days.[4] These events intimidated and silenced most opponents of the military both inside and outside the government. All political parties were effectively muzzled, then disbanded by government order in 1941.

When the League of Nations condemned the Japanese invasion of China in 1933, Japan walked out of the organization. Faced with growing international isolation, Japan formed a military alliance with Nazi Germany in 1936, joined by Fascist Italy the following year. In the summer of 1937, the Japanese army began a full-scale invasion of China and, the following winter, unleashed a murderous rampage against civilians in the capital of China, an incident now known as the "Rape of Nanking." The United States responded by nullifying its trade agreement with Japan in 1939. Thus cut off from a major source of raw materials essential to the survival of its industrial economy, Japan moved its troops into French Indochina (Vietnam, Laos, and Cambodia) in July 1941 in search of alternative sources of supplies. In response, Washington froze Japanese-owned assets in the United States and banned the sale of oil to Japan.

Faced with the prospect of running out of its limited fuel reserve, the Japanese government, now led by General Tojo Hideki, decided to start a war against the United States. On December 7, 1941, Japanese naval air units executed a carefully planned surprise attack on the U.S. naval base at Pearl Harbor in Hawaii. The United States immediately declared war on Japan.

Japan had some notable military successes early in the war, but it soon began to lose one major battle after another in the Pacific Ocean. By late 1944, its effort was reduced to a desperate defense of its homeland from increasingly frequent and devastating air raids by U.S. bombers. In August 1945, Japan's resistance ended when the first atomic bombs used in war annihilated two major cities, Hiroshima and Nagasaki. On August 15, Japan surrendered unconditionally to the Allied Powers.

zaibatsu

Giant holding companies in pre–World War II Japan, each owned and controlled by members of a particular family. The largest were divided into a number of independent firms under the democratization program during the postwar occupation but were later revived as *keiretsu*, although no longer under the control of any of the original founding families.

The Birth and Evolution of a Pacifist Democracy (1945–Present)

The Allied Occupation of Japan transformed an authoritarian militarist state into a pacifist democracy.[5] The occupation, which lasted from 1945 to 1952, was formally a joint operation by the major Allies: the United States, the British Commonwealth, the Soviet Union, and China. In practice, the United States, represented by General

Hiroshima in the wake of the atomic bombing in August 1945.

AP Images/Stanley Troutman

Supreme Commander for the Allied Powers (SCAP)

The official title of General Douglas MacArthur between 1945 and 1951 when he led the Allied Occupation of Japan.

Douglas MacArthur, who held the position of the **Supreme Commander for the Allied Powers (SCAP)**, played the predominant role.

During the first year and a half of the occupation, SCAP pursued twin central goals: the complete demilitarization and democratization of Japan. The Japanese armed forces were swiftly dismantled, military production was halted, and wartime leaders were either arrested or purged from their public positions. Seven of them, including General Tojo, were executed for war crimes. Militaristic and antidemocratic institutions and practices were banned. At the same time, workers' right to organize was recognized, women were given the vote, and major *zaibatsu* were dissolved. Only the government bureaucracy was left largely intact.

The authoritarian Meiji Constitution was replaced by a democratic constitution, drafted by a handful of American lawyers. The new constitution granted the emperor only a purely symbolic role and transferred all his political powers to the people. It also made the bicameral Diet the state's sole law-making body. All its members, including those in the reorganized and renamed upper house, the House of Councilors, were to be directly elected by the people. Article 9, known as the "peace clause," defined the new Japan as a permanently disarmed pacifist nation.

The Allied Powers and Japan signed a peace treaty in September 1951, in the midst of the Korean War that had broken out in June 1950. In order to protect the disarmed nation from a potential military threat posed by the ongoing war, the United States and Japan also signed a bilateral security treaty at the same time. The latter treaty allowed the United States to continue to use military bases and keep its troops in Japan, an arrangement renewed in 1960 and still in place today. To assist the U.S. military, a quasi-military force of Japan's own, originally named the National Police Reserve and subsequently renamed the **Japan Self-Defense Forces (JSDF)**, was created and has since grown into a fully-fledged, but so far strictly defensive, military force.

The 1960 revision and extension of the United States–Japan Security Treaty provoked fierce opposition both in the Diet and in the streets of Tokyo and other major cities. The opponents warned that the treaty would make Japan a semipermanent military dependency of the United States and an enemy of Japan's closer neighbors, China and the Soviet Union. The conservative Liberal Democratic Party (LDP) government nonetheless rammed the revised treaty through the Diet, an action that provoked such a violent public reaction that President Eisenhower's scheduled state visit to Japan was canceled and the cabinet of Prime Minister Kishi Nobusuke resigned.

The experience of the 1960 political crisis led Kishi's successors to eschew controversial constitutional and security policy issues and concentrate on economic problems. This change in the LDP's strategy ushered in a quarter century of political stability and phenomenal economic growth. In the late 1980s, however, Japan's fiscal and monetary policy-makers let a rampant speculative bubble in the nation's real estate and stock markets develop, then burst, plunging the nation into a deep and long recession. Despite repeated government interventions to jump-start the stagnant economy over the last two decades, the nation remains mired in economic stagnation to this day.

Demonstrators against renewal of U.S.–Japan Mutual Security Treaty in front of Diet Building in Tokyo, May 1960.

AP Images/Nobuyuki Masaki

The Four Themes and Japan

Japan in a Globalized World of States

The modern world Japan joined in the late nineteenth century appeared to its leaders to be divided between economically and technologically advanced and militarily powerful Western imperialist states on one hand, and backward, powerless, and often conquered non-Western states, on the other. To survive in such a world as an independent nation, Japan had to quickly catch up with and join the first group of states. Meiji Japan did so and emerged as the first modern Asian imperialist power by the late 1920s. A little over a decade later, it even launched a war against the United States. The devastating experience of the war, however, led most Japanese to abandon their faith in military force as a means of their nation's survival and seek peaceful international cooperation as a better alternative.

Postwar Japan joined the United Nations in 1956. It has been elected a non-permanent member of the Security Council ten times since 1958. It has also been

Japan Self-Defense Forces (JSDF)

Inaugurated in Japan as a police reserve with 75,000 recruits in August 1950, following the outbreak of the Korean War. Today, it consists of approximately 250,000 troops equipped with sophisticated modern weapons.

the second largest contributor, next to the United States, to the operating budgets of not only the UN but also the International Monetary Fund (IMF) and the World Bank. In the Asia-Pacific region, it has been the largest contributor to the Asian Development Bank (ADB) and provided all of its presidents. It is a founding member and a major promoter of the Asia-Pacific Economic Cooperation (APEC) forum and an active supporter of the Association of Southeast Asian Nations (ASEAN).

Governing the Economy

Meiji Japan successfully built a modern industrial economy virtually from scratch, thanks importantly to careful and comprehensive strategic planning and guidance by the state, an approach later known as industrial policy. This approach was spectacularly successful not only in pre–World War II Japan but also in postwar Japan, and has been copied by many other nations. The policy, however, ceased to work in the increasingly globalized world of the late twentieth and early twenty-first centuries.

The Democratic Idea

Japanese encountered the idea of democracy for the first time early in the Meiji period. Once the nation was exposed to the idea, a number of groups around the nation began to call for creation of political institutions embodying the idea. The Meiji oligarchy responded to their demand by, first, creating a system of partially elective prefectural legislatures (assemblies), then promulgating a Western-style constitution and instituting a partially elective national legislature, the Imperial Diet.

Japan thus entered the twentieth century as a formally constitutional monarchy with national and local legislatures and multiple vocal political parties. Its leaders and most of its people at that time were far more interested in rapid industrialization and military buildup than in democracy. Nonetheless, its encounter and experiment with democratic politics in the pre–World War II period prepared the nation for far more serious and successful democratization after the war. The democratic idea has now become a core element of Japanese political culture.

The Politics of Collective Identity

The leaders of the ancient Japanese state, all or most of whom had left Korea and moved to the archipelago probably due to conflicts back home, claimed their new state to be a land of "the Rising Sun," separate and independent from both Korea and China. Among common people, however, the sense of a Japanese ethnic or national identity remained weak and poorly articulated until the late thirteenth century, when the nation was attacked twice by naval forces sent by the Mongolian emperor of China, Kublai Khan. The invasion attempts failed both times, thanks to timely typhoons, which were translated as "divine winds" and used to reinforce the myth that Japan was a divine nation. The myth was subsequently systematically and effectively harnessed by leaders of Meiji and early Showa Japan to their aggressive foreign and military policies, which eventually led to the Pacific War.

The war devastated the nation not only physically but also spiritually. However, it did not seriously affect its people's national identity. Despite the presence of a few minority groups with considerable grievances (see Section 4), virtually all Japanese continue to share a deep and strong sense of common national identity and destiny.

Themes and Comparisons

Japan shares certain geographical features and historical experiences more with some European nations than with its Asian neighbors. For example, Britain is not only an archipelagic nation like Japan, but is also known, like Japan, to have been inhabited by modern humans since about 30,000 years ago. Britain was connected to continental Europe until the end of the Ice Age, as Japan was once connected to the Asian mainland. The form and practice of feudalism in medieval Japan and medieval Britain were very similar, if not identical. Until the eleventh century, however, Britain had been repeatedly invaded by peoples from the continent, first by Romans, then Germanic tribes, and finally Normans, while Japan was spared such large-scale foreign invasions after the sixth century. Both are also old monarchies. These geographical and historical similarities and differences may help explain some aspects of their contemporary political institutions and culture.

Modern Germany, too, resembles modern Japan in some ways. Both entered the modern world at about the same time in the mid-nineteenth century, became a major industrial and military power by the early twentieth century; started and lost World War II; were occupied, disarmed, and democratized by their wartime enemies; and reemerged as two of the postwar-world's most economically powerful and politically stable democracies.[6] Postwar Germany has, however, not only made genuine and durable peace with its neighbors, whom it had invaded, occupied, and brutalized during the war. Postwar Japan, by comparison, has failed to achieve genuine reconciliation with its neighbors, especially China and Korea, whom it had invaded, occupied, and brutalized, and continues to anger and antagonize them to this day. These remarkable similarities and differences may teach us some important lessons about the role of political culture and leadership.

Where Do You Stand?

Is Japan a particularly exceptional nation in the modern world? Why or why not?

Is Japan a particularly good subject of comparative politics because it is so different from or so similar to some other nations or both?

POLITICAL ECONOMY AND DEVELOPMENT

SECTION 2

State and Economy

In pre–World War II Japan, the state with its slogan of "rich country, strong army" played a central role in achieving rapid industrialization and economic development in the resource-poor nation. The Meiji government founded and operated munitions factories, mines, railroads, telegraph and telephone services, and textile mills, until it sold them at token prices to private entrepreneurs, some of whom later became heads of *zaibatsu* conglomerates.[7] These corporate empires spearheaded the rapid expansion

▼ **Focus Questions**

• In what ways is the historical pattern of the evolution of the modern Japanese political economy unique?

• Why and in what ways has it served as a model for other developing nations, particularly for those in East Asia?

of the Japanese economy, significantly helped by government subsidies, tax breaks, tariff protection, and infrastructure construction.

The Sino-Japanese War (1894–1895) and the Russo-Japanese War (1904–1905) also spurred the growth of Japan's heavy industries. World War I brought about a wartime boom in Japanese export trade and left its trade balance in the black for the first time since the Meiji Restoration.[8] Thanks also to the entrepreneurial talent and initiative of its business leaders and a highly motivated and increasingly skilled workforce, Japan's economy grew steadily by about 3 percent per year from 1868 through the early twentieth century. In the 1930s, now under nearly total control by the state, it grew at more than 5 percent per year.[9] By the beginning of World War II, Japan had thus become one of the world's fastest-growing and most competitive economic powers.

Following its defeat in that war, Japan recovered remarkably quickly, thanks importantly to the assistance provided by the U.S.-led Occupation in combating the postwar political and social chaos and rebuilding the ruined economy. Such assistance included donation of a variety of relief goods, policy advice and guidance, especially on fiscal and monetary policy issues, and permission to resume foreign trade. Even more important in the long run was, however, a set of drastic reforms implemented under the Occupation, including the dissolution of the *zaibatsu* conglomerates and wholesale redistribution of landlord-owned agricultural land to tenant cultivators. By significantly reducing the concentration of wealth and economic power, these reforms prepared Japan for vast expansion of its middle class and domestic consumer markets. The Occupation's demilitarization program freed Japan from the burden of military spending and enabled it to devote its capital, labor, and technology exclusively to the production of civilian goods and services.

After the Occupation ended in 1952, the United States continued to assist Japan's economic recovery by opening its own markets to Japanese exports and granting Japanese firms access to advanced industrial technology developed by U.S. firms. The United States also supported Japan's admission to the United Nations, the International Monetary Fund (IMF), the World Bank, and the General Agreement on Tariffs and Trade (GATT), which later became the World Trade Organization (WTO). Membership in such international organizations enabled Japanese manufacturers to gain access to overseas raw materials, merchandise, and capital markets, and advanced industrial technologies. Thanks to these circumstances, the Japanese economy grew at an average annual rate of 10 percent from the mid-1950s to the early 1970s, until it became one of the most dynamic and competitive economies in the postwar world.

Japan also significantly benefitted from the Korean War in the 1950s and the Vietnam War in the 1960s, in both of which it served as the main regional supplier of goods and services for the U.S. military. The Cold War in general also helped Japan both economically and politically by dramatically shifting American policy goals from the country's total demilitarization and democratization to its swift economic recovery and incorporation into the U.S.-led Cold War bloc.

The Japanese state continued to play the role of the patron and guardian for domestic industries, as it had been doing since the Meiji period. Under its refined and expanded industrial policy programs, the government provided investment funds and tax breaks and allocated foreign exchange and foreign technologies to targeted industries. The 1973 Oil Crisis dealt a severe blow to Japan, which then depended on Arab oil for more than three-quarters of its total crude oil imports, and its economic growth substantially slowed down. Prompted by the government, however, the Japanese manufacturing industry shifted its emphasis from the raw materials-intensive sectors, such as chemicals and metals, to the assembly and knowledge-intensive sectors, and managed to substantially reduce its energy consumption.

The production and export of automobiles and electronics subsequently expanded rapidly, largely thanks to the development of energy-saving and anti-pollution technologies, such as numerically controlled machine tools and industrial robots. By the 1980s, the surging Japanese exports had made Japan the world's largest creditor nation, and the United States had begun to view Japanese imports as a serious threat to its own industries. This led to the 1985 Plaza Accord, a joint decision by representatives of the U.S., Japanese, and European finance ministers to bring about a drastic devaluation of the U.S. dollar in order to make Japanese and German exports more expensive and less competitive.

Alarmed by the potentially crippling effects of the Plaza Accord on the nation's export-driven economy, the Japanese government eased its monetary policy, even while trade surpluses continued to increase money supply. The excess money supply then led many banks and companies to invest in land and stocks, giving rise to uncontrolled asset inflation ("bubble"). The stock price average tripled and the urban land price index quadrupled in the 1985–1989 period. In late 1989, the government belatedly and abruptly tightened lending regulations and raised interest rates. This sudden policy reversal burst the bubble and touched off a protracted recession that continues to this day.

Protection of domestic agriculture is another case of Japan's failed economic policy. Until the early 1990s, Japan maintained a total ban on the import of foreign rice, under the pressure of a powerful interest group network, an iron triangle (see Section 3) of farmers organized in agricultural cooperatives, Diet members from rural districts, and Ministry of Agriculture bureaucrats. The protection of rice farmers at the expense of crop diversification and broad productivity improvement led to a sharp decline in Japan's calorie-based food self-sufficiency rate from about 80 percent in 1960 to 40 percent in 2007.

Japan's financial sector also has been under strong state control and protection. An informal system of government control known as **administrative guidance** has led the nation's major banks and securities firms to form tight networks of mutual cooperation and assistance, backed by an implicit government commitment to bail out their members in trouble. This so-called convoy system helped weak and uncompetitive financial institutions survive, until many of them, saddled with bad loans accumulated in the days of the bubble economy, went bankrupt in the 1990s and early 2000s. Those that survived stopped lending, especially to small businesses, effectively starving them of investment funds and aggravating the recession. The government set up a Financial Services Agency in 2001 to help banks and securities firms rid themselves of bad loans and begin to lend again. The agency has since mediated a series of bank mergers to create some of the largest financial institutions in the world. These moves, however, have done little to lift Japan out of the interminable recession.

Since its inauguration in December 2012, the Japanese government led by Prime Minister Abe Shinzo has been attempting to revive the sick economy through the so-called Abenomics with "three arrows": (1) aggressive monetary easing with a 2-percent target inflation rate, so as to devalue the yen and stimulate exports; (2) massive fiscal spending with expanded public works and tax breaks for corporations financed with government bonds; and (3) deregulation and structural reforms. The third and last "arrow" had been not only on the ruling LDP's policy agenda for some time, but also on that of the main opposition, the Democratic Party of Japan (DPJ). However, it had failed to materialize, due mainly to the resistance of the entrenched iron triangles (see Section 3). Abenomics includes both Keynesian measures, such as expansion of public works, and neoliberal actions, such as welfare-spending cuts, tax reductions for corporations and the wealthy, participation in the regional free-trade

administrative guidance

Informal guidance, usually not based on statute or formal regulation, that is given by a government agency, such as a ministry and its subdivisions, to a private organization, such as a firm, or a lower-level government. The lack of transparency of the practice makes it subject to the criticism that it is a disguised form of collusion between a government agency and a firm.

regime, known as the Trans-Pacific Partnership (TPP), and labor market deregulation to make it easier to lay off employees in hard times.

As of late 2013, some economic indicators have improved but most consumers are facing the rising costs for imported energy and foodstuffs along with stagnant wages. Critics warn that if this third arrow should fail to raise productivity, wages, and the economic growth rate, the already enormous public debt will further pile up to an unsustainable level and worsening income inequality could undermine social cohesion and even the legitimacy of the existing institutions and practices of democratic politics and policy-making.

Society and Economy

The private industrial sector of the Japanese economy is characterized by interdependence and networking among a small number of large enterprises, on one hand, and a vast number of small and medium enterprises (SMEs), on the other. In this "dual structure" system, a great deal of critical technological innovation occurs in SMEs, many of which are subcontractors to and innovate on behalf of larger firms. The average SME pays its employees about 30 percent less than the average large firm pays its employees and generally offers poorer working conditions and job security than the latter.

keiretsu

A group of closely allied Japanese firms that have preferential business relationships and often interlocking directorates and stock-sharing arrangements.

Several huge business alliances, known as *keiretsu*, have been formed by some of the large firms. As exemplified by the Mitsubishi Group, a typical *keiretsu* consists of a major bank and several large manufacturing, trading, shipping, construction, and insurance companies that are horizontally linked with one another. There are also vertically structured *keiretsu*, like the Toyota Group, in which one large firm is tied to a number of smaller firms that serve as contractors and subcontractors to provide all or most parts needed to produce final products. A large firm affiliated with a vertical *keiretsu* may also belong to a horizontal *keiretsu*.

Since the late 1990s, both types of *keiretsu* have met increasing challenges of the accelerating process of globalization, such as the overseas relocation of manufacturing bases and the multinationalization of firms resulting from cross-border mergers and acquisitions (M&A) and business alliances. This process has weakened some *keiretsu* links, but Japanese managers and employees by and large tend to stick with their own firms and *keiretsu*.

Since the Meiji era, the traditional patriarchal family has been used as the model of the state and many other types of organization. The Japanese employment system has been thus known for its paternalistic practices, such as lifetime employment, seniority-based wages, company-based labor unions, and hiring and promotion practices that discriminate against women. These practices all contribute to the persistent gender gaps in wages and seniority rankings in Japanese firms.

During the early postwar period, Japan was rocked by a series of violent labor disputes between intransigent management and employees led by radical union leaders. During the three and a half decades of rapid economic growth that followed, however, steadily rising wages eroded the appeal of militant labor unionism, until it virtually disappeared by the mid-1980s.

While the Japanese economy was booming in the 1970s and 1980s, most Japanese regarded themselves as members of the "middle class," thanks to a relatively egalitarian pattern of income distribution. This situation, however, began to change as the Japanese economy started to shrink in the 1990s. Although Japan's unemployment rate remains relatively low even today, hovering around 4 percent, its rate of relative poverty—defined as the percentage of households with incomes lower than 60 percent of the median household income in the given country—rose to one of the highest levels among Organization for Economic Cooperation and Development (OECD) member states by the mid-2000s, due notably to an increase in the number of nonregular workers, from about 16 percent in the mid-1980s to over 30 percent in the mid-2000s. These are part-time or temporary employees with few, if any, benefits. Many firms' recession-induced cost-cutting and the "deregulation" of the Labor Standard Law and other labor-related laws in the late 1990s contributed to the growth of this group of workers, but an underlying long-term cause is a structural change from a manufacturing-centered to a service-centered economy. Thus, a new cleavage between regular and nonregular employees has been added to the traditional division between large firms and SMEs. This new labor market duality overlaps gender gaps to compound the inequalities in Japanese society.

Although Japanese women are as highly educated as Japanese men, gender gaps in Japan are among the worst in the world with little sign of improvement. An Equal Employment Opportunity Law was enacted in 1987, but it has had little impact. Women account for about three-quarters of the nation's nonregular workers and the average female employee is paid about 60 percent of what the average male employee is paid. Japan also ranks among the lowest even in Asia in the ratio of female senior officials and managers, at about 10 percent. The prewar notion of the ideal family with a male bread-earner and a "good wife and wise mother" homemaker still pervades Japanese society and corporate employment policies, making it extremely difficult for women to pursue a managerial career and manage child-rearing at the same time. The rapid aging of Japan's population, however, makes it imperative to promote female participation in all fields of life and at all levels of seniority in each field by reforming the tax and social welfare systems, increasing affordable childcare, and ending the outdated corporate practices.

The 1947 constitution mandates the development of a comprehensive national social welfare system. Today, the Japanese system is comparable to the United States' but compares poorly with those in most Western nations. While Japan's total public

Japan's New National Symbol

Source: Roger Dahl, "Dahl's Japan," *Japan Times*, March 14, 2010, http://www.japantimes.co.jp /life/cartoons/ca20100314ed.html.

social welfare spending matches the OECD average of 22 percent of GDP, the redistributive impacts of Japan's tax and social welfare systems are among the lowest in the OECD and its social welfare spending is concentrated in pensions and health care for the elderly.[10] Although virtually all Japanese are provided with some social welfare benefits, the amounts of these benefits are hardly sufficient to meet the needs of most citizens. This situation creates a vicious circle: swelling the ranks of those unable or reluctant to spend their diminished or diminishing incomes on anything but essential necessities of life, aggravating the persistent deflation, and prolonging the recession. A key to cut this vicious circle would be expansion of the social welfare programs, which would encourage consumption. Social welfare spending, however, is already the largest government budget item. The rapidly aging population automatically ratchets it up each year, while tax revenue remains stagnant or is even declining.

The recession-induced decline in tax revenue and private sector investment has been made up mostly by the issue of government bonds. As a result, the national debt rose to 1,000 trillion yen (about US$10 trillion) in 2013, or 230 percent of Japan's GDP, by far the highest ratio among OECD nations, to further deepen the Japanese citizen's sense of insecurity for the future. How to restore fiscal health, while stimulating the economy to create jobs and improving the social welfare system is thus one of the biggest challenges faced by the Japanese government and people.

Environmental Issues

As early as the mid-nineteenth century, the government-sponsored introduction and development of modern industries, mainly mining, textiles, and iron works, caused considerable environmental damage. Under a regime committed to building a "rich nation with a strong army," however, most victims silently endured the consequences of the government policy.

Postwar Japan's frantic effort to repair and rebuild its war-ravaged economy, then to catch up and compete with the leading economies of the postwar world, caused far more serious and widespread environmental problems, as illustrated by the cases known as the **Four Great Pollution Trials**. In the face of widespread public protests, the Diet passed a series of stiff antipollution laws in the late 1960s and early 1970s.[11]

Four Great Pollution Trials

Include mercury poisoning in Minamata City, thus known as the Minamata Disease, a very similar case in another city, thus known as the Second Minamata Disease, cadmium poisoning known as the *itai-itai* (ouch-ouch) disease, and severe asthma caused by inhalation of sulfur dioxide that occurred in Yokkaichi City, hence known as the Yokkaichi Asthma.

Japan has since been spared human-made environmental disasters as serious as any of the Four Great cases, except those caused by nuclear power plants. The nation hosted the 1997 Conference of the Parties to the United Nations Framework Convention on Climate Change (UNFCCC), which adopted the Kyoto Protocol with a view to reducing greenhouse gas emissions around the world. In the post-bubble "lost decades" of the 1990s and 2000s, however, public attention in Japan shifted away from environmental issues toward more pressing economic problems, even while the nation was blanketed by pollutants from increasingly diverse sources, such as home appliances, plastics, and food preservatives.

The top priority of the Japanese government at the turn of the millennium was the resuscitation of its stagnant economy and a key to the success of its effort was access to a reliable and affordable source of energy to fuel the nation's industry. It had found such a source in nuclear plants built and operated in Japan itself. With the development of breeder reactor technology, a domestic nuclear power plant could keep generating electric power indefinitely, at least in theory. On such an assumption, the first Japanese nuclear reactor had been built in the mid-1960s and, despite a fatal accident that occurred in 1999 at the hub of the nation's nuclear power industry, **Tokai Village**, as many as fifty had been built and were in operation by 2012, supplying about 30 percent of the electric power used in the nation.

Tokai Village

A seaside community lying about ninety miles northeast of Tokyo that is Japan's major nuclear research center with nuclear fuel reprocessing and enrichment facilities.

The March 2011 disaster at a nuclear plant in Fukushima Prefecture called this assumption into question. More than three years later, the level of radioactivity at the damaged reactors remains so high that they cannot be directly inspected, much less repaired, while some of the 1,000 or so steel tanks built to store radiated cooling water are leaking radioactive waste water into the ground and the sea. The waters off the Fukushima coast remain indefinitely closed to fishing and some 280,000 "nuclear refugees" are under government orders not to return to their contaminated homes. The nation's fifty nuclear reactors are all offline. Japan is thus faced now with an excruciatingly difficult choice between the imperatives of energy security, on the one hand, and environmental protection, on the other.

Japan in the Global Economy

Following the 1868 Meiji Restoration, Japan pursued rapid industrialization, initially by exporting relatively cheap products of labor-intensive industries, such as textiles, and then increasingly higher-value-added products of more capital-intensive industries, including iron and steel, shipbuilding, and machinery. After World War II, especially since the 1960s, this export-led development strategy has been followed by other East Asian nations and led them to achieve what the World Bank called an "economic miracle."

In the 1960s and 1970s, Japan's exports increased even faster, taking advantage of reduced trade barriers, thanks to the U.S.-led expansion of the GATT-based free trade regime. Japan's booming exports resulted also from the price competitiveness of Japanese products in earlier years and their greatly improved quality and reputation in later years, thanks to well-timed structural changes and accelerating innovation in manufacturing technology, often spurred by external pressure.

As the Japanese exports to the United States grew, however, Washington began to charge Tokyo with unfair trade practices. The U.S. complaints and criticism shifted from Japan's high tariffs to protect domestic industries in the 1950s to **nontariff barriers (NTBs)** in the 1960s and, in the 1980s, to structural impediments to foreign imports and investments, such as a complex and opaque domestic distribution system, collusive business practices among *keiretsu* companies, and financial practices that artificially raised land prices.[12] In response, Japan has removed or significantly reduced the tariff and nontariff import barriers and the other alleged unfair practices. Meanwhile, rapidly growing China has replaced Japan as the U.S. trading partner with the largest bilateral trade balance surplus and the largest foreign exchange reserves in the world, to some extent diverting American attention away from Japan.

nontariff barriers (NTBs)

Policies—such as import quotas, health and safety standards, packaging and labeling rules, and unique or unusual business practices—designed to limit foreign imports and protect domestic industries. A form of protectionism that does not use tariffs.

Meanwhile, increasing international competition and rising wage levels at home led many Japanese manufacturers to relocate their plants to developing countries, especially China and nations in Southeast and South Asia. Some

GLOBAL CONNECTION

Japan and the Regional Political Economy

The Asia-Pacific region has been of special economic and strategic interest to modern Japan throughout its history. In the lead-up to and during the Pacific War, the region was the primary target of Japanese imperialism. Today, Japan is a leading partner in the evolving framework of regional cooperation. It has concluded economic partnership agreements (EPAs) with seven ASEAN member states plus India, Mexico, Chile, Peru, and Switzerland. The current LDP government is a party to the ongoing U.S.-led Trans-Pacific Partnership (TPP) negotiation to create an Asia-Pacific free trade zone.

The 2008 financial crisis triggered by the bankruptcy of Lehman Brothers gave rise to a broad consensus among leaders in the region on the need to construct a more self-reliant regional economic structure based on local supply and demand by raising living standards of the people in the region, so that more industrial goods produced in Asia are consumed in Asia. Trading and investment activities by private firms in the region have since steadily increased, giving rise to multiple networks of intraregional cross-border transactions, especially in intermediate goods, such as steel and automobile parts. Intraregional trade now accounts for nearly 60 percent of foreign trade for the thirteen "ASEAN Plus Three" nations, namely, the ten ASEAN members plus China, Japan, and South Korea.

A particularly important area where the process of regional economic integration has gained notable momentum in recent years has been environment-related trade, investment, and cooperative projects. A world leader in the design and production of environment-related products, Japan exports antipollution and energy-saving equipment and infrastructure and promotes regional and bilateral efforts to reduce transborder air and marine pollution. For example, despite their ongoing disputes over territorial issues, Japan, China, and South Korea agreed in May 2013 to initiate a trilateral policy dialogue on the transborder air pollution from sources in China.

MAKING CONNECTIONS How has Japanese foreign direct investment (FDI) affected the development and integration of national economies in Asia, as well as Japan's own economy?

Japanese firms have also begun to invest in development of oil, natural gas, and other energy-related resources abroad. While contributing to the development and integration of Asia-Pacific economies, these actions have also contributed to the "hollowing out" of Japan's own manufacturing industry by transferring jobs and technology overseas.

Meanwhile, inward foreign direct investment in Japan itself remains at the lowest level among the OECD nations. There is growing pressure for further integration of Japan into the world economy from the nation's business sector and mainstream media. There is, however, a countervailing pressure exerted by groups critical of and opposed to the current thrust of globalization based on neoliberal ideas. Many of these groups are led by women and envision the construction of a more equitable, self-reliant, and ecology-friendly economy with a more effective system of income redistribution and control of wasteful consumption and energy use. This type of anti-globalization movement, while still fragmented, has grown considerably stronger and more credible since the 2011 Fukushima "triple disaster."

Where Do You Stand?

Should Japan continue to rely on industrial policy to achieve a high growth rate of its economy, as it did in the earlier years? Why or why not?

Some Japanese call for actions to accelerate the globalization of the Japanese economy, while others oppose such actions because they believe the current push for globalization to be based on pernicious neoliberal ideas. Which view do you support and why?

GOVERNANCE AND POLICY-MAKING

Organization of the State

Focus Questions ⍰

- Are the widely publicized activities of powerful iron triangles compatible with democratic government and politics in Japan, or anywhere else?

- What factors or circumstances have most significantly constrained the exercise of political leadership by Japanese prime ministers and their cabinets in the last two decades?

Japan is a constitutional monarchy and a parliamentary democracy, much like Britain and Sweden. The monarch (the emperor) is the symbolic head of state, but the people exercise sovereign power through their elected representatives in the national parliament, the Diet. Unlike the presidential system of the United States, the Japanese constitution allows a considerable degree of fusion of powers between legislative and executive branches, although the judiciary is an independent third branch, like its U.S. counterpart. While the constitution gives the Diet the power to elect the prime minister, enact laws, approve the government budget, ratify international treaties, and audit the financial transactions of the state, in practice, the cabinet rather than the Diet initiates most legislation and makes most laws. Decision making by the cabinet, in turn, is strongly influenced by the nonelected national bureaucracy.

Unlike the United States, Japan is a unitary state where subnational governments can only exercise powers delegated by the national government. All local chief executives, namely, prefectural governors and municipal mayors, and members of prefectural and municipal assemblies are popularly elected, but they are, to an important extent, politically subordinate to and financially dependent on the national government. Their independent decision-making power is far more limited than is the case with their counterparts in federal states, such as the United States, Canada, Germany, and Australia.

Japan is divided into forty-seven prefectures (provinces), which are subdivided into about 1,720 municipalities as of January 2013, ranging from large cities like metropolitan Tokyo with about 8.5 million residents and Yokohama with about 3.7 million residents, to half a dozen villages with no more than a few hundred inhabitants.

A distinctive feature of the Japanese polity is its constitutional pacifism (Article 9) introduced under the rule of the postwar Allied Occupation, the initial goals of which were the complete demilitarization and democratization of Japan (see Section 1). This constitutional commitment radically changed the structure of and power relations in the executive branch: the abolition of the powerful military greatly expanded the jurisdiction and power of the civilian bureaucracy, in particular the economic bureaucracy in charge of the reconstruction and redevelopment of the war-torn nation's economic and social infrastructure.

Despite persistent controversy over its origins in drafts prepared by the Occupation authorities, especially its pacifist clause, the present Japanese constitution has never been amended since its enactment in 1947. The issue of constitutional revision, however, has been around since the beginning and recently brought back onto the front burner among both political parties and the general public, as tension has risen over territorial disputes with China and South Korea and the North Korean military threat. The LDP and a minor new party highlighted the issue in their 2013 upper house election manifestoes.

Recent public opinion polls show that the majority of Japanese now support some revisions of the constitution. The reasons for their support vary, however. In addition to the alleged anachronism of the pacifist clause, Article 9, they include, among others, the need to replace the current parliamentary election of the prime minister by direct popular election, so as to strengthen central leadership, and the consolidation of the forty-seven prefectures into ten or so larger regional units, so as to empower local governments, promote decentralization of policy-making power, and increase administrative and fiscal efficiency.

The Executive

The Prime Minister and the Cabinet

Under the Japanese constitution, the prime minister is elected by the Diet and is, in practice, the leader of the party that controls a majority or plurality of seats in the lower house. Each house elects a candidate for prime minister. If different candidates are elected by the two houses, the one elected by the lower house becomes prime minister. The prime minister must be a current Diet member and retains his or her seat in the Diet while serving as the head of the executive branch. He or she has the constitutional rights to submit bills to the Diet in the name of the cabinet, control and supervise the national civil service, and, in rare cases, suspend a cabinet member's constitutionally guaranteed immunity from an adverse legal action during his or her tenure in office. The prime minister is also the commander-in-chief of Japan's military, the JSDF, and may order, subject to the Diet's consent, JSDF troops to take appropriate actions in a national emergency.

If the lower house passes a vote of no confidence against a cabinet, the prime minister must either resign, in which case the ruling party will choose a new party leader and prime minister, or dissolve the house and call a new election. A Japanese prime minister may also resign for a variety of other reasons, such as poor health, loss of support from important elements of his party, a personal scandal, and, increasingly, loss of support among the general public, as measured by public opinion polls frequently taken by government offices, polling companies, and mass media. As a result, the average tenure in office of prime ministers in postwar Japan has been just a little over two years, with several serving for less than a year. The frequent turnover of cabinets seriously impairs their ability to implement their policy plans and also damages public trust in government. Not surprisingly, in the public discourse, the cabinet has long been depicted as a body simply to rubber-stamp decisions made by the bureaucracy and approved in advance by administrative vice ministers, that is, senior bureaucrats, at their periodic meetings. These meetings were officially abolished by the DPJ government in 2009, but have since been informally reinstated.

In the period from 1955, when the LDP was founded and formed its first government, to the end of 2013, all but five of Japan's twenty-eight prime ministers were LDP leaders. They were first chosen as the party's president, formally by election, but, more commonly, by consensus forged in advance through behind-the-scenes negotiations among leaders of the several intraparty factions. This process usually produced a prime minister who had previously held important cabinet and/or party positions, in accordance with the rules of a seniority-based promotion system and intraparty factional balance. All but two of the ten LDP presidents and prime ministers who served during the last two decades were so-called hereditary Diet members, who were elected to their Diet seats formerly held by relatives, typically their own fathers. Most turned out to be ineffectual as party and government leaders and served very short terms.

The only notable exception to this rule was Koizumi Junichiro, who served as prime minister from April 2001 to September 2006. Although he "inherited" his

Diet seat from his father, his rise to the top party position was due mainly to his own personal popularity for his aggressive antiestablishment populist posture. His neoliberal reforms pushed under a slogan, "no pain, no gain," helped to boost the Japanese economy in the short run. The "gain" failed to last, however: it led to a sharp rise in the ranks of nonregular employees without improvement in social welfare programs to reduce the "pain" of the deregulation. The "Koizumi boom" also demonstrated the limits of personal leadership based solely on a prime minister's popularity in achieving a lasting change that is fiercely opposed by powerful vested interests allied with politicians in the ruling party itself and bureaucrats in the key government ministries.

The National Bureaucracy

At the core of the Japanese state are eleven national government ministries, each with virtually exclusive jurisdiction over a specific area or areas of public policy. A ministry's mandate, as defined by law and practice, includes exercise of both regulatory and custodial powers over both individuals and organizations. The regulatory power is exercised mainly through the enforcement of legal and quasi-legal requirements for licenses, permits, or certificates for virtually any kind of activity with actual or

📇 PROFILES

The Japanese Monarchy

KURITA KAKU/Gamma-Rapho/ Getty Images

Japan has the oldest surviving monarchy in the world with the reign of the first legendary emperor dating back to the mid-seventh century BCE and that of the first documented emperor to the late seventh century CE. According to tradition, Akihito, the present occupant of Japan's Chrysanthemum Throne—so-called after the flower chosen as the crest of the imperial family in 1868—is the 125th in an unbroken line of Japanese emperors and empresses. His ancestors were Japan's actual rulers from the late seventh through the early tenth centuries and thereafter remained the nation's titular rulers until after the end of World War II. Under the Meiji Constitution (1889–1947), the emperor was not only Japan's sovereign ruler but also a demigod. The 1947 Constitution, however, relegated the emperor to the status of a symbol of the Japanese state in which the people became sovereign.

The Japanese imperial family today consists of twenty-two members, most prominently Emperor Akihito and Empress Michiko; the emperor's oldest son and heir apparent, Crown Prince Naruhito, his wife, Masako, and their daughter, Aiko.

Succession to the Chrysanthemum Throne is governed by strict traditional rules of patrilineage, and only male heirs are entitled to succeed to the throne. Under these rules, Prince Akishino, the crown prince's younger brother, is second and his young son, Prince Hisahito, third in the current line of succession. Until Prince Hisahito was born in September 2006, no son had been born to any branch of the imperial family since Akishino's birth in 1965. This situation had given rise to intense and emotional debates both inside and outside the government over the need to amend the law to allow a female heir to succeed to the throne—a standard practice among contemporary European monarchies. Once the potential male heir was born, however, the highly charged debates ended almost overnight.

Compared to his aloof and enigmatic father, Hirohito, who at least figuratively led Japan into and out of the disastrous world war and whose role in that war remains controversial, Emperor Akihito is a far more down-to-earth monarch. An eleven-year-old boy at war's end, he lived through the austere early postwar years as an impressionable young man, mingled freely with classmates from commoner families, learned English from an American Quaker woman, and married a businessman's daughter. Nonetheless, with the rigidly patrilineal succession rule in place, the Japanese monarchy remains an extraordinarily tradition-bound institution.

MAKING CONNECTIONS Does monarchy in general and the Japanese monarchy in particular serve or harm democracy in any way? If so, how?

potential effects on the public interest. The custodial power is used to provide various types of public assistance to private citizens and groups, including subsidies and tax exemptions for particular industries. There has been persistent criticism of excessive control and use of discretionary power by bureaucrats, often in violation of the spirit of the laws and regulations on which such control and power are based.

Each ministry is headed by a minister, one to three parliamentary vice ministers, and one or two administrative vice ministers. The core organization of a ministry consists of a minister's secretariat; several staff bureaus, which are concerned mainly with broad policy issues; and several line bureaus, which are responsible for the implementation of specific policies and programs. Each bureau is subdivided into several divisions and departments. These core components are supplemented, as a rule, by several auxiliary agencies, commissions, committees, and institutes.

The vertically divided administration and an entrenched tradition of ministerial autonomy have often seriously interfered with cooperation among ministries. For example, in the aftermath of the devastating earthquake that hit Kobe City in January 1995, ministerial egoism and parochialism were widely blamed for long delays, often with tragic consequences, in the national government's response to the disaster.

The Japanese national civil service entrance examinations are highly competitive, especially in the fast-track or "career" category, officially called Class I. In principle, civil servants serve in one particular ministry for life, a factor contributing to inter-ministerial rivalries that breed intense jurisdictional disputes as well as fostering the tendency for officials to seek ministerial interests over public interests.

The standard mandatory retirement age for Japanese national civil servants is 60, but, by custom, most career officials retire at a younger age, usually about 55, with fairly modest retirement benefits. These circumstances lead them to seek postretirement jobs and many find high-paying positions in public or semipublic organizations or major private firms. This way of gaining postretirement employment is known as *amakudari* (descent from heaven), which constitutes an important link in an "iron triangle" of bureaucrats, politicians, and leaders of the major interest groups, including private business (see below).

amakudari

A Japanese practice, known as "descent from heaven," in which government officials retiring from their administrative positions take jobs in public corporations or private firms with which their own ministry has or recently had close ties.

The "descent" is usually arranged in advance between the ministry ("heaven") from which the official is retiring and a public or semipublic organization or private enterprise within the circle of the ministry's clientele. The civil service law forbids employment of a retired civil servant within two years of his or her retirement by a private enterprise that has had a close business relationship with the government office where the retired official has been employed in the last five years. This restriction, however, may be lifted at the National Personnel Authority's discretion, as it is routinely done for several dozen retiring senior bureaucrats each year. Moreover, there are no legal restrictions on the "descent" of a retired official to a public or semipublic organization.

In the 1970s and 1980s, Japan's government bureaucracy was greatly admired, both at home and abroad, as the exceptionally intelligent, energetic, and dedicated architect of the nation's post–World War II economic miracle. By the end of the 1990s, however, its enviable reputation had largely dissipated. First, the depressed state of the Japanese economy was blamed on the bureaucrats. Second, a series of headline-grabbing scandals involving officials in some of the traditionally most powerful and prestigious ministries tainted the reputation of Japanese bureaucrats as unselfish, public-minded, and incorruptible mandarins. Third, politicians began to claim a greater share of policy-making power at the expense of bureaucrats. Fourth, diminishing tax revenue and tighter spending discipline spelled a shrinking war chest for bureaucrats to tap into for greasing their relationships with politicians and special interest groups,

Table 6.2	Cabinet Positions (September 2013)
Prime Minister	
Deputy Prime Minister and Minister of Finance	
Minister of Internal Affairs and Communications	
Minister of Justice	
Minister of Foreign Affairs	
Minister of Education, Culture, Sports, Science, and Technology	
Minister of Health, Labor, and Welfare	
Minister of Agriculture, Forestry, and Fisheries	
Minister of Economy, Trade, and Industry	
Minister of Land, Infrastructure, Transport, and Tourism	
Minister of Environment	
Minister of Defense	
Chief Cabinet Secretary	
Minister for Reconstruction	
Minister in Charge of Support for Women's Empowerment and Child-Rearing	
Minister for Okinawa and Northern Territories Affairs	
Minister in Charge of Economic Revitalization	
Minister in Charge of Administrative Reform	
Chairman of the National Public Safety Commission	

thus seriously eroding their influence. Finally, largely as a result of these developments, many bureaucrats lost their self-confidence and sense of mission. Still, they continue to exercise enormous power in Japanese policy-making and implementation processes.

In addition to the national government ministries and agencies, there were, as of 2010, about 7,000 public and semipublic enterprises funded wholly or substantially by the central government. Their activities ranged from energy resource development to promotion of international cooperation and oversight of publicly managed gambling. Many had outlived their usefulness and served primarily as destinations of retiring bureaucrats' lucrative descent from heaven. They were among the main targets of the short-lived DPJ government's civil service reform campaign, which fizzled out as the inexperienced ministers in charge were easily and quickly outmaneuvered by redoubtable veteran bureaucrats. On this score, the DPJ prime ministers' leadership did not measure up even to their mostly ineffectual LDP predecessors', not to mention Koizumi's,

In 2012, Japan's national government, including its auxiliary organizations and JSDF staff and troops, had on its payroll about 560,000 people, or 0.6 percent of the approximately 63 million gainfully employed people in the country. The Japanese national civil service costs about 5.2 percent of the national government's annual budget and 0.8 percent of Japan's GDP. It is difficult to compare the efficiency of different nations' public bureaucracies, but it is probably reasonable to call Japan's civil service relatively lean and thrifty.

Other State Institutions

The Military

Prewar Japan's military establishment was totally dismantled by the Allied Occupation authorities after World War II, and the nation was forbidden to rearm by the peace clause of the 1947 Constitution. Nonetheless, the outbreak of the Korean War in 1950 led the Japanese government, with strong American prompting, to launch a rearmament program. Initially, a so-called national police reserve was created, to avoid provoking controversy over its constitutionality. By 1954, this force had evolved into the JSDF. In 1959, the Supreme Court ruled that Article 9 of the constitution did not forbid Japan to take necessary measures to defend itself as an independent state. The JSDF is now accepted by the Japanese public as a legitimate component of the Japanese state.

The JSDF is today roughly equal, both in operational capability and in physical size, to the armed forces of the major Western European nations. Although Japan spends only about 1 percent of its GDP on defense, its $59.2 billion defense budget in 2012 was the sixth largest in the world, after those of the United States, China, Russia, France, and Britain. Nevertheless, its alliance with the United States is the keystone of Japan's security policy.

Following the enactment of the International Peace Cooperation (IPC) Law in 1992, JSDF troops began to participate in limited noncombat UN peacekeeping operations, such as medical, refugee repatriation, logistic support, infrastructural reconstruction, election-monitoring, and policing operations. Beginning with election watch duties in Angola in 1992, JSDF troops, along with civilian Japanese, have participated in more than a dozen peacekeeping operations in a number of nations and regions around the world, including Cambodia, Mozambique, El Salvador, Rwanda, Syria/Golan Heights, Bosnia/Herzegovina, East Timor, and South Sudan. They have been also active in disaster relief operations both in Japan and abroad. Domestic public support for JSDF has grown dramatically since its search and rescue operations in the 2011 "triple disaster." The troops' discipline and professionalism were highly acclaimed and nearly 90 percent of respondents in a 2012 government survey supported the dispatch of JSDF troops abroad for similar activities.

Amid the heightened public concern about the territorial dispute with China over a tiny group of islands in the East China Sea, called Senkaku by Japanese and Diaoyu by Chinese, and with North Korea over its nuclear program, Prime Minister Abe has begun to maneuver for relaxation of the current restrictions on JSDF's operations and an eventual revision of the constitution with a view to allowing Japan to participate in collective defense actions. In an August 2013 *Asahi Shimbun* poll, however, only 27 percent of respondents supported and 59 percent opposed such moves for fear of stoking militarism at home and further provoking Asian neighbors.

THE U.S. CONNECTION

U.S.-Japan Alliance and the Japan Self-Defense Forces

When Japan signed the peace treaty with the Allied Powers in 1951 to end their occupation of the nation, it also signed a mutual security treaty with the United States. By virtue of this treaty, which was revised and extended indefinitely in 1960, the United States has maintained an extensive network of military bases and troops in Japan, the bulk of them in Okinawa.

Following the outbreak of the Korean War in 1950, Japan created a small military, later named the Japan Self-Defense Forces (JSDF). Now a full-fledged conventional military force, the JSDF operates as a key auxiliary to the U.S. Forces Japan (USFJ). As Figure 6.2 shows, however, Japan spends a far smaller portion of its GDP for military defense than the United States. Not surprisingly, the United States has been demanding a larger defense effort by Tokyo. Japan has responded not by increasing its defense spending, an action both financially and politically difficult, but by expanding JSDF's participation in UN-sponsored and/or U.S.-led "peacekeeping" operations.

Following the September 11, 2001, terrorist attacks on the United States, Japan dispatched a half-dozen warships to the Indian Ocean to assist the U.S. forces in their operations in and around Afghanistan. In 2011, Japan relaxed its ban on Japanese firms' participation in joint development of weapons systems with United States and other nations' counterparts.

As tensions have risen between Japan and its neighbors in recent years, over North Korea's nuclear weapons program, China's military modernization and expansion, and, especially, territorial disputes with China and South Korea, the Japanese concern about the reliability of the U.S. "nuclear umbrella" has deepened, fueling the push among conservative politicians and pundits, led by the right-wing nationalist LDP prime minister, Abe Shinzo, and his cabinet since December 2012, for the relaxation of the constitutional restrictions on Japanese rearmament. This movement in Japan in turn further arouses the neighboring nations' suspicions and wariness about the alleged revival of Japanese militarism, leading to a spiral of mutual distrust and hostility, and increasingly reckless brinkmanship on both sides. This development poses a troublesome moral hazard problem for the United States at the end of 2013. It does not immediately threaten the six-decade-old U.S.-Japan alliance, but has led many people in both nations to reassess its costs and benefits.

FIGURE 6.2 Military Expenditures as Percentages of Gross Domestic Product, 2012

Source: Information from the Stockholm International Peace Institute (SIPRI): http://milexdata.sipri.org/files/?file=SIPRI+milex+data+1988-2012+v2.xlsx

MAKING CONNECTIONS How have the purpose and role of the U.S.-Japan security alliance changed since the early 1950s as the strategic conditions have radically changed in the world and, especially, in the Asia-Pacific region?

The Judiciary

The judicial branch of the Japanese government operates according to the rules set by the Supreme Court, which consists of the chief judge and fourteen other judges. All Japanese judges are appointed by the cabinet, except for the chief judge of the Supreme Court, who is nominated by the cabinet and formally appointed by the emperor. Supreme Court judges are subject to a popular review and potential recall in the first lower house election following their appointment and every ten years thereafter. None, however, has ever been recalled as a result of the popular review.

The Supreme Court, eight higher (regional) courts, and fifty district (prefectural-level) courts possess, and occasionally use, the constitutional power of judicial review. But the Supreme Court has been extremely reluctant to declare an existing law unconstitutional. Since its institution in 1947, it has declared only twenty-one existing laws, all politically insignificant, unconstitutional. This apparent proclivity for inaction may be attributed mainly to the influential legal opinion that holds that the judiciary should not intervene in decisions of the legislative or executive branch of government, which represents the people's will more directly than the judiciary.

Until May 2009, professional judges alone handled all cases brought to court. A quasi-jury system has now been introduced, however, under which even a major criminal case is heard and a decision made by a panel composed of three professional judges and six randomly chosen citizens. Many consider the introduction of this **"Lay Judge System"** (*saiban-in-seido*) one of the most radical government reforms in post–Occupation Japan and a major step toward democratizing its legal system.

The Police

The organization and operation of the Japanese police are under the control of prefectural governors and prefectural public safety commissions. The National Police Agency exercises largely nominal supervisory and coordinating authority. This decentralized system was created by the postwar Allied Occupation and has since been maintained, with some modifications, in reaction against prewar Japan's notoriously abusive national police.

Until the 1980s, the Japanese police enjoyed a reputation, both at home and abroad, as a highly disciplined, efficient, and effective guardian of law and order in the nation. Since then, however, that reputation has been damaged by a growing incidence of mediocre performance, low motivation, and widespread corruption.

Nonetheless, Japan remains a relatively crime-free society, with less than half as many victims of criminal offenses per capita in 2005 as Britain, a little over half as many as the United States, and substantially fewer than either France or Germany. When it comes to the percentage of offenders apprehended, Japan's record of 32 percent in 2007 was higher than the United States' 20 percent and Britain's 28 percent, but lower than France's 36 percent and Germany's 55 percent. Once a case comes to trial, on the other hand, Japan boasts a virtually 100 percent conviction rate.

The extraordinarily high conviction rate is achieved largely by prosecutors' heavy reliance on confessions. Confessions are often obtained by abusive interrogation methods employed within the confines of "substitute prisons" where suspects can be detained for up to twenty-two days by police and prosecutors, and are given very restricted access to their lawyers, in apparent violation of the constitutional guarantee (Article 34) of all citizens' right to counsel and habeas corpus. The criminal justice system in Japan has therefore been frequently criticized for the alleged abuse of prisoners and suspects, and the arbitrary and often inhumane way prisons are run.

Since the quasi-jury system was introduced in May 2009, some efforts have been made to open the judicial system to greater public scrutiny and help reduce human rights abuses. For example, the Ministry of Justice's specialist advisory group, the Legislative Council, has been discussing the use of videotaping and recording of the actual scenes of interrogations with a view to increasing the transparency and accountability of the prosecutorial procedures.

Subnational Government

The Japanese prefectures and their subdivisions are under the administrative and financial control of the national government and enjoy very limited independent decision-making authority. The national government collects about two-thirds of the taxes levied by all levels of governments, funds about one-third of local government

---

"Lay Judge System"
(*saiban-in-seido*)

The quasi-jury system for major criminal cases that was introduced into Japan's judicial system in May 2009. Guilt or innocence of the accused—and, if convicted, the sentence—are determined by a judicial panel composed of three professional judges and six laypersons.

operations and projects, and wields decision-making power roughly proportional to the lopsided division of the taxing and funding power. In this respect, Japan differs from most other industrial democracies, where subnational levels of government have much greater autonomy and capabilities.

The 1947 Constitution of Japan devotes its last substantive chapter to local self-government and refers to "the principle of local autonomy." There has always been a broad consensus among Japanese scholars and a large segment of the general public that robust local autonomy is an essential element of modern democracy. This academic and public opinion has been increasingly embraced by the national associations of prefectural and local politicians as a variety of local issues, such as social welfare, local economy, and environmental protection, have become too many and too diverse for the central government alone to adequately deal with. A Local Decentralization Promotion Law was enacted by the Diet in 1995 and has been followed by a series of similar legislative and executive actions under both the LDP and DPJ governments. In 2009, the DPJ government even appointed a blue-ribbon group with a grandiose title "Local Sovereignty Strategy Conference," which drew up an ambitious plan of reforms to be undertaken.

The enthusiasm for decentralization, however, has waned and the blue-ribbon panel was abolished by the new LDP government in March 2013. Decentralization has thus remained more rhetoric than action, due to strong opposition among LDP Diet members, unwilling to lose an important source of funding for favored local projects, and senior bureaucrats, averse to see their turfs and perks shrink, as well as the very short tenures of most prime ministers and cabinets.

The Policy-Making Process

Policy-making in postwar Japan has long been dominated by the dynamics of politics played by and among the "iron triangles" of LDP politicians, bureaucrats, and leaders of the major interest groups. Draft bills were reviewed and approved by the LDP's Policy Research Council, which operated through a dozen standing committees, each corresponding to a government ministry, and a host of ad hoc committees. The recommendations of these committees were presented to the Council's executive committee and then to the party's Executive Council. If approved by both bodies, the recommendations usually became government policies to be implemented through legislative actions of the Diet or administrative actions of the bureaucracy.

Most LDP policy committees were led by veteran Diet members experienced and knowledgeable in specific policy areas. Over the years, they formed close personal relationships with senior bureaucrats and leaders of special interest groups. These LDP legislative leaders formed closely knit networks, popularly known as *zoku* (tribes), and worked in cooperation with allied bureaucrats and interest groups through the "iron triangles." Such tribes and iron triangles dominated policy-making in all major policy areas, but were especially prominent in agriculture, construction, education, telecommunications, and transportation.

The iron triangles promoted special interests favored by politicians and bureaucrats. Bureaucrats had their turfs protected and often expanded by allied politicians, and politicians had their election campaigns financed by contributions of allied interest groups. The LDP tribes were the principal actors in Japan's widespread **pork-barrel politics** and the major sources of political corruption. Big businesses, small shop owners, farmers, builders, insurers, and doctors were all represented by their own tribes that protected them against those who threatened their interests, whether they were Japanese consumers, insurance policy holders, patients, or foreign producers and exporters.

zoku

Members of the Japanese Diet (parliament) with recognized experience and expertise in particular policy areas such as agriculture, construction, and transportation, and close personal connections with special interests in those areas.

pork-barrel politics

A term originally used by students of American politics to refer to legislation that benefits particular legislators by funding public works and projects in their districts. More broadly, the term refers to preferential allocation of public funds and other resources to particular districts or regions so as to give electoral advantage to particular politicians or political parties.

The power of the vested interests has been vividly illustrated by "the nuclear village," a network of the institutional and individual advocates of nuclear power in the utility and manufacturing industries, the Diet, government bureaucracy, financial institutions, the mass media, and academia. This network has dominated Japan's energy policy-making ever since the LDP government found in nuclear power an answer to the problem of post–Oil Crisis power supply in the early 1970s, and, since the early 1980s, the best way to reduce greenhouse gas emissions as well. A critical factor in the Fukushima disaster was the corruption of the government regulators by the nuclear village, which had for long provided them with postretirement jobs, as well as generous political funds to allied politicians. Despite the intense public criticism it faced in the wake of the 2011 "triple disaster," the village has survived and is thriving under the pronuclear power LDP government.

The actions of the entrenched iron triangles, all working to protect their own interests and often at cross purposes with each other, make Japanese politics look like a downtown intersection in a perennial traffic gridlock, stymie periodic reformist efforts, and ensure the perpetuation of the status quo. Old and outdated policies, practices, and procedures survive and help only to aggravate already bad situations, such as the protracted economic slump and the mounting public debt. In the absence of effective political leadership with an inspiring vision of the future, the situation breeds pessimism and political alienation and suppresses citizen participation and activism.

Where Do You Stand?

When a national disaster occurs as a result of a private firm's action or actions subsidized and supervised by government, such as the 2011 Fukushima nuclear disaster, who should be held responsible and pay for it, the firm or the government, that is, taxpayers?

What action or actions and by whom might bring about effective structural reforms to end the policy-making stalemate in Japan?

SECTION 4

REPRESENTATION AND PARTICIPATION

The Legislature

According to the Japanese constitution, the Diet is the state's highest and sole law-making organ. It consists of a House of Councilors (upper house) and a House of Representatives (lower house). The lower house is the larger and more powerful of the two, with the power to override the decision of the upper house contrary to its own regarding the government budget, ratification of international treaties, and the election of a new prime minister. The full term of office for the 480 lower house members is four years, but this house may be and frequently is dissolved and a new election held at the discretion of the cabinet. The 242 upper house members serve a fixed term of six years. Their terms are staggered and half of them are elected every three years.

An ordinary session of the Diet lasts for 150 days each year, but may be extended once. An extraordinary session may be called at any time by the cabinet or by one-quarter or more of the members of either house. As in the U.S. Congress, the bulk of legislative work is done in a number of standing and ad hoc committees in each house.

A bill must be passed by both houses to become a law. An ordinary bill may be introduced either by the cabinet or a group of twenty or more lower house members or ten or more upper house members. A budget bill may be introduced either by the cabinet or fifty or more lower house members or twenty or more upper house members. Until the early 2000s, far more cabinet bills were introduced and passed than members' bills. During the last decade, the numbers of the two types of bills introduced have become more equal, but a much higher percentage of cabinet bills have been passed than members' bills.

A bill approved by a committee of either house is referred to and debated by the whole house and, if approved, transmitted to the other house, where the same process is repeated. An ordinary bill is passed or rejected by a simple majority in a committee of either house, then by the whole house, but an amendment of the constitution requires the consent of two-thirds or more of all members in each house and a majority of voters in a national referendum.

An ordinary bill already passed by the lower house, then rejected by the upper house, may be voted on again and into law by a two-thirds majority of lower house members present and voting. A budget bill must be introduced first to the lower house and may be passed by that house alone, regardless of the upper house's action. Ratification of an international treaty may be introduced to either house, but, if the two houses disagree, the decision of the lower house prevails. Unlike members of the U.S. Congress, but like legislators in other parliamentary democracies, Japanese Diet members normally vote strictly along party lines.

The overwhelming majority of Japanese legislators are men. At the end of 2013, there were thirty-eight women members in each house, accounting for 8 percent and 16 percent, respectively, of the lower and upper house members. An April 2013 survey by the Inter-Parliamentary Union ranked Japan 161st among 189 nations in the percentage of women in a unicameral parliament or the lower house of a bicameral parliament.

Focus Questions ▽

- How have the Japanese party and electoral systems changed during the last two decades?

- How do the political status and socioeconomic conditions of minority groups in Japan compare with those of their counterparts in China and the United States?

Political Parties and the Party System

For a decade following the end of World War II, several political parties, mostly formed by surviving members of prewar parties, divided themselves into three loosely knit ideological groupings: the Liberals on the right, the Democrats in the middle, and the Socialists (Japan Socialist Party: JSP) and the Communists (Japan Communist Party: JCP) on the left. The Liberals were in power for the better part of the Allied Occupation of Japan. In 1955, the Liberals and Democrats merged into a Liberal Democratic Party (LDP). For the next three and a half decades, the LDP dominated Japanese politics both at the national and local levels.

The LDP's de facto one-party rule began to unravel in the late 1980s, due partly to a series of political corruption scandals, which implicated a number of party leaders and over which a group of dissidents deserted the party to form a new Democratic Party of Japan (DPJ) with defectors from the JSP. As a result, the LDP lost the 1993 lower house election for the first time in its 38-year history and yielded control of government to a coalition of opposition parties. The LDP, however, came back into power in less than a year and stayed in power for the next fourteen years, in coalition, initially with the JSP—renamed the Social Democratic Party (SDP) in 1996—and, subsequently, with the Buddhist Clean Government Party (CGP) founded in the mid-1960s. The LDP-CGP coalition lost the 2007 upper house and the 2009 lower house elections and yielded government to a rival DPJ-led coalition. Due, however, partly to its ineffectual response to the 2011 "triple disaster" and partly to its failure to pull the nation out of the long recession, the DPJ-led coalition was roundly beaten by the LDP and CGP in the 2012 lower house and 2013 upper house elections (see Table 6.3).

In recent years, a number of minor parties have come and gone. Three of them, named the Japan Restoration Party, Your Party, and Tomorrow Party of Japan, won more seats than the SDP in the 2012 lower house election and the first two did so in the 2013 upper house election as well. None of them, however, is likely to survive for more than a few years.

The five better-established parties continue to stick to their familiar positions on most domestic and foreign policy issues. On the issue of constitutional change, the LDP remains committed to its revisionist position, especially with regard to Article 9, a position adopted at its founding in 1955 and reaffirmed with renewed urgency by the party's current leadership. The LDP's longtime coalition partner, the CGP, on the other hand, remains antirevisionist, albeit with increasing ambivalence. So do the DPJ, JCP, and SDP. On another controversial issue of whether resident foreigners, mainly Koreans, should be granted the right to vote in local elections, the LDP opposes and the other four support their enfranchisement with varying degrees of enthusiasm.

When it comes to the territorial disputes with neighboring nations, all parties are agreed on the legitimacy of the Japanese claim to the three island groups in dispute: the Northern Islands with Russia; Senkaku with China; and Takeshima (Dokdo in Korean) with South Korea. Moreover, all but the SDP implicitly support the LDP's tacit commitment to defend them by force, if necessary. The SDP alone calls for the resolution of all territorial disputes strictly by negotiation. Similarly, all agree that jump-starting the stagnant economy is a more pressing need than curbing the mounting government debt and generally support expansionary monetary and fiscal policies.

Table 6.3	Japan's Political Parties			
			Diet Seats	
Ideology	**Party Name**	**Year Founded**	**Lower House 2012 Election**	**Upper House 2013 Election (Total Seats)**
Right	Liberal Democratic Party (LDP)	1955	294	65 (115)
Center	Clean Government Party (CGP)	1964	31	11 (20)
	Democratic Party of Japan (DPJ)	1998	57	17 (59)
Left	Social Democratic Party (SDP)	1955	2	1 (3)
	Japan Communist Party (JCP)	1945	8	8 (11)
	Others & Independents		88	19 (34)
Total			480	121 (242)

On the future of nuclear power plants in the wake of the 2011 "triple disaster," all but the LDP call for their shutdowns by 2030 or sooner.

All Japanese political parties are primarily groups of Diet and prefectural assembly members with token grassroots memberships. In a nation with an electorate of well over 100 million in 2013, the LDP had about 790,000 registered grassroots members, the CGP 440,000, the JCP 320,000, the DPJ 220,000, and the SDP 17,000.

Under a political reform law passed in 1994 with a view to reducing their susceptibility to corruption due to fund-raising pressures, Japan's national parties are subsidized by the state treasury. Each party receives an amount that equals 250 yen (¥) multiplied by Japan's current population, in proportion to the sum of the number of seats it currently holds in the two houses and the average share of the vote it has won in the most recent lower house and the two most recent upper house elections. According to this formula, the LDP received in 2013 about ¥14.6 billion ($146 million), the DPJ ¥8.5 billion, CGP ¥2.6 billion, and SDP ¥500 million. The JCP alone refuses to accept this handout from the government.

Japanese local government and politics are generally nonpartisan. All of the current forty-seven prefectural governors and nearly all of the 1,737 mayors are independents, and so are over 70 percent of municipal assembly members. The only exception is prefectural assembly members, more than 80 percent of whom are affiliated with one or another major national party, about half with the LDP.

Elections

Diet election campaigns are also partially funded by the state treasury. Candidates receive free posters, stamped postcards, space in the official gazette, radio and television advertisements, use of public halls for campaign rallies and speeches, and free passes for public means of transportation during the legally defined campaign periods.

Under the system in effect from the mid-1920s to 1994, all lower house members, as well as some of the upper house members, were elected in multimember districts by the **single non-transferrable vote (SNTV)** method. This system tended to pit candidates of the same party against each other within each district and led most candidates to focus on their records of constituency services, rather than their views of and positions on broader policy issues. Constituency service activities were carried out primarily by the candidate's personal campaign organization, generically known as *koenkai* (support association).

In 1994, the SNTV system for lower house elections was replaced by a mixed member proportional (MMP) system that combines a **single-member district (SMD)** and proportional representation (PR) systems. Three hundred members are elected in single-member districts and 180 in eleven regional constituencies by a party-list PR method. To field a candidate or candidates in a PR district, a party must have at least five incumbent Diet members, or have won at least 2 percent of the vote in the most recent Diet election, or have at least ten candidates running in the current election. Each voter casts two ballots in a lower house election, one for a candidate in a single member district and one for a party in a PR district.

The 242 members of the upper house are elected to six-year terms. Unlike the lower house, the upper house cannot be dissolved and elections occur regularly every three years. Ninety-six members (forty-eight in each triennial election) are elected by a party-list PR method in a nationwide competition. The remaining 146 members (seventy-three every three years) are elected from prefectures, between two and ten per prefecture, by the SNTV method.

single non-transferable vote (SNTV)

A method of voting used in a multimember election district system. Each voter casts only one ballot for a particular candidate and that vote may not be transferred to another candidate even of the same party. As many candidates with the most votes are elected as the number of seats allocated to each district.

koenkai

A candidate's personal campaign organization, consisting mainly of his or her relatives, friends, fellow alumni, coworkers, and their acquaintances. An effective *koenkai* is expensive to maintain and conducive to political corruption.

single-member district (SMD)

An electoral district in which only one representative is elected, most commonly by the first-past-the-post method, i.e., whoever wins the most votes.

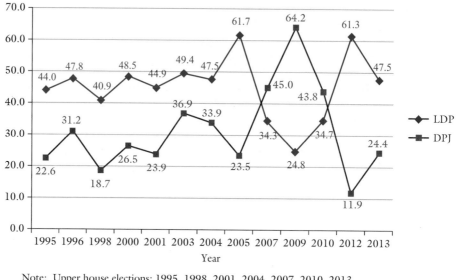

Note: Upper house elections: 1995, 1998, 2001, 2004, 2007, 2010, 2013.
Lower house elections: 1996, 2000, 2003, 2005, 2009, 2012.

FIGURE 6.3 LDP and DPJ Percentage Shares of Diet Seats, 1995–2013 Elections

The LDP dominated Diet elections under the pre-1994 lower house electoral system and continued to do so for a decade under the new system. As Figure 6.3 shows, however, the DPJ-led opposition beat the LDP-led ruling coalition in the 2007 upper house election, while the LDP held a two-thirds majority in the lower house. Because, as a rule, a bill must be passed by both houses to become a law, this situation led to a constant legislative gridlock. Then, in the 2009 lower house election, the DPJ won a landslide victory and formed the first non-LDP government since 1994. In the July 2010 upper house election, the DPJ won more seats than the LDP, but, when the numbers of seats won by the parties allied with each were counted, not enough to keep control of the house. This created a reverse divided, and gridlock-prone, Diet. Finally, the LDP won decisive victories both in the 2012 lower house and 2013 upper house elections, regaining control of both houses for the first time since 2007. It is premature, however, to regard this latest development as a sure sign of the return of a stable **predominant-party regime** under the LDP's rule.

predominant-party regime

A multiparty political system in which one party maintains a predominant position in parliament and control of government for a long period of time.

Until the late 1980s, voter turnout in Diet elections fluctuated between 68 and 77 percent in lower house elections and 57 and 75 percent in upper house elections. Turnout rates hit low points in the mid-1990s, a period characterized by a series of political corruption scandals, at about 60 percent in lower house elections and 45 percent in upper house elections. The rates subsequently recovered to 69 percent in the 2009 lower house election and 58 percent in the 2010 upper house election, but fell back to 59 percent in the 2012 lower house election and 53 percent in the 2013 upper house election. These numbers indicate a significant increase in the last few years in political alienation or disenchantment, if not apathy, among Japanese voters and their tepid support for the current state of party and legislative politics.

As Figure 6-4 shows, nonvoting has been particularly widespread among younger voters. Over the last two decades, the turnout rates of voters under the age of 40, and particularly those under 30, have been conspicuously and consistently lower than the older cohorts', especially those in their 60s. We will explore the problem of younger voters' apparent alienation and nonparticipation in a later section.

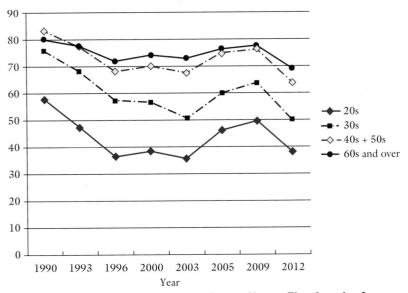

FIGURE 6.4 Voter Turnout Rates in Lower House Elections by Age Cohort, 1990–2012

Source: Akarui Senkyo Suishin Kyokai (Association for Promoting Fair Elections), *Nendaibetsu Tohyoritsu no Suii* (Changes in Voter Turnout Rates by Age Cohort), http://www.akaruisenkyo.or.jp/070various/071syugi/693/

Political Culture, Citizenship, and Identity

As the process of globalization has intensified in the last few decades, Japanese society, like many others around the world, has become increasingly diversified. Compared with most nations of North America and Western Europe, however, Japan remains far more closed to and insulated from foreign immigrants and their social and cultural influences. The number of resident foreigners in Japan in 2012, for example, was only slightly over 2 million, or about 1.6 percent of Japan's total population. Moreover, nearly a third of these foreigners were Chinese, a little over a quarter Koreans, and about 12 percent Japanese Brazilians and Peruvians. In other words, nearly three-quarters of resident foreigners shared ethnic and cultural backgrounds with native Japanese.

Today's Japan is inundated with all manners of information purveyed by both print and electronic media. Its mainstream mass media are, however, far less openly partisan than their U.S. counterparts, due importantly to the institution and influence of "press clubs." A press club consists of one or more reporters from each accredited member newspaper, television station, radio station, or news service agency.[13] Each club is provided with office space by the organization it covers, and its members gather information mainly from the organization's official spokespersons. A reporter who seeks and makes public unofficial information risks losing good standing with the host organization and even club membership. The system works to suppress publication of news critical of the organizations concerned, such as a government ministry or a major firm. Moreover, all major Japanese newspapers and privately owned television and radio stations depend heavily on advertisements and tend to avoid publishing information that might offend and alienate their advertisers.

Interest Groups, Social Movements, and Protest

Former Outcaste Class

The discrimination against and physical segregation of Japan's outcaste class dates back to the pre-Tokugawa era. For centuries, members of the class were condemned to pariah status and lived in ghettos, popularly known as the *buraku* (hamlets). The discrimination and segregation were legally abolished in the wake of the Meiji Restoration, but persisted in practice.[14]

In 1922, a group of young activists from a "hamlet" in Nara Prefecture, near Kyoto, founded a National Levelers Association, named after the famous egalitarian movement in seventeenth-century England. The original organization was disbanded in 1940, on the eve of the Pacific War, but a successor organization was founded in 1955 under the name of the Buraku Liberation League. Under its pressure, a series of laws was passed by the Diet in the 1970s to help eliminate the approximately 4,600 "hamlets" that still existed and integrate the more than 1 million residents into the broader national community. Since then, considerable improvement has been made in the economic conditions of former outcaste communities, but complete equality and full integration into the national community remain ideals yet to be realized and the Liberation League, with a current membership of about 60,000, continues its campaign for elimination of the residual discriminatory practices related mainly to employment and marriages.

Women's Movement

The movement to improve the social and political status of women in Japan also dates back to the early part of the Meiji period. Japan's first major women's organization was the Tokyo Women's Temperance Union, founded in 1886, which campaigned mainly for the abolition of prostitution. The Bluestocking Society, formed in 1911 by a group of younger women writers inspired by the eighteenth-century English namesake, attacked the traditional patriarchal family system and called for the expansion of educational and professional opportunities for women, but with little immediate success.

The Taisho Democracy era after World War I saw the birth of women's organizations more explicitly committed to achieving gender equality in politics. The Society of New Women founded in 1920 successfully lobbied the Imperial Diet to amend the Peace and Police Law, a 1900 law that prohibited women's participation in political parties and other political organizations. This was followed by the formation of Japan's first suffragist organization in 1924 and its first openly socialist women's organization in 1929. In the militarist climate of the 1930s, however, all of these liberal women's organizations were disbanded and replaced by organizations espousing the traditional status and role of women as good homemakers, wives, and mothers.

The political emancipation of women was one of the central goals of the postwar reforms undertaken by the Allied Occupation. Japanese women were enfranchised for the first time and began to participate actively in politics as voters. Informal, but widespread, discrimination against women, however, remains a conspicuous characteristic of contemporary Japanese society and politics. According to the 2013 edition of the United Nations *Human Development Report* (*HDR*), Japan ranked tenth out of 186 countries in the Human Development Index (HDI), which measures overall quality of economic and physical life. But, according to the 2013 edition of the World Economic Forum's *Global Gender Gap Report*, which measures degrees of gender equality, Japan ranked 105th among 136 nations. Japan is thus one of the most

'THREE STEPS BEHIND'

EU & US GENDER EQUALITY

JAPAN

Rogerdahl@aol.com

Roger Dahl

"Japan Lagging in Gender Equality" (An old Japanese adage says that a good woman walks three steps behind her husband.)

Source: Roger Dahl, "Dahl's Japan" *Japan Times*, October 24, 2010: http://www.japantimes .co.jp/life/cartoons/ca20101024ed.html.

gender-unequal nations in today's world and by far the most gender-unequal among today's highly industrialized nations.

Ethnic Minorities: Ainu, Okinawans, Koreans, and New Immigrants

Japanese are ethnically more homogenous than most other nations, but identity issues have been of considerable concern to the ethnic minority known as the Ainu, Okinawans, and Koreans and other resident foreigners.

The Ainu are descendants of some of the earliest immigrants to the Japanese archipelago, known as the *Jomon* (rope-patterned), from the common decorative pattern found on pottery left by them, who once inhabited the greater part of the northern regions of the country. With their distinctive language and culture, including the concept of land as communal, as opposed to personal, property, the Ainu were treated as a quasi-foreign people before the Meiji Restoration. As they subsequently began to be treated as members of the Japanese nation, they were systematically robbed of their land by new immigrants from other regions of the country and, like Native Americans in the United States and Aboriginals in Australia, routinely abused and condemned to abject poverty. As an increasing number of immigrants have arrived in their home territory, intermarriage has increased. According to a 2006 survey, there were about 24,000 self-identified Ainu in Hokkaido in that year. There are no reliable statistics available on the Ainu population in the nation as a whole, but it is estimated to be about 200,000.

Until the late 1990s, the Ainu were, in theory, protected by an 1899 law, but, in practice, nearly totally ignored by the Japanese government and most Japanese citizens. In 1994, an Ainu scholar and author filled a vacancy in the upper house of the Diet left by a deceased JSP member and was instrumental in the enactment of a 1997 Law to Promote Ainu Culture, which replaced the old Meiji law and has helped bring more government and public attention to the plight of this minority group. Prompted by the adoption of the Declaration on the Rights of Indigenous Peoples by the United Nations General Assembly in 2007, the Diet declared the Ainu the indigenous people of Japan in 2008.

Okinawans are also believed to be descendants mainly of the *Jomon* people. Before the Meiji Restoration, they were subjects of the Kingdom of the Ryukyus, a state under Chinese suzerainty until the early seventeenth century, when it was invaded and occupied by a military force sent by the lord of a Japanese feudal domain in southern Kyushu and came under ambiguous dual suzerainty of Qing China and Tokugawa Japan. The Meiji government unilaterally incorporated the island kingdom into Japan's newly created system of local administration in 1879.

Like the Ainu, Okinawans, with their own distinctive language and culture, have faced prejudice and discrimination. Throughout its history, Okinawa has remained the poorest prefecture in the country in terms of per capita income. In the three-month-long Battle of Okinawa, by far the bloodiest fought between Japanese and U.S. forces within Japanese territory at the end of World War II, about two-thirds of the approximately 190,000 Japanese killed or missing were Okinawans and nearly 80 percent of them were civilians.

After the war ended in August 1945, Okinawa was administratively separated from the rest of the country, placed under U.S. military rule, and turned into a key outpost of U.S. forces during the Cold War. The island prefecture was returned to Japanese administration in 1972, but it remains home to three-quarters of the U.S. military bases in Japan. These bases take up 10 percent of Okinawa's land area, which accounts for only 0.6 percent of Japan's territory. Moreover, it still ranks at the bottom of the nation's forty-seven prefectures in per capita income. The Okinawan identity as an ethnic minority has considerably weakened over the years, but neither their collective historical memories nor their grievances about their present economic conditions and, especially, the U.S. military bases have significantly declined.

After the Meiji Restoration and especially after Japan annexed Korea in 1910, many Koreans migrated to Japan. Initially, most came voluntarily. By the 1930s, however, they were increasingly drafted under duress to work in some of the nation's most poorly equipped and accident-prone factories and mines. At the end of World War II, more than 2 million Koreans were living in Japan. A majority returned to Korea, but approximately 650,000 stayed in Japan.[14]

A "human chain" formed by opponents of U.S. military bases in Okinawa.
Kyodo News/Newscom

Unlike some other countries, such as the United States, that grant citizenship, as a rule, to any person born within their territories regardless of their parents' citizenship status based on the *jus soli* ("right of the soil") principle, Japan grants citizenship to anyone born of a parent who is a Japanese citizen regardless of where he or she is born, but to nobody else except through naturalization based on the *jus sanguinis* ("right of blood") principle. Moreover, Japan does not permit dual citizenship in principle. Most of the half million or so ethnic Koreans who currently live in Japan were born of Korean parents and therefore were denied Japanese citizenship at birth. A minority of them have applied for and acquired Japanese citizenship after they reached the legally required age of 20, but the majority remain resident aliens. About 380,000, or three-quarters, are recognized as having been colonial Japanese citizens before 1945 or their descendants and are entitled to permanent residence in Japan. Like other alien residents, however, these Koreans cannot vote in Japanese elections, nor receive publicly funded social security or pension benefits.

Labor

Introduced as an integral component of the Occupation-sponsored democratization program, the postwar Japanese labor movement was initially led by left-leaning public service unions allied with the Socialist and Communist parties. At the peak of its strength in 1949, the movement boasted 35,000 unions with 6.6 million members, representing about 55 percent of the nation's total urban labor force, engaging in frequent, and often violent, actions against management, and winning major concessions over wages and working conditions for the members. As the nation's postwar economic reconstruction progressed and its living conditions steadily improved in the next few decades, until most Japanese families came to identify themselves as middle class, the labor movement lost not only its militancy but its effective grip on rank-and-file workers.

The rate of unionization had fallen to one-third of the total urban labor force by the mid-1970s, to one-quarter by the mid-1990s, and to less than one-fifth by 2010. The number of labor disputes involving organized strikes or walkouts lasting for more than a half day, or four hours, peaked in the mid-1970s at about 5,200 per year, and plummeted thereafter, until it fell below 100 by the first year of the twenty-first century. Acrimonious, not to mention violent, labor disputes have been virtually absent from the Japan of the "Lost Decades," when over a third of the nation's urban labor force consists of nonunion temporary and part-time employees.

The Political Impact of Technology

A total novice in, but an eager and enthusiastic student of, modern industrial and military technologies when it entered the mid-nineteenth-century Eurocentric world, Japan had grown into a major technological power by the early twentieth century. On the eve of World War II, the nation was capable of building some of the most sophisticated military hardware at the time, including the world's largest warships and most agile warplanes.

Under the Allied Powers' control following its surrender in 1945, Japan was stripped of all its military technology, as well as its armed forces and arsenal. Within the next two decades, however, the nation reemerged as one of the postwar world's leading technological powers, although with the use of its power formally limited to the production of civilian goods and services.

The designer, builder, and user of the world's first high-speed rail, known as the Bullet Train since its inauguration in 1964, Japan's cutting-edge industrial products, especially automobiles, electronics, new materials, and machine tools, dominated export markets around the world in the next two decades, in competition with their U.S. and European counterparts. Subsequently, however, Japan's technological edge in the civilian goods export markets began to be challenged by others, notably South Korea and Taiwan in the 1990s, followed by mainland China in the 2000s.

As has happened elsewhere, social media have become an increasingly common mode of communication in Japanese society, enabling people with shared political views to form virtually instant online networks of the like-minded. According to studies by some Japanese scholars, this trend tends to sharpen and harden partisan divisions among Japanese voters. In the 2013 House of Councilors election, when the use of social media in election campaigns was legalized for the first time, both the right-wing LDP and the left-wing JCP made significant gains, while the middle-of-the-road DPJ and SDP both suffered significant losses. The alleged divisive political impact of social media has ominous implications in a nation known for its strong concern for national unity and social harmony.

Since the mid-1950s, Japanese industries have developed potentially dual-use technologies in a number of fields, including nuclear power, aerospace, new materials, and biological engineering. Some have been also involved in the development of more overtly military technologies, such as missiles and drones, within the framework of joint design and production projects with U.S. counterparts. A nation constitutionally demilitarized and pacifist, however, Japan permits its weapons industry to produce only enough to supply its own Self-Defense Forces and maintains its ban on the export of weapons dating back to the mid-1960s, at least for now.

Where Do You Stand?

Is the current Japanese parliamentary election system a good one? If so, in what sense? If not, how could it be improved?

Is the Japanese political party system better or worse than the United States' and how so?

SECTION 5

JAPANESE POLITICS IN TRANSITION

Focus Questions

- How has the March 2011 "triple disaster" affected Japanese politics and political economy?

- What is the most serious problem that Japan faces today? Why is it so serious?

Japan is still struggling with both physical and mental damages left by the 2011 "triple disaster." It depressed Japan's GDP growth to –0.6 percent in 2011 just as it had begun an encouraging rise to 4.7 percent the previous year following more than a decade of lackluster performance. In 2012 and 2013, GDP growth climbed back to about 2 percent. In 2012, Japan's GDP per capita on a purchasing power parity was $35,900, comparable to Britain and France, but well below that of the United States ($51,700). Most Japanese, however, are not seriously concerned about post-disaster changes in their personal economic situations, much less about the rankings of Japan's GDP or GDP per capita among the nations of the world, which have not changed much since long before the 2011 disaster.

In 2010, when Japan's international rankings were just about where they are today, a government survey found about two-thirds of respondents satisfied with their current personal economic conditions. By comparison, an *Asahi Shimbun* poll taken about the same time found an overwhelming 90 percent of respondents already deeply concerned and pessimistic about the future of their nation. This existing glum national mood has been significantly reinforced by the 2011 disaster, especially by how, and how ineffectually, the government responded to it. The result has been a substantial increase in the distrust of government and political alienation, as manifested in the low voter turnout in the most recent Diet elections.

In a June 2012 survey by Japan's public broadcaster, NHK, the most important objective in the wake of the "triple disaster" was to live peacefully with their family members and close friends for three-quarters of respondents, to freely enjoy their everyday life for another 20 percent, and to make the world better in cooperation with other people for a minuscule 4 percent. It is difficult to predict at this point whether this national mood is going to last or just passing. If lasting, it may do serious damage to postwar Japan's democratic political culture.

Political Challenges and Changing Agendas

On top of the continuing impacts of the 2011 "triple disaster," Japan faces several long-term and serious social, economic, and political challenges. The rapid aging of the nation's population is one of the most important and intractable. Japan's average life expectancy at birth of 84 in 2013 is among the longest in the world and its birthrate of 8.23 per 1,000 persons among the lowest in the world. As a result of these two trends, Japan now has a higher percentage of citizens 65 years old and over than any other major advanced industrial nation. This has led to a sharp rise in the cost of health care for elderly people and a significant shortfall in the number of younger, productive workers.

The May 2011 monthly demographic report of the Japanese Ministry of Internal Affairs and Communications showed that the number of minors under 15 years old was 13.1 percent of Japan's total population. The percentage share of this age group had been steadily declining over the last several decades. Back in 1950, this group accounted for more than one-third of the nation's total population. Its ranks fell below those of 65 years old and over for the first time in 1997. Today, the elderly account for a little over 23 percent of the total population, or about 10 percent more than minors. This makes Japan the fastest aging nation in the world. The question many Japanese ask is: Who will be providing for the rapidly growing ranks of the elderly and how?

Prompted by a widespread public shock over the fall of the total fertility rate to a historical low of 1.57 in 1990—thus known as the "1.57 shock"—the Japanese government set up a special cabinet-level task force in 1994 to devise and implement a series of legislative, budgetary, and administrative steps to reverse, or at least halt, the alarming trend. These initially emphasized financial support for the construction and maintenance of local day care centers and nursery schools, but have subsequently been expanded to include a variety of assistance to mothers and would-be mothers, such as providing free or subsidized prenatal and postnatal care and services. Since the turn of the millennium, prefectural and municipal governments have begun to initiate a number of similar programs on their own, such as funding special discounts for pregnant women at designated retail stores. The national and local governments together now spend well over $1 billion each year on the "birthrate decline" problem. All these efforts, however, have failed to reverse the long-term demographic change.

The increasing public spending for birthrate-boosting efforts substantially adds to the national and local governments' overall annual spending for social welfare–related programs and to the mounting government debt, which is another extremely serious challenge the nation faces. Over the last two decades, Japan's GDP has grown by 19 percent, its annual national government's budget by 27 percent, and the annual government spending for social welfare–related programs by 116 percent. Meanwhile, the Japanese government budget has been chronically in deficit, which has been routinely covered by newly issued government bonds, the accumulated amount of the public debt has steadily increased, and debt service has risen to claim nearly a quarter of the 2013 budget. The outstanding national government debt in 2013 stood at about 225 percent of Japan's GDP, or about $60,000 per citizen, which is a bit above that of the United States ($54,000).

Recent cabinets have therefore tried hard to increase revenue and cut spending. In 1989, the effort to increase revenue led to the introduction of a 3 percent national value-added tax, officially called the consumption tax. The rate was raised to 5 percent in 1997 and to 8 percent in April 2014. It is scheduled to be further increased to 10 percent in October 2015. A serious effort to cut spending has also been under way since the 1980s, but has so far failed to make a tangible dent in the enormous government debt problem.

The sorry state of Japan's economy and government finance inevitably affects its international economic role and status. Once touted as the world's most dynamic industrial economy, Japan ranked only twenty-fourth on the 2013 *World Competitiveness Scoreboard* of sixty nations, compiled by the International Institute for Management Development (IMD) of Lausanne, Switzerland. Japan was the largest donor of official development assistance (ODA) funds throughout the 1990s, but fell to the fifth place in 2007, below the United States, France, Germany, and Britain, and has stayed there since then.

These difficult, and apparently worsening, problems, compounded by the impacts of the 2011 "triple disaster," breed a widespread sense of helplessness and doubt about government's ability to solve them, which in turn keeps a large segment of the Japanese electorate from voting in Diet, and also local, elections. This growing nonparticipatory mood poses another serious challenge and threat to the future of Japanese democracy.

Youth Politics and the Generational Divide

As we saw in Section 4, the turnout rates of Japanese youth under the age of 30 in recent Diet elections have been consistently and significantly lower than that of any older age cohort. There are a number of plausible reasons for this apparent reluctance of Japanese youth to participate in the most basic form of democratic politics. Lack of political interest, however, does not seem to be an important reason in light of the results of a recent government survey.

Every five years since 1972, the Japanese government has been conducting "World Youth Consciousness Surveys," in which some 1,000 randomly chosen youth in Japan and their counterparts in several foreign nations were interviewed and asked a battery of questions about their views of wide-ranging social and political issues. In the 2008 survey, the latest the results of which are available, they were asked whether they were interested in the current politics of their nation. Fifty-eight percent of the Japanese youth answered in the affirmative, as compared to 55 percent of U.S., 50 percent of South Korean, 43 percent of French, and 33 percent of British respondents. The percentage of the Japanese youth dissatisfied with their political system (48 percent) was marginally lower than their South Korean counterparts' (49 percent), but significantly higher than their U.S. (32 percent), French (31 percent), and British

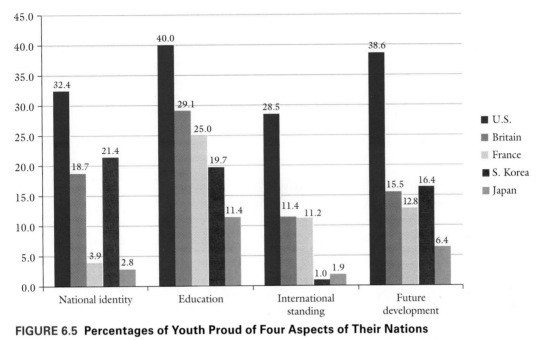

FIGURE 6.5 Percentages of Youth Proud of Four Aspects of Their Nations

Source: Cabinet Office, Government of Japan, *8th World Youth Consciousness Survey,* 2009, http://www8.cao.go.jp/youth/kenkyu/worldyouth8/html/mokuji.html

(22 percent) counterparts'. The most striking findings of this survey, however, were their diverse responses to questions asking whether they were proud of their own nation for its standard of education, international influence and standing, sense of national identity, and possibility of development in the future. As Figure 6.5 shows, the percentages of the Japanese youth who were proud of these aspects of their nation were conspicuously lower than those of their foreign counterparts', except on the question of their nation's international standing, where the percentage of the proud Japanese youth was marginally higher than that of their South Korean counterparts.

All this suggests that Japanese youth are politically more pessimistic than apathetic and that the pervasive pessimism lies behind the significantly and consistently low turnout of Japanese youth in recent elections. This interpretation is reinforced by the findings of a 2009 Japan Youth Research Institute study, which showed that 72 percent of Japanese lower secondary school students and 81 percent of Japanese upper secondary school students, as compared to 34 and 43 percent, respectively, of their U.S. counterparts, felt that they as individuals could not make any significant difference to government decisions.

Japanese Politics in Comparative Perspective

Japan thus faces a number of complex and very difficult political, economic, and social challenges. In broader comparative perspective, however, few of them are unique to Japan. Its aging population problem is acute, but the same problem is nearly as serious in most advanced and emerging industrial nations, including China. Japan's economic and fiscal problems, such as low and falling growth rates and growing budget deficits, are also widely shared by most high-income nations. Natural disasters such as earthquakes and tsunamis, and even those caused by humans, such as accidents at nuclear power plants, occur also in many other nations.

Among the nearly 200 nations in today's globalized world, however, Japan is a unique nation with a pacifist constitution written by foreigners in the wake of the bloodiest war in human history started, in part, by Japan itself. The LDP and LDP governments have been pushing for the revision of the "imposed" constitution, but public opposition has so far blocked their move. Whether and how much longer Japan will remain the world's only pacifist democracy is the most important and interesting question for us to keep asking in the years to come.

Where Do You Stand?

Do you think that today's Japanese youth are understandably pessimistic about the present state and future of their own nation or unreasonably so? How does this compare to your own feelings about your country?

Should Japan revise its present constitution, fully rearm itself, and become more like most other advanced industrial nations in that regard?

Chapter Summary

We began this chapter with a brief review of the continuing domestic and international impacts of the "triple disaster" that hit Japan in 2011, a sobering reminder of the precarious geographical position the nation occupies on this planet and its special vulnerability to both natural hazards and human errors. We then touched on the main watershed events in its history from the arrival of its first human inhabitants some 35,000 years ago to the present time: the birth of the Japanese monarchy under the powerful influence of its closest neighbors, China and Korea; the rise of the warrior class and the isolationist Tokugawa shogunate; its fall under the United States military pressure and the Meiji Restoration, leading to a short period of democratic government, then the rise of militarism and the plunge into the disastrous Pacific War. We then reviewed the critical junctures in the evolution of the demilitarized and democratized postwar Japan through the phase of an economic "miracle" under the Liberal Democrats' one-party rule, followed by one of prolonged recession, in which the nation still remains mired.

Section 2 tracked the trajectory of the development of Japan's modern industrial economy since the Meiji period, nurtured and protected by the state under its industrial policy. We considered in particular the impacts of the demilitarization and democratization reforms on the spectacular performance of postwar Japan's trade-dependent economy in the late 1950s through the early 1970s, then the effects of the 1985 Plaza Accord and the Japanese government's ill-conceived response, which led, first, to the growth of a bubble economy, then its burst

and the onset of an endless period of recession, compounded by the rapid aging of the Japanese population and the increasingly intense competition with the emerging economies in the region.

Section 3 sketched the characteristics of governance and policy-making in a unitary state where the central government wields a disproportionate amount of political and financial power at the expense of local governments. We pointed out that, apart from the predominant power and role of the central government common to most unitary states, Japan has the world's oldest surviving monarchy, albeit allowed only a symbolic role today, and a military of ambiguous constitutionality. We reviewed the practice of policy-making during the LDP's four-decade-long control of government, effectively under the control of the "iron triangles" of politicians, bureaucrats, and interest groups in all major policy areas with a nonassertive judiciary reluctant to use its constitutional power of judicial review against actions of the legislative and executive branches. We saw that the recent changes of government have made no significant difference to the role and power of either the central government or the "iron triangles" in the basic structure of governance and policy-making in Japan.

In Section 4, we discussed, first, the structure and operation of the Diet, noting that it resembles the U.S. Congress in some respects, such as its bicameral structure and committee-centered operation, and that it is, also like the U.S. Congress but unlike most other national legislatures in today's world, an exceptionally male-dominated institution. We then described the party system characterized by the conservative LDP's dominant position, pointed out that all Japanese parties are primarily groups of Diet and prefectural assembly members with very small grassroots membership, and explained the extremely complicated rules of Diet elections. Our discussion extended to the important features of Japanese political culture and society, such as the small number of resident foreigners, the nonpartisan mass media, and the types, status, and organized movements of the cultural and ethnic minorities. The section ended with a brief overview of the growing role and influence of technology in Japanese politics.

Section 5 recapitulated the lingering physical and psychological effects of the 2011 "triple disaster" and briefly referred to the challenges of the aging population and the rising social welfare costs and government debt. We then focused on the challenges the Japanese youth face and their responses, as seen especially in their voting, or nonvoting, behavior and in international comparisons. We characterized them as a singularly pessimistic and alienated bunch.

Key Terms

administrative guidance
amakudari
Four Great Pollution Trials
Japan Self-Defense Forces (JSDF)
keiretsu
koenkai
"Lay Judge System"
　(*saibanin-seido*)

nontariff barriers (NTBs)
pork-barrel politics
predominant-party regime
samurai (*bushi*)
shogun
single non-transferable
　vote (SNTV)
single-member district (SMD)

Supreme Commander for the
　Allied Powers (SCAP)
Taisho democracy
Tokai Village
zaibatsu
zoku

Suggested Readings

Barnhart, Michael A. *Japan Prepares for Total War: The Search for Economic Security, 1919–1941*. Ithaca, NY: Cornell University Press, 1987.

Curtis, Gerald L. *The Logic of Japanese Politics: Leaders, Institutions, and the Limits of Change*. New York: Columbia University Press, 1999.

Dower, John. *Embracing Defeat: Japan in the Aftermath of World War II*. London: Penguin Books, 1999.

Gluck, Carol. *Japan's Modern Myths: Ideology in the Late Meiji Period*. Princeton, NJ: Princeton University Press, 1985.

Haddad, Mary Alice. *Building Democracy in Japan*. Cambridge: Cambridge University Press, 2012.

Hall, John Whitney, et al., eds., *The Cambridge History of Japan*, 6 vols. Cambridge: Cambridge University Press, 1988–1993.

Lockwood, William W. *The Economic Development of Japan: Growth and Structural Change, 1868–1938*. Princeton, NJ: Princeton University Press, 1954.

Martin, Sherry. *Popular Democracy in Japan: How Gender and Community Are Changing Modern Electoral Politics*. Ithaca, NY: Cornell University Press, 2011.

Samuels, Richard J. *Securing Japan: Tokyo's Grand Strategy and the Future of East Asia*. Ithaca, NY: Cornell University Press, 2007.

Upham, Frank K. *Law and Social Change in Postwar Japan*. Cambridge, MA: Harvard University Press, 1987.

Suggested Websites

Asahi Shimbun, a newspaper
www.asahi.com/english

Cabinet Office, Government of Japan
www.cao.go.jp/index-e.html

Daily Yomiuri Online, a newspaper
www.yomiuri.co.jp/dy

Japan Guide
jguide.stanford.edu

Japan Times
http://www.japantimes.co.jp

Portal Site of Official Statistics of Japan
http://www.e-stat.go.jp/SG1/estat/eStatTopPortalE.do

Prime Minister of Japan and His Cabinet
http://kantei.go.jp/foreign/index-e.html

The Mainichi Daily News, a newspaper
http://mdn.mainichi.jp

7 India

Atul Kohli and Amrita Basu

Official Name: Republic of India (Bharat)

Location: South Asia

Capital City: New Delhi

Population (2014): 1.23 billion

Size: 3,287,590 sq. km.; slightly more than one-third the size of the United States

THE MAKING OF THE MODERN INDIAN STATE

Politics in Action

Focus Questions ▽

- What accounts for India's ability to maintain democratic institutions for most of its post-independence history?

- What lessons does India hold for the prospects of establishing democracy in multiethnic societies?

"Going Hungry Gets Results Mostly," proclaims a *New York Times* article on fasts in India. It continues: "In India it seems the only way to get heard is to go hungry. But would-be-fasters better get in line: anyone with an axe to grind or cause to promote appears ready to starve to get their way." Although clearly going hungry is not always politically effective, fasts are indeed an important mode of resistance in India. Political fasts, also known as hunger strikes, contest the Indian state's right and ability to control the body politic. Anyone can fast, regardless of their physical or material resources.

India experienced a massive, well publicized movement against corruption by high-ranking state and party officials. Anna Hazare, the movement's leader, began a 98-day fast in New Delhi in April 2011 to demand passage of a strong anticorruption bill with stiff penalties. While he ended his fast after Prime Minister Manmohan Singh agreed to support such a bill, he threatened to undertake an indefinite fast if the government did not enact the bill within two weeks. The government arrested Hazare but released him when protests spread throughout the country. Hazare immediately resumed his fast, which ended when he struck a compromise with the government eight days later.

Hazare's fasts reveal the extent to which the Gandhian tradition of self-sacrifice to challenge unjust state practices continues to inspire public protest. Mohandas Karamchand Gandhi did more than any other leader in India or the world to publicize fasts and imbue them with moral and political significance. From 1922–1947, Gandhi engaged in innumerable fasts of restricted duration and seventeen fasts unto death; the longest one lasted twenty-one days. Hazare's movement headquarters in rural Maharashtra resembles Gandhi's Phoenix Farm and Sabarmati ashram. Hazare describes his movement as the second freedom struggle, campaigns against untouchability and alcoholism and has sought to make his personal example the basis for his larger political claims. The Aam Admi Party (Ordinary People's Party), that grew out of the anticorruption movement, claims fidelity to Gandhi's conception of *swaraj*, which emphasizes self-governance, community building, and government accountability.

However, if Gandhian direct action tactics appealed to impoverished peasants, the anticorruption movement has attracted the globalized, professional urban middle classes through Facebook, twitter, and SMS campaigns. One observer notes that the spectacle of Hazare fasting at a prominent park in India's capital became Indian television's most successful reality show, with record-setting ratings for its nonstop coverage.

Debates about the ethics and efficacy of fasting and protest against corruption reveal a tension between two democratic principles in India. The first principle values direct democracy and popular political engagement outside institutional arenas.

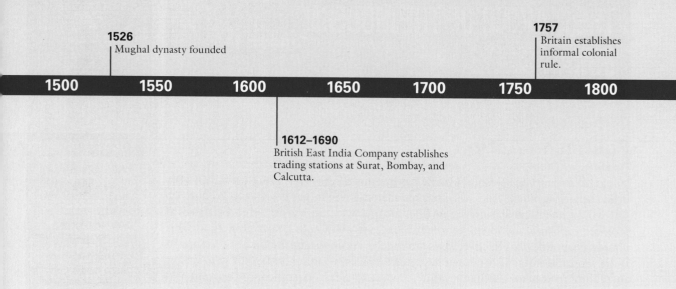

1526
Mughal dynasty founded

1757
Britain establishes informal colonial rule.

| 1500 | 1550 | 1600 | 1650 | 1700 | 1750 | 1800 |

1612–1690
British East India Company establishes trading stations at Surat, Bombay, and Calcutta.

Supporters of the anticorruption movement are proud that a civil society movement put the state on notice and forced political parties to address rampant corruption. The second principle measures the success of democracy by the strength of established political institutions and fears the disruptive, unaccountable, coercive character of fasts. This perspective is best captured by Balasaheb Ambedkar, the author of the Indian Constitution, who famously argued, "Where constitutional methods are open, there can be no justification for these unconstitutional methods. These methods are nothing but the grammar of anarchy and the sooner they are abandoned, the better for us." India's first prime minister, Jawaharlal Nehru, echoing Ambedkar's views, argued that fasting to achieve administrative or political change was antithetical to democratic principles. Critics allege that Hazare's fasts hold the state hostage to movements that are less accountable than elected leaders and established institutions. They contend that the movement encouraged the emergence of leaders of lesser moral eminence than Hazare, who engaged in fasts against corruption to build their own following. They also point out that the powerful, centralized anticorruption agency proposed by the anticorruption movement is undemocratic. While there is no easy solution to the debate about the appropriate relationship of social movements to democratic institutions, the anticorruption movement testifies to the vitality of Indian democracy.

Geographic Setting

India is the seventh-largest country in the world and the third-largest country in Asia. It is called a subcontinent because of its large and distinct land mass. India's rich geography includes three diverse topographic zones (the mountainous northern zone, the basin formed by the Ganges River, and the peninsula of southern India) and a variety of climates (cold in the northern mountain range; dry and hot in the arid, northern plateau; and subtropical in the south). Along with Pakistan and Bangladesh,

1857
Britain establishes formal colonial rule in response to Indian Rebellion.

1947
India achieves independence from Britain; India and Pakistan are partitioned; modern Indian state is founded.

1966–1984
Indira Gandhi is prime minister (except for a brief period from 1977 to 1980).

1850	1885	1920	1955	1990	2025

1885
Indian National Congress is created.

1947–1964
Jawaharlal Nehru is prime minister.

2014
A BJP-led government under the leadership of Narendra Modi came to power.

2009–present
Congress-dominated United Progressive Alliance government

2004–present
Congress Party-dominated coalition government, the United Progressive Alliance

1999–2004
Bharatiya Janata Party-dominated coalition government

Construction Site for the 2010 Commonwealth Games
AP Images/Kevin Frayer

India is separated from the rest of Asia by the Himalayas to the north and the Indian Ocean to the east, south, and west. Only the northwest frontier is easily passable and has been used for thousands of years.

With 1.23 billion people, India's population is second only to its neighbor China. Although the Indian economy is growing rapidly, so is its population. Population growth strains physical infrastructure and increases the need for social services, especially because so many children are born into poverty. The Indian government's family planning policies have been meager and ineffective.

India is the world's largest democracy and the oldest democracy in Asia, Africa, and Latin America. It has had democratic institutions since it became an independent country in 1947 after nearly two centuries of British colonial rule. The durability of Indian democracy is impressive considering the country's huge population and enormous social and regional diversity. India has twenty-two official national languages. Hindi, the largest, is spoken by about 30 percent of the population. There are also numerous regional dialects. India contains many ethnic groups, regionally concentrated tribal groups, and followers of every major religion in the world. While Hindus represent 79.5 percent of the population, India includes Muslims, **Sikhs**, Christians, Jains, Buddhists, and several tiny Jewish communities. India's 176,000,000 Muslims are the third-largest Muslim population in the world, after Indonesia and Pakistan.

Indian society, especially Hindu society, is divided into numerous caste groupings. Mainly based on occupation, castes tend to be closed social groups into which people are born, marry, and die. Historically, the **caste system** compartmentalized and ranked the Hindu population through rules governing daily life, such as eating, marriage, and prayer. Caste hierarchy conceptualizes the world as divided into realms of purity and impurity. Each hereditary and endogamous group (that is, a group into which one is born and within which one marries) constitutes a *jati*, which is itself organized by *varna*, or shades of color. The four main *varnas* are the **Brahmin**, or

Sikhs

Sikhs, a religious minority, constitute less than 2 percent of the Indian population and 76 percent of the state of Punjab. Sikhism is a monotheistic religion that was founded in the fifteenth century.

caste system

According to the Hindu religion, society is divided into castes. Membership in a caste is determined at birth. Castes form a rough social and economic hierarchy.

Brahmin

The highest caste in the Hindu caste system.

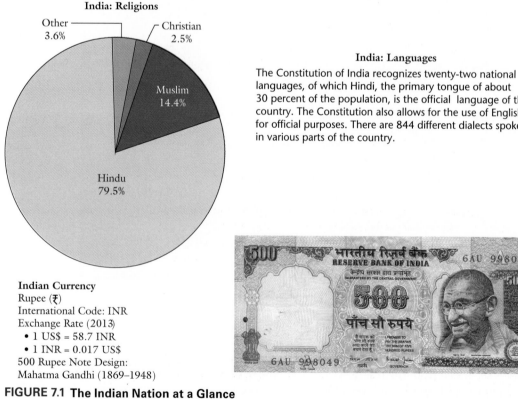

India: Religions

- Other 3.6%
- Christian 2.5%
- Muslim 14.4%
- Hindu 79.5%

India: Languages

The Constitution of India recognizes twenty-two national languages, of which Hindi, the primary tongue of about 30 percent of the population, is the official language of the country. The Constitution also allows for the use of English for official purposes. There are 844 different dialects spoken in various parts of the country.

Indian Currency
Rupee (₹)
International Code: INR
Exchange Rate (2013)
- 1 US$ = 58.7 INR
- 1 INR = 0.017 US$
500 Rupee Note Design:
Mahatma Gandhi (1869–1948)

FIGURE 7.1 The Indian Nation at a Glance
© Steve Estvainik/Shutterstock.com (for photo)

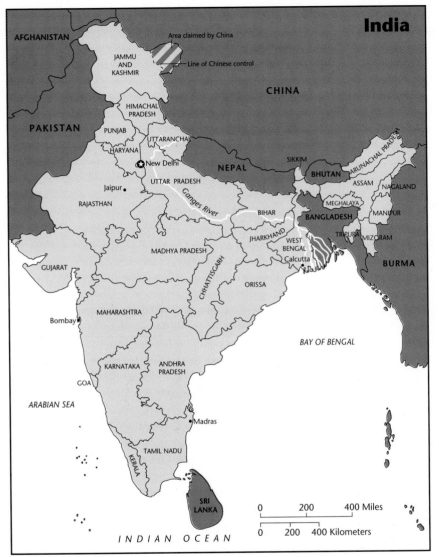

© Cengage Learning®

priestly caste; the *Kshatriya*, or warrior and royal caste; the *Vaishyas*, or trading caste; and the *Shudra*, or artisan caste. Each *varna* is divided into many *jatis* that correspond to occupational groups (such as potters, barbers, and carpenters).

Sixty-nine percent of the Indian population lives in far-flung villages in the countryside. However, the major cities, Bombay (renamed Mumbai), Calcutta (renamed Kolkata), and New Delhi, the national capital, are among the largest and most densely populated cities in the world. (See Figure 7.1.)

Critical Junctures

Indian civilization dates back to the Indus Valley Civilization of the third millennium BCE. The subcontinent, comprising present-day Pakistan, India, and Bangladesh, has witnessed the rise and fall of many civilizations and empires. Alexander the Great's invasion of northwestern India in 326 BCE introduced trade and communication with

Table 7.1	Political Organization
Political System	Parliamentary democracy and a federal republic.
Regime History	In 2014 the government was formed by the BJP, with Narendra Modi as the prime minister. The BJP and the Congress are two of India's main national parties.
Administrative Structure	Federal, with twenty-eight state governments.
Executive	Prime minister, leader of the party or coalition with the most seats in the parliament.
Legislature	Bicameral, upper house elected indirectly and without much substantial power; lower house, the main house, with members elected from single-member districts, winner-take-all.
Judiciary	Independent constitutional court with appointed judges.
Party System	Multiparty system. The Bharatiya Janata Party (BJP) is the dominant Party; the Congress Party is the major opposition party.

western Asia. The Maurya dynasty (322–185 BCE) under Emperor Ashoka united separate kingdoms in northern India into a single empire. The Mughal kingdom (early sixteenth century to mid-nineteenth century) further expanded to include most of the Indian subcontinent and parts of what are now Afghanistan.

As the Mughal Empire declined, several states expanded and new states emerged. The most important formed the Maratha Empire, which, at its height, controlled most of central and northern India. Other important regimes in the post-Mughal period included the Sikh Empire in the north, and the Mysore kingdom and state of Hyderabad in the south.

Pre-colonial India was mostly divided into princely states. However, the power of princely rulers was limited by a dominant social order that they were unable to change.

The Colonial Legacy (1757–1947)

The British began gaining control of the subcontinent in the late seventeenth century when the East India Company, a large English trading organization, developed commercial interests in India. With strong backing from the British Crown, it played off one Indian prince against another. After the **Indian Rebellion** of 1857, also known as the Sepoy Rebellion and the Mutiny of 1857, a large-scale revolt by Indian soldiers, Britain assumed direct control from the East India Company.

The British described India, its most valuable colonial possession, as the "jewel in the [British] crown." India provided Britain with raw materials, notably cotton, and a profitable market for Britain's growing industry, especially textiles. (Britain dismantled India's own textile industry to create demand for British products.) Colonial rule ended shortly after World War II in 1947, when the Indian nationalist movement succeeded in expelling the British and made India an independent country. India was among the first colonies in the developing world to gain independence.

Indian Rebellion

An armed uprising by Indian soldiers against expansion of British colonialism in India in 1857.

In order to control the subcontinent, the British created a relatively efficient administrative structure consisting of an all-India civil service, police force, and army. At first, only British nationals were permitted to serve in these institutions. Eventually, some educated Indians were permitted to join. These institutions continue to be organized along the principles the British colonialists established in the nineteenth and twentieth centuries. Britain started constructing a railway system in east India in the 1840s; by 1880 there were over 9,000 miles of rail lines throughout the country. The rail system continued to expand throughout the twentieth century. It is currently the largest in Asia and continues to be an important means for transporting people and freight.

The Nationalist Movement and Partition (1885–1947)

British rulers and traditional rural Indian elites became allies of sorts, squeezing resources from the peasantry to maintain the bureaucratic state and support the luxurious lifestyle of a parasitic landlord class. However, this exploitative pattern generated increasing opposition. The growth of commerce, education, and urbanization gave rise to urban, educated upper-caste Indians who resented being treated as second-class citizens. They formed the Indian National Congress (INC) in 1885.

In its early years, the INC periodically met and petitioned British rulers for a greater voice in administering India's affairs. They sought political equality and access to higher administrative offices. Eventually, their requests turned into demands. Some nationalists resorted to violence; others adopted a strategy of nonviolent mass mobilization. Thanks to the brilliant and inspiring leadership of Mohandas Karamchand Gandhi, the INC was able to preserve a fragile unity. Gandhi led India's nationalist movement for decades, and his strategy of militant but nonviolent protest has set a high standard for political activists. In the United States, civil rights leader Martin Luther King, Jr., for example, was deeply inspired by Gandhi.

As support for the INC grew, the British had to repress it or make concessions. They tried both. The turning point occurred when Britain's struggle against Nazi Germany increased the costs of maintaining control over India. To gain Indians' support for the war effort, Britain promised to grant India independence. In August 1947, soon after the war ended, India became a sovereign nation.

The euphoria of Indian independence was tempered by the human tragedy that accompanied the partition of the subcontinent. Influential members of India's minority Muslim elite regarded the Hindu-dominated INC with suspicion, in part because of the legacies of colonial divide-and-rule policies. When the INC refused to concede to their demands for separate political rights, they demanded the creation of an independent Muslim state in northern India, which had a large Muslim population. Britain divided the subcontinent into two sovereign states in 1947—the Muslim state of Pakistan and the secular state of India, the majority of whose citizens were Hindu. Partition, as it was called, was turbulent and destructive. Millions of Muslims fled from India to Pakistan, and millions of Hindus fled the other way. More than 10 million people migrated and nearly a million died in interethnic violence. The Muslim population of India declined from 24 percent before independence to 10 percent thereafter.

Three features of the nationalist movement greatly influenced Indian state building and democracy. First, the INC created a broad tent within which political, ethnic, and religious conflicts could play out. This helped India to form and maintain a relatively stable political system. However, second, Hindu-Muslim tensions, which gave rise to Partition, resulted in enduring hostilities between the neighboring states of India and Pakistan. The two countries have fought three wars since Partition. Although some recent initiatives have defused tensions, there remains the possibility of war between these two nuclear powers.

Third, the nationalist movement laid the foundations for democracy in India. Many of the INC's prominent leaders, like Gandhi and Jawaharlal Nehru, were educated in England and were committed democrats. Moreover, the INC chose its leaders through internal elections, participated in provincial elections, and ran democratic governments, albeit with limited powers, in British-controlled Indian provinces. These pre-independence democratic tendencies were valuable future resources.

The Nehru Era (1947–1964)

After independence, India adopted a Westminster model of British-style parliamentary democracy. The INC transformed itself from an opposition movement into a political party, the Congress Party. It was highly successful in the first years of independence, both because of its popularity in having led India to independence and because the Congress government created a nationwide **patronage system** that rewarded supporters with posts and resources.

patronage system

A political system in which government officials appoint loyal followers to positions rather than choosing people based on merit.

Jawaharlal Nehru wanted India to play a global role. Together with other leaders of newly independent countries in Asia and Africa, he initiated what became known as the **nonaligned bloc**, a group of countries seeking autonomy from the two superpowers. He attempted to set India on a rapid road to industrialization by promoting heavy industry. He was also committed to redistributing wealth through land reform. However, much of India's land remained concentrated in the hands of traditional rural elites. While Nehru and the Congress Party proclaimed pro-poor, socialist commitments, they generally failed to deliver on their promises. To this day, India remains divided between a small affluent elite and hundreds of millions of poor peasants and urban workers. In recent years, India's economic growth has created a sizeable middle class between these two extremes. Nonetheless, the majority of Indians in both cities and countryside remain poor. Despite India's amazingly fast economic growth in the past two decades, the per capita income of its citizens places India among the poorest countries in the world.

nonaligned bloc

Countries that refused to ally with either the United States or the USSR during the Cold War years.

An important change in the decade following independence was the creation of states based on the principal language in the region. Many non-Hindi language speakers feared domination by Hindi speakers and demanded that the Indian union be reorganized into linguistically defined states. Nehru reluctantly agreed to the creation of fourteen such states in 1957. In later years, additional states were carved out of existing ones, and there are now twenty-eight major states within India.

The Indira Gandhi Era (1966–1984)

When Nehru died in 1964, the Congress Party was divided over the choice of a successor and hastily selected a compromise candidate, mild-mannered Lal Bahadur Shastri, as prime minister. When Shastri died in 1966, rivalry among potential successors broke out. Party elites chose another compromise candidate, Nehru's daughter, Indira Gandhi (no relation to Mohandas Gandhi). They calculated that, as Nehru's daughter, she would help the Congress Party garner sufficient electoral support to remain in power. They also thought that she would be a weak woman whom they could manipulate. Their first calculation was correct; the second was wholly inaccurate.

Indira Gandhi was India's second longest-serving prime minister. Her father was the longest-serving. She held office from 1966 to 1984, except 1977 to 1980. Her rule produced several long-term legacies for contemporary Indian democracy. She quickly consolidated control over the Congress Party, replacing existing leaders with loyal allies. Gandhi also adopted a populist rhetoric that was popular with India's poor. However, she failed to translate it into real gains. Like her father, she failed to redistribute agricultural land from large landowners to small farmers and agricultural laborers or to generate employment, provide welfare, and broaden access to education and medical services.

Indian politics became increasingly turbulent under Indira Gandhi. As her power grew, so did opposition to her. In 1974, the political situation in India became quite unstable. When the opposition organized strikes and demonstrations, Gandhi declared a State of Emergency in 1975. She suspended many democratic rights, arrested most opposition leaders, and ruled by decree. The **Emergency** lasted nearly two years, the only period since independence in 1947 that India did not function as a democracy (see Table 7.2 for a list of Indian prime ministers).

Gandhi ended the Emergency in 1977 and called for national elections, confident that she would be reelected. However, opposition groups hastily formed an umbrella organization, the Janata Party. Gandhi and the Congress Party were soundly defeated. For the first time since independence, a non-Congress government briefly occupied power. Soon after the elections, Janata leaders became factionalized, and the government collapsed. Indira Gandhi regained power in the 1980 parliamentary elections.

Indira Gandhi's tenure in power between 1980 and 1984 was marked, as it had been when she governed earlier, by a personal and populist political style, an increasingly centralized political system, failure to implement antipoverty policies, and political turbulence. However, Gandhi departed from her previous approach in two ways. First, she abandoned a socialist commitment and started embracing India's private sector as a means to improve its poor economic performance. Second, she abandoned secularism and began using religious appeals to mobilize India's Hindu majority. Gandhi contributed to polarization and conflict by depicting Punjabi Sikhs' grievances as religious rather than territorial. She also covertly encouraged the rise of an extremist faction among Sikhs. The movement turned violent and took over the holiest Sikh temple in Amritsar. In 1984, Gandhi made the fatal mistake of dispatching troops to root out the militants. Sikhs were outraged when the operation badly damaged the temple and left many dead and injured. Months later, Gandhi was assassinated by her Sikh bodyguards. Immediately after her death, groups of Hindus, led by members of the Congress Party, murdered 3,700 Sikhs in New Delhi and other north Indian cities. Some of the people responsible for the carnage were convicted decades later.

Under Indira Gandhi's leadership, Indian politics became more personalized, populist, and nationalist. While her foreign policies strengthened India's international position, her domestic policies weakened democratic institutions. For example, whereas during the Nehru era, local elites had helped select the Congress Party's higher political officeholders, Gandhi directly appointed national and regional-level party officials. Although this enabled her to gain a firm grip over the party, it also isolated her from broader political forces and eroded the authority of regional leaders.

Indira Gandhi's death ushered in a new generation of the Nehru–Gandhi dynasty, when her son Rajiv Gandhi became prime minister and served until 1989. Rajiv Gandhi won a landslide victory in the elections that followed his mother's death as a result of the sympathy that his mother's assassination generated. He came to office promising clean government, a high-tech economy that would carry India into the next century, and reduced ethnic conflict. He was somewhat successful in easing tensions in the Punjab. But he inflamed relations between Hindus and Muslims by

Emergency (1975–1977)

The period when Indian prime minister Indira Gandhi suspended many formal democratic rights and ruled in an authoritarian manner.

Table 7.2	Prime Ministers of India, 1947–Present	
	Years in Office	**Party**
Jawaharlal Nehru	1947–1964	Congress
Lal Bahadur Shastri	1964–1966	Congress
Indira Gandhi	1966–1977	Congress
Morarji Desai	1977–1979	Janata
Charan Singh	1979–1980	Janata
Indira Gandhi	1980–1984	Congress
Rajiv Gandhi	1984–1989	Congress
V. P. Singh	1989–1990	Janata
Chandra Shekhar	1990–1991	Janata (Socialist)
Narasimha Rao	1991–1996	Congress
Atal Bihari Vajpayee	1996 (13 days)	BJP & Allies
H. D. Deve Gowda	1996–1997	United Front
I. K. Gujral	1997–1998	United Front
Atal Bihari Vajpayee	1998–1999	BJP & Allies
Atal Bihari Vajpayee	1999–2004	BJP & Allies
Manmohan Singh	2004–2014	Congress & Allies
Narendra Modi	2014–present	BJP & Allies

sponsoring a law that sharply limited the rights of Muslim women. His leadership was also marred by allegations of corruption.

Coalition Governments (1989 to the Present)

For the first three decades after independence, many parties competed for office. However, none came close to rivaling Congress, particularly in national politics. The Congress Party led all governments from 1947 to 1989, except for one brief interlude (1977–1980). The decline of the Congress Party ushered in an era of instability with no clearly dominant party. In each national election since 1989, coalition governments have depended on the support of other state-based parties. The BJP-dominated National Democratic Alliance (1999–2004) depended heavily on regional allies.

However, in 2004 the Congress coalition government gained a stronger mandate than it had in many years. The leader of Congress was Sonia Gandhi, widow of slain Prime Minister Rajiv Gandhi. Although she had demonstrated her ability to lead Congress, party elites feared that her Italian background made her a risky choice as prime minister. Instead they named Manmohan Singh, a respected former cabinet minister, prime minister.

For the first time, a politician who was neither leader of his own party nor that of the ruling alliance became prime minister. Although not a charismatic figure, Manmohan Singh initially proved to be a highly capable and popular prime minister. His Congress-led coalition government was reelected to power in 2009 by a larger margin than in 2004. However, as described below, his reputation became tarnished when he failed to address widespread corruption by Congress government officials. Narendra Modi of the BJP party was elected as India's prime minister in the 2014 election. His electoral majority was significant. Only developments in the future will tell whether this new national election marks the end of the phase of coalition governments or not.

September 11th and Its Aftermath

India was deeply affected by the September 11, 2001, attacks on the World Trade Center in New York and on the Pentagon in Washington. Although none of the al Qaeda terrorists who hijacked the planes on September 11th was from India or neighboring Pakistan, the global network of violence that flourished after 9/11 cast a shadow over Indo-Pakistan relations. On the Pakistani side, high-level units of Pakistan's powerful and shadowy intelligence organization, the Inter-Services Intelligence (ISI), provided support for groups linked to al Qaeda. For years before 9/11, these groups carried out attacks on Indian armed forces and civil officials in the part of Kashmir controlled by India but claimed by Pakistan.

After 9/11, militants based in Pakistan, and supported by the ISI, began to launch attacks on the Indian heartland. Two incidents were especially dramatic. First, militants bombed and damaged the Indian Parliament in Delhi on December 13, 2001, killing fifteen people. In November 2008, ten Pakistani members of the terrorist organization Lashkar-e-Taiba stormed Mumbai's most iconic and busiest sites, including the Taj Intercontinental Hotel and the Chhatrapati Shivaji Terminus. With guns blazing, they barricaded themselves in the hotel and executed scores of guests (selecting Westerners as their

One hundred sixty-four people were killed and 308 people were injured in the November 29, 2008, bombing of the Taj Hotel in Mumbai. The Lashkar-e-Taiba claimed responsibility for this attack.

AP Images/Lefteris Pitarakis

prime target). For three horrifying days, television stations around the world portrayed the standoff at the hotel. The crisis ended when Indian elite forces stormed the hotel and killed all but one militant; 164 people were killed and 308 people were injured during the several-day crisis. The lone surviving gunman was tried and sentenced to death in May 2010.

Tensions between India and Pakistan dramatically escalated when the surviving militant provided details of the ISI's involvement in the massacre. Although Prime Minister Singh avoided a war with Pakistan, the Mumbai attack inflamed relations between the two countries.

Ties between India and the United States have become closer since 9/11. The United States accorded India an important role in strengthening the Afghan president Hamid Karzai's government following its decision to withdraw troops from Afghanistan and its discovery of Osama Bin Laden in Pakistan. The United States has increased weapons' sales to India and the Indian government has signed a strategic partnership agreement with Karzai that provides for Indian training of Afghan security forces and increased trade and cultural exchanges.

The Four Themes and India

India in a Globalized World of States

India is well positioned, by its large size, growing wealth, democratic legitimacy, and geographic location, to play a powerful role in world affairs. Yet for this to occur, Indian leaders must prevent domestic pressures from escalating into international conflicts and must nurture peaceful relations with India's powerful neighbors, Pakistan and China.

Governing the Economy

In the years following independence, Indian policy-makers first sought to achieve economic self-sufficiency through state-led industrialization focused on satisfying the needs of India's large internal market. This economic strategy required protectionist measures (such as high tariffs) to shield India from foreign economic competition. It succeeded in creating some important basic industries but also generated extensive inefficiencies and failed to reduce severe poverty. Like many developing nations, India later adjusted its economic strategy to meet the demands of competitive and interdependent global markets. During the 1980s, these reforms consisted mainly of government incentives to India's private sector to increase production. Since 1991, reforms have opened the Indian economy to the outside world. The results include both a growing economy and growing inequalities. Among the daunting challenges facing Indian leaders is how to ensure sustained growth while sponsoring measures to reduce poverty and economic inequalities.

The Democratic Idea

India has become more democratic in some ways but less democratic in others. A larger number of people, with more diverse identities, are participating in politics. The Indian political class is no longer recruited from a single region, caste, and class. However, business leaders wield much more political influence than do the far more numerous poor. The growth of Hindu majoritarianism has challenged minority rights and resulted in attacks on Muslims and Christians.

The Politics of Collective Identity

Democracy is supposed to provide a level playing field in which diverse interests and identities seek to resolve their differences. India demonstrates that an incredibly large and diverse country can generally process conflicts peacefully and democratically. However, it also demonstrates the recurrent danger of political forces instigating violence, often for electoral purposes.

Implications for Comparative Politics

India's fascinating profile can deepen our understanding of comparative politics. First, it is a poor yet vibrant democracy. Despite widespread poverty and illiteracy, most Indians value their citizenship rights and exercise them vigorously. Against great odds, India became and remains a thriving democracy, an especially striking achievement given the authoritarian fate of most newly independent countries in Asia and Africa.

Second, the Indian state has managed to remain fairly cohesive and stable at the national level—although political violence has occurred in a variety of states and regions. Third, with well over a billion people of diverse cultural, religious, and linguistic identities, Indian democracy is an excellent arena for analyzing various theories and dilemmas of comparative politics. At its best, India offers instructive lessons in multiethnic democracy. At its worst, it can provide lessons in how democracy can be misused.

Fourth, theorists of democratic change in Latin America and Eastern Europe have puzzled over what constitutes a consolidated democracy and how to achieve it. Here, a comparison between India and Pakistan is instructive. Whereas the two countries were formed at the same moment, India has functioned as a democracy for all but three years since 1947, whereas Pakistan has been an authoritarian state for most of the same period.

Fifth, comparativists have explored whether democracy and social equity can be achieved simultaneously in poor countries. The case of Kerala, a state in southern India, suggests that the answer is a cautious yes. Although one of the poorest states in India, Kerala has achieved near-total literacy, long life expectancy, low infant mortality, and widespread access to medical care. Kerala's development indicators compare favorably with the rest of India, other low-income countries, and even wealthy countries like the United States.

Finally, comparativists have long engaged in a lively debate about the impact of democracy on economic growth. While cross-national evidence remains inconclusive, India's record of steady per capita growth of 4–5 percent annually in the past thirty years powerfully demonstrates how successful economic management can occur within a democratic framework. At the same time, India's failure to adequately redistribute its economic resources provides a more sobering lesson.

Where Do You Stand?

Would India have been better off with a more authoritarian system?

Is democracy really meaningful for those who do not have enough to eat and may not be able to read and write?

SECTION 2

POLITICAL ECONOMY AND DEVELOPMENT

▼ Focus Questions

- What have been two major achievements and two major failures of Indian economic development strategy?

- How successfully has India managed to balance the goals of promoting economic efficiency and social equity? Suggest one or more ways that the trade-off could be improved.

At independence, India had a poor, largely agricultural economy. Although a majority of Indians, especially the poor, still work and live in the countryside, India has developed a substantial industrial base, a booming service sector, and a vibrant middle class. Since the Congress government introduced economic liberalization policies in 1991, all governments have supported economic reforms to reduce heavy-handed state economic direction that discouraged private initiative. Support of the private sector has helped spur rapid economic growth. For example, although per capita income in India grew less than 1 percent a year during the decade 1970–1979, it grew 5.5 percent annually during 2000–2009.

However India's economic growth rates declined significantly, from 8–9 percent in the past decade to less than half that amount in recent years. High inflation, decreased consumer spending, and increased borrowing costs have slowed industrial growth. The year 2013 also witnessed an unprecedented fall in the rupee's value that further contributed to capital flight. The global credit rating agency, Moody, has warned that the current combination of low growth and high inflation are unsustainable.

Prime Minister Singh attributed the economic decline to United States fiscal and monetary policies and the outflow of capital for the purchase of gold and oil. Accordingly, the Indian government has raised interest rates to curb inflation, reduced fuel subsidies, and boosted capital controls on both corporations and individuals. Additional reasons for the economic downturn are India's failure to develop a vibrant export-oriented industrial base because of the high costs of real estate and electricity and poor infrastructural facilities. Sustained economic growth requires improved basic education and health services, and the construction of more ports, roads, bridges, and power plants.

State and Economy

The Economy after Independence

One of the central tasks that Indian leaders faced after 1947 was to modernize the sluggish economy. During Nehru's rule, India's model of development emphasized the creation of public enterprises and state guidance of private economic activity. Nehru created a powerful planning commission that established government investment priorities. Unlike the planning process in communist states, Indian plans included a large role for private entrepreneurs. Some large, private family-owned firms in industries like steel were a powerful force in the Indian economy. But the government also limited the start-up and expansion of private industries. It imposed high tariffs, arguing that newly created Indian industries required protection from foreign competitors.

This government-planned mixed economy enabled India to create an impressive industrial base but did little to help the poor. The protected industries were quite inefficient by global standards, and were hindered from acting boldly by the mountains of red tape that government bureaucrats generated.

Given the predominantly rural character of India, the highly unequal distribution of agricultural land presented a particularly significant challenge. Although the government passed legislation in the early 1950s reducing the size of landholdings, it reallocated little of the reclaimed land to poor tenants and agricultural laborers. Most land remained in the hands of medium- to large-sized landowners, who became part of the Congress political machine. This weakened the Congress Party's socialist commitment and its ability to assist the rural poor.

Rather than fulfilling its promise to enact substantial land reforms, the government adopted an alternative strategy in the late 1960s. Known as the **green revolution**, it aimed to increase agricultural production by providing farmers with improved seeds, subsidized fertilizer, and irrigation. The green revolution made India self-sufficient in food and even a food exporter. This represented a sharp contrast with the past, when famines resulted in mass starvation.

However, the benefits of the green revolution were highly uneven. While production increased sharply in the Punjab, for example, other regions (and especially poor farmers in less favored regions) were left behind. The very success of the green revolution created other long-term problems. In particular, intensive use of fertilizers depleted the soil. Purchasing costly agricultural machinery forced farmers to borrow large sums—often from money-lenders at high interest rates. In recent years, the states that were the standard bearers of the green revolution have experienced a severe agricultural crisis. One tragic result has been a wave of suicides by farmers who are unable to repay massive debts.

To summarize, the period between 1950 and 1980 consisted of **state-led economic development** that expanded the public sector, protected the domestic sector from foreign competition and closely supervised private sector activity. Political leaders hoped to strengthen India's international position by promoting self-sufficient industrialization. This policy was somewhat successful. State-led development insulated the Indian economy from global influences. The strategy resulted in modest economic growth, whose main beneficiaries were the business classes, medium and large landowning farmers, and political and bureaucratic elites. A substantial urban middle class also developed. By 1980, India was a significant industrial power that produced its own steel, airplanes, automobiles, chemicals, military hardware, and many consumer goods. Although land reform failed, the green revolution greatly increased food production.

However, state-led development also had substantial flaws. Shielded from competition, industry was often inefficient, and the entire economy grew at a slow pace. The elaborate rules and regulations controlling private economic activity encouraged corruption, as entrepreneurs bribed bureaucrats to evade the rules. And the focus on heavy industry meant that most investment involved purchasing machinery rather than creating jobs: 40 percent of India's population, primarily poor tenant farmers and landless laborers, were unable to escape poverty; indeed, the number of desperately poor people increased substantially.

Economic Liberalization

Political and economic elites became increasingly dissatisfied with India's inadequate economic performance compared with that of other Asian countries. For example, during the 1970s, whereas India's economy grew at the rate of 3.4 percent annually, South Korea's grew at 9.6 percent. India's business and industrial classes began to regard government regulation of the economy as a hindrance rather than a help. They became aware that poverty limited the possibility for expanding domestic markets. A turning point occurred in the 1980s and accelerated after 1991, when India moved toward **economic liberalization**. Under the leadership of Finance Minister

green revolution

A strategy for increasing agricultural (especially food) production, involving improved seeds, irrigation, and abundant use of fertilizers.

state-led economic development

The process of promoting economic development using government machinery.

economic liberalization

The removal of government control and regulation over private enterprise.

(and later prime minister) Manmohan Singh, the Indian government loosened its tight grip on the economy by eliminating price controls, reducing state intervention in day-to-day economic affairs, easing import regulations, reforming the tax system, and eliminating many state-run monopolies. As a result, the private sector grew rapidly, foreign investment poured into the country, and the economy grew rapidly.

India's economic performance has been highly impressive since then, with growth rates maintaining a pace of 5–7 percent annually. This record is especially noteworthy compared to the dismal performance of many debt-ridden African economies. An important reason for this success is that Indian entrepreneurs have been able to operate better with fewer government restrictions. Since 1991, the reduction of tariffs and other restrictions has further integrated India into the global economy.

However, this pattern of economic growth required borrowing capital from abroad to expand productive equipment. The need to repay foreign loans exerted enormous pressure on the government. In the 1990s, India was forced to borrow from the International Monetary Fund (IMF) and the World Bank to repay past loans. In return, these international organizations required the Indian government to reduce subsidies to the poor and sell government shares in public enterprises. Government policies reduced the workforce in public enterprises and reduced public spending and deficits.

Reforms in Agriculture

Since the 1990s, governments have reduced subsidized food supplies in order to limit public spending. In order to comply with the dictates of the World Trade Organization (WTO), the government removed restrictions on imports. Although industrialized countries have maintained trade barriers on agricultural products and continue to subsidize their domestic farmers, India's safety net has shrunk as its agricultural economy has opened up to global forces.

There are substantial successes on the positive side of the economic ledger. Some industries, such as information technology, have taken off. The service sector is expanding and contributes significantly to economic growth. Liberalization policies have accelerated industrial expansion. The stock of modern technology continues to grow, and the closer relationship between government and business has encouraged substantial domestic and foreign investment. At the same time, India has yet to devise an adequate balance between economic development, environmental

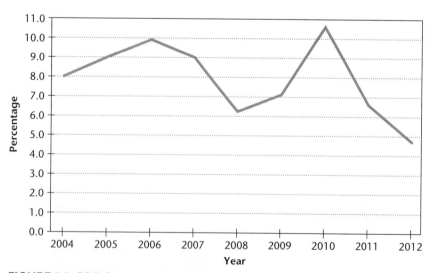

FIGURE 7.2 GDP Growth, 2004–2012

Source: World Bank GDP Growth, http://data.worldbank.org/indicator/NY.GDP.MKTP.KD.ZG/countries/IN-8s?display=graph.

protection, and social equity. The booming economy consumes enormous amounts of scarce resources and further burdens the Indian and global ecosystem.

Society and Economy

Inequality and Social Welfare Policy

India is deeply stratified by class and income. At the top of the income pyramid, a small group of Indians have made incredible fortunes in business and industry. The wealth of the Ambanis, Tatas, and Birlas rivals that of the richest corporate tycoons in the world. About 100 million Indians are relatively well off and enjoy a standard of living comparable to that of middle or upper-middle-class people anywhere in the world. Moreover, thanks to a large pool of low-wage labor, middle-class Indians generally employ at least one full-time domestic worker.

India's lower-middle classes, about half the population, are mainly self-employed business owners, small farmers, and urban workers. India has the largest number of poor people in the world, though measures of poverty differ. According to the Indian government's definition of poverty, 22 percent of the population was living in poverty in 2011–2012. Many observers believe that these numbers seriously underestimate the level of poverty in India. The World Bank measures poverty by the number of people in a country who live on $1.25 per day or less; by that standard nearly 33 percent of Indians lived in poverty in 2010 (the last year for which the World Bank data is readily available). If one employs the measures used by the Indian government, the proportion of those who are defined as poor has halved since independence. However, India's rapid population growth has increased the absolute number of the poor: from about 200 million in the 1950s to about 300 million currently.

About three-quarters of the poor live in India's thousands of villages. Most are landless laborers. The urban poor are concentrated in giant slums with few public services, such as electricity and indoor plumbing. Although the economic boom has improved conditions for hundreds of millions, many more Indians are mired in poverty, and their children have little prospect of leading a better life.

The sizable number of poor people encourages many Indian politicians to adopt populist or socialist electoral platforms—although often in name only. However, there are some important exceptions. For example, the states of West Bengal and Kerala have a long history of radical politics; the poor in these states are well organized and periodically elect left-leaning state governments. These governments have redistributed land to the poor and implemented antipoverty programs. The poor have also fueled many social movements. The **Naxalite** revolutionary movement is an important example. Influenced by Maoist ideals, it has organized the landless poor to engage in land seizures and attacks on the state and dominant classes.

Over the years, Indian governments have pursued various poverty alleviation programs. The last Congress government (2000–2014) initiated the Employment Guarantee Scheme to provide the poor with jobs constructing roads and bridges, and cleaning agricultural waterways. Because the rural poor are unemployed for nearly half the year when agricultural jobs are not available, these schemes have become an important source of off-season jobs and income. In an effort to reduce high malnutrition rates, the Indian parliament passed a Food Security Bill that provides rice and grain at heavily subsidized prices to the country's poor. Two-thirds of India's population qualifies for subsidized food under the bill.

Naxalite

The Naxalite movement emerged as a breakaway faction of the CPM in West Bengal in 1967. It is a radical, often violent, extra-parliamentary movement.

However, overall, India has a poor record of reducing poverty. Antipoverty programs and land reforms have generally failed to reduce economic inequality and help the poor. India has few Western-style welfare programs, such as unemployment insurance and comprehensive public health programs. Especially noteworthy is that India does not provide universal primary education. Thus, only 75 percent of boys and men are literate. The situation is far worse for girls and women, of whom only 51 percent are literate. This increases the likelihood that poverty will be perpetuated in future generations.

A variety of inequalities in India have increased over the last two decades, notably between Indian regions as well as across Indian cities and the countryside. For example, the average per capita income of a resident of India's richer states, such as Gujarat, is four times higher that of an individual living in the poor state of Bihar. An average citizen living in a village is also likely to be much poorer than someone living in a city. Class inequalities within cities have also become more skewed.

India's population continues to grow at a rapid pace—double the rate of China. Before long it will be the world's largest country. India's democratic government, unlike China's authoritarian system, has generally resisted coercive population control policies. But it has also failed to practice more progressive ways to reduce population growth. For example, although literate women are more likely to marry later in life and engage in family planning, the Indian government has failed to make education a priority, and as noted above, girls and women are especially likely to be illiterate. Since India has more people than it can use productively, a growing population hinders economic growth.

India is one of the few countries in the world with a lower percentage of females than males. Evidence that Indian society favors boys over girls can be inferred from such social indicators as lower female literacy, nutrition levels, and survival rates of female infants. Prejudice against girls is reinforced through traditions like the dowry system (the Hindu custom of giving the groom and his family substantial money and goods at a daughter's wedding). Although dowries are illegal, they have grown alongside increased materialism and aspirations for upward social mobility, particularly among the urban middle and lower-middle classes.

India has the world's largest population of child labor, though this has been declining in recent years. Children are employed in agriculture, match production, rug weaving, and selling refreshments at train stations. Children often work long hours at low wages. Because they cannot attend school, they have limited prospects for upward mobility. The problem of child labor is closely related to India's failure to provide universal primary education (see Figure 7.3).

Many Indian elites claim that compulsory primary education is an unaffordable luxury in a poor country like India. However, this argument is false; many poor African countries have higher rates of primary school enrollment than India. The more likely obstacle to universal primary education is poverty and caste inequality. Many poor families see large families as a form of insurance, for they depend on their children's labor for support. And many upper-caste elites do not consider educating lower-caste children a priority. Over the last two decades, the government has increased public spending on primary education, and enrollments have increased sharply. The Indian Constitution stated that within a ten-year period the state would endeavor to provide free and compulsory education for children. However, not until 2010 did the Right of Children to Free and Compulsory Education Act make education for children between the ages of 6 and 14 a fundamental right. The Act requires elementary schools to improve their infrastructure, teacher qualifications and student–teacher ratio, and requires private schools to reserve 25 percent of seats for poor children (to be reimbursed by the state). Although the Act is a landmark achievement, critics contend that the government lags in its implementation. The quality of education in government schools remains poor.

Those who suffer most are at the bottom of the caste hierarchy: the **untouchables**. The Indian census classifies nearly 10 percent of India's population as belonging to the untouchables—or **scheduled castes**, as they are officially known. Untouchables engage in occupations such as cleaning and leather work, which is considered "unclean," and they are not considered members of organized Hindu society. The members of this group are stigmatized and excluded from meaningful participation in social and economic life.

The caste system has a destructive impact on Indian social and economic life. By assigning people to specific occupations at birth, it limits individual choice and impedes social and economic mobility. Although the link between caste and occupation has weakened, especially in urban areas, it remains an important organizing principle for employment. Caste groups sometimes re-designate their caste identities to achieve group mobility without undermining the principles governing caste hierarchies. In the political arena, voting blocs are often organized on a caste basis. Caste divisions among the lower classes in rural India make it difficult for the poor to defend their class interests.

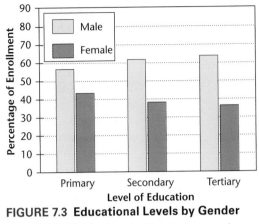

FIGURE 7.3 Educational Levels by Gender

Source: UNESCO Institute for Statistics, www.uis.unesco.org/en/stats/stats.

untouchables

The lowest caste in India's caste system, whose members are among the poorest and most disadvantaged Indians.

scheduled castes

The lowest caste in India; also known as untouchables.

Environmental Issues

India's patterns of production and consumption coupled with inadequate and ineffective government regulation have created serious environmental problems. India's lakes and rivers are polluted by sewage and factory waste. Industrial overuse has created a drinking water shortage. By the Indian government's own estimates, water from over half of India's rivers is too polluted to drink and the water from more than a quarter of rivers is too polluted to bathe in. Yet rivers remain the main source of drinking water for millions of Indians, with resulting diseases and illnesses. Some of the world's most polluted cities are in India. It is common to see a thick haze enveloping Indian metropolitan areas. New Delhi's air pollution readings are twice as high as Beijing's.

Urbanization, commercial logging, and using wood for fuel have caused deforestation, droughts, floods, and cyclones. Illegal deforestation costs the Indian government hundreds of millions of dollars annually. Illegal mining has caused massive environmental damage.

India will likely experience severe consequences from global climate change due to its long coastline and reliance on seasonal monsoons for agricultural production. The emission of carbon dioxide has already created an increase in temperature, rise in the sea level, and destruction of coastal croplands and fisheries.

Yet environmental issues rarely drive the country's politics. In 2013, India's minister of state for environment and forests resigned amidst complaints by big business that environmental regulations were delaying industrial projects. The petroleum minister assumed her responsibilities and immediately approved several polluting industries in environmentally sensitive regions. The national government has generally favored large infrastructure projects that ensure economic growth at the expense of the environment. Although it recognizes a trade-off between preserving the environment and achieving high economic growth, the poor state of the environment reduces India's growth potential. The World Bank estimates that environmental degradation costs India $80 billion a year, or 5.7 percent of its GDP.

Although the government adopted a National Action Plan on climate change in 2008 to reduce its carbon footprint, it has resisted pressures from Western countries to reduce greenhouse gas emissions. At the 2009 United Nations Climate Change Conference in Copenhagen, for example, India opposed drastic carbon-cutting steps unless developed countries took them first and provided monetary assistance to help developing countries do the same. India strenuously resisted pollution limits in global climate talks in Warsaw in November 2013.

The one institution that has taken a pro-active role in environmental protection is India's Supreme Court. It has included in the right to life and liberty, a fundamental constitutional right to a healthy environment. As a result, an individual can approach the Court directly when the public interest is jeopardized by environmental harm. Acting on a Public Interest Litigation to curb industrial pollution of water bodies, for instance, the Court issued notices to the Union government, Central Pollution Control Board, and nineteen states to implement pollution control norms and the "polluter pays" principle.

The Supreme Court has issued notices and directives to the central and state governments on multiple environmental issues, such as freezing production licenses granted to manufacturers of endosulfan pesticide, relocating hazardous industries from the national capital region, limiting noise pollution, and requiring civic bodies to manage plastic waste. Under the Environmental Protection Act (1986) various projects require clearance by the state or central environment ministries. The Court required the central government to appoint a national environment regulator to evaluate the environmental impact of projects.

The Supreme Court has ordered a variety of environmental safeguards. In 1998, it ordered that all Delhi's public diesel-powered vehicles convert to natural gas. The Court has investigated illegal mining in the states of Orissa and Jharkhand. In 2013 it required village councils to approve mining projects that encroach on tribal settlements.

Inspired by Public Interest Litigation and sheer survival concerns, the poor have engaged in struggles protesting environmental destruction. The Chipko movement, which emerged in the early 1970s in the Himalayas, is one of the best-known and oldest movements against deforestation. It has influenced similar forms of activism in other regions. In 1984, a gas leak in a Union Carbide plant in Bhopal caused an explosion that resulted in thousands of deaths and injuries. It generated movements demanding greater compensation for victims of the gas leak, as well as the adoption of environmental regulations to prevent similar disasters in the future. There have been large-scale protests against India's efforts to expand power generation through investing in nuclear reactors.

One of India's largest environmental movements has opposed the construction of a dam that it claimed would benefit prosperous regions to the detriment of poor regions, as well as displace millions of people, mostly tribals who do not possess land titles. The Narmada Bachao Andolan (Save the Narmada Struggle) galvanized a large movement to engage in nonviolent protest against the construction of the giant Sardar Sarvodaya Dam in western India in 1986. Although it caused the World Bank to rescind promised loans, the Indian government completed the project.

India in the Global Economy

Although for decades starting in the 1950s India provided leadership to the non-aligned bloc, it sought to minimize global economic exchange. When India's economy was relatively closed to outside influences, powerful groups had vested interests in preventing change. Many bureaucrats accepted bribes from business executives to issue licenses or evade regulations. Moreover, labor unions, especially in government-controlled factories, supported inefficient operations because this kept employment at high levels. These well-entrenched groups resisted liberalization and threatened to support opposition parties if the government sponsored a decisive policy shift.

By the 1980s, the negative effects of this pattern finally forced a change. When the government opened the economy, foreign investment soared from $100 million a year to nearly $4 billion annually between 1992 and 1998, and to nearly $8 billion annually in 2006–2007. However, foreign investment in India remains several times lower than in China and Brazil. Furthermore, it is concentrated in industries producing for the domestic market; it has not facilitated export promotion, a major source of hard currency.

One high-tech sector in which India excels is computer software. Indian firms and multinational corporations employ large numbers of highly skilled, low-cost, English-speaking scientific and engineering talent to make India a world leader in the production of software. India boasts the equivalent of California's Silicon Valley in Bangalore in southern India, home to a large number of software firms. Furthermore, transnational corporations have recently hired graduates of India's superb higher institutions of engineering and technology.

For the same reason, India has become a prime destination for corporate call centers, tech support, and back office operations of banks, insurance companies, and financial firms. Scores of high-rise office buildings, shopping malls, and housing complexes have sprung up outside Delhi and Mumbai, graphic evidence of the new India. However, because they are so cut off from traditional Indian society, they further intensify the country's extreme social fragmentation.

India's integration within the global economy has increased as a result of a WTO agreement on trade in services, which requires the government to ease restrictions on banking, insurance, and other services. More than forty foreign banks have opened in India, and the government has also opened up the insurance sector to private and foreign investment. This has been a mixed blessing. For example, foreign banks focus on retail banking in profitable urban areas and ignore less lucrative areas of lending.

GLOBAL CONNECTIONS

India in the Global Economy

India's economy has globalized since 1991. Tariffs on trade have come down. India's exports and imports have grown rapidly. Laws on foreign investment have also become more liberal. While direct foreign investment is significantly lower in India than in China, foreign investment into India has continued to grow over the last two decades. Foreign monies in the form of portfolio investments have also flown into India, buoying the stock markets but also adding volatility.

In terms of financial markets, India is not as well integrated into the global economy as many Latin American and some East Asian economies. While criticisms of this selective integration abound, India suffered a lot less during a variety of global financial crises than other developing markets.

MAKING CONNECTIONS What are the pros and cons of a country like India being integrated in the global economy?

This reduces the possibilities for farmers and small-scale industrialists in rural and poorer regions to obtain loans.

Because India has compiled an enviable growth record in the last decade, it has become an attractive destination for foreign investment. India has catapulted into the first ranks of large developing countries. It is a charter member of the so-called BRIC countries: Brazil, Russia, India, and China—a bloc of developing countries that wields significant clout in the international arena.

Where Do You Stand?

Will economic growth on its own solve the problem of poverty in India?

There is an old argument that democracies are no good at promoting growth. What does the India case teach you about this argument?

SECTION 3

GOVERNANCE AND POLICY-MAKING

Organization of the State

The 1950 constitution, adopted soon after India gained independence, created a democratic republic with a parliamentary system and a weak, mostly ceremonial, president. India's political system is federal, and states have substantial autonomy, power, and responsibilities. For much of the period since 1947, India has been a stable, democratic country with universal suffrage and periodic local, state, and national elections. This record of democratic stability is remarkable among developing countries. Indian democracy has proved so durable because its political institutions have been able to accommodate many challenges. (See Table 7.1 for an outline of Indian political organization.)

Unlike the British constitution, which it resembles in many respects, the Indian constitution is a written document that has been periodically amended. Because the Indian constitution is highly detailed, it leaves less room for interpretation than many other national constitutions. Three special features are worth noting. First, unlike many constitutions, the Indian constitution directs the government to promote social and economic equality and justice. The constitution thus outlines policy goals, rather than simply enumerating formal procedures of decision making and allocating powers among political institutions. Although the impact of these constitutional provisions on welfare and social justice is limited, political parties and movements have appealed to them when seeking reforms.

Second, the Indian constitution, like the U.S. constitution, provides for freedom of religion and defines India as a secular state. And third, the constitution allows for the temporary suspension of many democratic rights under emergency conditions. These provisions were used, for understandable reasons, during wars with Pakistan and China. But they have also been invoked, more disturbingly, to deal with internal political threats, most dramatically during the national Emergency from 1975 to 1977.

Further, the constitution specifies that, in the event that state governments are unable to function in a stable manner, the national government is authorized to declare

⊞ PROFILE

The Nehru–Gandhi Dynasty

Jawaharlal Nehru was a staunch believer in liberal democratic principles. When India became independent in 1947, Nehru became prime minister and retained that position until his death in 1964. Nehru was a committed nationalist and social democrat. He sought to strengthen India's autonomy and national economy and improve the lives of the Indian poor. He tried to establish a socialist, democratic, and secular state, although India often failed to live up to these lofty ideals. Nehru attempted to set India on a rapid road to industrialization by promoting heavy industry. He advocated redistributing wealth through land reform, although much of India's land remained concentrated in the hands of traditional rural elites. Finally, Nehru championed democratic and individual rights, including the right to private property. Upon his death, India inherited a stable polity, a functioning democracy, and an economy characterized by a large public sector and a complex pattern of state control over the private sector.

Indira Gandhi became prime minister shortly after the death of her father, Jawaharlal Nehru, and dominated the Indian political scene until her assassination in 1984. While her foreign policies strengthened India's international position, her domestic policies weakened democratic institutions. Her tendency to centralize and personalize authority within the Congress contributed to the erosion of the party. She engaged in repressive measures to curtail growing political opposition. After she ordered the army to invade the Golden Temple, the Sikhs' most revered temple, she was assassinated by her Sikh bodyguards.

MAKING CONNECTIONS Some observers have suggested that having one family dominate Indian politics for many years promoted political stability. Others claim that it made a mockery of Indian democracy. Who is correct?

President's Rule, which involves suspending the elected state government and administering the state's affairs from Delhi. President's Rule was designed to be used as a last resort to temporarily curb unrest in federal states. However, by 1989 the central government had declared President's Rule sixty-seven times. The Congress government, particularly under Indira Gandhi's leadership, used President's Rule to remove governments formed by opposition parties and to strengthen its own control. Under pressure from the opposition, Indira Gandhi created the Sarkaria Commission in 1983 to review center-state relations. It reported in 1987 that President's Rule had been necessary only twenty-six of the sixty-seven times it had been used and urged the central government to exercise restraint in imposing it. A landmark 1994 Supreme Court ruling affirmed the Sarkaria Commission findings, called for judicial review of central government decisions to impose President's Rule, and affirmed the possibility of the courts striking it down. The coalition governments that have held office since 1989 have been reluctant to invoke President's Rule. An important reason is that parties in national governing coalitions oppose the national government suspending state governments that they lead.

In India's federal system, the central government controls most essential government functions, such as defense, foreign policy, taxation, public expenditures, and economic planning. State governments formally control agriculture, education, and law and order. However, because states are heavily dependent on the central government for funds to finance programs in these policy areas, their actual power is limited.

The *Lok Sabha*, or House of the People, is the lower chamber of parliament and the *Rajya Sabha*, the upper house. (India's parliament will be described in Section 4.) Following elections to the *Lok Sabha*, the leader of the political party with the most seats becomes the prime minister. Effective power is concentrated in the prime minister's office. The prime minister in turn nominates members of the cabinet, mostly members of parliament belonging to the ruling coalition. The prime minister and cabinet members also head various ministries.

Lok Sabha

The lower house of parliament in India, where all major legislation must pass before becoming law.

Rajya Sabha

India's upper house of parliament; considerably less politically powerful than the *Lok Sabha*.

The Executive

The Prime Minister and Cabinet

The prime minister governs with the help of the cabinet, which periodically meets to discuss important issues, including new legislative proposals. Because the cabinet directs the majority party coalition in parliament, passing a bill is less complicated than it can be in a presidential system. The permanent bureaucracy, especially senior- and middle-level bureaucrats, is responsible for policy implementation. As in most parliamentary systems, such as Britain, Germany, and Japan, there is considerable overlap between the executive and the legislative branches of the government.

The Prime Minister

The prime minister directs India's Council of Ministers, and is therefore in charge of all government ministries. As such, the prime minister is ultimately responsible for all the daily activities of the central government. Among other things, the prime minister has the power to appoint individuals to various government offices, establish policy on significant issues, and administer the civil service. From 1947 to 1984, except for several brief interludes, India had only two prime ministers: Jawaharlal Nehru and Indira Gandhi (see Table 7.2). This is nearly unique among democracies; it underlines the powerful hold that the Nehru–Gandhi family had on India's political destiny. With the election of Narendra Modi as India's prime minister in 2014 one wonders if the dynastic rule by the Nehru-Gandhi party has come to an end.

THE U.S. CONNECTION

Comparing Chief Executives in India and the United States

In the U.S. presidential system, the positions of head of state and chief executive are combined in one office: the president. The president thus both symbolizes the unity of the entire country and is a political party leader and head of government.

This pattern is quite unusual. In most countries, there are two offices. The head of state is mostly a ceremonial office, occupied by a monarch or a president indirectly elected by the legislature or an electoral college. In India, the president is elected for a five-year term by an electoral college composed of elected representatives from the national and state governments. The president symbolizes the unity of India and is expected to rise above partisan conflicts. However, presidential approval is necessary for most parliamentary bills to become laws. Presidents can veto bills by refusing assent or delaying their enactment. Presidents can also name the prime minister when parliamentary elections do not produce a clear verdict as to which party should lead the new government.

By combining the functions of head of state and head of government, the United States concentrates enormous power in one person. The Indian system assigns the two functions to different officials, thus leaving the president generally above the political fray and making the prime minister a more partisan figure. What are the strengths and weaknesses of each system?

MAKING CONNECTIONS Which is preferable and why: the Indian system in which the functions of head of state (president) and head of government (prime minister) are assigned to different officials? Or the American system of combining the two functions within the single office of the president?

The Cabinet

The prime minister chooses the cabinet, mostly from among the governing party's senior members of parliament. Being named to the cabinet is among the most sought-after prizes in Indian politics. The main criteria guiding a prime minister's choice are seniority, competence, and personal loyalty. Regional and caste representation are also considered. With the advent of coalition governments, representatives from each political party in the coalition must be named to the cabinet. The result is that cabinets nowadays are often large, unwieldy, and divided.

Cabinet ministers have three roles. First, they are members of the government and participate in shaping its general policy orientation. Second, they are leaders of their own parties and must try to maintain party cohesion and support for the government. This may be difficult, especially if the government pursues a policy that is unpopular with the party's members. Third, cabinet ministers direct a ministry responsible for a particular policy area. They must thus supervise the ministry's civil servants and try to ensure that the department performs competently. Complicating a minister's situation is that what brings success in one area may detract from success in another.

The Bureaucracy

The prime minister and cabinet ministers supervise the bureaucracy in close collaboration with senior civil servants. Each senior minister oversees a sprawling department staffed by some highly competent, overworked, senior civil servants and many not-so-competent, underworked, lowly bureaucrats.

The **Indian Administrative Service (IAS)**, an elite corps of top bureaucrats, constitutes a critically important but relatively thin layer at the top of India's bureaucracy. Recruitment occurs through a highly competitive examination. Many more candidates compete than are chosen, since IAS appointments provide lifetime tenure, excellent pay, and great prestige. In 2009, for example, out of the nearly 600,000 applicants for IAS civil service posts, just 7,000 were selected for an interview, and 2,500 were appointed. Whereas political leaders come and go, senior civil servants stay—and accumulate a storehouse of knowledge and expertise that makes them powerful and competent.

Many of India's most talented young men and women were attracted to the IAS in the decades after independence because of the prestige that came with service in national government. The attraction of the IAS has declined, however, and many of India's most talented young people now go into engineering and business administration, or leave the country for better opportunities abroad. Government service has become tarnished by corruption, and the level of professionalism within the IAS has declined as politicians increasingly prefer loyalty over merit and seniority when making promotions. Nevertheless, the IAS continues to recruit highly talented young people, many of whom become dedicated senior civil servants who constitute the backbone of the Indian government.

Below the IAS, the level of talent and professionalism drops sharply. The national and state-level Indian bureaucracy is infamous for corruption and inefficiency. Civil servants are powerfully organized and, thanks to lifetime tenure, free to resist orders coming from their superiors. There has been a marked decline in the competence and integrity of the Indian bureaucracy through the years. Its lack of responsiveness and accountability pose a major problem for Indian democracy. These problems contribute to the gap between good policies and their poor implementation at the local level.

Indian Administrative Service (IAS)

India's civil service, a highly professional and talented group of administrators who run the Indian government on a day-to-day basis.

Other State Institutions

The Military and the Police

With more than 1.3 million well-trained and well-equipped members, the Indian military is a highly powerful and professional organization. It has never intervened directly in politics. Over the years, the continuity of constitutional, electoral politics and a relatively apolitical effective military have come to reinforce and strengthen each other. Civilian politicians provide ample resources to the armed forces and, for the most part, encourage them to function as a professional organization. The armed forces, in turn, accept direction from democratically elected civilian leaders.

The Indian police forces have never been as professionalized as the armed forces. The police come under the jurisdiction of state governments, not the central government. Because state governments are generally less effective and honest than the national government, the Indian police are not neutral civil servants. State-level politicians regularly interfere in police personnel issues, and police officers in turn regularly oblige politicians. The police are easily bribed and often allied with criminals or politicians. The police generally favor dominant social groups such as landowners, upper castes, and the majority Hindu religious community. A large, sprawling, and relatively ineffective police service remains a problematic presence in Indian society.

In addition to the national army and the state-level police, the national government controls paramilitary forces that number nearly half a million men. As Indian politics became more turbulent in the 1980s, paramilitary forces steadily expanded. Because the national government calls on the army only as a last resort to manage internal conflicts, and because state-level police forces are generally unreliable, paramilitary forces are often used to maintain order.

The Judiciary

An independent judiciary is another component of India's state system. The major judicial authority is the Supreme Court, comprising a chief justice and seventeen other judges. The president appoints judges on the advice of the prime minister. Once appointed, judges cannot be removed from the bench until retirement at age 65.

The main political role of the Supreme Court is to ensure that legislation conforms to the constitution. The Supreme Court has acted as a bulwark against state abuses of power in some landmark civil rights judgments. It introduced a system of public interest litigation that allows anyone to file a petition in the High Court against a violation of the legal or constitutional right(s) of any person or class of persons whose fundamental rights have been breached. This has resulted in judicial activism against executive wrongdoing.

A principal source of conflict is that the constitution simultaneously protects private property yet also directs the government to pursue social justice. Indian leaders have often promulgated socialist legislation, for example, requiring the redistribution of agricultural land. The Supreme Court considers legislation of this nature because it potentially violates the right to private property. For instance, during the early years of independence, the courts overturned state government laws to redistribute land from **zamindars** (traditional landowners) on the grounds that the laws violated *zamindars'* fundamental rights. Parliament retaliated by amending the constitution to protect the executive's authority to promote land redistribution. But matters did not end there. The Supreme Court responded that parliament lacked the power to abrogate fundamental rights. During the Emergency period, Indira Gandhi directed

zamindars

Landlords who served as tax collectors in India under the British colonial government. The *zamindari* system was abolished after independence.

parliament to pass an amendment limiting the Supreme Court's right of judicial review to procedural issues. After the Emergency ended, the newly elected government reversed the change.

Over the years, the Supreme Court has clashed head-on with the parliament as a result of the contradiction between constitutional principles of parliamentary sovereignty and judicial review. For example, it has required central and state governments to prevent starvation by releasing food stocks and to promote education by providing school lunches and daycare facilities.

Like other Indian political institutions, the judiciary suffers from institutional decay. The caseload on the Supreme Court, as with much of the Indian legal system, is extremely heavy, and there is a significant backlog of cases. When cases drag on for years, public confidence in the judiciary crumbles. Still the Supreme Court remains a powerful and valuable institution.

Compared to other large, multiethnic democracies, India has generally protected fundamental civil rights, including an independent judiciary, universal suffrage, and a free and lively press. India's media, especially its newspapers and magazines, are as free as any in the world. The combination of a vocal intellectual stratum and a free press is a cherished element in India's democracy.

Nevertheless, the tradition of a strong, interventionist state has enabled the government to violate civil liberties. After September 11, the Indian parliament passed the Prevention of Terrorism Act (POTA), which provided a vague definition of terrorism and allowed a citizen to be charged without having committed a specific act. Grounds included conspiring, attempting to commit, advocating, abetting, advising, or inciting terrorism. Penalties included harsh prison sentences and death. Confessions made to police officers were admissible as evidence in courts, contrary to ordinary law, and the police used torture to extract confessions. The government used POTA in a highly arbitrary manner. The largest number of arrests took place in India's newest state, Jharkhand, where members and supporters of radical groups were incarcerated under POTA. The government also portrayed pro-independence groups in Kashmir and Muslim groups throughout India as terrorists.

Shortly after Manmohan Singh became prime minister in 2004, the cabinet repealed POTA on grounds that it had been misused. Instead, it amended existing laws to tackle terrorism. However, Singh's government did not dismiss charges against those previously arrested under POTA.

Subnational Government

The structure of India's twenty-eight state governments parallels that of the national government. Each state has a government, headed by a chief minister who leads the party with most seats in the lower house of the state legislature. The chief minister appoints cabinet ministers who head various ministries staffed by a state-level, permanent bureaucracy. The quality of government below the national level is often poor.

Each state has a governor appointed by the national president. Governors are supposed to serve under the direction of the chief minister. However, in practice they often become independently powerful, especially in states that have unstable governments or are at odds with the national government. Governors can dismiss elected state governments and proclaim temporary Presidential Rule if they determine that the state government is ineffective.

There is an ongoing power struggle between state and central governments. States often demand more resources from the central government. They have also demanded greater power and recognition of their distinctive cultural and linguistic identities. When conflicting political parties are in power at the national and state levels, center-state relations can be inflamed by political and ethnic conflicts.

Indian politics has become increasingly regionalized in recent years. States have become more autonomous economically and politically. State parties play an increasingly important role in national governance and with economic liberalization have sought foreign investment independent of the national government. One consequence is that regional inequalities are widening.

India has an elaborate system of local governance. The *panchayats* are locally elected councils at the local, district, and state levels. They were strengthened in 1992 by a constitutional amendment that stipulated that *panchayat* elections should be held every five years, and required that one-third of seats on the *panchayats* should be reserved for women and that scheduled castes and tribes should be represented in proportion to their numbers in the locality. Most states have met the 33 percent women's **reservations** at all three levels and several have exceeded it.

The resources and planning capabilities of the *panchayats* are relatively limited. State legislatures determine how much power and authority they can wield. Most *panchayats* are responsible for implementing but not devising rural development schemes. Although *panchayats* are provided with considerable resources, they have little discretion over how to allocate funds. Corruption is common because local political elites, bureaucrats, and influential citizens often siphon off public funds. Thus, many of the funds spent on poverty alleviation programs have been wasted.

panchayats

Elected bodies at the village, district, and state levels that have development and administrative responsibilities.

reservations

Jobs or admissions to colleges reserved by the government of India for specific underprivileged groups.

The Policy-Making Process

The government in New Delhi formulates major policies. Senior civil servants play an important role identifying problems, synthesizing data, and presenting political leaders with alternative solutions. Because the prime minister usually commands a majority in parliament, passage of most legislation is ensured.

The real policy drama in India occurs when major bills are debated in parliament and implemented. Consider the policy shift to economic liberalization. The new course was formulated by a handful of senior ministers and bureaucrats. To reach the decision, however, a fairly complex set of political activities took place. Decision-makers at the highest level of government consulted important interest groups, such as associations of Indian businessmen and representatives of international organizations like the World Bank and IMF. Groups that opposed the reform made their positions known. Organized labor, for example, called a one-day general strike to oppose privatizing the public sector. Newspapers, magazines, and intellectuals weighed in. Political parties announced their positions. Members of the ruling party, Congress in this case, did not necessarily support their own leaders at the early stage. Opposition parties highlighted the harm that the reform might inflict. These pressures modified the policy that the government eventually adopted.

After policies have been adopted, their implementation is far from assured. Regarding liberalization, some aspects of the new policy package proved easier to implement than others. Changing the exchange rate was relatively easy because the policy decision and its implementation required the actions of only a handful of politicians and bureaucrats. By contrast, simplifying the procedures for creating new business enterprises proved far more complicated. Implementation required the cooperation of many bureaucrats—whose power would be reduced from the change. Consequently, many tried to sabotage the newly simplified procedures.

Where Do You Stand?

Is India too centralized?

The poor quality of local bureaucracy in India is not a problem because active civil society groups can solve local problems. Discuss.

REPRESENTATION AND PARTICIPATION

SECTION 4

The Legislature

Focus Questions ❡

- How effectively does India's parliament represent the country's diverse interests?

- What are the causes and consequences of the shift from a one-party system dominated by the Congress Party to the emergence of a multi-party system?

The Indian parliament is bicameral, consisting of the *Lok Sabha* and the *Rajya Sabha*. *Lok Sabha* elections are of vital importance. First, the outcome determines which party coalition will control the government. Second, although members of parliament cannot shape policies, they enjoy considerable status, access to resources, and influence over allocations of government funds.

Elections to the *Lok Sabha* are held at least every five years. However, as in other parliamentary systems, the prime minister may choose to call elections earlier. India is divided into 544 electoral districts of roughly equal population, each of which elects one representative to the national parliament by a first-past-the-post electoral procedure. Since party leaders control nominations, most legislators are beholden to them for securing a party ticket. Given the importance of the party label for nominations, members of parliament support party leaders and maintain strong voting discipline in the *Lok Sabha*.

The main tasks of the *Lok Sabha* are to elect the prime minister (that is, the leader of the winning party coalition), pass legislation, and debate government actions. Although any member of parliament can introduce bills, the government sponsors most of those that are eventually passed and become laws. After bills are introduced, they are assigned to parliamentary committees for detailed study and discussion. The committees report the bills back to the *Lok Sabha* for debate, possible amendment, and preliminary votes. They are then sent to the *Rajya Sabha*, which generally approves bills passed by the *Lok Sabha*. Most members of the *Rajya Sabha* are elected indirectly by state legislatures. The *Rajya Sabha* is much weaker than the *Lok Sabha* because its assent is not required for the passage of spending measures that the *Lok Sabha* approves, it cannot introduce no-confidence motions, and it is much smaller than the *Lok Sabha*. After the *Rajya Sabha* votes on (and possibly amends) bills, they return to the *Lok Sabha* for a third reading, after which the final text is voted on by both houses. If passed, it is sent to the president for approval.

Although the *Lok Sabha* can make and unmake governments (by voting to bring them down), it does not play a significant role in policy-making. Keep in mind that (1) the government generally introduces new legislation; (2) most legislators are politically beholden to party leaders; and (3) all parties maintain tight discipline to ensure voting along party lines.

Changes in Parliament's social composition do not have significant policy consequences. Whether members of parliament are business executives or workers, men

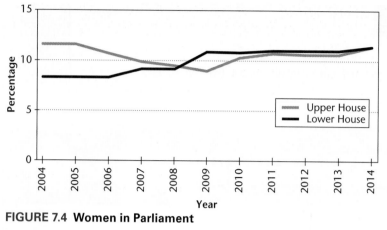

FIGURE 7.4 Women in Parliament

http://www.ipu.org/wmn-e/classif.htm.

or women, or members of upper or lower castes is unlikely to significantly influence policy. Nevertheless, groups in society derive symbolic recognition from having one of their own in parliament.

The typical member of parliament is a male university graduate between 40 and 60 years old. Over the years, there have been some changes in the social composition of legislators. For example, legislators in the 1950s were likely to be urban men and were often lawyers and members of higher castes. Today, nearly half of all members of parliament come from rural areas, and many have agricultural backgrounds. Members of the middle castes (the so-called backward castes) are also well represented today. These changes reflect some of the broad shifts in the distribution of power in Indian society. By contrast, the proportion of women and of poor, lower-caste individuals in parliament remains low. The representation of women in parliament has gradually increased from 4.4 percent (or twenty-two women) in the first parliament (1952–1957) to 10.8 percent (fifty-eight women) in 2009. (See Figure 7.4.) The small number of women MPs reflects party biases toward nominating female candidates. Only 7 percent of the candidates in the 2009 general election were women.

Following many years of deliberation and debate, the upper house of parliament approved a constitutional amendment in 2010 reserving at least 33 percent seats in parliament and the legislative assemblies for women; it awaits a decision by the lower house.

Political Parties and the Party System

Political parties and elections are where much of the real drama of Indian politics occurs. Since parties that control a majority of seats in the national and state parliaments form the government and control public resources, parties devote substantial political energy to contesting elections. Since independence, the party system has evolved from being dominated by Congress to one in which Congress is merely one of the major parties. Following the most recent election in 2014 the Congress is in danger of becoming a minor party (see Table 7.3). What thus began as a virtually one-party system has evolved into a real multiparty system with three main political tendencies: centrist, center-left, and center-right.

India's major national parties are ideologically diverse. As a centrist party, the Congress stands for secularism, economic liberalization, and mild redistribution of wealth. The Bharatiya Janata Party (BJP) favors private enterprise and supports secularism in principle but not in practice. In addition to these two main contenders, other major competitors include the Janata, the all-India CPM, and forty regional parties.

The Indian party system has changed dramatically since 1989. A multiparty system has emerged following the decline of Congress and growth of state parties. Taken together, the forty officially recognized state parties have significant weight in Indian politics. Some are regional powerhouses and control state governments.

Table 7.3		Major Party Election Results												
	1991		**1996**		**1998**		**1999**		**2004**		**2009**		**2014**	
	%	Seats	%	Seats	%	Seats	%	Seats	%	Seats	%	Seats	%	Seats
Congress	37.3	225	29	143	25.4	140	28.4	112	26.69	145[a]	28.55		19.3%	44
BJP & Allies	19.9	119	24	193	36.2	250	41.3	296	35.9	1.189	24.63		31%	282
Janata	10.8	55	Joined with UF		Joined with UF		1	1	Joined with Congress		0		Ran separately —	
United Front	—	—	31	180	20.9	98	—	—	—	—	—	—	—	—
Communists[b]	—	48	Joined with UF		Joined with UF		5.4	32	7.0	53	1.43		3.2%	9
Others							23.9	107	19.9	78	34.71			208

[a]The more relevant figures in 2004 for Congress and allies were 35.82 and 219, respectively.
[b]Includes both the CPM and the CPI.
Source: India Today, July 15, 1991, March 16, 1998; *Economic Times* website, economictimes.indiatimes.com; and *The Hindu*, May 20, 2004.

State parties have largely determined the outcome of the last three elections and participated in every coalition government since 1989. Even in the 2009 elections, which were commonly seen as a victory for the national Congress party, state parties won 29.2 percent of the vote. During the 2014 elections the BJP won a solid majority of seats with 31 percent of the popular vote. With the Congress and the Communists winning only 22.5 percent of the vote between the two of them, nearly half the popular vote was secured by regional parties. As one would expect, there are feverish negotiations among coalition parties over the allocation of cabinet positions and the policies that the governing coalition will pursue. While the fragmentation of the party system enables the representation of multiple interests, it also deters the government from acting decisively. Cabinets are large, unwieldy, and cautious. If the government acted boldly, it could lose the support of one or more coalition partners, forfeit its parliamentary majority, and be forced to resign.

In recent elections, the two major contenders have been a coalition led by the left of center Congress Party and another led by the Hindu right-wing Bharatiya Janata Party (BJP).

Although polls have often predicted a "hung Parliament," where one coalition gets a plurality but no clear majority to form a government on its own, thus far the electoral performances of the Congress Party and the BJP have been sufficiently strong to enable them to govern. BJP's clear majority in the 2014 election may well be the beginning of a new trend.

The Congress Party

Following independence, with Nehru at its helm, Congress was the unquestioned ruling party of India. Over the years, especially since the mid-1960s, this hegemony came to be challenged. By the time Indira Gandhi assumed power in 1966, the Congress Party had begun to lose its political sway, and anticolonial nationalism was fading. Soon, many poor, lower-caste citizens became independent from the political guidance of village big men. As a result, numerous regional parties started challenging the Congress Party's monopoly on power.

Indira Gandhi sought to reverse the decline in Congress's electoral popularity by mobilizing the poor, who were India's vast majority. Her promise to end poverty struck a popular chord and propelled Gandhi to the top of India's political pyramid. Her personal success, however, split the party. Indira Gandhi replaced the party's decentralized bottom-up structure with a centralized organization that enabled leaders to control the party, but was a major liability in achieving grassroots support.

Whereas during the 1970s Congress had a left-of-center, pro-poor political platform, beginning in 1984 it became centrist under Rajiv Gandhi (see Section 2). For much of the 1980s and 1990s, the Congress Party tilted right of center, championing economic efficiency, business interests, and limited government spending on health, education, and welfare. However, its victories in the 2004 and 2009 national elections were based on a platform of secularism and limited redistribution. The lack of ideological clarity hurt Congress party in the 2014 election, when it lost decisively.

The Janata Party and Janata Dal

The Janata Party was created in 1977 when several small parties formed an alliance to oppose Indira Gandhi's Emergency. It was not a cohesive political party but a changing coalition of small parties and factions. It had a weak organizational structure, and lacked a distinctive, coherent political platform. To distinguish itself from Congress, it claimed fidelity to Mahatma Gandhi's vision of modern India as decentralized and village-oriented. The Janata Party primarily represented small, rural agriculturalists who generally fall in the middle of the rigid caste hierarchy between Brahmins and untouchables.

Much to everyone's surprise, Janata won the 1977 elections and, with support from other parties, formed the national government. This loose coalition lasted only a little over two years, when conflicting leadership ambitions tore it apart. The Janata Party maintained a small presence in a few Indian states. In 2013 it merged with the BJP. (See below.)

Mandal Commission

A government-appointed commission headed by B. P. Mandal to consider seat reservations and quotas to redress caste discrimination.

The most important successor to the Janata Party was the Janata Dal, which was formed in 1988. Under the leadership of V. P. Singh, the Janata Dal came to power in 1989 in a coalition known as the National Front. VP Singh took the audacious step of supporting a proposal by the **Mandal Commission**, an official government agency, that recommended quotas in government jobs and admissions to universities for what are known as other backward classes, generally, the middle, rural castes. The policy is known as reservation, similar to the policy of reserving seats for women in the *panchayats* described above, and to affirmative action programs in the United States. The **other backward classes**, who became beneficiaries of reservations constitute between 32 and 52 percent of the population. Prime Minister Singh's attempt to garner electoral support backfired when upper castes organized demonstrations, riots, and political violence that contributed to the downfall of Singh's government.

other backward classes

The middle or intermediary castes in India that have been accorded reserved seats in public education and employment since the early 1990s.

The Janata Dal returned to power briefly in 1996, as head of a United Front coalition, with outside support from the Congress. However, the government collapsed when Congress withdrew support for the coalition less than a year later. The Janata Dal has since split into a large number of parties.

The Bharatiya Janata Party (BJP)

The rise of the Bharatiya Janata Party (BJP), which began as the small and marginal Jan Sangh to become one of the two major national parties and ruling party (1999–2004) and again in 2014, is among the most important developments in Indian politics in the past quarter century. The BJP is a right-leaning, Hindu-nationalist party, the first major Indian party to seek support on the basis of religious identity. Unlike Congress and Janata, the BJP is highly centralized and well organized. Its disciplined party members become party cadres only after long apprenticeship.

The BJP differs from Congress and the Janata Party in another respect. It has close ties to a large non-parliamentary organization, the Rashtriya Swayam Sevak Sangh (RSS). The RSS recruits young people (especially educated youth in urban areas) by championing a chauvinistic reinterpretation of India's "great Hindu past." The BJP also has close ties with another RSS affiliated group, a religious organization, the Visva Hindu Parishad (VHP).

Until the late 1980s, the Jana Sangh and the BJP were mainly supported by the urban, lower-middle classes, especially small traders and commercial groups. Since their numbers were relatively small, the BJP was a minor actor on the Indian political scene. The party widened its base of support in the late 1980s by appealing to Hindu nationalism. The BJP found in Indian Muslims a convenient scapegoat for the frustrations of various social groups.

In the 1989 elections, the BJP emerged as the third-largest party after the Congress and Janata parties. In 1991, it gained the second-largest number of seats in parliament. The BJP sought Hindu support by allying with the RSS and VHP to challenge the legitimacy of a Muslim mosque (the babri masjid) located at Ayodhya, in northern India. BJP and VHP leaders claimed that centuries ago, a Muslim ruler had destroyed a Hindu temple at the birth place of the Hindu god Ram to construct the mosque. The BJP, RSS, and VHP organized a nationwide campaign, which culminated in the destruction of the mosque on December 6, 1992. Seventeen hundred people, mostly Muslim, were killed in the aftermath of the campaign.

After the BJP was twice defeated in parliamentary elections following the destruction of the mosque at Ayodhya, it shelved contentious issues that favored the interests of Hindus. Its efforts succeeded when it helped form a coalition, the National Democratic Alliance, which took office briefly (March–April 1999) followed by a full term (October 1999–January 2004). With the formation of the NDA government, the BJP renounced some of its chauvinist positions and distanced itself from the RSS and the VHP at the national level. However, it retained close ties to the anti-minority RSS and VHP: all top-ranking BJP leaders are RSS members.

The BJP, in alliance with the VHP, continued to engage in anti-minority violence in several states. The most important instance was in Gujarat in February–March 2002, when the BJP state government orchestrated a campaign of terror against the Muslim population, which resulted in 2,000 deaths. The BJP capitalized on Hindu electoral support to return to office in Gujarat in 2002 and 2007.

The BJP suffered consecutive defeats in the 2004 and 2009 general elections. Its 2009 defeat revealed its weaknesses in key federal states, where it failed to compensate for the loss of important coalition partners who feared that they would lose minority votes by remaining part of the NDA in the aftermath of the Gujarat violence. Further, the BJP's image of a cohesive and disciplined party was tarnished by conflicts among its leaders.

The 2009 elections also revealed the lack of popular support for Hindutva. The Congress government's rejection of sectarian religious appeals and at least verbal support for improving the situation of minorities has contributed to its repeated electoral victories. This may be a reason why the BJP has downplayed its Hindu-nationalist platform in recent years. The BJP's handsome electoral victory in 2014 was propelled by a promise to renew India's economic growth and promote development. In practice, the BJP ran elections by combining themes of Hindutava, caste politics and promise of good performance. The success of the party was also substantially propelled by support from the business community and business controlled media.

The Communist Party of India (CPM)

India is one of the few democratic countries in the world with a self-proclaimed communist party. Although the CPM is communist in name, it has evolved into a social democratic (or center-left) party that accepts democracy and the limits of a market economy. At the same time, it seeks to obtain greater benefits for the poor. The CPM's political base today is concentrated in two Indian states, West Bengal and Kerala. CPM candidates are often elected to the *Lok Sabha* from these states, and the CPM has frequently run their state governments.

The CPM is a disciplined party, with party cadres and a hierarchical authority structure. Within the national parliament, CPM members often strongly criticize government policies that are likely to hurt the poor. CPM-run state governments in West Bengal and Kerala have provided relatively honest and stable administration. They have sponsored moderate reforms that seek to provide services to shantytown dwellers, channel public investments to rural areas, and ensure the rights of agricultural tenants (for example, by preventing landlords from evicting them).

However, in recent years, the CPM has sought to attract foreign investment through the creation of Special Economic Zones, which offer tax breaks and other subsidies to multinational corporations. The CPM government's acquisition of farmland in one such zone, Nandigram in West Bengal in 2007, provoked widespread protests that the CPM government violently repressed. The CPM's relatively poor showing in the 2009 elections can partly be explained by the crackdown and, more generally, by the CPM's sponsorship of SEZs. In 2011, the CPM lost control of the state governments of both Kerala and West Bengal. The performance of the CPM in 2014 elections was quite dismal.

The Aam Admi Party

The Aam Aadmi Party (translation: *Common Man Party*; abbreviated as AAP) was created by Arvind Kejriwal, a former bureaucrat and political activist who demanded passage of the Right to Information Act and a crackdown on corruption. Kejriwal's anticorruption campaign targeted a number of prominent politicians.

Kejriwal formed the AAP in 2011 after splitting with Anna Hazare, the anticorruption movement's other major leader. Unlike Hazare, Kejriwal believed that the movement needed to contest elections. The AAP's platform for elections in Delhi included creating an agency to investigate charges of corruption against public officials, decentralization, improving the quality of health care and government schools, rehabilitating slum dwellers, and reducing consumers' electricity bills by 50 percent. The AAP party engaged in grassroots organizing to communicate its empathy for popular concerns.

The AAP stunned the political class by placing second in the Delhi elections. The BJP won the largest number of seats. With no party obtaining an overall majority, the AAP formed a minority government with support from the Congress Party and Arvind Kejriwal became Chief Minister of Delhi.

Kejriwal made a splash by shunning the trappings of wealth and power. He refused the services of a Personal Security officer and an official residence. His swearing in ceremony took place at the Ram Lila *maidan*, the site of Anna Hazare's fast. The ministers who attended the ceremony traveled there by metro.

The AAP government quickly implemented some campaign promises. It provided subsidies to reduce electricity bills for low income households and established an antigraft helpline for the citizens to report corrupt officials. However, the Delhi government was soon involved in a scandal related to sex trafficking and drug racketeering. Another problem resulted from the AAP lack of a majority in the Legislative Assembly. When Kejriwal failed to pass the promised bill creating an anticorruption agency, he resigned from the post of Chief Minister 49 days after assuming office. The electoral performance of the AAP party in the 2014 elections was spectacularly poor, suggesting that it may have been a flash in the pan.

The major contenders in the 2014 parliamentary elections were the BJP and Congress dominated coalitions. The BJP selected Narendra Modi as its candidate for prime minister when he was Chief Minister of Gujarat. The BJP's campaign highlighted Modi's personal popularity, particularly among youth and the middle classes, who consider him incorruptible and efficient in delivering economic growth. Meanwhile, Congress delayed announcing its candidate for prime minister perhaps in part because its leadership is filled with uncharismatic septuagenarians who lack Modi's charisma. Rahul Gandhi, the young heir of the Nehru-Gandhi dynasty, is not very popular and naming him candidate for prime minister early would have highlighted the Congress Party's reliance on dynastic politics; eventually Rahul Gandhi was a leader of sorts of the Congress party and fared very poorly.

Corruption, inflation, and slowing economic growth rates were the major issues in the 2014 elections. These factors, along with the Congress Party's unimpressive election campaign, resulted in a landslide victory for the BJP in the recent parliamentary elections. After several decades of coalition governments India now has a majority government in power. The BJP, however, is a controversial and a polarizing force in Indian politics. While its supporters are clearly ecstatic at its performance, many remain apprehensive, both about its anti-Muslim politics and its pro-business policy preferences.

Elections

Elections in India are a colossal event. Nearly 500 million people are eligible to vote, and close to 300 million cast ballots. The turnout rate is far higher than in the United States. Although television plays an important role, campaigning still often involves personal contacts between politicians and voters. Senior politicians fly around the country making speeches at election rallies amid blaring music. Lesser politicians and party supporters travel the dusty streets in tiny villages and district towns. Political messages boom from loudspeakers.

Given India's low literacy rates, pictures of party symbols are critical: a hand for Congress; lotus flower for the BJP; hammer and sickle for the CPM; and broom for the Aam Aadmi Party. Illiterate voters vote by putting a thumb mark on the preferred symbol.

Members of parliament are elected by a single-member district first-past-the-post system. Many candidates compete in each electoral district; the candidate with a plurality wins the seat. This system privileges the major political parties.

A pillar of Indian democracy is the fact that elections are open, competitive, and honest. Much of the credit goes to the independent Election Commission, which has been highly successful in protecting the integrity of the electoral process.

Political Culture, Citizenship, and Identity

Several aspects of Indian political culture are noteworthy. First, the political/public and private spheres are not sharply differentiated. One undesirable result is corruption, since politicians frequently seek personal and family enrichment through public office. A more attractive result is a high level of citizens' political involvement. Second, the Indian elite is extremely factionalized. Personal ambition prevents leaders from pursuing collective goals, such as forming cohesive parties, running stable governments, or giving priority to national development. Unlike many East Asian countries, for example, where consensus is powerful and political negotiations take place behind closed doors, politics in India involves open conflicts.

Third, regions are highly differentiated by language and culture, villages are poorly connected with each other, and communities are stratified by caste. Some observers regard group fragmentation as playing a positive role in promoting political stability. Others believe that it obstructs implementing national reforms to improve the lot of the poor.

India's highly open style of democracy often fuels political conflicts involving identity groups. Ethnic conflicts were minimal when Nehru stressed secular nationalism and Indira Gandhi's poor-versus-rich cleavage were core political issues. In the 1980s and 1990s, however, the decline of the Congress Party and developments in telecommunications and transportation accentuated group differences. As a result, identity-based political conflicts have mushroomed. Two are especially significant, First, caste conflicts, that were formerly local and regional, have become national in character. V. P. Singh initiated this process when he introduced reservations for other backward classes. This gave rise to political parties that sought to advance the interests of lower caste groups and to increasing caste-based contestation.

Second, identity-based conflicts pit Hindus against Muslims. For most of the post-independence period, Hindu-Muslim conflicts were triggered by tensions on the local level. However, in the mid-1980s and 1990s, the BJP provoked anti-Muslim emotions in an effort to attract Hindu support. Although anti-Muslim violence has not occurred on a national scale, it has occurred in many regions.

Interest Groups, Social Movements, and Protest

India has a vibrant tradition of political activism that has both enriched and complicated the workings of democracy. Social movements, non-governmental organizations (NGOs), and trade unions have pressured the state to address the interests of underprivileged groups and check authoritarian tendencies. Recent welfare and civil rights legislation, including the Right to Information, Rural Employment Guarantee Act, Forest Act, and Land Acquisition and Rehabilitations Act, were passed in response to the demands of civil society activists.

Labor has played a significant role. Unions frequently engage in strikes, demonstrations, and a technique called *gherao*, when workers hold executives of a firm hostage to press their demands. Labor unions are politically fragmented, particularly at the national level. Instead of the familiar model of one union/one factory, unions allied to different political parties often organize within a single factory. Rival labor organizations compete for workers' support at higher levels as well. The government generally stays out of labor–management conflicts.

Social movements date back to the mid-1970s. Prime Minister Indira Gandhi distrusted voluntary organizations and movements, and sought to restrict their activities. During the national Emergency (1975–1977), the government imprisoned members of the opposition. However, activists reacted by forming political parties and social movements. Socialist leader Jai Prakash Narain organized the most influential movement opposing Emergency rule. It helped bring about the downfall of Congress and the election of the Janata Party. A decade later, V. P. Singh resigned from Congress and formed the *Jan Morcha* (Peoples' Front), a movement that brought new groups into politics and helped elect the National Front in 1989.

There was a significant growth in the number of NGOs after the 1980s. Over the years, the government's financial support for NGOs has steadily increased.

The large number and extensive activities of social movements make India quite distinctive among developing countries. The most significant social movements include the women's movement, the environment movement, the farmers' movement, the *dalit* movement, and the anticorruption movement. The term *dalit* means oppressed. It is widely used today in preference to the terms "scheduled castes" or "untouchables."

dalit

The *dalit* movement is organized by untouchables or scheduled caste against caste discrimination and oppression.

The roots of the *dalit* movement lie in a reform movement among Hindus that began in 1875. The modern *dalit* movement was inspired by Dr. Bhimrao Ramji Ambedkar, the *dalit* author of the Indian constitution, who formed the Republican Party in the late 1960s. When the party disintegrated, it was succeeded by the Dalit Panthers, a movement that demanded that *dalits* be treated with dignity and provided with better educational opportunities. Today, the *dalit* movement seeks a greater share of electoral power and public office. Among its most notable successes is the Bahujan Samaj Party (BSP), created in 1989 with the goal of increasing *dalits'* political representation. The BSP grew rapidly in the 1990s by championing *dalit* empowerment while appealing to a broad cross-caste base of support. The BSP succeeded in forming coalition governments with other political parties in Uttar Pradesh (UP), India's most populous state. It held office (2007–2012) independently, with its powerful female leader, Mayavati (known by one name only), as UP's chief minister.

The 1980s witnessed the formation of many autonomous urban women's organizations in major cities. They engaged in campaigns against female feticide (facilitated by the use of amniocentesis), media misrepresentation of women, harmful contraception dissemination, coercive population policies, rape in police custody, dowry murders and *sati* (the immolation of widows on their husbands' funeral pyres).

sati

Sati, or widow immolation, was outlawed by the British in the nineteenth century. *Satis* have occurred, although they are uncommon, in post-Independence India.

After a lull in activism around sexual violence, 2012 witnessed massive protests by young men and women in response to the horrific gang rape and subsequent death of Jyoti Singh, a 23-year-old student in Delhi. People demonstrated in Delhi and elsewhere in the days that followed, outraged at the brutality against Jyoti Singh, her poor medical treatment, and the faulty investigation of the crime. The protest reflected the same frustration with the state that fuelled the anticorruption movement. The scale and duration of protest against rape demonstrated that activists were determined to prevent sexual violence from being ignored.

The government's response demonstrated the ability of progressive activists to hold it accountable. It appointed a judicial committee to submit a report and recommend amendments to criminal law concerning sexual assault. The committee's report proposed substantial changes in rape laws. The government created fast-track courts for prosecuting rape and Parliament passed the Criminal Law (Amendment) Act in 2013 to stiffen penalties for sexual offences. Critics charged that the law failed to criminalize marital rape and prosecute military personnel accused of sexual offences under criminal law.

Four important developments have influenced the character and trajectory of social movements in recent years. First, many social movements have developed close relationships to the state and to electoral politics. In the past, social movements tended to be community-based and issue-specific. Once a movement achieved some success, for example, limiting deforestation, stopping the construction of a dam, or obtaining higher agricultural subsidies, it would dissolve. Although many social movements remain limited in focus, duration, and geographic reach, some have sought to overcome these difficulties by engaging in electoral politics. The *dalit* movement, Hindu nationalist, and anticorruption movement are important examples. Other movements have sought to work with the state. The women's movement, for example, has worked closely with the bureaucracy and the courts.

Second, the growth of the religious right has confronted left-wing social movements with a serious challenge. Although the religious right and the secular left disagree on most issues, they have adopted the same stance on some questions, like opposing economic liberalization and globalization. This poses the dilemma of whether groups fundamentally opposed on some issues should form tactical alliances around other issues.

Third, as the state has abandoned its socialist commitments, social movements and political parties have also ceased to focus on poverty and class inequality. The most important exception is the Naxalites. Although they have strong support among some of India's poorest communities, their use of violence has repelled many social activists.

Fourth, many NGOs and social movements have developed extensive transnational connections. The consequences have been double-edged. On the positive side, funding from foreign sources has been vital to the survival of NGOs and social movements. However, NGOs that receive foreign funding are often viewed with suspicion. Moreover, foreign funding has created a division between activists with and without access to foreign donors.

Crowds gathered to protest the construction of the Sardar Sarovar Dam.

AP Images/Sebastian John

The Political Impact of Technology

The growth of technologies of communication has had important implications for politicians, political parties, and relations between citizens and the state. The cell phone and Internet have revolutionized communications in India. Although only 28 million of 1.2 billion Indians have access to landline telephones, 880 million people have cell phones. India has over 200 million Internet users, the third largest user base after China and the United States. Urban youth are the primary users of cell phones and the Internet, although a sizable 40 percent of cell phone users live in rural areas.

Political parties and social movements have used the Internet to galvanize support, politicize issues, and raise funds within India and among diasporic groups. The BJP's Narendra Modi is an ardent proponent of social media and has extensively employed Twitter and Facebook in his election campaign. The Aam Aadmi Party raised over $3 million through the Internet in its first few months of existence. Social movements protesting rape and corruption have used social media to organize protests and disseminate information.

Technological innovations have also influenced India's military weaponry and strategy. It has invested in Unmanned Ariel Vehicles (UAVs) and is planning to bolster its cyber security credentials. Some military analysts have been critical of India's lack of preparedness in combating cyber terrorism, as Indian government websites have been the target of several cyber attacks, probably from China.

Both citizens and the state have employed technology to monitor each other. Citizens have used the Internet to expose government corruption, seek greater transparency and achieve better access to government services. The Indian government plans to provide electronic IDs to every Indian citizen, which should improve service delivery but might also enable the government to increase surveillance. India began an ambitious cyber surveillance program in 2009. Aside from accessing cell phone records and intercepting phone calls, the program allows the government to access Internet data. In 2012, Research in Motion, the company manufacturing Blackberries, provided the Indian government with encryption keys that allowed it to retrieve emails and messages on its phones.

Where Do You Stand?

Since democracy is about preventing the abuse of power, fragmentation of power in India is a good thing. Discuss.

Based on what you have learned about Indian politics and the BJP, do you think the election of Narendra Modi is a good, new direction for India?

INDIAN POLITICS IN TRANSITION

SECTION 5

Political Challenges and Changing Agendas

India has come a long way in the more than six decades since independence. On the positive side of the ledger, Indians can justly be proud of the fact that this large, poor, and incredibly diverse country has survived intact. The fact that India has been fairly well governed during this period represents another achievement. The disturbing record of failed states in far smaller countries provides a reason to celebrate the fact

▼ Focus Questions

• Identify two major challenges confronting India. How well equipped are Indian political institutions to meet these challenges?

• In what ways does India provide a useful model of economic and political development for other countries?

that the Indian state is reasonably effective. A further achievement is that India has been a well-functioning democracy for virtually its entire existence and has generally upheld the rule of law and protected civil rights, notably those of minorities. Finally, despite unevenness, India is leapfrogging into the twenty-first century. By scoring sustained and rapid economic growth for the last three decades, India has become a leader of the world's emerging economies.

However, these are the impressive features of the proverbially half-filled glass. We conclude the chapter by highlighting some pressing challenges that India must surmount to fulfill its rich and promising potential.

The Challenge of Ethnic Diversity

The future of Indian democracy is closely bound up with how the country confronts the growing politicization of ethnic identities, that is, the attempt by organized ethnic groups to obtain state power and state-controlled economic resources. Caste, language, and religion are the basis for political mobilization. Democracy can encourage political parties and leaders to manipulate group identities for electoral purposes.

Political struggles in India are simultaneously struggles for identity, power, and wealth. Identity politics is characterized by two distinct trends: the tendency for a variety of diverse non–class-based regional and ethnic groups to make demands on parties and governments; and pressure on political parties to broaden their electoral appeals to the middle and lower strata of Indian society. If India's growth dividend is sufficiently large, it may be possible to satisfy both sets of demands. However, this requires an unusually favorable set of circumstances, including continued economic growth, skillful political leadership, and a commitment to distributing economic gains broadly enough to satisfy all significant groups.

Political Violence

In recent years, India has experienced the growth of two forms of violence in addition to Hindu nationalist violence described earlier. The first is fueled by the poor and dispossessed, who have participated in the Naxalite-led insurgency in thirteen out of India's twenty-eight states. Prime Minister Singh has characterized the "Maoist rebels" as India's major "law and order problem." The Naxalite-led insurgency has produced 5,000 deaths since 2009.

Second, India has become a prime site of terrorist violence in recent years. In the 1990s, most attacks were linked to regional conflicts in the Punjab, Kashmir, and the Northeast. While violent attacks continue in Kashmir, they have extended to other parts of the country. The sources of terrorist attacks have also become more varied. Organizations with links to the RSS have planned several of them, although they have been made to appear the work of Muslim militants. Pakistan's ISI and other transnational Islamic networks have been responsible for many others.

India-Pakistan Tensions

From the moment that India and Pakistan became separate states, their relations have varied from tense to violent, including three wars, simmering tensions over Kashmir, and periodic violence between their armed forces. Indo-Pakistani conflict is a major reason for the two countries' high military expenditures.

The attack on the Indian parliament in 2001 sent tensions between the two countries to the boiling point. India charged that the attacks were orchestrated by the Pakistani government and assembled over 1 million troops at the Pakistani border. The threat of nuclear war was a distinct possibility. Intense intervention by the United States helped defuse the situation, and the two countries withdrew most of their troops from the border.

Relations since then have ebbed and flowed. They improved in 2005, when the Indian and Pakistani governments initiated bus service across the cease-fire line for the first time in fifty years. However, the attack on the Taj in Mumbai in 2008 once again escalated tensions. A high point in their relations occurred during the Asian semifinals of the Cricket World Cup tournament in 2011, which pitted India against Pakistan and was played in India. Prime Minister Singh took the unprecedented step of inviting the Pakistani prime minister Asaf Ali Zardari to India as his guest and Zardari accepted the invitation. This was followed by additional meetings in 2011–2012, when both countries agreed that they would extend for five years an agreement to reduce the risk of accidents involving nuclear weapons. They also supported measures to enhance cross-border trade and travel across the Line of Control in Jammu and Kashmir. Still, India remains suspicious that Pakistan is harboring terrorist organizations and remains dissatisfied with its refusal to prosecute the perpetrators of the 2008 Mumbai attacks.

Manmohan Singh has been responsible for constructive diplomatic overtures to Pakistan. It is not clear whether Narendra Modi will do the same. Inviting the head of the state of Pakistan to his inauguration may be a good beginning, though it is too early to tell. A key issue is whether India can prevent conflict with Pakistan from spiraling into nuclear war. The fact that both countries possess nuclear weapons makes the stakes incredibly high. Moreover, India has tense relations with not one but two nuclear-armed neighbors. Conflict with China, its powerful neighbor to the North and East, is never far from the surface.

Nuclear Weapons

Soon after the BJP was first elected to power in May 1998, it fulfilled an electoral promise by gate-crashing the nuclear club. Although it cited threats from China and Pakistan as the key reason to develop nuclear weapons, the BJP's decision can also be traced to electoral considerations. The Hindu bomb, as the BJP described it, was an excellent way to mobilize Indians' national pride and thereby deflect attention from domestic, economic, and political problems.

After India detonated a nuclear bomb, Pakistan responded in kind, triggering fears of a nuclear arms race in South Asia. Worldwide condemnation and sanctions on both India and Pakistan swiftly followed. The Manmohan Singh government took a dramatic step toward defusing tensions over the nuclear issue in 2004 when it proclaimed India's commitment to preventing the proliferation of weapons of mass destruction. As a result of this commitment, the United States and India signed an agreement in 2005 that authorized India to secure international help for its civilian nuclear reactors while retaining its nuclear arms. The agreement was followed by the removal of a U.S. ban on selling nuclear technology to India. The Indo-U.S. nuclear treaty provides for cooperation on nuclear issues despite India's continuing violation of nonproliferation norms. (For example, India has refused to sign the Comprehensive Test Ban Treaty and the Nuclear Nonproliferation Treaty.) In a major policy shift in 2012, the United States dropped its demand that India sign an agreement authorizing the United States to inspect the weapons it has sold to India.

Kashmir in a World of States

The roots of the conflict over Kashmir go back to the origins of India and Pakistan. In 1947, the Maharaja of Kashmir agreed to annex the territory to India. India agreed to hold a plebiscite to determine whether Kashmiris in Indian-controlled Kashmir wanted to remain part of the Indian nation. The status of Kashmir—whether it should be part of India, part of Pakistan, or an independent state—was unresolved in 1947 and remains unresolved today. Tensions have often been attributed to the ethnic and religious diversity of the state's population, which is roughly 65 percent Muslim and 35 percent Hindus and other minorities. Most of the non-Muslim minorities—Hindus, Sikhs, and Buddhists, concentrated in the areas of the state called Jammu and Ladakh—prefer living under Indian sovereignty. A large proportion of Muslims feel otherwise. However, the political sources of tensions are far more significant than religious and ethnic differences.

One reason for the persistence of tensions involving Kashmir have to do with the different interests and perspectives of the three major regional powers. Mutual distrust between India and Pakistan, growing tensions between India and China, and a strategic partnership between Pakistan and China have made a peaceful resolution on Kashmir all but impossible. China occupies part of a disputed area of Kashmir. Pakistan has escalated hostilities by violating a UN-sponsored ceasefire, refusing to withdraw its troops and supporting militants who have engaged in terrorist attacks against moderate Kashmiris. India has aggravated the situation by refusing to hold a plebiscite (until Pakistan withdraws its troops) and by preventing other powers from helping resolve the dispute. The Indian Army routinely employs repression to curb political dissent in Kashmir. In past years the Indian government installed unrepresentative and unpopular governments in Kashmir that were favorable to India. On the positive side, elections in Kashmir in recent years have become more open and inclusive and the Indian government has increased investments in Kashmir for economic development and job creation.

India's Regional Relations

India's relations with regional powers have been inconsistent historically. Relations with China have been especially tumultuous. Although the two countries fought only one war, in 1962, recurrent border disputes reflect their competition for regional and international influence. Since 2005, Indo-Chinese relations have been more cooperative around economic than around territorial matters. New Delhi and Beijing signed a series of political and economic agreements, signaling a move toward greater cooperation. Today China is India's major trading partner. Bilateral trade was $75 billion in 2012, and should exceed $100 billion by 2015.

By contrast, Indo-Chinese relations have been strained over territorial issues. China continues to claim sizable portions of territory in Kashmir that India considers its own. China has made border incursions into the volatile northeastern state of Arunachal Pradesh. India has opposed Beijing's growing investments in Pakistan-occupied Kashmir and in the neighboring Gilgit-Baltistan area. Tensions between the two countries increased in 2011 when China discovered an Indian naval vessel in the South China Sea, which it claims is under its jurisdiction and India considers international waters. That same year, China opposed an agreement between an Indian company and the Vietnamese government to prospect for oil in Vietnam's offshore waters. However, balanced against these tensions are certain shared interests vis-à-vis the West on global trade, climate change, and other issues. In 2012 President Hu Jintao declared the "Year of India-China Friendship and Cooperation" and Chinese Defense Minister General Liang Guanglie visited India to strengthen strategic cooperation between the two countries.

Although India and Nepal established strong economic and political ties through the 1950 Indo-Nepal Treaty of Peace and Friendship, relations between the two countries have sometimes been fraught. Tensions between the two countries escalated after Nepal became an absolutist monarchy in 2005. Relations have improved since the king was deposed and democracy reestablished in Nepal in 2008.

India's relations with Sri Lanka and Bangladesh have been deeply influenced by their shared ethnic compositions. India is home to 55 million Tamils, who live in the southern state of Tamil Nadu. The Liberation Tigers of Tamil Eeelam (LTTE), which waged a secessionist movement in Sri Lanka resulting in a prolonged civil war, acquired significant support from Indian Tamils. India sent troops to Sri Lanka to disarm the LTTE in 1987 but actually enflamed the conflict. India withdrew its troops in 1990. Since the end of the civil war in Sri Lanka, the two countries have strengthened trade relations through the Indo-Sri Lanka Free Trade Agreement. They have also strengthened security ties. In 2013, India, Sri Lanka, and the Maldives signed a trilateral security pact to combat piracy and terrorism in the Indian Ocean. However, the end of the civil war has also witnessed disputes between India and Sri Lanka over water rights. Despite negotiations, both navies continue firing on fishing boats that cross the International Maritime Boundary Line (IMBL) and imprisoning their crews.

The creation of Bangladesh as a predominantly Bengali nation that seceded from Pakistan in 1971 was in good measure a result of India's intervention. India's Bengali population strongly identified with Bangladesh's claims to nationhood, and India's military helped engineer Bangladesh's breakaway from Pakistan. However, Bangladesh has expressed resentment at trade imbalances, India's control over water resources, and Indian army incursions into its territory. Since 2010, the two countries have taken steps toward improving trade relations and resolving border disputes.

Economic Performance

India's economic experience is neither a clear success nor clear failure. India has maintained strong and steady economic growth rate for decades. As a result, from being held up as an example of economic failure, India has recently emerged as a leader of developing countries. Several factors are responsible. The first involves the relationship between political governance and economic growth. India has been fortunate to have enjoyed relatively good government: its democratic system is mostly open and stable, most political leaders are public spirited, and top bureaucrats are well trained and competent.

The second factor concerns India's strategy for economic development. In the 1950s, India chose to insulate its economy from global forces, limiting trade and foreign investment and emphasizing the government's role in promoting self-sufficiency in heavy industry and agriculture. The positive result was that India grew enough food to feed its large and growing population and produced a vast range of industrial goods. This strategy, however, was not without costs. India sacrificed the additional economic growth that might have come from competing effectively in global markets. Moreover, during this period it made little effort to alleviate its staggering poverty: land redistribution failed, job creation by heavy industries was minimal, and investment in the education and health of the poor was limited. In addition to the terrible human and social costs of this neglect, the poor became a drag on economic growth because they were unable to buy goods and stimulate demand for increased production; an uneducated and unhealthy labor force is not a productive labor force.

Yet the sluggish phase is now long past, and the Indian economy has grown briskly over the last three decades. However, India's numerous poor are not benefiting sufficiently from growth. Cuts in public spending on education and health services have been especially hard on the poor. The government has not succeeded in distributing the gains of growth to reduce poverty and inequality.

International Power and Domestic Prosperity

India's attempts to become a strong regional and international power are shaped and constrained by the international environment. The increasing interdependence of the global economies was illustrated by the 2008 economic crisis. India's growth rate declined as did the demand for its exports and foreign investments, and the fiscal deficit rose to nearly 7 percent of GDP. However, the Indian economy quickly regained strength, and soon began to surge ahead again.

Institutional Decay

Institutional decay is at the root of many of India's other challenges. Competent, honest, and responsive institutions are required to deal with the far-ranging problems identified above, including Indo-Pakistan relations, ethnic diversity, and economic performance. Yet such institutions are in short supply. Disturbing evidence periodically surfaces of corruption that tarnishes key sectors of the state, such as the police, civil service, and political parties. Official corruption is not limited to accepting bribes in exchange for favors. For example, in 2010, it became evident that cabinet ministers and their associates had received kickbacks from India's purchase of weaponry and the sale of telecommunication rights. India's telecom minister was accused of selling licenses to use Indian airwaves to cell phone operators at extremely low prices, costing the Indian government $40 billion in lost revenues. The incident led to further investigations, which revealed corruption at the highest levels of the central government. Although there was no evidence that Prime Minister Singh was directly involved, his refusal for months to launch an official investigation undermined his authority. Without a thorough housecleaning to eliminate institutional decay, India will make little progress in dealing with its many other pressing challenges.

In brief, India has an enviable array of resources and a daunting host of challenges. How well it will use its resources to confront these challenges is an open question. Will it be able to capitalize on its positive achievements, such as the long-standing democratic ethos framed by functioning institutions, a vibrant media and civil society, and a growing and ambitious middle class? Or will it be crippled by ethnic hostility resulting in inaction at best and disintegration of the country at worst?

The alleviation of poverty and class inequality remains a pressing challenge. So too does the Naxalite insurgency. The state's repressive response to Naxalism has only contributed to its growth. Tensions with Pakistan and instability in Kashmir continue to simmer. Understanding how India meets—or fails to meet—these challenges will be of enormous interest to students of comparative politics in the years to come. How India reconciles its national ambitions, domestic demands for greater economic redistribution, and global pressures for an efficient economy will affect its influence on regional and global trends.

Youth Politics and the Generational Divide

India is one of the youngest countries in the world; over half of all Indians are under the age of 25. Economists believe that when this group joins the workforce, it will contribute to significant economic growth. However, this potential requires a major investment in education and the creation of jobs. The government reported that in 2013 the unemployment rate for the population as a whole was 4.7 percent whereas for the age group 15–29 it was 13.3 percent.

Youth play an important role in Indian politics. Young people have been active in struggles against corruption and antiquated rape laws. They are also deeply concerned about inflation and unemployment. Young people significantly influence elections. According to the 2011 census, 149 million of the 725-million electorate of India in the 2014 election were first-time voters.

There are significant differences in the employment opportunities and life styles of urban and rural youth. The unemployment rate for high school graduates among 15- to 29-year-olds is 36.6 percent in the rural areas and 26.5 percent in the urban areas.

Inadequate rural employment opportunities have resulted in large-scale youth migration from villages to cities. Youth migrants represent three-quarters of the total internal migrants in India, up from two-thirds two decades ago. Young migrants add pressure to the already weak infrastructure in urban areas. If they lack documents that establish their identity and residency rights, they are not eligible for social benefits and often live in squalor.

By contrast, urban middle-class youth represent the face of globalizing India and often incur the resentment of the lower middle classes. Class tensions have generated social tensions that Hindu nationalists have magnified. Some militant Hindu nationalists have sought to impose dress codes on female college students, assaulted "loose pub-going women," and attacked couples who celebrate Valentine's day.

Indian Politics in Comparative Perspective

India provides an incredibly interesting and important laboratory for studying issues in comparative politics. Consider the issue of democratic consolidation. Although democracy was introduced to India by its elites, it has established firm roots within society. A clear example is when Indira Gandhi declared Emergency rule (1975–1977) and curtailed democratic freedoms. In the next election, in 1977, Indian citizens decisively voted Gandhi out of power, registering their preference for democratic rule. Most Indians value democracy and advance their claims within democratic institutions, even when those institutions are flawed.

Comparativists debate whether democracy or authoritarianism is better for economic growth. In the past, democratic India's economic performance did not compare well with the success stories of authoritarian regimes in East Asia and China. However, India's impressive economic growth in recent years suggests that the returns are not yet in. India provides a fine laboratory for studying the relationship of democratic institutions and economic performance.

Another issue within Indian politics with important comparative implications involves the relationship between democratic institutions and multiethnic societies. By studying India's history, particularly the post-1947 period, comparativists can explore how cleavages of caste, religion, and language have been contained and their destructive consequences minimized. Yet the repeated instances of ethnic violence in India suggest the need for caution. Comparativists have also puzzled over the conditions under which multiple and contradictory interests within a democratic framework can generate positive economic and distributional outcomes. Here, the variable performance of different regions in India can serve as a laboratory. For instance, what can be learned from studying two communist-ruled states, Kerala and West Bengal, which sponsored land redistribution policies and extensive social welfare programs? Many scholars have praised the Kerala model because it abolished tenancy and landlord exploitation, provided effective public food distribution of subsidized rice to low-income households, enacted protective laws for agricultural workers and pensions for retired agricultural laborers, and provided extensive government employment for low-caste communities.

Another question engaging comparativists is whether success in providing education and welfare produces success in the economic sphere. Again, the case of Kerala provides pointers for further research. Kerala scores high on human development indicators such as literacy and health, and its economy has also grown in recent years. At the same time, Kerala remains one of the poorest states in India.

It is not yet clear whether India will be able to build upon and extend its achievements or will fail to cope with many severe challenges in coming years. Political scientists will doubtless find much to learn from studying India's future development. The results will be of vital importance to over 1 billion Indian citizens. And, given India's immense size and strategic importance, developments in Indian politics will affect the fate of people throughout the world.

Where Do You Stand?

Religious groups in India should not have separate laws governing such issues as marriage or inheritance. All these issues should be covered under a single law applicable to all Indians. Discuss.

India's lowest castes have gained in dignity and, even though poor, now feel more included in the Indian political system. Discuss.

Chapter Summary

Democracy in India has endured for more than six decades, nearly as long as it has in Germany or Japan. Given the record of democratic failures in the developing world, this is one of India's major achievements. Related to this is another political achievement: the creation of a multiethnic, federal polity. Once again, countries such as the old Soviet Union and Yugoslavia were unable to hold together their diverse ethnic groups. India's success on this front is thus noteworthy. And finally, on the positive side of the ledger, one also needs to add that India's economy has grown at a reasonably impressive rate since 1980. An ethnically plural democracy that can sustain economic growth is a country that is worth studying and understanding.

Against these positive achievements, however, are fairly impressive failures that have also been discussed above. The most glaring of these is the failure to improve the living conditions of those who live at the bottom of the society. While India has experienced considerable economic growth, the fruits of this growth have been shared disproportionately. Not only then does India house a very large percentage of poor people, but nearly half the children in that country are undernourished and literacy is widespread. Recent incidences of rape also underline the precarious position of women in Indian society. And finally, Indian cities are highly polluted and lack of planning and organization make them less-than-livable environments.

While India's democracy is vibrant, the quality of governance offered by Indian democracy is often poor. This is at the root of numerous shortcomings in India's development record. The government in India reacts to short-term electoral incentives and often fails to take actions on pressing problems of long run significance. The quality of bureaucracy in India also declines sharply toward the bottom. As a result, even good intentions and policies do not get implemented. Narendra Modi won the 2014 election promising to overcome such obstacles and to put India on a rapid growth trajectory. Whether Modi will facilitate inclusive development or introduce new problems by excluding minorities and the poor from frutits of development will only become clear over the next decade.

Key Terms

Brahmin
caste system
dalits
economic liberalization
Emergency (1975–1977)
green revolution
Indian Administrative Service
 (IAS)

Indian Rebellion
Lok Sabha
Mandal Commission
Naxalite
nonaligned bloc
other backward classes
panchayats
patronage system

Rajya Sabha
reservations
sati
scheduled castes
Sikh
state-led economic development
untouchables
zamindars

Suggested Readings

Basu, Amrita. *Violent Conjunctures in Democratic India: The Case of Hindu Nationalism* (forthcoming, Cambridge University Press).

Basu, Amrita, and Srirupa Roy, eds. *Violence and Democracy in India*. Calcutta: Seagull Books, 2006.

Chandra, Kanchan. *Why Ethnic Parties Succeed: Patronage and Ethnic Head Counts in India*. Cambridge: Cambridge University Press, 2007.

Chatterjee, Partha. *Lineages of Political Society: Studies in Postcolonial Democracy*. New York: Columbia University Press, 2011.

Frankel, Francine. *India's Political Economy, 1947–2004: The Gradual Revolution*. New Delhi: Oxford University Press, 2005.

Guha, Ramachandran. *India after Gandhi: The World's Largest Democracy*. New York: Harper Perennial, 2008.

Hasan, Zoya. *Politics of Inclusion: Caste, Minority and Representation in India*. Delhi: Oxford University Press, 2009.

Jayal, Niraja Gopal. *Citizenship and its Discontents: An Indian History*. Cambridge, MA: Harvard University Press, 2013

Jayal, Niraja Gopal, and Pratap Mehta, eds. *The Oxford Companion to Politics in India*. New Delhi: Oxford University Press, 2010.

Kohli, Atul. *Poverty Amid Plenty in the New India*. Cambridge: Cambridge University Press, 2012.

Panagariya, Arvind. *India: The Emerging Giant*. New York: Oxford University Press, 2008.

Sen, Amartya. *The Argumentative Indian*. London: Allen Lane, 2005.

Varshney, Ashutosh. *Ethnic Conflict and Civic Life: Hindus and Muslims in India*. New Haven: Yale University Press, 2002

Suggested Websites

Indian National Congress
http://www.inc.in/

Bharatiya Janata Party (BJP)
www.bjp.org

Aam Aadmi Party (AAP)
http://www.aamaadmiparty.org/

Times of India
http://timesofindia.indiatimes.com/
 international-home

Economic and Political Weekly, a good source of information on Indian politics
www.epw.in/

Frontline, a magazine with coverage of Indian politics
http://www.frontline.in/

The Hindu, an English daily paper in India
http://www.thehindu.com/

Hindustan Times
www.hindustantimes.com

Directory of Indian government websites
goidirectory.nic.in

Sabrang Communications, providing coverage of human rights issues in India
www.sabrang.com

8 The United States

Louis DeSipio

Official Name: United States of America

Location: North America, between Canada and Mexico

Capital City: Washington, D.C.

Population (2014): 318.9 million

Size: 9,826,630 sq. km.; about half the size of South America; slightly larger than China

THE MAKING OF THE MODERN AMERICAN STATE

Barack Obama's election in 2008 saw the largest presidential victory margin in recent elections (a margin not repeated in 2012). His 2008 victory was accompanied by increases in the size of the Democratic majorities in the U.S. House and Senate. Having one party in control of both houses of Congress and the presidency was unusual in contemporary politics. The sizes of Democratic majorities in the House and Senate were also substantial. Obama used these majorities to pass a series of major bills including two economic stimulus bills, the Affordable Care Act (ACA) (discussed later), civil rights legislation focusing on workplace discrimination, and reform of the financial services industry. The Senate also confirmed two members of the U.S. Supreme Court nominated by President Obama.

The 2010 and 2012 elections changed the balance of political power in Washington and reduced the likelihood that the Obama administration would be able to continue to promote its agenda. Democratic losses in 2010 in the U.S. House gave control of that body to the Republicans. Democrats maintained a slight majority in the U.S. Senate, but not a sufficient majority to overcome Republican filibusters (a parliamentary procedure to slow debate) on major issues. The divided government of the period after 2010 is more the norm in contemporary U.S. politics and limits the ability of the United States to execute its responsibilities among the globalized world of states or to its own citizens.

Focus Questions ▽

- Based on your reading of the issues that led to the previous critical outcomes and their resolutions, what do you think will be the trigger of the next critical juncture and its outcome?

- How does geographic setting shape the governing structures that have emerged in the United States over the past 225 years?

Politics in Action

In 2013, the U.S. federal government shut down for sixteen days and ceased most of its routine activities. This shutdown resulted from the failure of the U.S. Congress to fulfill its constitutional responsibility and pass an appropriations bill to fund the federal government for the president's review. This failure resulted from a deep-seated disagreement between the Republican-controlled U.S. House of Representatives and the Democrat-controlled U.S. Senate. In the past, most disagreements like this were resolved with short-term appropriations bills that allowed the government to continue to operate while Congress worked out its differences. In 2013, however, some Republican leaders—including members of the Tea Party caucus (discussed later)—felt that it was better to pass no bill and shut down the government than to compromise with Democrats and the president.

Such behavior made little sense to many in the United States. The president's approval ratings improved throughout the shutdown. It made even less sense to U.S. allies and other nations who look to the United States for global military and economic leadership. During the shutdown, U.S. embassies and consulates had to partially close and U.S. economic support for other countries stopped.

After sixteen days, cooler heads prevailed and Congress passed an appropriations bill. Although there were certainly some short-term economic costs to the country and the global economy from the congressional bickering, the long-term consequence is probably greater. The United States showed how the design of U.S. national government is structured to impede policy-making, particularly in political eras like the present in which the division between the two parties is narrow. With the shutdown,

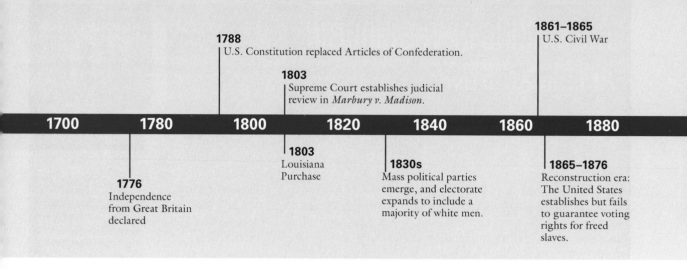

CHRONOLOGY of U.S. Political Development

1788
U.S. Constitution replaced Articles of Confederation.

1803
Supreme Court establishes judicial review in *Marbury v. Madison.*

1861–1865
U.S. Civil War

| 1700 | 1780 | 1800 | 1820 | 1840 | 1860 | 1880 |

1776
Independence from Great Britain declared

1803
Louisiana Purchase

1830s
Mass political parties emerge, and electorate expands to include a majority of white men.

1865–1876
Reconstruction era: The United States establishes but fails to guarantee voting rights for freed slaves.

the United States sent a signal to its own citizens and the world that it cannot always be relied upon to fulfill its role as a global leader. A longer shutdown would undoubtedly have had a more profoundly negative effect on the global economy and the authority with which the United States can speak on international affairs.

For many in the United States, the effect was somewhat more muted because of another feature in the constitutional design—**federalism**. The primary contact between most U.S. residents and government is with their state and local governments. Federalism is a system of governance with twin sovereigns—the federal government and state governments in the case of the United States. A short-term shutdown of the federal government does not lead to any change in the activities of state governments. A longer-term shutdown would likely impede state government functioning as in implementing many federal programs and expecting the federal government to pay for these programs, something it could not do if shutdown.

federalism

A system of governance in which political authority is shared between the national government and regional or state governments. The powers of each level of government are usually specified in a federal constitution.

Geographic Setting

The United States occupy nearly half of North America. Its only two neighbors, Mexico and Canada, do not present a military threat and are linked in a comprehensive trade agreement: the North American Free Trade Agreement (NAFTA). U.S. territory is rich in natural resources, arable land, navigable rivers, and protected ports. This abundance has led Americans to assume they will always have enough resources to meet national needs. Finally, the United States has always had low population densities and has served as a magnet for international migration.

European colonization led to the eventual unification of the territory that became the United States under one government and the expansion of that territory from the Atlantic to the Pacific Oceans. This process began in the early 1500s and reached its peak in the nineteenth century, when rapid population expansion was reinforced by an imperialist national ideology (**manifest destiny**) to expand all the way to the Pacific. Native Americans were pushed aside. The United States experimented with colonialism around 1900, annexing Hawaii, Guam, the Northern Marianas Islands, and Puerto Rico.

Puerto Rico is a colony of the United States with limited autonomy in trade and foreign policy. Puerto Ricans are U.S. citizens by birth and can travel freely to the

manifest destiny

The public philosophy in the nineteenth century that the United States was not only entitled but also destined to occupy territory from the Atlantic to the Pacific.

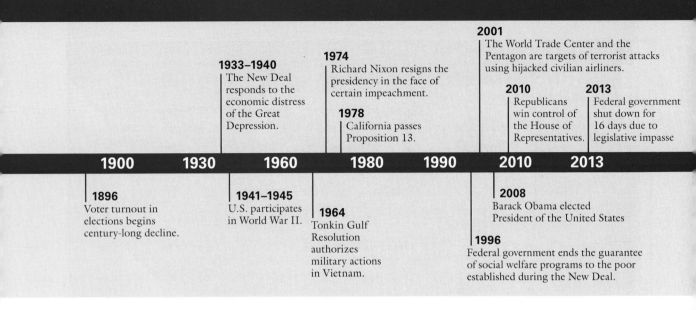

1933–1940
The New Deal responds to the economic distress of the Great Depression.

1974
Richard Nixon resigns the presidency in the face of certain impeachment.

1978
California passes Proposition 13.

2001
The World Trade Center and the Pentagon are targets of terrorist attacks using hijacked civilian airliners.

2010
Republicans win control of the House of Representatives.

2013
Federal government shut down for 16 days due to legislative impasse

1900   1930   1960   1980   1990   2010   2013

1896
Voter turnout in elections begins century-long decline.

1941–1945
U.S. participates in World War II.

1964
Tonkin Gulf Resolution authorizes military actions in Vietnam.

2008
Barack Obama elected President of the United States

1996
Federal government ends the guarantee of social welfare programs to the poor established during the New Deal.

United States. Although some in Puerto Rico seek independence, most want either a continuation of Commonwealth status or statehood. Guam is an "unincorporated territory" (a U.S. territory that is not on the road to statehood and does not have all of the protections of the U.S. Constitution).

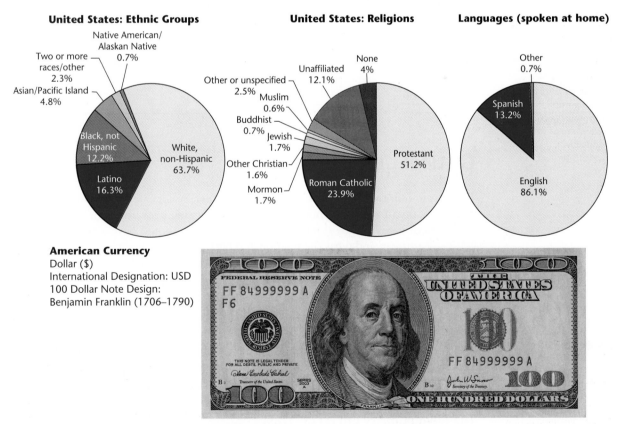

FIGURE 8.1 The American Nation at a Glance
© Sai Yeung Chan/Shutterstock.com (for photo)

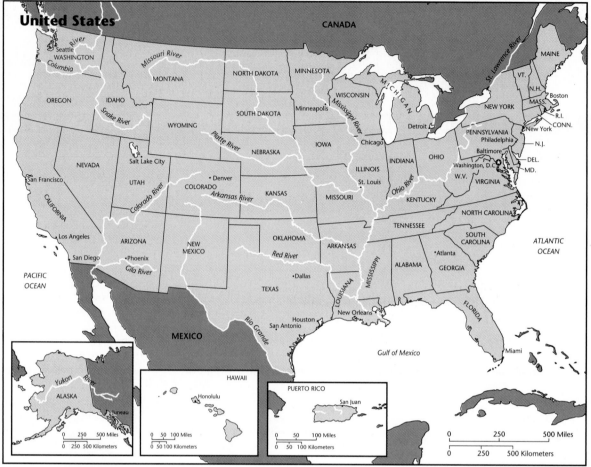

© Cengage Learning®

Critical Junctures

The first four critical junctures in U.S. political history appeared at points when mass discontent organized itself enough to change governing institutions or relationships. Each juncture challenged dominant ideas about who should have a voice in democratic government and what the relationship between government and citizen should be. Four periods of focused popular demand are explored here:

1. From the beginning of the American Revolution through the ratification of the Constitution and Bill of Rights
2. The Civil War and Reconstruction
3. The New Deal
4. The contemporary period of routinely divided national government and frequent shifts in which party controlled the presidency, the Senate, and the House of Representatives that began with the 1968 national elections

The Revolutionary Era (1773–1789)

Mass and elite discontent with British colonial rule sparked the American Revolution and the signing of the **Declaration of Independence**. Mass interests wanted to keep

Declaration of Independence

The document asserting that the British colonies in what is now the United States had declared themselves independent from Great Britain. The Declaration of Independence was signed in Philadelphia on July 4, 1776.

Table 8.1	Political Organization
Political System	Presidential system.
Regime History	Representative democracy, usually dated from the signing of the Declaration of Independence (1776) or the Constitution (1787).
Administrative Structure	Federalism, with powers shared between the national government and the fifty state governments; separation of powers at the level of the national government among legislative, executive, and judicial branches.
Executive	President, "directly" elected (with Electoral College that officially elects president and vice president) for four-year term; the cabinet is an advisory group of heads of major federal agencies and other senior officials selected by president to aid in decision making but with no formal authority.
Legislature	Bicameral. Congress composed of a lower house (House of Representatives) of 435 members serving two-year terms and an upper house (Senate) of 100 members (two from each state) serving six-year terms; elected in single-member districts (or, in the case of the Senate, states) by simple plurality (some states require a majority of voters).
Judiciary	Supreme Court with nine justices nominated by president and confirmed by Senate, with life tenure; has specified original and appellate jurisdiction and exercises the power of judicial review (can declare acts of the legislature and executive unconstitutional and therefore null and void).
Party System	Essentially two-party system (Republican and Democrat), with relatively weak and fractionalized parties; more than in most representative democracies, the personal following of candidates remains very important.

government close to home, in each colony, and wanted each colony to have substantial independence from the others. Elite interests advocated a national government with control over foreign policy, national assumption of state Revolutionary War debts, and the ability to establish national rules for commerce.

Mass interests won the first round of this battle. From 1777 to 1788, the **Articles of Confederation** governed the nation. Because the national government could not implement foreign or domestic policy, raise taxes, or regulate trade between the states without the cooperation of the individual states, elite interests gained support for replacing the Articles with the Constitution. The limited powers of the national government under the Articles rested in a legislature, but the states had to ratify most key decisions. States also established their own foreign policies, often different from each other. They also established their own fiscal policies and financed state budgets through extensive borrowing.

The Constitution maintained most power with the states but granted the federal (or national) government authority over commerce and foreign and military policy. It also gave the federal government a source of financing independent of the states. And, most important, it created a president, who had powers independent of the legislature. The Constitution delegated specific, but limited, powers to the national government. These included establishing post offices and roads, coining money, promoting the progress of science, raising and supporting an army and a navy, and

Articles of Confederation

The first governing document of the United States, agreed to in 1777 and ratified in 1781. The Articles concentrated most powers in the states and made the national government dependent on voluntary contributions of the states.

establishing a uniform rule of naturalization. These powers (Article I, Section 8 of the Constitution) tended to give the federal government the power to create a national economy. Finally, the Constitution limited citizens' voice in government. Presidents were elected indirectly, through the Electoral College, a body of political insiders from each state who are elected on election day and meet the following month to formally elect the president. Members of the Senate were originally elected by state legislatures. Only the members of the House of Representatives were elected by the people, but the states determined who could vote for members of the House. At first, only property-holding men held the vote in most states. By the 1840s, most white adult men could vote. Women did not receive voting rights nationally until 1920.

As popular support for ratifying the Constitution grew, many who had supported the Articles of Confederation made a new demand: The newly drafted U.S. Constitution should include enumerated protections for individuals from governmental power. Meeting this demand for a **Bill of Rights** was necessary to ensure the ratification of the Constitution. Because federal judges had to interpret these rights, the federal courts later played a growing role in the national government, particularly in the twentieth century.

Bill of Rights

The first ten amendments to the U.S. Constitution (ratified in 1791), which established limits on the actions of government. Initially, the Bill of Rights limited only the federal government. The Fourteenth Amendment and subsequent judicial rulings extended the provisions of the Bill of Rights to the states.

The Civil War and Reconstruction (1861–1876)

The morality of slavery convulsed the nation before the war, but the war itself began over the question of whether the states or the national government should be dominant. Many states believed they could reject specific federal laws. Any time Congress threatened to pass legislation to restrict slavery in the South, one or more southern state legislatures would threaten to nullify it. Many believed that if any state could nullify federal laws, the union would be put at risk. The Civil War resolved this issue in favor of the indivisibility of the union. The war also established an enforceable national citizenship to supplement state citizenship, which had existed even before the Constitution.[1] Establishing national citizenship began a slow process that culminated in the New Deal, as citizens looked to the federal government to meet their basic needs in times of national crisis.

To establish full citizenship for the freed slaves, Congress revisited the question of individual liberties and citizenship. These post–Civil War debates on the relationship of citizens to the national government established several important principles in the Fourteenth Amendment to the Constitution (1868). First, it extended the protections of the Bill of Rights to cover actions by states as well as by the federal government. Second, it extended citizenship to all persons born in the United States. This made U.S. citizens of freed slaves and also guaranteed that U.S.-born children of immigrants who migrated would become U.S. citizens at birth. Third, Congress sought to establish some federal regulation of voting and to grant the vote to African Americans. When the federal government failed to continue enforcing black voting rights, African Americans, particularly in the South, could not routinely exercise the vote until the Voting Rights Act in 1965. These fundamental guarantees that ensure electoral opportunities today limit prerogatives recognized as the states' responsibilities in the Constitution.

The New Deal Era (1933–1940)

The third critical juncture in U.S. political development was the New Deal, the Roosevelt administration's response to the economic crisis of the Great Depression. The federal government tapped its constitutional powers to regulate interstate commerce in order to vastly expand federal regulation of business. It also established a nationally guaranteed safety net, which included such programs as **Social Security** to provide monthly payments to the elderly who had worked and programs to provide housing for the working poor and food subsidies for children in poor households. The federal government also subsidized agriculture and protected farmers against the cyclical nature of demand. The legislative and judicial battles to establish such policies represent a fundamental expansion of the role of the federal government.

The federal government now asserted dominance over the states in delivering services to the people. Equally important, during the New Deal the presidency asserted dominance over the Congress in policy-making. The New Deal president, Franklin D. Roosevelt, found powers that no previous president had exercised. All post–New Deal presidents remain much more powerful than any of their predecessors, except perhaps for Abraham Lincoln, who served during the Civil War. Beginning in the 1960s, however, Congress began to challenge growth in executive power. Although the New Deal programs represented a significant change from the policies that preceded the Great Depression, they also reflected underlying American political values (see Section 4). Even in the New Deal era, class-based politics was kept to a minimum.

As the Depression came to a close, the United States geared up for its involvement in World War II. Although the United States had previously been involved in international conflicts beyond its borders, the experience of World War II was different at the beginning of U.S. involvement and at the end. The United States entered the war after U.S. territory was attacked. After the war, the United States was at the center of a multilateral strategy to contain the Soviet Union.

Divided Government, Frequently Shifting Partisan Dominance, and Political Contestation of the Scope of Government (1968 to the Present)

The fourth critical juncture, which began with the 1968 presidential election, is ongoing today. This critical juncture has two dimensions. First, the national government has been routinely divided between the two political parties with dominance of each branch of government shifting regularly. This division exacerbates the inefficiency that was designed into the American constitutional order and increases popular distrust of government (see Section 3).

In 1968 Richard Nixon (a California Republican) became president. Through Nixon's term and that of his Republican successor, Gerald Ford, the Democrats maintained control of both houses of Congress. In the period since 1968, one of the parties has controlled the presidency, the U.S. Senate, *and* the U.S. House of Representatives only five times. The Democrats controlled all three from 1977 to 1980, from 1993 to 1994, and from 2009 to 2010. The Republicans controlled all three from late January to June 2001 and again from 2003 to 2007. One party has replaced the other in the presidency five times since 1968. This division of the federal government between the parties and the routine shift in party control of the Congress or the presidency slow government response to controversial policy issues.

The second ongoing dimension of the contemporary critical juncture emerges from the apparent inefficiency caused by divided government. Many in the United States began to question the steady increase in the scope of governmental services. The electoral roots of this popular discontent can be found in the passage of Proposition 13 by California voters in 1978, which limited California's ability to increase **property taxes**.

Social Security

National systems of contributory and noncontributory benefits to provide assistance for the elderly, sick, disabled, unemployed, and others similarly in need of assistance. The specific coverage of social security, a key component of the welfare state, varies by country.

property taxes

Taxes levied by local governments on the assessed value of property. Property taxes are the primary way in which local jurisdictions in the United States pay for the costs of primary and secondary education. Because the value of property varies dramatically from neighborhood to neighborhood, the funding available for schools—and the quality of education—also varies from place to place.

The passage of Proposition 13 began an era that continues today, in which many citizens reject the expansion of government.

Popular discontent in the contemporary era is not limited to taxes; it also focuses on the scope of government. This period saw popular mobilization to reshape government's involvement in "values" issues, such as abortion, same-sex marriage, and the role of religion. Advocates on all sides of these issues want government to protect their interests, while condemning government for allegedly promoting the interests of groups with opposing positions. Ultimately, the courts become the venue to shape government policies on social issues.

While divided government had become the norm in 1968, the division became even more razor thin in the late 1990s. Each election raises the possibility of a switch in partisan control of the Senate or the House and the intense focus of both parties and **interest groups** on winning the handful of seats that could switch from one party to the other.

interest groups

Organizations that seek to represent the interests—usually economic—of their members in dealings with the government. Important examples are associations representing people with specific occupations, business interests, racial and ethnic groups, or age groups in society.

A jet crashes into the World Trade Center on September 11, 2001.
Source: AP Images/Moshe Bursuker.

September 11, 2001, and Its Aftermath

It is in this environment that the United States responded to the terrorist attacks of September 11. Initially, Congress and the populace rallied behind the president to increase the scope of federal law enforcement powers and to provide financial assistance for New York City, the families of the victims of the attack, and the airlines.

Popular support for President Bush and his administration's initial efforts to respond to the challenges of September 11 continued as the administration prepared for an invasion of Afghanistan. The United States also experienced a period of international support immediately following the September 11, 2001, attacks. In addition to immediate offers of humanitarian assistance, initial U.S. military responses to the attacks won widespread backing around the world.

The initial domestic cohesion and international support for the United States dissipated quickly. U.S. efforts to extend the war on terrorism to Iraq became the focus of many of the objections to growing U.S. power and unilateralism in international affairs.

Domestically, Bush saw steadily declining popular support. A sizeable minority of the U.S. population opposed the U.S. invasion of Iraq without the support of the United Nations or other international bodies. This opposition grew in the period after the military phase of the war ended when it became evident that the peace would be harder fought than the war. Bush's policies and overall stridency in domestic and foreign policy returned the country to the near-even partisan division that had characterized the country in the 1990s.

The Four Themes and the United States

The United States in a Globalized World of States

The constitutional structure of the U.S. government may now be at a disadvantage relative to other governing systems that can react more quickly and decisively to societal needs and shifts in public opinion. In parliamentary systems, even when they are burdened by the compromises necessary to maintain coalition governments, prime ministers can exercise power in a way that a U.S. president or Congress can never expect to do. In the United States, elections are held on a regular cycle, regardless of the popularity of the president. The presidency and Congress are routinely controlled by the two opposing parties. Federalism further slows government action.

Until the New Deal and World War II, the United States pursued a contradictory policy toward the rest of the world of states: It sought isolation from international politics but unfettered access to international markets. World War II changed the first of these stances, at least at elite levels (see Section 2): The United States sought to shape international relations through multilateral organizations and military force. It designed the multilateral organizations so that it could have a disproportionate voice (for example, in the United Nations Security Council). With the end of the Cold War, some now call for a reduced role of the U.S. government in the world of states or, at a minimum, a greater willingness to use a unilateral response to international military crises. This decline in mass interest in the U.S. role in the world among some U.S. citizens in the decade since the 9/11 attacks and the wars in Iraq and Afghanistan reflects the fact that foreign policy has never been central to the evolution of U.S. politics and governance.

Governing the Economy

The conflict between the president and Congress, the centralization of federal power in the twentieth century, and the growing concern about the cost and scope of government represent the central challenge to predicting the future direction of U.S. politics. Each part of this conflict speaks to questions of how much the United States and the states should regulate the economy. There will be no quick resolution; the Constitution slows resolution by creating a system of federalism and **separation of powers** (see Section 3).

The federal government and the states have sought to manage the economy by building domestic manufacturing, exploiting the nation's natural resources, and regulating the banking sector, while interfering little in the conduct of business (see Section 2). This hands-off attitude toward economic regulation can come at a price.

The Democratic Idea

The democratic idea in the U.S. context was one of an indirect, representative democracy with checks on democratically elected leaders. The emergence of a

separation of powers

An organization of political institutions within the state in which the executive, legislature, and judiciary have autonomous powers and no one branch dominates the others. This is the common pattern in presidential systems, as opposed to parliamentary systems, in which there is a fusion of powers.

strong national government after the New Deal era meant that national coalitions could often focus their demands on a single federal government, rather than always having to target a host of state governments as well. The decline in mediating institutions that can channel these demands reduces the ability of individual citizens to influence the national government (see Section 4). In the contemporary era, however, many in U.S. society challenge the size and scope of the federal government and seek a return to the state-focused polity that characterized the United States before the New Deal.

The Politics of Collective Identity

As a nation of immigrants, the United States must unite immigrants and descendants of immigrants from Europe, Africa, Latin America, and Asia with the established U.S. population. Previous waves of immigrants experienced only one to two generations of political and societal exclusion. Whether today's immigrants (particularly those who enter the United States without legal immigrant status) experience the same relatively rapid acculturation remains an open question. Preliminary evidence indicates that the process may be even quicker for immigrants who possess skills and education but slower for those who do not.[2] The United States has never fully remedied its longest-lasting difference in collective identities with full economic and political incorporation of African Americans, which was central to the Civil War and Reconstruction era and remains a challenge to today's U.S. politics.

Themes and Comparisons

single-member-plurality (SMP) electoral system

An electoral system in which candidates run for a single seat from a specific geographic district. The winner is the person who receives the most votes, whether or not they amount to a majority. SMP systems, unlike systems of proportional representation, increase the likelihood that two national coalition parties will form.

Scholars of U.S. politics have always had to come to terms with the idea of American exceptionalism—the idea that the United States is unique and cannot easily be compared to other countries. In several respects, the United States *could* be considered exceptional: Its geography and natural resources offer it advantages that few other nations can match; its experience with mass representative democracy is longer than that of other nations; it has been able to expand the citizenry beyond the descendants of the original citizens; and U.S. society has been much less divided by class than have the societies of other states.[3]

The U.S. Constitution, for all of its limitations, has served as the model for the constitutions of many newly independent nations. Some form of separation of powers (see Section 3) has become the norm in democratic states. Similarly, district-based and **single-member-plurality (SMP) electoral systems** (see Section 4) have been widely adapted to reduce conflict in multiethnic states, of which the United States was the first large-scale example. Through its active role in multilateral institutions, the United States also attempts to impose its will on other nations.

Where Do You Stand?

The balance between the powers of the federal and state governments has shifted considerably. Where should the balance of power rest for different government responsibilities?

Can the United States afford to continue to be the world's policeman?

POLITICAL ECONOMY AND DEVELOPMENT

State and Economy

When national leaders present the accomplishments of the United States, they often claim that by governing the economy less, the United States allows the private economy to thrive. In this simplified version of this story, the private sector is the engine of national growth, and this private sector is most successful when left alone by government. Economic success, then, is tied to the **free market**—*the absence of government regulation* and the opportunity for entrepreneurs to build the nation's economy.

Relative to other advanced democracies, the U.S. economy is much less regulated. The U.S. government has traditionally taken a laissez-faire attitude toward economic actors. This absence of regulation allowed for the creation and expansion of many new types of production that subsequently spread throughout the world, but it also can come at a cost. U.S. policy-makers cede power to private actors who are not concerned with the impact of their activities on the broader economy, such as the mortgage lenders who built the subprime lending industry or the investment banks that bought the subprime loans.

The Constitution reserves for the federal government authority to regulate *inter*-state commerce and commerce with foreign nations. As a result, state and local governments are limited in their ability to shape the economy. Over time, however, states have established the ability to regulate workplace conditions as part of their **police powers** or of jurisdiction over public health and safety.

Except for agriculture, higher education, and some defense-related industries, the size of various sectors of the economy is almost entirely the result of the free market. The federal government does try to incubate some new industries, but it primarily uses grants to private agencies—often universities—to accomplish this end. The United States also occasionally supports ailing industries.

Since the New Deal, the federal government has guaranteed minimum prices for most agricultural commodities and has sought to protect agriculture by paying farmers to leave some land fallow. It has also considerably reduced the costs of production and risks associated with agriculture by providing subsidized crop insurance, canals and aqueducts to transport water, and flood control projects. It has subsidized the sale of U.S. agricultural products abroad and purchased some surplus agricultural production for storage and distribution in the United States. Although a less explicit form of subsidy, weak regulation of U.S. immigration laws has ensured a reliable, inexpensive labor supply.

The federal government has also limited its own ability to regulate the economy. With the formation of the **Federal Reserve Board** in 1913, it removed control of the money supply from elected officeholders. Today, unelected leaders on the Federal Reserve Board, many with ties to the banking industry, control the volume of money in the economy and the key interest rates that determine the rates at which banks lend money to businesses and individuals. As the United States slid toward recession in 2008, the Federal Reserve was the central U.S. policy-making agency seeking to avert recession. It provided direct subsidies and low-cost loans to banks, allowing

Focus Questions ▽

- What principles guide U.S. governmental decisions about economic regulation?

- How does federalism shape U.S. decision making on protections for workers and social welfare programs for citizens?

free market

A system in which government regulation of the economy is absent or limited. Relative to other advanced democracies, the United States has traditionally had less market regulation.

police powers

Powers that are traditionally held by the states to regulate public safety and welfare. Police powers are the form of interaction with government that citizens most often experience. Even with the growth in federal government powers in the twentieth century, police powers remain the primary responsibility of the states and localities.

Federal Reserve Board

The U.S. central bank established by Congress in 1913 to regulate the banking industry and the money supply. Although the president appoints the chair of the board of governors (with Senate approval), the board operates largely independently.

them to survive. The Federal Reserve also purchased government bonds owned by banks to keep interest rates low in the expectation that the banks would use their newly available cash to lend to private borrowers. Congressional challenges to the Federal Reserve's autonomy raise concerns among other nations that the United States will be less able to act as a global banker and lender of last resort in the future.

The U.S. government does not regulate the flow of capital. As a result, many large U.S.-based firms have evolved into multinational corporations, removing themselves from a great deal of U.S. government regulation and taxation.

It is important to recognize that from the nation's earliest days, the federal government promoted agriculture and industry, spurred exports, and (more recently) sought to stabilize the domestic and international economy. These promotional efforts included tariffs, which sought to disadvantage products that competed with U.S. manufactures; roads and canals, so that U.S.-produced goods could be brought to market cheaply and quickly; the distribution of federally owned lands in the West to individuals and to railroads, so that the land could contribute to national economic activity; and large-scale immigration, so that capital would have people to produce and consume goods (see Section 3). Efforts to promote U.S. industry often came at the expense of individual citizens, who are less able to organize and make demands of government. Tariffs, for example, kept prices high for domestic consumers.

Through much of the nation's history, the United States used its diplomatic and military resources to establish and maintain markets for U.S.-produced commodities and manufactured goods abroad. The United States, for example, uses its position in the world economy and on multilateral lending institutions to open markets, provide loans for nations facing economic distress, and protect some U.S.-produced goods from foreign competition. Despite national rhetoric to the contrary, the United States has consistently promoted economic development, though not by regulating production or spurring specific industries.

The U.S. economy has increasingly come to rely on two unintentional forms of international subsidy. First, it has built up a steadily increasing international trade deficit. In other words, the United States has bought much more abroad than it has sold. Although some aspects of these trade deficits could well reflect a strength in the U.S. economy (for example, being able to purchase goods produced inexpensively abroad), continuing deficits of this level act as a downward pressure on the U.S. dollar (see Figure 8.2). Slowing this downward pressure for the time being is

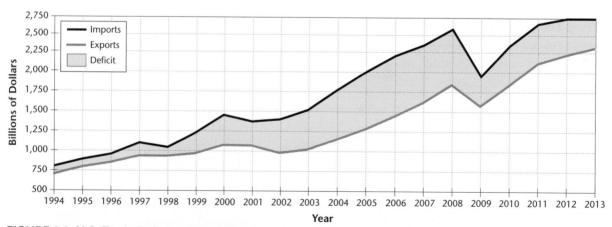

FIGURE 8.2 U.S. Trade Deficit, 1994–2013

Source: U.S. Bureau of the Census. 2014. "U.S. Trade in Goods and Services—Balance of Payments (BOP) Basis," http://www.census.gov/foreign-trade/statistics/historical/gands.pdf (accessed March 9, 2014).

the second form of international subsidy: The U.S. dollar is the international reserve currency. This means that many nations and individual investors keep their reserves (their savings) in dollars. By doing this, they keep demand for the dollar up, reducing the downward pressure that comes from trade deficits. The euro, the European common currency, however, is increasingly serving as a reserve currency. The long-term stability of the U.S. economy and the value of the dollar as a reserve currency are being challenged by an increasing national debt (discussed later in this chapter) and market concerns about unfunded liabilities in federal and state pension, health care, and insurance programs.

In the twentieth century, the U.S. government took on new responsibilities to protect citizens and to tax businesses, in part, to provide government-mandated services for workers. The government also expanded regulation of workplace safety, pension systems, and other worker–management relations issues (see Section 3). Despite this expansion of the government role in providing protections to workers, the United States offers fewer guarantees to its workers than do other advanced democracies.

The public sector has traditionally been smaller in the United States than in other advanced democracies. Nevertheless, the U.S. government and the states conduct activities that many believe could be better conducted by the private sector. The federal government operates hospitals for veterans, provides water and electrical power to Appalachian states, manages lands in the West and Alaska, runs the civilian air traffic control system, and, after September 11, manages passenger and luggage screening at commercial airports. Roads have traditionally been built and maintained by the state and federal governments, and waterways have been kept navigable (and open to recreational use) by the federal government.

Often left out of the story of the development of the U.S. economy is the role of its natural resources and the environment. The nation's territory is diverse in terms of natural resources and environments, stretching from tropical to arctic. The territory includes arable land that can produce more than enough year round for the domestic market as well as for extensive exports. The United States has protected ports and navigable rivers, and few enemies can challenge U.S. control over these transportation resources. For more than a century, it was able to expand trade while not investing in a large standing military to defend its trade routes.

Society and Economy

The United States adheres more strictly to its laissez-faire ideology in terms of the outcomes of the economic system. The distribution of income and wealth is much more unequal in the United States than in other advanced democracies, and that gap has been steadily widening over the past 30 years. In 2012, the top 5 percent alone earned more than 22.3 percent of the total amount earned (see Figure 8.3). Wide differences exist between women and men and between racial groups. Women, on average, earned $14,000 annually less than men. Non-Hispanic whites earned an average of $44,000 in 2012 compared to $48,000 for Asian Americans, $31,000 for blacks, and $29,000 for Hispanics.

The United States has tolerated these conditions and sees them as an incentive for people at the lower end of the economic spectrum. Wealth and income have become more skewed since 1980. The mere mention in an election of the class implications of a policy, particularly tax policy, will usually lead to the charge of fomenting class warfare.

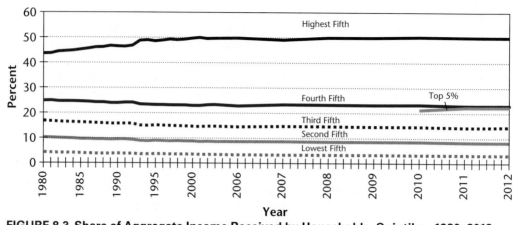

FIGURE 8.3 Share of Aggregate Income Received by Households, Quintiles, 1980–2012

Source: U.S. Bureau of the Census. 2013. "Historical Income Table—Households" Table H-2. Share of Aggregate Income Received by Each Fifth and Top 5 Percent of Households. http://www.census.gov/hhes /www/income/data/historical/household/index.html (accessed March 9, 2014).

Federal income taxation of individuals is progressive, with higher-income people paying a higher share of their income in taxes. Rates range from 0 percent for individuals with incomes less than $8,925 to 39.6 percent for individuals with incomes exceeding approximately $406,750. The progressive nature of federal taxes is reduced considerably by two factors. Upper-income taxpayers receive a much higher share of their income from investments, which are taxed at lower rates. Second, all taxpayers with salary income are subject to a regressive tax for Social Security and disability benefits. The tax for Social Security and Medicare is currently 7.65 percent paid by the worker and 7.65 percent paid by the employer. The Social Security share of this tax is imposed only on the first $117,000 of income and not at all on higher incomes.

State and local taxes tend to be much less progressive. Most states levy a sales tax. This is a flat tax, ranging between 2.9 and 8.25 percent depending on the state. Many states levy a state income tax. No state has an income tax that is as progressive as the federal income tax. The final major form of individual taxation is property taxes. Governments in the United States have increasingly supplemented taxes with user fees charged for the provision of specific services.

Thus, the gap between rich and poor in the United States is not remedied by progressive taxation. This gap might well have led to the emergence of class-based political movements, but immigration policy, which also promoted economic development, focused workers' attention away from class and toward cultural differences that reduced the salience of class divisions in U.S. society. Unions, which could also have promoted class-based politics and focused workers' attentions on income inequalities, have traditionally been weak in the United States. This weakness reflects individual-level antipathy toward unions, but also state and federal laws that limit the abilities of unions to organize and collectively bargain.

The U.S. economy could not have grown without the importation of immigrant labor. The United States has generally sought to remedy labor shortages with policies that encouraged migration. Today, the United States is one of just four countries that allow large-scale migration of those who do not already have a cultural tie to the receiving nation. Immigration to the United States numbers approximately 1,100,000 people annually, who immigrate under the provisions of the law to a permanent status that allows for eventual eligibility for U.S. citizenship (see Figure 8.4).[4]

Until the economy soured in 2008, these legal immigrants were joined by as many as 500,000 additional unauthorized migrants annually.[5]

Although the United States tolerates the unequal distribution of income and wealth, in the twentieth century, it intervened directly in the free market to establish protections for workers and, to a lesser degree, to guarantee the welfare of the most disadvantaged in the society. The programs for workers, which are primarily **distributive policies**, receive much more public support than do programs to assist the poor, which are primarily **redistributive policies**. Distributive policies allocate resources into an area that policy-makers perceive needs to be promoted without a significant impact on income or wealth distribution. Redistributive policies take resources from one person or group in society and allocate them to a more disadvantaged group in the society. Most worker benefits, such as health insurance, childcare, and pensions, are provided by private employers, if they are provided at all, but are regulated by the government.

Best known among the federal programs aimed toward workers is Social Security, which taxes workers and their employers to pay for benefits for retired and disabled workers (and nonworker spouses). In the past, retirees almost always received more than they had paid into the system (a form of intergenerational redistribution), but it will take significant reforms to guarantee that this outcome continues when today's workers reach retirement age. Actuarial estimates indicate that the Social Security Trust Fund will be exhausted in 2033 if there are no changes to the tax used to pay for Social Security or the benefit rates or age of eligibility. Medicare—the government health plan for the elderly—will run out of funds in 2024. The U.S. government faces the dilemma of having to lower benefits for each of these programs, raising taxes, or paying benefits out of general revenues. Changing the tax basis of Social Security and Medicare now (or lowering benefits now) would delay this point of reckoning.

distributive policies

Policies that allocate state resources into an area that lawmakers perceive needs to be promoted. For example, leaders today believe that students should have access to the Internet. In order to accomplish this goal, telephone users are being taxed to provide money for schools to establish connections to the Internet.

redistributive policies

Policies that take resources from one person or group in society and allocate them to a different, usually more disadvantaged, group. The United States has traditionally opposed redistributive policies to the disadvantaged.

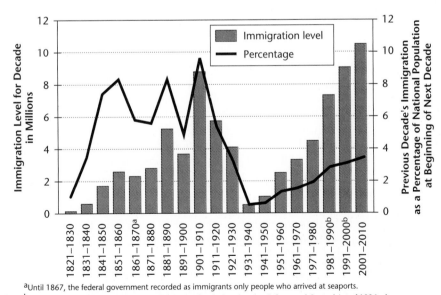

aUntil 1867, the federal government recorded as immigrants only people who arrived at seaports.

bThese figures include recipients of legalization under the Immigration Reform and Control Act of 1986 who immigrated to the United States prior to 1982 but were recorded as having entered in the year in which they received permanent residence.

FIGURE 8.4 Immigration to the United States, 1821–2010

Source: Adopted from DeSipio, Louis, and Rodolfo O. de la Garza, *Making Americans/ Remaking America: Immigration* and Immigrant Policy (Boulder, CO: Westview Press, 1998), Table 2.1.

In 2010, in response to growing numbers of uninsured Americans and spiraling health care costs, Congress created a new national health care program for U.S. citizens and permanent residents—the Affordable Care Act. The ACA is largely distributive in nature with some additional subsidies (redistribution) for low-income individuals. It builds on the private health insurance that many Americans receive through their employers or unions. The ACA will not be fully implemented until 2020 at the earliest; it is controversial for several reasons. Some fear that it will undermine the incentive for employers, particularly small employers, to provide insurance. Governments would then have to provide a higher share of insurance and assume costs currently paid by employers. Others resent that government is not more central to the provision of insurance and that private insurance, with its overhead costs and quest for profits, will absorb health care expenditures that could go to providing better treatments. When the national health care bill was debated, some in Congress called for government to replace the role of private insurers (the so-called single-payer option). States are concerned that they will have to provide insurance to residents who are not otherwise able to get private insurance and that they will have to assume at least 10 percent of the costs of providing this insurance (the federal government will pay the rest). Finally, some feel that the new mandate that all Americans have health insurance or be fined violates the Constitution (the Supreme Court rejected this assertion in 2013).

The government also established a minimum wage and a bureaucratic mechanism to enforce this wage. Some states and localities have established higher minimum wages than the federal minimum wage.

The states regulate worker–employer relations through unemployment insurance and insurance against workplace injuries. Benefits and eligibility requirements vary dramatically by state, although the federal governmental mandates that all workers be eligible for twenty-six weeks of unemployment benefits (assuming the worker has been employed for more than six months).

Beginning in the 1930s, the United States also established social welfare programs to assist the economically disadvantaged. As one would expect in a system organized around the free market, these programs have never been as broad-based or as socially accepted as in other economies. The states administered these programs—which provide food, health care, housing assistance, some job training, and some cash assistance to the poor—with a combination of federal and state funds. Eligibility and benefit levels varied dramatically from state to state.

In today's economy, public benefits and public employment are increasingly limited to U.S. citizens. Over time, these policies could enhance differences between the non-Hispanic white and black populations, on the one hand, and ethnic groups with large shares of immigrants, such as Latinos and Asian Americans, on the other.

Both the federal and state governments are facing gaps between income and expenditures. The federal government can continue to run a large annual deficit. The sum of these deficits—the national debt—totals nearly $17.5 trillion. Most states do not have this option and must either raise revenues or cut services annually.

Deficits can have a salutary effect on the national economy during weak economic times because the federal government can more easily borrow and then spend this money to stimulate the economy and support individuals who are out of work. In the long run, however, this federal debt absorbs money that could be invested in private sector activities and will slow national economic growth. In 2014, the federal government will pay approximately $233 billion in interest on its debt, an amount that will increase considerably when interest rates rise.

Environmental Issues

One area in which the United States has taken a limited role in regulating the activities of private actors in the American economy is environmental regulation. When the environment first became an issue in international politics, the United States took aggressive action to clean the air and the nation's oceans and navigable waterways. In each of these regulatory areas, federal legislation had dramatic impacts. Emissions standards have made the air much healthier, even in the nation's most car-focused cities. Waterways that were dangerous to the touch are now open to swimming. New lands were added to the national park system.[6] The visible successes of the early environmental **regulations** reduced the salience of environmental issues. These 1970s-era environmental regulations have not been followed by a continuing national commitment to environmentalism.

The United States has fewer environmental regulations than other advanced democracies and has been less willing to engage in multilateral agreements on environmental issues than on issues such as international security and economic cooperation. The United States, for example, is a signatory to the Kyoto Protocols to limit climate change (primarily through the reduction of greenhouse gases), but the treaty was never ratified by the U.S. Senate and is nonbinding on the United States. At least nine U.S. states and 740 U.S. cities have passed emissions caps that broadly follow Kyoto guidelines (though often less rapidly than Kyoto would mandate). Unlike an international treaty, however, these state and city efforts can be amended with a majority vote in a legislature and are more difficult to enforce.

Early in his term, President Obama proposed "cap and trade" energy regulation that would have set limits on carbon emissions while allowing factories and other carbon emitters to sell unused carbon emissions to create incentives for conversion to renewable energy sources. Despite some early bipartisan support, this legislation ultimately failed, losing support from all Senate Republicans and some Democrats.

Environmental issues are not central to the agendas of either U.S. political party. In an era of routinely divided government (see Section 4), new legislation to protect the environment is unlikely to pass in the U.S. Congress. Using his executive authority, President Obama has expanded the number of national parks and wilderness areas.

regulations

The rules that explain the implementation of laws. When the legislature passes a law, it sets broad principles for implementation; how the law is actually implemented is determined by regulations written by executive branch agencies. The regulation-writing process allows interested parties to influence the eventual shape of the law in practice.

The United States in the Global Economy

Since colonial times, the United States has been linked to world trade. By the late twentieth century, the United States had vastly expanded its role in international finance and was an importer of goods produced abroad (often in low-wage countries that could produce goods less expensively than U.S. factories) as well as an exporter of agricultural products.

After World War II, the United States reversed its traditional isolationism to take a leading role in regulating the international economy. The increasing interdependence of global economies was the result, in part, of conscious efforts by world leaders at the end of World War II, through the Bretton Woods Agreement, to establish and fund multinational lending institutions. Chief among these institutions were the World Bank and the International Monetary Fund. Since their establishment in the 1940s, they have been supplemented by a network of international lending and regulatory agencies and regional trading agreements.

The United States is also part of regional trading networks, such as NAFTA with Canada and Mexico. After its passage, the United States also entered into an agreement with neighboring countries in the Caribbean to reduce tariffs on many goods.

The U.S. government plays a central role in the international political economy. It achieves this through its domination of international lending agencies and regional defense and trade organizations. But these efforts are ultimately limited by domestic politics. Thus, while presidents may promote an international agenda, Congress often limits the funding for international organizations. The United States then appears to many outside the country as a hesitant and sometimes resentful economic leader.

In recent years, another multilateral institution has emerged that can potentially challenge U.S. economic dominance. The European Union (EU) is much more than a trading alliance. It is an organization of twenty-seven European nations with growing international influence. Eighteen EU members share a common currency, the euro. As the euro came into widespread use, the dollar faced its first challenge in many years as the world's dominant trading currency.

The United States also funds binational international lending through such agencies as the Export-Import Bank and the Overseas Private Investment Corporation. These agencies make loans to countries and private businesses to purchase goods and services from U.S.-owned businesses. The United States also provides grants and loans to allies to further U.S. strategic and foreign policy objectives or for humanitarian reasons.

"Well, they look pretty undocumented to me."

Immigration has been central to the development of the United States economy from its earliest days. Native populations have long been suspicious of the newcomers.

J.B. Handelsman The New Yorker Collection/The Cartoon Bank

THE GLOBAL CONNECTION

Arizona SB 1070 and U.S. Relations with Mexico

Many issues divide the United States and Mexico: trade disputes, migration, drug smuggling and violence, and gun smuggling among others. In 2010, Arizona added to this list. Reflecting popular concerns over Congress's failure to reform immigration, it passed a law requiring police to verify the legal immigration status of people arrested or detained by the police. The law, SB 1070, also criminalized giving assistance to an unauthorized alien, such as allowing a unauthorized immigrant family member to live in your home.

Many in the United States were concerned by these requirements. Under the Constitution, regulation of immigration is an enumerated power of the federal government. Aside from this constitutional concern, many raised concerns of racial profiling. Would police in Arizona verify the legal status of all people detained or just of those who were Latino or Asian American? Mexico also objected

to SB 1070 asserting that its nationals will be subject to harassment in Arizona. In 2012, the Supreme Court held much of SB 1070 to be unconstitutional, but left in place provisions that allowed for immigration status checks during law enforcement activities.

Arizona's enactment of the law made it more difficult for the U.S. government to negotiate with Mexico on issues of joint importance. SB 1070 demonstrates the inherent difficulty in a federalist system for the making of foreign policy. Ultimately, the United States cannot prevent any state from passing legislation that can muddy binational relations.

MAKING CONNECTIONS Should the regulation of immigrants be a state responsibility like other police powers or federal responsibility related to the establishment of national immigration policy?

The United States has slowly, and grudgingly, adapted to a world where it can no longer simply assert its central role. Thus, the U.S. government and, more slowly, the American people have seen their problems and needs from a global perspective. The separation of powers between the executive and legislative branches, and the local constituencies of members of Congress, ensures continuing resistance to this new international role (see The Global Connection: Arizona SB 1070 and U.S. relations with Mexico).

Where Do You Stand?

What services and protections should the United States guarantee to each of its citizens?

The United States has seen its national debt grow dramatically over the past decade and will probably not be able to rely on borrowing at comparable levels in the future. Should taxes be raised to meet the level of federal expenditures or should programs be cut? If you believe that programs should be cut, which programs should be cut?

GOVERNANCE AND POLICY-MAKING

SECTION 3

Organization of the State

The U.S. Constitution was drafted in 1787 and ratified the following year. The Constitution established a central government that was independent of the states but left the states most of their preexisting powers (particularly police powers and public

▼ **Focus Questions**

• How have twentieth-century presidents been able to expand these powers of the presidency?

• Can citizens more effectively influence the policy-making process through anti-party movements like the Tea Party or through traditional mainstream party mobilization?

safety). Although it had limited powers, the new U.S. government exercised powers over commerce and foreign policy that were denied to the states.

The Constitution has been amended twenty-seven times since 1787. The first ten of these amendments (ratified in 1791) make up the Bill of Rights, the set of protections of individual rights that were a necessary compromise to ensure that the Constitution was ratified. The remaining seventeen amendments have extended democratic election practices and changed procedural deficiencies in the original Constitution that came to be perceived as inconsistent with democratic practice. Examples of amendments to extend democratic election practices are the extension of the vote to women and to citizens between the ages of eighteen and twenty (the Nineteenth and Twenty-Sixth Amendments, respectively) or the prohibition of poll taxes, a tax that had to be paid before an individual could vote (the Twenty-Fourth Amendment). Changes to procedural deficiencies included linking presidential and vice presidential candidates on a single ticket, replacing a system where the candidate with the most votes in the Electoral College won the presidency and the second-place candidate won the vice presidency (the Twelfth Amendment), and establishing procedures to replace a president who becomes incapacitated (the Twenty-Fifth Amendment).

Each amendment requires three-quarters of the states to agree to the change. Although the Constitution allows states to initiate amendments, all twenty-seven have resulted from amendments initially ratified by Congress. When Congress initiates an amendment to the Constitution, two-thirds of the members of the House and the Senate must vote in favor of the amendment before it is sent to the states. States set their own procedures for ratifying constitutional amendments

Two guiding principles anchor the American system of government: federalism and separation of powers.[7]

Federalism is the division of authority between multiple levels of government in the United States, between the federal and state governments. Separation of powers is an effort to set government against itself by vesting separate branches with independent powers so that any one branch cannot permanently dominate the others.

These two characteristics of American government—federalism and separation of powers—were necessary compromises to guarantee the ratification of the Constitution. They are more than compromises, however. They reflect a conscious desire by the constitutional framers to limit the federal government's ability to control citizens' lives. To limit what they perceived as an inevitable tyranny of majorities over numerical minorities, the framers designed a system that set each part of government against all the other parts. Each branch of the federal government could limit the independent action of the other two branches, and the federal government and the states could limit each other.

Federalism and separation of powers have a consequence that could not be fully anticipated by the framers of the Constitution: U.S. government is designed to be inefficient. Because each part of government is set against all others, policy-making is difficult. No single leader or branch of government can unequivocally dominate policy-making as the prime minister can in a parliamentary system. Although a consensus across branches of government can sometimes appear in times of national challenge, such as in the period immediately after the 9/11 attacks, this commonality of purpose quickly dissolves as each branch of government seeks to protect its prerogatives and position in the policy-making process.

Federalism establishes multiple sovereigns. A citizen of the United States is simultaneously a national citizen and a citizen of one of the states. Each citizen has responsibilities to each of these sovereigns and can be held accountable to the laws of each. Over the nation's history, the balance of power has shifted, with the federal government gaining power relative to the states, but to this day, states remain responsible for many parts of citizens' lives and act in these areas independently of the federal government.

Many powers traditionally reserved to the states have shifted to the federal government. The most rapid of these shifts occurred during the New Deal, when the federal government tapped its commerce regulation powers to create a wide range of programs to address the economic and social needs of the people. In part, the court challenges to the ACA focused on the questions of federalism: whether Congress had the authority to mandate individual health coverage or to require the states to establish insurance pools for their residents who could not buy insurance from private insurers as part of Congress's authority to regulate interstate commerce.

The second organizing principle of American government is separation of powers. Each of the three branches of the federal government—the executive, the legislative (see Section 4), and the judiciary—shares in the responsibilities of governing and has some oversight over the other branches. In order to enact a law, for example, Congress must pass the law, and the president must sign it. The president can block the action of Congress by vetoing the law. Congress can override the president's veto through a two-thirds vote in both houses of Congress. The courts can review the constitutionality of laws passed by Congress and signed by the president. Congress and the states acting in unison can reverse a Supreme Court ruling on the constitutionality of a law by passing a constitutional amendment by two-thirds votes in each house that is subsequently ratified by three-quarters of the states. The Senate must ratify senior appointments to the executive branch, including members of the cabinet, as well as federal judges. The president nominates these judges, and Congress sets their salaries and much of their jurisdiction (except in constitutional matters). In sum, separation of powers allows each branch to limit the others and prevents any one branch from carrying out its responsibilities without the others' cooperation. It also allows for the phenomenon of divided government in which different political parties control the executive and legislative branches of government. This complexity encourages an ongoing competition for political power.

The Executive

The Presidency

The American presidency has grown dramatically in power since the nation's first days. The president, who is indirectly elected, serves a fixed four-year term and is limited to two terms by a constitutional amendment ratified in 1951. The president is both head of state and head of government.

Through much of U.S. political history, the president was not at the center of the federal government. Quite the contrary: The Constitution established Congress as the central branch of government and relegated the president to a much more poorly defined role whose primary responsibilities are administering programs designed and funded by Congress. Even now, the structural weaknesses of the presidency remain. The president must receive ongoing support from Congress to implement his agenda. But the president cannot control Congress except to the degree that public opinion (and, to a much lesser degree, party loyalty) encourages members of Congress to support the president. U.S. presidents are far weaker than prime ministers in parliamentary systems; they can, however, stay in office long after they have lost popular support.

The president is the commander-in-chief of the military and may grant pardons, make treaties (with the approval of two-thirds of the Senate), and make senior appointments to the executive branch and to judicial posts (again with the Senate's concurrence). The president is required to provide an annual state of the union report to Congress and may call Congress into session. Finally, the president manages the bureaucracy, which at the time of the Constitution's ratification was small but has subsequently grown in size and responsibility. In terms of formal powers, the president is far weaker than Congress.

With one exception, presidents until the turn of the twentieth century did not add considerably to the delegated powers. The exception was Abraham Lincoln, who dominated Congress during the Civil War. His example was one that twentieth-century presidents followed. He became a national leader and was able to establish his own power base directly in the citizenry. Lincoln realized that each member of Congress depended on a local constituency (a district or state), and he labeled their activities as being local or sectional. Lincoln created a national power base for the presidency by presenting himself as the only national political leader, an important position during the Civil War. He had an advantage in being commander-in-chief during wartime; however, the foundation of his power was not the military but his connection to the people.

In the twentieth century, presidents discovered that they had a previously untapped resource. Beginning with Theodore Roosevelt, twentieth-century presidents used the office of the president as a bully pulpit to speak to the nation and propose public policies that met national needs. No member of Congress or the Senate could claim a similar national constituency.

Later in the twentieth century, presidents found a new power. As the role of the federal government expanded, they managed a much larger federal bureaucracy that provided services used by nearly all citizens. Thus, a program like Social Security connects most citizens to the executive branch. Beginning with the New Deal, presidents proposed programs that expanded the federal bureaucracy and, consequently, the connection between the people and the president. Some congressional opposition to the ACA focused on the creation of another program that linked the individual welfare of all Americans to an executive branch program.

Finally, twentieth-century presidents learned another important lesson from the experience of Abraham Lincoln. The president has an authority over the military that places the office at the center of policy-making in military and international affairs. Thus, in the period from World War II to the collapse of the Soviet Union, the presidency gained strength from the widely perceived need for a single decision-maker.

Although the presidency gained powers in the twentieth century, the office remains structurally weak relative to Congress. Presidential power is particularly undercut by the norm of divided government: Presidents have little power over Congresses controlled by the other party. Since Congress retains the power to appropriate funds, the president must ultimately yield to its will on the design and implementation of policy.

Until the election of Barack Obama, all presidents had been white men. All but one (John F. Kennedy) have been Protestant. In today's politics having served as a governor works to a candidate's advantage. Despite a common assumption, only four vice presidents have been elected to the presidency immediately at the end of their terms. It is more common for vice presidents to move to the presidency on the death of the president.

PROFILE

Barack Obama

Source: Official White House Photo by Pete Souza.

Barack Obama's 2008 and 2012 elections to the presidency surprised many observers of U.S. society and politics. Obama self-identifies as, and is understood to be, African American in a society that has persistently discriminated against blacks. Many observers felt that this would prevent many white Americans from supporting his candidacy. In the end, the majority of white voters opposed Obama, but his victory was sealed by strong support from African Americans, Latinos, and Asian Americans. Obama's African roots come from his father, who migrated to the United States as a student in the early 1960s.

Obama's preparation for his candidacy and for the presidency included service as a community organizer and later as a civil rights attorney. On many other dimensions, Obama shared characteristics with people recently elected to the presidency. He is trained as a lawyer, is married, and held elective office at the time of his candidacy.

President Obama began his administration facing greater challenges than most of his predecessors. The United States was engaged in two ground wars abroad as well as the war on terrorism. Obama's resources to address these international challenges were limited by a collapse in the global economy that worsened in the months before his election. A collapse in the financial services sector spurred a recession that more than doubled unemployment rates and the federal deficit. Personal bankruptcies and home foreclosures grew to new record levels.

During his first two years in office, President Obama had a resource that few of his predecessors did—sizeable Democratic majorities in the Senate and House of Representatives. The result was an ambitious agenda that saw the passage of more major pieces of legislation than any president since Lyndon Johnson had been able to pass, including: the ACA, two economic stimulus bills to help the nation recover from the recession, a bill to regulate the financial services industry, ratification of an arms control treaty with Russia, the end of the military's restrictions on gay and lesbian service members, civil rights legislation focusing on the workplace, and the confirmation of two Supreme Court justices, one of whom was the first Latino on the high court.

MAKING CONNECTIONS President Obama's first two years in office saw many legislative successes. What resources did Obama have to achieve his goals? What limits do presidents face?

The Cabinet and the Bureaucracy

To manage the U.S. government, the president appoints (and the Senate confirms) senior administrators to key executive branch departments. The chief officers at each of the core departments make up the president's cabinet. The U.S. cabinet has no legal standing, and presidents frequently use it only at a symbolic level. The president is also free to extend membership to other senior appointed officials (such as the U.S. ambassador to the United Nations), so the number of cabinet members fluctuates from administration to administration.

The senior officers of the executive branch agencies manage a workforce of approximately 2.2 million civilian civil servants (the bureaucracy). Although formally part of the executive branch, the bureaucracy must also be responsive to Congress. The presidential appointees who lead the federal agencies establish broad policy objectives and propose budgets that can expand or contract the responsibilities of executive-branch offices. Congress must approve these budgets, and it uses this financial oversight to encourage bureaucrats to behave as their congressional monitors wish.

Arguably, the inability of either Congress or the president to control the bureaucracy fully should give it some independence. But the bureaucracy as a rule does not have the resources to collect information and shape the laws that guide its operations.

Interest groups have steadily filled this informational role, but the information comes at a cost. Bureaucracies often develop symbiotic relations with the interests that they should be regulating. The interest groups have more access to Congress and can shape the operations of the regulatory agencies. These **iron triangle relationships** (among a private interest group, a congressional committee or subcommittee overseeing the policy in question, and a federal agency implementing the policy) often exclude new players who represent alternative views on how policies should be implemented. Without an independent source of authority, the bureaucracy must depend on both the elected branches and also on interest groups.

iron triangle relationships

A term coined by students of American politics to refer to the relationships of mutual support formed by particular government agencies, members of congressional committees or subcommittees, and interest groups in various policy areas.

Other State Institutions

Besides the presidency and the Congress (see Section 4), several other institutions are central to the operation of U.S. government: the military, national security agencies, the judiciary, and state and local governments.

The Military

The U.S. Army, Navy, Marine Corps, Coast Guard, and Air Force include approximately 1.4 million active-duty personnel plus an additional 900,000 reserve and national guard troops. The president is commander-in-chief of the U.S. military, but on a day-to-day basis, U.S. forces serve under the command of a nonpolitical officer corps.

Because of the unique geographic resources of the United States, the military has had to dedicate few of its resources to defending U.S. territory. Beginning with the new U.S. geopolitical role after World War II, the military was given new responsibilities to support U.S. multilateral and regional defense agreements.

The United States increasingly looks to its allies to support U.S. military objectives abroad. In preparation for war with Iraq, U.S. military leaders designed an invasion force of 130,000, with 100,000 ground troops and the remainder in support positions abroad. These 100,000 U.S. military ground troops were supported by at least 15,000 British ground troops. They were supplemented by approximately 160,000 contractors.[8]

Many of the traditional responsibilities of the military, such as support of troops and specialized technical activities, have been transferred to reserve units and to private firms who work under contract to the Defense Department. Reserve troops are now called to active duty more frequently. They were required to serve multiple long-term commitments in Iraq and Afghanistan and were prohibited from leaving the reserves at the end of their commitments.

With the increased expectations for the military came increased reliance on defense technologies. U.S. nuclear weapons, intelligence technologies, and space-based defense technologies, as well as the maintenance of conventional weaponry and troop support, have significantly raised the cost of maintaining the military. This has led to ongoing national debates about the cost of the military and whether defense resources should go to technology or for troops. Industries have emerged to provide goods and services to the military. Proposals to cut defense spending often face opposition from these industries.

National Security Agencies

The September 11, 2001, attacks focused the attention of policy-makers on domestic security. Agencies with responsibility in this area had been dispersed throughout the federal government. They were now concentrated in the Department of Homeland Security under a single cabinet secretary. Although it took somewhat longer, intelligence-gathering agencies were placed under the administrative control of a director of national intelligence. Funding for domestic security and international intelligence gathering increased by approximately one-third.

Legislation passed in the months after September 11, 2001, also subjected U.S. citizens and permanent residents to greater levels of government scrutiny and to potential violations of civil rights. The Bush administration asserted (and the courts rejected) a position that suspected terrorists could be seized and held indefinitely, without charges.

The Judiciary

Of the three branches of federal government, the courts are the most poorly defined in the Constitution. Initially, it was unclear what check the courts had on other branches of government. Equally important, the courts were quite dependent on the president, who appointed judges, and on Congress, which approved the nomination of judges and set the jurisdictional authority of the courts.

In 1803, the Supreme Court established the foundation for a more substantial role in federal policy-making. It ruled in *Marbury v. Madison* that the courts inherently had the right to review the constitutionality of the laws. This ruling, though used rarely in the nineteenth century, gave the judiciary a central place in the system of **checks and balances**.

Even with the power of judicial review, the judicial branch remained weaker than the other branches. In addition to Congress's ability to establish court jurisdiction in nonconstitutional cases and the president's ability to fill the courts with people of his choosing, the courts have other weaknesses. They must rely on the executive branch to enforce their decisions. Enforcement proves particularly difficult when a court's rulings are not in line with public opinion, such as when the courts ruled that busing should be used as a tool to accomplish racial integration in the schools.

Beginning in the second half of the twentieth century, the federal courts gained power relative to the other branches of government. In part, this came from expanding the rules of standing so that groups as well as individuals could challenge laws, policies, or government actions and by maintaining longer jurisdiction over cases as a tool to establish limited enforcement abilities. The courts also gained relative power because of the expansion of federal regulatory policy. Unclear laws and regulations, often requiring technical expertise to implement, placed the courts at the center of many policy debates. The courts have also gained power because they became a venue for individuals and groups whose interests were neglected by the democratically elected institutions but who could make claims based on constitutional guarantees of civil rights or civil liberties. African Americans, for example, received favorable rulings from federal courts before Congress and the president responded to their demands. Since the 9/11 attacks, the executive branch and majorities in Congress showed that they were willing to limit individual rights in a search for collective security. Courts—including the Supreme Court—have been more cautious.

The power of the courts ultimately rests with their ability to persuade the citizenry that their procedures are fair and their judgments are based on the Constitution and the law. This may become more difficult in the future as the courts and particularly the Supreme Court have moved steadily to the ideological right. Analysis in 2010, at the time of the retirement of longtime Justice John Paul Stevens, demonstrated that each of the current nine justices is more conservative than his or

Marbury v. Madison

The 1803 U.S. Supreme Court ruling that the federal courts inherently had the authority to review the constitutionality of laws passed by Congress and signed by the president. The ruling, initially used sparingly, placed the courts centrally in the system of checks and balances.

checks and balances

A governmental system of divided authority in which coequal branches can restrain each other's actions. For example, the U.S. president must sign legislation passed by Congress for it to become law. If the president vetoes a bill, Congress can override that veto by a two-thirds vote of the Senate and the House of Representatives.

Supreme Court nominee Sonia Sotomayor prepares to testify before the Senate Judiciary Committee as part of her confirmation process.

AP Images/J. Scott Applewhite

her predecessor on the Court and that majority opinions have become more conservative, on average, than under any of the three previous chief justices. With the courts increasingly involved in contentious national issues, the Senate has taken its role in reviewing appointments more seriously and has slowed the confirmation of appointees, leaving some judicial circuits severely short of judges.

The steady increase in judicial power in the twentieth century should not obscure the fundamental weaknesses of the courts relative to the elected branches. The courts are more dependent on the elected branches than the elected branches are on them.

Subnational Government

State governments serve as an important part of government in the United States. Their responsibilities include providing services to people more directly than does the federal government. Most important among these is education, which has always been a state and local responsibility in the United States.

States and localities are able to experiment with new policies. If a policy fails in a single state, the cost is much lower than if the entire country had undertaken a new policy that eventually failed. Successes in one state, however, can be copied in others or nationally.

In addition to state governments, citizens pay taxes to, and receive services from, local governments that include counties, cities, and districts for special services such as water and fire protection, and townships. These local entities have a different relationship to the states, however, than do states to the federal government. The local entities are statutory creations of the state and can be altered or eliminated by the state (and are not a form of federalism).

Local governments provide many of the direct services that the citizenry receives from the government. Because states and localities have different resources (often based on local property taxes) and different visions of the responsibilities of government, people in the United States may receive vastly different versions of the same government service, depending simply on where they live.

The Policy-Making Process

Because of separation of powers and constitutional limits on each branch of government, the federal policy-making process has no clear starting or ending point. Instead, citizens and organized interests have multiple points of entry and can fight outcomes through multiple points of attack. Without centralization, policies often conflict with each other. The United States, for example, subsidizes tobacco cultivation but seeks to hamper tobacco companies from selling cigarettes through high taxes, health warnings, and limits on advertising. Federalism further complicates policy-making. Each state sets policy in many areas, and states often have contradictory policies. In sum, policy advocates have many venues in which to propose new policies or to change existing policies: congressional committees, individual members of Congress, executive-branch regulatory agencies, state governments, and, in some states, direct ballot initiatives.

With so many entrance points, there are equally many points at which policies can be blocked. Once Congress passes a law, executive-branch agencies must issue regulations to explain specifically how the law will be implemented. Subtle changes can be inserted as part of this process. On controversial issues, senior political appointees set policy for the writing of regulations.

Furthermore, people or interest groups that feel disadvantaged by the regulations can fight regulations in the courts. They also can contest the law itself, if they can find a way to claim that the law is unconstitutional or conflicts with another law or with state government responsibilities. Once a policy is in place, it can be opposed or undermined by creating a competing policy in another agency or at the state level.

The Constitution gives no guidance about the origins and outcomes of policy initiatives. The president must present an annual report to Congress on the state of the nation. This has evolved into an organized set of policy proposals. Without presidential leadership in policy-making, Congress partially filled the void. Enumerated powers in the Constitution direct Congress to take action in specific policy areas, such as establishing a post office or building public roads. Once Congress established committees to increase its efficiency (see Section 4), these committees offered forums for discussion of narrow policy. These committees, however, are not mandated in the Constitution and are changed to reflect the policy needs of each era. Thus, while presidents can propose policies (and implement them), only Congress has the ability to deliberate about policy and pass it into law.

Beginning in the 1970s some federal courts experimented with initiating policy as a way of maintaining jurisdiction in cases brought before them. These efforts, such as court-mandated control over state prison or mental health care systems, spurred much national controversy and caused the judiciary to decline in public opinion. Today, the courts are much more likely to block or reshape policies than to initiate them.

Without any clear starting point, individual citizens have great difficulty when they seek to advocate a new policy. Into this void have come extragovernmental institutions, some with narrow interests and some promoting collective interests.

Prominent or wealthy individuals or groups can get Congress's or the president's attention through campaign contributions and other types of influence.

Mediating institutions have also emerged to represent mass interests. Political parties organize citizen demands and channel them to political leaders. The parties balance the needs of various interests in society and come as close as any other group in society to presenting comprehensive policy proposals (often summarized in the parties' platforms). Group-based interests also organize to make narrow demands. In the twentieth century, as both federal and state governments began to implement more widespread distributive and redistributive policies, more organized interest groups appeared. These interest groups have become the dominant form of mediating institution in U.S. politics (see Section 4). Unlike political parties, however, interest groups represent only a single issue or group of narrowly related issues.

Where Do You Stand?

With the new role assumed by the United States among the globalized world of states after World War II, could the United States be led by the presidency of the nineteenth century envisioned in the Constitution?

Separation of powers and federalism impede the policy-making process in the United States relative to other nations. What constitutional changes would you propose to improve the policy-making process in the United States?

SECTION 4

REPRESENTATION AND PARTICIPATION

▽ Focus Questions

• How do Congress's constitutional powers and its organizational structure ensure that it is the most powerful branch of the U.S. government?

• Who votes and who doesn't in U.S. politics? Why?

The Legislature

Of the three branches in the federal government, the founders envisioned that Congress would be at the center and would be the most powerful. They concentrated the most important powers in it and were most explicit about its responsibilities. For most of the nation's history, their expectations for the powers of Congress have been met.

One of the most important compromises of the Constitutional Convention involved the structure of Congress. States with large populations wanted seats in the national legislature to be allocated based on population. Small states feared they would be at a disadvantage under this system and wanted each state to have equal representation. The compromise was a **bicameral** system with two houses, one allocated by population—the House of Representatives—and the other with equal representation for each state—the Senate. This compromise has remained largely uncontested for the past 225 years despite the growing gap in population between large and small states. The senatorial vote of each resident of Wyoming has sixty-six times the impact of each Californian.

The two legislative bodies are structured differently. The House has 435 members and is designed to be more responsive to the popular will. Terms are short (two years), and the districts are smaller than Senate seats except in the smallest states. The average House seat has approximately 716,000 constituents and will continue to grow. The Senate has 100 members and is designed to be more deliberative, with six-year, staggered terms. Although unlikely, it is possible every two years to vote out an entire House of Representatives; the Senate could see only one-third of its members unseated during any election year.

Membership in the U.S. House of Representatives is more diverse than the people who have held the presidency, although most members are white male Protestants. In the 112th Congress (2013–2015), approximately 19 percent of House members were women, 10 percent were African American, 7 percent were Latino, and 2 percent were Asian American. Most members, regardless of gender, race, or ethnicity, are highly educated professionals. Law is the most common profession. The Senate is less racially diverse but has a comparable share of women to the House: Two African Americans, three Latinos, two Asian Americans, and twenty women served in the Senate in 2014.

The two central powers of Congress are legislation and oversight. For a bill to become law, it must be passed in the same form by both the House and the Senate and signed by the president. Equally important, Congress has the ability to monitor the implementation of laws that it passes. Since it continues to control the appropriation of funds for programs each year, Congress can oversee programs being administered by the executive branch and shape their implementation through allocations of money or by rewriting the law.

Congress has organized itself to increase its efficiency. Discussion and debate take place primarily in committees and subcommittees. The committee system permits each member to specialize in specific areas of public policy. Committees are organized topically, and members often seek to serve on committees that are of particular interest to their constituencies—for instance, a member of Congress from a rural area may seek to serve on the Agriculture Committee. All members seek to serve on committees that have broad oversight of a wide range of government activities, such as the Appropriations Committee, through which all spending bills must pass. Specialization allows each member to have some influence while not requiring that she or he know the substance of all facets of government.

For a bill to become law, it must be reviewed by the committee and subcommittee that have responsibility for the substantive area that it covers. When a member proposes a bill, it goes to a committee based on its subject matter and usually never gets any further. In each session, relatively few bills receive hearings before a subcommittee or committee. The House and Senate leadership (the Speaker of the House, the Senate Majority Leader, and committee chairs) are central to deciding which bills receive hearings. If the bill receives support from the committee, it must then be debated by the body as a whole. In the House, this may never occur because that institution has another roadblock: the Rules Committee, which determines what can be debated on the floor and under what terms. Only in the Senate can debate be unlimited (although it can be limited by cloture, a vote of sixty senators to limit debate). These hierarchical structures strengthen the powers granted to the House and the Senate in the Constitution because they allow Congress to act efficiently and to use its powers to investigate federal programs, even though it does not administer them. As a result, Congress places itself at the center of the policy-making process. This specialization and hierarchy ensure that congressional leaders are more central to the design and oversight of policy than are members of European parliaments.

This tension between the constitutional powers of Congress and the national focus on the president as the national leader became evident in the federal government's response to the 9/11 attacks. Initially, President Bush shaped the public

bicameral

A legislative body with two houses, such as the U.S. Senate and the U.S. House of Representatives. Just as the U.S. Constitution divides responsibilities between the branches of the federal government and between the federal government and the states, it divides legislative responsibilities between the Senate and the House.

policy response. As Bush administration policies evolved and the response came to focus on structural changes in the federal government, however, Congress began to reassert its constitutional prerogatives. Congress also ensured that the National Commission on Terrorist Attacks on the United States, unofficially known as the 9/11 Commission, would be formed, funded, and given sufficient time to conduct its investigation and write its report. The commission documented executive-branch intelligence-gathering failures and provided the political pressure necessary to force the Bush administration to create a new federal official—the Director of National Intelligence—who would oversee most U.S. intelligence-gathering agencies.

Congressional oversight of presidential leadership in the U.S. response to September 11 and the wars in Afghanistan and Iraq demonstrate that Congress has not yielded as the president gained power. It passed legislation to undermine presidential power and, equally important, applied its authority to investigate federal programs to weaken the presidency. These investigations of presidents and their senior appointees weaken the connection between the presidency and the people and weaken not just the presidents as individuals, but also the presidency as an office.

Political Parties and the Party System

The roots of two-party politics can be found both in the nation's political culture and in the legal structures that govern elections. The Democrats can trace their origins to the 1800 election, while the Republicans first appeared in 1854. Despite the fact that today's parties have consistently competed against each other, the coalitions that support them (and which they, in turn, serve) have changed continually.

Today, the Republicans depend on a coalition of upper-income voters, social conservatives, small-business owners, residents of rural areas, and evangelical Christians. They receive more support from men than from women and are strongest in the South and the Mountain West.

The Republicans have tried to make inroads in minority communities but have been largely unsuccessful, with the exception of Cuban Americans and some Asian American groups (see Table 8.2). For Republicans to win Latino (or African American) votes on a wider scale, the party would have to be willing to alienate some core Republican constituencies.

The contemporary Democratic coalition includes urban populations, the elderly, racial and ethnic minorities, workers in export-oriented businesses, unionized labor, and, increasingly, working women. Suburban voters have increasingly joined the Democratic coalition. Today's Democrats are concentrated in the Northeast and on the West Coast. The Democrats have built a steady advantage among women voters.

Democratic partisanship grew steadily over the Bush years and declined slightly in the first Obama term. In 2014, Democrats made up 30 percent of the electorate, Republicans 23 percent, and Independents 45 percent. Although the Independents have seen the most growth over the past two decades, they tend to lean reliably toward one party or the other. When these "leaners" are accounted for, the Democrats maintain the advantage—roughly 47 percent to 40 percent. Generally, Democrats, who are more likely to be poor, less educated, and younger than Republican voters, are less likely to turn out on Election Day, particularly in "off-year" (nonpresidential) elections. After the 2012 election, the Republicans controlled governorships in twenty-nine states, and the Democrats controlled twenty-one. In 2014, the Republicans hold a majority of seats in the House of Representatives (234 to 199, with two vacancies). Democrats hold the majority in the Senate (55 to 45).

Table 8.2	**Democratic Party Share of Two-Party Vote, Presidential Elections 1992–2012**					
	1992 Percent	**1996 Percent**	**2000 Percent**	**2004 Percent**	**2008 Percent**	**2012 Percent**
Whites	49.4	48.3	43.8	41.4	43.9	39
Blacks	89.2	87.5	91.8	88.9	96.0	93
Hispanics	70.9	77.4	68.4	56.6	68.9	71
Asian Americans	36.0	47.3	56.8	56.0	63.9	73

Note: These calculations exclude votes for candidates other than Democratic and Republican candidates.
Source: Author's calculations based on *New York Times.* 2008. "Election Results 2008." http://elections.nytimes.com/2008/results/president/national-exit-polls.html (accessed February 15, 2010) and *New York Times.* 2012. "President Exit Polls." http://elections.nytimes.com/2012/results/president/exit-polls?action=click&module=Search&region=searchResults%230&version=&url=http%3A%2F%2Fquery.nytimes.com%2Fsearch%2Fsitesearch%2F%23%2F2012%2Belection%2Bpoll%2F (accessed March 9, 2014).

These majorities will likely be in flux for the next several elections. The electorate is much more evenly divided than the U.S. House or the governorships suggest; both saw Democratic gains in 2006, 2008, and 2012 and gains for the Republicans in 2010. Of the two parties, the Republicans have a more fragile coalition. Beginning in the 1990s, internal conflicts grew in the Republican Party. Moral conservatives and fiscal conservatives each wanted the party to focus on their interests and jettison the others' issues as a way of expanding the party's base of support. In 2010, this division manifested itself in the emergence of the Tea Party activists who sought to move the Republican Party to the right out of concerns that the federal government was spending too much and usurping powers that should be held by the states (see U.S. Connection: The Tea Party).

These party divisions lead to speculation that new parties might emerge. But the political culture of the United States dampens the likelihood that a faction of one of the parties will break off and form a party that competes in election after election. Instead, two coalitional parties are the norm, an unusual pattern among advanced democracies.

Electoral law reinforces this situation. Most U.S. elections are conducted under a single-member-plurality election system in district-based elections. Single-member district-based elections reward coalitional parties and diminish opportunities for single-issue parties or narrowly focused parties, such as the Green Party or the Tea Party, should it break off from the Republican Party. Broad coalitional parties can contest seats in election after election, while smaller parties in the United States are likely to dissolve after several defeats.

There are more than 600,000 elected offices in the United States. To compete regularly in even a small percentage of these, a party must have a national presence and a national infrastructure. Most third parties fail long before they are able to compete in more than a few hundred races.

Finally, the heterogeneity of the U.S. population and the range of regional needs and interests rewards parties that can form coalitions prior to elections, as does a system with just two political parties. The Constitution-driven inefficiency of the U.S. government

U.S. CONNECTION

The Tea Party

The 2010 U.S. elections saw the emergence of a new political movement—the Tea Party. Despite its name, it is a social movement not a party, and largely organizes within the Republican Party. Tea Party activism emerged in response to anger in the electorate over federal government spending and growing federal budget deficits, to Federal Reserve actions to support the banking sector and to keep interest rates low, and to the enactment of the ACA. Tea Party activism is highly decentralized, so there is no single Tea Party, and it rejects centralized leadership.

Various Tea Party organizations and chapters endorsed candidates for the House of Representatives and Senate in the 2010, 2012, and 2014 elections. In several cases, Tea Party candidates defeated the preferred candidates of Republican leaders in party primaries. Although the Tea Party saw some major victories in the U.S. House of Representatives, several Tea Party candidates who defeated establishment Republicans in primaries went on to defeat in the general election. Had the mainstream Republicans been their party's candidate in 2010 or 2012, it is likely that they would have won the general election. Had all won, Republicans would have controlled the Senate in 2011 and 2013.

Today's Tea Party reflects the latest in a long line of U.S. populist movements that appear in eras when the national government is perceived to be distant and out of touch. Over time, its energy will likely dissipate. Its rejection of formal organization and leadership structures make it difficult to sustain the high levels of citizen involvement seen in the period leading up to the 2010 and 2012 elections. That said, it will undoubtedly be a force in the 2014 and 2016 elections. Candidates for the 2016 Republican presidential nomination will need to win support from the activists who have been mobilized by the Tea Party movement and local Tea Party members will challenge incumbent moderate Republicans in party primaries. Whether or not the Tea Party survives as an independent movement, its organizing principles of reducing the size and scope of the federal government will likely be part of U.S. political debates for the foreseeable future.

MAKING CONNECTIONS What groups in the U.S. electorate does the Tea Party movement speak to and mobilize? Are these groups likely to be a larger or smaller share of the overall electorate twenty years from now?

would become all the more dramatic if multiple parties (rather than two that must, by their nature, be coalitions) were competing in legislatures to shape outcomes.

Elections

As an example of its commitment to democratic norms, the United States points to the frequency of elections and the range of offices filled through elections. Unlike the case in parliamentary systems, these elections are conducted on a regular schedule: presidential elections every four years, Senate elections every six years, House of Representatives elections every two years. States and localities set the terms of state and local offices, but almost all have fixed terms.

Fundamental to understanding U.S. elections is federalism. States set the rules for conducting elections and for who can participate and how votes are counted. When the country was founded, this authority was almost complete, since the Constitution said little about elections. At the country's founding, most states limited electoral participation to white male landholders. By the 1830s, many states had eliminated the property-holding requirement, in part in response to the emergence of competitive political parties that sought to build membership.

Further expansion of the U.S. electorate required the intervention of the federal government and amendment of the Constitution to reduce state authority in determining voter eligibility. The first of the efforts to nationalize electoral rules was initially a failure. This was the effort to extend the franchise to African Americans after the Civil

War through the Fourteenth and Fifteenth Amendments. More successful was the Nineteenth Amendment, ratified in 1920, which extended the vote to women.[9] The Civil War amendments finally had an impact with the passage of the Voting Rights Act (VRA) in 1965, which secured African Americans access to the ballot box. In 1975, Congress extended the VRA to other ethnic and racial groups who had previously seen their right to vote abridged because of their origin or ancestry—Hispanics, Asian Americans, Native Americans, and Alaskan Natives. In 1971, the Twenty-Sixth Amendment gave the vote to all citizens aged eighteen and older.

States continue to regulate individual participation in elections through their control of voter registration. In most advanced democracies, the national government is responsible for voter registration rather than the individual. Individual registration prescreens potential voters to ensure they meet the state's requirements for voting: residence in the jurisdiction for a set amount of time and, in many states, the absence of felony convictions. While this may appear minimal and necessary to prevent voter fraud such as an individual's voting multiple times in the same election, the requirement to register in advance of the election prevents many from being able to vote.[10]

There is a second consequence of federalism on U.S. elections: The responsibility for holding elections, deciding which nonfederal offices are filled through elections, and determining how long nonfederal officeholders will serve before again having to be elected is the responsibility of the states and, if the states delegate the power, to localities. Thus, a local office that is elected in one state could be an appointed office in another. Terms for state and local offices, such as governors, vary. Elections are held at different points throughout the year. Finally, federalism shapes elections by delegating to the states responsibilities for determining how votes are collected and how they are counted, even in elections to national office.

What are the consequences of this federalist system of elections? At a minimum, it leads to confusion and burnout among potential voters. Many voters are unaware of elections that are not held on the same schedule as national elections. Others who are aware become overloaded with electoral responsibilities in jurisdictions that have frequent elections and so choose not to vote in local races.

One result of this decentralized system with a legacy of group-based exclusion is that increasing numbers of citizens do not vote. In the late 1800s, for example, turnout in national elections exceeded 80 percent of those eligible to vote, and the poor participated at rates comparable to the rich. By 1996, turnout in the presidential election dropped below 50 percent (returning to 62 percent in 2012). In state and local races, turnouts in the range of 10 to 20 percent are the norm. Perhaps more important, turnout varies dramatically among different groups in society. The poor are less likely to vote than the rich, the young less likely than the old, and the less educated less likely than the more educated.[11] Because blacks and Hispanics are more likely to be young, poor, and have lower levels of formal education, they are less likely to vote than are whites. Hence, political institutions are less likely to hear their demands and respond to their needs.

These class- and age-driven differences in participation are not entirely the result of federalism and variation in the rules for individual participation and the conduct of elections. Declining party competitiveness

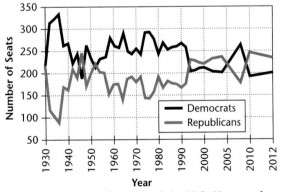

FIGURE 8.5 Party Control of the U.S. House of Representatives, 1930–2012

Source: U.S. House of Representatives, Office of the Clerk. 2013. "Party Divisions of the House of Representatives (1789 to Present)." http://clerk.house.gov/art_history /house_history/partyDiv.html (accessed March 9, 2014).

at the state level also plays a role. Nevertheless, the steady elimination of formal group-based exclusion has been replaced by the marginalization of the majority of some groups, such as Asian Americans and Hispanics. The United States has yet to live up to its democratic ideals.

This declining participation should not obscure the dramatic changes in leadership and issues addressed that result from elections (see Figure 8.5). In 2006, the Democrats regained control of the Senate and House of Representatives and elected the first woman to serve as Speaker of the House (Nancy Pelosi). In 2010, the Republicans gained control of the House as well as many governorships and state house majorities. These Republican majorities in many state governments allowed them to guide redistricting that determined congressional and state legislative seats for the remainder of the decade.

Political Culture, Citizenship, and Identity

The United States is a large country with distinct regional cultures, ongoing immigration leading to distinct languages and cultures, class divisions, and a history of denying many Americans their civil rights. Despite these cleavages, the United States has maintained almost from its first days a set of core political values that has served to unify the majority of the citizenry. These values are liberty, equality, and democracy.

Liberty, as it is used in discussions of U.S. political culture, refers to liberty from restrictions imposed by government. A tangible form of this notion of liberty appears in the Bill of Rights, which provides for the rights of free speech, free assembly, free practice of religion, and the absence of cruel and unusual punishment. Support for liberty takes a second form: support for economic liberty and free enterprise. Property and contract rights are protected at several places in the Constitution. Furthermore, Congress is empowered to regulate commerce.

Clearly, these liberties are not mutually exclusive. But protections of the Bill of Rights often conflict with each other: Economic liberties reward some in the society at the cost of economic opportunities for others. Nevertheless, the idea that citizens should be free to pursue their beliefs and their economic objectives with only limited government interference has been a unifying element in U.S. political culture.

Equality is the second unifying American political value. In the Declaration of Independence, it is "self-evident" that "all men are created equal." At various times in the nation's history, women, Native Americans, African Americans, Mexican Americans, Chinese Americans, Japanese Americans, and naturalized citizens have been excluded from membership in the polity and, consequently, from access to this equality. But each of the excluded groups, such as African Americans during the civil rights movement, used the widespread belief in equality to organize and demand that the United States live up to its ideals.

It is important to observe what this belief in equality is not. The equality that has long been sought is equality of opportunity, not equality of result, such as that sought in the communist states. There is support for the notion that people should have an equal opportunity to compete for economic rewards, not that they should end up at the same point.

The final unifying value is representative democracy. Throughout the nation's history, there has been a belief that government is legitimate only to the degree that it reflects the popular will. As with the notion of equality, the pool of citizens whose voices should be heard has changed over time, from white male property holders at

"*Warning: offer void in some states.*"

State regulation of marriage ensures that same-sex marriage rulings that apply to one state do not immediately translate into a national policy recognizing same-sex marriage.

Christopher Weyant The New Yorker Collection/The Cartoon Bank

the time of the founding to most citizen adults today (convicted felons are excluded from the franchise in many states).

The United States has never had a national religion and, at times in the nation's history, conflicts between Protestants and Catholics have been divisive. In contemporary society, division over religion is more between those for whom religion provides routine guidance in politics and social interactions and those for whom religion is a private matter that does not shape political activities.

In 2013, 50 percent of U.S. adults were Protestant, 24 percent were Roman Catholic, and 2 percent were Jewish or Mormon. Less than 1 percent were Muslim. Nearly 17 percent of U.S. adults reported no religious preference. Despite the fact that there is no national religion in the United States, religion plays a more central role in U.S. politics than it does in the politics of European democracies. Moral issues—such as abortion and LGBTQ rights—guide the votes of a sizeable minority of the population. Many elected leaders are overt in their religiosity to a degree that would not be acceptable in European politics (and would not have been in U.S. politics as recently as thirty years ago).

Values are very much at the heart of contemporary political debates. Leaders have marshaled these values throughout the nation's history to reduce potential cleavages in U.S. society. Since the United States cannot look to a common ethnicity of its people (as, for example, Germany can), to a sovereign with a historical tie to the citizenry (as in a monarchy like the United Kingdom), or to a purported common religion or ideology among its citizens (as does Iran or Cuba), the belief in these values has been used to unify the diverse peoples of the United States.[12]

Interest Groups, Social Movements, and Protest

In the United States, political participation has long included activities other than elections and party politics. In the nation's story about its origins, protest proves central; the Revolution was spurred by acts of civil disobedience such as the Boston Tea Party. Similarly, protest and social movements repeatedly forced the United States to live up to its democratic ideals. From the woman's suffrage movement of the nineteenth century to the civil rights movement of the 1950s and 1960s, people defined as being outside the democratic community organized to demand that they be included.

These protest movements have also been able to tap the willingness of Americans to become involved in collective action. This voluntarism and civic involvement have long been identified as stronger in the U.S. democracy than in other advanced democracies.

In recent years, however, observers of U.S. politics have noted a decline in civic involvement, a decline that has also appeared in the other advanced democracies. Although social movements remain, they have become much more driven by elites than were their predecessors. Voluntarism and civic involvement have declined, and the likelihood of participation has followed the patterns of voting, with the more educated, wealthier, and older generally more likely to volunteer and be civically engaged.[13] This decline in civic involvement in U.S. politics has serious long-term implications for society. As civic involvement declines, Americans talk about politics less with their peers and have a lessened sense that they can shape political outcomes. They are less likely to be part of networks that allow for collective political action. Political scientist Robert Putnam has identified this as the "bowling alone" phenomenon in which social capital—the networks of relationships with norms of behavior, trust, and cooperation that increase the likelihood that society will function effectively—is in decline.[14] Americans traditionally had many social venues, such as bowling leagues, where they had an outlet to talk about politics and, potentially, to organize when they were frustrated with political outcomes. There are fewer of these today (people are busier, have more job responsibilities, and spend more time watching television). The decline in civic engagement has led to reduced political efficacy and greater frustration with the course of politics.

Protest, of course, remains an option for people who feel neglected by the political order. In 2006, for example, as many as 5 million immigrants, their families, and their supporters took to the streets to protest anti-immigrant legislation in the U.S. House of Representatives. Mass protests such as these, however, are very much the exception. Despite the fact that many in the United States oppose immigration at current levels, the social movement organizations that have formed to promote this cause—most notably the Minuteman organization—have rarely been able to generate much mass participation. National polling indicates that for the population as a whole—who neither joined the street protests nor the militias—immigration is an area of continuing concern. Each of the last five Congresses has sought to reform immigration in a comprehensive manner, but has failed, suggesting that neither the street protests, nor the anti-immigrant militias were of sufficient gravity or organization to pressure Congress into action on immigration.

The twentieth century saw the rise of a new form of organized political activity: interest groups. Like political parties and candidates for office, these organizations try to influence the outcome of public policy by influencing policy-makers. They differ, however, in that they are usually organized to influence a single issue or a tightly related group of issues. Also unlike social movements, they rely on money and professional staff rather than on committed volunteers. Interest groups increased in prominence as the federal and state governments increasingly implemented distributive and redistributive policies. Beginning in the 1970s, a specialized form of interest group, the **political action committee (PAC)**, appeared to evade restrictions on corporations and organized labor to make financial contributions to political candidates and political parties.

Interest groups are so numerous in U.S. politics that it is not possible to even venture a guess as to their number. They include national organizations, such as the National Rifle Association, as well as local groups, such as associations of library patrons who seek to influence city council appropriations. They include mass organizations, such as the American Association of Retired Persons, and very narrow interests, such as oil producers seeking to defend tax protections for their industry.

Although interest groups and PACs are now much more common than social movements in U.S. politics, they do not replace one key function traditionally fulfilled by the social movements, which seek to establish accountability between citizens and government. Interest groups by definition protect the needs of a cohesive group in the society and demand that government allocate resources in a way that benefits the interests of that group. They usually include as members people who already receive rewards from government or are seeking new benefits. Their membership, then, tends to include more socially, financially, and educationally advantaged members of U.S. society. There is no place in the network of interest groups for individuals who are outside the democratic community or whose voices are ignored by the polity. The key role that social movements and protest have played in U.S. politics is being replaced by a more elite and more government-focused form of political organization.

political action committee (PAC)

A narrow form of interest group that seeks to influence policy by making contributions to candidates and parties in U.S. politics.

The Political Impact of Technology

An open question for scholars of U.S. politics is the degree to which technology, and particularly social media, can serve as a resource to share political information and to mobilize those who are not fully engaged in civic and political life, in other words to counter the growing bowling alone phenomenon. Social media ensure that most Americans are in more frequent contact with friends, family, and colleagues than they have been in the recent past. Just as a bowling league did once, this contact can allow for the easy transfer of political information and the subtle (and, sometimes, not so subtle) encouragement to participate.

Candidates, parties, and interest groups are certainly aware of technology's potential value in generating more mass engagement. The 2008 and 2012 Obama campaigns, for example, focused an unprecedented effort on using social media, both in the party primaries and the general election. Analysts credit these efforts with turning out higher than expected turnout from young voters and for the high levels of support they gave to Obama. Few candidates (or parties or interest groups) can delicate the level of resources and cutting-edge technologies that the Obama campaign did. Future campaigns (and social movement activism and interest group activity) will find new strategies—and probably more effective strategies—to use technology to reach potential supporters, but this process will generally be slower than the development of new communications technologies.

Technology, however, should not be seen as a panacea for reinvigorating community engagement in U.S. civic and political life. Not all in society have equal access to technologies and some of the gaps in access to technology overlap with the groups least likely to participate in politics. Ultimately, technology is a means to communicate and it is up to leaders to develop a message that will resonate with potential supporters, however that message is delivered.

Where Do You Stand?

The nation's founders wanted the U.S. Congress at the center of government and the policy-making process. Would you give it the same powers and responsibilities if you were writing the Constitution today? Why or why not?

Should voting in U.S. national elections be made mandatory?

SECTION 5

UNITED STATES POLITICS IN TRANSITION

⑦ Focus Questions

- In what ways can effective mediating institutions overcome the roadblocks to governance built into the U.S. Constitution?

- How has the U.S. role in global governance and global institutions changed in the period since World War II?

The election of Barack Obama signaled a significant transition for U.S. electoral politics. Had only non-Hispanic whites voted, John McCain and Mitt Romney would have easily won the presidency. Obama's victories should not, however, obscure the fact that the U.S. electorate has a dramatically lower share of minority participants than does the population as a whole. Latinos, for example, made up 17 percent of the population in 2012, but just 8 percent of the electorate; Asian Americans made up 5 percent of the population and 3 percent of the electorate.

Without question, some of these gaps will narrow over time. Minority populations tend to be younger, for example, than non-Hispanic whites, and voting increases with age. The minority voting gap, nevertheless, presents an ongoing challenge for the American democracy, one that will likely grow in the short term. The gap is even greater in the states with large minority populations. At the state level, the pool of regular voters is dominated by older upper-income white voters; this population is more resistant to pay for the services needed by many of the minority nonvoters, such as K–12 education, social services, and adult education. Candidates and office holders, however, often speak to the needs of voters over the societal need to ensure that all Americans have access to the resources they need to succeed.

Political Challenges and Changing Agendas

The United States today faces some familiar and some new challenges that result from the nation's new place in the world of states. Primary among the continuing challenges is the need to live up to its own definition of the democratic idea and to balance this goal of representative government elected through mass participation with the divergent economic outcomes that result from its laissez-faire approach to governing the economy. The United States must address these challenges with a system of government that was designed to impede the actions of government and a citizenry that expects much of government but frequently does not trust it to serve popular needs.

The United States has assumed a relatively new role and set of responsibilities in the world of states, at least new as far as the past seventy years; U.S. governing institutions must now respond not just to their own people, but more broadly to an international political order that is increasingly interconnected and seeks rapid responses to international security, political, and economic crises. The institutional arrangements of U.S. government hamper quick responses and increase the likelihood of parochial responses that the rest of the world can hear as isolationism or unilateralism. These institutional arrangements are reinforced by a citizenry that for the most part cares little about foreign policy (except when war threatens), expects quick and often painless solutions to international crises, and has little respect, and sometimes open animosity, for multinational political and economic institutions such as the UN and the IMF. Despite the citizenry's continued focus on domestic concerns, U.S. jobs and national economic well-being are increasingly connected to international markets and to the willingness of governments and individuals to buy U.S. bonds. Over time, many in the United States may come to resent this economic integration.

Economics is not the only role that the United States plays in the world of states, as has been brought home in the period since the 9/11 attacks. Although the citizenry has demonstrated a willingness to pay the financial cost of a global military, it has been much less willing to sacrifice lives. As a result, U.S. leaders must continually balance their military objectives and responsibilities to allies and international organizations with an inability to commit U.S. forces to conflicts that might lead to substantial casualties.

This tension between U.S. reliance on a global economic order among developed nations and a willingness to pursue a unilateral military and defense policy appeared repeatedly after the 9/11 attacks. The initial approach of national leaders as well as the citizenry was to pursue military actions against Afghanistan and Iraq alone if necessary. Although alliances formed for each military engagement, this threat of unilateral action made the building of long-term multilateral alliances all the more difficult.

In addition to its economic and military roles, the United States exports its culture and language throughout the world. This process contributes to economic development in the United States; equally important, it places the United States at the center of an increasingly homogenizing international culture. But this process also creates hostility in countries that want to defend their national and local cultures.

The substantial changes in the U.S. connections to the world of states have not been matched by equally dramatic changes in the U.S. role in governing the economy. Laissez-faire governance continues. The United States tolerates income and wealth disparities greater than those of other advanced democracies. Business is less regulated and less taxed in the United States than in other democracies. Few in the polity contest this system of economic regulation.

Since the Great Depression, the United States has seen an expansion of redistributive programs to assist the poor. In the period of divided government, however, the United States has reduced its commitment to assisting the poor and has established time limits for any individual to collect benefits. It seems highly unlikely that the United States will develop targeted programs to assist citizens in need that compare to those of other advanced democracies.

Distributive programs targeted to the middle class, such as Social Security, Medicare, and college student loans, have also been implemented in the twentieth century. These have much more support among voters and are harder to undermine, even if they challenge traditional laissez-faire approaches. The costs of these programs, however, are putting an increasing long-term burden on the federal budget and, because of deficit spending, on the national economy. There is little political will to deal with these long-term costs. Divided government, with routinely shifting Democratic and Republican majorities, adds to this complexity; each party must treat each election as the opportunity to reenter the majority.

The U.S. government faces a challenge to its sense of its own democratic idea that is more dramatic than that faced by other advanced democracies. The 62 percent of the electorate who turned out in 2012 represented a slight decline from 2008. Turnout in non–presidential-year elections is even lower—approximately 42 percent in 2010. Participation is not spread evenly across the population: older, more affluent, and more educated citizens are much more likely to vote than are the young, the less educated, and the poor. Elected representatives are receiving less guidance from a narrower subset of the people.

The breadth of nonelectoral politics is also narrowing. Previous study of the United States found rich networks of community-based organizations, voluntary organizations, and other forms of nonelectoral political activity. Community politics in the United States, however, began to decline in the 1950s (roughly when electoral turnout began to decline) and appears to be at record lows today.

The politics of collective identities has always been central to U.S. politics because the country has been a recipient of large numbers of immigrants through much of its history. Each wave of immigrants has differed from its predecessors in terms of culture and religion. These differences forced the country to redefine itself in order to live up to its democratic idea. The "old" group of each era also perceived the "new" group as a threat to the political values of the nation. Today, Asian and Hispanic immigrants are seen as a challenge by the descendants of European immigrants.

The United States has experienced a long period of sustained high levels of immigration since 1965. The current period of high immigration has seen higher levels of overall immigration than the previous period of sustained high immigration (beginning after the Civil War and extending to the 1920s). Many in Congress today are proposing legislation to further deter undocumented migration, but there have been few proposals to reduce the opportunities for legal immigration.

Without strong political parties, mediating institutions, and nonelectoral community politics, the political integration of these immigrants and their children may stall. The preliminary evidence is that naturalization rates are increasing, but that naturalized citizens vote and participate in other forms of politics at lower levels than comparably situated U.S.-born citizens. If these patterns continue, the United States faces a new risk: Contemporary immigrants and their children may not be represented in the political order, even when these immigrants become U.S. citizens.

In the past, institutional arrangements and mediating institutions could partly overcome the weaknesses of the U.S. constitutional system. Congress dominated the executive until the New Deal era, after which the president dominated Congress until Watergate. This institutional dominance reflected the framers' intent through the Great Depression and after, at least in terms of the dominance of one branch. It is unclear that the framers envisioned a system where two, and occasionally all three, branches of government would compete for dominance and where the Congress and the presidency would be routinely controlled by different political parties.

Mediating institutions once played a role that they cannot tackle today. Once the political parties formed as mass institutions in the 1830s, they served a necessary role in unifying popular opinion and forcing elite compromise. Today, parties are in decline and have been replaced by a distinct type of mediating institution that does not seek compromise across issues and instead promotes narrow interests. Interest groups connect the citizenry to political institutions, but they only advance a narrow agenda.

The United States faces the same challenges it has always faced, and it is still limited by a governing system that seeks to inhibit government activity. In the past, it has overcome these challenges when citizens participated actively, often working through mediating institutions and mobilizing new groups to active political participation. With citizen participation becoming more selective and mediating institutions less broadly based, the United States will have trouble facing challenges. Because of our central position in the world economy, if we cannot meet our challenges, the whole world will suffer with us.

Youth Politics and the Generational Divide

Increasingly, the group asked to resolve these tensions in American governance, define the place of the United States in the world, and pay for the long-term costs of underfunded social welfare programs for the elderly are today's young adults and those who are not yet of voting age. This youth population is a very different population along many dimensions than today's likely voters. The under-30 population in the United States is much more likely to be non-white and more likely to be either an immigrant or the child of an immigrant. They are much less likely to live in rural areas than is today's electorate and (at least for those who are in their 20s) are likely to have higher levels of formal education. Perhaps most troubling for a nation like the United States that premises its legitimacy on the democratic idea, the youth population has a high share of long-term unauthorized immigrants who have no way to adjust their immigration status (and only limited connections to their countries of birth).

The differences between today's youth population and older members of U.S. society are not simply compositional. Today's young adults have come of age in an era of sustained economic uncertainty and geopolitical change. They have grown up in a world in which the United States was attacked on September 11, 2001; the threat of global terror has shaped their understandings of safety and the role of government in their lives. Their likely future participatory and partisan trajectories and their understandings of the U.S. role in the world are not yet fully formed (particularly for those under 18). It is safe to say that based on composition and experiences alone, however, that they will be very different from today's voters and leaders in terms of the issues that shape their connection to politics and their expectations for what government can realistically deliver.

Ultimately, the position of today's youth in tomorrow's politics will depend on the degree to which they organize, that political institutions mobilize them, and they feel that government is responsive to their needs. Youth are probably most affected by the bowling alone phenomenon, so they have lower than average rates of civic and electoral participation. The Obama campaigns made clear than youth can be better mobilized. Even without specific mobilization, today's youth will likely follow the paths of previous generations and increase their civic and political engagement as they age. The incentive for institutions to mobilize today's youth will only increase in the future as today's regular participants die off. While the nearly even partisan divide impedes governance, it creates a huge incentive to educate the citizenry and mobilize supporters. Young adults already benefit from this environment and, so far at least, have served as a resource for the Democrats. Finally, today's youth need to feel a sense of political efficacy, that government is responsive to them. Evidence suggests that young adults are somewhat less efficacious, but they share the American values discussed here and will increasingly want to have their voices heard as they and their families come to seek more from government in order to thrive in U.S. society.

United States Politics in Comparative Perspective

From the perspective of the study of comparative politics, the United States may well remain an enigma. Its size, wealth, unique experiences with immigration, history of political isolation from the world, and reliance on separation of powers and federalism do not have clear parallels among other advanced democracies. This distinctness comes through perhaps most clearly in the way the United States engages its international political responsibilities. While the president has traditionally directed the scope of U.S. foreign policy, Congress, as it reasserts power relative to the president, will likely play an increasing role. Members of Congress, who represent narrow geographic districts and are more directly connected to mass interests, are less likely to take an internationalist perspective than the president does. When Congress speaks on international issues, it is often with multiple voices, including some that oppose U.S. involvement in multilateral organizations. This conflict over control and direction of foreign policy has increased since the end of the Cold War.

The relationship of the United States to Cuba offers an example. Since the Cuban revolution (1959), the United States has not recognized Cuba and has imposed economic sanctions in an effort to remove Fidel and, now, Raul Castro from power and to encourage economic reforms. Increasingly, however, interests in the United States across the ideological spectrum (agricultural producers, recent Cuban émigrés, the travel and tourism industry, and liberals who never supported the sanctions) have sought to expand opportunities for trade with Cuba. These efforts, however, have been effectively blocked by Cuban American leaders, who raise the prospect of Cuban American voters fleeing a candidate who supports a change in policy, and by Cuban American members of Congress who use leadership positions to slow policy change. In the 112th Congress (2011–2013), Cuban American Ileana Ros-Lehtinen chaired the U.S. House Foreign Affairs Committee. Her position on the committee and in the Republican leadership blocked any change in U.S. economic sanctions on Cuba.

The impact of the constitutionally mandated structural and institutional weaknesses of U.S. government is not limited to the American people. The United States plays a dominant role in the world economy, as well as a central political role in international organizations. Thus, the inefficiencies and multiple entry points into U.S. policy-making shape the ability of the United States to respond to crises and develop coherent long-term policies in conjunction with its allies. In 1998, for example, as the world economy declined, the president, with the support of the chair of the Federal Reserve, proposed that the United States increase its contribution to the IMF by $18 billion. Congress initially balked at this request for several reasons, none of which were apparent to the U.S. allies. While the power of intransigence and horse trading makes sense to analysts of U.S. politics, analysts abroad cannot so easily understand the seeming failure of the United States to act in a time of crisis. Eventually Congress passed the added IMF appropriation.

In sum, despite its central role in the international economic system and in multilateral organizations, the United States often remains reluctant to embrace fully the international system that it helped shape. This hesitancy appears despite the active role of U.S. economic interests abroad and the importance of international trade to the U.S. economy. The United States does not hesitate to impose its will abroad when it perceives its security threatened, or when it perceives that the rules made by the international organizations undermine its economic or political interests. Thus, despite its central role in the world of states, the United States is sometimes a hesitant leader. The post–9/11 world makes this a much more difficult position to sustain. The challenge of the contemporary era is not states—as it was in the Cold War era—but instead international non–state-based networks. These cannot so easily be controlled through economic dominance and multilateral political alliances. As the United States faces the new challenges of a post–9/11 world, it must again reexamine the degree to which it is willing to act unilaterally and to pay the price for global concern about its occasional unilateralism.

Where Do You Stand?

Thinking about likely changes to demographic composition of the United States and the electorate over the next fifty years, do you expect the United States to have more or less engagement in the globalized world of states in the future? Why?

Should the United States rely on its geographic isolation and economic power to reduce its leadership role in the multilateral organizations that it helped create after World War II?

Chapter Summary

The U.S. democratic model remains a powerful force in the world of nations. It has survived for over two centuries and has adapted to the pressures of an increasingly globalized world. It faces the ongoing challenge of meeting the demands of its citizens and other nations with a system of governance designed over two centuries ago to limit government and to set the institutions of government against each other. Reinforcing this challenge is the stark partisan division in the populace that has emerged over the past twenty years. This division came to a head in the 2013 federal government shutdown.

Mass organization can significantly change the focus and direction of government. In recent elections, however, coalitions on the left (2008) and on the right (2010) have emerged victorious each offering a vision of change that resonates with and mobilizes different segments of

the electorate. The constitutional system may slow the influence of this mass mobilization on policy-making, but ensures that the citizenry's voice will be heard every two years and that governing institutions will change to reflect changing demands among voters and other organized interests in U.S. society.

This internal debate over the size and scope of the U.S. government presents an ongoing challenge for the globalized world of states. The long-term health of the U.S. economy (and consequently U.S. society) requires the health of the global economy. Frequent changes in the leadership role that the United States is willing to play in the world and its willingness to work with multinational institutions that it created make it harder in the long run for the United States to maintain the role of a global leader that it has occupied since the end of World War II.

Key Terms

Articles of Confederation	Declaration of Independence	free market
bicameral	distributive policies	interest groups
Bill of Rights	Federal Reserve Board	iron triangle relationships
checks and balances	federalism	manifest destiny

Marbury v. Madison	redistributive policies	single-member-plurality (SMP)
police powers	regulations	electoral system
political action committee (PAC)	separation of powers	social security
property taxes		

Suggested Readings

Amar, Akhil Reed. *The Bill of Rights: Creation and Reconstruction.* New Haven, CT: Yale University Press, 1998.

Dawson, Michael C. *Black Visions: The Roots of Contemporary African-American Political Ideologies.* Chicago: University of Chicago Press, 2002.

Deering, Christopher J., and Steven S. Smith. *Committees in Congress,* 3rd ed. Washington, DC: Congressional Quarterly Books, 1997.

The Federalist Papers. Edited by Clinton Rossiter. New York, Mentor, 1961.

Hartz, Louis. *The Liberal Tradition in America.* New York: Harvest/HBJ, 1955.

Judis, John B., and Ruy Teixeira. *The Emerging Democratic Majority.* New York: Scribner, 2002.

Kupchan, Charles. *The End of the American Era: U.S. Foreign Policy and the Geopolitics of the Twenty-First Century.* New York: Knopf, 2002.

Verba, Sidney, Kay Lehman Schlozman, and Henry Brady. *Voice and Equality: Civic Voluntarism in American Politics.* Cambridge: Harvard University Press, 1995.

Wilson, Woodrow. *Congressional Government: A Study in American Politics.* Baltimore: Johns Hopkins University Press, 1885.

Zolberg, Aristide. *A Nation by Design: Immigration Policy in the Fashioning of America.* Cambridge: Harvard University Press, 2006.

Suggested Websites

The 9/11 Commission Report
http://www.gpoaccess.gov/911/index.html

Find Law—Cases and Codes: U.S. Constitution
findlaw.com/casecode/constitution/

New York Times
www.nytimes.com

Thomas—Legislative Information from the Library of Congress
thomas.loc.gov

U.S. Census Bureau
www.census.gov

White House
www.whitehouse.gov

9 Brazil

Alfred P. Montero

Official Name: Federative Republic of Brazil (Republica Federativa do Brasil)

Location: Eastern South America

Capital City: Brasília

Population (2013): 202.7 million

Size: 8,511,965 sq. km.; slightly smaller than the United States

1822
Dom Pedro I declares himself emperor of Brazil, peacefully ending three hundred years of Portuguese colonial rule.

1888
Abolition of slavery

1930
Getúlio Vargas gains power after a coup led by military and political leaders. His period of dictatorship (1937–1945) is known as the New State.

1950
Vargas is elected president. Scandals precipitate his suicide in 1954.

1960
Jânio Quadros becomes president.

| 1700 | 1800 | 1850 | 1900 | 1930 | 1950 | 1960 |

1824
Constitution drafted

1891
A new constitution establishes a directly elected president.

1889
Dom Pedro II, who assumed throne in 1840, is forced into exile; landowning elites establish an oligarchical republic.

1945
Vargas calls for general elections. General Eurico Dutra of the Social Democratic Party wins.

1956
Juscelino Kubitschek becomes president.

SECTION 1
THE MAKING OF THE MODERN BRAZILIAN STATE

Focus Questions

- How has the authority of the national government varied over the history of Brazil from independence to the present?

- In what major ways has Brazilian democracy been limited since independence?

Politics in Action

Four years after the International Olympic Committee's (IOC) decision to award Rio de Janeiro the 2016 Summer Games and a year before Brazil prepared to host the 2014 World Cup of Football (Soccer), massive street protests galvanized world attention on the streets of major Brazilian cities. The protestors, many of them young and college educated, fiercely criticized the actual and projected costs of hosting these international events. They contrasted the billions of dollars spent on soccer stadiums with the meager funds spent on glaring needs in public health care, education, and infrastructure. These protests surprised many observers who expected that the limelight of the World Cup and the Olympics would allow Brazil to burnish its success in recent years as an emerging economy, the world's fifth-largest (up from ninth just ten years before). These expectations were buoyed following the discovery in 2007 of over 60 billion barrels worth of oil buried in deep wells off of the coast of Rio de Janeiro state. Yet Brazil is a country of many contradictions, where the riches promised by oil exploitation and rising median household incomes due to recent periods of high growth contrast with notorious levels of inequality and decaying public services. The mass protests preceding the World Cup reflected Brazilians' rising expectations and their frustrations that more cannot be done to attend to the challenges of development.

1964
A military coup places power in the hands of successive authoritarian regimes.

1984
Diretas Já!, a mass mobilization campaign, calls for direct elections.

1988
A new constitution grants new social and political rights.

1992
Collor is impeached; Vice President Itamar Franco assumes presidency.

2002
Lula da Silva is elected president.

1998
Cardoso is reelected.

2010
Dilma Rousseff, Lula's former chief-of-staff, is elected Brazil's first woman president.

| 1970 | 1985 | 1990 | 1995 | 2000 | 2010 |

1961
Quadros resigns. João Goulart gains presidency despite an attempted military coup.

1985
Vice-presidential candidate José Sarney becomes president on the sudden death of elected president Tancredo Neves.

1989
Fernando Collor is elected president.

1994
Fernando Henrique Cardoso is elected president after his Real Plan controls inflation.

1999
The Real Plan weathers a financial crisis.

2006
Lula is reelected after surviving a corruption scandal.

Geographic Setting

Larger than the continental United States, Brazil occupies two-thirds of South America. Its 192 million inhabitants are concentrated in the urban southern and southeastern regions; the northern Amazon region, with 5.3 million, is sparsely populated.

Brazil includes thick rain forest in the Amazon valley, large lowland swamps (the *pantanal*) in the central western states, and vast expanses of badlands (the *sertão*) in the north and northeast. Brazil is rich in natural resources and arable land. The Amazon has an abundance of minerals and tropical fruit; the central and southern regions provide iron ore and coal; offshore sources of petroleum are significant and will become even more so as they are exploited. Brazil's farmlands are highly fertile. The Amazon's climate is wet, the *sertão* is dry, and the agricultural areas of the central, southeastern, and southern regions are temperate. Natural resource exploitation make the fragile ecology of the Amazon a matter of international concern.

Immigration of Europeans and Africans has contributed to an ethnically mixed society. Approximately 48 percent of the population is white, 43 percent *pardo* (brown or mulatto), 8 percent black, and 0.5 percent Asian.[1] These numbers probably ignore people of mixed race, who are sometimes classified erroneously as being white or *pardo*. The indigenous people of the Amazon basin are estimated to number 250,000. The Asian population, which numbers just over 1 million, is dominated by people of Japanese descent who immigrated from 1908 through the 1950s.

Brazil is a blend of different cultural influences, although Portuguese as the common language helps keep Brazilians united. Brazilians are not greatly divided over religious differences. About 65 percent of Brazilians profess Roman Catholicism, though the Church plays only a secondary role in politics and society (see Section 4). Evangelical Protestants have recently made inroads. Protestants now compose about 22.2 percent of the population. Afro-Brazilian and indigenous religions also operate alongside the Catholic liturgy (see Figure 9.1 and Table 9.1).

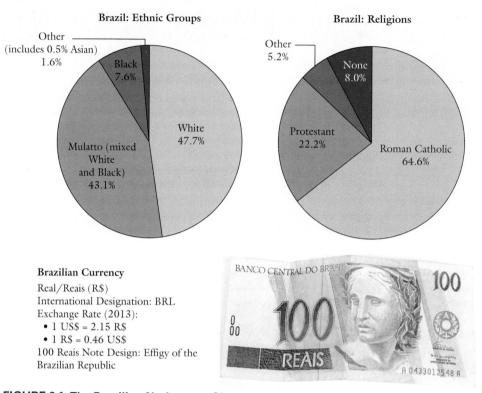

Brazilian Currency

Real/Reais (R$)
International Designation: BRL
Exchange Rate (2013):
- 1 US$ = 2.15 R$
- 1 R$ = 0.46 US$

100 Reais Note Design: Effigy of the
Brazilian Republic

FIGURE 9.1 The Brazilian Nation at a Glance

© Vinicius Tupinamba/Shutterstock.com (for photo)

Critical Junctures

The Brazilian Empire (1822–1889)

Brazil was a Portuguese colony, not a Spanish one, and it escaped the violent wars of independence that afflicted the Spanish colonial system. Brazilian independence was declared peacefully by the Crown's own agent in the colony in 1822.

To control its sprawling territory, Brazil centralized authority in the emperor, who acted as a **moderating power** (*poder moderador*), mediating conflicts among the executive, legislative, and judicial branches of government and powerful landowning oligarchy. This centralization contrasted with other postcolonial Latin American states, which suffered numerous conflicts among territorially dispersed strongmen (*caudillos*).

Imperial Brazil enjoyed several features of representative democracy: regular elections, alternation of parties in power, and scrupulous compliance with the constitution. Liberal institutions only regulated political competition among rural, oligarchical elites, leaving out most Brazilians who were neither enfranchised nor politically organized.

The Old Republic (1889–1930)

In 1889 came the peaceful demise of the empire, the exile of Emperor Dom Pedro II, and the emergence of a republic ruled by the landowning oligarchy. The decline of slavery and the rise of republicanism ended the empire. Liberal political values in opposition to centralized political authority took root among the coffee oligarchy.

**moderating power
(poder moderador)**

A term used in Brazilian politics to refer to the situation following the 1824 constitution in which the monarchy was supposed to act as a moderating power, among the executive, legislative, and judicial branches of government, arbitrating party conflicts, and fulfilling governmental responsibilities when nonroyal agents failed.

Table 9.1	Political Organization
Political System	Federal republic, presidential with separation of powers.
Regime History	Democratic since 1946 with periods of military authoritarianism, especially 1964–1985.
Administrative Structure	Federal, with twenty-six states plus the Federal District, which also functions as a state. Subnational legislatures are unicameral. State governments have multiple secretariats, the major ones commonly being economy, planning, and infrastructure. The states are divided into municipalities (about 5,564), with mayors and councillors directly elected.
Executive	President, vice president, and cabinet. The president and vice president are directly elected by universal suffrage in a two-round runoff election for four-year terms. Since 1998, the president and vice president may run for a second term.
Legislature	Bicameral: The Senate is made up of three senators from each state and from the Federal District, elected by plurality vote for an eight-year term; the Chamber of Deputies consists of representatives from each state and from the Federal District, elected by proportional vote for a four-year term.
Judiciary	Supreme Court, High Tribunal of Justice, regional courts, labor courts, electoral courts, military courts, and state courts. Judiciary has financial and administrative autonomy. Most judges are appointed for life.
Party System	Multiparty system including several parties of the right, center-left, and left. Elections are by open-list proportional representation. There is no restriction on the creation and merging of political parties.

As these elites grew suspicious of attempts to centralize power, they discounted the need for a moderating power in the national state.

The Old Republic (1889–1930) was based on the influence of coffee growers and a small urban industrial and commercial class linked to the coffee trade. The constitution of 1891, inspired by the U.S. model, established a directly elected president, guaranteed separation of church and state, and gave the vote to all literate males (about 3.5 percent of the population before 1930). The legitimacy of the republican political system was established on governing principles that were limited to a privileged few, but no longer determined by the hereditary rights of the emperor. The states gained greater authority to formulate policy, spend money, levy taxes, and maintain their own militias.

Although the constitution expressed liberal ideas, most Brazilians lived in rural areas where the landed oligarchy squashed dissent. As in the southern United States and in Mexico, landed elites manipulated local politics. In a process known as *coronelismo*, these elites, or colonels, manipulated their poor workers so they would vote to elect officials favored by the elite.

These ties between patron (landowner) and client (peasant) became the basis of modern Brazilian politics. In return for protection and occasional favors, the client did the bidding of the patron. As cities grew and the state's administrative agencies expanded, the process of trading favors and demanding political support in return became known as **clientelism**.

clientelism

An informal aspect of policy-making in which a powerful patron (for example, a traditional local boss, government agency, or dominant party) offers resources such as land, contracts, protection, or jobs in return for the support and services (such as labor or votes) of lower-status and less powerful clients; corruption, preferential treatment, and inequality are characteristic of clientelist politics.

© Cengage Learning®

In contrast to the centralized empire, the Old Republic consecrated the power of local elites. Governors and mayors were empowered to control areas of economic policy delegated by the federal government.

The 1930 Revolution

interventores

In Brazil, allies of Getúlio Vargas (1930–1945, 1950–1952) picked by the dictator during his first period of rulership to replace opposition governors in all the Brazilian states except Minas Gerais. The *interventores* represented a shift of power from subnational government to the central state.

As world demand for coffee plummeted during the Depression of the 1930s, the coffee and ranch elites faced their worst crisis. Worker demonstrations and the Brazilian Communist Party challenged the legitimacy of the Old Republic. Among the discontented political elites, a figure emerged who transformed Brazilian politics forever: Getúlio Vargas (see "Profile: Getúlio Dornelles Vargas" in Section 3).

Vargas came to power as the head of a new "revolutionary government" that swiftly crushed middle-class and popular dissent. He built a political coalition around a new project of industrialization led by the central government and based on central state resources. Unlike the Old Republic, Vargas controlled regional governments by replacing all governors (except in Minas Gerais) with handpicked allies (**interventores**). The center of gravity of Brazilian politics swung back to the national state. Vargas, as "father of the people," could not be upstaged by competing political images and organizations. Brazilian society would be linked directly to the state and to Vargas as the state's primary agent.

Vargas believed he could win the support of landed elites, commercial interests, bureaucrats, and the military by answering their demands in a controlled way. They were allowed to participate in the new political order, but only as passive members of state-created and state-regulated unions and associations. This model of **state corporatism** rejects the idea of competition among social groups by having the state arbitrate all conflicts. For instance, when workers requested increases in their wages, state agencies determined to what extent such demands would be met and how business would pay for them.

By 1937, Vargas had achieved a position of virtually uncontested power. During the next eight years, he consolidated his state corporatist model with labor codes, the establishment of public firms to produce strategic commodities such as steel and oil, and paternalistic social policies. These policies were collectively called the New State (*Estado Nôvo*).

The Populist Republic (1945–1964)

The ever-growing mobilization of segments of the working and middle classes, and U.S. diplomatic pressure forced Vargas to call for full democratic elections to be held in 1945. Three political parties competed in these elections: The Social Democratic Party (PSD) and the Brazilian Labor Party (PTB) were pro-Vargas, while the National Democratic Union (UDN) stood against him. The PSD and the PTB, which operated in alliance, were both creations of the state, while the UDN brought together regional forces that wanted a return to liberal constitutionalism. The campaign was so bitter that the military forced Vargas to resign, two months before the general election.

The turn to democracy in 1946 did not break with the past. The new constitution guaranteed periodic elections, but the most important economic and social policies were still decided by the state bureaucracy, not by the national legislature.

Populism, but not democracy, defined the new political order. In Brazil, the terms *populist* and *populism* refer to politicians, programs, or movements that seek to expand citizenship to previously disenfranchised sectors of society in return for political support. Populist governments grant benefits to guarantee support, but discourage lower-class groups from creating their own organizations. Populists do not consider themselves accountable to the people.

Brazilian workers supported Vargas for his promises to improve the social insurance system, and elected him in 1950. However, economic limitations and opposition claims that he was preparing a new dictatorship made Vargas politically vulnerable. He was soon swept up in a bizarre scandal involving the attempted assassination of a popular journalist. During the crisis, accusations of Vargas's complicity in the assassination increasingly wore on him, leading him to kill himself on August 24, 1954. Under Vargas's democratic successor, Juscelino Kubitschek (1956–1960), the economy improved. Brazilian industry expanded tremendously. Kubitschek was a master of political symbolism and **nationalism**, promoting images of a new, bigger Brazil that could create "fifty years of development in five." This was symbolized by his decision to move the capital from Rio de Janeiro to a planned city called Brasília—a utopian city that rallied support for Kubitschek's developmentalist policies.

The presidents after Kubitschek proved much less competent. João Goulart, for instance, began an ill-fated campaign for structural reforms, mainly in education and agriculture. In response, peasant league movements, students, and professional organizations organized protests, strikes, and illegal seizures of land. As right-wing organizations battled leftist groups in the streets of the capital, the military ended Brazil's experiment with democratic populism in March 1964.

state corporatism

A system of interest representation in which the constituent units are organized into a limited number of singular, compulsory, noncompetitive, hierarchically ordered, and functionally differentiated categories, recognized or licensed (if not created) by the state and granted a representational monopoly within their respective categories in exchange for observing certain controls in their selection of leaders and articulation of demands and supports.

populism

Gaining the support of popular sectors. When used in Latin American politics, this support is often achieved by manipulation and demagogic appeals.

nationalism

An ideology seeking to create a nation-state for a particular community; a group identity associated with membership is such a political community. Nationalists often proclaim that their state and nation are superior to others.

The Rise of Bureaucratic Authoritarianism (1964–1985)

The military government installed what the Argentine political sociologist Guillermo O'Donnell termed **bureaucratic authoritarianism (BA)**.[2] Such regimes respond to severe economic crises and are led by the armed forces and key civilian allies, most notably by professional economists, engineers, and administrators. BA limited civil rights and other political freedoms, sometimes going so far as wholesale censorship of the press, torture of civilians, and imprisonment without trial, all for the sake of economic development.

The military government first planned a quick return to civilian rule and even allowed limited democratic institutions to continue. After being purged in 1964 of the BA's opponents, the national congress continued to function, and direct elections for federal legislators and most mayors (but not the president or state governors) took place at regular intervals. In November 1965, the military replaced all existing political parties with only two: the National Renovation Alliance (ARENA) and the Brazilian Democratic Movement (MDB). ARENA was the military government's party, and MDB was the "official" party of the opposition. Former members of the three major parties joined one of the two new parties.[3]

The powers of these democratic institutions were severely limited. The military government used institutional decrees to legislate the most important matters,

Brazil's capital, Brasília. The planned city was designed by the world-famous Brazilian architect Oscar Niemeyer.

George Holton/Science Source

preventing the congress from having an important voice. Few civilian politicians could speak out directly against the military for fear of being removed from office.

In economic policy, the military reinforced the previous pattern of state interventionism. The government promoted **state-led economic development** by creating hundreds of state corporations and investing enormous sums in established public firms. Brazil implemented one of the most successful economic development programs among newly industrialized countries. Termed the "Brazilian miracle," these programs demonstrated that, like France, Germany, and Japan in earlier periods, a developing country could create its own economic miracle.

The Transition to Democracy and the First Civilian Governments (1974–2001)

After the oil crisis of 1973 set off a wave of inflation around the world, the economy began to falter. Increasing criticism from Brazilian business led the last two ruling generals, Geisel and Figueiredo, to begin a gradual process of democratization. Initially, these leaders envisioned only a liberalizing, or opening (*abertura*), of the regime to allow civilian politicians to compete for political office. As was later the case with Gorbachev's *glasnost* in the Soviet Union, however, control over the process of liberalization gradually slipped from military hands and was captured by organizations within civil society. In 1974, the opposition party, the MDB, stunned the military government by increasing its representation in the Senate from 18 to 30 percent and in the Chamber of Deputies from 22 to 44 percent. Although the party did not have a majority in Congress, it did capture a majority in both chambers of the state legislatures in the most important industrialized southern and southeastern states.

In the following years, the opposition made successive electoral gains and obtained concessions from the government. The most important were the reestablishment of direct elections for governors in 1982, political amnesty for dissidents, the elimination of the government's power to oust legislators from political office, and the restoration of political rights to those who had previously lost them. In the gubernatorial elections of November 1982, the opposition candidates won landslide victories in the major states.

The military wanted to maintain as much control over the succession process as possible and preferred to have the next president selected within a restricted electoral college. But mass mobilization campaigns demanded the right to elect the next president directly. The *Diretas Já!* ("Direct Elections Now!") movement, comprising an array of social movements, opposition politicians, and labor unions, expanded in size and influence in 1984. Although the movement failed to achieve its goal of making the founding elections of the new democracy direct, the effort inspired a generation of movement leaders with gender, racial, religious, and issue-based orientations. More immediately, the military lost supporters, who backed an alliance (the Liberal Front) with Tancredo Neves, the candidate of the opposition PMDB, the Party of the MDB. Neves's victory in 1984, however, was marred by his sudden death on the eve of the inauguration. Vice President José Sarney became the first civilian president of Brazil since 1964.

The events leading to Sarney's presidency disappointed those who had hoped for a clean break with the authoritarian past. Most of the politicians who gained positions of power in the new democracy hailed from the former ARENA or its misleadingly named successor, the Democratic Social Party (PDS). Most of these soon joined Sarney's own PMDB or its alliance partner, the Party of the Liberal Front (PFL). A political transition that should have produced change led to considerable continuity.

---

state-led economic development

The process of actively promoting economic development through government policy, usually involving indicative planning and financial subsidization of industries.

---

abertura

(Portuguese for "opening"; *apertura* in Spanish) In Brazil, refers to the period of authoritarian liberalization begun in 1974 when the military allowed civilian politicians to compete for political office in the context of a more open political society.

A chance for fundamental change appeared in 1987 when the national Constituent Assembly met to draft a new constitution. Given the earlier success of the opposition governors in 1982, state political machines became important players in the game of constitution writing. The state governments petitioned for the devolution of new authority to tax and spend. Labor groups also exerted influence through their lobbying organizations. Workers demanded constitutional protection of the right to strike and the right to create their own unions without authorization from the Ministry of Labor.[4]

Soon after Sarney's rise to power, annual rates of inflation began to skyrocket. The government sponsored several stabilization plans, but without success. Dealing with runaway inflation and the removal of authoritarian politicians became the key issues in the 1989 presidential elections, the first direct contests since the 1960s.

Once again, Brazilians would be disappointed. Fernando Collor de Mello, became president after a grueling campaign against Lula da Silva, the popular left-wing labor leader and head of the Workers' Party (*Partido dos Trabalhadores*, or PT). Collor's administration embraced structural reform, such as privatization of state enterprises and deregulation of the economy, but it failed to solve the nagging problem of inflation. Collor was eventually impeached in late 1992 due to his involvement in bribery and influence peddling.

Collor's impeachment brought Itamar Franco to the presidency. Franco's most important decision was naming Fernando Henrique Cardoso, his finance minister. In July 1994, Cardoso's Real Plan finally stopped inflation by creating a new currency, the *real* that would be managed closely by the Central Bank (see Section 2).

Cardoso rode the success of the Real Plan to the presidency, beating out Lula and the PT in 1994 and again in 1998. He proved adept at keeping inflation low and consolidating some of the structural reforms first started by Collor. But Brazil's budget and trade deficits increased, and financial crises in Asia and Russia in 1997 and 1998 eventually led to a crisis in the Real Plan. In January 1999, the value of the *real* collapsed. But the currency soon stabilized, and hyperinflation did not return. The Cardoso administration was also able to pass the Law of Fiscal Responsibility in 2000, which addressed many of the pernicious effects of runaway spending by state and municipal governments.

Brazil after September 11, 2001

September 11 and the collapse of the Argentine economy that same year produced a fundamental crisis of confidence in Brazil. In particular, Argentina's crisis threatened to destabilize the recovery of the *real*. Meanwhile, Washington's war on terror threatened to displace social and economic priorities in Brazil's relations with the United States. Diplomacy with Washington became particularly bitter over the Bush administration's insistence on going to war with Iraq and its heavy-handed approach to dealing with foreigners.

The election of Lula da Silva as president in October 2002 stemmed from a popular desire to put the social agenda ahead of the American focus on security. Lula's election also reflected the maturation of democracy. Once a proponent of socialism, Lula embraced Cardoso's reform agenda. He passed major social security reforms in 2003 and 2004, but, similar to his predecessor's difficulties, his reforms became stalled in congress during the run-up to municipal elections in late 2004. Worse still, PT-led municipal governments, once a model of good governance in Latin America, were accused of procuring kickbacks to fund electoral activities. PT leaders surrounding Lula were implicated in a second scandal involving the purchase of votes in the congress for reform legislation. However, Lula won reelection in 2006 anyway, and he continued to garner high presidential approval ratings well into his second term. He expanded public expenditures on infrastructure and industry as part of his Plan for the Acceleration of Growth.

Improved growth, higher median incomes, and decreased inequality set the stage for Lula to promote the election of his chief-of-staff, Dilma Rousseff, as his successor in 2010. Dilma became Brazil's first woman president. Her election caps off perhaps the most meteoric of political careers, though one completely dependent on Lula. A former militant against the authoritarian regime, Dilma was jailed and tortured in 1970 and 1972. After finishing her degree in economics, she ventured again into politics during the New Republic but as an appointee in municipal and state government in Rio Grande do Sul and its capital, Porto Alegre. She joined the PT late in her career, in 2000, and was plucked from obscurity by Lula in 2002 to become his Minister of Energy and later his chief of staff. Having no real experience in elected office, her first experience as an elected leader was the presidency.

Dilma's government expanded public spending, including over $127 billion in new investments by the public oil company, Petrobras, which sought to exploit off-shore reserves. But the continued slow growth of advanced economies and the prospect of slower growth in China, a prominent purchaser of Brazilian agricultural and iron ore exports, limited how far Dilma could push spending in preparation for the 2014 World Cup and the 2016 Summer Olympic Games. Public protests prior to these events also pressured the government to allocate more to social policy. In the post 9/11 world, Brazilian politics continued to focus more on development and democracy and less on security.

The Four Themes and Brazil

Brazil in a Globalized World of States

Both international and domestic factors have influenced the Brazilian state's structure, capacity, and relations with society. During the empire, international opposition to slavery forced powerful oligarchs to turn to the state for protection. The coffee and ranch economies provided the material base for the Old Republic and were intricately tied to Brazil's economic role in the world. Even the *Estado Nôvo*, with its drive to organize society, was democratized by the defeat of fascism in Europe. The return to democracy during the 1980s was part of a larger global experience, as authoritarian regimes gave way all over Latin America, Eastern Europe, southern Europe, and the Soviet Union. As Brazil's economy has grown in size, it faces greater responsibilities in the globalized world of states, both in foreign economic and security policy.

Governing the Economy

The entry of the working and middle classes as political actors reshaped the Brazilian state during the twentieth century. Vargas's New State mobilized workers and professionals. Populist democracy later provided them protection from unsafe working environments, the effects of eroding wages, and the prohibitive expense of health care. Public firms employed hundreds of thousands of Brazilians and transformed the development of the country. During the 1980s and 1990s, neoliberal reforms dramatically altered the role of the Brazilian state (see Section 2). Brazil's governance of the economy highlights the strategic role of the state in the maintenance of growth.

State-led growth built the foundation for governing the economy, and developmentalism moved Brazil from a predominantly agrarian economy into an industrialized one. The country's high growth trajectory in recent years has generated a positive pattern, but it also presents numerous challenges. Policy-makers must find better ways of adjusting policy to the needs of a larger economy and a society that demands decreasing levels of poverty and inequality; trends that build on the successes of wise social policy-making in recent years.

The Democratic Idea

personalist politicians

Demagogic political leaders who use their personal charisma to mobilize their constituency.

Brazil certainly has the institutions of a democracy, but patrimonialism, populism, corporatism, and corruption undermine them. Brazilian politicians typically cultivate personal votes (**personalist politicians**) that challenge the creation of strong parties and alliances (see Section 4). But despite its shortcomings, Brazilians appreciate that democracy gives them more say in policy-making. Thousands of new political groups, social movements, civic networks, and economic associations have emerged in recent years. The Brazilian state is highly decentralized into twenty-six states, a federal district, and 5,564 municipalities. Each center of power is a locus of demand-making by citizens and policy-making by elites. Although centralized rule is no longer desirable, Brazilians still struggle with the coordination and governability of a complex state and political system.

The Politics of Collective Identity

In assessing the politics of collective identity, the first question to answer is who are the Brazilians? This has always been a vexing issue, especially because heavy flows of international commerce, finance, and ideas have made Brazil's borders obsolete. One common answer is that the symbols of the Brazilian nation still tie Brazilians together: carnival, soccer, samba, and bossa nova. Even though these symbols have become more prevalent, they have lost some of their meaning because of commercialization. Catholicism is a less unifying force today, as Pentecostalism and evangelism have eaten into the church's membership. Women have improved their social position and political awareness as gender-based organizations have become important resources of civil society. Yet even here, Brazil remains extremely patriarchal: women are expected to balance motherhood and other traditional roles in the household, even while economic needs pressure them to produce income.

Race remains the most difficult issue to understand. Racial identity continues to divide Brazilians, but not in the clear-cut manner it divides blacks and whites in the United States. Categories are multiple, especially since racial mixing defies the kind of stark, black–white segregation in the United States.

Class continues to separate Brazilians due to high income inequality. Like India, Brazil's social indicators consistently rank near the bottom in the world, though these indicators are improving. Income disparities mirror racial differences. The poor are mostly blacks and mulattos, while the rich are mostly white.

Themes and Comparisons

As a large, politically decentralized, and socially fragmented polity, Brazil presents several extraordinary challenges to the study of comparative politics. First, the Brazilian state has varied in its degree of centralization, producing distinct capacities for promoting development, democracy, and social distribution. Although political centralization has made the French state strong, decentralized states such as the United States and Germany have proven successful as well. The Brazilian case provides lessons for how other large, decentralized states in the developing world, such as India, might reconcile the needs of development and democracy.

The challenges posed by Brazil's democratic institutions represent other matters of concern to comparative politics. Along with Russia, Brazil demonstrates how the lack of coherent party systems and electoral institutions can endanger democracy. Paradoxically, as Brazil developed economically and made its way back to democracy in the 1980s, it also became a more socially unequal country. Other democracies have also found that democratization does not improve the distribution of wealth. The complex divisions afflicting Brazilians' collective identities also challenge all attempts to address the country's problems. In this regard, Brazil presents a puzzle for theories about collective identities: How has such a socially fragmented society remained a coherent whole while sustaining democracy?

Where Do You Stand?

The *Estado Nôvo* and the bureaucratic authoritarian periods were associated with the industrial development of Brazil. Do you think that this suggests that economic development may sometimes require authoritarian rule?

Supporters of Cardoso and Lula disagree on which leader did the most for Brazil. Which one would you say did the most to address the needs of democracy, the economy, and social development?

> **export-led growth**
>
> Economic growth generated by the export of a country's commodities. Export-led growth can occur at an early stage of economic development, in which case it involves primary products, such as the country's mineral resources, timber, and agricultural products; or at a later stage, when industrial goods and services are exported.

POLITICAL ECONOMY AND DEVELOPMENT

SECTION 2

Like most developing countries, Brazil's politics has always been shaped by the quest for economic and social development. Two processes have left enduring legacies: the pattern of state intervention in the domestic market and the effects of external economic change. External economic crises have compelled the state to intervene through protection, subsidies, and even the production of goods it previously imported. These policies have made Brazil one of the faster-growing newly industrialized countries of the world, alongside India and China. But it must continually navigate the balance between state intervention and market-based adjustment as the challenges of globalization change.

State and Economy

Brazil's economic development prior to the New State depended on **export-led growth**, that is, on the export of agricultural products. During the Old Republic, international demand for Brazilian coffee gave Brazil a virtual global monopoly. Cotton, sugar, and cereals also continued to be important export products.

Coffee linked Brazil to the world market with minimal state involvement in the period before the Great Depression. Export receipts provided a reservoir of capital to build railroads, power stations, and other infrastructure. These investments then

> **Focus Questions** ▽
>
> • How did the Brazilian state's role in promoting development change as the country moved from import-substitution to market-oriented reform?
>
> • Identify some of the persisting problems of Brazilian economic development and how progress has been made during the New Republic in addressing them.

interventionist

An interventionist state acts vigorously to shape the performance of major sectors of the economy.

import substitution industrialization (ISI)

Strategy for industrialization based on domestic manufacture of previously imported goods to satisfy domestic market demands.

state technocrats

Career-minded bureaucrats who administer public policy according to a technical rather than a political rationale. In Mexico and Brazil, these are known as the *técnicos*.

spurred the growth of light industries, mostly in textiles, footwear, and clothing. Public finance had a minor role.

The state became far more **interventionist** during the 1930s when international demand for coffee declined. As exports fell, imports of manufactured goods also declined. These forces prompted **import substitution industrialization (ISI)**, a model of development that promoted domestic production of previously imported manufactured goods. At first, Brazil did not need large doses of state intervention. This so-called light, or easy, phase of ISI focused on products that did not require much capital or sophisticated technology. Most of these industries were labor intensive and created jobs.

At the end of World War II, the ISI model expanded through the promotion of heavy industry and capital-intensive production. A new generation of **state technocrats**, inspired by the United Nations Economic Commission for Latin America (ECLA), sought to "deepen" ISI by promoting capital-intensive sectors through industrial policies including planning, subsidies, and financial support, state agencies promoted the quick growth of these industries.

During the 1950s Brazil was a prime example of ECLA-style **developmentalism**, the ideology and practice of state-sponsored growth. The state promoted private investment by extracting and distributing raw materials for domestic industries at prices well below the international market. Other firms, if they were linked to sectors of the economy receiving these supports, would benefit in a chain reaction.

Growth rates achieved impressive levels, especially during the 1970s (see Table 10.2), but the first serious contradictions of ISI emerged by this time. Protection led to non-competitive, inefficient production in which growing industries depended too heavily on public subsidies. ISI also became import-intensive. Businesses used subsidized finance to import technology and machinery, since the government overvalued the currency to make import prices cheaper. But this overvaluation hurt exports, by making them more expensive. Because the export sector could not supply much-needed revenues to sustain growth, the government printed money, which in turn led to inflation.

The failures of ISI during the 1960s inspired many Brazilian academics to adopt the view, then popularized as the "dependency school," that underdeveloped or "peripheral" countries could not achieve sustained levels of industrialization and growth in a world dominated by "core" economies in North America and Western Europe. ISI's failures, it was argued, were due to the ill-fated attempt to adjust marginally the inherently exploitative structure of world markets. The dependency school advocated de-linking Brazil from the world economy, but this view remained mostly academic and did not become a basis for policy.

From 1964 to 1985, the state continued to promote industrialization, especially durable consumer goods for the domestic market. Multinational firms also invested and transferred technology. Industry became 40 percent of the GDP by 1980.

Table 9.2	Governing the Economy: GDP Growth Rates
1940–1949	5.6%
1950–1959	6.1%
1960–1969	5.4%
1970–1979	12.4%
1980–1989	1.5%
1990–1996	2.1%
1997–2000	0.8%
2001–2003	1.0%
2004–2007	3.2%
2008–2010	5.7%
2011–2013	1.9%

Source: IBGE and the World Bank.

Parastatals (public or state firms) played a crucial role in the ISI development model. Large-scale projects were financed and managed by bureaucratic agencies, state firms, and foreign companies. Peter Evans characterized these complex relations among the state, foreign investors, and domestic capitalists as a "triple alliance."[5] But the state remained the dominant partner.

The Fiscal System

As the Brazilian economy became more complex after the 1960s, new opportunities for evading taxes emerged. An **informal economy** of small firms, domestic enterprises, street vendors, and unregistered employees proliferated, outside the taxable economy. Economists estimate that the informal economy could be as large as 20 percent of Brazil's gross domestic product ($420 billion), it may employ about 40 to 60 million people, and it may represent a loss of $70 billion annually in forgone tax revenues.

The new constitution of 1988 allowed states and municipalities to expand their collection of taxes and to receive larger transfers of funds from Brasília. Significant gaps then emerged in tax collection responsibilities and public spending. Although the central state spent less than it collected in taxes between 1960 and 1994, Brazil's 5,564 municipal governments spent several times more than they collected. Subnational governments also gained more discretion over spending, since the federal government required few earmarks. The governors also used public banks held by the state governments to finance expenditures, thus expanding their debt.

The Cardoso administration had the most success in recovering federal tax revenues and reducing the fiscal distortions of Brazil's federal structure. The Fiscal Responsibility Law of 2000 set strict limits on federal, state, and municipal expenditures. But with large civil service payrolls, governments are hard-pressed to implement the law. Despite these problems, improved tax collection and economic growth have reduced the public debt from 60 percent of GDP in 2002 to 38 percent in 2012 (see Figure 9.2).

In 2003, Lula's government passed a simplified tax code and a tax reform permitting increases in federal taxes. But it postponed legislation to address fiscal competition among the states, the simplification and unification of the states' value-added tax, and efforts to reduce the overall tax burden on business. The government also failed to do something about the weight of sales taxes that fall more heavily on the poor.

The Problem of Inflation

Inflation accompanied state-led development because the state, business, and unions all distorted the value of goods and services by manipulating prices, interest rates, and wages. Successive attempts to control inflation fell apart as different interest groups attempted to retain these controls. No fewer than seven "stabilization" plans between 1985 and 1994 collapsed, sometimes generating "hyperinflation" (600 percent or more annual inflation). Figure 9.3 illustrates this terrible track record.

Only Cardoso's Real Plan proved successful. The Real Plan anchored the *real*, the new currency, to the dollar. It did not fix the *real* to the dollar strictly but

---

developmentalism

An ideology and practice in Latin America during the 1950s in which the state played a leading role in seeking to foster economic development through sponsoring vigorous industrial policy.

parastatals

State-owned, or at least state-controlled, corporations, created to undertake a broad range of activities, from control and marketing of agricultural production to provision of banking services, operating airlines, and other transportation facilities and public utilities.

informal economy

That portion of the economy largely outside government control in which employees work without contracts or benefits. Examples include casual employees in restaurants and hotels, street vendors, and day laborers in construction or agriculture.

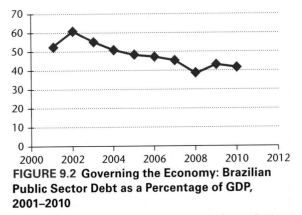

FIGURE 9.2 Governing the Economy: Brazilian Public Sector Debt as a Percentage of GDP, 2001–2010

Source: Based on numbers produced by the Central Bank of Brazil.

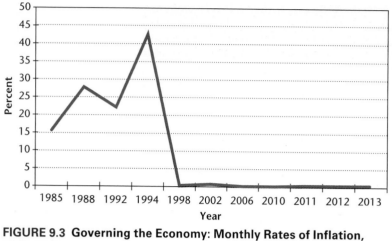

FIGURE 9.3 Governing the Economy: Monthly Rates of Inflation, 1985–2013

Source: Author's design based on Brazilian Central Bank figures, accessed in January 2014.

allowed it to float within a range set by the Central Bank, allowing more flexibility in the exchange rate. From 1995 until 1999, the *real* became overvalued, making exports more expensive abroad by raising the costs of production, and making imports cheaper. Brazil's trade deficit rose by more than 140 percent. The *real* then fell by more than 50 percent against the dollar in January 1999. Despite the devaluation, hyperinflation did not return, and the government moderated growth in public spending. Renewed growth and good fiscal management by the Lula administration began to reduce the massive public debt. Under the Dilma government, rising public spending have jeopardized this record of stability with rising wage rates, higher deficits and public debt. Average annual inflation is 6 percent, which is slightly worse than the average in developing countries.

Society and Economy

Between 1950 and 1980, employment in industry jumped from 14 percent to 24 percent, while employment in agriculture declined from 60 percent to 30 percent. Nevertheless, the jobs created in industry did not begin to absorb the huge number of unemployed. Many new jobs required skilled and semiskilled specialized labor. In the late 1980s and 1990s, even skilled workers faced losing their jobs because of intense industrial restructuring that caused manufacturing to employ 48 percent fewer workers. With the rapid expansion of the economy during the 2000s, urban unemployment fell dramatically from 18 percent to 5.4 percent by 2012, though about half of all workers remain employed in the informal sector where they are paid less and receive few benefits.

Industrialization also failed to eradicate the racial inequalities inherited from slavery. Despite the impressive industrial development of Brazil, Afro-Brazilians continued to make less than their white colleagues and had fewer opportunities for upward mobility. According to one study, nonwhite men and women in Brazil have made real gains in their income because of improvements in education and occupation, but the gap separating nonwhite income from white income remains significant.[6] On average, blacks make 41 percent and mulattos make 47 percent of what whites make.

Women make up 28 percent of the economically active population and continue to enter the labor market in record numbers. Working women typically have more years of schooling than men, but they still receive lower salaries for the same job. Brazilian women make only 70 percent of what men make, and black women do even worse at 40 percent. In rural areas, women are substantially disadvantaged in the granting of land titles. Female heads of families are routinely passed over by official agencies distributing land titles to favor oldest sons, even when these are minors. Thirty-four percent of illiterate women earn the minimum wage or less, versus 5 percent of illiterate

Table 9.3	Governing the Economy: Brazilian Income Distribution in Comparative Perspective			
Country	10% Richest	20% Richest	20% Poorest	10% Poorest
Brazil	43.0	58.7	3.0	1.1
Mexico	41.3	56.4	3.8	1.2
Chile	41.7	56.8	4.1	1.6
China	31.4	47.8	5.7	2.4
Nigeria	32.4	48.6	5.1	2.0
India	31.1	45.3	8.1	3.6
United States	29.9	45.8	5.4	1.9
United Kingdom	28.5	44.0	6.1	2.1
France	25.1	40.2	7.2	2.8
Russia	34.3	50.2	5.6	2.2

Source: World Bank, *World Development Indicators 2013* (Washington, DC: World Bank, 2013).

males. Although recent economic growth and rising median incomes have begun to reverse decades of worsening inequality, income remains more poorly distributed in Brazil than it is in most other developing countries (see Table 9.3).

The Welfare System

In a country of startling social inequalities, welfare policy plays a remarkably small role, even though expenditures on health care and education stand at 25 percent of GDP. The effects of this spending are uneven. Salaried formal sector workers receive most benefits, including pensions and the best access to both private and public health care. Workers in the informal sector generally do not collect welfare since the federal government does not consider them employed. Corruption, clientelism, and outright waste prevent benefits from going to the people who need them the most.[7]

More people need welfare than actually contribute to the welfare state. That means the government must finance the shortfall. More serious is the unevenness of the system. More than 70 percent of all income transfers are retirement benefits that go to middle-class and upper-class individuals. The indigent receive only 1.5 percent of these funds. Informal workers and the unemployed must use public health services, while formal sector workers access the public health care system for expensive procedures and retain private insurance for less expensive care.

The Cardoso administration laid some of the groundwork for reversing poverty and inequality. In addition to several programs to provide grants directly to poor families to improve their health and the education of their children, Cardoso also targeted the rural poor. The Family Health Program, for instance, provides community health workers for areas that have historically been underserved. Some studies have shown that this program has accelerated the decline in infant mortality and, along with other programs, has improved prenatal care and family reproductive medicine, including reductions in the rates of HIV/AIDS.[8]

The Lula administration focused even more on social reform. In the fall of 2003, the government passed a social security reform that raised the minimum retirement age, placed stricter limits on benefit ceilings, reduced survivor benefits, and taxed pensions and benefits. Issues including the taxation of social security benefits for judges and military officers and the reduction of survivor benefits for the latter group became stumbling blocks in cross-party negotiations. The government made concessions on these and other issues, but the total annual savings were less than half of the original target.

The most notable social reform is *Bolsa Família* (the Family Grant Program), which consolidated three programs started by the Cardoso government. Lula expanded the funding of *Bolsa Família*, which grants modest monthly sums to families that keep their children in school and see the doctor for regular vaccinations and checkups. Since 2003, 11.1 million families or 20 percent of the Brazilian population (46 million people) have benefited from *Bolsa Família*, though the program consumes less than 3 percent of total social spending.[9] Both Cardoso's and Lula's sustained efforts in social welfare have generated some aggregate results: Poverty rates have fallen since 1994 and other improvements such as reduced illiteracy, particularly in the poorest regions, have been recorded in recent years.

Agrarian Reform

Landownership is terribly concentrated in Brazil with only 1 percent of landowners (about 58,000 individuals) holding a parcel equal to the size of Venezuela and Colombia combined. Over 3 million other farmers survive on only 2 percent of the country's land.

favelas

A Portuguese-language term for the shantytowns that ring many of the main cities in Brazil. The shantytowns emerge where people can invade unused land and build domiciles before the authorities can remove them. Unfinished public housing projects can also become the sites of *favelas*. *Favelas* expanded after the 1970s as a response to the inadequate supply of homes in urban centers to meet the demand caused by increasing rural–urban migration.

The Cardoso administration expropriated some unproductive estates and settled 186,000 families on them. Despite Lula's earlier rhetoric concerning land reform, his administration failed to initiate anything close to a land reform. The issue was one that enlivened the presidential campaign in 2010 of a former PT member, Marina Silva, of the small Green Party, whose 19 percent share of the first-round vote reflected how neglected social issues involving land and ecology still remain salient issues in Brazilian politics.

The landless poor have swelled the rings of poverty around Brazil's major cities. During the 1950s and 1960s, the growth of industry in the south and southeast enticed millions to migrate in the hopes of finding new economic opportunities. By 1991, 75 percent of Brazil's population was living in urban areas.

The pressures on Brazilian cities for basic services overwhelmed the budgets of municipalities and state governments. Squatters soon took government land, settling on the outskirts of the major cities. They built huge shantytowns called *favelas* around cities like Rio and São Paulo.

Regional disparities in income have remained stark. The nine states of the Northeast have a per capita GDP half of the national average. The Northeast has 28 percent of the national population but it accounts for only 13.8 percent of the GDP. By contrast, the Southeast has 42.6 percent of the population and 55.2 percent of the GDP. The agglomeration of industry in the South and Southeast and the persistence of poverty in the Northeast have created pressures for land reform or at least poverty-alleviating policies. These pressures will deepen as Dilma Rousseff and her successors depend on electoral support from this region.

Environmental Issues

The environmental limits of Brazil's development model have only become more apparent over time. During the height of the ISI period, the central and southern states of São Paulo, Minas Gerais, Rio de Janeiro, and Rio Grande do Sul became sites of environmental degradation. In the 1970s Guanabara Bay and the Paraiba do Sul River basin, both in Rio de Janeiro state, approached the brink of biological death. Urban pollution in São Paulo devastated the Tietê River, threatening the health of millions. In Cubatão, an industrial city east of metropolitan São Paulo, conditions became so bad that by 1981, one city council member reported that he had not seen a star in twenty years.

Big development projects reached the Amazon River basin in the 1970s. These industrial projects threatened the tropical forests, as did cattle ranching, timber extraction, and slash-and-burn agriculture by poor farmers. By the 1980s, it was clear that the primary result of these practices was the deforestation of the Amazon. The annual rate of deforestation during the 1990s approached alarming levels, with 29,059 km^2 lost in 1995 alone. After a decline during the late 1990s, the rate shot up again to 27,423 km^2 in 2004.

Partly due to the return to democracy in 1984, new environmental movements within and outside Brazil began to influence official and public opinion. The national environmental movement in Brazil gained its strongest initial attention as ecological groups mobilized at the United Nations Earth Summit, hosted in Rio de Janeiro in 1992. In the years that followed, international advocacy networks established a presence in Brazil, led by the World Wildlife Fund and Greenpeace. These and domestic groups pressured the government to make commitments to reduce carbon emissions and to reduce deforestation, which undermines the capacity of the planet to absorb excess CO_2. By clamping down on illegal natural resource extraction and unsustainable slash-and-burn agriculture, the Brazilian state has been able to slow the deforestation rate to 6,900 km^2, the lowest levels recorded since 1970. Yet improved policing via satellite and follow-up on the ground are necessary to keep these rates low and falling.

Under the Lula and Dilma administrations, Brazil made substantial commitments to address environmental problems. Brazil signed and ratified all of the major multilateral conventions on species depletion, climate change, toxic waste, as well as the environmental framework agreement for Mercosul, making the customs union a notable presence in international environmental legislation. Brazil has also agreed to reduce its carbon dioxide emissions by 36.1–38.9 percent below what they would otherwise be in 2020. Conservation efforts have also increased, with a total of over 60 million hectares under legal protection from exploitation.

But these commitments may also be undermined by the dominant economic development model with its emphasis on extraction of natural resources, and especially off-shore oil. Dilma Rousseff's government has been most enthusiastic about the most environmentally questionable projects, including the massive Belo Monte Dam in Pará. Governmental and non-governmental environment impact statements note that the project will cause loss of habitat, affect fish migration routes, disrupt water supply on the Xingú river, and violate the cultural and human rights of indigenous groups

Brazilian President Luiz Inacio Lula da Silva is shown in this photo attending a reelection campaign wearing a cap of the Landless Movement (MST).

AP Images/Victor R. Caivano

in the area. By the time the Belo Monte dam is finished, it will be the second largest in Brazil, behind Itaipú, and the world's third largest after China's Three Gorges Dam.

Brazil in the Global Economy

Brazil has maintained strategic relations with the global market. The financing needs of state-led industrialization required Brazil to pursue international sources of credit, making it the largest debtor country in Latin America during the 1980s.[10] When soaring inflation in the industrialized countries ratcheted up interest rates on the debt, Brazilian growth slowed under the weight of higher interest payments.

Unlike the other large Latin American countries, Brazil rejected the reform agenda proposed by the International Monetary Fund (IMF). Although the Collor and Cardoso governments implemented some of this agenda by reducing tariffs and privatizing some state companies, Brazil's economy retained much of its autonomy in the global market. Tariff rates are among the highest in the developing world, the state still owns golden shares in several large, privatized firms, and the state engages in industrial policy, particularly through the National Development Bank (BNDES). As its trade relations have changed, Brazil has even turned away from some of its commitments to hemispheric trade agreements (see Global Connection: Governing the Economy in a World of States: The Rise of China and Brazilian Trade).

GLOBAL CONNECTION

Governing the Economy in a World of States: The Rise of China and Brazilian Trade

Although no more than 14 percent of Brazil's GDP is represented by exports, the roles of trade and foreign economic policy have become more central elements of Brazil's development. Soon after China joined the World Trade Organization (WTO) in October 2001, it became Brazil's largest trade partner, surpassing the United States and the European Union. Brazilian exports of soy and iron ore have proven strategic to China's economic boom and Chinese demand, in turn, helped sustain the longest period of economic growth in Brazil since the 1970s. Total Brazilian exports to China increased from $7.7 billion in 2005 to $46.5 billion by 2011 or 18 percent of Brazil's total exports.

The expansion of trade with China coincided with a reorientation of Brazil's foreign economic policy. During the 1990s, Brazil led its neighbors, Argentina, Paraguay, and Uruguay, to create the Common Market of the South (MERCOSUL). Under the Treaty of Asunción (1995), the partners agreed to reduce tariffs on imports from signatories and impose a common external tariff (CET) ranging from 0 to 23 percent of imports by non-members. As Brazil's trade with China and other parts of the world have increased, trade with MERCOSUL partners declined after 2006. This reality coincided with Brazil's interests under the Lula and Dilma administrations to diversify

(continued)

trade relations by cultivating more South–South trade in South Asia, Africa, and East and Southeast Asia. Brazil currently supplies 37 percent of all Latin American exports to Asia.

MERCOSUL remains active, but the signatories have failed to deepen it into a more effective common market along the lines of the European Union. Brazil's reorientation toward trade, spurred by China's rise, has also made it less interested in pursuing a hemispheric free trade accord led by the United States. Indeed, Brazil is more likely than

it was in the past to engage in trade rows with the United States before the WTO and to pursue a more aggressive posture with its neighbors in trade conflicts.

MAKING CONNECTIONS Does the linkage between Brazilian growth and the rise of China empower or limit the capacity of the Brazilian government to control the economy?

Source: Alfred P. Montero, *Brazil: Reversal of Fortune* (Cambridge: Polity Press, 2014), Chapter 7.

Nevertheless, Brazil's commitment to the international free-trade system will likely expand with the growing importance of its export sector. Maintaining a healthy trade surplus will continue to be a major component in the country's formula for growth, especially as commodity prices for soy, oranges, wheat, coffee, and other products increase. At the same time, Brazil cannot depend on the occasional "commodity boom" to sustain growth. It is becoming one of the major manufacturing and agrindustry nodes in the globalized system of production and consumption with ties to East Asia becoming more important as a target market for exports but also outward-oriented Brazilian companies such as the airplane manufacturer, Embraer. A frequent user of the WTO dispute resolution apparatus, Brazil will increasingly employ the rules governing international trade to protect these interests and secure market access.

Where Do You Stand?

Neoliberals recognize that the state has played an important role in the development of Brazil, but they point to the failures of ISI to show that more market-oriented policies are necessary. Do you agree more with the neoliberals or with the statists?

Brazilians like to say that the size of their economy gives Brazil the right to exercise its influence around the world. Do you agree?

politics of the governors

In Brazil, refers to periods of history in which state governors acquire extraordinary powers over domains of policy that were previously claimed by the federal government. The term refers most commonly to the Old Republic and the current state of Brazilian federalism.

GOVERNANCE AND POLICY-MAKING

SECTION 3

Organization of the State

Brazilian state institutions have changed significantly since independence. Even so, a number of institutional legacies continue to shape Brazilian politics. The most important is the centralization of state authority in the executive. This process began with the rise of Getúlio Vargas and the New State during the 1930s (see "Profile: Getúlio Dornelles Vargas"). Yet old tendencies such as the **politics of the governors** helped shape the constitution of 1988, not to preserve the centralization of presidentialism but to reestablish the decentralization of federalism.

The Brazilian state has traditionally placed vast power in the hands of the executive. The directly elected president is the head of state, head of government, and commander-in-chief of the armed forces. Although the executive is one of three branches of government (along with the legislature and the judiciary), Brazilian presidents have traditionally been less bound by judicial and legislative constraints than most of their European or North American counterparts. Brazilian constitutions have granted more discretion to the executive than to the other branches in enforcing laws or making policy. But central power has been secular. The Catholic Church has never controlled any portion of the state apparatus or directly influenced national politics as it has in other Catholic countries.

Brazil's executive and the bureaucracy manage most of the policy-making and implementation functions of government. The state lacks the checks and balances of the U.S. government system. It differs also from the semipresidentialism of France. Both the Brazilian federal legislature and state governments look to the president and to the minister of the economy for leadership on policy. The heads

---

📇 PROFILE

Getúlio Dornelles Vargas

Getúlio Vargas as president in 1952.

Source: Keystone/Stringer/ Hulton Archive/Getty Images.

Getúlio Dornelles Vargas (1883–1954) came from a wealthy family in the cattle-rich southernmost state of Rio Grande do Sul. Vargas's youth was marked by political divisions within his family between federalists and republicans, conflicts that separated Brazilians during the Old Republic and particularly in Rio Grande do Sul. Political violence, which was common in the state's history, also affected Vargas's upbringing. His two brothers were each accused of killing rivals, one at the military school in Minas Gerais that Getúlio attended with one of his older siblings. After a brief stint in the military, Vargas attended law school in Porto Alegre, where he excelled as an orator.

After graduating in 1907, he became a district attorney. Later, he served as majority leader in the state senate. In 1923, Vargas was elected federal deputy for Rio Grande do Sul, and in 1924 he became leader of his state's delegation in the Chamber of Deputies. In 1926, he became finance minister. He served for a year before winning the governorship of his home state. Never an ideologue, Vargas practiced a highly pragmatic style of governing that made him one of Brazil's most popular politicians.

Vargas's position as governor of Rio Grande do Sul catapulted him into national prominence in 1929. The international economic crisis forced several regional economic oligarchies to unite in opposition to the coffee and pro-export financial policies of the government and in favor of efforts to protect their local economies. The states, including the state of São Paulo, divided their support between two candidates for the presidency: Julio Prestes, who was supported by President Luis, and Vargas, head of the opposition. The two states of Minas Gerais and Rio Grande do Sul voted as a bloc for Vargas, but he lost the 1930 election. Immediately afterward, a coup by military and political leaders installed Vargas in power.

The reforms of Vargas's New State after 1937 established the revised terms that linked Brazilian society to the state. Even today, his political legacy continues in the form of state agencies designed to promote economic development and laws protecting workers and raising living standards for families so that they do not suffer from poverty and hunger.

MAKING CONNECTIONS In what ways was Vargas's embrace of pragmatism reflected in the institutions that he created to govern the Brazilian political system and the economy?

Source: Robert M. Levine, *Father of the Poor? Vargas and His Era* (New York: Cambridge University Press, 1998).

of the key agencies of the economic bureaucracy—the ministers of the economy and of planning, the president of the Central Bank, and the head of the national development bank—have more discretion over the details of policy than the president does. Recent presidents have also had little choice but to delegate authority to the bureaucracy, given the growing complexity of economic and social policy. Ultimate authority nevertheless remains in the hands of the president, who may replace cabinet ministers.

Although the Brazilian president is the dominant player among the three branches of government, the powers of the legislature and the judiciary have become stronger. The 1988 constitution gave many oversight functions to the legislature and judiciary, so that much presidential discretion in economic and social policy is now subject to approval by either the legislature or the judiciary, or both (see Table 9.1).

The Executive

Although the adoption of parliamentarism was briefly considered following the 1987 National Constituent Assembly, Brazil remained presidential. Even so, rules designed to rein in the federal executive found their way into the 1988 constitution. Partly in reaction to the extreme centralization of executive authority during military rule, the delegates restored some congressional prerogatives from before 1964, and they granted new ones, including oversight of economic policy and the right to be consulted on executive appointments. Executive decrees, which allowed the president to legislate directly, were replaced by "provisional measures" (also known as "emergency measures"). Provisional measures preserved the president's power to legislate for sixty days, at the end of which congress can pass, reject, or allow the provisional law to expire. But consistent with the assertion of congressional power, new restrictions on provisional measures passed both houses of Congress in 2001. Since especially the Fernando Henrique Cardoso presidency, presidents and the leaders of the largest parties in the Congress have haggled over the details of legislation with each branch requiring patronage from the other to secure passage. Nevertheless, Brazilian presidents through their prerogative in initiating annual budgets and employing provisional measures for other legislation retain considerable powers to legislate.[11]

The president is elected for a four-year term with the opportunity to stand for re-election in a consecutive term. The major presidential candidates since the Cardoso presidency have tended to be prominent government ministers or governors from states such as São Paulo and Rio de Janeiro. These elites often capture party nominations with the organizations to which they are already affiliated, making national conventions nothing less than coronations. Political allies then shift resources to those candidates they believe will most likely win and shower patronage back at supporters once in government. Though there are parallels with the U.S. presidency, Brazilian presidents are institutionally empowered differently (see "The U.S. Connection: The Presidency").

Since the beginning of the military governments, the ministry of economy has had more authority than any other executive agency of the state. These powers grew in response to the economic problems of the 1980s and 1990s. As a result of their control of the federal budget and the details of economic policy, recent ministers of the economy have had levels of authority typical of a prime minister in a parliamentary system. This power is shared somewhat with the head of the Central Bank, which coordinates monetary authority and financial regulations with the presidency.

U.S. CONNECTION

The Presidency

Like the American president, the Brazilian president is the only executive elected by all eligible voters throughout the country. He or she is the figure that the voters most identify as the head of government and head of state. Yet the Brazilian presidency has powers that exceed those of the American president. Over 85 percent of all bills before congress emerge from the Palácio do Planalto, home of the president's offices in Brasília. The most important bill is the annual budget, which is crafted by the chiefs of the economic bureaucracy and the presidency and then sent to congress. The Senate and the Chamber of Deputies may amend legislation, but that is usually done with an eye to what the president will accept. Like the American president, the Brazilian president maintains a pocket veto and like forty-three governors but not the U.S. president, also has a line-item veto. Brazilian presidents may also impound approved funds, which makes legislators mindful of enacting policies in ways not favored by the president. Brazilian presidents can issue executive orders that take the force of law, but these decrees can operate in areas normally reserved for the congress. "Provisional measures," as they are called in Brazil, are employed regularly and with little judicial oversight, though they are often the focus of negotiations with congressional leaders, who since 2001 have more of a say in their ratification.

Given the Brazilian state's extensive bureaucratic apparatus, the president has extensive powers of appointment. During the New Republic, presidents have had the power to appoint upwards of 48,000 civil servants, eight times more than the 6,000 appointed by American presidents. Of these, only ambassadors, high court justices, the solicitor general, and the president of the Central Bank are subject to Senate approval.

Similar to the American president, the Brazilian president is the commander-in-chief of the armed forces. In practice, however, the military branches have retained some prerogatives over internal promotion, judicial oversight, and the development of new weapons systems. Brazilian presidents since Collor have exerted their authority over the military, restricting the autonomy of the armed forces over some of these areas.

MAKING CONNECTIONS How is the Brazilian presidency stronger than the American presidency and in what ways is it weaker?

The Bureaucracy: State and Semipublic Firms

Bureaucratic agencies and public firms have played a key role in Brazilian economic and political development. After 1940, the state created a large number of new agencies and public enterprises. Many of these entities were allowed to accumulate their own debt and plan development projects without undue influence from central ministries or politicians. Public firms became a key part of the triple alliance of state, foreign, and domestic capital that governed the state-led model of development. By 1981, the federal government owned ten of the top twenty-five enterprises in Brazil, and state governments owned eight others. Public expenditures as a share of GDP increased from 16 percent in 1947 to more than 32 percent in 1969, far higher than in any other Latin American country except socialist Cuba.

Much of this spending (and the huge debt that financed it) was concentrated on development projects, many of gigantic proportions. Key examples include the world's largest hydroelectric plant, Itaipú; Petrobrás's petroleum processing centers; steel mills such as the gargantuan National Steel Company in Volta Redonda, Rio de Janeiro; and Vale do Rio Doce (today known only as Vale), which maintains interests in sectors as diverse as mining, transport, paper, and textiles. On the eve of the debt crisis in 1982, the top thirty-three projects accumulated U.S. $88 billion in external debt, employed 1.5 million people, and contributed $47 billion to the GDP.

Managing the planning and finance of these projects calls for enormous skill. Recruitment into the civil service requires passage of exams, with advanced degrees required of those who aspire to management positions in the more technical economic and engineering agencies. For example, the National Bank for Economic and Social Development (BNDES) remains the most important financier of development projects in Brazil. Founded in the early 1950s, the BNDES plays a key role in channeling public funds to industrial projects such as the automobile sector and domestic suppliers of parts and labor. The experience of the BNDES demonstrated that despite Brazil's clientelist legacies, the Brazilian bureaucracy could function effectively. Meritocratic advancement and professional recruitment granted these agencies some autonomy from political manipulation.[12] BNDES's technocracy took on larger responsibilities during the Cardoso, Lula, and Dilma presidencies. At present, the bank manages an array of investment and development projects that make it a larger development bank than the World Bank.

Juridical changes represent some of the most important ways in which the role of the bureaucracy has changed. The 1988 constitution initially reinforced certain bureaucratic monopolies. For example, the state's exclusive control over petroleum, natural gas, exploration of minerals, nuclear energy, and telecommunications was protected constitutionally. But this began to change with the adoption of structural reforms during the 1990s, beginning with the Collor government's National Destatization Program (*Programa Nacional de Destatização*; PND). Under the PND, public firms, amounting to a total value of $39 billion, were sold ($8.5 billion in the steel sector alone). The Cardoso administration went even further. It convinced Congress to amend the constitution to remove the public monopoly on petroleum refining, telecommunications, and infrastructure, making these sectors available for auction or licensing arrangements with private firms. In 1998, much of the public telecommunications sector was privatized, bringing in about $24 billion. Under Lula and Dilma, state-controlled entities such as Petrobras and BNDES have reasserted their role in the economy. The National Development Bank has been assertive in adopting a clear mission of providing long-term finance and even venture capital to promote productivity-enhancing investments such as new technology.

Other State Institutions

The Judiciary

Brazil has a network of state courts, with jurisdiction over state matters, and a federal court system, not unlike the one in the United States, which maintains jurisdiction over federal crimes. A supreme court (the Supreme Federal Tribunal), similar in jurisdiction to the U.S. Supreme Court acts as the final arbiter of court cases. The Supreme Federal Tribunal's eleven justices are nominated by the president and confirmed by an absolute majority of the Senate. The Superior Court of Justice, with thirty-three sitting justices, operates beneath the Supreme Federal Tribunal as an appeals court. The Supreme Federal Tribunal decides constitutional questions. The military maintains its own court system.

The judiciary adjudicates political conflicts as well as civil and social conflicts. The Electoral Supreme Tribunal (*Tribunal Supremo Eleitoral*, TSE) has exclusive responsibility to organize and oversee all issues related to elections. The TSE has the power to investigate charges of political bias by public employees, file criminal charges against persons violating electoral laws, and validate electoral results. In addition to these constitutional provisions, the TSE monitors the legal compliance of electoral campaigns and executive neutrality in campaigns. Political candidates with pending charges are allowed to run for office, but they are prohibited from taking their elected seats if they do not resolve the charges. Dozens of "dirty record" (*ficha suja*) candidates have been prevented from running for office, reinforcing the power that the TSE and its regional electoral courts have to oversee all elections.

As in the rest of Latin America, penal codes established by legislation govern the powers of judges. This makes the judiciary less flexible than in North America, which operates on case law, but it provides a more effective barrier against judicial activism—the tendency of the courts to render broad interpretations of the law. The main problem in the Brazilian system has been the lack of judicial review. Lower courts do not have to follow the precedents of the STF or STJ, though that has been changing due to judicial reforms passed since 2004.

In recent years, the judiciary has been severely criticized for its perceived unresponsiveness to Brazil's social problems and persistent corruption in the lower courts. In rural areas, impoverished defendants are often denied the right to a fair trial by powerful landowners, who have undue influence over judges and procedures. Courts have also refused to hear cases prosecuting those who organize child prostitution, pornography, and murder of street urchins.

Corruption in the judiciary is an important and high-profile issue. The federal police has initiated a number of investigations since 2003 to root out corrupt judges. Typically, these cases expose criminal rings that implicate state and federal judges, police officers, and other agents of the court system.

Restructuring the judiciary continues to receive attention. In December 2004, Congress passed a comprehensive reform meant to increase the capacity of the STF and STJ to set precedent and reduce the number of appeals. The reform established a National Judicial Council to regulate the lower courts, where judges are more tolerant of nepotism and conflict of interest. Some critics view these reforms as inadequate, on the grounds that the structure of the judiciary and its approach to interpreting and implementing laws are the central obstacles to accomplishing policy goals. Observers applaud the professionalization of prosecutorial and investigatory offices, especially the Public Ministry, the federal and state prosecutors, and the auditing agencies of the federal and state treasuries. Strict civil service guidelines, meritocratic admission and advancement, and much oversight provided by these agencies may induce further reforms within the judiciary and the wider bureaucracy as cases of corruption by elected and appointed official come to light.

Subnational Government

Like Germany, Mexico, India, and the United States, the Brazilian state has a federal structure. The country's twenty-six states are subdivided into 5,564 municipal governments. The structure of subnational politics in Brazil consists of a governor; his or her chief advisers, who also usually lead key secretariats such as economy and planning; and a unicameral legislature often dominated by the supporters of the governor. Governors serve four-year terms and are limited to two consecutive terms in office.

By controlling patronage through their powers of appointment and spending, governors and even some mayors can wield extraordinary influence.[13] The 1982 elections were the first time since the military regime when Brazilians could elect their governors directly. This lent legitimacy to the governors' campaign to decentralize fiscal resources. In recent years, attempts to mollify this subnational constituency have watered down key pieces of reform legislation. Political decentralization further fragmented the Brazilian polity, but it also empowered some subnational governments to create innovative new policies.[14] The 1988 constitution accelerated this process by giving the states and municipalities a larger share of tax revenues. During the early to mid-1990s, this process went too far, allowing states and cities to go deeply into debt. The Cardoso administration went the farthest to slow down this unsustainable process of debt-led subnational spending. The federal government required states and municipalities to finance a larger share of social spending. The Central Bank took over bankrupt state banks and privatized most of them. The Fiscal Responsibility Law of 2000 introduced new penalties for profligacy by subnational governments.

Nevertheless, governors and mayors remain significant actors in policy-making. These politicians remain leaders in their parties as they are key hubs for the distribution of patronage to lower-ranked politicians. At the same time, these leaders have sometimes demonstrated the capacity for good government. One study of the state of Ceará has demonstrated that even the most underdeveloped subnational governments can promote industrial investment, employment, and social services.[15]

The Military and the Police

Like many other South American militaries, the Brazilian armed forces retain substantial independence from civilian presidents and legislators. Brazil has suffered numerous coups; those in 1930 and 1964 were critical junctures, while others brought in caretaker governments that eventually yielded to civilian rule. The generals continue to maintain influence in Brazilian politics, blocking policies they do not like and lobbying on behalf of those they favor.

The military's participation in Brazilian politics became more limited, if still quite expansive, following the transition to democracy. Several laws gave the military broad prerogatives to "guarantee internal order" and to play a "tutelary role" in civilian government. During the Sarney administration, members of the armed forces retained cabinet-level rank in areas of importance to the military, such as the ministries of the armed forces and the nuclear program. Most important, the military succeeded in securing amnesty for human rights abuses committed during the preceding authoritarian regime. In an effort to professionalize the armed forces, the Collor government slashed the military budget, thereby reducing the autonomy that the military enjoyed during the authoritarian period. Collor also replaced the top generals with officers who had few or no connections to the authoritarian regime and were committed to civilian leadership. Cardoso introduced a new security strategy that thoroughly professionalized the armed forces, leaving them out of civilian processes controlling the defense budget.

In recent years, the militarization that most Brazilians see involves their local police forces. The state police consists of two forces: the civil police force, which acts as an investigative unit, and the uniformed military police force, which maintains order. The military police do not just regulate military personnel but civilians as well. They often partake in specialized commando-type operations in urban areas, especially in the *favelas*, and they engage in riot control. These forces are only nominally controlled by state governors; they are, in fact, trained, equipped, and managed by the armed forces, which also maintain a separate judicial system to try officers for wrongdoing.

Rising urban crime rates produced a movement to "pacify" and hold areas that had once been ceded de facto to drug gangs. "Pacification units" of specialized police forces routinely invade and patrol *favelas* in Rio, São Paulo, Recife, and other major cities with destitute urban rings. The specter of criminal violence has shocked Brazilians into voting for politicians who promise better police security. But Brazilians have learned that police forces themselves are often part of the problem.

Despite official oversight of police authorities, in practice the military and civil police forces in many cities of the northeast, in São Paulo, and in Rio de Janeiro often act abusively. Cases of arbitrary detention, torture, corruption, and systematic killings by Brazilian police have been the focus of periodic human rights investigations.[16] The police are also targets of violence, as organized crime syndicates, especially in São Paulo, have become more brazen in their attacks on police installations.

The federal police force is a small unit of approximately 3,000 people. It operates like a combined U.S. Federal Bureau of Investigation, Secret Service, Drug Enforcement Agency, and Immigration and Naturalization Service. Despite its limited size, the federal police force has been at the center of every national investigation of corruption. Thanks to the federal police and the Public Ministry, the official federal prosecutor with offices in each of Brazil's states and the federal district, the federal government's capacity for investigation and law enforcement has expanded considerably.

The Policy-Making Process

Although policy-making continues to be fluid and ambiguous, certain domains of policy are clearly demarcated. Foreign policy, for example, is exclusively the responsibility of the executive branch. Political parties and the Congress still have only inconsistent power over investment policies. Bureaucratic agencies retain command over the details of social and economic policies.

Clientelism injects itself at every stage of policy-making, from formulation and decision making to implementation. Established personal contacts often shape who benefits from policy-making. Quid pro quos, nepotism, and other kinds of favoritism, if not outright corruption, regularly obstruct or distort policy-making.[17] Complex formal and informal networks link the political executive, key agencies of the bureaucracy, and private interests. These networks are the chief players in clientelist circles. Cardoso described these clientelistic networks as **bureaucratic rings**. He considered the Brazilian state to be highly permeable, fragmented, and therefore easily colonized by private interests that make alliances with midlevel bureaucratic officers to shape public policy to benefit themselves.

One example of the role of bureaucratic rings is the creation of large development projects. Governors and mayors want lucrative public projects to be placed in their jurisdictions; private contractors yearn for the state's business; and politicians position themselves for all the attendant kickbacks, political and pecuniary.[18]

Among the key sources of influence outside the state is organized business. Unlike business associations in some Asian and West European countries, Brazilian business groups have remained independent of corporatist ties to the state. Business associations have also remained aloof from political parties. Lobbying by Brazilian entrepreneurs is common, and their participation in bureaucratic rings is legendary. Few major economic policies are passed without the input of the Federation of São Paulo Industries (*Federação das Industrias do Estado de São Paulo*, or FIESP).

The country's labor confederations and unions have had less consistent access to policymaking. Although unions were once directly organized and manipulated by the corporatist state, they gained autonomy in the late 1970s and the 1980s. From then on, they sought leverage over policy-making through outside channels, such as the link between the *Central Única dos Trabalhadores* (CUT, Workers' Singular Peak Association) and Lula da Silva's Workers' Party. Attempts to bring labor formally into direct negotiations with business and the state have failed, in part due to widening

bureaucratic rings

A term developed by the Brazilian sociologist and president Fernando Henrique Cardoso that refers to the highly permeable and fragmented structure of the state bureaucracy that allows private interests to make alliances with midlevel bureaucratic officers. By shaping public policy to benefit these interests, bureaucrats gain the promise of future employment in the private sector. While in positions of responsibility, bureaucratic rings are ardent defenders of their own interests.

cleavages within the union movement due to their sector's orientation toward trade, technology, and remuneration.

Debate and lobbying do not stop in Brazil once laws are enacted. Policy implementation is a subject of perpetual bargaining. One salient example is "the Brazilian way" (*o jeito brasileiro*)—a social convention that allows any Brazilian to ask for a temporary suspension of a rule for the sake of expediency. Although *jeito* is used only for relatively minor rules, it delivers the message that the rule of law is not to be entirely respected either by the rich or by the poor.

Where Do You Stand?

Would you consider the Brazilian state "strong"?

Does clientelism in policy-making have redeeming qualities?

REPRESENTATION AND PARTICIPATION

SECTION 4

The fragmentation of legislative politics, the weaknesses of political parties, and the interests of particular politicians and their clientelistic allies make enacting reform on behalf of the national interest extremely difficult. Politicians and parties that can best dispense patronage and cultivate clientele networks are the most successful. More often than not, the main beneficiaries are a small number of elite economic and political interests who develop ongoing relationships with legislators, governors, and presidents.

The transition to democracy, however, coincided with an explosion of civil society activism and mobilization. The expansion of voting rights and the involvement of gender and ethnic groups, urban social movements, and environmental and religious organizations in Brazilian politics have greatly expanded the range of political participation. Just the same, political institutions have failed to harmonize the demands of conflicting forces.

Focus Questions ❓

- In what ways do Brazilian political institutions impede representation and elite accountability?

- How does the mobilization of civil society in Brazil enhance the country's democratic governance?

The Legislature

The 594-member national legislature has an upper house, the Senate, with 81 members, and a lower house, the Chamber of Deputies, with 513 members. Every state and the federal district elect three senators by simple majority. Senators serve for eight-year terms and may be reelected without limit. Two-thirds of the Senate is elected at one time, and the remaining one-third is elected four years later. Senatorial elections are held at the same time as those for the Chamber of Deputies, all of whose members are elected on a four-year cycle. Federal deputies may be reelected without limits. Each state is allowed a minimum of eight and a maximum of seventy deputies, according to population. This introduces severe malapportionment in the allocation of seats. Without the ceiling and floor on seats, states with large populations, such as São Paulo, would have more than seventy deputies, and states in the underpopulated Amazon, such as Roraima, would have fewer than eight.

The two houses of the legislature share equal authority to make laws, and both must approve a bill for it to become law. Each chamber can propose or veto legislation passed by the other. When the two chambers pass bills on a given topic that contain different provisions, they go back and forth between houses without going through a joint conference committee, as in the United States. Once a bill is passed by both houses in identical form, the president may sign it into law, reject it as a whole, or accept some and reject other parts of it. The legislature can override a presidential veto by a majority vote in both houses during a joint session, but such instances are rare. Constitutional amendments must be passed twice by three-fifths of the votes in each house of congress. Amendments may also be passed by an absolute majority in a special constituent assembly proposed by the president and created by both houses of congress. The Senate is empowered to try the president and other top officials, including the vice president and key ministers and justices, for impeachable offenses. It also approves the president's nominees to high offices, including justices of the high courts, heads of diplomatic missions, and directors of the Central Bank.

Legislators view their service primarily as a means to enhance their own income, thanks to generous public pensions and kickbacks earned from dispensing political favors. Election to the federal legislature is often used as a stepping stone to even more lucrative, especially executive, posts. After the presidency, the most coveted positions are the governorships of industrialized states. Most members of Congress come from the middle or upper-middle classes; most of these have much to gain if they can step into well-paid posts in the executive and the parastatal enterprises following their congressional service. A mere 3 percent of seats in Congress are held by Afro-Brazilians. Only 9 percent of the seats in the Chamber and 14 percent of those in the Senate are held by women.

The many deficiencies of the Brazilian legislature were highlighted in recent years by several corruption scandals. Vote buying in the Congress by the Lula government is the most prominent example, but kickbacks from public contracts are even more common. With the matter of corruption very much in the news cycle in Brazil, Congress is often criticized for its lack of accountability. One response to legislative corruption has been to use parliamentary commissions of inquiry to review allegations of malfeasance by elected officials. Although these temporary committees have demonstrated some influence, they have rarely produced results. The temporary committees work alongside sixteen permanent legislative committees that treat issues as diverse as taxation and human rights. These committees, however, are not nearly as strong as the major committees in the U.S. Congress. Legislative committees, both temporary and permanent, often fail to conclude an investigation or find solutions to persistent dilemmas in policy.

Political Parties and the Party System

Many of the traditional weaknesses of the party system were reinforced after the transition to democracy, making parties anemic. Politicians switched parties nearly at will to increase their access to patronage, sometimes during their terms in office. A Supreme Court decision in 2007 ruled against this practice but allowed switching prior to elections. Other rules of the electoral system create incentives for politicians to ignore party labels. Brazil's experience with proportional representation (PR), which is used to elect federal and state deputies, is particularly important in this regard. Proportional representation may be based on either a closed-list or an open-list system. In closed-list PR, the party selects the order of politicians, and voters cannot cross party lines. Because voters are effectively choosing the party that best represents them, this system encourages party loyalty among both the electorate and individual politicians. In an open-list PR system, the voters have more discretion and can cross party lines. Brazil's PR system is open-list. On electronic voting machines, voters cast their ballots for individuals not parties by inputting the candidate's electoral number. The geographic boundaries of electoral districts in Brazil for state and federal deputies are entire states. There are few limits on how many individuals and parties may run in the same electoral district. Crowded fields discourage party loyalty and emphasize the personal qualities of candidates, who must stand out in the minds of voters. Worse still, the open-list PR system creates incentives for politicians to ignore party labels, because voters can cross party lines with ease.

With so much emphasis on the personal qualities of politicians, ambitious individuals can ignore the established party hierarchies while achieving elected office. As a result, Brazil has the most fragmented party system in Latin America and one of the most fragmented in the world. This makes parties extremely poor vehicles for representing political alternatives. Brazil's electoral system further fragments power because state, not national, parties select legislative candidates. In most cases, Brazilian governors exert tremendous influence over nominations.

Given the political fragmentation of the legislature and the weakness of the party system, presidents struggle to maintain majority alliances in Congress. Since the Cardoso presidency, the distribution of cabinet ministries to the leaders or notables of other parties has been a primary means of crafting congressional alliances. Some political scientists have argued that this system of "coalitional presidentialism" is stable and has enabled the political system to become more governable. That may be true, but it is also the case that the system is confusing and can easily become the focus of corruption as it did when Lula's government was exposed for organizing a vote-buying scheme in 2005.

Fundamental to the confusing nature of the Brazilian political system is the number of political organizations that have emerged over the last few years. These parties can be defined ideologically, although the categories are not as internally consistent or cut and dry as they might seem (see Table 9.4).

Political parties on the right currently defend neoliberal economic policies designed to shrink the size of the public sector. They support the reduction and partial privatization of the welfare state. On constitutional reform, right-wing parties are fairly united in favor of rolling back social spending; they also advocate electoral reform—specifically, the establishment of a majority or mixed, rather than purely proportional, district voting system.

A loose set of conservative parties currently struggles for the mantle of the right. In front of the pack is the PFL (Party of the Liberal Front), which was refounded in 2007 as the Democrats (DEM). PFL/DEM is one of the larger parties in the Senate and the Chamber and has generally opposed President Lula. Many small parties have allied with right-wing and center-right parties or advocated right-wing issues, such as the Brazilian Labor Party (PTB), the Progressive Party (PP), and the evangelistic Liberal Party/Party of the Republic (PL/PR).

The two other largest parties in congress are the PMDB (Party of the Brazilian Democratic Movement, the successor to the old MDB) and the PSDB. These parties, while having disparate leftist and rightist elements, tend to dominate the center and center-left segments of the ideological spectrum. Along with the PFL/DEM, these have been the key governing parties during the democratic era. There is agreement

Table 9.4	The Democratic Idea: The Major Parties in Brazil
Conservative/Right-Wing Parties	
PFL/DEM	*Partido da Frente Liberal* (Party of the Liberal Front) (refounded as the *Democratas* (Democrats) in 2007)
PL/PR	*Partido Liberal (Liberal Party)* (refounded as the Party of the Republic in 2007)
PP	*Partido Progressista* (Progressive Party)
Centrist Parties	
PMDB	*Partido do Movimento Democrático Brasileiro* (Party of the Brazilian Democratic Movement)
PSDB	*Partido da Social Democracia Brasileira* (Party of Brazilian Social Democracy)
Populist/Leftist Parties	
PT	*Partido dos Trabalhadores* (Workers' Party)
PSB	*Partido Socialista Brasileiro* (Brazilian Socialist Party)
PCdoB	*Partido Comunista do Brasil* (Communist Party of Brazil)
PDT	*Partido Democrático Trabalhista* (Democratic Labor Party)
PPS	*Partido Popular Socialista (ex-Partido Comunista Brasileiro)* (Popular Socialist Party)

that these parties have become more cohesive in favor of neoliberal reform, and hence they can be characterized as being on the right or center-right.[19]

Political parties on the left advocate reducing deficits and inflation but also maintaining the present size of the public sector and improving the welfare state. Left-oriented parties want to expand the state's role in promoting and protecting domestic industry. On constitutional reform, they support the social rights guaranteed by the 1988 constitution.

The Workers' Party (PT) has been the most successful of the leftist parties, having elected Luiz Inácio "Lula" da Silva twice to the presidency followed by Dilma Rousseff. The PT was founded by workers who had defied the military government and engaged in strikes in São Paulo's metalworking and automobile industries in 1978 and 1979. Although the PT began with a working-class message and leftist platform, its identity broadened and moderated during the 1980s and early 1990s. Under Lula's leadership the party increasingly sought the support of the middle class, rural and urban poor, and even segments of business and the upper classes. In the years preceding Lula's presidency, the party moderated its criticism of capitalism, ultimately accepting many of the economic reforms that Cardoso implemented. During Lula's presidency, the PT moved further to the center, leaving its left-most flank exposed in elections. Former PT member Marina Silva's third-place showing in the 2010 presidential race and her probable challenge to Dilma will incite others, possibly Eduardo Campos, the popular governor of Pernambuco, whose PSB has allied with the PT but may consider leading the leftist challenge to the PT.

Currently, no party has more than 25 percent of the seats in either house of Congress (see Figures 9.4 and 9.5). Cardoso's multiparty alliance of the PSDB-PFL-PTB-PPB controlled 57 percent of the vote in the lower house and 48 percent in the upper house. Lula failed to organize a similar "governing coalition"; his government depended on enticing centrist and center-right parties to vote for his legislation. His successor, Dilma Rousseff, enjoys a larger support base in Congress than Lula or even Cardoso, given the erosion of conservative parties' seat shares.

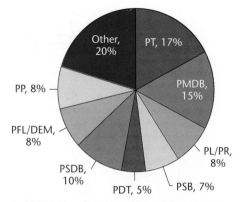

FIGURE 9.4 Share of Seats of the Major Parties in the Chamber of Deputies, Based on October 2010 Election Results

Source: Data from final TSE numbers.

Elections

The Brazilian electorate stands at 135 million with an average turnout well above 80 percent. These figures make it the largest and most participatory electorate in Latin America. Compulsory voting, improved literacy, and efforts by political parties, especially on the left, to educate citizens on the value of participation have expanded the electorate impressively.

Yet given the multiplicity of parties, unbalanced apportionment of seats among the states, and the sheer size of some state-sized electoral districts, candidates often have few incentives to be accountable to their constituencies. In states with hundreds of candidates running in oversized electoral districts, the votes obtained by successful candidates are often widely scattered, limiting the accountability of those elected. In less-populated states, there are more seats and parties per voter; the electoral and party quotients are lower. As a result, candidates often alter their legal place of residence immediately before an election in order to run from a safer seat, compounding the lack of accountability.

With the *abertura*, political parties gained the right to broadcast electoral propaganda on radio and television. All radio stations and TV channels are required to carry, at no charge, two hours of party programming each day during a campaign season. The parties are entitled to an amount of time on the air proportional to their number of votes in the previous election. But some candidates gain more access through private channels and community radio stations that family members may own.

Despite the short-comings, Brazilians have voted in larger numbers and have avoided the kinds of anti-system protests seen in other Latin American countries. Nevertheless, participation is not enough. Relatively few Brazilians identify with a political party, and the vast majority of those who do are aligned to the PT. Most Brazilians have no clear left-right ideology, so there is little to align political representatives and voters other than material interests.

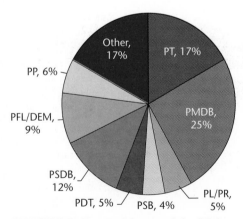

FIGURE 9.5 Share of Seats of the Major Parties in the Senate, Based on October 2010 Election Results

Source: Data from final TSE numbers.

Luiz Inácio "Lula" da Silva, founder of the Workers' Party and Brazilian president (2002–2006)

© iStockphoto.com/EdStock

Not surprisingly, Brazilians remain disappointed with the results of democracy. The weakness of political parties, coupled with the persistence of clientelism and accusations of corruption against even previously squeaky clean parties such as the PT, have disillusioned average Brazilians and have generated support for occasional protests that call attention to systemic problems without calling for a change of the regime itself.

Political Culture, Citizenship, and Identity

The notion of national identity describes a sense of national community that goes beyond mere allegiance to a state, a set of economic interests, regional loyalties, or kinship affiliations. A national identity gains strength through a process of nation building during which a set of national symbols, cultural terms and images, and shared myths consolidate around historical experiences that define the loyalties of a group of people.

Several developments made Brazilian nation building possible. Unlike nation formation in culturally, linguistically, and geographically diverse Western Europe, Africa, and Asia, Brazil enjoyed a homogeneous linguistic and colonial experience. As a result, Brazilian history largely avoided the ethnic conflicts that have become obstacles to nation building in Eastern Europe, Nigeria, and India. Immigrants added their ideas and value systems at the turn of the century, but they brought no compelling identities that could substitute for an overarching national consciousness. Regional secessionist movements were uncommon in Brazilian history and were short-lived episodes when they did emerge in the twentieth century.

Despite Brazil's rich ethnic makeup, racial identities in Brazil have seldom been the basis for political action. Brazilians often agreed on the spurious idea that Brazil was a racial democracy. Even in the face of severe economic and political oppression of native peoples, Afro-Brazilians, and Asians, the myth of racial democracy has endured in the national consciousness.

Like the myth of racial democracy, the major collective political identities in Brazilian history have sought to hide or deny the real conflicts in society. For example, the symbols and images of political nationalism tended to boost the quasi-utopian visions of the country's future development. Developmentalists under the military governments and democratic leaders such as Kubitschek espoused optimism that "Brazil is the country of the future." (More cynical Brazilians quipped afterwards that Brazil is the country of the future, and will always be.)

The persistence of optimistic myths about the country in the face of socioeconomic and political realities often leads to angry disengagement from politics. Slow improvements in primary and secondary education have not been enough to produce a more engaged and knowledgeable electorate. Yet avenues for participation have

Carnival in Brazil, the world's largest floor show, is also an insightful exhibition of allegories and popular myths about the country, its people, and their culture.
Reuters/Corbis

proliferated in the democratic period, creating the hope that new identities that are more empowering might develop.

During the redemocratization process, new trends in Brazilian political culture emerged. Most segments of Brazilian society came to embrace "modernization with democracy," even if they would later raise doubts about its benefits. One prominent example is the role played by the Catholic Church in promoting democracy. During the transition, a number of Catholic political organizations and movements aided by the church organized popular opposition to the military governments. After the transition, archbishops of the Catholic Church helped assemble testimonials of torture victims. The publication of these depositions in the book *Nunca Mais* (*Never Again*) fueled condemnation of the authoritarian past. In this way, an establishment that previously had been associated with social conservatism and political oppression became a catalyst of popular opposition to authoritarianism. One well-known outcome of these changes was the development of liberation theology, a doctrine that argued that religion should seek to free people not only from their sins but from social injustice. By organizing community-based movements to press for improved sanitation, clean water, basic education, and, most important, freedom from oppression, Catholic groups mobilized millions of citizens. Among the Brazilian church's most notable accomplishments was the development of an agrarian reform council in the 1970s, the Pastoral Land Commission. The commission called for extending land ownership to poor peasants. The Brazilian church also created ecclesiastical community movements to improve conditions in the *favelas*. Pentecostal and other evangelical movements have fed off of the demand for such organization, producing a more fragmented religious market that has continued to empower Brazilians but without the need to turn to Roman Catholicism.

These trends have coincided with a growing but still tempered distrust of the state. Early during the regime transition, business groups assailed the failures of state-led development, while labor unions claimed that corporatist management of industrial relations could not satisfy the interests of workers. But such distrust was never taken too far. The democratic period has enjoyed a consensus among journalists, economists, politicians, intellectuals, and entrepreneurs that national institutions can be adjusted incrementally to strengthen democracy and promote economic growth. Constitutional, administrative, and economic reform are the focus of those who call for change, including the street protestors that commanded the attention of the world preceding the World Cup.

Those who see Brazilian democracy as holding promise can take comfort from the fact that political transitions since Cardoso's election have been without institutional disruption. When Lula's turn came to occupy the presidential office, he managed to end his presidency with much higher approval ratings than any of his predecessors. Such support came largely from popular social policies such as the Bolsa Família. Lula's success then led voters to elect his handpicked successor, Dilma Rousseff, in 2010. One hopeful lesson from this is that more than Lula's personal charisma was at play in Dilma's election. The policies of Lula's government probably contributed to the 2010 election results. The challenge of selling a complex set of policies to a population with weak political socialization and poor general education has become central to gaining and maintaining political power in Brazil.

Unlike the situation in the United States, the events of 9/11 did not fundamentally change Brazilian political culture or increase the nation's sense of vulnerability. Having suffered the military regime's torture and arbitrary killings—a kind of state terrorism—in their own country, Brazilians are well aware that democracy and decency have enemies capable of the greatest cruelty. Many Brazilians also live with everyday terrors—poverty, hunger, disease, and violence—that they regard as far more dangerous than terrorism.

Interest Groups, Social Movements, and Protest

Despite much disengagement from and distrust of politics, Brazil has a highly participatory democracy. In the mid-1970s, Brazil witnessed an explosion of social and political organization: grassroots popular movements; new forms of trade unionism; neighborhood movements; professional associations of doctors, lawyers, and journalists; entrepreneurial associations; and middle-class organizations. At the same time, a host of non-governmental organizations (NGOs) became more active in Brazil; among them were Amnesty International, Greenpeace, and native Brazilian rights groups. Domestic groups active in these areas increasingly turned to the NGOs for resources and information, adding an international dimension to what was previously an issue of domestic politics.

By the 1980s, women were participating in and leading popular initiatives on a wide variety of issues related to employment and the provision of basic services. Many of these organizations enlisted the support of political parties and trade unions in battles over women's wages, birth control, rape, and violence in the home. Although nearly absent in employers' organizations, women are highly active in rural and urban unions. In recent years, Brazilian women have created more than 3,000 organizations to address issues of concern to women. A good example includes special police stations *(delegacias de defesa da mulher*, DDMs) dedicated to addressing crimes against women, adolescents, and children. The DDMs have been created in major Brazilian cities, and particularly in São Paulo state.

Women's groups have been given a boost as more women have joined the workforce. More than 20 percent of Brazilian families are supported exclusively by women. Social policies such as Bolsa Família reinforce the importance of women in society by focusing their resources on women as the heads of households. Women have also made strides in representative politics and key administrative appointments. Ellen Gracie Northfleet became the first woman to head the Supreme Court until her retirement in 2011; Lula appointed a second woman to the court in 2006. A woman was also named to the board of directors of the Central Bank. Women in formal politics have in recent years become mayors of some major cities, such as São Paulo, and Marina Silva, now with Eduardo Campos's PSB, regularly figures into national conversations about presidential elections. Although in recent years, the number of women with seats in congress has nearly doubled, the rate remains one of the lowest in Latin America.

In contrast to the progress of women's movements, a movement to address racial discrimination has not emerged. Only during the 1940s did some public officials and academics acknowledge that prejudice existed against blacks. At that time, the problems of race were equated with the problems of class. Attacking class inequality was thus considered a way to address prejudice against blacks. This belief seemed plausible because most poor Brazilians are either *pardo* (mulatto) or black. But it might be just as logical to suggest that they are poor because they are black. In any case, the relationship between race and class in Brazil is just as ambiguous as it is in the United States and other multiethnic societies.

Both gender and race are often encompassed in organizational politics that take on social and class-based issues. Conflicts over housing policy, sanitation, transport, health, and education involve not only movements but non-governmental organizations and municipal government. Thousands of Brazilian towns and cities sponsor popular councils and policy-specific conferences that involve a variety of civil societal organizations. Health councils have become the most common, with local citizens debating with organizations and their elected representatives how resources for medical care should be spent. Such processes are said to undercut clientelism by investing in pluralism.

The strength of Brazilian civil society is evident in urban settings, but it has been only sporadically available in the more sparsely populated areas of the Amazon basin. Over the past half-century, large-scale and poorly regulated economic development of the Amazon has threatened the cultures and lives of Indians. Miners, loggers, and land developers typically invade native lands, often with destructive consequences for the ecology and indigenous people. For example, members of the Ianomami, a tribe living in a reserve with rich mineral resources, are frequently murdered by miners. During the military government, the national Indian agency, FUNAI, turned a blind eye to such abuses, claiming that indigenous cultures represented "ethnic cysts to be excised from the body politic."[20] With the *abertura*, many environmental NGOs defended the human rights of indigenous people as part of their campaign to defend the Amazon and its people. As the matter of global warming and the importance of the Amazon as the "green lung of the planet" has focused attention on the region, transnational movements and NGOs have become more involved in publicizing the plight of indigenous peoples and the ecological costs of development.

The Political Impact of Technology

Technology has fundamentally affected the way that Brazilians interact with the political system. The organized media fundamentally affects the choices that voters make. Beyond the large national broadcasters, 2,168 community radio stations, many owned by politicians or family members, exert influence over how citizens think about the issues. More than 78 percent of all towns in Brazil have no other source of radio. In poor areas, such as the Northeast, 35 percent of all stations are controlled by politicians who use them to mobilize their own voters. This form of manipulation of the ideas citizens hear has been dubbed by journalists as *coronelsimo eletrônico* (electronic clientelism)—a high-tech form of the old clientelist networking.

In other ways, technology has improved elite accountability to voters. Electronic voting was adopted nationally a few years after the transition to democracy. The technology, which provides a paper trail, has been effective in eliminating ballot-stuffing, miscounting, and other forms of electoral fraud and incompetence. The creation of an electronic record of voting has also facilitated the work of the National Electoral Court as it investigates cases of attempted fraud around the country.

Social media and politics have mixed in Brazil like in no other country. Brazil maintains the largest population of Facebook and Twitter users outside of the United States. These social media played a fundamental role in the protests that affected 430 cities throughout the country in June 2013. Organizers coordinated their planning and selected timing and location using social media. Like protests such as the various Occupy movement events, these events were leaderless and nonpartisan with various groups employing competing Twitter feeds and Facebook pages to take ownership of the protests. The technological inflections of the protests fit neatly with the youthful element of largely educated, middle-class, white Brazilians that formed much of the vanguard. These participants used social media not only to coordinate the events themselves but to gather video footage and share tips on dealing with tear gas (vinegar was a key ingredient). Of course, the broader the range of participants and their involvement the more the set of issues that motivated the protests expanded to encompass everything from a hike in transport fees to the costs of soccer stadiums and the role of corruption in politics. Technology enhances the organization of protests but does not necessarily make their politics more focused.

Brazil has the world's fastest rate of Internet user growth. The government, through its efforts to deepen the quality of education through modified curricula and the use of standardized tests to identify schools in need, has redoubled its efforts to expand Internet access and computer literacy to the poorest Brazilians. At the same time, the federal government and the states and many cities have made ample use of the Internet to disseminate information and interact with their citizens, especially through social policies in health care, poverty alleviation, and pensions. Brazil presently has perhaps the most transparent system of access to data on government expenditures and policies than any Latin American country. And recent freedom of information legislation has legally empowered regular citizens to open up access to government data even further.

Where Do You Stand?

Supporters of "coalitional presidentialism" see the Brazilian political system as progressively more governable. Do you agree?

Are strong parties necessary in order to make civil societal groups in Brazil more influential in policy-making?

BRAZILIAN POLITICS IN TRANSITION

Political Challenges and Changing Agendas

Focus Questions ▼

• What are some of the legacies of the Lula presidency that have shaped Dilma Rousseff's presidency?

• Is Brazil prepared to be considered a global power?

The contrast between Lula's campaign to become president in 2002 and the Brazil led by Lula that captured the right to stage the 2014 World Cup and the 2016 Olympic Summer games, could not be more stark. In 2002, investment banks and even some policy-makers around the world worried out loud that a Lula presidency would reject capitalism and lead the country to default on its external debt. The giant Wall Street firm, Goldman Sachs, even published a "Lulameter" to inform clients about the probability of a Lula victory and, therefore, impending economic disaster in South America. We now know that those fears were misplaced. Not only did Lula continue Cardoso's market-oriented reforms, he expanded the social policies of his predecessor. High annual growth rates, rising median incomes, and a fall in poverty and inequality levels are Lula's legacy after eight years in office. Far from his being what one investment firm called "Da Lula Monster" of anticapitalism, Lula led Brazil through its most prosperous period since the days of Juscelino Kubitschek and the military's "miracle" economy. With the World Cup and Olympics within view, and the promise of growth in future years based on the exploitation of oil and other natural resources, Brazil can even claim to be a rising world power on a par with China, India, and Russia.

The central challenges of Dilma's presidency have involved the laborious practice of currying center-right support by embracing the very mechanisms of clientelism that create a deadlock in the country's democratic institutions. Institutional obstacles such as the need for 60 percent majorities for major reform legislation have undercut the president's ambitions. Given the focus of the 2013 protests, political reform remains the top priority for the Dilma government if any headway is going to be made. The open-list electoral system should be replaced by a closed-list system to increase the internal discipline of parties. Public financing of campaigns should replace private spending, which reinforces the clientelist networks that too often interfere with the representative function.

Making Brazil's economic development more inclusive is another challenge. Lula was able to make many more poor Brazilians feel included in the economy, especially with the *Bolsa Família* program's targeting of social benefits to lift millions out of poverty. But moving more of these Brazilians into self-sustaining employment in the formal sector will require the creation of jobs. Part of the answer is to mobilize public resources to promote private investment and the exploitation of natural resources. But these strategies face fiscal and ecological limits. More promising is Dilma's efforts to rapidly increase spending on education, particularly in areas such as science, mathematics, and information technology.

The environmental limits of Brazil's economic growth model present systematic concerns. The fact that many of Brazil's exports are still extractive (such as iron ore and lumber), or agricultural commodities (such as soy), place ever more pressure on the country's ecology. Deforestation of the Amazon and international climate change are intricately linked. A key issue is whether Brazil can help preserve the rain forest and reduce its own production of greenhouse gases at the same time that it maintains a brisk rate of economic growth.

The Brazilian state has moved decisively back into a leadership role in promoting economic growth with macroeconomic stability. Sustained by large capital inflows, Lula's government was able to redirect substantially more resources to the National Development Bank. The BNDES is now the largest development bank in the world, and it handles a range of loan programs to finance everything from the biggest infrastructure projects to innovations by small firms. In other ways, the central state has become a far more passive agent. Brazilian workers no longer negotiate labor issues with state mediation, as they still do in Germany. This allows the interests of business to usually prevail. The lack of welfare for informal workers represents another important gap in the social safety net.

Brazilian democracy will continue to confront notable challenges. The political system must find a way to address the interests of the poor, who are the least likely members of civil society to participate collectively. For many, this sense of disengagement has turned into open doubt about the utility of democracy itself. Annual polls by Latinobarómetro continue to show that Brazilians have one of the weakest levels of support for democracy in Latin America. The weakness of political party loyalties and well-documented instances of corruption involving organizations such as the PT help to explain these negative views of democracy.

Although Brazil is one of the world's key platforms for agricultural production and manufacturing, Brazilian firms and workers (not to mention the public sector) struggle to become competitive in a rapidly changing global marketplace. While Brazil is benefiting from strong demand for its natural resource exports, commodity booms do not tend to last. Gains from capital inflows must be put to work in the form of investment for the future in everything from road-building and port modernization to education.

As globalization and democratization have made Brazilian politics less predictable, older questions about what it means to be Brazilian have re-emerged. Brazil highlights the point made in the Introduction that political identities are often reshaped in changed circumstances. What it means to be Brazilian has become a more complex question. Democracy has given ordinary Brazilians more of a voice, but they have become active mostly on local issues, not at the national level. Women, non-governmental organizations, Catholics, Pentecostals, blacks, landless peasants, and residents of *favelas* have all organized in recent years around social and cultural issues. On the one hand, these movements have placed additional pressure on an already weakened state to deliver goods and services. On the other hand, these groups have supplied alternatives to the state by providing their own systems of social services and cultural support.

One recent development involves the way that Brazilian elites see the role of their country in forging a counterweight to the hegemonic power of the United States. Under Lula, Brazil pursued a policy of "benign restraint" of the United States. Following this policy, Brazil opposed the United States on issues such as the war in Iraq and American agricultural subsidies, but it cooperated with Washington in the war against terrorism and regional integration. Under Dilma, Brazil has pursued a less conflictual policy that has focused more on the country's access to natural resources and foreign markets. The relationship with the United States remains in flux, especially following the scandal in 2013 involving surveillance of government officials by the U.S. National Security Agency. This unpleasant discovery, which was made possible by Edward Snowden, put pressure on Dilma's government to make a starker choice between a foreign policy that aligns with the United States or challenges it more directly. After Snowden's release of the data on Brazil, Dilma cancelled a state visit to Washington and expressed the view that the Americans would have to work hard to restore close ties to Brazil.

Youth Politics and the Generational Divide

The generation of young people in their late teens and twenties in Brazil is a social group that has no memory of the hyperinflationary period of the late 1980s and 1990s. They have only known a democratic Brazil and one with improving governability. Their country is no longer a young democracy with modest expectations but an established democracy with abundant resources in which perennial problems of poverty, inequality, and poor governance deserve to be the priorities of public policy. This clash of youthful expectations and lingering problems was at the center of the protests that erupted in June 2013. With the doubling of the national population of university students over the past decade, these actors played a key role in coordinating the protests, using social media in most cases. Their demand for cleaner government is a salient concern of this generation, which has witnessed multiple major corruption scandals during the past few years.

Young Brazilians have proven to be far from apathetic about politics. They vote and mobilize often, though the degree of engagement is a function of the level of education with the college educated acting most consistently. Access to technology and available time are two other factors that facilitate the activism of middle-class youth. Although college students do not often feel the problems of workers and informal sector employees because they tend not to use public health care and other government services, they do use public transport. This is one reason why a sudden spike in transport costs sparked the protests of 2013. Young people could identify with the poor in this context.

Demographically, Brazil remains a young country that is not aging as rapidly overall as countries such as China or Japan. The Brazilian pension system, for example, remains on a sound demographic footing with 5.6 workers sustaining each current pensioner. By 2030, there will be 3.1 workers per pensioner. Improvements in educational quality and access mean that these workers will be more productive over time. If these benefits are distributed more equally to include more women and Afro-Brazilians, they promise to transform society over the long term.

Brazilian Politics in Comparative Perspective

The most important lesson that Brazil offers for the study of comparative politics is that fragmented polities threaten democracy, social development, and nation building. The Brazilian political order is fragmented on several levels. The central state is fragmented by conflicts between the executive and the legislature, divided alliances and self-interested politicians in Congress, decentralized government, and an indecisive judiciary with a complicated structure and an uncertain mission. Political parties are fragmented by clientelism and electoral rules that create incentives for politicians and voters to ignore party labels. Finally, civil society itself is fragmented into numerous, often conflictual, organizations, interest groups, professional associations, social movements, churches, and, most important, social classes and ethnic identities.

In some socioeconomically fragmented societies, such as the United States and India, institutions have been more successful in bridging the gap between individualistic pursuits and the demand of people for good government. Political parties, parliaments, and informal associations strengthen democracy in these countries. Where these institutions are faulty, as they are in Brazil, fragmentation exacerbates the weakness of the state and the society.

A weak state deepens the citizenry's sense that all politics is corrupt. Moreover, police brutality, human rights violations, judicial incompetence, and the unresponsiveness of bureaucratic agencies further discourage citizens from political participation. These problems reinforce the importance of creating systems of accountability. Unfortunately, the English word *accountability* has no counterpart in either Portuguese or Spanish. Given Brazil's (and Latin America's) long history of oligarchical rule and social exclusion, the notion of making elites accountable to the people is so alien that the languages of the region lack the required vocabulary. Systems of accountability must be built from the ground up; they must be nurtured in local government and in community organizations, and then in the governments of states and the central state. The judiciary, political parties, the media, and organizations of civil society must be able to play enforcement and watchdog roles. These are the building blocks of accountability that are the fulcrum of democracy.

Without a system of elite accountability, representation of the citizenry is impossible. In particular, the poor depend on elected officials to find solutions to their problems. Brazilian politicians have shown that through demagoguery and personalism, they can be elected. But being elected is not the same as representing a constituency. For this to occur, institutions must make political elites accountable to the people who elected them.

The notable successes of social policy under Cardoso, Lula, and Dilma have made substantial changes in the lives of millions of poor Brazilians, but sustaining these efforts requires great political unity. Collective identities, by definition, require mechanisms that forge mutual understandings among groups of people. Fractured societies turn to age-old ethnic identities that can produce destructive, internecine conflict, as the India–Pakistan and Nigerian experiences demonstrate. In Brazil, such extreme conflict has been avoided, but the divisive effects of a fragmented polity on collective identities are serious nonetheless. Divided by class, poor Brazilians continue to feel that politics holds no solutions for them, so they fail to mobilize for their rights. Blacks, women, and indigenous peoples share many interests. Yet few national organizations have been able to unite a coalition of interest groups to change destructive business practices. Finally, all Brazilians are harmed by the clearing of rain forests, pollution of rivers and lakes, and destruction of species; yet the major political parties and Congress seem incapable of addressing these issues consistently.

Perhaps the most serious effect of political fragmentation on Brazil has involved the struggle to defend the country's interests in an increasingly competitive, global marketplace. While globalization forces all countries, and particularly developing countries, to adapt to new technology, ideas, and economic interests, it also provides states with the opportunity to attract investment. Given the weakness of the Brazilian state, the social dislocation produced by industrial restructuring (such as unemployment), and the current instability of the international investment climate, Brazil maintains only an ambiguous vision of its role in the global capitalist order. Although Brazilian business, some unions, and key political leaders speak of the need to defend Brazil's interests in the international political economy, the country has few coherent strategies. But dealing with these issues requires a consistent policy created by a political leadership with clear ideas about the interests of the country. In Brazil's fragmented polity, developing such strategies is difficult.

In the world since September 11, 2001, issues of security outpaced matters of equity and development. Dilma's government has followed Lula's lead in its commitment to fighting terrorism at the same time that it has sought to pursue social justice and refused to bend to the security policies of the United States. Brazil's successful bids to host the World Cup and the Olympics are evidence that it does not seek to isolate itself from the world. If Brazil becomes an increasingly fair and just nation, it will prove to be influential simply through its example to other developing countries. Finally, Brazil's experience with economic restructuring and democratization will continue to influence other countries undergoing similar transformations in Latin America and elsewhere. As a large and resource-rich country, Brazil presents a useful case for comparison with other big developing countries such as Mexico, Russia, India, and China. Among the dimensions on which useful comparisons can be made are its evolving federal structure, as well as its efforts to manage its resources while dealing with environmental costs.

As a transitional democracy, Brazil can provide insights into governance systems. As a negative example, Brazil's ongoing experiment with presidentialism, multiparty democracy, and open-list PR may well confirm the superiority of alternative parliamentary systems in India and Germany or presidentialism in France and the United States. As a positive example, Brazil's ability to keep a diverse country united through trying economic times has much to teach Russia and Nigeria, since these countries too are weighed down by the dual challenges of economic reform and nation building.

Within Latin America, Brazil continues to consolidate its position as the preeminent economy of the region. Brazil exercises regional leadership on commercial questions, and with its continued dominance of the Amazon basin, the country commands the world's attention on environmental issues in the developing world. Brazil's experiences with balancing the exigencies of neoliberal economic adjustment with the sociopolitical realities of poverty will keep it at center stage. Brazil may not be "the country of the future," but it is a country with a future. None of the problems of Brazilian politics and social development are immune to improvement. If political reform is consolidated in the next few years, the groundwork will have been laid for transforming Brazil into a country that deserves the respect of the world.

Where Do You Stand?

Should Brazil exert its influence in the world even if it means growing conflicts with the United States?

Do you think that Brazil is "the country of the future"?

Chapter Summary

Brazil is a country of continental size with a long history of building a national state and, in recent decades, a more democratic system of government. Both processes have been shaped at different points by presidents such as Vargas, Cardoso, and Lula. Central characteristics of Brazilian politics such as clientelism, personalism, and corporatism have endured and adapted to the modernization of the state and the economy. Brazilian democracy has survived and prospered since 1985, and it now does so in the context of heightened expectations concerning development and its role in the world.

During the past three decades, Brazil has emerged from being an inward-oriented industrializer dependent on the state and foreign credit to becoming a market-oriented industrialized country that has achieved an enviable new competitive position in the world. Old problems of inflation and runaway government debt have been brought under control. Even persistent social inequalities and poverty are now improving and the objects of more efficiently targeted social policies. The ecological and land-ownership dimensions of development will continue to be areas for improving the quality of life for more of

Brazil's people. The economy is now more interconnected with other markets than at any other time in the country's history. So navigating domestic and international priorities in foreign economic policy will become more prominent tasks for the current government of Dilma Rousseff and her successors.

The Brazilian state is a mixture of professionalism and clientelism, and both of these dimensions have remained even as the country has democratized and developed. Brazilian democracy has strengthened law enforcement as the prosecutorial, oversight and investigative functions of the state have become more adept at detecting corruption. But accountability requires that the guilty be punished and that the courts adjudicate more efficiently and without excusing lawbreaking by privileged groups.

The Brazilian political system suffers from weak partisan identities among voters, low discipline within political parties, and inconsistent relations between the presidency and Congress. The open-list PR electoral system makes these tendencies worse, and further confuses voters. At the same time, civil society remains actively engaged in politics, often in sustained and organized ways. The election of Dilma Rousseff continued a tendency to rely on ad hoc alliances with Congress, but the advent of mass protests and increasing pressure from a more participatory citizenry, will continue to exert pressure on Dilma to embrace political reforms.

Despite the persistence of institutional impediments to reform and more efficient democratic governance, Brazil is poised to make the most of its increasing prosperity to address erstwhile social problems and emerge on the global stage as a power to be respected. Much depends on the quality of the country's leadership, which will work with Lula's legacy of good social and economic policy performance. To the extent that voters come to identify and reward good government, the incentives of Brazilian politics, which currently favor particular interests, will come to embrace the provision of good policies. The same expectations can provide support for efforts under the Dilma Rousseff presidency for political reform.

Key Terms

abertura
bureaucratic authoritarianism (BA)
bureaucratic rings
clientelism
developmentalism
export-led growth
favelas

import substitution industrialization (ISI)
informal economy
interventionist
interventores
legitimacy
moderating power (*poder moderador*)

nationalism
parastatals
personalist politicians
politics of the governors
populism
proportional representation (PR)
state corporatism
state technocrats

Suggested Readings

Ames, Barry. *The Deadlock of Democracy in Brazil: Interests, Identities, and Institutions in Comparative Politics.* Ann Arbor: University of Michigan Press, 2001.

Hochstetler, Kathryn, and Margaret Keck. *Greening Brazil: Environmental Activism in State and Society.* Durham, NC: Duke University Press, 2007.

Hunter, Wendy. *The Transformation of the Workers' Party in Brazil, 1989–2009.* New York: Cambridge University Press, 2010.

Kingstone, Peter R., and Timothy J. Power, eds. *Democratic Brazil Revisited.* Pittsburgh: University of Pittsburgh Press, 2008.

Mainwaring, Scott. *Rethinking Party Systems in the Third Wave of Democratization: The Case of Brazil.* Stanford: Stanford University Press, 1999.

Montero, Alfred P. *Brazil: Reversal of Fortune.* Cambridge, UK: Polity Press, 2014.

Samuels, David J. *Ambition, Federalism, and Legislative Politics in Brazil.* New York: Cambridge University Press, 2003.

Skidmore, Thomas E. *The Politics of Military Rule in Brazil, 1964–85.* New York: Oxford University Press, 1988.

Stepan, Alfred. *Rethinking Military Politics: Brazil and the Southern Cone.* Princeton, NJ: Princeton University Press, 1988.

Weyland, Kurt. *Democracy Without Equity: Failures of Reform in Brazil.* Pittsburgh: University of Pittsburgh Press, 1996.

Suggested Websites

LANIC database, University of Texas—Austin, Brazil Resource page
lanic.utexas.edu/la/brazil/

YouTube, President Lula da Silva's 2007 address at Davos
http://www.youtube.com/watch?v=RqsDMU3ASgo

The U.S. Library of Congress Country Study Page for Brazil
lcweb2.loc.gov/frd/cs/brtoc.html

SciELO Brazil, Searchable Database of Full-Text Articles on Brazil
www.scielo.br

National Development Bank of Brazil, Searchable Database of Documents on Brazilian Economy and Development (many in English)
http://www.bndes.gov.br/SiteBNDES/bndes /bndes_en/

10 Mexico

Halbert Jones

Official Name: United Mexican States (Estados Unidos Mexicanos)

Location: Southern North America

Capital City: Mexico City

Population (2014): 120.3 million

Size: 1,972,550 sq. km.; slightly less than three times the size of Texas

AP Images/Gregory Bull

© Cengage Learning®

THE MAKING OF THE MODERN MEXICAN STATE

Politics in Action

Early on the morning of February 22, 2014, Mexican marines raided an apartment in the Pacific resort of Mazatlán and detained Joaquín Guzmán, the powerful head of the Sinaloa drug cartel. Known as "El Chapo"—or "Shorty"—on account of his diminutive stature, Guzmán had built a massive fortune over several decades through his control of the flow of narcotics through Mexico and into the United States. His escape from a maximum-security prison in 2001 and his success in evading arrest for more than a decade thereafter made him a symbol of the weaknesses and shortcomings of the Mexican state. After running his criminal empire from a lavish jail cell for several years, Guzmán bribed his way out of prison, and even after President Felipe Calderón launched an offensive against the cartels in 2006, he managed to stay at least one step ahead of the authorities. Mexicans were left to wonder if the security forces simply could not find "El Chapo" or if corrupt officials were allowing him to remain free. Neither scenario gave citizens much cause for confidence in their leaders. Guzmán's arrest therefore had considerable symbolic importance as an indication that the Mexican government has both the will and the capacity to uphold the rule of law.

Successes like the capture of "El Chapo" have helped to counter exaggerated fears, voiced as Calderón's campaign against the cartels triggered intense violence in some parts of the country, that Mexico was in danger of becoming a "failed state." Nonetheless, the threats posed by criminal organizations both to public safety and to the authority of the government remain major preoccupations for Mexican leaders. Although Enrique Peña Nieto, Mexico's president since 2012, would prefer to focus the attention of the world and of his people on his country's economic potential rather than on security issues, he was obliged in January 2014 to assert federal control over law enforcement operations in the state of Michoacán, where the rise of vigilante groups in opposition to a local cartel had led to concerns about the absence or ineffectiveness of the legitimately constituted authorities. While Mexican officials face the need to develop institutions that can take on criminal elements and win the trust of Mexican citizens, unfortunately the activities of drug trafficking organizations are likely to remain a challenge for Mexico for as long as there is a large market for illegal narcotics next door in the United States.

Meanwhile, President Peña Nieto has sought since taking office to demonstrate that the Mexican government is capable of bold and effective action in other areas. His election in July 2012 as the candidate of the Institutional Revolutionary Party (PRI) was a milestone in Mexican history. The PRI dominated the country's politics for most of the twentieth century, but when it lost the presidency to an opposition party in 2000, many observers doubted that it would ever recover. However, after more than a decade of legislative paralysis, and as the country reeled from drug-related violence that had claimed some 60,000 lives over six years, voters turned again

Focus Questions ▽

- In what ways have the critical junctures of Mexican history grown out of the country's relations with other countries, especially the United States?

- What factors contributed to Mexico's democratic transition at the end of the twentieth century?

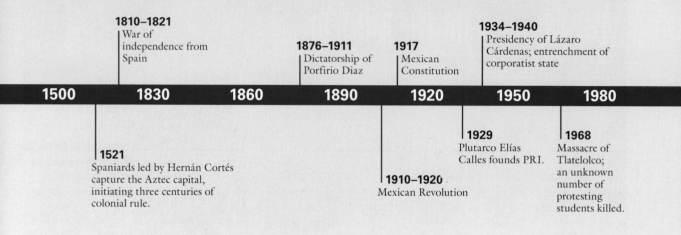

1810–1821 War of independence from Spain

1876–1911 Dictatorship of Porfirio Diaz

1917 Mexican Constitution

1934–1940 Presidency of Lázaro Cárdenas; entrenchment of corporatist state

| 1500 | 1830 | 1860 | 1890 | 1920 | 1950 | 1980 |

1521 Spaniards led by Hernán Cortés capture the Aztec capital, initiating three centuries of colonial rule.

1910–1920 Mexican Revolution

1929 Plutarco Elías Calles founds PRI.

1968 Massacre of Tlatelolco; an unknown number of protesting students killed.

to the PRI in the 2012 presidential election. To overcome the structural difficulties created by partisan divisions in the legislature, the new president signed an accord with party leaders that committed them to an ambitious program of reforms. The impact of these changes will be felt for years to come, and as these measures are being drafted and implemented, the dynamics of Mexican politics are being redefined. A long-ruling, formerly authoritarian party is learning to govern in the context of the competitive, multiparty system that has taken shape over the past several decades. To understand how Mexican politics is likely to evolve in the future, it will be necessary to study closely the development and structure of this system.

Geographic Setting

mestizo

A person of mixed white, indigenous, and sometimes African descent.

indigenous groups

Population descended from the original inhabitants of the Americas, present prior to the Spanish Conquest.

Mexico includes coastal plains, high plateaus, fertile valleys, rain forests, and deserts within an area slightly less than three times the size of Texas. Two imposing mountain ranges run the length of Mexico: the Sierra Madre Occidental to the west and the Sierra Madre Oriental to the east. Mexico's geography has made communication and transportation between regions difficult and infrastructure expensive. Mountainous terrain limits large-scale commercial agriculture to irrigated fields in the north, while the center and south produce a wide variety of crops on small farms. The country is rich in oil, silver, and other natural resources, but it has long struggled to manage those resources wisely.

Mexico is the second-largest nation in Latin America after Portuguese-speaking Brazil and the largest Spanish-speaking nation in the world. Sixty percent of the population is *mestizo*, or people of mixed indigenous and Spanish ancestry. About 30 percent of the population claim descent from Mexico's original inhabitants, although only 6.5 percent speak an indigenous language. The largest **indigenous groups** are the Maya in the south and the Náhuatl in the central regions, with well over 1 million members each. Although Mexicans take great pride in their nation's pre-Columbian heritage, issues of race and class divide society.

1982
Market reformers come to power in PRI.

1988
Carlos Salinas is elected amid charges of fraud.

1997
Opposition parties advance nationwide; PRI loses absolute majority in congress for first time in its history.

2009
PRI makes major gains in congressional elections as the country faces a wave of drug-related violence.

1985   **1990**   **1995**   **2000**   **2005**   **2010**   **2020**

1978–1982
State-led development reaches peak with petroleum boom and bust.

1989
First governorship is won by an opposition party.

1994
NAFTA goes into effect; uprising in Chiapas; Colosio assassinated.

2000
PRI loses presidency; Vicente Fox of PAN becomes president, but without majority support in congress.

2006
Felipe Calderón of PAN takes office as president; no party has a majority of seats in congress.

2012
Enrique Peña Nieto of the PRI elected to the presidency; his administration pursues an ambitious reform program.

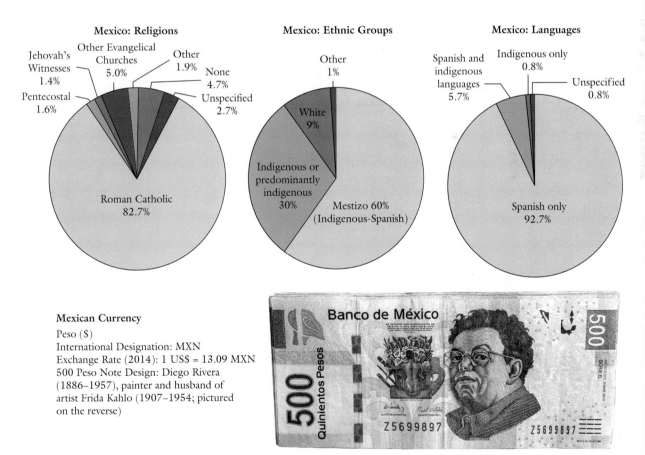

Mexico: Religions

Jehovah's Witnesses 1.4%
Pentecostal 1.6%
Other Evangelical Churches 5.0%
Other 1.9%
None 4.7%
Unspecified 2.7%
Roman Catholic 82.7%

Mexico: Ethnic Groups

Other 1%
White 9%
Indigenous or predominantly indigenous 30%
Mestizo 60% (Indigenous-Spanish)

Mexico: Languages

Spanish and indigenous languages 5.7%
Indigenous only 0.8%
Unspecified 0.8%
Spanish only 92.7%

Mexican Currency

Peso ($)
International Designation: MXN
Exchange Rate (2014): 1 US$ = 13.09 MXN
500 Peso Note Design: Diego Rivera (1886–1957), painter and husband of artist Frida Kahlo (1907–1954; pictured on the reverse)

FIGURE 10.1 The Mexican Nation at a Glance

Javier Correa/Alamy (for photo)

Table 10.1	Political Organization
Political System	Federal republic
Regime History	Current constitution in force since 1917
Administrative Structure	Federal system with thirty-one states and a federal district (Mexico City)
Executive	President, elected by direct election with a six-year term of office; reelection not permitted
Legislature	Bicameral Congress. Senate (upper house) and Chamber of Deputies (lower house); elections held every three years. There are 128 senators, 3 from each of the thirty-one states, 3 from the federal (capital) district, and 32 elected nationally by proportional representation for six-year terms. The 500 members of the Chamber of Deputies are elected for three-year terms from 300 electoral districts, 300 by simple majority vote and 200 by proportional representation.
Judiciary	Independent federal and state court system headed by a Supreme Court with eleven justices appointed by the president and approved by the Senate.
Party System	Multiparty system. One-party dominant (Institutional Revolutionary Party) system from 1929 until 2000. Major parties: National Action Party, Institutional Revolutionary Party, and the Party of the Democratic Revolution.

Mexico became a largely urban country in the second half of the twentieth century, and Mexico City is one of the world's largest metropolitan areas, with about 20 million inhabitants. Migration both within and beyond Mexico's borders has become a major issue. Greater economic opportunities in the industrial cities of the north lead many women and men to seek work there in the *maquiladoras*, or assembly industries. Many job seekers continue on to the United States. On Mexico's southern border, many thousands of Central Americans look for better prospects in Mexico and beyond.

maquiladoras

Factories that produce goods for export, often located along the U.S.–Mexican border.

Critical Junctures

Independence, Instability, and Dictatorship (1810–1910)

After a small band of Spanish forces led by Hernán Cortés toppled the Aztec Empire in 1521, Spain ruled Mexico for three centuries. Colonial policy was designed to extract wealth from New Spain, as the territory was known, ensuring that economic benefits flowed to the mother country.

In 1810, a parish priest in central Mexico named Miguel Hidalgo began the first of a series of wars for independence. Although independence was gained in 1821, Mexico struggled to create a stable government for decades afterward. Liberals and conservatives, monarchists and republicans, and federalists and centralists were all engaged in the battle to shape the new nation's future. Between 1833 and 1855, thirty-six presidential administrations came to power, and in many regions, local strongmen, or *caudillos*, exercised more authority than the national government.

caudillos

Charismatic populist leaders, usually with a military background, who use patronage and draw upon personal loyalties to dominate a region or a nation.

© Cengage Learning®

During this chaotic period, Mexico lost half its territory. Central America rejected rule from Mexico City in 1823, and the northern territory of Texas won independence in 1836. After Texas became a U.S. state in 1845, a border dispute led the United States to declare war on Mexico in 1846. U.S. forces invaded the country and occupied Mexico City. An 1848 treaty recognized the loss of Texas and gave the United States title to what later became the states of New Mexico, Utah, Nevada, Arizona, California, and part of Colorado for about $18 million, leaving a legacy of deep resentment toward the United States.

After the war, liberals and conservatives continued their struggle over issues of political and economic order. The Constitution of 1857 incorporated many of the goals of the liberals, such as a somewhat democratic government, a bill of rights, and limitations on the power of the Roman Catholic Church. In 1861, Spain, Great Britain, and France occupied Veracruz to collect debts owed by Mexico. The French army continued on to Mexico City, where it installed a European prince as the Emperor Maximilian (1864–1867). Conservatives welcomed this respite from liberal rule. Benito Juárez returned to the presidency in 1867 after defeating and executing Maximilian. Juárez is still hailed in Mexico today as an early proponent of more democratic government.

In 1876, a popular retired general named Porfirio Díaz came to power. He established a dictatorship—known as the *Porfiriato*—that lasted thirty-four years and was at first welcomed by many because it brought sustained stability to the country.

Díaz imposed an authoritarian system to create political order and economic progress. Over time, he relied increasingly on a small clique of advisers, known as

GLOBAL CONNECTION

Conquest or Encounter?

The year 1519, when the Spanish conqueror Hernán Cortés arrived on the shores of the Yucatán Peninsula, is often considered the starting point of Mexican political history. The land that was to become Mexico was home to extensive and complex indigenous civilizations that were advanced in agriculture, architecture, and political and economic organization. By 1519, diverse groups had fallen under the power of the militaristic Aztec Empire, which extended throughout what is today central and southern Mexico.

Cortés and the colonial masters who came after him subjected indigenous groups to forced labor; robbed them of gold, silver, and land; and introduced flora and fauna from Europe that destroyed long-existing ecosystems. They also brought alien forms of property rights and authority relationships, a religion that viewed indigenous practices as the devil's work, and an economy based on mining and cattle—all of which soon overwhelmed existing structures of social and economic organization. Within a century, wars, exploitation, and the introduction of European diseases reduced the indigenous population from an estimated 25 million to 1 million or fewer. Even so, the Spanish never constituted more than a small percentage of the total population, and massive racial mixing among the Indians, Europeans, and to a lesser extent Africans produced a new *raza*, or *mestizo* race.

What does it mean to be Mexican? Is one the conquered or the conqueror? While celebrating indigenous achievements in food, culture, the arts, and ancient civilization, middle-class Mexico has the contradictory sense that to be "Indian" nowadays is to be backward. But perhaps the situation is changing, with the upsurge of indigenous movements from both the grassroots and the international level striving to promote ethnic pride, defend rights, and foster the teaching of Indian languages.

The collision of two worlds still resonates. Is Mexico colonial or modern? Third or First World? Southern or Northern? Is the United States an ally or a conqueror? Many Mexicans at once welcome and fear full integration into the global economy, asking themselves: Is globalization a new form of conquest?

MAKING CONNECTIONS How does Mexico's experience as a colony of Spain compare with the history of other countries that once were part of European empires?

---

científicos (scientists), who wanted to adopt European technologies and values to modernize the country. Díaz and the *científicos* encouraged foreign investment and presided over a period of rapid growth and development. Social tensions grew, however, as many poorer Mexicans found themselves forced off their lands, and as many members of the middle and upper classes came to resent the Porfirians' monopoly on political power.

The Revolution of 1910 and the Sonoran Dynasty (1910–1934)

The most formative event in the country's modern history was the Revolution of 1910, which ended the *Porfiriato* and was the first great social revolution of the twentieth century. The revolution was fought by a variety of forces for a variety of reasons, which made the consolidation of power that followed as significant as the revolution itself.

Díaz had promised an open election for president, and in 1910, Francisco Madero presented himself as a candidate. Madero and his reform-minded allies hoped that a new class of politically ambitious citizens would move into positions of power. When this opposition swelled, Díaz tried to repress growing dissent, but the clamor for change forced him into exile. Madero was elected in 1911, but he was soon using the military to put down revolts by reformers and reactionaries alike. When Madero was assassinated during a **coup d'état** in 1913, political order collapsed.

coup d'état

A forceful, extra-constitutional action resulting in the removal of an existing government.

At the same time that middle-class reformers struggled to displace Díaz, a peasant revolt that focused on land claims erupted in central and southern regions. This revolt had roots in legislation that made it easy for wealthy landowners and ranchers to claim the lands of peasant villagers. Villagers joined forces under a variety of local leaders. The most famous was Emiliano Zapata. His manifesto, the Plan de Ayala, became the cornerstone of the radical agrarian reform that became part of the Constitution of 1917.

In the north, the governor of Coahuila, Venustiano Carranza, placed himself at the head of an army that pledged to restore constitutional governance after Madero's murder, while Francisco (Pancho) Villa's forces combined military maneuvers with banditry, looting, and warlordism. In 1916, troops from the United States entered Mexico to punish Villa for an attack on U.S. territory. The presence of U.S. troops on Mexican soil resulted in increased hostility toward the United States.

The Mexican Constitution of 1917 was forged out of the diverse and often conflicting interests of the various factions that arose during the 1910 Revolution. It established a formal set of political institutions and guaranteed citizens a range of progressive social and economic rights: agrarian reform, social security, the right to organize in unions, a minimum wage, an eight-hour workday, profit sharing for workers, a secular public education system, and universal male suffrage. Despite these socially advanced provisions, the constitution did not provide suffrage for women, who had to wait until 1953 to vote in local elections and 1958 to vote in national elections. To limit the power of foreign investors, restrictions were placed on the ability of non-Mexicans to own land or exploit natural resources. Numerous articles severely limited the power of the Catholic Church, long a target of liberals who wanted Mexico to be a secular state. Despite such noble sentiments, violence continued as competing leaders sought to assert power and displace their rivals.

Power was gradually consolidated in the hands of a group of revolutionary leaders from the north of the country. Known as the Sonoran Dynasty, after their home state of Sonora, these leaders were committed to a capitalist model of economic development. Eventually, one of the Sonorans, Plutarco Elías Calles, emerged as the *jefe máximo*, or supreme leader. After his presidential term (1924–1928), Calles managed to select and dominate his successors from 1929 to 1934.

In 1929, Calles brought together many of the most powerful contenders for leadership to create a political party. The bargain he offered was simple: Contenders for power would accommodate each other's interests in the expectation that without political violence, the country would prosper and they would be able to reap the benefits of even greater power and economic spoils. For the next seven decades, Calles's bargain ensured nonviolent conflict resolution among elites and the uninterrupted rule of the Institutional Revolutionary Party (PRI) in national politics.

Lázaro Cárdenas, Agrarian Reform, and the Workers (1934–1940)

In 1934, Calles handpicked Lázaro Cárdenas as the official candidate for the presidency. He fully anticipated that Cárdenas would go along with his behind-the-scenes management of the country. To his surprise, Cárdenas executed a virtual coup that established his own supremacy.[1] Even more unexpectedly, Cárdenas mobilized peasants and workers in pursuit of the more radical goals of the revolution. During his administration, more than 49 million acres of land were distributed, nearly twice as much as had been parceled out by all the previous postrevolutionary governments combined. Most of these lands were distributed in the form of *ejidos* (collective land grants) to peasant groups. Recipients of these grants provided an enduring base of

ejido

Land granted by Mexican government to an organized group of peasants.

support for the government. Cárdenas also encouraged workers to form unions to demand higher wages and better working conditions. In 1938, he wrested the petroleum industry from foreign investors and placed it under government control.

During the Cárdenas years (1934–1940), the bulk of the Mexican population was incorporated into the political system. Organizations of peasants and workers, middle-class groups, and the military were added to the official party. In addition, Cárdenas's presidency witnessed a great expansion of the role of the state as the government encouraged investment in industrialization, provided credit to agriculture, and created infrastructure.

The Politics of Rapid Development (1940–1982)

In the decades that followed, Cárdenas's successors used the institutions he created to counteract his reforms. Gradually, the PRI developed a huge patronage machine, characterized by extensive chains of personal relationships based on the exchange of favors. These exchange relationships, known as clientelism, became the cement that built loyalty to the PRI and the political system.

PROFILE

Lázaro Cárdenas

As president from 1934 to 1940, Lázaro Cárdenas arguably did more than any other Mexican leader to make possible the longevity of the political system that emerged from the Revolution of 1910. Through his reforms, Cárdenas won the loyalty and admiration of many Mexicans, convincing them of the legitimacy of the revolutionary regime.

Cárdenas was very much a product of the Revolution. Born in 1895 in the small town of Jiquilpan, Michoacán, he was only 15 years old when fighting broke out in 1910. As armed groups marched across west-central Mexico, the young Cárdenas joined the revolutionary forces, leaving behind the printshop where he had been working to support his widowed mother and seven siblings. Thanks to his literacy and penmanship, he received a commission as an officer on the staff of a local commander, and he rose quickly through the ranks. As part of the Constitutionalist Army, Cárdenas served under General Plutarco Elías Calles, a mentor who would later become a rival.

While on campaign, Cárdenas became more deeply aware of the hardships endured by Mexico's indigenous and rural populations and of their struggles for land. Later, in the 1920s, as the regional military commander in the country's most important oil-producing zone, he saw how foreign companies disregarded local regulations and flouted Mexican sovereignty. These experiences played a significant role in shaping his political outlook.

After serving as governor of his native state (1928–1932) and in the cabinet as defense minister (1933), Cárdenas was selected by his old patron Calles as the ruling party's presidential candidate in the 1934 elections. After taking office, however, Cárdenas shook off his predecessor's influence and launched wide-ranging reforms. His policies made him unpopular with business leaders, landowners, and social conservatives, but many more Mexicans felt that he was the first president to concern himself with their well-being. Cárdenas also won widespread admiration for his personal honesty and morality.

After stepping down from the presidency, Cárdenas watched with concern as subsequent administrations turned to the right, adopting more conservative policies even as they continued to claim to represent the ideals of the Revolution. The venerable ex-president sought to use his standing within the PRI and in Mexican society to press for more progressive policies. In the early 1960s, for example, he praised Fidel Castro's Cuban Revolution and signaled his support for renewed reform within Mexico. Nonetheless, he ultimately remained loyal to the system he had played such an important role in constructing.

Though Lázaro Cárdenas died in 1970, his name continues to carry great weight. Both the PRI and the PRD—founded by his son Cuauhtémoc—lay claim to his legacy, and countless Mexicans identify Cárdenas as the president they admire most.

MAKING CONNECTIONS Given his role in the nationalization of the oil industry, what effect might Cárdenas's iconic status have on current debates in Mexico over the future of the energy sector?

This kind of political control reoriented the country's development away from the egalitarian social goals of the 1930s toward a development strategy in which the state actively encouraged industrialization and the accumulation of wealth. Growth rates were high from the 1940s through the 1960s, but protests against the regime's authoritarian tendencies were beginning to arise by 1968, when government forces brutally suppressed a student movement in the capital's Tlatelolco district. Moreover, by the 1970s, Mexico's economic strategy was faltering.

Just as the economy faced a crisis in the mid-1970s, vast new amounts of oil were discovered in the Gulf of Mexico. Soon, extensive public investment programs were fueling rapid growth in virtually every sector of the economy. The boom was short-lived, however. International petroleum prices plunged in the early 1980s, forcing Mexico to default on its national debt in 1982 and plunging the country into a deep economic downturn.

Crisis and Reform (1982–2000)

This crisis led two presidents, Miguel de la Madrid (1982–1988) and Carlos Salinas (1988–1994), to introduce the first major reversal of the country's development strategy since the 1940s. New policies were put in place to limit the government's role in the economy and to reduce barriers to international trade. This period marked the beginning of a new effort to integrate Mexico into the global economy. In 1993, President Salinas signed the North American Free Trade Agreement (NAFTA), which committed Mexico, the United States, and Canada to the elimination of trade barriers between them. These economic reforms were a turning point for Mexico and meant that the country's future development would be closely tied to international economic conditions.

After a "lost decade" of stagnant growth following the 1982 default, the economic volatility that continued to afflict the country through much of the 1990s came to be accompanied by worrying signs of political instability. In 1994, a guerrilla movement, the Zapatista Army of National Liberation (EZLN), seized four towns in the southern state of Chiapas. The group demanded land, democracy, indigenous rights, and the immediate repeal of NAFTA. Many citizens throughout the country openly supported the aims of the rebels. Following close on the heels of the rebellion came the assassination of the PRI's presidential candidate, Luis Donaldo Colosio, an event that shocked all citizens and shook the political elite deeply.

With the election of replacement candidate Ernesto Zedillo in August 1994, the PRI remained in power, but these shocks provoked widespread disillusionment and frustration with the political system. At the same time, reforms to the country's electoral processes and institutions made it easier for opposition groups to challenge the ruling party and gave the public greater confidence in the fairness of elections. In 1997, for the first time in modern Mexican history, the PRI lost its majority in the lower house of the national congress. The 2000 election of Vicente Fox as the first non-PRI president in seven decades was the culmination of this electoral revolution.

Since 2000: Mexico as a Multiparty Democracy

After taking office in December 2000, Vicente Fox found it difficult to bring about the changes that he had promised to the Mexican people. Proposals for reform went down to defeat, and the president was subjected to catcalls and heckling when he made his annual reports to the congress. The difficulties faced by Fox as he attempted to implement his ambitious agenda arose in part because he and his administration lacked experience. However, a bigger problem for the president was that he lacked the compliant congressional majority and the close relationship with his party that his PRI predecessors had enjoyed.

With his legislative agenda stalled, Fox hoped that achievements in international policy would enhance his prestige at home. He was particularly hopeful that a close connection with the U.S. president, George W. Bush, would facilitate important breakthroughs in relations with the United States. The events of September 11, 2001, dramatically changed the outlook, however. The terrorist attacks on the United States led officials in Washington to seek to strengthen border security and to shift much of their attention away from Mexico and Latin America and toward Afghanistan and the Middle East. As a result, Mexican hopes for an agreement under which a greater number of their citizens would legally be able to migrate to and work in the United States were dashed. Thus, Fox found both his domestic and international policy priorities largely blocked.

As Fox's term in office came to a close, his National Action Party (PAN) turned to Felipe Calderón as its candidate in the 2006 presidential election. His main opponent was Andrés Manuel López Obrador of the Party of the Democratic Revolution (PRD). When Calderón won by a small margin, López Obrador refused to concede defeat. This defiant response had the unintended effect of dividing the opposition and allowing Calderón to consolidate his hold on power. By far the greatest challenge Mexico faced as Calderón took office was the increasing cost of fighting the war on drugs and organized crime. The new president relied on the army and federal police to launch military offensives against drug cartels throughout the country. Calderón secured the support of the United States for his strategy through the Mérida Initiative, which offered U.S. security assistance to Mexico and to Central American countries fighting transnational criminal organizations. The offensive resulted in the apprehension or killing of many leading drug traffickers, but it also touched off a wave of violence that has claimed tens of thousands of lives, damaged the country's image abroad, and undermined the confidence of many Mexicans in the ability of their government to maintain order and assure their safety.

In recent years, Mexican authorities have moved forcefully against the country's drug-trafficking organizations, which had amassed considerable resources through their criminal activities.

SUSANA GONZALEZ/dpa/Corbis

In the 2012 presidential election, Mexicans turned to the PRI in the hope that the party that had maintained stability in the country for so many years would be able to control the violence and govern effectively. Voters chose Enrique Peña Nieto, the young former governor of the state of Mexico, over the PRD's López Obrador and Josefina Vázquez Mota of the PAN (the first female presidential candidate nominated by a major party). López Obrador again made allegations of electoral fraud, but in contrast to the situation after the very close election of 2006, official results showed that Peña Nieto had won by a clear margin. Another orderly and peaceful transfer of power between parties, this time from the PAN back to the PRI, took place on December 1, 2012.

The return of the formerly dominant party to the presidency did not amount to a restoration of the old political system, however. Unlike his PRI predecessors, Peña Nieto faced a divided legislature and a citizenry that had become accustomed to questioning presidential authority and to having its say. To overcome the partisan divisions in congress that had created so many problems for Fox and Calderón, Peña Nieto moved quickly to capitalize on his mandate, entering into a "Pact for Mexico" with the major party leaders to press ahead on needed reforms. The agenda has included an overhaul of the education system, a revamping of tax policy, and—perhaps most controversially in a country in which Cárdenas's expropriation of the oil industry is remembered as a national triumph—the opening of the energy sector to foreign investment. Though the new administration has so far been successful in steering many of its initiatives through the legislative process, it has also faced intense protests. The fate of its program and of its approach to governing Mexico therefore remains to be determined.

The Four Themes and Mexico

Mexico in a Globalized World of States

Mexico's history has been deeply marked by its place in the world economy, its interactions with foreign powers, and its weakness relative to its powerful neighbor to the north. Through much of the nineteenth century, it faced pressure and intervention not just from the United States but also from European powers seeking to dominate the country. When stability was finally achieved under Porfirio Díaz, it was foreign investment that fueled development and growth, even as foreign domination of some sectors of the economy contributed to the resentments that would explode in the Revolution of 1910. Through much of the twentieth century, Mexico sought to protect its interests by developing its own industries to serve a domestic market and by asserting its economic and ideological independence from the world's great powers. After the early 1980s, the government rejected this position in favor of rapid integration into the global economy.

Since taking the strategic decision to open its economy, Mexico has embraced the opportunities and confronted the challenges presented by globalization. Mexican leaders calculated that by securing access to the vast U.S. and Canadian markets, they would allow the country to maintain a competitive position in an increasingly interconnected global economy. NAFTA did lead to a dramatic rise in the level of trade between Mexico and its North American neighbors, but the increased exposure to the world economy also left Mexico more vulnerable to abrupt shifts in international capital flows and to financial crises. After one such crisis hit at the end of 1994, for example, the Mexican economy contracted sharply, inflation soared, and taxes rose while wages were frozen. Mexico was likewise deeply affected by the global economic crisis of 2008, largely because of its strong links with the hard-hit U.S. economy.

Governing the Economy

Mexico's development from the 1930s to the 1980s was marked by extensive government engagement in the economy. During this period, the country industrialized and became primarily urban. At the same time, the living conditions of most

Mexicans improved, and standards of health, longevity, and education grew. Yet, along with these achievements, development strategies led to industrial and agricultural sectors that were often inefficient and overly protected by government, inequalities in the distribution of income and opportunities increased, and growth was threatened by a combination of domestic policies and international economic conditions. In the 1980s, the earlier model of development collapsed in crisis, and more market-oriented policies have significantly reduced the role of government in the economy and opened the country up to global economic forces. Yet growth has been slow under the new policies and inequalities have increased further. The larger questions of whether the current development strategy can generate growth, whether Mexican products can find profitable markets overseas, whether investors can create job opportunities for millions of unemployed and part-time workers, and whether the confidence of those investors can be maintained over the longer term continue to challenge the country.

The Democratic Idea

The Mexican people's pursuit of the ideal of democratic governance has been another important historical theme. Indeed, Madero launched the Revolution of 1910 with a call for "effective suffrage" and competitive elections, and his slogans were adopted by the postrevolutionary regime. Under the PRI, however, the country opted not for true democracy but for representation through government-mediated organizations within a **corporatist state**, in which interest groups became an institutionalized part of state structure rather than an independent source of advocacy. Although the democratic forms specified in the constitution were observed, the ruling party dominated the electoral process at all levels of government, and opposition groups were co-opted, marginalized, or (as a last resort) repressed. The system was referred to as a "perfect dictatorship," because of its ability to perpetuate itself and maintain stability, generally without having to resort to violence.

corporatist state

A state in which interest groups become an institutionalized part of the state structure.

Over the last several decades of the twentieth century, however, the legitimacy of PRI rule was increasingly called into question. Demands for a more democratic system led to electoral reforms and the emergence of a more open political landscape. In the more competitive political environment that developed as a result, opposition parties won governorships, seats in congress, and, in 2000, the presidency. Though the PRI returned to power (via the ballot box) in 2012, democratic practices are now well established. However, many Mexicans are frustrated that democratic governance has not delivered security and sustained growth. The country's future stability depends on the ability of a more democratic system to guarantee public safety and provide economic opportunities.

The Politics of Collective Identity

A fundamental underlying strength of the Mexican nation is a strong sense of identity forged through more than two centuries of resistance to foreign interventions and invasions and through the shared experience of the Mexican Revolution. Mexico's identity is also strongly reinforced by the country's proximity to the United States. Though commercial links, migration, popular culture, and many other forces tie Mexico closely to the "colossus of the north," Mexicans are keenly aware of what sets them apart from their American neighbors, and they are determined to maintain their own traditions and values.

While patriotism and a common cultural background bind together citizens from all walks of life, Mexican society is also marked by deep divisions. The EZLN's 1994 rebellion reflected the fact that rural Mexico in general, the south of the country in particular, and indigenous groups most of all had been left behind by policies promoting industrial development and integration into the world economy. Huge disparities in the distribution of wealth and income also create potentially explosive divisions between economic and social classes throughout the country. Though the PRI was able to maintain stability by using patronage and clientelism to mediate between a diverse range of interest groups for decades, in a more democratic system political appeals directed at particular classes might well become increasingly effective.

Themes and Comparisons

Mexico's modern history resembles that of Russia and China in that it has been framed by a social revolution that overturned the preexisting order, but the ideology that drove the Mexican revolutionary process was not communism. Instead, the Revolution of 1910 reflected concerns that arose from social conditions and historical experiences that were particular to Mexico. A diverse, often fractious revolutionary coalition called for democratic government, social justice, and national control of the country's resources. In the years after the revolution, the state created conditions for political and social peace. By incorporating peasants and workers into party and government institutions, by providing benefits to low-income groups during the 1930s, and by presiding over considerable economic growth after 1940, the regime became widely accepted as legitimate. In a world of developing nations wracked by political turmoil, military coups, and regime changes, the PRI established a strong state with enduring institutions. The party presided over decades of political stability and sustained (if unequally distributed) growth. Only in the face of economic crisis did this system begin to crumble toward the end of the twentieth century.

By moving since the 1980s to develop a more open and competitive political system, while embracing globalization as a development strategy, Mexico has followed a path chosen by a number of other Latin American nations, such as Brazil and Chile. Unlike those countries, though, Mexico made a transition away from civilian authoritarian rule rather than military dictatorship, and the democratic nature of the institutions provided for in the 1917 constitution meant that no major reform was required to bring about a change in regime. In the twenty-first century, the Mexican government is more transparent and accountable to its citizens than it was in the past, and there is much greater scope than before for **civil society** activism and for independent political activity. Mexicans value the new opportunities for political participation that they have won, but they have discovered that democratic institutions do not necessarily provide more efficient and effective governance. The rise of drug cartels as a significant threat to public security in recent years has also shaken Mexicans' confidence in their institutions. Though these criminal organizations do not pursue explicitly political ends in the way that guerrilla insurgencies and terrorist groups in other nations might, their wealth and the powerful economic forces that sustain them make them in some ways harder to fight. Given the capacity that these groups have to corrupt public officials and to carry out acts of violence, Mexicans fear the influence they might have on their country's politics. Finally, though Mexico has achieved an impressive degree of industrialization and economic development, it

civil society

Refers to the space occupied by voluntary associations outside the state, for example, professional associations (lawyers, doctors, teachers), trade unions, student and women's groups, religious bodies, and other voluntary association groups.

continues to face the challenge of overcoming deep inequalities between regions and social classes and of providing opportunities for millions of citizens living in poverty.

Where Do You Stand?

How would you assess the meaning and legacy of the Mexican Revolution? To what extent were the promises of the revolution fulfilled?

In recent years, both the resiliency and the fragility of the Mexican state have been on display, as the country has experienced both a peaceful political transition to competitive democracy and a wave of violence as the government has confronted criminal organizations. Do you see Mexico's institutions as fundamentally strong or fundamentally weak?

SECTION 2

POLITICAL ECONOMY AND DEVELOPMENT

▼ Focus Questions

- What accounts for the Mexican government's decision to seek greater integration into the global economy?

- In what ways have global linkages helped or harmed the lives of various social groups?

state capitalism

An economic system that is primarily capitalistic but in which there is some degree of government ownership of the means of production.

State and Economy

In light of the central role played by the Mexican state in the development of the national economy over the course of more than a century, a more thorough discussion of that history is necessary to understand the relationship between state and economy today.

During the *Porfiriato* (1876–1911), policy-makers believed that Mexico could grow rich by exporting raw materials. Their efforts to attract international investment encouraged a major boom in the production and export of products such as henequin (for making rope), coffee, cacao (cocoa beans), cattle, oil, silver, and gold. Soon, the country had become so attractive to foreign investors that large amounts of land, the country's petroleum, its railroad network, and its mining wealth were largely controlled by foreigners. Nationalist reaction against these foreign interests played a significant role in the tensions that produced the Revolution of 1910.

After the revolution, this nationalism combined with a sense of social justice inspired by revolutionary leaders such as Zapata. The country adopted a strategy in which the government guided industrial and agricultural development. This development strategy, often called **state capitalism**, relied heavily on government actions to encourage private investment and reduce risks for private entrepreneurs. At the same time, many came to believe that Mexico should begin to manufacture the goods that it was then importing.

Import Substitution and Its Consequences

Between 1940 and 1982, Mexico pursued a form of state capitalism and a model of development known import substitution industrialization (ISI). Like Brazil and other Latin American countries during the same period, the government provided incentives and assistance to promote industries that would supply the domestic market.

Between 1940 and 1950, GDP grew at an annual average of 6.7 percent, while manufacturing increased at an average of 8.1 percent. In the 1950s, manufacturing

Table 10.2	Mexican Development, 1940–2010						
	1940	**1950**	**1960**	**1970**	**1980**	**1990**	**2010**
Population (millions)	19.8	26.3	38.0	52.8	70.4	88.5	117.9
Life expectancy (years)	–	51.6	58.6	62.6	67.4	68.9	76.7
Infant mortality (per 1,000 live births)	–	–	86.3	70.9	49.9	42.6	14.7
Illiteracy (% of population age 15 and over)	–	42.5	34.5	25.0	16.0	12.7	6.9
Urban population (% of total)	–	–	50.7	59.0	66.4	72.6	77.8
Economically active population in agriculture (% of total)	–	58.3	55.1	44.0	36.6	22.0	13.1
	1940–1949	**1950–1959**	**1960–1969**	**1970–1979**	**1980–1989**	**1990–1999**	**2000–2009**
GDP growth rate (average annual percent)	6.7	5.8	7.6	6.4	1.6	3.4	1.3
Per capita GDP growth rate	–	–	3.7	3.3	–0.1	1.6	0.3

Sources: World Bank, World Development Indicators; Central Intelligence Agency.

achieved an average of 7.3 percent growth annually, and in the 1960s, that figure rose to 10.1 percent. Agricultural production also grew as new areas were brought under cultivation and new technologies were adopted on large farms. Even the poorest Mexicans believed that their lives were improving, and key statistical indicators reflected a real rise in standards of living (see Table 10.2). So impressive was Mexico's economic performance that it was referred to internationally as the "Mexican Miracle."

During this period, business elites, unionized workers, and wealthy commercial farmers benefitted from state policies and provided a strong base of support for the apparently successful ISI model. Government policies eventually limited the potential for further growth, however.[2] Industrialists who received subsidies and were protected from competition had few incentives to produce efficiently. The domestic market was also limited by poverty; many Mexicans could not afford the sophisticated manufactured products the country would need to produce in order to keep growing under the import substitution model.

Indeed, as the economy grew, many were left behind. The ranks of the urban poor grew steadily, particularly from the 1960s. By 1970, a large proportion of Mexico City's population was living in inner-city tenements or squatter settlements surrounding the city.[2] Mexico developed a sizable informal sector—workers who produced and sold goods and services at the margin of the economic system and faced extreme insecurity.

Also left behind in the country's development after 1940 were peasant farmers. Their lands were often the least fertile, plot sizes were minuscule, and access to markets was impeded by poor transportation and exploitive middlemen. Increasing disparities in rural and urban incomes, coupled with high population growth rates, contributed to the emergence of rural guerrilla movements and student protests in the mid- and late 1960s.

Sowing the Oil and Reaping a Crisis

In the early 1970s, Mexico faced the threat of social crisis brought on by rural poverty, chaotic urbanization, high population growth, and the questioning of political legitimacy. The government responded by investing in infrastructure and public industries, regulating the flow of foreign capital, and increasing social spending. It was spending much more than it generated, causing the public debt to grow rapidly.

Just as the seriousness of this unsustainable economic situation was being recognized, vast new finds of oil came to the rescue. Between 1978 and 1982, Mexico became a major oil exporter. The government embarked on a policy to "sow the oil" in the economy and "administer the abundance" with vast investment projects in virtually all sectors and with major new initiatives to reduce poverty and deal with declining agricultural productivity.

Oil accounted for almost four-fifths of the country's exports, causing the economy to be extremely vulnerable to changes in oil prices. And change they did. Global overproduction led to a steep drop in petroleum prices in 1982. At the same time, access to foreign credit dried up. In August 1982, the government announced that the country could not pay the interest on its foreign debt, triggering a crisis that reverberated around the world.

The economic crisis had several important implications for structures of power and privilege in Mexico. The crisis convinced even the most diehard believers that import substitution created inefficiencies in production, failed to generate sufficient employment, cost the government far too much in subsidies, and ultimately increased dependency on industrialized countries. In addition, the power of privileged interest groups and their ability to influence government policy declined.

A wide variety of interests began to organize outside the PRI to demand that government do something about the situation. Massive earthquakes in Mexico City in September 1985 proved to be a watershed for Mexican society. Severely disappointed by the government's failure to respond to the disaster, hundreds of communities organized rescue efforts, soup kitchens, shelters, and rehabilitation initiatives. A surging sense of political empowerment developed, as groups long accustomed to dependence on government learned that they could solve their problems better without it.[3]

The elections of 1988 became a focus for protest against the economic dislocation caused by the crisis and the political powerlessness that most citizens felt. For the first time in decades, the PRI was challenged by the increased popularity of opposition political parties, one of them headed by Cuauhtémoc Cárdenas, the son of the country's most revered president. When the votes were counted, it was announced that Carlos Salinas, the PRI candidate, had received a bare majority of 50.7 percent, as opposition parties claimed widespread electoral fraud.

New Strategies: Structural Reforms and NAFTA

Between 1988 and 1994, the mutually dependent relationship between industry and government was weakened as new free-market policies were put in place. Deregulation gave the private sector more freedom to pursue economic activities and less reason to seek special favors from government. The private sector also came to control much more of the economy as the government sold off state enterprises as part of its reform program. In the countryside, a constitutional revision made it possible for *ejidos* to be divided into individually owned plots; this made farmers less dependent on government but more vulnerable to losing their land.

Among the farthest-reaching initiatives was the North American Free Trade Agreement (NAFTA). This agreement with Canada and the United States created the basis for gradual introduction of free trade among the three countries. However, the liberalization of the Mexican economy and opening of its markets to foreign competition increased Mexico's vulnerability to changes in international economic conditions. These factors, as well as mismanaged economic policies, led to a major economic crisis for the country at the end of 1994 and profound recession in 1995. NAFTA has meant that the fate of the Mexican economy is increasingly linked to the health of the U.S. economy.

The Mexican Economy Today

Under the influence of NAFTA, the Mexican economy has become increasingly oriented toward production for the North American market, and the manufacturing sector in particular has grown in importance. In addition to the traditional *maquiladora* industries along the northern border, Mexico is taking advantage of the large number of engineers trained by its universities to develop more advanced industries. Querétaro, in central Mexico, for example, is emerging as a center for the aerospace industry. The country also plays an integral part in a manufacturing process for automobiles that has become continental in scale, with parts from the United States, Canada, and Mexico moving between plants in the three countries as new cars are assembled. These developments give the country an economic profile that is quite distinct from that of many of its Latin American neighbors, many of which still rely more heavily on exports of agricultural products and raw materials.

Remittances reflect another close economic link with the United States. Mexican migrants abroad sent some $22 billion home to relatives in 2013, with 98 percent of those funds coming from the United States (see The U.S. Connection: Mexican Migration to the United States). This sum represents 2 percent of Mexico's GDP, not an insignificant figure, and though the volume of remittances has declined somewhat since the economic crisis of 2008, these transfers provide a vital economic lifeline to many communities in central and southern Mexico, some of which send almost all of their adult men to the United States to work.[4]

Oil production also remains important to the economy, particularly since the national petroleum company, PEMEX, continues to provide a substantial proportion of government revenues. However, the government's reliance on oil revenues

remittances

Funds sent by migrants working abroad to family members in their home countries.

THE U.S. CONNECTION

Mexican Migration to the United States

Mexicans began moving to the United States in substantial numbers late in the nineteenth century, and their ranks grew as many fled the conditions created by the Revolution of 1910. Most settled in the border states of California and Texas, where they joined preexisting Mexican communities that had been there since the days when the American southwest had been part of Mexico. Even greater numbers of migrants began to arrive during World War II, when the U.S. government allowed Mexican workers, known as *braceros*, to enter the country to help provide much-needed manpower for strategic production efforts. After the *bracero* program came to an end in 1964, Mexicans continued to seek work in the United States, despite the fact that most then had to enter the country illegally.

To a large extent, the U.S. government informally tolerated the employment of undocumented migrants until the 1980s, when policy-makers came under pressure to assert control over the border. The 1986 Immigration Reform and Control Act (IRCA) allowed migrants who had been in the United States for a long period of time to gain legal residency rights, but it called for tighter controls on immigration in the future. IRCA and subsequent efforts to deter illegal immigration turned a pattern of seasonal migration into a flow of migrants that settled permanently north of the border. Before 1986, most Mexican migrant workers left their families at home and worked in the United States for only a few months at a time before returning to their country with the money they had earned. The money that these migrants send back to Mexico helps to sustain not just their own families but entire regions that have been left behind by the migrants who gained amnesty under IRCA and then sent for their families to join them, creating a more permanent immigrant community. Also, as increased vigilance and new barriers making the crossing of the border more difficult, more of the migrants who arrived in the United States decided to remain there rather than risk apprehension by traveling back and forth

between the two countries. High-profile efforts to patrol the border around urban areas such as San Diego and El Paso led migrants to use more remote crossing points, and although the number of Mexicans who died trying to reach the United States rose as many attempted to travel through the desolate deserts of Arizona, the overall rate of illegal immigration was not affected by the government's crackdown.

In the 1990s and 2000s, growing Mexican communities in the United States spread into areas such as North Carolina, Georgia, Arkansas, and Iowa, where few Mexicans had lived before. They also became increasingly mobilized politically as they organized to resist anti-immigrant voter initiatives such as Proposition 187 in California in 1994 and Proposition 200 in Arizona in 2004, both of which threatened to cut off social services for undocumented migrants. At the same time, their political importance in Mexico has reached unprecedented heights as officials at all levels of government there recognize the critical importance to the Mexican economy of the remittances received from migrants working in other countries. Mexican governors, mayors, and federal officials now regularly visit representatives of migrant groups in the United States, often seeking their support and funding for projects at home. Moreover, a 1996 law allowing Mexicans to hold dual citizenship makes it possible for many Mexican migrants to have a voice in the governance of both the country of their birth as well as the country where they now reside. In 2005, Mexican legislators finally approved a system under which registered Mexican voters living abroad could participate in federal elections. Although levels of electoral participation by Mexicans abroad have so far been relatively modest, this huge group could play a decisive role in future contests.

MAKING CONNECTIONS How might debates over immigration policies in the United States affect the politics and foreign relations of Mexico?

has starved the state oil monopoly of the capital it would need to invest in new technologies and seek out new deposits. As the output of existing oilfields has begun to decline, the politically sensitive question of reform in the energy sector has therefore become unavoidable. Peña Nieto's energy reform will allow foreign companies to enter into joint ventures in Mexico with PEMEX, a development that could revitalize the sector but could also inflame nationalist resentments if Mexico is not seen to benefit from new discoveries.

Society and Economy

Mexico's economic development has had a significant impact on social conditions in the country. Overall, standards of living and quality of life rose markedly after the 1940s. Provision of health and education services expanded until government cutbacks on social expenditures in the early 1980s and has been extended further in recent years as modest economic growth has resumed. Among the most important consequences of economic growth was the development of a large middle class, most of whom live in Mexico's numerous large cities.

These achievements reflect well on the ability of the economy to increase social well-being in the country. But in terms of standard indicators of social development—infant mortality, literacy, and life expectancy—Mexico fell behind a number of Latin American countries that grew less rapidly but provided more effectively for their populations. Costa Rica, Colombia, Argentina, Chile, and Uruguay had lower over-all growth but greater social development in the period after 1940. These countries paid more attention to the distribution of the benefits of growth than did Mexico.

In part, because of the specific way in which Mexico has pursued economic growth, there is also a regional dimension to disparities in social development. The northern areas of the country are significantly better off than the southern and central areas. In the north, large commercial farms using modern technologies grow fruits, vegetables, and grains for export. Moreover, urban industrial centers such as Monterrey and Tijuana provide steady employment for skilled and unskilled labor. Along the border, *maquiladoras* provide many jobs, particularly for young women who are seeking some escape from the burdens of rural life or the constraints of traditional family life.

In the southern and central regions of the country, the population is denser, the terrain more difficult, and the number of farmers eking out subsistence greater. Investment in irrigation and transportation infrastructure has been lacking in many areas. Most of the 26 million Mexicans who continue to live in rural areas, and most of the country's remaining indigenous groups live in the southern regions, often in remote zones where they have been forgotten by government programs and exploited by regional bosses for generations.

The general economic crisis of the 1980s had an impact on social conditions in Mexico as well. Wages declined by about half, and unemployment soared as businesses collapsed and the government laid off workers. The informal sector expanded rapidly. Here, people manage to make a living by hawking chewing gum, umbrellas, candy, shoelaces, and many other items in the street; jumping in front of cars at stoplights to wash windshields and sell newspapers; producing and repairing cheap consumer goods; and selling services on a daily or hourly basis. The economic crisis also reduced the quality and availability of social services, as the government imposed austerity measures. Though economic recovery has been slow and fitful in recent decades, the Mexican government has begun to fill the void left by cuts in social spending during the depths of the crisis. Recent years have seen the launch of successful programs that provide vastly expanded access to basic health care and cash grants to poor families that keep their children in school.

Environmental Issues

With its varied landscapes, including long coastlines, extensive coral reefs, towering mountain peaks, tropical rain forests, and arid deserts, Mexico is a country of tremendous biodiversity, with many fragile ecosystems that have been badly damaged by insensitive economic development. Though a tradition of conservation stretches back at least to the 1930s, when Lázaro Cárdenas established a national park system, for many years the pursuit of economic development and industrialization was given priority over the enforcement of environmental regulations. One result was that Mexico City became one of the most polluted cities in the world, and in some rural areas oil exploitation left devastating environmental damage.[5]

When residents of Mexico City and other parts of the country began to mobilize outside of the PRI in the 1980s to pressure the government to address the issues that mattered most to their communities, environmental concerns were an important item on their agenda, and much stricter controls on automobile and industrial emissions have helped to make the capital's air more breathable since that time. As Mexico has sought a place in the global economy since the late 1980s, pressure from abroad also played a vital role in bringing about a strengthening of the state's commitment to environmental protection. When critics of NAFTA threatened to block the agreement in the United States on the grounds that Mexico failed to live up to international environmental standards, the Mexican government signed onto side agreements providing for greater environmental oversight in order to secure the ratification of the free-trade accord. The government also signalled that it was assigning greater importance to environmental concerns by creating a ministry for the environment and natural resources in 1994; more than coincidentally, the new cabinet department came into existence in the same year that NAFTA went into effect.

Although many concerns remain, the will and the capacity of the Mexican state to act to protect the environment have been significantly enhanced over the past two decades. Moreover, in an increasingly interconnected world, Mexican civil society organizations with an interest in these issues have benefitted greatly from the connections they have developed with international networks of environmental groups.

Mexico in the Global Economy

The crisis that began in 1982 altered Mexico's international economic policies. In response to that crisis, the government relaxed restrictions on the ability of foreigners to own property, reduced and eliminated tariffs, and did away with most import licenses. Foreign investment was courted in the hope of increasing the manufacture of goods for export. The government also introduced a series of incentives to encourage the private sector to produce goods for export. In 1986, Mexico joined the General Agreement on Tariffs and Trade (GATT), a multilateral agreement that sought to promote freer trade among countries and that later became the basis for the World Trade Organization (WTO). In the 1990s and 2000s, Mexico signed trade pacts with many countries in Latin America, Europe, and elsewhere.

The government's effort to pursue a more outward-oriented development strategy culminated in the ratification of NAFTA in 1993, with gradual implementation beginning on January 1, 1994. In 2013, 77.6 percent of the country's exports were sent to the United States, and 50.1 percent of its imports came from that country, making Mexico's northern neighbor its most important trading partner by a wide margin.[6] Access to the U.S. market is essential to Mexico and to domestic and foreign investors. NAFTA signaled a new period in U.S.–Mexican relations by making closer integration of the two economies a certainty.

NAFTA also entails risks for Mexico. Domestic producers worry about competition from U.S. firms. Farmers worry that Mexican crops cannot compete effectively with those grown in the United States; for example, peasant producers of corn and beans have been hard hit by the availability of lower-priced U.S.-grown grains.[7] In addition, many believe that embracing free trade with Canada and the United States indicates a loss of sovereignty. Certainly, Mexico's economic situation is now more vulnerable to the ebb and flow of economic conditions in the U.S. economy. Indeed, after the United States plunged into a deep recession in 2008, Mexico's economy contracted by more than 7 percent, despite the fact that the crisis was not of its own making. Moreover, some in Mexico are also concerned with evidence of "cultural imperialism" as U.S. movies, music, fashions, and lifestyles increasingly influence consumers. Indeed, for Mexico, which has traditionally feared the power of the United States in its domestic affairs, internationalization of political and economic relationships poses particularly difficult problems of adjustment.

On the other hand, the United States, newly aware of the importance of the Mexican economy to its own economic growth and concerned about instability on its southern border, hammered together a $50 billion economic assistance program composed of U.S., European, and IMF commitments to support its neighbor when economic crisis struck in 1994. The Mexican government imposed a new stabilization package that contained austerity measures, higher interest rates, and limits on wages. Remarkably, by 1998, Mexico had paid off all of its obligations to the United States.

Globalization is also stripping Mexico of some of the secrecy that traditionally surrounded government decision making, electoral processes, and efforts to deal with political dissent. International attention increasingly focuses on the country, and investors want clear information on what is occurring in the economy. The government can no longer respond to events such as the peasant rebellion in Chiapas, alleged electoral fraud, or the management of exchange rates without considering how such actions will be perceived in Tokyo, Frankfurt, London, or Washington.

Where Do You Stand?

Mexico is recognized by investors as an important emerging economy, but can its development strategy be considered a success when some regions of the country and some economic sectors are being left behind? What can be done to address the disparities being exacerbated by uneven growth?

Taking into account the full range of effects that NAFTA has had on Mexico, do you think the free trade agreement has been good or bad for the country?

GOVERNANCE AND POLICY-MAKING

SECTION 3

Organization of the State

Under the Constitution of 1917, Mexico's political institutions resemble those of the United States. There are three branches of government, and a set of checks and balances limits the power of each. The congress is composed of the Senate and the

sexenio

The six-year term in office of Mexican presidents.

Chamber of Deputies. One hundred twenty-eight senators are elected, three from each of the country's thirty-one states; three from the Federal District, which contains the capital, Mexico City; and another thirty-two elected nationally by proportional representation (PR). The 500 members of the Chamber of Deputies are elected from 300 electoral districts—300 by simple majority vote and 200 by proportional representation. State and local governments are also elected. The president, governors, and senators are elected for six years, an important institutional feature of Mexican politics referred to as the *sexenio*. Congressional deputies (representatives in the lower house) and municipal officials are elected for three years.

In practice, the Mexican system is very different from that of the United States. The constitution is a long document that can be easily amended. It lays out the structure of government and guarantees a wide range of human rights, including familiar ones such as freedom of speech and protection under the law, but also economic and social rights such as the right to a job and the right to health care. In practice, these rights do not reach all of the population. Although there has been some decentralization, the political system is still much more centralized than that of the United States. Since the democratic transition of 2000, congress has become more active as a decision-making arena and as a check on presidential power, but the executive remains central to initiating policy and managing political conflict.

The Executive

The President and the Cabinet

The presidency is the central institution of governance and policy-making in Mexico. Until the 1990s, the incumbent president always selected who would run as the PRI's next presidential candidate, appointed officials to all positions of power in the government and the party, and often named the candidates who almost automatically won elections as governors, senators, deputies, and local officials.[8] Even after the transition to a more competitive political system, the president continues to set the broad outlines of policy for the administration and has numerous resources to ensure that those policy preferences are adopted. Until the mid-1970s, Mexican presidents were considered above criticism in national politics and revered as symbols of national progress and well-being. While the crises of the 1980s and 1990s diminished presidential prestige, the extent of presidential power remains a legacy of the long period of PRI dominance.

Mexican presidents have a set of formal powers that allows them to initiate legislation, lead in foreign policy, create government agencies, make policy by decree or through administrative regulations and procedures, and appoint a wide range of public officials. More importantly, informal powers allow them to exert considerable control. The president manages a vast patronage machine for filling positions in government and initiates legislation and policies that were, until recently, routinely approved by the congress.

Mexican presidents, though powerful, are not omnipotent. They must, for example, abide by a deeply held constitutional norm by stepping down at the end of their term, and they must adhere to tradition by removing themselves from the political limelight to allow their successors to assume full presidential leadership. All presidents, regardless of party, must demonstrate their loyalty to the myths and symbols of Mexican nationalism, and they must make a rhetorical commitment to social justice and sovereignty in international affairs.

President Enrique Peña Nieto (left) is congratulated by his predecessor, Felipe Calderón, at his inauguration on December 1, 2012.

AP Images/Alexandre Meneghini

In the 1990s, President Zedillo gave up a number of the traditional powers of the presidency. He announced, for example, that he would not select his PRI successor but would leave it up to the party to determine its candidate. This created considerable tension as the PRI had to take on unaccustomed roles and as politicians sought to fill the void left by the "abandonment" of presidential power. Fox, Calderón, and Peña Nieto inherited a system in which the president is expected to set the policies and determine the priorities for a very wide range of government activity, yet needs a strong party in congress and experienced people in his administration to enact legislation and implement policies.

Until the democratic transition of 2000, presidents were almost always members of the outgoing president's cabinet. With the victory of the PAN in 2000, this long tradition came to an end. Prior to running for president, Vicente Fox had been in business and had served as the governor of the state of Guanajuato. Calderón, although he had served briefly as energy minister, was not the candidate within the PAN that Fox had initially favored. In this respect, Calderón's victory in 2006 continued a trend toward greater independence of parties from presidential preferences. As the PRI candidate in 2012, Peña Nieto obviously had not served in the cabinets of Fox or Calderón; instead, he had just completed a term as the governor of the populous state of Mexico, which includes many of the suburbs of Mexico City. His candidacy reflected the prominence that state governors had attained in the PRI during the years that the party had been out of power at the national level.

Mexican presidents since the mid-1970s have had impressive educational credentials and have tended to be trained in economics and management rather than in the traditional field of law. Most presidents since López Portillo have had postgraduate training at elite institutions in the United States. By the 1980s, a topic of great debate

technocrats

Career-minded bureaucrats who administer public policy according to a technical rather than a political rationale.

in political circles was the extent to which a divide between *políticos* (politicians) and *técnicos* (**technocrats**) had emerged within the national political elite. Having studied law and attended Mexican universities, Peña Nieto's educational background differs from that of his immediate predecessors.

Once elected, the president moves quickly to name a cabinet. Before 2000, he usually selected those with whom he had worked over the years as he rose to political prominence. He also used cabinet posts to ensure a broad coalition of support; he might, for example, appoint people with close ties to the labor movement, business interests, or some of the regional strongholds of the PRI. Only in rare exceptions were cabinet officials not active members of the party. When the PAN assumed the presidency, the selection of cabinet members became more difficult. Until then, the PAN had elected officials only to a few state and local governments and to a relatively small number of seats in congress. As a consequence, the range of people with executive experience to whom Fox could turn was limited. He appointed U.S.-trained economists for his economic team and business executives for many other important posts. Few of these appointees had close ties to the PAN or prior experience in government. By contrast, Calderón filled his cabinet positions with longtime members of the PAN who had a longer history of political engagement, but after so many years in opposition, many of these appointees also lacked extensive experience in government. Over the years, few women have been selected for ministry-level posts. Initially, they only presided over agencies with limited influence over decision making, like the ministries of tourism and fisheries. More recently, however, women have served as foreign minister and as attorney general. Peña Nieto has followed the traditions of the PRI by naming a number of aides from his term as governor of Mexico state, as well as allies from key regions, to his cabinet. At the same time, he has looked beyond his party to fill some posts. He named Rosario Robles, a woman and the former president of the left-of-center Party of the Democratic Revolution (PRD), as minister for social development, and he appointed a member of Calderón's cabinet as foreign minister.

The president has the authority to fill numerous other high-level positions, which allows him to provide policy direction and keep tabs on what is occurring throughout the government. The range of appointments that a chief executive can make means that the beginning of each administration is characterized by extensive turnover of positions. Progress on the president's policy agenda can therefore be slow toward the beginning of each *sexenio* as newly appointed officials learn the ropes and assemble their staff, though this effect was not noticeable during Peña Nieto's very active first year in office. The president's power to make appointments allows him to build a team of like-minded officials in government and ensure their loyalty.

The Bureaucracy

Mexico's executive branch is large and powerful. Almost 1.5 million people work in the federal bureaucracy, most of them in Mexico City. An additional 1 million work in state-owned industries and semiautonomous agencies of the government. State and local governments employ over 1.5 million people.

Officials at lower levels in the bureaucracy are unionized and protected by legislation that gives them job security and a range of benefits. At middle and upper levels, most officials are called "confidence employees"; they serve as long as their bosses have confidence in them. These officials have been personally appointed by their superiors at the outset of an administration. Their modest salaries are compensated for by the significant power that they can have over public affairs. For aspiring young professionals, a career in government is often attractive because of the challenge of dealing with important problems on a daily basis. Some employees also benefit from opportunities to take bribes or use other means to promote their personal interests.

The Parastatal Sector

The parastatal sector—composed of semiautonomous or autonomous government agencies, many of which produce goods and services—was extremely large and powerful in Mexico prior to the 1990s. As part of its post-1940 development strategy, the government engaged in numerous activities that in other countries are carried out by the private sector. Thus, until the Salinas administration, the country's largest steel mill was state-owned, as were the largest fertilizer producer, sugar mills, and airlines. In addition, the national electricity board still produces energy, which it supplies to industries at subsidized prices. The state-owned petroleum company, PEMEX, grew to enormous proportions in the 1970s and 1980s under the impact of the oil boom. NAFIN, a state investment corporation, provides a considerable amount of investment capital for the country. At one point, a state marketing board called CONASUPO was responsible for the importation and purchase of the country's basic food supplies, and in the 1970s, it played a major role in distributing food, credit, and farm implements in rural areas.

This large parastatal sector was significantly trimmed by the economic policy reforms that began in the 1980s. Concerted efforts were then made to privatize many of these enterprises, including the telephone company, the national airlines, and the nationalized banks. Many strategic industries thus passed into a small number of private hands, and much of the banking sector came under the control of foreign corporations. However, some core components of the parastatal sector will likely remain in government hands for the foreseeable future because an influential bloc of nationalist political actors insists on the symbolic importance of public ownership of key industries. For example, even with reforms taking effect to allow foreign investment in the energy sector, PEMEX is likely to remain a state enterprise with a key position in the petroleum industry.

Other State Institutions

The Military

Mexico is one of only a few countries in the developing world, particularly in Latin America, to have successfully marginalized the military from centers of political power. Although former military leaders dominated Mexican politics during the decades immediately after the Revolution of 1910, Calles and Cárdenas laid the groundwork for civilian rule by introducing the practice of rotating regional military commands so that generals could not build up geographic bases of power. In addition, postrevolutionary leaders made an implicit bargain with the military leaders by providing them with opportunities to engage in business so that they did not look to political office as a way of gaining economic power. After 1946, the military no longer had institutional representation within the PRI and became clearly subordinate to civilian control. No military officer has held the presidency since that time.

This does not mean that the military has operated outside politics. It has been called in from time to time to deal with domestic unrest: in rural areas in the 1960s, in Mexico City and other cities to repress student protest movements in 1968, and in

Chiapas beginning in 1994. When the PAN government made it possible for citizens to gain greater access to government information, it was discovered that the military had been involved in political repression, torture, and killing in the 1970s and 1980s. The scandal created by such revelations lowered its reputation, though polls show that Mexicans continue to have more confidence in the armed forces than many other institutions, including the police forces, which are widely regarded as corrupt and ineffective.

In recent years, the military has been heavily involved in efforts to combat drug trafficking, and rumors have at times arisen about deals struck between military officials and drug barons. The military continues to be used to fight drug cartels and organized crime. In some regions particularly hard-hit by drug-related violence, the military took over many policing functions. Though the army is seen as less corrupt than many of the local police forces they have replaced, concerns about their ongoing presence on the streets of Mexican cities have arisen, particularly as allegations of civil and human rights violations by soldiers have emerged in some areas.

Whenever the military is called in to resolve domestic conflicts, some Mexicans become concerned that the institution is becoming politicized and may come to play a larger role in political decision making. Thus far, such fears have not been realized, and many believe that as long as civilian administrations are able to maintain the country's tradition of stability, the military will not intervene directly in politics.

The Judiciary

Unlike Anglo-American legal systems, Mexico's law derives from the Roman and Napoleonic tradition and is highly formalized. Because Mexican law tends to be very explicit and because there are no punitive damages allowed in court cases, there are fewer lawsuits than in the United States. One important exception to this is the *amparo* (protection), whereby individual citizens may ask for a writ of protection, claiming that their constitutional rights have been violated by specific government actions or laws.

There are both federal and state courts in Mexico. The federal system is composed of the Supreme Court, which decides the most important cases; circuit courts, which take cases on appeal; and district courts, where cases enter the system. As in the United States, Supreme Court justices are nominated by the president and approved by the Senate. Since most of the important laws in Mexico are federal, state courts have played a subordinate role. This is changing, however. As Mexican states become more independent from the federal government, state law has been experiencing tremendous growth. In addition, there are many important specialized federal courts, such as labor courts, military courts, and electoral courts.

Like other government institutions in Mexico, the judiciary was for many decades politically, though not constitutionally, subordinate to the executive. The courts occasionally slowed the actions of government by issuing *amparos*; however, in almost every case in which the power of the state was at stake, the courts ruled on the side of the government. The Zedillo administration tried to change this by emphasizing the rule of law over that of powerful individuals. Increasing interest in human rights issues by citizens' groups and the media added pressure to the courts to play a stronger role in protecting basic freedoms.

Although the judicial system remains the weakest branch of government, reforms continue to be proposed. In 2008, in response to concern for the rights of defendants who fall victim to police and prosecutorial misconduct, constitutional amendments called for the introduction of public trials with oral testimony and the presumption of innocence. When fully implemented, the reforms will represent one of the most significant changes to the judiciary in modern Mexican history. The northern state of Chihuahua was the first to adopt the new system, but the new procedures have been controversial there, and progress elsewhere in the country has been slow.

Subnational Government

As with many other aspects of the Mexican political system, regional and local government in Mexico is quite different from what is described in the constitution. Under Mexico's federal system, each state has its own constitution, executive, unicameral legislature, and judiciary. Municipalities (equivalent to U.S. counties) are governed by popularly elected mayors and councils. But most state and municipal governments are poor. Most of the funds they command are transferred to them from the central government, and they have little legal or administrative capacity to raise their own revenue. States and localities also suffer greatly from the lack of well-trained and well-paid public officials. As at the national level, many jobs in state and local governments are distributed as political patronage, but even officials who are motivated to be responsive to local needs are generally ill equipped to do so. In light of these weaknesses, it is not surprising that local governments have been particularly susceptible to the ability of wealthy, heavily armed drug cartels to corrupt and intimidate public officials, especially in poor and remote regions.

Since the early 1990s, the government has made several serious efforts to decentralize and devolve more power to state and local governments. At times, governors and mayors have resisted such initiatives because they meant that regional and local governments would have to manage much more complex activities and be the focus of demands from public sector workers and their unions. Local governments were also worried that they would be unable to acquire the budgetary resources necessary to carry out their new responsibilities.

Until 1989, all governors were from the PRI, but since then politics at the state level has become competitive in almost every region of the country. During the 25 years since the first PAN governor took office in Baja California, approximately three-quarters of Mexico's states have had at least one non-PRI administration. Municipalities have also increasingly been the focus of authentic party competition. As opposition parties came to control these levels of government, they were challenged to improve services such as police protection, garbage collection, sanitation, and education. PRI-dominated governments have also tried to improve their performance because they are now more threatened by the possibility of losing elections.

The Policy-Making Process

The Mexican system is very dependent on the quality of its leadership and on presidential understanding of how economic and social policies can affect the development of the country. As indicated throughout this chapter, the president's single six-year term of office, the *sexenio*, is an important fact of political life in Mexico. New presidents can introduce extensive change in positions within the government. They are able to bring in "their" people, who build teams of "their" people within ministries, agencies, and party networks. This generally provides the president with a group of high- and middle-level officials who share the same general orientation toward public policy and are motivated to carry out his goals. When the PRI was the dominant party, these officials believed that in following presidential leadership, they enhanced their chances for upward political mobility. In such a context, even under a single party, it was likely that changes in public policies could be introduced every six years, creating innovation or discontinuity, or both.

Together with the bureaucracy, the president is the focal point of policy formulation and political management. Until 1997, the legislature always had a PRI majority and acted as a rubber stamp for presidentially sponsored legislation. Since then, the congress has proven to be a more active policy-maker, blocking and forcing the negotiation of legislation, and even introducing its own bills. The president's skills in negotiating, managing the opposition, using the media to acquire public support, and maneuvering within the bureaucracy can be important in ensuring that his program is fully endorsed.

Significant limits on presidential power occur when policy is being implemented. At times, policies are not implemented because public officials at the lower levels disagree with them or make deals with affected interests in order to benefit personally. This is the case, for example, with taxes that remain uncollected because individuals or corporations bribe officials to overlook them. In other cases, lower-level officials may lack the capacity to implement some policies, such as those directed toward improving education or rural development services. For various reasons, Mexican presidents cannot always deliver on their intentions. Traditionally, Mexican citizens have blamed lower-level officials for such slippage, but exempting the president from responsibility for what does or does not occur during his watch has become much less common since the 1970s.

Where Do You Stand?

Should Mexico lift its constitutional ban on presidential reelection, as a number of other Latin American countries have done in recent years? Would having to face the voters for reelection make officials more accountable, or might allowing them to stay in office for more than one term open the door to a return to authoritarianism?

With the decline in the deference given to presidential preferences in recent years, more voices have been heard and taken into account as policies have been formulated, but the process has become more contentious and less efficient. On balance then, is it good for Mexico that the authority of the president has diminished over the past two decades?

SECTION 4 REPRESENTATION AND PARTICIPATION

How do citizen interests get represented in Mexican politics, given the high degree of centralization, presidentialism, and, until recently, single-party domination? Is it possible for ordinary citizens to make demands on government and influence public policy? In fact, Mexico has had a relatively peaceful history since the revolution, in part because the political system offers some channels for representation and participation. Throughout this long history, the political system has emphasized compromise among contending elites, behind-the-scenes conflict resolution, and distribution of political rewards to those willing to play by the formal and informal rules of the game. It has also responded, if only reluctantly and defensively, to demands for change.

Often, citizens are best able to interact with the government through a variety of informal means rather than through the formal processes of elections, campaigns, and interest group lobbying. Interacting with government through the personal mechanisms of clientelism usually means that the government retains the upper hand in deciding which interests to respond to and which to ignore. For many interests, this has meant "incorporation without power."[9] Increasingly, however, Mexican citizens are organizing to alter this situation, and the advent of truly competitive elections has increased the possibility that citizens who organize can gain some response from government.

The Legislature

Students in the United States are frequently asked to study complex charts explaining how a bill becomes a law because the formal process of lawmaking affects the content of legislation. Under the old reign of the PRI in Mexico, while there were formal rules that prescribed such a process, studying them would not have been useful for understanding how the legislature worked. Because of the overwhelming dominance of the ruling party, opposition to presidential initiatives by Mexico's two-chamber legislature, the Senate and the Chamber of Deputies, was rarely heard. If representatives did not agree with policies they were asked to approve, they counted on the fact that policy implementation was flexible and allowed for after-the-fact bending of the rules or disregard of measures that were harmful to important interests.

Representation in congress has become more diverse since the end of the 1980s. Between 1988 and 2006, the PRI's grip on the legislature steadily weakened. By the end of that period, the party had fewer representatives in the Chamber of Deputies than either of its two main rivals. The PRI subsequently made large gains in mid-term legislative elections in 2009, and it is once again the largest party in the both houses of congress, but today the legislature is divided between strong PRI, PAN, and PRD blocs, with no single party able to dominate proceedings. In large part because the PRI has lost its stranglehold on congressional representation, the role of

Focus Questions ▽

• Since the early 1980s, how has the balance of power shifted between the legislative and executive branches of government? How do these shifts correspond to changes in the overall political landscape?

• What are the power bases of the main political parties in Mexican politics? What factors made it possible for the PAN to unseat the long-dominant PRI in 2000? What accounts for the success of the PRI in returning to power in 2012?

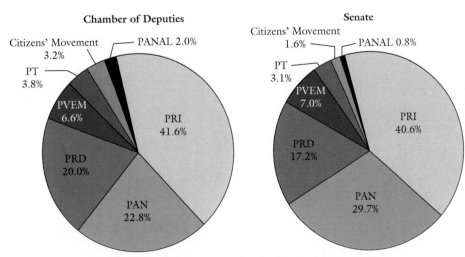

FIGURE 10.2 Congressional Representation by Party, 2014

Source: CIA World Factbook, www.cia.gov/library/publications/the-world-factbook/geos /mx.html#Govt; see also www.senado.gob.mx and www.camaradediputados.gob.mx.

the legislature in the policy process has been strengthened considerably since the late 1990s.[10] The cost of greater power sharing between the executive and the legislature, however, has been a slow-down in the policy process. The biggest change, therefore, has been that the congress has evolved from a rubber-stamp institution to one that must be negotiated with by the executive branch.

Political Parties and the Party System

Even under the long reign of the PRI, a number of political parties existed in Mexico. By the mid-1980s, some of them were attracting more political support, a trend that continued into the 1990s and 2000s (see Table 10.3). Electoral reforms introduced by the PRI administrations between the 1970s and the 1990s made it easier for opposition parties to contest and win elections. In 1990, an electoral commission was

Table 10.3	Voting for Major Parties in Presidential Elections, 1934–2012			
Year	Votes for PRI Candidate	Votes for PAN Candidate	Votes for PRD Candidate	Voter Turnout (% of eligible adults)
1934	98.2	—	—	53.6
1940	93.9	—	—	57.5
1946	77.9	—	—	42.6
1952	74.3	7.8	—	57.9
1958	90.4	9.4	—	49.4
1964	88.8	11.1	—	54.1
1970	83.3	13.9	—	63.9
1976	93.6	—	—	29.6
1982	71.0	15.7	—	66.1
1988	50.7	16.8	31.0	49.4
1994	50.1	26.7	16.6	77.3
2000	36.1	42.5	16.6	64.0
2006	22.3	35.9	35.3	58.6
2012	38.2	25.4	31.6	63.1

Source: From *Comparative Politics Today: A World View*, 4th ed., Gabriel Almond and G. Bingham Powell, Jr. © 1988. Reprinted by permission of Addison-Wesley Educational Publishers, Inc. For 1988: *El Universal*, "Resultados Electorales," graficos.eluniversal .com.mx/tablas/presidente/presidentes.htm. For 1994: Instituto Federal Electoral, *Estadística de las Elecciones Federales de 1994, Compendio de Resultados* (México, D.F., 1995). For 2000–2012: Instituto Federal Electoral, www.ife.org.mx.

created to regulate campaigns and elections, and in 1996 it became fully independent of the government. Now all parties receive funding from the government and have access to the media.

The PRI

Mexico's Institutional Revolutionary Party (PRI) was founded by a coalition of political elites who agreed that it was preferable to work out their conflicts within an overarching structure of compromise than to continue to resort to violence. In the 1930s, the forerunner of the PRI (the party operated under different names until 1946) incorporated a wide array of interests, becoming a mass-based party that drew support from all classes in the population. Over seven decades, its principal activities were to generate support for the government, organize the electorate to vote for its candidates, and distribute jobs and resources in return for loyalty to the system.

Until the 1990s, party organization was based largely on the corporatist representation of class interests. Labor was represented within party councils by the Confederation of Mexican Workers (CTM), which included industry-based unions at local, regional, and national levels. Peasants were represented by the National Peasant Confederation (CNC), an organization of *ejido* and peasant unions and regional associations. The so-called popular sector, comprising small businesses, community-based groups, and public employees, had less internal cohesion but was represented by the National Confederation of Popular Organizations (CNOP). Of the three, the CTM was consistently the best organized and most powerful. Traditionally, the PRI's strongest support came from the countryside, where *ejidatarios* and independent small farmers were dependent on rewards of land or jobs. As the country became more urbanized, the support base provided by rural communities remained important to the PRI, but produced many fewer votes than were necessary to keep the party in power.

Within its corporatist structures, the PRI functioned through extended networks that distributed public resources—particularly jobs, land, development projects, and access to public services—to lower-level activists who controlled votes at the local level. In this system, those with ambitions to hold public office or positions within the PRI put together networks of supporters from above (patrons), to whom they delivered votes, and supporters from below (clients), who traded allegiance for access to public resources. For well over half a century, this system worked extremely well. PRI candidates won by overwhelming majorities until the 1980s. Of course, electoral fraud and the ability to distribute government largesse are central explanations for these numbers, but they also attest to an extremely well-organized party.

By the 1980s, new generations of voters were less beholden to patronage-style politics and much more willing to question the party's dominance, and the PRI began to be challenged by parties to the right and left. Outcomes were hotly contested by the opposition, which claimed fraudulent electoral practices. As the PRI faced greater competition from other parties and continued to suffer from declining popularity, efforts were made to restructure and reform it. Party conventions were introduced in an effort to democratize the internal workings of the party, and some states and localities began to hold primaries to select PRI candidates, a significant departure from the old system of selection by party bosses.

After the PRI lost the presidency in 2000, the party faced a difficult future. At the dawn of the twenty-first century, Mexico's voters were younger, better educated, and more middle class than they were during the period of PRI dominance. They were also more likely to live in urban areas than they were in the days of the party's greatest success. With the vast majority of the country's population living in cities, the PRI faced the challenge of winning the support of more urban voters.

Nonetheless, the PRI remained a strong political force. It did not, as some predicted, dissolve once it lost the ability to control the presidency. As one of the largest blocs in a divided congress between 2000 and 2012, PRI representatives could often exercise significant control over the legislative agenda. Just as importantly, the party continued to control most subnational governments, and state governors emerged as some of the most influential figures in the party. The PRI is still the only party that has a presence in every region of the country, and after the violence and legislative gridlock of recent years, some Mexicans clearly hope that the party will be able to draw upon its long experience in government to offer a greater degree of order and stability.

The PAN

anticlericalism

Opposition to the power of churches or clergy in politics. In some countries, for example, France and Mexico, this opposition has focused on the role of the Catholic Church in politics.

The National Action Party (PAN) was founded in 1939 to represent interests opposed to the centralization and **anticlericalism** of the PRI. It was established by those who believed that the country needed more than one strong political party and that opposition parties should oppose the PRI through legal and constitutional actions. Historically, this party has been strongest in northern states, where it has drawn upon a regional tradition of resistance to central authority. It has also been primarily an urban party of the middle class and is closely identified with the private sector. The PAN has traditionally campaigned on a platform endorsing greater regional autonomy, less government intervention in the economy, reduced regulation of business, clean and fair elections, rapprochement with the Catholic Church, and support for private and religious education. When PRI governments of the 1980s and 1990s moved toward market-friendly and export-oriented policies, the policy differences between the two parties were significantly reduced. Nevertheless, a major difference of perspectives about religion continued to characterize the two parties.

For many years, the PAN was able to elect only about 10 percent of all deputies to the national congress and to capture control of just a few municipal governments. Beginning in the 1980s, it was able to take advantage both of the damage done to the PRI by economic crises and the opportunities provided by political reforms to increase its power. A PAN candidate was elected as the first opposition state governor in many years in 1989, and the party built up a sizeable bloc in both houses of congress during the 1990s. The PAN's victory in the 2000 presidential election was a historic breakthrough. Its triumph that year and in 2006 made the PAN the nation's governing party for 12 years.

In nominating Vicente Fox for the presidency in 2000, the party was taking an unusual step, for Fox was not a long-standing member of the party. Many party insiders considered him to be an opportunistic newcomer. Though Fox won the presidential election, the PAN organization was weak and not at all united in backing him. His inability to capitalize on his electoral victory and push forward a more ambitious package of reforms allowed the party insiders to regain control of the nominating process and advance the candidacy of Felipe Calderón in 2006. Unlike Fox, he was a lifelong member of the PAN and was the son of one of the PAN's founding members. In 2012, the party nominated a former education and social development minister, Josefina Vázquez Mota, as its presidential candidate. Her third-place showing indicated the country was ready for a change, and though the party continues to hold several governorships and the second-largest number of seats in both houses of congress, the PAN has struggled since its defeat to overcome internal divisions over its future.

The PRD

Another group that has played a key role in the construction of a more competitive political system in Mexico is the Party of the Democratic Revolution (PRD), which emerged in the late 1980s as a populist, nationalist, and leftist alternative to the PRI. Its candidate in the 1988, 1994, and 2000 elections was Cuauhtémoc Cárdenas, the son of Mexico's most revered president. In the 1988 elections, Cárdenas was officially credited with winning 31.1 percent of the vote. He benefited from massive political defection from the PRI and garnered support from workers disaffected with the boss-dominated unions, as well as from peasants who remembered his father's concern for the welfare of the poor.

Even while the votes were being counted, the party began to denounce widespread electoral fraud and claim that Cárdenas would have won if the election had been honest. The party challenged a number of vote counts in the courts and walked out on the inaugural speech given by the PRI's Salinas. Considerable public opinion supported the party's challenge. After the 1988 elections, then, it seemed that the PRD was a strong contender to become Mexico's second-most-powerful party. It was expected to have a real chance in future years to challenge the PRI's "right" to the presidency.

Nevertheless, in the aftermath of these elections, the party was plagued by internal divisions over its platform, leadership, organizational structure, and election strategy. By 1994, it still lagged far behind the PRI and the PAN in establishing and maintaining the local constituency organizations needed to mobilize votes and monitor the election process. In addition, the PRD found it difficult to define an appropriate left-of-center alternative to the market-oriented policies carried out by the government. In the 1994 and 2000 elections, Cárdenas won less than 17 percent of the vote.

Under the leadership of a successful grassroots mobilizer named Andrés Manuel López Obrador, who was elected to head the party in 1996 and who subsequently served as mayor of Mexico City, the PRD began to stage a turnaround. PRD administrations in several states, many municipalities, and, most importantly, in the Federal District, showed that the party could take on the challenges of governance. Under López Obrador, the PRD's prospects for the 2006 elections looked good. Indeed, for most of 2005, polls indicated that López Obrador was the clear favorite to win the presidency. In early 2006, however, Calderón was able to shift the focus of his campaign and raise fears that a López Obrador presidency would threaten the stability of Mexico's economy. The election was hard fought and characterized by growing animosity. In the end, Calderón was able to win by a narrow margin. López Obrador refused to concede defeat and staged several protests, including a shadow inauguration where he declared himself the "legitimate" president of Mexico.

López Obrador's response to the outcome of the 2006 election split public opinion and created another debilitating divide in the PRD, this time between those who supported their candidate's claims and more pragmatic party leaders who favored looking to the future. These divisions deepened in the aftermath of the 2012 elections, when López Obrador again claimed fraud in the wake of his defeat. With some in the PRD signaling a willingness to work with the incoming Peña Nieto administration as a constructive opposition party, López Obrador took steps to break away and began the process of forming a new party, the National Regeneration Movement (MORENA). Though the PRD continues to govern the Federal District and a few states, the factionalism that has characterized the party make its future prospects uncertain.

Other Parties

There are a number of smaller parties that contest elections in Mexico. In 2014, the most important small parties were the Citizens' Movement, the Labor Party (PT), the Green Party (PVEM), and the New Alliance Party (PANAL). Since Mexican law requires parties to receive at least 2.5 percent of the vote to be able to compete in future elections, the long-term viability of some of these organizations is doubtful. Small parties, however, usually do win a few of the seats in the Chamber of Deputies and the Senate that are filled by proportional representation.

These small parties sometimes have an impact on national politics by forming alliances with the larger parties, either endorsing their candidates in national and state elections or backing a single slate of candidates for congress. For example, in 2012, the Citizens' Movement and the PT formed an alliance with the PRD to support the presidential candidacy of Andrés Manuel López Obrador, and the PRI and the PVEM jointly backed Peña Nieto. For its part, the New Alliance Party, generally seen as the political arm of the powerful national teachers' union, withdrew from the coalition supporting Peña Nieto and sought to influence the electoral process by nominating its own presidential candidate (who won just over 2 percent of the vote). The Green Party and the Citizens' Movement also hold one state governorship each, though in both cases their members were elected to office thanks to alliances with larger parties.

Elections

Each of the three main political parties draws voters from a wide and overlapping spectrum of the electorate. Nevertheless, a typical voter for the PRI is likely to be from a rural area or small town, to have less education, and to be older and poorer than voters for the other parties. A typical voter for the PAN is likely to be from a northern state, to live in an urban area, to be a middle-class professional, to have a comfortable lifestyle, and to have a high school or even a university education. A typical voter for the PRD is likely to be young, to be a political activist, to have an elementary or high school education, to live in one of the central states, and to live in a small town or an urban area. As we have seen, the support base for the PRI is the most vulnerable to economic and demographic changes in the country, though disillusionment with the status quo allowed the party to overcome this challenge in 2012.

Since 1994, elections have been more competitive and much fairer than they were during decades of PRI dominance, and subsequent congressional, state, and municipal elections reinforced the impression that electoral fraud is on the wane in many areas. The PAN's victory in 2000 substantially increased this impression. When López Obrador claimed in 2006 and 2012 that he had been robbed of victory, the legitimacy of the federal electoral authorities was questioned, but no evidence of wide-scale fraud or election tampering was uncovered.

Political Culture, Citizenship, and Identity

Most Mexicans have a deep familiarity with how their political system works and the ways in which they might be able to extract benefits from it. They understand the informal rules of the game in Mexican politics that have helped maintain political stability despite extensive inequalities in economic and political power. Clientelism has long been a form of participation in the sense that through their connections, many people, even the poorest, are able to interact with public officials and get something out of the political system. This kind of participation emphasizes how limited resources, such as access to health care, can be distributed in a way that provides maximum political payoff. This informal system is a fundamental reason that many Mexicans continued to vote for the PRI for so long. However, new ways of interacting with government are emerging, and they coexist along with the clientelistic style of the past. An increasing number of citizens are seeking to negotiate with the government on the basis of citizenship rights, not personal patron–client relationships.

As politics and elections became more open and competitive, the roles of public opinion and the mass media have become more important. Today, the media play an important role in forming public opinion in Mexico. As with other aspects of Mexican politics, the media began to become more independent in the 1980s, enjoying a "spring" of greater independence and diversity of opinion.[11] There are currently several major television networks in the country, and many citizens have access to global networks. The number of newspapers and news magazines is expanding, as is their circulation. To be sure, there is some concern that many of the most important and influential media outlets in the country are controlled by a small number of individuals and corporations. Also, violence against and intimidation of Mexican journalists by drug trafficking organizations has limited the ability of the press to report on the important issues raised in the context of the fight against organized crime in recent years. Nonetheless, citizens in Mexico today hear a much wider range of opinion and much greater reporting of debates about public policy and criticism of government than at any time previously.

Interest Groups, Social Movements, and Protest

The Mexican political system has long responded to groups of citizens through pragmatic **accommodation** to their interests. This is one important reason that political tensions among major interests have rarely escalated into the kind of serious conflict that can threaten stability. Where open conflict has occurred, it has generally been met with efforts to find some kind of compromise solution. Accommodation has been particularly apparent in response to the interests of business. Mexico's development strategy encouraged the growth of wealthy elites in commerce, finance, industry, and agriculture.

Labor has been similarly accommodated within the system. Wage levels for unionized workers grew fairly consistently between 1940 and 1982, when the economic crisis caused a significant drop in wages. At the same time, labor interests were attended to through concrete benefits and limitations on the rights of employers to discipline or dismiss workers. Union leaders controlled their rank and file in the interest of their own power to negotiate with government, but at the same time, they sought benefits for workers who continued to provide support for the PRI. The power of the union bosses has declined, in part because the unions are weaker than in the past, in part because union members are demanding greater democratization, and in part because the PRI no longer monopolizes political power. Likewise, in the countryside, rural organizations have gained greater independence from the government. Indigenous groups have also emerged to demand that government be responsive to their needs and respectful of their traditions.

accommodation

An informal agreement or settlement between the government and important interest groups in response to the interest groups' concerns for policy or program benefits.

Mexicans are accustomed to making demands on their leaders, and protest is an established feature of Mexican political culture. Here, protesters march into Mexico City's central square, the Zócalo.

AP Images/Gregory Bull

Despite the strong and controlling role of the PRI in Mexico's political history, the country also has a tradition of civic organizations that operate at community and local levels with considerable independence from politics. Urban popular movements, formed by low- and modest-income (popular) groups, gained renewed vitality in the 1980s.[12] When the economic crisis resulted in drastic reductions of social welfare spending and city services, working- and middle-class neighborhoods forged new coalitions and greatly expanded the national discussion of urban problems. The Mexico City earthquake of 1985 encouraged the formation of unprecedented numbers of grassroots movements in response to the slow and poorly managed relief efforts of the government. Subsequent elections provided these groups with significant opportunities to press candidates to respond to their needs.

Urban popular movements bring citizens together around needs and ideals that cut across class boundaries. Neighborhood improvement, the environment, local self-government, economic development, feminism, and professional identity have been among the factors that have forged links among these groups. Women have begun to mobilize in many cities to demand community services, equal pay, legal equality, and opportunities in business that have traditionally been denied to them.

Traditionally, much activism has focused on questions of economic redistribution rather than divisive social issues, but this has recently begun to change. Political issues that are commonly discussed in the United States, such as abortion and gay rights, have recently begun to be debated publicly in Mexico. In April 2007, the PRD-controlled legislative assembly of Mexico City voted to decriminalize abortions in the first trimester (in the rest of Mexico abortion continues to be illegal except in cases of rape or severe birth defects, although in fact gaining access to a legal abortion even under these circumstances is difficult). And in November 2006, the Federal District's PRD-led government legalized gay civil unions. Reflecting its background as a largely Catholic, socially conservative party, the PAN remains vehemently opposed to these measures. For example, in 2000 the PAN-dominated legislature of Guanajuato voted to ban abortion even in the case of rape, and established penalties of up to three years in prison for women who violated the law.

Although President Fox was opposed to abortion, he did attempt to distance himself from the Guanajuato law and for the most part avoided discussing contentious social and cultural subjects. But under his administration condom use was encouraged and a campaign against homophobia was launched. In 2004, he caused a furor within his own party when his administration approved the distribution of the morning-after pill in public clinics. These policies were denounced by Calderón, who came from a more traditionalist wing of his party. He vowed in his 2006 campaign to ban the use of this pill and openly expressed his opposition to abortion and gay rights. President Peña Nieto has so far largely sought to avoid confronting these contentious social issues. He has described himself as personally opposed to abortion but also opposed to its criminalization, and he has said that the question of same-sex unions should be left to Mexico's states.

The Political Impact of Technology

As in other countries, changes in communications technology over the past two decades or so have had a major impact on the ways in which citizens organize themselves and on the ways in which politicians and political parties seek to reach their constituents. Young, highly educated, and urban groups in particular are heavy users of social media, and even many poorer Mexicans and residents of smaller towns and rural areas have mobile telephones and some degree of access to the Internet. During the 2012 presidential campaign, therefore, all of the major candidates actively sought to attract Twitter followers and to project a positive image on Facebook. They also found themselves subject to embarrassment when footage of their gaffes on the campaign trail was circulated widely on social media. A viral video in which Peña Nieto struggled to name three books that had influenced him reinforced some voters' suspicion that the PRI candidate was not a deep thinker, and footage of Josefina Vázquez stumbling over prepared remarks damaged her efforts to make up ground in the polls.

Social media even gave rise to a movement that changed the narrative of the 2012 campaign for a time. After candidate Peña Nieto was confronted by protesters during an appearance at a Mexico City university in May 2012, the media reported that the protesters had been agitators from outside the campus rather than students at the institution, prompting 131 of the protesters to post a video online in which they displayed their university identification cards. Thousands of other social media users who also saw television and other media coverage of the campaign as biased toward Peña Nieto expressed their support by posting, "Yo soy 132," or "I am the 132nd [student]." The online movement led to marches and rallies, calling for a deepening of democracy in Mexico.

Communications technology has also taken on political significance in Mexican citizens' response to the drug-related violence that has affected the country in recent years. In regions in which local journalists were effectively silenced by threats from the cartels, some users of social media relied on that outlet to broadcast information on the danger posed by criminal activities in specific locations. When Twitter users in Veracruz circulated what turned out to be an inaccurate report of a shootout at a school, state authorities prosecuted them for terrorism. Though the governor issued a pardon in that case, the state legislature proceeded to pass a new law to make it a crime to use social media to undermine public order. Thus, the place of new communications technologies in Mexican politics and society continues to be negotiated and to evolve.

Where Do You Stand?

Through public funding and guaranteed broadcasting airtime, political parties in Mexico are given a privileged position as recognized vehicles for the representation of citizens' interests, but increasingly Mexicans are mobilizing for political change outside of party structures, through civil society organizations, popular movements, and social media. How should government policies respond to these developments?

Should public funding of political parties be curtailed, or would that simply create an opening for wealthy private interests to exert greater influence in politics?

SECTION 5
MEXICAN POLITICS IN TRANSITION

Focus Questions ▼

- What challenges does the process of globalization pose to Mexicans' strong sense of national identity?

- How successful has Mexico been in confronting the legacy of authoritarian rule? To what extent have recent administrations been able to make the government more accountable and transparent?

The Mexican political landscape has been transformed over the past twenty years, as a long period of dominance by a single party has given way to a competitive multiparty system. The country's institutions, leaders, and citizens are still adjusting to this ongoing process of change. While most Mexicans are proud that their political system has become more democratic, many also lament that the division of power between political parties and branches of government at times seems to make the state less efficient and possibly less able to address effectively the challenges of development and governance faced by Mexico.

One particularly dramatic illustration of how much Mexican politics has changed can be seen on September 1 of each year, when, in accordance with Article 69 of the Constitution, the executive branch delivers a report on the state of the nation to congress at the opening of its annual session. For decades, this date was known informally as the "Day of the President," as the ritual surrounding the address highlighted the prestige and authority of the chief executive. The president would don his ceremonial red, white, and green sash before traveling to the legislative chambers from the National Palace, the symbolic seat of power in Mexico since the days of the Spanish viceroys. While delivering his *informe* (report), the president could count on a respectful hearing from an attentive audience of deputies and senators who were overwhelmingly drawn from the ranks of his own party. Though the spectacle of the *informe* during the heyday of PRI dominance excluded dissenting voices, it projected an image of a strong, stable political system. Even in 1982, when President José López Portillo broke into tears while reporting on his failure to avert a debt crisis that sent the country into an economic tailspin, legislators dutifully applauded.

That deference to the president began to break down in 1988, however. After a contentious presidential election marred by allegations of fraud, a legislator who had broken away from the PRI to support opposition candidate Cuauhtémoc Cárdenas dared to interrupt President Miguel de la Madrid's speech. More recently, after members of the PRD charged that Felipe Calderón's election in 2006 was illegitimate, outgoing President Vicente Fox was prevented from even reaching the rostrum when he arrived to give his address on September 1 of that year. He complied with his constitutional mandate by submitting a printed copy of his report and then left the building without delivering his speech. In 2007, President Felipe Calderón likewise appeared before a deeply divided legislature only long enough to hand over a printed version of his *informe*, and new rules introduced in 2008 eliminated the requirement that the president deliver his report in person. Since then, the annual report of the executive branch has been transmitted by a government minister to the legislature, where representatives of the parties represented in Congress deliver a response. In 2013, plans for Peña Nieto to make a public presentation of his first *informe* at a large military parade ground had to be scaled back in the face of massive protests by a dissident teachers' union that had paralyzed Mexico City. Instead the president shared his report with a much smaller audience at his official residence. These incidents show how many more voices, besides the president's, are heard on important national issues in Mexico today, though to many the fact that the chief executive is no longer able to find a respectful audience for his report suggests that the capacity of the state has been diminished.

Political Challenges and Changing Agendas

As Mexicans adjust and adapt to the dramatic political transition of recent years, they are conscious that their nation faces many challenges, and they are struggling to build a political system that will be both democratic and effective. They are calling upon the state to be open about abuses of authority in the past and to protect citizens from such abuses in the future. They seek to address long-standing inequalities in Mexican society, in part by ensuring that women and ethnic minorities have access to economic opportunities and social services. They also hope to preserve Mexican identity while realizing the economic benefits of integration into global networks.

Mexico today provides a testing ground for the democratic idea in a state with a long history of authoritarian institutions. The democratic ideas of citizen rights to free speech and assembly, free and fair elections, and responsive government are major reasons that the power of the PRI came under so much attack beginning in the 1980s. As part of its commitment to delivering a sharp change from the practices of the past, the administration of Vicente Fox (2000–2006) pledged to make government more transparent and to improve the state of human rights in Mexico. In the past, the government had been able to limit knowledge of its repressive actions, use the court system to maintain the political peace, and intimidate those who objected to its actions. Fox appointed human rights activists to his cabinet and ordered that secret police and military files be opened to public scrutiny. He instructed government ministries to supply more information about their activities and about the rights that citizens have to various kinds of services. The government also sought to protect the rights of Mexicans abroad, and the United States and Mexico established a working group to improve human rights conditions for migrants.

The results of these actions have been dramatic. For the first time, Mexicans learned of cases of hundreds of people who had "disappeared" as a result of police and military actions. In addition, citizens have come forward to announce other disappearances, ones they were unwilling to report earlier because they feared reprisals. In 2002, former president Luis Echeverría was brought before prosecutors and questioned about government actions against political dissent in 1968 and 1971, a kind of accountability unheard of in the past. The National Human Rights Commission has been active in efforts to hold government officials accountable and to protect citizens from repetitions of the abuses of the past.

Yet challenges to human rights accountability remain. Opening up files and setting up systems for prosecuting abusers needs to be followed by actions to impose penalties on abusers. The Mexican judicial system is weak and has little experience in human rights cases. In addition, action on reports of disappearances, torture, and imprisonment has been slowed by disagreement about civil and military jurisdictions. Human rights activists claimed that police and military personnel, in particular, still had impunity from the laws, and human rights concerns have grown as the military has taken a more direct role in law enforcement in the context of the Calderón administration's effort to dismantle drug trafficking organizations. Human rights advocates point to recent alleged abuses by members of the armed forces and call for greater accountability from an institution that is still shielded from much civilian scrutiny. Although human rights are much more likely to be protected than in the past, the government still has a long way to go in safeguarding the rights of indigenous people, political dissidents, migrants, gays and lesbians, and poor people whose ability to use the judicial system is limited by poverty and lack of information.

Mexico is also confronting major challenges in adapting newly democratic institutions to reflect ethnic and religious diversity and to provide equity for women in economic and political affairs. The past two decades have witnessed the emergence of more organized and politically independent ethnic groups demanding justice and equality from government. These groups claim that they have suffered for nearly 500 years and that they are no longer willing to accept poverty and marginality as their lot. The Catholic Church, still the largest organized religion in the country, is losing members to Protestant sects that appeal particularly to the everyday concerns of poor Mexicans. Women are becoming more organized, but they still have a long way to go before their wages equal those of men or they have equal voice in political and economic decisions.

Another significant challenge for Mexico today is reconciling its strong sense of national identity with the strains placed on a country's sovereignty by the process of global economic integration. Mexicans define themselves in part through a set of historical events, symbols, and myths that focus on the country's troubled relationship with the United States. The myths of the Revolution of 1910 emphasize the uniqueness of the country in terms of its opposition to the capitalists and militarists of the northern country. This view stands in strong contrast to more recent perspectives touting the benefits of an internationally oriented economy and the undeniable post-NAFTA reality of information, culture, money, and people flowing back and forth across borders.

The country's sense of national identity is also affected by international migration. Every year, large numbers of Mexicans enter the United States as workers. Many return to their towns and villages with new values and new views of the world. Many stay in the United States, where Hispanics have become the largest ethnic minority population in the country. Although they may believe that Mexico is a better place to nurture strong family life and values, they are nevertheless strongly influenced by U.S. mass culture, including popular music, movies, television programs, fast food, and consumer goods.

The inability of the Mexican economy to create enough jobs pushes additional Mexicans to seek work in the United States, and the cash remittances that migrants abroad send home to their families and communities are now almost as important a source of income for Mexico as PEMEX's oil sales. However, the issues surrounding migration have become even more complex since the attacks of September 11, 2001. Hopes for a bilateral accord that would permit more Mexicans to enter and work in the United States legally evaporated after U.S. officials suddenly found themselves under greatly increased pressure to control the country's borders. Whether or not the U.S. government approves, the difference in wages between the United States and Mexico will persist for a long time, which implies that migration will also persist.

There is disagreement about how to respond to the economic challenges that Mexico faces. Much of the debate surrounds the question of what integration into a competitive international economy really means. For some, it represents the final abandonment of Mexico's sovereignty. For others, it is the basis on which future prosperity must be built. Those who are critical of the market-based, outward-oriented development strategy are concerned about its impact on workers, peasants, and national identities. They argue that the state has abandoned its responsibilities to protect the poor from shortcomings of the market and to provide for their basic needs. They believe that U.S. and Canadian investors have come to Mexico only to find low-wage labor for industrial empires located elsewhere. They see little benefit in further industrial development based on importation of foreign-made parts, their assembly in Mexico, and their export to other markets. Those who favor closer integration with Canada and the United States acknowledge that some foreign investment does not promote technological advances or move the workforce into higher-paying and more skilled jobs. They emphasize, however, that most investment will occur because Mexico has a relatively well-educated population, the capacity to absorb modern technology, and a large internal market for industrial goods.

Inequality represents another daunting challenge for Mexican society. While elites enjoy the benefits of sumptuous lifestyles, education at the best U.S. universities for their children, and luxury travel throughout the world, large numbers of Mexicans remain ill-educated, poorly served with health care, and distant from the security of knowing that their basic needs will be met. As in the United States, some argue that the best solutions to these problems are economic growth and expanded employment. They believe that the achievement of prosperity through integration into the global economy will benefit everyone in the long run. For this to occur, however, they insist that education will have to be improved and made more appropriate for developing a well-prepared workforce. From their perspective, the solution to poverty and injustice is fairly clear: more and better jobs and improved education.

For those critical of the development path on which Mexico embarked in the 1980s and 1990s, the problems of poverty and inequity are more complex. Solutions involve understanding the diverse causes of poverty, including not only lack of jobs and poor education but also exploitation, geographic isolation, and discriminatory laws and practices, as well as the disruptive impact of migration, urbanization, and the tensions of modern life. In the past, Mexicans looked to government for social welfare benefits, but their provision was deeply flawed by inefficiency and political manipulation. Thus, although many continue to believe that it is the responsibility of government to ensure that citizens are well educated, healthy, and able to make the most of their potential, the populace is deeply suspicious of the government's capacity to provide such conditions fairly and efficiently.

Youth Politics and the Generational Divide

Young people have long played a central role in driving political change in Mexico. The student movement of 1968 helped to begin the process of questioning the legitimacy of PRI rule, and younger voters played a disproportionally important part in bringing about the democratic transition of 2000. The younger generation is also heavily overrepresented in the social media world from which future political campaigns and initiatives are likely to arise, as the "Yo soy 132" movement did in 2012.

Another fundamental reason for the importance of young people in Mexican politics is that they currently account for a very high proportion of the country's population. Unlike Japan or many European countries, Mexico is not a rapidly aging country, with a large share of its population over 65. Instead, more than half of the population is under 30. This means that very many voters in the 2012 elections cast their ballots with little memory of the PRI's "perfect dictatorship." Having grown up in a democratic Mexico with a competitive political environment, these voters are perhaps unlikely to be interested in a return to the PRI's old style of politics, but the party preferences and affiliations of younger Mexicans remain to be defined. Given the demographic significance of Mexico's younger population, the development of those preferences will shape Mexican politics for a long time to come.

Mexican Politics in Comparative Perspective

Mexico faces many of the same challenges that beset other countries: creating equitable and effective democratic government, becoming integrated into a global economy, responding to complex social problems, and supporting increasing diversity without losing national identity. The legacies of its past, the tensions of the present, and the innovations of the future will no doubt evolve in ways that continue to be uniquely Mexican.

Mexico represents a pivotal case of political and economic transition for the developing world. If it can successfully bridge the gap between its past and its future and move from centralization to effective local governance, from regional vulnerability to global interdependence, and from the control of the few to the participation of the many, it will set a model for other countries that face the same kind of challenges.

Where Do You Stand?

Does Mexico offer lessons for other countries moving from authoritarian forms of governance to more democratic ones? What might Mexico learn from the experience of some of the other countries you are studying?

If you were a young person in Mexico today, what issues do you think would be most important to you? Which political party (if any) would you support, and why?

Chapter Summary

The Mexican political system is unique among developing countries in the extent to which it managed to institutionalize and maintain civilian political authority for a very long time. The country's development has been shaped by the revolutionary ideals that arose from its distinctive historical experience, by its proximity to the United States, and by its ongoing efforts to find a place in an interconnected global economy. Currently, Mexico is undergoing significant political change, transforming itself from a corporatist state to a democratic one. At the same time, Mexican society is experiencing high levels of violence as the state confronts drug trafficking organizations that represent a challenge to its authority and to the rule of law.

While Mexico's development from the 1930s to the 1980s was marked by extensive government engagement in the economy, since that time the country has opened its economy and pursued prosperity through market reforms and free trade. But while links with the U.S. economy have deepened, growth has been slow under the new policies. Industry and oil give the country a per capita income higher than those of most other developing nations, but the country suffers from great inequalities in how wealth is distributed, and poverty continues to be a grim reality for millions. The way the country promoted economic growth and industrialization is important in explaining why widespread poverty has persisted and why political power is not more equitably distributed.

On paper, Mexico's government resembles that of the United States, with three branches of government, checks and balances among them, and federalism defining the relationship between national, state, and local governments. In practice, however, the country developed a political system that concentrated most power in the hands of the president and the executive branch and managed political conflict through a dominant party. Much of the power of the president and the PRI was based on their capacity to use patronage to respond to political conflicts. This system is undergoing rapid change, as the legislature and court systems develop more independent roles, state and local governments acquire more independence, and multiple parties compete for power.

Mexico's democratic transition took place gradually, as Mexican citizens developed the capacity to question the dominance of the PRI regime and as the government introduced important changes that opened up opportunities for opposition parties to develop and for people to vote more easily for these parties. Since the election of 2000 demonstrated that a transition of power from a civilian authoritarian regime to a more democratic one could take place peacefully, Mexico has had considerable experience with democratic politics. This experience has been marked both by pride in the country's democratic path and frustration that democratic institutions have not been able to pass needed reforms, to create jobs, and to guarantee security.

What will the future bring? How much will the pressures for change affect the nature of the political system? In 1980, few people could have foreseen the extensive economic policy reforms and pressures for democracy that Mexico would experience in the next three decades. Few would have predicted the defeat of the PRI in the elections of 2000, much less its return to power in 2012. In considering the future of the country, it is important to remember that Mexico has a long tradition of relatively strong institutions. It is not a country that will easily slip into sustained political instability. Despite real challenges faced as Mexico confronts criminal organizations and seeks to reform its police forces and judicial system, the country is not in danger of collapse, as some outside observers have been tempted to suggest. A tradition of constitutional government, a strong presidency, a political system that has incorporated a wide range of interests, little military involvement in politics, and a deep sense of national identity—these are among the factors that need to be considered in understanding the political consequences of democratization, economic integration, and greater social equality in Mexico.

Key Terms

accommodation
anticlericalism
caudillos
civil society
corporatist state

coup d'état
ejidos
indigenous groups
maquiladoras
mestizo

remittances
sexenio
state capitalism
technocrats

Suggested Readings

Call, Wendy. *No Word for Welcome: The Mexican Village Faces the Global Economy.* Lincoln: University of Nebraska Press, 2011.

Camp, Roderic Ai. *The Metamorphosis of Leadership in a Democratic Mexico.* Oxford: Oxford University Press, 2010.

Davidow, Jeffrey. *The U.S. and Mexico: The Bear and the Porcupine.* Princeton, NJ: Markus Wiener Publishers, 2004.

Délano, Alexandra. *Mexico and its Diaspora in the United States: Policies of Emigration since 1848.* New York: Cambridge University Press, 2011.

Eisenstadt, Todd A. *Politics, Identity, and Mexico's Indigenous Rights Movements* (Cambridge Studies in Contentious Politics). New York: Cambridge University Press, 2011.

Grayson, George. *Mexico: Narco-Violence and a Failed State?* Piscataway, NJ: Transaction Publishers, 2009.

Henderson, Timothy J. *Beyond Borders: A History of Mexican Migration to the United States.* New York: Wiley-Blackwell, 2011.

Preston, Julia, and Samuel Dillon. *Opening Mexico: The Making of a Democracy.* New York: Farrar, Straus and Giroux, 2004.

Selee, Andrew, and Jacqueline Peschard. *Mexico's Democratic Challenges: Politics, Government, and Society.* Stanford, CA: Stanford University Press, 2010.

Speed, Shannon. *Rights in Rebellion: Indigenous Struggle and Human Rights in Chiapas.* Stanford, CA: Stanford University Press, 2007.

Suggested Websites

Office of the President (in Spanish and English)
www.presidencia.gob.mx

Secretariat of Foreign Relations (in Spanish and English)
www.sre.gob.mx

Mexican Embassy to the United States
http://embamex.sre.gob.mx/usa/

Office of Mexican Affairs, U.S. Department of State
http://www.state.gov/p/wha/ci/mx/

The Mexico Project, National Security Archive
www2.gwu.edu/~nsarchiv/mexico

11 South Africa

Tom Lodge

Location: Southern Africa, at the southern tip of the continent of Africa

Capital City: Pretoria (administrative capital); Cape Town (legislative capital); Bloemfontein (judicial capital)

Population (2013): 51.8 million

Size: 1,219,090 sq. km.; nearly twice the size of Texas

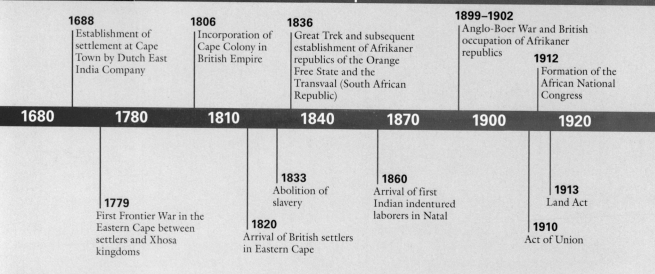

1688
Establishment of settlement at Cape Town by Dutch East India Company

1806
Incorporation of Cape Colony in British Empire

1836
Great Trek and subsequent establishment of Afrikaner republics of the Orange Free State and the Transvaal ("South African Republic)

1899–1902
Anglo-Boer War and British occupation of Afrikaner republics

1912
Formation of the African National Congress

| 1680 | 1780 | 1810 | 1840 | 1870 | 1900 | 1920 |

1779
First Frontier War in the Eastern Cape between settlers and Xhosa kingdoms

1833
Abolition of slavery

1820
Arrival of British settlers in Eastern Cape

1860
Arrival of first Indian indentured laborers in Natal

1913
Land Act

1910
Act of Union

THE MAKING OF THE MODERN SOUTH AFRICAN STATE

SECTION 1

Politics in Action

▽ Focus Questions

- Why did institutionalized racism become such a central characteristic of South African social life in the twentieth century?

- In which ways does racial inequality persist in South Africa?

On August 12th 2012, 500 policemen took up positions confronting a crowd of striking mineworkers. The workers had gathered on Nkaneng hill, a rocky outcrop near their workplace, the Marikana platinum mine in North West Province, South Africa. The workers had been on an illegal ("wildcat") strike for several days. They were carrying spears, machetes, and sticks. After police advanced on the strikers, attempting to corral them into a confined area, chanting strikers began marching up and down the police line. Police used tear gas but this failed to scatter the crowd. When one of the workers fired a handgun and a group charged the police, police opened fire with automatic weapons and chased strikers across the rocky terrain. Thirty-four workers were killed in a few minutes. Most were shot in the back, the majority more than 300 yards from the original police line. Several of the bodies were photographed by journalists; it was evident they had been shot at close range or even crushed by police vehicles. Several of the dead were handcuffed. The carnage that day at Marikana represented the single most lethal confrontation between police and protestors since the Sharpeville massacre in 1960, when up to 80 demonstrators were shot dead.

The strike began on August 10th, and was led by "Rock Drill Operators," who soon persuaded their workmates to join them in striking. They demanded a 200 percent pay raise. Over the next days a series of confrontations helped set the stage for the events on the 16th. On the 11th the workers marched on the offices of the National Union of Mineworkers (NUM) to protest the union's failure to support the

1923
Native Urban Areas Act codifies urban racial segregation.

1960
Sharpeville massacre and prohibition of the two main African nationalist organizations, the ANC and the PAC.

1976
Soweto uprising.

1992
Opening of constitutional negotiations.

1996
Adoption of final constitution.

2008
Thabo Mbeki resigns from the presidency after criticism for putting pressure on the Directorate for Public Prosecutions.

1925 1950 1980 1990 2000 2010

1922
Rand Rebellion by white mineworkers

1926
Institution of job reservation for white workers in the Mines and Works Amendment Act

1948
Election into power of National Party and the inception of Apartheid program

1986
Repeal of the pass laws

1999
Thabo Mbeki succeeds Nelson Mandela as president.

1994
First universal suffrage election under a transitional constitution

1990
Unbanning of the ANC and the PAC and release of political prisoners

2010
South Africa hosts the World Cup Soccer tournament, a recognition of the country's transition from apartheid to democracy.

2009
ANC wins fourth victory in national elections. Jacob Zuma becomes president.

strike call. Indeed, NUM officials fired on the demonstration. By the 14th, sporadic violence had claimed nine lives including two police and two security guards. Strikers also attacked NUM shop stewards. The strike leaders belonged to a new union, the Association of Mineworkers and Construction Union (AMCU). For months the ACMU had been challenging the NUM's status as the recognized union in the platinum mines in the region. AMCU leaders accused the NUM of being a "sweetheart" formation, allied with management; these accusations seem to have resonated among mineworkers, 150,000 of whom nationally joined the new union.

After the massacre, most of the 28,000 workers at Marikana stayed out on strike. Protests spread to other mines and by October 75,000 workers had participated in strikes. Two hundred and seventy of the Marikana workers were arrested and charged with murder, charges that were dropped subsequently. In mid-September, workers were persuaded to accept only slightly more than the managers had been offered previously. For Lonmin, the company owning the mine, it was back to business as usual. But the political effects of this confrontation extended beyond the mining industry.

The workers' demands reflected deteriorating conditions. Migrant mine workers used to live in company hostels. Since 1994 workers have been moving from company-supplied accommodation into shanty settlements; accepting instead a modest "living out" allowance. Most underground workers at Marikana originate from the Eastern Cape and maintain two households and two families, one near the mine where they live and one at the rural home they visit on annual holidays. Wage increases have lagged behind prices and household indebtedness has doubled in the last five years. Meanwhile, the "official" union, the NUM, a long-term ally of the ruling party, the African National Congress, is increasingly led by white-collar surface workers, that is clerical staff who don't work underground. At Marikana, the social gulf between NUM members and underground workers is accentuated by the tendency for surface workers to live in company housing or in Rustenberg suburbs, not the shanty settlements. The underground workers are rural Xhosas who bring with them to the workplace beliefs and customs that relate to rural village culture. The strikers protected themselves with *muti*, traditional medicine, and in assembling at Nkaneng Hill they were enacting a historic communal response to crisis, when village householders used to gather at defensible mountain

Table 11.1	Political Organization
Political System	Parliamentary democracy and federal republic.
Regime History	Governed by an African National Congress–led coalition from 1994. Between 1910 and 1994 governments were formed by parties representing a white minority and were elected through racially restricted franchises.
Administrative Structure	Nine regional governments sharing authority with a national administration. Regional governments can be overridden on most significant issues by national legislatures.
Executive	President elected by parliament. President selects cabinet.
Legislature	National assembly and regional legislatures elected on the basis of party list proportional representation. National Council of Provinces made up by delegations from each regional government serves as a second chamber.
Judiciary	Independent constitutional court with appointed judges.
Party System	Multiparty system. African National Congress predominates.

locations. By contrast, NUM officials at Marikana tended to have urban backgrounds and were to have grown up in the surrounding Batswana community.

The massacre initially elicited a divided response from government and the ruling party, with cabinet members alternately criticizing and supporting the police action. The Communist Party, well represented in President Zuma's cabinet, called for the arrest of ACMU leaders, a demand echoed by the Congress of South African Trade Unions, of which the NUM is a key affiliate. Later it became known that the ANC's deputy leader, Cyril Ramaphosa, himself a Lonmin director, had emailed the police the day before the massacre urging them to halt what he called the strikers' "dastardly criminal" behavior. President Zuma ordered an official investigation; its report had not been issued by early 2014. In December 2013, the National Union of Metalworkers, another major COSATU affiliate, announced that it would refuse to support the ANC in the general election, accusing the ruling party of betraying workers. At the end of 2013 opinion polling found that ANC support had dropped by 10 percent from one year earlier—from the mid 60s to 53 percent. Respondents cited Marikana as the key reason for their disaffection with the ruling party. Even for more dispassionate observers, these bloody developments were a grim reminder that in a deeply unequal society, the prospects of brutally violent disorder are never very far away.

Geographic Setting

South Africa is about twice the size of Texas. In the 2011 census the population totaled 51.8 million. Two-thirds of this population is urban. Government statistics divide the population into four main race groups: 41 million Bantu-language-speaking *Africans*, who are descended from migrants from Central Africa. The first European settlers arrived in the seventeenth century. Their descendants make up nearly 4.6 million *Whites*. The 4.6 million *Coloureds* (the term used universally in South Africa) represent a group whose ancestry includes the earliest indigenous hunter-gatherers, as well as slaves from

Africans

South African usage refers to Bantu language speakers, the demographic majority of South African citizens.

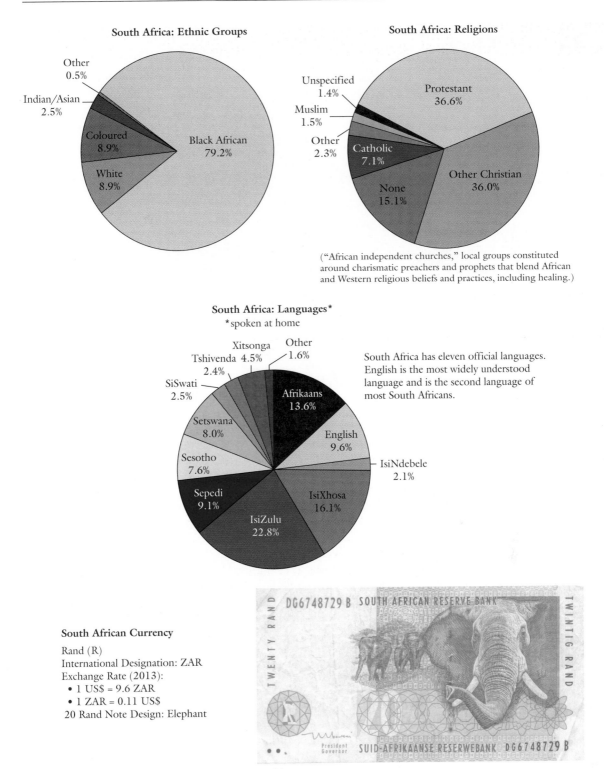

South Africa: Ethnic Groups

- Other 0.5%
- Indian/Asian 2.5%
- Coloured 8.9%
- White 8.9%
- Black African 79.2%

South Africa: Religions

- Unspecified 1.4%
- Muslim 1.5%
- Other 2.3%
- Catholic 7.1%
- None 15.1%
- Protestant 36.6%
- Other Christian 36.0%

("African independent churches," local groups constituted around charismatic preachers and prophets that blend African and Western religious beliefs and practices, including healing.)

South Africa: Languages*
*spoken at home

- Other 1.6%
- Xitsonga 4.5%
- Tshivenda 2.4%
- SiSwati 2.5%
- Setswana 8.0%
- Sesotho 7.6%
- Sepedi 9.1%
- IsiZulu 22.8%
- IsiXhosa 16.1%
- IsiNdebele 2.1%
- English 9.6%
- Afrikaans 13.6%

South Africa has eleven official languages. English is the most widely understood language and is the second language of most South Africans.

South African Currency

Rand (R)
International Designation: ZAR
Exchange Rate (2013):
- 1 US$ = 9.6 ZAR
- 1 ZAR = 0.11 US$
20 Rand Note Design: Elephant

FIGURE 11.1 The South African Nation at a Glance

© Jonathan Noden-Wilkinson/Shutterstock.com (for photo)

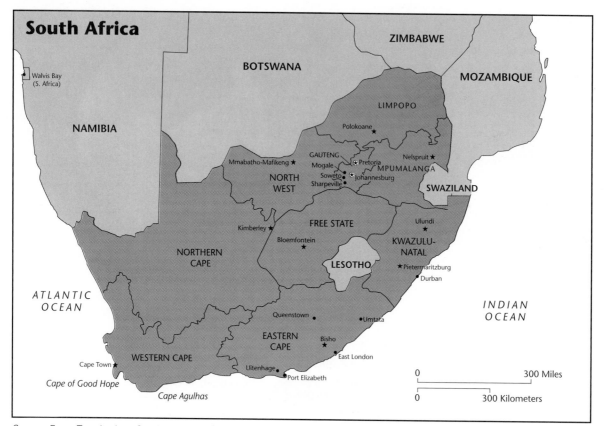

Source: From Tom Lodge, *South African Politics Since 1994*, pp. vi–vii. Reprinted with permission.

Indonesia and offspring from unions between white settlers and these groups. Nearly 1.3 million Indians are mostly descendants of indentured laborers brought from India. Under the apartheid regime (1948–1993), of racial segregation, each group had a different legal status. While racial segregation is no longer the law today, the communal identities created by official racial classification still influence social life. Most blacks still live in historically segregated ghetto-like neighborhoods, and most whites live in the more comfortable suburbs. (See Figure 11.1 for the South African nation at a glance.) A rapidly expanding black middle class is joining whites to live in the suburbs, though. Realtors in Johannesburg and Pretoria reported in 2012 that around half the home buyers in historically white suburbs were middle-class Africans.

Critical Junctures

Settlement, 1688–1911

Afrikaner

Descendants of Dutch, French, German, and Scots settlers speaking a language (Afrikaans) derived heavily from Dutch. They were politically mobilized as an ethnic group through the twentieth century.

In 1652 the Dutch East India Company established a reprovisioning station at the southern tip of Africa. The Dutch settlers were not the first to arrive. Africans had settled in the region at least 2,000 years previously, when Bantu speakers drove away or merged with earlier San and the Khoi-Khoi hunter-gatherers and pastoralists.

By the eighteenth century Dutch settlers in South Africa called themselves **Afrikaners**. They spoke a Dutch dialect called Afrikaans. In 1806, Britain added the territory to its empire. Because they resented British policies (including Britain's abolition of slavery), about one-tenth of the Afrikaner population—the *voortrekkers*—migrated northwards between 1836 and 1840. The *voortrekkers* established the Orange Free State in 1852 and the Transvaal in 1854.

Dynamics of the Frontier, 1779–1906

White settlement quickly displaced the Khoi-San. The settlers encountered more formidable adversaries among Xhosa-speaking Africans along the eastern coast. The frontier wars between 1779 and 1878 fixed the boundaries between white farmers and the Xhosa kingdoms.

The strongest African resistance arose in the heavily militarized Zulu Kingdom. The wars that created the Zulu state in the early nineteenth century forced other peoples to migrate. They based their own states on the Zulu model. But huge areas had been depopulated, and were thus available for white settlers. While white settlers usually preserved some precolonial African institutions, these played a subordinate role in colonial administrations.

In 1843, Britain annexed Natal, which had been part of the Zulu kingdom. From 1860, British immigrants established sugar plantations and began recruiting Indian labor. Today about 80 percent of South Africa's Indian population lives in this province, known as KwaZulu-Natal.

Imperialists against Republicans, 1867–1910

After gold was discovered in the Witwatersrand region of the Transvaal in 1886, a massive mining industry grew up. By 1898 the mine owners, mainly British, increasingly objected to the Afrikaner government in Pretoria, the Transvaal capital, mostly because the government tended to favor landholders over mine owners in official programs to recruit African labor. By the late 1890s, the British government had become receptive to the mine owners, or "Randlords," since global rivalries had increased the strategic value of the Transvaal gold reserves. War between Britain and the Afrikaner republics was declared on October 11, 1899. The savage Anglo-Boer War (1899–1902) was prolonged by the guerrilla campaign launched against the British by Afrikaner farmers, called **Boers**.

But Britain prevailed. Casualties included 28,000 Afrikaner civilians who died in concentration camps. Africans served in armies on both sides and 14,000 Africans died in internment camps. Voting was already color-blind in the British Cape Colony region, and Africans hoped that after the war they would be able to vote throughout the country. But during the peace negotiations, the British prioritized good relations between the Afrikaners and the English over Africans. An African elite retained the vote in the Cape, but elsewhere the agreement denied the franchise to Africans.

Britain's ascendency in South Africa was confirmed by its victory in the Anglo-Boer War. Under the new British administration, officials constructed an efficient bureaucracy. A customs union between the four territories—the Cape, Natal, Travsvaal, and the Orange Free State—eliminated tariffs. A new Native Affairs Department reorganized labor recruitment. In 1910, under the Act of Union the four territories became provinces of the Union of South Africa, which became a self-governing dominion of the British empire. Africans outside the Cape were excluded from voting.

The Origins of Modern Institutionalized Racism, 1910–1945

These arrangements confirmed the essential features of racist order. The need to coerce African labor—in order to control African workers and keep wages low—guided policy. In gold mining, profits depended on very cheap labor. The mines used a closed

voortrekkers

Pastoralist descendants of Dutch settlers in South Africa who moved north from the British-controlled Cape in 1836 to establish independent republics; later regarded as the founders of the Afrikaner nation.

Boer

Literally "farmer"; modern usage is a derogatory reference to Afrikaners.

compound system, which was originally developed to stop smuggling in the diamond fields, but on the Witwatersrand became a totalitarian system of control. Given low wages and harsh conditions, recruiting workers needed to be repressive. Beginning with the 1913 Land Act, new laws enforced racial discrimination. These laws were designed to meet the needs of a mining economy, which needed cheap labor that could not rebel. The Land Act allowed Africans to own land only inside a patchwork of native reserves.

In the 1880s Afrikaner nationalists constructed a supposedly traditional community based on language standardization and literary culture. This community attracted white people who had been forced off the land during the Anglo-Boer War. During a white miners' armed insurrection in 1922, Afrikaner workers resurrected a Boer commando system.

The miners protested because their employers were giving to Africans certain semi-skilled jobs previously reserved for whites. One hundred fifty-three people were killed during the suppression of the rebellion. Two years later, a coalition government of the Labour Party and the (Afrikaner) National Party set up a "civilized labor" policy. It specified that all whites, even unskilled ones, should earn enough to maintain "civilized" standards. To ensure this, even certain unskilled jobs were reserved for whites. The new government also invested in public industries. The pace of industrialization accelerated after 1933. Currency devaluation prompted fresh waves of foreign investment.

Apartheid and African Resistance, 1945–1960

In 1934, a United Party was created by a fusion between the National Party and the pro-British South African Party led by Jan Smuts, who became prime minister in 1939. The United Party favored a broader conception of white South African nationhood than many Afrikaner nationalists. With respect to Africans its leaders were generally segregationist though a minority held more liberal views. Social tensions prompted two different sets of political challenges to Smuts' United Party administration.

After moderate Afrikaner nationalists joined Jan Smuts in the United Party, hard-liners formed a Purified National Party. Meanwhile, Afrikaner nationalism became a mass movement under the direction of a secret *Broederbond* (Brotherhood) that sponsored savings banks, trade unions, and voluntary organizations. From 1940, the National Party developed a program around the idea of **apartheid** (separateness). This emphasized even stricter racial separation than already existed in South Africa. Apartheid would restrict Indians and Coloureds, and confine Africans to menial labor. This appealed to white workers who feared African competition. The National Party also drew support from farmers, who found it difficult to recruit labor. The National Party won a narrow electoral victory in 1948, marking the formal beginning of the apartheid era in South African history. More racist legislation followed. **Pass laws** required all Africans to carry internal passports at all times and interracial sex was banned. Blacks needed special permits to travel to or live in towns.

African politics also became a mass movement in the 1940s. Although the African National Congress had been founded in 1912, it was not very active until the 1940s. In 1945 the Natal Indian Congress, an organization first formed in 1894 by Mohandas Gandhi to protest discrimination against Indians, led a nonviolent resistance movement that inspired ANC leaders.

The Sharpeville Massacre and Grand Apartheid, 1960–1976

In the 1950s, African politicians reacted to fresh restrictions and segregation with civil disobedience, general strikes, and consumer boycotts. After the Communist Party was prohibited in 1950, the ANC and allied Indian and Coloured organizations

apartheid

In Afrikaans, "separateness." The term was first used in 1929 to describe Afrikaner nationalist proposals for strict racial separation and "to ensure the safety of the white race."

pass laws

Laws in apartheid South Africa that required Africans to carry identity books in which officials stamped the permits required for Africans to travel between the countryside and cities.

became more radical, as communists began to play a more assertive role in their leadership. White communists remained active in black trade unions.

On March 21, 1960, South Africa police killed approximately eighty people who had peacefully assembled outside a police station at the **township** of Sharpeville to protest the pass laws. After the Sharpeville massacre, the authorities banned the ANC and a more militant offshoot, the Pan-Africanist Congress, which had organized the antipass protests.

While the African liberation movements reorganized in exile and prepared for guerrilla warfare, National Party governments under Hendrik Verwoerd and John Vorster ratcheted up their program of racial separation in what became known as "Grand Apartheid."[1] The 1970 Black Homeland Citizenship Act specified that

township

In South Africa, a segregated residential area reserved for Africans; during apartheid, tightly controlled and constituted mainly by public housing.

PROFILE

Nelson Mandela

Colin McConnell/Toronto Star/ Getty Images

Born in a Transkei village in 1918, Nelson Mandela claimed royal lineage. After he rebelled against an arranged marriage and was suspended from Fort Hare University, he traveled to Johannesburg to begin work as a legal clerk. He joined the ANC in 1942 and helped to establish the Youth League. This group wanted to radicalize the ANC's moderate philosophy in favor of a militant, racially exclusive nationalism. By 1951, however, Mandela had become friends with Indian activists and white Communists. This led him to revise his belief that African nationalists should not cooperate across race lines. That year, Mandela helped plan a "defiance campaign" against "unjust laws." Thereafter, as the ANC's deputy president, Mandela, played a major role as an ANC strategist. In 1952, he founded a law firm with his comrade Oliver Tambo.

Following the Sharpeville massacre in March 1960, Mandela was detained for five months, and the ANC was outlawed. These events prompted him to join the Communist Party briefly while retaining his leadership in the ANC. In May 1961, he led a nationwide general strike. In October, he helped form *Umkhonto-we-Sizwe* (the armed wing of the ANC). Mandela left South Africa in January 1962 to seek support for the ANC abroad. When he returned in July, he was arrested, convicted of sabotage, and sentenced to life in prison.

During nearly thirty years of imprisonment, often involving hard labor that permanently damaged his vision, Mandela maintained his authority over successive generations of convicted activists. Beginning in 1985, he began a secret series of meetings with government leaders to urge constitutional negotiations with the ANC.

On February 11, 1990, Mandela was released. As ANC president from 1991, his leadership was crucial in curbing the expectations of his organization's often unruly following. He shared the Nobel Peace Prize in 1993 with President F. W. De Klerk. After the ANC's electoral victory in 1994, he served as South African president until 1999. His personal achievements during this period included symbolic acts of reconciliation with the Afrikaner minority. He continued to play an elder statesman role within the ANC and appeared at an ANC rally before the 2009 election, his final political act. He died on December 5, 2013.

Nelson Mandela contributed significantly to the ANC's ideological formation in the 1950s. He was a powerful proponent of the multiracial Congress Alliance. Although influenced by Marxism, he maintained an admiration for British parliamentary democracy. Maintaining his social connections with the rural aristocracy, Mandela skillfully balanced his pronouncements to the various constituencies within the ANC's following. After 1960, his personal courage and theatrical style were vital in keeping rank-and-file militants loyal to the ANC. He pioneered the ANC's transformation to a clandestine insurgent body and led its second transformation into an electoral political party. His speech at his trial in 1964, in which he declared that he was "prepared to die" for his "ideal of a democratic and free society," increased his stature making him, in the words of the *London Times*, "a colossus of African nationalism."

MAKING CONNECTIONS In which ways did Mandela contribute to the making of the modern South African state?

homelands

Areas reserved for exclusive African occupation, established through the 1913 and 1936 land legislation and later developed as ethnic states during the apartheid era.

migrant laborers

Laborers who move to another location to take a job, often a low-paying, temporary one.

Umkhonto-we-Sizwe

Zulu and Xhosa for "Spear of the Nation," the armed wing of the African National Congress, established in 1961.

all Africans would become citizens of supposedly sovereign states within the territory of South Africa. Blacks would no longer be citizens of South Africa. The ten **homelands** became increasingly overcrowded as 1.4 million farm workers were resettled within them. In addition, several hundred thousand city dwellers were deported to the homelands. African urban workers would become permanent **migrant laborers**, forced to renew their contracts every year and leave their families in the homelands.

To prepare for this change, the central government took control of the administration of the African townships in the cities. Construction of family housing for Africans in the major cities was halted. Instead, the authorities built huge dormitory-like hostels for "bachelor" workers. A program of Bantu education, stressing menial training introduced into primary schools in 1954, was extended to African secondary schooling. Restrictions were placed on African, Indian, and Coloured enrollment in the major universities. Special segregated colleges were established. New laws allowed detention without trial made it easier to torture prisoners. Through a network of informers, the police located most of the cells responsible for brief campaigns of sabotage and insurgency that had been mounted by the ANC and the Pan-Africanist Congress. By 1965, most significant African leaders who had not left the country were beginning life sentences on Robben Island, a prison and former leper colony offshore from Cape Town. These leaders included Nelson Mandela, ANC deputy president and commander-in-chief of its armed wing, ***Umkhonto-we-Sizwe*** (Spear of the Nation).

Armed police stand by their Nyala (antelope) armoured vehicle awaiting orders to disperse the striking mineworkers assembled in front of them, on Nkaneng hill, 12 August 2012.

Antonio Muchave/Sowetan/Gallo Images/Getty Images

During this era of Grand Apartheid, foreign capital and public investment built up strategic industries such as armaments and synthetic fuels, in anticipation of international **sanctions** that were beginning to be imposed on South Africa because of its racist policies. The country experienced substantial economic growth and modernization.

As Africans moved into semiskilled manufacturing jobs created by the expanding economy, black workers obtained new leverage. Wildcat strikes broke out in 1973 as a combative trade union movement gained strength. Daily tabloid newspapers aimed at township readers had appeared in the mid-1960s, responding to mass literacy. They publicized a new generation of political organizations influenced by the U.S. black power movement and led influenced by the expanding numbers of graduates from the segregated universities.

sanctions

International embargos on economic and cultural contracts with a particular country; applied selectively to South Africa by various governments and the United Nations from 1948 until 1994.

Generational Revolt and Political Reform, 1976–1990

In the mid-1970s, the collapse of Portuguese colonial power in Angola and Mozambique inspired South African anti-apartheid activists. The ideas of the racially assertive black consciousness movement percolated down to secondary schools, quickly finding followers in an educational system that discriminated terribly against Africans.

The Education Ministry rashly decided that half the curriculum in black schools should be taught in Afrikaans. This provoked demonstrations on June 16, 1976, in the townships around Johannesburg. The police fired into a crowd of 15,000 children. In the following days, the revolt spread to fifty Transvaal centers. The next year saw street battles, strikes, and classroom boycotts. At least 575 protesters died. Several thousand more from outside the country crossed into South Africa to join the liberation organizations.

By the mid-1970s, Afrikaner nationalism had changed. Two-thirds of Afrikaners were now white-collar workers and hence less likely to be worried by African competition for their jobs. Afrikaner firms were now among the most advanced manufacturers. Their directors were increasingly bothered by apartheid regulations that restricted the mobility of black labor. Reflecting this change, African workers gained collective bargaining rights. Black trade unions won legal recognition. The year 1986 saw the repeal of the pass laws and other means of **influx control** that had been used to regulate black migration to the cities.

influx control

A system of controls that regulated African movement between towns and the countryside, enforcing residence in the homelands and restricting Africans' choice of employment.

In 1983, the United Democratic Front (UDF) was formed by anti-apartheid organizations drawn from the student movement, trade unions, and township-based civic associations. They proclaimed their loyalty to the ANC's "nonracial" ideology. UDF affiliates were conspicuous in the insurrectionary protest that developed in the townships in late 1984 in response to rent hikes. Township rioting, military repression, guerrilla warfare, and conflict between supporters of liberation movements and the adherents of homeland regimes all contributed to a new bloody phase of South Africa's political history. Between 1984 and 1994, politically motivated killings claimed 25,000 lives.

The South African Miracle, 1990–1999

On February 12, 1990, a new president, F. W. De Klerk, created a bombshell when he announced the repeal of prohibitions on the ANC and other proscribed organizations. He also announced that Nelson Mandela would be released unconditionally from prison. De Klerk was a conservative, but he was disturbed by the prospect of tightening economic sanctions and was encouraged by the collapse of the Eastern European communist governments, which had previously been important supporters of the ANC. He hoped that through abandoning apartheid and beginning negotiations for power-sharing, the National Party could build black support. He also believed that an anti-ANC coalition could prevail built around a powerful political movement based on the KwaZulu homeland authority, the Inkatha Freedom Party, led by a Zulu prince, Chief Mangosuthu Buthelezi. ANC leaders, in turn, were willing to make concessions because they calculated that they could not seize power through revolution while opinion polls assured them that they enjoyed growing public support.

At the time, it seemed miraculous that such bitter adversaries could be ready to collaborate so closely in designing a new political system. Their success was even more remarkable because political hostilities continued between their supporters. Between 1990 and 1994, 14,000 people died in violent conflicts between the ANC, Inkatha, and various state-sponsored vigilante groups. By 1993, two years of bargaining had produced a transitional constitution in which the main parties would hold cabinet positions in accordance with their shares of the vote in proportional representation elections. All participants in politically motivated violence, including torture of prisoners and terrorist attacks, could obtain immunity from prosecution. Even senior public servants (mostly white) would keep their jobs. Power would be divided between a national assembly and nine provincial legislatures. These legislatures would absorb the homeland bureaucracies. Parliament would sit as a constitutional assembly to draw up a final constitution, which would have to follow the fundamental principles agreed to in the 1993 document.

On April 27, 1994, with just over 62 percent of the ballot, the ANC achieved an overwhelming majority among black voters except in KwaZulu-Natal, where Inkatha obtained a narrow victory. With 20 percent of the national vote, De Klerk's New National Party received substantial support from Coloureds and Indians, as well as most white voters. Eight more parties achieved parliamentary representation. On May 10, the Government of National Unity (GNU) took office, led by Nelson Mandela and including representatives of the ANC, the National Party, and the Inkatha Freedom Party. For many observers South Africans had achieved an astonishing historical turnaround, nearly unprecedented

Nelson Mandela walks through the gates of Pollsmoor Prison on the day of his release, hand in hand with his wife, Winnie. Mandela insisted on leaving the prison on foot, rather than being driven.

Peter Turnley/CORBIS

in terms of the relatively peaceful transformation from the white-dominated repressive regime to a multiracial democracy.

In office, the GNU began the Reconstruction and Development Programme (RDP), a plan drawn up by the ANC's labor ally, the Congress of South African Trade Unions (COSATU). The RDP emphasized "people-driven development" including fairer allocation between blacks and whites of spending on education, health, and welfare. But their actual policies were surprisingly moderate. Under both Mandela and his successor, Thabo Mbeki, ANC-led administrations attempted to address the basic needs of poor people. Social expenditure was limited, however, by tight budgets. By adopting the Growth, Employment, and Redistribution policy (GEAR) in 1996, the ANC leadership went even further by embracing free-market reforms, including privatization and tariff reduction, despite stiff objections from trade unionists. In 2007, Mbeki's opponents succeeded in electing his deputy Jacob Zuma to replace him as the ANC's party leader and shortly thereafter Mbeki resigned from the state presidency. Mbeki's resignation followed the dismissal of corruption charges against Zuma, charges that the judge suggested were instigated from the president's office.

Jacob Zuma became South Africa's head of state in 2009 after the ANC's fourth electoral victory. He rewarded his left-wing allies with key cabinet positions. Rising public investments in roads and railway renewal, together with the construction of stadiums for the soccer World Cup, held in South Africa in 2010, and an oil pipeline from Maputo helped raise the fiscal deficit and increase foreign borrowing by 2012 four times the level inherited from Apartheid. Construction expanded employment between 2009 and 2011 but unemployment began rising again in 2012. By the end of 2013 the officially recorded unemployment rate was close to 26 percent, 3 percent more than in 2009; among school dropouts, joblessness was much higher. Rising public social spending partially offsets the resulting poverty but also contributes to the fiscal deficit.

South Africa has lived with high levels of unemployment and very acute social inequality for decades but increasingly visible displays of wealth by venal politicians have accentuated political resentments. Public anger at the decision to spend R250 million (USD $25 million) on fortifying the president's luxurious homestead at Inkandla found expression in December 2013 at Nelson Mandela's memorial service when Zuma was jeered mid-speech by an invited audience of ANC members.

The Four Themes and South Africa

South Africa in a Globalized World of States

Ever since the Anglo-Boer War, South Africa has attracted an unusual degree of international attention. Its political economy has been shaped by inflows of capital and population. Throughout the twentieth century the economy depended on imported technology, which made it vulnerable to international pressure. Hence, the sanctions imposed when the country's institutionalized racial segregation attracted unanimous censure within the post–World War II world of states proved quite effective, when combined with internal pressure, in ending apartheid.

External influences have complicated South Africa's relationship with the rest of Africa. As a **settler state**, South Africa was perceived by pan-African politicians as a colonial leftover, a perception reinforced by apartheid South Africa's alignment with

settler state

Colonial or former colonial administrations controlled by the descendants of immigrants who settled in the territory.

Western powers during the Cold War. Even after democracy's advent, South Africa's status as the most developed country in Africa excited resentment as much as admiration. As the continent's leading economy in 1999, South Africa became the only African member of the G20 grouping, an annual convention of finance ministers and heads of reserve banks from the world's biggest economies.

Governing the Economy

State-directed industrialization in South Africa was encouraged with the establishment in 1928 of the Iron and Steel Corporation. The expansion of public enterprise accelerated during apartheid. The threat of foreign trade embargoes prompted increases in protective trade tariffs to encourage import substitution industrialization during the 1960s. However, between 1993 and 2001 South Africa removed about two-thirds of these tariffs to meet conditions of membership in the World Trade Organization. Tariff reform affected some industries very harshly.

The Democratic Idea

South African democracy is the product of many traditions. Immigrants contributed key features of South African political culture. In the twentieth century, this included a lineage of militant socialism that accompanied the arrival of English and Australian workers before World War I. Baltic Jewish refugees included in their numbers veterans of Russian revolutionary movements. Communists, working with African nationalists, helped ensure that black opposition to apartheid was led by advocates of racially inclusivity. Nonracial themes in South African politics were also shaped by the heritage of liberal institutions promoted by earlier arrivals from Europe, for example, the influential network of Methodist-sponsored secondary schools and colleges attended by ANC leaders. Modern South African democratic thought reflects each of these legacies, as well as the social ethics derived from indigenous African statecraft, with its traditions of consensual decision making and the etiquette of kinship.[2]

Modern democracy in South Africa is also influenced by the ideas of an African trade union movement that was built in the late 1970s and that emphasized accountable leadership. South Africa's adoption of a constitutionally entrenched bill of rights was partially influenced by other countries. The negotiators who devised a path from apartheid to democracy were inspired by the succession of transitions from authoritarian regimes that unfolded in many parts of the world in the 1980s and 1990s.

Collective Identity

In nine parliamentary and municipal elections since 1994, post-apartheid South African voters continue to appear to be influenced by feelings of racial identity. Africans overwhelmingly support African nationalist parties. Despite the conspicuous presence of whites in the ANC's leadership, only tiny numbers of white South Africans support the party. Among all groups, material interests may reinforce notions of racial community. Virtually all very poor South Africans are African; they find it difficult to feel any sense of shared social identity with generally affluent white South Africans. The prospects for democratic progress are limited when racial solidarities are so decisive.

Themes and Comparisons

Most comparative analyses of South African politics emphasize its significance as a relatively successful example of **democratization**. Post-apartheid politics in South Africa offers useful insights into the factors that build and consolidate democratic life: These factors include a pattern of economic growth in which the construction of a modern economy happened before universal enfranchisement; the role played in making democracy work by a vigorous civil society; as well as the effects of a set of state institutions carefully designed to promote social inclusion and reward consensus. South Africa also offers an encouraging model of a racially segmented society that has succeeded in nurturing stable and democratic political institutions.

democratization

Transition from authoritarian rule to a democratic political order.

Where Do You Stand?

What accounts for the fact that the South African system of apartheid was such an exceptionally oppressive system before 1994?

From what you have read so far, how significant have been the changes brought about by South Africa's democratic transition?

POLITICAL ECONOMY AND DEVELOPMENT

SECTION 2

State and Economy

Apartheid Economics

For over half a century, economic and social policy was directed to promoting the apartheid regime. From 1952, laws prohibited Africans from living in any town unless they had been born there or had worked for the same employer for ten years. Migrant workers without urban residential rights had to live in tightly controlled hostels. By the mid-1960s, repression had eliminated most of the militant African trade unions. In 1968 the Armaments Development and Manufacturing Corporation (Armscor) was created. This greatly expanded the scope of public industrial enterprise.

Apartheid economics was buttressed by a welfare state, although one that functioned in a racially discriminatory fashion. Public construction of African housing began on a significant scale with the inception of a vast township—later named Soweto (the acronym for southwestern township) outside Johannesburg during the 1930s. The need for African labor during wartime industrialization led the government to suspend pass laws. During the 1940s, as Africans rapidly moved to the cities, illegal shanty settlements mushroomed on the fringes of most cities. Although after 1948 governments restricted further African urbanization, they funded a rapid expansion of public housing to accommodate Africans who were permitted to live in towns. In 1971, African public housing totaled more than 500,000 family dwellings. During the 1960s, official policy increasingly favored single workers' hostel construction instead of family housing. Most townships included bleak barracks-like hostels

Focus Questions

- In what ways has the state's role in the economy changed since 1970 and especially since the end of apartheid?

- How did international sanctions affect the South African apartheid economy and what role did they play in hastening the end of apartheid?

in which African migrant workers slept in bunks and used communal bathrooms and kitchens.

In the 1960s, the state extended its control over African educational institutions. But it also increased school enrolment massively. By the end of the decade, most children were at school, although there were huge inequalities in the amount of public money spent per capita on white and black children. Pension payments between the races were equalized only in 1993. South Africa's universal public pension, together with its range of welfare payments, remain unusual in sub-Saharan African states today.

Liberalization and Deregulation

economic deregulation

The lifting or relaxation of government controls over the economy, including the reduction of import taxes and the phasing out of subsidized prices.

The dismantling of apartheid was accompanied by **economic deregulation**. By 1984, most official employment discrimination had been removed. In the mid-1980s, the government began to dismantle the protections and subsidies for white agriculture. Parallel to these developments, the Iron and Steel Corporation was privatized. In the late 1980s, rising defense spending and expanding public debt brought fresh reasons to deregulate and privatize. When the government abolished the restrictive pass laws in 1986, this should have opened up the labor market. But by this time the main labor shortages were in skilled sectors because generations of Africans had not been able to receive industrial training and technical education. Once Africans were allowed to move to the cities, urban growth escalated and since 1990 most South African towns have doubled in population.

Since 1994, ANC governments have expanded the liberal economic policies of the late apartheid era. Redistributive policies attempt to expand the scope of private ownership rather than broaden the public sector. For instance, between 1994 and 2013 the government helped to finance the construction of more than 3.3 million low-cost houses through grants to impoverished families that enable them to buy their own houses, built by private contractors on cheap former public land. For many township residents, home ownership was more expensive than public rented housing or the payments they had made to "shacklords" in squatter camps: The housing subsidies usually did not cover construction costs, and poor families who moved into the houses often ended up paying more on mortgage repayments than they had paid on rents. Moreover, rural urban migration and demographic pressure combined to increase the figures for the "housing backlog": Today, at least another 2.1 million houses need to be built to meet the needs of shanty dwellers.

In 1994, the government agreed to reduce industrial tariffs by two-thirds by 2001 and agricultural tariffs by 36 percent within a decade as a condition for joining the World Trade Organization. In 1997, industries stopped receiving export incentive subsidies. Currency exchange controls were substantially relaxed as well to promote foreign investment.

Since 1994, privatization policies have had their most profound effect on municipal administration. Heavily indebted local authorities now contract out basic services such as water supply and garbage collection to private companies. To put the railroad network on a commercial footing, most smaller rural stations were closed. Effectively, the state abandoned a major share of its former duty to provide cheap, subsidized public transport. Even so, the transport corporation remains wholly state-owned after successive failures to attract foreign investors and local black empowerment groups. Indeed, since 2004, government has stopped selling public assets partly because difficulties in negotiating the telephone utility. Telkom's sale made it obvious that black South Africans would not be the main beneficiaries of any further "core" privatization. Black businessmen cannot mobilize sufficient capital by themselves to purchase major stakes and in most of the privatizations up to 2004 they assumed a junior partnership.

Society and Economy

South Africa remains one of the most unequal societies in the world despite efforts to alleviate poverty. Measured through the Gini coefficient statistical measure of income inequality in which 0 is "perfectly equal" income and 1 is "perfectly unequal," South Africa inequality in 2012 was a disturbingly high .63—well above the end of apartheid level (.56 in 1995). To be sure, large numbers of Africans have been joining the richer population: Those living in the top fifth of income earners rose from 0.4 million in 1994 to 1.9 million in 2008, though this also means that income inequality among Africans has increased dramatically. Unemployment, chiefly affecting Africans, remains very high at 26 percent at the end of 2013, compared to 23.4 percent in 1996.[3]

South African inequality is, to a large extent, the historic product of government policies that enabled whites to move ahead economically at the expense of Africans. Racial inequities in government expenditure were especially obvious in education. In the 1950s, more whites than Africans were trained as teachers, even though five times as many African children were of school-going age. The 1960s saw a swift expansion of African enrollment, but as late as 1984, only a fraction of Africans compared to most white students completed high school. In 1985, although there were five times more African than white students, the government was still spending half its educational budget on white schools.

After elections ushered in an African-controlled government in 1994, public policies attempted to equalize entitlements and allocations as well as broaden access to public goods, but without dramatic expansion in public spending. Today, public expenditure on education has become equitable. Africans now outnumber other racial groups attending universities. More people receive welfare grants, 16 million today, up from 3 million in 1994. Measures to alleviate poverty include providing running water for about a third of the rural population. In 1999, municipalities began to implement free water and electricity allowances. During the 1990s, the electricity network expanded massively to embrace poorer rural communities. In addition, 1,300 new clinics have given free public health care to millions of pregnant women and children. However, hospitals in the main urban centers have deteriorated.

Have these efforts resulted in less poverty? Certainly since 1994, poor people have benefited from government services and public support. However, their absolute numbers have not changed much. Since 2000, poverty may have declined slightly but in 2012, 41 percent of the population was still living below the poverty line. Sharp increases in the provision of welfare grants, whose cost rose from 2 percent of GDP in 2001 to 3.5 percent in 2010, may have helped alleviate poverty.[4] However, a dramatic increase in economic growth is needed to reduce poverty significantly.

Unemployment has undermined the government's efforts to address poverty. The manufacturing workforce shrank by 400,000 in ten years after 1988, a 25 percent fall. At the same time 500,000 workers left farms. More recently, however, the number of manufacturing jobs has stabilized, and the numbers employed on commercial farms have increased. Public sector employment shrank only slightly, a reflection of the leverage exercised by public sector trade unions. By the late 1990s they were the major players in the still powerful union movement. Despite unemployment, union membership grew rapidly. In 2013 overall union membership was 2.8 million. Unemployment is concentrated among school dropouts and rural people. Africans are still much more likely to be unemployed than other groups.

Between 1996 and 2011, as a consequence of wider access to public health facilities, infant mortality fell slightly from 51 per 1,000 to 47 per 1,000. However life expectancy also fell from 64 in 1996 to 51 in 2007 though in 2013 it had risen to nearly 60. Falling life expectancy reflected the devastating impact of HIV/AIDS, which, according to South Africa's Medical Research Council, was responsible for 25 percent of deaths in 2000. Rising life expectancy reflects the government's efforts to expand treatment of AIDS since 2007. Official statistics indicate that between 1990 and 2010 around 4.5 million South Africans died of AIDS. South Africa's rate of HIV/AIDS infection remains among the highest in the world. In the late 1980s and early 1990s, accelerating urbanization combined with structural unemployment, political violence, and labor migration loosened social cohesion in poor communities, accentuating their vulnerability to the illness.[5]

Black Empowerment

Enlarging the share of black ownership in the economy remains a policy priority. In the words of Thabo Mbeki "the struggle against racism in our country must include the objective of creating a black bourgeoisie [that is, middle class]." A series of laws enacted since 1999 promote black business. The Preferential Procurement Act that regulates the awarding of government contracts requires winning companies to allocate shares to "previously disadvantaged" people. The Promotion of Equality Act set up a monitoring system to record how well companies were "deracializing" their managements. The National Empowerment Fund Act reserves 2 percent of the proceeds from the sale of public corporations to finance black shareholding in these concerns, although as we have seen, since 2004, privatization has largely halted because of the absence of black business groups who can purchase majority stakes. Mining and energy, though, have traditionally benefited from government protection and subsidies. Here the government has extracted corporate commitments to black empowerment and has been providing black entrepreneurs about 2.5 billion rand ($375 million) a year of start-up capital.

How successful has been the program to "deracialize" South African capitalism? Measured by the proportion of black-owned companies on the Johannesburg stock exchange, the share of the economy owned by a "black bourgeoisie" remains quite modest. In 2012, 21 percent of the shares of the top 100 companies traded on the Johannesburg Stock Exchange were held by black South Africans, according to the Exchange's own research.

However, black participation in the economy is not limited to black share ownership. Political pressure has prompted all major companies to appoint black people to their boards: In 2002, for example, more than 11 percent of South African company directors were black. In the real estate business, the number of black realtors was almost nonexistent in 1990; it now matches the numbers of white realtors—a telling instance of the proliferation of property ownership in black communities. Within companies the proportion of black people in management has also been rising steadily. For example, in 2012, 44 percent of senior managers and 71 percent of middle managers in the Standard Bank, one of South Africa's largest banks, were black.[6]

Whether black empowerment has made South Africa more socially stable is another question. Given the rising black share of economic ownership the government certainly has an incentive to maintain business-friendly policies. To be sure, most of those who have benefited most from these measures have been politically well-connected, especially former activists. However, it is also true that political pressure has prompted companies to promote black managers, and this has promoted a rapid expansion of a black middle class. At the same time, black empowerment by itself has not reduced black poverty; what reduction has occurred has been an effect of extending social welfare. Indeed black empowerment may have promoted economic inefficiencies that have curbed growth and job creation. To most poor black South Africans, wealth still appears predominantly white.

Environmental Issues

The government is also beginning to expand its authority over environmental issues. By the beginning of the 1990s, trade union opposition to unsafe working conditions was expanding into a broader concern with the effects of industrial pollution. The environmental movement acquired a popular base as it embraced "brown" issues of the urban landscape, such as poor access to clean water and unsafe waste disposal, as well as the more traditional interests of "green" conservationism like vehicle emissions and energy efficiency.

In 1993, ANC negotiators insisted on including clauses on environmental health and ecological sustainability in the constitution. Since 1994, government policies have attempted to integrate ecological concerns with the requirements of social justice. A series of court cases have produced settlements in which historically dispossessed communities have signed "comanagement" agreements with the National Parks Board. The 1998 Marine Living Resources Act has opened up fishing grounds to impoverished villagers. In return, villagers are expected to keep the size of their catches sustainable.

More ambitious measures are needed, though, to cope with the scale of today's environmental hazards. Key features of South Africa's political economy make the country and its inhabitants especially vulnerable in a context in which climate change is generating tough challenges. This became evident after a series of severe floods devastated crowded settlements on marginal land. The Department of Health estimated that nearly 2,000 people died as a consequence of floods between 1980 and 2010 and more than 18 million were affected in other ways. For example, flooding is believed to have caused upsurges in malaria, diarrhea, and cholera. In South Africa's main industrial region, poor regulation of the mining industry has generated huge quantities of acidic waste, which poses a major threat to national water supplies as the waste pollutes reservoirs. Water demand in an arid country is stressed by increasing reliance on coal-fired power stations to match rising electricity consumption. Because of the need to cool these power stations, the Electricity Supply Commission is now South Africa's biggest water purchaser.

In response, the government plans bolder measures to curb industrial pollution. In 2010 a special Green Economy Summit promised expansion of clean energy supplies. Domestic solar water hearing units are now visible features in low-cost housing schemes, and officials plan to accelerate their local production. Replacing coal with bio-ethanol fuel is another goal, but this development will impose its own ecological costs as it will require additional water for irrigating fields, which undermines local food production. Trade unions have opposed biofuel production, arguing that in effect South Africa will be substituting high-paid jobs in petrol refining for menial work in crop production.

Meanwhile, environmental protests have increasingly attracted mass participation. In Johannesburg, a busy local chapter of Earthlife Africa has helped make acid mine drainage a policy concern, though politicians continue to maintain that the risks are "exaggerated." Activists also encounter wider opposition. When nongovernmental organizations oppose industrial development, they sometimes provoke strong hostility from local people suffering from unemployment. This happened in Saldanha Bay in 1998, when environmentalists opposing building a new steel factory were accused of elevating the welfare of penguins over the livelihoods of people. Environmental groups object to plans to build an additional nuclear reactor at the existing facility at Koeberg, just 30 kilometers from Cape Town. It is the only nuclear power station on the entire continent of Africa. To date, efforts to halt the building of a second reactor have been confined to relatively decorous public meetings. Greenpeace activists did scale the walls of the Koeburg compound to post a placard in 2002, but since then, there has been no militant protest. However, there remains evident public anxiety, particularly as residential settlement has extended closer to the power station. The Nuclear Regulator issued a defensively phrased statement in the wake of the Fukushima disaster, pointing out that designs for both the existing and projected reactors at Koeberg were intended to withstand level 7 earthquakes and eight meter tidal waves. And in 2011, a government-sponsored "Green Paper" addressing climate change pledged construction of a new "nuclear power station fleet."

South Africa in the Global Economy

From the mid-1940s, protectionist policies promoted manufacturing for the domestic market. These policies, together with restrictions on the use of black labor, caused growing inefficiencies, which economists believe constrained growth by the early 1970s.[7]

Protectionist policies favored the manufacture of consumption rather than capital goods. This helps explain why, in contrast to other middle-income developing countries, South Africa lagged behind in producing machines and equipment. In comparison to most primary commodity producers, high gold prices and well-diversified markets for exports helped South Africa maintain a trade surplus throughout most of the apartheid era, despite the rising cost of oil imports.

One important consequence of the international sanctions campaign was that the government began to invest in local branches of production, fearing that sanctions might become more effective. For example, during the 1960s, threats of an oil embargo stimulated a petrochemical industry that remains one of South Africa's more competitive export sectors.

More significant in its political effect than trade sanctions on South African policy-makers was the impact of divestment and credit denial by companies and banks, principally American, in reaction to the state of emergency that was imposed in 1985. Divestment was a direct response to threats by U.S. colleges as well as state and local governments to sell their holdings in companies with South African interests. The divestment campaign culminated in the passage by the U.S. Congress of the Comprehensive Anti-Apartheid Act in October 1986. Divestment did not directly hurt South African economic activity since South African domestic capital was the major source of investment in the economy. However, the prospect of future limitations on the country's ability to secure foreign loans was extremely alarming to the government. By 1987, South African industrialists were dismayed about the difficulties they anticipated in obtaining access to advanced technology.[8]

Traditionally, South Africa dominated its regional economy through such arrangements as the South African Customs Union (which linked South Africa and its neighbors in a free-trade and revenue-sharing zone). During the 1980s, however, the region's economic significance as a trading partner with South Africa substantially increased at the same time that labor migration from the region into South Africa slackened. In the early 1980s, at a time of balance-of-payments difficulties, regional annual trade surpluses in South Africa's favor reached $1.8 billion. South Africa's regional trading partners bought 40 percent of its manufacturing exports. By the end of the decade, however, regional trade was contracting because of the warfare that intensified when South Africa sponsored insurgencies against Marxist governments in neighboring Angola and Mozambique. Such destabilization created growing unease within industrial circles, as well as disagreements within government itself.

The effects of South Africa's post-1994 reintegration into the international economy were initially disheartening. Through the rest of the decade, growth levels remained modest—2.3 percent increases in GDP while foreign investors remained wary. The ending of sanctions helped to increase South African trade with other African countries, but also prompted an outflow of South African investment into countries with lower labor costs. WTO-mandated tariff reductions exposed hitherto protected industries to foreign competition with heavy job losses resulting in textiles and clothing factories. After 2000, though, growth began to accelerate, reaching levels above 5 percent from 2005 until 2008, but then dipping to around between 2.5 and 3.5 percent from 2008 to the present. As noted above, public investments, mainly funded by foreign lending stimulated other sectors of the economy and created nearly half a million new jobs. Export-oriented manufacturing has expanded though not as much as the government hoped: The most buoyant export sector is in energy in which South Africa sells electricity to African neighbors and coal to the rest of the world. Local industries continue to encounter fierce foreign competition in the domestic market, however, particularly from the growing volume of Chinese imports.

GLOBAL CONNECTION

South Africa in BRICS

BRICS stands for Brazil, Russia, India, China, and South Africa, an informal alliance of the world's largest developing economies. The foreign ministers of four of these countries began holding meetings in 2006 and then formed a formal association in 2008. At China's urging, South Africa was invited to join the group in 2010. The association seeks to use its members' combined economic strength to shift the distribution of global economic power in their favor. Accordingly the group has called for a new reserve currency and to work for the creation of a development bank to rival the International Monetary Fund.

For Jacob Zuma's administration, BRICS membership is perceived as welcome recognition of South Africa's status as Africa's most advanced economy. In reality, South Africa is a small power compared to its partners. Its economy is less than a quarter the size of India's and an even smaller fraction of China's. Its importance to the group is a consequence of its mining industry as well as its sophisticated infrastructure that enables it to perform gateway functions for the African continent. South Africa takes its membership in the group very seriously. At World Trade

(continued)

Organization summits, South Africa aligns with its partners in arguing that developing countries should be able to maintain protectionist tariffs. Similarly, South Africans tend to join the Chinese, Brazilians, and Indians in opposing cuts to energy emissions.

Meanwhile South African trade with the BRICS group has expanded five times since 2005, although, in contrast to its still larger trade with the European Union, South Africa's trade balance with the BRICS group is negative. China has become a bigger export market for South Africa than the United States and its fastest-growing investor.

BRICS cooperation is intended to reach beyond global flows of trade and finance. As already noted, South Africa has aligned itself with its partners in international negotiations about climate change. Such diplomatic alignments have engendered anxiety among human rights activists. In 2013, the Dalai Lama was denied a visa to visit South Africa after being invited to speak at a conference in Pretoria. In global forums nowadays, South Africa generally takes its cues from its BRICS partners. For example, during South Africa's second term on the UN Security Council, it sided with China and abstained from voting on a Western powers-sponsored resolution on Syria.

MAKING CONNECTIONS South African policy-makers argue that diplomatic and economic alignment with developing countries as in BRICS is in their national interest. Are they right?

Where Do You Stand?

South African social inequality has increased since 1994. Why does this matter politically?

Is poverty in today's South Africa mainly an effect of Apartheid?

SECTION 3

GOVERNANCE AND POLICY-MAKING

Focus Questions

- Why is the executive branch of government so powerful in South Africa?

- Why is public confidence in the legal system so limited?

Organization of the State

South Africa's modern state organization emerged from protracted bargaining between 1992 and 1996 as apartheid crumbled. A transitional constitution settled how South Africa would be governed after the first democratic elections, which were held in 1994. Parliament, acting as a constitutional assembly, drafted a document that incorporated key principles adopted at the earlier multiparty talks. This ensured that certain minority concerns would receive enduring protection. A bill of rights supplies safeguards ranging from traditional civil liberties to environmental protections and sexual choice. Most clauses of the constitution can be changed through a two-thirds vote in the National Assembly, the lower house of parliament. However, an opening section of the Constitution lists a set of key values that require a 75 percent majority for amendment.

Since 1994, the South African state has been a quasi-federal system. The national government has the power to override laws passed by nine provincial regional legislatures. The provincial administrations depend on funds allocated by the central government.

Between 1994 and 1999, the transitional constitution specified that the executive of the Government of National Unity had to be composed of a coalition of party representatives, with posts being distributed proportionately among parties that achieved more than 5 percent of the popular vote. The National Party, the former ruling group during apartheid, withdrew from the GNU in 1996, partly because of its failure to persuade the drafters of the 1996 constitution to retain **power sharing** after 1999.

The Executive

Although the South African system of government has inherited many features of the Westminster model, the South African president is considerably more powerful than the British prime minister. South African governments are formed by the president, who must be a member of the National Assembly. After being elected by the Assembly, the president vacates his or her parliamentary seat and appoints and subsequently chairs a cabinet of ministers. The president, who can only serve two five-year terms, also chooses a deputy president.

South Africa's first president after elections in 1994 was Nelson Mandela, who served one term and declined to serve another on grounds of age. His single term was decisive in establishing the prestige of the new government both abroad, and more importantly, at home. His successor, Thabo Mbeki, followed Mandela's example in taking care to cultivate strong personal relationships with members of the Afrikaner elite. Prior to becoming president of the Republic, both Mandela and Mbeki had been elected at ANC delegate conferences to head the party. The president can be impeached or removed from office by a two-thirds vote of the National Assembly, but only on grounds of disability or serious misconduct.

power sharing

Constitutional arrangements to ensure that the major political parties share executive authority. These can include mandatory coalitions and allocation of senior official positions between parties.

Dressed in his warrior kilt (Ishebu), Jacob Zuma demonstrates his mastery of traditional dance steps while his supporters sing his anthem from the Umkhonto camps, Umshini Wami, My Machine Gun.

AP Images

As Mandela's deputy president, Mbeki was largely responsible for the day-to-day management of the administration as well as managing the cabinet. After he became president in 1999, the office accumulated new functions and resources. Although he was elected to a second term in 2004, Mbeki lost his party's support in ANC leadership elections at the end of 2007, a consequence both of unpopular economic policies and personal animosities that alienated powerful party personalities. He resigned the following year, to be replaced by his deputy, Kgalema Motlanthe. After the 2009 election, the new National Assembly elected Jacob Zuma as president and Motlanthe reassumed his former role as deputy.

To his opponents within the ANC, Jacob Zuma's lack of a formal education and his tangles with the law made him unsuited for office. In truth, though, even Zuma's legal difficulties helped to generate public approval. In 2007, he faced charges for accepting bribes offered during the negotiation of weapons purchases. The previous year, he was acquitted in a rape case in which his defence was that his accuser, a houseguest, had signalled her availability, by wearing a short skirt and failing to cross her legs, wanton behavior from the standpoint of decorous Zulu convention. If he was mistaken, Zuma told the court, he would "have his cows ready" if his accuser agreed to marry him. The judge found him not guilty for other reasons, but Zuma's explanation of his actions resonated with the honor code of many of his supporters—socially marginalized young men who remained rooted in a rural patriarchal culture.

However, these were not his only supporters. Zuma's continued Communist Party membership encouraged trade unionists to think that he was a champion of their concerns. More generally, his warm manner and down-to-earth style endeared him to ordinary ANC members. His efforts in the early 1990s to broker peace in KwaZulu Natal earned him respect and trust outside the ANC.

Yet the corruption charges against Zuma were serious. In the 2005 trial of Shabir Shaik, Zuma's former financial adviser, prosecutors demonstrated that Shaik had negotiated a bribe from a French contractor on Zuma's behalf. According to the evidence accepted by the court in Shaik's trial, Jacob Zuma was an active accomplice in corrupt practices. However, under pressure from the president's office, the Directorate of Public Prosecutions made various procedural errors in their efforts to prosecute him. As a result, a high court dismissed the case against Zuma in 2008 on technical grounds. His reelection as president in 2009 was now inevitable. In office, however, Zuma's political support base, which consisted of an uneasy alliance between different disaffected groups within the ANC, began to fragment and various scandals weakened his personal authority.

Unlike the president, cabinet ministers remain members of parliament and are accountable to it through question-time sessions. These are regularly scheduled occasions, in which ministers must reply to queries from backbenchers. Ministers are also accountable to various parliamentary standing committees. Parliamentarians lose office if they are expelled from membership by their parties. This gives the executive great power. Elected by a parliamentary majority, the president will normally be a political party leader, enjoying a controlling influence over the makeup of parliamentary representation. Given the president-as-party-leader's de facto power over parliamentary office holding, a revolt by ruling party backbenchers is extremely unlikely. In 1999, Thabo Mbeki could appoint his cabinet without any restrictions. He chose, however, to include members of the Inkatha Freedom Party, which had been a fierce rival of the ANC. In 2004 Mbeki made room in his cabinet for Marthinus van Schalwyk, the leader of the National Party, who became Minister for the Environment and Tourism. In 2009, Jacob Zuma appointed to his cabinet Pieter Mulder, the leader of the Freedom Front, which is the main representative of Afrikaner communalist politics. Although there is no formal requirement for socially representative cabinets, ANC governments embody a racial cross section. Of thirty-four cabinet ministers fourteen are women, a reflection of the ANC's commitment to gender equity, which has also ensured that at least one-third of ANC parliamentarians are female.

There are few checks other than constitutional restraints on the leadership of the ruling party. Certainly, Thabo Mbeki attempted to impose his personal authority more frequently than his predecessor. For example, he dictated the choice of the leaders of the provincial governments to the ANC regional organization. In 1998, an ANC "deployment committee" was set up. This was intended to decide on key appointments in parastatal organizations, as well as to have the final say over the makeup of the party's electoral lists. Since Zuma's accession to the presidency, however, the management of political patronage has become increasingly personalized, and the party's deployment committee has been sidelined by the president's office.

Unlike Mandela's charismatic and unquestioned authority within the ANC, the accession of both Mbeki and Zuma to the party leadership was contested. Accordingly, leaders are now expected to reward their political allies. Both Mbeki and Zuma used their powers of appointment to favor trusted associates and displace rivals. Such political patronage has resulted in a proliferation of factionalism within the ANC, impeding the development of competent public administration and feeding corruption. Estimates of the annual cost of public corruption suggest that as much as 4 billion rand ($600 million) a year is lost through corruption and waste, much of it through procurements in which politically well-connected suppliers cooperate with officials in charging inflated prices. In 2010, investigators discovered that 6,000 civil servants failed to disclose their business interests, often involving companies with government contracts.

In contrast to previous administrations, Zuma's government has expanded deficit-funded expenditure, partly because of increasingly generous social welfare provisions but also through employing more public servants, mainly nurses and teachers as well as policemen, 250,000 of whom have been added to a bureaucracy of around 1.3 million. The government now spends double the salaries as it did in 2007. This bureaucracy is partly controlled by the central government and partly by the provinces. Certain departments—defense, security, justice, finance, trade and industry, and home affairs—are administered in a centralized fashion by national government ministries. For other departments—education, social services, and

THE U.S. CONNECTION

Organization of the State: South Africa Compared to the United States

In South Africa, as in the United States, the Constitution lays down the essential features of state organization. In the United States, the Supreme Court has the final say on constitutional interpretation. In South Africa, the Constitutional Court performs this function. In both countries the president appoint the judges, but in South Africa, Constitutional Court judges hold office for fixed terms whereas in the United States, Supreme Court judges are appointed for life. In South Africa, it is easier to amend the constitution. Most changes require only a two-thirds vote in parliament. In the United States, three-fourths of the fifty states must approve constitutional amendments, which also require two-thirds votes in Congress.

South Africa follows the Westminster system in which the party winning parliamentary elections sets up the executive. This is different from the American separation

(continued)

of presidential and legislature elections. American presidents have formidable powers, but Congress can check these powers to some degree. In South Africa the parliament tends to defer to the presidency. South African executive authority has grown through the use of national list proportional representation for legislative elections, which centralizes party organization and empowers party leaders. Unlike in the United States parliamentarians do not represent particular districts.

In both countries, presidents may serve only two terms, and in both, presidents can be removed from office through impeachment. In South Africa, political parties can use any method they want to choose presidential candidates and all other candidates for elected public offices. The relative weakness of American political parties is partly a result of the primary elections that give ordinary citizens such an important role in deciding who runs for office. Cabinet ministers remain subject to the normal rules of parliamentary accountability, but because one party (the ANC) dominates the political system, the executive enjoys considerable autonomy. In both countries executive power derives partly from a spoils system in which politicians appoint senior officials in the civil service.

Both countries are federal systems, but in South Africa the nine provinces depend almost entirely upon the central government for their budgets. Provincial governments can pass legislation, but the National Assembly can override their laws. This is very different from the considerable powers that American states, cities, and towns exercise in areas such as welfare and education. The United States possesses a relatively accessible political system with many places where citizens and lobbies can affect policy-making. This openness is the result of several factors: federalism, a decentralized party system, separation of powers, and the fact that office holders are personally accountable to the voters. In comparison, the South African political system is less open and more centralized.

MAKING CONNECTIONS What are the key political effects of constitutional differences between South Africa and the United States?

health—provincially elected governments enjoy considerable discretion. Certain central ministries are extremely efficient—finance, for example, especially with respect to tax collection; but others have reputations for corruption and incompetence.

Other State Institutions

The Judiciary and the Police

All judges are appointed through a constitutional process that limits executive discretion. Court judgments demonstrate robust judicial independence, despite complaints by cabinet ministers that judges are trying to make themselves policy-makers. Senior levels of the judiciary are freer of political influence than they were during apartheid.

Judicial independence has been especially obvious with respect to the Constitutional Court. In key judgments in 2001 and in 2002 the court ruled on how the government should allocate public resources to meet its constitutional duty to supply shelter for a group of forcibly evicted squatters in Grootboom near Cape Town and to provide antiretroviral medication for HIV/AIDS patients. In 2009, the Court again showed its assertiveness by granting voting rights to certain groups of foreign residents, a decision that probably benefited the ANC's opponents in upcoming elections.

Public respect for legal institutions needs to be based on more than their autonomy and integrity. For most citizens, courts are inaccessible and inefficient. Huge caseloads make legal proceedings extremely slow. Nearly half of South Africa's prisoners are awaiting trial. Several thousand cases a year do not reach trial because criminal syndicates bribe court officials to destroy dockets.

South Africa has one of the highest crime rates in the world, a consequence of gross social inequalities, a violent political history, and a general disrespect for the law that apartheid engendered. Unfortunately, rising rates of youth unemployment supply a more contemporary explanation for crime.

Overall, conviction rates in South Africa, at 8 percent in 2002, represent one of the lowest levels in the world. This is a reflection of poor police work. Up to the 1990s judges tolerated routine use of torture to extract confessions, even in petty criminal cases. Today, although judges are much more discerning, reports suggest that the police still torture suspected criminals quite routinely. Between March 2008 and April 2009, the Independent Complaints Directorate investigated 828 cases of assaults by police officers on people held in their custody; many were sufficiently severe to rate as torture. In 2011 and 2012 nearly 500 people were killed in armed police operations, according to the Independent Complaints Directorate.

Since 1994, despite efforts at reform, police competence remains patchy. Policy choices since the mid-1990s have downgraded the detective services in favor of public order and patrol policing and placed detectives under local uniformed station managers.[9] Rapid expansion of the force—between 2008 and 2013, its size doubled—accentuated inefficiencies. One reason that conviction rates are low is that semiliterate constables ignore basic rules of evidence. Pay scales for rank-and-file police officers are the lowest in the public sector, which makes the force exceptionally prone to corruption. In 2010, Jackie Selebi, a one-time head of Interpol (International Criminal Police Organization), and South Africa's most senior police officer, was convicted on

In February 2013 Mido Macia, a Mozambican taxi driver was arrested by police for a minor traffic violation. Spectators filmed on their cell phone images that were subsequently broadcast on local and international TV networks. They showed policemen handcuffing Macia to the back of their van and then driving away dragging him along the road. Macia later died of his injuries in a police cell. Eight officers were put on trial for murder in November 2013.

corruption charges and sentenced to fifteen years in prison. His successor, General Bheki Cele also lost his position after corruption accusations in 2011—but not before he had presided over an aggressive "shoot to kill" approach, which continues to shape police behavior, as was so tragically evident at Marikana. In 2013, police were filmed by journalists handcuffing to their vehicle a Mozambican taxi driver arrested for a parking violation. After dragging him along the ground for a few hundred yards, the police took him to the police station, where he subsequently died.

National Security Organizations

The South African military is not in better shape. The South African National Defence Force (SANDF) employed 70,000 soldiers, sailors, and airmen in 2012, less than half the size of the police force. One reason that South Africa is reluctant to play a major role in continental peacekeeping operations is the poor quality of its armed forces. In 1998, the government committed itself to ambitious expenditures on military aircraft, submarines, and light destroyers for the navy, while recruitment was to be increased by 10,000 annually. However, well over a decade later, the Defence Force remains too underequipped and undermanned to play even the fairly confined defensive role envisaged for it in the 2009 Defence White paper. The shortcomings are most evident in the air force, where half the combat pilot positions are unfilled as are a similar proportion of the posts allocated to technical support. In any case, even if there were enough pilots to fly aircraft, the air force is unable to provide basic supplies. Press reports in 2013 cited internal SANDF documentation indicating that 60 percent of the helicopter fleet and all new fighter-trainers were grounded. One consequence of the helicopter groundings was that aerial anti-poaching operations in the Kruger Park were halted. The army continues to use obsolete equipment, some of it over thirty years old. Budgetary increases in 2009 intended for recruitment and material were absorbed in a major pay increase awarded when soldiers joined civil servants in striking for a 10 percent pay raise. With expenditure on the SANDF equaling 1.3 percent of GDP, experts agree that South African defense is underfunded.

Subnational Government

A more serious limitation on the power of the South African state than its military weakness is shortcomings of the subnational governments, both in provincial administrations and in municipal authorities.

The nine provincial governments are led by premiers, who are limited to two terms in office. In principle, premiers are elected by their legislatures, but in the seven provinces in which the ANC predominates, such elections are formalities. Premiers are in reality appointed and dismissed by the president.

Each premier appoints a minicabinet, called an executive council. Provincial revenues derive mainly from central government. In addition, provinces receive conditional grants for particular projects from the national ministries. Provincial administrations are supposed to allocate their expenditure between departments in accordance with national budgetary guidelines. In practice, they enjoy considerable financial discretion, for example, in contracting for services and equipment.

In the beginning, provinces had to amalgamate several civil services from different homelands or from the separate establishments that existed for white, Coloured, and Indian people. The new provincial boundaries brought together rival elites who sometimes remained jealous of each other's influence. In many of the former homelands, bureaucratic systems had suffered considerable degeneration. Because

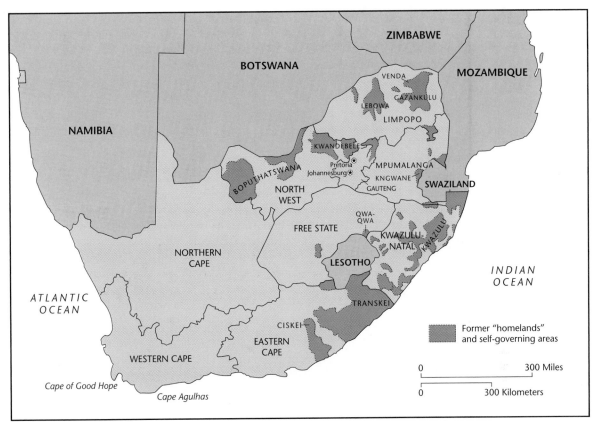

© Cengage Learning®

governments did not have strong accountability mechanisms, provincial administrations were often short of key skills such as financial record keeping, and civil servants were as a consequence often very corrupt.

Reforming such administrations was extremely difficult, particularly because it was impossible to dismiss public servants during the Mandela era—a consequence of the transition guarantees in the 1993 constitution. Additionally, militant public service unions affiliated to COSATU, the ANC's ally, often protect identifiably corrupt officials. Most of the new provincial governments lacked basic information, even about the number of their employees or the location of public property. Finally, South Africa's current public administration inherited hierarchical and authoritarian traditions from the apartheid regime, which in practice have proved very difficult to change.

In any case, as social reforms have expanded citizen entitlements, including free prenatal health care, abortions on demand, housing subsidies, and a wider range of welfare grants—the bureaucracy has acquired a whole range of new tasks, even though it was already badly managed and poorly qualified. Public service managers in regional departments often find it difficult to interpret and understand policy designed in national ministries.

Partly because of the failings of the provincial administrations, from 1999 onwards national policy-makers increasingly turned to municipal government as the key agency in the delivery of development projects. Because of their taxation powers, local governments in many respects have greater discretionary power than provincial administrations, especially in the case of the metropolitan councils in South Africa's six main cities. Although the big cities derive most of their revenues from local taxes, the smaller local authorities remain heavily dependent on government grants. Today about 75 percent of South Africa's cities are governed by ANC-dominated administrations.

However, there has been very low voter turnout in local elections, and heavy criticism of the way local councils were performing. The public was clearly disappointed with the first decade of democratic local government. The Ministry of Provincial and Local Government has invested considerable effort to train councillors as well as to set up a system of ward committees to improve accountability and public participation in planning. But reforms do not seem to have improved the quality of representation in local government. Corruption is especially entrenched in local government. Municipal administration personnel also lack basic skills. For example in 2007, one-third of city governments employed no engineers, an effect of the exodus during the preceding decade of white apartheid-era officials. As the cabinet minister responsible for municipalities conceded in 2010, outside the big cities, local government was "not working."

The Policy-Making Process

Before it came to power in 1994, the ANC appeared to be committed to participatory ways of making policy. This was reflected in the way the post-apartheid Reconstruction and Development Programme (RDP) was adopted and the new government's rhetoric about "stakeholder" consultation in development planning and institutional accountability.

The early Mandela administration seemed to put this approach into practice when it came to making policy. Assertive parliamentary committees and ministers who were prepared to work closely with these committees made the process more open to interest groups and the infant lobbying industry. Departments conscientiously circulated Green Papers and White Papers (successive drafts of policy proposals) to all interested parties, and they encouraged public feedback at policy presentations up and down the country.

The announcement by the minister of finance of the essential tenets of an official Growth, Employment, and Redistribution (GEAR) policy in 1996 represented an abrupt turnaround. From then on, the minister warned, macroeconomic management would stress deficit reduction, the removal of tariff protection, government downsizing, privatization, exchange control relaxation, and setting wage increases below rates of productivity growth. The ANC's trade union allies clearly could not endorse these objectives. After a currency crisis in late 1995, government announced that the private sector would henceforth be the main engine for job creation and social progress. The government itself, the minister warned, was not in the business of creating jobs.

The minister announced, immediately after GEAR's publication, that its content was nonnegotiable. This made it different from any other official policy announcements. The announcement of GEAR set the tone for the new style of policy-making in South Africa. Since 1996, policy shifts have typically occurred in sudden fashion, without elaborate consultative procedures. The surest way to influence policy from outside government has become through direct access to the president's office and the informal networks that surround it.

Successive ANC governments, including Jacob Zuma's, have retained rhetorical commitment to fiscally conservative policies, although Zuma has expanded public employment. This has put economic issues at the center of political conflict. COSATU hostility to GEAR has been expressed in several national strikes. Other kinds of dissent, both by unions and the broader public, involve opposition to official financial policies. Trade unions joined civic associations to mobilize popular protest against contracting out municipal services to private firms as well to challenge the moral right of municipalities to evict delinquent tenants and withdraw services from payment defaulters. The austerity produced by GEAR's economies has had an especially severe effect on municipalities, which have received less and less funding from the central government. At the beginning of the Mandela government, ANC leaders hoped to maintain their activist traditions in the ways in which they made decisions and exercised power. In South African democracy's second decade, the worlds of policy decision making and popular political activism have become increasingly insulated from each other.

Where Do You Stand?

The changes in 1994 were a compromise. Did they leave South Africa's administration stronger or weaker?

Did the ANC make unwise concessions during the negotiations? If so, what were they and why were they made? If not, why do you reject the criticisms made of the compromise?

REPRESENTATION AND PARTICIPATION

SECTION 4

The Legislature

South Africa's legislature consists of a 400-member National Assembly located in Cape Town, as well as the National Council of Provinces, an upper house of parliament? Parliamentarians can take the initiative in drafting and enacting laws but in practice most legislation since 1994 has been drafted by government ministers and officials, not by ordinary members of parliament. Draft laws must be read in the National Assembly before portfolio committees review their content. These committees usually call for public recommendations on the bill before calling for revision, acceptance, or rejection of the law. Once a bill has received its second reading in the National Assembly, it can be enacted. Parliamentary committees also review the work of different government departments. Standing Committees on Public Accounts and Public Finance monitor general public spending, and they can summon ministers and public servants to appear before them.

The second chamber, the National Council of the Provinces has ninety members made up of nine equal delegations drawn from the provincial legislatures. To encourage consensus within provincial delegations, each province can cast only one vote within the Council. The National Council for the Provinces reviews all legislation. But for most laws its functions are only advisory.

Much of what happens in parliament depends on the ANC caucus, which represents nearly two-thirds of the votes in the National Assembly. On the whole, ANC parliamentarians tend to defer to the executive. This is partly because of the country's

Focus Questions

- Why has the South African National Assembly been so ineffective in checking executive power?

- What factors encourage parties to take up moderate positions during elections?

electoral system. In general elections, parties compete for National Assembly seats by offering single lists of candidates rather than by running candidates in individual districts or constituencies. If a ruling party's leadership predominates within the executive branch, as is the case with the ANC, then the executive branch's power over parliament is much greater than in most other systems in which the executive branch is accountable to parliament. This is because MPs hold their seats at the will of party leadership, not through being personally elected. The list system through which MPs hold their seats at the discretion of party leaders means that MPs who defy party policy or leadership directives risk incurring heavy penalties, including losing their seat in parliament at the next election.

During the Mandela presidency ANC MPs were occasionally willing to confront the executive branch. During the Mbeki administration, parliamentary committees became much less assertive, and government ministers treated committees scornfully. In any case, ANC parliamentarians may have other priorities than ensuring executive accountability. The fact that in 2007, 40 percent of the ANC caucus listed themselves as company directors suggests that many ANC MPs devote significant time to private business pursuits.

In 2001, the ANC established a political committee to monitor the hearings of the Select Committee on Public Accounts (SCOPA), which was investigating allegations of corrupt arms contracting. SCOPA's inquiry followed allegations that a former defense minister had accepted an 11 million rand ($1.6 million) bribe. SCOPA was chaired according to convention by an opposition MP but it contained a majority of ANC members. Initially SCOPA followed its investigation energetically but after an early clash with the President's office the leader of the ANC group within SCOPA, Andrew Feinstein, was demoted and subsequently resigned, complaining of ministerial efforts to circumscribe the inquiry.[10] Following Feinstein's departure, SCOPA ceased to play any further role in the efforts to identify bribe-takers. For its critics, SCOPA's inability to investigate the arms purchases was proof enough of the ANC leadership's tight control of parliament. To be fair, on several occasions since the arms inquiry, over the last ten years, SCOPA and the various portfolio committees have occasionally attempted to challenge the executive, but usually without much support from the ANC contingent on each committee.[11]

Political Parties and the Party System

Today, South Africa's party system is still shaped by old racial divisions. The main parties that emerged as the leading groups in the 1994 election were well-established organizations during the apartheid era: the African National Congress founded in 1912 and in 1994 supported by most Africans and the (Afrikaner) National Party founded in 1914 and in 1994 voted for by a majority of whites. In 1994, most of the parties competing in the election drew support mainly from a different ethnic or racial group. Even after apartheid, the pattern of racial or ethnic bloc voting has changed only slightly. This has helped to ensure the African National Congress's predominance.

The African National Congress

The ANC began in a conference of African notables that assembled in 1912 to protest the impending South African Land Act. Years later, during World War II, the ANC began to build a mass membership. By this time, several of its leaders were also members of the Communist Party. Within the ANC, both Communists and Africanists (racially assertive African nationalists) who formed the Youth League influenced the ANC to embrace more aggressive tactics. The Communist Party was banned in 1950; its members then worked within the ANC and allied organizations. Communist influence and older liberal traditions nurtured by Methodist schools, which trained most African political leaders, ensured that although the ANC's membership remained exclusively African, it defined its program on a broader basis. In 1956, the ANC's Freedom Charter proposed a democratic future in which all races would enjoy equal rights. A "Defiance Campaign" of civil disobedience against new apartheid laws swelled membership.

A breakaway movement, the Pan-Africanist Congress (PAC), formed in 1959 as a more radical alternative to the ANC. After the uproar that followed the Sharpeville massacre in March 1960, the government banned both the ANC and the PAC. Moving underground and into exile, they began planning armed insurgencies.

During its thirty years in exile, the ANC strengthened its alliance with the Communist Party. Partly because of this alliance, it opened its ranks to whites, Indians, and Coloureds. Because survival in exile required discipline and authority, the ANC patterned its internal organization on the centralized model of communist parties.

After 1976, ANC guerrillas attracted attention with attacks on symbolic targets. A charismatic cult developed around the ANC's imprisoned leaders on Robben Island, especially Nelson Mandela. Mandela's stature helped the ANC achieve international recognition and acceptance. By the late 1980s, meetings between its leaders and Western statesmen underlined its status as a government-in-waiting. The ANC established secret contacts with South African officials in the mid-1980s. After the party was unbanned and Mandela was released from prison in 1990, the international recognition the ANC had obtained in exile brought the financial resources needed to build a sophisticated mass organization in South Africa.

Today, the ANC's overwhelming predominance in South African political life is partly a result of its legitimacy as a national liberation movement in the struggle against apartheid. Its political authority also results from an extensive political organization, represented through local branches throughout the country. In every election since 1994 it has enjoyed a preponderant majority of voter support, at around two-thirds in parliamentary polls. In 2014, the ANC's 62.15 percent share of the vote resulted in an allocation of 249 seats in the National Assembly.

Even in its first terms in office, authoritarian tendencies within the ANC hardened. In 1997, amendments to the party constitution endorsed centralism and prohibited factionalism. This was supposed to make it difficult for caucuses to emerge around a policy position at odds with that of the leadership. Party officials also tried to promote authoritarian patterns of party discipline by appealing to a new Africanist advocacy of deference and respect for elders in society. However, the rank and file rebellion against Thabo Mbeki's effort to secure a third term as party president at its national conference in 2007 may have helped strengthen the ANC's commitment to internally democratic procedures.

Smaller Parties

In the most recent election, in May 2014, twelve opposition parties won votes. Of these only two will represent significant challenges to the ANC's parliamentary predominance. In the poll the Democratic Alliance continued its steady expansion of support, this time obtaining over 22 percent of the ballot and eighty-nine seats.

A new formation, positioning itself to the left of the ANC, the Economic Freedom Front obtained twenty-five seats with 6 percent of the vote. Meanwhile the ANC's old rival among Zulu-speaking voters in Kwa-Zulu Natal, Inkatha, continued its decline, losing support to a breakaway group, the National Freedom Party. The eight other parties that won seats in parliament each received less than one percent of the votes. Since 1994 the most conspicuous trend in opposition politics has been the expansion of the Democrats as well as the disappearance of the old ruling party during apartheid, the National Party. The National Party obtained more than 20 percent of the vote in 1994. In the next two polls, most of its support was captured by the Democrats. The National Party itself disbanded in 2006 and some of its leaders joined the ANC. The Inkatha Freedom Party's support also declined from its 1994 high point of 10 percent of the vote. A Congress of the People (COPE) was constituted by disaffected members of the ANC at the end of 2008 after the very divisive leadership election in which delegates voted to replace Thabo Mbeki with his former deputy, Jacob Zuma, and in the 2009 poll it obtained seven percent of the vote. Over the years other parties have included right-wing Afrikaner groups, parties drawing upon political networks established in the ethnic homelands during apartheid, and various fringe socialist and "black conscious" or "Africanist" nationalist groupings.

A common perception about South African elections is that their results reflect a racial or ethnic "census" with racial and ethnic identity supplying the main consideration in promoting voter choice. From this perspective, the ANC as the historic agency of black South African political emancipation can count on emotional loyalty among most black voters. Correspondingly, in this view, the ANC's main opponent, the Democratic Alliance draws its most firm adherents from middle-class voters in the white minority. This is changing, though. Black politics is not monolithic and the Democrats' electoral base includes significant shares of African and Coloured voters. Moreover, voters no longer identify quite so emotionally with parties. People are less likely to believe that they "belong" to a party or that it is "theirs," considerations that used to favor the ANC.[12]

The Democratic Alliance can trace its origins to an opposition group in the all-white parliament, twelve dissenting MPs who supported African enfranchisement. They formed the Progressive Party in 1959. Only one survived the 1961 election, Helen Suzman, and she became a lonely parliamentary opponent of apartheid and the ruling National Party as well as an advocate of civil rights until she was joined by six other MPs who were elected in 1974. Thereafter, the renamed Progressive Federal Party (PFP) became increasingly influential among white South Africans.

The PFP was criticized by black anti-apartheid groups for supporting an educational requirement for voting eligibility and its opposition to sanctions. But from 1984 onwards it began to recruit and form political alliances within the black and Coloured communities. The PFP renamed itself the Democratic Party in 1987 and subsequently absorbed into its parliamentary following several breakaway groups from the National Party. Campaigning principally around human rights issues in 1994, the Democratic Party (DP) performed badly, winning only seven seats with 1.73 percent of the vote. Five years later, the DP's "Fight Back" campaign capitalized on white and to a certain extent Indian and Coloured voters' anxieties arising from rising crime rates and affirmative action in favor of black people. The party won thirty-eight seats, capturing much of the NNP's former support. In 1995, the DP joined forces with the National Party as the Democratic Alliance to contest local elections. A merger was agreed but remained incomplete in 2001 when the NNP leadership announced its decision to support and participate in the government. Not all National Party members followed their leaders and the Democratic Alliance continued to claim that it represented most of the NNP's branches and fought the 2004 elections under the same name.

The Inkatha Freedom Party was established ostensibly as a Zulu cultural organization in 1975 by the KwaZulu homeland chief minister, Chief Mangosuthu Buthelezi. It won all the seats in the KwaZulu legislative assembly elections in 1978 and thenceforth ruled the homeland until KwaZulu's incorporation into the province of KwaZulu-Natal in 1994. Unlike other homeland parties, though, Inkatha projected itself as a militant liberation movement and enjoyed mass support among Zulu migrant communities around Johannesburg. It secured control of the KwaZulu-Natal provincial administration in 1994 and 1999, losing its dominance in 2004 though its members continue to serve in a coalition administration with the ANC. In all elections it presents itself as a national party, not an ethnic group and its parliamentary representation has substantially included non-Zulus. Programmatically, it shares many of the ANC positions except with respect to what it considers to the rights and prerogatives of "traditional leaders" as well as its emphasis on "self-help" and "self–reliance." Ideologically, party officials view their organization as conservatively predisposed and to the right of the ANC. Inkatha lost more ground in the 2014 election. Very much an organization constructed around the charismatic qualities of its founder and president, Mangosuthu Buthelezi, its reluctance to renew its leadership is one ingredient in its decline. Chief Buthelezi, now in his eighties, remains the movement's leader and continues to represent his organization in parliament. Divisions over the leadership issue contributed to the breakaway of the National Freedom Party. IFP's electoral support is mainly in rural districts within the Zulu royal kingdom but even here it is challenged by the ANC, particularly as Jacob Zuma's public persona is constructed around the same "traditionalist" Zulu values that Inkatha claims to defend: patriarchy, deference to age, martial virtues, and cattle-based pastoralism.

The Congress of the People (COPE) was the product of the first really significant disaffection within the modern ANC. In his efforts to win the ANC leadership Jacob Zuma derived substantial support from the ANC's Youth League, whose activists were drawn largely from unemployed youngsters. But he was also backed by the trade unions and the Communist Party. The Communist Party functions as a militant grouping within the ANC and it does not contest parliamentary elections, preferring instead to win influence as an ANC faction. Mbeki's resignation from the presidency, and the subsequent reshuffling of party offices and cabinet positions promoted the move to form a breakaway party by figures who had lost power in this contest and who believed that under Zuma, pushed by his supporters, the ANC would move away from centrist positions to embrace more radical policies. The new party took its name from the Congress of the People, the assembly in 1955 where the ANC adopted its Freedom Charter. In its ideological professions it would simultaneously lay claim to the Congress's heritage and also pose itself as a constitutional, law-abiding, and centrist alternative to the ANC. On the ground, though, it was personal loyalties that counted most among its supporters: in its Eastern Cape heartland COPE was constituted by breakaway ANC branches. Zuma's victory in the ANC succession contest had displaced a dominant group of notables with Eastern Cape origins associated with Mbeki and certainly loyalty to Mbeki was strongest in this province. But COPE did quite well elsewhere as well, garnering support mainly from former ANC voters, especially in the main urban centers.

After the 2009 election, Cope's fortunes foundered. Leadership quarrels over the use of party finances diverted attention from the task of building a structured organization. In two years its organized following halved. More tellingly, in the 2011 local elections it obtained a meager 2.2 percent of votes nationally. A succession of defections of party leaders was encouraged by the ANC strategy of welcoming COPE defectors back into its fold.

In the 2011 municipal elections, the DA won in excess of 24 percent of the vote countrywide. In doing this it was taking votes not just from rival opposition groups but also from the ANC, particularly in the main cities. It remains likely that black votes still constitute a minority of the party's support but they now represent a substantial and growing share. By the party's own calculations, 750,000 Africans voted for the DA in 2014. The Democrats are now led in parliament by Mmusi Maimane, very representative of the younger black middle class achievers who are the prime target of the DA's efforts to expand its vote. Maimane was born in Soweto in 1980. Educated a private Catholic secondary schools he obtained two masters degrees before lecturing at a business school. Helen Zille as the party's senior leader serves as premier of the Western Cape for in this province for a decade now, the Democratic Alliance has exercised executive power in running one of South Africa's wealthiest regional governments. In this province in which black Africans still constitute a minority the DA enjoys majority support. The party also controls Cape Town's metropolitan administration.

Zille is white but she speaks Xhosa fluently and since the inception of her premiership, the Democrats began making modest inroads even into the core ANC urban bases in working-class townships in the Western Cape and elsewhere. In fact, the DA has been trying since 2000 to cross the racially segmentary lines that appeared to confine party support in the 1994 election. In the area around Johannesburg, the DA had established by 2003 thirty-two branches in what it termed "emergent areas," that is, black townships or squatter camps. In 2003, DA and ANC local leaders traded accusations in newspaper letter columns that their opponents were disrupting their party's activities in Alexandra, traditionally an ANC stronghold. This indirectly confirmed that the DA was expanding into fresh territory. Since then, though, DA strategy has changed. Rather than concentrating on building organization in black townships, undertakings that in any case invite aggressive attention from ANC activists, DA planners now favor "relying on public relations as the primary driver of the party's popularity with voters" and they assign a low priority to the task "of establishing membership structures on the ground."[13] What has changed, of course, since the early 2000s, is the introduction of electronic social media as an instrument in communicating political messages. This is a medium in which the DA has played a pioneering role in South Africa.

What are its messages? Programmatically, the DA is somewhat to the right of the ANC, maintaining a firm commitment to free market economics. Hence, it is critical of the ANC's restrictive management of the economy, especially with respect to contractual rights accorded to workers that in its view curb job growth. It also opposes the government's enforcement of affirmative action though this is an issue on which there is disagreement within the party leadership between older white leaders and younger African middle-class democrats. But the party's appeal to voters probably derives from two main considerations. First, its often highly experienced parliamentarians have been in the forefront of efforts to exercise oversight with respect to official corruption and this has helped to make the party popular at a time when the ANC's venality has become much more conspicuous. The DA has exploited President Zuma's vulnerability on this score with relish. Helen Zille led a delegation to his ostentatious homestead at Inkandla "to inspect the project," a move that provoked outrage from local chiefs who told reporters "… we have arrived at a point where we say enough of this disrespectful white girl."[14]

The second source of the DA's electoral appeal and a consideration that differentiates it from any other opposition group is that the DA itself commands executive power, for it runs administrations in one provincial government and in several municipalities. In office, it has gained a reputation for honesty and effectiveness in the provision of public services both to middle-class households and to poorer communities. It was in the Western Cape under a DA administration that the first mass provision of antiretroviral medication was made available for HIV/AIDS patients at a time when the ANC national government was opposing such treatment. Incumbency in government also brings to the DA the power of patronage. Its ability to allocate funding and resources as well as make public appointments may well enhance its appeal to new supporters as well as help it to recruit plausible black leaders.

In the 2014 election, it is likely that most of the DA's million or so new votes came from Africans. The DA's gains were concentrated in Gauteng and Western Cape. Geographical analysis of the DA vote's distribution indicates that it is finally making significant inroads into certain African "township" neighborhoods; in the more middle class districts in Soweto, for example. Here its emphasis on its own black leadership as well as invective directed at corrupt ANC leaders appeared to have paid off.

The other main contender for African votes are the Economic Freedom Fighters. The Freedom Fighters purport to represent a left-wing alternative to the ANC. They advocate industrial nationalization and land seizures, although its left-wing credentials are belied by the lavish lifestyle and habits of its founder, Julius Malema, a millionaire beneficiary of preferential public contracting. Malema was expelled from the ANC after embarrassing its leaders by attacking what he called the "imperialist puppet" government of Botswana. As the president of the ANC's Youth League he had been very popular. Surveys have indicated that his new movement may attract a significant proportion of younger better-educated Black South Africans, university students for example, especially those frustrated by the continuing predominance white South Africans exercise over the professions. In the election EFF did comparatively well as one might expect in Malema's home province, in Limpopo. But they also drew significant support from the shanty settlements on Johanensburg's outskirts, a mongst the poorest and most recently urbanized. Between now and the next election, if the EFF holds together and strengthens its organization, it may well block the DA's advance toward becoming a major force within the ANC's traditional heartland.

Elections

South African elections are generally judged to be free and fair, and in certain respects they have become more so. All the available evidence suggests that voters are confident about ballot secrecy as well as the integrity of the count. Most importantly, it has become easier for candidates of all parties to canvass voters outside the areas where their core supporters live. In 1994, there were "no go" areas in which canvassers from certain parties were forcibly excluded by their competitors' activists and supporters. By 2004, though, each of the main parties were routinely deploying door-to-door canvassers in the same neighborhoods, sometimes at the same time. Low levels of voter registration remain a concern, though, with nearly a quarter of the eligible electorate unregistered. In 2013, the Independent Electoral Commission

Table 11.2	South African General Elections, 1994–2014				
Party	1994	1999	2004	2009	2014
African Christian Democratic Party	88,104 (0.45%)	228,976 (1.43%)	250,272 (1.60%)	142,658 (0.81%)	104,039 (0.57%)
African Independent Congress	–	–	–	–	97,642 (0.53%)
AgangSA	–	–	–	–	52,350 (0.28%)
ANC	12,237,655 (62.55%)	10,601,330 (66.35%)	10,880,915 (69.69%)	11,650,748 (65.90%)	11,650,000 (62.15%)
African People's Convention	–	–	–	–	30,076 (0.17%)
Congress of the People	–	–	–	1,311,027 (7.42%)	123,235 (0.67%)
Democratic Party/ Alliance	338,426 (1.73%)	1,527,337 (9.56%)	1,931,201 (12.37%)	2,945,829 (16.66%)	4,091,584 (22.23%)
Freedom Front	424,555 (2.17%)	127,217 (0.80%)	139,465 (0.89%)	146,796 (0.83%)	165,715 (0.90%)
Inkatha	2,058,294 (10.94%)	1,371,477 (8.58%)	1,088,664 (6.97%)	804,260 (4.55%)	441,854 (2.40%)
National Freedom Party	–	–	–	–	288,742 (1.57%)
New National Party	3,983,690 (20.39%)	1,098,215 (6.87%)	257,824 (1.65%)	–	–
Pan-Africanist Congress	243,478 (1.25%)	113,125 (0.71%)	113,512 (0.35%)	48,530 (0.27%)	37,784 (0.21%)
United Democratic Movement	–	546,790 (3.42%)	355,717 (2.28%)	149,680 (0.85%)	184,636 (1.00%)
Others	149,296 (0.81%)	362,676 (2.19%)	595,101 (3.80%)	480,416 (2.73%)	176,389 (0.96%)
Total Votes	**19,533,498**	**15,977,142**	**15,612,671**	**17,680,729**	**18,654,457**
Turnout of registered voters	–	89.30%	76.70%	77.30%	73.43%
Turnout of voting age population	86%	71.80%	57.80%	59.80%	59.3%

held a registration drive in which it hoped to match its performance in 2009, when it registered 2 million new voters. Again, around 2 million new voters joined the roll in 2009 but registration among young voters remained poor, with just under half the 20–29 age group registered to vote. The considerations that dissuade younger voters will be discussed in Section 5.

Both in the 2009 and in the 2014 elections a disturbing recent trend has been an increased tendency for ruling party speakers at mass meetings to suggest that electoral support will be rewarded with grants or other benefits. In 2014, on one or two occasions, the official agency responsible for distributing welfare benefits allocated food parcels at ANC rallies. Moreover in the run-up to formal campaigning, observers have noted an increased incidence of "robust" electioneering, including attacks on rival activists. There were twelve politically motivated killings between January 2013 and February 2014, mostly in KwaZulu Natal and mainly the effect of strife in the workers' hostels between Inkatha and the breakaway group, the National Freedom Party. The election season itself featured no real violence, though in their campaigning, leaders occasionally used inflammatory or threatening language. The DA's Helen Zille told one meeting that the ANC was "like a snake" and a DA leaflet suggested that the ANC wanted to stop coloured people getting jobs in the Western Cape. The ANC's Fikile Mbalula characterized the DA government in the Western Cape as "witches" that were "oppressing us." Not to be outdone, ANC deputy president Cyril Ramaphosa warned villagers in Limpopo, his home region, that a vote for the DA would be a vote for the return of the "boers" and Apartheid. In general, though, the weight of evidence suggests that the ANC continues to win victories through persuasive campaigning rather than as a consequence of coercion, threats, or untoward inducements.

Arguably, South Africa's electoral system promotes the formation of socially inclusive political parties and civil electioneering. South Africa uses a national list system of proportional representation. In national and provincial elections (held simultaneously every five years), parties nominate lists of candidates—one list for the National Assembly and one for each of the nine provinces. Voters use two ballot papers, one for the Assembly and one for their provincial legislature, on which they indicate their preferred party. In this way, voters can divide their support between two parties. Names of candidates do not appear on the ballot papers. Seats are allocated in proportion to each party's share of the votes. In South Africa, this electoral system in which the nation serves as a single national constituency for the parliament contains strong incentives for moderation because the electorate is so spread out. All parties are encouraged to seek votes outside their core support or base areas, a consideration that helps to encourage them to adopt programs with broad social appeal. Party leaders put people on their lists who might not win electoral contests that were focused around individual candidates: members of racial minorities or women, for example. As we have noted, though, the drawback is that parliamentarians hold their seats at the will of party leaders, and this has produced a parliament that tends to be unduly deferential toward the executive.

Political Culture, Citizenship, and Identity

Relatively high turnout rates in four out of five national elections were encouraging signs of strong citizenship identity among South Africans. Turnout fell sharply in 2004 but rose subsequently. During the Mandela administration, there were rising levels of approval and satisfaction with democracy, although opinion polls suggest such sentiments are less widely shared today. All pollsters agree that people are more likely to trust the national government than provincial or local authorities.

Opinion polls indicate that South Africans tend to believe that race relations have improved since 1994. But racial divisions continue to affect patterns of political support. Although public schools and middle-class neighborhoods have become desegregated, most black people still live in ghetto-like townships or in the historical homeland areas; racial distinctions still remain very conspicuous in South African social geography. However, since 1994, new patterns of public behavior seem to have created more conciliatory attitudes among South Africans. A national survey in 2004 found that 60 percent of South Africans believed that race relations were improving, and 30 percent thought they remained the same. Blacks were more likely than other groups to think that race relations were better. In general, perceptions about the future are becoming more optimistic among all groups.[15]

Even so, there remain sources of racial tension. The government is critical of what it takes to be the slow progress of black business, and ANC leaders routinely blame the absence of quicker social change on "white economic selfishness" (Thabo Mbeki's phrase). Class-based politics was generally quite comfortably accommodated within the ANC's fold during the anti-apartheid struggle, since most of its active followers were workers and their families, and the war against apartheid could be considered an offensive against capitalism. Even today, union leaders hold back from organizing a workers' party separately from the ANC, recognizing that many workers are likely to retain the loyalties fostered by decades of nationalist politics. However, populist racial invective directed against white privilege and wealth remains politically compelling, especially for leaders of the ANC's Youth League, with their constituency among unemployed school dropouts.

In the 1950s, a powerful women's movement developed within the ANC to oppose extending the pass laws to African women. More and more women were heading single-parent households, and many women were moving into industrial occupations and higher education, which led to feminist movements. One of the first major social reforms enacted by Mandela's government was legalizing abortion on demand. In general, the ANC's female members have forced the party to pay at least some attention to women's rights and entitlements.

Interest Groups, Social Movements, and Protest

Social movements continue to be unusually well organized for a developing country. Although participation at union meetings may have dwindled, labor unions have extensive financial resources, since dues are automatically deducted from workers' wages, and unions often organize entire economic sectors. The ranks of organized labor include 2.8 million.

In townships, residents' associations have created an impressive associational network. Surveys suggest that more people participate in civic associations than in political parties. From 2002, a new generation of local single-issue movements began to address the problems of landlessness, electricity cut-offs, and evictions of bond or municipal tax defaulters. Around these concerns a strong vein of assertive protest has gathered momentum in which the activist repertoire often includes forceful behavior that borders on the violent: damage to public buildings, tire-burning, and skirmishing with police. The frequency of "major service delivery protests" as monitored by the authorities has risen for a decade. Since 2007, research shows that between 2007 and 2012 the number of protests quintupled, peaking in 2012 with nearly 250 protests.[16] Participants tend to be young, often unemployed school dropouts. The focus of their anger is often the venality of local politicians, but the aggression can direct itself at more vulnerable targets. In 2008, sixty immigrants, mainly from Mozambique and Zimbabwe, were killed by xenophobic rioters in a series of incidents around Johannesburg. These murders were spurred by the widely shared conviction that foreigners were depriving local people of their jobs. Protest tends to be concentrated in the bigger cities, in poor neighborhoods, but by no means the most under-resourced, and often in areas that express electoral support for the ruling party. This suggests that forceful and even violent protest has become part of a bargaining repertoire in which citizens "alternate the brick (protest) and the pro-ANC ballot."[17] Official responses to such protests have recently deployed heavily armed police ready to fire into crowds: Marikana was an extreme version of confrontational public order enforcement favored by Jacob Zuma's police commanders.

Such behavior contrasts with gentler predispositions that seem to prevail in South African associational life. For example, surveys confirm that about half the population does voluntary work for charitable organizations. The proportion is higher among younger people.[18] With the exception of COSATU, which invites white participation, associational life remains racially segregated, however. Business organizations, for example, continue to represent white and black firms separately. The larger corporations are still perceived to represent white privilege. Churches may have racially integrated hierarchies, but most South Africans worship in racially exclusive congregations. Only black South Africans attend soccer games in significant numbers to watch the multiracial teams in the Premier Soccer League. Rugby and cricket fans remain predominantly white despite efforts within the sports administrations to make the teams more diverse. South African democracy is still weakened by divisions between ethnic groups that prevent people from recognizing common interests and shared enthusiasms.

The Political Impact of Technology

Most South Africans possess cell phones. This means that a majority of the population can access online information through using mobile phones, despite the uneven spread of broadband services. South Africa usage of social media and social networks is the highest on the continent. South Africans are among the top thirty nations signed up to Facebook.

This has yet to have the transformative political impact that information and communications technology (ICT) is believed to have achieved in other African political settings. In the "Arab Spring" of 2011, Facebook and other online networks played a key role in assembling people without previous activist experience. South of the Sahara, ICT-facilitated political activism is strongest in Kenya. For example, the *Huduma* group has developed "crowd sourcing" Internet platforms to encourage poor communities to complain about bad services. Crowd-sourced electoral monitoring was used during the Nigerian elections in 2011 to enable citizens to report any intimidation on their phones and this has helped to lower the customary level of electoral violence. Such usage of Internet communication aims to enhance democracy, but not all technology-driven activism is benign. In the bloody aftermath of the 2007 Kenyan elections, texting supplied a major channel for communicating hate messages and, in the fighting that followed, attacks were coordinated through cell phones.

In South Africa, political parties have been swift to open Facebook and Twitter accounts as well as draw upon a local social media network, Mxit, which can be accessed by people without smart phones. All parties tried to communicate with supporters through social media during the 2009 campaigning but the networks had a more telling effect in 2014. For the DA in particular, Facebook has become a major channel of communication with potential supporters, whereas the ANC still depends heavily on face-to-face canvassing, demonstrating its physical presence within core support localities. Election monitoring in South Africa is now facilitated by tablets and mobile phone communication, as in Nigeria, and development agencies have been using social media networks to reach vulnerable groups. For example the *UmNyango* project in KwaZulu Natal has encouraged rural women to report and act against domestic violence. New social movements that seek to mobilize the "militant poor," such as the shack dwellers' *Abahlali baseMjondolo*, use Facebook. However, social media in South Africa has yet to facilitate the networks that underpin nationally coordinated protest movements; insurgent activism remains localized.

Where Do You Stand?

What have been the ANC's main achievements as the ruling party since 1994?

What are the benefits and what are the shortcomings of one party predominating politically for such a long time?

SECTION 5

SOUTH AFRICAN POLITICS IN TRANSITION

▼ Focus Questions

- What are likely to be the long-term effects of HIV/AIDS in South Africa?

- In certain respects it has been easier to institute and consolidate democracy in South Africa than in many other developing countries that underwent democratic transitions in the 1980s and 1990s. Why?

Political Challenges and Changing Agendas

The impact of AIDS on South African society is hard to overestimate. More that 10 percent of the population is currently HIV-positive, 5.7 million people, according to UN figures. Four and a half million South Africans have already died of HIV/AIDS. Its victims tend to be between the ages of fifteen and fifty—the most economically active members of the population. Poor households that support AIDS patients can spend up to two-thirds of their income on the cost of care.[19]

South Africa's initial efforts to combat the spread of AIDS and deal with its effects were tentative and confused. Belatedly, a public education program, including the free distribution of condoms, began to promote awareness of the disease toward the end of the Mandela presidency. At the beginning of the program, however, education was presented as an alternative to medical treatment. Surveys suggested that AIDS awareness was not enough. It did not reduce the sexual behavior that spreads the disease.

In October 1998, the minister of health announced that the government would cease supplying antiretroviral drugs to hospitals that until then had prescribed them to pregnant women to prevent mother-to-child transmission of AIDS. The 80 million rand ($12 million) saving would be used instead for distributing 140 million contraceptives and training 10,000 teachers in life skills. One month later, Thabo Mbeki, who then was chairman of a ministerial committee on AIDS, defended the minister's decision by claiming that the drug concerned, azidothymidine (AZT), was "dangerously toxic." This was patently false.

Hostility to the public prescription of drugs stemmed from more complicated considerations, however. President Mbeki began expressing doubts about the scientific status of the disease in late 1999. He believed that conventional explanations about the disease's causes stemmed from racial prejudice. In 2001, Mbeki referred to the "insulting" theory that AIDS originated in Africa. In reality, Mbeki contended, South Africans who were dying of the illnesses that immune deficiency exposed them to (tuberculosis for example) were not victims of a virus; they were instead the casualties of poverty. Mbeki was aligning himself with a tiny minority of dissident scientists who have either denied AIDS' existence altogether or have disputed the causal link between HIV and AIDS. In 2000, the president established a panel to investigate the scientific evidence about the causes of AIDS.

Mbeki's skepticism about AIDS certainly undermined attempts to combat the pandemic. Between 1998 and 2001, public hospitals were prevented from using antiretroviral drugs, including nevirapine, a much cheaper alternative to AZT—even for treating rape victims. But several provinces, including two ANC administrations in the Eastern Cape and Gauteng, resumed using nevirapine quite widely during 2001. However, most provincial health ministers loyally maintained the ban, firing doctors who questioned such policy. Taking their cue from the president, cabinet ministers began questioning AIDS statistics and projections, suggesting that these derived from faulty sampling procedures. After the Treatment Action Campaign successfully obtained a Constitutional Court judgment compelling the government to use nevirapine, ANC nominees on the Medical Control Council began warning that the drug might need to be deregistered on grounds of toxicity. Although in August 2002, in response to internal pressures within the ANC, the cabinet appeared to commit itself to provision of antiretroviral treatment, the health ministry resisted. The Treatment Action Campaign organized a civil disobedience protest during 2003 against the delay.

Full compliance with the Court's decision only began after Mbeki's fall from power. By 2009, with a new health minister in charge, 850,000 patients were receiving medication and around 2 million are today, about two-thirds of those who need it, at an annual cost of R18 billion (US$ 1.8 billion). Today the major challenges are administrative: to manage the scale of the treatment required, the health service has recruited 50,000 new workers and health spending increased from 11.9 percent of the budget in 2009/10 to 13.1 percent in 2012/13. But despite additional resources, clinics and hospitals remain overcrowded and poorly equipped. Treatment and the necessary counseling that ensure patient adherence to the drugs regime depends on the services of 60,000 auxiliary community health workers. They are paid token gratuities of R1000 a month and have become increasingly disaffected. But after Zuma himself publically underwent an AIDs test, the leadership's support for an effective program to counter the pandemic is no longer in doubt. This political turnaround has apparently helped to change public behavior: within one year, 10 million people had undergone testing. Infection rates have been on the decline, especially among younger South Africans since 2006, a consequence, experts believe, of increased condom usage and more successful preventive education. Even so, 300,000 additional people every year become HIV-positive, and millions of South Africans will remain acutely dependent on effective public health care for decades to come.

Economic Challenges

Despite increasing death rates among the economically active, high-level unemployment is likely to persist. HIV/AIDS cuts already low saving rates and accentuates the shortages of skilled workers. Every year, half a million students leave high school without graduating. When they enter the labor market without skills, they ensure that unemployment will remain at high levels for a long time.

Modern governments are not in the business of creating jobs, Mbeki's ministers used to claim that the removal of subsidies and tariffs would encourage more competitive industries. In their view, South Africa had adopted the "correct macro financial policy fundamentals." Critics replied that one factor that deterred investors—high crime rates—was partly the result of the government's failure to undertake thorough police reform. Fairly modest levels of public debt compared to that of most other developing countries prompted left-wing economists to suggest that heavier foreign borrowing might finance higher levels of public investment in services and fighting poverty, as well as stimulate the kinds of growth rates needed to reduce unemployment significantly. This advice may have had some impact. After 2004, during Mbeki's second term, foreign loan–funded investment in infrastructure did help to expand employment, although mainly in short-term construction jobs.

Government social expenditure has helped to soften the effects of poverty, but social inequality is more acute than it was in 1994. Absolute poverty has probably receded a little given the construction of nearly 3 million houses now inhabited by poor people and the much wider distribution of welfare grants.

Agricultural landownership is one domain, however, in which white privileges remain especially visible, and so far the government has made only gradual progress to change racial patterns of landholding. Since 2000, a succession of illegal land occupations has underlined how volatile landlessness can be as a political issue, especially when many Africans bitterly remember being forced off the land. South African land reform is based on a principle of paying market-level prices to landowners. Even when historically dispossessed communities win back their original land rights, the process of restitution is subject to protracted negotiations over compensation.

The prospects for South Africa's transitional democracy will be fragile if its political institutions are too frequently used to protect property rights. On the other hand, it is also possible that constitutional arguments help the poor and helpless by raising awareness of their circumstances. Defending and extending democracy may become much more challenging, however, if resources available for public services become scarcer and it becomes more difficult to decide who should receive them. Polls confirm that the South African public's ideas of democracy emphasize improvements in living conditions. In other words, people associate democracy with the provision of livelihoods and basic necessities. They attach less importance to its institutional and political dimensions. In this sense, the challenges of governing the economy and deepening the democratic idea come together in ways that define politics in South Africa today.

Youth Politics and the Generational Divide

Young South Africans are becoming better educated: The 2011 Census indicated that the proportion of population aged 20 years and older with no schooling had halved between 1996 and 2011 and those completing secondary education had nearly doubled. Overall, about half the population is below the age of 24, though the youngest group—aged between 0 and 14—has proportionately decreased, a finding that suggests a slowing growth rate. For the last decade the proportion of young people aged 15 to 24 seeking work is steadily increasing, totaling around 53 percent in 2011. South Africa has one of the highest rates of youth unemployment in the world. Recent opinion polls show higher rates of distrust of politicians and lower levels of party identification among the youngest South Africans who are eligible for voting. For example, nearly two-thirds of youth believed corruption had increased sharply during 2012.[20]

This is South Africa's first "born free" generation, that is, the first cohort entering adulthood who grew up in the decades following the democratic transition. They attach less political significance to anti-apartheid history. As noted above, registration statistics suggest that the 18–24 age group is the least inclined to vote. When members of this group do vote, they are likely to change their support from one party to another between elections.

Contradicting the more general trend of disengagement with organized politics among young people has been the expansion within the ANC of its Youth League's influence. Much of its membership is young men in their early 20s who live in the poorest districts, often in the countryside. The League supported Jacob Zuma's ascendency but it turned against Zuma when top ANC leaders opposed its calls for mining nationalization and land redistribution, the most important demands in the Economic Freedom Fighters' program. The EFF's Facebook page is reported to have the largest impact of any party, with an estimated 56,000 users in 2013.

Young people are conspicuously in the forefront of a new mass-based shack dwellers movement, *Abahlali baseMjondolo*, based in the townships around Durban, which claims a following of 10,000; there is certainly potential space to the left of the ANC for youth activism.

South African Politics in Comparative Perspective

Unlike many of the countries that moved from authoritarian regimes to democratic governments in the late 1980s and early 1990s, South Africa's political economy was developed through a settler minority that became a permanent part of its population. This made the transition to democracy both easier and more challenging.

Between two world wars, a politically independent settler state could invest the revenues from the local production of primary commodities to develop a relatively diversified industrial economy. It expropriated land from its African subjects and recruited some of their members to create a modern working class. Later, unlike many former colonial countries in Africa, well-organized social forces could mobilize to support democratization, in particular the African trade unions, whose members worked on industrial assembly lines even under apartheid. Democratic politics within the white settler minority prompted wider kinds of political organization across the population almost from the beginning of South Africa's Act of Union in 1910. Today, the organizations represented in the South African parliament are among the oldest political parties in the developing world. Ironically, despite its often brutal efforts during the apartheid era to promote ethnic division, the South African state probably was a more decisive influence in stimulating a national identity throughout most of the twentieth century than was the case for many more benign governments elsewhere in the colonial and postcolonial world.

Nevertheless, South African society was deeply divided in the 1990s, at the beginning of democratization. Except for the churches, most institutions and organizations were segmented, separated, or stratified by race. In addition, economic inequalities between rich and poor were among the most extreme in the world, and this injustice was reinforced by the fact that inequalities ran along racial lines.

In certain respects, South African democratization represents a success story. The national government has created trust among citizens. Its political procedures are recognized to be fair, and political leaders have generally observed its rules. A constitution that was designed to be socially inclusive has fostered widely representative institutions. Popular support of the government is partly a result of its efforts to extend services to poor people, distribute resources fairly, and expand and improve infrastructure and education. Relatively well-managed public finance encouraged a revival of GDP growth, earning for South Africa recognition as one of the most important emerging economies.

One reason that democratization since 1994 has brought about more effective governance is that it was preceded by a long process of political and economic reform. The dismantling of the tariffs and subsidies that nurtured and protected industry and commercial agriculture began more than a decade before the universal right to vote. Unlike in the countries of the post-communist world, the coming of democracy did not bring sudden exposure to the harsh shocks of international competition. Economic liberalization has continued at a relatively measured pace compared to the experience of many Third World countries, which have been compelled to undergo very rapid structural adjustment of their economies. The welfare state created under apartheid has maintained many of its provisions and even extended some of them, in sharp contrast to the shrinking scope of social services offered by most governments in the developing world.

Similarly, political liberalization preceded universal enfranchisement over a relatively long period. Industrial relations reform enabled black trade unions to participate in institutionalized collective bargaining through the 1980s. This encouraged the growth of well-structured associational life, both inside and outside the workplace, which reinvigorated older political organizations. Elsewhere, new democracies have been fragile because they have not had strong representative movements and parties. In South Africa, constitutional negotiations did not take place in a political vacuum or in a situation of near state collapse. Until the 1994 elections, the apartheid state retained effective authority, and because the negotiations that moved the country toward democracy unfolded over several years, the settlement elicited a high degree of consensus.

Will South Africa manage to deal with its economic challenges under democratic conditions? To redress poverty and reduce inequality significantly, the state will have to make much more serious inroads into minority privileges. Although the constitution obligates government to meet basic needs of citizens, it was also designed to reassure economically dominant groups that their interests would be safeguarded under democracy. It is likely that the constitution will become increasingly challenged if the government attempts to address inequality through expanding the scope of administrative regulation, for example, through compulsory purchases to accelerate land reform, for example. Meanwhile, increasing social inequality supplies a setting in when poor people confront authority officials can respond with extreme violence, as was so evident at Marikana.

Where Do You Stand?

What are the prospects for South African political stability?

Why does South Africa's social inequality matter?

Chapter Summary

A unified South Africa was established in the aftermath of the Anglo-Boer War of 1899–1902. A modern administration was geared to providing cheap labor to the gold mining industry and restricted African access to land. In the decades following Union, white workers succeeded in gaining privileges as citizens, but the status of black South Africans deteriorated. Afrikaner nationalists held office from 1948 and established a strict regime of racial apartheid. Popular African resistance was suppressed in 1960. In exile, the main African movements embraced guerrilla warfare. From 1976 onwards, urbanization, industrialization, and mass literacy prompted powerful challenges to white minority rule. In 1990, in response to insurgency and international pressure, the South African political leadership lifted the ban on the main African political organizations and began to negotiate a political settlement. In 1994 a democratically elected government began attempting to reduce poverty and inequality while also encouraging economic regeneration.

Racial segregation required considerable state intervention in the economy. In particular until 1986 the state restricted Africans' mobility, in order to ensure adequate supplies of cheap black labor for mining and agriculture. State-owned enterprises, however, helped to develop a substantial manufacturing sector. From the 1970s, external anti-apartheid pressures as well as shortages of crucial skills began to prompt liberalization. Even before the advent of universal suffrage in 1994, most apartheid restrictions had been dismantled. Since then, democratic governments have continued to expand economic liberalization, reducing tariffs and selling public enterprises. Rising unemployment, partly a consequence of market reform, constrains the government's efforts to reduce poverty.

For the post-apartheid transition period, between 1994 and 1999, a power-sharing coalition helped to reassure racial minorities. Nine provincial governments give South African politics a quasi-federal character and offer smaller political parties the possibility of executive office. Despite such safeguards, the ruling party and its leaders are very powerful because of large ANC majorities in the National Assembly. Presidential authority gains strength from an electoral system that makes members of parliament very dependent on the party leadership. Continuing shortcomings in the police, the judicial system, and the provincial administrations effectively limit executive power. Meanwhile policy-making has become increasingly centralized.

On the whole, members of the post-apartheid parliament within the ruling party have failed to exercise formal oversight. The African National Congress inherited from an eighty-year liberation struggle a tightly centralized organizational structure and a mass following that was grouped into an extensive network of branches. It remains the predominant organization among black South Africans. Any effective challenge to its authority will require smaller parties, historically based among racial or ethnic minorities, to draw away significant numbers of the ANC's core support. This is only now beginning to happen. South Africa may represent a racially divided dominant-party democracy, but elections are fair, and strong social movements increase the prospects of democratic consolidation.

The four main challenges to South Africa's political leadership are HIV/AIDS, unemployment, social inequality, and political disaffection among young people. Extreme social inequality as well as official venality may reduce public support for democracy and open up opportunities for populist authoritarian politics. Government efforts to alleviate poverty with high social spending may be difficult to sustain if growth levels remain modest.

Key Terms

Africans
Afrikaner
apartheid
Boer
democratization
economic deregulation

homelands
influx control
migrant laborers
pass laws
power sharing
sanctions

settler state
township
Umkhonto-we-Sizwe
voortrekkers

Suggested Readings

Booysen, Susan. *The African National Congress and the Regeneration of Political Power*. Johannesburg: Wits University Press, 2011.

Calland, Richard. *The Zuma Years: South Africa's Changing Face of Power*. Cape Town: Zebra Press, 2013.

Feinstein, Andrew. *After the Party: Corruption, the ANC and South Africa's Uncertain Future*. London: Verso, 2009.

Fourie, Pieter. *The Political Management of HIV and AIDS in South Africa*. New York: Palgrave Macmillan, 2006.

Gibson, James L. *Overcoming Apartheid: Can Truth Reconcile a Divided Nation?* New York: Russell Sage Foundation, 2004.

Gumede, William Mervin. *Thabo Mbeki and the Battle for the Soul of the ANC.* Cape Town: Zebra Press, 2005.

Lodge, Tom. *Sharpeville: An Apartheid Massacre and its Consequences.* Oxford: Oxford University Press, 2011.

Mandela, Nelson. *Long Walk to Freedom.* New York: Little, Brown, 1994.

Marx, Anthony. *Making Race and Nation: A Comparison of the United States, South Africa and Brazil.* Cambridge: Cambridge University Press, 1998.

Seekings, Jeremy. *The UDF: A History of the United Democratic Front in South Africa, 1983–1991.* Athens: Ohio University Press, 2000.

Welsh, David. *The Rise and Fall of Apartheid.* Charlottesville: University of Virginia Press, 2009.

Suggested Websites

Electoral Institute for Sustainability of Democracy in Africa
http://www.eisa.org.za

South African Institute of Race Relations
http://www.sairr.org.za

Statistics South Africa
http://beta2.statssa.gov.za/

12 Nigeria

Darren Kew and Peter Lewis

Official Name: Federal Republic of Nigeria

Location: Western Africa

Capital City: Abuja

Population (2014): 177.2 million

Size: 923,768 sq. km.; slightly more than twice the size of California

CHRONOLOGY | of Nigerian Political Development

1960
| Independence. Nigeria consists of three regions under a Westminster parliamentary model. Abubakar Tafawa Balewa, a northerner, is the first prime minister.

January 1966
| Civilian government deposed in coup. General Aguiyi Ironsi, an Igbo, becomes head of state.

1967–1970
| Biafran civil war

July 1975
| Military coup deposes Gowan; led by General Murtala Muhammed, a northerner.

February 1976
| Murtala Muhammed assassinated in failed coup led by Middle Belt minorities. Muhammed's second-in-command, General Olusegun Obasanjo, a Yoruba, assumes power.

October 1979
| Elections held. A majority in both houses is won by NPN, led by northern/Hausa-Fulani groups. Alhaji Shehu Shagari is elected Nigeria's first executive president.

June 12, 1993
| Moshood Abiola wins presidential elections, but Babangida annuls the election eleven days later.

July–September 1994
| Prodemocracy strike by the major oil union, NUPENG, cuts Nigeria's oil production by an estimated 25 percent. Sympathy strikes ensue, followed by arrests of political and civic leaders.

| 1960 | 1965 | 1970 | 1975 | 1980 | 1985 | 1990 | 1995 |

July 1966
Countercoup is led by General Yakubu Gowan (an Anga, from the Middle Belt) with aid from northern groups.

November 1993
Defense Minister General Sani Abacha seizes power in a coup. Two years later he announces a three-year transition to civilian rule, which he manipulates to have himself nominated for president in 1998.

August 1993
Babangida installs Ernest Shonekan as "interim civilian president" until new presidential elections could be held later that autumn.

August 1985
Buhari is overthrown by General Ibrahim B. Babangida, a Middle Belt Muslim, in a palace coup. Babangida promises a return to democracy by 1990, a date he delays five times before being forced from office.

December 1983
Military coup led by General Muhammadu Buhari, a northerner

September 1978
New constitution completed, marking the adoption of the U.S. presidential model in a federation with 19 states

Spring 2002

The Supreme Court passes several landmark judgments, overturning a PDP-biased 2001 electoral law, and ruling on the control of offshore oil and gas resources. In November the Court opens the legal door for more parties to be registered.

April–May 2007

The ruling PDP again takes a vast majority of election victories across the nation amid a deeply compromised process. Umaru Musa Yar'Adua becomes president. Yar'Adua promises reform, but spends his first year trying to solidify his tenuous hold on power.

June 1998

General Abacha dies; succeeded by General Abdulsalami Abubakar, a Middle Belt Muslim from Babangida's hometown. Abubakar releases nearly all political prisoners and installs a new transition program. Parties are allowed to form unhindered.

May 2006

President Obasanjo tries to amend the constitution to allow himself a third term in office, but is defeated by the National Assembly.

April 2011

Jonathan wins the presidential election despite opposition from Northern factions for violating an informal ethnic rotation principle. The PDP again takes the majority of contests, but improved elections under a reformist chairman allow opposition parties to make some inroads.

February 2015

Nationwide elections are scheduled, promising a titanic struggle between the PDP and APC at all levels of government.

1999	2000	2005	2007	2011	2012	2020

1999

Former head of state Olusegun Obansanjo and his party, the Peoples Democratic Party (PDP), sweep the presidential and National Assembly elections, adding to their majority control of state and local government seats. The federation now contains thirty-six states.

August 2002

The National Assembly begins impeachment proceedings against President Obasanjo over budgetary issues. The matter ends by November, with the president apologizing.

2011

A formerly minor Islamist movement, dubbed Boko Haram by the media, resurfaces with even greater tactical sophistication in the northeast after being crushed by the military in 2009, and launches a stunning bombing campaign across the northeast, even striking the UN headquarters in Abuja. President Jonathan declares a state of emergency in three northeast states in 2013, and a military counteroffensive hems the insurgency inside its core area of operations around Borno and Yobe states, but military scorched-earth tactics result in heavy civilian casualties.

2013

The four main opposition parties merge to form the All Progressives Congress (APC), creating the first major threat to PDP rule since the start of the Fourth Republic in 1999. Six PDP governors defect, giving the APC control of nearly have the state governments and federal House seats, and a majority in the federal Senate.

November 1999

Zamfara state in the north is the first of twelve to institute the *shari'a* criminal code, resulting in Muslim-Christian communal conflicts in several of these states over the next two years. That same month, President Obasanjo sends the army to the Niger Delta town of Odi to root out local militias, leveling the town in the process. The military remains engaged in regular skirmishes with Niger Delta militias throughout the next decade, until President Yar'Adua reaches an agreement with the militants and offers them amnesty in 2009.

January 2012

Massive public demonstrations, which civil society activists call Occupy Nigeria, peacefully fill the streets of Lagos, Kano, Abuja, and other major urban areas to protest the president's removal of a fuel price subsidy. Social media plays a key role for the organizers, many of who are from the nation's growing middle class professionals. Trade unions, however, form the key muscle for strikes that bring the nation to a standstill for two weeks, and when the unions agree to a partial restoration of the fuel subsidy, the demonstrations collapse.

May 2010

President Yar'Adua dies in office, after several months incapacitated in a Saudi hospital. Vice President Goodluck Jonathan assumes the presidency.

THE MAKING OF THE MODERN NIGERIAN STATE

Politics in Action

- What are some of the key impacts that colonialism and military rule left on the development of the Nigerian state?

- What role has ethnicity played in the development of Nigeria's political parties, and in the collapse of Nigeria's First Republic and descent into civil war?

In late November 2009, President Umaru Musa Yar'Adua collapsed for at least the third time since coming to office in 2007 from an ailment that he had never fully explained to the nation. He was rushed unconscious to a hospital in Saudi Arabia, and only his wife and a handful of his closest advisors saw him directly. For over three months, Nigerians had no direct evidence that their president was conscious or alive, and even his own ministers and a delegation of senators were refused access. Government activity at the federal level ground to a halt.

Shockingly, for the first two months, neither the National Assembly nor the cabinet raised any public concern that the nation in effect had no president. The First Lady and the president's inner circle released occasional statements that the president was recovering well, but prevented any direct contact with him and blocked all attempts to have Vice President Jonathan step in as acting president as the constitution directs. Finally, under both international pressure and the threat of a military coup, the National Assembly declared Jonathan Acting President in February 2010. President Yar'Adua returned to the country shortly thereafter, but was clearly too ill to govern, and he passed away in May 2010. Goodluck Jonathan then was sworn in as president.

The fact that Nigeria could persist for months without a functioning president, during which time his wife and a few advisors could seek to run the country themselves—and that they would go largely unchallenged—speaks volumes about the state of the nation's politics. Democratization in Nigeria—15 years after the exit of the military from power—has yet to produce good governance. Instead, authoritarian rule has given way to competitive oligarchy, in which an increasingly greedy, oil-rich political elite fight to expand their power, while more than 90 percent of Nigerians struggle to survive on less than two U.S. dollars per day. This impoverished majority is so disenfranchised by the state that their president could disappear for months, and a small cabal could hold the nation hostage, without much public outcry.

Under the surface of this fiasco, however, were some important signs that a decade of democracy has had some impact. First and foremost, throughout the crisis, as opposition grew it insisted on the constitution as the framework for resolving the dispute. Ultimately, elites turned to the National Assembly, not the military, and military leaders rejected pressure from some junior officers to stage a coup.

Nigeria thus encapsulates many characteristics that more broadly identify Africa, as the young democracy faces the challenge of managing the country's contentious ethnic and religious diversity in conditions of scarcity and weak institutions, while facing the constant struggle between **authoritarian** and democratic governance, the push for development amidst persistent underdevelopment, the burden of public corruption, and the pressure for accountability. Nigeria, like most other African countries, has sought to create a viable nation-state out of the incoherence created by its

authoritarian

A system of rule in which power depends not on popular legitimacy but on the coercive force of the political authorities.

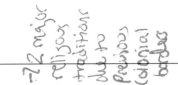

colonial borders. More than 250 competing ethnic groups, crosscut by two major religious traditions, have repeatedly clashed over economic and political resources. The result: a Nigeria with low levels of popular legitimacy and **accountability,** and a persistent inability to meet the most basic needs of its citizens. Nigeria today remains an **unfinished state** characterized by instabilities and uncertainties. Will Nigeria return to the discredited path of authoritarianism and greater underdevelopment, or will the civilian leadership rise to achieve a consolidated democracy and sustainable growth?

Geographic Setting

Nigeria, with 160 million people inhabiting 356,669 square miles, is the most populous nation in Africa. A center of West African regional trade, culture, and military strength, Nigeria borders four countries—Benin, Niger, Chad, and Cameroon. Nigeria, like nearly all African states, is barely over a half-century old.

Nigeria was a British colony from 1914 until 1960. Nigeria's boundaries had little to do with the borders of the precolonial African societies, and merely marked the point

accountability

A government's responsibility to its population, usually by periodic popular elections, transparent fiscal practices, and by parliament's having the power to dismiss the government by passing a motion of no confidence. In a political system characterized by accountability, the major actions taken by government must be known and understood by the citizenry.

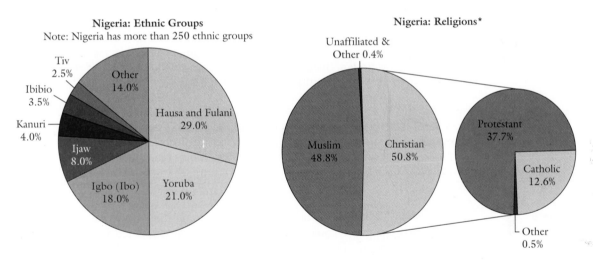

Languages: English (official), Hausa, Yoruba, Igho (Ibo), Fulani, 100–200 additional indigenous

Nigerian Currency

Niara (₦)
International Designation: NGN
Exchange Rate (2010): 1 US$ = 150.88 NGN
500 Naira Note Design: Aliyu Mai-Bornu (1919–1970) and Clement Isong (1920–2000), economists and governors of the Central Bank of Nigeria

FIGURE 12.1 The Nigerian Nation at a Glance
© iStockphoto.com/Johnny Greig (for photo)

Table 12.1	Political Organization
Political System	Federal republic
Regime History	Democratic government took office in May 1999, after sixteen years of military rule. The most recent national elections were held in 2011.
Administrative Structure	Nigeria is a federation of thirty-six states, plus the Federal Capital Territory (FCT) in Abuja. The three tiers of government are federal, state, and local. Actual power is centralized under the presidency and the governors.
Executive	U.S.-style presidential system, under Goodluck Jonathan
Legislature	A bicameral civilian legislature was elected in April 2011. The 109 senators are elected on the basis of equal representation: three from each state, and one from the FCT. The 360 members of the House of Representatives are elected from single-member districts.
Judiciary	Federal, state, and local court system, headed by the Federal Court of Appeal and the Supreme Court, which consists of fifteen appointed associate justices and the chief justice. States may establish a system of Islamic law (*shari'a*) for cases involving only Muslims in customary disputes (divorce, property, etc.). Most Nigerian states feature such courts, which share a Federal Court of Appeal in Abuja. Non-Muslim states may also set up customary courts, based on local traditional jurisprudence. Secular courts retain supreme jurisdiction if conflict arises between customary and secular courts.
Party System	Nearly fifty parties have been registered by the Nigerian electoral commission since 2002. The largest are the People's Democratic Party (PDP) and the All Progressives Congress (APC), which together control all but two states of the federation. PDP won the presidency and a slight majority of governorships, but defections from the PDP have given the APC control of the Senate.

unfinished state

A state characterized by instabilities and uncertainties that may render it susceptible to collapse as a coherent entity.

where British influence ended and French began. Britain ruled northern and southern Nigeria as two separate colonies until 1914, when it amalgamated its Northern and Southern Protectorates. In short, Nigeria was an arbitrary creation reflecting British colonial interests. This forced union of myriad African cultures and ruling entities under one political roof remains a central feature of Nigerian political life today.

Nigeria is a hub of regional activity. Its population is nearly 60 percent of West Africa's total. Nigeria's gross domestic product (GDP) typically represents more than half of the total GDP for the entire subregion. It is one of the few countries in the world that is evenly divided religiously, half Muslim and half Christian.

Nigeria includes six imprecisely defined "zones." The Hausa, Nigeria's largest ethnic group, dominate the northwest (or "core North"). The northeast consists of minority groups, the largest of whom are the Kanuri. Both northern regions are predominantly Muslim. The Middle Belt includes minority groups, both Muslim and Christian. The southwest is dominated by the country's second-largest ethnic group, the Yoruba, who are approximately 40 percent Muslim, 50 percent Christian (primarily Protestant), and 10 percent practitioners of Yoruba traditional beliefs. The southeast is the Igbo homeland, Nigeria's third largest group, who are primarily Christian. Between the Yoruba and Igbo regions is the southern minority zone, which stretches across the Niger Delta areas and east along the coast as far as Cameroon.

Critical Junctures

Nigeria's recent history reflects influences from the precolonial period, the crucial changes caused by British colonialism, the postcolonial alternation of military and civilian rule, and the economic collapse from 1980 to 2000, caused by political corruption and overreliance on the oil industry, which has been reinforced by the post–2003 oil boom.

The Precolonial Period (800–1900)

In contrast to the forest belt to the south, the more open terrain in the north, with its need for irrigation, encouraged the early growth of centralized states. Such states from the eighth century included Kanem-Bornu and the Hausa states. Another attempt at state formation led to the Jukun kingdom, which by the end of the seventeenth century was a subject state of the Bornu Empire.

Trade across the Sahara Desert with northern Africa shaped developments in the savanna areas of north. Trade brought material benefits as well as Arabic education and Islam, which gradually replaced traditional spiritual, political, and social practices. In 1808, the Fulani, from lands west of modern Nigeria, fought a holy war (*jihad*), and established the Sokoto Caliphate, which used Islam and a common

jihad

Literally "struggle." Although often used to mean armed struggle against unbelievers, it can also mean to fight against sociopolitical corruption or a spiritual struggle for self-improvement.

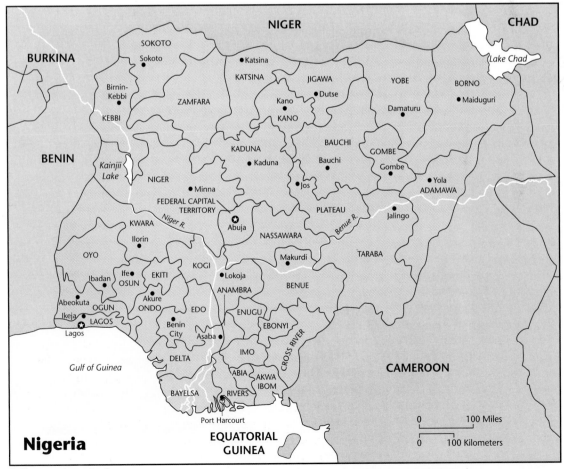

Nigeria

© Cengage Learning®

language, Hausa, to unify the disparate groups in the north. The Fulani Empire held sway until British colonial authority was imposed on northern Nigeria by 1900.

Toward the southern edge of the savanna, politics generally followed kinship lines. Political authority was so diffuse that later Western contacts described them as "stateless," or **acephalous societies**. Because such groups as the Tiv lacked complex political hierarchies, they escaped much of the upheaval experienced under colonialism by the centralized states, and retained much of their autonomy.

Southern Nigeria included the highly centralized Yoruba empires and the kingdoms of Oyo and Ife; the Edo kingdom of Benin in the Midwest; the acephalous societies of the Igbo to the east; and the trading city-states of the Niger Delta and its hinterland, peopled by a wide range of ethnicities.

Several precolonial societies had democratic elements that might have led to more open and participatory polities had they not been interrupted by colonialism. Governance in the Yoruba and Igbo communities involved principles of accountability and representation. Among the Islamic communities of the north, political society was highly structured, reflecting local interpretations of Qur'anic principles. Leadership structures were considerably more hierarchical than those of the south, and women were typically consigned to subordinate political status. The Islamic Fulani Empire was a confederation in which the rulers, emirs, owed allegiance to the sultan, who was the temporal and spiritual head of the empire. The sultan's powers, in turn, were limited by his duty to observe Islamic principles.

acephalous societies

Literally "headless" societies. A number of traditional Nigerian societies, such as the Igbo in the precolonial period, lacked executive rulership as we have come to conceive of it. Instead, the villages and clans were governed by committee or consensus.

[handwritten margin note: colonialism ruined many chances at open/democratic polities]

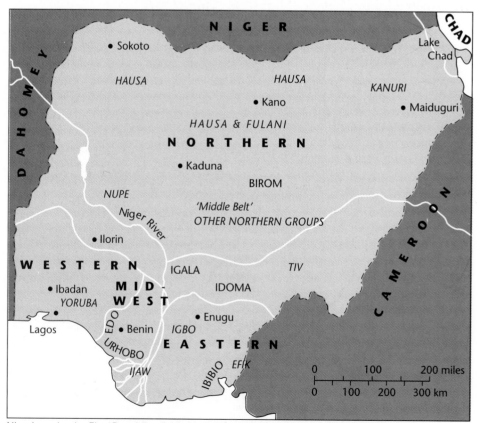

Nigeria under the First Republic, divided into four regions, with the massive Northern Region encompassing two-thirds of the nation's territory and more than half its population.

© Cengage Learning®

Colonial Rule and Its Impact (1860–1945)[1]

Competition for trade and empire drove the European imperial powers further into Africa. Colonial rule deepened the extraction of Nigeria's natural resources and the exploitation of Nigerian labor. Colonialism left its imprint on all aspects of Nigeria's political and economic systems.

Where centralized monarchies existed in the north, the British ruled through **indirect rule**, which allowed traditional structures to persist as subordinates to the British governor and a small administrative apparatus. With more dispersed kingships, as among the Yoruba, or in acephalous societies, particularly among the Igbo and other groups in the southeast, the colonizers either strengthened the authority of traditional chiefs and kings or appointed **warrant chiefs** (who ruled by warrant of the British Crown), weakening the previous practices of accountability and participation.

The British played off ethnic and social divisions to keep Nigerians from developing organized political resistance to colonial rule. When resistance did develop, the colonizers were not afraid to employ repressive tactics, even as late as the 1940s. Yet the British also promoted the foundations of a democratic political system. This dual standard left a conflicted democratic idea: formal democratic institutions within an authoritarian political culture. Colonialism also strengthened the collective identities of Nigeria's multiple ethnic groups by fostering political competition among them, primarily among the three largest: the Hausa, Yoruba, and Igbo.

Divisive Identities: Ethnic Politics under Colonialism (1945–1960)

Based on their experience under British rule, leaders of the anticolonial movement came to regard the state as an exploitative instrument. Its control became an opportunity to pursue personal and group interests rather than broad national interests. When the British began to negotiate a gradual exit from Nigeria, the semblance of unity among the anticolonial leaders soon evaporated. Intergroup political competition became increasingly fierce.

Nigerian leaders quickly turned to support. The three largest ethnic groups, the Hausa, Igbo, and Yoruba, though each a numeric minority, together comprise approximately two-thirds of Nigeria's population. They have long dominated the political process. By pitting ethnic groups against each other for purposes of divide and rule, and by structuring the administrative units of Nigeria based on ethnic groups, the British ensured that ethnicity would be the identification and mobilization.

With the encouragement of ambitious leaders, however, these groups took on a more political character. Nigeria's first political party, the National Council of Nigeria and the Cameroons (later the National Convention of Nigerian Citizens, NCNC), initially drew supporters from across Nigeria. As independence approached, however, elites began to divide along ethnic lines to mobilize support for their differing political agendas.

In 1954, the British divided Nigeria into a federation of three regions with elected governments. Each region soon fell under the domination of one of the major ethnic groups and their respective parties. The Northern Region came under the control of the Northern People's Congress (NPC), dominated by Hausa-Fulani elites. In the southern half of the country, the Western Region was controlled by the Action Group (AG), which was controlled by Yoruba elites. The Igbo, the numerically dominant group in the Eastern Region, were closely associated with the NCNC, which became the ruling party there.

Chief Obafemi Awolowo, leader of the AG, captured the sentiment of the times when he wrote in 1947, "Nigeria is not a nation. It is a mere geographical expression. There are no 'Nigerians' in the same sense as there are 'English,' 'Welsh,' or 'French.'

indirect rule

A term used to describe the British style of colonialism in Nigeria and in India in which local traditional rulers and political structures were used to help support the colonial governing structure.

warrant chiefs

Leaders employed by the British colonial regime in Nigeria. A system in which "chiefs" were selected by the British to oversee certain legal matters and assist the colonial enterprise in governance and law enforcement in local areas.

The word 'Nigerian' is merely a distinctive appellation to distinguish those who live within the boundaries of Nigeria from those who do not."[2]

The First Republic (1960–1966)

The British granted Nigeria independence in 1960. Nigerians adopted the British Westminster model at the federal and regional levels, with the prime minister chosen by the majority party or coalition. Northerners came to dominate the federal government by virtue of their greater population. The ruling coalition for the first two years quickly turned into a northern-only grouping when the NPC achieved an outright majority in the legislature. Having benefited less from the economic, educational, and infrastructural benefits of colonialism, the northerners who dominated the First Republic set out to redistribute resources to their benefit. This NPC policy of "northernization" brought them into direct conflict with their southern counterparts, particularly the Yoruba-based AG and later the Igbo-dominated NCNC.

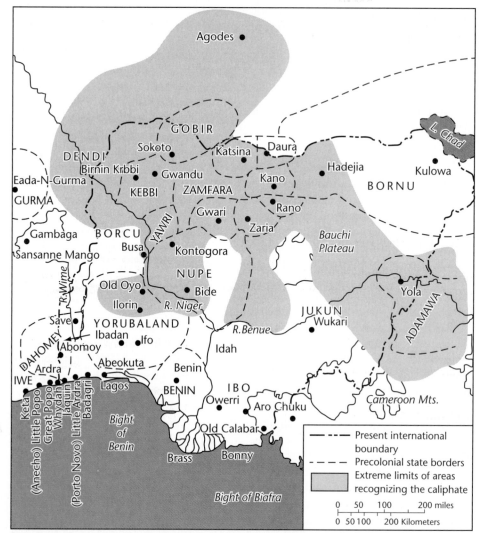

Precolonial Nigeria, showing the Sokoto Caliphate at its greatest extent in the early nineteenth century. The British conquest brought many nations under one roof.

© Cengage Learning®

Rivalries intensified as the NPC sat atop an absolute majority in the federal parliament with no need for its former coalition partner, the NCNC. Nnamdi Azikiwe, the NCNC leader who was also president in the First Republic (then a largely symbolic position), and Tafawa Balewa, the NPC prime minister, separately approached the military to ensure that if it came to conflict, they could count on its loyalty. Thus, "in the struggle for personal survival both men, perhaps inadvertently, made the armed forces aware that they had a political role to play."[3]

Civil War and Military Rule (1966–1979)

With significant encouragement from contending civilian leaders, a group of largely Igbo officers seized power in January 1966. General Aguiyi Ironsi, also an Igbo, was killed in a second coup in July 1966, which brought Yakubu Gowon, a Middle Belt Christian, to power as a consensus head of state among the non-Igbo coup plotters.[4]

Because many northern officials had been killed in the initial coup, a tremendous backlash against Igbos flared in several parts of the country. Ethnic violence sent many Igbos fleeing to their home region in the east. By 1967, the predominantly Igbo population of eastern Nigeria attempted to secede and form its own independent country, named Biafra. Gowon built a military-led government of national unity in what remained of Nigeria (the north and west) and, after a bloody three-year war of attrition and starvation tactics, defeated Biafra in January 1970. The conflict claimed at least a million deaths.

After the war, Gowon presided over a policy of national reconciliation, which proceeded fairly smoothly with the aid of growing oil revenues. Senior officers reaped the benefits of the global oil boom in 1973–1974, however, and corruption was widespread. Influenced by the unwillingness of the military elite to relinquish power and the spoils of office, Gowon postponed a return to civilian rule, and was overthrown in 1975 by Murtala Muhammad, who was assassinated before he could achieve a democratic transition. General Olusegun Obasanjo, Muhammad's second-in-command and successor, peacefully ceded power to an elected civilian government in 1979, which became known as the Second Republic. Obasanjo retired but would later reemerge as a civilian president in 1999.

The Second and Third Republics, and Predatory Military Rule (1979–1999)

The president of the 1979–1983 Second Republic, Shehu Shagari, and his ruling National Party of Nigeria (NPN, drawn largely from the First Republic's northern-dominated NPC), did little to reduce the mistrust between the various parts of the federation, or to stem rampant corruption. The NPN captured outright majorities in the 1983 state and national elections through

Olusegun Obasanjo ruled Nigeria first as military head of state from 1976 to 1979 and then as civilian president from 1999 to 2007. As president, he instituted a number of important reforms, but also tried—and failed—to change the constitution to extend his term in office.

Issouf Sanogo/Staff/AFP/Getty Images

massive fraud and violence. The last vestiges of popular tolerance dissipated, and a few months later the military, led by Major General Muhammadu Buhari, seized power.

When General Buhari refused to pledge a rapid return to democratic rule and failed to revive a plummeting economy, his popular support wavered, and in August 1985 General Ibrahim Babangida seized power. Babangida and his cohort quickly announced a transition to democratic rule, then stalled and subsequently annulled the presidential election of June 1993. In stark contrast to all prior elections, the 1993 election was relatively fair and was evidently won by Yoruba businessman Chief Moshood Abiola. The annulment provoked angry reactions from a population weary of postponed transitions, lingering military rule, and the deception of rulers. Babangida resigned, and his handpicked successor, Ernest Shonekan, led a weak civilian caretaker government. General Sani Abacha, who had been installed by Babangida as defense minister, soon seized power but delayed implementation, cracked down on opposition and civil liberties and fomented corruption on a massive scale. Only Abacha's sudden death in June 1998 saved the country from certain crisis. General Abdulsalami Abubakar, Abacha's successor, quickly established a new transition program and promptly handed power to an elected civilian government led by President Olusegun Obasanjo and the People's Democratic Party (PDP) in May 1999.

The Fourth Republic (1999 to the Present)

Obasanjo was called out of retirement by the leaders of the PDP to run for president. Obasanjo, although a Yoruba, handed over power as military head of state in 1979 to the northerner Shehu Shagari at the dawn of the Second Republic. The northern political establishment had concluded that Obasanjo was a Yoruba candidate they could trust. In addition, many perceived that an ex-military leader could better manage to keep the armed forces in the barracks once they left power.

Obasanjo claimed a broad mandate to arrest the nation's decline by reforming the state and economy. Within weeks, he electrified the nation by retiring all the military officers who had held positions of political power under previous military governments, seeing them as the most likely plotters of future coups.

Obasanjo targeted the oil sector for new management and lobbied foreign governments to forgive Nigeria's massive debts. The minimum wage was raised significantly, a "truth and reconciliation" commission was set up to address past abuses. Civil society groups thrived on renewed political freedom, corruption returned with a vengeance. Narrowly avoiding impeachment, Obasanjo secured renomination from his party (the PDP) in the 2003 elections, cutting deals with party barons, such that the PDP political machine succeeded while public confidence plummeted and reform was stymied. Faced with increasing political turmoil and social conflict, the president called a National Political Reform Conference in early 2005, which achieved little. The president chose a little-known, reclusive governor from the north with health problems to be his successor: Umaru Musa Yar'Adua of Katsina state.

Obasanjo misjudged both the Nigerian people and Yar'Adua. Despite local and international condemnation of the April 2007 polls, the public did not erupt, and Obasanjo had little choice but to hand over to leadership to Yar'Adua in May 2007. Instead of focusing on his campaign promises, Yar'Adua spent most of his energies solidifying his control of the PDP, which became a perpetual guiding principle of politics throughout this era. The president's sudden collapse and evacuation to Saudi Arabia in November 2009 showed that he was dying. Normal government activity all but ceased while a small circle of advisors usurped presidential powers and secured government contracts. International pressure grew. Coup threats surfaced. Finally Vice President Goodluck Jonathan, from the oil-rich Niger Delta, moved cautiously to assure Northern powerbrokers that they could work with him. His deft political efforts, backed in part by support from former President Obasanjo, ensured a smooth transition when President Yar'Adua at last passed away in May 2010.

Like Obasanjo and Yar'Adua, President Jonathan came to office without control of his own party, the PDP, and moved quickly to establish his control, using the largesse of Nigeria's massive state-controlled oil wealth. Within several months, he made clear his intention to run for president in April 2011. In stark contrast to his predecessors, however, President Jonathan pressed electoral reform.

The 2011 elections were much improved from the disastrous 2007 contests, but the PDP still utilized its massive resource advantages to buy votes. Expectations of cleaner elections sparked leading to over 800 deaths in post-election riots.

Many northern factions also remained antagonistic over the shift of power back to a southerner. This antagonism soon led to a massive struggle within the PDP, which the president eventually won, but at great cost. Six governors—five from the disgruntled northern bloc—decamped in 2013 for the new opposition party, the All Progressives Congress (APC). The APC had formed earlier in 2013 when leaders of the four main opposition parties recognized the limits of their smaller, largely regional parties, and sensed opportunity in the PDP's internal battles.

Jonathan took the oath of office in 2011 promising reforms, but his administration soon fell victim to massive corruption. A growing Islamist insurgency in the northeast, led by a group called Boko Haram, drew attention away from reform and development and toward increased security concerns and expenditures.

[Handwritten margin note: Obasanjo ↓ Yar'Adu (died) ↓ Goodluck Jonathan]

The Four Themes and Nigeria

Nigeria in a Globalized World of States

Federalism and democracy have been important strategies in the effort to build a coherent nation-state in Nigeria out of more than 250 different ethnic groups. The legacy of colonial rule and many years of military domination, however, left a nearly unitary system in federal guise: a system with an overly powerful central government surrounded by weak and largely economically dependent states.

When the military returned to the barracks in 1999, it left an overdeveloped executive arm at all levels of government—federal, state, and local—at the expense of weak legislative and judicial institutions. Unchecked executive power has encouraged the arbitrary exercise of authority and patronage politics, which sap the economy and undermine the rule of law of the national executive.

Nigeria in the Globalized World of States
Nigeria, with its natural riches, has long been regarded as a potential political and economic giant of Africa. Nigerian leaders have long aspired to regional leadership, undertaking several peacekeeping operations and an ambitious diplomatic agenda—through the United Nations, the African Union, and on its own—to broker peace initiatives and to foster democracy in some instances. Recent efforts include Sudan's troubled Darfur region, Côte d'Ivoire, and Zimbabwe.

Governing Nigeria's Economy Nigeria's economy has largely depended on unpredictable oil revenues, sparse external loans, and aid. Owing to neglect of agriculture, Nigeria moved from self-sufficiency in basic foodstuffs in the mid-1960s to heavy dependence on imports less than twenty years later. Manufacturing activities, after a surge of investment by government and foreign firms in the 1970s, suffered from disinvestment for decades. Since 2003, however, this decline has reversed in the south—particularly Lagos—and many areas of the economy outside of oil also begin to expand rapidly. High oil and gas prices have spurred growth but done little to reduce poverty.

Democratic Ideas amid Colonialism and Military Rule The Nigerian colonial state was conceived and fashioned as **interventionist**, with administrative controls and significant ownership of the economy.

interventionist

An interventionist state acts vigorously to shape the performance of major sectors of the economy.

After independence in 1960, Nigeria's civilian and military rulers alike expanded the interventionist state. Although colonial rulers left Nigeria with the machinery of parliamentary democracy, they socialized the population to be passive subjects rather than responsive participants. Colonialism bequeathed an authoritarian legacy to independent Nigeria. Military rule continued this pattern from 1966 to 1979 and again from 1983 to 1999.

This dualism promoted two public realms to which individuals belonged: the communal realm, in which people identified by ethnic or subethnic groups (Igbo, Tiv, Yoruba, and others), and the civic realm in which citizenship was universal.[5] Nigerians came to view the state as the realm where resources were plundered (see Section 4). Morality was reserved for the ethnic or communal realm. Military rule reinforced this pattern and the democratic idea in Nigeria has also been filtered through deep regional divisions.

The south experienced the benefits and burdens of colonial occupation. The coastal location of Lagos, Calabar, and their surrounding regions made them important hubs for trade and shipping activity, around which the British built the necessary infrastructure—schools (promoting Christianity and Western education), roads, ports, and the like—and a large African civil service to facilitate colonialism. In northern Nigeria, the British used indirect rule and used local structures, left intact Islamic institutions, and prohibited Christian missionary activity. The north consequently received few infrastructural benefits, but its traditional administration was largely preserved.

Thus, at independence the south enjoyed the basis for a modern economy and exposure to democratic institutions, but the north remained largely agricultural and monarchical. Even throughout even the darkest days of military rule, these institutions persevered. Nigeria's incredible diversity continually demands involves constant processes to advances democracy promises.

Nigeria's Fragile Collective Identity This division between north and south is overlaid with hundreds of ethnic divisions across the nation, which military governments and civilians alike have been prone to manipulate for selfish ends. These many cultural divisions have been continually exacerbated by the triple threats of clientelism, corruption, and unstable authoritarian governing structures, which together stir up ethnic group competition and hinder economic potential.[6] Clientelism is the practice by which particular individuals or segments receive disproportionate policy benefits or political favors from a political patron, usually at the expense of the larger society. In Nigeria, patrons are often linked to clients by

different form of colonial rule enhanced the division of the future nations in the south the North

ethnic, religious, or other cultural ties, but these ties have generally benefited only a small elite. By fostering political competition along cultural lines, clientelism tends to undermine social trust and political stability, which are necessary conditions for economic growth.

Nevertheless, the idea of Nigeria has taken root among the country's ethnic groups over 50 years after independence. Most Nigerians enjoy many personal connections across ethnic and religious lines, and elites in both the north and the south have significant business activities throughout the country. Even so, ethnicity remains a critical flashpoint.

Themes and Comparisons

Nigeria is by far the largest country in Africa and among the ten most populous countries in the world. One out of every five black Africans is Nigerian. Unlike most other African countries, Nigeria has the human and material resources to overcome the vicious cycle of poverty and **autocracy**. Hopes for this breakthrough, however, have been regularly frustrated over five decades of independent rule.

autocracy

A government in which one or a few rulers has absolute power, thus, a dictatorship.

Nigeria remains the oldest surviving federation in Africa, and it has managed through much travail to maintain its fragile unity. That cohesion has come under increasing stress, however, and a major challenge is to ensure that Nigeria does not ultimately collapse. Nigeria's past failures to sustain democracy and economic development also render it an important case for the study of resource competition and the perils of corruption, and its experience demonstrates the interrelationship between democracy and development. Democracy and development depend on leadership, political culture, institutional autonomy, and the external economic climate; Nigeria has much to teach us on all these topics.

Where Do You Stand?

Many Nigerians feel that the British bringing together so many ethnicities and religions under one political roof was a terrible mistake, because the diversity is just too great for Nigeria to hold together as a single nation. Do you agree?

After all the problems caused by military rule, do you see any advantages to it? Why might it have been appealing?

POLITICAL ECONOMY AND DEVELOPMENT

SECTION 2

Colonialism bequeathed Nigeria an interventionist state, and governments after independence continued this pattern. The state became the central fixture in the Nigerian economy, stunting the private sector and encumbering industry and commerce. As the state began to unravel in the late 1980s and 1990s, leaders grew more predatory, plundering the petroleum sector, and preventing the nation's vast economic potential from being realized.

State and Economy

Focus Questions

- What were some of the key impacts of the oil boom on Nigeria's political economy?
- What efforts has Nigeria made to try to address poverty and spur development?

The Nigerian state plays the central role in economic decision making. Most of the nation's revenues, and nearly all of its hard currency, are channeled through the government, which control these earnings, known as **rents**. Winning government contracts becomes a central economic activity, with lucrative results.[7] Those left out must try to survive on petty trade and subsistence agriculture (the informal sector economy) in which taxes and regulation rarely reach and accounts for about one-fifth of the entire Nigerian GDP.

rents

Economic gains that do not compensate those who produced them and do not contribute to productivity, typically associated with government earnings that do not get channeled back into either investments or policies that benefit the public good. Pursuit of economic rents (or "rent-seeking") is profit seeking that takes the form of nonproductive economic activity.

Origins of Economic Decline

agriculture → nonfood export crops → oil → oil collapse (need to import oil)

In the colonial and immediate postcolonial periods, Nigeria's economy was centered on agricultural production for domestic consumption and export. Nigeria was self-sufficient in food production. In the 1960s, emphasis shifted to the development of nonfood export crops through large-scale enterprises.

Small farmers received scant government support. Food production suffered.[8] The Biafran War (1967–1970), severe drought, and the development of the petroleum industry reduced agricultural production, which plummeted from 80 percent of exports in 1960 to just 2 percent by 1980.[9] External debt skyrocketed, and corruption increased. The economic downturn of the 1980s created even greater incentives for government corruption. Within three years of seizing power in 1993, General Abacha allowed all of Nigeria's oil refineries to collapse, forcing this giant oil-exporting country into the absurd situation of having to import petroleum. Scam artists proliferated, especially on the Internet, which earned perhaps $100 million annually.

From 1985 to the Present: Deepening Economic Crisis and the Search for Solutions

structural adjustment program (SAP)

Programs established by the World Bank intended to alter and reform the economic structures of highly indebted Third World countries as a condition for receiving international loans. SAPs often involve the necessity for privatization, trade liberalization, and fiscal restraint, which typically requires the dismantling of social welfare systems.

Structural Adjustment The year 1985 marked a turning point for the Nigerian state and economy. Within a year of wresting power from General Buhari in August 1985, the Babangida regime developed an economic **structural adjustment program (SAP)** with the active support of the World Bank and the IMF (also referred to as the **international financial institutions**, or **IFIs**). The decision to embark on the SAP was made against a background of increasing economic constraints arising from the continued dependence of the economy on waning oil revenues, a growing debt burden, **balance of payments** difficulties, and lack of fiscal discipline.[10]

The large revenues arising from the oil windfall enabled the state to increase its involvement in direct production. Beginning in the 1970s, the government created a number of parastatals (state-owned enterprises; see Section 3), including large shares in major banks and other financial institutions, manufacturing, construction, agriculture, public utilities, and various services. Although the government has since sold many of its parastatals, the state remains the biggest employer as well as the most important source of revenue, even for the private sector.

Privatization, which is central to Nigeria's adjustment program, means that state-owned businesses would be sold to private (nonstate) investors, domestic or foreign to generate revenue and improve efficiency, but both domestic and foreign investors were for many years hesitant to risk significant capital in light of persistent instability, unpredictable economic policies, and endemic corruption. Recently, however, attractive areas such as telecommunications, utilities, and oil and gas are drawing significant foreign capital.

Economic Policy President Obasanjo opened his second term in office in 2003 with a renewed focus on economic reform and development. Nigeria stabilized its macroeconomic policy, restructured the banking sector, and established a new anticorruption agency, the Economic and Financial Crimes Commission (EFCC). Unfortunately, many of these ambitious goals were followed by lackluster implementation, and President Jonathan has continued this trend. Buoyant oil revenues have helped to spur the economy higher since 2003, but poverty has not significantly diminished.

Perhaps Obasanjo's greatest economic achievement was paying off most of Nigeria's heavy foreign debt (see Table 12.3). On taking office in 1999 he promptly undertook numerous visits to Europe, Asia, and the United States to urge the governments of those countries to forgive most of Nigeria's obligations. After persistent international lobbying, along with progress on economic reforms during Obasanjo's second term, Nigeria eventually secured an agreement for a substantial reduction of the country's debt. In June 2005, the Paris Club of official creditors approved a package of debt repayments, repurchases, and write-offs that reduced Nigeria's external debt by 90 percent.

international financial institutions (IFIs)

This term generally refers to the International Bank for Reconstruction and Development (the World Bank) and the International Monetary Fund (IMF), but can also include other international lending institutions.

balance of payments

An indicator of international flow of funds that shows the excess or deficit in total payments of all kinds between or among countries. Included in the calculation are exports and imports, grants, and international debt payments.

GLOBAL CONNECTION

From Vision 2010 to NEEDS

In the early 1990s, concerned with the nation's economic decline, a number of the larger Nigerian businesses and key multinational corporations decided to pursue new initiatives, including the first Economic Summit, a high-profile conference that advocated numerous policies to move Nigeria toward becoming an "emerging market" that could attract foreign investment along the lines of the high-performing states in Asia.

Through Vision 2010, the government pledged to adopt a package of business-promoting economic reforms, while business pledged to work toward certain growth targets consistent with governmental priorities in employment, taxation, community investment, and the like. Along with government and business leaders, key figures were invited to participate from nearly all sectors of society, including the press, non-governmental organizations, youth groups, market women's associations, and others. Government-owned media followed Vision 2010's pronouncements with great fanfare, while the private media reviewed them with a healthy dose of skepticism regarding Abacha's intentions and the elitist nature of the exercise. Vision 2010's final report called for:

- Restoring democratic rule
- Restructuring and professionalizing the military
- Lowering the population growth rate
- Rebuilding education
- Meaningful privatization
- Diversifying the export base beyond oil
- Supporting intellectual property rights
- Central bank autonomy

Presidents Obasanjo and Yar'Adua both adopted the core goals of Vision 2010, announcing his own Vision 2020 and a Seven Point Agenda that included economic reforms. President Jonathan encompassed these in his own plan, called Vision 20:2020, which set many similar goals as the previous plans, and suffered similar problems of poor implementation.

MAKING CONNECTIONS What elements of Vision 2010 do you see evident in the economic policies of Nigerian presidents after 1999?

Source: Vision 2010 Final Report, September 1997; Federal Government of Nigeria, the *National Economic Empowerment and Development Strategy,* March 2004.

Table 12.2	Selected Economic Indicators, 1980–2009		
Years	Real GDP (in billions)	GDP %Growth	Inflation Rate % (CPI)
1980	64.2	4.2	9.97
1985	28.4	9.7	7.44
1990	28.5	8.2	7.36
1993	21.4	2.2	57.17
1995	28.1	2.5	72.84
1997	36.2	2.7	8.53
1999	34.8	1.1	6.62
2000	46	5.4	6.93
2001	48	3.1	18.87
2002	59.1	1.55	12.88
2003	67.7	10.3	14.03
2005	112.2	5.4	17.86
2007	165.9	6.45	5.38
2008	207.1	6	11.58
2009	173	5.6	11.54
2011	245.7	5.1	10.8
2012	262.6	6.7	12.2

Source: World Bank. Some data compiled by Evan Litwin and Mukesh Baral.

President Yar'Adua vowed to continue President Obasanjo's reforms, but made marginal progress. While this massive corruption around the oil industry has continued unabated, however, Nigeria's small private sector has been quietly expanding rapidly. Although the last three administrations have not followed through on the expansive development policies they promised, they have largely left much of the private sector to its own designs, and there has been a boom in the private sector and significant infrastructure development.

Social Welfare The continued decline in Nigeria's economic performance since the early 1980s has caused great suffering, and the recent rise of the private sector has yet to take a significant bite out of poverty for the majority of Nigerians.

Since 1986, there has been a marked deterioration in the quantity and quality of social services, complicated by a marked decline in household incomes. The SAP program and subsequent austerity measures emphasizing the reduction of state expenditures have forced cutbacks in spending on social welfare, Nigeria's provision of basic education, health care, and other social services—water, education, food, and shelter—remain woefully inadequate. In addition to the needless loss of countless lives to preventable and curable maladies, the nation is fighting to stave off an AIDS epidemic of catastrophic proportions. The government has made AIDS a secondary priority, leaving much of the initiative to a small group of courageous but underfunded nongovernmental organizations.

Society and Economy

Because the central government controls access to most resources and economic opportunities, the state has become the major focus for competition among ethnic, regional, religious, and class groups.[11]

Table 12.3	Nigeria's Total External Debt (millions of US$ at current prices and exchange rates)	
Years	**Total Debt /GDP**	**Total Debt Service/ Exports**
1977	8.73	1.04
1986	109.9	38.03
1996	88.97	14.79
1997	78.54	8.71
1999	83.76	7.54
2000	68.18	8.71
2001	64.67	12.9
2002	51.55	8.13
2003	51.16	5.96
2007	5.2	1.79
2008	5.55	0.67
2009	4.53	0.81
2012	18.37	.3

Source: World Bank. Recent data compiled by Evan Litwin and Mukesh Baral.

Ethnic and Religious Cleavages

Nigeria's ethnic relations have generated tensions that sap the country's economy of much-needed vitality.[12] The dominance of the Hausa, Igbo, and Yoruba in the country's national life, and the conflicts among political elites from these groups, distort economic affairs.

Government ineptitude (or outright manipulation), and growing Islamic and Christian assertion, have also heightened conflicts.[13] Christians have perceived past northern-dominated governments as being pro-Muslim in their management and distribution of scarce resources, some of which jeopardized the secular nature of the state. These fears have increased since 1999, when several northern states instituted expanded versions of the Islamic legal code, the *shari'a*. For their part, Muslims feared that President Obasanjo, a born-again Christian, tilted the balance of power and thus the distribution of economic benefits against the north, and such fears are again on the rise under President Jonathan, also a Christian. Economic decline has contributed to the rise of Christian and Muslim fundamentalisms, which have spread among unemployed youths and others in a society suffering under economic collapse.

women work agriculture/business but can't own land or shop T

Northers mong clan due to lack of water → religious conflict T

Gender Differences

Although the Land Use Act of 1978 stated that all land in Nigeria is ultimately owned by the government, land tenure in Nigeria is still governed by traditional practice, which is largely patriarchal. Despite the fact that women, especially from the south and Middle Belt areas, have traditionally dominated agricultural production and form the bulk of agricultural producers, they are generally prevented from owning land, which remains the major means of production. Trading, in which women feature prominently, is also controlled in many areas by traditional chiefs and local government councilors, who are overwhelmingly male.

Women's associations in the past tended to be elitist, urban based, and mainly concerned with issues of trade, children, household welfare, and religion.[14] Women are grossly underrepresented at all levels of the governmental system; only 19 (of 469) national legislators are women.

Reflecting the historical economic and educational advantages of the south, women's interest organizations sprouted in southern Nigeria earlier than in the north. Although these groups initially focused generally on nonpolitical issues surrounding women's health and children's welfare, they are now also focusing on explicit political goals, such as getting more women into government and increasing funds available for education.

Environmental Issues

Northern Nigeria is located on the edge of the Sahel, the vast, semi-arid region just south of the Sahara desert that is farmable but often troubled with fragile water supplies. Although much of the north enjoys seasonal rains that come from the tropical southern part of Nigeria, the northern edges of the country have been suffering the growing effects of climate change, as water supplies dry up. Most dramatic has been the drying of Lake Chad in the northeast, which has shrunk to roughly a fifth of its size in the 1960s. As desertification pressures spread in the north, nomadic Fulani herdsman have been forced to move their cattle toward the more temperate south, causing growing numbers of local conflicts with farmers. These disputes can take on religious tones when the Fulani, who are predominantly Muslim, move into lands settled by Christian farmers.

The environment is also a major issue in the Niger Delta, but for a different reason. Here, years of pollution from the oil industry has killed off much of the local fish stock that communities in the region depended upon for their livelihoods, and gas flaring from the oil wells light up the night and make the air toxic to breathe. A small ethnic group in one of the oil-producing communities, the Ogoni, formed an environmental rights organization in 1990 that pushed for peaceful action to clean up the damage and give the Ogoni greater control over the oil wealth. The military, however, clamped down on the movement and hung its key leaders. Thereafter, protests across the region increased, and many turned violent, devolving into the militant insurgency that plagues the Niger Delta today.

Finally, Nigeria's environment faces growing pressures from the nation's population explosion. Sprawling megacities are stretching across Nigeria's urban areas, especially from the commercial hub of Lagos, whose entire urban stretch has absorbed as far as Ibadan to the north and is estimated to include over 20 million people. At the same time, Lagos is rapidly losing its coastline to the rising sea levels, putting increased pressure on the limited space.

Nigeria in the Global Economy

The Nigerian state has remained comparatively weak and dependent on foreign industrial and financial interests. The country's acute debt burden was dramatically reduced in 2005, but started growing again by 2014, and Nigeria is still reliant on the developed industrial economies for finance capital, production and information technologies, basic consumer items, and raw materials. Mismanagement, endemic corruption, and the vagaries of international commodity markets have squandered the country's economic potential. Apart from its standing in global energy markets, Nigeria receded to the margins of the global economy. The recent economic boom centered in Lagos has attracted increasing international investment, but this must be matched with serious development and anti-corruption policies at the federal level, which has so far been lacking.

Nigeria and the Regional Political Economy

Nigeria's aspirations to be a regional leader in Africa have not been dampened by its declining position in the global political economy. Nigeria was a major actor in the formation of the **Economic Community of West African States (ECOWAS)** in 1975 and has carried a disproportionately high financial and administrative burden for keeping the organization afloat. Under President Obasanjo's initiative, ECOWAS voted in 2000 to create a parliament and a single currency for the region as the

> **Economic Community of West African States (ECOWAS)**
>
> The West African regional organization, including fifteen member countries from Cape Verde in the west to Nigeria and Niger in the east.

THE U.S. CONNECTION

Much in Common

[handwritten annotation: U.S → buys lots of oil → pretty good / Nigerians moving to U.S. relationship]

Since the 1970s Nigeria has had a strong relationship with the United States. Most of Nigeria's military governments during the Cold War aligned their foreign policies with the West, although they differed over South Africa, with Nigeria taking a strong anti-apartheid stance. Beginning with the Second Republic constitution, Nigeria closely modeled its presidential and federal systems on those of the United States, and Nigerian courts will occasionally turn to American jurisprudence for legal precedents. Since President Carter's visit to Nigeria in 1978, Washington has supported Nigerian efforts to liberalize and deepen democratic development.

Overwhelmingly, however, the key issue in U.S.–Nigerian relations has been oil. The United States buys roughly 8 percent of its petroleum imports from Nigeria and has repeatedly pushed Abuja to increase production of its "sweet crude," the especially high quality oil Nigeria offers. Nigeria also discovered massive gas reserves off its coasts. Nigeria's military governments used America's oil addiction to force it to moderate its pressure on Abuja to democratize. The civilian governments since 1999 have also largely ignored U.S. complaints over declining election quality, and the Yar'Adua administration cultivated ties

with China after the United States suspended high-level diplomatic relations over the farcical 2007 elections.

Shortly thereafter, the Bush administration welcomed President Yar'Adua to Washington. President Jonathan, however, came to office in part with the help of U.S. pressure, and he has cultivated close ties with the Obama administration and featured his meetings with President Obama strongly in his 2011 and 2015 election campaigns.

Nigeria and the United States also share strong societal ties. Since the 1960s, Christian Nigerians have been avid consumers of American Pentecostalism, sprouting thousands of new churches over the years and infusing them with a uniquely Nigerian flare, such that many of these churches are now opening satellites in the United States and around the globe. In addition, a growing number of Nigerians have migrated to the United States, such that nearly 300,000 are now U.S. citizens. Since 2000, this diaspora has begun to exercise some influence over U.S. policy, and they have also used their financial resources to support development projects and exercise political influence in Nigeria.

MAKING CONNECTIONS Does American oil addiction give Nigeria more influence over the United States in the end?

next step toward a European Union–style integration. The currency was never implemented, but ECOWAS citizens are able to travel and trade across member state borders relatively freely.

Nigeria was also the largest contributor of troops to the West African peacekeeping force to Liberia from 1990 to 1997 to restore order and prevent the Liberian civil war from destabilizing the subregion. Nigeria under President Obasanjo also sought to mediate crises in Guinea-Bissau, Togo, and Ivory Coast, and in Darfur (Sudan), Congo, and Zimbabwe outside the ECOWAS region. President Jonathan has continued to support Nigerian peacekeeping commitments abroad, taking a particularly strong stand against the 2012 coup and Islamist rebellion in Mali through ECOWAS. The growing Boko Haram insurgency within Nigeria, however, has absorbed much of Nigeria's military resources since 2011 and left less for its international commitments.

Nigeria and the Political Economy of the West

Shortly after the 1973–1974 global oil crisis, Nigeria's oil wealth was perceived by the Nigerian elite as a source of strength.[15] By the 1980s, however, the global oil market had become a buyers' market. Thereafter, it became clear that Nigeria's dependence on oil was a source of weakness. The depth of Nigeria's international weakness became more evident with the adoption of structural adjustment in the mid-1980s. Given the enormity of the economic crisis, Nigeria was compelled to seek IMF/World Bank support to improve its balance of payments and facilitate economic restructuring and debt rescheduling, and it has had to accept direction from foreign agencies ever since.

Nigeria remains a highly visible and influential member of the Organization of Petroleum Exporting Countries (OPEC), selling on the average more than 2 million barrels of petroleum daily and contributing approximately 8 percent of U.S. oil imports. Nigeria's oil wealth and its great economic potential have tempered the resolve of Western nations in combating human rights and other abuses, notably during the Abacha period from 1993 to 1998.

The West has been supportive of the return of Nigerian leadership across Africa. Together with President Thabo Mbeki of South Africa, President Obasanjo was instrumental in convincing the continent's leaders to transform the OAU into the African Union (AU) in 2002, modeled on European-style processes to promote greater political integration across the continent.

Despite its considerable geopolitical resources, Nigeria's economic development profile remains harsh. Nigeria is listed very close to the bottom of the UNDP's Human Development Index (HDI), 153 out of 174, behind India and Tanzania. GDP per capita in 2014 was rising rapidly at $2258, but the wealth remains extremely poorly distributed, and less than 1 percent of GDP was recorded as public expenditures on education and health, respectively.

Where Do You Stand?

Has oil been a blessing or curse for the Nigerian economy?

Many Nigerians feel they have ample natural resources to develop the nation, but that they have been plagued with poor leadership to make it happen. Do you see evidence of this?

GOVERNANCE AND POLICY-MAKING

The rough edges of what has been called the "unfinished Nigerian state" appears in its institutions of governance and policy-making. What seemed like an endless political transition under the Babangida and Abacha regimes was rushed through in less than a year by their successor, Abdulsalami Abubakar. President Obasanjo thus inherited a government that was close to collapse, riddled with corruption, unable to perform basic tasks of governance, yet facing high public expectations to deliver rapid progress. He delivered some important economic reforms over his eight years as president, but he gradually succumbed to the "Big Man," prebendal style of corrupt clientelist networks, and tried to change the Constitution to allow himself to stay in power indefinitely. The Nigerian public, however, rejected his ambitions, providing his political opponents, civil society, and the media a strong base to mobilize and force him to leave in May 2007. President Yar'Adua, like Obasanjo, came to power without a client network of his own and immediately set out to build one. President Jonathan also took office without much of a network, and quickly turned Nigeria's massive state resources to the task of getting himself elected in 2011 and keeping control of the ruling party thereafter.

Focus Questions ❓

• What is the "National Question," and how have Nigerians tried to resolve it?

• What is prebendalism, and how has the "Big Man" problem played out in the civilian governments since 1999?

Organization of the State

The National Question and Constitutional Governance

After almost five decades as an independent nation, Nigerians are still debating the basic political structures of the country, who will rule and how, and in some quarters, if the country should even remain united. They call this fundamental governance issue the "national question." How is the country to be governed given its great diversity? What should be the institutional form of the government? How can all sections of the country work in harmony and none feel excluded or dominated by the others? Without clear answers to these questions, Nigeria has stumbled along since independence between democracy and constitutionalism, on the one hand, and military domination on the other. The May 2006 rejection of President Obasanjo's third-term gambit, and the fact that most elites insisted on a constitutional solution to the crisis over President Yar'Adua's incapacitation and death suggest, however, that Nigeria may have turned a corner in terms of a growing respect for constitutional rule.

Nigerian constitutions have suffered under little respect from military or civilian leaders, who have often been unwilling to observe legal and constitutional constraints. Governance and policy-making in this context are conducted within fragile institutions that are swamped by personal and partisan considerations.

Federalism and State Structure

Nigeria's First Republic experimented with the British-style parliamentary model, in which the prime minister is chosen directly from the legislative ranks. The First

Republic was relatively decentralized, with more political power vested in the three federal units: the Northern, Eastern, and Western Regions. The Second Republic constitution, which went into effect in 1979, adopted a U.S.-style presidential model. The Fourth Republic continues with the presidential model: a system with a strong executive who is constrained by a system of formal checks and balances on authority, a bicameral legislature, and an independent judicial branch charged with matters of law and constitutional interpretation.[16]

Like the United States, Nigeria also features a federal structure comprising 36 states and 774 local government units empowered, within limits, to enact their own laws. The judicial system also resembles that of the United States, with a network of local and appellate courts as well as state-level courts. Unlike the United States, however, Nigeria also allows customary law courts to function alongside the secular system, including *shari'a* courts in Muslim communities. Nigerian citizens have the right to choose which of these court systems that they wish to use, but if the disputants cannot agree, then the case goes to the secular courts by default.

In practice, however, military rule left an authoritarian political culture that remains despite the formal democratization of state structures. The control of oil wealth by this centralized command structure has further cemented economic and political control in the center, resulting in a skewed federalism in which states enjoy nominal powers, but in reality most are highly dependent on the central government. Another aspect of federalism in Nigeria has been the effort to arrive at some form of elite accommodation to moderate some of the more divisive aspects of cultural pluralism. The domination of federal governments from 1960 to 1999 by northern Nigerians led southern Nigerians, particularly Yoruba leaders, to demand a "power shift" of the presidency to the south in 1999, leading to the election of Olusegun Obasanjo. Northerners then demanded a shift back to the north in 2007, propelling Umaru Yar'Adua, a northern governor, into office. This ethnic rotation principle is not formally found in the constitution, but all the major political parties recognize it as a necessity. Moreover, the parties practice ethnic rotation at the state and local levels as well.[17]

A central issue in both the 2009–2010 crisis over Yar'Adua's incapacitation and the 2011 election of President Jonathan, a southerner from the Niger Delta, is that Jonathan's ascension has broken the ethnic rotation principle. Northern factions argued that under this rule the presidency should have stayed with them for two terms until 2015. These factions were, however, unable to unite and block Jonathan from winning the PDP nomination and election in 2011. Consequently, northern groups tried to wrest control of the PDP in 2012 from the president, and when they failed, they turned to the opposition in order to attempt to bring the presidency back to their region in 2015.

This informal norm of ethnic rotation has built upon an older, formal practice, known as "federal character." Federal character calls for ethnic quotas in government hiring practices, and was introduced into the public service and formally codified by the 1979 constitution. Although this principle is regarded by some as a positive Nigerian contribution to governance in a plural society, its application has also intensified some intergroup rivalries and conflicts. Some critics have argued that it is antidemocratic, encouraging elite bargaining at the expense of public votes. President Jonathan's breaking of this principle through his election in 2011 raised significant tensions in the PDP primaries and was partly responsible for the election riots that killed 800 people, and propelled northern factions of his party into the opposition by 2013.

The Executive

The Executive under Military Rule

The leadership styles among Nigeria's seven military heads of state varied widely but, in general, under military administrations, the president, or head of state, made appointments to most senior government positions.[18] Since the legislature was disbanded, major executive decisions (typically passed by decrees) were subject to the approval of a ruling council of high-level military officers, although by Abacha's time this council had become largely a rubber stamp for the ruler. Although the military became increasingly repressive, nearly all the juntas spoke of transiting to democracy in order to gain legitimacy.

Given the highly personalistic character of military politics, patron–client relationships flourished. The military pattern of organization, with one strongman at the top and echelons of subordinates below in a pyramid of top-down relationships, spread throughout Nigerian political culture and subcultures.

Having been politicized and divided by these patron–client relationships, the military was structurally weakened during its long years in power. While there have been reports of coup plots on a number of occasions during the Fourth Republic, especially during President Yar'Adua's final days, the military establishment has so far remained loyal and generally within its constitutional security roles.

President Obasanjo paid close attention to keeping the military professionally oriented—and in the barracks. U.S. military advisers and technical assistance were invited to redirect the Nigerian military toward regional peacekeeping expertise—and to keep them busy outside of politics. So far, this strategy has been effective, but the military remains a threat. Junior and senior officers threatened coups over the farcical 2007 elections and the refusal of Yar'Adua's advisors to hand power to Jonathan in 2009–2010, and could do so again if the 2015 election proves deeply contentious.

The Fourth Republic: The Obasanjo, Yar'Adua, and Jonathan Administrations

President Obasanjo's first six months in office were marked by initiatives to reform the armed forces, revitalize the economy, address public welfare, and improve standards of governance. The president sought to root out misconduct and inefficiency in the public sector. Soon, however, familiar patterns of clientelism and financial kickbacks for oil licenses resurfaced. Obasanjo proposed an anticorruption commission with sweeping statutory powers to investigate and prosecute public officials. Delayed in its establishment, the commission had little impact. A second anticorruption commission, however, the Economic and Financial Crimes Commission (EFCC), has since its founding in 2003 had an impressive record of indictments.

Nonetheless, a major impediment to reform came from the ruling party itself. The PDP is run by a collection of powerful politicians from Nigeria's early governments, many of whom grew rich from their complicity with the Babangida and Abacha juntas. With a difficult reelection bid in 2003, these fixers again delivered a victory for the president and the PDP, accomplished through massive fraud in a third of Nigeria's states and questionable practices in at least another third of the country.

After the 2003 election President Obasanjo appeared convinced that he needed to build his own prebendal network if he were to govern and if he were to pursue his ambition to stay in office past two terms. He and his supporters soon moved to gain control of the PDP, offering benefits for loyalty, and removing allies of rival Big Men in the party. The president then signaled the EFCC to investigate his rivals, arresting some and forcing others to support his plans. When Obasanjo's third-term amendment was quashed by the National Assembly in May 2006, the president then had himself named "Chairman for Life" of the PDP, with the power to eject anyone from the party, even his successor as president.

Not surprisingly, President Yar'Adua spent his first year in office trying to gain control over the PDP. He halted many of the last-minute privatizations of state assets into the hands of Obasanjo loyalists and replaced the chairman on the EFCC. The Yar'Adua administration also did nothing to prevent the National Assembly from instigating a series of investigations into the Obasanjo administration that unearthed massive corruption, including the discovery that more than $10 billion had been sunk into the power sector that had produced no results. President Yar'Adua also assisted many of the PDP governors—twelve of whom had their elections overturned by the courts—to retain their seats in rerun elections. By 2009, Yar'Adua had greater control of the PDP, and Obasanjo was on the decline. Yar'Adua's incapacitation later that year and death thereafter, however, reversed Obasanjo's fortunes, and he threw his support behind Goodluck Jonathan at the key moment when Yar'Adua loyalists were preventing him from becoming acting president.

With Obasanjo's support, Jonathan moved to build other alliances to gain influence in the PDP, particularly with the powerful state governors. Their support, bought with the massive resources in the hands of the presidency, won him the PDP nomination and swept him to victory in April 2011. As President Jonathan moved to take control of the PDP, however, his relationship soured with President Obasanjo, who then turned his support to Jonathan's opponents in the PDP. Within months, the party had divided, with six governors defecting in 2013 to the newly formed opposition party, the All Progressives Congress (APC).

These developments demonstrated the continuing deficits of legitimacy for the government as well as the democratic system. As Nigeria's political elites continue to flout the rules of the system, it is inevitable that patronage, coercion, and personal interest will drive policy more than the interests of the public. President Jonathan followed this pattern of "Big Man" prebendal politics—with one important exception: he appointed a credible chairman of the nation's electoral commission, Attahiru Jega. Jega had only a few months to prepare for the April 2011 election, but his reforms assured a more credible outcome than 2007, and hold the promise of significant change for 2015 as more reforms within the commission begin to take hold.

The Bureaucracy

As government was increasingly "Africanized" before independence, the bureaucracy became a way to reward individuals in the prebendal system (see below). Individuals were appointed on the basis of patronage, ethnic group, and regional origin rather than merit.

It is conservatively estimated that federal and state government personnel increased from 72,000 at independence to well over 1 million by the mid-1980s. The salaries of these bureaucrats presently consume roughly half of government expenditures. Several of President Obasanjo's progressive ministers undertook extensive reforms within their ministries, with some successes, but which the bureaucracy fought at every turn.

Semipublic Institutions

Among the largest components of the national administration in Nigeria are numerous state-owned enterprises, usually referred to as parastatals. In general, parastatals are established for several reasons. First, they are intended to furnish public facilities, including water, power, telecommunications, ports, and other transportation, at lower cost than private companies. Second, they were introduced to accelerate economic development by controlling the commanding heights of the economy, including steel production, petroleum and natural gas production, refining, petrochemicals, fertilizer, and certain areas of agriculture. Third, there is a nationalist dimension that relates to issues of sovereignty over sectors perceived sensitive for national security.

Prebendalism

Prebendalism is the disbursing of public offices and state rents to one's ethnic clients. It is an extreme form of clientelism that refers to the practice of mobilizing cultural and other sectional identities by political aspirants and officeholders for the purpose of corruptly appropriating state resources. Prebendalism is an established pattern of political behavior that justifies the pursuit of and the use of public office for the personal benefit of the officeholder and his clients. The official public purpose of the office becomes a secondary concern. As with clientelism, the officeholder's clients comprise a specific set of elites to which he is linked, typically by ethnic or religious ties. Thus, clients or supporters perpetuate the prebendal system in a pyramid fashion with a "Big Man" or "godfather" at the top and echelons of intermediate Big Men and clients below.[19]

prebendalism

Patterns of political behavior that rest on the justification that official state offices should be utilized for the personal benefit of officeholders as well as of their support group or clients.

Other State Institutions

Other institutions of governance and policy-making, including the federal judiciary and subnational governments (incorporating state and local courts), operate within the context of a strong central government dominated by a powerful chief executive.

The Judiciary

At one time, the Nigerian judiciary enjoyed relative autonomy from the executive arm. Aggrieved individuals and organizations could take the government to court and expect a judgment based on the merits of their case. This situation changed as each successive military government demonstrated a profound disdain for judicial practices, and eventually it undermined not only the autonomy but also the very integrity of the judiciary as a third branch of government.

The Buhari, Babangida, and Abacha regimes, in particular, issued a spate of repressive decrees disallowing judicial review. Through the executive's power of appointment of judicial officers to the high bench, as well as the executive's control of judicial budgets, the government came to dominate the courts. In addition, the once highly competent judiciary was undermined severely by declining standards of legal training and bribery. The decline of court independence reached a low in 1993 when the Supreme Court placed all actions of the military executive beyond judicial review. The detention and hanging of Ken Saro-Wiwa and eight other Ogoni activists in 1995 underscored the politicization and compromised state of the judicial system.

With the return of civilian rule in 1999, however, the courts have slowly begun to restore some independence and credibility. In early 2002, for instance, the Supreme Court passed two landmark judgments on election law and control of the vast offshore gas reserves. Since the farcical 2007 elections, the courts have overturned twelve gubernatorial races and a host of legislative contests, and the Supreme Court reviewed the 2007 and 2011 presidential elections as well.

State and Local Judiciaries The judiciaries at the state level are subordinate to the Federal Court of Appeal and the Supreme Court. Some of the states in the northern part of the country with large Muslim populations maintain a parallel court system based on the Islamic *shari'a* (religious law). Similarly, some states in the Middle Belt and southern part of the country have subsidiary courts based on customary law. Each of these maintains an appellate division. Otherwise, all courts of record in the country are based on the English common law tradition, and all courts are ultimately bound by decisions handed down by the Supreme Court.

How to apply the *shari'a* has been a source of continuing debate in Nigerian politics. For several years, some northern groups have participated in a movement to expand the application of *shari'a* law in predominantly Muslim areas of Nigeria, and some even have advocated that it be made the supreme law of the land. Prior to the establishment of the Fourth Republic, *shari'a* courts had jurisdiction only among Muslims in civil proceedings and in questions of Islamic personal law. In November 1999, however, the northern state of Zamfara instituted a version of the *shari'a* criminal code that included cutting off hands for stealing and stoning to death for those (especially women) who committed adultery. Eleven other northern states adopted the criminal code by 2001, prompting fears among Christian minorities in these states that the code might be applied to them. Two thousand people lost their lives in Kaduna in 2000 when the state installed the *shari'a* criminal code despite a population that is half Christian.

Although the *shari'a* criminal code appears to contradict Nigeria's officially secular constitution, President Obasanjo refused to challenge it, seeing the movement as a "fad." His refusal to challenge *shari'a* saved the nation from a deeply divisive policy debate and gave northern political and legal systems time to adjust. In fact, although the *shari'a* systems in these states have created more vehicles for patronage, they have also opened up new avenues for public action to press government for accountability and reform. In addition, women's groups mobilized against several questionable local *shari'a* court decisions to challenge them at the appellate level, winning landmark decisions that helped to extend women's legal protections under the code.

State and Local Government

Nigeria's centralization of oil revenues has fostered intense competition among local communities and states for access to national patronage. Most states would be insolvent without substantial support from the central government. About 90 percent of state incomes are received directly from the federal government, which includes a lump sum based on oil revenues, plus a percentage of oil income based on population. In all likelihood, only the states of Lagos, Rivers, and Kano could survive on their own. Despite attempted reforms, most local governments have degenerated into prebendal patronage outposts for the governors to dole out to loyalists. For the most part, they do little to address their governance responsibilities.

The federal, state, and local governments have the constitutional and legal powers to raise funds through taxes. However, Nigerians share an understandable unwillingness to pay taxes and fees to a government with such a poor record of delivering basic services. The result is a vicious cycle: government is sapped of

---

shari'a

Islamic law derived mostly from the Qur'an and the examples set by the Prophet Muhammad in the Sunnah.

resources and legitimacy and cannot adequately serve the people. Communities, in turn, are compelled to resort to self-help measures to protect these operations and thus withdraw further from the reach of the state. Very few individuals and organizations pay taxes, the most basic government functions are starved of resources.

The Policy-Making Process

Nigeria's prolonged experience with military rule has resulted in a policy process based more on top-down directives than on consultation, political debate, and legislation. A decade of democratic government has seen important changes, as the

---

PROFILE

President Goodluck Jonathan

President Goodluck Jonathan, casting his vote in his Bayelsa state village and wearing a traditional hat common to many Niger Delta communities. He was elected vice president in 2007, named Acting President by the National Assembly on the incapacitation of President Yar'Adua in 2010, and elected president in 2011.

Pius Utomi Ekpei/AFP/ Getty Images

The story goes that President Jonathan's father, a canoe maker from Bayelsa state, had an innate sense that his son was born lucky, and so named him Goodluck. Whether the story is truth or legend, events certainly support its conclusion: fortune has so far smiled on the president, rocketing him from humble beginnings in the Niger Delta to the center of Nigerian politics. Jonathan worked as both a lecturer and an environmental official while finishing his Ph.D. in zoology. In 1998 he joined the PDP and won the office of deputy governor of Bayelsa state. He then became governor in 2005 when his predecessor was impeached for corruption. When President Obasanjo picked the little-known Yar'Adua as the 2007 presidential candidate for the PDP, he sought to balance the ticket with someone from the Niger Delta. The other regional governors—having been in office longer—were richer and deemed more powerful, so Obasanjo turned to Jonathan for the vice presidency. As President Yar'Adua's health failed, Jonathan found himself acting president in February 2010 and then president when Yar'Adua passed away in May 2010.

Given this quick ascent, the fact that the president chose a cautious approach based on continuity of the policies of his predecessors is not surprising. Unfortunately for Nigerians, however, President Jonathan has also continued the practices of promising bold policies and not implementing them, and of focusing his efforts on gaining control of the corrupt PDP machine. His administration is accused of levels of corruption higher than any of his predecessors. Bayelsa politics, where he started his ascent, is infamous for corruption and militant activity, and militias dynamited Jonathan's house the night he was elected vice president in 2007. His wife, Patience, was accused by the EFCC of money laundering in 2006 and forced to return $13.5 million, although she was never prosecuted, and her extravagant spending is a constant topic in the media, such as gold-plated iPhones for attendees at his daughter's wedding in 2014. His ambitions to be reelected in 2015 have split the PDP, such that power politics have dominated his tenure and sidelined most major policy initiatives. He did, however, name a respected civil society leader to head the electoral commission early in his time in office.

President Jonathan is the first Nigerian head of state to have a Facebook page (http://www.facebook.com/jonathangoodluck), and is even believed to take the time to write some of the postings himself.

MAKING CONNECTIONS What do you see as President Jonathan's most important contributions and failings so far?

legislatures, courts, and state governments have begun to force the presidency to negotiate its policies and work within a constitutional framework. But military rule and its "loyalty pyramids"[20] has left indelible marks on policy-making in Nigeria and its networks of corruption.[21]

Where Do You Stand?

The three presidents since 1999 all came to power promising reform, but soon succumbed to the dominant corrupt patterns of prebendalism set by the military years ago. Is corruption just too ingrained in Nigeria for any politician to resist?

Does Nigeria's parallel system of *shari'a* and customary courts alongside its secular ones seem like a good idea to accommodate the nation's diversity, or does it perpetuate ethnic and religious differences that divide the country?

SECTION 4

REPRESENTATION AND PARTICIPATION

Representation and participation are two vital components of modern democracies. Nigerian legislatures have commonly been sidelined or reduced to subservience by the powerful executive, while fraud, elite manipulation, and military interference have marred the formal party and electoral systems. Thus, we also emphasize unofficial methods of representation and participation through the institutions of civil society, which are sometimes more important than the formal institutions.

▼ Focus Questions

- What have been the benefits and costs of the move from ethnic parties under the early republics to the multiethnic parties of the Fourth Republic?

- What role has civil society played in resisting military rule and voicing the public interest under civilian government?

The Legislature

Nigeria's legislature has been a primary victim of the country's political instability. Legislative structures and processes historically suffered abuse, neglect, or peremptory suspension by the executive. Until the first coup in 1966, Nigeria operated its legislature along the lines of the British Westminster model, with an elected lower house and a smaller upper house composed of individuals selected by the executive. For the next thirteen years of military rule, a Supreme Military Council performed legislative functions by initiating and passing decrees at will. During the second period of civilian rule, 1979–1983, the bicameral legislature was introduced similar to the U.S. system, with a Senate and House of Representatives (together known as the National Assembly) consisting of elected members, which is the model still in use.

More women now, but still not many

Election to the Senate is on the basis of equal state representation, with three senators from each of the thirty-six states, plus one senator from the federal capital territory, Abuja. The practice of equal representation in the Senate is identical to that of the United States, except that each Nigerian state elects three senators instead of two. Election to the Nigerian House of Representatives is also based on state representation but weighted to reflect the relative size of each state's population, again after the U.S. example. Only eight women were elected in 1999 to sit in the Fourth

Republic's National Assembly; by 2011 this number rose slightly to nineteen, but still constituting only 4 percent of the legislature's membership.

Political Parties and the Party System

An unfortunate legacy of the party and electoral systems after independence was that political parties were associated with particular ethnic groups.[22] The three-region federation created by the British, with one region for each of the three biggest ethnic groups (Hausa, Yoruba, and Igbo), created strong incentives for three parties—one dominated by each group—to form. This in turn fostered a strong perception of politics as an ethnically zero-sum (or winner-takes-all) struggle for access to scarce state resources. This encouraged the political and social fragmentation that ultimately destroyed the First Republic and undermined the Second Republic.

In addition to the three-region structure of the federation at independence, Nigeria's use of a first-past-the-post plurality electoral system produced legislative majorities for these three parties with strong ethnic identities. During subsequent democratic experiments, many of the newer parties could trace their roots to their predecessors in the first civilian regime. Consequently, parties were more attentive to the welfare of their ethnic groups than to the development of Nigeria as a whole. In a polity as potentially volatile as Nigeria, these tendencies intensified political polarization and resentment among the losers.

In the Second Republic, the leading parties shared the same ethnic and sectional support, and often the same leadership, as the parties that were prominent in the first civilian regime. In his maneuvering steps toward creating the civilian Third Republic, General Babangida announced a landmark decision in 1989 to establish only two political parties by decree.[23] The state provided initial start-up funds, wrote the constitutions and manifestos of these parties, and designed them to be "a little to the right and a little to the left," respectively, on the political–ideological spectrum. Interestingly, the elections that took place under these rules from 1990 to 1993 indicated that the two parties cut across the cleavages of ethnicity, regionalism, and religion, demonstrating the potential to move beyond ethnicity.[24] The Social Democratic Party (SDP), which emerged victorious in the 1993 national elections, was an impressive coalition of Second Republic party structures, including elements of the former UPN, NPP, PRP, and GNPP. The opposing National Republican Convention (NRC) was seen as having its roots in northern groups that were the core of the National Party of Nigeria (NPN).

Elections

Table 12.4 shows historical trends in electoral patterns and communal affiliations. As clearly outlined, northern-based parties dominated the first and second experiments with civilian rule. Given this background, it is significant that Moshood Abiola was able to win the presidency in 1993, the first time in Nigeria's history that a southerner electorally defeated a northerner. Abiola, a Yoruba Muslim, won a number of key states in the north, including the hometown of his opponent. Southerners therefore perceived the decision by the northern-dominated Babangida regime to annul the June 12 elections as a deliberate attempt by the military and northern interests to maintain their decades-long domination of the highest levels of government.

Table 12.4	Federal Election Results in Nigeria, 1959–2011

Presidential Election Results, 1979–2011

	Victor (% of the vote)	Leading Contender (% of the vote)
1979	Shehu Shagari, NPN (33.8)	Obafemi Awolowo, UPN (29.2)
1983	Shehu Shagari, NPN (47.3)	Obafemi Awolowo, UPN (31.1)
1993	M.K.O. Abiola, SDP (58.0)	Bashir Tofa, NRC (42.0)
1999	Olusegun Obasanjo, PDP (62.8)	Olu Falae, AD/APP alliance (37.2)
2003	Olusegun Obasanjo, PDP (61.9)	Mohammadu Buhari, ANPP (31.2)
2007	Umaru Yar'Adua, PDP (69.8)	Mohammadu Buhari, ANPP (18.7)
2011	Goodluck Jonathan, PDP (58.9)	Mohammadu Buhari, CDC (32.0)

Parties Controlling the Parliament/National Assembly (Both Houses) by Ethno-Regional Zone, First to Fourth Republics

		Northwest	North-Central	Northeast	Southwest	South-South	Southeast
First	1959	**NPC**	**NPC** (NEPU)	**NPC**	*AG*	AG	NCNC*
	1964–1965	**NPC**	**NPC**	**NPC**	NNDP* (AG)**	NNDP* (AG)**	*NCNC*
Second	1979	**NPN**	PRP **(NPN, UPN)**	GNPP **(NPN)**	*UPN* **(NPN)**	**NPN** *(UPN)*	NPP*
	1983	**NPN**	**NPN** (PRP)	**NPN**	*UPN* **(NPN)**	**NPN**	NPP**
Third	1992	**NRC**	*SDP* **(NRC)**	*SDP* **(NRC)**	*SDP*	**NRC** *(SDP)*	**NRC**
Fourth	1999	**PDP** *(APP)*	**PDP**	**PDP** *(APP)*	AD **(PDP)**	**PDP** *(APP)*	**PDP**
	2003	*ANPP* **(PDP)**	*ANPP* **(PDP)**	**PDP** *(ANPP)*	**PDP** AD	**PDP** *(ANPP)*	**PDP** (APGA)
	2007	*ANPP* **(PDP)**	**PDP** ANPP	**PDP** ANPP	**PDP** AC	**PDP**	**PDP** PPA
	2011	**PDP** CDC	**PDP** CDC	**PDP** ANPP	*ACN* **PDP**	**PDP** ACN	**PDP** ACN

Boldfaced: Ruling party
Italicized: Leading opposition
*: Coalition with ruling party
**: Coalition with opposition

(continued)

Table 12.4 | (continued)

National Assembly and State-Level Elections

Senate	1999	2003
PDP	63	73
APP/ANPP	26	28
AD	20	6

House	1999	2003
PDP	214	213
APP/ANPP	77	95
AD	69	31
Other		7

Governorships	1999	2003
PDP	21	28
APP/ANPP	9	7
AD	6	1

State Houses of Assembly	1999	2003
PDP	23	28
APP/ANPP	8	7
AD	5	1

2007 election results:

Parties	House of Representatives		Senate	
	Votes %	Seats	Votes %	Seats
People's Democratic Party	54.5	223	53.7	76
All Nigeria People's Party	27.4	96	27.9	27
Action Congress	8.8	34	9.7	6
Others	2.8	7	2.7	–

Governorships		State Assemblies	
26	PDP	28	PDP
5	ANPP	5	ANPP
2	PPA	1	PPA
2	AC	2	AC
1	APGA		

2011 Elections

Party	House Votes %	House Seats	Senate Votes %	Senate Seats	Governorships	State Assemblies
PDP	54.4	152	62.4	53	23	26

(continued)

Table 12.4		(continued)				
ACN	19.0	53	21.2	18	6	5
CDC	11.1	31	7.1	6	1	0
Others	15.4	43	9.4	8	6	5

List of Acronyms Used in Table 12.4

AC (later ACN)	Action Congress (of Nigeria)	NPN	National Party of Nigeria
AG	Action Group	NPP	Nigerian People's Party
AD	Alliance for Democracy	NRC	National Republican Convention
ANPP	All Nigerian People's Party (formerly APP)	PPA	Progress People's Alliance
APGA	All People's Grand Alliance	PRP	People's Redemption Party
APP	All People's Party	PDP	People's Democratic Party
CDC	Congress for Democratic Change		
GNPP	Great Nigerian People's Party	SDP	Social Democratic Party
NAP	Nigerian Advance Party	UPN	Unity Party of Nigeria
NCNC	National Convention of Nigerian Citizens (formerly National Council of Nigeria and the Cameroons)		
NEPU	Northern Elements Progressive Union		
NNDP	Nigerian National Democratic Party		
NPC	Northern People's Congress		
NPF	Northern Progressive Front		

Old Roots and New Alignments: The PDP and the Other Parties of the Fourth Republic

Nigerians generally reacted with anger to General Abacha's 1993 coup and his subsequent banning of the SDP and NRC. With the unions crushed and Abiola in jail by the end of 1994, democracy deteriorated. In late 1996, the Abacha government registered only five parties,[25] all of which endorsed Abacha as president for elections scheduled in August 1998, and opposition increased. A group of former governors and political leaders from the north (many former NPN and PRP members) publicly petitioned Abacha not to run for president and human rights and prodemocracy groups protested. Even General Babangida voiced his opposition to Abacha's continuing as president. The only real obstacle to Abacha's plan for "self-succession" was whether the military would allow it.

The G-34, the prominent group of civilian leaders who had condemned Abacha's plans to perpetuate his power, created the People's Democratic Party (PDP) in late August, minus most of their Yoruba members, who joined the Alliance for Democracy

(AD). At least twenty more parties applied for certification to the electoral commission (INEC); many of them were truly grassroots movements, including a human
rights organization and a trade union party.

To escape the ethnic-based parties of the First and Second Republics, INEC
required that parties earn at least 5 percent of the votes in twenty-four of the thirty-
six states in local government elections in order to advance to the later state and federal levels. This turned out to be an ingenious way of reducing the number of parties,
while obliging viable parties to broaden their appeal. The only parties to meet INEC's
requirements were the PDP, AD, and the All People's Party (APP). To assuage the
Yoruba over Abiola's lost 1993 mandate, the PDP turned to retired General Obasanjo,
who went on to defeat an AD/APP alliance candidate in the 1999 presidential contest.

The parties of the Fourth Republic are primarily alliances of convenience among
prebendal Big Men from across Nigeria. Their sole purpose is to gain power. They
have no ideological differences or policy platforms that distinguish them, such that
politicians who lose in one party will frequently shift to another. Yet these parties do
feature one terribly important innovation that distinguishes them from those of the
First and Second Republics: the PDP, the old APP (later ANPP), and now the APC
and other leading parties of the Fourth Republic are multiethnic. They rely on elite-
centered structures established during previous civilian governments and transition
programs, and demonstrate the cross-ethnic alliances that developed over the last
quarter-century. The PDP includes core members of the northern established NPN,
the northern progressive PRP, and the Igbo-dominated NPP of the Second Republic,
as well as prominent politicians from the Niger Delta. The APP (later ANPP) was
also a multiethnic collection, drawing from the Second Republic's GNPP, a party
dominated by the northeastern-based Kanuri and groups from the Middle Belt, and
also features politicians who had prominent roles in the Abacha-sponsored parties.
The ANPP also included northwestern politicians of royal lineage, Igbo business
moguls, and southern minority leaders. The AD, however, was as Yoruba-centered as
its predecessors, the UPN in the Second Republic and the AG in the First Republic.
The party would later pay at the polls for its lack of national appeal, however, and
would join with breakaway factions of the PDP to form the Action Congress (AC,
later ACN; see below). In 2013, the ANPP and ACN would join with two other
opposition parties and six defecting governors from the PDP to form the APC, a
truly multiethnic, national party to rival the PDP.

This rise of multiethnic political parties is one of the most significant democratic
developments of the Fourth Republic. In multiethnic parties there is a strong incentive for politicians to bargain and bridge their ethnic differences *within* the party, so
that they may then compete with the other parties in the system, which would preferably be multiethnic as well.[26] In Nigeria, ethnic divisions—supported by prebendal
networks—still dominate national politics, but the multiethnic parties have at least
done fairly well at bridging these many divides during election periods and at fostering a climate of compromise during particularly divisive national debates.

The main vehicle whereby other African countries like Ghana have begun to
rise out this elite corruption trap is through the rise of a unified, viable political
opposition. Prior to 2013, the two main opposition parties, the ANPP and AD (later
ACN), never organized a working relationship or a serious policy challenge to the
PDP, except in the weeks prior to elections. ANPP leaders generally preferred to work
with the PDP in order to gain access to government largesse, and most of its governors actually left to join the PDP by 2010. The courts, however, overturned 2007
gubernatorial races in Edo, Osun, Ondo, Ekiti, Imo, and Abia, handing these seats
to several opposition parties and bringing their total number of states to thirteen.

The PDP took power again in 2011 with a massive majority across Nigeria, controlling the presidency, twenty-three governorships and twenty-six state assemblies, and more than half of the seats of the National Assembly. Yet it was also a party in disarray, with its northern factions under pressure from outrage over President Jonathan's breaking of the ethnic rotation principle, and southern leaders like former President Obasanjo angered by Jonathan's efforts to seize control of the PDP. Sensing both the limits of their small parties and opportunity in the growing rebellion within the PDP, leaders of the ANPP, ACN, and two other parties, including 2003–2011 opposition presidential candidate (and former military head of state) Muhammahu Buhari, agreed to merge to form the All Progressives Congress (APC) in 2013. Within months, they had attracted six PDP governors to their alliance, bringing their total number of states controlled to sixteen, with a majority in the Senate and near parity with the PDP in the House. Thus, for the first time in the Fourth Republic, the opposition under the APC has a serious chance at unseating the PDP in the 2015 elections. Yet the APC, like the PDP, is largely an alliance of convenience among the powerful personal networks of its "Big Men" politicians, and it will hold together only so long as it serves the interests of these powerbrokers.

Political Culture, Citizenship, and Identity

Military rule left Nigeria with strong authoritarian influences in its political culture. Most of the younger politicians of the Fourth Republic came of age during military rule and learned the business of politics from Abacha, Babangida, and their military governors. Nigeria's deep democratic traditions discussed in Section 1 remain vibrant among the larger polity, but they are in constant tension with the values imbibed during years of governance when political problems were often solved by military dictate, power, and violence rather than by negotiation and respect for law. This tension was manifest in the irony that the leading presidential contenders in 2003 were all former military men, one of whom—Buhari—was the ringleader of the 1983 coup that overthrew the Second Republic. Perhaps symbolic of a growing shift in Nigerian political culture away from its authoritarian past, however, Umaru Yar'Adua was the nation's first university graduate to become president, and Goodluck Jonathan has a Ph.D. in zoology.

Modernity versus Traditionalism

The interaction of Western (colonial) elements with traditional (precolonial, African) practices has created the tensions of a modern sociopolitical system that rests uneasily on traditional foundations. Nigerians straddle two worlds, each undergoing constant evolution. On the one hand, the strong elements in communal societies that promoted accountability have been weakened by the intrusion of Western culture oriented toward individuality, and exacerbated by urbanization. On the other hand, the modern state has been unable to free itself fully from rival ethnic claims organized around narrow, exclusivist constituencies.

As a result, exclusivist identities continue to dominate Nigerian political culture and to define the nature of citizenship.[27] Individuals tend to identify with their immediate ethnic, regional, and religious groups rather than with state institutions, especially during moments of crisis. Entirely missing from the relationship between state and citizen in Nigeria is a fundamental reciprocity—a working social contract—based on the belief that there is a common interest that binds them.

Religion

Religion has been a persistent source of comfort and a basis for conflict through-out Nigerian history. Islam began to filter into northeast Nigeria in the eleventh and twelfth centuries, spread to Hausaland by the fifteenth century, and greatly expanded in the early nineteenth century. In the north, Islam first coexisted with, then gradually supplanted, indigenous religions. Christianity arrived in the early nineteenth century, but expanded rapidly through missionary activity in the south. The amalgamation of northern and southern Nigeria in 1914 brought together the two regions and their belief systems.

These religious cultures have consistently clashed over political issues such as the secular character of the state. The application of the *shari'a* criminal code in the northern states has been a focal point for these tensions. For many Muslims, the *shari'a* represents a way of life and supreme law that transcends secular and state law; for many Christians, the expansion of *shari'a* law threatens the secular nature of the Nigerian state and their position within it. The pull of religious versus national identity becomes even stronger in times of economic hardship.

The nation is now evenly divided between Muslims and Christians, and the Middle Belt states where the fault line runs have often been particularly volatile. Communal conflicts frequently erupt in these areas, often between Fulani herdsmen, who are Muslim, and farmers, who in some instances may be Christian, or between farmers of the two religions over control of land or access to public funds. In most of these instances, religion is not the source of the conflict, but once disputes ignite they can quickly engage religious identities.

A handful of violent Islamist and Christian fundamentalist groups, how-ever, have become active in recent years, particularly in the northeast and the Middle Belt. Most violent among these has been the *Congregation of the People of Tradition for Proselytization and Jihad,* dubbed Boko Haram by the media, mean-ing "Western education is sinful," for the movement's rejection of the Western pedigrees of the Nigerian elite and the Western-created Nigerian state, mani-fest in its secular education system, that it views as corrupt and immoral. Boko Haram seeks to establish its idiosyncratic vision of an Islamist state in Nigeria and expresses common cause with global jihadist groups like al Qaeda. Much of its activities were focused in Borno and Yobe states in the northeast until 2011, at which point it received technical assistance from al Qaeda's Algerian affiliate and expanded its scope of operations across the northeast and north central region, attacking police stations and setting off bombs, including at the UN headquarters in Abuja. President Jonathan declared a state of emergency in three states, and a counteroffensive by the Nigerian military hemmed Boko Haram largely back within its Borno and Yobe base by 2014, but it remained capable of occasional attacks as far south as Abuja.

The Press

The plural nature of Nigerian society, with the potential to engender a shared political culture, can be seen in virtually all aspects of public life. The Nigerian press has long been one of the liveliest and most irreverent in Africa. The Abacha regime moved to stifle its independence, as had Babangida. In addition, mem-bers of the media are sometimes regarded as captives of ethnic and regional con-stituencies, a perception that has weakened their capacity to resist attacks on their rights and privileges. Significantly, much of the Nigerian press has been based in a Lagos-Ibadan axis in the southwestern part of Nigeria and has frequently been labeled "southern." Recently, however, independent television and radio stations have proliferated around the country, and forests of satellite towers now span Nigerian cities to support the boom in Internet cafés and telecommunications. Internet-based investigative journalists such as saharareporters.com have utilized the uncensored medium of the Internet to print stories that the mainstream newspapers have been afraid to publish, exposing the corrupt activities of some of Nigeria's biggest politicians.

Interest Groups, Social Movements, and Protest

Because the political machinery was in the hands of the military throughout the 1980s and 1990s, Nigerians sought alternative means of representation and protest. Historically, labor has played a significant role in Nigerian politics, as have student groups, women's organizations, and various radical and populist organizations. Business groups have frequently supported and colluded with corrupt civilian and military regimes. In the last year of the Abacha regime, however, even the business class, through mechanisms like Vision 2010, began to suggest an end to such arbitrary rule. The termination of military rule has seen civil society groups flourish across Nigeria.

Labor

Organized labor has played an important role in challenging governments during both the colonial and postcolonial eras in several African countries, Nigeria among them. Continuous military pressure throughout the 1980s and 1990s forced a decline in the independence and strength of organized labor in Nigerian politics. The Babangida regime implemented strategies of state corporatism designed to control and co-opt various social forces such as labor. When the leadership of the Nigerian Labour Congress (NLC), the umbrella confederation, took a vigorous stand against the government, the regime sacked the leaders and appointed conservative replacements. Prodemocracy strikes in mid-1994 by the National Petroleum Employees Union (NUPENG) and other sympathetic labor groups significantly reduced oil production and nearly brought the country to a halt, whereupon the Abacha regime arrested and disbanded its leadership.

The Nigerian labor movement has been vulnerable to reprisals by the state and private employers. The government has always been the biggest single employer of labor in Nigeria, as well as the recognized arbiter of industrial relations between employers and employees. Efforts by military regimes to centralize and co-opt the unions caused their militancy and impact to wane. Moreover, ethnic, regional, and religious divisions have often hampered labor solidarity, and these differences have been periodically manipulated by the state. Nevertheless, labor still claims an estimated 2 million members across Nigeria and remains one of the most potent forces in civil society. The unions have a great stake in the consolidation of constitutional rule in the Fourth Republic and the protections that allow them to organize and act freely on behalf of their members. The NLC has called national strikes on a number of occasions since 2000, typically over wages and fuel price hikes, including the Occupy Nigeria demonstrations of 2012 (see below).

The Business Community

Nigeria has a long history of entrepreneurialism and business development. This spirit is compromised by tendencies toward rent-seeking and the appropriation of state resources. Members of the Nigerian business class have been characterized as "pirate capitalists" because of the high level of corrupt practices and collusion with state officials.[28] Many wealthy individuals have served in the military or civilian governments, while others protect their access to state resources by sponsoring politicians or entering into business arrangements with bureaucrats.

Private interests have proven surprisingly resilient, as organized groups have emerged to represent the interests of the business class and to promote general economic development. There are numerous associations throughout Nigeria representing a broad variety of business activities and sectoral interests. National business associations, such as the Nigerian Association of Chambers of Commerce, Industry, Mines, and Agriculture (NACCIMA), the largest in the country, have taken an increasingly political stance, expressing their determination to protect their interests by advocating for better governance.

Other Social Groups

Student activism continues to be an important feature of Nigerian political life, and student unions have been major players in Nigerian politics since the 1960s. Since the 1990s, however, many universities have seen the rise of what are called "cults"— gangs of young men who are typically armed and sometimes do have cultish rituals associated with their groups. Many of these cultists "graduated" to join the militias and thugs of the politicians after 2000, while the cults are also often employed by elites for their power plays. In partial response to the cult phenomenon, religious movements have proliferated across Nigerian universities, providing students with an alternative way of life to these violent groups. Yet the religious groups on campuses have also provided vehicles for encouraging and recruiting both Christian and Muslim fundamentalists.

Overall, civil society groups are making substantial contributions to consolidating democracy in Nigeria. In particular, many groups have built good working relationships with the National Assembly and state legislatures, from which both sides have benefited. Their relationships with the political parties, however, remain distant. Nigeria's prospects for building a sustainable democracy during the Fourth Republic will depend, in part, on the willingness of many of these advocacy groups to increase their collaboration with the political parties, while avoiding cooptation and maintaining a high level of vigilance and activism.

The Political Impact of Technology

The dramatic rise of cellular phones in Nigeria since 2000—adding 100 million lines in a single decade—alongside a growing presence on the Internet have transformed the nation. Cellular phones are everywhere, including the latest models, and intense competition among service providers has produced ample coverage and one of the most efficient and lucrative industries in the country. The doubling in size of Nigeria's service sector during roughly the same period, as the nation's GDP grew on average over 6 percent annually since 2003, signals that the small but rapidly rising middle class is using this technology extensively.

Social media organizing large events →

Although middle-class professionals were using new technologies to monitor elections as early as 2003, the 2011 election marked an important watershed moment, as civil society activists used social media to track election violations across the country and plan a more extensive effort for 2015. Most impressive, however, were the protests that followed President Jonathan's removal of fuel subsidies in January 2012. In a movement inspired by the Arab Spring and Occupy Wall Street, thousands of Nigerians took to the streets for two weeks in what became known as Occupy Nigeria. Largely and loosely organized by concerned professionals working through social media sites like Facebook and Twitter, Occupy Nigeria brought peaceful demonstrations in cities across the nation, with the largest in Lagos, Abuja, and Kano, and within days attracted the attention of Nigerian Labour Congress (NLC), which in solidarity called for a general strike that brought economic activity to a halt.

Most impressively, the movement showed none of the ethnic, religious, or sectional elements so ever-present in Nigerian politics. In fact, interfaith cooperation was evident throughout, with breathtaking pictures of Christians forming a human shield around Muslims while they performed their required daily prayers, and Muslims escorting Christians to church, as just one example. What united the protesters was a common frustration with the massive corruption throughout Nigerian governance—a progressive agenda that seeks sweeping reform and broad-based development. The demonstrations collapsed after the NLC called off the strike as it reached a bargain with the Jonathan administration that restored half of the fuel subsidy, but many of the organizers continue to extend and consolidate their networks online, and promise to mobilize again at the next opportunity—most likely the 2015 elections.

Christians form a protective ring around Muslims while they conduct their afternoon prayers in Kano during Occupy Nigeria in 2012.

Ayemoba Godswill/Demotix/Demotix/Demotix/Corbis

Where Do You Stand?

What can the United States or other foreign governments do to support civil society groups and social media-based movements like Occupy Nigeria so they can transform Nigeria?

Do you agree that multiethnic parties are a good idea for political development? Can you think of examples from other countries that prove or disprove the point?

NIGERIAN POLITICS IN TRANSITION

SECTION

5

Despite the slow progress of the Fourth Republic, Nigerians overwhelmingly favor democratic government over military rule. About 70 percent of respondents in a recent survey said that they still prefer democracy to any other alternative, although popular frustration is growing with the slow pace of reform and continued corruption in politics.[29] This growing anger with the massive corruption is the one constant that transcends the nation, featuring strongly in the motives of groups as different as Boko Haram and the Niger Delta militias to Occupy Nigeria. Will democracy in Nigeria be consolidated sufficiently to meet minimal levels of public satisfaction, or will the nation again succumb to destructive authoritarian rule?

Nigerian politics must change in fundamental ways for democracy to become more stable and legitimate. First and foremost, the nation must turn from a system of politics dominated by "Big Men"—for all intents and purposes, a competitive oligarchy—to a more representative mode of politics that addresses the fundamental interests of the public. Second, Nigerians must conclusively settle the national question and commit to political arrangements that accommodate the nation's diversity. In short, Nigeria's Fourth Republic must find ways of moving beyond prebendal politics and develop a truly national political process in which mobilization and conflicts along ethnic, regional, and religious lines gradually diminish, and which can address Nigeria's true national crisis: poverty and underdevelopment.

Focus Questions

- What role can political opposition and civil society play in reversing prebendalism and the politics of the "Big Men"?

- What other reforms can help to settle the National Question and harness the strong democratic yearnings of the Nigerian public?

Political Challenges and Changing Agendas

Nigeria's fitful transition to democratic rule between 1985 and 1999 was inconclusive, largely because it was planned and directed from above. This approach contrasts sharply with the popular-based movements that unseated autocracies in Central and Eastern Europe or the Arab Spring. The military periodically made promises for democratic transition as a ploy to stabilize and legitimate their governments. General Abubakar dutifully handed power to the civilians in 1999, but only after ensuring that the military's interests would be protected under civilian rule and creating an overly powerful executive that reinforces prebendalism and its patronage system. The military's rapid transition program produced a tenuous, conflicted democratic government that faces daunting tasks of restoring key institutions, securing social stability, and reforming the economy. The continuing strength and influence of collective identities, defined on the basis of religion or ethnicity, are often more binding than national allegiances. The parasitic nature of the Nigerian economy is a further source of instability. Rent-seeking and other unproductive, often corrupt, business activities remain accepted norms of wealth accumulation.

Nonetheless, Nigerians are sowing seeds of change in all of these areas. Attitudes toward the military in government have shifted dramatically. Military attitudes themselves have changed significantly as well, as evidenced by the restraint shown by the armed forces during President Yar'Adua's incapacitation and long absence. The decline in the appeal of military rule can be attributed to the abysmal performances of the Babangida and Abacha regimes in economic oversight and governance. Many now recognize that the military, apart from its contributions to national security, is incapable of promoting economic and social progress in Nigeria. Yet frustrations with corruption and poor governance have grown to the point that others still see the military as possible solution, and may call on it to intervene in a future crisis, which could have catastrophic consequences. If, however, the armed forces can stay secure in their barracks, as still seems more likely, then the nature of the struggles among civilian political elites will decide the direction of political and economic change. Thus, democratic development may be advanced in the long run if stable coalitions appear over time in a manner that balances the power among contending groups, and if these key elites adapt to essential norms and rules of the political game.

Initially, members of the new political class confined their struggles within the constraints of the democratic system: using the courts, media, legislative struggles, and even legal expediencies such as impeachment. Political actors largely worked through formal institutions, contending openly and offsetting the power of a single group or faction. Since the 2003 elections, however, the political elite have also shown a growing willingness to use extra-systemic measures to forward their interests through election rigging, corruption, and militia-led violence. The Niger Delta has grown particularly violent, with increasingly well-armed militias that in some cases have shown a measure of independence from their political patrons. The rise of Boko Haram in the northeast has created an additional threat for the Nigerian state, which politicians have also been seeking to use for political gain.

The next critical step down the long road of democratic development for Nigeria is the creation of a viable, multiethnic opposition party that is also loyal, meaning that it plays by the rules of the system. Opposition parties help to reduce corruption in the system because they have an interest in exposing the misconduct of the ruling party, which in turn pressures them to restrain their own behavior. Furthermore, in order to unseat the ruling party and win elections, opposition parties need to engage the public to win their votes. In this manner, issues of interest to the public are engaged by the parties. This is the basis of the social contract: elites gain the privilege of power so long as they use it to promote the public interest.

The introduction of so many new parties after 2002 slowed the development of a viable, loyal opposition, further diluting it and allowing the PDP to govern largely unchecked. The PDP has also worked to absorb or co-opt opposition leaders when possible. The rise of the APC in 2013, however, at last offers a real chance for Nigeria to develop two national, multiethnic parties that can check and balance each other and offer the Nigerian public a serious alternative at the ballot box. If in their competition with each other the two parties reach out to civil society for support and vie for public attentions by offering real development policies they actually seek to implement, then Nigeria will finally turn the corner toward stability and growth, joining Ghana and other regional democratic leaders. Yet the political

Protests over federal exploitation of the oil-producing Niger Delta sparked a region-wide insurgency by 2003, with heavily armed militias engaged in both political disputes and criminal activities, cutting Nigeria's oil production by more than a quarter.

PIUS UTOMI EKPEI/AFP/Getty Images

bargains holding the APC together remain tenuous, and will face tremendous strain as the election approaches. Moreover, the moment when political opposition stands in striking distance of winning an election is one of the most dangerous points in political development, as ruling parties do not often give up power quietly. The PDP shows every intention of using rigging, bribery, and violence as in previous elections, and APC politicians are no strangers to these tactics either, raising the specter of massive instability and bloodshed for the 2015 contests if the situation spirals out of control. Meanwhile, the military watches closely from the sidelines.

The project of building a coherent nation-state out of competing nationalities remains unfinished. Ironically, because the parties of the Fourth Republic generally do not represent any particular ethnic interest—indeed, they do not represent anyone's interests except those of the leaders and their clients—ethnic associations and militias have risen to articulate ethnic-based grievances. Ethnic consciousness cannot—and should not—be eliminated from society, but ethnicity cannot be the main basis for political competition. If current ethnic mobilization can be contained within ethnic associations arguing over the agenda of the parties, then it can be managed. If, however, any of the ethnic associations captures one of the political parties or joins with the militias to foment separatism, instability will result. The same is true if the PDP comes to be seen as the Christian party of the south, and the APC the Muslim party of the north, which is a danger as the APC moves to nominate a northern Muslim presidential candidate to capitalize on the frustration there with President Jonathan. President Jonathan also stoked ethnic mobilization by convening a National Conference in March 2014, which was characterized primarily by the airing of ethnic and regional grievances. Meanwhile, the Niger Delta militias and Boko Haram have both threatened to divide the country.

Democratic development also requires further decentralization of power structures in Nigeria. The struggle on the part of the National Assembly and the state governors to wrest power from the presidency has advanced this process, as has the growing competence and role of the judiciary. Privatization of government parastatals could also reduce the power of the presidency over time, since it will no longer control all the primary sectors of the economy. A more decentralized system allows local problems to be solved within communities rather than involving national institutions and the accompanying interethnic competition. Decentralization also lowers the stakes for holding national offices, thereby reducing the destructive pressures on political competition and political office. The devolution of power and resources to smaller units, closer to their constituents, can substantially enhance the accountability of leaders and the transparency of government operations.

Civil society groups are the final link in democratic consolidation in Nigeria. These groups are critical players in connecting the Nigerian state to the Nigerian people. They aggregate and articulate popular interests into the policy realm, and they provide advocacy on behalf of their members. If the political parties are to reflect anything more than elite interests and clientelist rule, the parties must reach out and build alliances with the institutions of civil society. For opposition parties like APC to become a viable opposition movement capable of checking the power of the PDP, they will have to build alliances with civil society groups in order to mobilize large portions of the population, particularly labor unions. Foreign pressure also plays an important role in maintaining the quest for democracy and sustainable development. In recent years, major external forces have been more forthright in supporting civil society and democratization in Nigeria. The United States, Britain, and some member states of the European Union quite visibly exerted pressure on Babangida and Abacha to leave and applied modest sanctions in support of democracy. These same governments again pressed Nigerian leaders to name Jonathan acting president during the crisis over President Yar'Adua's incapacitation.

Nevertheless, the Western commitment to development and democracy in Africa is limited by the industrial powers' addiction to oil, which has blunted the impact of such pressure on Nigeria, and is now exacerbated by growing competition from China for energy resources. Much of the initiative for Africa's growth therefore needs to emerge from within. In Nigeria, such initiatives will depend on substantial changes in the way Nigerians do business. It will be necessary to develop a more sophisticated and far less corrupt form of capitalist enterprise and the development of entrepreneurial, particularly middle-class interests within Nigeria who will see their interests tied to the principles of democratic politics and economic initiative. Occupy Nigeria offers hope in this regard, signifying a rising progressive, multicultural movement of professionals seeking to fundamentally change the corrupt system.

Nigerian politics has been characterized by turmoil and periodic crises ever since the British relinquished colonial power. Over fifty years later, the country is still trying to piece together a fragile democracy, yet key signs of economic growth and political reform are at last on the horizon. Despite these positive trends, the nation continues to wrestle with overdependence of its economy on oil, enfeebled infrastructure and institutions, heightened sociopolitical tensions, an irresponsible elite, and an expanding mass culture of despondency and rage. Only responsible government combined with sustained civil society action can reverse this decline and restore the nation to what President Obasanjo called "the path to greatness."

Youth Politics and the Generational Divide

Much of this great choice between development or collapse facing Nigeria may well be decided by the nation's youth. With women averaging over five births each and yet a life expectancy of only 48 years, Nigeria's population is widely skewed toward youths, such that over 70 percent of Nigerians are under the age of 30, and over half are under the age of 19. At current rates, Nigeria's population is predicted to top 400 million by 2050, the fourth largest nation in the world that will be home to approximately 280 million or more youths under age 30.

The vast majority of these youths are and will be extremely poor, with more than half trying to eke out a living on less than a dollar per day. At least a fifth of them are officially unemployed, but the real figures are much worse, especially in the northern half of the country. A few are, however, wired into the global economy through cellular and Internet technology, and their numbers are growing alongside their political sophistication and organizing skills, which they demonstrated during Occupy Nigeria. Yet the fact that Nigeria is a youth-majority state underlines another massive political divide growing in the country: the domination of its elders. Septuagenarian and older politicians still play powerful roles in both the PDP and APC, and wealthy men in their 50s and 60s dominate the presidency, National Assembly, and governorships. On the other hand, Boko Haram, the Niger Delta militias, and other anti-state actors are dominated by the young. Which way will Nigeria's new faces turn? Much will depend upon the ability of the political parties to engage youth in their ranks, and to produce serious policies that foster broad-based development that offers opportunity and hope to the massive younger generation that is now rising.

Nigerian Politics in Comparative Perspective

The study of Nigeria has important implications for the study of African politics and, more broadly, of comparative politics. The Nigerian case embodies a number of key themes and issues that can be generalized. We can learn much about how democratic regimes are established and consolidated by understanding Nigeria's pitfalls and travails. Analysis of the historical dynamics of Nigeria's ethnic conflict helps to identify institutional mechanisms that may be effective in reducing ethnic conflict in other states. We can also learn much about the necessary and sufficient conditions for economic development, and the particular liabilities of oil-dependent states.

A Globalizing World of States

Nigeria exists in two "worlds" of states: one in the global political economy and the other within Africa. Economically, Nigeria was thrust into the world economy in a position of weakness, first as a British colony and later as an independent nation. Despite its resources and the potential of oil to provide the investment capital needed to build a modern economy, Nigeria has grown weaker. It lost much of its international clout, and in place of the international respect it once enjoyed as a developing giant within Africa, the country became notorious throughout the 1990s for corruption, human rights abuses, and failed governance. The return of democracy and soaring oil prices have restored some of Nigeria's former stature, but its economic vulnerability and persistent corruption keep it a secondary player in the world of states.

The future of democracy, political stability, and economic renewal in other parts of Africa, and certainly in West Africa, will be greatly influenced for good or ill by unfolding events in Nigeria, the giant of the continent. Beyond the obvious demonstration effects, the economy of the West African subregion could be buoyed by substantial growth in the Nigerian economy. In addition, President Obasanjo conducted very active public diplomacy across Africa, seeking to resolve major conflicts, promote democracy, and improve trade. President Yar'Adua was far less active in foreign policy, and cultivated stronger ties with China. President Jonathan has strong ties with the United States, and took a strong stance against the 2012 coup and insurgency in Mali, but has not articulated a comprehensive African policy or further abroad.

Until recently, international political and business attention shifted elsewhere on the continent, focusing on such countries as South Africa, Botswana, and Ghana. Insurgency in the Niger Delta also meant that Nigeria has fallen behind Angola as the largest oil producer on the continent. Moreover, the Boko Haram insurgency has placed Nigeria under watch by Western security agencies as a base of operations for Islamist terror groups. Yet a decade of steady economic growth, focused primarily in the south, is attracting growing investment and business interest.

Governing the Economy

Nigeria provides important insights into the political economy of underdevelopment. At independence in 1960, Nigeria was stronger economically than its Southeast Asian counterparts Indonesia and Malaysia. Independent Nigeria appeared poised for growth, with a wealth of natural resources, a large population, and the presence of highly entrepreneurial groups in many regions of the country. Today, Nigeria is among the poorest countries in the world in terms of human development indicators, while many of its Asian counterparts have joined the ranks of the wealthy countries. One critical lesson Nigeria teaches is that a rich endowment of resources is not enough to ensure economic development. In fact, it may encourage rent-seeking behavior that undermines more productive activities.[30] Sound political and institutional development must come first.

Other variables are critically important, notably democratic stability and a capable developmental state. A developmentalist ethic, and an institutional structure to enforce it, can set limits to corrupt behavior and constrain the pursuit of short-term personal gain at the expense of national economic growth. Institutions vital to the pursuit of these objectives include a professional civil service, an independent judiciary, and a free press. Nigeria has had each of these, but they were gradually undermined and corrupted under military rule. The public "ethic" that has come to dominate Nigerian political economy has been prebendalism. Where corruption is unchecked, economic development suffers accordingly.

Nigeria also demonstrates that sustainable economic development requires sound economic policy. Without export diversification, commodity-exporting countries are buffeted by the price fluctuations of one or two main products. Nigeria, by contrast, has substituted one form of commodity dependence for another, and it has allowed its petroleum industry to overwhelm all other sectors of the economy, and only recently has the non-oil sector begun to revive. Nigeria even became a net importer of products (for example, palm oil and palm nuts) for which it was once a leading world producer. Nigeria is even in the absurd position of being unable to feed itself, despite rich agricultural lands. In comparative perspective, we can see that natural resource endowments can be tremendously beneficial. The United States, for example, has parlayed its endowments of agricultural, mineral, and energy resources into one of the world's most diversified modern economies. Meanwhile, Japan, which is by comparison poorly endowed with natural resources, has one of the strongest economies in the world, achieved in large part through its unique developmental strategies. Each of these examples illustrates the primacy of sound economic policies implemented through consolidated political systems.

The Democratic Idea

Many African countries have experienced transitions from authoritarian rule.[31] With the end of superpower competition in Africa and the withdrawal of external support for Africa's despots, many African societies experienced a resurgence of popular pressures for greater participation in political life and more open forms of governance. Decades of authoritarian, single-party, and military rule in Africa left a dismal record of political repression, human rights abuses, inequality, deteriorating governance, and failed economies. A handful of elites acquired large fortunes through wanton corruption. The exercise of postcolonial authoritarian rule in Africa has contributed to economic stagnation and decline. The difficulties of such countries as Cameroon, Togo, and Zimbabwe in achieving political transitions reflects, in large part, the ruling elites' unwillingness to cede control of the political instruments that made possible their self-enrichment.

Nigeria exemplifies the harsh reality of authoritarian and unaccountable governance. Nigerians have endured six military regimes, countless attempted coups, and a bloody civil war that claimed more than 1 million lives. They have also seen a once-prospering economy reduced to a near shambles. Today, democracy has become a greater imperative because only such a system provides the mechanisms to limit abuses of power and render governments accountable.

Collective Identities

Nigeria presents an important case in which to study the dangers of communal competition in a society with deep cultural divisions. How can multiethnic countries manage diversity? What institutional mechanisms can be employed to avert tragedies such as the 1967–1970 civil war or the continuing conflicts that have brought great suffering to Rwanda and the former Yugoslavia? This chapter has suggested institutional reforms such as multiethnic political parties, decentralization, and a strengthened federal system that can contribute to reducing tensions and minimizing conflict.

Insights from the Nigerian experience may explain why some federations persist, while identifying factors that can undermine them. Nigeria's complex social map, and its varied attempts to create a nation out of its highly diverse population, enhances our understanding of the politics of cultural pluralism and the difficulties of accommodating sectional interests under conditions of political and economic insecurity. Federal character in Nigeria has become a form of ethnic and regional favoritism and a tool for dispensing patronage. Yet the country has benefited in some ways from the attention devoted to creating state and local governments, and from giving people in different regions a sense of being stakeholders in the entity called Nigeria.

Where Do You Stand?

Are you convinced that a viable political opposition—perhaps the new APC—supported by civil society could put Nigeria on the path to development, or do you think that Boko Haram, the Niger Delta militias, and prebendal "Big Man" politics will eventually push Nigeria to collapse?

Should the United States and other countries be pushing for more and deeper democracy in Africa, or does the example of Nigeria suggest it is too difficult?

Chapter Summary

Colonialism forced many nations under one political roof, ensuring that ethnic divisions would dominate the nation's politics after independence in 1960, leading to collapse and civil war. Military rule for nearly 30 years after the war, greased by rents from the oil industry, reunified Nigeria under a federal system, but also fed the prebendal pattern that has corrupted the politics of the Fourth Republic.

Nigeria's challenges reflect the frustrated hopes of its people for a better life, stable government, and a democratic political order, while suggesting the potential contributions that this country could make to the African continent and the wider international arena. Such potential depends upon responsive and capable democratic governance. If Nigeria cannot reverse the corrupt, prebendal status quo, however, then the specter will remain of military entrepreneurs, or ethnic and religious extremists, plunging Nigeria into another cycle of coups, decline, and possibly collapse.

Key Terms

accountability
acephalous societies
authoritarian
autocracy
balance of payments
clientelism
indirect rule
international financial institutions (IFIs)
interventionist
jihad
legitimacy
prebendalism
rents
shari'a
structural adjustment program (SAP)
unfinished state
warrant chiefs

Suggested Readings

Agbaje, Adigun. *The Nigerian Press: Hegemony and the Social Construction of Legitimacy, 1960–1983.* Lewiston, NY: Edwin Mellen Press, 1992.

Diamond, Larry. *Class, Ethnicity and Democracy in Nigeria: The Failure of the First Republic.* London: Macmillan, 1988.

Decalo, Samuel. *Coups and Army Rule in Africa,* 2nd ed. New Haven: Yale University Press, 1990.

Falola, Toyin. *Violence in Nigeria: The Crisis of Religious Politics and Secular Ideologies.* Rochester, NY: University of Rochester Press, 1999.

Joseph, Richard A. *Democracy and Prebendal Politics in Nigeria: The Rise and Fall of the Second Republic.* Cambridge: Cambridge University Press, 1987.

Kew, Darren. "Nigerian elections and the neopatrimonial paradox: In search of the social contract," *Journal of Contemporary African Studies* 28, no. 4 (2010): 499–521.

Lewis, Peter M. "Endgame in Nigeria? The Politics of a Failed Democratic Transition." *African Affairs* 93 (1994): 323–340.

Lubeck, Paul. *Islam and Urban Labor in Northern Nigeria.* Cambridge: Cambridge University Press, 1987.

Osaghae, Eghosa. *Crippled Giant: Nigeria since Independence.* Bloomington: Indiana University Press, 1998.

Suberu, Rotimi. *Federalism and Ethnic Conflict in Nigeria.* Washington, DC: U.S. Institute of Peace, 2001.

Suggested Websites

British Broadcasting Corporation: A 2002 interview with President Obasanjo
news.bbc.co.uk/2/hi/talking_point/1800826.stm

Gamji: A collection of news stories from Nigerian newspapers, as well as opinion pieces and other news links
www.gamji.com

The Guardian, Nigeria's leading daily newspaper
www.ngrguardiannews.com

Human Rights Watch reports
hrw.org/doc/?t=africa&c=nigeri

International Institute for Democracy and Electoral Assistance
archive.idea.int/frontpage_nigeria.htm

Stanford University's Center for African Studies
http://africanstudies.stanford.edu/

13 The Russian Federation

Joan DeBardeleben

Official Name: Russian Federation (Rossiiskaia Federatsiia)

Location: Eastern Europe/Northern Asia

Capital City: Moscow

Population (2014): 142.5 million

Size: 17,075,200 sq. km.; approximately 1.8 times the size of the United States

Aleshkovsky Mitya/Itar-Tass/
ABACA/Newscom

© Cengage Learning®

THE MAKING OF THE MODERN RUSSIAN STATE

SECTION 1

Politics in Action

Focus Questions ▽

• What are the most important critical junctures in recent Russian history? In what ways was each juncture a reaction to a recurring problem in Russian history?

• What were Russia's principal challenges in the 1990s and how have they changed since the year 2000?

On February 21, 2012, an unusual performance occurred in Christ the Savior Church in central Moscow. The punk rock group known as Pussy Riot displayed what it called a "punk prayer," protesting the Russian Orthodox Church's support for incumbent President Vladimir Putin in the upcoming presidential election. Formed in 2011, the group has described itself as feminist and in opposition to the Putin regime.[1] Although Pussy Riot had previously appeared at other venues, this performance elicited particular objection from the authorities, leading to the arrest and two-year sentencing of two members for "hooliganism, motivated by religious hatred." The ruling became a cause célèbre and focus of social media attention, interpreted as symbolic of the Kremlin's lack of tolerance of political opposition.

In December 2013, in a well-publicized move, the Russian legislative body (the State Duma) passed an amnesty law, supported by President Putin. Among those freed were the two imprisoned members of Pussy Riot. At a press conference following their release, the band members expressed continuing criticism of Putin, vowing

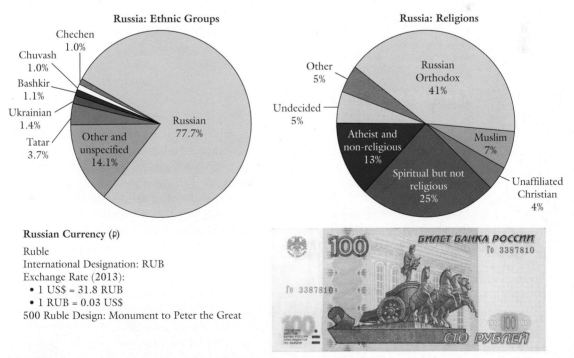

Russia: Ethnic Groups

Chechen 1.0%
Chuvash 1.0%
Bashkir 1.1%
Ukrainian 1.4%
Tatar 3.7%
Other and unspecified 14.1%
Russian 77.7%

Russia: Religions

Other 5%
Undecided 5%
Atheist and non-religious 13%
Spiritual but not religious 25%
Russian Orthodox 41%
Muslim 7%
Unaffiliated Christian 4%

Russian Currency (₽)

Ruble
International Designation: RUB
Exchange Rate (2013):
• 1 US$ = 31.8 RUB
• 1 RUB = 0.03 US$
500 Ruble Design: Monument to Peter the Great

FIGURE 13.1 The Russian Nation at a Glance

© 4780322454/Shutterstock.com (for photo)

CHRONOLOGY of Soviet and Russian Political Development

1918–1928
Civil war, war communism, and the New Economic Policy

1941–1945
Nazi Germany invades Soviet Union; "Great Patriotic War"

1965–1982
The Brezhnev era and bureaucratic consolidation

1982–1985
Leadership change after Brezhnev's death

1929–1953
Stalin in power

1915   1925   1935   1945   1955   1965   1985

1929–1938
Collectivization and purges

1956–1964
The Khrushchev era and de-Stalinization

1985–1991
The Gorbachev era and *perestroika*

1917
The Bolshevik seizure of power

1953–1955
Leadership change after Stalin's death

to maintain the political struggle, with a particular focus on prisoners' rights. The amnesty, which also freed other regime critics, was widely interpreted as an effort to bolster the tarnished human rights reputation of the Russian government and head off potential boycotts of the Winter Olympics, to be held in Sochi, Russia, in February 2014.

The Pussy Riot incident became a powerful symbol of the efforts of the Russian leadership to steer a path between tight-handed political control, on the one hand, and concessions to international pressure, on the other. At the same time, increases in visible protest in Russia and often-successful efforts by the regime itself to mobilize domestic public opinion revealed deep cultural and political rifts plaguing the country.

Geographic Setting

After the Soviet Union broke up in 1991, fifteen newly independent states emerged on its territory. This section focuses on the Russian Federation, the largest successor state and the largest European country in population (142.5 million in mid-2014)[2] and, in area, the largest country in the world, spanning eleven time zones.

Russia underwent rapid industrialization and urbanization under Soviet rule. Only 18 percent of Russians lived in urban areas in 1917, at the time of the Russian Revolution; 73 percent do now. Less than 8 percent of Russia's land is arable, while 45 percent is forested. Russia is rich in natural resources, concentrated in western Siberia and northern Russia. These include minerals (even gold and diamonds), timber, oil, and natural gas, which now form the basis of Russia's economic wealth.

Before the communists took power in 1917, Russia's czarist empire extended east to the Pacific, south to the Caucasus Mountains and the Muslim areas of Central Asia, north to the Arctic Circle, and west into present-day Ukraine, eastern Poland, and the Baltic states. In the USSR the Russian Republic formed the core of a multiethnic state.

1991
Collapse of the USSR
and establishment of
the Russian Federation
as an independent state

1998
Financial crisis and
devaluation of the ruble

2000–2008
Putin presidency, with
recentralization of
state power

2007–2008
Parliamentary and
presidential elections
establishing dominance of
United Russia and smooth
transition to the presidency
of Dmitry Medvedev

1990   1995   2000   2005   2010   2015

1993
Adoption of the new Russian
constitution by referendum; first
(multiparty) parliamentary elections in
the Russian Federation (December)

2004
Hostage-taking in
Beslan, southern
Russia; Putin
announces new
centralizing measures.

March 2014–
Russia takes control of the
Ukrainian region of Crimea
and annexes it to Russia.

March 2012–
Vladimir Putin elected as
president, after a four-year break

1991–1999
Yeltsin presidency, with market and
democratic reforms

December 2011–March 2012
State Duma elections and Presidential
elections, and protest demonstrations

Russia's ethnic diversity and geographic scope have made it a hard country to govern. Currently Russia faces pockets of instability on several of its borders, most notably in eastern Ukraine (since early 2014), in Tajikistan and Afghanistan in Central Asia, and in Georgia and Azerbaijan in the south. Besides Ukraine, Russia's western neighbors include Belarus, and several member states of the European Union (EU), namely Finland, Estonia,

Table 13.1	Political Organization
Political System	Constitutionally a semi-presidential republic
Regime History	Re-formed as an independent state with the collapse of communist rule in December 1991; current constitution since December 1993.
Administrative Structure	Constitutionally a federal system, with eighty-three subnational governments, plus two regions annexed from neighboring Ukraine in 2014 that are not recognized by most Western countries as being part of Russia; politically centralized.
Executive	Dual executive (president and prime minister). Direct election of president; prime minister appointed by the president with the approval of the lower house of the parliament (State Duma).
Legislature	Bicameral. Upper house (Federation Council) appointed by heads of regional executive and representative organs. Lower house (*State Duma*) chosen by direct election, with mixed electoral system involving single-member districts and proportional representation for a total of 450 deputies. Powers include proposal and approval of legislation, approval of presidential appointees.
Judiciary	Independent constitutional court with nineteen justices, nominated by the president and approved by the Federation Council, holding twelve-year terms with possible renewal.
Party System	Dominant establishment party (United Russia) within a multi-party system

Latvia, Lithuania, and Poland. Located between Europe, the Islamic world, and Asia, Russia's regional sphere of influence is now disputed.

Critical Junctures

The Decline of the Russian Tsarist State and the Founding of the Soviet Union

patrimonial state

A system of governance in which the ruler treats the state as personal property (patrimony).

Until 1917, an autocratic system headed by the tsar ruled Russia. Russia had a **patrimonial state** that not only ruled the country but also owned the land.[3] The majority of the peasant population was tied to the nobles, the state, or the church (through serfdom). The serfs were emancipated in 1861 as a part of the tsar's effort to modernize Russia and to make it militarily competitive with the West.

The key impetus for industrialization came from the state and from foreign capital. Despite some reforms, workers became increasingly discontented, as did liberal intellectuals, students, and, later, peasants, in the face of Russia's defeat in the Russo-Japanese war and continued tsarist repression. Revolution broke out in 1905. The regime maintained control through repression and economic reform until March 1917, during the height of World War I, when revolution deposed the tsar and installed a moderate provisional government. In November, the Bolsheviks, led by Vladimir Lenin, overthrew that government.

The Bolshevik Revolution and the Establishment of Soviet Power (1917–1929)

The Bolsheviks were Marxists who believed their revolution reflected the political interests of the proletariat (working class). Most revolutionary leaders, however, were not workers, but came from a more educated and privileged stratum, the intelligentsia. Their slogan, "Land, Peace, and Bread," appealed to both the working class and the discontented peasantry—over 80 percent of Russia's population.

democratic centralism

A system of political organization developed by V. I. Lenin and practiced, with modifications, by all communist party-states. Its principles include a hierarchical party structure.

The Bolshevik strategy was based on two key ideas: democratic centralism and vanguardism. **Democratic centralism** mandated a hierarchical party structure in which leaders were, at least formally, elected from below, but strict discipline was required in implementing party decisions once they were made. The centralizing elements of democratic centralism took precedence over the democratic elements, as the party tried to insulate itself from informers of the tsarist forces and later from real and imagined threats to the new regime. The concept of a **vanguard party** governed the Bolsheviks' relations with broader social forces. Party leaders claimed to understand the interests of working people better than the people did themselves. Over time, this philosophy was used to justify virtually all actions of the party and the state it dominated.

vanguard party

A political party that claims to operate in the "true" interests of the group or class that it purports to represent, even if this understanding doesn't correspond to the expressed interests of the group itself.

In 1922 the Bolsheviks formed the Union of Soviet Socialist Republics (USSR); they were the first communist party to take state power. Prior to this, the Bolsheviks had faced an extended civil war (1918–1921), when they introduced war communism, which involved state control of key economic sectors and forcible requisitioning of grain from the peasants. The *Cheka*, the security arm of the regime, was strengthened, and restrictions were placed on other political groups. By 1921, the leadership had recognized the political costs of war communism. In an effort to accommodate the peasantry, the New Economic Policy (NEP) was introduced in 1921 and lasted until 1928. Under NEP, state control over the economy was loosened so that private enterprise and trade were revived. The state, however, retained control of large-scale industry.

Gradually, throughout the 1920s, the authoritarian strains of Bolshevik thinking eclipsed the democratic elements. Lacking a democratic tradition and bolstered by the vanguard ideology of the party, the Bolshevik leaders were plagued by internal struggles following Lenin's death in 1924. These conflicts culminated in the rise of Joseph Stalin and the demotion or exile of other prominent figures such as Leon Trotsky and Nikolai Bukharin. By 1929 all open opposition, even within the party itself, had been silenced.

The Bolshevik revolution also initiated a period of international isolation. Western countries were hardly pleased with the revolutionary developments, which led to expropriation of foreign holdings and which represented the first successful challenge to the international capitalist order. Some of Russia's former Western allies from World War I sent material aid and troops to oppose the new Bolshevik government during the civil war.

The Stalin Revolution (1929–1953)

From 1929 until his death in 1953, Joseph Stalin consolidated his power as Soviet leader. He brought changes to every aspect of Soviet life. The state became the engine for rapid economic development, with state ownership of virtually all economic assets. By 1935, over 90 percent of agricultural land had been taken from the peasants and made into state or collective farms. **Collectivization** was rationalized as a means of preventing the emergence of a new capitalist class in the countryside. It actually targeted the peasantry as a whole, leading to widespread famine and the death of millions. Rapid industrialization favored heavy industries, and consumer goods were neglected. Economic control operated through a complex but inefficient system of central economic planning, in which the state planning committee (Gosplan) set production targets for every enterprise in the country. People were uprooted from their traditional lives in the countryside and catapulted into the rhythm of urban industrial life. Media censorship and state control of the arts strangled creativity as well as political opposition. The party/state became the authoritative source of truth; anyone deviating from the authorized interpretation could be charged with treason.

Gradually, the party became subject to the personal whims of Stalin and his secret police. Overall, an estimated 5 percent of the Soviet population was arrested at one point or another under the Stalinist system, usually for no apparent cause. Forms of resistance were evasive rather than active. Peasants killed livestock to avoid giving it over to collective farms.

Isolation from the outside world was a key tool of the Stalinist system of power. But the policy had costs. While it shielded Soviet society from the Great Depression of the 1930s, the Soviet economy, protected from foreign competition, also failed to keep up with the rapid economic and technological transformation in the West.

In 1941, Nazi Germany invaded the Soviet Union, and Stalin joined the Allied powers. Casualties in the war were staggering, about 27 million people, including 19 million civilians. War sacrifices and heroism have remained powerful symbols of pride and unity for Russians up through the present day. After the war, the other Allied powers allowed the Soviet Union to absorb new territories into the USSR itself (these became the Soviet republics of Latvia, Lithuania, Estonia, Moldavia, and portions of western Ukraine). The Allies also implicitly granted the USSR free rein to shape the postwar governments and economies in East Germany, Poland, Hungary, Czechoslovakia, Yugoslavia, Bulgaria, and Romania. Western offers to include parts of the region in the Marshall Plan were rejected under pressure from the USSR. Local Communist parties gained control in each country. Only in Yugoslavia were

collectivization

A process undertaken in the Soviet Union under Stalin from 1929 into the early 1930s and in China under Mao in the 1950s, by which agricultural land was removed from private ownership and organized into large state and collective farms.

indigenous Communist forces sufficiently strong to hold power largely on their own and thus later to assert their independence from Moscow.

The USSR emerged as a global superpower as the Soviet sphere of influence encompassed large parts of Central and Eastern Europe. In 1947, the American president Harry Truman proclaimed a policy to contain further Soviet expansion (later known as the Truman Doctrine). In 1949, the North Atlantic Treaty Organization (NATO) was formed involving several West European countries, the United States, and Canada, to protect against potential Soviet aggression. In 1955 the Soviet Union initiated the Warsaw Pact in response. These events marked the beginning of the Cold War, characterized by tension and military competition between the two superpowers, leading to an escalating arms race that was particularly costly to the Soviet Union.

The Soviet Union isolated its satellite countries in Central and Eastern Europe from the West and tightened their economic and political integration with the USSR. Some countries within the Soviet bloc, however, had strong historic links to Western Europe (especially Czechoslovakia, Poland, and Hungary). Over time, these countries served not only as geographic buffers to direct Western contacts but also as conduits for Western influence.

Attempts at De-Stalinization (1953–1985)

Even the Soviet elite realized that Stalin's terror could be sustained only at great cost. The terror destroyed initiative and participation, and the unpredictability of Stalinist rule inhibited the rational formulation of policy. From Stalin's death in 1953 until the mid-1980s Soviet politics became more regularized and stable. Terror abated, but political controls remained in place, and efforts to isolate Soviet citizens from foreign influences continued.

In 1956, Nikita Khrushchev, the new party leader, embarked on a bold policy of de-Stalinization, rejecting terror as an instrument of political control. The secret police (KGB) was subordinated to the authority of the Communist Party of the Soviet Union (CPSU), and party meetings resumed on a regular basis. However, internal party structures remained highly centralized, and elections were uncontested. Khrushchev's successor, Leonid Brezhnev (party head 1964–1982), partially reversed Khrushchev's de-Stalinization efforts. Controls were tightened again in the cultural sphere. Individuals who expressed dissenting views through underground publishing or publication abroad were harassed, arrested, or exiled. However, unlike in the Stalinist period, the political repression was predictable. People generally knew when they were transgressing permitted limits of criticism.

From the late 1970s onward, an aging political leadership was increasingly ineffective at addressing mounting problems. Economic growth rates declined, living standards improved only minimally, and opportunities for upward career mobility declined. To maintain the Soviet Union's superpower status, resources were diverted to the military sector, gutting the consumer and agricultural spheres. An inefficient economic structure raised the costs of exploiting new natural resources. High pollution levels and alcoholism contributed to health problems. At the same time, liberalization in some Eastern European states and the telecommunications revolution made it increasingly difficult to shield the Soviet population from exposure to Western lifestyles and ideas. Among a certain critical portion of the population, aspirations were rising just as the capacity of the system to fulfill them was declining.

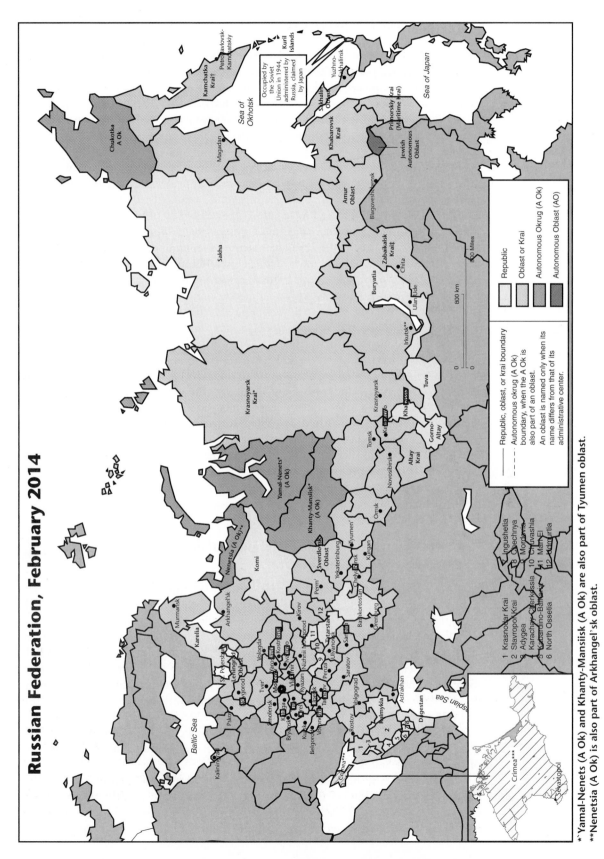

Russian Federation, February 2014

Legend:
- Republic
- Oblast or Krai
- Autonomous Okrug (A Ok)
- Autonomous Oblast (AO)

Republic, oblast, or krai boundary

Autonomous okrug (A Ok) boundary, when the A Ok is also part of an oblast.

An oblast is named only when its name differs from that of its administrative center.

Occupied by the Soviet Union in 1944, administered by Russia, claimed by Japan — Kuril Islands

800 km / 800 Miles

1 Krasnodar Krai
2 Stavropol Krai
3 Adygea
4 Karachay-Cherkessia
5 Kabardino-Balkaria
6 North Ossetia
7 Ingushetia
8 Chechnya
9 Mordovia
10 Chuvashia
11 Mari El
12 Udmurtia

*'Yamal-Nenets (A Ok) and Khanty-Mansiisk (A Ok) are also part of Tyumen oblast.

**Nenetsia (A Ok) is also part of Arkhangel'sk oblast.

***Note: Hatching indicates that these regions are contested, as their inclusion in Russia is not recognized by large parts of the international community.

© Cengage Learning®

Perestroika and *Glasnost* (1985–1991)

Mikhail Gorbachev took office as a Communist Party leader in March 1985. He endorsed a reform program that centered around four important concepts intended to spur economic growth and bring political renewal. These were *perestroika* (economic restructuring), *glasnost* (openness), *demokratizatsiia* (a type of limited democratization), and "New Thinking" in foreign policy. Gorbachev's reform program was designed to adapt the communist system to new conditions rather than to usher in its demise.

The most divisive issues were economic policy and demands for republic autonomy. Only half of the Soviet population was ethnically Russian in 1989. Once Gorbachev opened the door to dissenting views, demands for national autonomy arose in some of the USSR's fifteen union republics. This occurred first in the three Baltic republics (Latvia, Lithuania, and Estonia), then in Ukraine, Georgia, Armenia, and Moldova, and finally in the Russian Republic itself. Gorbachev's efforts failed to bring consensus on a new federal system that could hold the country together.

Gorbachev's economic policies failed as well. Half-measures sent contradictory messages to enterprise directors, producing a drop in output and undermining established patterns that had kept the Soviet economy functioning, although inefficiently. To protect themselves, regions and union republics began to restrict exports to other regions, despite planning mandates. In "the war of laws," regional officials openly defied central directives.

Just as his domestic support was plummeting, Gorbachev was awarded the Nobel Peace Prize, in 1991. Under his New Thinking, the military buildup in the USSR was halted, important arms control agreements were ratified, and many controls on international contacts were lifted. In 1989, Gorbachev refused to prop up unpopular communist governments in the Soviet bloc in Central European countries. First in Hungary and Poland, then in the German Democratic Republic (East Germany) and Czechoslovakia, pressure from below pushed the communist parties out of power. To Gorbachev's dismay, the liberation of these countries fed the process of disintegration of the Soviet Union itself.

glasnost

Gorbachev's policy of "openness," which involved an easing of controls on the media, arts, and public discussion.

Collapse of the USSR and the Emergence of the Russian Federation (1991 to the Present)

In 1985 Mikhail Gorbachev drafted Boris Yeltsin into the leadership team as a nonvoting member of the USSR's top party organ, the Politburo. Ironically, Yeltsin later played a key role in the final demise of the Soviet Union. In June 1991 a popular election confirmed Yeltsin as president of the Russian Republic of the USSR (a post he had held since May of the previous year). In August 1991 a coalition of conservative figures attempted a coup d'état to halt Gorbachev's program to reform the Soviet system. While Gorbachev was held captive at his summer house (*dacha*), Boris Yeltsin climbed atop a tank loyal to the reform leadership and rallied opposition to the attempted coup. In December 1991, Yeltsin and the leaders of Ukrainian and Belorussian Republics declared the end of the Soviet Union, proposing to replace it by a loosely structured entity, the Commonwealth of Independent States.

As leader of the newly independent Russian Federation, Yeltsin took a more radical approach to reform than Gorbachev had done. He quickly proclaimed his commitment to Western-style democracy and market economic reform. However, that program was controversial and proved hard to implement. The executive and legislative branches of the government also failed to reach consensus on the nature of a new Russian constitution; the result was a bloody showdown in October 1993, after Yeltsin disbanded what he considered to be an obstructive parliament and laid siege to its premises, the Russian White House. The president mandated new parliamentary elections and a referendum on a new constitution, which passed by a narrow margin in December 1993.

Yeltsin's radical economic reforms confronted Russians with an increasingly uncertain future marked by declining real wages, high inflation, and rising crime. Yeltsin's initial popularity was also marred by an extended military conflict to prevent Chechnya, a southern republic of Russia, from seceding from the country. Concern that separatism could spread to other regions was an important motivation for the military intervention. Despite these problems, with the help of an active public relations effort, Yeltsin was reelected president in 1996, winning 54 percent of the vote against the Communist Party candidate, Gennady Zyuganov, in a second round of voting. During his second term in office Yeltsin was plagued by poor health and continuing failed policies. In 1998 a major financial crisis added to his problems.

In 1999, Yeltsin appointed Vladimir Putin prime minister and when Yeltsin resigned as president in December 1999 Putin became Acting President. In presidential elections that followed in March 2000 Putin won a resounding victory. Putin benefited from auspicious conditions. In 1999 the economy began a period of sustained economic growth that lasted until the 2008–2009 global financial crisis. High international gas and oil prices fed tax dollars into the state's coffers.

Just as economic growth revived, worries about security increased. Instability associated with the Chechnya problem underlay a string of terrorist attacks, beginning in 1999. One particularly tragic event involved a hostage-taking on the first day of school (September 1, 2004) in the town of Beslan in southern Russia, which ended in tragedy, with more than 300 hostages killed—the majority children. Meanwhile, in March 2003, Russian authorities tried to set Chechnya on a track of

[handwritten annotation: a region that wanted to succeed from Russia, but could not]

Opposition supporters stand in front of the stage during the "March of Millions" protest rally in Moscow, September 15, 2012.
MIKHAIL VOSKRESENSKY/Reuters /Landov

normalization, holding a referendum that would confirm Chechnya's status within the Russian Federation. However, intermittent violence continued.

Despite these problems, Putin recorded consistently high levels of popular support throughout his tenure and successfully managed the transition to his hand-picked successor as president, Dmitry Medvedev, who won the 2008 presidential elections handily. Putin introduced political reforms marked by increased political centralization, restrictions on political opposition, and the growing dominance of one political party, United Russia. Since 2000 Russia has been characterized by a drift to a form of **soft authoritarianism**, in which formal and informal mechanisms secure the dominance of the ruling group. When the economic-financial crisis took hold in 2008, a new source of insecurity arose. With the decline in oil and gas prices, Russia's main export commodities, the economic upturn was interrupted. In 2009 Russian President Medvedev announced a modernization program to address some of the imbalances in the Russian economy, but the momentum for reform proved to be weak. The December 2011 legislative elections reconfirmed the dominance of United Russia and elections in March 2012 reinstated Putin as president. However, charges of election fraud and unfair electoral conditions led to mass protests in major Russian cities and throughout the country.

soft authoritarianism

A system of political control in which a combination of formal and informal mechanisms ensure the dominance of a ruling group or dominant party, despite the existence of some forms of political competition and expressions of political opposition.

Themes and Comparisons

Following the collapse of the USSR in 1991, international support for the new reform-oriented government in Russia surged, with the proliferation of aid programs and international financial credits. However, in the 1990s, Russia's status as a world power waned, and the expansion of Western organizations (NATO, EU) to Russia's western border undermined its sphere of influence in Central and Eastern Europe. Russia's western neighbors began to look to Europe as a guidepost for the future. But Russia's economic recovery following 1998, the rise of energy prices, and Europe's dependence on imports of Russian energy resources fueled Russia's renewed international influence. Over time, despite American efforts to "reset" the relationship in a positive direction, tensions have reasserted themselves between Russia and the West. These have included differing position on issues such as the Syrian crisis, American intentions to install a missile shield in Central Europe to guard against a potential Iranian attack, and policies toward Russia's neighbors such as Ukraine and Georgia. In an effort to assert Russia's regional influence, in 2011 Putin announced the intent to create a Eurasian Union, as a counterpoint to the European Union; efforts have also increased to reinforce cooperation with other rising powers such as China. Shortly after the Sochi Olympics, in February 2014, a political crisis in neighboring Ukraine led to the removal of the Russia-leaning president, Victor Yanukovych, and put in place a pro-Western interim government; these changes elicited a Russian military takeover and quick annexation of Ukraine's southern region of Crimea, undoing much of the goodwill that Russia had won in hosting the Olympics. Western governments refused to recognize Russia's annexation of Crimea, and instituted sanctions to deter Russia from further violations of Ukraine's territorial sovereignty. In August 2014, Russia announced countersanctions that would restrict imports of some Western food products.

For nearly a decade after the collapse of the Soviet system, the Russian Federation was mired in a downward spiral of economic decline. After 1998, however, growth rates recovered, budget surpluses became routine, and the population experienced a marked increase in economic confidence. Questions arose, however, about the depth of the economic recovery. The temporary drop in energy prices associated with the 2008 financial crisis and ensuing global recession revealed that Russia's economic strategy, which relies heavily on the export of natural resources to support the state budget, makes the country vulnerable to fluctuations in the global economy. Although many important policy problems have been addressed, others remain unresolved, including inadequate levels of foreign investment, capital flight, continuing high levels of inequality, and a decline in the agricultural sector.

Concerns about the fate of Russian democracy have also become widespread in the West and have elicited increased public protests within Russia. While the constitution adopted in 1993 has gained a surprising level of public acceptance, domestic opponents express intensified concern that increasing centralization of power and institutional changes adopted after 2000 have undermined real political competition. The regime justifies these changes as necessary to ensure state capacity to govern and to secure continuing economic growth, but critics see Russia as moving in the direction of electoral authoritarianism, where political competition is "managed" by the president's office through a dominant political party, United Russia. High levels of corruption still pervade the Russian political and economic system, despite the proclaimed commitment of the political leadership to curtail them.

Finally, Russians continue to seek new forms of collective identity. The loss of superpower status, doubts about the appropriateness of Western economic and political models, and the absence of a widely accepted ideology have all contributed to uncertainty about what it means to be Russian. Russia itself suffers from internal divisions as well. Although overt separatism has been limited to the Republic of Chechnya, differing visions of collective identity have emerged in some of Russia's ethnic republics, particularly in Muslim areas. A revival of Russian nationalism, directed partly at the West and partly at non-Christian ethnic minority groups, is of increasing concern. Diverging views about gender roles and the legitimacy of diverse definitions of sexual orientation have become increasingly visible. A particular focus of international criticism relates to a Russian law passed in 2013 that imposes fines for "propagandizing" minors about nontraditional sexual relations.

Many countries have attempted a transition from authoritarian rule to democratic governance. In Russia's case, one of the most important factors affecting this process is the tradition of strong state control, stretching from tsarist times through the Soviet period, and now influencing present developments. In addition, the intertwined character of politics, economics, and ideology in the Soviet Union has made reform difficult. In effect, four transition processes were initiated simultaneously in the early 1990s: democratization, market reform, a redefinition of national identity, and integration into the world economy. Whereas other democratizing countries may have undergone one or two of these transitions, Russia initially tried to tackle all four at once. Because the former communist elites had no private wealth to fall back on, corrupt or illegal methods were sometimes used by Russia's emerging capitalist class to maintain former privileges. Citizens, confronted with economic decline and an ideological vacuum, have been susceptible to appeals to nationalism and for strong state control. No doubt, economic uncertainty has made the Russian public willing to accept strong leadership and limits on political expression that would be resisted in many Western countries. Russia's current "backsliding" from democratic development may, in part, reflect the difficulties of pursuing so many transitions at once.

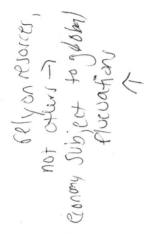

Some countries rich in natural resources, such as Norway, have achieved sustained economic growth and stable democratic systems. In other cases, and this perhaps applies to Russia, such dependence on natural resource wealth has produced a "resource curse," leaving other economic sectors underdeveloped and uncompetitive, with the country highly vulnerable to global economic fluctuations. In the Russian case, the concentration of economic power associated with the natural resource sector has also fed high levels of inequality and corruption.

Where Do You Stand?

Mikhail Gorbachev was awarded the Nobel Peace Prize in 1991 and is credited in the West with having brought a peaceful end to Soviet rule. However, most Russians hold Gorbachev in low regard. How do you evaluate the historical significance of Gorbachev?

Is the centralization of power that has occurred under President Vladimir Putin justified in order to foster economic stability and stable government?

SECTION 2

POLITICAL ECONOMY AND DEVELOPMENT

▼ Focus Questions

- What were Russia's most difficult problems in moving from the Soviet command economy to a market economy?

- How have social policies changed in Russia since the Soviet period?

The collapse of the Soviet system in late 1991 ushered in a sea change, radically reducing the state's traditionally strong role in economic development and opening the Russian economy to foreign influence. However, the process of market reform that the Russian government pursued after 1991 brought with it an immediate dramatic decline in economic performance as well as fundamental changes in social relationships. After experiencing an unprecedented period of economic depression from 1991 to 1998, Russia experienced renewed economic growth, but this growth was built largely on the country's wealth of energy and natural resources. With the economic/financial crisis of 2008–2009, prices of oil and natural gas declined but recovered relatively quickly, avoiding major economic impacts. The Russian economy remains, however, highly dependent on natural resource exports, which introduces long-term economic risks. Under Vladimir Putin, the role of the state in key government sectors has been strengthened so that Russia's market economic system has distinctive features compared to Western systems. Extreme levels of social inequality and corruption also characterize the system.

State and Economy

In the Soviet period, land, factories, and all other important economic assets belonged to the state. Short- and long-term economic plans defined production goals, but these were frequently too ambitious. Except in the illegal black market and peasant market, prices were controlled by the state and production was unresponsive to demand.

The Soviet economic model registered some remarkable achievements: rapid industrialization, provision of social welfare and mass education, relatively low levels of inequality, and advances in key economic sectors such as the military and space industries. Nonetheless, over time, top-heavy Soviet planning could neither sustain rising prosperity at home nor deliver competitive products for export. Gorbachev's efforts to adapt Soviet economic structures to meet these challenges were largely unsuccessful.

Following the collapse of the USSR, Russian president Boris Yeltsin endorsed a more radical policy of **market reform**. Four main pillars of his program were (1) lifting price controls, (2) encouraging small private businesses and entrepreneurs, (3) privatizing most state-owned enterprises, and (4) opening the economy to international influences. In January 1992, price controls on most goods were loosened or removed entirely. As a result, the consumer price index increased by about 2,500 percent between December 1991 and December 1992. Real wages declined by 50 percent. Economic troubles continued throughout most of the 1990s.

Privatization in Russia was rapid compared to most other post-communist countries. By early 1994, 80 percent of medium-sized and large state enterprises in designated sectors of the economy had privatized; however, they often did not achieve the desired result of improving efficiency and competitiveness. The most widely adopted method, called **insider privatization**, hampered reform of business operations and reduced the expected gains of privatization. Managers, many of whom did not have the skills needed to operate in a market environment, were reluctant to lay off excess labor or resisted overtures by outside investors who might gain control of the enterprise. Some managers extracted personal profit from enterprise operations rather than investing available funds to improve production. Productivity and efficiency did not increase significantly; unprofitable firms continued to operate. When the sale of shares was opened to outside investors, many firms were unattractive because backward technology would require massive infusions of capital. Some of the more attractive enterprises fell into the hands of developing financial–industrial conglomerates that had acquired their wealth through positions of power or connections in the government. At the same time, new ventures, which were generally more efficient than former state firms, faced obstacles: confusing regulations, high taxes, lack of capital, and poor infrastructure (transport, banking, communications).

Reform of agriculture was even less satisfactory. Large joint-stock companies and associations of individual households were created on the basis of former state and collective farms. These privatized companies operated inefficiently, and agricultural output declined. Foreign food imports also undercut domestic producers, contributing to a downward spiral in agricultural investment and production.

A key obstacle to the success of the market reform agenda in the 1990s was the weakness of state institutions. Without an effective tax collection system, for instance, the government could not acquire revenues to pay its own bills on time, provide essential services to the population, and ensure a well-functioning economic infrastructure (such as transportation, energy, public utilities). A weak state meant inadequate regulation of the banking sector and poor enforcement of health, safety, and labor standards. As the state failed to carry out these functions, businesses took matters into their own hands, for example, by hiring private security services for protection, or by paying bribes. Ineffective government fed corruption and criminality.

The central state in Moscow also had difficulty exerting its authority in relation to regional officials and in the face of increasing power of business **oligarchs**. These wealthy individuals benefited from privatization and often wielded significant political influence. Diverse methods of laundering money to avoid taxes became widespread. Corruption involving government officials, the police, and operators abroad fed a rising crime rate. Rich foreigners, Russian bankers, and outspoken journalists became targets of the Russian mafia.

A financial crisis in August 1998 brought the situation to a head. Following a sharp upturn in 1996–1997, in August 1998 the Russian stock market lost over 90 percent of its value. The government defaulted on its bonds. Many Russian banks, holders of the government's short-term bonds, faced imminent bankruptcy. The

market reform

A strategy of economic transformation that involves reducing the role of the state in managing the economy and increasing the role of market forces.

insider privatization

The transformation of formerly state-owned enterprises into joint-stock companies or private enterprises in which majority control is in the hands of employees and/or managers.

oligarchs

A small group of powerful and wealthy individuals who gained ownership and control of important sectors of Russia's economy in the context of privatization of state assets in the 1990s.

Russians shop at the Apraksin Dvor market in St. Petersburg.
Yadid Levy/Alamy

government began to print more of the increasingly valueless rubles, threatening to undermine the ruble's value further and thus intensify the underlying financial crisis.

The government finally allowed a radical devaluation of the ruble. Within a two-week period, the ruble lost two-thirds of its value against the U.S. dollar, banks closed or allowed only limited withdrawals, supplies of imported goods decreased,

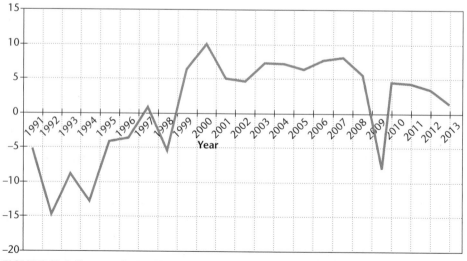

FIGURE 13.2 Economic Decline and Recovery (gross domestic product), as percent of previous year

Source: This figure is reproduced from *Introduction to Comparative Politics* (Cengage 6th edition, 2013) with addition of data from the Federal State Statistics Service of the Russian Federation website.

and business accounts were frozen—forcing some firms to lay off employees and others to close their doors. However, despite these effects, the 1998 financial crisis ushered in positive changes. First, the devalued ruble made Russian products more competitive with foreign imports. Firms were able to improve their products, put underused labor back to work, and thus increase productivity. The state budget benefited from improved tax revenues. Economic growth revived, beginning in 1999.

When Vladimir Putin became president in the year 2000, he set about strengthening the capacity of the state to maintain the growth impetus. He introduced a set of legislative reforms to spur recovery. A 13 percent flat income tax, deemed easier to enforce, was one very visible aspect of the package. A budget surplus replaced a deficit. By 2007 the Russian government had lowered its debt burden to 3 percent of GDP. Foreign reserves grew from just $12 billion (U.S.) in 1998 to about $500 billion (U.S.) in March 2008.[4] Putin also took measures to limit the power of economic oligarchs who used their financial positions to affect political outcomes. A prominent case involved Mikhail Khodorkovsky, the chief executive officer and major shareholder of the giant Russian oil company, Yukos. In 2003 Khodorkovsky was placed under arrest for fraud and tax evasion, and in May 2005 he was sentenced by a Russian court to nine years in prison. In December 2013 Khodorkovsky was pardoned and released from prison, a move that many observers interpreted as attempt to gain Western approval in the lead up to the February 2014 Winter Olympics in Sochi, Russia.

Despite Putin's successes in securing a revival of economic growth, corruption has remained a major obstacle to effective economic management. Transparency International's annual Corruption Perceptions index, based on a compilation of independent surveys, ranked Russia 127th out of the 177 countries surveyed in 2013,[5] indicating high levels of corruption and only a marginal improvement over previous ratings.

Society and Economy

The regime's social goals also produced some of the most marked achievements of the Soviet system. These achievements created a set of public expectations that continue to influence current policy choice. Benefits to the population in the Soviet period included free health care, low-cost access to essential goods and services, maternity leave (partially paid), child benefits, disability pensions, and mass education. In a short period of time, universal access to primary and secondary schooling led to nearly universal literacy under Soviet rule. Postsecondary education was free of charge, with state stipends provided to university students. Guaranteed employment and job security were other priorities. Almost all able-bodied adults, men and women alike, worked outside the home. Citizens received many social benefits through the workplace, and modest pensions were guaranteed by the state, ensuring a stable but minimal standard of living for retirement.

The Soviet system, however, was plagued by shortages and low-quality service. For example, advanced medical equipment was in limited supply. Sometimes under-the-table payments were required to prompt better-quality service. Many goods and services were scarce. Housing shortages restricted mobility and forced young families to share small apartments with parents. Productivity was low by international standards, and work discipline weak. Drunkenness and absenteeism were not unusual.

As a matter of state policy, wage differentials between the best- and worst-paid were lower than in Western countries. While having social benefits, this approach also reduced the incentive for outstanding achievements and innovation. Due to state ownership, individuals could not accumulate wealth in real estate, stocks, or businesses. Although political elites had access to scarce goods, higher-quality health care, travel, and vacation homes, these privileges were hidden from public view.

The Soviet experience led Russians to expect the state to ensure a social welfare network, but in the 1990s, budget constraints necessitated cutbacks, just when social needs were greatest. Although universal health care remained, higher-quality care and access to medicine depended more obviously on ability to pay. Benefits provided through the workplace were cut back, as businesses faced pressures to reduce costs. At the same time, some groups benefited from market reforms, including those with Western language skills and those employed in the natural resources, banking, and financial sectors. At the top of the scale are the super-wealthy, including people who appropriated benefits during the privatization process or engaged in successful business activity afterwards. However, losers have been more numerous. Poverty is highest among rural residents, the unemployed, children, the less educated, pensioners, and the disabled. As a result of low wage levels, the majority of those in poverty are the working poor.

Following the economic upturn that began in 1999, large differentials in income and wealth have persisted, but the portion of the population living below the subsistence level declined after 1999. In addition average real disposable income has increased. Beginning in 2000, levels of personal consumption began to rise, but many individuals still hold two to three jobs just to make ends meet. Social indicators of economic stress (such as a declining birthrate, suicide rate, and murder rate) began to decline after 2002, but only slowly. The economic-financial crisis of 2008–2009 introduced new economic uncertainties just when many Russians were beginning to feel that life was returning to normal.

In recent years, maintenance of existing levels of state support for social programs has been a contentious issue. Massive street demonstrations occurred in several Russian cities in early 2005 over changes to social welfare policy. Called "monetarization of social benefits," the reforms involved replacing certain services (such as public transport) that had been provided free to disadvantaged groups (pensioners, veterans, the disabled) with a modest monetary payment to the individual. Many Russians viewed the measures as involving direct reductions in social welfare benefits. After large-scale demonstrations, the government agreed to accompany the reforms by a modest increase in pensions and to restore subsidized transport. Learning from this experience the government has attempted to avoid cuts in social welfare measures and pensions since, even during the economic-financial crisis of 2008.

Russia saw a steady decline in population until 2009, mitigated to some extent by a positive inflow of immigrants, particularly from other former Soviet republics. Life expectancy in 2011 was estimated at 63 years for Russian men and 75 years for women, an improvement over the 1990s but still lower than in Western societies. Primary factors contributing to the high mortality rates include stress related to social and economic dislocation and unnatural causes of death (accidents, murders, suicides).

Both Putin and Medvedev introduced policies to encourage a rising birthrate, such as higher child support payments, and monetary and other benefits for women having two or more children. Birthrates had begun to rise already in 1999, so it is hard to know how much of the continuing increase is due to government policy. Although declining birthrates often accompany economic modernization, the extraordinary economic stresses of the 1990s exacerbated this tendency; the restoration of economic growth in the late 1990s may have reduced the reluctance of many couples to have children, but the birthrate still is well below levels of the 1980s. Women continue to carry the bulk of domestic responsibilities while also working

Wearing shirts that read "Is something wrong? Give birth," Russian pension-ers took part in a flash mob in Moscow's underground in May 2011. According to organizers, the goal of the action was to encourage Russian women to get pregnant and increase the nation's birthrate.

Denis Sinyakov/Landov

outside the home to boost family income. Many women take advantage of the per-mitted three-year maternity leave, which is only partially paid, but difficulties in reconciling home and work duties no doubt contribute to low birthrates as well.

Russia's ethnic and regional diversity also has economic implications. Levels of development vary greatly across the country's federal units, with major cities (such as Moscow and St. Petersburg), as well as regions rich in natural resources, being the most affluent.

Environmental Issues

In the Soviet period, an emphasis on economic growth at the expense of environ-mental protection resulted in high levels of air and water pollution, with associated health problems. Inadequate technological safeguards and an insufficient regulatory structure led to the disastrous nuclear accident at Chernobyl (now in Ukraine) in 1986, which produced long-lasting contamination of immense areas of agricultural land in Ukraine, as well as in some areas of Russia. Following the Chernobyl acci-dent, under Gorbachev's *glasnost* policy, citizen environmental awareness and activ-ism increased, often associated with assertions of national identity in the various republics of the USSR, including Russia. In 1988, under Gorbachev's leadership a specific environmental protection agency was created.

Following the collapse of the USSR, the newly independent Russian state was preoccupied with other problems, in the face of the major economic downturn of the 1990s. The country's heavy economic reliance on resource-extraction industries brought with it higher than average environmental impacts. In May 2000, the State Committee for Environmental Protection (the successor to the environmental agency created in 1988) was abolished with most of its responsibilities moved to a new ministry (now called the Ministry of Natural Resources and Ecology). This model of mixing oversight of use and protection of nature in a single agency may be an indicator of the low priority assigned to environmental protection, as compared to resource use.

A particular priority for the European Union was to gain Russian ratification of the Kyoto Protocol, an international agreement to reduce greenhouse gas emissions and to address the dangers of climate change. Given the failure of the United States to support the agreement, Russia's signature was needed to put the agreement into effect. Russia ratified the Kyoto Protocol in 2004. However, this involved minimal commitment since Russia's greenhouse gas emission levels had decreased as a result of production downturns of the 1990s. In 2012 Russia declined further commitments under a second phase of the agreement. However, the proportion of global carbon emissions from Russia exceeds it relative share of the global population and GDP.[6] The relatively low utilization of renewable energy sources and highly inefficient use of energy in Russia suggest that Russia's environmental performance has clear avenues for improvement, and the Russian government has expressed support for such measures, even if their implementation has so far been weak.

Russia in the Global Economy

During the Soviet period, the economy was largely isolated from outside influences, as foreign trade was channeled through central state organs. However, things changed after 1991. Over time, the ruble was allowed to respond to market conditions, and firms were permitted to conclude agreements directly with foreign partners. Western governments and international organizations such as World Bank, the International Monetary Fund (IMF), and the European Union (EU) contributed substantial amounts of economic assistance, often in the form of repayable credits. After the August 1998 crisis, the Russian government defaulted, first on the ruble-denominated short-term debt, and then on the former Soviet debt. Since then, debt repayments have been made on time. In 2001, the government decided to forgo additional IMF credits. By 2005, it had paid off its IMF debt.

Russia has also become more open to foreign investment. However, levels still remain low compared to other East European countries, despite improvements since 2004. The inflow of West European investment capital was negatively affected by the financial and economic crisis there since 2008, and is likely to be negatively impacted in the future by the crisis over Ukraine and associated Western sanctions against Russia. Major sources of foreign direct investment since 2000 have been Germany, the United States, and Cyprus (mainly recycled Russian capital, previously exported for tax reasons), but foreign investors are, since 2006, prevented from gaining a majority share in certain sectors of the economy that are identified as of strategic importance. After an extended accession process, in 2012 Russia was admitted to the World Trade Organization (WTO). Initial adaptation costs have included difficulties in some sectors, such as the agricultural and food industries, due to increased competition, as well as lost tariff revenue. However, it is expected that in the medium to long run WTO membership will contribute significantly to economic growth.

The geographic focus of Russia's foreign trade activity has shifted markedly since the Soviet period. Whereas in 1994 Ukraine was Russia's most important trading partner, in 2011 the top spots were filled by Germany (11.0 percent of imports to Russia), the Netherlands (receiving 10.8 percent of Russian exports), and China (the largest source of Russian imports, 14 percent). Overall in 2012 the EU provided 34 percent of Russian imports and 45 percent of its exports, while imports from Russia were only 11.9 percent of the EU's total, with exports to Russia making up 7.3 percent. A substantial portion (about three-quarters) of Russia's export commodities to Europe are mineral resources (including energy resources), while about half of the EU's exports to Russia are machinery and transport equipment, resulting in an assymetrical trade relationship.[7] In the face of increased tensions with the West, Russia is seeking to increase energy exports to China.

Russia's position in the international political economy remains undetermined. With a highly skilled workforce, high levels of educational and scientific achievement, and a rich base of natural resources, Russia has many of the ingredients necessary to become a competitive and powerful force in the global economy. However, if the country's industrial capacity is not restored, reliance on natural resource exports will leave Russia vulnerable to global economic fluctuations in supply and demand.

GLOBAL CONNECTIONS

Russia and International Organizations

Russia has achieved membership in many international and regional organizations such the World Bank, the International Monetary Fund, the Council of Europe, and the World Trade Organization. In other cases, Russia has forged partnerships with organizations for which membership is currently not foreseen (e.g., the European Union or the North Atlantic Treaty Organization, NATO). Relations with three regional organizations are profiled here:

The European Union (*EU*). Russia has not expressed a desire to join the European Union, but in 1997 a ten-year Partnership and Cooperation Agreement (PCA) between the EU and Russia went into effect, setting the basis for a "strategic partnership." Discussions to renew the agreement are still underway. In 2003 the EU and Russia agreed on four "Common Spaces" of cooperation, relating to economic relations; common borders; external security; and research, education, and culture. In 2007 the EU and Russia initiated a process to facilitate the issuance of visas for Russians wishing to visit the EU, and in 2010 they announced a Modernization Partnership. The conflict over Ukraine in 2014 introduced a setback to progress in these and other areas.

The Council of Europe (distinct from the European Union) is the major European vehicle for the defense of human rights, enforced through the European Court of Human Rights (ECHR) in Strasbourg, France. Russia acceded to the organization in 1996 and ratified the European Convention on Human Rights in 1998. In joining the Council of Europe, Russia subjected itself to periodic reviews and to the judgments of the ECHR, along with a number of other obligations. Thousands of human rights cases involving Russia have been brought to the ECHR, many related to the Chechnya conflict, and most judgments have gone against Russia.

The North Atlantic Treaty Organization (*NATO*) was originally formed after World War II to safeguard its members on both sides of the Atlantic from the Soviet threat. Following the collapse of the communist system, NATO has had to rethink its mandate and the nature of potential threats. Among its redefined duties are crisis management, peacekeeping, opposing international terrorism, and prevention of nuclear proliferation. Since 1999 many countries of Central and Eastern Europe have been admitted as members. Russia has objected to the expansion of NATO at each step. Russia has, nonetheless, over time, developed a stronger working relationship with the organization, including the agreement on the NATO-Russia Founding Act on Mutual Relations in 1997, formation of the NATO-Russia Council in 2002, and, an agreement in November 2010 to undertake a Joint Review of 21st Century Common Security Challenges. The conflict over Ukraine in 2014 may undermine these efforts.

MAKING CONNECTIONS How has NATO enlargement affected Russia's relations with the West?

In 2010, about 69 percent of exports were mineral products (i.e., fuels and energy resources), whereas only about 5.7 percent were machinery and equipment, with other resources such as metals and timber making up a large part of the balance.[8] Furthermore, levels of capital investment and technological innovation have not been adequate to fuel increased productivity; even in the lucrative energy sector, experts doubt whether, without significant foreign involvement, Russian firms will be able to develop new reserves adequate to meet both domestic needs and contractual obligations to foreign (at this point mainly European) consumers. At the same time, its wealth in natural resources has given Russia advantages compared to its neighbors, since these expensive materials do not need to be imported. Ultimately, Russia's position in the global economy will depend on the ability of the country's leadership to address domestic economic challenges and to facilitate differentiation of the country's export base.

Where Do You Stand?

Do you think that a strong role for the state in economic affairs makes sense in Russia, given the country's history?

What measures do you think could be taken to bring corruption under control in Russia?

SECTION 3

GOVERNANCE AND POLICY-MAKING

Focus Questions

• Why has the Russian leadership viewed centralization as necessary and what centralizing measures have been taken since 2000?

• What is the relationship between the prime minister and the president in Russia? How have the particular individuals who have filled these posts helped to shape this relationship?

In the 1990s the Russian leadership, under Boris Yeltsin, endorsed liberal democratic principles, and subsequent Russian presidents, both Vladimir Putin and Dmitry Medvedev, have reaffirmed their commitment to democracy. However, over time, the interpretation of how democratic governance should be interpreted to make it compatible with Russia's unique political tradition has become contested. Skeptics see Putin's measures to strengthen presidential power as undermining many of the Russian Federation's founding democratic principles. Protests reached a high point in late 2011 and early 2012, when large public demonstrations in Moscow and other major cities questioned the fairness of the legislative and presidential elections. In response, Vladimir Putin, reelected as president in March 2012 after a four-year interlude, endorsed a mix of concessions and heightened controls that elicited continuing debate about the fate of Russia's democratic experiment.

Organization of the State

In the Soviet period, before Gorbachev's reforms, top organs of the Communist Party of the Soviet Union (CPSU) dominated the state. The CPSU was hierarchical. Lower party bodies elected delegates to higher party organs, but elections were uncontested, and top organs determined candidates for lower party posts. The Politburo, the top party organ, was the real decision-making center. A larger body, the Central Committee, represented the broader political elite, including regional party leaders and representatives of various economic sectors. Alongside the CPSU were Soviet state structures, which formally resembled Western parliamentary systems but had little decision-making authority. The state bureaucracy had day-to-day responsibility in both the economic and political spheres but followed the party's directives in all matters. People holding high state positions were appointed through the *nomenklatura* system, which allowed the CPSU to fill key posts with politically reliable individuals. The Supreme Soviet, the parliament, was a rubber-stamp body.

The Soviet constitution was primarily symbolic, since many of its principles were ignored in practice. The constitution provided for legislative, executive, and judicial organs, but separation of powers was considered unnecessary because the CPSU claimed to represent the interests of society as a whole. When the constitution was violated (frequently), the courts had no independent authority to enforce or protect its provisions. Likewise, the Soviet federal system was phony, since all aspects of life were overseen by a highly centralized Communist Party. Nonetheless, the various subunits that existed within the Russian Republic of the USSR were carried over into the Russian Federation in an altered form.

Gorbachev introduced innovations into the Soviet political system: competitive elections, increased political pluralism, reduced Communist Party dominance, a revitalized legislative branch of government, and renegotiated terms for Soviet federalism. He also tried to bring the constitution into harmony with political reality. These changes moved the political system haltingly and unevenly closer to the liberal democratic systems of the West.

Likewise, even before the collapse of the USSR, political institutions began to change in the Russian Republic, which was only one of fifteen federal units that made up the Soviet Union. A new post of president was created, and on June 12, 1991, Boris Yeltsin was elected by direct popular vote as its first incumbent. Once the Russian Federation became independent in December 1991, a crucial turning point in its development was the adoption by referendum of a new Russian constitution in December 1993. This constitution provides the legal foundation for current state institutions and by now seems to have acquired broad-based popular legitimacy.

The document affirms many established principles of liberal democratic governance—competitive multiparty elections, separation of powers, an independent judiciary, federalism, and protection of individual civil liberties. At the same time, the president and executive branch are granted strong powers. Despite this, in reality, in the 1990s the state demonstrated only a weak capacity to govern, involving dysfunctional conflict between major institutions of government. Subnational governments demanded increased autonomy, even sovereignty, generating a process of negotiation and political conflict between the center and the regions that sometimes led to contradictions between regional and federal laws. The constitution made the executive dominant but still dependent on the agreement of the legislative branch to realize its programs. Under President Yeltsin, tension between the two branches of government was a persistent obstacle to effective governance. In addition, establishing real judicial independence remained a significant political challenge.

During Vladimir Putin's first term (2000–2008) the power of the presidency was augmented further in an effort to address the weakness of central state authority. Many observers feel, however, that Putin's centralizing measures have undermined the very checks and balances that were supposed to protect against reestablishment of authoritarian control. In addition, inadequate salaries, and lack of professionalism in the civil service have made it difficult to control widespread corruption and misuse of political power.

nomenklatura

A system of personnel selection in the Soviet period under which the Communist Party maintained control over the appointment of important officials in all spheres of social, economic, and political life.

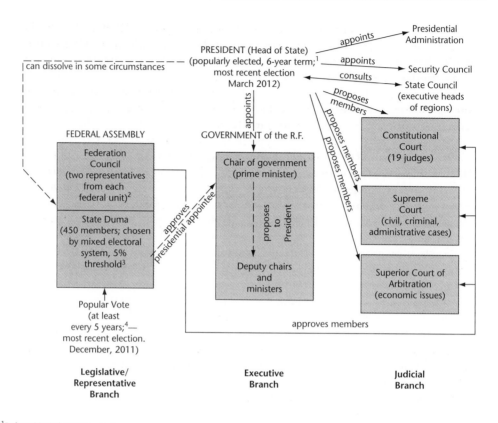

FIGURE 13.3 Political Institutions of the Russian Federation (R.F.) 2014

[1]Before 2012 the term was 4 years.
[2]One representative appointed by the regional legislature and one by the regional excutive.
[3]Was a nationwide proportional representation system from 2007–2013, with 7% threshold. Until 2007 half of seats were chosen in single-member-districts and half by proportional representation with a 5% threshold.
[4]Prior to 2011–2012 the term was 4 years.

The Executive

The constitution establishes a semi-presidential system, formally resembling the French system but with stronger executive power. As in France, the executive itself has two heads (the president and the prime minister), introducing a potential context for intrastate tension. The president is also the head of state, and, except between 1998 and 2000 and between 2008 and 2012, this office held primary power. The prime minister, appointed by the president but approved by the lower house of the parliament (the State Duma, hereafter Duma), is the head of government. As a rule of thumb, the president has overseen foreign policy, relations with the regions, and the organs of state security, while the prime minister has focused his attention on the economy and related issues. However, with Yeltsin's continuing health problems in 1998 and 1999, operative power shifted in the direction of the prime minister. In December 1999, Yeltsin resigned from office, making the prime minister, Vladimir Putin, acting president until he was himself elected president in March 2000.

One of the president's most important powers is the authority to issue decrees, which Yeltsin used frequently for contentious issues. Although presidential decrees may not violate the constitution or specific legislation passed by the bicameral legislature, policy-making by decree allows the president to ignore an uncooperative or divided parliament. Yeltsin's decision in 1994, and again in 1999, to launch the offensive in Chechnya was not approved by either house of parliament. Under Putin and Medvedev the power of decree has been used more sparingly, partly because both leaders have had strong support in the legislature.

The president can also call a state of emergency, impose martial law, grant pardons, call referendums, and temporarily suspend actions of other state organs if he deems them to contradict the constitution or federal laws. Some of these actions must be confirmed by other state organs (such as the upper house of the parliament, the Federation Council). The president is commander-in-chief of the armed forces and conducts affairs of state with other nations. Impeachment of the president involves the two houses of the legislative body (the Duma and the Federation Council), the Supreme Court, and the Constitutional Court. If the president dies in office or becomes incapacitated, the prime minister fills the post until new presidential elections can be held.

The Russian government is headed by the prime minister, flanked by varying numbers of deputy prime ministers. The president's choice of prime minister must be approved by the Duma. During Yeltsin's presidency, six prime ministers held office, the longest being Viktor Chernomyrdin, from December 1992 until March 1998, and the final one being Vladimir Putin, appointed in August 1999. After becoming acting president in December 1999, Putin had three prime ministers (and one acting prime minister) during his first two terms of office. The first of these, Mikhail Kasyanov (May 2000 to February 2004), later became an outspoken opposition figure. Following his election as president in 2008, Medvedev selected Putin as his prime minister, with the roles reversed in 2012.

The prime minister can be removed by the Duma through two repeat votes of no confidence passed within a three-month period. Even in the 1990s when there was tension with President Yeltsin, the Duma was unable or unwilling to exercise this power, presumably in part because this action could lead to dissolution of the Duma itself. Until 2008, the prime minister was never the leader of the dominant party or coalition in the Duma. This changed when Putin became prime minister in 2008 because he was also elected as chairperson of the dominant party, United Russia, in that year.

The National Bureaucracy

The state's administrative structure includes twenty-one ministries, and some twenty federal services and agencies (as of January 2014). Based on an administrative reform adopted in 2004, ministries are concerned with policy functions or political aspects, whereas other state organs undertake monitoring functions or implementation, as well as providing services to the public. Many observers agree that these administrative reforms have not improved bureaucratic efficiency or government responsiveness.

Some government bodies (such as the Foreign Affairs Ministry, the Federal Security Service, and the Defense Ministry) report directly to the president. The president has created various advisory bodies that solicit input from important political and economic actors and also co-opt them into supporting government policies. The most important are the Security Council and the State Council. Formed in 1992, the Security Council advises the president in areas related to foreign policy and security (broadly conceived); its membership and size has varied over time, but has generally included heads of the so-called power ministries such as Defense and the Federal Security Service, as well as the other key ministers and government officials. The 2009 State Security Strategy of the Russian Federation accorded the Security

PROFILES

President Vladimir Putin
(right) with Prime Minister
(and former President)
Dmitry Medvedev (left).

AP Images/ITAR-TASS,
Presidential Press Service,
Vladimir Rodionov

Vladimir Putin

Vladimir Putin, the current president, is no doubt the most powerful person in Russia; he has enjoyed a consistently high level of public support since his first election as president in March 2000, while at the same time being a controversial figure reviled by his critics for moving Russia in an authoritarian direction. For many ordinary Russians, Putin represents a reassertion of Russia's potential after painful years of economic decline, loss of international stature, and weak government in the 1990s. Projecting an image of masculine prowess, Putin has been captured in numerous alluring poses that contribute to his image of strength, for example while executing impressive judo moves, driving a three-wheeled Harley Davidson, and fishing topless in one of Russia's far-flung regions.

Putin was born in October 1952 in what is now St. Petersburg, Russia's second largest city. In the Soviet period, Putin pursued a career in the security services (the KGB) and was eventually assigned to duty in East Germany, where he remained until 1990 when the communist state there collapsed. Because of this career background, while in political office Putin has drawn many of his staff from the security forces.

Little known until 1999, Putin's rise to political prominence was swift and the rise in his popularity was equally meteoric. Upon returning to his home city of St. Petersburg in 1990, Putin gradually became involved in municipal government, moving to Moscow in 1996 to take up a political post. In 1999, Yeltsin appointed Putin prime minister and shortly thereafter acting president of the Russian Federation, when Yeltsin resigned from the presidential post. In February 2000 Putin won the presidential election with 56.7 percent of the vote, leaving his nearest competitor, Communist Party leader Gennady Zyuganov, behind with only 29 percent. Putin was reelected with over 71 percent of the vote in 2004.

Since the constitution limits a person to two consecutive terms as president, Putin hand-picked Dmitry Medvedev as the presidential candidate to succeed him for a four-year term from 2008 until 2012, but in September 2011 Putin and Medvedev announced that Putin, with Medvedev's support, would again seek the presidency in 2012. Putin reportedly indicated that the leadership deal had been arranged "several years back."[*] While parts of the Russian public did not react well to this preplanned "leadership swap," Putin was again elected president, this time for a six-year term, winning 63.6 percent of the vote.

Putin's domestic public approval rating has remained above 60 percent since the 2012 election, rising to above 80 percent in April 2014, a level most Western politicians would envy.[**] Some consider Putin to be a master tactician, who has managed to achieve a pragmatic mix of control and flexibility, weaving a political narrative that is contentious but persuasive to large parts of his domestic audience.

MAKING CONNECTIONS Why is Putin so popular with large parts of the Russian population?

[*] Reported by BBC World News, September 24, 2011.

[**] Levada Centre, Index of approval of the activities of Vladimir Putin and Dmitry Medvedev, http://www.levada.ru/indeksy (last accessed May 22, 2014).

Council a coordinating role in this area, but the body remains only advisory. The State Council, chaired by the president, was formed in September 2000 as part of Putin's attempt to redefine the role of regional leaders in federal decision making (see below) and includes the heads of Russia's constituent federal units. A smaller presidium, made up of seven of the regional heads selected by the president, meets monthly.

Ministers other than the prime minister do not require parliamentary approval. The prime minister makes recommendations to the president, who appoints these officials. Ministers and other agency heads are generally career bureaucrats who have risen through an appropriate ministry, although sometimes more clearly political appointments are made. Many agencies have been reorganized, often more than once. Sometimes restructuring signals particular leadership priorities. For example, in May 2008, Putin created a new Ministry of Energy, splitting off these functions from those of the Ministry of Industry and Trade. This move reflected the growing importance of this sector to Russia's economy.

Top leaders have also used restructuring to place their clients and allies in key positions. For example, Putin drew heavily on colleagues with whom he worked earlier in St. Petersburg or in the security establishment, referred to as *siloviki*, in staffing a variety of posts in his administration. **Clientelistic networks** continue to play a key role in both the presidential administration and other state organs. These linkages are similar to "old-boys' networks" in the West; they underscore the importance of personal loyalty and career ties between individuals as they rise in bureaucratic or political structures. While instituting a merit-based civil service system has been a state goal, it has not yet been achieved in reality. The Russian state bureaucracy continues to suffer low levels of public respect and continuing problems with corruption.

Despite efforts to reduce the size of the state bureaucracy during Putin's terms of office, its size increased substantially, in part through the creation of new federal agencies. As an apparent cost-cutting measure, in December 2010 Medvedev issued a presidential decree mandating further cuts in the size of the federal bureaucracy.

Public and Semipublic Institutions

In limited sectors of the economy, partial or complete state ownership has remained intact or even been restored after earlier privatization was carried out. Public or quasi-public ownership may take the form of direct state or municipal ownership of assets or majority control of shares in a "privatized" firm. Economic sectors more likely to involve public or semipublic ownership include telecommunications (the nonmobile telephone industry in particular), public transport (railways, municipal transport), the electronic media (television), and the energy sector. Prime examples from the energy sector are Gazprom, the natural gas monopoly, in which the federal government controls just over 50 percent of the shares, and Rosneft, operating in the petroleum industry, where the state owns nearly 70 percent. Several television channels are publicly owned. Indirect state influence is also realized through the dominant ownership share in many regional TV channels by Gazprom-Media, a subsidiary of the state-controlled natural gas company.

In other areas, such as education and health care, while some private facilities and institutions have emerged in recent years, these services are still primarily provided through tax-supported agencies. Some prestigious new private universities, often with Western economic support, have cropped up in major urban areas, but Russia's large historic universities remain public institutions. Likewise, a state-run medical care system assures basic care to all citizens, although private clinics and hospitals are increasingly servicing the more affluent parts of the population. In public transport, smaller private companies that provide shuttle and bus services have grown up alongside publicly owned transport networks. In general, public or semipublic agencies offer services at a lower price, but often also with lower quality.

Significant parts of the social infrastructure remain under public or semipublic control. In the Soviet period, many social services were administered to citizens through the workplace. These services included daycare, housing, medical care, and vacation facilities, as well as food services and some retail outlets. During the 1990s a process of divestiture resulted in the transfer of most of these assets and responsibilities to other institutions, either to private owners or, often, to municipalities. For

siloviki

Derived from the this refers to Russian word *sil*, meaning "force," this refers to Russian politicians and governmental officials drawn from the security and intelligence agencies, special forces, or the military, many of whom were recruited to important political posts under Vladimir Putin.

clientelistic networks

Informal systems of asymmetrical power in which a powerful patron (e.g., the president, prime minister, or governor) offers less powerful clients resources, benefits, or career advantages in return for support, loyalty, or services.

example, while many state- or enterprise-owned apartments were turned over to private ownership by their occupants, an important part of the country's housing stock was placed in municipal ownership.

Political authorities, including the president, are responsible for appointing executive officials in many public and semipublic institutions. This situation indicates a continuing close relationship between major economic institutions and the state, likely to remain in the future due to the Russian tradition of a strong state and the dismal economic results associated with privatization in the 1990s. Indicative of this trend, the overall share of GDP created in the non-state sector increased from 5 percent in 1991 to 70 percent in 1997, then fell from 70 percent in 1997 down to 65 percent in 2005–2006.[9]

Other State Institutions

The Judiciary

Concepts such as judicial independence and the rule of law were poorly understood in both pre-revolutionary Russia and the Soviet era. These concepts have, however, been embedded in the new Russian constitution and are, in principle, accepted both by the public and political elites. However, their implementation has been difficult and not wholly successful.

In Russia, a Constitutional Court was formed in 1991. Its decisions were binding, and in several cases even the president had to bow to its authority. After several controversial decisions, Yeltsin suspended the operations of the court in late 1993. However, the 1993 Russian constitution provided for a Constitutional Court again, with the power to adjudicate disputes on the constitutionality of federal and regional laws, as well as jurisdictional disputes between various political institutions. Judges are nominated by the president and approved by the Federation Council, a procedure that produced a political stalemate after the new constitution was adopted, so that the new court became functional only in 1995. Since 1995, the court has established itself as a vehicle for resolving conflicts involving the protection of individual rights and conformity of regional laws with constitutional requirements. The court has, however, been cautious in confronting the executive branch, and questions have been raised not only by critics but also by some justices themselves about the independence of the court from presidential influence.

Alongside the Constitutional Court is an extensive system of lower and appellate courts, with the Supreme Court at the pinnacle. These courts hear ordinary civil and criminal cases. In 1995, a system of commercial courts was also formed to hear cases dealing with issues related to privatization, taxes, and other commercial activities. The Federation Council must approve nominees for Supreme Court judgeships, and the constitution also grants the president power to appoint judges at other levels. Measures to shield judges from political pressures include criminal prosecution for attempting to influence a judge, protections from arbitrary dismissal, and improved salaries for judges. One innovation in the legal system has been the introduction of jury trials for some types of criminal offenses.

Subnational Governments

The collapse of the Soviet Union was precipitated by the demands of some union republics for more autonomy and, then, independence. After the Russian Federation became an independent state, the problem of constructing a viable federal structure resurfaced within Russia itself. Some of the federal units were very assertive in putting forth claims for autonomy or even sovereignty. The most extreme example is Chechnya, whose demand for independence led to a protracted civil war. The ethnic dimension complicates political relations with some other republics as well, particularly Tatarstan and Bashkortostan, which occupy relatively large territories in the center of the country and are of Islamic cultural background.

Putin's most controversial initiatives relating to Russia's regions were part of his attempt to strengthen what he termed the **power vertical**. This concept refers to an integrated structure of executive power from the presidential level down through to the local level. Critics have questioned whether this idea is consistent with federal principles, and others see it as undermining Russia's fledgling democratic system. A first step in creating the power vertical was the creation of seven, now nine, federal districts on top of the existing federal units. Although not designed to replace regional governments, the districts were intended to oversee the work of federal offices operating in these regions and to ensure compliance with federal laws and the constitution.

A second set of changes to create the power vertical involved a weakening of the independence of governors and republic heads (hereafter called governors). Beginning in 1996, the governors, along with the heads of each regional legislative body, sat as members of the upper house of the Russian parliament, the Federation Council. This arrangement gave the governors a direct voice in national legislative discussions and a presence in Moscow. In 2001, Putin gained approval for a revision to the composition of the Federation Council, removing regional executives. Now one regional representative is appointed by the regional executive and the other by the regional legislature. Some governors resisted this change, seeing it as an assault on their power. Putin made concessions to make the change more palatable, for example, giving governors the right to recall their representatives. The State Council was formed to try to assure the governors that they would retain some role in the federal policy-making arena.

power vertical

A term used by Vladimir Putin to describe a unified and hierarchical structure of executive power ranging from the national to the local level.

federal system

A political structure in which subnational units have significant independent powers; the powers of each level are usually specified in the federal constitution.

U.S. CONNECTION

Federalism Compared

Russia is a *federal system**, according to its constitution. This means that, at least in theory, powers are divided between the central government and Russia's constituent units. The number of federal units is disputed, as Russia claims to have eighty-five regions, including two regions in Crimea (Republic of Crimea and the city of Sevastopol), annexed from Ukraine in March 2014. However, most Western countries do not recognize the validity of the annexation.

In comparison to the American federal system, the Russian structure seems complicated. Some of Russia's federal units are called republics (21, or 22 including the Republic of Crimea), while others are *oblasts* (regions) (49), *krais* (territories) (6), one autonomous republic (1), autonomous *okrugs* (4), and cities of federal status (2, Moscow and St. Petersburg, or 3 with Sevastopol). Russia's size and

multiethnic population underlie this complexity. Because many ethnic groups are regionally concentrated in Russia, unlike in the United States, these groups form the basis for some federal units, notably the republics and okrugs, which are named after the ethnic groups that reside there.

In the 1990s, Russia's federal government had difficulty controlling what happened in the regions. Regional laws sometimes deviated from federal law. Bilateral treaties with the federal government granted some regional governments special privileges. During his term as president, Vladimir Putin put measures in place to ensure a greater degree of legal and political uniformity throughout the country.

Russia's federal units are represented in the upper house of the national legislature, the Federation Council. Just as the U.S. Senate includes two representatives from each state, in

(continued)

Russia each region also has two delegates in this body; however, their method of selection has varied over time. In 1993 they were elected directly, as in the United States. From the mid-1990s, the governor and the head of each regional legislature themselves sat on the Federation Council. Now the members of the Federation Council are appointed, one by the region's governor and the other by the region's legislature.

Russia's federal units depend on funding from the central government to carry out many of their functions, especially in the field of social welfare. Other informal mechanisms, such as use of political patronage through the United Russia party, reduce the independence of the regional executives. Although Russia does have a constitutional court to resolve disputes over the jurisdictions of the federal government and the regions, unlike in the United States the constitution does not provide a strong basis for regional power, since it places many powers in the hands of the central government while most others are considered "shared" jurisdictions.

MAKING CONNECTIONS Have centralizing measures in Russia undermined the federal nature of Russia's political system?

*Definitions of key terms in this boxed feature appear in the Glossary, which begins on p. 698.

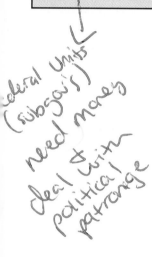

(handwritten margin note: federal units (subgov's) need money, deal with political patronage)

Following the Beslan terrorist attack in 2004, Putin identified corruption and ineffective leadership at the regional level as culprits in allowing terrorists to carry out the devastating school hostage taking. Accordingly, Putin proposed an additional reform that created the decisive element of central control over regional politics. This change eliminated the popular election of governors; rather, the president nominated them for approval by the regional legislature. The president's nominees were approved by the regional legislature in every case, usually with an overwhelming majority or even unanimously. In his first two years in office, Medvedev replaced eighteen incumbent governors in this way, apparently seeking individuals who would both be politically loyal and managerially competent.[10] Following the public protests against alleged fraud in the 2011 and 2012 elections, Medvedev proposed legislation reinstating gubernatorial elections, but with a "municipal filter" that requires a candidate's nomination to be supported by a certain number of local deputies or officials. The first elections under the law, held in October 2012 and September 2013, resulted in victories for the candidates of the dominant party, United Russia, in all cases. This outcome reflected both some restrictive features of the new law, informal mechanisms of influence exercised by the incumbent, and the failure of opposition forces to unite in support of viable candidates.

The distribution of tax revenues among the various levels of government has been another contentious issue. The Soviet state pursued a considerable degree of regional equalization, but regional differences have increased in the Russian Federation. Putin created a more regularized system for determining the distribution of revenues, taking account of both the regional tax base and differences in the needs of various regions (for instance, northern regions have higher expenses to maintain basic services). However, in fact, an increasing proportion of tax revenues are now controlled by Moscow, and regional governments are constantly faced with shortfalls in carrying out their major responsibilities, for example, in social policy. Economic disparities between rich and poor regions have reached dramatic proportions, with Moscow and areas rich in natural resources being the best off.

The Military and Security Organs

Because of Vladimir Putin's career background in the KGB, he drew many of his staff from this arena. Thus, while the formal status of the Federal Security Service (the successor to the KGB) has not changed, the security establishment has acquired increasing importance under Putin. A justification for the increasing role for security forces was a series of terrorist attacks, with targets including apartment buildings, schools, a popular Moscow theatre, public transport, and a Moscow airport. Attacks in Russia initially had indigenous roots in the separatist region of Chechnya, as terrorism was used by Chechen militants to counter Russian military efforts to defeat separatist forces. Over time, linkages between Russian terrorist groups and international Islamic fundamentalist organizations have become increasingly important. Since the September 11 attacks, cooperation between Russian and Western security agencies has increased.

Because many Russians are alarmed by the crime rate and terrorist bombings in the country, restrictions on civil liberties justified as guarding against the terrorist threat have not elicited strong popular concern. At the same time, there is widespread public cynicism about the honesty of the ordinary police. Many believe that payoffs can buy police cooperation in overlooking crimes or ordinary legal infractions such as traffic tickets.

The Soviet military once ranked second only to that of the United States. Russian defense spending declined in the 1990s, then increased again after 2000, but is still below Soviet levels. In 2012 military spending represented about 4.5 percent of GPD (roughly comparable to the proportion in the United States), but in absolute terms has risen due to economic growth following 1999. The Soviet and Russian military have never usurped civilian power. The Communist Party controlled military appointments and, during the August 1991 coup attempt, troops remained loyal to Yeltsin and Gorbachev, even though the Minister of Defense was among the coup plotters. Likewise, in October 1993, despite some apparent hesitancy in military circles, military units defended the government's position, this time firing on civilian protesters and shocking the country.

The political power and prestige of the military have suffered, in part as a result of its failure to deal effectively with Chechnya. Accordingly, the government increased the role of the Federal Security Service there instead of relying on the army alone. Reports of deteriorating conditions in some Russian nuclear arsenals have raised international concerns about nuclear security. The Russian Federation still maintains universal male conscription, but noncompliance and draftees rejected for health reasons have been persistent problems. In 2008 mandatory service was reduced from two years to one year; women have never been subject to the military draft. A law to permit alternative military service for conscientious objectors took effect in 2004. In 2013 the Defense Minister indicated that a military draft will remain necessary, alongside a professional army, but that soon draftees will not be used in combat.[11]

High crime rates indicate a low capacity of the state to provide legal security to its citizens. Thus, in addition to state security agencies, sometimes businesses and individuals turn to private security firms to provide protection. A network of intrigue and hidden relationships can make it hard to determine the boundaries of state involvement in the security sector, and the government's inability to enforce laws or to apprehend violators may create an impression of state involvement even where they may be none. A prominent example is the case of a former agent of the Russian Federal Security Service, Alexander Litvinenko, an outspoken critic of the Russian government, who took political asylum in the United Kingdom. In November 2006, Litvinenko was fatally poisoned in London with a rare radioactive isotope. On his deathbed, Litvinenko accused the Kremlin of being responsible for his death, an undocumented accusation. The United Kingdom's efforts to extradite Andrei Lugovoi, an ex-KGB agent and Russian politician, to stand trial for the murder were refused by the Russian government, citing a constitutional prohibition. The issue sparked tension between the two countries, including expulsion of diplomats on both sides. These kinds of incidents have generated an atmosphere reminiscent of Cold War spy novels.

The Policy-Making Process

Policy-making occurs both formally and informally. According to the constitution, the federal government, the president and his administration, regional legislatures, individual deputies, and some judicial bodies may propose legislation. In the Yeltsin era, conflict between the president and State Duma made policy-making contentious and fractious; under Putin and Medvedev, the State Duma has generally gone along with proposals made by the president and the government, and the proportion of legislation initiated by the executive branch has increased significantly.

In order for a bill to become law, it must be approved by both houses of the parliament in three readings and signed by the president. If the president vetoes the bill, it must be passed again in the same wording by a two-thirds majority of both houses in order to override the veto. Many policy proclamations have been made through presidential or governmental decrees, without formal consultation with the legislative branch. This decision-making process is much less visible and may involve closed-door bargaining rather than an open process of debate and consultation.

Informal groupings also have an important indirect impact on policy-making. During the Yeltsin period, business magnates were able to exert behind-the-scenes influence to gain benefits from the privatization of lucrative firms in sectors such as oil, media, and transport. Putin has attempted to reduce the direct political influence of these powerful economic figures, but at the cost of also reducing political competition.

A continuing problem is weak policy implementation. Under communist rule, the party's control over political appointments enforced at least some degree of conformity to central mandates. Under Yeltsin, fragmented and decentralized political power gave the executive branch few resources to ensure compliance. Pervasive corruption, including bribery and selective enforcement, hindered enforcement of policy decisions. Although Putin and Medvedev both have stated their commitment to restrict these types of irregularities, they continue to persist. However, the commitment to reestablishing order and a rule of law has been an important justification for the centralization of power.

Where Do You Stand?

Do you think a strong presidency, such as exists in Russia, is compatible with democracy? If the public supports such an arrangement, does that itself give it democratic legitimacy?

In a country as wide and diverse as Russia, is federalism a good idea, or is it likely to increase the risk of separatism and disunity?

SECTION 4

REPRESENTATION AND PARTICIPATION

civil society

A term that refers to the space occupied by voluntary associations outside the state, for example, professional associations, trade unions, and student groups.

Gorbachev's policies in the 1980s brought a dramatic change in the relationship between state and society, as *glasnost* sparked new public and private initiatives. Most restrictions on the formation of social organizations were lifted, and a large number of independent groups appeared. Hopes rose that these trends might indicate the emergence of **civil society**. Just a few years later, only a small stratum of Russian society was actually actively engaged; the demands of everyday life, cynicism about politics, and increasing controls on political opposition led many people to withdraw into private life. However, with hardships imposed by the economic crisis of 2008–2009 and allegations of election fraud in the December 2011 Duma elections, there is evidence of increasing political activism among a small but important sector of society.

The Legislature

The Federal Assembly came into being after the parliamentary elections of December 12, 1993, when the referendum ratifying the new Russian constitution was also approved. The upper house, the Federation Council, represents Russia's constituent federal units. The lower house, the State Duma (hereafter the Duma), has 450 members and involves a **mixed electoral system** (discussed below).

Within the Duma, factions unite deputies from the same party. In February 2013 there were four party factions representing the parties elected in the December 2011 vote; in January 2014, 237 (or 52.7 percent) of the 449 deputies in the State Duma were part of the faction of the dominant party, United Russia.[12] Other parties had, respectively 56 (Liberal Democratic Party of Russia), 92 (Communist Party of the Russian Federation), and 64 (A Just Russia) deputies. The Duma elects its own speaker (or chair); since December 2011, this has been Sergei Naryshkin of the United Russia party.

Compared to the communist period, deputies reflect less fully the demographic characteristics of the population at large. For example, in 1984, 33 percent of the members of the Supreme Soviet were women; after the 2007 Duma elections, 14 percent of deputies were women, but this dropped to 11 percent after the 2011 elections.[13] The underrepresentation of women, as well as of workers, in the present Duma indicates the extent to which Russian politics is primarily the domain of male elites.

The upper house of the Federal Assembly, the Federation Council, has two members from each of Russia's federal regions and republics. Many prominent businessmen are among the appointees, and in some cases the posts may be granted in exchange for political loyalty. Party factions do not play a significant role in the Federation Council. Deputies to the Federation Council, as well as to the Duma, are granted immunity from criminal prosecution.

The constitution grants parliament powers in the legislative and budgetary areas, but if there is conflict with the president or government, these powers can be exercised effectively only if parliament operates with a high degree of unity. In practice, the president can often override or bypass the parliament through mechanisms such as the veto of legislation or use of decrees. Each house of parliament has the authority to confirm certain presidential appointees. The Federation Council must also approve presidential decrees relating to martial law and state emergencies, as well as to deploying troops abroad.

Following electoral rebuffs in the 1993 and 1995 parliamentary elections, Yeltsin confronted a parliament that obstructed many of his proposed policies, but the parliament did not have the power or unity to offer a constructive alternative. Since the 2003 Duma election, however, parliament has cooperated with the president, since a majority of the deputies have been tied to the United Russia faction, closest to the president, and deputies from other parties have also often supported the president's initiatives. In general, the process of gaining Duma acceptance of government proposals has depended more on the authority of the president and on the particular configuration of power at the moment rather than on the presence of disciplined party accountability such as exists in some European countries.

mixed electoral system

A system of electoral representation in which a portion of the seats are selected in winner-take-all single-member districts, and a portion are allocated according to parties within multi-member constituencies, roughly in proportion to the votes each party receives in a popular election.

Society's ability to affect particular policy decisions through the legislative process is minimal. Parties in the parliament are isolated from the public at large, suffer low levels of popular respect, and the internal decision-making structures of parties are generally elite-dominated.

Political Parties and the Party System

One of the most important political changes following the collapse of communism was the shift from a single-party to a multiparty system. In the USSR, the Communist Party (CPSU) not only dominated state organs but also oversaw social institutions, such as the mass media, trade unions, youth groups, educational institutions, and professional associations. It defined the official ideology for the country, set the parameters for state censorship, and ensured that loyal supporters occupied all important offices. Approximately 10 percent of adults in the Soviet Union were party members, but there were no effective mechanisms to ensure accountability of the party leadership to its members.

As part of Gorbachev's reforms, national competitive elections were held in 1989, but new political parties were not formal participants in Russia until 1993. Since then, a confusing array of political organizations has run candidates in elections. For the December 2011 Duma elections only seven parties met conditions of legal registration. A change in the law governing political parties was adopted as a concession to popular protests after those elections; this loosened requirements for party registration. However, this has evoked concerns that one result might be fragmentation of opposition to United Russia.

In the 1990s, many parties formed around prominent individuals, making politics very personalistic. Furthermore, other than the Communist Party, Russian parties are young, so deeply rooted political identifications have not had time to develop. Finally, many citizens do not have a clear conception of how parties might represent their interests. In this context, image making is as important as programmatic positions, so parties appeal to transient voter sentiments.

While individual leaders play an important role in political life in Russia, some key issues have divided opinions in the post-1991 period. One such issue is economic policy. Nearly all political parties have mouthed support for creation of a market economy. However, communist/socialist groupings have been more muted in their enthusiasm and have argued for a continued state role in providing social protection and benefits for vulnerable parts of the population. The liberal/reform groupings, on the other hand, have advocated more rapid market reform, including privatization, free prices, and limited government spending. United Russia charts a middle ground, appealing to voters from a wide ideological spectrum.

Another dividing line relates to national identity. Nationalist/patriotic parties emphasize the defense of Russian interests over Westernization. They favor a strong military establishment and protection from foreign economic influence. Liberal/ reform parties, on the other hand, advocate integration of Russia into the global market and the adoption of Western economic and political principles. Again, the United Russia party has articulated an intriguing combination of these viewpoints, with its leaders identifying Europe as the primary identity point for Russia, but at the same time insisting on Russia's role as a regional power, pursuing its own unique path of political and economic development. Ethnic and regional parties have not had a significant impact on the national electoral scene.

Table 13.2	Election Results and Seats in the Russian State Duma, 2007–2014				
Party	Percent of 2007 party list vote	Percent of Duma seats 2007	Percent of party list vote 2011	Percent of Duma seats Feb 2014	Current party leader
Centrist					
United Russia	64.3	70.0	49.3	52.7	Dmitri Medvedev (since 2012, Vladimir Putin 2007–2012)
A Just Russia	7.7	8.4	13.3	14.3	Sergey Mironov
Communist/Socialist					
Communist Party of the Russian Federation	11.6	12.7	19.2	20.5	Gennady Zyuganov
Nationalist/Patriotic					
Liberal Democratic Party of Russia	8.1	8.9	11.7	12.5	Vladimir Zhirinovksy
Patriots of Russia	0.9	0	1.0	0	Gennady Semigin
Liberal/Westernizing					
Yabloko	1.6	0	3.4	0	Sergey Mitrokhin
Union of Rightist Force/Just Cause	1.0	0	0.6	0	Viacheslav Maratkanov

Russian political parties do not fit neatly on a left–right spectrum. Nationalist sentiments crosscut economic ideologies, producing the following party tendencies:

- The traditional left, critical of market reform and often mildly nationalistic
- Centrist "parties of power," representing the political elite
- Liberal/reform forces, supporting assertive Western-type market reform and political norms
- Nationalist/patriotic forces, primarily concerned with identity issues and national self-assertion

The most important parties in all four groupings have not challenged the structure of the political system but have chosen to work within it. Since 2000, liberal/reform parties have been marginalized and are no longer represented in political institutions. Of the four parties represented in the State Duma, two are centrist (United Russia and A Just Russia). The second-strongest party after United Russia, the Communist Party of the Russian Federation, is a traditional left party. The fourth party, the Liberal Democratic Party of Russia, is nationalist/patriotic.

The Dominant Party: United Russia

dominant party

A political party that manages to maintain consistent control of a political system through formal and informal mechanisms of power, with or without strong support from the population.

Since 2003, one political party, United Russia, has taken on clear dominance. Its predecessor, the Unity Party, rose to prominence, together with Vladimir Putin, in the elections of 1999 and 2000. While the Unity Party gained 23.3 percent of the vote in Duma elections in 1999, United Russia received 37.6 percent in 2003, 64 percent in 2007, but just over 49 percent in 2011. In April 2008, at a party congress, United Russia's delegates unanimously approved creation of a custom-made post for Vladimir Putin as party chairman, but with his election as president in 2012, Dmitry Medvedev, who became prime minister, took over that position, keeping the presidency formally distinct from the party leadership.[14] In fact, United Russia has served as a major source of political support for Putin.

What explains United Russia's success? An important factor is the association with Putin, but the party has also built a political machine to generate persuasive incentives for regional elites. The party is truly a party of power, focused on winning to its side prominent people, including heads of Russia's regions, who then use their influence to further bolster the party's votes. The party has a rather poorly defined program, which emphasizes the uniqueness of the Russian approach (as distinct from Western models), an appeal to values of order and law, and a continued commitment to moderate reform. The question now facing the party is whether it has adequate institutional strength to impose accountability on its leaders and whether it can develop an organizational footing in society.

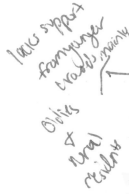

lacks support from younger crowds mainly

Older & rural residents

Other Parties Represented in the State Duma (2007–2011)

Many consider the Communist Party of the Russian Federation (CPRF) to be the only party that could be considered a real opposition force. The CPRF was by far the strongest parliamentary party after the 1995 elections, winning over one-third of the seats in the Duma. Since then its strength declined until 2011. With the second-strongest showing, after United Russia, in the 2011 Duma elections, the party's vote showed an increase from 11.6 percent in 2007 to 19.2 percent in 2011. The party defines its goals as being democracy, justice, equality, patriotism and internationalism, a combination of civic rights and duties, and socialist renewal. Primary among the party's concerns are the social costs of the market reform process.

The CPRF appears to represent those who have adapted less successfully to the radical and uncertain changes of recent years, as well as some individuals who remain committed to socialist ideals. Support for the party is especially strong among older Russians, the economically disadvantaged, and rural residents. The party's principal failures have been an inability to adapt its public position to attract significant numbers of new adherents, particularly among the young, as well as the absence of a charismatic and attractive political leader. Although one might expect Russia to offer fertile ground for social democratic sentiments like those that have been successful in the Scandinavian countries of Western Europe, the CPRF has not expanded its base of support, nor has it made room for a new social democratic party that could be more successful.

Two other parties were represented in the State Duma after the 2011 elections. The party called A Just Russia, founded in 2006, placed third, with 13.3 percent of the vote. Many observers consider that A Just Russia was formed with the Kremlin's support to demonstrate the competitive nature of Russia's electoral system, while undermining opposition parties that might pose a real threat to United Russia. The leadership espouses support for socialist principles, placing it to the left of United Russia on the political spectrum and offering a political magnet for dissatisfied supporters of the Communist Party. In highly exceptional cases, A Just Russia has been able to win mayoral elections in smaller cities; however, the party does not pose a real challenge to the position of United Russia and has generally supported the president and government.

The fourth party represented in the Duma, the Liberal Democratic Party of Russia (LDPR), is neither liberal nor particularly democratic in its platform; the party can be characterized as nationalist and populist. Its leadership openly appeals to the anti-Western sentiments that grew in the wake of Russia's decline from superpower status. Concern with the breakdown of law and order seems to rank high among its priorities. The party's leader, Vladimir Zhirinovsky, has garnered especially strong support among working-class men and military personnel. However, most often this party has not challenged the political establishment on important issues.

While these three parties, singly or combined, cannot challenge the power of United Russia, they have on occasion issued protests over what they consider to be unfair electoral procedures. For example, in October 2009 deputies from all three factions abandoned a session of the State Duma as a sign of protest against the results of regional elections, accusing United Russia of infringement of proper electoral procedures and demanding that the results be nullified. After consultations with the president, the demands were withdrawn.

The Liberal Democratic Parties: Marginalized

The liberal/reform parties (those that most strongly support Western economic and political values) have become marginalized since 2003, when they won only a handful of seats in the Duma. These groups have organized under a variety of party names since 1993, including Russia's Choice, the Union of Rightist Forces, and, most recently, Just Cause, as well as the Yabloko party. These parties have espoused a commitment to traditional liberal values, such as a limited economic role for the state, support for free-market principles, and the protection of individual rights and liberties. Prominent figures such as Boris Nemstov and Grigory Yavlinksy were visible and sometimes influential in the 1990s as representatives of reform policies, but they have since found it hard to build a stable and unified electoral base. Many Russians hold policies associated with these figures, such as rapid privatization and price increases, as responsible for Russia's economic decline in the 1990s. Often referred to as "democrats," their unpopularity also creates confusion as to what democracy really implies. An additional source of weakness has been their difficulty in running under a uniform and consistent party name or leadership figure. Mikhail Prokhorov, a Russian businessman and billionaire owner of the Brooklyn Jets, won support from a part of the liberal electorate in his bid for the presidency in 2012 (winning about 8 percent of the vote). He subsequently formed the party Civic Platform. Support for liberal/reform parties generally has been stronger among the young, the more highly educated, urban dwellers, and the well-off. Thus, ironically, those with the best prospects for succeeding in the new market economy have been the least successful in fashioning an effective political party to represent themselves.

Elections

Turnout in federal elections remains respectable, generally between 60 and 70 percent; it stood at 60 percent in the 2011 Duma election and close to 65 percent in the 2012 presidential vote, down from about 70 percent in 2008. National elections receive extensive media coverage, and campaign activities begin as long as a year in advance. The political leadership has also actively encouraged voter turnout, to give elections an appearance of legitimacy. Up until 2003, national elections since 1991 were generally considered to be reasonably fair and free. However, international observers have expressed serious concerns about the fairness of elections since 2003, related, for example, to slanted media coverage as well as electoral irregularities.

Until 2007, the electoral system for selecting the Duma combined proportional representation (with a 5 percent threshold) with winner-take-all districts. In addition, voters were given the explicit option of voting against all candidates or parties (4.7 percent chose this in 2003). In an interlude from 2007 until 2014, the single-member districts were abolished, so that all 450 deputies were elected on the basis of one national proportional representation district, with a minimum threshold for party representation raised to 7 percent. In February 2014 the electoral system was revised again, returning to a system similar to that which had existed prior to 2007; however, there are some additional requirements for registration of candidates in the winner-take-all districts. Parties are required to include regional representatives on their lists from across the country. A 2001 law on political parties created difficult thresholds for political parties to participate in elections, but these were relaxed in April 2012, so that now only 500 members are needed to register a party, although there must still be branches in half of Russia's federal regions. In 2006, national legislation removed the "against all" option from the ballot, but it was reinstated in 2012.

With the rapid ascent of United Russia since 1999, opposition parties have had difficulty offering an effective challenge to the dominant party. One reason is genuine popular support for Putin as well as the failure of the opposition parties to develop appealing programs or field attractive candidates. Media coverage has also strongly favored United Russia and the president. Administrative control measures and selective enforcement of laws have limited the scope of permissible political opposition, sometimes providing pretexts to disqualify opposition forces. In addition, the carrot-and-stick method has wooed regional elites, producing a bandwagon effect that builds on rewards for political loyalty.

Russia has yet to experience a real transfer of power from one political grouping to another, which some scholars consider a first step in consolidating democratic governance. Under the Russian constitution, presidential elections have been held every

Table 13.3	Russian Views on Political Systems												
	Nov97	**Mar00**	**Mar03**	**Dec06**	**Nov07**	**Feb08**	**Feb09**	**Feb10**	**Feb11**	**Jan12**	**Jan13**	**Jan14**
The Soviet one, which we had until the 1990s	38	42	48	35	35	24	38	34	33	29	36	39
The current system	11	11	18	26	17	36	25	28	19	20	17	19
Democracy like Western countries	28	26	22	16	19	15	18	20	23	29	22	21
Other	8	4	6	7	7	7	7	7	8	7	9	8
Hard to say	16	17	7	16	12	18	12	12	16	15	16	13

"What type of political system seems the best to you: the Soviet, the present system, or democracy of the type in Western countries?"

Source: Levada Center, http://www.levada.ru/24-02-2014/luchshaya-politicheskaya-i-ekonomicheskaya-sistema, accessed March 14, 2014.

four years, but beginning with the 2012 election the term is six years; the Duma mandate was extended from four to five years.

Political Culture, Citizenship, and Identity

Political culture can be a source of great continuity in the face of radical upheavals in the social and political spheres. Some attitudes toward government that prevailed in the Soviet period have endured with remarkable tenacity, including acceptance of strong political leadership and centralized power. At the same time, the Soviet development model glorified science, technology, industrialization, and urbanization; these values were superimposed on the traditional way of life of the largely rural population. When communism collapsed, Soviet ideology was discredited, and in the 1990s the government embraced Western political and economic values. Many citizens and intellectuals are skeptical of this "imported" culture, partly because it conflicts with other traditional civic values such as egalitarianism, collectivism, and a broad scope for state activity, and partly because it is viewed as an outside imposition. Public opinion surveys over time do, however, suggest at least general support for liberal democratic values such as an independent judiciary, a free press, basic civil liberties, and competitive elections, but at the same time a desire for strong political leadership. During Putin's presidency the leadership espoused a particular Russian concept of **sovereign democracy**, emphasizing the importance of adapting democratic principles to the Russian context.

sovereign democracy

A concept of democracy articulated by President Putin's political advisor, Vladimir Surkov, to communicate the idea that democracy in Russia should be adapted to Russian traditions and conditions rather than based on Western models.

In the USSR, just over 50 percent of the population was ethnically Russian. Since many ethnic minorities now reside in other Soviet successor states, according to the 2010 census Russians now make up 77.7 percent of the population of the Russian Federation. The largest minority group is the Tatars (3.7 percent), a traditionally Muslim group residing primarily in Tatarstan, one of Russia's republics. Other significant minorities are the neighboring Bashkirs (1.1 percent), various indigenous peoples of the Russian north, the many Muslim groups in the northern Caucasus region, and ethnic groups (such as Ukrainians and Armenians) of other former Soviet republics. There are over fifty languages spoken by at least 50,000 people in the Russian Federation,[15] although Russian is clearly the lingua franca. Some 25 million ethnic Russians reside outside of the Russian Federation in other former Soviet republics, which at times has provided a pretext for Russian intervention in regions adjacent to the country.

Because Russia is a multiethnic state, one important aspect of the state's search for identity relates to what it means to be Russian. The Russian language itself has two distinct words for Russian: *russkii*, which refers to an ethnicity, and *rossiiskii*, a broader civic concept referring to people of various ethnic backgrounds who make up the Russian citizenry. While the political foundation of the Russian Federation is based on a civic rather than ethnic definition of "Russianness," both anti-Semitic and anti-Muslim sentiments surface in everyday life. In recent years there have been increasing concerns about the rise of an exclusionary form of Russian nationalism among certain parts of the population. Official state policy, while explicitly opposing ethnic stereotypes, may, in some cases, have implicitly fed them.

Today, the Russian Orthodox Church appeals to many citizens who are looking for a replacement for the discredited values of the communist system. Although an important source of personal meaning and a strong social presence, religion has not emerged as a significant basis of political cleavage for ethnic Russians. A controversial law, directed primarily at Western proselytizers, was passed in 1997, making it harder for new religious groups to organize. Human rights advocates and foreign observers protested strongly, again raising questions about the depth of Russia's commitment to liberal democratic values.

Attitudes toward gender relations in Russia reflect traditional family values. It is generally assumed that women will carry the primary responsibility for child care and a certain standard of "femininity" is expected of women both inside and outside the workplace. Feminism is not popular in Russia, as many women consider it inconsistent with traditional notions of femininity or with accepted social roles for women. At the same time, a number of civil society organizations have sprung up to represent the interests of women; some of them advocate traditional policies to provide better social supports for mothers and families, while others challenge traditional gender roles and definitions.

Changing cultural norms affect gender relations in other ways as well. Images propagated in advertising and through the mass media often represent women as sex objects. Advertising also reinforces commercialized images of female beauty that may not correspond to cultural expectations or to healthy lifestyles. In the face of unemployment and the breakdown in traditional social linkages, increasing numbers of young women have turned to prostitution to make a living; HIV/AIDS rates are also increasing at a rapid rate, fueled by prostitution, low levels of information, and the rise of drug trafficking related to Russia's permeable eastern border.

Social class identity was a major theme in the Soviet period. The Bolshevik revolution was justified in the name of the working class, and the Communist Party of the Soviet Union claimed to be a working-class party. Because social class was a major part of the discredited Soviet ideology, in the post-communist period many Russians remain skeptical of claims made by politicians to represent the working class, and trade unions are weakly supported. Even the Communist Party of the Russian Federation does not now explicitly identify itself as a working-class party.

Interest Groups, Social Movements, and Protest

Since the collapse of the USSR, numerous political and social organizations have sprung up in every region of Russia, representing the interests of groups such as children, veterans, women, environmental advocates, pensioners, and the disabled. Many observers saw such blossoming activism as the foundation for a fledgling civil society that would nurture the new democratic institutions established since 1991. Despite limited resources and small staffs, these non-government organizations (NGOs) provided a potential source of independent political activity. However, there have been many obstacles to realizing this potential including inadequate resources and restrictions on their activities.

In January 2006 Putin signed legislation amending laws on public associations and noncommercial organizations. These controversial changes, protested widely by Western governments, placed new grounds for denying registration to such organizations, established new reporting requirements (particularly for organizations receiving funds from foreign sources), and increased government supervisory functions. Particular requirements are placed on foreign noncommercial nongovernmental organizations operating in Russia. A 2012 law requires NGOs that engage in political activity on the basis of foreign financing to register as "foreign agents" and submit to strict reporting requirements. Several Russian organizations have refused to comply;

some NGOs also filed a complaint with the European Court of Human Rights. The law reflects concern that foreign influence may spur political activism in the country that could challenge stability or the current structure of power.

At the same time, the government has attempted to channel public activism through official forums. These have included the Civic Forum, organized with government support in 2001, and more recently, the Public Chamber, created in 2005 by legislation proposed by the president. Based on voluntary participation by presidential appointees and representatives recommended by national and regional societal organizations, the organization is presented as a mechanism for public consultation and input, as well as a vehicle for creating public support for government policy. It likely involves an effort to co-opt public activists from more disruptive forms of self-expression, but also to mobilize the assistance of citizens' groups in delivering social services.

A variety of mass-based political organizations protest the current political direction of the government, but since 2007 the authorities have periodically tried to restrict use of public demonstrations and protests. The widespread protests that followed the 2011 Duma elections represented the most dramatic evidence of significant opposition sentiment in major urban centers. On December 10, 2011, an estimated 50,000 protesters participated, followed by equally large demonstrations leading up to the presidential election in March 2012. Just before a planned demonstration on June 12, 2012 (named the "march of millions"), Putin signed a new law that imposed high fines for participating in demonstrations that undermine public order or destroy public property; the homes of leading opposition figures were also searched.

In the context of the 2011-12 protests, new public figures emerged, the most notable being the 38-year-old anti-corruption blogger, Alexei Navalny. His depiction of United Russia as a "party of crooks and thieves" became an opposition rallying

The feminist rock punk group, Pussy Riot, undertakes a protest performance in Christ the Saviour Church, Moscow, in Feburary 2012

Aleshkovsky Mitya/Itar-Tass/ABACA/Newscom

call. After being arrested and convicted of alleged embezzlement that had occurred several years earlier, Navalny was sentenced to five years in prison. Surprisingly, Navalny was released pending an appeal and permitted to stand on the ballot in the newly reinstated Moscow mayoral race in October 2013. He won 27 percent of the vote against the incumbent mayor and Putin loyalist, Sergei Sobianin, who got just over 51 percent. In February 2014, Navalny was again placed under house arrest.

The official trade unions established under Soviet rule have survived under the title of the Federation of Independent Trade Unions (FITU). However, FITU has lost the confidence of large parts of the workforce. In some sectors, such as the coal industry, new independent trade unions have formed, mainly at the local level. Labor actions have, at various times, included spontaneous strikes, transport blockages, and even hunger strikes. Immediate concessions are often offered in response to such protests, but the underlying problems are rarely addressed. During the period of the financial-economic crisis that began in 2008, protests occurred across Russia, often focused on nonpayment of wages. More recently low wage levels have elicited some strikes. However, such local protest actions seem to be only weakly linked to the national political protests, referred to above, in Moscow and in other large cities.

The Political Impact of Technology

The media itself has an important impact on how interests are expressed. In the post-Soviet period, television has been the main source of news and political information for Russian citizens. Article 29 of the Russian constitution guarantees "freedom of the mass media" and prohibits censorship. However, Russia ranked 148th out of 179 countries in 2013 in terms of press freedom, according to *Reporters without Borders*.[16] A recent survey by a respected independent public opinion agency revealed that 69 percent of respondents acknowledged government censorship in the main Russian TV channels and 77 percent felt that a greater diversity of views expressed in TV media would be desirable.[17]

While much of the television coverage is subject to more or less direct influence by the government, some newspapers and independent journalists, as well as Internet sources, do offer a critical perspective on political developments. Independently minded journalists are exposed to significant risks due to the incapacity of the state to enforce law and order. An estimated fifty-two journalists have been murdered since 1992, making Russia the third-most-dangerous country for journalists in the world.[18] Many cases involved reporting in war-torn Chechnya; others are contract murders or assassinations

As in other countries, Internet usage has increased rapidly in the Russian Federation, and its use can have important political implications. In 2013 only 38 percent of survey respondents indicated that they did not make use of the Internet, and 37 percent reported using it almost every day, with 27 percent indicating use for finding news updates.[19] However, major uses of the Internet are social media and entertainment; the Russian corollary of Facebook, called *vKontake.ru*, is particularly popular with young people, as is the Russian Internet search engine Yandex. Internet use, as in other countries, is more widespread among the young. Contacts through social media and other Internet sources were important in mobilizing participation in demonstrations surrounding the 2011–2012 elections. Those who use the Internet to connect to opposition circles are often of a more critical political orientation, but the Internet has not provided a medium for creation of a sustained and unified opposition movement. Furthermore, the state has also made effective use of Internet communications to disseminate its interpretations of the news, [20] as well as creating relatively effective e-portals for government services.

The Russian government has also effectively used electronic media to project a positive image abroad through vehicles such as the global TV channel, RT (formerly Russia Today), and its associated Internet site (rt.com). In another widely publicized act, in August 2013 Russian authorities granted asylum to Edward Snowden, for whom the United States sought extradition in connection with Snowden's alleged release of classified security documents. Non-governmental sources in Russia have launched successful cyberattacks, most notably on a range of Estonian governmental and business sites in 2007, following an Estonian decision, sharply criticized by Russian authorities, to remove a pro-Soviet statue from central Tallinn.

While until recently government restrictions on domestic Internet usage have been minimal, in the context of the Sochi Olympics monitoring of e-communications was thorough-going, justified as needed to monitor security threats to the games. In early 2014, new legislation created instruments for closer monitoring of bloggers with large followings. More broadly Russian legislation provides security services with the authority to access citizens' online activity, as well as the obligation of Internet service providers to facilitate the collection of the information. As yet, this capacity has not been utilized in a systematic way to control opposition activities. The Internet still provides the attentive Russian public with access to a broad range of domestic and foreign opinion, even if most citizens do not utilize this opportunity to its full potential.

Where Do You Stand?

Is the Russian government justified in trying to limit the influence of foreign governments or international organizations on Russian domestic politics?

In a country with a history of radical ruptures, is it reasonable for the government to put limits on opposition protests in the name of stability and stable government?

SECTION 5

RUSSIAN POLITICS IN TRANSITION

Focus Questions

- What types of strategies has Russia pursued under Vladimir Putin's leadership in trying to reestablish itself as a regional and global power? How effective have these strategies been?

- What are the main challenges to political stability in Russia?

On March 1, 2014, the Russian Duma authorized President Putin to deploy military forces in Crimea, an autonomous region of the neighboring independent state of Ukraine, justified in order to protect the rights of Russians residing there. In the preceding days, Crimea had already effectively been brought under Russian military control due to the mobilization of forces of Russia's Black Sea Fleet based in Crimea under a long-term lease agreement with Ukraine. Russian control of the region was reinforced by the introduction of additional troops. A self-appointed pro-Russian regional government in Crimea held a contested referendum on March 16, with Russia's blessing, proposing that Crimea be annexed to Russia. Russia accepted Crimea into the Russian Federation the same week. The international community, especially the United States and the European Union, expressed sharp criticism of the Russian invasion and annexation, declaring it contrary to international law and the referendum illegal and invalid.

The Russian intervention was in response to a power turnover in Ukraine in late February 2014, which resulted from three months of massive popular demonstrations in Ukraine's capital, Kiev, against the incumbent president, Victor Yanukovych. Those protests were triggered by Yanukovych's decision, under heavy Russian pressure, to back away at the last minute from signing long-awaited free trade and association agreements with the European Union. When violence erupted, the crisis culminated in the collapse of Yanukovych's rule as he fled Ukraine. The new interim Ukrainian government, installed by the elected parliament, made a sharp pro-Western turn, with new presidential elections announced for May 25, 2014, which produced a clear victory for Petro Poroshenko, a pro-Western businessman. Moscow viewed events in Ukraine as undermining its efforts to draw Ukraine closer to Russia.

Russia's actions evoked a strong international reaction, as leaders of the United States, the European Union, and several European countries called upon Russia to refrain from violating Ukraine's territorial sovereignty Russia, along with the United States and the United Kingdom, had guaranteed that sovereignty in the 1994 Budapest Memorandum when Ukraine gave up its nuclear arsenal inherited from the Soviet period. Western governments and the EU instituted sanctions against Russia following the annexation of Crimea, claiming that Russia was continuing to foment unrest in eastern Ukraine by covertly encouraging takeovers of public buildings by armed separatist forces. The stationing of some 40,000 Russian troops near Ukraine's eastern border also fed fears that Russia might engage in further violations of Ukraine's territorial sovereignty. Although a portion of the troops were withdraw before the May 2014 election, Russia's actions fueled distrust of Russia in neighboring countries, and raised questions about the stability of the post-Soviet international order in Europe.

Political Challenges and Changing Agendas

Russia's future path continues to remain unclear. Will the country move "two steps forward, one step backward" toward a more democratic political system? Or is the country moving clearly in an authoritarian direction? Will Russia be able to reestablish a respected role as a regional and global power, to bring corruption under control, to establish trust in political institutions, and to diversify the economy? These are some of the key challenges facing the Russian Federation.

When the first edition of this book was published in 1996, five possible scenarios for Russia's future were presented:

1. A stable progression toward democratization
2. The gradual introduction of "soft authoritarianism"
3. A return to a more extreme authoritarianism of a quasi-fascist or communist variety
4. The disintegration of Russia into regional fiefdoms
5. Economic decline, civil war, and military expansionism

At the time of this writing, the "soft authoritarian" scenario seems to have taken hold; however, there are still significant forces that may move Russia back to a more democratic trajectory. Major questions also linger over Russia's regional and international aspirations in the wake of the 2014 events in Ukraine.

In the international sphere, Russia's flirtation with Westernization in the early 1990s produced ambiguous results, leading to a severe transitional recession and placing Russia in the position of a supplicant state requesting international credits and assistance from the West. Russia's protests against unpalatable international developments, such as NATO enlargement and NATO's bombing of Yugoslavia in

1999, revealed Moscow's underlying resentment against Western dominance, as well as the country's sense of powerlessness in affecting global developments. The events of September 11, 2001, however, provided an impetus for cooperative efforts in the battle against international terrorism, and Russia's economic revival imparted to the country a sense of greater power. Evidence of warmer relations included the formation of a NATO-Russia Council in May 2002, but new tensions arose around American withdrawal from the Anti-Ballistic Missile Treaty in 2002, Russian objections to the American incursion into Iraq in March 2003, American proposals to erect a missile defense system in Central Europe, a 2008 Russian incursion into Georgia, and most recently events surrounding developments in Ukraine in 2014.

One of Russia's main challenges has been to reestablish itself as a respected regional leader in neighboring countries, particularly those that were formerly part of the Soviet Union. The relationship to Ukraine has been fraught with particular difficulties. Ukraine's own internal political divisions have provided Russia with an opportunity to exert political leverage, as parts of the population desire closer ties with Russia, while others are oriented toward the West. Despite the country's declared aspiration for eventual membership in the European Union, Ukraine's economy remains closely linked to Russia's. Ukraine's role as a transit country for gas pipelines between Russia and the European Union has meant that tensions between Russia and Ukraine have sometimes led to the interruption of gas supplies to Western Europe.

The massive popular protests in Ukraine that followed the contested presidential election in 2004 (the Orange Revolution) elicited apprehension in Moscow, with Russia's leaders claiming they were nurtured by Western organizations. In February 2010 relations with Ukraine improved, as presidential elections in Ukraine saw the victory of the more pro-Russian candidate, Viktor Yanukovych, who subsequently concluded an agreement with Russia providing a twenty-five-year lease on a naval base in Ukraine's Crimea for use by Russia's Black Sea fleet in exchange for lower natural gas prices. However, as noted above, prospects for closer relations with the European Union in 2014 led Russia to increase the pressure on Ukraine to move closer to Russia, leading to an international crisis when Russia annexed Ukraine's region of Crimea. As a response to Russia's action, Ukraine and the European Union signed an Association Agreement in March 2014 and a comprehensive free trade agreement in June 2014, as the West strongly backed Ukraine's objections to Russia's move.

Relations with some other neighboring post-Soviet countries (e.g., Georgia) have been equally fraught with difficulties, as Russia has struggled to establish itself as a positive role model in the region. Efforts to form regional organizations to strengthen ties between these countries and Russia have taken a variety of forms. The largely ineffective Commonwealth of Independent States, formed in 1991 when the Soviet Union collapsed, was joined later by the Collective Security Treaty Organization (CSTO), the Eurasian Economic Forum, and the Shanghai Cooperation Organization (SCO, including China and the post-Soviet Central Asian states). Each of these organizations includes a subset of countries from the former Soviet space as members, but without Ukraine or Georgia. Most recently, Vladimir Putin announced the formation of the Eurasian Union, beginning with the formation of a Customs Union between Russia, Belarus and Kazakhstan. Putin's vision is for this to lead to more comprehensive integration, uniting several of the non-EU countries in the post-Soviet space under Russian leadership. However, concerns about Russian dominance and incompatibility with European aspirations have held back potential members, such as Ukraine, from signing on.

Russia's has also sought to establish itself as an equal partner with the United States and Europe. Following U.S. Secretary of State Clinton's effort to reset U.S.-Russian relations in March 2009, progress was made on key issues of conflict at a

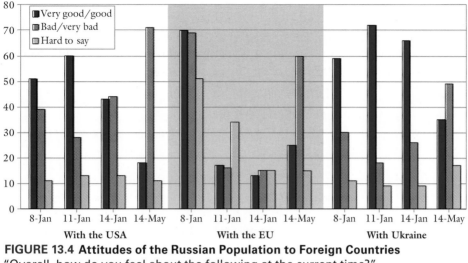

FIGURE 13.4 Attitudes of the Russian Population to Foreign Countries
"Overall, how do you feel about the following at the current time?"

Source: Data from Levada Center, http://www.levada.ru/26-02-2014/otnoshenie-rossiyan-k-drugim
-stranam, accessed March 14, 2014.

NATO-Russia Summit in Lisbon in November 2010. In the face of the expiration of the Strategic Arms Reduction Treaty in December 2009, a new agreement between the United States and Russia went into effect in January 2011. However, the decision of the United States to pursue installation of a missile defense system in Eastern Europe (in response to potential Iranian action) has continued to irritate Russia. Until 2014, progress in EU-Russia relations was more substantial, with a broad range of negotiating platforms, and movement toward eased visa regulations and enhanced trade; however, this process has largely halted in the face of the crisis over Crimea and the conflict in eastern Ukraine. Nonetheless, Russia remains the most important source of Europe's gas imports. However, experts believe that without increased Western investment and technological know-how, Russia will not be able to develop untapped deposits quickly enough to meet both domestic demands and export commitments. An major agreement regarding future Russian gas exports to China, signed in May 2014, is an indicator of Russia's intention of reducing its dependence on exports to Europe.

The 2008–2009 global financial-economic crisis sent a warning to Russia about the dangers of an economy dependent on energy exports. A sharp drop in gas and oil prices temporarily undercut the foundation of Russia's economic motor. From positive growth rates in the previous ten years, Russia moved to a dramatic fall by the first quarter of 2009. Because energy prices recovered fairly quickly and Russian had reserve funds to fall back on, the crisis did not push Russia back to the disastrous economic situation of the 1990s, but the dramatic shift in economic performance may have reminded both the Russian public and its leaders of the potential fragility of the economic recovery.

In November 2009 President Medvedev published a much-discussed article entitled "Go Russia" in which he called for a modernization program, primarily through the development of high-technology sectors.[21] However, with Putin's return to the presidency in 2012, the modernization program proved to be stillborn. Furthermore, hopes that political liberalization might accompany efforts to diversify the economy were also dashed. The continuing disjuncture between high personal support for Putin alongside a continuing lack of confidence in the ability of political institutions to address the country's problems suggests that the legitimacy of the system is still on thin ice. The more positive working relationship between the executive and legislative branches that emerged under the Medvedev-Putin tandem has been at the cost of permitting a real parliamentary opposition to function. Failed efforts to control corruption, mechanisms to exert control over the newly reinstated gubernatorial

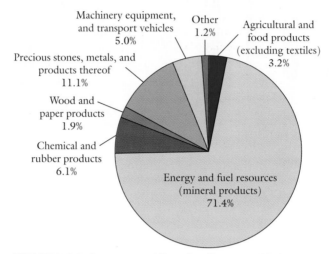

FIGURE 13.5 Structure of Russian Exports, 2012

Source: Data from the Russian State Statistical Service, *Russia in Figures 2013*, http://www.gks.ru/bgd/regl/b13_12/Main.htm, accessed 14 March 2014.

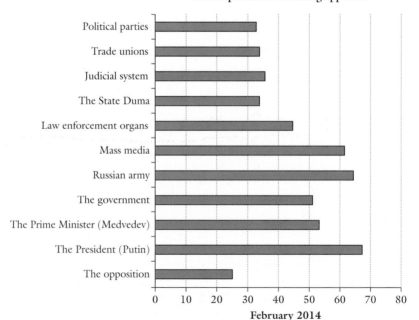

FIGURE 13.6 Approval Ratings of Various Offices and Institutions, % of Respondents Indicating Approval

Source: Data from the website of the Russian Public Opinion Research Center (VTsIOM), http://wciom.ru/ratings, accessed March 14, 2014.

elections and efforts to control political opposition already show signs of producing poor policy choices that may themselves reinforce public cynicism about the motives of politicians and the trustworthiness of institutions.

Despite changes in social consciousness, the formation of new political identities also remains unfinished business. Many people are still preoccupied by challenges of everyday life, with little time or energy to engage in new forms of collective action to address underlying problems. Under such circumstances, the appeal to nationalism and other basic sentiments can be powerful. The weakness of Russian intermediary organizations (interest groups, political parties, or associations) means that politicians can more easily appeal directly to emotions because people are not members of groups that help them to evaluate the political claims. These conditions reduce safeguards against authoritarian outcomes.

Nevertheless, the high level of education and increasing exposure to international media and the Internet may work in the opposite direction. Many Russians identify their country as part of Europe and its culture, an attitude echoed by the government. Exposure to alternative political systems and cultures may make people more critical of their own political system and seek opportunities to change it. Russia remains in what seems to be an extended period of transition. In the early 1990s, Russians frequently hoped for "normal conditions," that is, an escape from the shortages, insecurity, and political controls of the past. Now, "normality" has been redefined in less glowing terms than those conceived in the late 1980s. Russians seem to have a capability to adapt to change and uncertainty that North Americans find at once alluring, puzzling, and disturbing.

Youth Politics and the Generational Divide

Young people in Russia have grown up in political circumstances that differ dramatically from those that affected their parents. Whereas individuals born before 1970 (now middle-aged or older) were socialized during the period of communist rule, Russians between the ages of 18 and 30 had their formative experiences during a period of rapid political change following the collapse of the USSR. Whereas their elders were drawn into communist youth organizations and influenced by the dominance of a single party/state ideology, young people today are exposed to a wider range of political views, have greater freedom to travel abroad, and also have freer access to international contacts and viewpoints. These tendencies are reinforced even further by increased access to information through the Internet, which young people use more freely. It is, therefore, not surprising that age is associated with differing political orientations.

Generational experience also affects the ability to adapt. In the Soviet period, weak material incentives encouraged risk avoidance, low productivity, poor punctuality, absenteeism, lack of personal initiative, and a preference for security over achievement. However, young people in Russia are adapting to a new work environment. They are more flexible, in part due to their age, but also because of differing socialization experiences that have resulted in altered expectations. Consequently, they are inclined to support the market transition and are more oriented toward maximizing self-interest and demonstrating initiative. Nevertheless, many Russians of all age groups still question values underlying market reform, preferring an economy that is less profit driven and more oriented to equality and the collective good.

Despite generational differences, young people represent a wide range of political views in Russia, as elsewhere. A controversial phenomenon is the youth group, Nashi (Ours), formed in 2005. While claiming to oppose fascism in Russia, some observers see the group as nurturing intolerance and extremist sentiments. Nashi's goals include educating youth in Russian history and values, and forming volunteer groups to help maintain law and order. The group has been highly supportive of Putin, seeing him as a defender of Russia's national sovereignty. On the other hand, political critics of the Putin regime, such as those who initially participated in demonstrations in 2011, were disproportionately young, but over time they were joined by many middle-aged protesters. While support for Putin in the lead up to the presidential election of 2012 was relatively similar across age groups, those older than 40 were more likely to support the Communist Party, and more young people supported the non-establishment candidate, Mikhail Prokhorov. According to surveys carried out in December 2013, older respondents were far more likely to express regret about the collapse of the USSR (86 percent of those over 55, compared to only 24 percent of those 18–24).[22]

These indicators suggest that age does affect political orientations, but not strongly enough to predict a generational shift in voting patterns in the foreseeable future.

Russian Politics in Comparative Perspective

The way in which politics, economics, and ideology were intertwined in the Soviet period has profoundly affected the nature of political change in all of the former Soviet republics and generally has made the democratization process more difficult. How has Russia fared compared to some of the other post-communist systems that faced many of these same challenges, and what can we learn from these comparisons? A rule of thumb, simple as it seems, is that the further east one goes in the post-communist world, the more difficult and prolonged the transition period has been (with the exception of Belarus, which lies adjacent to the European Union but maintains an authoritarian system). This is partly because the more westerly countries of Central Europe that were outside the USSR (Poland, Hungary, Czech Republic, Slovakia), as well as the Baltic states (Estonia, Latvia, Lithuania), were able to accede to the European Union, producing a strong motivation to embark on fundamental reform. This illustrates the potentially powerful impact of international forces on domestic political developments, if domestic actors are receptive. Also these countries were under communist rule for a shorter period of time. In addition most of these countries had a history of closer ties and greater cultural exposure to Western Europe; ideas of liberalism, private property, and individualism were less foreign to citizens in countries such as Czechoslovakia, East Germany, Poland, and Hungary than in regions farther east, including Russia. Historical legacies and cultural differences do matter.

Russia's experience demonstrates the importance of strong political institutions if democracy is to be secured. Their weakness in the 1990s contributed to high levels of social dislocation, corruption, and personal stress, as well as to demographic decline and poor economic adaptation to the market. However, Russia's rich deposits of natural resources have sheltered it from difficulties facing some neighboring countries like Ukraine. At the same time, Russia's natural resource wealth has made it difficult to untangle economic and political power, reducing political accountability to the public. The "resource curse" produces economic hazards as well, including the so-called Dutch disease, in which heavy reliance on income from natural resource exports pushes the value of the currency up, making it more difficult for domestic producers to export successfully and feeding inflationary pressures.

In all of the post-Soviet states (except the Baltic states), the attempt to construct democratic political institutions has been characterized by repeated political crises, weak representation of popular interests, executive–legislative conflict, faltering efforts at constitutional revision, and corruption. In Russia, terrorist attacks persist, reinforcing a sense of insecurity and producing fertile ground for nationalist sentiments and a strong role for the security forces, which themselves enjoy a low level of popular legitimacy. Nonetheless, with the exception of the Chechnya conflict and its spillover into the neighboring areas in Russia's European south, Russia has escaped major domestic violence and civil war, unlike parts of the former Yugoslavia, Georgia, Moldova, the Central Asian state of Tajikistan, and, most recently, eastern Ukraine.

Will Russia be able to find a place for itself in the world of states that meets the expectations of its educated and sophisticated population? Even after the first decade of the new millennium, prospects are still unclear. One thing is certain: Russia will continue to be a key regional force in Europe and Asia by virtue of its size, its rich energy and resource base, its large and highly skilled population and its nuclear arsenal. However, Russia's leaders have had an ambivalent attitude toward accepting crucial norms that would underlie an effective and enduring partnership with the West.

If the Russian leadership gradually moves Russia on a path closer to liberal democratic development, then this may provide an example to other semiauthoritarian countries in Russia's neighborhood. On the other hand, if the continuation of existing authoritarian trends is associated with sustained economic growth and stability that benefits the majority of the population, then Russia may settle into an extended period of soft authoritarianism that reinforces the East–West divide, and that could, if not resisted by the political leadership, feed destructive nationalist tendencies. Finally, if the Russian leadership's insulation generates unpopular and ineffective policy outcomes, or if world energy prices trigger an economic downslide, this may stimulate a new process of reflection on Russia's future path and offer an opportunity for democratic forces to reassert themselves and find popular resonance.

Where Do You Stand?

Is Russia justified in taking strong action to assure that a neighboring country, such as Ukraine, stays within its "sphere of influence"?

Should Western countries make greater efforts to promote liberal democratic opposition groups in Russia?

Chapter Summary

Russian history has been characterized by a series of upheavals and changes that have often made life unpredictable and difficult for the citizen. The revolutions of 1917 replaced tsarist rule with a political system dominated by the Communist Party. In the Stalinist period, Communist rule involved a process of rapid industrialization, collectivization of agriculture, and purges of the party, followed by large losses of population associated with World War II. With the death of Stalin came another important transition, as Soviet politics was transformed into a more predictable system of bureaucratic authoritarianism, characterized by relative stability but without political competition or democratic control. The most recent transition, ushered in by the collapse of Communist Party rule in 1991, resulted in the emergence

of the Russian Federation as an independent state. When the Russian Federation was formed in 1991, new political structures needed to be constructed. A constitution was adopted in 1993, which involves a directly elected president with strong political powers.

Russia's political course since 1991 has been profoundly influenced by the fact that the country underwent simultaneous and radical transformations in four spheres: politics, economics, ideology, and geopolitical position in the world. Managing so much change in a short time has been difficult and has produced mixed results. Efforts to democratize the political system have been only partially successful, and experts disagree both about whether the political controls initiated by Putin were needed to ensure stability and under what conditions they might be reversed. In the economic sphere, after recovering from a period of deep economic decline in the 1990s, Russia's renewed growth depends largely on exports of energy and natural resources, making the country vulnerable to external shocks such as the 2008–2009 global crisis. The country faces the challenge of effectively using its natural resource wealth to rebuild other sectors of the economy. In terms of ideology, nationalism threatens to reinforce intolerance and undermine social unity. Continuing high levels of corruption also undermine popular confidence in state institutions. Whereas countries that have joined the European Union seem, for the most part, to have successfully established viable democratic systems with functioning market economies, other post-Soviet states in Eastern Europe and Central Asia face similar challenges to Russia's in consolidating democracy and market reform. Russia has sought to reassert its role as a regional and global force, but a revival of tension with the West in the face of Russia's annexation of Crimea and conflict over Ukraine threatens stability in Russia's neighborhood.

Key Terms

civil society
clientelistic networks
collectivization
democratic centralism
dominant party
federal system

glasnost
insider privatization
market reform
mixed electoral system
nomenklatura
oligarchs

patrimonial state
power vertical
siloviki
soft authoritarianism
sovereign democracy
vanguard party

Suggested Readings

Black, J. L. and Michael Johns, eds. *Russia After 2012: From Putin to Medvedev to Putin – Continuity, Change, or Revolution?* London and New York: Routledge, 2013.

Gel'man, Valdimir, and Cameron Ross, eds. *The Politics of Sub-National Authoritarianism in Russia*. Farnham, Surrey UK: Ashgate, 2010.

Hopf, Ted, ed. *Russia's European Choice*. New York: Palgrave MacMillan, 2008.

Hough, Jerry, and Merle Fainsod. *How the Soviet Union Is Governed*. Cambridge: Harvard University Press, 1979.

Ledeneva, Alena V. *Can Russia Modernize? Sistema, Power Networks and Informal Governance*. Cambridge: Cambridge University Press, 2013.

Mankoff, Jeffrey. *Russian Foreign Policy: The Return of Great Power Politics*. Lanham, MD: Rowman & Littlefield, 2012.

Oates, Sarah. *Revolution Stalled: The Political Limits of the Internet in the Post-Soviet Space*. Oxford: Oxford University Press, 2013.

Pipes, Richard. *Russia under the Old Regime*. New York: Scribner, 1974.

Remington, Thomas F. *Politics in Russia*, 7th ed. New Jersey: Pearson, 2012.

Sakwa, Richard. *Putin: Russia's Choice*. London and New York: Routledge, 2008.

Suggested Websites

The Carnegie Moscow Center
www.carnegie.ru/en/

Itar-TASS News Agency
http://en.itar-tass.com/

Johnson's Russia List
http://www.russialist.org/

Open Democracy (Russia)
http://www.opendemocracy.net/russia

Radio Free Europe/Radio Liberty
http://www.rferl.org/section/Russia/161.html

The Moscow News
www.mnweekly.ru

Russian Analytical Digest
http://www.laender-analysen.de/index
.php?topic=russland&url=http://www.res.ethz.ch
/analysis/rad/

Russia Today
rt.com

14 Iran

Ervand Abrahamian

Official Name: Islamic Republic of Iran (Jomhuri-ye Eslami-ye Iran)

Location: Middle East (West Asia)

Capital City: Tehran

Population (2014): 80.8 million

Size: approximately 1,648,000 sq. km.; slightly larger than Alaska

1925
Reza Khan establishes the Pahlavi dynasty.

1953
CIA-supported coup overthrows Mossadeq.

1941–1945
Allied occupation of Iran during World War II

1963
Shah launches "White Revolution."

1920   1940   1950   1960   1965   1970   1975

1921
Colonel Reza Khan's military coup

1941
Muhammad Reza Pahlavi becomes Shah of Iran.

1951
Nationalization of the oil industry by government of Prime Minister Mossadeq

1975
Shah establishes the Resurgence Party.

1905–1911
Constitutional Revolution

SECTION 1

THE MAKING OF THE MODERN IRANIAN STATE

Politics in Action

▽ Focus Questions

- To what extent does geography, language, history, religion, and religion give Iran a distinct identity?

- How did Muhammad Reza Shah come to power, and to what role did the United States play in supporting him?

ayatollah

Literally, "sign of God." A high-ranking cleric in Iran.

In 2013, Iran with a resounding vote elected Dr. Hassan Rouhani president of the Islamic Republic. Rouhani is a middle-ranking religious cleric, not an **ayatollah**, and prefers to be addressed as Dr.—a title he has from a university in Scotland where he obtained a Ph.D. in constitutional law. He won the election running on a reform platform, promising to remedy a "sick economy," strengthen the rule of law, and, most important of all, improve relations with the West, especially over the nuclear stand-off with the United States. The 2013 election was in many ways a replay of previous ones. In 1997, Muhammad Khatami, another middle-ranking reform cleric, had been elected president in a landslide victory. He was reelected in 2001 again with a landslide victory. But in 2005, after deteriorations of relations with the United States, he had been replaced by an ultraconservative populist named Mahmoud Ahmadinejad. Ahmadinejad had retained the presidency in 2009 after a hotly disputed election. Iran may lack many features of a true democracy. But it certainly does not lack fiercely contested elections.

These very different electoral outcomes illustrate the contradictory political forces at work in the Islamic Republic of Iran. Iran is a mixture of **theocracy** and democracy. Its political system is based on both clerical authority and popular sovereignty, on the divine right of the clergy and the rights of the people, on concepts derived from early Islam and from modern democratic principles. Iran

Timeline

1979 — Islamic Revolution; Shah forced into exile; Iran becomes an Islamic Republic; Ayatollah Khomeini becomes Leader.

March 1980 — Elections for the First Islamic *Majles* (parliament). Subsequent Majles elections every four years

June 1981 — President Bani-Sadr ousted by Khomeini, replaced by Muhammad Ali Rajai

2005 — Ultraconservative Mahmoud Ahmadinejad elected president

2013 — Dr. Hassan Rouhani elected President on reform platform

| 1979 | 1980 | 1985 | 1990 | 2000 | 2005 |

1979–1981 — Hostage crisis—52 U.S. embassy employees held by radical students

December 1979 — Referendum on the Islamic constitution

October 1981 — Ayatollah Ali Khamenei elected president

January 1980 — Abol-Hassan Bani-Sadr elected president

1980–1988 — War with Iraq

1989 — Khomeini dies; Khamenei appointed Leader; Rafsanjani elected president (reelected in 1993)

1997 — Muhammad Khatami elected president on reform platform (reelected in 2001)

2009 — Ahmadinejad re-elected; large-scale protests against alleged electoral fraud take place in Tehran and other cities.

---

has regular elections for the presidency and the *Majles* (Parliament), but the clerically dominated **Guardian Council** determines who can run. The president is the formal head of the executive branch. But he can be overruled, even dismissed, by the chief cleric, the **Leader** known in the West as the **Supreme Leader**. The president appoints the minister of justice, but the whole judiciary is under the supervision of the chief judge, who is appointed directly by the Leader. The *Majles* is the legislature, but bills do not become law unless the Guardian Council deems them compatible with Islam and the Islamic constitution. Thus, the Guardian Council—formed of twelve senior judges with six appointed by the Leader and six jointly by the Majles and the chief judge—has considerable judicial as well as legislative authority.

Geographic Setting

Iran is three times the size of France, slightly larger than Alaska, and much larger than its immediate neighbors. Most of its territory is inhospitable to agriculture. Rain-fed agriculture is confined mostly to the northwest and the provinces along the Caspian Sea. Only pastoral nomads can survive in the semiarid zones and in the high mountain valleys. Thus, 67 percent of the total population of a little over 80 million is concentrated on 27 percent of the land—mostly in the Caspian region, in the northwest provinces, and in the cities of Tehran, Mashed, Isfahan, Tabriz, Shiraz, and Qom.

Iran is the second-largest oil producer in the Middle East and the fourth-largest in the world, and oil revenues have made Iran an urbanized and partly industrialized country. Nearly 70 percent of the population lives in urban centers; 84 percent of the labor force is employed in industry and services; 85 percent of adults are literate; life expectancy has reached over seventy-three years; and the majority of Iranians enjoy a standard of living well above that found in most of Asia and Africa. Iran can no longer be described as a typically poor developing country. It

---

theocracy

A state dominated by the clergy, who rule on the grounds that they are the only interpreters of God's will and law.

Majles

The Iranian parliament, from the Arabic term for "assembly."

Guardian Council

A committee created in the Iranian constitution to oversee the *Majles* (the parliament.

Leader/Supreme Leader

A cleric elected to be the head of the Islamic Republic of Iran.

is a middle-income country with a GDP per capita above that of Brazil and South Africa. Recent UN economic sanctions have caused considerable hardship but have not reduced its general standing.

Iran lies on the strategic crossroads between Central Asia and Turkey, between the Indian subcontinent and the Middle East, and between the Arabian Peninsula and the Caucasus Mountains, which are often considered a boundary between Europe and Asia. This has made the region vulnerable to invaders.

The population today reflects these historic invasions. Some 53 percent speak Persian (**Farsi**), an Indo-European language, as a first language; the remainder of the population primarily speaks eight other languages. Use of Persian, however, has dramatically increased in recent years because of successful literacy campaigns. Over 90 percent of the population can now communicate in Persian, the national language. Although Iran shares many religious and cultural features with the rest of the Islamic Middle East, its Persian heritage gives it a national identity distinct from that of the Arab and Turkish world. Iranians by no means consider themselves part of the Arab world.

Islam, with over 1 billion adherents, is the second-largest religion in the world after Christianity. Islam means literally "submission to God," and a Muslim is someone who has submitted to God—the same God that Jews and Christians worship. Islam has one central tenet: "There is only one God, and Muhammad is His Prophet." Muslims, in order to consider themselves faithful, need to perform the following four duties to the best of their ability: give to charity; pray every day facing Mecca, where Abraham is believed to have built the first place of worship; make a pilgrimage at least once in a lifetime to Mecca, which is located in modern Saudi Arabia; and fast during the daytime hours in the month of Ramadan to commemorate God's revelation of the Qur'an (Koran, or Holy Book) to the Prophet Muhammad. These four, together with the central tenet, are known as the Five Pillars of Islam.

From its earliest days, Islam has been divided into two major branches: Sunni, meaning literally "followers of tradition," and Shi'i, literally "partisans of Ali." Sunnis are by far in the majority worldwide. Shi'is constitute less than 10 percent of Muslims worldwide and are concentrated in Iran, southern Iraq, Bahrain, eastern Turkey, Azerbaijan, and southern Lebanon.

Although both branches accept the Five Pillars, they differ mostly over who should have succeeded the Prophet Muhammad (d. 632). The Sunnis recognized the early dynasties that ruled the Islamic empire with the exalted title of caliph ("Prophet's Deputy"). The Shi'is, however, argued that as soon as the Prophet died, his authority should have been passed on to Imam Ali, the Prophet's close companion, disciple, and son-in-law. They further argue that Imam Ali passed his authority to his direct male heirs, the third of whom, Imam Husayn, had been martyred fighting the Sunnis in 680, and the twelfth of whom had supposedly gone into hiding in 941.

The Shi'is are also known as Twelvers since they follow the Twelve Imams. They refer to the Twelfth Imam as the *Mahdi*, the Hidden Imam, and believe him to be the Messiah who will herald the end of the world. Furthermore, they argue that in his absence, the authority to interpret the *shari'a* (religious law) should be in the hands of the senior clerical scholars—the ayatollahs. Thus, from the beginning, the Shi'is harbored ambivalent attitudes toward the state, especially if the rulers were Sunnis or lacked genealogical links to the Twelve Imams. For Sunnis, the *shari'a* is based mostly on the Qur'an and the teachings of the Prophet. For Shi'is, it is based also on the teachings of the Twelve Imams.

Farsi

Persian word for the Persian language. Fars is a province in Central Iran.

Table 14.1	Political Organization
Political System	A mixture of democracy and theocracy (rule of the clergy) headed by a cleric with the title of the Leader.
Regime History	Islamic Republic since the 1979 Islamic Revolution.
Administrative Structure	Centralized administration with 30 provinces. The interior minister appoints the provincial governor-generals.
Executive	President and his cabinet. The president is chosen by the general electorate every four years and is limited to two terms. The president chooses his cabinet ministers, but they need to obtain the approval of the *Majles* (parliament).
Legislature	Unicameral. The *Majles*, formed of 290 seats, is elected every four years. It has multiple-member districts with the top runners in the elections taking the seats. Bills passed by the *Majles* do not become law unless they have the approval of the clerically dominated Council of Guardians.
Judiciary	A Chief Judge and a Supreme Court independent of the executive and legislature but appointed by the Leader.
Party System	The ruling clergy restricts most party and organizational activities.

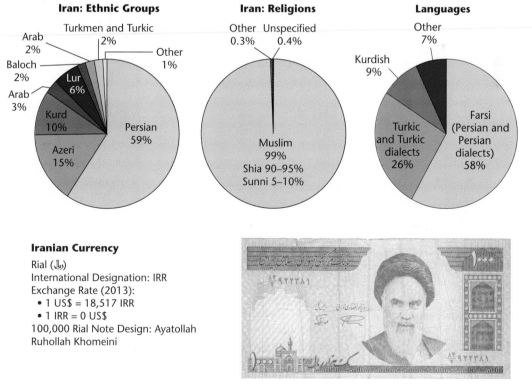

Iran: Ethnic Groups

Turkmen and Turkic 2%
Arab 2%
Baloch 2%
Arab 3%
Lur 6%
Kurd 10%
Azeri 15%
Persian 59%
Other 1%

Iran: Religions

Other 0.3%   Unspecified 0.4%
Muslim 99%
Shia 90–95%
Sunni 5–10%

Languages

Other 7%
Kurdish 9%
Turkic and Turkic dialects 26%
Farsi (Persian and Persian dialects) 58%

Iranian Currency

Rial (ریال)
International Designation: IRR
Exchange Rate (2013):
• 1 US$ = 18,517 IRR
• 1 IRR = 0 US$
100,000 Rial Note Design: Ayatollah Ruhollah Khomeini

FIGURE 14.1 The Iranian Nation at a Glance
© Oleg_Mit/Shutterstock.com (for photo)

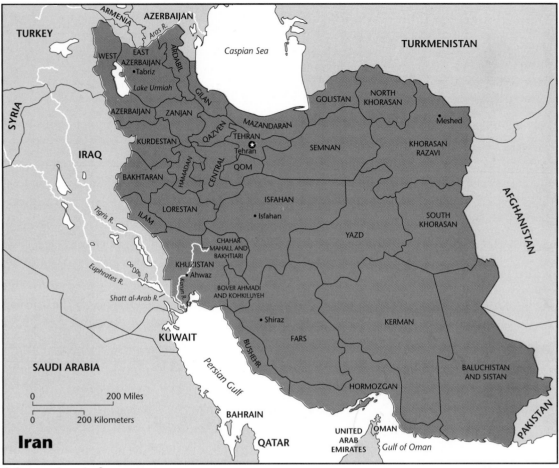

© Cengage Learning®

Critical Junctures

The Safavids (1501–1722)

The Safavid dynasty conquered the territory that is now Iran in the sixteenth century and forcibly converted their subjects to Shi'ism, even though the vast majority had been Sunnis. By the mid-seventeenth century, Sunnism survived only among the tribal groups at the periphery.

Safavid Iran also contained small communities of Jews, Zoroastrians, and Christians. The Safavids tolerated religious minorities as long as they paid special taxes and accepted royal authority. According to Islam, Christians, Jews, and Zoroastrians were to be tolerated as legitimate **People of the Book**, because they were mentioned in the Holy **Qur'an** and possessed their own sacred texts: the Bible, the Torah, and the Avesta.

The Safavids governed through Persian scribes and Shi'i clerics as well as through tribal chiefs, large landowners, city merchants, guild elders, and urban ward leaders. Their army was formed mostly of tribal cavalry led by tribal chieftains. Safavid revenues came mostly from land taxes levied on the peasantry. The Safavids claimed absolute power, but they lacked a central state and had to cooperate with many semi-independent local leaders.

People of the Book

The Muslim term for recognized religious minorities, such as Christians, Jews, and Zoroastrians.

Qur'an

The Muslim Bible.

The Qajars (1794–1925)

In 1722 Afghan tribesmen invaded the capital. After a half-century of civil wars the Qajars—a Turkic-speaking Shi'i tribe—reconquered much of Iran. They moved the capital to Tehran and re-created the Safavid system of central manipulation and court administration. They also declared Shi'ism to be the state religion, even though they, unlike the Safavids, could not boast of genealogical links to the Twelve Imams. Since these new shahs, or kings, did not pretend to wear the Imam's mantle, Shi'i clerical leaders could claim to be the main interpreters of Islam.

Qajar rule coincided with the peak of European imperialism in the nineteenth century. The Russians seized parts of Central Asia and the Caucasus region from Iran and extracted major economic concessions. The British Imperial Bank won the monopoly to issue paper money. The Indo-European Telegraph Company got a contract to extend communication lines throughout the country. Exclusive rights to drill for oil in the southwest were sold to a British citizen. Iranians increasingly felt their whole country had been auctioned off.

These resentments led to the constitutional revolution of 1905–1909. The 1906 constitution introduced elections, separation of powers, a legislative assembly, and the concepts of popular sovereignty and the nation (*mellat*). It retained the monarchy, but centered political power in a national assembly called the *Majles*.

The constitution gave the *Majles* extensive authority over all laws, budgets, treaties, concessions, and the makeup of the cabinet. The ministers were accountable to the *Majles*, not to the shah. The constitution also included a bill of rights guaranteeing equality before the law, protection of life and property, and freedom of expression and association.

Shi'ism was declared Iran's official religion. Clerical courts continued to implement the *shari'a*. A Guardian Council of senior clerics elected by the *Majles* had veto power over parliamentary bills it deemed un-Islamic.

The initial euphoria soon gave way to deep disillusionment. Pressures from the European powers continued, and a devastating famine after World War I took some 1 million lives, almost 10 percent of the total population. Internal conflicts polarized the *Majles* into warring liberal and conservative factions. Liberals, mostly members of the intelligentsia, championed social reforms, especially the replacement of the *shari'a* with a modern legal code. Conservatives, led by landlords, tribal chiefs, and senior clerics, vehemently opposed such reforms, particularly land reform, women's rights, and the granting of full equality to religious minorities.

The central government, without any real army, bureaucracy, or tax-collecting machinery, could not administer the provinces. During World War I, Russia and Britain formally carved up Iran into three zones. Russia occupied the north, Britain the south. Iran was left with a small middle "neutral zone."

By 1921, Iran was in complete disarray. According to a British diplomat, the propertied classes, fearful of communism, were anxiously seeking "a savior on horseback."[1]

The Pahlavis (1925–1979)

In February 1921 Colonel Reza Khan carried out a coup d'état. He replaced the cabinet and consolidated power in his own hands. Four years later, he deposed the Qajars and crowned himself Shah-in-Shah—King of Kings—and established the Pahlavi dynasty. This was the first nontribal dynasty to rule the whole of Iran. During the next sixteen years, he systematically modernized the country by building almost from scratch a highly centralized state with a standing army and a large administrative bureaucracy.

Reza Shah ruled with an iron fist until 1941, when the British and the Soviets invaded Iran to stop Nazi Germany from establishing a foothold there. Reza Shah promptly abdicated in favor of his son, Muhammad Reza Shah, and went into exile, where he soon died. In the first twelve years of his reign, the young Shah retained control over the armed forces but had to tolerate a free press, an independent judiciary, competitive elections, assertive cabinet ministers, and boisterous parliaments. He also had to confront two vigorous political movements: the communist Tudeh (Masses) Party and the National Front, led by the charismatic Dr. Muhammad Mossadeq (1882–1967).

The Tudeh drew its support mostly from working-class trade unions. The National Front drew its support mainly from the salaried middle classes and campaigned to nationalize the British company that controlled the petroleum industry. Mossadeq also wanted to sever the Shah's links with the armed forces. In 1951, Mossadeq was elected prime minister and promptly nationalized the oil industry. The period of relative freedom, however, ended abruptly in 1953, when royalist army officers overthrew Mossadeq and installed the Shah with absolute power. The coup was financed by the U.S. Central Intelligence Agency (CIA) and the British. This intensified anti-British sentiment and created a deep distrust of the United States. It also made the Shah appear to be a foreign puppet.

The Pahlavi dynasty continued to build a highly centralized state. The armed forces grew from 40,000 in 1925 to 124,000 in 1941, and to 410,000 in 1979. The armed forces were supplemented by a pervasive secret police known as SAVAK.

Iran's bureaucracy expanded to twenty-one ministries employing over 300,000 civil servants in 1979. The Education Ministry grew twentyfold. The powerful Interior Ministry appointed provincial governors, town mayors, district superintendents, and village headmen; it could even rig *Majles* elections and create rubber-stamp parliaments.

The Justice Ministry supplanted the *shari'a* with a European-style civil code and the clerical courts with a modern judicial system culminating in a Supreme Court. The Transport Ministry built an impressive array of bridges, ports, highways, and railroads known as the Trans-Iranian Railway. The Ministry of Industries financed factories specializing in consumer goods. The Agricultural Ministry became prominent in 1963 when the Shah made land reform the centerpiece of his "White Revolution." This White Revolution was an effort to promote economic development and such social reform as extending the vote to women. It also created a Literacy Corps for the countryside. This White Revolution from above—encouraged by the United States—was a concerted attempt to forestall a communist-led Red Revolution from below. Thus, by the late 1970s, the state had set up a modern system of communications, initiated a minor industrial revolution, and extended its reach into even the most outlying villages.

The state also controlled the National and the Central Banks; the Industrial and Mining Development Bank; the Plan Organization in charge of economic policy; the national radio-television network; and most important, the National Iranian Oil Company.

The dynasty's founder, Reza Shah, had used coercion, confiscation, and diversion of irrigation water to make himself one of the largest landowners in the Middle East. This wealth transformed the Shah's imperial court into a large military-monied complex, providing work for thousands in its numerous palaces, hotels, casinos, charities, and beach resorts. This patronage system grew under his son, Muhammad Reza

Shah, particularly after he established his tax-exempt Pahlavi Foundation, which eventually controlled 207 large companies.

The Pahlavi drive for secularization, centralization, industrialization, and social development won some favor from the urban propertied classes. But arbitrary rule; the 1953 coup that overthrew a popular prime minister; the disregard for constitutional liberties; and the stifling of independent newspapers, political parties, and professional associations produced widespread resentment. The Pahlavi state, like the Safavids and the Qajars, hovered over, rather than embedded itself into, Iranian society.

In 1975, the Shah formed the Resurgence Party. He declared Iran a one-party state and threatened imprisonment and exile to those refusing to join the party. The Resurgence Party was designed to create yet another organizational link with the population, especially with the **bazaars** (traditional marketplaces), which, unlike the rest of society, had managed to retain their independent guilds and thus escape direct government control. The Resurgence Party promptly established its own bazaar guilds as well as newspapers, women's organizations, professional associations, and labor unions. It also prepared to create a Religious Corps to teach the peasants "true Islam."

bazaar

An urban marketplace where shops, workshops, small businesses, and export-importers are located.

The Islamic Revolution (1979)

These grievances were best summed up by an exile newspaper in Paris on the very eve of the 1979 revolution. In an article entitled "Fifty Years of Treason," it charged the Shah and his family with establishing a military dictatorship; collaborating with the CIA; trampling on the constitution; creating SAVAK, the secret police; rigging parliamentary elections; organizing a fascistic one-party state; taking over the religious establishment; and undermining national identity by disseminating Western culture. It also accused the regime of inducing millions of landless peasants to migrate into urban shantytowns; widening the gap between rich and poor; funneling money away from the middle-class bourgeoisie into the pockets of the wealthy comprador bourgeoisie (entrepreneurs linked to foreign companies and multinational corporations); wasting resources on bloated military budgets; and granting new capitulations to the West.

These grievances took sharper edge when the leading opposition cleric, Ayatollah Ruhollah Khomeini—exiled in Iraq—formulated a drastically new version of Shi'ism. His version of Shi'ism has often been labeled Islamic fundamentalism. It would be better to call it **political Islam** or even more accurately as Shi'i populism. The term *fundamentalism*, derived from American Protestantism, implies religious dogmatism, intellectual inflexibility and purity, political traditionalism, social conservatism, rejection of the modern world, and the literal interpretation of scriptural texts. While Khomeinism shares some of these characteristics, Khomeini was not so much a social conservative as a political revolutionary who used populist rhetoric to rally the population against a decadent elite.

Khomeini was born in 1902 into a landed clerical family in central Iran. During the 1920s, he studied in the famous Fayzieh Seminary in Qom with the leading theologians of the day, most of whom were scrupulously apolitical. He taught at the seminary from the 1930s through the 1950s, avoiding politics even during the mass campaign to nationalize the British-owned oil company. His entry into politics did not come until 1963, when he, along with most other clerical leaders, denounced the White Revolution. Forced into exile, Khomeini taught at the Shi'i center of Najaf in Iraq from 1964 until 1978. During these years, Khomeini developed his own version

→ opposition to the shah

political Islam

A term for the intermingling of Islam with politics and often used as a substitute for Islamic fundamentalism.

of Shi'i populism by incorporating socioeconomic grievances into his sermons and denouncing not just the Shah but also the whole ruling class.

Khomeini denounced monarchies in general as part of the corrupt elite exploiting the oppressed masses. Oppressors were courtiers, large landowners, high-ranking military officers, wealthy foreign-connected capitalists, and millionaire palace dwellers. The oppressed were the masses, especially landless peasants, wage earners, bazaar shopkeepers, and shantytown dwellers.

Khomeini gave a radically new meaning to the old Shi'i term *velayat-e faqih* (jurist's guardianship). He argued that jurist's guardianship gave the senior clergy all-encompassing authority over the whole community, not just over widows, minors, and the mentally disabled (the previous interpretation). Only the senior clerics could understand the *shari'a*; the divine authority given to the Prophet and the Imams had been passed on to their spiritual heirs, the clergy. He further insisted the clergy were the people's true representatives, since they lived among them, listened to their problems, and shared their everyday joys and pains. He claimed that the Shah secretly planned to confiscate all religious endowment funds and replace Islamic values with "cultural imperialism."

In 1977–1978, the Shah tried to deal with a 20 percent rise in consumer prices and a 10 percent decline in oil revenues by cutting construction projects and declaring war against "profiteers," "hoarders," and "price gougers." Shopkeepers believed the Shah was diverting attention from court corruption and planning to replace them with government-run department stores. They also thought he was out to destroy the bazaar.

The Shah was also subjected to international pressure on the sensitive issue of human rights—from Amnesty International, the United Nations, and the Western press, as well as from the recently elected Carter administration in the United States. In 1977, the Shah gave the International Red Cross access to Iranian prisons and permitted political prisoners to have defense attorneys. This international pressure allowed the opposition to "breathe" again after decades of suffocation.[2]

This slight loosening of the reins sealed the fate of the Shah. Political parties, labor organizations, and professional associations—especially lawyers, writers, and university professors—regrouped after years of being banned. Bazaar guilds regained their independence. College, high school, and seminary students took to the streets—with each demonstration growing in size and vociferousness. On September 8, 1978, remembered in Iran as Black Friday, troops shot and killed a large but unknown number of unarmed civilians in central Tehran. This dramatically intensified popular hatred for the regime. By late 1978, general strikes throughout the country were bringing the whole economy to a halt. Oil workers vowed that they would not export petroleum until they had got rid of the "Shah and his forty thieves."[3]

In urban centers, local committees attached to the mosques and financed by the bazaars were distributing food to the needy, supplanting the police with militias known as *pasdaran* (Revolutionary Guards). They replaced the judicial system with ad hoc courts applying the *shari'a*. Anti-regime rallies were now attracting as many as 2 million protesters. Protesters demanded the abolition of the monarchy, the return of Khomeini, and the establishment of a republic that would preserve national independence and provide the downtrodden masses with decent wages, land, and a proper standard of living. The revolution was in full swing.

Although led by pro-Khomeini clerics, these mass rallies drew support from a broad variety of organizations: the National Front; the Lawyer's, Doctor's, and Women's associations; the communist Tudeh Party; the Fedayin, a Marxist guerrilla group; and the Mojahedin, a Muslim guerrilla group formed of lay intellectuals. The

jurist's guardianship

Khomeini's concept that the Iranian clergy should rule on the grounds that they are the divinely appointed guardians of both the law and the people.

pasdaran

Persian term for guards, used to refer to the army of Revolutionary Guards formed during Iran's Islamic Revolution.

rallies also attracted students, from high schools and colleges, as well as shopkeepers and craftsmen from the bazaars. A secret Revolutionary Committee in Tehran coordinated protests throughout the country. This was one of the first revolutions to be televised worldwide. Many would later feel that these demonstrations inspired the 1980s revolutions that swept through Eastern Europe.

Confronted by this opposition and by increasing numbers of soldiers who were deserting to the opposition, the Shah decided to leave Iran. A year later, when he was in exile and dying of cancer, many speculated that he might have mastered the upheavals if he had been healthier, possessed a stronger personality, and received full support from the United States. But even a man with an iron will and full foreign backing would not have been able to deal with millions of angry demonstrators, massive general strikes, and debilitating desertions from his own armed forces.

On February 11, 1979, a few hours of street fighting provided the final blow to the fifty-four-year-old dynasty that claimed a 2,500-year-old heritage.

The Islamic Republic (1979–present)

Returning home triumphant in the midst of the Iranian Revolution after the Shah was forced from power, Khomeini was declared the Imam and Leader of the new Islamic Republic. In the past, Iranian Shi'is, unlike the Arab Sunnis, had reserved the special term *Imam* only for Imam Ali and his eleven direct heirs, whom they deemed infallible, and, therefore, almost semidivine. For many Iranians in 1979, Khomeini was charismatic in the true sense of the word: a man with a special gift from God. Khomeini ruled as Imam and Leader of the Islamic Republic until his death in 1989.

Seven weeks after the February revolution, a nationwide referendum replaced the monarchy with an Islamic Republic. Liberal and lay supporters of Khomeini, including Mehdi Bazargan, his first prime minister, had hoped to offer the electorate the choice of a *democratic* Islamic Republic. But Khomeini overruled them. He declared the term was redundant since Islam itself was democratic. Khomeini was now hailed as the Leader of the Revolution, Founder of the Islamic Republic, Guide of the Oppressed Masses, Commander of the Armed Forces, and most potent of all, Imam of the Muslim World.

A new constitution was drawn up in late 1979 by the **Assembly of Experts** (*Majles-e Khebregan*). Although this seventy-three man assembly was elected by the general public, almost all secular organizations as well as clerics opposed to Khomeini boycotted the elections because the state media were controlled, independent papers had been banned, and voters were being intimidated by club-wielding vigilantes known as the *Hezbollahis*("Partisans of God"). The vast majority of those elected were pro-Khomeini clerics, including forty *hojjat al-Islams*(middle-ranking clerics) and fifteen ayatollahs. They drafted a highly theocratic constitution vesting much authority in the hands of Khomeini in particular and the clergy in general—all this over the strong objections of Prime Minister Bazargan, who wanted a French-style presidential republic that would be Islamic in name but democratic in structure.

When Bazargan threatened to submit his own constitution to the public, television controlled by the clerics showed him shaking hands with U.S. policy-makers. Meanwhile, Khomeini denounced the U.S embassy as a "den of spies" plotting a repeat performance of the 1953 coup. This led to mass demonstrations, a break-in at the embassy, the seizure of dozens of American hostages, and eventually the resignation of Bazargan. Some suspect the hostage crisis had been engineered to undercut Bazargan.

Assembly of Experts

Group that nominates and can remove the Leader. The assembly is elected by the general electorate, but almost all its members are clerics.

Hezbollahis

Literally "partisans of God." In Iran, the term is used to describe religious vigilantes. In Lebanon, it is used to describe the Shi'i militia.

hojjat al-Islam

Literally, "the proof of Islam." In Iran, it means a medium-ranking cleric.

A month after the embassy break-in, Khomeini submitted the theocratic constitution to the public and declared that all citizens had a divine duty to vote; 99 percent of those voting endorsed it.

In the first decade after the revolution, a number of factors helped the clerics consolidate power. First, few people could challenge Khomeini's overwhelming charisma. Second, the invasion of Iran in 1980 by Saddam Hussein's Iraq rallied the Iranian population behind their endangered homeland. Third, international petroleum prices shot up, sustaining Iran's oil revenues. The price of a barrel of oil, which had hovered around $30 in 1979, jumped to over $50 by 1981. This enabled the new regime, despite war and revolution, to continue to finance existing development programs.

The second decade after the revolution brought the clerics serious problems. Khomeini's death in June 1989 removed his decisive presence. His successor, Ali Khamenei, lacked not only his charisma but also his scholastic credentials and seminary disciples. The 1988 UN-brokered cease-fire in the Iran-Iraq War ended the foreign danger. A drastic fall in world oil prices, which plunged to less than $10 a barrel by 1998, placed a sharp brake on economic development. Even more serious, by the late 1990s, the regime was facing a major ideological crisis, with many of Khomeini's followers, including some of his closest disciples, now stressing the importance of public participation over clerical hegemony, of political pluralism over theological conformity, and of civil society over state authority—in other words, of democracy over theocracy.

Iran after 9/11

The terrorist attacks in the United States on September 11, 2001, and the subsequent American invasions of Afghanistan in October 2001 and Iraq in March 2002, had

The Shah's statue on the ground, February 1979.
Abbas/Magnum Photos

profound consequences for Iran. At first, the American war on terror brought Iran and the United States closer together since Iran for years had seen both the Taliban and Saddam Hussein as its own mortal enemies. Saddam Hussein was hated for the obvious reason; he had waged an eight-year war on Iran. The Taliban was hated in part because it had massacred a large number of Shi'i Afghans; and in part because it was financed by Sunni Wahhabi fundamentalists in Saudi Arabia who consider Shi'ism as well as all innovations since the very beginnings of Islam to be unacceptable heresies. In fact, these Sunni fundamentalists consider Shi'is to be as bad if not worse than non-Muslim infidels. Not surprisingly, Iran helped the United States depose the Taliban in 2001. It also used its considerable influence among the Iraqi Shi'is to install a pro-American government in Baghdad in 2003. It offered the United States in 2003 a "grand bargain" to settle all major differences, including those over nuclear research, Israel, Lebanon, and the Persian Gulf.

These hopes, however, were soon dashed—first, because in his State of the Union address in January 2002, President George W. Bush named Iran (along with Iraq and North Korea) as part of an "Axis of Evil" supporting terrorism and developing weapons of mass destruction. Moreover, after the occupation of Iraq, the United States surrounded Iran with military bases in the Persian Gulf, Turkey, Azerbaijan, Georgia, Afghanistan, and Central Asia. Bush also refused to enter serious negotiations until Iran unconditionally stopped nuclear research. These hard-line actions played a major role in both undermining the Iran's liberal President Khatemi and paving the way for the electoral victory of the bellicose Ahmadinejad in 2005. Reformers did not want to be associated with an American administration that not only insisted Iran should not have a nuclear program but also aggressively advocated regime change in Tehran. For most Iranians, this again resurrected memories of the 1953 CIA coup. These issues increased tensions and brought Iran and the United States closer to a diplomatic, if not military, stand-off. The United States insisted—at least, until the election of President Obama—that it would not negotiate with Iran unless it stopped its nuclear enrichment program. Iran, in turn, insisted that its nuclear program had no military purpose and that it conformed to guidelines set by international treaties.

The Four Themes and Iran

Iran in a Globalized World of States

By denouncing the United States as an "arrogant imperialist," canceling military agreements with the West, and condoning the taking of U.S. diplomats as hostages, Khomeini asserted Iranian power in the region but also inadvertently prompted Saddam Hussein to launch the Iraq-Iran War in 1980.

Khomeini's policies made it difficult for his successors, including the current President Rouhani, from normalizing relations with the West. Khomeini had called for revolutions throughout the Muslim world, denouncing Arab rulers in the region, particularly in Saudi Arabia, as the "corrupt puppets of American imperialism." He strengthened Iran's navy and bought nuclear submarines from Russia. He launched a research program to build medium-range missiles and nuclear power—possibly even nuclear weapons. He denounced the proposals for Arab-Israeli negotiations over Palestine. He sent money as well as arms to Muslim dissidents abroad, particularly Shi'i groups in Lebanon, Iraq, and Afghanistan. He permitted the intelligence services to assassinate some one hundred exiled opposition leaders living in Western Europe. These policies isolated Iran not only from the United States but also from

THE GLOBAL CONNECTION

The Nuclear Power Issue

For Iran, nuclear technology—always defined as a "civilian program"—is a non-negotiable right of an independent nation, essential not only for its long-term energy needs but also to attain the hallmark of a developed country. It sees nuclear power as a matter of both sovereignty and modernity.

For the United States and the other Western powers, any nuclear technology—even for peaceful purposes—in the hands of Iran is fraught with many risks. They argue that such technology could be expanded into a weapons program, and nuclear weapons could then be used on Israel or passed on to "terrorist organizations." It seems that the only way to resolve the issue is for the West to accept Iran's civilian program, and Iran, in return, to provide verifiable guarantees that its program would not trespass into the military realm. Under the George W. Bush administration, negotiations broke down since the United States demanded that Iran cease forthwith all enrichment.

Furthermore, Iran's plans to develop nuclear power have been delayed because the United States has persuaded Europe not to transfer the technology needed to do so to Iran and by a successful joint U.S.-Israeli cyber-sabotage program that injected a software "worm" into the computers used to control the production of enriched uranium.

Under the Obama administration, the United States has implicitly accepted Iran's right to enrich so long as it provides verifiable guarantees that it would not enrich to the point of producing weapons. To pressure Iran to provide such guarantees, the Obama administration has persuaded the UN to place economic sanctions on Iran—especially on the Revolutionary Guards and elite members of the regime. In 2014, the Obama and the Rouhani administrations began serious negotiations to resolve these differences.

MAKING CONNECTIONS What are the main differences between Shi'i and Sunni Islam?

the European Community, human rights organizations, and the United Nations. Reforming presidents, especially Khatami and Rouhani, have done their best to rectify this damage.

The Islamic Republic is determined to remain dominant in the Persian Gulf and to play an important role in the world of states. It has one of the biggest but outdated conventional armies in the region, a large land mass, considerable human resources, a respectable gross domestic product (GDP), and vast oil production.

Governing the Economy

In the early years of the Islamic Republic in the 1980s, peasants continued to migrate to the cities because of the lack of both agricultural land and irrigation. Industry suffered from lack of investment capital. Inflation and unemployment were high. The population steadily increased, and real per capita income fell due to forces outside state control. To deal with these problems, some leaders favored state-interventionist strategies. Others advocated laissez-faire market-based strategies. Such differences over how to govern the economy are still being debated in Iran and are the source of much political contention.

The Democratic Idea

Khomeini argued that Islam and democracy were compatible since the vast majority of people in Iran respected the clerics as the true interpreters of the *shari'a*, and wanted them to oversee state officials. Islam and the democratic idea, however, appear less reconcilable now that much of the public has lost its enthusiasm for clerical rule. Khomeinism has divided into two divergent branches in Iran: political liberalism and clerical conservatism. These ideological currents, which will be discussed later in this chapter, are at the heart of Iranian politics today.

Democracy is based on the principles that all individuals are equal, especially before the law, and that all people have inalienable natural rights. The *shari'a* is based on inequalities—between men and women, between Muslims and non-Muslims, between legitimate minorities, known as the People of the Book, and illegitimate ones, known as unbelievers. Moderate clerics, however, advocate reforming the *shari'a* to make it compatible with individual freedoms and human rights.

The Politics of Collective Identity

The state emphasis on Shi'ism has to some extent alienated the 10 percent of Iranians who are Sunnis. In addition, the regime's insistence on a theocratic constitution antagonized some important clerics as well as lay secular Muslims, who lead most of the political parties. Similarly, the strong association of Shi'ism with the central, Persian-speaking regions of the country could alienate the important Turkic minority in Azerbaijan province. All of these trends put some strain on Iran's collective national identity.

Themes and Comparisons

The Khomeinist movement culminating in the 1979 revolution helped expand Islam from a personal religion concerned with the individual's relations with God into an all-encompassing ideology that dealt with political, legal, social, and economic matters as well as personal ones. The slogan of the revolution was "Islam is the Solution." This expanded interpretation of Islam became known as **Islamism** and political Islam. The direct product of this Islam is the creation of an Islamic Republic that is theocratic—a regime in which the clergy claim special authority on grounds that as experts on theology they have a better understanding of religion and therefore greater expertise than laymen in supervising the running of the state. This authority is based not on the claim they enjoy direct communications with God—they do not claim such privilege—but that they have scholarly knowledge of the scriptures and God's laws—the *shari'a*. This makes the Islamic Republic a unique political system in the modern world.

Islamism

The use of Islam as a political ideology. Similar to political Islam and Islamic fundamentalism.

Although this was the main contribution of the Islamic Republic to comparative politics, the reform movement of the 1990s and early 2000s did its best to counter it. The leading reformers, who label themselves the new Muslim intellectuals, argue that their intellectual fathers, the revolutionary generation, had mistakenly "bloated religion" and expanded it from personal ethics into an all-encompassing political ideology. In other words, they had turned faith into a total system of thought similar to twentieth-century European totalitarian ideologies—the other major isms. The new Muslim intellectuals set themselves the task of slimming down, narrowing, and lightening this overbloated system of thought. In short, they have turned away from Islamism back to a more conventional understanding of Islam.

It is this two contrasting interpretations of Islam that help explain the bitter conflict in contemporary Iran between reformers and conservatives, between so-called fundamentalists and liberal pragmatists, between supporters of Khatami-Rouhani and those of Ahmadinejad, between the generation that made the 1979 revolution and the new generation that came of age during the same revolution. They both consider themselves Islamic but have sharply different interpretations of Islam—especially when it comes to politics, including the relations with the West and the United States.

Where Do You Stand?

Some see revolutions as dawns of hope; others as unmitigated disasters. How would you assess the Iranian Revolution?

Some describe Khomeini as a conservative fundamentalist; others as a radical populist. How would you describe him?

SECTION 2

POLITICAL ECONOMY AND DEVELOPMENT

▼ Focus Questions

• What impact did the Shah's economic policies have on Iranian society?

• What role do oil revenues play in integrating Iran into the global economy?

rentier state

A country that obtains much of its revenue from the export of oil or other natural resources.

State and Economy

British prospectors struck oil in Iran's Khuzistan province in 1908, and the British government in 1912 decided to fuel its navy with petroleum rather than coal. It also decided to buy most of its fuel from the Anglo-Iranian Oil Company. Iran's oil revenues increased modestly in the next four decades, reaching $16 million in 1951. After the nationalization of the oil industry in 1951 and the agreement with a consortium of U.S. and British companies in 1955, oil revenues rose steadily, from $34 million in 1955 to $5 billion in 1973 and, after the quadrupling of oil prices in 1974, to over $23 billion in 1976. Between 1953 and 1978, Iran's cumulative oil income came to over $100 billion.

Oil financed over 90 percent of imports and 80 percent of the annual budget and far surpassed total tax revenues. Oil also enabled Iran not to worry about feeding its population. Instead, it could undertake ambitious development programs that other states could carry out only if they squeezed scarce resources from their populations. In fact, oil revenues made Iran into a **rentier state**, a country that obtains a lucrative income by exporting raw materials or leasing out natural resources to foreign companies. Iran as well as Iraq, Algeria, and the Gulf states received enough money from their oil wells to be able to disregard their internal tax bases. The Iranian state thus became relatively independent of society. Society, in turn, had few inputs into the state. Little taxation meant little representation.

From the 1950s through the 1970s, Muhammad Reza Shah tried to encourage other exports and attract foreign investment into non-oil ventures. Despite some increase in carpet and pistachio exports, oil continued to dominate. In 1979, on the eve of the Islamic Revolution, oil still provided 97 percent of the country's foreign exchange. Foreign firms invested no more than $1 billion in Iran—and much of this was not in industry but in banking, trade, and insurance. In Iran, as in the rest of the Middle East, foreign investors were deterred by government corruption, labor costs, small internal markets, potential instability, and fear of confiscation.

Despite waste and corruption, there was significant growth in many modern sectors of the economy under the Shah. (See Table 14.2.) GNP grew at an average rate of 9.6 percent per year from 1960 to 1977. This made Iran one of the fastest-growing economies in the world. Land reform created over 644,000 moderately prosperous farms. The number of modern factories tripled. The Trans-Iranian Railway was completed. Roads were built connecting most villages with the provincial cities. Iran was seen as having started an economic "take-off" into modernization.

Iran's Economy under the Islamic Republic

Iran's main economic problem has been instability in the world oil market. Oil revenues, which continued to provide the state with much of its income, fell from $20 billion in 1978 to less than $10 billion in 1998. They did not improve until the early 2000s increasing to $17 billion in 2000, $44 billion in 2005, and over $55 billion per year by the late 2000s. This increase was due not to a rise in production—in fact, total production in 2005 was a third less than in 1975—but

Table 14.2	Industrial Production	
Product	**1953**	**1977**
Coal (tons)	200,000	900,000
Iron ore (tons)	5,000	930,000
Steel (tons)	–	275,000
Cement (tons)	53,000	4,300,000
Sugar (tons)	70,000	527,000
Tractors (no.)	–	7,700
Motor vehicles (no.)	–	109,000

Source: E. Abrahamian, "Structural Causes of the Iranian Revolution," *Middle East Research and Information Project*, no. 87 (May 1980), 22.

to the dramatic rise in the price of oil in the international market. A barrel of oil jumped from $14 in 1998 to $30 in 2000, $56 in 2005, and over $100 in 2013–14. Ironically, the impressive growth in private cars and public transport has strained the refineries and forced Iran to become more dependent on imported gasoline. What is more, the oil revenues enabled the government to allocate as much as $100 billion a year subsidizing essential goods such as bread, heating fuel, gasoline, sugar, rice, milk, and cooking oil. In 2011–14, it made bold moves trimming these subsidies, and, instead, giving cash directly to the poor.

Although contemporary Iran is awash in oil money, the country's economic situation has been complicated by a population explosion, the Iran–Iraq War, and the emigration of some 3 million Iranians. The annual population growth rate, which was 2.5 percent in the late 1970s, jumped to over 4 percent in the early 1980s, one of the highest rates in the world. The war with Iraq wrought on Iran as much as $600 billion in property damage and over 218,000 dead. The Islamic Revolution itself frightened many professionals and highly skilled technicians, as well as wealthy entrepreneurs, and industrialists into fleeing to the West.

The overall result was a twenty-year economic crisis lasting well into the late 1990s. The value of real incomes, including salaries and pensions, dropped by as much as 60 percent. Unemployment hit 20 percent; over two-thirds of entrants into the labor force could not find jobs. Peasants continued to flock to urban shantytowns. Tehran grew from 4.5 million to 12 million people. The total number of families living below the poverty level increased. By the late 1990s, over 9 million urban dwellers lived below the official poverty line.[4] Shortages in foreign exchange curtailed vital imports, even of essential manufactured goods. What is more, the regime that came to power advocating self-sufficiency now owed foreign banks and governments over $30 billion, forcing it to renegotiate foreign loans constantly. In the 2005 presidential elections, these problems helped explain the strong victory of Ahmadinejad, the conservative populist candidate. But the United States imposed sanctions on the Ahmadinejad administration compounded these economic problems, causing spiraling inflation, shortage of imported goods, and increasing brain drain to the West.

Nevertheless, the Islamic Republic has over the years scored some notable economic successes. The Reconstruction Ministry built 30,000 miles of paved roads, 40,000 schools, and 7,000 libraries. It brought electricity and running water to more than half of the country's 50,000 villages. The number of registered vehicles on the roads increased from 27,000 in 1990 to over 3 million in 2009. More dams and irrigation canals were built, and the Agricultural Ministry distributed some 630,000 hectares of confiscated arable land to peasants and gave farmers more favorable prices.

The government has exercised control over most of Iran's economy for the entire history of the Islamic Republic. Reformist president Khatami took steps to reduce the role of the state in governing the economy by allowing privatization in some sectors of the economy (including banking) and relaunching a stock market to sell shares of government businesses to private investors. Even Ayatollah Khamenei, the chief religious leader, and former conservative president Ahmadinejad have endorsed privatization. Ahmadinejad initiated a program to give "justice shares" of state-owned industries to low-income citizens. Nevertheless, about 70 percent of the Iranian economy continues to be under state control.

Society and Economy

During the Shah's reign, a huge amount of state investment went into social welfare. Enrollment in primary schools grew from fewer than 750,000 to over 4 million; in secondary schools from 121,000 to nearly 740,000; in vocational schools from 2,500 to nearly 230,000; and in universities from under 14,000 to more than 154,000. Between 1963 and 1977, the number of hospital beds increased from 24,126 to 48,000; medical clinics from 700 to 2,800; nurses from 1,969 to 4,105; and doctors from 4,500 to 12,750. These improvements, together with the elimination of epidemics and famines, lowered infant mortality and led to a population explosion.

The Shah's approach to development, however, increased his unpopularity with many sectors of Iranian society. The Shah believed that if economic growth benefited those who were already better off, some of the wealth would gradually trickle down to the lower levels of society. But these benefits got stuck at the top and never trickled down.

In fact, wealth trickled up: In 1972, the richest 20 percent of urban households accounted for 47.1 percent of total urban family expenditures; by 1977, it accounted for 55.5 percent. In 1972, the poorest 40 percent accounted for 16.7 percent of urban family expenditures; by 1977, this had dropped to 11.7 percent. In Iran's cities, the rich were getting richer, and the poor were getting poorer.

The new factories drew criticism that they were mere assembly plants that used inexpensive labor and were poor substitutes for real industrial development that would benefit the nation. The Shah's public health programs still left Iran with one of the worst doctor–patient ratios and child mortality rates in the Middle East. The per capita income in the richest provinces was ten times more than in the poorest ones. The ratio of urban to rural incomes was 5 to 1. Land reform created a small layer of prosperous farmers but left the vast majority of peasants landless or nearly landless (see Table 14.3). By the mid-1970s, Iran was one of the most unequal countries in the world.[5]

These inequalities created a **dual society**—on one side the modern sector, headed by elites with close ties to the oil state, on the other side the traditional sector, the clergy, the bazaar middle class, and the rural masses. Each sector, in turn, was sharply stratified into unequal classes (see Figure 14.2).

The upper class—the Pahlavi family, the court-connected entrepreneurs, the military officers, and the senior civil servants—made up less than 0.01 percent of the population. In the modern sector, the middle class—professionals, civil servants, salaried personnel, and college students—formed about 10 percent of the population. The bottom of the modern sector—the urban working class, factory workers, construction laborers, peddlers, and unemployed—constituted over 32 percent. In the traditional sector, the middle class—bazaar merchants, small retailers, shopkeepers, workshop owners, and well-to-do family farmers—made up 13 percent; the rural masses 45 percent.

These inequalities fueled resentments, which were expressed more in cultural and religious terms than in economic and class terms. Among the fiercest critics

Table 14.3	Land Ownership in 1977
Size (Hectares)	**Number of Owners**
200+	1,300
51–200	44,000
11–50	600,000
3–10	1,200,000
Landless	700,000

Note: One hectare is equal to approximately 2.47 acres.
Source: E. Abrahamian, "Structural Causes of the Iranian Revolution," *Middle East Research and Information Project*, no. 87 (May 1980).

dual society

A society and economy that are sharply divided into a traditional, usually poorer, and a modern, usually richer, sector.

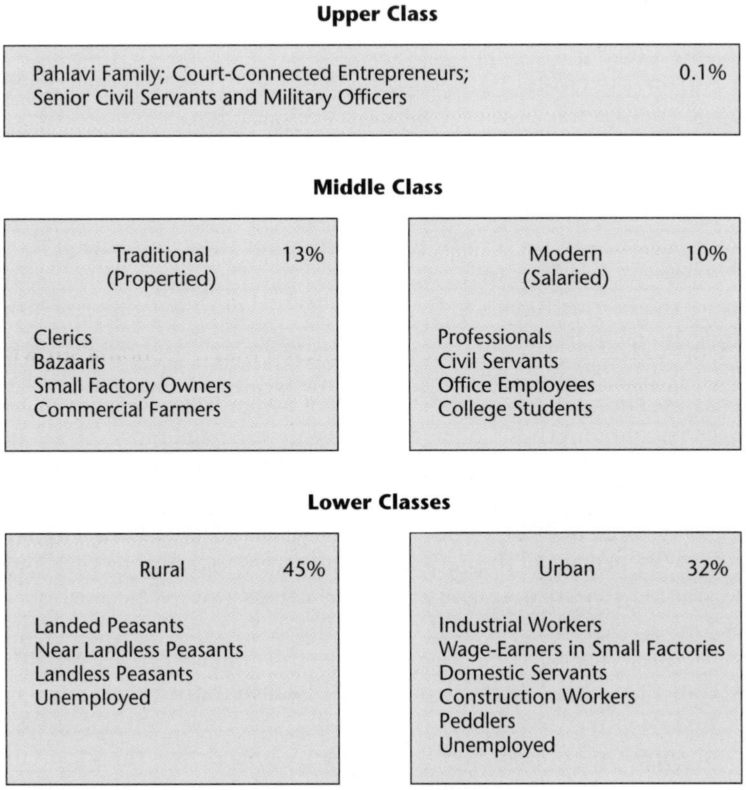

Upper Class

Pahlavi Family; Court-Connected Entrepreneurs; Senior Civil Servants and Military Officers	0.1%

Middle Class

Traditional (Propertied)	13%	Modern (Salaried)	10%
Clerics Bazaaris Small Factory Owners Commercial Farmers		Professionals Civil Servants Office Employees College Students	

Lower Classes

Rural	45%	Urban	32%
Landed Peasants Near Landless Peasants Landless Peasants Unemployed		Industrial Workers Wage-Earners in Small Factories Domestic Servants Construction Workers Peddlers Unemployed	

FIGURE 14.2 Iran's Class Structures in the Mid-1970s.
Iranian society was divided sharply not only into horizontal classes, but also into vertical sectors—the modern and the transitional, the urban and the rural. This is known as a dual society.

was Jalal Al-e Ahmad (1923–1969). He argued that the ruling class was destroying Iran by mindlessly imitating the West; neglecting the peasantry; showing contempt for popular religion; worshipping mechanization, regimentation, and industrialization; and flooding the country with foreign ideas, tastes, luxury items, and mass-consumption goods. He stressed that developing countries such as Iran could survive this "plague" of Western imperialism only by returning to their cultural roots and developing a self-reliant society, especially a fully independent economy. Al-e Ahmad is deemed to be not only the main intellectual critic of the old order but also the founder of the "back to roots" movement that brought about the Islamic Revolution.

Al-e Ahmad's ideas were developed further by another young intellectual named Ali Shariati (1933–1977). Studying in Paris during the 1960s, Shariati was influenced by Marxist sociology, Catholic liberation theology, the Algerian revolution, and, most important, Frantz Fanon's *Wretched of the Earth* (1961), which urged colonial peoples to use violence to liberate themselves from imperial rule.

Shariati argued that history was a continuous struggle between oppressors and oppressed. Each class had its own interests, its own interpretations of religion, and its own sense of right and wrong. God periodically sent down prophets, such as Abraham, Moses, Jesus, and Muhammad. Muhammad had been sent to launch a dynamic community in "permanent revolution" toward the ultimate utopia: a perfectly classless society.

Although Muhammad's goal, claimed Shariati, had been betrayed by his illegitimate successors, his radical message had been preserved by the Shi'i Imams, especially by Imam Husayn, who had been martyred to show future generations that human beings had the moral duty to fight oppression in all places at all times. According to Shariati, the contemporary oppressors were the imperialists, the modern-day feudalists, the corrupt capitalists, and their hangers-on. He criticized the conservative clerics who had tried to transform revolutionary religion into an apolitical public opiate. Shariati died on the eve of the revolution, but his prolific works were so widely read and so influential that many felt that he, rather than Khomeini, was the true ideologue of the Islamic Revolution.

Despite setbacks in the 1980s, life improved for most Iranians in the 1990s. On the whole, the poor in Iran are better off now than their parents had been before the founding of the Islamic Republic. By the late 1990s, most independent farmers owned radios, televisions, refrigerators, and pickup trucks. The extension of social services narrowed the gap between town and country and between the urban poor and the middle classes. The adult literacy rate grew from 50 percent to 83 percent, and by 2000 the literacy rate among those in the six to twenty-nine age range hit 97 percent. The infant mortality rate has fallen from 104 per 1,000 in the mid-1970s to 39 per 1,000 in 2013. Life expectancy climbed from fifty-five years in 1979 to sixty-eight in 1993 and to seventy-three in 2013—one of the best in the Middle East. The UN estimates that by 2000, 94 percent of the population had access to health services and safe water.

The Islamic Republic also made major strides toward population control. At first, it closed down birth control clinics. But it reversed direction once the ministries responsible for social services felt the full impact of this growth. In 1989, the government declared that Islam favored healthy rather than large families and that one literate citizen was better than ten illiterate ones. It reopened birth control clinics, cut subsidies to large families, and announced that the ideal family should consist of no more than two children. It even took away social benefits from those having more than two children. The current population growth rate is 1.3 percent. The government is now toying with the idea of reversing policy and encouraging population growth.

Environmental Issues

Iran faces a horrendous environment problem. The ago-old problem of aridity and lack of regular rainfall has been compounded in recent years by a series of droughts and dry winters—most probably caused by climate change and global warming. Water levels have fallen; major rivers—such Sefid Rud in Isfahan—have turned into streams; and lakes such as Urmiah in Azerbaijan are drying up into ponds. The impressive numbers of dams built in the last fifty years have added to the problem since such concentrations of water inadvertently increase evaporation. These problems are prevalent throughout the Middle East and contribute to what is now known as the "Arab Spring"—especially in Syria.

The environmental issue comes in the form of a horrendous air pollution problem in Tehran where the city is flanked by a high mountain range that blocks the air currents and thus traps the polluted air. Much of this pollution comes from the increasing use of private cars. By 2000 Tehran had the reputation of having one of the world's worst air pollution problems. This problem has been further compounded by the recent UN sanctions. These sanctions have prevented Iran from importing properly refined gasoline. Instead, Iran has been producing its own poorly refined gasoline that seriously pollutes the air and endangers public health. The Department of Environment revealed that in 2013 some 45,000 deaths were directly or indirectly caused by air pollution. On a number of days the municipality warned citizens not to venture out unless they had to.

The environmental issue has been articulated by the reform movement—especially by the educated youth who supported President Khatami, the failed candidacy of Mousavi, and now President Rouhani. It is significant that Mousavi's supporters named their organization the Green Movement giving it a double meaning since green is traditionally the color of Shi'i Islam. There have also been public protests in Azerbaijan against the plight of Lake Urmiah.

Various administrations—both reform and conservative—have taken some measures to address the problem. They have channeled considerable resources into solar and nuclear energy—the avowed rational for the latter is that it will provide cleaner energy for industrial and home electrical use. They have supported reforestation and water conservation—especially in the cities. They have encouraged citizens in Tehran to use public transport especially city buses rather than private cars and taxis. What is more, they have built an extensive subway network in Tehran linking much of the suburbs—even the distant ones—to the central city. For the first time Tehran has a modern metro system worthy of the best ones in the West.

The core environmental problems, however, are harder to address. Car pollution will not diminish until vehicles and gasoline are cleaner. And these issues cannot be really addressed until the nuclear stand-off with the United States is resolved. And even more serious, the problem of increasing aridity and global warming cannot be addressed unless it is done on a worldwide scale. Iran, like other countries, is intimately interconnected with the rest of world—whether it likes it nor not.

Iran in the Global Economy

The integration of Iran into the world of states began in the latter half of the nineteenth century. Several factors account for this integration: concessions granted to the European powers; the Suez Canal and the Trans-Caspian railway; telegraph lines across Iran linking India with Britain; the outflow of capital from Europe after 1870; and, most important, the Industrial Revolution in Europe and the subsequent export

Organization of Petroleum Exporting Countries (OPEC)

An organization dedicated to achieving stability in the price of oil, avoiding price fluctuations, and generally furthering the interests of the member states.

resource curse

The concept that revenue derived from abundant natural resources, such as oil, often bring unforeseen ailments to countries.

of European manufactured goods to the rest of the world. In the nineteenth century, Iran's foreign trade increased tenfold.

Economic dependency resulted, a situation common in much of the developing world. Less-developed countries become too reliant on developed countries; poorer nations are vulnerable to sudden fluctuations in richer economies and dependent on the export of raw materials, whose prices often stagnate or decline, while prices for the manufactured products they import invariably increase.

Cash crops, especially cotton, tobacco, and opium, reduced the acreage for wheat and other edible grains in Iran. Many landowners stopped growing food and turned to commercial export crops. This led to disastrous famines in 1860, 1869–1872, 1880, and 1918–1920.

Furthermore, many local merchants, shopkeepers, and workshop owners in the bazaars now formed a national propertied middle class aware of their common interests against both the central government and the foreign powers. This new class awareness played an important role in Iran's constitutional revolution of 1905.

Under the Shah, Iran became the second-most-important member (after Saudi Arabia) of the **Organization of Petroleum Exporting Countries (OPEC)**; Iran could cast decisive votes for raising or moderating oil prices. At times, the Shah curried Western favor by moderating prices. At other times, he pushed for higher prices to finance his ambitious projects and military purchases. These purchases rapidly escalated once President Richard Nixon began to encourage U.S. allies to take a greater role in policing their regions. Moreover, Nixon's secretary of state, Henry Kissinger, argued that the United States should finance its ever-increasing oil imports, by exporting more military hardware to the Persian Gulf. Arms dealers joked that the Shah read their technical manuals the same way that some men read *Playboy*. The Shah's arms buying from the United States jumped from $135 million in 1970 to a peak of $5.7 billion in 1977. In addition to these vast military expenditures, the oil revenues had other unforeseen consequences: high labor costs; lack of incentives for competing industries; and the easy import of agricultural and manufactured goods. It is for this reason that some economists often describe oil as a **resource curse**.

This military might gave the Shah a reach well beyond his immediate boundaries. Iran occupied three small but strategically located Arab islands in the Strait of Hormuz, thus controlling the oil lifeline through the Persian Gulf but also creating distrust among his Arab neighbors. The Shah talked of establishing a presence well beyond the Gulf on the grounds that Iran's national interests reached into the Indian Ocean.

In the mid-1970s, the Shah dispatched troops to Oman to help the local sultan fight rebels. He offered Afghanistan $2 billion to break its then

The clerical regime relies on two crutches of power: the bayonet and the oil well.

Courtesy Mojahed (in exile).

close ties with the Soviet Union, a move that probably prompted the Soviets to intervene militarily in that country. A U.S. congressional report declared: "Iran in the 1970s was widely regarded as a significant regional, if not global, power. The United States relied on it, implicitly if not explicitly, to ensure the security and stability of the Persian Gulf sector and the flow of oil from the region to the industrialized Western world of Japan, Europe, and the United States, as well as to lesser powers elsewhere."[6]

These vast military expenditures, as well as the oil exports, tied Iran closely to the industrial countries of the West and to Japan. Iran was now importing millions of dollars' worth of rice, wheat, industrial tools, construction equipment, pharmaceuticals, tractors, pumps, and spare parts, the bulk of which came from the United States. Trade with neighboring and other developing countries was insignificant.

The oil revenues thus had major consequences for Iran's political economy, all of which paved the way for the Islamic Revolution. They allowed the Shah to pursue ambitious programs that inadvertently widened class and regional divisions within the dual society. They drastically raised public expectations without necessarily meeting them. They made the rentier state independent of society. Economic slowdowns in the industrial countries, however, could lead to a decline in their oil demands, which could diminish Iran's ability to buy such essential goods as food, medicine, and industrial spare parts.

One of the major promises made by the Islamic Revolution was to end this economic dependency on oil and the West. The radical followers of Ayatollah Khomeini, the founder of the Islamic Republic, once denounced foreign investors as imperialist exploiters and waxed eloquent about economic self-sufficiency.

But in 2002, Iran contemplated a dramatically new law permitting foreigners to own as much as 100 percent of any firm in the country, to repatriate profits, to be free of state meddling, and to have assurances against both arbitrary confiscations and high taxation. To maintain oil production, Iran needs new deep-drilling technology that can be found only in the West. This goes a long way toward explaining why the regime now is eager to attract foreign investment and to rejoin the world economy.

Where Do You Stand?

Some see Iran as divided into socioeconomic class. Others see it as a dual society divided into a modern and a traditional sector. How would you describe it?

Some see abundant oil revenues as a resource curse; others as a means for rapid development. Which description do you find more apt?

GOVERNANCE AND POLICY-MAKING

SECTION 3

Organization of the State

The political system of the Islamic Republic of Iran is unique. It is a theocracy with important democratic features. It is a theocracy (from the Greek, "divine rule") because the religious clerics control the most powerful political positions. But the system also contains elements of democracy with some high government officials,

▼ Focus Questions

• In what ways do the clergy have extraordinary powers in Iran?

• How do they control the government of the Islamic Republic?

including the president, elected directly by the general public. All citizens, both male and female, over the age of eighteen now have the right to vote.

The state rests on the Islamic constitution implemented immediately after the 1979 revolution and amended between April and June 1989 during the last months of Khomeini's life by the Council for the Revision of the Constitution, which was handpicked by Khomeini himself. The final document is a highly complex mixture of theocracy and democracy.

The preamble affirms faith in God, Divine Justice, the Qur'an, the Day of Judgment, the Prophet Muhammad, the Twelve Imams, the eventual return of the Hidden Imam (the Mahdi), and, of course, Khomeini's doctrine of jurist's guardianship that gives supreme power to senior clergy. All laws, institutions, and state organizations must conform to these "divine principles."

The Executive

The Leader and Major Organizations of Clerical Power

The constitution named Khomeini to be the Leader for Life on the grounds that the public overwhelmingly recognized him as the "most just, pious, informed, brave, and enterprising" of the senior clerics—the grand ayatollahs. It further described him as the Leader of the Revolution, the Founder of the Islamic Republic, and, most important, the Imam of the Muslim Community. It stipulated that if no single Leader emerged after his death, then all his authority would be passed on to a leadership council of senior clerics.

After Khomeini's death in 1989, however, his followers distrusted the other senior clerics so much that they did not set up such a council. Instead, they elected one of their own, Ali Khamenei, a middle-ranking cleric, to be the new Leader.

Khamenei was born in 1939 in Mashed into a minor clerical family originally from Azerbaijan. He studied theology with Khomeini in Qom and was briefly imprisoned by the Shah's regime in 1962. Active in the anti-Shah opposition movement in 1978, he was given a series of influential positions immediately after the revolution, even though he held only the rank of *hojjat al-Islam*. He became Friday prayer leader of Tehran, head of the Revolutionary Guards, and, in the last years of Khomeini's life, president of the republic. After Khomeini's death, he was elevated to the rank of Leader even though he was neither a grand ayatollah nor a recognized senior expert on Islamic law. He had not even published a theological treatise. The government-controlled media, however, began to refer to him as an ayatollah. Some ardent followers even referred to him as a grand ayatollah qualified to guide the world's whole Shi'i community. After his elevation, he built a constituency among the regime's more diehard elements: traditionalist judges, conservative war veterans, and anti-liberal ideologues.

The Islamic Republic has often been described as a regime of the ayatollahs (high-ranking clerics). It could be more aptly called a regime of the *hojjat al-Islams* (middle-ranking clerics), since few senior clerics want to be associated with it. None of the grand ayatollahs and few of the ordinary ayatollahs subscribed to Khomeini's notion of jurist's guardianship. In fact, most disliked his radical populism and political activism.

The constitution gives wide-ranging powers to the Leader, who is elected now by an eighty-six member Assembly of Experts. As the vital link between the three branches of government, the Leader can mediate between the legislature, the executive, and the judiciary. He can "determine the interests of Islam," "supervise the implementation of general policy," and "set political guidelines for the Islamic Republic." He can eliminate presidential candidates and dismiss the duly elected president. He can grant amnesty. As commander-in-chief, he can mobilize the armed forces, declare war and peace, and convene the Supreme Military Council. He can appoint and dismiss the commanders of Revolutionary Guards as well as those of the regular army, navy, and air force.

The Leader has extensive power over the judicial system. He can nominate and remove the chief judge, the chief prosecutor, and the revolutionary tribunals. He can dismiss lower court judges. He also nominates six clerics to the powerful twelve-man Guardian Council, which can veto parliamentary bills. This Council has also obtained (through separate legislation) the right to review all candidates for elected office, including the presidency and the national legislature, the *Majles*. The other

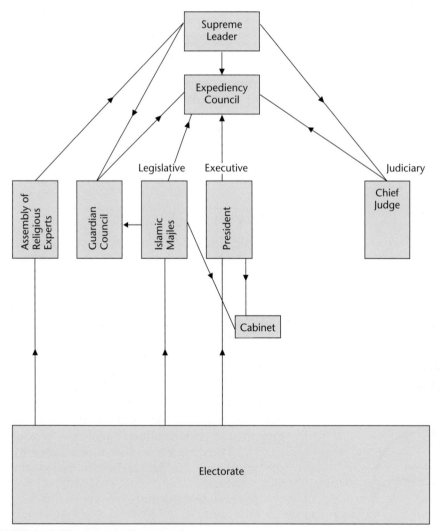

FIGURE 14.3 The Islamic Constitution
The general public elects the *Majles*, the president, and the Assembly of Experts. But the Leader and the Guardian Council decide who can compete in these elections.

Expediency Council

A committee set up in Iran to resolve differences between the *Majles* (parliament) and the Guardian Council.

Imam Jum'ehs

Prayer leaders in Iran's main urban mosques.

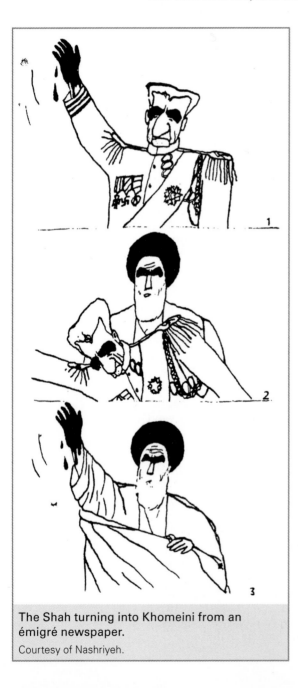

The Shah turning into Khomeini from an émigré newspaper.

Courtesy of Nashriyeh.

six members of the Guardian Council are jurists nominated by the chief judge and approved by the *Majles*. Furthermore, the Leader appoints more than two-thirds of the some fifty man **Expediency Council**, which has the authority to resolve differences between the Guardian Council and the *Majles* (the legislature) and to initiate laws on its own. This Council includes the most important personages in the Islamic Republic—the Guardian Council, the heads of the three branches of government, representatives of the cabinet, and individuals chosen by the Leader.

The Leader also fills a number of important non-government posts: the preachers (*Imam Jum'ehs*) at the main city mosques, the director of the national radio-television network, and the heads of the main religious endowments, especially the **Foundation of the Oppressed** (see below). By 2001, the Office of the Leader employed over six hundred in Tehran and had representatives in most sensitive institutions throughout the country. The Leader has obtained more constitutional powers than ever dreamed of by the Shah.

The Assembly of Experts is elected every eight years by the general public. Its members must have an advanced seminary degree, so it is packed with clerics. The Assembly has the right to oversee the work of the Leader and to dismiss him if he is found to be "mentally incapable of fulfilling his arduous duties." It has to meet at least once a year. Its deliberations are closed. In effect, the Assembly of Experts has become a second chamber to the *Majles*, the parliament of the Islamic Republic.

The Government Executive

The constitution of the Islamic Republic reserves important executive power for the president. The president is described as the highest state official after the Leader. The office is filled every four years through a national election. If a candidate does not win a majority of the vote in the first round of the election, a run-off chooses between the two top vote-getters. The president cannot serve more than two terms.

The constitution says the president must be a pious Shi'i faithful to the principles of the Islamic Republic, of Iranian origin, and between the ages of 25 and 75. The president must also demonstrate "administrative capacity and resourcefulness" and have "a good past record." There has been some dispute about whether the language used in the constitution restricts the presidency to males.

The president has the power to

- Conduct the country's internal and external policies, including signing all international treaties, laws, and agreements;
- Chair the National Security Council, which is responsible for defense matters;

- Draw up the annual budget, supervise economic matters, and chair the state planning and budget organization;
- Propose legislation to the *Majles*;
- Appoint cabinet ministers, with a parliamentary stipulation that the minister of intelligence (the state security agency) must be from the ranks of the clergy;
- Appoint most other senior officials, including provincial governors, ambassadors, and the directors of some of the large public organizations, such as the National Iranian Oil Company, the National Electricity Board, and the National Bank.

Iran has no single vice president. Instead the president may select " presidential deputies" to help with "constitutional duties." Often there are as many as ten such vice presidents. One is designated as the "first vice president." The others have specific responsibilities, such as presiding over veteran's, women's, or energy issues.

During the revolution, Khomeini often stressed that in his Islamic Republic trained officials and not clerics—also known as mullahs or akhunds—would administer the state. But in actual fact, four of the six presidents in the Islamic Republic have been clerics: Khamenei, Rafsanjani, Khatami, and now Rouhani. The first president, Abol-Hassan Bani-Sadr, a lay intellectual was ousted in 1981 precisely because he denounced the regime as "a dictatorship of the mullahtariat," comparing it to a communist-led "dictatorship of the proletariat." Ahmadinejad, the last lay president, was an urban planner, and was elected initially because of strong support from ultra-conservative clerics. But he eventually lost this support and was eased out of influence. He jeopardized this support by stressing the evangelical rather than the academic-theological side of Shi'i Islam. He insinuated that as a true believer he had privileged access to the hidden knowledge of the Hidden (Absent) Imam.

The Bureaucracy

As chief of the executive branch of the government, the president heads a huge bureaucracy. In fact, this bureaucracy continued to proliferate after the revolution, even though Khomeini had often criticized the Shah for having a bloated government. It expanded, for the most part, to provide jobs for the many college and high school graduates. On the eve of the revolution, the state ministries had 300,000 civil servants and 1 million employees. By the early 1990s, they had over 600,000 civil servants and 1.5 million employees.

Among the most important ministries of the Islamic Republic are Culture and Islamic Guidance, which has responsibility for controlling the media and enforcing "proper conduct" in public life; Intelligence, which has replaced the Shah's dreaded SAVAK as the main security organization; Heavy Industries, which manages the nationalized factories; and Reconstruction, which has the dual task of expanding social services and taking "true Islam" into the countryside. Its main mission is to build bridges, roads, schools, libraries, and mosques in the villages so that the peasantry will learn the basic principles of Islam. "The peasants," declared one cleric, "are so ignorant of true Islam that they even sleep next to their unclean sheep."[7]

The clergy dominate the bureaucracy as well as the presidency. They have monopolized the most sensitive ministries—Intelligence, Interior, Justice, and Culture and Islamic Guidance—and have given posts in other ministries to relatives and protégés. These ministers appear to be highly trained technocrats, sometimes with advanced degrees from the West. In fact, they are often fairly powerless individuals dependent on the powerful clergy—chosen by them, trusted by them, and invariably related to them.

Foundation of the Oppressed

A clerically controlled foundation set up after the revolution in Iran.

📇 PROFILE

President Dr. Hassan Rouhani

President Rouhani with his foreign minister at the General Assembly meeting of the United Nations in 2013.

Chris Ratcliffe/Bloomberg /Getty Images

Hassan Rouhani, a consummate regime insider but running on a clearly moderate ticket, won an easy victory in the 2013 presidential elections. Born in 1948, he had grown up in a nonclerical household in a village a hundred miles east of Tehran. His father, surnamed Fereydun, was a carpenter-turned-farmer who had moved out of Tehran after World War II. At the age of twelve, Hassan enrolled in a seminary in Qum where he soon participated in anti-Shah activities and to confuse the police adopted the name Rouhani (literally meaning "Clerical"). Graduating from the seminary, he performed his military service and then enrolled in the Faculty of Law in Tehran University where he specialized in criminal justice. As the revolution began to unfold, he was one of the first young clerics to rush off to Paris to vow allegiance to Khomeini.

After the revolution, Rouhani held a series of high posts: as parliamentary deputy from his home province; as clerical representative on committees to reorganize the chiefs of staff and the radio-television network; as member of the Assembly of Experts and Expediency Council; as long-standing member of the National Security Council; as trouble-shooting ambassador to France, Syria, and North Korea; and, most important of all, President Khatami's chief nuclear negotiator with the United Nations and the United States. He had offered the UN a compromise solution that had been acceptable to most of the other parties, especially the United Kingdom, but had been rejected by the George W. Bush administration. After the Khatami era, he had headed the main think-tank for foreign policy named the Centre for Strategic Studies; had written a number of book on Islamic law; and somehow had managed to find time to complete a doctorate in law from Caledonian University in Glasgow.

He ran the 2013 election on a reform platform. He emphasized the need for "cautious realism," "moderation," "prudence," and "hope"; "economic well-being" and a higher standard of living; greater interaction with the outside world and "normalization of relations," especially with the United States and the West; as well as the importance of citizen's rights and gender equality. He took the previous Ahmadinejad administration to task—sometimes implicitly, sometimes explicitly—for "extremism"; for weakening the economy through mismanagement, inflation, and high unemployment; and bringing down on the nation the horrendous U.S.-UN sanctions by refusing to be more transparent on the nuclear program, by denying the Holocaust, and thereby by unnecessarily antagonizing the West. He was clearly courting voters who in previous elections had overwhelmingly supported political liberals like Khatami and economic reformers such as Rafsanjani. Not surprisingly, both Khatami and Rafsanjani enthusiastically endorsed Rouhani. For his part, the Leader remained above the fray—unlike the previous election when he had endorsed Ahmadinejad. He had probably concluded that the economic sanctions necessitated a more compromising foreign policy. His refusal to back the conservative candidates ensured that the revolutionary guards and the conservative clerical institutions would not interfere with the elections.

MAKING CONNECTIONS Why did Rouhani win the presidential elections in 2013?

Other State Institutions

The Judiciary

The constitution makes the judicial system the central pillar of the state, overshadowing the executive and the legislature. It also gives the Leader and the clergy wide-ranging powers over the judiciary. Laws are supposed to conform to the religious law, and the clergy are regarded as the ultimate interpreters of the *shari'a*. Bills passed by the *Majles* are reviewed by the Guardian Council to ensure that they conform to the *shari'a*. The minister of justice is chosen by the president but needs the approval of both the *Majles* and the chief judge.

The judicial system itself has been Islamized down to the district-court level, with seminary-trained jurists replacing university-educated judges. The Pahlavis purged the clergy from the judicial system; the Islamic Republic purged the university educated.

The penal code, the Retribution Law, is based on a reading of the *shari'a* that was so narrow that it prompted many modern-educated lawyers to resign in disgust, charging that it contradicted the United Nations Charter on Human Rights. It permits injured families to demand blood money on the biblical and Qur'anic principle of "an eye for an eye, a tooth for a tooth, a life for a life." It mandates the death penalty for a long list of "moral transgressions," including adultery, homosexuality, apostasy, drug trafficking, and habitual drinking. It sanctions stoning, live burials, and finger amputations. It divides the population into male and female and Muslims and non-Muslims and treats them unequally. For example, in court, the evidence of one male Muslim is equal to that of two female Muslims. The regime also passed a "law on banking without usury" to implement the *shari'a* ban on all forms of interest taking and interest giving.

Although the law was Islamized, the modern centralized judicial system established under the Shah was not dismantled. For years, Khomeini argued that in a truly Islamic society, the local *shari'a* judges would pronounce final verdicts without the intervention of the central authorities. Their verdicts would be swift and decisive. This, he insisted, was the true spirit of the *shari'a*. After the revolution, however, he discovered that the central state needed to retain ultimate control over the justice system, especially over life-and-death issues. Thus, the revolutionary regime retained the appeals system, the hierarchy of state courts, and the power to appoint and dismiss all judges. State interests took priority over the spirit of the *shari'a*—although religious authorities have ultimate control over the state.

Practical experience led the regime to gradually broaden the narrow interpretation of the *shari'a*. To permit the giving and taking of interest, without which modern economies would not function, the regime allowed banks to offer attractive rates as long as they avoided the taboo term *usury*. To meet public sensitivities as well as international objections, the courts rarely implemented the harsh penalties stipulated by the *shari'a*. They adopted the modern method of punishment, imprisonment, rather than the traditional one of corporal public punishment. By the early 1990s, those found guilty of breaking the law were treated much as they would be in the West: fined or imprisoned rather than flogged in the public square. Those found guilty of serious crimes, especially murder, armed violence, terrorism, and drug smuggling, were often hanged. Iran, after China, has the highest number of executions per year, and the highest per capita executions in the world. This has created a major issue for Iran at the UN.

The Military

The clergy have taken special measures to control Iran's armed forces—both the regular army of 370,000, including 220,000 conscripts, and the new forces formed of 120,000 Revolutionary Guards established immediately after 1979, and 200,000 volunteers in the Mobilization of the Oppressed (*Basej-e Mostazafin*), a volunteer militia created during the Iraqi war. The Leader, as commander-in-chief, appoints the chiefs of staff as well as the top commanders and the defense minister. He also places chaplains in military units to watch over regular officers. These chaplains act very much like the political commissars who once helped control the military in the Soviet Union and still do in China's People's Liberation Army.

After the revolution, the new regime purged the top ranks of the military, placed officers promoted from the ranks of the Revolutionary Guards in command positions over the regular divisions, and built up the Revolutionary Guards as a parallel force with its own uniforms, budgets, munitions factories, recruitment centers, and even small air force and navy. According to the constitution, the regular army defends the external borders, whereas the Revolutionary Guards protect the republic from internal enemies.

Political sentiments within the regular military remain unknown, if not ambivalent. In recent years, the *Basej* have been placed under the authority of the Revolutionary Guards. Although the military, especially the Revolutionary Guards, form an important pillar of the Islamic Republic, they consume only a small percentage of the annual budget. In fact, the republic spends far less on the armed forces than did the Shah. In the last years of the Shah's rule, military purchases accounted for 17 percent of the GDP; they now account for 2 percent. In 2012, Iran spent $6.2 billion on arms, whereas Turkey spent $18.1 billion, Saudi Arabia $21 billion, and the tiny United Arab Emirates $14.4 billion. It is this change of priorities that helps to explain how the Islamic Republic has been able to extend social services to the general population and has managed to survive for all these decades.

Subnational Government

Although Iran is a highly centralized unitary state, it is divided administratively into provinces, districts, subdistricts, townships, and villages. Provinces are headed by governors-general, districts by governors, subdistricts by lieutenant governors, towns by mayors, and villages by headmen.

The constitution declares that the management of local affairs in every village, town, district, and province will be under the supervision of councils whose members would be elected directly by the local population. It also declares that governors-general, governors, and other regional officials appointed by the Interior Ministry have to consult local councils.

Because of conservative opposition, no steps were actually taken to hold council elections until 1999 when Khatami, the new reform-minded president, insisted on holding the country's very first nationwide local elections. Over 300,000 candidates, including 5,000 women, competed for 11,000 council seats—3,900 in towns and 34,000 in villages. Khatami's supporters won a landslide victory taking 75 percent of the seats, including twelve of the fifteen in Tehran. The top vote getter in Tehran was Khatami's former interior minister, who had been impeached by the conservative *Majles* for issuing too many publishing licenses to reform-minded journals and newspapers. Conservatives did well in the 2003 local elections, due largely to widespread voter abstention, but moderates and reformers made a comeback in 2006 when the turnout was about 60 percent of voters. With the 2009 crackdown on the reforms now known as the Green Movement, the conservatives won. But with Rouhani's victory in 2013, the reformers are likely to make a comeback in the near future.

Semipublic Institutions

The Islamic Republic has set up a number of semipublic institutions. They include the Foundation of the Oppressed, the Alavi Foundation (named after Imam Ali), the Martyrs Foundation, the Pilgrimage Foundation, the Housing Foundation, the Foundation for the Publication of Imam Khomeini's Works, and the Fifteenth of Khordad Foundation, which commemorates the date (according to the Islamic calendar) of Khomeini's 1963 denunciation of the White Revolution. Although supposedly autonomous, these foundations are directed by clerics appointed personally by the Leader. According to some estimates, their annual income may be as much as half that of the government.[8] They are exempt from state taxes and are allocated foreign currencies, especially U.S. dollars, at highly favorable exchange rates subsidized by the oil revenues. Most of their assets are property confiscated from the old elite.

The largest of these institutions, the Foundation for the Oppressed, administers over 140 factories, 120 mines, 470 agribusinesses, and 100 construction companies. It also owns the country's two leading newspapers, *Ettela'at* and *Kayhan*. The Martyrs Foundation, in charge of helping war veterans, controls confiscated property that was not handed over to the Foundation for the Oppressed. It also receives an annual subsidy from the government. These foundations together control $12 billion in assets and employ over 400,000 people. The recent moves to "privatize" state enterprises have tended to strengthen these foundations since these semipublic organizations are well placed and well enough financed to be able to buy shares in these new companies. Their main competitors in winning government contracts and buying privatized enterprises have been the Revolutionary Guards. Indeed, "privatization" is a misleading term in the Iranian context since it invariably means transfer of state enterprises to semi-state foundations.

The Policy-Making Process

Policy-making in Iran is highly complex in part because of the cumbersome constitution and in part because factionalism within the ruling clergy has resulted in more amendments, which have made the original constitution even more complicated. Laws can originate in diverse places, and they can be modified by pressures from numerous directions. They can also be blocked by a wide variety of state institutions. In short, the policy-making process is highly fluid and diffuse, often reflecting the regime's factional divisions.

The clerics who destroyed Iran's old order remained united while building the new one. They were convinced that they alone had the divine mandate to govern. They followed the same leader, admired the same texts, cited the same potent symbols, remembered the same real and imaginary indignations under the Shah, and, most important, shared the same vested interest in preserving the Islamic Republic. Moreover, most had studied at the same seminaries and came from the same lower-middle-class backgrounds. Some were even related to each other through marriage and blood ties.

But once the constitution was in place, the same clerics drifted into two loose but identifiable blocs: the Society (*Majmu'eh*) of the Militant Clergy, and the Association (*Jam'eh*) of the Militant Clergy. The former can be described as statist reformers or populists, and the latter as laissez-faire (free-market) conservatives. The reformers hoped to consolidate lower-class support by using state power for redistributing wealth, eradicating unemployment, nationalizing enterprises, confiscating large estates, financing social programs, rationing and subsidizing essential goods, and placing price ceilings on essential consumer goods. In short, they espoused the creation of a comprehensive welfare state. The conservatives hoped to retain middle-class support, especially in the bazaars, by removing price controls, lowering business taxes, cutting red tape, encouraging private entrepreneurs, and balancing the budget, even at the cost of sacrificing subsidies and social programs. In recent years, the statist reformers have begun to emphasize the democratic over the theocratic features of the constitution, stressing the importance of individual rights, the rule of law, and government accountability to the electorate. In many ways, they have become

THE U.S. CONNECTION

Conservatives versus Liberals

In both the United States and Iran, conservative politicians—calling themselves "compassionate conservatives" in the United States and "principalists" in Iran—have a core base limited to less than 30 percent of the electorate. To win national elections, they have to reach out to others while continuing to energize their supporters to vote. To reach out, they both resort to patriotic and populist language—stressing "national security," accusing "weak-kneed liberals" for not standing up to foreign enemies, claiming to represent the "ordinary folks" and appealing to cultural values. In 2005, Ahmadinejad won the presidential elections in part because he presented himself as a "man of the people." He also won partly because his liberal opposition was badly divided. But the biggest reason for the conservative victory was probably because he projected himself as a tough patriot who could better defend the nation from foreign threats—especially after President George W. Bush named Iran as a member of the "Axis of Evil" in 2002 . Conversely, Rouhani won the 2013 elections by arguing that the conservative administration had stifled economic aspirations by unnecessarily antagonizing the United States, by underestimating the costs of UN sanctions, and by grossly mismanaging finances, especially through printing of money and thus causing of inflation. He held out the hope that normalization of relations with the United States would lead to improved standard of living.

MAKING CONNECTIONS Why has the nuclear issue become such a major problem between Iran and the United States?

like social democrats such as those in Britain's Labour Party. Since Khomeini had vehemently denounced liberalism as anti-Islamic, few describe themselves as liberals. They prefer the label reformers or progressives.

The conservatives in Iran were originally labeled middle-of-the-roaders and traditionalists. The statists were labeled progressives, seekers of new ideas, and Followers of the Imam's Line. The former liked to denounce the latter as extremists, leftists, and pro-Soviet Muslims. The latter denounced the free-marketers as medievalists, rightists, capitalists, mafia bazaaris, and pro-American Muslims. Both could bolster their arguments with apt quotes from Khomeini.

This polarization created a major policy-making gridlock, since the early Islamic *Majles* was dominated by the reformers, whereas the Guardian Council was controlled by the conservatives appointed by Khomeini. Between 1981 and 1987, over one hundred bills passed by the reformer-dominated *Majles* were vetoed by the Guardian Council on the grounds that they violated the *shari'a*, especially the sanctity of private property. The vetoed legislation included a labor law, land reform, nationalization of foreign trade, a progressive income tax, control over urban real estate transactions, and confiscation of the property of émigrés whom the courts had not yet found guilty of counterrevolutionary activities. Introduced by individual deputies or cabinet ministers, these bills had received quick passage because reformers controlled the crucial *Majles* committees and held a comfortable majority on the *Majles* floor. Some ultraconservatives had countered by encouraging the faithful not to pay taxes and instead to contribute to the grand ayatollahs of their choice. After all, they argued, one could find no mention of income tax anywhere in the *shari'a*.

Both sides cited the Islamic constitution to support their positions. The conservative free-marketers referred to the long list of clauses protecting private property, promising balanced budgets, and placing agriculture, small industry, and retail trade in the private sector. The reformers referred to an even longer list promising education, medicine, jobs, low-income housing, unemployment benefits, disability pay, interest-free loans, and the predominance of the public sector in the economy.

To break the gridlock, Khomeini boldly introduced into Shi'ism the Sunni Islamic concept of *maslahat*—that is, "public interest" and "reasons of state." Over the centuries, Shi'i clerics had denounced this as a Sunni notion designed to bolster illegitimate rulers. Khomeini now claimed that a truly Islamic state could safeguard the public interest by suspending important religious rulings, even over prayer, fasting, and the pilgrimage to Mecca. He declared public interest to be a primary ruling and the others mere secondary rulings. In other words, the state could overrule the views of the highest-ranking clerics. In the name of public interest, it could destroy mosques, confiscate private property, and cancel religious obligations. Khomeini added that the Islamic state had absolute authority, since the Prophet Muhammad had exercised absolute (*motalaq*) power, which he had passed on to the Imams and thus eventually to the Islamic Republic. Never before had a Shi'i religious leader claimed such powers for the state, especially at the expense of fellow clerics.

As a follow-up, Khomeini set up a new institution named the Expediency Council for Determining the Public Interest of the Islamic Order—known as the Expediency Council. He entrusted it with the task of resolving conflicts between the Islamic *Majles* and the Guardian Council. He packed it with thirteen clerics, including the president, the chief judge, the Speaker of the *Majles*, and six jurists from the Guardian Council. The Expediency Council eventually passed some of the more moderate bills favored by the reformers. These included a new income tax, banking legislation, and a much-disputed labor law providing workers in large factories with a minimum wage and some semblance of job security.

Constitutional amendments introduced after Khomeini's death institutionalized the Expediency Council. The new Leader could now not only name its members but also determine its tenure and jurisdiction. Not surprisingly, Khomeini's successor Khamenei, packed it with his supporters—none of them prominent grand ayatollahs. He also made its meetings secret and allowed it to promulgate new laws rather than restrict itself to resolving legislative differences between the Guardian Council and the *Majles*. The Expediency Council is now a secretive body that is accountable only to the Leader. It stands above the constitution. In this sense, it has become a powerful policy-making body rivaling the Islamic *Majles*, even though it did not exist in the original constitution.

maslahat

Arabic term for "expediency," "prudence," or "advisability," now used in Iran to refer to reasons of state or what is best for the Islamic Republic.

Where Do You Stand?

Iran is often described as a theocracy. Would you agree?

Khomeini claimed there were no contradictions between democracy and Islam. Would you agree?

REPRESENTATION AND PARTICIPATION

SECTION 4

Although the Islamic Republic is a theocracy, it incorporates some features of a democracy. According to the constitution, the voters directly choose the president and the Assembly of Experts, which in turn chooses the Leader. What is more, the elected legislature, the *Majles*, exercises considerable power. According to one of the founders of the regime, the *Majles* is the centerpiece of the Islamic constitution.[9]

? Focus Questions

- What are the powers and limitations of Iran's parliament?

- What social groups are most likely and least likely to support the Islamic Republic?

Another architect of the constitution has argued that the people, by carrying out the Islamic Revolution, implicitly favored a type of democracy confined within the boundaries of Islam and the guardianship of the jurist.[10] But another declared that if he had to choose between democracy and power of the clergy as specified in the concept of jurist's guardianship, he would not hesitate to choose the latter, since it came directly from God.[11] On the eve of the initial referendum, Khomeini himself declared: "This constitution, which the people will ratify, in no way contradicts democracy. Since the people love the clergy, have faith in the clergy, want to be guided by the clergy, it is only right that the supreme religious authority oversee the work of the [government] ministers to ensure that they don't make mistakes or go against the Qur'an."[12]

The Legislature

According to Iran's constitution, the *Majles* "represents the nation" and possesses many powers, including making or changing ordinary laws (with the approval of the Guardian Council), investigating and supervising all affairs of state, and approving or ousting the cabinet ministers. In describing this branch of government, the constitution uses the term *qanun* (statutes) rather than *shari'a* (divine law) so as to gloss over the fundamental question of whether legislation passed by the *Majles* is derived from God or the people. It accepts the reasoning that God creates divine law (*shari'a*) but elected representatives can draw up worldly statutes (*qanuns*).

The *Majles* has 290 members and is elected by citizens over the age of eighteen. It can pass *qanuns* as long as the Guardian Council deems them compatible with the *shari'a* and the constitution. It can choose, from a list drawn up by the chief judge, six of the twelve-man Guardian Council. It can investigate at will cabinet ministers, affairs of state, and public complaints against the executive and the judiciary. It can remove cabinet members—with the exception of the president—through a parliamentary vote of no confidence. It can withhold approval for government budgets, foreign loans, international treaties, and cabinet appointments. It can hold closed debates, provide members with immunity from arrest, and regulate its own internal workings, especially the committee system.

The *Majles* plays an important role in everyday politics. It has changed government budgets, criticized cabinet policies, modified development plans, and forced the president to replace some of his ministers. In 1992, 217 deputies circulated an open letter that explicitly emphasized the powers of the *Majles* and thereby implicitly downplayed those of the Leader. Likewise, the Speaker of the House in 2002 threatened to close down the whole *Majles* if the judiciary violated parliamentary immunity and arrested one of the liberal deputies.

Political Parties and the Party System

Iran's constitution guarantees citizens the right to organize parties, and a 1980 law permits the Interior Ministry to issue licenses to parties. But political parties were not encouraged until Khatami was elected president in 1997. Since then, three major parties have been active: the Islamic Iran Participation Front and the Islamic Labor Party, both formed by Khatami reformist supporters, and the more centrist Servants of Reconstruction created by *Hojjat al-Islam* Ali-Akbar Hashemi Rafsanjani, the former president and now chairman of the Expediency Council.

In general, formal parties are less important in Iranian politics than reformist and conservative coalitions and groups that form along ideological and policy lines. For example, former president Ahmadinejad had his initial power base in the Alliance of Builders of Islamic Iran, a coalition of several conservative political parties and organizations that delivered votes very effectively in local (2003), parliamentary (2004), and presidential (2005) elections.

According to the Interior Ministry, licenses have been granted to some seven hundred political, social, and cultural organizations, but all are led by people considered politically acceptable by the regime. Real political opposition has been forced into exile, mostly in Europe. The most important opposition groups are:

The Liberation Movement

Established in 1961 by Mehdi Bazargan, the Islamic Republic's first prime minister. Bazargan had been appointed premier in February 1979 by Khomeini himself, but had resigned in disgust ten months later when the Revolutionary Guards had permitted students to take over the U.S. embassy. The Liberation Movement is a moderate Islamic party. Despite its religious orientation, it is secular and favors the strict separation of mosque and state.

The National Front

Originating in the campaign to nationalize the country's oil resources in the early 1950s, the National Front remains committed to nationalism and secularism, the political ideals of Muhammad Mosaddeq, the prime minister who was overthrown in the CIA-supported coup in 1953. Because the conservative clergy feel threatened by the National Front's potential appeal, they have banned it.

The Mojahedin

Formed in 1971 as a guerrilla organization to fight the Shah's regime, the Mojahedin tried to synthesize Marxism and Islam. It interpreted Shi'i Islam as a radical religion favoring equality, social justice, martyrdom, and redistribution of wealth. Immediately after the revolution, the Mojahedin opposed the clerical regime and attracted a large following among students. The regime retaliated with mass executions forcing the Mojahedin to move their base of operations to Iraq. Not unexpectedly, the Mojahedin became associated with a national enemy and thereby lost much of its appeal.

The Fedayin

Also formed in 1971, the Fedayin modeled itself after the Marxist guerrilla movements of the 1960s in Latin America, especially those inspired by Che Guevara and the Cuban revolution. Losing more fighters than any other organization in the struggle against the Shah, the Fedayin came out of the revolution with great mystique and popular urban support. But it soon lost much of its strength because of massive government repression and a series of internal splits.

The Tudeh (Party of the Masses)

Established in 1941, the Tudeh is a mainstream, formerly pro-Soviet communist party. Although the Tudeh initially supported the Islamic Republic as a "popular anti-imperialist state," it was banned, and most of its organizers were executed during the 1980s. Some members now call for the overthrow of the regime; other call for its reform.

Elections

The constitution promises free elections. In practice, however, *Majles* elections, which are held every four years, have varied from relatively free but disorderly in the early days of the Islamic Republic to controlled and highly unfair in the middle years; back to relatively free, but orderly in the late 1990s; and back again to highly controlled—even rigged—in 2009. In 2013, however, they were surprisingly free permitting the victory of the reform candidate Rouhani. He won 52 percent of the vote, thus avoiding a run-off. His main rival, the well-known mayor of Tehran, obtained only 17 percent. The other four candidates—all well-known conservatives—mustered together no more than 30 percent. Ahmadinezad's candidate received a mere 11 percent. Rouhani's carried all the main cities with the exception of Qom with its large seminaries. He also carried the Sunni provinces as well as in his home Caspian region. Over 72 percent of the some 50 million eligible voters participated. The Islamic Republic needs such elections, especially with high voter turnout, to retain a modern form of political legitimacy.

In the 1980s, ballot boxes were placed in mosques with Revolutionary Guards supervising the voting. Neighborhood clerics were on hand to help illiterates complete their ballots. Club-wielding gangs assaulted regime opponents. Now electoral freedom is restricted by the government-controlled radio-television network, the main source of information for the vast majority of citizens. The Interior Ministry can ban dissident organizations, especially their newspapers on the grounds they are anti-Islamic. Moreover, the electoral law, based on a winner-take-all majority system rather than on proportional representation, is designed to minimize the voice of the opposition.

But the main obstacle to fair elections has been the Guardian Council with its powers to approve all candidates. For example, the Council excluded some 3,500 candidates (nearly half of the total) from running in the parliamentary elections of 2004 by questioning their loyalty to the concept of jurist's guardianship. The purge of reformers was facilitated both by President George W. Bush's labeling of Iran as a member of the global "Axis of Evil" in 2002 and by the American military occupation of Afghanistan and Iraq. Reluctant to rock the boat at a time of apparent and imminent "national danger," most reformers restrained themselves and withdrew from active politics. Not surprisingly, the conservatives won a hollow victory in the 2004 *Majles* elections. They received a clear majority of the seats, but the voter turnout was less than 51 percent, and in Tehran only 28 percent. This was the worst showing since 1979. For a regime that liked to boast about mass participation, this was seen as a major setback—even as a crisis of legitimacy. There was a bit of an upturn, to about 60 percent, in the turnout in both rounds of the presidential election of 2005. Still this was a sharp downturn from the more than 80 percent that had voted in the 1997 presidential contest that brought the reformist Khatami to power. The 2009 elections, by reactivating the reform movement, may well have produced another record turnout, but because of government interference in tallying the vote, the facts remain unclear.

Political Culture, Citizenship, and Identity

In theory, the Islamic Republic of Iran should be a highly viable state. After all, Shi'ism is the religion of both the state and the vast majority of the population. Shi'ism is the central component of Iranian popular culture. Also, the constitution guarantees basic rights to religious minorities as well as to individual citizens. All citizens, regardless of race, language, or religion, are promised the rights of free expression, worship, and organization. They are guaranteed freedom from arbitrary arrest, torture, and police surveillance.

The constitution extends additional rights to the recognized religious minorities: Christian Armenians, Christian Assyrians, Jews, and Zoroastrians. Although they form just 1 percent of the total population, they are allocated five *Majles* seats. They are permitted their own community organizations, including schools, their own places of worship, and their own family laws. The constitution, however, is ominously silent about Sunnis and Baha'is. Sunni Muslims are treated in theory as full citizens, but their actual status is not spelled out. Bahai'is, followers of a nineteenth-century preacher in Iran who emphasized the spiritual unity of all humankind, are considered heretics because their founder had proclaimed his own teachings to supersede that of not only the Old and New Testaments but also of the Qur'an and the Shi'i Imams. Moreover, some ultraconservative Shi'is deem Baha'is to be part of the "international Zionist conspiracy" on the grounds their main shrine is located in modern-day Israel. In fact, the shrine long predates the establishment of the state of Israel.

The constitution also gives guarantees to non-Persian speakers. Although 83 percent of the population understands Persian, thanks to the educational system, over 50 percent continue to speak non-Persian languages at home. The constitution promises them rights unprecedented in Iranian history. It states: "local and native languages can be used in the press, media, and schools." It also states that local populations have the right to elect provincial, town, and village councils. These councils can watch over the governors-general and the town mayors, as well as their educational, cultural, and social programs.

These generous promises have often been honored more in theory than in practice. The local councils—the chief institution that protected minorities—were not held until twenty years after the revolution. Subsidies to non-Persian publications and radio stations remain meager. Jews have been so harassed as "pro-Israeli Zionists" that more than half—40,000 out of 80,000—have left the country since the revolution. Armenian Christians had to end coeducational classes, adopt the government curriculum, and abide by Muslim dress codes, including the veil. The Christian population has declined from over 300,000 to fewer than 200,000.

The Baha'is, however, have borne the brunt of religious persecution. Their leaders have been executed as "heretics" and "imperialist spies." Adherents have been fired from their jobs, had their property confiscated, and been imprisoned and tortured to pressure them to convert to Islam. Their schools have been closed, their community property expropriated, and their shrines and cemeteries bulldozed. It is estimated that since the revolution, one-third of the 300,000 Baha'is have left Iran. The Baha'is, like the Jews and Armenians, have migrated mostly to Canada and the United States.

The Sunni population, which forms as much as 10 percent of the total, has its own reasons for being alienated from Iran's Islamic Republic. The state religion is Shi'ism, and high officials have to be Shi'i. Citizens must abide by Khomeini's concept of jurists' guardianship, a notion derived from Shi'ism. Few institutions cater to Sunni needs. There is not a single Sunni mosque in the whole of Tehran. It is not surprising that the newborn republic in 1979 faced most stiff opposition in regions inhabited by Sunni Kurds, Arabs, Baluchis, and Turkmans. It crushed the opposition by sending in Revolutionary Guards from the Persian Shi'i heartland of Isfahan, Shiraz, and Qom. Sunnis invariably now vote for reform candidates. For example, Rouhani won 81 percent of the vote in the Kurdish region of Baneh.

Azeris, who are Shi'i but not Persian speakers, are well integrated into Iran. In the past, the Azeris, who form 24 percent of the population and dwarf the other minorities, have not posed a serious problem to the state. They are part of the Shi'i community, and have prominent figures in the Shi'i hierarchy—most notably the current Leader, Khamenei. What is more, many Azeri merchants, professionals, and workers live and work throughout Iran.

But the 1991 creation of the Republic of Azerbaijan on Iran's northeastern border following the disintegration of the Soviet Union has raised new concerns, since some Azeris on both sides of the border have begun to talk of establishing a larger unified Azerbaijan. It is no accident that in the war between Azerbaijan and Armenia in the early 1990s, Iran favored the latter. So far, the concept of a unified Azerbaijan appears to have limited appeal among Iranian Azeris.

Interest Groups, Social Movements, and Protest

In the first two decades after its founding, the government of the Islamic Republic often violated its own constitution. It closed down newspapers, professional associations, labor unions, and political parties. It banned demonstrations and public meetings. It imprisoned tens of thousands without due process. It systematically tortured prisoners to extract false confessions and public recantations. And it executed some 25,000 political prisoners, most of them without due process of law. The United Nations, Amnesty International, and Human Rights Watch all took Iran to task for violating the UN Human Rights Charter as well its own Islamic constitution. Most victims were Kurds, military officers from the old regime, and leftists, especially members of the Mojahedin and Fedayin.

Although the violation of individual liberties affected the whole population, it aroused special resentment among three social groups: the modern middle class, educated women, and organized labor. The modern middle class, especially the intelligentsia, has been secular and even anticlerical ever since the 1905 revolution. Little love is lost between it and the Islamic Republic. Not surprisingly, the vast majority of those executed in the 1980s were teachers, engineers, professionals, and college students.

Educated women in Iran also harbor numerous grievances against the conservative clerics in the regime, especially in the judiciary. Although the Western press often dwells on the head-scarf, Iranian women consider the veil one of their less important problems. Given a choice, most would probably continue to wear it out of personal habit and national tradition. More important are work-related grievances: employment, job security, pay scales, promotions, maternity leave, and access to prestigious professions. Despite patriarchal attitudes held by the conservative clergy, educated women have become a major factor in Iranian society. They now form 60 percent of college students, 47 percent of doctors, 28 percent of government employees, and 33 percent of the general labor force, up from 8 percent in the 1980s. They have established their own organizations and journals reinterpreting Islam to conform

Executions in Kurdestan, 1979.

Jahangir Razmi/Magnum Photos

to modern notions of gender equality. Their main organization is known as the Women's One Million Signature Campaign. Women do serve on local councils and in the *Majles* (there are nine in the current parliament, 3.1 percent of the total). One grand ayatollah has even argued that they should be able to hold any job, including president, court judge, and even Leader.

Factory workers in Iran are another significant social group with serious grievances. Their concerns deal mostly with high unemployment, low wages, declining incomes, lack of decent housing, and an unsatisfactory labor law, which, while giving them mandatory holidays and some semblance of job security, denies them the right to call strikes and organize independent unions. Since 1979, wage earners have had a Workers' House—a government-influenced organization—and its affiliated newspaper, *Kar va Kargar* (*Work and Worker*), and since 1999 the Islamic Labor Party has represented their interests. In most years, the Workers' House flexes its political muscle by holding a May Day rally. In 1999, the rally began peacefully with a greeting from a woman reform deputy who had received the second-most votes in the 1996 Tehran municipal elections. But the rally turned into a protest when workers began to march to parliament denouncing conservatives who had spoken in favor of further watering down of the Labor Law. On May Day 2006, an estimated 10,000 workers marched to demand that the labor minister resign. Bus drivers in Tehran, who had been active in earlier protests, went on strike in January 2006 to protest the arrest and maltreatment of one of their leaders. Workers also protested the contested presidential elections of 2009 by participating in the mass demonstrations. The leader of the 2006 bus strike went into exile in Turkey and is now in North America.

The Political Impact of Technology

The regime places great importance on scientific, especially technological, education. It channels the top high school graduates into scientific fields, and generously nourishes Sharif University, the MIT of Iran—so much so that its top students are often recruited by North American universities even before graduating.

This interest is driven in part by security concern and in part by deep-seated cultural values. Such education provides not only the physicists needed for the nuclear projects and the lesser known space program, but also technicians to monitor the Internet and prevent cyber attacks on its nuclear installations. The desire to monitor the Internet and cell phones was greatly intensified after the 2009 mass protests over the presidential elections. The opposition made full use of the social media and cell phones—most urban households now have access to either cell phones or the Internet. The regime countered by making full use of the same to monitor and disrupt the opposition. Once the opposition had been crushed, many reformist journalists emigrated abroad where they started websites and blogs—often with the help of Western governments and NGOs. The security services in Iran have done their best to prevent citizens from gaining easy access to these sites.

The national culture also places great value on scientific education. Ever since the state set up an educational system, the top high school graduates have gravitated toward the sciences—not the arts and humanities. Science—and now nuclear science—is seen as the cutting edge of modernity. What is more, the prevalent view in Iran is that the Muslim Civilization had flourished in the distant past because of its scientific achievements, and, therefore, the key to recapturing the lost grandeur is through technology. When Reza Shah abolished traditional titles, college graduates with science-oriented degrees became generally known as "Engineers." Those with nonscientific ones became known as "Doctors." In recent years, a new title has appeared—that of Engineer Hojjat al-Islam—signifying the person has a science degree as well as a seminary education. We may well soon hear of His Excellency Engineer Grand Ayatollah.

Where Do You Stand?

The regime in Iran is known as the Islamic Republic. Would you describe it as more Islamic or republican?

The regime places great emphasis on elections. Why do you think it does so?

IRANIAN POLITICS IN TRANSITION

The recent mass demonstrations that brought down the presidents of Tunisia, Yemen, and Egypt have had repercussions in Iran. The Leader praised them claiming they replicated the Islamic Revolution of 1979 in Iran. The reform movement countered that these demonstrations were inspired by the 2009 protests against the rigged elections and that they showed such protests—if continued for length of time—could bring down other autocratic regimes. The Leader categorized Mubarek of Egypt and Bin Ali of Tunisia as versions of the Shah of Iran who was deposed by the Islamic Revolution of 1979. The reformers categorized Mubarek and Bin Ali as typical autocrats who rigged and manipulated elections. Despite these polemics, there are two major differences between Iran and these nearby countries. First, the latter, as well as the Shah, ultimately fell from power because of the defection of their armed forces. The former has survived in part because it retains the critical support of the armed forces. Second, the Islamic Republic—despite its democratic shortcomings—does hold regular elections. The others, however, had tried to transform republics into "hereditary republics"—an oxymoron that has enflamed public outrage.

Focus Questions

• What are the most important challenges facing the Islamic Republic?

• In what ways is Iran different from other developing countries?

Political Challenges and Changing Agendas

Contemporary Iran faces both major internal and challenges. Internally, the Islamic Republic continues to struggle with the troubling question of how to combine theocracy with democracy, and clerical authority with mass participation. After several years, when Iran's reformers seemed to be on the political rise, the conservative clerics and their supporters, who already controlled the judiciary, took over the *Majles* in 2004 and the executive in 2009. In 2013, however, they lost the presidency to the moderate Rouhani and may well lose the *Majles* in the near future.

Many observers feel that the conservatives have lost touch with the grassroots of Iranian society and that their political base is probably less than 30 percent of the electorate. It is estimated that some 70 percent of the public favors the reformers, and that much of this majority, if not offered real choices, will, at a minimum, protest by staying home on election days. In fact, conservatives do best when the turnout is low, reformers benefit when it is high. The conservatives, including the Leader Khamenei, now face the challenge of how to maintain some semblance of legitimacy.

This challenge is troubling to the clerical leadership since the country has in recent decades gone through a profound transformation in political values, with much of the population embracing key aspects of the democratic idea including political pluralism, mass participation, civil society, human rights, and individual liberties. Even conservatives have begun to use such terms, openly describing themselves as "neoconservatives," "constructivists," and "pragmatists."

Meanwhile, those in the general public who feel excluded from national politics remain active in influential non-governmental organizations that make up an important part of Iranian civil society. The most visible of these is a human rights group headed by Shirin Ebadi, the winner of the Nobel Peace Prize in 2003. Ms. Ebadi has been a lawyer, judge (until the Islamic Republic barred women from holding such positions), writer, teacher, and prominent activist in the struggle to protect the rights of women and children. Even if excluded from the political arena, such activists will remain committed to using legal, nonviolent means to promote change. But they do not want to be associated with American projects for "regime change."

The development of the democratic idea in Iran has been constricted by theocracy. Some argue that Islam has made this inevitable. But Islam, like the other major religions, can be interpreted in ways that either promote or hinder democracy. Some interpretations of Islam stress the importance of justice, equality, and consultation as political principles. Islam also has a tradition of tolerating other religions, and the *shari'a* explicitly protects life, property, and honor. In practice, Islam has often separated politics from religion, government legal statutes from holy laws, spiritual affairs from worldly matters, and the state from the clerical establishment.

Moreover, theocracy in Iran originates not in Islam itself but in the very specific concept of the jurist's guardianship as developed by Khomeini. On the whole, Sunni Islam considers clerics to be theological scholars, not a special political class. This helps explain why the Iranian regime has found it difficult to export its revolution to other parts of the Muslim world. The failure of the democratic idea to take deeper root in Iran should be attributed less to anything intrinsic in Islam than to the combination of crises between 1979 and 1981 that allowed a particular group of clerics to come to power. Whether they remain in power depends not so much on Islamic values but on how they handle socioeconomic problems and especially the demands for political participation.

Politics in the Islamic Republic of Iran is sharply divided over the question of how to govern an economy beset by rising demands, wildly fluctuating petroleum revenues, and the nightmarish prospect that in the next two generations, the oil wells will run dry. Most clerics favor a rather conventional capitalist road to development, hoping to liberalize the market, privatize industry, attract foreign capital, and encourage the propertied classes to invest. Others envisage an equally conventional statist road to development, favoring central planning, government industries, price controls, high taxes, state subsidies, national self-reliance, and ambitious programs to eliminate poverty, illiteracy, slums, and unemployment. Some are hoping to find a third way, combining elements of state intervention with free enterprise.

Economic problems like those that undermined the monarchy could well undermine the Islamic Republic, particularly if there was another sharp drop in oil prices. The country's collective identity has also come under great strain in recent years. The emphasis on Shi'ism has antagonized Iran's Sunnis as well as its non-Muslim citizens. The emphasis on clerical Shi'ism has further alienated all secularists, including lay liberals and moderate nationalists, to say nothing of a large majority of Iranians who live abroad. Furthermore, the official emphasis on Khomeini's brand of Shi'ism has alienated those Shi'is who reject the whole notion of jurist's guardianship. The elevation of Khamenei as the Leader has also antagonized many early proponents of jurist's guardianship on the grounds that he lacks the scholarly qualifications to hold the position that embodies the sacred and secular power of the Islamic Republic.

Iran's ruling clerical regime has gradually eroded the broad social base that brought it to power in the Islamic Revolution nearly three decades ago. The country's collective identity, although strong in religious terms, is strained to some extent by other internal fault lines, especially those of class, ethnicity, gender, and political differences. Growing discontent may be expressed through apolitical channels, such as apathy, emigration, inward-looking religion, or even drug addiction. There is also a possibility that those seeking change may turn to radical action if they cannot attain their goals through legal reformist movement. Those who want to understand the possibilities for political change in Iran would do well to remember that the country produced two popular upheavals in the twentieth century that fundamentally transformed the political system: the constitutional (1905) and the Islamic (1979) revolutions.

The Islamic Republic's first attempt to enter the world of states as a militant force to spread its theocratic version of Islam proved counterproductive. This effort diverted scarce resources to the military and contributed to the disastrous war with Iraq. It drove Saudi Arabia and the Gulf sheikdoms into a closer relationship with the United States. It prompted the United States to isolate Iran, discouraged foreign investment, and prevented international organizations from extending economic assistance. Iran's militancy also alarmed nearby secular Islamic states such as Turkey, Tadzhikistan, and Azerbaijan. During the Khatami years, however, the regime managed to repair some of this damage. It won over many Arab states and established cordial relations with its neighbors. It also managed to repair some bridges to the European Community. This repair work, however, was seriously undone by the Ahmadinejad administration. The Rouhani administration is now trying to again repair the damage, return to Khatami's policies, and, if possible, normalize relations with the Gulf states, especially Saudi Arabia.

The major external challenge to the Islamic Republic comes from the United States. The George W. Bush administration, by naming Iran as a member of the "Axis of Evil" in 2002 and openly calling for "regime change" (and promoting such change by military means in neighboring Afghanistan and Iraq) dramatically increased pressures on Iran beyond those that already existed because of American economic sanctions, lack of diplomatic relations, and the successful barring of Iran from the World Trade Organization. The Bush administration accused Iran of sabotaging the Arab-Israeli peace process, helping terrorist organizations, especially Hamas in Palestine and Hezbollah in Lebanon, and "grossly violating" democratic and human rights of its own citizens. It also accused Iran of transforming its nuclear program into a nuclear weapons program and thus violating the UN Non-Proliferation Treaty.

The conservatives who then dominated Iranian politics were able to transform this external threat into a political asset. They intimidated many reformers into toning down their demands for domestic change, even silencing them, by declaring that the country was in danger, that the enemy was at the gates, and that any opposition to the government in such times would play into the hands of those who wanted to do harm to Iran. Political commentators even in the United States suspected that the Bush administration was seriously planning military action against Iran—perhaps a preemptive air strike against its nuclear reactors. Such suspicions fed rumors of war. Few Iranians are willing to appear unpatriotic by openly criticizing their government at a time of external danger.

The Obama administration has followed a more nuanced policy. Before his election, Obama offered an olive branch and implicitly accepted Iran's right to enrich uranium so long as it gave verifiable guarantees it would not produce nuclear weapons. After the election, he continued to hold out an olive branch but at the same time imposed through the UN stringent economic sanctions to bring Iran into serious negotiations. Such negotiations started in 2013—immediately after Rouhani's elections. Rouhani, who, as chief nuclear negotiator under Khatami, had himself earlier offered olive branches to Washington, quickly took up Obama's offer.

Both the Obama and the Rouhani administrations were eager for a compromise: the former because it did not want another war and was eager to wind down its entanglements in the Middle East; the latter in part because of the sanctions, in part because it had always favored transparency, and in part because its aim had always been not to develop actual nuclear weapons, but instead to attain the theoretical capacity to be able to develop such weapons in the long-term future if necessity ever required it—such as another Saddam Hussein invading Iran and unleashing weapons of mass destruction. To have such a capacity, Iran needs the scientific knowledge, the centrifuges, and the ability to enrich uranium to a high level required for weapons.

The negotiations are formally between Iran and the Permanent Five Members of UN Security Council plus 1 (United States, United Kingdom, France, Russia, and China, plus Germany). But in reality, they were between Iran and the United States. Behind closed doors negotiators tackled the hard technical issues of how much uranium Iran would be permitted to enrich, how many centrifuges it could retain, whether it could experiment with plutonium as well as uranium, and how much it would open up its facilities to UN inspections. The outline of a general settlement was there, but reaching a mutually satisfactory agreement will be a challenge.

Youth Politics and the Generational Divide

Iran's youth, especially college students, are a force to be reckoned with: Over half the current population was born after 1979 and as many as 1.15 million are enrolled in higher education. In 1999, eighteen different campuses, including Tehran University, erupted into mass demonstrations against the chief judge, who had closed down a reformist newspaper. Revolutionary Guards promptly occupied the campuses, killing or seriously injuring an unknown number of students. Again in late 2002, thousands of students protested the death sentence handed down to a reformist academic accused of insulting Islam. But in 2004, when the Guardian Council barred thousands of reformers from the parliamentary elections, the campuses remained quiet, partly out of fear, partly out of disenchantment with the reformers for failing to deliver on their promises, and partly because of the concern about the looming danger from the United States military presence in Iraq. Students, however, returned to active politics in large numbers during the 2009 presidential elections between Ahmadinejad and the reform candidates, and even more so in the mass demonstrations protesting these contested elections. Of course, they also played an important role in the 2013 election of Rouhani. Youth's major concern is the lack of jobs for the college educated. The "Brain Drain"—an international term coined to describe the exodus of professions from Iran in the 1960s—continues to plague twenty-first century Iran.

Iran, thus, has a generational gap similar to that in many developing and even developed counties. The young generation—especially college graduates—have difficulty finding appropriate jobs. They have to settle either for less suitable ones or emigrate to the West. They have difficulty buying or renting homes. They consequently delay leaving their parents and getting married. Despite these similarities with other parts of the world, Iran so far has not shown the typical symptoms of the generational conflict—conflicts over bread-and-butter issues as such pensions, medical benefits, and old-age care. Such concerns are easily alleviated by the abundant income coming from oil and the anticipated revenue expected from the untapped gas reserves. Oil—not youth—is expected to carry the "burden" of the older generation.

Iranian Politics in Comparative Perspective

Unlike most developing countries, Iran was never formally colonized by the European imperial powers and has always been independent. It is, in many ways, an old state with many institutions that date back to ancient times. Furthermore, while many other developing world states have weak connections with their societies, Iran has a religion that links the elite with the masses, the cities with the villages, the government with the citizenry. Shi'ism, as well as Iranian national identity, serves as social and cultural cement, which gives the population a strong collective identity.

Although Shi'ism gives Iran this asset, it also helps explain why the county is unique in the world in that it has a semi-theocratic state. Despite these theocratic features, Iran still has much in common with many other fast-developing countries in Asia and Latin American—especially Brazil, Mexico, Venezuela, India, and

Indonesia. In some ways, it is better off. It no longer fits the stereotype of the Third World. It has overcome the worst aspects of backwardness—dire poverty, hunger and malnutrition, illiteracy, highly infant mortality, high death rates, and low life expectancy. It has an impressive educational system, and with it a burgeoning middle class that feels quite at home in the modern world. It has large oil revenues and resources, and even larger gas reserves ready to be tapped—once UN sanctions are lifted and Iran return fully to the global economy. What is more, Iran—unlike some oil states such as Nigeria—has a functioning state that is capable of effectively distribution to the general population the benefits of the oil revenues as well as administering quite effectively the whole country. The Islamic Republic is by no mean a failed state.

Where Do You Stand?

Iran is often described with the neighboring countries, especially the Arab countries, as part and parcel of the Middle East. Would you agree with this description?

Iran's nuclear program has been very controversial in the international community. Do you think that Iran has good persuasive reasons to scale down this program?

Chapter Summary

The Iranian state—unlike many others in the Middle East—is viable and well established. It has a long history. Its official religion—Shi'ism—binds the elite with the masses, the government with the governed, the rulers with the ruled. Its ministries are embedded deep into society, providing multiple social services. It has substantial oil revenues, which, although fluctuating, provide the government the means to finance the ever-growing ministries. What is more, the recent past—especially the Islamic Revolution and the eight-year war with Iraq—has helped create a strong sense of national solidarity against the outside world—not just against the West but also much of the Sunni Muslim World.

It has often been said that oil is a resource curse of the producing countries. It has been blamed for creating "rentier states," "dual societies," autocratic governments, unpredictable budgets, and retardation of other economic activities. Although this may be true in some parts of the world, in Iran oil has been the main engine driving state development and social modernization. It is mainly due to oil that Iran enters the twenty-first century with a strong state and a fairly modernized society in which almost all citizens have access to schools, medical clinics, modern sanitation, piped water, electricity, radios, televisions, and basic consumer goods.

The clergy exercise authority over elected officials in three separate ways: the Leader, a cleric, supervises the three branches of government; the Guardian Council can veto legislation passed by parliament; and the same Council can vet all candidates running for high office. Despite these restrictions, the constitution—in theory—has the possibility of moving away from theocracy toward

democracy. After all, the constitution enshrines the public's right to elect parliament, president, and even the Leader. The constitution even endows the public with the authority to amend the constitution. The main obstacle to democracy is the vetting process, which grants ultimate power to the Leader, not the constitution itself.

The George W. Bush administration liked to denounce Iran as a "totalitarian state" tyrannized by unelected unpopular leaders. While Iran is no liberal democracy, it hardly fits the "totalitarian" category. The clergy, despite opposition from the intelligentsia, continue to rule in part because they still enjoy some legitimacy—especially among the bazaars, rural population, and urban poor; in part because they have brought economic benefits to the wider population; and in part because they have left some room for civil society and have permitted interest groups to function so long as they do not violate red lines and directly question the clergy's legitimacy. They have also been greatly helped by the perceived notion that the nation is under siege—even under imminent threat—from the United States.

Iran could meet its internal challenge by becoming more flexible, liberalizing, giving greater scope to civil society, and allowing more public participation and competitive elections—in short, strengthening the democratic as opposed to the theocratic features of the constitution. If it did so, it would transform itself closer to democracy. If it does not, it could freeze up, alienate the public, lose legitimacy, and thereby make itself vulnerable to destruction. Iran could also meet its external challenge by following a cautious foreign policy, going slow on its nuclear program, providing verifiable guarantees that it was not building nuclear weapons, toning down its rhetoric, and assuring its neighbors as well as the United States that it was a "normal state" uninterested in exporting revolution. If it does not, it could well end up with a confrontation with the United States—a confrontation that would be disastrous for both countries. A window of opportunity has now been opened up with the negotiations between the Obama and Rouhani administrations.

Key Terms

Assembly of Experts
ayatollah
bazaar
dual society
Expediency Council
Farsi
Foundation of the Oppressed
Guardian Council
Hezbollahis
hojjat al-Islam

Imam Jum'ehs
Islamism
jurist's guardianship
Leader/Supreme Leader
Majles
maslahat
Organization of Petroleum
    Exporting Countries (OPEC)
pasdaran
People of the Book

political Islam
Qur'an
rentier state
resource curse
theocracy

Suggested Readings

Abrahamian, Ervand. *A History of Modern Iran*. New York: Cambridge University Press, 2008.

———. *The Coup: 1953, The CIA, and the Roots of Modern U.S.-Iranian Relations*. New York: The New Press, 2013.

Beeman, William O. *The "Great Satan" vs. the "Mad Mullahs": How the United States and Iran Demonize Each Other*. New York: Praeger, 2005.

Ebadi, Shirin, and Azadeh Moaveni. *Iran Awakening: A Memoir of Revolution and Hope*. New York: Random House, 2006.

Gheissari, Ali, and Vali Nasr. *Democracy in Iran: History and the Quest for Liberty*. New York: Oxford University Press, 2006.

Keddie, Nikki. *Modern Iran: Roots and Results of Revolution*, updated ed. New Haven, CT: Yale University Press, 2006.

Moin, Baqer. *Khomeini: Life of the Ayatollah*. New York: Thomas Dunne Books, 2000.

Nafisi, Azar. *Reading Lolita in Tehran: A Memoir in Books*. New York: Random House, 2003.

Pollack, Kenneth. *The Persian Puzzle: The Conflict between Iran and America*. New York: Random House, 2005.

Satrapi, Marjaneh. *Persepolis*. New York: Pantheon, 2003.

Suggested Websites

University of Texas—Iran Maps
www.lib.utexas.edu/maps/iran.html

Columbia University—The Gulf/2000 Project's Map Collection
gulf2000.columbia.edu/maps.shtml

The Story of the Revolution, British Broadcasting Corporation
www.bbc.co.uk/persian/revolution

Iranian Mission to the United Nations
www.un.int/iran

Iran Report, Radio Free Europe
www.rferl.org/reports/iran-report

News Related to Iran
www.farsinews.net

www.onlinenewspapers.com/iran.htm

15 China

William A. Joseph

Official Name: People's Republic of China
(Zhonghua Remin Gongheguo)

Location: East Asia

Capital City: Beijing

Population (2014): 1.35 billion

Size: 9,596,960 sq. km.; slightly smaller than the United States

China Photos/Getty Images

© Cengage Learning®

1912
Sun Yat-sen founds the Nationalist Party (*Guomindang*) to oppose warlords who have seized power in the new republic.

1927
Civil war between Nationalists (now led by Chiang Kai-shek) and Communists begins.

1937
Japan invades China, marking the start of World War II in Asia.

| 1700 | 1900 | 1910 | 1920 | 1930 | 1940 | 1950 |

1911
Revolution led by Sun Yat-sen overthrows 2,000-year-old imperial system and establishes the Republic of China.

1921
Chinese Communist Party (CCP) is founded.

1934
Mao Zedong becomes leader of the CCP; formally elected chairman in 1943.

1949
Chinese Communists win the civil war and establish the People's Republic of China.

SECTION 1
THE MAKING OF THE MODERN CHINESE STATE

Focus Questions

- How did the Communist Party come to power in China?

- How has China changed—and remained the same—since the Communist Party came to power?

Politics in Action

In the early morning hours of June 4, 1989, Chinese soldiers began an assault to clear pro-democracy demonstrators from Tiananmen Square in Beijing. One of the protestors described what happened when he and others joined hands on the outskirts of the square to form a human chain to halt the army's advance:

> …without warning, the troops opened fire on us. People cursed, screamed and ran. In no time, seventy or eighty people had collapsed all around me. Blood spattered all over, staining my clothes.

At a nearby intersection, he saw "several hundred bodies, mostly young people, including some children."

> As the army continued to move toward the square, an angry crowd of over ten thousand surged forward to surround the troops. This time the soldiers turned on the people with even greater brutality. The fusillades from machine guns were loud and clear. Because some of the bullets used were the kind that explode within the body, when they struck, the victims' intestines and brains spilled out. I saw four or five such bodies. They looked like disemboweled animal carcasses.[1]

By the time dawn broke, Tiananmen Square had indeed been cleared. A unknown number of civilians had been killed. In the days that followed, a wave of government repression spread throughout the country. Thousands of Chinese citizens were

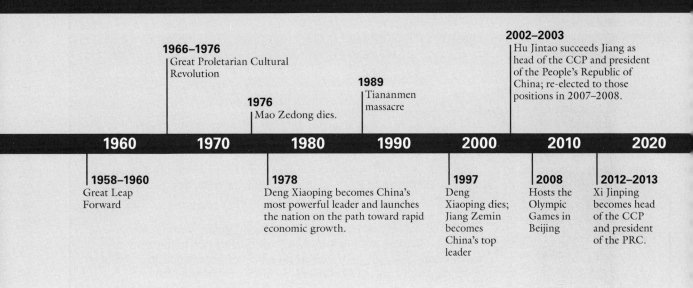

1966–1976
Great Proletarian Cultural Revolution

1976
Mao Zedong dies.

1989
Tiananmen massacre

2002–2003
Hu Jintao succeeds Jiang as head of the CCP and president of the People's Republic of China; re-elected to those positions in 2007–2008.

1960   1970   1980   1990   2000   2010   2020

1958–1960
Great Leap Forward

1978
Deng Xiaoping becomes China's most powerful leader and launches the nation on the path toward rapid economic growth.

1997
Deng Xiaoping dies; Jiang Zemin becomes China's top leader

2008
Hosts the Olympic Games in Beijing

2012–2013
Xi Jinping becomes head of the CCP and president of the PRC.

arrested for their participation in the demonstrations in Beijing and other cities, and there were several well-publicized executions.

June 4, 2014, marked the twenty-fifth anniversary of the Beijing massacre. In the weeks prior to that anniversary, dozens of political activists, artists, and lawyers were detained by the Chinese authorities to ensure that they would not try

Ethnic Groups

55 other nationalities, including Zhuang, Manchu, Hui, Miao, Uyghur, Mongal, Tibetan, and Korean, 8.5%

Han Chinese 91.5%

Chinese Currency
Renminbi(RMB)("People's Currency"); also called yuan
International Designation: CNY
Exchange Rate (2013):
- 1 US$ = 6.1 CNY
- 1 CNY = 0.16 US$
100 RMB Note Design: Mao Zedong (1893–1976), Chairman of Chinese Communist Party (1943–1976)

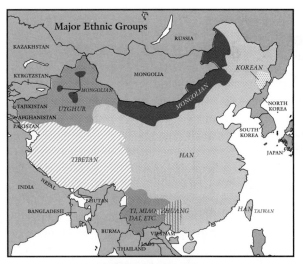

Languages: Standard Chinese (Mandarin) based on the Beijing dialect; other major dialects include Cantonese and Shanghaiese. Also various minority languages, such as Tibetan and Mongolian.

Religions: Officially atheist; Buddhist 18.2%, Christian 5.1%, Muslim 1.8%, folk religion 21.9%, other .08%, unaffiliated 52.2%

FIGURE 15.1 The Chinese Nation at a Glance

© Cengage Learning® (for map)

© G2019/Shutterstock.com (for photo)

Table 15.1	Political Organization
Political System	Communist party–state; officially, a socialist state under the people's democratic dictatorship.
Regime History	Established in 1949 after the victory of the Chinese Communist Party (CCP) in the Chinese civil war.
Administrative Structure	Unitary system with twenty-two provinces, five autonomous regions, four centrally administrated municipalities, and two Special Administrative Regions (Hong Kong and Macao).
Executive	Premier (head of government) and president (head of state) formally elected by legislature, but only with approval of CCP leadership; the head of the CCP, the general secretary, is in effect the country's chief executive, and serves concurrently as president of the PRC.
Legislature	Unicameral National People's Congress; about 3,000 delegates elected indirectly from lower-level people's congresses for five-year terms. Largely a rubber-stamp body for Communist Party policies, although in recent years has become somewhat more active in policy-making.
Judiciary	A nationwide system of people's courts, which are constitutionally independent but, in fact, largely under the control of the CCP; a Supreme People's Court supervises the country's judicial system and is formally responsible to the National People's Congress, which also elects the court's president.
Party System	A one-party system, although in addition to the ruling Chinese Communist Party, there are eight politically insignificant "democratic" parties.

to commemorate it in any way. What happened in Tiananmen in 1989 cannot be mentioned in the press. It is not taught in schools. The Internet police scrub any reference to it in blogs and tweets. No official accounting of the number of dead has been given.

The People's Republic of China (PRC) has changed dramatically in many ways in the quarter century since so much blood was spilled on the streets of the country's capital. The country is much more prosperous and deeply integrated into the global economy. Its stature as a rising world power had increased enormously. The Chinese people enjoy greater economic, social, and cultural freedoms. In 1989, fewer than ten thousand Chinese students were studying abroad; by 2014 there were nearly 400,000.

But much has not changed. The Chinese Communist Party (CCP) still rules China with an iron political grip. Most people do not feel the coercive weight of that grip in their daily lives, but the party still crushes individual or collective action it judges as a challenge to the party's authority. For all of its truly remarkable economic progress, the PRC remains one of the world's harshest dictatorships. The rift between China's authoritarian political system and its increasingly modern and globalized society remains deep and ominous.

Geographic Setting

China is located in the eastern part of mainland Asia, at the heart of one of the world's most strategically important regions. It is slightly smaller than the United States in land area, and is the fourth-largest country in the world, after Russia, Canada, and the United States.

The north is much like the U.S. plains states in its weather and topography. This wheat-growing area is also China's industrial heartland. Southern China has a much warmer climate. In places it is even semitropical, which allows year-round agriculture and intensive rice cultivation. The vast, sparsely populated western part of the country is mostly mountains, deserts, and high plateaus.

China is the most populous nation in the world with about 1.35 billion people. A little more than half of those live in urban areas. The PRC has nearly 160 cities with a population of a million or more. Beijing, the capital, has 20.7 million residents, while Shanghai, the economic heart of the country, has 23.5 million. Nevertheless, 650 million people still live in the countryside, which continues to play a very important role in China's economic and political development.

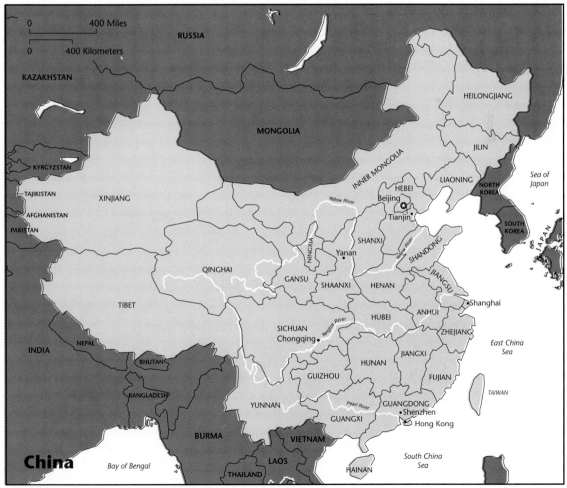

Although China and the United States are roughly equal in area, China's population of 1.35 billion is more than four times greater. Less than 15 percent of its land, however, can be used for agriculture. The precarious balance between people and the land needed to feed them has been a dilemma for centuries. It remains one of the government's major concerns.

In 1997, the former British colony of Hong Kong, one of the world's great commercial centers, became a Special Administrative Region (SAR) of the PRC. Hong Kong and China's other SAR, Macau, a former Portuguese colony with a thriving casino economy that became part of the PRC in 1999, have a great deal of autonomy from the government in Beijing in most matters other than foreign relations and defense.

About 92 percent of China's citizens are ethnically Chinese. The remaining 8 percent is made up of fifty-five ethnic minority groups. Most of these minority peoples live in the country's geopolitically sensitive border regions, including Tibet and Xinjiang, which has a large Muslim population. The often uneasy relationship between some of China's minorities and the central government in Beijing is a crucial and volatile issue in Chinese politics today.

Critical Junctures

From 221 BCE to 1912 CE, China was ruled by a series of family-based dynasties headed by an emperor. The Chinese empire went through extensive geographic expansion and other significant changes during this time. But the basic political and social organization remained remarkably consistent. One of its most distinctive aspects was a national bureaucracy chosen on the basis of merit, which developed much earlier than similar government institutions in Europe. Imperial officials were appointed by the emperor only after they had passed a series of very difficult examinations that tested their mastery of the teachings of Confucius (551–479 BCE), a philosopher who emphasized obedience to authority, respect for superiors and elders, and the responsibility of rulers to govern benevolently.

The Chinese empire was fatally weakened in the nineteenth century by an unprecedented combination of poor governance, a population explosion that led to economic stagnation and deepening poverty, internal rebellions, and external aggression by European powers, including the Opium War (1839–1842), which was fought over British demands that they be allowed to sell the narcotic in China. Many efforts were made to reform the imperial government. But these efforts were not enough to save the 2000-year-old imperial system, and in 1912, a revolution toppled the ruling dynasty and established the Republic of China.

Warlords, Nationalists, and Communists (1912–1949)

Dr. Sun Yat-sen*, who was partly educated in Hawaii, became the first president of the Republic. But he was unable to hold on to power, and China quickly fell into a lengthy period of conflict and disintegration. Rival military leaders, known as warlords, ruled large parts of the country. Sun founded the Nationalist Party, which he hoped would be able to reunify the country.

In 1921, a few intellectuals, inspired by the 1917 Russian revolution, established the Chinese Communist Party (CCP). They were looking for a more radical solution to China's problems than that offered by the Nationalist Party. They initially joined

---

*In Chinese, the family name come first.

with the Nationalists to fight the warlords. But in 1927, Chiang Kai-shek, who had become the head of the Nationalist Party after Sun's death in 1925, turned against the communists, who were nearly wiped out in a bloody crackdown. Chiang then unified the Republic of China under his personal and increasingly authoritarian rule.

The Communist Party relocated its headquarters deep within the remote countryside. This retreat created the conditions for the eventual rise to power of Mao Zedong, who led the CCP to nationwide victory two decades later. Mao had been one of the junior founders of the Communist Party. Coming from a peasant background, he had strongly urged the CCP to pay more attention to China's suffering rural masses. "In a very short time," he wrote in 1927, "several hundred million peasants will rise like a mighty storm, like a hurricane, a force so swift and violent that no power, however great, will be able to hold it back."[2] While the CCP was based in the rural areas, Mao began his climb to the top of the party leadership.

Under pressure from Chiang Kai-shek's army, in 1934 the communists were forced to embark on a year-long, 6,000-mile journey called the Long March, which took them across some of the most remote parts of China. Although only about 8,000 of the original 80,000 Long Marchers finished the trek, the communists were able to established a base in an impoverished area of northwest China in October 1935. It was there that Mao consolidated his control of the CCP. He was a brilliant political and military leader, but he also sometimes used ruthless means to gain power. He was elected party chairman in 1943, a position he held until his death in 1976.

Japan's invasion of China in 1937 had a major impact on the Chinese civil war. Chiang Kai-shek's government fled into the far southwestern part of the country, which effectively eliminated them as an active combatant against Japanese aggression. In contrast, the CCP base in the northwest was on the front line against Japan's troops. The Communists successfully mobilized the peasants to use **guerrilla warfare** to fight the invaders. This resistance to Japan gained the CCP a strong following among the Chinese people.

After Japan surrendered in 1945, the Chinese civil war quickly resumed. Communist forces won a decisive victory over the U.S.-backed Nationalists. Chiang Kai-shek and his supporters retreated to the island of Taiwan, 90 miles off the Chinese coast. On October 1, 1949, Mao Zedong declared the founding of the People's Republic of China (PRC).

Mao Zedong in Power (1949–1976)

The Communist Party came to power in China on a wave of popular support because of its reputation as social reformers and patriotic fighters. The CCP quickly turned its attention to some of the country's most glaring problems. A land reform campaign redistributed property from the rich to the poor and increased agricultural production. Highly successful drives eliminated opium addiction and prostitution from the cities. A national law greatly improved the legal status of women. The CCP often used violence to achieve its objectives and silence opponents. Nevertheless, the party gained considerable legitimacy among many parts of the population because of its successful policies during the early years of its rule.

Between 1953 and 1957, the PRC, with aid from the Soviet Union, implemented a **centrally planned economy** and took decisive steps toward **socialism**. Private property was almost completely eliminated through the takeover of industry by the government and the collectivization of agriculture. The Chinese economy grew significantly during this period. But Mao disliked the expansion of the government bureaucracy and the persistence of inequalities, especially those between the urban and rural areas.

guerrilla warfare

A military strategy based on small, highly mobile bands of soldiers (the guerrillas, from the Spanish word for war, *guerra*) who use hit-and-run tactics like ambushes to attack a better-armed enemy.

centrally planned economy

An economic system in which the state directs the economy through bureaucratic plans for the production and distribution of goods and services. The government, rather than the market, is the major influence on the economy. Also called a command economy.

socialism

A system in which the state plays a leading role in organizing the economy, owns most productive resources and property, and actively promotes equality.

GLOBAL CONNECTION

The Republic of China on Taiwan

After the Nationalists fled to Taiwan, communist forces would probably have taken over the island if the United States had not intervened to prevent an invasion. More than six decades later, Taiwan remains politically separate from the People's Republic of China and still formally calls itself the Republic of China.

Chiang Kai-shek and the Nationalists imposed a harsh dictatorship on Taiwan. This deepened the sharp divide between the Mainlanders who had arrived in large numbers with Chiang in 1949 and the native Taiwanese majority, whose ancestors had settled there centuries before and who spoke a distinctive Chinese dialect.

With large amounts of U.S. aid and advice, the Nationalist government promoted rural development, attracted foreign investment, and presided over impressive economic growth by producing globally competitive exports. Health and education levels were quickly raised and now are among the best in the world. Taiwan's GDP per capita ($39,600) is higher than that of Britain or France.

After Chiang died in 1975, his son, Chiang Ching-kuo, became president of the Republic of China and head of the Nationalist Party. He permitted some political opposition and gave important government and party positions, previously dominated by Mainlanders, to Taiwanese. When he died in 1988, the Taiwanese vice president, Lee Teng-hui, became president.

Under President Lee, Taiwan made great strides toward democratization. Laws used to imprison dissidents were revoked, the media was freed of all censorship, and multiparty elections were held. An opposition political party won presidential and parliamentary elections in 2000 to 2004. The Nationalists have been in power since 2008.

The most controversial political issue in Taiwan is whether the island should work toward reunification with the mainland or declare independence from China. Most people in Taiwan prefer the status quo in which the island is, for all intents and purposes (including its own strong military), independent of the PRC, but is not an internationally recognized country.

The PRC regards Taiwan as a rightfully part of China and has refused to renounce the use of force if the island moves toward independence. Nevertheless, the two have developed extensive economic relations and other connections. The Taiwan Straits—the ocean area between the island and the mainland—is still considered one of the world's most volatile areas in terms of the potential for military conflict.

MAKING CONNECTIONS Why would Taiwan be reluctant to reunify with the PRC?

---

communism

According to Marxism, the stage of development that follows socialism and in which all property is publically owned, economic production is coordinated for the common good, and a radical degree of equality has been achieved.

These concerns led Mao to launch the Great Leap Forward (1958–1960). The Great Leap was a utopian effort to speed up the country's development so rapidly that China would catch up economically with Britain and the United States in just a few years. It also aimed to propel China into an era of true **communism** in which there would be almost complete economic and social equality. These goals were to be achieved by mobilizing the labor power and revolutionary enthusiasm of the masses under the leadership of the CCP.

But irrational policies, wasted resources, poor management, and the suppression of any criticism combined with bad weather to produce a famine in the rural areas that claimed 30–40 million lives. An industrial depression followed the collapse of agriculture. China suffered a terrible setback in economic development.

In the early 1960s, Mao took a less active role in day-to-day decision making. Two of China's other top leaders at the time, Liu Shaoqi and Deng Xiaoping, were put in charge of reviving the economy. They completely abandoned the radical strategy of the Great Leap and used a combination of government planning and market-oriented policies to stimulate production.

This approach did help the Chinese economy. But by the mid-1960s, Mao had concluded that the policies of Liu and Deng had led to a resurgence of elitism and inequality. He thought they were threatening his communist goals by setting the country on the road to capitalism. China also broke relations with the Soviet Union, which Mao had concluded was no longer a truly socialist country.

The Great Proletarian Cultural Revolution (1966–1976) was Mao's ideological crusade designed to jolt China back toward his vision of communism. Its main goal was the political purification of the nation through struggle against alleged class enemies. Using his unmatched political clout and charisma, Mao put together a potent coalition of radical party leaders, loyal military officers, and student rebels (called Red Guards) to support him and attack anyone thought to be guilty of betraying his version of communist ideology, known as Mao Zedong Thought. The Cultural Revolution led to widespread destruction of historical monuments, the psychological and physical persecution of millions of people, and a series of disruptive power struggles within the top leadership of the CCP.

Mao died in September 1976 at age eighty-two. A month later, a group of relatively moderate leaders arrested their radical rivals, the so-called Gang of Four, led by Mao's widow, Jiang Qing. This marked the end of the Cultural Revolution.

Deng Xiaoping and the Transformation of Chinese Communism (1977–1997)

To repair the damage caused by the Cultural Revolution, China's new leaders restored to power many veteran officials who had been purged by Mao and the radicals. These included Deng Xiaoping. By 1978, Deng had clearly become the country's most powerful leader, although he never took for himself the formal positions of head of either the Communist Party or the Chinese government. Instead he appointed younger, loyal men to those positions.

Deng's policies were a profound break with the Maoist past. State control of the economy was significantly reduced, and market forces were allowed to play an increasingly important role. After decades of stagnation, the Chinese economy began to experience high levels of growth in the 1980s. Chinese artists and writers were allowed much great freedom. Better-educated officials were recruited to modernize the PRC government. Deng Xiaoping gathered global praise for his leadership of the reforms that were transforming nearly every aspect of life in China.

Then came Tiananmen.

Large-scale demonstrations began in Beijing in the early spring of 1989 and quickly spread to other cities. Most of the initial protesters were university students who were expressing their discontent about inflation, corruption, and slow pace of political reform. Over time, they became more vocal in their demands for democratization, although they never called for the overthrow of the Communist Party. At one point, more than a million people from all walks of life gathered in and around Tiananmen Square to show support for the students.

For a while the CCP leadership did little more than denounce the demonstrators as trouble-makers and issue vague warnings about dire consequences. But a small group of mostly elderly leaders, including Deng Xiaoping, who was 85 at the time, ran out of patience. The army was ordered to end the "counter-revolutionary rebellion" and restore order in Beijing. It did so with brutal violence on June 4th. The PRC government continues to insist that it did the right thing in the interests of national stability.

Following the Beijing massacre, China went through a couple of years of intense political crackdown and a slowdown in the pace of economic change. In early 1992, Deng Xiaoping took bold steps to accelerate reform of the economy. He did so partly because he hoped economic progress would enable China to avoid the collapse of the communist party–state such as had happened just the year before in the Soviet Union.

From Revolutionaries to Technocrats (1997 to the Present)

In mid-1989, Deng Xiaoping had promoted Jiang Zemin, the mayor and Communist Party leader of Shanghai, to become the head of the CCP. Although Deng remained the power behind the throne, he gradually turned over greater authority to Jiang, who

PROFILES

A Tale of Two Leaders

Chinese Communist leaders Mao Tse-tung and Deng Xiaoping in 1959.

Bettmann/CORBIS

Mao Zedong (1893–1976) and Deng Xiaoping (1904–1997) had much in common. They were both born in rural China and joined the Chinese Communist Party in their early 20s. Both participated in the CCP's Long March in 1934–1935 to escape annihilation by Chiang Kai-shek's Nationalist army. When Mao consolidated his power as the undisputed leader of the CCP in the 1940s, Deng became one of his most trusted comrades. After the founding of the PRC, Deng rose to the highest levels of party leadership. And both men transformed China in ways that mark them as two of the most important figures in all of Chinese—and perhaps world—history.

But, in some ways, Mao and Deng were very different. Most importantly, Deng was a pragmatist—someone who acts to get things done rather than dwelling on abstract ideas. Mao was an idealist who thought about the future in utopian terms and then tried to find ways to make reality fit his vision. Mao twice removed Deng from power during the Cultural Revolution because he concluded that Deng's economic pragmatism was taking China down "the capitalist road" and away from his communist ideals.

Less than a year after Mao died and his radical followers were purged in the fall of 1976, Deng made his way back to the inner circle of power. By 1978, he was clearly China's most powerful leader. Deng used his power to lead the country toward spectacular economic growth by taking the PRC in a very un-Maoist capitalist direction.

But another thing that Mao and Deng had in common was an unshakeable belief that communist party leadership of China should not be challenged. Mao initiated a number of ruthless movements to squash dissent. The brutal crackdown on the Beijing pro-democracy protests in June 1989 was Deng's response to those who questioned party rule.

Today both Mao Zedong and Deng Xiaoping are revered in China. Mao's legacy is tarnished by the tragic human cost of his utopian campaigns. But he is lauded for restoring China's sovereignty and dignity after more than a century of humiliation at the hands of foreign powers. Deng is seen as the architect of China's economic miracle. Few people associate him with the 1989 Beijing massacre since that remains a forbidden topic in the PRC.

MAKING CONNECTIONS How do you think history will judge the achievements and shortcomings of Mao Zedong and Deng Xiaoping?

---

also became president of the PRC in 1993. When Deng Xiaoping died in February 1997, Jiang was secure in his position as China's top leader.

Under Jiang Zemin's leadership, China continued its economic reforms and remarkable growth. The PRC became an even more integral part of the global economy. But the country also faced widening gaps between the rich and the poor, environmental degradation, and pervasive corruption. Overall, China was politically stable during the Jiang era. But the CCP still repressed any individual or group it perceived as challenging its authority.

Jiang Zemin was succeeded as head of the CCP in November 2002 and PRC president in March 2003 by Hu Jintao. The transfer of power from Jiang to Hu was remarkably predictable and orderly. Jiang had retired after two terms in office, as required by new party rules, and Hu had, for several years, been expected to succeed Jiang.

Both Jiang and Hu also represented a new kind of leader for the PRC. Mao and Deng had been involved in communist politics almost their whole adult lives. They had participated in the CCP's long struggle for power dating back to the 1920s. They were among the founders of the communist regime in 1949. In contrast, Jiang and Hu were technocrats. They had technical university training (as engineers) before working their way up the ladder of success in the party bureaucracy by a combination of professional competence and political loyalty.

Another smooth and predictable leadership transition took place when Xi Jinping (b. 1953) ascended to the top party position in November 2012 and the presidency of the PRC in March 2013. Xi is also technocrat (with a degree in chemical engineering). There is little reason to expect he will deviate significantly from the combination of economic reform and political repression that has been the CCP's formula for retaining power since the days of Deng Xiaoping.

This cartoon captures the contradiction between economic reform and political repression that characterized China under the leadership of Deng Xiaoping and his successors.

Tribune Media Services, Inc. All Rights Reserved. Reprinted with permission.

The Four Themes and China

China in a Globalized World of States

When the PRC was established in 1949, China occupied a very weak position in the international system. For more than a century, its destiny had been shaped by interventions from abroad that it could do little to control. Mao made many tragic and terrible blunders during his years in power. But one of his great achievements was to build a strong state able to affirm and defend its sovereignty. Although still a relatively poor country by many per capita measures, the sheer size of its economy makes the PRC an economic powerhouse. Its foreign trade policies have a significant effect on many other countries and on the global economy. China is a nuclear power with the world's largest conventional military force. It is an active and influential member of the world's most important international organizations, including the United Nations, where it sits as one of the five permanent members of the Security Council. China has become a major player in the world of states.

Governing the Economy

Throughout its history the PRC has experimented with a series of very different approaches to governing the economy: a Soviet-style planning system in the early 1950s, the radical egalitarianism of the Maoist model, and the market-oriented policies implemented by Deng Xiaoping and his successors. Ideological disputes over these development strategies were the main cause of the ferocious political struggles within the CCP during the Mao era. Deng began his bold reforms in the late 1970s with the hope that improved living standards would restore the legitimacy of the CCP, which had been badly tarnished by the economic failings and political chaos of much of the previous three decades. The remarkable success of China's recent leaders in governing the economy has sustained the authority of the CCP at a time when most of the world's other communist regimes have disappeared.

The Democratic Idea

Any hope that the democratic idea might take root in the early years of communist rule in China quickly vanished by the mid-1950s with the building of a one-party communist state and Mao's unrelenting campaigns against alleged enemies of his revolution. The Deng era brought much greater economic, social, and cultural freedom, but time and again the CCP has strangled the stirrings of the democratic idea, most brutally in Tiananmen Square in 1989. Deng's successors have been faithful disciples. They have vigorously championed economic reform in China. They have also made sure that the CCP retains its firm hold on political power.

The Politics of Collective Identity

Because of its long history and ancient culture, China has a very strong sense of collective national identity. Memories of past humiliations and suffering at the hands of foreigners still influence the international policies of the PRC. The CCP places great emphasis on nationalism as a means to rally the Chinese people behind the government, especially because faith in communist ideology has weakened as the country embraces capitalist economic policies. The enormous inequalities between those that have benefited from those policies and those left behind have led to the emergence socioeconomic class as a growing source of collective identity in contemporary China. China's cultural and ethnic homogeneity has also spared it the widespread communal violence that has plagued so many other countries. The exception has been in the border regions where there is a large concentration of minority peoples, including Tibet and Xinjiang.

In an act of outrage and protest, an unarmed citizen stood in front of a column of tanks leaving Tiananmen Square the day after the Chinese army had crushed the prodemocracy demonstration in 1989. This "unknown hero" disappeared into the watching crowd. Neither his identity nor his fate is known.

AP Images/Jeff Widener

Theme and Comparisons

The People's Republic of China can be compared with other **communist party-states** with which it shares many political and ideological features. This raises several intriguing questions: Why has China's communist party–state proven more durable than that of the Soviet Union and nearly all other similar regimes? By what combination of reform and repression has the CCP held on to power? What signs are there that it is likely to hold power for the foreseeable future? What signs suggest that communist rule in China may be weakening? What kind of political system might emerge if the CCP were to lose or relinquish power?

China is also part of the developing world as measured by the average standard of living of its population, but its record of growth in the past several decades has far exceeded that of almost all other developing countries. Furthermore, the educational and health levels of the Chinese people are quite good for a country at its level of development. How has China achieved such relative success in its quest for economic development? By contrast, much of the developing world has become more democratic in recent decades. How and why has China resisted this wave of democratization? What does the experience of other developing countries say about how economic modernization might influence the prospects for democracy in China?

Where Do You Stand?

The Chinese Communist Party says that Mao's achievements far outweighed his shortcomings. What do you think?

Is a government ever justified in using massive force against unarmed demonstrators who are occupying a huge public space in the national capital, as happened in Tiananmen Square on June 4, 1989?

POLITICAL ECONOMY AND DEVELOPMENT

SECTION 2

State and Economy

When the Chinese Communist Party came to power in 1949, China's economy was suffering from more than a hundred years of rebellion, invasion, civil war, and bad government. The country's new communist rulers almost immediately seized most property from wealthy landowners, rich industrialists, and foreign companies. They then set up a centrally planned economy based on the Soviet model. The state owned or controlled most economic resources. Government planning and commands, not market forces, drove economic activity, including setting prices for almost all goods.

China's planned economy yielded impressive results in terms of increased production. But it also created huge bureaucracies and new kinds of inequalities, especially between the heavily favored industrial cities and the investment-starved rural areas. Both the Great Leap Forward (1958–1961) and the Cultural Revolution (1966–1976)

Focus Questions ▽

- What have been the major changes in China's approach to governing the economy since the Maoist era?

- What have been the major social consequences of China's rapid economic growth over the last three decades?

embodied the unique and radical Maoist approach to economic development that was intended to be less bureaucratic and more egalitarian than the Soviet model.

Under Mao, the PRC built a strong industrial base. The people of China became much healthier and better educated. But the Maoist economy was plagued by political interference, poor management, and ill-conceived projects. This led to wasted resources of truly staggering proportions. Overall, China's economic growth rates, especially in agriculture, barely kept pace with population increases. The average standard of living changed little between the mid-1950s and Mao's death in 1976.

China Goes to Market

In a 1962 speech about how to recover from the Great Leap Forward famine, Deng Xiaoping had remarked, "It doesn't matter whether a cat is white or black, as long as it catches mice."[3] He meant that the CCP should not be overly concerned about whether a particular policy was socialist or capitalist if it helped the economy. Such sentiments got Deng in trouble with Mao. They made Deng one of the principal targets of the Cultural Revolution.

Once he emerged as China's foremost leader in the aftermath of Mao's death in 1976, Deng let the cat loose. He launched what is referred to as the "Reform and Opening Up" policy to transform the Chinese economy. "Reform" meant letting market forces play a greater role, while reducing government control, whereas "Opening Up" meant dramatically increasing China's engagement with the global economy. Authority for making economic decisions passed from bureaucrats to families, factory managers, and even the owners of private businesses. Individuals were encouraged to work harder and more efficiently to make money rather than to "serve the people" as had been the slogan during the Maoist era.

In most sectors of China's economy today, the state no longer dictates what to produce and how to produce it. Almost all prices are now set according to supply and demand, as in a capitalist economy, rather than by administrative decree. Most government monopolies have given way to fierce competition between state-owned and non-state-owned firms. But there are still many thousands of **state-owned enterprises (SOEs)** with tens of millions of employees in China. Although vastly outnumbered by private business that employ many more workers and account for about 60 percent of China's Gross Domestic Product (GDP), SOEs still dominate critical sectors of the economy such as steel, petroleum, telecommunications, and transportation.

state-owned enterprises (SOEs)

Companies in which a majority of ownership control is held by the government.

But even SOEs must now respond to market forces. Some have become very profitable, modern enterprises. But many others are overstaffed economic dinosaurs with outdated facilities and machinery. The state-owned sector remains a severe drain on the country's banks (largely government-controlled), which are still sometimes required to bail out financially failing SOEs. These large loans are rarely, if ever, paid back. Many economists think that even more drastic SOE reform is needed. But the country's leaders have been unwilling to relinquish control of these important industries. They also fear the political and social turmoil that could boil up from a massive layoff of industrial workers.

The results of the PRC's move from a planned toward a market economy have been phenomenal (see Figure 15.2). China has been one of the fastest-growing economies in the world for more than twenty years. Gross Domestic Product (GDP) grew at an average rate of 10.3 percent per year from 1992 to 2012. During the same period, India's GDP growth averaged 6.7 percent, Brazil's was 3.1 percent, and the United States 2.6 percent. Although growth has slowed (to 7.7 percent in 2013), China weathered the global recession of 2008–2009 far better than any other major economy largely because of a huge government stimulus package.

Nevertheless, China's GDP per capita (a measure of the average standard of living) is still very low when compared to that of more developed countries. In 2013, GDP per capita in the United States was $52,800. In the PRC, it was $9,900; but in 1980, it was only $250, which again reflects how spectacular China's economic growth has been in recent decades.

Rising incomes have also led to a consumer revolution in China. In the late 1970s, people in the cities could only shop for most consumer goods at state-run stores. These carried a very limited range of often shoddy products. Today, China's urban areas are shopping paradises. There are privately owned stores of all sizes, gigantic malls, fast-food outlets, and a great variety of entertainment options. A few decades ago, hardly anyone owned a television. Now most households have a color TV. Cell phones are everywhere. In the cities, a new middle class is starting to buy houses, condominiums, and cars. China is even developing a class of "super-rich" millionaires and billionaires.

Despite these changes, economic planning has by no means disappeared. Officially, the PRC says it has a **socialist market economy**. While allowing a considerable degree of capitalism, national and local bureaucrats continue to exercise a great deal of control over the production and distribution of goods, resources, and services. Market reforms have gained substantial momentum that would be nearly impossible to reverse. But the CCP still ultimately determines the direction of China's economy.

Remaking the Chinese Countryside

One of the first revolutionary programs launched by the Chinese Communist Party when it came to power in 1949 was land reform that confiscated the property of landlords and redistributed it as private holdings to the poorer peasants. But in the mid- to late 1950s the state reorganized peasants into collective farms and communes in which the village, not individuals, owned the land, and local officials directed all production and labor. Individuals were paid according to how much they worked on the collective land. Most crops and other farm products had to be sold to the state at low fixed prices. Collectivized agriculture was one of the weakest links in China's command economy because it was very inefficient in the way

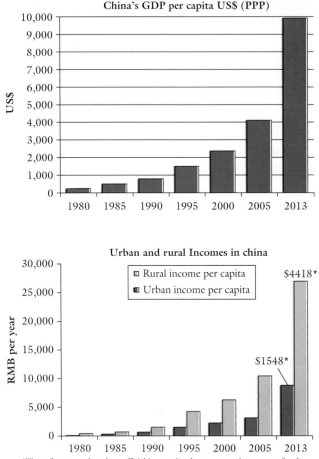

*These figures are based on official international currency exchange rates for the US$ and the Chinese RMB. If purchasing power parity (PPP) figures were available, the US$ amount would be about three times higher.

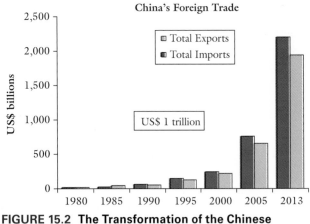

FIGURE 15.2 The Transformation of the Chinese Economy since 1980

Source: China Statistical Yearbooks; CIA World Factbook; World Bank World Development Indicators.

socialist market economy

The term used by the government of China to refer to the country's current economic system that mixes elements of both socialism and capitalism.

household responsibility system

The system put into practice in China beginning in the early 1980s in which the major decisions about agricultural production are made by individual farm families based on the profit motive rather than by a commune or the government.

iron rice bowl

A feature of China's socialist economy during the Maoist era (1949–1976) that provided guarantees of lifetime employment, income, and basic cradle-to-grave benefits to most urban and rural workers.

floating population

Migrants from the rural areas who have moved to the cities to find employment.

it used resources, including labor, and undermined incentives for farmers to work hard to benefit themselves and their families. Per capita agricultural production and rural living standards were stagnant from 1957 to 1977.

After Mao's death in 1976, some commune leaders experimented with giving farmers more freedom to plant what they wanted, consume or sell what they produced, and engage in other economic activities, such as raising poultry, in order to increase their incomes. China's leaders not only allowed these experiments, but embraced them as national policy to be implemented throughout the country. Collective farming was abolished. It was replaced by the **household responsibility system**, which remains in effect today. Under this system, the village still owns the farmland. But it is contracted out by the local government to individual families, which take full charge of the production and marketing of crops. Largely because farmers are now free to earn income for themselves, agricultural productivity has sharply increased. There are still many very poor people in the Chinese countryside, but hundreds of millions have risen out of extreme poverty in the last two and a half decades because of expanded economic opportunities.

Economic life in the rural China has also been transformed by the expansion of rural industry and commerce. Rural factories and businesses range in size from a handful of employees to thousands. They employ more than 160 million people and have played a critical role in absorbing the vast pool of labor that is no longer needed in agriculture.

Society and Economy

Economic reform has made Chinese society much more diverse and open. People are vastly freer to choose jobs, travel about the country and internationally, practice their religious beliefs, join non-political associations, and engage in a wide range of other activities that were prohibited or severely restricted during the Maoist era. But economic change has also caused serious social problems.

Economic reform has created significant changes in China's basic system of social welfare. The Maoist economy provided almost all workers with what was called the **iron rice bowl**. As in other communist party–state economies, such as the Soviet Union, the government guaranteed employment and basic cradle-to-grave benefits to most of the urban and rural labor force. The workplace was more than just a place to work and earn a living. It also provided housing, health care, day care, and other services.

China's economic reformers believed that guarantees like these led to poor work motivation and excessive costs. They implemented policies designed to break the iron rice bowl. Income and employment are no longer guaranteed. They are now directly tied to individual effort.

An estimated 60 million workers have been laid off from state-owned enterprises since the early 1990s. Many are too old or too unskilled to find good jobs in the modernizing economy. They are now the core of a very large stratum of urban poor that has become a fixture in even China's most glittering cities. The PRC has very little unemployment insurance or social security for its displaced workers.

Economic changes have opened China's cities to a flood of rural migrants. After agriculture was decollectivized in the early 1980s, many peasants, no longer held back by the strict limits on internal population movement enforced in the Mao era, headed to the urban areas to look for jobs. This so-called **floating population** of about 240 million people is the biggest human migration in history. In Shanghai more than one-third of the population of 23.5 million is made up of migrants. Migrant workers are mostly employed in low-paying jobs and live in substandard housing, but fill an

The futuristic skyline of Shanghai's Pudong district reflect the spectacular modernization of China's most prosperous areas in recent decades.

© Cuiphoto/Shutterstock.com

important niche in China's changing labor market, particularly in boom areas like export industries and construction.

The benefits of economic growth have reached most of China. But the market reforms and economic boom have created sharp class differences, and inequalities between people and parts of the country have risen significantly. A huge gap separates the average incomes of urban residents from those in the countryside (see Figure 15.2). The gap is also widening between the prosperous coastal regions and most inland areas. In the Maoist era, China was one of the world's most egalitarian countries; today it ranks with Brazil and South Africa as among the most unequal. Surveys show that most Chinese don't resent such inequality as long as their lives are improving and they believe their children's lives will be even better.[4] But if economic growth slows significantly and people find their rising expectations dashed, glaring socioeconomic inequalities could become a source of discontent and instability.

Some steps have been taken to improve the lot of the less well-off. In 2006, the government abolished taxes on agriculture, which had been in effect in some form in China for 2,600 years. By 2012, health insurance had been expanded to cover more than 90 percent of the population. But for most people the coverage is pretty minimal, and out-of-pocket expenses can be financially ruinous or deter the sick from seeking care.

China's economic boom and mixed state-private economy have also created enormous opportunities for corruption. Officials still control numerous resources and retain power over many economic transactions from which large profits can be made. The CCP has repeatedly launched well-publicized campaigns against official graft, with harsh punishment, even execution, for serious offenders. But corruption remains one of the biggest sources of public criticism of the government and seriously undermines the political legitimacy of the Communist Party.

The social status, legal rights, employment opportunities, and education of women in China have improved enormously since the founding of the PRC in1949. Women have also benefited from rising living standards and economic modernization in the post-Mao era. But the trend toward a market economy has not benefited men and women equally. Although China has one of the world's highest rates of female participation in the labor force (70 percent), "[w]omen's incomes are falling relative to men's; traditional attitudes are relegating women to the home; and women's net wealth may be shrinking." Women's annual income is 67.3 percent of men's in urban areas; in the rural areas it is just 56 percent.[5]

In the early 1980s, China implemented a policy that limited couples to having just one child. The government claimed that this was necessary for the country's economic development. The population growth rate was, indeed, sharply reduced but the means used to achieve this goal were sometimes coercive, including forced abortions and sterilization. The strong preference for sons in Chinese culture also led to female infanticide and the abandonment of girl babies. In recent years, the availability of inexpensive ultrasound screenings has given rise to widespread gender specific abortions. The policy has been relaxed to allow some couples to have a second child, but the fact is that the state still claims the right to determine individual reproductive decisions.

Environmental Issues

One of the biggest downsides of China's spectacular economic growth has been the serious damage caused to the environment. Industrial expansion has been fuelled primarily by highly polluting coal. The air in China's cities is among the dirtiest in the world. The tops of ultra-modern skyscrapers are frequently obscured by dense smog. The pollution is so bad in Beijing that breathing the air is equivalent to smoking two packs of cigarettes per day. Many residents wear industrial-strength facemasks as they go about their daily business. Pollution has been linked to lower life expectancy in northern China. Private automobile use is just starting to take off and is expanding rapidly, which will greatly add to urban pollution in addition to further snarling already horrendous traffic. China has surpassed the United States as the world's largest source of carbon dioxide (CO_2) emissions, although per capita emissions remain much lower than in most developed countries. Pollution from China, much of it from export-producing industries, carries across the Pacific Ocean and contaminates air quality in the Western United States.

Soil erosion, wetland destruction, deforestation, and desertification (the loss of arable land to deserts) from unsustainable farming practices are at crisis levels. Roughly 70 percent of China's rivers and lakes are badly polluted. The government does little to regulate the dumping of garbage and toxic wastes. Nearly a quarter of the population (300 million people) does not have access to safe drinking water.

Northern China also faces a severe water shortage due to decreased rainfall, industrial expansion, and urbanization. To remedy this situation, the PRC has undertaken a multi-decade project to divert water from the Yangtze River in central China to the Yellow and two other rivers in the north. At a current estimated cost of over $60 billion, it is one of most expensive engineering projects in history. It has also raised concerns among environmentalists that the diverted water will be so polluted by factories along its route that it will be unfit for use.

The water diversion project is an example of what one scholar has called PRC's preference for an "engineering fix" to its energy needs and environmental problems.[6] So, too, is the Three Gorges dam on the Yangtze River, the world's largest and most costly ($28 billion) hydroelectric dam. The dam generates electric power equivalent to fifteen nuclear reactors and has also greatly expanding commercial shipping navigation of the river deep into China's southwest region. But the project resulted in significant ecological damage and over 1.5 million people had to be relocated.

The PRC is critical of rich countries that press it (and other developing countries) to slow down economic growth or invest in expensive pollution controls when those countries paid little heed to the environmental damage caused by their own industrial revolutions. Nevertheless, the Chinese government realizes that environmental degradation is so severe that it could threaten its modernization drive and has been paying more attention to environmental protection. China has also become a leader in the development of alternative clean energy, including wind and solar power.

China in the Global Economy

At the end of the Maoist era in 1976, the PRC was not deeply involved in the global economy. Total foreign trade was less 10 percent of GDP. Foreign direct investment (FDI) in China was minuscule. Mao's policy of "self-reliance" was intended to make sure that the PRC was not economically dependent on any foreign country. Furthermore, the stagnant economy, political instability, and heavy-handed bureaucracy were not attractive to potential investors from abroad.

In the early 1980s, as part of its "Reform and Opening Up," China embarked on a strategy of using trade to promote economic development. This followed the model of export-led growth pioneered by Japan, South Korea, and Taiwan, which takes advantage of low-wage labor to produce goods that are in demand internationally. It then uses the export earnings to modernize the economy.

The PRC is now the world leader in exports, ahead of the United States, Germany, and Japan, and is after the United States, the second largest importer of goods and services. Foreign trade accounted for 60 percent of the PRC's GDP in 2005–2012, with a relatively equal balance between imports and exports. As Table 15.2 shows, China is much more economically dependent on trade than is the United States or Japan; but, in comparison with other major economies, it is less or comparably dependent.

China is often referred to as the "factory to the world," because so many countries import large quantities of products

Table 15.2	Trade Dependency (2005–2012 Average)		
	Imports (% of GDP)	Exports (% of GDP)	Total Trade (% of GDP)
Germany	44.1	46.8	90.9
South Africa	31.3	29.6	60.9
Britain	31.4	29.2	60.6
China	27.3	32.7	60.0
Russia	21.5	30.9	52.4
India	26.5	21.8	48.3
Japan	15.1	15.5	30.6
United States	16.1	11.9	28.0
Brazil	12.2	12.9	25.1

Source: World Bank World Development Indicators.

made in the PRC. What makes these products competitive is the low cost of production, particularly wages. In 2009, according the U.S. Bureau of Labor Statistics, the average factory job in China paid $1.34 per hour compared with $32.00 per hour in the United States.

But wages are rising in China because of a labor shortage due largely to the one-child policy. It is facing increasing competition for overseas investment from Vietnam, Bangladesh, and other developing countries with lower labor costs. Long-term growth will depend on a combination of exporting more sophisticated, less labor-intensive products and focusing the production of goods and services more on the domestic market.

Where Do You Stand?

There are those who say that China's economy under Mao Zedong was better in some ways than that under Deng Xiaoping and his successors. In what ways might this be true?

Do you see the rise of China as a threat to American interests or as an opportunity for cooperation in areas of mutual interest?

THE U.S. CONNECTION

U.S.–China Relations

Shortly after the founding of the People's Republic, the United States and China fought each other in the Korean War (1950–1953). From then until the early 1970s, the two countries had very little contact because of the Cold War.

In 1972, Richard Nixon became the first U.S. president ever to visit China. Formal diplomatic relations between Washington and Beijing were established in 1979. Since then ties have deepened, despite some disruptions, such as following the Tiananmen massacre in 1989, and recurring tensions over trade, human rights, and other issues. Many believe that U.S.–China relations are the most important bilateral diplomatic relationship in the world.

China now trades with the United States more than with any other country, while China is America's second-largest trading partner (after Canada). Many in the United States think that cheap Chinese imports means lost jobs for Americans and that American firms can't compete with Chinese companies because labor costs in China are so much lower. They also say that the PRC engages in unfair trade practices, exploits sweatshop labor, and suppresses independent union activity. Some see the fact that China owns $1.2 trillion of U.S. government debt (which it bought with part of the vast reserves of U.S. dollars earned from exports) as having made the United States dangerously dependent on the PRC. Critics of Sino-American economic relations want the U.S. government to put more restrictions on trade and financial dealings with China.

On the other side, many say that the benefits of U.S. trade with China far outweigh the negative impacts. First of all, consumers benefit greatly by the availability of a large variety of less-expensive products. In fact, although most of the things sold by companies like Walmart and Target are made in China, overall, only 2.7 percent of consumer spending in 2010 by Americans was on goods and services from China; 88.5 percent were from the United States. Furthermore, some argue that the United States should focus on developing more high-tech businesses to create jobs rather than trying to compete with China and other countries in "old-fashioned" labor-intensive industries. They also point out that many American firms have huge investments in China, which will grow—as will demand for American products—as that country becomes more prosperous. U.S. government debt is the result of American overspending, and several other countries besides the PRC own large chunks of it, including Japan and Britain. Finally, those who oppose restrictions on Sino-American economic engagement see it as one important way to promote not only the free market in China but also a more open society and democracy.

MAKING CONNECTIONS Why and how have U.S.–China relations improved since the end of the Cold War?

GOVERNANCE AND POLICY-MAKING

Organization of the State

In the early 1980s, about two dozen countries in Africa, Asia, Europe, and Latin America, with more than one-third of the world's population, were ruled by communist parties. Today, China, Cuba, Vietnam, North Korea, and Laos are the only remaining communist party–states. The political systems of these countries are characterized by the existence of an official state ideology based on Marxism-Leninism, communist party domination of all government and social institutions, and the suppression of all opposition parties and movements. Ruling communist parties claim that only they can govern in the best interests of the entire nation and therefore have the right to exercise the "leading role" throughout society.

Communist ideology is much less important in China today than it was during the Mao era when there was a great emphasis on enforcing ideological correctness. But even though the PRC has moved sharply toward a market economy in recent decades, the CCP still asserts that it is building socialism with the ultimate objective of creating an egalitarian and classless communist society. Ideology also sets the boundaries for what is permissible in politics since the party does not allow open opposition to its doctrines.

The preamble of the PRC's constitution states that the country is under "the leadership of the Communist Party of China." Article 1 defines the PRC as "a socialist state under the people's democratic dictatorship." It also declares that "disruption of the socialist system by any organization or individual is prohibited." Such provisions imply that the Chinese "people" (implicitly, supporters of socialism and the leadership of the Communist Party) enjoy democratic rights and privileges under CCP guidance. But the constitution also gives the CCP authority to exercise dictatorship over any person or organization that, it believes, opposes socialism and the party.

The Executive

The government of the People's Republic of China (the "state") is organizationally and functionally distinct from the Chinese Communist Party. Each has an executive branch, although the Communist Party exercises direct or indirect control over all government organizations and personnel. The government of the PRC acts as the administrative agency for enacting, implementing, and enforcing policies made by the party. In order to fully understand governance and policy-making in China, it is necessary to look at the structure of both the Chinese Communist Party and the government of the People's Republic of China and the relationship between the two.

CCP Organization

According to the CCP constitution (a wholly different document from the constitution of the PRC), the "highest leading bodies" of the party are the **National Party Congress** and the **Central Committee** (see Figure 15.3). But neither is as powerful as the much smaller CCP executive organizations.

National Party Congress

The symbolically important meeting, held every five years for about one week, of about 2,100 delegates representatives of the Chinese Communist Party, who endorse policies and the allocation of leadership positions that have been determined beforehand by the party's much smaller ruling bodies.

Central Committee

The top 370 or so leaders of the Chinese Communist Party. It meets annually for about two weeks and is charged with carrying on the business of the National Party Congress when it is not in session.

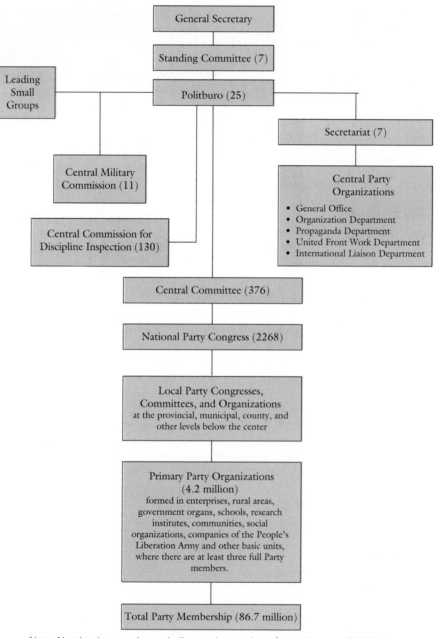

Note: Number in parentheses indicates the number of members as of 2013-14.

FIGURE 15.3 Organization of the Chinese Communist Party

The National Party Congress meets for only one week every five years, and it has more than 2,200 delegates. This reflects the fact that the role of the Congress is more symbolic than substantive. The essential function of the National Party Congress is to approve decisions already made by the top leaders and to provide a showcase for the party's current policies. There is little debate and no seriously contested voting of any consequence.

The Central Committee (with 376 full and alternate members) consists of CCP leaders from around the country who meet annually for about a week in the late fall. Members are elected for a five-year term by the National Party Congress by secret ballot, with a very limited choice of candidates. The overall composition of the Central Committee is closely controlled by the top leaders to ensure compliance with their policies.

In principle, the Central Committee directs party affairs when the National Party Congress is not in session. But its size and short, infrequent meetings (called plenums) greatly limit its effectiveness. However, the plenums do represent significant gatherings of the party elite and can be an important forum for discussion. The announcements following the meetings are a way of telling the public of important policy changes, such as the relaxation in the one-child policy announced in November 2013 that will allow more couples to have a second child.

The most powerful political organizations in China's communist party–state are two small executive bodies at the very top of the CCP's structure: the **Politburo** (or Political Bureau), and its even more exclusive **Standing Committee**. These bodies are formally "elected" for five-year terms by the Central Committee from among its own members under carefully controlled conditions and with no choice among candidates. The slate of candidates is determined through a secretive process of negotiation and bargaining within the party elite. The first that most Chinese citizens know of the full composition of the Politburo and the Standing Committee is when they are presented on stage in rank order at the conclusion of the National Party Congress every five years. The current Politburo has twenty-five members, seven of whom also sit on the Standing Committee, the apex of power in the CCP.

Before 1982, the leading position in the party was the chairman of the Politburo's Standing Committee, which was occupied by Mao Zedong (hence *Chairman* Mao) for more than three decades until his death in 1976. The title of chairman was abolished in 1982 to symbolize a break with Mao's highly personal and often arbitrary style of rule. Since then, the party's leader has been the **general secretary**, who presides over the Politburo and the Standing Committee. Xi Jinping was elected to his first term as general secretary in 2012.

The Politburo and Standing Committee are not accountable to the Central Committee or any other institution in any meaningful sense. Although there is now somewhat more openness about the timing of and subjects covered in their meetings, the operations of the party's executive organizations are generally shrouded in secrecy. Top leaders work and often live in a huge walled compound called Zhongnanhai ("Middle and Southern Seas") on lakes in the center of Beijing adjacent to Tiananmen Square. Zhongnanhai is not only heavily guarded, as any government executive headquarters would be, but it also has no identifying signs on its exterior other than some party slogans, nor is it identified on public maps.

Two other executive organizations of the party deserve brief mention. The Secretariat manages the day-to-day work of the Politburo and Standing Committee and coordinates the party's complex and far-flung structure with considerable authority in organizational and personnel matters. The Central Commission for Discipline Inspection (CCDI) is in charge of investigating corruption within the party and other violations of party rules. Its investigations and hearings are conducted behind closed doors. If someone is found guilty, they may be demoted or even expelled from the party and, in some cases, turned over to the state judicial system for trial and, if appropriate, for punishment.

The Communist Party has an organized presence throughout Chinese society. CCP organizations in provinces, cities, and counties are headed by a party committee. There are also about 4.2 million primary party organizations, usually

Politburo

The committee made up of the top twenty-five leaders of the Chinese Communist Party.

Standing Committee

A subgroup of the Politburo, currently with seven members. The most powerful political organization in China.

general secretary

The formal title of the head of the Chinese Communist Party. From 1942 to 1982, the position was called "chairman" and was held by Mao Zedong until his death in 1976.

called branches. These are found, for example, in workplaces, government offices, schools, urban neighborhoods, rural towns, villages, and army units. Local and primary organizations extend the CCP's reach throughout Chinese society. They are also designed to ensure coordination within the vast and complex party structure and subordination to the central party authorities in Beijing.

Under Mao and Deng, power within the CCP was highly concentrated in one individual. No important policy decision was made without their consent. No Chinese leader since has had the personal authority or charisma of Mao or Deng. They have governed as a "first among equals" within a collective leadership that includes their fellow members on the Standing Committee and Politburo.

Party politics at the top has also become more institutionalized. Not only are the leaders limited to two five-year terms, they are also ineligible to be reelected if they will reach age 68 while in office. Term and age limits add considerable predictability to the leadership succession.

The route to the very top has also become more predictable. In 2007, when Xi Jinping was not only elevated to the Standing Committee, but was also given other positions, including vice president of the PRC and head of the school for training party leaders, it was clear that he had been anointed to become general secretary in 2012 and would be reelected in 2017. His predecessor, Hu Jintao, followed the same political trajectory.

In the Mao and Deng eras, few CCP leaders had an education beyond high school. Today, twenty of the twenty-five members of the Politburo (and six of the seven who sit on the Standing Committee) have a university-level degree. Two members of the Standing Committee have a BA in engineering, including Xi Jinping; others studied law, history, economics, and statistics. Almost all of China's leaders have also gained decades of experience working in party and government posts outside the capital. In fact, the only route to the top of the CCP is through the provinces. Prior to being elevated to the central leadership, Xi Jinping held key positions in four different provinces and Shanghai, where he served as both mayor and party secretary.

PRC Organization

National People's Congress (NPC)

The legislature of the People's Republic of China. It is under the control of the Chinese Communist Party and is not an independent branch of government.

State authority in China is formally vested in a system of people's congresses that begins at the top with the **National People's Congress (NPC)**, which is a completely separate organization from the National Party Congress. The NPC is China's national legislature and is discussed in more detail in Section 4.

The National People's Congress formally elects the president and vice president of China. But there is only one candidate, chosen by the top leadership of the Communist Party, for each office. The president's term is concurrent with that of the congress (five years). There is a two-term limit. As China's head of state, the president meets and negotiates with other world leaders. But the office of president is largely ceremonial and has little executive power.

The president of the PRC has always been a high-ranking CCP leader. Since the early 1990s, the general secretary of the Communist Party has served concurrently as the country's president. Thus, Xi Jinping is both General Secretary Xi and President Xi, though the source of his power clearly lies in the former position.

The premier (prime minister) of the People's Republic has authority over the government bureaucracy and policy implementation. The premier is formally appointed by the president with the approval of the National People's Congress. But in reality, the Communist Party leadership decides which of its members will serve as premier.

The premier directs the **State Council**, which is something like the cabinet in a presidential or parliamentary system. In addition to the premier, the State Council includes several vice premiers, the heads of government ministries and commissions, and a few other senior officials. Most State Council members run functionally specific departments, such as the Ministry of Foreign Affairs and the National Health and Family Planning Commission.

State Council

The highest organization in the state administration, directed by the premier. It also includes several vice premiers, the heads of government ministries and commissions, and a few other senior officials.

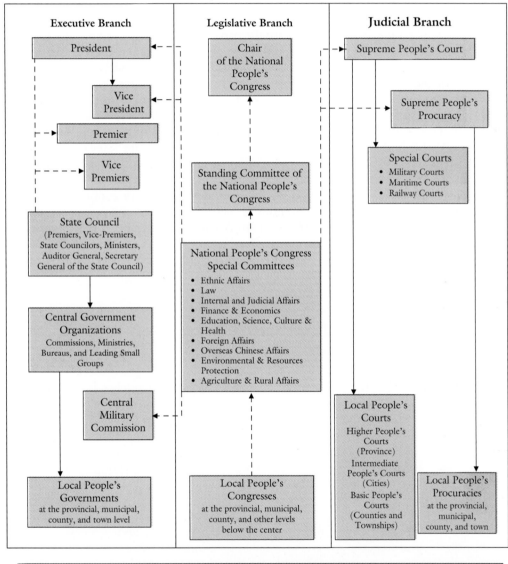

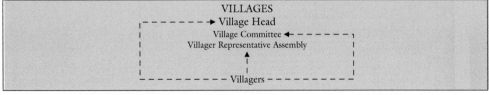

FIGURE 15.4 Organization of the People's Republic of China

cadre

A person who exercises a position of authority in a communist party–state; cadres may or may not be Communist Party members.

China's party–state is immense in size and in the scope of its reach throughout the country. The total number of cadres—people in positions of authority paid by the government or party—in the PRC is around 40 million. The term **cadre** applies to both the most powerful leaders as well as to local-level bureaucrats. Not all cadres are party members, and not all party members are cadres. The vast majority of cadres work below the national level, and a minority work directly for the government or the CCP. The remainder occupies key posts in economic enterprises, schools, and scientific, cultural, and other institutions.

The CCP uses a weblike system of organizational controls to make sure that the government complies with the party's will in policy implementation. In the first place, almost all key government officials are also party members. Furthermore, the CCP exercises control over the policy process through party organizations that parallel government agencies at all levels of the system. For example, each provincial government works under the watchful eye of a provincial party committee. In addition, the Communist Party maintains an effective presence inside every government organization through a "leading party group" that is made up of key officials who are also CCP members.

nomenklatura

A system of personnel selection under which the Communist Party maintains control over the appointment of important officials in all spheres of social, economic, and political life.

The CCP also influences the policy process by means of the "cadre list," or as it was known in the Soviet Union where the practice was developed, the *nomenklatura* system. The cadre list covers millions of important positions in the government and elsewhere (including institutions such as universities, banks, trade unions, and newspapers). Any personnel decision involving an appointment, promotion, transfer, or dismissal that affects a position on this list must be approved by a party organization department, whether or not the person involved is a party member. The *nomenklatura* system is one of the major instruments by which the CCP tries to "ensure that leading institutions throughout the country will exercise only the autonomy granted to them by the party."[7]

Other State Institutions

The Judiciary

China has a four-tiered system of "people's courts" that reaches from a Supreme People's Court down through higher (provincial-level), intermediate (city-level), and grassroots (county- and township-level) people's courts. The Supreme People's Court supervises the work of lower courts and the application of the country's laws, but it does not exercise judicial review over state policies and therefore is not a truly independent branch of government. It also does not interpret the country's constitution as it applies to laws or legislation.

At the end of the Maoist era, there were only 3,000 (poorly trained) lawyers in China; now there are more than 200,000 (compared to more than a million lawyers in the United States), with an increasingly high level of professionalism. Chinese courts can provide a real avenue of redress to the public for a wide range of nonpolitical grievances, including loss of property, consumer fraud, and even unjust detention by the police. Citizen mediation committees based in urban neighborhoods and rural villages play an important role in the judicial process by settling a majority of civil cases out of court.

China's criminal justice system is swift and harsh. Great faith is placed in the ability of an official investigation to find the facts of a case. The outcome of cases that actually do come to trial is pretty much predetermined. The conviction rate is 98–99 percent for all criminal cases. Prison terms are long and subject to only cursory appeal. A variety of offenses in addition to murder—including, in some cases, rape and especially major cases of embezzlement and other "economic crimes"—are subject to capital punishment. The number of annual executions is considered a state secret in China, but it is certainly in the thousands, and the PRC executes more people each year than the rest of the world combined.

Although the PRC constitution guarantees judicial independence, China's courts and other legal bodies remain under Communist Party control. The appointment of all judicial personnel is subject to party approval. At all levels of the system, party political and legal committees keep a close watch on the courts. Lawyers who displease officials are often harassed in various ways, their licenses to practice law might not be renewed, and they themselves are sometimes arrested.

China has become a country where there is rule *by* law, which means that the party–state uses the law to carry out its policies and enforce its rule. But it is still far from having established the rule *of* law, in which everyone and every organization, including the Communist Party, is accountable and subject to the law.

Subnational Government

China (like France and Japan) is a unitary state in which the national government exercises a high degree of control over other levels of government. It is not a federal system (like the United States and India) that gives subnational governments considerable policy-making and financial autonomy.

Under the central government, the PRC has twenty-two provinces, four very large centrally administered cities (Beijing, Shanghai, Tianjin, and Chongqing), five **autonomous regions**, which are areas of the country with large minority populations (such as Tibet).

Each level of subnational government has a people's congress that meets infrequently and plays a limited, but increasingly active, role in supervising affairs in its area. In theory, these congresses (the legislative branch) are empowered to supervise the work of the "people's governments" (the executive branch) at the various levels of the system. But in reality, subnational government executives (such as provincial governors and city mayors) are more accountable to Communist Party authority than to the people's congresses.

Despite considerable economic decentralization, the central government retains the power to intervene in local affairs when and where it wants. This power of the central authorities derives not only from their ability to set binding national priorities, but also from their control over the military and the police, the tax system, critical energy resources, and construction of major infrastructure projects.

Under the formal layers of state administration are China's 640,000 or so rural villages, which are home to a little less than half of the country's population. These villages, with an average population of 1,000, are technically self-governing and are not formally responsible to a higher level of state authority. In recent years, village leaders have been directly and competitively elected by local residents, and village representative assemblies have become more vocal. However, the most powerful organization in the village is the Communist Party committee, and the single most powerful person is the local Communist Party leader (the party secretary).

The Military, Police, and Internal Security

China's **People's Liberation Army (PLA)**, which encompasses all of the country's ground, air, and naval armed services, is, according to the PRC Ministry of Defense, "a people's army created and led by the Communist Party of China."

autonomous region

A territorial unit that is equivalent to a province and contains a large concentration of ethnic minorities. These regions, for example, Tibet, have some autonomy in the cultural sphere but in most policy matters are strictly subordinate to the central government.

People's Liberation Army (PLA)

The combined armed forces of the People's Republic of China, which includes land, sea, air, and strategic missile forces.

The PLA is the world's largest military force, with about 2.3 million active personnel (down from nearly 4 million in 1989). On a per capita basis, the PRC has 1.7 active military personnel per 1,000 of its population, compared with the U.S. ratio of 4.5 per 1,000. The PLA also has a formal reserve force of about 500,000. A people's militia of 8 million minimally trained civilians can be mobilized and armed by local governments in the event of war or other national emergency.

The key organization in charge of the Chinese armed forces is the **Central Military Commission (CMC)**. There are currently eleven members of the CMC, ten of whom are military officers. The one civilian is CCP general secretary and PRC president, Xi Jinping, who chairs the committee. The chair of the CMC is, in effect, the commander-in-chief of China's armed forces and has always been the most powerful leader of the communist party.

China's internal security apparatus consists of several different organizations. The 600,000 strong People's Armed Police (PAP) guards public officials and buildings and carries out some border patrol and counterterrorism functions. It has also been called in to quell public disturbances, including worker, peasant, and ethnic unrest. The Ministry of State Security, with a force of about 1.7 million, is responsible for combating espionage and gathering intelligence at home and abroad.

The Ministry of Public Security is the main policing organization in the PRC and is responsible for the prevention and investigation of crimes and for surveillance of Chinese citizens and foreigners in China suspected of being a threat to the state. Local public security bureaus, which carry out day-to-day police work, are under the command of the central ministry in Beijing.

Central Military Commission (CMC)

The most important military organization in the People's Republic of China, headed by the general secretary of the Chinese Communist Party, who is the commander-in-chief of the People's Liberation Army.

The Policy-Making Process

At the height of Mao Zedong's power from the 1950s through much of the 1970s, many scholars described policy-making in China as a simple top-down "Mao-in-command" system. Since the late 1980s, terms such as "fragmented authoritarianism"[8] have been used to convey that although power is still highly concentrated in the top leadership organizations of the Chinese Communist Party, there are now many other sources of influence in the policy-making process. This model sees policy as evolving not only from commands from above, but also as a complex interplay of cooperation, conflict, and bargaining among political actors at various levels of the system. The focus on economic development has also led to the growing influence of nonparty experts, the media, and non-governmental organizations within the policy-making loop.

At the national level, flexible issue-specific task forces called "leading small groups" bring together top officials from various ministries, commissions, and committees in order to coordinate policy-making and implementation on matters that cross the jurisdiction of any single organization. Some groups, for example, the Central Leading Group on Foreign Affairs, are more or less permanent fixtures in the party–state structure, while others may be convened on an ad hoc basis to deal with short-term matters like a natural disaster or an epidemic. Since most of the members are high-ranking CCP officials, they are also a means to ensure party supervision of policy in that particular area.

China's parliament, the National People's Congress, formally passes legislation that gives policy the force of law. But it takes its cues from the Communist Party leadership and cannot be considered an independent actor in the policy-making process.

Because the PRC is a unitary system, subnational levels of government have little policy-making autonomy. The central authorities pass along policy guidelines through a network of party leadership teams to be found in every locality and important government offices, and those teams closely monitor compliance with party directives. Nevertheless, the decentralization of power that has accompanied economic reform has given local governments considerable clout in policy implementation.

The policy process in China is much more institutionalized and smoother as well as less personalized and volatile than it was in the Maoist era. But it is still highly secretive, and leaders of the People's Republic are not accountable to the people of China. The unchallengeable power of the Communist Party is still the most basic fact of political life in the People's Republic of China.

Where Do You Stand?

One of the characteristics of a communist party–state is its commitment to Marxism-Leninism as the official ideology. Does the United States have an ideology?

Because of the dominant role of a single political party, China's policy-making process certainly doesn't suffer from political paralysis. Do you think that's a good thing?

socialist democracy

The term used by the Chinese Communist Party to describe the political system of the People's Republic of China. The official view is that this type of system, under the leadership of the Communist Party, provides democracy for the overwhelming majority of people and suppresses (or exercises dictatorship over) only the enemies of the people.

REPRESENTATION AND PARTICIPATION

The Chinese Communist Party claims that it represents the interests of all the people of China and describes the People's Republic as a **socialist democracy**. In the CCP's view, this is superior to democracy in capitalist countries where wealthy individuals and corporations dominate politics and policy-making despite multiparty politics. China's *socialist* democracy is based on the unchallengeable role of the CCP as the country's only ruling party and should not be confused with the *social* democracy of Western European center-left political parties, which is rooted in a commitment to competitive politics.

Focus Questions

- What are the powers and limitations of China's National People's Congress as the legislative branch of government?

- What kinds of protests take place in China, and how does the party-state respond?

The Legislature

The Chinese constitution grants the National People's Congress (NPC) the power to enact and amend the country's laws, approve and monitor the state budget, and declare and end war. The NPC is also empowered to elect (and recall) the president and vice president, the chair of the state Central Military Commission, the head of China's Supreme Court, and the procurator-general (in charge of national-level investigation and prosecution of crime). The NPC has final approval over the selection of the premier and members of the State Council. On paper, China's legislature certainly looks to be the most powerful branch of government. In fact, these powers, which are not insignificant, are exercised only as allowed by the Communist Party.

The National People's Congress is a unicameral legislature with nearly 3,000 members (called "deputies") who meet only for about two weeks every March. When the NPC is not in session, its powers are exercised by a 175-member Standing Committee (not to be confused with the CCP Standing Committee), which convenes every other month. A council of about fifteen members conducts the day-to-day business of the NPC. The chair of the NPC is always a high-ranking Communist Party leader.

NPC deputies are elected for five-year terms. Except for those from the People's Liberation Army, they are chosen from lower-level people's congresses in China's provinces, autonomous regions, major municipalities, and a few other constituencies.

Deputies are not full-time legislators, but remain in their regular jobs and home areas except for the brief time when the congress is in session. A large majority of the deputies to the NPC are members of the CCP, but many belong to one of China's eight noncommunist (and powerless) political parties (see below) or have no party affiliation. Workers and farmers make up less than 15 percent of NPC deputies; the remainder are government and party cadres, military personnel, intellectuals, professionals, celebrities, and business people.

Despite great fanfare in the press as examples of socialist democracy in action, most legislation is passed and all state leaders are elected by the NPC by overwhelming majorities and with little substantive debate. The annual sessions are largely taken up by the presentation of very long reports by the premier and other state leaders. The NPC never deals with sensitive political issues. The CCP also monitors the election process to make sure that no outright dissidents are elected as deputies.

Nevertheless, some deputies have become a bit more assertive on issues like corruption and environmental problems. Minor government legislative initiatives have occasionally been defeated or tabled. Major bills may take years to draft and be amended as a result of committee hearings, consultation with experts, and discussion among deputies. The media is not allowed to cover the legislative process in any detail or to print editorial opinions on the issues.

Political Parties and the Party System

The Chinese Communist Party

With 86.7 million members at the end of 2013 million members, the Chinese Communist Party is by far the largest political party in the world. But its membership makes up a very small minority of the population (less than 10 percent of those over eighteen, the minimum age for joining the party). This is consistent with the CCP's view that it is a "vanguard" party that admits only those who are truly dedicated to the communist cause. Joining the Communist Party is a time-consuming process that can last as long as two years and involves a lengthy application, interviews, references, a background check, and a probation period.

The social composition of CCP membership has changed profoundly since the party came to power in 1949. In the mid-1950s, peasants made up nearly 70 percent of party members. Figure 15.5 shows the composition of the CCP as of late 2012. The party now claims that rather than representing just workers and peasants, it represents the interests of the overwhelming majority of people in China and is open to all those who are committed to promoting national development and are willing to accept party leadership in achieving that goal.

The CCP welcomes members from what it calls the "new social stratum" that has emerged in the process of market reform and globalization of the Chinese economy. The new social stratum includes private business owners ("entrepreneurs")

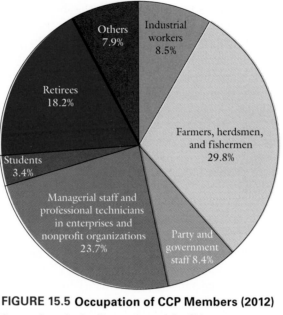

FIGURE 15.5 Occupation of CCP Members (2012)

Source: Organization Department of the Chinese Communist Party

and managerial-level staff in private or foreign-funded companies. This is a dramatic change from the Maoist era when any hint of capitalism was crushed.

Women make up only 23.8 percent of the CCP membership as a whole and just 4.9 percent of the full members of the Central Committee elected in 2012. The Politburo has two female members. No woman has ever served on the party's most powerful organization, the Politburo Standing Committee.

Between 1.5 and 3.0 million people join the CCP each year. Even though many Chinese believe that communist ideology is irrelevant to their lives and the nation's future, being a party member remains a prerequisite for advancement in many careers, particularly in government.

China's Non-Communist "Democratic Parties"

China is rightly called a one-party system because the country's politics are so thoroughly dominated by the Chinese Communist Party. But, in fact, China has eight political parties in addition to the CCP. These are officially referred to as China's "democratic parties," which is said to be another example of socialist democracy in the PRC. Each non-communist party represents a particular group in Chinese society, such as overseas Chinese who have returned to live in the country. But these parties, all of which were established before the founding of the PRC in 1949 and accept the "guidance" of the CCP, have a total membership of only a little over half a million. They provide advice to the CCP on nonpolitical matters and generate support within their particular constituencies for CCP policies. Individual members of these parties may assume important government positions. But politically, these parties are relatively insignificant and function as little more than "a loyal non-opposition."[9]

New political parties are not allowed to form. When a group of activists who had been part of the 1989 Tiananmen protests tried to establish a China Democracy Party in 1998 to promote multiparty politics, they were arrested or forced into exile abroad, and the party was banned.

Elections

Most elections in the PRC are mechanisms to give the communist party–state greater legitimacy by allowing large numbers of citizens to participate in the political process under very controlled circumstances. But elections, especially at the local level, are becoming somewhat more democratic and more important in providing a way for citizens to express their views and hold some local officials accountable.

Most elections in China are *indirect*. In other words, the members of an already elected or established body elect those who will serve at the next-highest level in the power structure. For example, the deputies of a provincial people's congress, not all the eligible citizens of the province, elect deputies to the National People's Congress. A comparable situation would exist in the United States if members of Congress were selected by and from state legislatures rather than by popular vote (as was the case with the Senate before the Seventeenth Amendment to the Constitution was enacted in 1907).

Direct elections in which all voters in the relevant area cast ballots for candidates for a particular position are most common in China's rural villages. Elections for village head and other leaders are generally multicandidate with a secret ballot. Villagers have used elections to remove leaders they think are incompetent or corrupt. The village CCP committee closely monitors such grassroots elections. In many cases, the local Communist Party leader has been chosen to serve simultaneously as the village head in a competitive election. This is often because the Communist Party leader is a well-respected person who has the confidence and support of the villagers. Some observers believe direct elections at the village-level could be the seeds of real democracy that will spread to higher levels of the political system. Others see them as a façade to appease international critics and give the rural population a way to express discontent without challenging the country's fundamental political organization. In any case, village elections have given residents some measure of meaningful input into local governance.

Many direct and indirect elections in China now have multiple candidates and open nominations, with the winner chosen by secret ballot. A significant number of independently nominated candidates have defeated official nominees, although even independent candidates also have to be approved by the CCP. And the most powerful positions in the government, such as city mayors and provincial governors, are appointed, not elected. Recent electoral reform has certainly increased popular representation and participation in China's government. But elections in the PRC still do not give citizens a means by which they can exercise effective control over those who have the most power to affect their lives. Top Chinese communist leaders, from Mao to now, have repeatedly claimed that multiparty democracy is unsuited to China's traditions and socialist principles.

Political Culture, Citizenship, and Identity

From Communism to Consumerism

Marxism-Leninism is still important in Chinese politics, since the Communist Party proclaims that it is China's official ideology. Serious challenges to that ideology are not permitted. The CCP also tries to keep communist ideology viable and visible by efforts to influence public opinion and values through its control of the media, the arts, and education. Political study is still a required but now relatively minor part of the curriculum at all levels of the school system, and more than 80 percent of China's students between the ages of 7 and 14 belong to the Young Pioneers, an organization designed to promote good social behavior, community service, patriotism, and loyalty to the party. The Communist Youth League, which serves to foster commitment to socialist values and generate support for party policies, has about 90 million members between the ages of 14 and 28.

Alternative sources of socialization and belief are growing in importance in China. These do not often take expressly political forms, however, because of the threat of repression. In the countryside, peasants have replaced portraits of Mao and other Communist heroes with statues of folk gods and ancestor worship tablets. The influence of extended kinship groups such as clans often outweighs the formal authority of the party in the villages. In the cities, popular culture, including gigantic rock concerts, shapes youth attitudes much more profoundly than party propaganda. Consumerism ("buying things") is probably the most widely shared value in China today. Many observers have spoken of a moral vacuum in Chinese society, which is not uncommon in countries undergoing such rapid, multifaceted change.

Freedom of religion is guaranteed by the PRC constitution (as is the freedom not to believe in any religion). Organized religion, which was ferociously suppressed during the Mao era, is attracting an increasing number of adherents. Buddhist temples, Christian churches, and other places of worship operate more freely than they have in decades. The government says there are 18 million Protestants and 6 million Catholics in China. But unofficial estimates of Christians put the figure at several times that and as high as 70–100 million.

Religious life, however, is strictly controlled and limited to officially approved organizations and venues. Clergy of any religion who defy the authority of the party–state are still imprisoned. The Chinese Catholic Church is prohibited from recognizing the authority of the pope and appoints its own bishops and cardinals.

Clandestine Christian communities, called house churches, have sprung up in many areas among people who reject the government's control of religious life and are unable to worship in public. Although local officials sometimes tolerate these churches, in numerous cases house church leaders and laypeople have been arrested and the private homes where services are held have been bulldozed.

China's media is much livelier and more open than during the Maoist period when it did little other than convey party messages. There is now much greater leeway to publish more entertainment news, human-interest stories, and some nonpolitical investigative journalism in areas that are consistent with party objectives. But all media outlets are under direct or indirect party control, and the state does shut down those that provoke its political displeasure. In 2013, China was ranked 173 out of 179 countries in the Press Freedom Index compiled annually by Reporters Without Borders.

In terms of political restrictions, the arts are the area of life that has seen the greatest change in China in recent years. Books, movies, plays, and other art forms are sometimes banned, but much of the artistic censorship is now self-imposed by creators who know the limits of what is acceptable to the party–state.

The views of Chinese citizens about what makes them part of the People's Republic of China—their sense of national identity—are going through a profound and uncertain transformation. Party leaders realize that most citizens are skeptical or dismissive of communist ideology and that appeals to socialist goals and revolutionary virtues no longer inspire loyalty. The CCP has turned increasingly to patriotic themes to rally the country behind its leadership. The official media put considerable emphasis on the greatness and antiquity of Chinese culture. They send the not-so-subtle message that it is time for China to reclaim its rightful place in the world order—and that only the CCP can lead the nation in achieving this goal.

In the view of some scholars and others, such officially promoted nationalism could lead to a more aggressive foreign and military policy. The party–state has fanned nationalist sentiment among Chinese citizens to garner support for its disputes with nearby countries over claims to uninhabited islands in the strategically important Sea of Japan and the potentially oil-rich South China Sea.

Of course, it is the cultural tie of being "Chinese" that is the most powerful collective identity that connects citizen to the nation. The Chinese people are intensely proud of their ancient culture and long history. Their enthusiasm for hosting the 2008 Olympics in Beijing reflected this cultural pride. They can also be very sensitive about what they consider slights to their national dignity. Many Chinese feel that Japan has not done enough to acknowledge or apologize for the atrocities its army committed in China during World War II. This has been a strain in relations between the two countries and has sometimes led to spontaneous anti-Japanese demonstrations by Chinese students.

China's Non-Chinese Citizens

The PRC calls itself a multinational state with fifty-six officially recognized ethnic groups, one of which is the Chinese majority, called the Han people (Han being the name of one of China's earliest dynasties). The Han make up 91.5 percent of the total population. The defining elements of a minority group involve some combination of language, culture (including religion), and race that distinguish it from the Han. The fifty-five non-Han minorities number a little more than 100 million, or about 8.5 percent of the total population. These groups range in size from 16 million (the Zhuang of southwest China) to about 2,000 (the Lhoba in the far west). Most of these minorities have come under Chinese rule over many centuries through the expansion of the Chinese state rather than through migration into China.

China's minorities are highly concentrated in the five autonomous regions of Guangxi, Inner Mongolia, Ningxia, Tibet, and Xinjiang. Only in the latter two, however, do minority people outnumber Han Chinese, who are encouraged to migrate to the autonomous regions. The five autonomous regions are sparsely populated, yet they occupy about 60 percent of the total land area of the PRC. Some of these areas are resource rich. All are located on strategically important borders of the country, including those with Vietnam, India, and Russia.

The Chinese constitution grants autonomous regions the right of self-government in certain matters. But they remain firmly under the control of the central authorities. Minority peoples enjoy some latitude to develop their local economies as they see fit. The use of minority languages in the media and literature is encouraged, as is, to a certain extent, bilingual education. Minority religions can be practiced, though only through state-approved organizations.

The most extensive ethnic conflict in China has occurred in Tibet. Tibet is located in the far west of China and has been under Chinese military occupation since the early 1950s. Tibetans practice a unique form of Buddhism, and most are fiercely loyal to the Dalai Lama, a priest they believe is the incarnation of a divine being. China has claimed authority over Tibet since long before the Communist Party came to power. Tibetans have always disputed that claim and resisted Chinese rule, sometime violently, including in 1959, when the Dalai Lama fled to exile in India following the failure of a rebellion by his followers.

During the Maoist era, traditional Tibetan culture was suppressed by the Chinese authorities. Since the late 1970s, Buddhist temples and monasteries have been allowed to reopen, and Tibetans have gained a significant degree of cultural freedom; the Chinese government has also significantly increased investment in Tibet's economic development. However, China still considers talk of Tibetan political independence to be treason, and Chinese troops have crushed several anti-China demonstrations in Lhasa, the capital of Tibet.

There are 20–30 million Muslims in China. They live in many parts of the country and belong to several different ethnic minority groups. The highest concentration of Muslims is in the far west of China in the Ningxia Hui and Xinjiang Uyghur autonomous regions.

The more secular Hui (about 10.5 million) are well assimilated into Han Chinese society. But there is growing unrest among Uyghurs (about 10 million) in Xinjiang, which borders several Islamic nations, including Pakistan and Afghanistan. Tensions between Uyghurs and Han Chinese exploded in Xinjiang in mid-2010, resulting in about 150 deaths and a thousand injuries. The government forcefully restored order and then arrested more than 1,500 people (almost all Uyghurs) in connection with the riots, twelve of whom were sentenced to death.

The Chinese government also has clashed with Uyghur militants who want to create a separate Islamic state of "East Turkestan" and have sometimes used violence, including bombings and assassinations, to press their cause. In March 2014, Uyghur separatists used knives to attack people in a train station in southwest China, killing 29 and injuring more than 140 before being killed or captured by police. The government referred to this attack as "China 9/11" but also urged that the public not blame Uyghurs as a whole for the mayhem.

China's minority population is relatively small and geographically isolated. Ethnic unrest has been sporadic and easily quelled. Therefore, the PRC has not had the kind of intense identity-based conflict experienced by countries with more pervasive religious and ethnic cleavages, such as India and Nigeria. But it is possible that domestic and global forces will make ethnic identity a more visible and volatile issue in Chinese politics.

Interest Groups, Social Movements, and Protest

Truly independent interest groups and social movements are not permitted to influence the political process in the PRC in any significant way. The CCP supports official **mass organizations** as a means to provide a way for interest groups to express their views on policy matters—within strict limits.

mass organizations

Organizations in a communist party–state that represent the interests of a particular social group, such as workers or women, but which are controlled by the communist party.

Total membership of mass organizations in China is in the hundreds of millions. Two of the most important are the All-China Women's Federation, the only national organization representing the interests of women in general, and the All-China Federation of Trade Unions (ACFTU), to which more than 250 million Chinese workers belong. Neither constitutes an autonomous political voice for the groups they are supposed to represent. But they sometimes do act as an effective lobby in promoting the nonpolitical interests of their constituencies. For example, the Women's Federation has become a strong advocate for women on issues ranging from domestic violence to economic rights. The Trade Union Federation successfully pushed for legislation to reduce the standard workweek from six to five days. The ACFTU also represents individual workers with grievances against management, although its first loyalty is to the communist party.

Since the late 1990s, there has been a huge increase in the number of non-governmental organizations (NGOs) less directly subordinate to the CCP than the official mass organizations. There is an enormous variety of national and local NGOs. These include ones that deal with the environment, health, charitable work, and legal issues. NGOs must register with the government, but they have considerable latitude to operate within their functional areas without direct party interference *if* they steer clear of politics and do not challenge official policies.

China has certainly loosened up politically since the days of Mao Zedong, and the spread of private enterprises, increasing labor and residential mobility, and new forms of informal association and communication are just some of the factors that are making it much harder for China's party–state to control its citizens as closely as in the past. But it is still very effective in monitoring dissent and preventing the formation of organizations that might challenge the CCP's authority. For example, in 2013, leaders of the New Citizens Movement, which has protested official corruption and advocated for constitutional government, were arrested on charges of illegal assembly in order to stop the movement from spreading.

Protest and the Party–State

The Tiananmen massacre of 1989 showed the limits of protest in China. The party leadership was particularly alarmed at signs that several autonomous student and worker grassroots organizations were emerging from the demonstrations. The brutal suppression of the democracy movement was meant to send a clear signal that neither open political protest nor the formation of independent interest groups would be tolerated.

Repression has not stopped all forms of citizen protest. The Falun Gong movement has carried out the biggest and most continuous demonstrations against the party–state. Falun Gong (FLG) is a spiritual movement with philosophical and religious elements drawn from Buddhism and Taoism along with traditional Chinese physical exercises (similar to *tai chi*) and meditation. It claims 70 million members in China and 30 million in more than seventy other countries. Its promise of inner tranquility and good health has proven very appealing to a wide cross section of people in China as a reaction to some of the side effects of rapid modernization.

The authorities began a crackdown on the FLG in 1999, which intensified after approximately 10,000 of its followers staged a peaceful protest in front of CCP headquarters in the center of Beijing. The authorities have destroyed FLG books and tapes, jammed websites, and arrested thousands of practitioners. Despite a few small FLG demonstrations, the crackdown seems to have been successful.

Each year, China experiences tens of thousands of so-called "mass incidents" that involve anywhere from a few dozen to more than a thousand people protesting against a wide range of grievances. These are almost always directed against local targets, not the party–state as a whole, and are often accommodated by higher-levels who see them as a way to find out about and problems before they become even more explosive.

Strikes and demonstrations by retired industrial workers protesting the non-payment of pensions or severance packages are among the most common type of mass incident in the urban areas. Employees at some foreign-owned enterprises have gone on strike against unsafe working conditions or low wages. Such actions at plants that produce most of the world's iPhones and iPads led Apple to enhance its initiative that monitors working conditions at its supplier plants in China and elsewhere.

The countryside has also seen an upsurge of protests over corruption, exorbitant taxes and extralegal fees, and environmental damage that impairs both human health and agricultural production. Illegal land seizures by greedy local officials working in cahoots with developers who want to build factories, expensive housing, or even golf courses is one of the major sources of rural mass incidents.

Urban and rural protests in China have not spread beyond the locales where they started. They have focused on the protestors' immediate material concerns, not on grand-scale issues like democracy, and most often are aimed at corrupt local officials or unresponsive employers, not the Communist Party. By responding positively to farmer and worker concerns, the party–state can win support and turn what could be regime-threatening activities into regime-sustaining ones.

The Political Impact of Technology

Internet access is exploding in China, with more than 600 million users by the end of 2013. That represents about 45 percent of the population, which is quite high for a country at China's level of economic development. By contrast, under 20 percent of people in India use the Internet.

The Chinese party–state knows that cutting-edge technology is critical to its modernization plans and wants citizens to become computer literate. But, as with so much else in China, the party–state wants to define the way and dictate the rules. Web access in China is tightly controlled by the licensing of a small number of Internet Service Providers who are responsible for who uses their systems and how. The government has invested huge sums to develop the Golden Shield Project, which operates under the auspices of the Ministry of Public Security and is charged with monitoring and censoring the Internet, including shutting out what it deems as objectionable foreign websites such as *The New York Times*. In early 2011, the authorities moved quickly to stifle social networking calls for peaceful gatherings in several Chinese cities to show support for the democracy movements in the Middle East and North Africa during the Arab Spring.

Nevertheless, the rapid spread of the Internet and social media—especially Twitter like blogs—has empowered citizens by providing a forum for communication and a flow of information that is difficult for the party–state to proactively control. There have been numerous large-scale online postings that have exposed corrupt officials, environmental problems, and child labor exploitation—and even poked fun at the heavy-handed government control of the Internet. The Internet has also been a means of mobilizing citizen action as in the aftermath of the hugely destructive and deadly earthquake that struck Sichuan province in May 2008 when relief funds were raised and blood drives organized online.

Where Do You Stand?

China claims it is a socialist democracy. Can socialism and democracy co-exist?

Do you think Tibet can be called a colony of China? Why or why not?

CHINESE POLITICS IN TRANSITION

⊽ Focus Questions

- What are the major economic and political challenges facing the CCP?

- Why has the Chinese communist party–state been more durable than other regimes of its type?

Political Challenges and Changing Agendas

In late 2011, China passed a milestone in its history. For the first time, more people lived in cities than in the countryside. At the end of the Maoist era in the late 1970s, the rural areas accounted for over 80 percent of the population; in 2014, that was down to about 46 percent. The pace of urbanization is expected to accelerate, and by 2030, nearly three-quarters of China's population—a billion people—will live in cities, more than 200 of which will have a million or more inhabitants. The flow of farmers to the cities in search of better job opportunities—the "floating population"—has been and will continue to be the major source of the new urban population.

Rapid urbanization is a measure of China's progress in modernization, but it also presents the country's leadership with monumental challenges. Migrants mostly work in very low-paying jobs, including export industries, hotels and restaurants, and construction, that offer no security or benefits. They live in substandard housing, often hastily constructed and jam-packed dwellings called "urban villages" located on former farmland that has been incorporated into the municipality.

Perhaps their greatest vulnerability is that their presence in the cities is technically illegal. Beginning in the late 1950s, all Chinese were given either a rural or an urban **household registration** (*hukou*) that was pegged to a specific location. They were not permitted to live or work in any other area. This system prevented the kind of uncontrolled rural flight that occurred in many other developing countries and led to the establishment of vast urban slums. But, by limiting the mobility of farmers, it also became the basis of deeply entrenched inequality between city and countryside.

The authorities allowed the recent wave of migrants to move to the cities despite their rural *hukous* because their labor was crucial to economic expansion. But the migrants have no rights in the urban areas, including access to health care or education for their children, and can be evicted if the government chooses to do so.

The new leadership under Xi Jinping that took over in China in 2012–2013 has given high priority to promoting what is called "people-centered" urbanization. The government has announced that urban registration will be extended to 100 million migrants currently living in cities while another 100 million will be moved to urban areas between 2014 and 2020. The government will also invest heavily in housing, schools, hospitals, and public transportation to meet the needs of the new city dwellers. This is a hugely ambitious undertaking that will have an enormous impact the country's economic development. But China's leaders are well aware of the political implications of a project that will profoundly affect the lives of hundreds of millions of people.

China's planned urbanization is just one part of the multifaceted challenge that its leaders face in trying to sustain and effectively manage the economic growth that has not only significantly improved the lives of most of citizens, but also is the basis of public support for the ruling Communist Party. The CCP is gambling that continued solid economic performance will literally buy it legitimacy and that most citizens will care little about democracy or national politics if their material lives continue to get better. So far this gamble seems to have paid off.

household registration (*hukou*)

In China, the system that registers each citizen as entitled to work and to live in a specific urban or rural location.

But the global financial crisis of 2008 brought a significant slowdown to China's GDP annual growth rate, largely because of deceased demand for Chinese exports in developed countries. For more than two decades prior, the economy had grown at an average of better than 10 percent per year. In 2007, the Chinese economy grew at over 14 percent. In 2008, it plummeted nearly five points, and by 2012–2013, economic growth was at 7.7 percent. By post-recession world standards, that was quite enviable, but still raised the specter of seriously dashed expectations among a population that had grown accustomed to rapidly improving standards of living, especially if growth rates dips even more. That could spell political trouble for the CCP.

The government of the PRC needs to find ways to restructure the economy so that it is less dependent on export-led growth, which is very vulnerable to shifts in the global market. This will involve promoting industries that produce for the domestic economy and its huge untapped consumer market. At the same time, the Chinese government is encouraging its citizens to spend more and save less (in a way, the opposite of America's dilemma) in order to stimulate the domestic economy.

Another major economic challenge for the Chinese leadership is to deepen reform of the country's banking system, which is still almost entirely state-owned and largely immune from market forces, by allowing more room for both private and foreign investors. And, if China is to truly become a mature, modern, and globally competitive economy, it must move beyond being the "factory of the world" and become a more innovative economy that produces international-caliber, leading-edge products of its own design.

The enormous class, regional, and urban-rural inequalities that so clearly mark modernizing China so far have not become the source of major social instability. But that could change, particularly if there is further economic contraction, which would hurt the less well-off much more than the wealthy, who are increasingly sending their assets—and their children—abroad.

Corruption affects the lives of most people much more directly than political repression. Despite well-publicized campaigns and often-harsh punishments for offenders, corruption is still so blatant and widespread that it is probably the single most corrosive force eating away at the legitimacy of the Chinese Communist Party. Environmental problems may not be far behind as a source of dissatisfaction with the political status quo.

China and the Democratic Idea

The PRC has evolved in recent decades toward a system of what has been called "Market-Leninism,"[10] a combination of increasing economic openness (a market economy) and continuing political rigidity under the leadership of a Leninist ruling party that adheres to a remodeled version of communist ideology. The major political challenges now facing the CCP and the country emerge from the sharpening contradictions and tensions of this hybrid system.

As the people of China become more secure economically, better educated, and more connected to the outside world, they will also likely become more politically active. Business owners may want political clout to match their rising economic and social status. Scholars, scientists, and technology specialists may become more outspoken about the limits on intellectual freedom. The many Chinese who travel or study abroad may find the political gap between their party–state and the world's democracies to be increasingly intolerable.

What are the prospects for democratization in China? On the one hand, China's long history of bureaucratic and authoritarian rule and the hierarchical values of still-influential Confucian culture seem to be heavy counterweights to democracy. And, although some aspects of its social control have broken down, the coercive power of China's communist party–state remains formidable. The PRC's relatively low per capita standard of living, large rural population and vast areas of extreme poverty, and state-dominated media and means of communications also impose some impediments to the spread of the democratic idea. Finally, many in China are apathetic about politics or fearful of the violence and chaos that radical political change might unleash. They are quite happy with the status quo of economic growth and overall political stability of the country under the CCP.

On the other hand, the impressive success of democratization in Taiwan in the past decade, including free and fair multiparty elections from the local level up to the presidency, strongly suggests that the values, institutions, and process of democracy are not incompatible with Confucian culture. And though it is still a developing country, China has a high literacy rate, extensive industrialization and urbanization, and a burgeoning middle class—conditions widely seen by social scientists as favorable to democracy.

Despite the CCP's continuing tight hold on power, there have been a number of significant political changes in China that could be harbingers of democracy: the enhanced political and economic power of local governments; the setting of a mandatory retirement age and term limits for all officials; the rise of younger, better educated, and more worldly leaders; the increasingly important role of the National People's Congress in the policy-making process; the introduction of competitive elections in rural villages; the strengthening and partial depoliticization of the legal system; tolerance of a much wider range of artistic, cultural, and religious expression; and the important freedom (unheard of in the Mao era) for individuals to be apolitical.

Furthermore, the astounding spread of the democratic idea around the globe has created a trend that will be increasingly difficult for China's leaders to resist. The PRC has become a major player in the world of states, and its government must be more responsive to international opinion in order to continue the country's deepening integration with the international economy and growing stature as a responsible and mature global power.

One of the most important political trends in China has been the resurgence of civil society, a sphere of independent public life and citizen association, which, if allowed to thrive and expand, could provide fertile soil for future democratization. The development of civil society among workers in Poland and intellectuals in Czechoslovakia, for example, played an important role in the collapse of communism in East-Central Europe in the late 1980s by weakening the critical underpinnings of party–state control.

The Tiananmen demonstrations of 1989 reflected the stirrings of civil society in post–Mao China. But the brutal crushing of that movement showed the CCP's determination to thwart its growth before it could seriously contest the party's authority. But as economic modernization and social liberalization have deepened in the PRC, civil society has begun to stir again. Some stirrings, like the Falun Gong movement, have met with vicious repression by the party–state. But others, such as the proliferation and growing influence of non-governmental organizations that deal with *non-political* matters such as the environment, have been encouraged by the authorities. The relatively new and rapidly growing phenomenon of online activism by China's netizens also suggests the emergence of a "digital civil society" that may well become a source of pressure for democratization.[11]

At some point, the leaders of the CCP will face the fundamental dilemma of whether to accommodate or, as they have done so often in the past, suppress organizations, individuals, and ideas that question the principle of party leadership. Accommodation would require the party–state to cede some of its control over society and allow more meaningful citizen representation and participation. But repression would likely derail the country's economic dynamism and could have terrible costs for China.

Youth Politics and the Generational Divide

In most developing countries, the under-30 age group is the fastest-growing segment of the population. By contrast, in China, it is the over-60-year-olds that account for the most rapidly expanding age group. This group numbered about 185 million (13.7 percent of the population) in 2010; that will grow to 284 million (21.0 percent) by 2025 and 440 million (34.6 percent) by 2050. This demographic trend is the result of a combination of factors, including longer life expectancy and, especially, the one-child policy that was introduced in the early 1980s and only modestly relaxed in 2013.

China's "graying population" presents the country with the challenge of supporting this growing cohort of senior citizens. The burden will fall particularly heavily on the shrinking younger generation, which will bear much of the responsibility for caring for elderly parents. Since both the husband and wife in a married couple are likely to be only-children, they will wind up caring for both sets of parents for what could be a decade or two. Other countries face a similar dilemma, but almost all of them (e.g., Japan) have a much higher per capita income and much more developed pension and health care systems. In other words, China's intragenerational challenge is complicated by the fact that it is "getting old before getting rich."[12]

Higher education has expanded rapidly in China over the last three decades, but still only about 20 percent of the age-relevant population is in college. Most of that population doesn't even apply since they lack the necessary high school education. For those who do want to apply, admission is extremely competitive, with just three out of five prospective students passing the required national college entrance examination. For jobs other than in the low-wage sectors of the economy, a college degree is a necessity, and, even for a substantial portion of China's 7 million college graduates each year (compared to 1.5 million in the United States), finding suitable employment has become a challenge. These unemployed or underemployed college-educated youth have become a fixture in many Chinese cities. They've come to be known as the "Ant Tribe" because they often share crowded apartments and pass the time by hanging out together. If China's economy were to slow down even more, the ranks of the Ant Tribe could grow in size and become increasingly unhappy about their situation. Unemployed educated youth have been a source of social unrest and political protest in many countries and were a major factor in launching the Arab Spring revolutions that began in 2011.

Chinese Politics in Comparative Perspective

China as a Communist Party–State

The fact that the Chinese Communists won power through an indigenous revolution with widespread popular backing and did not depend on foreign military support for their victory sets China apart from the situation of most of the now-deposed Eastern European communist parties. Despite some very serious mistakes over the six decades of its rule in China, the CCP still has a deep reservoir of historical legitimacy among large segments of the population.

The PRC has also been able to avoid the kind of economic crises that greatly weakened other communist systems, including the Soviet Union, through its successful market reforms that have dramatically improved the lives of most Chinese. CCP leaders believe that one of the biggest mistakes made by the last Soviet communist party chief, Mikhail Gorbachev, was that he went too far with political reform and not far enough with economic change, and they are convinced that their reverse formula is a key reason that they have not suffered the same fate.

But China also has much in common with other communist party–states past and present, particularly the insistence on the unchallengeable principle of party leadership in any way that the party chooses to exert that leadership. Stalinist Russia and Maoist China were classified as examples of **totalitarianism** because of the communist party's claim to exercise nearly total control of not just politics and ideology, but the economy, culture, and society as well. Under totalitarian regimes (which also included Nazi Germany), the distinction between public and private pretty much disappears, and the party–state enforces its authority through a combination of propaganda (extended to education and the media), coercion, and terror.

China is much less totalitarian than it was during the Maoist era. To promote economic development, the CCP has relaxed its grip on many areas of life. Citizens can generally pursue their private interests without interference by the party–state as long as they avoid sensitive political issues and are not seen as challenging the Communist Party's right to rule.

The PRC can now be considered a "consultative authoritarian regime" that "increasingly recognizes the need to obtain information, advice, and support from key sectors of the population, but insists on suppressing dissent … and maintaining ultimate political power in the hands of the Party."[13] By moderating, if not totally abandoning some its Maoist totalitarian features, the Chinese Communist Party has shown remarkable adaptability that so far has allowed it to both carry out bold economic reform and sustain a dictatorial political system.

China as a Developing Country

The development of the PRC raises many issues about the role of the state in governing the economy. It also provides an interesting comparative perspective on the complex and much-debated relationship between economic and political change in the developing world.

When the Chinese Communist Party came to power in 1949, China was a desperately poor country, with an economy devastated by a century of civil strife and world war. It was also in a weak and subordinate position in the post–World War II international order. Even at the end of the Maoist era in the late 1970s, the PRC was among the poorest nations in the and little more than a regional power. Measured against these starting points, China has made remarkable progress in improving the well-being of its citizens, building a strong state, and enhancing the country's global role.

Why has China been more successful than so many other nations in meeting some of the major challenges of development? Those with political power in the developing world have often served narrow class or foreign interests more than the national interest. The result is that governments of many developing countries have become **predatory states** that prey on their people and the nation's resources to enrich the few at the expense of the many. They become defenders of a status quo

totalitarianism

A political system in which the state attempts to exercise total control over all aspects of public and private life, including the economy, culture, education, and social organizations, through an integrated system of ideological, economic, and political control. Totalitarian states rely on extensive coercion, including terror, as a means to exercise power.

predatory state

A state in which those with political power prey on the people and the nation's resources to enrich themselves rather than using their power to promote national development.

built on extensive inequality and poverty rather than agents of needed change. In contrast, the PRC's recent rulers have been quite successful in creating a **developmental state**, in which government power and public policy are used effectively to promote national economic growth. In this very important way, China has become a leader among developing nations.

But, in an equally important way, China is lagging behind many other countries in Africa, Asia, and Latin America. Whereas much of the developing world has been heading toward democracy, the PRC has stood firm against that wave of democratization. According to the 2012 edition of the annual Democracy Index produced by the highly respected magazine, *The Economist*, China ranked just six places from the bottom among 167 countries according to a survey that uses a variety of measures, including the fairness of elections, political participation, and civil liberties.[14]

There is a sharp and disturbing contrast between the harsh political rule of the Chinese communist party–state and its remarkable accomplishments in improving the material lives of the Chinese people. The CCP's tough stance on political reform is in large part based on its desire for self-preservation. But in keeping firm control on political life while allowing the country to open up in other important ways, Chinese Communist Party leaders also believe they are wisely following the model of development pioneered by the newly industrializing countries (NICs) of East Asia such as South Korea and Taiwan.

The lesson that the CCP draws from the NIC experience is that only a strong government can provide the political stability and social peace required for rapid economic growth. According to this view, democracy—with its open debates about national priorities, political parties contesting for power, and interest groups squabbling over how to divide the economic pie—is a recipe for chaos, particularly in a huge and still relatively poor country.

But another of the lessons from the East Asian NICs—one that most Chinese leaders have been reluctant to acknowledge—is that economic development, social modernization, and global integration also create powerful pressures for political change from below and abroad. In both South Korea and Taiwan, authoritarian governments that had presided over economic miracles in the 1960s and 1970s gave way in the 1980s and 1990s to democracy.

China is in the early to middle stages of a period of growth and modernization that are likely to lead it to NIC status within two or three decades. In terms of the extent of industrialization, per capita income, the strength of the private sector of the economy, and the size of the middle and professional classes, China's level of development is still below the level at which democracy succeeded in Taiwan and South Korea. Before concluding that China's communist rulers will soon yield to the forces of democratization, it is important to remember that "authoritarian governments in East Asia pursued market-driven economic growth for decades without relaxing their hold on political power."[15]

But economic reform in China has already created social groups at home and opened up the country to ideas from abroad that are likely to grow as sources of pressure for more and faster political change. And the experiences of many developing countries suggest that such pressures will intensify as the economy and society continue to modernize. Therefore, at some point in the not-too-distant future, the Chinese Communist Party is likely to again face the challenge of the democratic idea. How China's new generation of leaders responds to this challenge is perhaps the most important and uncertain question about Chinese politics in the early decades of the twenty-first century.

developmental state

A nation-state in which the government carries out policies that effectively promote national economic growth.

Where Do You Stand?

Do you think that the Chinese Communist Party will still be in power in 2049, one hundred years after the founding of the People's Republic?

Do you think China is ready for democracy? Would democracy be good for China?

Chapter Summary

For more than 2000 years, China was a hereditary monarchy headed by an emperor until it was overthrown by a revolution in 1912. From then until 1949 it was known as the Republic of China, but the central government was never in full control. Warlords ruled various parts of the country, a civil war broke out between the American-backed Nationalist Party government and the Chinese Communist Party, and Japan occupied almost all of eastern China during World War II. In 1949, the civil war ended with the victory of the Communist Party under Mao Zedong and the establishment of the People's Republic of China. From then until his death in 1976, Mao launched several radical campaigns that had a disastrous political and economic impact on China. Deng Xiaoping became China's most powerful leader in 1978. He implemented major reforms that helped make China the fastest-growing major economy in the world. But he also made it very clear that he would not tolerate any challenges to the authority of the Communist Party. Deng's successors have largely followed his model of economic reform and political repression.

During the Maoist era (1949–1976), the state thoroughly dominated the economy through a system of central planning in which government bureaucrats determined economic policies. Any kind of private economic activity was suppressed. This approach achieved some success in promoting industrialization and raising the educational and health standards of the Chinese people. But, overall, it left China as a very poor country with little involvement in the global economy. Under Deng Xiaoping and his successors, the state has given up much of its control of the economy and encouraged free-market forces, private ownership, international trade, and foreign investment. Living standards, modernization, and globalization have all increased dramatically. But serious problems, such as socioeconomic inequality and pollution, are a challenge for China's current leaders.

China is one of the few remaining countries in the world still ruled by a communist party. Even though the CCP has moved China in the direction of a capitalist economy, it still proclaims it is following communist ideology. The CCP insists it is the only political party that can lead the country toward economic development and maintain stability, and it prohibits any serious challenge to its authority. Power is highly concentrated in the

top two dozen or so leaders of the CCP, who are chosen through secretive inner-party procedures. The government of the People's Republic of China is technically separate from the CCP, and political reform in China has brought some autonomy to government institutions, such as the national legislature and the judiciary. But, in fact, the government and policy-making operates under the close supervision of the Communist Party and almost all high-ranking government officials are also members of the Communist Party.

Representation of citizen interests and political participation in China are carried out under the watchful eye of the Chinese Communist Party. The National People's Congress, the legislature of the PRC, has become more active as the country's focus has shifted from revolutionary politics to economic development. Elections, particularly at the local level, have become more democratic. The Communist Party has also changed significantly, not just welcoming workers, peasants, and political activists into its ranks, but even recruiting members from among China's growing capitalist class of private business owners. Although they are much more open than during the Maoist era, the media, the arts, and education are still ultimately under party supervision. Communist ideology is declining as a unifying force for China's citizens, and the ability of the communist party–state to control and influence its citizens is weakening. The Internet, religion, consumerism, and popular culture are growing in influence. These all present a challenge to the CCP, which now emphasizes Chinese nationalism as a source of citizen identity. Some of the greatest political tensions in China are in parts of the country with high concentrations of non-Chinese ethnic minorities, such as in Tibet and among Muslims in Xinjiang. Protests by farmers and industrial workers with economic grievances have been on the increase, but these have not become large scale or widespread.

The legitimacy of the Chinese Communist Party to rule China rests heavily on the fact that it has presided over three decades of phenomenal economic growth that have dramatically improved the lives of most people in the country. Party leaders face major challenges in continuing to manage the economy, especially in light of the global financial of 2009. These challenges include rapid urbanization, reform of the banking system, and the transition from an export-led model of growth to one that depends more on domestic consumption and innovation. The CCP is also very likely to face increasing demands for a political voice from different sectors of society as its citizens become more prosperous, well educated, and worldly. In comparative perspective, China has proven more economically successful and politically adaptable than other communist party–states, including the Soviet Union, which collapsed in 1991. China has also been much more successful than most other developing countries in promoting economic growth, but so far resisted the wave of democratization that has spread to so many other parts of the world.

Key Terms

autonomous region
cadre
Central Committee
Central Military Commission (CMC)
centrally planned economy
communism
developmental state
floating population
general secretary
guerrilla warfare
household registration (*hukou*)
household responsibility system
iron rice bowl
mass organizations

National Party Congress
National People's Congress (NPC)
nomenklatura
People's Liberation Army (PLA)
Politburo
predatory state
socialism
socialist democracy
socialist market economy
Standing Committee
State Council
state-owned enterprises (SOEs)
totalitarianism

Suggested Readings

Davin, Delia. *Mao: A Very Short Introduction.* New York: Oxford University Press, 2013.

Fenby, Jonathan. *The Penguin History of Modern China: The Fall and Rise of a Great Power, 1850 to the Present.* New York: Penguin Global, 2013.

Gao Yuan. *Born Red: A Chronicle of the Cultural Revolution.* Stanford, CA: Stanford University Press, 1987.

Joseph, William A., ed. *Politics in China: An Introduction*, 2nd edition. New York: Oxford University Press, 2014.

Kraus, Richard Kurt. *The Cultural Revolution: A Very Short Introduction.* New York: Oxford University Press, 2012.

Lampton, David M. *Following the Leader: Ruling China, from Deng Xiaoping to Xi Jinping.* Berkeley, CA: University of California Press, 2014.

McGregor, Richard. *The Party: The Secret World of China's Communist Rulers.* New York: Harper, 2010.

Nathan, Andrew J., Larry Diamond, and Marc F. Plattner, eds. *Will China Democratize?* Baltimore, MD: The Johns Hopkins University Press, 2013.

Schell, Orville, and John Delury. *Wealth and Power: China's Long March to the Twenty-First Century.* New York: Random House, 2013.

Wasserstrom, Jeffery. *China in the 21st Century: What Everyone Needs to Know*, 2nd edition. New York: Oxford University Press, 2013.

Suggested Websites

The Central Government of the People's Republic of China
http://www.gov.cn/english/

China Brief (The Jamestown Foundation)
http://www.jamestown.org/programs/chinabrief/

China in the News
http://chinapoliticsnews.blogspot.com/

China Leadership Monitor (Hoover Institution)
http://www.hoover.org/publications/
   china-leadership-monitor

International Department of the Communist Party of China
http://www.idcpc.org.cn/

News of the Communist Party of China
http://english.cpc.people.com.cn/

China Digital Times (University of California at Berkeley)
http://chinadigitaltimes.net/

Endnotes

Chapter 1

[1]See Philippe Schmitter, "Comparative Politics," in Joel Krieger, ed., *The Oxford Companion to Comparative Politics* (New York: Oxford University Press, 2013), pp. 223–231. For a collection of articles in the field of comparative politics, see Mark Kesselman, ed., *Readings in Comparative Politics*, 2nd ed. (Boston: Wadsworth, 2010).

[2]See, for example, Gerhard Loewenberg, Peverill Squire, and D. Roderick Kiewiet, eds., *Legislatures: Comparative Perspectives on Representative Assemblies* (Ann Arbor: University of Michigan Press, 2002).

[3]See, for example, Merilee S. Grindle, *Despite the Odds: The Contentious Politics of Education Reform* (Princeton: Princeton University Press, 2004), which compares education policies in several Latin American countries; and Paul F. Steinberg and Stacy D. VanDeveer, *Comparative Environmental Politics: Theory, Practice, and Prospects* (Cambridge, MA: MIT Press, 2012).

[4]See, for example, Benedict Anderson, *Imagined Communities: Reflections on the Origins and Spread of Nationalism*, rev. ed. (London: Verso, 1991); and James DeFronzo, *Revolutions and Revolutionary Movements*, 5th ed. (Boulder, CO: Westview Press, 2014).

[5]Peter A. Hall, *Governing the Economy: The Politics of State Intervention in Britain and France* (New York: Oxford University Press, 1986); and Mark Blyth, *Great Transformations: Economic Ideas and Institutional Change in the Twentieth Century* (Cambridge: Cambridge University Press, 2002).

[6]See, for example, most of the chapters in William A. Joseph, ed., *Politics in China: An Introduction*, 2nd ed. (New York: Oxford University Press, 2014).

[7]For discussions of rational choice theory in the popular press, see "Political Scientists Debate Theory of 'Rational Choice,'" in the *New York Times*, February 26, 2000, B11; and Jonathan Cohn, "Irrational Exuberance: When Did Political Science Forget About Politics?" *New Republic*, October 25, 1999, 25–31.

[8]On democratic transitions, see for example, Samuel P. Huntington, *The Third Wave: Democratization in the Late Twentieth Century* (Norman: University of Oklahoma Press, 1993); Larry Diamond, Marc F. Plattner, and Philip J. Costopoulos, eds., *Debates on Democratization* (Baltimore: Johns Hopkins University Press, 2010); and Barbara Wejnert, *Diffusion of Democracy: The Past and Future of Global Democracy* (Cambridge: Cambridge University Press, 2014).

[9]See Joel Krieger, ed., *Globalization and State Power: A Reader* (New York: Pearson/Longman, 2006).

[10]This term is borrowed from Peter A. Hall, *Governing the Economy.*

[11]Peter A. Hall and David Soskice, eds., *Varieties of Capitalism: The Institutional Foundations of Comparative Advantage* (New York: Oxford University Press, 2001). See also David Coates, ed., *Varieties of Capitalism, Varieties of Approaches* (Basingstoke, UK: Palgrave/Macmillan, 2005).

[12]See, for example, Chalmers Johnson, *MITI and the Japanese Miracle: The Growth of Industrial Policy* (Stanford: Stanford University Press, 1982); Meredith Woo-Cummings, ed., *The Developmental State* (Ithaca, NY: Cornell University Press, 1999); Robert Wade, *Governing the Market: Economic Theory and the Role of Government in East Asian Industrialization* (Princeton: Princeton University Press, 2003); Dwight H. Perkins, *East Asian Development: Foundations and* Strategies (Cambridge, MA: Harvard University Press, 2013); and Linda Yueh, *China's Growth: The Making of an Economic Superpower* (New York: Oxford University Press, 2013).

[13]Adam Przeworski et al., *Democracy and Development: Political Institutions and Well-Being in the World, 1950– 1990* (Cambridge: Cambridge University Press, 2000).

[14]Amartya Sen, "Democracy as a Universal Value," *Journal of Democracy* 10, no. 3 (July 1999): 3–17. This article is included in Kesselman, *Readings in Comparative Politics*. For a study that finds a positive correlation between democracy and economic growth, see Daron Acemoglu, Suresh Naidum, Pascual Restrepo, and James A. Robinson, "Democracy Does Cause Growth," Working Paper 20004 (Cambridge, MA: National Bureau of Economic Research, 2014).

[15]Freedom House's annual Freedom in World Reports are available at www.freedomhouse.org.

[16]Sen, "Democracy as a Universal Value," 3.

[17]Andrew Roberts, "Review Article: The Quality of Democracy," *Comparative Politics* 37, no. 3 (April 2005), 357.

[18]For contrasting views on this debate, see Samuel P. Huntington, *Political Order in Changing Societies* (New Haven: Yale University Press, 1968); and Mark Kesselman, "Order or Movement?: The Literature of Political Development as Ideology," *World Politics* 26 (1973), 139–154.

[19]Przeworski et al., *Democracy and Development*.

[20]Alfred Stepan, *Arguing Comparative Politics* (New York: Oxford University Press, 2001), 184.

Chapter 2

[1]Inman, Phillip, "Minority Ethnic Workers in UK Twice as Likely to Be Unemployed as Whites." *The Guardian.* Guardian News and Media, January 9, 2014. Web. May 15, 2014.

[2]UK Office of National Statistics, 2014.

[3]Richard Heffernan, Philip Cowley, and Colin Hay. Developments in British Politics Bk. 9. Basingstoke: Palgrave Macmillan, 2011.

[4]Philip Norton, *The British Polity*, 3rd ed. (New York: Longman, 1994), p. 59.

[5]Stephen Haseler, "Britain's Ancient Régime," *Parliamentary Affairs* 40, no. 4 (October 1990): 418.

[6]See Bill Jones and Philip Norton, *Politics UK*, 7th ed. (New York: Longman, 2010), pp. 475–476.

[7]Ivor Crewe, "Great Britain," in I. Crewe and D. Denver, eds., *Electoral Change in Western Democracies* (London, Croom Helm, 1985), p. 107.

[8]See Gabriel A. Almond and Sidney Verba, *The Civic Culture: Political Attitudes and Democracy in Five Nations* (Princeton, NJ: Princeton University Press, 1963); Almond and Verba, eds., *The Civic Culture Revisited* (Boston: Little, Brown, 1980); and Samuel H. Beer, *Britain Against Itself: The Political Contradictions of Collectivism* (New York: Norton, 1982), pp. 110–114.

[9]See Chris Howell, *Trade Unions and the State* (Princeton, NJ: Princeton University Press, 2005), esp. Ch. 6.

[10]Bhiku Parekh et al., *The Future of Multi-Ethnic Britain: The Parekh Report* (London: Profile Books, 2000), p. 10.

[11]Peter Riddell, *The Thatcher Decade* (Oxford: Basil Blackwell, 1989), p. 289.

[12]Tony Blair, "Doctrine of the International Community," speech to the Economic Club of Chicago, Hilton Hotel, Chicago, April 22, 1999.

Chapter 3

[1]*Le Monde*, March 20, 2007.

[2]James B. Collins, *The State in Early Modern France*, 2nd ed. (New York: Cambridge University Press, 2009), pp. 211 and 209.

[3]Tony Chafer and Emmanuel Godin, eds., *The End of the French Exception?* (New York: Palgrave Macmillan, 2010), p. 2.

[4]Henri Mendras with Alistair Cole, *Social Change in Modern France: Towards a Cultural Anthropology of the Fifth Republic* (Cambridge: Cambridge University Press, 1991), p. 1.

[5]Jonah D. Levy, "The Return of the State? French Economic Policy under Nicolas Sarkozy," unpublished paper presented at the 106th Annual Meeting of the American Political Science Association," Washington, DC, September 2–5, 2010, p. 5.

[6]Vivien A. Schmidt, *From State to Market? The Transformation of French Business and Government* (Cambridge: Cambridge University Press, 1996), p. 442.

[7]*Financial Times*, December 16, 2013.

[8]See Paul Krugman's columns in the *New York Times*, November 11, 2013, and January 16, 2014, and his *New York Times* opinion blog posted March 9, 2014.

[9] *Le Monde*, February 6, 2014.

[10] *Métro*, March 15, 2007.

[11] Katrin Bennhold, "For Women in France, Dim Outlook on Equality," *New York Times*, October 12, 2010.

[12] Richard Balme, "France, Europe and the World: Foreign Policy and the Political Regime of the Fifth Republic," in Sylvain Brouard, Andrew M. Appleton, and Amy G. Mazur, eds., *The French Fifth Republic at Fifty: Beyond Stereotypes* (New York: Palgrave Macmillan, 2009), p. 141.

[13] John T. S. Keeler and Alec Stone, "Judicial-Political Confrontation in Mitterrand's France: The Emergence of the Constitutional Council as a Major Actor in the Policy-making Process," in Stanley Hoffmann, George Ross, and Sylvia Malzacher, eds., *The Mitterrand Experiment: Continuity and Change in Mitterrand's France* (New York: Oxford University Press, 1987), p. 176.

[14] Emiliano Grossman, "Governments under the Fifth Republic: The Changing Instruments/Weapons of Executive Control," in Sylvain Brouard, Andrew M. Appleton, and Amy G. Mazur, eds., *The French Fifth Republic at Fifty: Beyond Stereotypes* (New York: Palgrave Macmillan, 2009), p. 51.

[15] *Libération*, July 5, 2010.

[16] *Le Monde*, July 5, 2011.

[17] Joan Wallach Scott, *The Politics of the Veil* (Princeton, NJ: Princeton University Press, 2007), p. 40.

[18] Pierre Birnbaum, *The Idea of France* (New York: Hill & Wang, 2001), pp. 278–279.

[19] Data from the Pew Research Center, cited by Martin A. Schain, *The Politics of Immigration in France, Britain, and the United States: A Comparative Study* (New York: Palgrave Macmillan, 2008), pp. 19–20.

[20] Sophie Meunier, "Free-Falling France or Free-Trading France?" *French Politics, Culture and Society* 22, no. 1 (Spring 2004): 98–107.

[21] Peter A. Hall, "Introduction: The Politics of Social Change in France," in Pepper D. Culpepper, Peter A. Hall, and Bruno Palier, eds., *Changing France: The Politics That Markets Make* (New York: Palgrave Macmillan, 2006), p. 1.

Chapter 4

[1] Simon Bulmer, Charlie Jeffery, and Stephen Padgett, eds., *Rethinking Germany and Europe: Democracy and Diplomacy in a Semi-Sovereign State* (London: Palgrave, 2010).

[2] Ralf Dahrendorf, *Society and Democracy in Germany* (Garden City: Anchor, 1969).

[3] Steven Silvia, *Holding the Shop Together* (Ithaca: Cornell University Press, 2013).

[4] Peter Hall and David Soskice, *Varieties of Capitalism: The Institutional Foundations of Comparative Advantage* (Oxford: Oxford University Press, 2001).

[5] Christopher Allen, "Trade Unions, Worker Participation, and Flexibility: Linking the Micro to the Macro" *Comparative Politics* 22, no. 3 (1990): 253–272.

[6] Hans-Werner Sinn, *Can Germany Be Saved? The Malaise of the World's First Welfare State* (Cambridge: MIT Press, 2009).

[7] Peter Katzenstein, *Policy and Politics in West Germany: The Growth of a Semi-Sovereign State* (Philadelphia: Temple University Press, 1987).

[8] Kathleen Thelen, *How Institutions Evolve: The Political Economy of Skills in Germany, Britain, the United States and Japan* (Cambridge: Cambridge University Press, 2004).

[9] Marc Morjé Howard, *The Politics of Citizenship in Europe* (Cambridge: Cambridge University Press, 2009); and Simon Green, *The Politics of Exclusion: Institutions and Immigration Policy in Contemporary Germany* (Manchester: Manchester University Press, 2004).

[10] Joyce Mushaben, "Challenging the Maternalist Presumption: Gender and Welfare Reform in Germany and the United States," in Ulrike Liebert and Nancy Hirschman, eds., *Women and Welfare: Theory and Practice in the U.S. and Europe* (Rutgers: Rutgers University Press, 2001).

[11] Carolyn Moore and Wade Jacoby, eds., *German Federalism in Transition: Reforms in a Consensual State* (London: Routledge, 2009).

[12] Jonathan Rodden, *Hamilton's Paradox: The Promise and Peril of Fiscal Federalism* (New York: Cambridge University Press, 2006).

[13] Daniel Kelemen, *Eurolegalism: The Transformation of Law and Regulation in the European Union* (Cambridge: Harvard University Press, 2011).

[14]Cas Mudde, *Populist Radical Right Parties in Europe* (New York: Cambridge University Press, 2007).

[15]Katzenstein, *Policy and Politics in West Germany*, p. 372.

[16]Katzenstein, *Policy and Politics in West Germany*, p. 58.

[17]Kirschbaum, Erik. *Rocking the Wall: Bruce Springsteen: The Untold Story of a Concert in East Berlin That Changed the World*. New York: Berlinica, 2013.

[18]Emily Schultheis, "German Parties Eye Obama's Web-Savvy Campaign," *Politico*, September 12, 2013.

Chapter 6

[1]George Sansom, *A History of Japan, 1334–1615* (Stanford, CA: Stanford University Press, 1961); A. L. Sadler, *A Short History of Japan* (Sydney: Angus & Robertson, 1963), chs. 4–6.

[2]Ronald P. Dore, *Education in Tokugawa Japan* (London: Athlone, 1965).

[3]Sadako N. Ogata, *Defiance in Manchuria: The Making of Japanese Foreign Policy, 1931–1932* (Berkeley: University of California Press, 1964), pt. II.

[4]Ben-Ami Shillony, *Revolt in Japan: The Young Officers and the February 26, 1936 Incident* (Princeton, NJ: Princeton University Press, 1973).

[5]Robert E. Ward and Sakamoto Yoshikazu, eds., *Democratizing Japan: The Allied Occupation* (Honolulu: University of Hawaii Press, 1987); John Dower, *Embracing Defeat: Japan in the Aftermath of World War II* (London: Penguin Books, 1999).

[6]Bernd Martin, *Japan and Germany in the Modern World* (Providence, RI: Berghahn Books, 1995).

[7]William W. Lockwood, *The Economic Development of Japan: Growth and Structural Change, 1868–1938* (Princeton, NJ: Princeton University Press, 1954), pp. 14–15.

[8]Lockwood, *Economic Development of Japan*, pp. 38–39

[9]Hugh Patrick and Henry Rosovsky, "Japan's Economic Performance: An Overview," in *Asia's New Giant: How the Japanese Economy Works*, ed. Hugh Patrick and Henry Rosovsky (Washington, DC: Brookings Institution, 1976), pp. 7–9; Takafusa Nakamura, "'Yakushin nihon' no uraomote" (The appearance and reality of the 'advancing Japan'), in *Showa keizaishi* (An economic history of the Showa period), ed. Hiromi Arisawa (Tokyo: Nihon keizai shimbunsha, 1976), pp. 108–111; Hugh Borton, *Japan's Modern Century: From Perry to 1970*, 2nd ed. (New York: Ronald Press Co., 1970), p. 305, Table 5.

[10]OECD, *OECD Economic Surveys Japan Overview 2013*, p. 36, http://www.oecd.org/eco/surveys/Overview%20 Japan%202013%20English.pdf

[11]Frank K. Upham, *Law and Social Change in Postwar Japan* (Cambridge: Harvard University Press, 1987), ch. 2.

[12]Stephen D. Cohen, *Uneasy Partnership: Competition and Conflict in U.S.-Japanese Trade Relations* (Cambridge, MA: Ballinger Publishing Company, 1985); Leonard J. Schoppa, *Bargaining with Japan: What American Pressure Can and Cannot Do* (New York: Columbia University Press, 1997).

[13]Susan J. Pharr and Ellis S. Krauss, eds., *Media and Politics in Japan* (Honolulu: University of Hawaii Press, 1996); Laurie Anne Freeman, *Closing the Shop: Information Cartels and Japan's Mass Media* (Princeton, NJ: Princeton University Press, 2000).

[14]George Hicks, *Japan's Hidden Apartheid: Korean Minority and the Japanese* (Brookfield, VT: Ashgate, 1997).

Chapter 8

[1]Rogers Smith, *Civic Ideals: Conflicting Visions of Citizenship in U.S. History* (New Haven, CT: Yale University Press, 1997).

[2] S. Karthick Ramakrishnan, *Democracy in Immigrant America: Changing Demographics and Political Participation* (Stanford, CA: Stanford University Press, 2005), chapters 4 and 5.

[3]Louis Hartz, *The Liberal Tradition in America* (New York: Harvest/HBJ, 1955).

[4]Randall Monger, *U.S. Legal Permanent Residents: 2009* (Washington, DC: Office of Immigration Statistics, U.S. Department of Homeland Security, 2010).

[5]Jeffrey S. Passel, *The Size and Characteristics of the Unauthorized Migrant Population in the U.S.: Estimates Based on the March 2005 Current Population Survey* (Washington, DC: Pew Hispanic Center, 2006).

[6]Gary C. Bryner, *Blue Skies, Green Politics: The Clean Air Act of 1990 and Its Implementation* (Washington, DC: CQ Press, 1995).

[7]See *The Federalist Papers*, ed. Clinton Rossiter (New York: Mentor, 1961), particularly *Federalist* Nos. 10 and 51.

[8]Deborah Avant, *The Market for Force: The Consequences of Privatizing Security* (New York: Cambridge University Press, 2005).

[9]Kristi Anderson, *After Suffrage: Women in Partisan and Electoral Politics Before the New Deal* (Chicago: University of Chicago Press, 1996), chapters 2 and 3.

[10]Ruy A. Teixeira, *The Disappearing American Voter* (Washington, DC: Brookings Institution, 1992).

[11]Raymond Wolfinger and Steven Rosenstone, *Who Votes?* (New Haven, CT: Yale University Press. 1980), chapters 2 and 3.

[12]Sanford Levinson, *Constitutional Faith* (Princeton, NJ: Princeton University Press, 1988).

[13]Sidney Verba, Kay Lehman Schlozman, and Henry Brady, *Voice and Equality: Civic Voluntarism in American Politics* (Cambridge: Harvard University Press, 1995).

[14]Robert D. Putnam, *Bowling Alone: The Collapse and Revival of American Community* (New York: Simon and Schuster, 2000).

Chapter 9

[1]IBGE (Instituto Brasileiro de Geografia e Estatística), *Censo 2010 (2010 Census)*, http://censo2010.ibge.gov.br /en/, (accessed November 26, 2013).

[2]Guillermo O'Donnell, *Modernization and Bureaucratic Authoritarianism: Studies in South American Politics* (Berkeley: Institute of International Studies, University of California, 1973).

[3]Thomas E. Skidmore, *The Politics of Military Rule in Brazil, 1964–85* (New York: Oxford University Press, 1988), p. 49.

[4]Margaret Keck, "The New Unionism in the Brazilian Transition," in Stepan, *Democratizing Brazil*, 284.

[5]Peter B. Evans, *Dependent Development: The Alliance of Multinational, State, and Local Capital in Brazil* (Princeton, NJ: Princeton University Press, 1979).

[6]Morsch, E., N. Chavannes, M. van den Akker, H. Sa, G. J. Dinant, "The Effects of the Family Health Program on Child Health in Ceará State, Northeastern Brazil," *Arch Public Health* 59 (2001), 151–165.

[7]Wendy Hunter and Natasha Sugiyama, "Democracy and Social Policy in Brazil: Advancing Basic Needs, Preserving Privileged Interests," *Latin American Politics and Society* 49 (2009), 29–58.

[8]See Morsch et al., "The Effects of the Family Health Program."

[9]Kathy Lindert, Anja Linder, Jason Hobbs, and Benedicte de la Briere, "The Nuts and Bolts of Brazil's *Bolsa Família* Program: Implementing Conditional Cash Transfers in a Decentralized Context," Social Protection Discussion Paper No. 0709, May 2007, pp. 18–19.

[10]Jeffry A. Frieden, *Debt, Development, and Democracy: Modern Political Economy and Latin America, 1965–1985* (Princeton, NJ: Princeton University Press, 1991), pp. 54–65.

[11]David Samuels, *Ambition, Federalism, and Legislative Politics in Brazil* (New York: Cambridge University Press, 2003).

[12]Peter B. Evans, "Predatory, Developmental, and Other Apparatuses: A Comparative Political Economy Perspective on the Third World State," *Sociological Forum* 4, no. 4 (1989), 561–587.

[13]See Samuels, *Ambition, Federalism, and Legislative Politics in Brazil*.

[14]Alfred P. Montero, *Shifting States in Global Markets: Subnational Industrial Policy in Contemporary Brazil and Spain* (University Park: Pennsylvania State University Press, 2002).

[15]Judith Tendler, *Good Government in the Tropics* (Baltimore: Johns Hopkins University Press, 1997).

[16]Human Rights Watch, *Police Brutality in Urban Brazil* (New York: Human Rights Watch, 1997), p. 13.

[17]Ben Ross Schneider, *Politics within the State: Elite Bureaucrats and Industrial Policy in Authoritarian Brazil* (Pittsburgh: University of Pittsburgh Press, 1991).

[18]Barry Ames, *The Deadlock of Democracy in Brazil: Interests, Identities, and Institutions in Comparative Politics* (Ann Arbor: University of Michigan Press, 2001).

[19]See Timothy J. Power, *The Political Right in Postauthoritarian Brazil: Elites, Institutions, and Democratization* (University Park: Pennsylvania State University Press, 2000).

[20]Turner, "Brazil: Indigenous Rights vs. Neoliberalism," p. 67.

Chapter 10

[1]An excellent history of this event is presented in Wayne A. Cornelius, "Nation-Building, Participation, and Distribution: The Politics of Social Reform Under Cárdenas," in Gabriel A. Almond, Scott Flanagan, and Robert J. Mundt (eds.), *Crisis, Choice and Change: Historical Studies of Political Development* (Boston: Little, Brown, 1973).

[2]A classic anthropological study on the urban poor left behind by the "Mexican Miracle" is Oscar Lewis, *The Children of Sánchez: Autobiography of a Mexican Family* (New York: Random House, 1961).

[3]Joe Foweraker and Ann L. Craig (eds.), *Popular Movements and Political Change in Mexico* (Boulder, CO: Lynne Rienner, 1989).

[4]Cohn, D'Vera, Ana Gonzalez-Barrera and Danielle Cuddington, "Remittances to Latin America Recover—but Not to Mexico," (Washington, DC: Pew Research Center, November 2013), available at http://www.pewhispanic.org/files/2013/12/Remittances_11-2013_FINAL.pdf.

[5]Roger Hansen, *The Politics of Mexican Development* (Baltimore: Johns Hopkins University Press, 1971), 75.

[6]World Trade Organization, *Trade Profiles: Mexico*, http://stat.wto.org/CountryProfile/WSDBCountryPFView.aspx?Language=E&Country=MX.

[7]For a recent study arguing that many Mexican farmers have been hurt by NAFTA, see Timothy A. Wise, "Agricultural Dumping Under NAFTA: Estimating the Costs of U.S. Agricultural Policies to Mexican Producers," Mexican Rural Development Research Report No. 7 (Washington, DC: Woodrow Wilson International Center for Scholars, 2010).

[8]For a description of how Mexican presidents went about the process of selecting their successors during the period of PRI dominance, see Jorge G. Castañeda, *Perpetuating Power: How Mexican Presidents Were Chosen* (New York: New Press, 2000).

[9]Daniel Levy and Gabriel Székely, *Mexico: Paradoxes of Stability and Change* (Boulder, CO: Westview Press, 1983), p. 100.

[10]See Luis Carlos Ugalde, *The Mexican Congress: Old Player, New Power* (Washington, DC: Center for International and Strategic Studies, 2000).

[11]See Chapell H. Lawson, *Building the Fourth Estate: Democratization and the Rise of a Free Press in Mexico* (Berkeley: University of California Press, 2002).

[12]Susan Eckstein (ed.), *Power and Popular Protest: Latin American Social Movements* (Berkeley: University of California Press, 1989).

Chapter 11

[1]David Welsh, *The Rise and Fall of Apartheid*, (Charlottesville: University of Virginia Press, 2009), 67–85.

[2]Andrew Nash, "Mandela's Democracy," *Monthly Review* (April 1999): 18–28.

[3]Most statistics used in this chapter are from the official census agency, *Statistics South Africa*. Its three monthly *Labour Force Surveys* enable comparisons over time.

[4]Servaas van der Berg, "Current poverty and income distribution in the context of South African history," Department of Economics, University of Stellenbosch, 2010.

[5]Pieter Fourie, *The Political Management of HIV and AIDS in South Africa* (Basingstoke: Palgrave-Macmillan, 2006), 50–64.

[6]Standard Bank, *2012 Black Empowerment Report*, Johannesburg, 2012, p. 6. http://sustainability.standardbank.com/downloads/bee-2012.pdf

[7]Terence Moll, "Did the Apartheid Economy fail?" *Journal of Southern African Studies* 17, no. 2 (1991): 289–291.

[8]Neta Crawford and Audie Klotz, *How Sanctions Work: Lessons from South Africa* (New York: St Martin's Press, 1999).

[9]Antony Altbeker, *A Country at War with Itself: South Africa's Crisis of Crime* (Johannesburg: Jonathan Ball, 2007), 142–143.

[10]Andrew Feinstein, *After the Party: Corruption, the ANC and South Africa's Uncertain Future* (London and New York: Verso, 2009), 180–184.

[11]Richard Calland, *The Zuma Years: South Africa's Changing Face of Power* (Cape Town: Zebra Press, 2013), 139–149.

[12]Robert Mattes, "Public Opinion since 1994" in Jessica Piombo and Liz Nijzink, eds., *Electoral Politics in South Africa: Assessing the First Democratic Decade* (New York: Palgrave-Macmillan, 2005), p. 55.

[13]Setumo Stone, "DA not creating home-grown members," *Business Day* (Johannesburg), 5 November 2012.

[14]Mandla Zuma, "Zille told: We will defend Zuma's home," *Sunday Times* (Johannesburg), 4 November 2012.

[15]Markinor, "SABC/Markinor Opinion 2004—Racial Relations in South Africa," (November 18, 2004), http://www.biz-community.com/Article .aspx?c511&5196&ai55200

[16]Multi-Level Government Initiative, Service Delivery Barometer, Community Law Centre, University of the Western Cape, 2012, http://www.mlgi.org.za/baromters /service-delivery-protest-barometer

[17]Susan Booysen, *The African National Congress and the Regeneration of Political Power* (Johannesburg: Wits University Press, 2011) p. 485.

[18]"Volunteer Statistics in South Africa," *The Star* (Johannesburg), December 11, 2004.

[19]Jeffrey Lewis, "Assessing the Demographic and Economic Impact of HIV/AIDS," in Kyle Dean Kaufmann and David L. Lindauer, eds., *AIDS and South Africa: The Social Expression of a Pandemic* (Basingstoke, UK: Palgrave Macmillan, 2004), p. 111.

[20]Ryland Fisher, "The ANC and South Africa's Youth Vote," *SA Reconciliation Barometer Blog*, Institute for Justice and Reconciliation, Cape Town, 21 January 2013.

Chapter 12

[1]Much of this context is recounted in James S. Coleman, *Nigeria: Background to Nationalism* (Berkeley: University of California Press, 1958).

[2]Obafemi Awolowo, *Path to Nigerian Freedom* (London: Faber and Faber, 1947), pp. 47–48.

[3]Billy Dudley, *An Introduction to Nigerian Government and Politics* (Bloomington: Indiana University Press, 1982), p. 71.

[4]Robin Luckham, *The Nigerian Military: A Sociological Analysis of Authority and Revolt 1960–67* (Cambridge: Cambridge University Press, 1971).

[5]Peter Ekeh, "Colonialism and the Two Publics in Africa: A Theoretical Statement," *Comparative Studies in Society and History* 17, no. 1 (January 1975).

[6]Richard A. Joseph, *Democracy and Prebendal Politics in Nigeria: The Rise and Fall of the Second Republic* (Cambridge: Cambridge University Press), pp. 55–58.

[7]Gavin Williams and Terisa Turner, "Nigeria," in John Dunn, ed., *West African States: Failure and Promise* (Cambridge: Cambridge University Press, 1978), pp. 156–157.

[8]Michael J. Watts, *State, Oil and Agriculture in Nigeria* (Berkeley: University of California Press, 1987), p. 71.

[9]Watts, *State Oil and Agriculture in Nigeria*, p. 67.

[10]Tom Forrest, *Politics and Economic Development in Nigeria*, 2nd ed. (Boulder, CO: Westview Press, 1995), pp. 207–212.

[11]Dele Olowu, "Centralization, Self-Governance, and Development in Nigeria," in James S. Wunsch and Dele Olowu, eds., *The Failure of the Centralized State: Institutions and Self-Governance in Africa* (Boulder, CO: Westview Press, 1991), p. 211.

[12]Robert Melson and Howard Wolpe, *Nigeria: Modernization and the Politics of Communalism* (East Lansing: Michigan State University Press, 1971).

[13]Toyin Falola, Violence in Nigeria: *The Crisis of Religious Politics and Secular Ideologies* (Rochester, NY: University of Rochester Press, 1998).

[14]Pat A. Williams, "Women and the Dilemma of Politics in Nigeria," in Crawford Young and Paul Beckett, eds., *Dilemmas of Democracy in Nigeria* (Rochester, NY: University of Rochester Press, 1997), pp. 219–241.

[15]Anthony Kirk-Greene and Douglas Rimmer, *Nigeria since 1970: A Political and Economic Outline* (London: Hodder and Stoughton 1981), p. 49.

[16]Rotimi Suberu, *Federalism and Ethnic Conflict in Nigeria* (Washington, DC: U.S. Institute of Peace, 2001).

[17]Suberu, *Federalism and Ethnic Conflict in Nigeria*, pp. 119–120.

[18]Henry Bienen, *Armies and Parties in Africa* (New York: Africana Publishing, 1978), pp. 193–211.

[19]Richard Joseph, *Democracy and Prebendal Politics in Nigeria: The Rise and Fall of the Second Republic* (Cambridge: Cambridge University Press, 1987), 55–68.

[20]Samuel DeCalo, *Coups and Army Rule in Africa* (New Haven, CT: Yale University Press, 1976), p. 18.

[21]Joseph, *Democracy and Prebendal Politics in Nigeria*, pp. 52–53.

[22]Richard Sklar, *Nigerian Political Parties* (Princeton: Princeton University Press, 1963).

[23]Babafemi Badejo, "Party Formation and Party Competitition," in Larry Diamond, Anthony Kirk-Greene, and Oyeleye Oyediran, eds., *Transition without End: Nigerian Politics and Civil Society under Babangida* (Boulder, CO: Lynne Rienner Publishers, 1997), p. 179.

[24]Eghosa Osaghae, *Crippled Giant: Nigeria since Independence* (Bloomington: Indiana University Press 1999), pp. 233–239.

[25]Peter M. Lewis, Barnett Rubin, and Pearl Robinson, *Stabilizing Nigeria: Pressures, Incentives and Support for Civil Society* (New York: Council on Foreign Relations, 1998), p. 87.

[26]Donald L. Horowitz, "Making Moderation Pay: The Comparative Politics of Ethnic Conflict Management," in Joseph V. Montville, ed., *Conflict and Peacemaking in Multiethnic Societies* (New York: Lexington Books, 1991), chapter 25.

[27]Rotimi Suberu, *Public Policies and National Unity in Nigeria*, Research Report No. 19 (Ibadan: Development Policy Centre, 199), pp. 9–10.

[28]Sayre Schatz, "'Pirate Capitalism' and the Inert Economy of Nigeria," *Journal of Modern African Studies* 22, no. 1 (March 1984): 45–57.

[29]Peter Lewis, Etannibi Alemika, and Michael Bratton, *Down to Earth: Changes in Attitudes to Democracy and Markets in Nigeria*, Afrobarometer Working Paper No. 20, Michigan State University, August 2002.

[30]See Terry Lynn Karl, *The Paradox of Plenty* (Berkeley: University of California Press, 1997); and Michael Ross, "The Political Economy of the Resource Curse," *World Politics* 51 (January 1999), 297–322.

[31]Michael Bratton and Nicolas van de Walle, *Democratic Experiments in Africa* (Cambridge: Cambridge University Press, 1997).

Chapter 13

[1]http://pussy-riot.livejournal.com/11352.html (accessed January 1, 2014).

[2]State Statistical Service of the Russian Federation, http://www.gks.ru/bgd/free/b13_00/IssWWW.exe /Stg/dk11/8-0.htm (accessed August 13, 2014).

[3]Richard Pipes, *Russia under the Old Regime* (London: Widenfeld & Nicolson, 1974), pp. 22–24.

[4]The Economist Intelligence Unit, *Country Profile Russia* (London, 2008), pp. 49–50.

[5]Transparency International, Corruption Perceptions Index Results 2013, http://cpi.transparency.org/cpi2013 /results/#myAnchor1 (accessed May 21, 2014).

[6]Jan Burck, Franziska Marten, and Christoph Bals, *The Climate Change Performance Index: Results* (Bonn: Germanwatch, 2014), p. 6.

[7]Russian Statistical Agency, gks.ru; and the European Commission, "European Union: Trade in Goods with Russia," http://trade.ec.europa.eu/doclib/docs/2006 /september/tradoc_113440.pdf pp. 7, 10, 11 (accessed May 21, 2014).

[8]Federal State Statistics Service of the Russian Federation, http://www.gks.ru/bgd/regl/B11_58/IssWWW.exe /Stg/d2/06-09.htm (accessed May 22, 2014).

[9]*EBRD Transition Report*, 2006.

[10]See Joan DeBardeleben and Mikhail Zherebtsov, "The Transition to Managerial Patronage in Russia's Regions," in *The Politics of Sub-national Authoritarianism in Russia*, edited by Vladimir Gel'man and Cameron Ross (Aldershot: Ashgate, 2010).

[11]http://rt.com/politics/defense-draft-russia-shoigu-529 (accessed November 11, 2013).

[12]State Duma of the Russian Federation, http://www .duma.gov.ru/structure/all/. One seat was apparently vacant (accessed March 1, 2014).

[13]David Lane, *State and Politics in the USSR* (Oxford: Blackwell, 1985), pp. 184–185; and Andrea Chandler, "Has the tandem improved women's rights?," in J. L. Black and Michael Johns, *Russia After 2012* (Routledge, 2013), p. 80.

[14]*Rossiiskaia gazeta*, May 28, 2012, http://www .rg.ru/2012/05/26/partiya-site.html (accessed May 21, 2014).

[15]Stefan Oeter, "International norms and legal status of minority languages in Russia," in *Managing Ethnic Diversity in Russia*, eds. Oleh Protsyk and Benedikt Harzl (Routledge, 2013), p. 38.

[16]Reporters without Borders, Press Freedom Index, http://en.rsf.org/press-freedom-index-2013,1054.html (accessed May 21, 2014).

[17]Levada Center, "Rossiiane o SMI," February 18, 2014, http://www.levada.ru/28-02-2014/rossiyane-o-smi (accessed May 21, 2014).

[18] Committee to Protect Journalists, "56 Journalists Killed in Russia since 1992," http://cpj.org/killed/europe/russia/ (accessed March 1, 2014).

[19] Levada Center, "Internet i SMI," September 9, 2013, http://www.levada.ru/19-09-2013/internet-i-smi (accessed May 21, 2014).

[20] Sarah Oates, *Revolution Stalled: The Political Limits of the Internet in the Post-Soviet Sphere* (Oxford University Press, 2013), p. 63, Ch. 7.

[21] Dmitry Medvedev, "Rossiia Vpered" (*Go Russia*, September 10, 2009), http://www.kremlin.ru/news/5413 (accessed January 30, 2011).

[22] Levada Center, "Vybory prezidenta" March 27, 2012, and "Rossiiane o raspade SSSR," Jan. 14, 2014, http://www.levada.ru/27-03-2012/vybory-prezidenta-kak-golosovali-sotsialnye-gruppy, http://www.levada.ru/14-01-2014/rossiyane-o-raspade-sssr (accessed May 21, 2014).

Chapter 14

[1] British Financial Adviser to the Foreign Office in Tehran, *Documents on British Foreign Policy, 1919–39* (London: Her Majesty's Stationery Office, 1963), First Series, XIII, 720, 735.

[2] M. Bazargan, "Letter to the Editor," *Ettela'at*, February 7, 1980.

[3] *Iran Times*, January 12, 1979.

[4] Cited in H. Amirahmadi, *Revolution and Economic Transition* (Albany: State University of New York Press, 1960), p. 201.

[5] International Labor Organization, "Employment and Income Policies for Iran" (unpublished report, Geneva, 1972), Appendix C, 6.

[6] U.S. Congress, *Economic Consequences of the Revolution in Iran,* 5.

[7] Cited in *Iran Times*, July 9, 1993.

[8] J. Amuzegar, *Iran's Economy under the Islamic Republic* (London: Taurus Press, 1994), p. 100.

[9] A. Rafsanjani, "The Islamic Consultative Assembly," *Kayhan*, May 23, 1987.

[10] S. Saffari, "The Legitimation of the Clergy's Right to Rule in the Iranian Constitution of 1979," *British Journal of Middle Eastern Studies* 20, no. 1 (1993): 64–81.

[11] Ayatollah Montazeri, *Ettela'at*, October 8, 1979.

[12] O. Fallaci, "Interview with Khomeini," *New York Times Magazine*, October 7, 1979.

Chapter 15

[1] Timothy Brook, *Quelling the People: The Military Suppression of the Beijing Democracy Movement* (Stanford, CA: Stanford University Press, 1999), p. 129.

[2] "Report on an Investigation of the Peasant Movement in Hunan Province," *Selected Works of Mao Zedong*, Vol. 1. (Beijing: Foreign Languages Press, 1965).

[3] "Restore Agricultural Production," *Selected Works of Deng Xiaoping (1938–1965)* (Beijing: Foreign Languages Press, 1984).

[4] Martin King Whyte, *Myth of the Social Volcano: Perceptions of Inequality and Distributive Injustice in Contemporary China* (Stanford, CA: Stanford University Press, 2010).

[5] Isabelle Attané, "Being a Woman in China Today: A Demography of Gender." *China Perspectives*, no. 4 (2012): pp. 5–15.

[6] Katherine Morton, "Environmental Policy," in William A. Joseph, ed., *Politics in China: An Introduction*," 2nd ed. (New York: Oxford University Press 2014), p. 360.

[7] John P. Burns, *The Chinese Communist Party's Nomenklatura System: A Documentary Study of Party Control of Leadership Selection, 1979–1984* (Armonk, NY: M. E. Sharpe, 1989), pp. ix–x.

[8] See Kenneth Lieberthal and Michel Oksenberg, *Policy Making in China: Leaders, Structures, and Processes* (Princeton, NJ: Princeton University Press, 1988); and Andrew Mertha, "'Fragmented Authoritarianism 2.0': Political Pluralization in the Chinese Policy Process," *China Quarterly*, no. 200 (December 2009), pp. 995–1012.

[9] James D. Seymour, *China's Satellite Parties* (Armonk, NY: M.E. Sharpe, 1987), p. 87.

[10] Nicholas D. Kristof, "China Sees 'Market-Leninism' as Way to Future," *New York Times*, September 6, 1993.

[11] Guobin Yang, "Internet and Civil Society," in William Tay and Alvin So, eds., *Handbook of Contemporary China* (Singapore: World Scientific Press, 2011), p. 443.

[12] "China's Predicament: 'Getting Old before Getting Rich,' " *The Economist*, June 25, 2009.

[13] Harry Harding, *China's Second Revolution: Reform after Mao* (Washington, DC: Brookings Institution, 1987), p. 200.

[14] *The Economist* Intelligence Unit, Democracy Index 2012, http://eiu.com/democracy.

[15] Nicholas Lardy, "Is China Different? The Fate of Its Economic Reform," in Daniel Chirot, ed., *The Crisis of Leninism and the Decline of the Left* (Seattle: University of Washington Press, 1991), p. 147.

Glossary

5 percent clause This rule obliges a German political party to get at least 5 percent of the "second votes" in order for its candidates to enter the *Bundestag* (or the state parliaments). This rule depresses votes for "splinter" parties unlikely to meet this threshold. Again, the term second votes will be wholly opaque at this point.

A

abertura (Portuguese for "opening"; *apertura* in Spanish) In Brazil, refers to the period of authoritarian liberalization begun in 1974 when the military allowed civilian politicians to compete for political office in the context of a more open political society.

absolute veto In areas that directly affect the German states, the *Bundesrat* can veto any bill passed by the *Bundestag*.

accommodation An informal agreement or settlement between the government and important interest groups in response to the interest groups' concerns for policy or program benefits.

accountability A government's responsibility to its population, usually by periodic popular elections, transparent fiscal practices, and by parliament's having the power to dismiss the government by passing a motion of no confidence. In a political system characterized by accountability, the major actions taken by government must be known and understood by the citizenry.

acephalous societies Literally "headless" societies. A number of traditional Nigerian societies, such as the Igbo in the precolonial period, lacked executive rulership as we have come to conceive of it. Instead, the villages and clans were governed by committee or consensus.

administrative guidance Informal guidance, usually not based on statute or formal regulation, that is given by a government agency, such as a ministry and its subdivisions, to a private organization, such as a firm or a lower-level government. The lack of transparency of the practice makes it subject to criticisms as a disguised form of collusion between a government agency and a firm.

Africans South African usage refers to Bantu language speakers, the demographic majority of South African citizens.

Afrikaner Descendants of Dutch, French, German, and Scots settlers in South Africa speaking a language (Afrikaans) derived heavily from Dutch and politically mobilized as an ethnic group through the twentieth century.

amakudari A Japanese practice, known as "descent from heaven," in which government officials retiring from their administrative positions take jobs in public corporations or private firms with which their own ministry has or recently had close ties.

ancien régime The monarchical regime that ruled France until the Revolution of 1789, when it was toppled by a popular uprising.

anticlericalism Opposition to the power of churches or clergy in politics. In some countries, for example, France and Mexico, this opposition has focused on the role of the Catholic Church in politics.

apartheid In Afrikaans, "separateness." The term was first used in 1929 to describe Afrikaner nationalist proposals for strict racial separation and "to ensure the safety of the white race."

Articles of Confederation The first governing document of the United States, agreed to in 1777 and ratified in 1781. The Articles concentrated most powers in the states and made the national government largely dependent on voluntary contributions of the states.

Assembly of Experts Group in Iran that nominates and can remove the Leader. The assembly is elected by the general electorate, but almost all its members are clerics.

austerity policies Spending cuts, layoffs, and wage decreases meant to address budget problems.

authoritarian A system of rule in which power depends not on popular legitimacy but on the coercive force of the political authorities.

authoritarianism Political systems in which power (or authority) is highly concentrated in a single individual, a small group of people, or a single political party, ethnic group, region, or institution. Furthermore, those with power are not selected by competitive elections, they claim an exclusive right to govern, and they use arbitrary force, among other means, to impose their will and policies on all who live under their authority.

authoritarian regime A system of rule in which power depends not on popular legitimacy but on the coercive force of the political authorities. Hence, there are few personal and group freedoms. It is also characterized by near absolute power in the executive branch and few, if any, legislative and judicial controls.

autocracy A government in which one or a few rulers has absolute power, thus, a dictatorship.

autonomous region A territorial unit in China that is equivalent to a province and contains a large concentration of ethnic minorities. These regions, for example, Tibet, have some autonomy in the cultural sphere but in most policy matters are strictly subordinate to the central government.

ayatollah Literally, "sign of God." A high-ranking cleric in Iran.

B

balance of payments An indicator of international flow of funds that shows the excess or deficit in total payments of all kinds between or among countries. Included in the calculation are exports and imports, grants, and international debt payments.

Basic Law The 1949 proto-constitution of the Federal Republic of Germany, which continues to function today.

bazaar An urban marketplace in Iran where shops, workshops, small businesses, and export-importers are located.

bicameral A legislative body with two houses, such as the U.S. Senate and the U.S. House of Representatives. Just as the U.S. Constitution divides responsibilities between the branches of the federal government and between the federal government and the states, it divides legislative responsibilities between the Senate and the House.

Bill of Rights The first ten amendments to the U.S. Constitution (ratified in 1791), which established limits on the actions of government. Initially, the Bill of Rights limited only the federal government. The Fourteenth Amendment and subsequent judicial rulings extended the provisions of the Bill of Rights to the states.

Blitzkrieg German battle tactics used in World War II that begin with aerial assaults to destroy enemy forces and infrastructure, followed quickly by a massive invasion of armored troops, with ordinary infantry mopping up resistance.

Boer Literally "farmer"; modern usage is a derogatory reference to South African Afrikaners.

Brahmin The highest caste in the Hindu caste system of India.

bureaucracy An organization structured hierarchically, in which lower-level officials are charged with administering regulations codified in rules that specify impersonal, objective guidelines for making decisions.

bureaucratic authoritarianism A term developed by Argentine sociologist Guillermo O'Donnell to interpret the common characteristics of military-led authoritarian regimes in Brazil, Argentina, Chile, and Uruguay in the 1960s and 1970s. According to O'Donnell, bureaucratic authoritarian regimes led by the armed forces and key civilian allies emerged in these countries in response to severe economic crises.

bureaucratic rings A term developed by the Brazilian sociologist and president Fernando Henrique Cardoso that refers to the highly permeable and fragmented structure of the state bureaucracy that allows private interests to make alliances with midlevel bureaucratic officers. By shaping public policy to benefit these interests, bureaucrats gain the promise of future employment in the private sector. While in positions of responsibility, bureaucratic rings are ardent defenders of their own interests.

C

cabinet The body of officials (e.g., ministers, secretaries) who direct executive departments presided over by the chief executive (e.g., prime minister, president).

cabinet government A system of government in which most executive power is held by the cabinet, headed by a prime minister.

cadre A person who exercises a position of authority in a communist party-state; cadres may or may not be communist party members.

caste system According to the Hindu religion, society is divided into castes. Membership in a caste is determined at birth. Castes form a rough social and economic hierarchy in India.

caudillos Charismatic populist leaders, usually with a military background, who use patronage and draw upon personal loyalties to dominate a region or a nation in Latin America.

causal theories An influential approach in comparative politics that involves trying to explain why "if X happens, then Y is the result."

Central Committee The top 370 or so leaders of the Chinese Communist Party. It meets annually for about two weeks and is charged with carrying on the business of the National Party Congress when it is not in session.

Central Military Commission (CMC) The most important military organization in the People's Republic of China, headed by the general secretary of the Chinese Communist Party, who is the commander-in-chief of the People's Liberation Army.

centrally planned economy An economic system in which the state directs the economy through bureaucratic plans for the production and distribution of goods and services. The government, rather, than the market, is the major influence on the economy. Also called a command economy.

chancellor An old German title now used by the German head of government and essentially the same as "prime minister."

checks and balances A governmental system of divided authority in which coequal branches can restrain each other's actions. For example, the U.S. president must sign legislation passed by Congress for it to become law. If the president vetoes a bill, Congress can override that veto by a two-thirds vote of the Senate and the House of Representatives.

citizen initiative Clause in 2009 Lisbon Treaty allowing citizens to propose referendums to initiate EU legislation, provided 1 million legal signatures have been obtained in a "significant number" of different EU member states.

citizen action groups Nonparty and often single-issue initiatives, often focused on concrete problems such as the environment, traffic, housing, or other social and economic issues.

civil servants Employees of federal, state, and municipal governments.

civil society Refers to the space occupied by voluntary associations outside the state, for example, professional associations (lawyers, doctors, teachers), trade unions, student and women's groups, religious bodies, and other voluntary association groups.

clientelism An informal aspect of policy-making in which a powerful patron (for example, a traditional local boss, government agency, or dominant party) offers resources such as land, contracts, protection, or jobs in return for the support and services (such as labor or votes) of lower-status and less powerful clients; corruption, preferential treatment, and inequality are characteristic of clientelist politics.

clientelistic networks Informal systems of asymmetrical power in which a powerful patron (e.g., the president, prime minister, or governor) offers less powerful clients resources, benefits, or career advantages in return for support, loyalty, or services.

co-determination The legal right of representatives of employees to help determine the direction of the company in which they work. Co-determination often takes place through elected works councils in each firm or factory.

cohabitation The term used by the French to describe the situation when a president and prime minister belong to opposing political coalitions.

Cold War The hostile relations that prevailed between the United States and the Soviet Union from the late 1940s until the demise of the USSR in 1991.

collective identities The groups with which people identify, including gender, class, race, region, and religion, and which are the "building blocks" for social and political action.

collectivization A process undertaken in the Soviet Union under Stalin from 1929 into the early 1930s and in China under Mao in the 1950s, by which agricultural land was removed from private ownership and organized into large state and collective farms.

Common Foreign and Security Policy (CFSP) Commitment in the Maastricht Treaty for deeper cooperation in international affairs and defense in the EU.

communism According to Marxism, the stage of development that follows socialism and in which all property is publically owned, economic production is coordinated for the common good, and a radical degree of equality has been achieved.

communist party–state A type of nation-state in which the communist party attempts to exercise a complete monopoly on political power and controls all important state institutions.

community method The EU method of making decisions in which the European Commission proposes, the Council of Ministers and European Parliament decide, and the European Court of Justice reviews European law.

comparative politics The field within political science that focuses on domestic politics and analyzes patterns of similarity and difference among countries.

comparativist A political scientist who studies the similarities and differences in the domestic politics of various countries.

conservative The belief that existing political, social, and economic arrangements should be preserved.

consolidated democracies Democratic political systems that have been solidly and stably established for an ample period of time and in which there is relatively consistent adherence to the core democratic principles.

constitutional monarchy System of government in which the head of state ascends by heredity but is limited in powers and constrained by the provisions of a constitution.

constructive vote of no confidence This measure requires the German *Bundestag* to elect a new chancellor by an absolute majority in order to oust the current one.

corporatist state A state in which interest groups become an institutionalized part of the state structure.

Corruption Perceptions Index A measure developed by Transparency International that ranks countries in terms of the degree to which corruption is perceived to exist among public officials and politicians.

country A territorial unit controlled by a single state.

coup d'état A forceful, extra-constitutional action resulting in the removal of an existing government.

critical juncture An important historical moment when political actors make critical choices, which shape institutions and future outcomes.

D

dalits The *dalit* movement is organized by untouchables or scheduled caste against caste discrimination and oppression.

decentralization Policies that aim to transfer some decision-making power from higher to lower levels of government.

Declaration of Independence The document asserting that the British colonies in what is now the United States had declared themselves independent from Great Britain. The Declaration of Independence was signed in Philadelphia on July 4, 1776.

democracy From the Greek *demos* (the people) and *kratos* (rule). A political system that featuring: selection to public offices through free and fair elections; the right of all adults to vote; political parties that are free to compete in elections; government that operates by fair and relatively open procedures; political rights and civil liberties; an independent judiciary (court system); civilian control of the military.

democratic centralism A system of political organization developed by V.I. Lenin and practiced, with modifications, by all communist party-states. Its principles include a hierarchical party structure.

democratic corporatism A bargaining system in which important policies are established and often carried out with the participation of trade unions and business associations.

democratic transition The process of a state moving from an authoritarian to a democratic political system.

democratization Transition from authoritarian rule to a democratic political order.

dependent variable The variable symbolized by Y in the statement that "If X happens, then Y will be the result"; in other words, the dependent variable is the outcome of X (the independent variable).

deregulation The process of dismantling state regulations that govern business activities.

developmental state A nation-state in which the government carries out policies that effectively promote national economic growth.

developmentalism An ideology and practice in Latin America during the 1950s in which the state played a leading role in seeking to foster economic development through sponsoring vigorous industrial policy.

dictatorships A form of government in which power and political control are concentrated in one or a few rulers who have concentrated and nearly absolute power.

distributional politics The use of power, particularly by the state, to allocate some kind of valued resource among competing groups.

distributive policies Policies that allocate state resources into an area that lawmakers perceive needs to be promoted. For example, leaders today believe that students should have access to the Internet. In order to accomplish this goal, telephone users are being taxed to provide money for schools to establish connections to the Internet.

dominant party A political party that manages to maintain consistent control of a political system through formal and informal mechanisms of power, with or without strong support from the population.

dual society A society and economy that are sharply divided into a traditional, usually poorer, and a modern, usually richer, sector.

E

Economic and Monetary Union The 1991 Maastricht Treaty federalized EU monetary policy, created a European Central Bank and founded the Eurozone and its single currency, the euro.

Economic Community of West African States (ECOWAS) The West African regional organization, including fifteen member countries from Cape Verde in the west to Nigeria and Niger in the east.

economic deregulation The lifting or relaxation of government controls over the economy, including the reduction of import taxes and the phasing out of subsidized prices.

economic liberalization The removal of government control and regulation over private enterprise.

ejido Land granted by Mexican government to an organized group of peasants.

Emergency (1975–1977) The period when Indian prime minister Indira Gandhi suspended many formal democratic rights and ruled in an authoritarian manner.

Energiewende A policy to shift German energy consumption from fossil fuels and nuclear to sustainable sources such as wind, solar, hydro, and biomass.

Environmental Performance Index A measure of how close countries come to meeting specific benchmarks for national pollution control and natural resource management.

European Commission The EU executive, which has a legal monopoly on proposing EU legislation and overseeing its implementation as "guardian of the treaties."

European Council An EU institution made up of heads of state and government of EU member states that meets periodically to provide general EU strategy.

European Court of Justice EU Supreme Court that decides the legality of EU legislation and its implementation.

European Parliament The Parliament of the European Union, which meets in Strasbourg and Brussels, "co-decides" EU law with the Council of Ministers, but it cannot initiate legislation.

European single market Official title of the EU's barrier-free economic space created after 1985.

Eurozone crisis Crisis of sovereign debt within Eurozone that broke out after 2009 that led to frantic emergency efforts by Eurozone members and the European Council to bail out Greece, Ireland, and Portugal and reconfigure EMU rules.

Eurozone The 18 members of the EU (out of 28 total members) who share a common currency, the euro.

executive The agencies of government that implement or execute policy.

Expediency Council A committee set up in Iran to resolve differences between the *Majles* (parliament) and the Guardian Council.

export-led growth Economic growth generated by the export of a country's commodities. Export-led growth can occur at an early stage of economic development, in which case it involves primary products, such as the country's mineral resources, timber, and agricultural products; or at a later stage, when industrial goods and services are exported.

F

Farsi Persian word for the Persian language. Fars is a province in Central Iran.

favelas A Portuguese-language term for the shantytowns that ring many of the main cities in Brazil. The shantytowns emerge where people can invade unused land and build domiciles before the authorities can remove them. Unfinished public housing projects can also become the sites of *favelas*. *Favelas* expanded after the 1970s as a response to the inadequate supply of homes in urban centers to meet the demand caused by increasing rural–urban migration.

Federal Reserve Board The U.S. central bank established by Congress in 1913 to regulate the banking industry and the money supply. Although the president appoints the chair of the board of governors (with Senate approval), the board operates largely independently.

federal states The 16 subnational units that make up the Federal Republic of Germany.

federal system A political structure in which subnational units have significant independent powers; the powers of each level are usually specified in the federal constitution.

federalism A system of governance in which political authority is shared between the national government and regional or state governments. The powers of each level of government are usually specified in a federal constitution.

floating population Migrants from the rural areas of China who have moved temporarily to the cities to find employment.

foreign direct investment Ownership of or investment in cross-border enterprises in which the foreign investor plays a direct managerial role.

Foundation of the Oppressed A clerically controlled foundation set up after the revolution in Iran.

Four Great Pollution Trials Include a mercury poisoning case in Minamata City, thus known as the Minamata Disease, a very similar case in another city, thus known as the Second Minamata Disease, a cadmium poisoning case known as the *itai-itai* (ouch-ouch) disease, and a case of severe asthma caused by inhalation of sulfur dioxide that occurred in Yokkaichi City, hence known as the Yokkaichi Asthma.

framework regulations Laws that set broad parameters for economic behavior but that require subsequent elaboration, often through formal agreements between employers and employees.

free market A system in which government regulation of the economy is absent or limited. Relative to other advanced democracies, the United States has traditionally had less market regulation.

Freedom in the World rating An annual evaluation by Freedom House of the state of freedom in countries around the world measured according to political rights and civil liberties.

fundamentalism A term recently popularized to describe extremist religious movements throughout the world.

fusion of powers A constitutional principle that merges the authority of branches of government, in contrast to the principle of separation of powers.

G

Gastarbeiter (**guest workers**) Workers who were recruited to join the German labor force in the 1960s and early 1970s, generally from Italy, Yugoslavia, and especially Turkey.

general secretary The formal title of the head of the Chinese Communist Party. From 1942 to 1982, the position was called "chairman" and was held by Mao Zedong until his death in 1976.

glasnost Gorbachev's policy of "openness," which involved an easing of controls on the media, arts, and public discussion in Russia in the 1980s.

Global Gender Gap A measure of the extent to which women in 58 countries have achieved equality with men.

globalization The intensification of worldwide interconnectedness associated with the increased speed and magnitude of cross-border flows of trade, investment and finance, and processes of migration, cultural diffusion, and communication.

grandes écoles Prestigious and highly selective schools of higher education in France that train top civil servants, engineers, and business executives.

grand corps Elite networks of graduates of selective training schools in France.

grassroots democracy The idea that real democracy requires participation from rank-and-file members and not merely from organizational leaders.

green revolution A strategy for increasing agricultural (especially food) production, involving improved seeds, irrigation, and abundant use of fertilizers.

gross domestic product (GDP) The total of all goods and services produced within a country that is used as a broad measure of the size of its economy.

gross national product (GNP) GDP plus income earned by the country's residents; another broad measure of the size of an economy.

Guardian Council A committee created in the Iranian constitution to oversee the *Majles* (the parliament).

guerrilla warfare A military strategy based on small, highly mobile bands of soldiers (the guerrillas, from the Spanish word for war, *guerra*) who use hit-and-run tactics like ambushes to attack a better-armed enemy.

H

health insurance funds Semipublic institutions that administer insurance contributions from employees and employers and thus pay for health care for covered participants.

heavy industries The coal, iron, and steel sectors and the machinery, railroad, and armaments production associated with them.

hegemonic power A state that can control the pattern of alliances and terms of the international order and often shapes domestic political developments in countries throughout the world.

hegemony The capacity to dominate the world of states and control the terms of trade and the alliance patterns in the global order.

Hezbollahis Literally "partisans of God." In Iran, the term is used to describe religious vigilantes. In Lebanon, it is used to describe the Shi'i militia.

hojjat al-Islam Literally, "the proof of Islam." In Iran, it means a medium-ranking cleric.

homelands Areas reserved for exclusive African occupation, established through the 1913 and 1936 land legislation and later developed as ethnic states during the apartheid era.

household responsibility system The system put into practice in China beginning in the early 1980s in which the major decisions about agricultural production are made by individual farm families based on the profit motive rather than by a people's commune or the government.

household registration (hukou) In China, the system that registers each citizen as entitled to work and to live in a specific urban or rural location.

Human Development Index (HDI) A composite number used by the United Nations to measure and compare levels of achievement in health, knowledge, and standard of living.

hung parliament A situation after an election when no single party comprises a majority in the British House of Commons.

Glossary

I

Imam Jum'ehs Prayer leaders in Iran's main urban mosques.

import substitution industrialization (ISI) Strategy for industrialization based on domestic manufacture of previously imported goods to satisfy domestic market demands.

independent variable The variable symbolized by X in the statement that "If X happens, then Y will be the result"; in other words, the independent variable is a cause of Y (the dependent variable).

Indian Administrative Service (IAS) India's civil service, a highly professional and talented group of administrators who run the Indian government on a day-to-day basis.

Indian Rebellion An armed uprising by Indian soldiers against expansion of British colonialism in India in 1857.

indicative planning A term that describes a national plan identifying desirable priorities for economic and social development.

indigenous groups Population descended from the original inhabitants of the Americas, present prior to the Spanish Conquest.

indirect rule A term used to describe the British style of colonialism in Nigeria and India in which local traditional rulers and political structures were used to help support the colonial governing structure.

industrial policy A policy that uses state resources to promote the development of particular economic sectors.

Industrial Revolution A period of rapid and destabilizing social, economic, and political changes caused by the introduction of large-scale factory production, originating in England in the middle of the eighteenth century.

influx control A system of controls that regulated African movement between cities and between towns and the countryside in South Africa, enforcing residence in the homelands and restricting African's choice of employment.

informal economy That portion of the economy largely outside government control in which employees work without contracts or benefits. Examples include casual employees in restaurants and hotels, street vendors, and day laborers in construction or agriculture.

insider privatization The transformation of formerly state-owned enterprises into joint-stock companies or private enterprises in which majority control is in the hands of employees and/or managers.

institutional design The institutional arrangements that define the relationships between executive, legislative, and judicial branches of government and between the national government and subnational units such as states in the United States.

interest groups Organizations that seek to represent the interests—usually economic—of their members in dealings with the government. Important examples are associations representing people with specific occupations, business interests, racial and ethnic groups, or age groups in society.

international financial institutions (IFIs) This term generally refers to the International Bank for Reconstruction and Development (the World Bank) and the International Monetary Fund (IMF), but can also include other international lending institutions.

International Monetary Fund (IMF) The "sister organization" of the World Bank, which also has more than 180 member states. It describes its mandate as "working to foster global monetary cooperation, secure financial stability, facilitate international trade, promote high employment and sustainable economic growth, and reduce poverty." It has been particularly active in helping countries that are experiencing serious financial problems. In exchange for IMF financial or technical assistance, a country must agree to a certain set of conditions that promote economic liberalization.

interventionist An interventionist state acts vigorously to shape the performance of major sectors of the economy.

interventores In Brazil, allies of Getúlio Vargas (1930–1945, 1950–1952) picked by the dictator during his first period of rulership to replace opposition governors in all the Brazilian states except Minas Gerais. The *interventores* represented a shift of power from subnational government to the central state.

iron rice bowl A feature of China's socialist economy during the Maoist era (1949–1976) that provided guarantees of lifetime employment, income, and basic cradle-to-grave benefits to most urban and rural workers.

iron triangles A term coined by students of American politics to refer to the relationships of mutual support formed by particular government agencies, members of congressional committees or subcommittees, and interest groups in various policy areas.

Islamism The use of Islam as a political ideology. Similar to political Islam and Islamic fundamentalism.

J

Japan Self-Defense Forces (JSDF) Inaugurated in Japan as a police reserve with 75,000 recruits in August 1950, following the outbreak of the Korean War. Today, it consists of approximately 250,000 troops equipped with sophisticated modern weapons.

jihad Literally "struggle." Although often used to mean armed struggle against unbelievers, it can also mean to fight against sociopolitical corruption or a spiritual struggle for self-improvement.

judicial review The ability of a high court to nullify actions by the executive and legislative branches when it judges that they violate the constitution.

judiciary One of the primary political institutions in a country; responsible for the administration of justice and in some countries for determining the constitutionality of state decisions.

Junkers The land-owning nobility of Prussia, who were the grain (rye)-growing component of Bismarck's "marriage of iron and rye."

jurist's guardianship Khomeini's concept that the Iranian clergy should rule on the grounds that they are the divinely appointed guardians of both the law and the people.

Justice and Home Affairs (JHA) Engagements to make legal and regulatory changes to allow free movement of EU citizens throughout the EU.

K

keiretsu A group of closely allied Japanese firms that have preferential trading relationships and often interlocking directorates and stock-sharing arrangements.

Keynesianism Named after the British economist John Maynard Keynes, an approach to economic policy in which state economic policies are used to regulate the economy in an attempt to achieve stable economic growth. During a recession, state budget deficits are used to expand demand in an effort to boost both consumption and investment, and to create employment. During periods of high growth when inflation threatens, cuts in government spending and a tightening of credit are used to reduce demand.

koenkai In Japanese politics, a candidate's personal campaign organization, consisting mainly of his or her relatives, friends, fellow alumni, coworkers, and their acquaintances. An effective *koenkai* is expensive to maintain and conducive to political corruption.

Kulturkampf Bismarck's fight with the Catholic Church over his desire to subordinate church to state in Prussia.

L

laissez-faire A term taken from the French, which means, "to let do," in other words, to allow to act freely. In political economy, it refers to the pattern in which state management is limited to such matters as enforcing contracts and protecting property rights, while private market forces are free to operate with only minimal state regulation.

"Lay Judge System" (*saibanin-seido*) The quasi-jury system for major criminal cases that was introduced into Japan's judicial system in May 2009. Guilt or innocence of the accused—and, if convicted, the sentence—are determined by a judicial panel composed of three professional judges and six laypersons.

Leader/Supreme Leader A cleric elected to be the head of the Islamic Republic of Iran.

legislature One of the primary political institutions in a country, in which elected or appointed members are charged with responsibility for making laws and usually providing for the financial resources for the state to carry out its functions.

legitimacy A belief by powerful groups and the broad citizenry that a state exercises rightful authority.

liberal rights Basic citizenship rights of speech, assembly, petition, religion, and so forth.

Lisbon Treaty After a decade of efforts to redesign EU institutions in light of enlargement to Central and Eastern Europe, the treaty created new positions of the President of the European Council and High Representative for foreign and security policy and increased the powers of the European Council and European Parliament.

Lok Sabha The lower house of parliament in India, where all major legislation must pass before becoming law.

M

Maastricht Treaty Treaty renegotiations (ratified in 1993) that gave the EU its present name, created the EMU and the CFSP, and granted the European Parliament power to "co-decide" EU legislation.

macroeconomic policy Policy intended to shape the overall economic system by concentrating on policy targets such as inflation and growth.

Majles The Iranian parliament, from the Arabic term for "assembly."

Mandal Commission A government-appointed commission headed by B.P. Mandal to consider seat reservations and quotas to redress caste discrimination in India.

manifest destiny The public philosophy in the nineteenth century that the United States was not only entitled but also destined to occupy territory from the Atlantic to the Pacific.

maquiladoras Factories that produce goods for export, often located along the U.S.–Mexican border.

Marbury v. Madison The 1803 U.S. Supreme Court ruling that the federal courts inherently had the authority to review the constitutionality of laws passed by Congress and signed by the president. The ruling, initially used sparingly, placed the courts centrally in the system of checks and balances.

market reform A strategy of economic transformation that involves reducing the role of the state in managing the economy and increasing the role of market forces.

maslahat Arabic term for "expediency," "prudence," or "advisability," now used in Iran to refer to reasons of state or what is best for the Islamic Republic.

mass organizations Organizations in a communist party–state that represent the interests of a particular social groups, such as workers or women but which are controlled by the communist party.

mestizo A person of mixed white, indigenous (Amerindian), and sometimes African descent.

middle-level theory Seeks to explain phenomena in a limited range of cases, in particular, a specific set of countries with particular characteristics, such as parliamentary regimes, or a particular type of political institution (such as political parties) or activity (such as protest).

migrant laborers Laborers who move to another location to take a job, often a low-paying, temporary one.

mixed electoral system A system of electoral representation in which a portion of the seats are selected in winner-take-all single-member districts, and a portion are allocated according to parties within multi-member constituencies, roughly in proportion to the votes each party receives in a popular election.

mixed member system An electoral system in which about half of deputies are elected from direct constituencies and the other half are drawn from closed party lists. The German *Bundestag* uses the mixed member system, which is basically a form of proportional representation.

mixed systems Countries whose political systems exhibit some democratic and some authoritarian elements.

moderating power (*poder moderador*) A term used in Brazilian politics to refer to the situation following the 1824 constitution in which the monarchy was supposed to act as a moderating power, among the executive, legislative, and judicial branches of government, arbitrating party conflicts, and fulfilling governmental responsibilities when nonroyal agents failed.

monetarism An approach to economic policy that assumes a natural rate of unemployment, determined by the labor market, and rejects the instruments of government spending to run budgetary deficits for stimulating the economy and creating jobs.

N

National Party Congress The symbolically important meeting, held every five years for about one week, of about 2,100 delegates representatives of the Chinese Communist Party, who endorse policies and the allocation of leadership positions that have been determined beforehand by the party's much smaller ruling bodies.

National People's Congress (NPC) The legislature of the People's Republic of China. It is under the control of the Chinese Communist Party and is not an independent branch of government.

nationalism An ideology seeking to create a nation-state for a particular community; a group identity associated with membership is such a political community. Nationalists often proclaim that their state and nation are superior to others.

nationalization The policy by which the state assumes ownership and operation of private companies.

nation-state Distinct, politically defined territory in which the state and national identity, that is, a sense of solidarity and shared values based on being citizens of the same country coincide.

Naxalite The Naxalite movement emerged as a breakaway faction of the CPM in the Indian state of West Bengal in 1967. It is a radical, often violent, extra-parliamentary movement.

Nazi A German abbreviation for the National Socialist German Workers' Party, the movement led by Hitler.

neoliberal A term used to describe government policies that aim to promote private enterprise by reducing government economic regulation, tax rates, and social spending. The term *liberal* in Europe usually refers to the protection of individual political and economic liberty; in the United States, it often refers to government policies to distribute resources to low income groups.

neoliberalism A term used to describe government policies aiming to promote free competition among business firms within the market, including reduced governmental regulation and social spending.

nomenklatura A system of personnel selection under which the communist party maintains control over the appointment of important officials in all spheres of social, economic, and political life.

nonaligned bloc Countries that refused to ally with either the United States or the USSR during the Cold War years.

nontariff barriers (NTBs) Policies—such as quotas, health and safety standards, packaging and labeling rules, and unique or unusual business practices—designed to prevent foreign imports in order to protect domestic industries. A form of protectionism that does not use formal tariffs.

North American Free Trade Agreement (NAFTA) A treaty among the United States, Mexico, and Canada implemented on January 1, 1994, that largely eliminates trade barriers among the three nations. NAFTA serves as a model for an eventual Free Trade Area of the Americas zone that could include most nations in the Western Hemisphere.

O

oligarchs A small group of powerful and wealthy individuals who gained ownership and control of important sectors of Russia's economy in the context of privatization of state assets in the 1990s.

Organization of Petroleum Exporting Countries (OPEC) An organization dedicated to achieving stability in the price of oil, avoiding price fluctuations, and generally furthering the interests of the member states.

Ostpolitik The policy developed by the West Germany's Willy Brandt to promote contact and commerce with the Soviet Union and its communist allies during the Cold War.

other backward classes The middle or intermediary castes in India that have been accorded reserved seats in public education and employment since the early 1990s.

P

panchayats Elected bodies at the village, district, and state levels that have development and administrative responsibilities in India.

parastatals State-owned, or at least state-controlled, corporations, created to undertake a broad range of activities, from control and marketing of agricultural production to provision of banking services, operating airlines, and other transportation facilities and public utilities.

parity law A French law passed in 2000, following the adoption of a constitutional amendment in 1999, and subsequently extended, that directs political parties to nominate an equal number of men and women for many elections.

parliamentary democracy System of government in which the chief executive is answerable to the legislature and may be dismissed by it.

parliamentary sovereignty The doctrine that grants the legislature the power to make or overturn any law and permits no veto or judicial review.

party democracy The constitutional guarantee that political parties have a privileged place in German politics, including generous subsidies for building party organizations.

pasdaran Persian term for guards, used to refer to the army of Revolutionary Guards formed during Iran's Islamic Revolution.

pass laws Laws in apartheid South Africa that required Africans to carry identity books in which officials stamped the permits required for Africans to travel between the countryside and the cities.

patrimonial state A system of governance in which the ruler treats the state as personal property (patrimony).

patronage system A political system in which government officials appoint loyal followers to positions rather than choosing people based on merit.

People of the Book The Muslim term for recognized religious minorities, such as Christians, Jews, and Zoroastrians.

People's Liberation Army (PLA) The combined armed forces of the People's Republic of China, which includes land, sea, air, and strategic missile forces.

personalist politicians Demagogic political leaders who use their personal charisma to mobilize their constituency.

police powers Powers that are traditionally held by the states to regulate public safety and welfare. Police powers are the form of interaction with government that citizens most often experience. Even with the growth in federal government powers in the twentieth century, police powers remain the primary responsibility of the states and localities.

Politburo The committee made up of the top twenty-five leaders of the Chinese Communist Party.

political action committee (PAC) A narrow form of interest group that seeks to influence policy by making contributions to candidates and parties in U.S. politics.

political economy The study of the interaction between the state and the economy, that is, how the state and political processes affect the economy and how the organization of the economy and strategic choices made by the government and state actors affect political processes.

political Islam A term for the intermingling of Islam with politics and often used as a substitute for Islamic fundamentalism.

populism Gaining the support of popular sectors. When used in Latin American politics, this support is often achieved by manipulation and demagogic appeals.

pork-barrel politics A term originally used by students of American politics to refer to legislation that benefits particular legislators by funding public works and projects in their districts. More broadly, the term refers to preferential allocation of public benefits or resources to particular districts or regions so as to give electoral advantage to particular politicians or political parties.

power sharing Constitutional arrangements to ensure that the major political parties share executive authority. These can include mandatory coalitions and allocation of senior official positions between parties.

power vertical A term used by Russian president, Vladimir Putin to describe a unified and hierarchical structure of executive power ranging from the national to the local level.

prebendalism Patterns of political behavior that rest on the justification that official state offices should be utilized for the personal benefit of officeholders as well as of their support group or clients.

predatory state A state in which those with political power prey on the people and the nation's resources to enrich themselves rather than using their power to promote national development.

predominant-party regime A multiparty political system in which one party maintains a predominant position in parliament and control of government for a long period of time.

prefects French administrators appointed by the minister of the interior to coordinate state agencies and programs within France's territorial subdivisions known as *départements.*

privatization The sale of state-owned enterprises or services to private companies or investors.

procedural democracy A system with formal procedures for popular choice of government leaders (especially free party competition) but which may lack other democratic elements.

property taxes Taxes levied by local governments on the assessed value of property. Property taxes are the primary way in which local jurisdictions in the United States pay for the costs of primary and secondary education. Because the value of property varies dramatically from neighborhood to neighborhood, the funding available for schools—and the quality of education—also varies from place to place.

proportional representation (PR) A system of political representation in which seats in the legislature are allocated to parties in proportion to the votes each party receives. In contrast, the single-member district system tends to favor larger parties and thus reduces the number of parties represented in legislature.

purchasing power parity (PPP) A method of calculating the value of a country's currency based on the actual cost of buying goods and services in that country rather than how many U.S. dollars the currency is worth.

Q

qualified majority voting Method in the Council of Ministers for deciding most EU legislation that weights member state voting power depending upon size and defining how many votes constitute a majority.

quangos Acronym for quasi-nongovernmental organizations, the term used in Britain for nonelected bodies that are outside traditional governmental departments or local authorities.

Qur'an The Muslim Bible.

R

Rajya Sabha India's upper house of parliament; considerably less politically powerful than the *Lok Sabha.*

rational choice theory An approach to analyzing political decision making and behavior that assumes that individual actors rationally pursue their aims in an effort to achieve the most positive net result. Rational choice is often associated with the pursuit of selfish goals, but the theory permits a wide range of motivations, including altruism.

redistributive policies Policies that take resources from one person or group in society and allocate them to a different, usually more disadvantaged, group. The United States has traditionally opposed redistributive policies to the disadvantaged.

referendum An election in which citizens are asked to approve (or reject) a policy or law.

regulations The rules that explain the implementation of laws. When the legislature passes a law, it sets broad principles for implementation: how the law is actually implemented is determined by regulations written by executive branch agencies. The regulation-writing process allows interested parties to influence the eventual shape of the law in practice.

remittances Funds sent by migrants working abroad to family members in their home countries or by urban migrants to their families in rural areas.

rentier state A country that obtains much of its revenue from the export of oil or other natural resources.

rents Economic gains that do not compensate those who produced them and do not contribute to productivity, typically associated with government earnings that do not get channeled back into either investments or policies that benefit the public good. Pursuit of economic rents (or "rent-seeking") is profit seeking that takes the form of nonproductive economic activity.

republic In contemporary usage, a political regime in which leaders are not chosen on the basis of their inherited background (as in a monarchy).

reservations Jobs or admissions to colleges reserved by the government of India for specific underprivileged groups.

resource curse The concept that revenue derived from abundant natural resources, such as oil, often bring unforeseen ailments to countries.

revolution The process by which an established political regime is replaced (usually by force and with broad popular participation) by a new regime that introduces radical changes throughout society.

S

samurai The warrior class in medieval Japan, also known as *bushi*. The class emerged around the tenth century, and a dominant band of its members established Japan's first warrior government in the twelfth century. The last samurai government was overthrown in the Meiji Restoration of the mid-nineteenth century.

sanctions International embargos on economic and cultural contracts with a particular country; applied selectively to South Africa by various governments and the United Nations from 1948 until 1994.

sati *Sati*, or widow immolation, was outlawed by the British in the nineteenth century. *Satis* have occurred, although they are uncommon, in post-Independence India.

scheduled castes The lowest caste in India; also known as the untouchables.

Schengen area EU area, named after small city in Luxembourg, where freedom of transnational movement without border controls was first agreed in 1985. Schengen now includes all EU members except Romania, Bulgaria, Croatia, the United Kingdom, and Ireland. It also includes non-EU countries Norway, Iceland, and Switzerland.

separation of powers An organization of political institutions within the state in which the executive, legislature, and judiciary have autonomous powers and no one branch dominates the others. This is the common pattern in presidential systems, as opposed to parliamentary systems, in which there is a fusion of powers.

settler state Colonial or former colonial administrations controlled by the descendants of immigrants who settled in the territory.

sexenio The six-year term in office of Mexican presidents.

shari'a Islamic law derived mostly from the Qur'an and the examples set by the Prophet Muhammad in the Sunnah.

shogun The title, meaning general, assumed by a succession of hereditary leaders of the three military dynasties—the Minamotos, the Ashikagas, and the Tokugawas—that ruled Japan one after another from the late twelfth century to the mid-nineteenth century. Their government was called the shogunate.

Sikhs A religious minority, constitute less than 2 percent of the Indian population and 76 percent of the state of Punjab. Sikhism is a monotheistic religion that was founded in the fifteenth century.

siloviki Derived from the Russian word *sil*, meaning "force," Russian politicians and governmental officials drawn from the security and intelligence agencies, special forces, or the military, many of whom were recruited to important political posts under Vladimir Putin.

single-member district (SMD) An electoral district in which only one representative is elected, most commonly by the first-past-the-post method, that is, whoever gets most votes.

single-member plurality (SMP) electoral system An electoral system in which candidates run for a single seat from a specific geographic district. The winner is the person who receives the most votes, whether or not they amount to a majority. SMP systems, unlike systems of proportional representation, increase the likelihood that two national coalition parties will form.

single non-transferable vote (SNTV) A method of voting used in a multimember election district system. Each voter casts only one ballot for a particular candidate and that vote may not be transferred to another candidate even of the same party. As many candidates with the most votes are elected as the number of posts to be filled in each district.

social class A group whose members share common world views and aspirations determined largely by occupation, income, and wealth.

social market economy A system that aims to combine the efficiency of market economies with a concern for fairness for a broad range of citizens.

social movements Large-scale grassroots action that demands reforms of existing social practices and government policies.

Social Progress Index A composite measurement of social progress in countries that takes into account basic needs, their food, shelter, and security; access to health care, education, and a healthy environment; and the opportunity for people to improve their lives.

social security National systems of contributory and noncontributory benefits to provide assistance for the elderly, sick, disabled, unemployed, and others similarly in need of assistance. The specific coverage of social security, a key component of the welfare state, varies by country.

socialism A system in which the state plays a leading role in organizing the economy, owns most productive resources and property, and actively promotes equality.

socialist democracy The term used by the Chinese Communist Party to describe the political system of the People's Republic of China. The official view is that this type of system, under the leadership of the Communist Party, provides democracy for the overwhelming majority of people and suppresses (or exercises dictatorship over) only the enemies of the people.

socialist market economy The term used by the government of China to refer to the country's current economic system that mixes elements of both socialism and capitalism.

socialist The doctrine stating that the state should organize and direct the economy in order to promote equality and help low-income groups.

soft authoritarianism A system of political control in which a combination of formal and informal mechanisms ensure the dominance of a ruling group or dominant party, despite the existence of some forms of political competition and expressions of political opposition.

sovereign democracy A concept of democracy articulated by President Putin's political advisor, Vladimir Surkov, to communicate the idea that democracy in Russia should be adapted to Russian traditions and conditions rather than based on Western models.

special relationship Refers to relations between the United States and Britain and is meant to convey not only the largely positive, mutually beneficial nature of the relationship but also the common heritage and shared values of the two countries.

Standing Committee A subgroup of the Politburo, currently with seven members. The most powerful political organization in China.

state The most powerful political institutions in a country, including the executive, legislative, and judicial branches of government, the police, and armed forces.

state capitalism An economic system that is primarily capitalistic but in which there is some degree of government ownership of the means of production.

state corporatism A system of interest representation in which the constituent units are organized into a limited number of singular, compulsory, noncompetitive, hierarchically ordered, and functionally differentiated categories, recognized or licensed (if not created) by the state and granted a representational monopoly within their respective categories in exchange for observing certain controls in their selection of leaders and articulation of demands and supports.

State Council The highest organization in the state administration, directed by the premier. It also includes several vice premiers, the heads of government ministries and commissions, and a few other senior officials.

state formation The historical development of a state, often marked by major stages, key events, or turning points (critical junctures) that influence the contemporary character of the state.

state-led economic development The process of actively promoting economic development through governmental policy, usually involving indicative planning and financial subsidization of industries.

state-owned enterprises Companies in which a majority of ownership control is held by the government.

state technocrats Career-minded bureaucrats who administer public policy according to a technical rather than a political rationale. In Mexico and Brazil, these are known as the *técnicos*.

statism A doctrine advocating firm and extensive state direction of the economy and society.

structural adjustment program (SAP) Programs established by the International Monetary Fund and the World Bank intended to alter and reform the economic structures of highly indebted developing countries as a condition for receiving international loans. SAPs often require privatization, trade liberalization, and fiscal restraint, which typically requires the dismantling of social welfare systems.

subsidiarity Principle consecrated by the 1991 Maastricht Treaty that the EU should seek decision making at the level of the lowest effective jurisdiction.

Supreme Commander for the Allied Powers (SCAP) The official title of General Douglas MacArthur between 1945 and 1951 when he led the Allied Occupation of Japan.

suspensive veto In policy areas with no direct effect on the states, the German *Bundesrat* has the prerogative to make the *Bundestag* pass a bill a second time.

sustainable development An approach to promoting economic growth that seeks to minimize environmental degradation and depletion of natural resources.

T

Taisho democracy A reference to Japanese politics in the period roughly coinciding with Emperor Taisho's reign, 1912–1926. The period was characterized by the rise of a popular movement for democratization of government by the introduction of universal manhood suffrage and the reduction of the power and influence of authoritarian institutions of the state.

technocrats Career-minded bureaucrats who administer public policy according to a technical rather than a political rationale.

theocracy A state dominated by the clergy, who rule on the grounds that they are the only interpreters of God's will and law.

Tokai Village A seaside community lying about ninety miles northeast of Tokyo that is Japan's major nuclear research center with reprocessing and enrichment facilities.

totalitarianism A political system in which the state attempts to exercise total control over all aspects of public and private life, including the economy, culture, education, and social organizations, through an integrated system of ideological, economic, and political control. Totalitarian states rely on extensive coercion, including terror, as a means to exercise power.

township In apartheid South Africa, a segregated residential area reserved for Africans that were tightly controlled and constituted mainly by public housing.

typology A method of classifying by using criteria that divide a group of cases into smaller cases with common characteristics.

U

Umkhonto-we-Sizwe Zulu and Xhosa for "Spear of the Nation," the armed wing of the African National Congress, established in 1961 in South Africa.

unfinished state A state characterized by instabilities and uncertainties that may render it susceptible to collapse as a coherent entity.

unitary state In contrast to a federal system, a system of government in which no powers are reserved for subnational units of government.

untouchables The lowest caste in India's caste system, whose members are among the poorest and most disadvantaged Indians.

V

vanguard party A political party that claims to operate in the "true" interests of the group or class that it purports to represent, even if this understanding doesn't correspond to the expressed interests of the group itself.

voortrekkers Pastoralist descendants of Dutch settlers in South Africa who moved north from the British-controlled Cape in 1836 to establish independent republics; later regarded as the founders of the Afrikaner nation.

W

warrant chiefs Leaders employed by the British colonial regime in Nigeria. A system in which "chiefs" were selected by the British to oversee certain legal matters and assist the colonial enterprise in governance and law enforcement in local areas.

Weimar Republic The constitutional system of Germany between the end of World War I in 1918 and the Nazi seizure of power in 1933. So-named because the assembly to write the constitution occurred in the German city of Weimar.

welfare state A set of public policies designed to provide for citizens' needs through direct or indirect provision of pensions, health care, unemployment insurance, and assistance to the poor.

Westminster model A form of democracy based on the supreme authority of Parliament and the accountability of its elected representatives; named after the Parliament building in London.

works councils Firm employees elected by their coworkers to represent the workforce in negotiations with management at that specific shop or company.

World Bank (officially the International Bank for Reconstruction and Development) The World Bank provides low-interest loans, no-interest credit, policy advice, and technical assistance to developing countries with the goal of reducing poverty. It is made up of more than 180 nations. All members have voting rights within the Bank, but these are weighted according to the size of each country's financial contribution to the organization.

World Trade Organization (WTO) A global international organization that oversees the "rules of trade" among its member states. The main functions of the WTO are to serve as a forum for its members to negotiate new agreements and resolve trade disputes. Its fundamental purpose is to lower or remove barriers to free trade.

Z

zaibatsu Giant holding companies in pre–World War II Japan, each owned and controlled by members of a particular family. The largest were divided into a number of independent firms under the democratization program during the postwar occupation but were later revived as *keiretsu*, although no longer under the control of any of the original founding families.

zoku Members of the Japanese Diet (parliament) with recognized experience and expertise in particular policy areas such as agriculture, construction, and transportation, and close personal connections with special interests in those areas.

About the Editors and Contributors

Ervand Abrahamian is Distinguished Professor of History at Baruch College and the Graduate Center of the City University of New York. He was elected Fellow of the American Academy of the Arts and Sciences. His publications include *Khomeinism: Essays on the Islamic Republic* (University of California Press, 1993), *Tortured Confessions: Prisons and Public Recantations in Modern Iran* (University of California Press, 1999), *A History of Modern Iran* (Cambridge University Press, 2008), and *The Coup: 1953, The CIA and the Roots of Modern U.S.-Iranian Relations* (The New Press, 2013).

Amrita Basu is the Paino Professor of Political Science and Sexuality, Women's and Gender Studies at Amherst College. Her main areas of interest are social movements, religious nationalism, and gender politics in India. She is the author of *Violent Conjunctures: Hindu Nationalism in Democratic India* (Cambridge University Press, 2014)

Joan DeBardeleben is Chancellor's Professor in the Institute of European, Russian, and Eurasian Studies (EURUS) and Director of the Centre for European Studies (EU Centre of Excellence) at Carleton University in Ottawa, Canada. Her research work deals with EU–Russian relations, the EU's policy toward its eastern neighbors, and electoral politics in Russia. Her recent publications include *Economic Crisis in Europe: What It Means for the EU and Russia*, co-editor and contributor (with Crina Viju) (Palgrave Macmillan, 2013); "New EU-Russian borders after enlargement: From local to transnational linkages," in *Shifting Priorities in Russia's Foreign and Security Policy*, Roger E. Kanet and Remi Piet, eds. (Ashgate, 2013); and "The 2011–2012 Russian elections: The next chapter in Russia's post communist transition?," in J. L. Black and Michael Johns, eds., *From Putin to Medvedev to Putin – Continuity, Change or Revolution?* (Routledge, 2013).

Louis DeSipio is a Professor of Political Science and Chicano/Latino Studies at the University of California, Irvine, where he directs the Center for the Study of Democracy. His research interests include Latino politics, the process of political incorporation of new and formerly excluded populations into U.S. politics, and public policies shaping immigrant incorporation such as immigration, immigrant settlement, naturalization, and voting rights. His most recent book is *U.S. Immigrant and Immigration Policies in the Twenty-First Century: Making Americans, Remaking America* (Westview Press, 2015).

Shigeko N. Fukai is Professor Emeritus of Okayama University and Visiting Professor at Chiba University (Japan). She has written a book in Japanese on a sustainable world order and a series of articles and chapters in both English and Japanese on sustainability, Japan's land problems and land policy-making, Japan's role in the emergent regional economic order in East Asia, and Japanese electoral and party politics.

Haruhiro Fukui is Professor Emeritus in the Department of Political Science, University of California, Santa Barbara. His most recent publications include "Japan: From deterrence to prevention," in Emil J. Kirchner and James Sperling, eds., *National Security Cultures: Patterns of Global Governance* (2010), "Japan," in Joel Krieger, ed., *The Oxford Companion to Comparative Politics* (2013), and "East Asian Studies: Politics," in James D. Wright, ed., *The International Encyclopedia of Social and Behavioral Sciences*, 2nd ed. (forthcoming).

Wade Jacoby is Mary Lou Fulton Professor of Political Science at Brigham Young University, where he also directs the Center for the Study of Europe. He teaches classes on European and comparative politics. He is co-editor of the journal *German Politics*, and the author of *Imitation and Politics: Redesigning Modern Germany* (Cornell University Press, 2001) and *The Enlargement of the European Union and NATO: Ordering from the Menu in Central Europe* (Cambridge University Press, 2006).

Halbert Jones is a senior research fellow at St Antony's College, University of Oxford, where he directs the North American Studies Programme. His research interests include U.S.–Latin American relations, the international relations of North America, and twentieth-century Mexican political history. He is the author of *The War Has Brought Peace to Mexico: World War II and the Consolidation of the Post-Revolutionary State* (University of New Mexico Press, 2014). He wishes to acknowledge the role of Professor Merilee S. Grindle of Harvard University in the development of the chapter on Mexico in previous editions.

William A. Joseph is professor of political science and chair of the department at Wellesley College. He is also an associate in research of the John King Fairbank Center for Chinese Studies

709

at Harvard University. His major areas of academic interest are contemporary Chinese politics and ideology, comparative revolutionary movements, and the Vietnam War. He is the editor of and a contributor to *Politics in China: An Introduction*, 2nd edition (Oxford University Press, 2014).

Mark Kesselman is Senior Editor of the *International Political Science Review* and Professor Emeritus of political science at Columbia University. His research focuses on the political economy of French and European politics. His publications include *The Ambiguous Consensus: A Study of Local Government in France* (Knopf, 1967), *The French Workers Movement: Economic Crisis and Political Change* (HarperCollins, 1984), *The Politics of Globalization: A Reader* (Houghton Mifflin, 2012), and *The Politics of Power: The Politics of Power: A Critical Introduction to American Government* (with Alan Draper), 7th edition (W.W. Norton, 2013). His articles have appeared in the *American Political Science Review, World Politics*, and *Comparative Politics*.

Darren Kew is Associate Professor of Conflict Resolution and Executive Director of the Center for Peace, Democracy, and Development at the University of Massachusetts, Boston. He studies the relationship between conflict resolution methods and democratic development in Africa. Much of his work focuses on the role of civil society groups in this development. He also monitored the last three Nigerian elections and the 2007 elections in Sierra Leone. Professor Kew is author of numerous works on Nigerian politics and conflict resolution, including the book: *Democracy, Conflict Resolution, and Civil Society in Nigeria* (Syracuse University Press, 2015).

Atul Kohli is the David Bruce Professor of International Affairs at Princeton University. He specializes in the study of development, with a special interest in India. His most recent book is, *Poverty amid Plenty in the New India* (Cambridge University Press, 2012).

Joel Krieger is the Norma Weilenz Hess Professor of Political Science at Wellesley College. He is author of *Reagan, Thatcher, and the Politics of Decline* (Oxford University Press, 1986) and *British Politics in the Global Age* (Oxford University Press, 1999). Prof. Krieger is the Editor in Chief of the *Oxford Companion to Comparative Politics* (2013) and *The Oxford Companion to International Relations* (2014).

Peter M. Lewis is Director of African Studies and Associate Professor at the Johns Hopkins University, School of Advanced International Studies (SAIS). His work focuses on economic reform and political transition in developing countries, with particular emphasis on governance and development in Sub-Saharan Africa. He has written extensively on questions of economic adjustment, democratization, and civil society in Africa; democratic reform and political economy in Nigeria; public attitudes toward reform and democracy in West Africa; and the comparative politics of economic change in Africa and Southeast Asia. His book, *Growing Apart: Politics and Economic Change in Indonesia and Nigeria* (2007) is concerned with the institutional basis of economic development, drawing upon a comparative study.

Tom Lodge is Dean of the Arts Faculty at the University of Limerick (Ireland). He taught politics at the University of the Witwatersrand in Johannesburg, South Africa, between 1978 and 2005. He has written extensively about South African developments and his most recent book is *Sharpeville: An Apartheid Massacre* (Oxford University Press, 2011).

Alfred P. Montero is the Frank B. Kellogg Chair of Political Science at Carleton College. His main research areas are the political economy of South American countries and the quality of democracy. He is the author of *Shifting States in Global Markets: Subnational Industrial Policy in Contemporary Brazil and Spain* (Penn State University Press, 2002), *Brazilian Politics: Reforming a Democratic State in a Changing World* (Polity Press, 2006), and *Brazil: Reversal of Fortune* (Polity Press, 2014). He is also co-editor (with David J. Samuels) of *Decentralization and Democracy in Latin America* (University of Notre Dame Press, 2004). Prof. Montero's research has been published in several scholarly journals and he is the editor of the refereed journal, *Latin American Politics and Society*.

George Ross, ad personam Chaire Jean Monnet, Université de Montréal. Author of *The European Union and Its Crises* (Palgrave-Macmillan, 2011), *Jacques Delors and European Integration* (Oxford UP 1995), co-editor of *Euros and Europeans* (Cambridge University Press 2004) and *What's Left of the Left?* (Duke University Press, 2011).

Index

A

Aam Admi Party (India), 265
Abacha, General Sani, 506, 510, 511, 528
abertura, **365**, 393
Abiola, Moshood, 506
absolute veto, **159**
Abubakar, General Abdulsalami, 506
accommodation, **437**
accountability, **499**
acephalous societies, **502**
Action Group (AG), 503
Adenauer, Konrad, 135, 160–161
Affordable Care Act (U.S.), 51, 313, 328, 333, 335, 344
Afghanistan, 90, 276
African National Congress (ANC), 449, 455–458, 460, 465, 469, 471, 476, 478–479
Africans, **450**
Afrikaner, **452**
AG. *see* Action Group (AG)
agriculture
    Brazil reforms in, 374
    in China, 655
    Mexican reforms in, 409
    in Russia and, 557
    in United States, 319, 323–324
Ahmadinejad, Mahmoud, 596, 609, 629
Ainu, 255–256
Alexander the Great, 270
Algeria, 87
Allied Occupation of Japan, 227
amakudari, **242**
American Revolution, 316
Amsterdam Treaty, 210
ANC. *see* African National Congress ANC
ancien régime, **85**, 85
anticlericalism, **434**
anti-nuclear movements, 169
    in Germany, 169
    in the U.S., 169
apartheid, **454**
    South Africa, 454, 486
apartheid economics
    South Africa, 461
Arab Spring, 211, 214
Articles of Confederation, **317**
Assembly of Experts, **605**, 618
Auschwitz, 161
austerity policies, **137**
authoritarianism, **86**, **498**
authoritarian regimes, 22
autocracy, **509**
autonomous regions, **667**
ayatollah, **596**

B

BA. *see* bureaucratic authoritarianism (BA)
Babangida, General Ibrahim, 506
balance of payments, **511**
Barroso, Jose, profile of, 191
Basic Law, **149**
bazaar, **603**
Berlin Wall, 135, 168, 187
Bharatiya Janata Party (BJP), 294
Biafran War, 510
bicameral, **341**
Bill of Rights (U.S), **318**, 346
bin Laden, Osama, 276
Bismark, Otto von, 129–130
black empowerment, South Africa
    South Africa, 464
Black Homeland Citizenship Act (South Africa), 455
Blair, Tony, 43–44, 48, 55, 57, 60, 66–67, 72, 76
Blitzkrieg, **134**
BNDES. *see* National Bank for Economic and Social Development (BNDES)
Boers, **453**
Boko Haram, 507, 516, 531, 535, 538–539
Bolshevik revolution, 548–549
Brahmin, 268
Brandt, WIlly, 135, 161
Brazil, 357–400
    agrarian reform, 374
    BA rise in, 364
    BNDES in, 381, 396
    Brazilian Empire, 360
    bureaucracy, 380
    bureaucracy in, 364
    collective identities, 368
    comparative politics, 397
    critical historical junctures of, 360–366
    democracy in, 364, 368
    economic development, 369–376
    economy, 369–374
    elections in, 389
    environmental and energy issues, 375
    ethnic and racial groups in, 360, 368, 372, 385, 393
    executive institutions in, 379–380
    the Fiscal system, 371
    generation gap, 397
    geographic setting of, 350
    globalization and, 376
    Governance and Policy-Making (Section 3), 377–384
    governing the economy, 367

    import substitution industrialization (ISI) in, 369–370, 375
    industrialization and, 363, 372
    inflation, 371
    inflation in, 371
    informal economy in, 371
    Iraq war and, 396
    judiciary in, 381
    labor movement in, 366
    legislature in, 385
    Mercosul and, 375
    military and the police, 383
    national identity and citizenship in, 390–391
    Old Republic, 360
    organization of the state, 377–378
    other state institutions, 381–383
    policy-making process in, 384
    political challenges and changing agenda of, 395–396
    political culture in, 390
    political development of, 358–368
    political economy in, 369–376
    political impact of technology in, 394
    political parties in, 386–388
    political themes in, 367–378
    politics in action, 358
    politics in transition, 395–398
    populism in, 363
    the Populist Republic, 363
    PTB in, 363
    public and semipublic institutions, 380
    religions in, 359, 391
    representation and participation in, 385–394
    revolution of 1930 in, 362
    September 11 terrorist attack and aftermath, 366
    social activism in, 392–393
    Social Democratic Party (SPD) in, 363
    society in, 371–374
    state, 369–371
    subnational government, 382
    themes and comparisons, 368
    trade with China, 376–377
    UDN in, 363
    United States and, 379, 396
    U.S. presidency compared to, 379
    welfare system, 373
    women in, 368, 372, 392–393
    world of states theme, 367
Brazilian Democratic Movement (MDB), 364
Brazilian Labor Party (PTB), 363
Bretton Woods, 182, 185, 329
Brezhnev, Leonid, 550